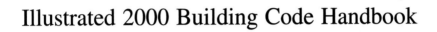

Illustrated 2000 Building Code Handbook

Illustrated 2000 Building Code Handbook

Terry L. Patterson, NCARB
University of Oklahoma

McGraw-Hill

New York San Francisco Washington, D.C.
Auckland Bogota Caracas Lisbon London
London Madrid Mexico City Milan
Montreal New Delhi San Juan Singapore
Sydney Tokyo Toronto

Library of Congress Cataloging-in-Publication Data

Patterson, Terry L.
    Illustrated 2000 building code handbook / Terry L. Patterson.
       p. cm.
    Includes index.
    ISBN 0-07-049437-1
      1. Building—Standards. I. Title.

    TH420 .P38 2000
    721'.02'18—dc21

                                         00-063834

McGraw-Hill

A Division of The McGraw·Hill Companies

The sponsoring editor for this book was Wendy Lochner, the editing supervisor was Sally Glover, and the production supervisor was Cheryl Souffrance. It was set in Graphite MM, Lucida Math, and Times by Jennie M. Patterson.

Printed and bound by R. R. Donnelly & Sons Company.

This book is printed on recycled, acid-free paper containing a minimum of 50% recycled, de-inked fiber.

To my father, Bert Patterson, Jr.

Contents

	Page
Preface	xxxvii
Acknowledgments	xxxix
Introduction	xliii
Chapter 1: Administration	1
106 Construction Documents	2
106.1.1 Means of egress	2
106.1.3 Exterior wall envelope	2
106.2 Site plan	3
Chapter 2: Definitions	5
202 Definitions	6–7
Chapter 3: Use and Occupancy Classification	9
302 Classification	10
302.1 General	10
302.1.1 Incidental use areas	11–12
302.1.1.1 Separation	12
302.2 Accessory use area	13
302.3.1 Two or more uses	13
302.3.2 Nonseparated uses	14
302.3.3 Separated uses	14–29
303 Assembly Group A	30
303.1 Assembly Group A	30–31
304 Business Group B	32
304.1 Business Group B	32
305 Educational Group E	34

305.1 Educational Group E   34
305.2 Day care   34
306 Factory Group F   35
306.1 Factory Industrial Group F   35
306.2 Factory Industrial F-1 Moderate-Hazard Occupancy   35
306.3 Factory Industrial F-2 Low-Hazard Occupancy   36
307 High-Hazard Group H   37
307.1 Hazardous Group H   37
307.3 Group H-1 structures   37
307.4 Group H-2 structures   37
307.5 Group H-3 structures   38
307.6 Group H-4 structures   38
307.7 Group H-5 structures   38
307.9 Exceptions   39–41
308 Institutional Group I   42
308.1 Institutional Group I   42
308.2 Group I-1   42
308.3 Group I-2   43
308.3.1 Child care facility   43
308.4 Group I-3   43
308.4.1 Condition 1   44
308.4.2 Condition 2   44
308.4.3 Condition 3   44
308.4.4 Condition 4   44
308.4.5 Condition 5   45
308.5 Group I-4, day care facilities   45
308.5.1 Adult care facility   45
308.5.2 Child care facility   45
309 Mercantile Group M   46
309.1 Mercantile Group M   46
309.2 Quantity of hazardous materials   46
310 Residential Group R   47
310.1 Residential Group "R"   47
311 Storage Group S   48
311.1 Storage Group S   48
311.2 Moderate-hazard Storage, Group S-1   48
311.3 Low-hazard storage, Group S-2   49
312 Utility and Miscellaneous Group U   50
312.1 General   50

Chapter 4: Special Detailed Requirements Based on Use and Occupancy   53
402 Covered Mall Buildings   54
402.1 Scope   54
402.2 Definitions   54
402.4 Means of egress   55
402.4.1 Determination of occupant load   55

402.4.1.1 Occupant formula   55
402.4.1.2 OLF range   55
402.4.1.3 Anchor buildings   55
402.4.1.4 Food courts   55
402.4.2 Number of means of egress   56
402.4.3 Arrangements of means of egress   56
402.4.3.1 Anchor building means of egress   56
402.4.4 Distance to exits   56
402.4.5 Access to exits   56
402.4.5.1 Exit passageway enclosures   57
402.4.6 Service areas fronting on exit passageways, and corridors   57
402.5 Mall width   57
402.5.1 Minimum width   57
402.6 Types of construction   58
402.7 Fire-resistance-rated separation   58
402.7.1 Attached garage   58
402.7.2 Tenant separations   59
402.7.2.1 Openings between anchor building and mall   59
402.8 Automatic sprinkler system   59
402.8.1 Standpipe system   59
402.9 Smoke control   60
402.10 Kiosks   60
402.11 Security grilles and doors   60
402.12 Standby power   60
402.13 Emergency voice/alarm communication system   61
402.14 Plastic signs   61
402.14.1 Area   61
402.14.2 Height and width   61
402.14.3 Location   61
402.14.4 Plastics other than foam plastics   62
402.14.4.1 Encasement   62
402.14.5 Foam plastics   62
402.14.5.1 Density   62
402.14.5.2 Thickness   62
402.15 Fire department access to equipment   62
403 High-Rise Buildings   63
403.1 Applicability   63
403.2 Automatic sprinkler system   63
403.3 Reduction in fire-resistance rating   64
403.3.1 Type of construction   64
403.3.2 Shaft enclosures   64
403.4 Emergency escape and rescue   64
403.5 Automatic fire detection   65
403.6 Emergency voice/alarm communication   65
403.7 Fire department communications system   65
403.8 Fire command   65

403.10.1 Standby power — 66
403.10.1.1 Fuel supply — 66
403.10.1.2 Capacity — 66
403.10.1.3 Connected facilities — 67
403.10.2 Separate circuits and fixtures — 67
403.10.2.1 Other circuits — 67
403.10.3 Emergency systems — 68
403.11 Stairway door operation — 68
403.11.1 Stairway communications system — 68
404 Atriums — 69
404.1 General — 69
404.1.1 Definition — 69
404.2 Use — 69
404.3 Automatic sprinkler protection — 70
404.4 Smoke control — 70
404.5 Enclosure of atriums — 70–71
404.6 Automatic fire detection system — 71
404.7 Standby power — 71
404.8 Interior finish — 71
404.9 Travel distance in atriums — 71
406 Motor-Vehicle-Related Occupancies — 72
406.1 Private garages and carports — 72
406.1.1 Classification — 72
406.1.2 Area increase — 72
406.2 Parking garages — 73
406.2.1 Classifications — 73
406.2.2 Clear height — 73
406.2.3 Guards — 73
406.2.4 Vehicle barriers — 75
406.2.5 Ramps — 75
406.2.6 Floor surfaces — 75
406.2.7 Mixed separation — 75
406.2.8 Special hazards — 76
406.2.9 Attached to rooms — 76
406.3 Open parking garages — 76
406.3.1 Scope — 76
406.3.2 Definitions — 76–77
406.3.3 Construction — 77
406.3.3.1 Openings — 77
406.3.4 Uses — 78
406.3.5 Area and height — 78–79
406.3.6 Area and height increases — 79–80
406.3.7 Location on property — 81
406.3.8 Stairs and exits — 81
406.3.9 Standpipes — 82
406.3.10 Sprinkler systems — 82

406.3.11 Enclosure of vertical openings   82
406.3.12 Ventilation   82
406.3.13 Prohibitions   83
406.4 Enclosed parking garages   83
406.4.1 Heights and areas   83
406.4.2 Ventilation   83
406.5 Motor vehicle service station   83
406.5.1 Construction   83
406.5.2 Canopies   84
407 Group I-2   85
407.1 General   85
407.2 Corridors   85
407.2.1 Spaces of unlimited area   85
407.2.2 Nurses' stations   86
407.2.3 Mental health treatment areas   86
407.2.4 Gift shops   86
407.3 Corridor walls   86
407.3.1 Corridor doors   87
407.3.2 Locking devices   87
407.4 Smoke barriers   88
407.4.1 Refuge area   88
407.4.2 Independent egress   88
407.5 Automatic sprinkler system   89
407.6 Automatic fire detection   89
408 Group I-3   90
408.1 General   90
408.2 Mixed occupancies   90
408.3 Means of egress   90
408.3.1 Door width   90
408.3.2 Sliding doors   90
408.3.3 Spiral stairs   91
408.3.4 Exit discharge   91
408.3.5 Sallyports   91
408.3.6 Vertical exit enclosures   91
408.4.1 Remote release   92
408.4.2 Power-operated doors and locks   92
408.4.3 Redundant operation   93
408.4.4 Relock capability   93
408.5 Vertical openings   93
408.6 Smoke barrier   94
408.6.1 Smoke compartments   94
408.6.2 Refuge area   95
408.6.3 Independent egress   95
408.7.1 Occupancy conditions 3 and 4   95
408.7.2 Occupancy condition 5   95
408.7.3 Openings in room face   96

408.7.4 Smoke-tight doors   96
408.8 Windowless buildings   96
410 Stages and Platforms   97
410.2 Definitions   97–98
410.3.1 Stage construction   99
410.3.2 Galleries, gridirons, catwalks and pinrails   100
410.3.3 Exterior stage doors   100–101
410.3.4 Proscenium wall   101
410.3.5 Proscenium curtain   101
410.3.7 Scenery   101
410.4 Platform construction   102
410.4.1 Temporary platforms   102
410.5.1 Separation from stage   103
410.5.2 Separation from each other   103
410.5.3 Opening protectives   104
410.5.4 Stage exits   104
410.6 Automatic sprinkler system   104–105

Chapter 5: General Building Heights and Areas   107
502 Definitions   108
502.1 Definitions   108–109
503 General Height and Area Limitations
503.1 General   110–114
503.1. Basements   115
503.1.2 Special industrial occupancies   115
503.1.3 Buildings on same lot   115
503.1.4 Type I construction   116
503.2 Party walls   116
503.3 Area determination   116
504 Height Modifications   117
504.1 General   117
504.2 Automatic sprinkler increase   117–120
504.3 Roof structures   121–122
505 Mezzanines   123
505.1 General   123
505.2 Area limitations   123
505.3 Egress   124
505.4 Openness   124–125
505.5 Industrial equipment platforms   125
505.5.1 Area limitations   126
505.5.2 Fire suppression   126
505.5.3 Guards   126
506 Area Modifications   127
506.1 General   127
506.1.1 Basements   127
506.2 Frontage increase   127–132

506.2.1 Width limits — 133
506.2.2 Open space limits — 133
506.3 Automatic sprinkler system increase — 134–135
507 Unlimited Area Buildings — 136
507.1 Unsprinklered, one-story — 136
507.2 Sprinklered, one-story — 136
507.3 Two-story — 137
507.4 Reduced open space — 137
507.5 High-hazard use groups — 139
507.7 Group E buildings — 139

Chapter 6: Types of Construction — 141
602 Construction Classification — 142
602.1 General — 142–153
602.1.1 Minimum requirements — 154
602.2 Type I and II — 154
602.3 Type III — 154
602.4 Type IV — 155
602.4.1 Columns — 155
602.4.2 Floor framing — 155
602.4.3 Roof framing — 156
602.4.4 Floors — 157
602.4.5 Roofs — 158
602.4.6 Partitions — 158
602.4.7 Exterior structural members — 158
602.5 Type V — 158
603 Combustible Material in Types I and II Construction — 160
603.1 Allowable uses — 160–163

Chapter 7: Fire-Resistant-Rated Construction — 165
702 Definitions — 166
702.1 Definitions — 166–176
704 Exterior Walls — 177
704.2 Projections — 177
704.2.1 Types I and II construction — 179
704.2.2 Types III, IV and V construction — 180
704.2.3 Combustible projections — 180
704.3 Buildings on the same property and buildings containing courts — 181
704.4 Materials — 181
704.5 Fire-resistance ratings — 182–186
704.6 Structural stability — 187
704.7 Unexposed surface temperature — 187–190
704.8 Allowable area of openings — 191–192
704.8.1 Automatic sprinkler system — 193
704.8.2 First story — 194
704.9 Vertical separation of openings — 194

704.10 Vertical exposure 196
704.11 Parapets 196–197
704.11.1 Parapet construction 197
704.12 Opening protection 198
704.12.1 Unprotected openings 199
704.13 Joints 199
704.13.1 Voids 199
705 Fire Walls 200
705.1 General 200
705.2 Structural stability 200
705.3 Materials 200
705.4 Fire-resistance rating 200
705.5 Horizontal continuity 201
705.5.1 Exterior walls 201
705.5.2 Horizontal projecting elements 202
705.6 Vertical continuity 203–204
705.6.1 Stepped buildings 205
705.7 Combustible framing in fire walls 205
705.8 Openings 206
706 Fire Barriers 207
706.1 General 207
706.2 Materials 207
706.3.1 Vertical exit enclosure 207
706.3.2 Exit passageway 207
706.3.3 Horizontal exit 208
706.3.4 Incidental use areas 208
706.3.5 Separation of occupancies 208
706.4 Continuity 208–209
706.5 Exterior walls 209
706.6 Openings 210
706.7.1 Prohibited penetrations 210
707 Shaft and Vertical Exit Enclosures 211
707.1 General 211
707.2 Shaft enclosure required 211–213
707.3 Materials 213
707.4 Fire-resistance rating 214
707.5 Continuity 214
707.6 Exterior walls 214
707.7 Openings 215
707.7.1 Prohibited openings 215
707.8 Penetrations 215
707.8.1 Prohibited penetrations 215
707.10 Enclosure at the bottom 215–217
707.12 Enclosure at the top 217
707.13 Refuse and laundry chutes 217
707.13.1 Refuse and laundry chute enclosures 218

707.13.2 Materials   218
707.13.3 Refuse and laundry chute access rooms   219
707.13.4 Termination room   219
707.13.6 Automatic fire sprinkler system   220
707.14 Elevator and dumbwaiter shafts   220
707.14.1 Elevator lobby   221
708 Fire Partitions   222
708.1 General   222
708.2 Materials   222
708.3 Fire-resistance rating   222–223
708.4 Continuity   223–225
708.5 Exterior walls   225
709 Smoke Barriers   226
709.2 Materials   226
709.3 Fire-resistance rating   226
709.4 Continuity   226
709.5 Openings   228
710 Horizontal Assemblies   229
710.2 Materials   229
710.3 Fire-resistance rating   229
710.3.1 Ceiling panels   229
710.3.1.1 Access doors   229
710.3.2 Unusable space   230
710.4 Continuity   230
711 Penetrations   231
711.1 Scope   231
711.2 Installation details   231
711.3 Fire-resistance-rated walls   231
711.3.1 Through penetrations   231–232
711.3.1.1 Fire-resistance-rated assemblies   232
711.3.1.2 Through-penetration firestop system   232
711.3.2 Membrane penetrations   233
711.3.3 Ducts and air transfer openings   234
711.3.4 Dissimilar materials   234
711.4 Horizontal assemblies   234
711.4.1 Through penetrations   235–236
711.4.1.1 Fire-resistance-rated assemblies   236
711.4.1.2 Through-penetration firestop system   236–237
711.4.2 Membrane penetrations   237–238
711.4.3 Nonfire-resistance-rated assemblies   238
711.4.3.1 Noncombustible penetrating items   239
711.4.3.2 Penetrating items   239
711.4.4 Ducts and air transfer openings   239
711.4.5 Dissimilar materials   239
711.4.6 Floor fire doors   239
714 Opening Protectives   240

714.2 Fire door and shutter assemblies   240
714.2.4.1 Glazing in door   241
714.2.6 Glazing material   241
714.2.6.1 Size limitations   241
714.3.2 Wired glass   243
714.3.3 Nonwired glass   244
714.3.4 Installation   244
714.3.5 Window mullions   244
714.3.6 Interior fire window assemblies   244
714.3.6.1 Where permitted   244
714.3.6.2 Size limitations   245
714.3.7 Exterior fire window assemblies   245–246
716 Concealed Spaces   247
716.1 General   247
716.2 Fireblocking   247
716.2.1 Fireblocking materials   248
716.2.1.1 Double stud walls   248
716.2.2 Concealed wall spaces   248
716.2.3 Connections between horizontal and vertical spaces   249
716.2.4 Stairways   249
716.2.5 Ceiling and floor openings   249
716.2.6 Architectural trim   250
716.2.7 Concealed sleeper spaces   250
716.3 Draftstopping in floors   251
716.3.1 Draftstopping materials   251
716.3.2 Groups R-1, R-2, R-3 and R-4   251
716.3.3 Other groups   252
716.4 Draftstopping in attics   252
716.4.1 Draftstopping materials   252
716.4.1.1 Openings   252
716.4.2 Groups R-1 and R-2   253
716.4.3 Other groups   254
716.5 Combustibles in concealed spaces in Types I and II construction   254
717 Fire-Resistance Requirements for Plaster   256
717.1 Thickness of plaster   256
717.2 Plaster equivalents   256
717.3 Noncombustible furring   256
717.4 Double reinforcement   256
717.5 Plaster alternatives for concrete   256
718 Thermal- and Sound-Insulating Materials   257
718.1 General   257
718.2 Concealed installation   258
718.2.1 Facings   258
718.3 Exposed installation   258
718.3.1 Attic floors   259
718.4 Loose-fill insulation   259

718.5   Roof insulation   259
718.6   Cellulose loose-fill insulation   260
718.7   Insulation and covering on pipe and tubing   260
719 Prescriptive Fire Resistance   261
719.1   General   261–324
719.1.1   Thickness of protective coverings   261
719.1.2   Unit masonry protection   261
719.1.3   Reinforcement for cast-in-place concrete column protection   325
719.1.4   Plaster application   325
719.1.5   Bonded prestressed concrete tendons   325

Chapter 8: Interior Finishes   327
801 General   328
801.1   Scope   328
801.1.1   Interior finishes   328
801.1.2   Decorative materials and trim   328
801.1.3   Applicability   329
801.2   Application   329
801.2.1   Windows   329
801.2.2   Foam plastics   329
802 Definitions   330
802.1   General   330–331
803 Wall and Ceiling Finishes   332
803.1   General   332
803.2   Stability   332
803.3.1   Direct attachment and furred construction   332
803.3.2   Set-out construction   333
803.3.3   Heavy timber construction   333
803.3.4   Materials   334
803.4   Interior finish requirements based on group   334–338
803.5   Textiles   339
803.5.1   Textile wall coverings   339
803.5.2   Textile ceiling finish   339
803.6   Expanded vinyl wall coverings   340
803.8.1   Materials and installation   340
803.8.1.1   Suspended acoustical ceilings   340
803.8.1.2   Fire-resistance-rated construction   340
804 Interior Floor Finish   341
804.1   General   341
804.2   Classification   341
804.3   Testing and identification   341
804.4   Application   342
804.4.1   Subfloor construction   342
804.4.2   Wood finish flooring   342
804.4.3   Insulating boards   343
804.5.1   Minimum critical radiant flux   343

805 Decorations and Trim   344
   805.1 General   344
   805.1.1 Noncombustible materials   344
   805.1.2 Flame-resistant materials   344
   805.2 Acceptance criteria and reports   344
   805.4 Pyroxylin plastic   345
   805.5 Trim   345

Chapter 9: Fire Protection Systems   347
903 Automatic Sprinkler Systems   348
   903.1.1 Alternate protection   348
   903.2.1 Group A   348
   903.2.1.1 Group A-1   348
   903.2.1.2 Group A-2   348
   903.2.1.3 Group A-3   348
   903.2.1.4 Group A-4   349
   903.2.1.5 Group A-5   349
   903.2.2 Group E   349
   903.2.3 Group F-1   349
   903.2.3.1 Woodworking operations   349
   903.2.4.1 General   350
   903.2.4.2 Group H-5 occupancies   350
   903.2.4.3 Pyroxylin plastics   350
   903.2.5 Group I   350
   903.2.6 Group M   351
   903.2.7 Group R-1   351
   903.2.8 Group R-2   351
   903.2.9 Group R-4   351–352
   903.2.10 Group S-1   352
   903.2.10.1 Repair garages   352
   903.2.11 Group S-2   352
   903.2.11.1 Commercial parking garages   352
   903.2.12.1 Stories and basements without openings 353
   903.2.12.1.1 Opening dimensions and access   353
   903.2.12.1.2 Openings on one side only   353
   903.2.12.1.3 Basements   354
   903.2.12.2 Rubbish and linen chutes   354
   903.2.12.3 Buildings over 55 feet in height   354
   903.2.15 Other required suppression systems   355
   903.3.1.1 NFPA 13 sprinkler systems   356
   903.3.1.1.1 Exempt locations   356–357
   903.3.1.2 NFPA 13R sprinkler systems   357
   903.3.1.3 NFPA 13D sprinkler systems   357
   903.3.2 Quick-response and residential sprinklers 358
   903.3.3 Obstructed locations   359
   903.3.4 Actuation   359

Chapter 10: Means of Egress   361
  1002 Definitions   362
    1002.1 Definitions   362–371
  1003 General Means of Egress   372
    1003.2.1 Multiple occupancies   372
    1003.2.2 Design occupant load   374
    1003.2.2.1 Actual number   374
    1003.2.2.2 Number by Table 1003.2.2.2   374–375
    1003.2.2.3 Number by combination   375
    1003.2.2.6 Exiting from multiple levels   378
    1003.2.2.7 Egress convergence   379
    1003.2.2.8 Mezzanine levels   379
    1003.2.2.9 Fixed seating   380
    1003.2.2.10 Outdoor areas   381
    1003.2.3 Egress width   383
    1003.2.3.1 Door encroachment   386
    1003.2.4 Ceiling height   387
    1003.2.5.1 Headroom   387
    1003.2.5.2 Freestanding objects   391
    1003.2.5.3 Horizontal projections   391
    1003.2.5.4 Clear width   391
    1003.2.6 Floor surface   391
    1003.2.7 Elevation change   394
    1003.2.8 Means of egress continuity   396
    1003.2.9 Elevators, escalators, and moving walks 396
    1003.2.10.1 Where required   396
    1003.2.10.2 Graphics   399
    1003.2.10.3 Stairway exit signs   400
    1003.2.10.4 Exit sign illumination   400
    1003.2.10.5 Power source   400
    1003.2.11 Means of egress illumination   400
    1003.2.11.1 Illumination level   401
    1003.2.11.2 Illumination emergency power   401
    1003.2.12 Guards   402–403
    1003.2.12.1 Height   403
    1003.2.12.2 Opening limitations   404
    1003.2.13 Accessible means of egress   404
    1003.2.13.1 General   406
    1003.2.13.1.1 Buildings with four or more stories 406
    1003.2.13.2 Enclosed stairways   408
    1003.2.13.3 Elevators   408
    1003.2.13.4 Platform lifts   410
    1003.2.13.5 Areas of refuge   410
    1003.2.13.5.1 Size   412
    1003.2.13.5.2 Separation   412
    1003.2.13.5.3 Two-way communication   412

1003.2.13.5.4 Instructions   414
1003.2.13.5.5 Identification   414
1003.2.13.6 Signage   414
1003.3.1 Doors   414
1003.3.1.1 Size of doors   415
1003.3.1.1.1 Projections into clear width   415
1003.3.1.2 Door swing   416
1003.3.1.3.1 Revolving doors   417
1003.3.1.3.1.1 Egress component   417
1003.3.1.3.1.2 Other than egress component   418
1003.3.1.3.2 Power-operated doors   418–419
1003.3.1.3.3 Horizontal sliding doors   419
1003.3.1.3.4 Access-controlled egress doors   421
1003.3.1.3.5 Security grilles   421
1003.3.1.4 Floor elevation   422
1003.3.1.5 Landings at doors   423
1003.3.1.6 Thresholds   425
1003.3.1.7 Door arrangement   425
1003.3.1.8.3 Hardware height   426
1003.3.2 Gates   427
1003.3.2.1 Stadiums   428
1003.3.2.2 Educational uses   428
1003.3.3.1 Stairway width   430
1003.3.3.2 Headroom   431
1003.3.3.3 Stair treads and risers   431–432
1003.3.3.3.1 Dimensional uniformity   432
1003.3.3.3.2 Profile   433
1003.3.3.4 Stairway landings   433
1003.3.3.5 Stairway construction   434
1003.3.3.5.1 Stairway walking surface   434
1003 3.3.5.2 Outdoor conditions   434
1003.3.3.6 Vertical rise   434
1003.3.3.7 Circular stairways   436
1003.3.3.8 Winders   437
1003.3.3.9 Spiral stairways   437
1003.3.3.10 Alternating tread devices   437
1003.3.3.10.1 Handrails of alternating tread devices   438
1003.3.3.10.2 Treads of alternating tread devices   438
1003.3.3.11 Handrails   438
1003.3.3.11.1 Height   439
1003.3.3.11.2 Intermediate handrails   439
1003.3.3.11.3 Handrail graspability   439
1003.3.3.11.4 Continuity   440
1003.3.3.11.5 Handrail extensions   440
1003.3.3.11.6 Clearance   441
1003.3.3.11.7 Stairway projections   441

1003.3.3.12 Stairway to roof   441
1003.3.3.12.1 Roof access   441
1003.3.4 Ramps   441
1003.3.4.1 Slope   442
1003.3.4.2 Cross slope   442
1003.3.4.3 Rise   442
1003.3.4.4.1 Width   442
1003.3.4.4.2 Headroom   442
1003.3.4.4.3 Restrictions   442
1003.3.4.5 Landings   442
1003.3.4.5.1 Slope   443
1003.3.4.5.2 Width   443
1003.3.4.5.3 Length   443
1003.3.4.5.4 Change in direction   443
1003.3.4.5.5 Doorways   443
1003.3.4.6 Ramp construction   443
1003.3.4.6.1 Ramp surface   443
1003.3.4.6.2 Outdoor conditions   444
1003.3.4.7 Handrails   444
1003.3.4.8 Edge protection   444
1003.3.4.8.1 Railings   445
1003.3.4.8.2 Curb or barrier   445
1003.3.4.9 Guards   445
1004 Exit Access   446
1004.2.1 Exit or exit access doorways required   446
1004.2.1.1 Three or more exits   446
1004.2.2 Exit or exit access doorway arrangement   446
1004.2.2.1 Two exit or exit access doorways   448
1004.2.2.2 Three or more exits or exit access doorways   448
1004.2.3 Egress through intervening spaces   450
1004.2.3.1 Multiple tenants   450
1004.2.3.2 Group I-2   457
1004.2.4 Exit access travel distance   457–458
1004.2.5 Common path of egress travel   463
1004.3.1 Aisles   465
1004.3.1.1 Public areas Group B and M   465
1004.3.1.2 Nonpublic areas   466
1004.3.1.3 Seating at tables   466
1004.3.1.3.1 Aisle accessway for tables and seating   467
1004.3.1.3.2 Table and seating accessway width   468
1004.3.1.3.3 Table and seating aisle accessway length   468
1004.3.2.2 Corridor width   470
1004.3.2.3 Dead ends   470
1004.3.2.5 Corridor continuity   473
1004.3.3 Egress balconies   473
1004.3.3.1 Wall separation   473

1004.3.3.2 Openness	473
1005 Exits	474
1005.1 General	474
1005.2.1 Minimum number of exits	474
1005.2.1.1 Open parking structures	474
1005.2.2 Buildings with one exit	476–477
1005.2.3 Exit continuity	479
1005.3.1 Exterior exit doors	479
1005.3.1.1 Detailed requirements	479
1005.3.1.2 Arrangement	479
1005.3.2 Vertical exit enclosures	479–480
1005.3.2.1 Vertical enclosure exterior walls	480–481
1005.3.2.2 Enclosures under stairways	481
1005.3.2.3 Discharge identification	483
1005.3.2.4 Stairway floor number signs	483
1005.3.2.5 Smokeproof enclosures	483
1005.3.2.5.1 Enclosure exit	484
1005.3.2.5.2 Enclosure access	484
1005.3.3 Exit passageway	484
1005.3.3.1 Width	485
1005.3.3.2 Construction	485
1005.3.4 Openings and penetrations	486
1005.3.4.1 Penetrations	486
1005.3.5 Horizontal exits	487
1005.3.5.1 Separation	487
1005.3.5.2 Opening protectives	488
1005.3.5.3 Capacity of refuge area	488
1005.3.6 Exterior exit stairways	488
1005.3.6.1 Use in a means of egress	488
1005.3.6.2 Open side	489
1005.3.6.3 Side yards	489
1005.3.6.4 Location	489
1005.3.6.5 Exterior stairway protection	491
1006 Exit Discharge	492
1006.1 General	492
1006.2.1 Exit discharge capacity	492
1006.2.2 Exit discharge location	492
1006.3 Exit discharge components	492
1006.3.1 Egress courts	492
1006.3.1.1 Width	495
1006.3.1.2 Construction and openings	495
1007 Miscellaneous Means of Egress Requirements	496
1007.1 Boiler, incinerator and furnace rooms	496
1007.2 Refrigeration machinery rooms	496
1007.3 Refrigerated rooms or spaces	497
1007.4 Cellulose nitrate film handling	497

1007.5 Stage means of egress 497

1007.5.1 Gallery, gridiron, and catwalk means of egress 498

1008 Assembly 499

1008.1 Assembly main exit 499

1008.2 Assembly other exits 499

1008.3 Foyers and lobbies 500

1008.4 Interior balcony and gallery means of egress 500

1008.4.1 Enclosure of balcony openings 500

1008.5 Width of means of egress for assembly 500

1008.5.1 Without smoke protection 502

1008.5.2 Smoke-protected seating 503–505

1008.5.2.1 Smoke control 505

1008.5.2.2 Roof height 505

1008.5.2.3 Automatic sprinklers 506

1008.5.3 Width of means of egress for outdoor smoke-protected assembly 506

1008.6 Travel distance 507

1008.7 Assembly aisles are required 507–508

1008.7.1 Minimum aisle widths 508

1008.7.2 Aisle width 508

1008.7.3 Converging aisles 508

1008.7.4 Uniform width 508

1008.7.5 Assembly aisle termination 509

1008.7.6 Assembly aisle obstructions 510

1008.8 Clear width of aisle accessways serving seating 510

1008.8.1 Dual access 511–513

1008.8.2 Single access 513–515

1008.9 Assembly aisle walking surface 515

1008.9.1 Treads 515

1008.9.2 Risers 515

1008.9.3 Tread contrasting marking stripe 516

1008.10 Seat stability 516

1008.11 Handrails 516

1008.11.1 Discontinuous handrails 517

1008.11.2 Intermediate handrails 517

1008.12.1 Cross aisles 518

1008.12.2 Sightline-constrained guard limits 518

1008.12.3 Guards at end of aisles 518

1008.13 Bleacher footboards 520

1008.14 Bench seating 520

1009 Emergency Escape and Rescue 521

1009.1 General 521

1009.2 Minimum size 521

1009.2.1 Minimum dimension 521

1009.3 Maximum height from floor 522

1009.4 Operational constraints 522

1009.5 Window wells 522

1009.5.1 Minimum size	522
1009.5.2 Ladders or steps	523
Chapter 11: Accessibility	525
1102 Definitions	526
1102.1 General	526
1103 Scoping Requirements	527
1103.1 Where required	527
1103.2.2 Existing buildings	527
1103.2.3 Work areas	527
1103.2.4 Detached dwellings	527
1103.2.5 Utility buildings	527
1103.2.6 Construction sites	528
1103.2.7 Raised areas	528
1103.2.8 Limited access spaces	528
1103.2.9 Equipment spaces	529
1103.2.10 Single occupant structures	529
1103.2.11 Residential Group R-1	529
1103.2.12 Fuel-dispensing systems	529
1104 Accessible Route	530
1104.1 Site arrival points	530
1104.2 Within a site	531
1104.3 Connected spaces	531
1104.4 Multilevel buildings and facilities	531–533
1104.5 Location	533
1105 Accessible Entrances	534
1105.1 Required	534
1105.2 Multiple accessible entrances	534
1106 Parking and Passenger Loading Facilities	535
1106.1 Required	535
1106.2 Groups R-2 and R-3	537
1106.3 Rehabilitation facilities and outpatient physical therapy facilities	537
1106.4 Van spaces	539
1106.5 Location	539
1106.6.1 Medical facilities	539
1106.6.2 Valet parking	539
1107 Special Occupancies	540
1107.2.1 Services	540
1107.2.2 Wheelchair spaces	540
1107.2.2.1 Wheelchair space clusters	542
1107.2.3 Dispersion of wheelchair space clusters	543
1107.2.3.1 Multilevel assembly seating areas	543
1107.2.3.2 Separation between clusters	543
1107.2.4 Assistive listening systems	543
1107.2.4.1 Receivers	544
1107.2.5 Dining areas	544

1107.2.5.1 Fixed or built-in seating or tables   545
1107.2.5.2 Dining counters   545
1107.3.1 Group I-1   545
1107.3.2 Group I-2   546
1107.3.3 Group I-3   546
1107.4 Care facilities   547
1107.5.1 Accessible sleeping accommodations   547–548
1107.5.2 Accessible spaces   549
1107.5.3 Dispersion   549
1107.5.4 Accessible dwelling units   549–550
1107.5.5 Accessible route   550–551
1107.5.6 Accessible spaces   551
1107.5.7 Group R-4   551
1107.6 Self-service storage facilities   552
1107.6.1 Dispersion   552
1108 Other Features and Facilities   553
1108.1 General   553
1108.2 Toilet and bathing facilities   553–554
1108.2.1 Unisex toilet and bathing rooms   555
1108.2.1.1 Standard   555
1108.2.1.2 Unisex toilet rooms   555
1108.2.1.3 Unisex bathing rooms   556
1108.2.1.4 Location   556
1108.2.1.5 Prohibited location   556
1108.2.1.6 Clear floor space   556
1108.2.1.7 Privacy   556
1108.2.2 Water closet compartment   557
1108.3 Sinks   557
1108.4 Ktichens, kitchenettes and wet bars   559
1108.5 Drinking fountains   559
1108.6 Elevators   559
1108.7 Lifts   559
1108.8 Storage   561
1108.8.1 Lockers   561
1108.8.2 Shelving and display units   561
1108.8.3 Coat hooks and folding shelves   562
1108.11 Seating at tables, counters and work surfaces   562
1108.11.1 Dispersion   562
1108.12.1 Dressing, fitting and locker rooms   563
1108.12.2 Check-out aisles   563
1108.12.3 Point of sales and service counters   564
1108.12.4 Food service lines   564
1108.12.5 Queue and waiting lines   564
1108.13 Controls, operating mechanisms and hardware   564
1108.13.1 Operable windows   565
1108.14.1 Groups R-2 and R-3   565

    1108.14.2 Other occupancies   565
  1109 Signage   566
    1109.1 Signs   566
    1109.2 Directional signage   566
    1109.3 Other signs   568

Chapter 12: Interior Environment   571
  1202 Ventilation   572
    1202.1 General   572
    1202.2 Attic spaces   572
    1202.2.1 Openings into attic   574
    1202.3 Under-floor ventilation   574
    1202.3.1 Openings for under-floor ventilation   575
    1202.3.2 Exceptions   577
    1202.4 Natural ventilation   577
    1202.4.1 Ventilation area required   578
    1202.4.1.1 Adjoining spaces   578
    1202.4.1.2 Openings below grade   578
    1202.4.2.1 Bathrooms   578
  1204 Lighting   579
    1204.1 General   579
    1204.2 Natural light   579
    1204.2.1 Adjoining spaces   579
    1204.2.2 Exterior openings   579
    1204.3 Artificial light   580
  1205 Yards or Courts   581
    1205.1 General   581
    1205.2 Yards   581
    1205.3 Courts   581–582
    1205.3.1 Court access   582
    1205.3.2 Air intake   582
    1205.3.3 Court drainage   582
  1206 Sound Transmission   584
    1206.1 Scope   584
    1206.2 Air-borne sound   584
    1206.3 Structure-borne sound   584
  1207 Interior Space Dimensions   585
    1207.1 Minimum room widths   585
    1207.2 Minimum ceiling heights   585
    1207.2.1 Furred ceiling   587
    1207.3 Room area   587
    1207.4 Efficiency dwelling units   587
  1208 Access to Unoccupied Spaces   588
    1208.1 Crawl spaces   588
    1208.2 Attic spaces   588
    1208.3 Mechanical appliances   588

1209 Surrounding Materials — 590
1209.1 Floors — 590
1209.2 Walls — 590
1209.3 Showers — 592
1209.4 Waterproof joints — 592
1209.5 Toilet rooms — 592

Chapter 13: Energy Efficiency — 595
1301 General — 596
1301.1.1 — 596

Chapter 14: Exterior Walls — 599
1403 Performance Requirements — 600
1403.1 General — 600
1403.2 Weather protection — 600–601
1403.3 Vapor retarder — 601
1403.6 Flood resistance — 602
1405 Installation of Wall Coverings — 603
1405.2 Weather protection — 603
1405.3 Flashing — 603
1405.3.1 Exterior wall pockets — 609
1405.3.2 Masonry — 610
1405.4 Wood veneers — 610
1405.5.1 Support — 611
1405.6 Stone veneer — 611–612
1405.7 Slab-type veneer — 612–613
1405.8 Terra cotta — 613–614
1405.9.1.1 Interior masonry veneers — 614
1405.10 Metal veneers — 615
1405.10.1 Attachment — 615
1405.10.2 Weather protection — 616
1405.11 Glass veneer — 616
1405.11.1 Length and height — 616
1405.11.2 Thickness — 616
1405.11.3 Application — 617
1405.11.4 Installation at sidewalk level — 617
1405.11.4.1 Installation above sidewalk level — 617
1405.11.5 Joints — 618
1405.11.6 Mechanical fastenings — 618
1405.11.7 Flashing — 618
1406 Combustible Materials on the Exterior Side of Exterior Walls — 619
1406.2.2 Architectural trim — 619
1406.2.3 Location — 619
1406.2.4 Fireblocking — 619–620
1406.3 Balconies and similar projections — 620–621

Chapter 15: Roof Assemblies and Rooftop Structures   625

  1503   Weather Protection   626

     1503.2   Flashing   626

     1503.2.1   Locations   626

     1503.3   Coping   626

     1503.4.1   Gutters   627

  1505   Fire Classification   628

     1505.2   Class A roof assemblies   628

     1505.3   Class B roof assemblies   628

     1505.4   Class C roof assemblies   628

     1505.7   Special purpose roofs   628

  1507   Requirements for Roof Coverings   629

     1507.2.1   Deck requirements   629

     1507.2.2   Slope   630

     1507.2.8   Underlayment application   630

     1507.2.8.2   Ice dam protection   631

     1507.2.9.1   Base and cap flashing   631

     1507.2.9.2   Valleys   632

     1507.2.9.3   Drip edge   632–633

     1507.3.1   Deck requirements   633

     1507.3.2   Deck slope   633

     1507.3.3.1   Low slope roofs   633

     1507.3.3.2   High slope roofs   634

     1507.3.9   Flashing   634

     1507.4.1   Deck requirements   635

     1507.4.2   Deck slope   635

     1507.5.1   Deck requirements   635

     1507.5.2   Deck slope   635

     1507.5.6   Flashing   638

     1507.6.1   Deck requirements   638

     1507.6.2   Deck slope   638

     1507.6.3   Underlayment   639

     1507.7.1   Deck requirements   639

     1507.7.2   Deck slope   639

     1507.7.3   Underlayment   639

     1507.7.5   Application   640

     1507.7.6   Flashing   640

     1507.8.1   Deck requirements   642

     1507.8.1.1   Solid sheathing required   642

     1507.8.2   Deck slope   642

     1507.8.3   Underlayment   642

     1507.8.6   Application   642

     1507.8.7   Flashing   644

     1507.9.1   Deck requirements   644

     1507.9.1.1   Solid sheathing required   644

     1507.9.2   Deck slope   645

1507.9.3 Underlayment	645
1507.9.7 Application	645
1507.9.8 Flashing	646–647
1507.10.1 Slope	647
1507.12.1 Slope	647
1507.13.1 Slope	647
1507.14.1 Slope	647
1507.15.1 Slope	647
1509 Rooftop Structures	648
1509.2 Penthouses	648
1509.2.1 Type of construction	649
1509.5 Towers, spires, domes and cupolas	650
1509.5.1 Noncombustible construction required	650–651
1509.5.2 Towers and spires	651

Chapter 16: Structural Design — 653

1604 General Design Requirements	654
1604.3.6 Limits	654–655
1607 Live Loads	656
1607.3 Uniform live load	656–658
1607.4 Concentrated loads	659
1607.5 Partition loads	659
1607.7.1 Handrails and guards	660
1607.7.1.1 Concentrated load	660
1607.7.1.2 Components	660
1607.7.2 Grab bars, shower seats and dressing room bench seats	660

Chapter 17: Structural Tests and Special Inspections — 663

1703 Approvals	664
1703.5 Labeling	664
1703.5.1 Testing	664
1703.5.2 Inspection and identification	664
1703.5.3 Label information	664

Chapter 18: Soils and Foundations — 667

1803 Excavation, Grading and Fill	668
1803.3 Site grading	668
1805 Footings and Foundations	669
1805.1 General	669
1805.2.1 Frost protection	669
1805.2.2 Isolated footings	670
1805.3.1 Building clearance from ascending slopes	670
1805.3.2 Footing setback from descending slope surface	671
1805.3.3 Pools	671
1805.3.4 Foundation elevation	672
1805.3.5 Alternate setback and clearance	672

1805.4.1 Design	672
1805.4.2 Concrete footings	673
1805.4.2.3 Plain concrete footings	673
1805.4.3 Masonry-unit footings	673
1805.4.3.1 Dimensions	679
1805.4.3.2 Offsets	679
1805.4.4 Steel grillage footings	679
1805.5 Foundation walls	680
1805.5.1.1 Thickness based on walls supported	680
1805.5.1.2 Thickness based on soil loads, unbalanced backfill height and wall height	681
1805.5.1.3 Rubble stone	681
1805.5.3 Alternative foundation wall reinforcement	681
1805.5.4 Hollow masonry walls	707
1805.5.6 Pier and curtain wall foundations	707–708
1806 Dampproofing and Waterproofing	709
1806.1 Where required	709
1806.1.1 Story above grade	709
1806.1.2 Underfloor space	710
1806.1.2.1 Flood hazard areas	710
1806.1.3 Ground-water control	711
1806.2 Dampproofing required	711
1806.2.1 Floors	712
1806.2.2 Walls	712
1806.2.2.1 Surface preparation of walls	713
1806.3 Waterproofing required	713
1806.3.1 Floors	713
1806.3.2 Walls	714
1806.3.2.1 Surface preparation of walls	714
1806.4 Subsoil drainage system	715
1806.4.1 Floor base course	715
1806.4.2 Foundation drain	715
Chapter 19: Concrete	717
1907 Details of Reinforcement	718
1907.5.2.1 Depth and cover	718
1907.5.2.2 Bends and ends	719
1907.7.1 Cast-in-place concrete (nonprestressed)	719
1909 Structural Plain Concrete	722
1909.6.1 Basement walls	722
1909.6.2 Other walls	723
1909.6.3 Openings in walls	724
1910 Seismic Design Provisions	725
1910.4.4.2 Footings	725
1911 Minimum Slab Provisions	727
1911.1 General	727

1914 Shotcrete 729
 1914.4.1 Size 729
 1914.4.2 Clearance 729
1915 Reinforced Gypsum Concrete 730
 1915.2 Minimum thickness 730
1916 Concrete-Filled Pipe Columns 731
 1916.4 Reinforcement 731
 1916.5 Fire-resistance-rating protection 732

Chapter 20: Aluminum 735
2002 Materials 736
 2002.1 General 736

Chapter 21: Masonry 739
2103 Masonry Construction Materials 740
 2103.5 Glass unit masonry 740
2104 Construction 741
 2104.1.2.1 Bed and head joints 741
 2104.1.2.1.1 Open-end units 741
 2104.1.2.2 Hollow units 742
 2104.1.2.3 Solid units 743
 2104.1.2.4 Glass unit masonry 744
 2104.1.3 Installation of wall ties 744
 2104.1.4 Chases and recesses 746
 2104.1.5 Lintels 746
 2104.1.8 Weep holes 747
 2104.2 Corbelled masonry 748
2106 Seismic Design 749
 2106.4.1.2 Masonry partition walls 749
 2106.4.1.3 Reinforcement requirements for masonry elements 750
 2106.4.2.3.1 Minimum reinforcement requirements for masonry shear walls 752
 2106.5.2 Minimum reinforcement requirements for masonry walls 754–757
 2106.5.3.1 Shear wall reinforcement requirements. 758
 2106.5.4 Minimum reinforcement for masonry columns 759
 2106.6.1 Design of elements that are not part of the lateral force-resisting system 759–760
 2106.6.2 Design of elements that are part of the lateral-force-resisting system 760–761
2107 Working Stress Design 762
 2107.2.2 ACI 530/ASCE 5/TMS 402, Section 59 762
2108 Strength Design of Masonry 764
 2108.9.2.1 Reinforcing bar size 764
 2108.9.2.2 Joint reinforcement 765
 2108.9.2.3 Clear distance between parallel bars 766
 2108.9.2.4 Clear distance between vertical bars in columns and piers 766
 2108.9.2.5 Clear distance between spliced bars 766
 2108.9.2.6 Bundling of reinforcing bars 767
 2108.9.2.7 Reinforcing bar cover 767

2108.9.2.8 Standard hooks	768
2108.9.2.9 Minimum bend diameter for reinforcing bars	769
2108.9.3.8 Dimensional limits	771–772
2108.9.6.3.3 Minimum clear span	773
2108.9.6.3.4 Beam depth	773
2108.9.6.3.5 Beam width	775
2108.9.6.6.2 Parallel column dimension	776
2108.9.6.6.3 Height-to-depth ratio	776
2108.9.6.6.4 Height-to-depth ratio	776
2109 Empirical Design Of Masonry	777
2109.2.1.1 Shear wall thickness	777
2109.2.1.2 Cumulative length of shear walls	777
2109.2.1.3 Maximum diaphragm ratio	779
2109.4.1 General	780–781
2109.4.2 Thickness	782
2109.4.3 Lateral support	783
2109.5.2 Minimum thickness	784
2109.5.3 Rubble stone walls	784
2109.5.4 Change in thickness	785
2109.5.5.1 Minimum thickness	785
2109.6.2.1 Solid units	786
2109.6.2.2 Hollow units	789
2109.6.2.3 Masonry bonded hollow walls	789
2109.6.3.1 Bonding with wall ties	790
2109.6.3.1.1 Bonding with adjustable wall ties	793
2109.6.3.2 Bonding with prefabricated joint reinforcement	794
2109.6.4.1 Ashlar masonry	795
2109.6.4.2 Rubble stone masonry	797
2109.6.5.1 Masonry laid in running bond	798
2109.6.5.2 Masonry laid in stack bond	799
2109.7.2.1 Bonding pattern	800
2109.7.2.2 Steel connectors	801
2109.7.2.3 Joint reinforcement	801
2109.7.2.4 Interior nonloadbearing walls	803
2109.7.3.1 Wood floor joists	804
2109.7.3.2 Steel floor joists	805
2109.7.3.3 Roof diaphragms	805
2109.7.4 Walls adjoining structural framing	806
2110 Glass Unit Masonry	807
2110.2.1 Standard units	807
2110.2.2 Thin units	807
2110.3.1 Exterior standard-unit panels	808–811
2110.3.2 Exterior thin-unit panels	812
2110.3.3 Interior panels	813
2110.3.4 Solid units	813
2110.3.5 Curved panels	814

2110.4.3 Lateral   815
2110.7 Reinforcement   816

Chapter 22: Steel   819
  2211 Wind and Seismic Requirements for Light-Framed Cold-Formed Steel Walls   820
    2211.1 General   820
    2211.2.1 Limitations for systems in tables 2211.1(1), 2211.1(2) and 2211.1(3)   829
    2211.3.1 Shear values   830
    2211.3.2 Orientation   830
    2211.3.3 Attachment   831
    2211.4.2 Orientation   832
    2211.4.3 Attachment   832
    2211.5.2 Orientation   833
    2211.5.3 Attachment   833

Chapter 23: Wood   835
  2304 General Construction Requirements   836
    2304.6.1 Wall sheathing   836
    2304.7.1 Structural floor sheathing   838
    2304.7.2 Structural roof sheathing   847
    2308.9.1 Size, height and spacing   857
    2308.9.3 Bracing   862–868

Chapter 24: Glass and Glazing   871
  2403 General Requirements for Glass   872
    2403.3 Framing   872
    2403.4 Interior glazed areas   872
    2403.5 Louvered windows or jalousies   872
  2405 Sloped Glazing and Skylights   873
    2405.1 Scope   873
    2405.2 Allowable glazing materials and limitations   873
    2405.3 Screening   874–875
    2405.4 Framing   875
  2406 Safety Glazing   877
    2406.2 Hazardous locations   877–880

Chapter 25: Gypsum Board and Plaster   883
  2502 Definitions   884
    2502.1 Definitions   884
  2504 Vertical and Horizontal Assemblies   886
    2504.1.1 Wood framing   886
    2504.1.2 Studless partitions   886
  2509 Gypsum Board in Showers and Water Closets   887
    2509.2 Base for tile   887
    2509.3 Limitations   887
  2510 Lathing and Furring for Cement Plaster (Stucco)   888

2510.5.1 Support of lath 888
2510.5.2.1 Use of gypsum board as a backing board 888
2510.5.2.2 Use of gypsum sheathing backing 888
2510.5.3 Backing not required 888
2510.6 Weather-resistant barriers 888
2511 Interior Plaster 889
2511.2 Limitations 889
2511.3 Grounds 889
2511.5.1 Wet areas 889
2512 Exterior Plaster 890
2512.1.2 Weep screeds 890
2512.3 Limitations 890
2512.5 Second coat application 890

Chapter 26: Plastic 893
2603 Foam Plastic Insulation 894
2603.4 Thermal barrier 894
2603.4.1.1 Masonry or concrete construction 895
2603.4.1.2 Cooler and freezer walls 895
2603.4.1.3 Walk-in coolers 896
2603.4.1.4 Exterior walls — one-story buildings 897
2603.4.1.5 Roofing 898
2603.4.1.6 Attics and crawl spaces 898
2603.4.1.7 Doors not required to have a fire-protection rating 900
2603.4.1.8 Exterior doors in buildings of Groups R-2 or R-3 900
2603.4.1.9 Garage doors 901
2603.4.1.10 Siding backer board 902
2604 Interior Finish and Trim 903
2604.2.2 Thickness 903
2604.2.3 Area limitation 903
2605 Plastic Veneer 904
2605.2 Exterior use 904
2606 Light-Transmitting Plastics 905
2606.7.1 Support 905
2606.7.3 Size limitations 905
2606.7.5 Electrical lighting fixtures 906
2606.12 Solar collectors 909
2607 Light-Transmitting Plastic Wall Panels 910
2607.3 Height limitation 910
2607.4 Area limitation and separation 911
2607.5 Automatic sprinkler system 915
2608 Light-Transmitting Plastic Glazing 917
2608.2 Buildings of other types of construction 917
2609 Light-Transmitting Plastic Roof Panels 919
2609.2 Separation 919
2609.3 Location 920

2609.4 Area limitations   921–926
2610 Light-Transmitting Plastic Skylight Glazing   927
2610.2 Mounting   927
2610.3 Slope   928
2610.4 Maximum area of skylights   930
2610.5 Aggregate area of skylights   931–933
2610.6 Separation   935
2611 Light-Transmitting Plastic Interior Signs   936
2611.2 Aggregate area   936
2611.3 Maximum area   936
2611.4 Encasement   937

Chapter 27: Electrical   939
2702 Emergency and Standby Power Systems   940
2702.2 Where required   940

Chapter 28: Mechanical Systems   943
2801 General   944
2801.1 Scope   944

Chapter 29: Plumbing Systems   947
2902 Minimum Plumbing Facilities   948
2902.1 Minimum number of fixtures   948–966
2902.2 Separate facilities   968
2902.3 Number of occupants of each sex   968
*2902.4 Location of employee toilet facilities in occupancies other than assembly
         or mercantile*   968–969
2902.4.1 Travel distance   969
*2902.5 Location of employee toilet facilities in mercantile and assembly
         occupancies*   969
2902.6 Public facilities   969
2902.6.1 Covered malls   970

Chapter 30: Elevators and Conveying Systems   973
3002 Hoistway Enclosures   974
3002.2 Number of elevator cars in a hoistway   974
3002.3 Emergency signs   975
3002.4 Elevator car to accommodate ambulance stretcher   976

Chapter 31: Special Construction   979
3104 Pedestrian Walkways and Tunnels   980
3104.5 Fire barriers between pedestrian walkways and buildings   980–981
3104.8 Width   982
3104.9 Exit access travel   982
3106 Marquees   983
3106.5 Construction   983

3109 Swimming Pool Enclosures 984
    3109.3 Public swimming pools 984
    3109.4.1 Barrier height and clearances 984
    3109.4.1.1 Openings 985
    3109.4.1.2 Solid barrier surfaces 985
    3109.4.1.3 Closely spaced horizontal members 986
    3109.4.1.4 Widely spaced horizontal members 986
    3109.4.1.5 Chain link dimensions 987
    3109.4.1.6 Diagonal members 988
    3109.4.1.7 Gates 989

Chapter 32: Encroachments into the Public Right of Way 991
3202 Encroachments 992
    3202.1.1 Structural support 992
    3202.2 Encroachments above grade and below 8 feet in height ... 993
    3202.2.1 Steps 993
    3202.2.2 Architectural features 994
    3202.2.3 Awnings 995
    3202.3.1 Awnings, canopies, marquees and signs 995
    3202.3.2 Windows, balconies, architectural features and mechanical equipment ... 997
    3202.3.3 Encroachments 15 feet or more above grade ... 999
    3202.3.4 Pedestrian walkways 1000
    3202.4 Temporary encroachments 1000

Chapter 33: Safeguards During Construction 1003
3304 Site Work 1004
    3304.1 Excavation and fill 1004
    3304.1.1 Slope limits 1004
    3304.1.2 Surcharge 1004

Chapter 34: Existing Structures 1007
3402 Additions, Alterations or Repairs 1008
    3402.4 Stairways 1008
    3407.8 Accessibility for existing buildings 1009
    3408.7.4 Ramps 1009
    3408.8.5 Ramps 1010

Chapter 35: Referenced Standards 1013–1020

Appendix A: List of Abbreviations 1025–1024
Appendix B: List of Symbols 1027
Appendix C: List of Tables 1029–1035
Index A: Tables 1039–1043
Index B: Subject 1045–1066

Preface

Every effort has been made to provide accurate clarifications of the code sections selected. To this end, I attended the public hearings on the Working Draft and have examined hundreds of proposals for changes that were subsequently approved or disapproved since that first issue. Proposal reasoning and comments of the technical committees were studied for additional insight to intentions. Dozens of professionals have been queried regarding the model codes on which the new code is based. I attended BOCA seminars to get a better grasp of that code, which has a dominant presence in the new code. Every section of the handbook was traced back to its origin in a model code or change proposal to verify accuracy and intent. Commentaries for all three model codes were studied. Some section sources located in other standards such as accessibility regulations, fire codes, and BCMC (Board for the Coordination of the Model Codes) reports were examined. Every cited reference that is included was examined for content and accuracy. Through this research it has become apparent that in spite of the best intentions of the code sponsors, there will be differences of opinion regarding interpretation. The individual who proposed the original version of a section is not the person providing the official interpretation. Original intent is easily obscured in the several stages of review, modification, and approval that occur between the first proposal to the final interpretation at the local level. Consequently, the meaning imparted by the actual phrasing in the code dominates original intent. This problem will be greater than ever before in the new code given the varying traditions of building officials in enforcing their own model codes.

If interest is sufficient, alternative interpretations will be provided in the next edition of this handbook. Settling on a single interpretation for every section in every jurisdiction will be difficult if users work in isolation. Learning how others view the code will be helpful to all concerned. Where your interpretation differs from any in this handbook, you are invited to inform me at an address listed below. Any contributions published will be appropriately credited.

Many actual building projects are used in the handbook to illustrate how real buildings comply with new code requirements. This has been done for two reasons. It is intended to bring a sense of reality to students studying the code who otherwise would find it remote from their life experience.

It also provides an opportunity to explore code intent as related to complex building circumstances. This is not possible using only imaginary examples having simple rectangular shapes that neatly fit into conditions described in the code. If you have a real project which illustrates an interesting or difficult code requirement, you are invited to contact me at an addresses listed below to discuss its possible publication in the next edition of the handbook. Such projects may be built under a model code as they are similar to the new code.

The usefulness of future editions will be enhanced if readers provide feedback on this work. You are invited to tell me which entry of the book is the most helpful and which is the least. You are also encouraged to tell me what should be added to the handbook to make it more useful. I can be reached by e-mail at tpatterson@ou.edu or fax at 405-325-7558. Comments can also be mailed to me at the College of Architecture, University of Oklahoma, Norman, Oklahoma 73019.

Terry L. Patterson
Norman Oklahoma

Acknowledgments

A large work such as this handbook cannot be the result of a single person's efforts. Many people provided important assistance. First, I thank my wife, Jennie M. Patterson, for her significant and lengthy effort on this project. Jennie produced virtually all of the graphics for the examples from architectural firms, all the tables and supporting calculations, the list of tables, the index, and the table of contents. She edited the whole work and developed the raw manuscript into a camera-ready format. She kept the computers running with the necessary maintenance and software management. This handbook would not be possible without Jennie's competent and timely contributions.

I am indebted to David B. Pendley, C.B.O., E.I.T., for his indispensable help to me in understanding *The BOCA® National Building Code* and the *Uniform Building Code*. David is the Building Official for the City of Norman, Oklahoma. He presently provides code interpretations, technical assistance, and building code administration to architects, engineers, inspectors, and builders, using the BOCA and International Building Codes within the Norman jurisdiction. David also acts as the city's commercial plan reviewer. He graduated from the University of Nebraska School of Engineering and Technology in Lincoln, Nebraska, with a B.S. degree in Construction Management. David's experience includes that of serving as the Building Official for Beatrice, Nebraska, and serving as the Chief Plans Examiner of the City of Fort Worth, Texas. David is a CABO Certified Building Official, ICBO Building Plans Examiner, an ICBO Building Inspector, an ICBO Plumbing Inspector, an ICBO Mechanical Inspector, and is licensed as a Engineer Intern in Texas and Oklahoma. David's extensive and competent assistance with the model codes in no way incurs responsibility on his part for my interpretations of the *2000 International Building Code* in this handbook. Any errors or misunderstandings are entirely my responsibility as the sole author of the handbook.

Many thanks go to my graduate assistants for their important help. Srdan Kalajdzic of Norman, Oklahoma, was especially helpful in identifying examples from architectural working drawings that illustrate code requirements. He also produced a large number of the generic details for the handbook. Srdan performed his tasks with his usual high level of dependability and competence. Many thanks to Rene Spineto of Guthrie, Oklahoma, who produced a large number of generic details and some graphics for the architectural project examples. Thanks to Arvind Vishnu Ram of Norman, Oklahoma, for his high-quality graphic production of numerous generic details. Thanks to Dana A. Templeton of Norman, Oklahoma, for her administrative help and some graphic work on the architectural project examples. Thanks to Kevin Zhou of Norman, Oklahoma for his help with the production of generic details. Joel K. Dietrich, AIA has my gratitude for his assistance as director of the Division of Architecture. His kind consideration of this project in his assignment of my academic work and his assignment of graduate assistants were key to the timely completion of the handbook. Thanks to James L. Kudrna for his help as director of the Division of Architecture in his assignment of graduate assistants and his support in the final stages of this work. I am also grateful for the continued support of the University of Oklahoma College of Architecture for my publishing efforts.

Casey B. Huse of Boise, Idaho, who recently graduated first in his class, contributed the excellent project design and artwork used on the cover of this handbook. Thanks go to Casey for his creative contribution and for his computer preparation of the work for publication.

Many thanks are due the following architectural firms who generously permitted me to select examples from their work to illustrate methods of compliance with the new code.

Alt Breeding Schwarz
   Architects, LLC
209 Main Street
Annapolis, MD 21401

Ankrom Moisan
   Associated Architects
6720 S.W. Macadam
Portland, OR 97219

C. Allen Mullins, Architect
P.O. Box 21
Bear Creek, PA 18602

Cromwell Architects Engineers
101 South Spring St.
Little Rock, AR 72201

David Woodhouse Architects
811 West Evergreen Avenue
Chicago, IL 60622

Gossen Livingston
   Associates, Inc.
420 South Emporia
Wichita, KS 67202

HKS, Inc.
1919 McKinney Avenue
Dallas, TX 75201

HKT Architects, Inc.
35 Medford Street
Somerville, MA 02143

The Hollis and Miller
   Group, Inc.
220 NW Executive Way
Lee's Summit, MO 64063

Overland Partners, Inc.
5101 Broadway St.
San Antonio, TX 78209

PBK Architects, Inc.
11 Greenway Plaza
Houston, TX 77046

Perkins Eastman Architects, P.C.
115 Fifth Avenue
New York, NY 10003

Phillips Metsch Sweeney Moore
   Architects
Marc A. Phillips, Proj. Architect
Santa Barbara, CA 93103

Spencer Godfrey Architects
1106 S. Mays
Round Rock, Texas 78664

Stephen Wen + Associates,
   Architects, Inc.
77 North Mentor Avenue
Pasadena, CA 91106

Vogt Architectural Services
9000 Old Cedar Avenue
Bloomingtron, MN 55420

Watkins Hamilton Ross
  Architects, Inc.
20 Greenway Plaza, Suite 450
Houston, Texas 77046
713-665-5665

Wilson Darnell Mann, P.A.
105 N. Washington
Wichita, KS 67202

Thanks to Carl Mileff & Associates, Inc., Building Code Services, 5070 N. Sixth Street, Suite 103, Fresno, CA 93710, (http://www.cmapc.com) for the use of their software, CodeBuddy™ Version 2.0. The software provides quick access to the Uniform Building Code requirements for "R" occupancy buildings. Its summaries and illustrations helped my understanding of those sections of the UBC. I also appreciate this company's sponsorship of the internet "Building Code Discussion Group" (http://www.delphi.com/buildingcode) where I was able to get code questions answered and where numerous discussions of code-related topics were available for my review.

I thank the following people for their helpful responses to my surveys and questions regarding various sections of model codes in their jurisdictions. This group bears no responsibility for my use and interpretation of data provided to me. Such responsibility is entirely my own. Thanks also go to the many respondents to my inquiries who declined acknowledgment by name for their help.

Gene Abbot
Building Official
City of Lakeville
20195 Holyoke Avenue
Lakeville, MN 55044

Thomas Anderson
ICBO Director
Chief Building Inspector
City of Hopkins
1010 S First Street
Hopkins, MN 55343

Dick Bower
Building Official
City of Soldotna
177 N. Birch Street
Soldotna, AK 99669

Christopher Caruso
Building Official
Drawer W
Clinton, PA 15026

Kenneth Elsberry
Building Official
City of Dallas
120 Main Street
Dallas, GA 30132

John Graber
Civil Engineering Technician
USDA Forest Service
Suite 680
310 W. Wisconsin Avenue
Milwaukee, WI 53203

Robert Hegner
Building Official
City of Northfield
801 S. Washington St.
Northfield, MN 55057

Frank P. Hodge, Jr.
Building Official
Town of Hilton Head Island
1 Town Center Ct.
Hilton Head Island, SC 29928

Charles M. Huss, R.C.I.
Project Specialist
Maniilaq Health Center
P.O. Box 256
Kotzebue, AK 99752

Douglas Lalim
Building Official
City of Williston
1011 18th St., West
Williston, ND 58801

Clayton Larson
Chief Building Official
City of Coon Rapids
11155 Robinson Drive, NW
Coon Rapids, MN 55433

Duane Lasley
Building Official
City of Duluth
City Hall, Room 210
411 West First
Duluth, MN 55802

John J. Mayo
Building Official
Certified Building Inspector
Certified
  Environmental Inspector
Lac Du Flambeau, WI 54538

Rick Murray
Building Official
City of Fulton
City Hall
Fulton, MO 65251

Aslam Rana
Building Inspector Services
  Director
City of Dothan
126 N. Saint Andrews, Rm 315
Dothan, AL 36303

Donald Ranes
Building Official
County of Natrona
Suite 200
120 West First Street
Casper, WY 82601

Jerry Ratzlaff
Building Official
Ramsey County
524 Fourth Avenue, Suite 7
Devil's Lake, ND 58301

James Rich
Building Official
City of Hermantown
5255 Maple Grove Road
Hermantown, MN 55811

Bruce J. Spiewak, AIA
Consulting Architect
375 Morgan Lane, Unit 405
West Haven, CT 06516

J.P. Swanson
Building Official
City of Big Lake
802 Kjellbergs
Monticello, MN 55362

Murray Ward
Building Official
City of Grand Rapids
420 N. Pokgama
Grand Rapids, MN 55744

Many thanks go to Samuel Ray Moore, Architect of Oklahoma City and to John C. Womack, AIA, of the School of Architecture, Oklahoma State University for their help in launching this project. And, special thanks to Wendy Lochner, Senior Editor at McGraw-Hill, for her advice and help in seeing this handbook through to a successful conclusion, and for her continued support of my work.

Introduction

Purpose.

This handbook clarifies the sections of the *2000 International Building Code* that are the most useful to designers, detailers, estimators, and students. It is not directed to specifiers or engineers. It is not intended to be a substitute for the code, but an aid to understanding it.

The *2000 International Building Code* is owned by the International Code Council, Inc., of Falls Church, Virginia. This handbook is neither sponsored nor approved by this agency, which has no relationship to this project.

Code language.

In their analysis of proposed change 1005.1-1 to the "First Draft" of the *International Building Code,* the Means of Egress Technical Subcommittee rejected the language of the proposal as being "commentary, not code text." This single statement succinctly summarizes the problem with codes for many people who must comply with them.

"Code text" is the language of building codes, a pseudo-legal kind of language intended to minimize variations in interpretation and withstand legal challenges. As in legal documents, the penalty for this special style is clarity to people who are not specialists in the language. The difficult language might be justified if interpretations among users and officials were consistent. This is not the case, as a visit to any internet code-discussion site will verify. Code questions posted on such sites often generate conflicting responses from code officials and other knowlegeable parties.

Building codes have other readability problems. Sentences are often long and convoluted. Some items in the first part of a sentence affect some items in the second and third parts of the sentence but all items are not necessarily affected by all other items. Sorting out the relationships between words is complicated by the fact that some phrases affect previous or subsequent sentences and some do not. Too much substantive content is joined by too few words of clarification. Another problem in reading a code is letting expectations affect interpretation. The logic on which the code is based is not always accessible to the user and does not always reflect the experience of the professional. Statistics, tests, tradition, and other data and trends in life safety on which codes are based may not be available to the average user. In most cases, taking the literal meaning of code statements is more effective than applying common sense. Since this approach is not 100 percent reliable, however, doubt makes the mental discipline required for understanding even more challenging.

Handbook language.

The language of this handbook accommodates the needs of design and production professionals and students. It is one of illustrations, tables, outlines, and lists. Common phrasing is substituted for legalistic wording. Lengthy and convoluted code sentences are broken down into line items. Quick and easy readability is the goal.

Format.

Drawings and diagrams illustrate numerous requirements. Actual building projects as well as generic examples are included. Tables are provided, many of which are based on mathematical equations that would otherwise require computation by the user. Large code tables are broken down into smaller tables and reformatted to reduce the number of variables that must be reconciled. Footnotes are integrated into the body of each table or the body of the text which eliminates the fine print that is difficult to read and easily overlooked. Exceptions are integrated into the body of the basic requirements. This eliminates reversals of requirements where exceptions supercede the main text.

Several common-sense shortcuts were taken in the handbook to facilitate readability. First, the handbook refers to the *International Building Code* simply as the code. The code consistently modifies references to residential occupancies as follows: "R-3 as applicable in Section 101.2." This indicates that the *International Residential Code* governs 1- and 2- family dwellings and townhouses ≤ 3 stories. By use of this phrase, the code is indicating to which residential occupancies it applies. It is sufficient to understand that the code does not address residences governed by the *International Residential Code*. Consequently, the reference to 101.2 is omitted throughout the handbook. Where sprinklers are addressed, the code typically refers to section 903.3.1.1 or 903.3.1.2. These sections essentially require that sprinklers comply with NFPA 13 and 13R respectively. Instead of listing these sections as references in italics, the handbook simply refers to sprinklers with the phrase "as per NFPA 13" or "13R" in the body of the requirement. The code refers to sprinklers as being automatic. Since it is understood that all sprinklers are to be automatic, the handbook omits this term.

The code often refers to "buildings and structures" so as not to exclude constructions such as stadiums, which may not be considered buildings. The handbook usually refers only to "buildings," which must be understood to include all the structures that the code governs. The handbook utilizes mathematical and other symbols instead of words to the greatest extent possible so as to provide visual relief to the text. For example, the symbols $\geq$ and $\leq$ are substituted, where readibility is enhanced, for the terms "minimum" and "maximum." The code reports frequently that certain cases must comply with the code. Such comments are omitted, as it must be understood that every entry of the code requires compliance.

The shortcuts and plain language used by the handbook lack the legal precision of the code. The code attempts to provide regulations that cannot be circumvented. The handbook makes selected regulations more accessible to designers, detailers, and estimators. Consequently, common sense must be applied to the guidance provided.

The need to refer to other pages in order to grasp the concept of a code requirement is minimized. Numerical references to other code sections are eliminated from the main text. Descriptions of such referenced data, the data itself, or the subject of the referenced data is substituted. This provides a more easily read text without the disruption of numbers that add no apparent meaning to the paragraph. The cited section number along with its name are listed below the body of the requirement text in italics. Comments on the citation are added where necessary for clarification. The reader may turn to the cited section if desired. The following example illustrates the contrast in formats:

Code entry:
> **407.2 Corridors.** "Corridors in occupancies in Group I-2 shall be continuous to the exits and separated from other areas in accordance with Section 407.3 except spaces conforming to Sections 407.2.1 through 407.2.4."

Handbook clarification:
407.2 Corridors

- The enclosure of occupancy I-2 corridors is governed as follows:
  - Each corridor must be continuous to an exit.
  - Corridors may be open to the spaces indicated below where design and construction meet minimum requirements for fire safety:
    Waiting areas.
    Nurses stations.
    Mental health treatment areas.
    Gift shops.
  - Otherwise, corridors must be separated from other spaces for purposes of smoke protection.

Note: The following are cited as sources of requirements for the spaces opening to a corridor:
> *407.2.1, "Spaces of unlimited area," which addresses waiting rooms.*
> *407.2.2, "Nurses' stations."*
> *407.2.3, "Mental health treatment areas."*
> *407.2.4, "Gift shops."*
> *407.3, "Corridor walls," for walls required to separate corridors from other spaces.*

Focus for design.
The handbook focuses on code sections affecting design decisions at the schematic stage and design development phases such as in Chapters 3, 4, 5, 10, 11, 12, 30, and 32. Designers are provided with a clarification of requirements affecting floor plan configuration and building

massing. Required heights, widths, lengths, clearances, and distances are among the data clarified. These sections are of particular interest to students, as much studio work is schematic in nature.

Focus for detailing.

The handbook focuses on code sections affecting detailing decisions in the working drawing phase such as in Chapters 6, 7, 8, 9, 14, 15, 18, 19, 21, 22, 23, 24, 25, 26, and 31. Detailers are provided with a clarification of requirements affecting material choices and detail configuration. Clarification of these sections also helps the designer make spatially related decisions based on probable relative cost of the options as driven by fire protection requirements. These sections are of particular interest to students since they narrow the choices for material selection and detail composition.

Focus for cost estimating.

The handbook focus on code sections affecting detailing also helps estimators prepare construction bids. Where architectural working drawings require that the builder "meet current code requirements," this handbook can provide options for code compliance where certain detailing is vague or missing in the project drawings.

Sections de-emphasized.

Material that is solely specification oriented is generally omitted from the handbook. That is, requirements referring to only specifications, tests, procedures, administration, other codes and standards, and paragraphs not related to space planning or detailing are not addressed. Chapters 1, 17, 33 and parts of other chapters are this type. These subjects are typically the responsibility of professionals who are familiar with code language. Specification type data is included in the handbook only where it is mixed with design and detailing information.

Requirements that are engineering oriented are generally omitted. This refers mainly to Chapter 16. Engineers and architects with responsibilities in Chapter 16 typically have the experience to respond directly to code language. Certain loading requirements from Chapter 16 are included in the handbook, as they may be useful to students and production personnel who need to approximate member sizes for detailing purposes.

Within chapters addressed by the handbook, certain paragraphs are omitted that are administrative in nature and contain no technical content. For example, sections are distributed throughout the code that establish the applicability of subsequent subsections. For these to be useful, they must be referred to periodically as subsequent sections are studied. This requires turning pages, which interrupts concentration. In lieu of these scope-type paragraphs, the applicability of each subsection is reported in the handbook within the subsection itself, where such is not self-evident. Other sections are also omitted where they do not contribute to the needs of designers and detailers. Some of these are scattered and some are grouped. Theses various omissions result in occasional gaps in section numbering. When a numbered paragraph is selected for clarification, however, every item under the number is addressed.

In order to keep handbook chapter numbering continuous and consistent with the code, a few "place holder" pages are inserted to identify de-emphasized chapters that lack significant material of interest to designers, detailers, and estimators. Chapters 1, 2, 13, 17, 20, 27, 28, and 33 have such pages. For most of these, material of minor interest is included. For example, Chapter 17 deals with testing, a subject not featured in the handbook. Sections on performance labels for materials and assemblies were included on the Chapter 17 "place holder" page. Such label information is of general interest to the detailer and is of more value than would be an empty page. Code Chapters 13 and 28 merely refer to other codes with no further information, so the "place holder" pages for these chapters are correspondingly brief.

Code errors.

The *2000 International Building Code,* being the first printing of a first edition, can be expected to contain errors, which it does. These include common typographical errors in wording and tabular numbers, obsolete section reference numbers, quite a few mistranscribed names of referenced standards in Chapter 35, and a few errors that are more significant. For example, in code table 2304.7(4) the following phrase is omitted from the end of the last sentence in footnote a: "…(38mm) of approved cellular or lightweight concrete is placed over the subfloor, or finish floor is ¾" (19mm) wood strip." The phrase is provided in the working draft but was lost in transcription through subsequent drafts. Footnote c in code table 803.4 omits the word "not" in the third sentence phrase "shall be considered," thus, reversing the meaning of the sentence. This error was transcribed directly from section 803.4.3 in the *The BOCA® National Building Code,* where the same error exists. Table 1107.2.4.1 was incorrectly copied from its source, the proposed changes to the ADA (Americans with Disabilities Act) Accessibility Guidelines. Such mechanical errors where discovered are corrected in the handbook.

Any conceptual errors where found in the code are not corrected. A few of this type occur where an omission or conflict is apparent which does not result from a mechanical error but from an oversight in phrasing. It is not the purpose of this handbook to improve on the requirements of the code but only to clarify its wording. Such corrections should be effected by the code change process, which only the International Code Council can accomplish.

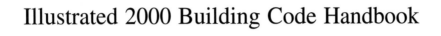

Illustrated 2000 Building Code Handbook

1

Administration

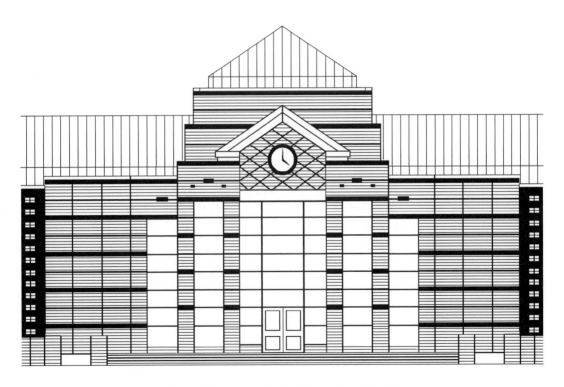

High School 6, Cypress-Fairbanks Independent School District.
Harris County, Texas. *(partial elevlation)*
PBK Architects, Inc. Houston, Texas.

106 Construction Documents

106.1.1 Means of egress

- Construction documents must show the following:
  - All parts of the means of egress as follows:
    Location.
    Construction.
    Size.
- For occupancies other than R-2 and R-3, the following is required:
  - Construction documents must show the number of occupants as follows:
    On every floor.
    In all rooms and spaces.

106.1.3 Exterior wall envelope

- Construction documents must describe the exterior wall envelope as follows:
  - Information must be adequate to verify code compliance, including the following:
    Wall intersections with dissimilar materials.
    Wall intersections with the roof.
    Wall intersections with eaves.
    Wall intersections with parapets.
    Means of drainage.
    Waster-resistive membrane.
    Details around openings.
    Flashing.
    Corners.
    End details.
    Control joints.
- Construction documents must include the following information:
  - Manufacturers' installation instructions and documentation verifying the following:
    That the following maintain weather resistance of the exterior wall envelope:
      Penetration and opening details.
  - Description of the exterior wall system as tested and the test method.

106 Construction Documents

106.2 Site plan

- Construction drawings submitted for approval must include a site plan showing the following:
  - Site plan must show to scale the following information:
    Size and location of the following:
    New and existing construction.
    Distances to lot lines.
    Established street grades and proposed finished grades.
  - Site plan must be prepared in accordance with a boundary line survey.
- Where demolition will occur, the site plan must show the following:
  - Construction to be demolished and to remain.
- The building official may waive the site plan requirement as follows:
  - For alteration or repair or where otherwise warranted.

NOTES

2

Definitions

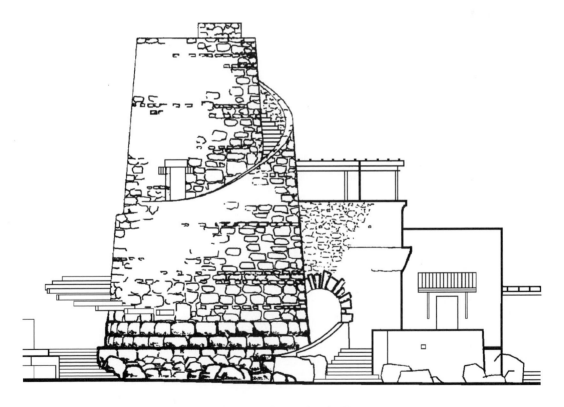

Lady Bird Johnson Wildflower Center. Austin, Texas. *(partial elevation)*
Overland Partners, Inc. San Antonio, Texas.

202 Definitions *(part 1 of 2)*

- **Court**
  - An uncovered space open to the sky.
  - Enclosed on ≥ 3 sides by one of the following:
    - Exterior building walls.
    - Other enclosing elements.

- **Dwelling**
  - A building containing one of the following:
    - 1 dwelling unit.
    - 2 dwelling units.
  - To be occupied for living purposes by one of the following means.

- **Dwelling unit**
  - A single unit as follows:
    - Provides complete independent living facilities.
    - For one or more persons.
    - Includes permanent provisions for the following:
      - Living.
      - Sleeping.
      - Eating.
      - Cooking.
      - Sanitation.

- **Grade floor opening**
  - One of the following:
    - Window.
    - Other opening.
  - Sill height is ≤ 44" from adjacent grade as follows:
    - Above finished grade.
    - Below finished grade.

- **Habitable space**
  - A space in a building for the following:
    - Sleeping.
    - Eating.
    - Cooking.
  - Does not include the following:
    - Bathrooms.
    - Toilet rooms.
    - Closets.
    - Halls.
    - Storage spaces.
    - Utility spaces.
    - Similar spaces.

202 Definitions *(part 2 of 2)*

- **Occupiable space**
  - A room or enclosed space.
  - Designed for human occupancy.
  - Where people congregate for the following:
    - Amusement.
    - Education.
    - Similar purposes.
    - Labor.
  - Has means of egress.
  - Has lighting.
  - Has ventilation.

- **Skylights and sloped glazing**
  - Any of the following:
    - Glass.
    - Transparent glazing material.
    - Translucent glazing material.
  - Installed at a slope $\geq 15°$ from vertical.
  - The following glazing is included:
    - In skylights.
    - In solariums.
    - In sun spaces.
    - In roofs.
    - In sloped walls.

- **Story**
  - The segment of a building between the following levels:
    - Upper surface of a floor.
    - Upper surface of the floor or roof directly above.
  - For floors other than the top floor, a story is measured in one of the following ways:
    - From top to top of successive tiers of beams.
    - From top to top of successive tiers of finished floor surfaces.
  - For the top floor, a story is measured as follows:
    - From top of finished floor to top of ceiling joists where there is a ceiling.
    - From top of finished floor to top of roof rafters where there is no ceiling.

- **Story above grade plane**
  - A story with its finished floor surface above the grade plane.
  - A basement with a finished floor surface at one of the following levels:
    - > 6' above grade plane.
    - > 6' above the finished ground level for > 50% of the building perimeter.
    - > 12' above the finished ground level at any point.

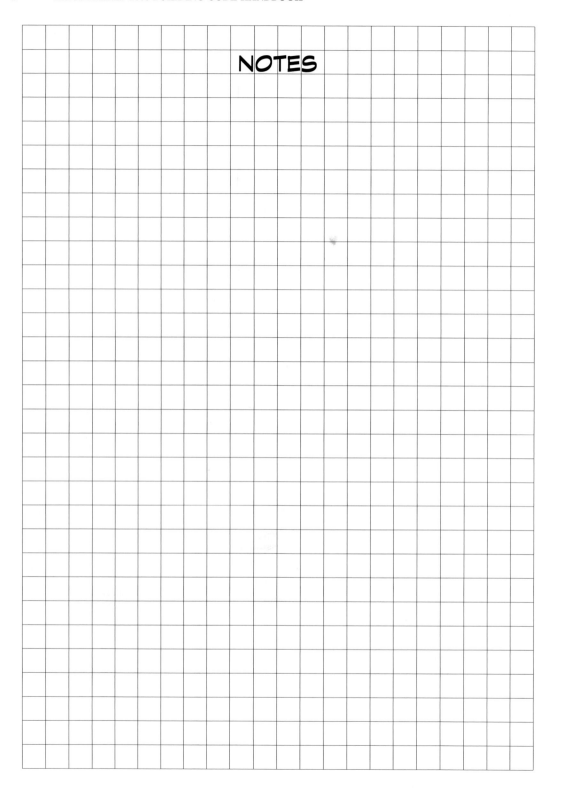

NOTES

3

Use and Occupancy Classification

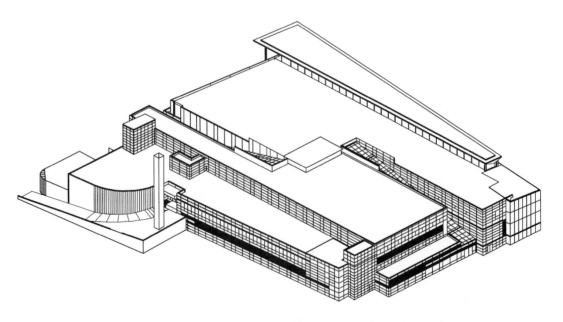

University of Connecticut New Downtown Campus at Stamford, Connecticut.
Perkins Eastman Architects, P.C. New York, New York.

302 Classification

302.1 General

- Buildings or parts of buildings are classified as one or more of the following occupancy categories:
  - A—Assembly:
    - A-1.
    - A-2.
    - A-3.
    - A-4.
    - A-5.
  - B—Business.
  - E—Educational.
  - F—Factory and Industrial:
    - F-1.
    - F-2.
  - H—High Hazard:
    - H-1.
    - H-2.
    - H-3.
    - H-4.
    - H-5.
  - I—Institutional:
    - I-1.
    - I-2.
    - I-3.
    - I-4.
  - M—Mercantile.
  - R—Residential:
    - R-1.
    - R-2.
    - R-3.
    - R-4.
  - S—Storage:
    - S-1.
    - S-2.
  - U—Utility and Miscellaneous.
- Buildings not listed in one of the occupancy categories by the code are to be assigned to the category with the most similar fire hazard.

302 Classification

302.1.1 Incidental use areas* *(part 1 of 2)*

- The following incidental use areas are not governed by this section:
  - Within and serving a dwelling unit.
- This section addresses incidental use areas as follows:
  - Protection required.
  - Separation from the rest of the building required.
- Occupancy classification of incidental use areas is as follows:
  - Same classification as the main occupancy in which they are located.
- The areas listed below require one of the following:
  - Requirement:
    - Separation with fire-resistance rating ≥ 1 hr.
    - Automatic fire-extinguishing system in the space.
  - Areas:
    - Furnace rooms:
      - With any equipment > 400,000 Btu/h input.
    - Boiler rooms:
      - With boilers > 15 psi and 10 horsepower.
    - Refrigerant machinery rooms.
    - The following spaces in occupancy E:
      - Laboratories where not classified as H.
      - Vocational shops not classified as H.
    - Laboratories in occupancy I-2:
      - Where not classified as H.
- The following areas require a separation with a fire-resistance rating ≥ 1 hr.
  - Laundry rooms > 100 sf.
  - Storage rooms > 100 sf.
  - I-3 padded cells.
  - Waste collection rooms > 100 sf.
  - Linen collection rooms > 100 sf.
- Automotive parking garages in other than R-3 require the following:
  - Separation with a fire-resistance rating ≥ 2 hr.
- Incinerator rooms require both the following:
  - Separation with a fire-resistance rating ≥ 2 hr.
  - Automatic fire-extinguishing system in the space.
- The following paint shops require one of the conditions listed below:
  - Paint shops:
    - Where not classified as H.
    - Where located in other than F.
  - Conditions:
    - Separation with a fire-resistance rating ≥ 2 hr.
    - Automatic fire-extinguishing system in the space.

Source: IBC Table 302.1.1.

302 Classification

302.1.1 Incidental use areas* *(part 2 of 2)*

- Battery systems with all the following characteristics require that listed below:
  - ○ Characteristics:
    Stationary lead-acid systems.
    Liquid capacity > 100 gallons.
    Used for any of the following:
    Facility standby power.
    Emergency power.
    Uninterrupted power supply.
  - ○ Requirements in B, F, H, M, S, U:
    Fire barriers with a fire-resistance rating ≥ 1 hr.
    Floor-ceiling assemblies with a fire-resistance rating ≥ 1 hr.
  - ○ Requirements in A, E, I, R:
    Fire barriers with a fire-resistance rating ≥ 2 hr.
    Floor-ceiling assemblies with a fire-resistance rating ≥ 2 hr.

302.1.1.1 Separation

This subsection addresses the fire-resistance-rated separations required for incidental use areas.

- Required separations are to be fire barriers.
- The following applies where a fire-extinguishing system is provided in lieu of a fire barrier:
  - ○ The space must be separated from the rest of the building with construction that resists the passage of smoke as follows:
    Partitions must extend from the floor to the underside of the following where applicable:
    The fire rated floor/ceiling assembly.
    The roof/ceiling assembly.
    The floor deck above.
    The floor deck above.
    Doors must close automatically when smoke is detected.
    Doors may not have openings which transfer air.
    Doors may not be undercut more than indicated below:

Table 302.1.1.1	Maximum Undercut of Doors	
Door type	Material below door	Clearance below door
Swinging, builders hardware	Rigid floor tile	$5/8$"
All types	Raised noncombustible sill	$3/8$"
All types	Floor with no sill	$3/4$"
All types	Floor covering	$1/2$"

Source: NFPA 80, "Fire Doors and Windows," Table 1-11.4.

Source: IBC Table 302.1.1

302 Classification

302.2 Accessory use area

- The following fire barriers are not governed by this section:
  - As required for accessory areas of occupancy H.
  - As required for incidental use areas.

  Note: The following are cited as the source of requirements for fire barriers that are not governed by this section:
  302.3.1, "Two or more uses," includes requirements for occupancy H.
  302.1.1, "Incidental use areas," lists separation requirements for selected incidental use areas.

- In other cases, fire barriers are not required for either of the following:
  - Uses occupying $\leq 10\%$ of any floor area.
  - Uses meeting both the following requirements:
    Height limits based on occupancy and construction type.
    Area limits based on occupancy and construction type.

  Note: IBC Table 503 lists height and area limitations based on occupancy and construction type.

302.3.1 Two or more uses

- This section addresses buildings containing uses in ≥ 2 occupancy classifications.

  Note: Section 508, "Special Provisions," is cited as the source of additional requirements for buildings with uses in ≥ 2 occupancy classifications. The separation of parking garages from other parts of a building is addressed.

- Separations for occupancy H are governed as follows:
  - Occupancy H-1 areas must be located in a building separate and detached from other occupancies.
  - Other H occupancies must be separated from other parts of the building by construction with a fire-resistance rating.

  Note: IBC Table 302.3.3, "Required Separation of Occupancies," lists fire-resistance rating requirements for separations between all occupancies.

- Other uses with mixed occupancy classifications must meet requirements based on one of the following separation conditions:
  - Mixed uses not separated by construction with a fire-resistance rating.
  - Mixed uses separated by construction with required fire-resistance ratings.

  Note: The following are cited as sources of requirements for the two separation conditions indicated above:
  302.3.2, "Nonseparated uses."
  302.3.3, "Separated uses."

302 Classification

302.3.2 Nonseparated uses

- Each area within a building is to have an occupancy classification based on use.
- Each building requires the most restrictive type of construction among the following:
  - That required based on limitations for each occupancy in the building as follows:
    Height limitations.
    Area limitations.
- Separations with a fire-resistance rating are not required between uses of mixed classification as follows:
  - Where not required by other provisions of the code.
- The following applies where mixed uses do not have separations with a fire-resistance rating:
  - In high-rise buildings, the following requirements govern the entire building:
    The most restrictive applicable high-rise provisions from among the mixed uses.
    The most restrictive fire-protection requirements from among the mixed uses.

  Note: Section 403, "High-Rise Buildings," contains provisions specific to such buildings.

  - In other buildings, each different use is governed by requirements specific to that use.

302.3.3 Separated uses *(part 1 of 15)*

This subsection applies where uses of mixed occupancy classifications are to be separated.

- Each area within a building is to have an occupancy classification based on use.
- Adjacent occupancies must be separated by construction as follows:
  - By one or both the following constructions with a fire-resistance rating specified herein:
    Fire barrier walls.
    Horizontal assemblies.
- Each fire area must comply with code requirements specific to its occupancy classification.
- Each fire area is required to meet height limitations based on the following:
  - Occupancy classification.
  - Construction type.

  Note: IBC Table 503, "Allowable Height and Building Areas," specifies height limitations based on occupancy and construction type.

- The sum of the following ratios in each story is required to be ≤ 1:
  - The area of each occupancy divided by its allowable area.
- The following applies to fire-resistance ratings for separations in sprinklered buildings:
  - Such rating is superseded by the rating required for floor construction based on construction type where the latter is higher.
- Occupancy H-1 separations are governed as follows:
  - A 4-hr fire-resistance rating is required for a separation subdividing an H-1 occupancy.

  Note: H-1 areas must be in a building separate and detached from other occupancies thus fire-resistance ratings for other than internal separation walls are not applicable.

Case study: Fig. 302.3.3. In order to separate the occupancy A-3 area (cafeteria and gymnasium) from the other occupancies in this building, a fire barrier is required at the perimter of the space. IBC Table 302.3.3 indicates that where A-3 is to be separated from E, such a barrier must have a 2-hr fire-resistance rating. The same rating is required for walls separating A-3 from B and S-2 occupancies which also occur in this plan. The gymnasium and cafeteria are separated from the adjacent B, S-2, and E occupancies by 2-hr walls. The A-3 space, therefore, is in its own fire area separate from the adjacent occupancies.

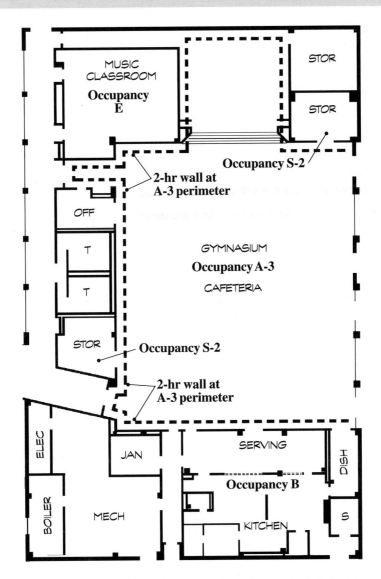

Fig. 302.3.3. Partial floor plan at cafeteria wing. New Jasper Pre-K–2nd Grade School. Jasper, Texas. PBK Architects, Inc. Houston, Texas.

302 Classification

302.3.3 Separated uses *(part 2 of 15)*

This part of the section governs fire-resistance ratings for separations of occupancy A.

- The following accessory spaces are not a separate occupancy from the area served:
  - A-3 assembly areas ≤ 750 sf.
  - Religious educational rooms with < 100 occupants.
  - Religious auditoriums with < 100 occupants.
  - Assembly spaces in occupancy E.
- A restaurant kitchen is not required to be separated from seating served.
- The table below shows separations required between A and the occupancies listed:

Table 302.3.3a   Occupancy A: Fire-Resistance Ratings for Occupancy Separations

Occupancies	Ratings in hrs
With sprinklers:	
A	1
B	1
E	1
F-1	2
F-2	1
H-2, H-5	4
H-3	3
H-4	2
I-1, I-3, I-4	1
I-2	2
M	1
R	1
S-1	2
S-2	1
U	1

A | 1 | A, B, E, F-2, I-1, I-3, I-4, M, R, S-2, U

A | 2 | F-1, H-4, I-2, S-1

A | 3 | H-3

A | 4 | H-2 H-5

Occupancies	Ratings in hrs
Without sprinklers:	
A	2
B	2
E	2
F-1	3
F-2	2
M	2
R	2
S-1	3
S-2	2
U	1

A | 1 | U

A | 2 | A, B, E, F-2, M, R, S-2

A | 3 | F-1 S-1

Source: IBC Table 302.3.3.

302 Classification

302.3.3 Separated uses *(part 3 of 15)*

This part of the section governs fire-resistance ratings for separations of occupancy B.

- Accessory storage areas with any of the following characteristics do not require separation from occupancy B:
  - Storage < 10% of floor area.
  - Storage < 1000 sf.
  - Storage with both the following:
    Area < 3000 sf.
    Area is sprinklered.
- The table below shows separations required between B and the occupancies listed:

Table 302.3.3b   **Occupancy B: Fire-Resistance Ratings for Occupancy Separations**

Occupancies	Ratings in hrs
With sprinklers:	
A	1
B	1
E	1
F-1	2
F-2	1
H-2	2
H-3, H-4, H-5	1
I-1, I-3, I-4	1
I-2	2
M	1
R	1
S-1	2
S-2	1
U	1

B — 1 — A, B, E, F-2, H-3, H-4, H-5, I-1, I-3, I-4, M, R, S-2, U

B — 2 — F-1, H-2, I-2, S-1

Occupancies	Ratings in hrs
Without sprinklers:	
A	2
B	2
E	2
F-1	3
F-2	2
M	2
R	2
S-1	3
S-2	2
U	1

B — 1 — U

B — 2 — A, B, E, F-2, M, R, S-2

B — 3 — F-1, S-1

Source: IBC Table 302.3.3.

302 Classification

302.3.3 Separated uses *(part 4 of 15)*

This part of the section governs fire-resistance ratings for separations of occupancy E.

- Accessory assembly uses in occupancy E are not separate occupancies.
- The table below shows separations required between E and the occupancies listed:

Table 302.3.3c   Occupancy E: Fire-Resistance for Occupancy Separations

Occupancies	Ratings in hrs
With sprinklers:	
A	1
B	1
E	1
F-1	2
F-2	1
H-2	4
H-3, H-5	3
H-4	2
I-1, I-3, I-4	1
I-2	2
M	1
R	1
S-1	2
S-2	1
U	1

E — 1 — A, B, E, F-2, I-1, I-3, I-4, M, R, S-2, U

E — 2 — F-1, H-4, I-2, S-1

E — 3 — H-3, H-5

E — 4 — H-2

Occupancies	Ratings in hrs
Without sprinklers:	
A	2
B	2
E	2
F-1	3
F-2	2
M	2
R	2
S-1	3
S-2	2
U	1

E — 1 — U

E — 2 — A, B, E, F-2, M, R, S-2

E — 3 — F-1, S-1

Source: IBC Table 302.3.3.

302 Classification

302.3.3 Separated uses *(part 5 of 15)*

This part of the section governs fire-resistance ratings for separations of occupancy F-1.

- The table below shows separations required between F-1 and the occupancies listed:

Table 302.3.3d   Occupancy F-1: Fire-Resistance Ratings for Occupancy Separations

Occupancies	Ratings in hrs
With sprinklers:	
A	2
B	2
E	2
F	2
H-2	2
H-3, H-4, H-5	1
I-1, I-3, I-4	2
I-2	3
M	2
R	2
S	2
U	2

Occupancies	Ratings in hrs
Without sprinklers:	
A	3
B	3
E	3
F	3
I	3
M	3
R	3
S	3
U	3

Source: IBC Table 302.3.3.

302 Classification

302.3.3 Separated uses *(part 6 of 15)*

This part of the section governs fire-resistance ratings for separations of occupancy F-2.

- The table below shows separations required between F-2 and the occupancies listed:

Table 302.3.3e   Occupancy F-2: Fire-Resistance Ratings for Occupancy Separations

Occupancies	Ratings in hrs
With sprinklers:	
A	1
B	1
E	1
F-1	2
F-2	1
H-2	2
H-3, H-4, H-5	1
I-1, I-3, I-4	1
I-2	2
M	1
R	1
S-1	2
S-2	1
U	1

F-2 | 1 | A, B, E, F-2, H-3, H-4, H-5, I-1, I-3, I-4, M, R, S-2, U

F-2 | 2 | F-1, H-2, I-2, S-1

Occupancies	Ratings in hrs
Without sprinklers:	
A	2
B	2
E	2
F-1	3
F-2	2
M	2
R	2
S-1	3
S-2	2
U	1

F-2 | 1 | U

F-2 | 2 | A, B, E, F-2, M, R, S-2

F-2 | 3 | F-1, S-1

Source: IBC Table 302.3.3.

302 Classification

302.3.3 Separated uses *(part 7 of 15)*

This part of the section governs fire-resistance ratings for separations of occupancies H-2 and H-3.

- The table below shows separations required between H-2 and the occupancies listed:

Table 302.3.3f   Occupancy H-2: Fire-Resistance Ratings for Occupancy Separations

Occupancies	Ratings in hrs
With sprinklers:	
A	4
B	2
E	4
F	2
H-2	4
H-3	1
H-4, H-5	2
I	4
M	2
R	4
S	2
U	1

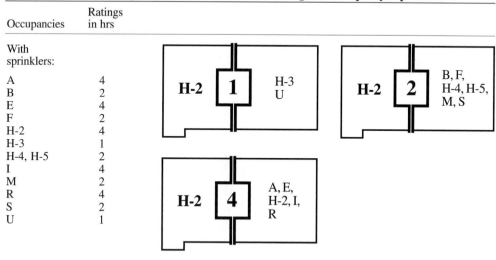

Source: IBC Table 302.3.3.

- The table below shows separations required between H-3 and the occupancies listed:

Table 302.3.3g   Occupancy H-3: Fire-Resistance Ratings for Occupancy Separations

Occupancies	Ratings in hrs
With sprinklers:	
A	3
B	1
E	3
F	1
H-3	3
H-2, H-4, H-5	1
I-1	4
I-2, I-3, I-4	3
M	1
R	3
S	1
U	1

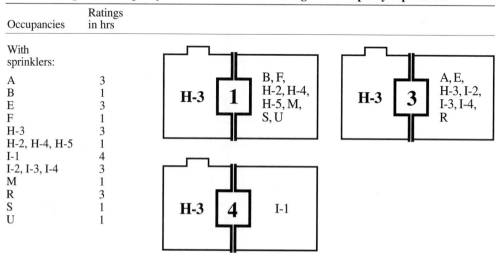

Source: IBC Table 302.3.3.

302 Classification

302.3.3 Separated uses *(part 8 of 15)*

This part of the section governs fire-resistance ratings for separations of occupancies H-4 and H-5.

- The table below shows separations required between H-4 and the occupancies listed:

Table 302.3.3h   Occupancy H-4: Fire-Resistance Ratings for Occupancy Separations

Occupancies	Ratings in hrs
With sprinklers:	
A	2
B	1
E	2
F	1
H-2, H-4	2
H-3, H-5	1
I	4
M	1
R	4
S	1
U	1

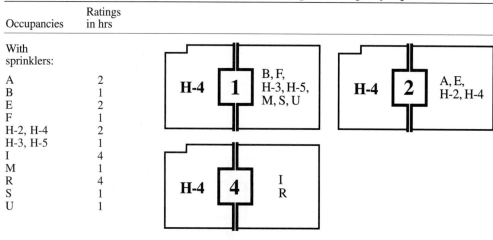

Source: IBC Table 302.3.3.

- The table below shows separations required between H-5 and the occupancies listed:

Table 302.3.3i   Occupancy H-5: Fire-Resistance Ratings for Occupancy Separations

Occupancies	Ratings in hrs
With sprinklers:	
A	4
B	1
E	3
F	1
H-2, H-5	2
H-3, H-4	1
I-1, I-2, I-3	4
I-4	3
M	1
R	4
S	1
U	3

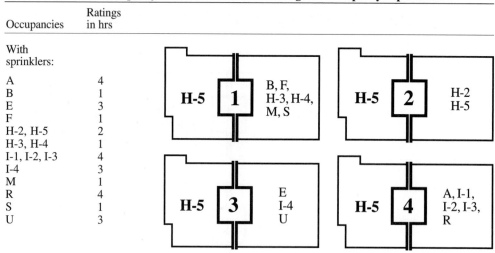

Source: IBC Table 302.3.3.

302 Classification

302.3.3 Separated uses *(part 9 of 15)*

This part of the section governs fire-resistance ratings for separations of occupancies I-1 and I-2.

- The table below shows separations required between I-1 and the occupancies listed:

Table 302.3.3j   **Occupancy I-1: Fire-Resistance Ratings for Occupancy Separations**

Occupancies	Ratings in hrs
With sprinklers:	
A	1
B	1
E	1
F-1	2
F-2	1
H-2, H-3, H-4, H-5	4
I-2	2
I-1, I-3, I-4	1
M	1
R	1
S-1	3
S-2	2
U	1

Source: IBC Table 302.3.3.

- The table below shows separations required between I-2 and the occupancies listed:

Table 302.3.3k   **Occupancy I-2: Fire-Resistance Ratings for Occupancy Separations**

Occupancies	Ratings in hrs
With sprinklers:	
A	2
B	2
E	2
F-1	3
F-2	2
H-3	3
H-2, H-4, H-5	4
I	2
M	2
R	2
S-1	3
S-2	2
U	1

Source: IBC Table 302.3.3.

302 Classification

302.3.3 Separated uses *(part 10 of 15)*

This part of the section governs fire-resistance ratings for separations of occupancies I-3 and I-4.

- The table below shows separations required between I-3 and the occupancies listed:

Table 302.3.3l   Occupancy I-3: Fire-Resistance Ratings for Occupancy Separations

Occupancies	Ratings in hrs
With sprinklers:	
A	1
B	1
E	1
F-1	2
F-2	1
H-3	3
H-2, H-4, H-5	4
I-1, I-3, I-4	1
I-2	2
M	1
R	1
S-1	2
S-2	1
U	1

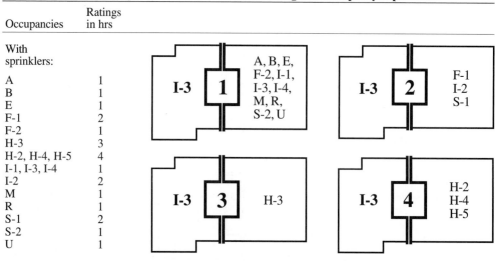

Source: IBC Table 302.3.3.

- The table below shows separations required between I-4 and the occupancies listed:

Table 302.3.3m   Occupancy I-4: Fire-Resistance Ratings for Occupancy Separations

Occupancies	Ratings in hrs
With sprinklers:	
A	1
B	1
E	1
F-1	2
F-2	1
H-2, H-4	4
H-3, H-5	3
I-2	2
I-1, I-3, I-4	1
M	1
R	1
S-1	2
S-2	1
U	1

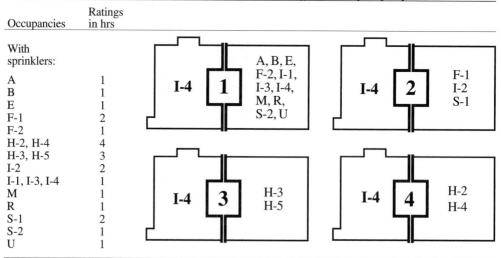

Source: IBC Table 302.3.3.

302 Classification

302.3.3 Separated uses *(part 11 of 15)*

This part of the section governs fire-resistance ratings for separations of occupancy M.

- Accessory storage areas with any of the following characteristics do not require separation from occupancy M:
  - Storage < 10% of floor area.
  - Storage < 1000 sf.
  - Storage with both the following:
    Area < 3000 sf.
    Area is sprinklered.
- The table below shows separations required between M and the occupancies listed:

Table 302.3.3n   Occupancy M: Fire-Resistance Ratings for Occupancy Separations

Occupancies	Ratings in hrs
With sprinklers:	
A	1
B	1
E	1
F-1	2
F-2	1
H-2	2
H-3, H-4, H-5	1
I-2	2
I-1, I-3, I-4	1
M	1
R	1
S-1	2
S-2	1
U	1

M | 1 | A, B, E, F-2, H-3, H-4, H-5, I-1, I-3, I-4, M, R, S-2, U

M | 2 | F-1, H-2, I-2, S-1

Occupancies	Ratings in hrs
Without sprinklers:	
A	2
B	2
E	2
F-1	3
F-2	2
M	2
R	2
S-1	3
S-2	2
U	1

M | 1 | U

M | 2 | A, B, E, F-2, M, R, S-2

M | 3 | F-1 S-1

Source: IBC Table 302.3.3.

302 Classification

302.3.3 Separated uses *(part 12 of 15)*

This part of the section governs fire-resistance ratings for separations of occupancy R.

- R-3 need not be separated from an occupancy U carport where the following applies:
  - The carport is 100% open on ≥ 2 sides and there is no enclosed use above the carport.
- R-3 and R-4 residences and their attics must be separated from a private garage as follows:
  - ≥ ½" gypsum board is required on garage side of wall.
  - Doors between residence and garage must be one of the following:
    - ≥ 1-³/₈" solid wood, solid steel, or honeycomb core steel door.
    - ≥ 20-minute-rated door assembly.
  - An opening between a sleeping room and a garage is not permitted.

  Note: 714.2.3, "Doors in corridors and smoke barriers," is cited as the source for additional door requirements.

- Ducts in a garage and ducts penetrating the walls or ceiling between a garage and a dwelling must be constructed of ≥ 26-gage sheet steel and may not open into the garage.
- The table below shows separations required between R and the occupancies listed:

Table 302.3.3o   Occupancy R: Fire-Resistance Ratings for Occupancy Separations

Occupancies	Ratings in hrs
With sprinklers:	
A	1
B	1
E	1
F-1	2
F-2	1
H-2, H-4, H-5	4
H-3	3
I-2	2
I-1, I-3, I-4	1
M	1
R	1
S-1	2
S-2	1
U	1
Without sprinklers:	
A	2
B	2
E	2
F-1	3
F-2	2
M	2
R	2
S-1	3
S-2	2
U	1

Source: IBC Table 302.3.3.

302 Classification

302.3.3 Separated uses *(part 13 of 15)*

This part of the section governs fire-resistance ratings for separations of occupancy S-1.

- Occupancy separation is not required for incidental storage areas in occupancy B or M if any of the following conditions apply:
  - Storage is < 10% of floor area.
  - Storage area is < 1000 sf.
  - Storage with both the following:
    Area < 3000 sf.
    Area is sprinklered.
- The table below shows separations required between S-1 and the occupancies listed:

Table 302.3.3p   Occupancy S-1: Fire-Resistance Ratings for Occupancy Separations

Occupancies	Ratings in hrs
With sprinklers:	
A	2
B	2
E	2
F	2
H-2	2
H-3, H-4, H-5	1
I-1, I-2	3
I-3, I-4	2
M	2
R	2
S	2
U	2
Without sprinklers:	
A	3
B	3
E	3
F	3
M	3
R	3
S	3
U	3

With sprinklers:

S-1 | 1 | H-3 H-4 H-5

S-1 | 2 | A, B, E, F, H-2, I-3, I-4, M, R, S, U

S-1 | 3 | I-1 I-2

Without sprinklers:

S-1 | 3 | A, B, E, F, M, R, S, U

Source: IBC Table 302.3.3.

302 Classification

302.3.3 Separated uses *(part 14 of 15)*

This part of the section governs fire-resistance ratings for separations of occupancy S-2.

- Occupancy separation is not required for incidental storage areas in occupancy B or M if any of the following conditions apply:
  - Storage is < 10% of floor area.
  - Storage area is < 1000 sf.
  - Storage with both the following:
    Area < 3000 sf.
    Area is sprinklered.
- Separation for areas used for private or pleasure vehicles may be reduced by 1 hr.
- The table below shows separations required between S-2 and the occupancies listed:

Table 302.3.3q   Occupancy S-2: Fire-Resistance Ratings for Occupancy Separations

Occupancies	Ratings in hrs
With sprinklers:	
A	1
B	1
E	1
F-1	2
F-2	1
H-2	2
H-3, H-4, H-5	1
I-1, I-2	2
I-3, I-4	1
M	1
R	1
S-1	2
S-2	1
U	1

S-2 — 1 — A, B, E, F-2, H-3, H-4, H-5, I-3, I-4, M, R, S-2, U

S-2 — 2 — F-1, H-2, I-1, I-2, S-1

Without sprinklers:	
A	2
B	2
E	2
F-1	3
F-2	2
M	2
R	2
S-1	3
S-2	2
U	1

S-2 — 1 — U

S-2 — 2 — A, B, E, F-2, M, R, S-2

S-2 — 3 — F-1, S-1

Source: IBC Table 302.3.3.

302 Classification

302.3.3 Separated uses *(part 15 of 15)*

This part of the section governs fire-resistance ratings for separations of occupancy U.

- An occupancy U carport is not required to be separated from R-3 where both the following conditions apply:
    - The carport is 100% open on ≥ 2 sides.
    - There is no enclosed use above the carport.
- The table below shows separations required between U and the occupancies listed:

Table 302.3.3r   Occupancy U: Fire-Resistance Ratings for Occupancy Separations

Occupancies	Ratings in hrs
With sprinklers:	
A	1
B	1
E	1
F-1	2
F-2	1
H-2, H-3, H-4	1
H-5	3
I	1
M	1
R	1
S-1	2
S-2	1
U	1
Without sprinklers:	
A	1
B	1
E	1
F-1	3
F-2	1
M	1
R	1
S-1	3
S-2	1
U	1

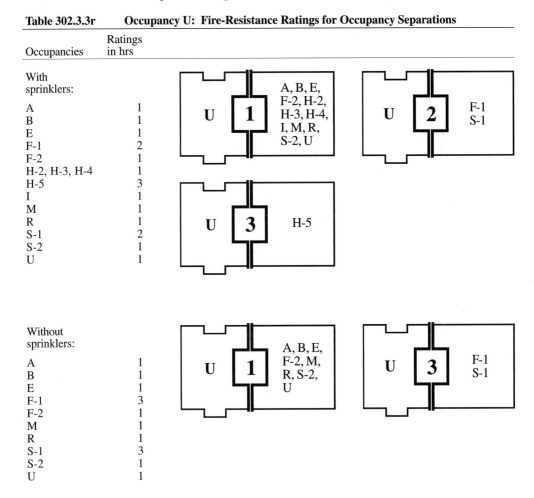

Source: IBC Table 302.3.3.

303 Assembly Group A

303.1 Assembly Group A *(part 1 of 2)*

- Buildings or parts of buildings where people gather for activities such as the following:
  Civic.
  Religious.
  Waiting for transportation.
  Social.
  Recreation.
  Consumption of food or drink.
- A gathering space is part of the occupancy served where both the following apply:
  - The gathering space has < 50 occupants.
  - The gathering space is accessory to the occupancy served.
- Assembly spaces are divided into the following designations:
  - A-1:
    For the production and viewing of the following:
      Performing arts.
      Motion pictures.
    Includes the following building types among others:
      Theaters and movie theaters.
      Television studios with audience seating.
      Radio studios with audience seating.
    Typically with fixed seating.
  - A-2:
    For the consumption of food and/or drink.
    Includes the following building types among others:
      Banquet halls.
      Taverns and bars.
      Night clubs.
      Restaurants.

303 Assembly Group A

303.1 Assembly Group A *(part 2 of 2)*

- A-3:
  - For the following functions:
    - Worship.
    - Recreation.
    - Amusement.
    - Gatherings not assigned to other assembly categories.
  - Includes the following building types among others:
    - Amusement arcades.
    - Funeral parlors.
    - Art galleries.
    - Gymnasiums.
    - Auditoriums.
    - Indoor swimming pools.
    - Bowling alleys.
    - Indoor tennis courts.
    - Churches.
    - Lecture halls.
    - Community halls.
    - Libraries.
    - Courtrooms.
    - Museums.
    - Dance halls.
    - Passenger waiting areas.
    - Exhibition halls.
    - Pool and billiard parlors.
- A-4:
  - Spaces for viewing indoor sporting activities with spectator seating, including the following:
    - Arenas.
    - Skating rinks.
    - Swimming pools.
    - Tennis courts.
- A-5:
  - For the following functions:
    - Participating in outdoor activities.
    - Viewing outdoor activities.
  - Includes the following building types among others:
    - Amusement park structures.
    - Bleachers.
    - Grandstands.
    - Stadiums.

304 Business Group B

304.1 Business Group B

- Includes buildings or parts of buildings used for the following:
  - Offices.
  - Professional transactions.
  - Service transactions.
  - Storage of records.
  - Storage of accounts.

- Includes the following building types among others:
  - Airport traffic control towers.
  - Electronic data processing.
  - Animal hospital, kennel.
  - Engineer's office.
  - Animal pound.
  - Fire station.
  - Architect's office.
  - Laboratories, testing and research.
  - Attorney's office.
  - Laundry pick-up/drop off.
  - Bank.
  - Laundry, self-service.
  - Barber shop.
  - Motor vehicle showroom.
  - Beauty shop.
  - Physician's office.
  - Car wash.
  - Print shop.
  - Civic administration.
  - Police station.
  - Clinic, outpatient.
  - Post Office.
  - Dentist.
  - Professional services.
  - Dry cleaning pick-up/drop off.
  - Radio station.
  - Dry cleaning, self service.
  - Telephone exchange.
  - Educational functions above 12th grade.
  - TV station.

Case study: Fig. 304.1. Because people gather in the conference room of the architect's office, it must be determined whether or not the space is to be designated as a business occupancy like the office in general or as an assembly occupancy. This is done by computing the number of occupants based on the use of the space, which is assembly in nature. According to IBC Table 1003.2.2.2, 15 sf per occupant are assigned for an assembly use having tables and chairs. This yields an occupant load of 19 for the room. Subsection 303.1 indicates that an accessory gathering space with < 50 occupants is considered to be same occupancy as that served. The conference room is designated, therefore, as occupancy B and must comply with means of egress requirements for a business.

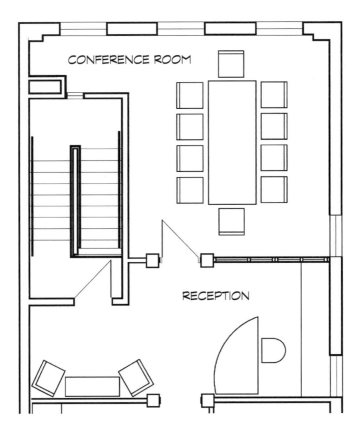

Fig. 304.1. Partial floor plan. Alterations to 209 Main Street, Annapaolis, Maryland. Alt Breeding Schwarz Architects, LLC. Annapolis, Maryland.

305 Educational Group E

305.1 Educational Group E

- Includes buildings or parts of buildings used as follows:
  - Buildings with both the following characteristics:
    - Serving 12th grade and lower.
    - Serving ≥ 6 people at one time.

305.2 Day care

- Occupancy E includes buildings or parts of buildings serving the following purposes with all the characteristics listed below:
  - Purposes:
    - Educational.
    - Supervisory.
    - Personal care.
  - Characteristics of services:
    - Serving > 5 children.
    - Serving children > 2½ years old.

306 Factory Group F

306.1 Factory Industrial Group F

- Includes buildings or parts of buildings used for any of the following functions, which are not classified as occupancy H:
  - Assembling.
  - Disassembling.
  - Fabricating.
  - Finishing.
  - Manufacturing.
  - Packaging.
  - Repair.
  - Processing operations.

306.2 Factory Industrial F-1 Moderate-Hazard Occupancy

- Includes factory and industrial functions not classified as F-2: Low Hazard including the following:

Aircraft	Recreational vehicles
Publishing	Athletic equipment
Bicycles	Rug making
Automobiles	Business machines
Bakeries	Boat fabrication
Electronics	Alcoholic beverages
Brushes	Motor vehicles
Rug cleaning	Photographic film
Brooms	Dry cleaning
Disinfectants	Construction and agricultural machinery
Dyeing	Food processing
Jute products	Musical instruments
Metals	Hemp products
Shoes	Cameras and Photo equipment
Printing	Canvas and fabric similar to canvas
Power houses	Leather products
Upholstering	Photographic equipment
Clothing	Optical products
Carpet making	Refuse incineration
Appliances	Cabinet making and door and sash millwork
Machinery	Engine manufacaturing and rebuilding
Trailers	Paper mills and paper products
Electric light plants	Soap and detergent
Furniture	Carpet cleaning
Textiles	TV and motion picture production
Laundries	Plastic products
Tobacco	Wood distillation

306 Factory Group F

306.3 Factory Industrial F-2 Low-Hazard Occupancy

- Includes factory and industrial functions as follows:
  - Use of noncombustible materials in the following:
    Manufacturing.
    Fabrication.
  - Does not cause a significant fire hazard in the following:
    Processing.
    Finishing.
    Packing.
  - Includes the following product types and processes:
    Nonalcoholic beverages.
    Ceramic products.
    Gypsum.
    Metal product fabrication.
    Brick and masonry.
    Foundries.
    Metal product assembly.
    Glass products.
    Ice.

307 High-Hazard Group H

307.1 Hazardous Group H

- Includes buildings or parts of buildings where materials of the following type are used as listed and are in the quantities indicated below:
  - Materials:
    Materials that pose a physical hazard.
    Materials that pose a health hazard.
  - Material use:
    Manufacturing.
    Processing.
    Generation of materials.
    Storage.
  - Quantities:
    In excess of limits defining significant hazard.

    Note: The following tables are cited as listing limits of hazardous materials.
        IBC Table 307.7(1), "Maximum Allowable Quantity Per Control Area of Hazardous Materials Posing a Physical Hazard."
        IBC Table 307.7(2), "Maximum Allowable Quantity Per Control Area of Hazardous Material Posing a Health Hazard."

307.3 Group H-1 structures

- Buildings containing detonation hazards.

  Note: The following common substances are in this category among others:

Initiating explosives	*Black powder*
Pellet powder	*Dynamite*
Detonating cord	*Ammunition*
Detonators	*Safety fuses*
Display fireworks	*Igniter fireworks*
Igniter cord	*TNT*
Nitroglycerine	

307.4 Group H-2 structures

- Buildings containing materials subject to the following hazards:
  - Extreme accelerated burning hazard.
  - Extremely rapid oxidation.

  Note: The following common substances are in this category among others:

Sawdust	*Coal dust*
Flour	*Grain dust*
Fertilizer dust	*Paper dust*
Plastic dust	*Cornstarch*
Cork dust	*Hydrogen*
Methane	*Carbon monoxide*

307 High-Hazard Group H

307.5 Group H-3 structures

- Buildings containing materials that readily support combustion.

    Note: The following common substances are in this category among others:

Excelsior	*Printing products*
Ozone	*Room freshener*
Defensive sprays	*Spray deodorant*
Magnesium	*Lacquer spray*
LP gas	*Insecticide spray*
Spray lubricants	*Spray cleaners*
Cocoa fiber	*Spray glass cleaner*
Spray paint	*Wastepaper*
Hair spray	*Bug spray*
Sulfur	*Consumer fireworks*
Butane	*Cotton*
Sisal	*Jute*
Hemp	*Rags*
Cloth	*Hay*
Straw	*Oxygen*

307.6 Group H-4 structures

- Buildings containing health hazards.

    Note: The following common substances are in this category among others:

Paint remover	*Battery acid*
Bleach	*Radioactive materials*
Lime	*Cement*
Iodine	*Calcium chloride*
Salts	*Fertilizer*
Ammonia	*Drain cleaner*
Pesticides	*Weed killer*
Oven cleaner	

307.7 Group H-5 structures

- Buildings containing the following:
  - Semiconductor fabrication.
  - Semiconductor research and development.
  - Hazardous production materials (HPM) including certain categories of the following:
    Flammable liquids.
    Combustible liquids.

307 High-Hazard Group H

307.9 Exceptions *(part 1 of 3)*

This subsection addresses buildings and parts of buildings containing hazardous materials that do not warrant an occupancy H classification.

- Materials in any quantity listed in this section must comply with the following:
  - They require the occupancy classification most compatible with their handling.
  - They must comply with applicable code requirements.

  Note: The following are cited as sources of applicable requirements:
  Section 414, "Hazardous Materials," and other pertinent sections of the IBC.
  International Fire Code.

- Buildings with quantities of hazardous materials < the limits defining a significant hazard.

  Note: The following tables are cited as defining limits of hazardous materials.
  IBC Table 307.7(1), "Maximum Allowable Quantity Per Control Area of
  Hazardous Materials Posing a Physical Hazard."
  IBC Table 307.7(2) , "Maximum Allowable Quantity Per Control Area of
  Hazardous Material Posing a Health Hazard."
  The International Fire Code is also cited as governing these materials.

- Buildings with control areas housing quantities of hazardous materials that are < the limits defining a significant hazard.

  Note: 414.2, "Control areas," is cited as providing requirements for such areas.

- Buildings housing the application of flammable finishes.

  Note: The following are included among others: flammable or combustible paint, varnish,
  lacquer, stain, fiberglass resins or other liquids applied by spray or dip tank;
  combustible powders applied by spray, electrostatic processes, or fluidized beds;
  dual-component coatings or flammable and combustible liquids applied by brush
  or roller in amounts > 1 gallon.
  The following are cited as governing these processes:
  Section 416, "Application of Flammable Finishes."
  NFPA 33, "Spray Application Using Flammable and Combustible Materials."
  NFPA 34, "Dipping and Coating Processes Using Flammable or Combustible
  Liquid."
  International Fire Code.

- Occupancy M storage and sale of flammable and combustible liquids.

  Note: The following are cited as governing these liquids:
  NFPA 30, " Flammable and Combustible Liquids Code."
  International Fire Code.

307 High-Hazard Group H

307.9 Exceptions *(part 2 of 3)*

- Building housing flammable or combustible liquids or gasses in closed systems for operating the following:
  - Machinery.
  - Equipment.
- Cleaning places using combustible liquid solvents of specified flash points and as follows:
  - Combustible solvents are contained in closed systems.
  - Equipment is listed by an approved testing agency.
  - The area is separated from the rest of the building as follows:
    By construction with a fire-resistance rating ≥ 1 hr.
- Cleaning places using combustible liquid solvents with specified flash points higher than the previous case.
- Distributors and stores selling liquor as follows:
  - No bulk storage.
- Buildings housing refrigeration systems.
- Storage or use of agricultural materials as follows:
  - Used on the property where stored.
- Buildings housing stationary batteries as follows:
  - Where used for any of the following:
    Facility emergency power.
    Uninterruptable power supply.
    Telecommunication facilities.
  - Where batteries comply with all the following:
    Batteries must have safety venting caps.
    Ventilation is provided.

  Note: International Mechanical Code is cited as governing ventilation requirements for the batteries.

- Buildings housing the following substances that are otherwise health hazards in occupancy H-4 are not designated as such where they have characteristics and applications as indicated below:
  - Substances:
    Corrosives.
    Irritants.
    Sensitizers.
  - Applications:
    Contained within common building materials.
    Used in retail display.
  - Characteristics as applicable:
    Personal products in their original packaging.
    Household products in their original packaging.

307 High-Hazard Group H

307.9 Exceptions *(part 3 of 3)*

- Buildings used for aerosol manufacturing are to be classified as follows as applicable and where conforming to pertinent standards:
  - F-1.
  - S-1.

    Note: The following standards are cited as governing this aerosol manufacturing:
    NFPA 30B, "Manufacture and Storage of Aerosol Products."
    International Fire Code.

- Buildings housing the display and storage of the following hazardous materials where the conditions listed below apply:
  - Materials:
    Nonflammable solid materials.
    Nonflammable liquids.
    Noncombustible liquids.
  - Conditions:
    Quantities are < than the limits defining significant hazard.
    In one of the following occupancies:
      M, S.

    Note: The following are cited as defining limits of hazardous materials.
    IBC Table 307.7(1), "Maximum Allowable Quantity Per Control Area of
    Hazardous Materials Posing a Physical Hazard."
    IBC Table 307.7(2), "Maximum Allowable Quantity Per Control Area of
    Hazardous Material Posing a Health Hazard."
    414.2.4, "Hazardous material in Group M display and storage areas and in
    Group S storage areas," is cited as governing these materials.

- Storage of materials as follows:
  - Industrial explosives in the following occupancies:
    B, F, M, S.
  - The following materials in the occupancies indicated below:
    Materials:
      Black powder.
      Smokeless propellant.
      Small arms primers.
    Occupancy:
      M, R-3.

    Note: The International Fire Code is cited as the governing quantity limits and other
    requirements for the explosive materials.

308 Institutional Group I

308.1 Institutional Group I

- Includes buildings or parts of buildings where occupants are physically limited as follows:
  - Occupants are served for the following due to health or age:
    Medical treatment.
    Other care.
    Other treatment.
  - Occupants are housed for penal or correctional purposes as follows:
    Occupants are detained.
    Liberty of occupants is restricted.

308.2 Group I-1

- Includes buildings or parts of buildings wherein people live in a residential environment as follows:
  - $\leq$ 16 occupants are housed for reasons related to the following:
    Age.
    Mental disability.
    Other reasons.
  - Occupants are able to respond to an emergency without physical assistance.
  - Personal care services are provided on the following basis:
    Occupants are supervised.
    Services are provided 24 hrs a day.
  - Facility types among others in this category:
    Residential board and care facilities.
    Assisted living facilities.
    Halfway houses.
    Group homes.
    Congregate care facilities.
    Social rehabilitation facilities.
    Alcohol and drug centers.
    Convalescent facilities.
- Similar facilities as follows are not classified as occupancy I-1:
  - Facilities with $\leq$ 5 people are classified as occupancy R-3.
  - Facilities with $\geq$ 6 people and $\leq$ 16 people are classified as occupancy R-4.

308 Institutional Group I

308.3 Group I-2

- Includes buildings or parts of buildings used for medical related purposes as follows:
  - Functions:
    Medical.
    Surgical.
    Psychiatric.
    Nursing.
    Custodial care.
  - Characteristics:
    > 5 persons are housed.
    Clients are housed 24 hrs a day.
    Clients are not capable of self-preservation.
  - Facility types include the following:
    Hospitals.
    Intermediate care nursing homes.
    Skilled care nursing homes.
    Mental hospitals.
    Detoxification facilities.
- Similar facilities are not classified as occupancy I-2 as follows:
  - Facilities serving $\leq$ 5 persons are classified as occupancy R-3.

308.3.1 Child care facility

- I-2 includes child care facilities as follows:
  - Care is provided 24 hrs a day.
  - > 5 children are served.
  - Children are $\leq$ 2-½ years old.

308.4 Group I-3

- Includes buildings wherein occupants are restrained for security purposes as follows:
  - > 5 restrained occupants.
  - Occupants are not capable of self-preservation due to security measures.
  - Facility types among others include the following:
    Prisons.
    Jails.
    Reformatories.
    Detention centers.
    Correctional centers.
    Prerelase centers.
  - Occupancy I-3 is subdivided into 5 conditions as follows:
    Degree of restraint is increased with each higher condition number.

308 Institutional Group I

308.4.1 Condition 1

This subsection addresses the least restrained condition of occupancy I-3.

- Includes buildings wherein detainees may move freely without restraint to the exterior from the following areas:
  - Sleeping areas.
  - Other spaces where detainees are permitted.
- Such buildings may be constructed as occupancy R.

308.4.2 Condition 2

This subsection addresses the occupancy I-3 condition of restraint at the next higher level above that of condition 1.

- Includes buildings in which detainees may move freely to ≥ 1 smoke compartments from the following areas:
  - Sleeping areas.
  - Other smoke compartments where detainees are permitted.
- Free egress to the exterior is prevented by locked exits.

308.4.3 Condition 3

This subsection addresses the occupancy I-3 condition of restraint at the next higher level above that of condition 2.

- Includes buildings in which detainees may move freely within individual smoke compartments such as the following:
  - A residential unit containing the following:
    Individual sleeping rooms.
    Group activity spaces.
- Egress between smoke compartments is impeded by remote-controlled locks.

308.4.4 Condition 4

This section addresses the occupancy I-3 condition of restraint at the next higher level above that of condition 3.

- Includes buildings in which movement between spaces occupied by detainees is restricted by remote-controlled locks as follows:
  - From the following within a smoke compartment:
    Sleeping areas.
    Activity spaces.
    Other spaces occupied by detainees.
  - Between smoke compartments.

308 Institutional Group I

308.4.5 Condition 5

This section addresses the most restrained condition of occupancy I-3.

- Includes buildings in which movement between occupied spaces is restricted by manual-release locks as follows:
  - From the following within a smoke compartment:
    - Sleeping areas.
    - Activity spaces.
    - Other spaces occupied by detainees.
  - Between smoke compartments.

308.5 Group I-4, day care facilities

- Care during religious functions at places of worship are not governed by this section.
- Buildings wherein persons receive custodial care as follows:
  - Occupants served may be of any age.
  - Care is < 24 hrs/day.
  - Care is by individuals other than the following:
    - Parents.
    - Guardians.
    - Relatives by blood.
    - Relatives by marriage.
    - Relatives by adoption.
  - Care is at a location other than the home of person receiving care.
- Similar facilities caring for ≤ 5 persons is classified as occupancy R-3.

308.5.1 Adult care facility

- A facility providing supervision and personal care for adults as follows:
  - Care is provided < 24 hrs/day.
  - Care is provided for > 5 adults.
  - Adults are unrelated.

308.5.2 Child care facility

- Day care service is classified as occupancy I-4 where the following apply:
  - Care is provided < 24 hrs/day.
  - Care is provided for > 5 children.
  - Children cared for are ≤ 2½ years old.
- Day care service is classified as occupancy E where all the following apply:
  - Care is provided < 24 hrs/day.
  - Care is provided for > 5 children.
  - Care is provided for ≤ 100 children.
  - Children cared for are ≤ 2½ years old.
  - Child-care rooms are on level of exit discharge.
  - Each child-care room has an exit door directly to the outside.

309 Mercantile Group M

309.1 Mercantile Group M

- Includes buildings or parts of buildings used for the display and sale of merchandise as follows:
  - Involves stocks of the following incidental items accessed by the public:
    Goods.
    Wares.
    Merchandise.
  - Includes the following functions:
    Department stores.
    Drug stores.
    Markets.
    Motor vehicle service stations.
    Retail stores.
    Wholesale stores.
    Sales rooms.

309.2 Quantity of hazardous materials

This section addresses hazardous materials stored or displayed in an occupancy M control area.

- The total amount of the following hazardous materials must be within permitted limits:
  - Nonflammable solids.
  - Nonflammable liquids.
  - Noncombustible liquids.

Note: *IBC Table 414.2.4, "Maximum Allowable Quantity Per Indoor and Outdoor Control Area in Group M and S Occupancies: Nonflammable Solids and Nonflammable and Noncombustible Liquids," is cited as listing quantity limitations.*

310 Residential Group R

310.1 Residential Group "R"

- Includes buildings or parts of buildings with sleeping accommodations as follows:
  - Those not classified as occupancy I.
- Residential spaces are divided into the following designations:
  - R-1:

    Buildings where residents are primarily transient as follows:

    Stay is < 30 days.

    Includes the following building types:

    Hotels.

    Motels.

    Transient boarding houses.
  - R-2:

    Buildings with > 2 dwelling units.

    Where residents are primarily permanent.

    Includes the following building types:

    Apartment houses.

    Dormitories.

    Fraternities.

    Sororities.

    Monasteries.

    Permanent boarding houses.

    Convents.
  - R-3:

    Buildings with ≤ 2 dwelling units.

    Residents are primarily permanent.

    Not classified as any of the following:

    R-1, R-2, I.

    Includes day care facilities as follows:

    Care is provided for ≤ 5 persons.

    Care is for persons of any age.

    Care provided < 24 hrs/day.
  - R-4:

    Residential Care /Assisted Living Facilities as follows:

    Number of residents served is > 5 and ≤ 16.

    Must meet height and area limitations based on the following:

    Occupancy.

    Type of construction.

    Otherwise, R-4 must meet the same construction requirements as does R-3.

Note: Section 503, "General Height and Area Limitations," is cited as governing these characteristics of R-4 buildings.

311 Storage Group S

311.1 Storage Group S

- Includes buildings or parts of buildings used for storage that are not classified as occupancy H.

311.2 Moderate-hazard storage, Group S-1

- Includes storage not classified as S-2.
- Includes the following types of storage:

Rattan	Furniture
Buttons	Burlap bags
Canvas belting	Books
Aircraft	Baskets
Paper bags	Leather belting
Boots	Bamboo
Shoes	Paper in rolls
Cardboard boxes	Glue
Cloth bags	Cordage
Wax candles	Paper in packs
Furs	Leather
Mucilage	Cardboard
Tobacco products	Grain
Linoleum	Horn
Woolen apparel	Noncelluloid combs
Paste	Lumber
Silk	Photo engraving
Resilient flooring	Sugar
Upholstery	Soap
Mattresses	Bulk tire storage

- Includes petroleum warehouses storing lubricating oils over a specified flash point.
- Includes motor vehicle repair garages containing limited hazardous materials.

  Note: The following are cited as governing repair garages:
  IBC Table 307.7(1), "Maximum Allowable Quantity Per Control Area of Hazardous Materials Posing a Physical Hazard."
  406.6, "Repair garages."

311 Storage Group S

311.3 Low-hazard storage, Group S-2

- Includes the storage of noncombustible materials as follows:
  - Packaging allowed for stored materials includes the following:
    On wood pallets.
    In paper cartons with single thickness divisions.
    In paper wrappings.
    In paper cartons without divisions.

  - Characteristics of all stored products:
    A negligible amount of the following plastic trim materials is allowed:
    Knobs.
    Handles.
    Film wrapping.
  - Items allowed to be stored, among others, are as follows:

Empty glass bottles	Frozen foods
Washers and dryers	Glass
Cement in bags	Gypsum board
Crayons	Metals
Electrical motors	Soapstones
Mirrors	Meats
Dry cell batteries	Food products
Pottery	Stoves
Electrical coils	Empty cans
Talc	Chalk
Open parking garages	Metal cabinets
Porcelain	Ivory
Closed parking garages	Inert pigments

Beer or wine ≤ 12% alcohol in metal, glass, and ceramic containers.
Dairy products in nonwaxed coated paper containers.
Foods in noncombustible containers.
Foods in noncombustible containers.
Fresh vegetables in nonplastic containers.
Fresh fruits in nonplastic containers.
Metal desks with plastic tops and trim.
Noncombustible liquids in glass bottles.
Oil-filled distribution transformers.
Other distribution transformers.

312 Utility and Miscellaneous Group U

312.1 General

- Occupancy U includes the following types of buildings and structures:
  - Accessory buildings.
  - Miscellaneous buildings not classified in another occupancy.
  - Building types and structures include the following:
    Agricultural buildings.
    Barns.
    Carports.
    Fences > 6' high.
    Stables.
    Tanks.
    Towers.
    Livestock shelters.
    Private garages.
    Greenhouses.
    Sheds.
  - Aircraft hangars are included as follows:
    Where accessory to a 1- or 2-family residence.

    Note: 412.3, "Residential aircraft hangars," is cited as governing these structures.

  - Grain silos are included as follows:
    Where accessory to a building in occupancy R.

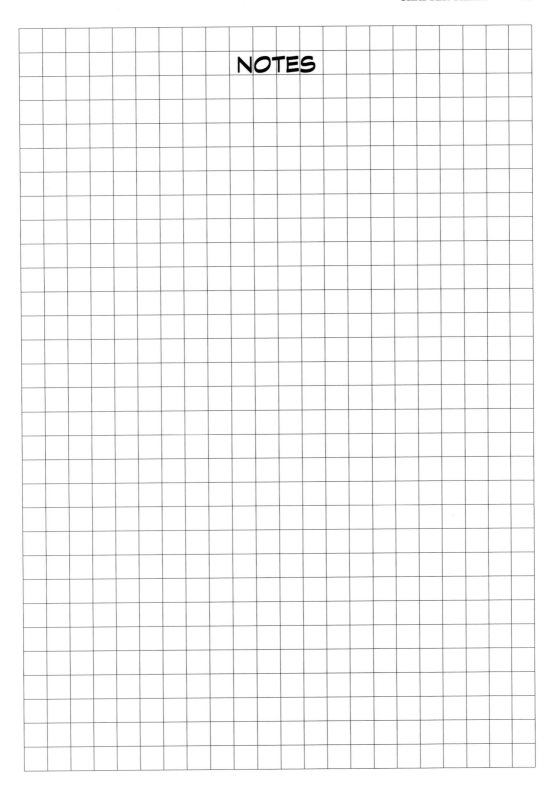

NOTES

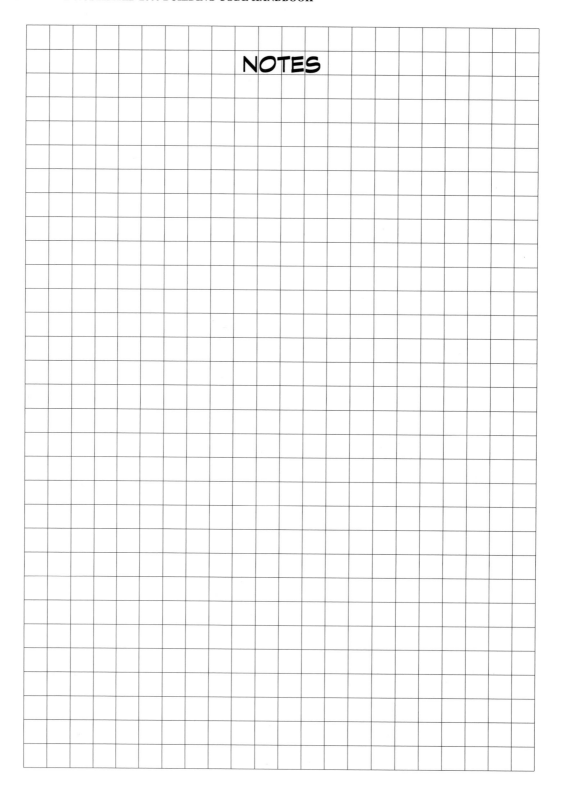

NOTES

4

Special Detailed Requirements Based on Use and Occupancy

Glad Tidings Assembly of God Church. Naticoke, Pennsylvania.
Mullins and Weida, Architect and Associate. Bear Creek, Pennsylvania.

402 Covered Mall Buildings

402.1 Scope

- This section does not apply to foyers and lobbies in the following occupancies:
  B, R-1, R-2.
- Otherwise, this section applies to covered mall buildings where both of the following apply:
  - Building is ≤ 3 floor levels at every location.
  - Building is ≤ 3 stories above grade.
- Covered mall buildings are required to meet one of the following sets of requirements:
  - Applicable sections of the code in total excluding this section.
  - This section plus applicable sections of the code other than those addressed by this section.

402.2 Definitions

- **Anchor building**
  - Located on the exterior perimeter of the mall building.
  - Is in an occupancy other than H.
  - Has direct access to a covered mall building.
  - Has required means of egress separate from the mall.

- **Covered mall building**
  - A single building housing tenants similar to the following types:
    Retail stores.
    Eating and drinking establishments.
    Entertainment and amusement facilities.
    Passenger transportation terminals.
    Offices.
    Similar functions.
  - ≥ 2 tenants have a main entrance into ≥ 1 mall areas.
  - Anchor buildings are not part of the covered mall building.

- **Food court**
  - A public seating area in the mall area.
  - Serves adjcent tenants that provide food preparation.

- **Gross leasable area**
  - Total floor area for tenant occupancy including tenant storage.
  - Area of tenant occupancy is measured to the following:
    To the outside of an individual tenant's walls.
    To the centerline of shared tenant walls.

- **Mall**
  - Covered common pedestrian area in a covered mall building.
  - Provides access for ≥ 2 tenants.
  - Has ≤ 3 levels open to each other.

402 Covered Mall Buildings

402.4 Means of egress

- Means of egress is required for the spaces listed below:
  - Each tenant space.
  - The covered mall building.
- Means of egress must comply with both of the following:
  - This section.
  - The code.
- Means of egress requirements of this section govern in the following case:
  - Where they conflict with requirements of other code sections.

402.4.1 Determination of occupant load

- Occupant load allowed in a tenant space is governed by the code.
- Means of egress requirements for a tenant space is based on the permitted occupant load of the space.

402.4.1.1 Occupant formula

This subsection addresses occupant load for means of egress in a covered mall building.

- The square feet required per occupant is calculated by the equation below as follows:
  - Gross leasable area does not include anchor buildings:

  Sf required per person = (0.00007 × gross leasable area in sf) + 25

  Note: Occupant load = gross leasable area ÷ sf required per person.

402.4.1.2 OLF range

This subsection addresses the range permitted for square feet per occupant as calculated for various sizes of covered mall buildings.

- The sf required per person in covered mall buildings must be ≤ 50.
- 30 sf per occupant may be used where the sf required per person is calculated to be < 30.

402.4.1.3 Anchor buildings

- The occupant load of a covered mall building does not include the following:
  - The occupant load of anchor buildings opening into the mall.

402.4.1.4 Food courts

- The occupant load of a food court is determined by requirements elsewhere in the code.
  Note: Section 1003, "Means of Egress," is cited as the source of requirements.
- The occupant load of the food court is added to the occupant load of the covered mall building as derived from gross leasable area.

402 Covered Mall Buildings

402.4.2 Number of means of egress

This section addresses tenant spaces in covered mall buildings.

- ● ≥ 2 means of egress are required in either of the following cases:
  - ○ Travel distance for other than employees from any point in a tenant space to the mall > 75'.
  - ○ Tenant space has an occupant load > 50.

402.4.3 Arrangements of means of egress

This subsection addresses assembly spaces in covered mall buildings.

- ● Assembly spaces with occupant loads ≥ 500 are governed as follows:
  - ○ Entrance to assembly space must be immediately adjacent to a main entrance of the mall.
  - ○ ≥ ½ the required means of egress for the assembly space must open directly to outside the mall building.

402.4.3.1 Anchor building means of egress

- ● The required means of egress for an anchor building is governed as follows:
  - ○ It must be separate from the means of egress for the mall.
- ● Means of egress requirements for the mall do not include the following:
  - ○ The occupant load of anchor buildings that open into the mall.
- ● Mall means of egress may not pass through anchor buildings.
- ● A mall terminating at an anchor building is a dead end in the following circumstance:
  - ○ Where at the termination there is no means of egress independent from the anchor building.

402.4.4 Distance to exits

This subsection addresses travel distance in a covered mall building.

- ● Travel distance must be ≤ 200' in the following cases:
  - ○ From any point in a tenant space to the mall.
  - ○ From any point in a tenant space to an exit.
  - ○ From any point in a mall to an exit.

402.4.5 Access to exits

- ● Dead ends are permitted in malls in the following case:
  - ○ Where dead-end length is ≤ 2 × its width at the narrowest point.
- ● Otherwise, where > 1 exit is required in a mall, the following applies:
  - ○ At all mall locations, travel in different directions to separate exits must be possible.
- ● The width of the following routes from a mall must be ≥ 66":
  - ○ Exit passageway.
  - ○ Exit access corridor.

402 Covered Mall Buildings

402.4.5.1 Exit passageway enclosures

This subsection addresses exit passageway enclosures that provide a secondary means of egress from a tenant space.

- Doors from a tenant space to such enclosures are governed as follows:
  - The doors must be 1-hr fire doors.
  - One of the following types of closing systems is required:
    The doors must be self-closing.
    The doors must be automatically closed by smoke detection.

402.4.6 Service areas fronting on exit passageways and corridors

- The following building services may open directly into exit passageways and corridors:
  - Where the enclosure fire-resistance rating is maintained as required:
    Mechanical rooms.
    Electrical rooms.
    Building service areas.
    Service elevators.

402.5 Mall width

- Malls are considered corridors for purposes of required egress.
- Requirements for mall widths and clearances specified in this section supercede those listed elsewhere in the code.

    Note: 1003.2.3, "Egress width," is cited as the section having requirements that are superceded by requirements in this section.

402.5.1 Minimum width

- Mall width must accommodate the occupant load served.
- Mall width must be ≥ 20'.
- A clear exit width ≥ 10' wide by ≥ 8' high is required in a mall between any projection of a tenant space and any of the following:
  - Kiosk.
  - Vending machine.
  - Bench.
  - Display opening.
  - Food court.
  - Other obstruction to means of egress travel.

402 Covered Mall Buildings

402.6 Types of construction

- The area of covered mall buildings including anchor buildings is governed as follows:
  - Area is not limited where the building meets both of the following requirements:
    The building must be one of the following construction types:
    Type I.
    Type II.
    Type III.
    Type IV.
    The following must be surrounded on all sides by permanent open space ≥ 60':
    Covered mall building.
    Attached anchor buildings.
    Parking structure.

402.7 Fire-resistance-rated separation

- A separation with a fire-resistance rating is not required between the following spaces:
  - Between a tenant space and the mall.
  - Between a food court and the mall.
  - Between a food court and adjacent tenant spaces.

402.7.1 Attached garage

- Where an open parking garage is located >10' away from a covered mall building, the following apply:
  - The walls separating the two structures must meet fire-resistance-rating requirements for exterior walls based on fire separation distance.
  - Pedestrian walkways and tunnels to the garage must meet applicable code requirements.

  Note: The following are cited as the source of applicable requirements:
  IBC Table 602, "Fire-Resistance Rating Requirements for Exterior Walls Based on Fire Separation Distance."
  3104, "Pedestrian walkways and tunnels."

- Attached parking garages are separate buildings from a covered mall building as follows:
  - Where the following are separated by a fire barrier with a fire-resistance rating ≥ 2 hours:
    Garages for vehicles carrying ≤ 9 passengers each.
    Open garages.

402 Covered Mall Buildings

402.7.2 Tenant separations

- Separations between tenant spaces are governed as follows:
  - They must be fire partitions.
  - They must have a fire-resistance rating ≥ 1 hr.

  Note: 708, "Fire Partitions," is cited as the source of applicable requirements.

- Separations between tenant spaces and the mall are governed as follows:
  - A separation with a fire-resistance rating is not required in the following case:
    Where a separation between occupancies is not required.

402.7.2.1 Openings between anchor building and mall

- This subsection does not apply to the following openings:
  - Between occupancy R-1 sleeping rooms and a mall.
- Openings between anchor buildings and the mall are governed as follows:
  - Openings are not required to be protected where anchor buildings have the following construction types:
    Type 1.
    Type 2.

402.8 Automatic sprinkler system

- Sprinklers are not required in open parking garages.

  Note: 406.2, "Parking garages," is cited as describing qualifying garages.

- Otherwise, covered mall buildings and connected buildings must be sprinklered as follows:
  - As per NFPA 13.
  - Prior to occupation by any tenant, the sprinkler system must be complete and operable throughout the covered mall building.
  - Empty tenant spaces must be protected with operable sprinklers as follows:
    Where approved alternative systems are not provided.
  - Mall sprinklers must be independent from the following:
    Sprinklers for tenant spaces.
    Sprinklers for anchor buildings.
  - Sprinklers of the same system serving more than one tenant are governed as follows:
    They must be controlled independently.

402.8.1 Standpipe system

- A standpipe system is required in covered mall buildings and connected buildings.

  Note: Section 905, "Standpipe Systems," is cited as governing such systems.

402 Covered Mall Buildings

402.9 Smoke control

- Smoke control is required in a covered mall building where it is required for atriums.

  Note: Section 404, "Atriums," is cited as the source of requirements for smoke control.

402.10 Kiosks

- This subsection governs kiosks and like structures in a mall as follows:
  - Temporary.
  - Permanent.
- Combustible kiosks must be constructed of fire-retardant-treated wood.
- Kiosks must have both of the following approved systems:
  - Fire detection.
  - Fire suppression.
- Kiosks must be separated ≥ 20' from other structures in a mall.
- Kiosks must be ≤ 300 sf in area.

402.11 Security grilles and doors

- Security grilles or doors of the following types in a required means of egress have requirements as indicated below:
  - Types:
    Horizontal sliding.
    Vertical.
  - Requirements:
    They must remain fully open during occupancy by the public.
    They may not be closed while the served space has the following conditions:
    Where > 10 persons occupy a space with 1 exit.
    Where > 50 persons occupy a space with >1 exit.
    They must be operable when the served space is occupied as follows:
    From inside the space.
    Without special knowledge or effort.
- Where ≥ 2 exits are required, the following applies:
  Security grilles or doors are limited to ≤ ½ the exits.

402.12 Standby power

- Standby power is required in mall buildings > 50,000 sf as follows:
  - Systems must be able to operate emergency voice/alarm systems.

402 Covered Mall Buildings

402.13 Emergency voice/alarm communication system

- Emergency voice/alarm systems are required in covered mall buildings > 50,000 sf of total floor area.
- Mall emergency voice/alarm systems must be accessible to the fire department as follows:
  - Where such systems are required.
  - Where such systems are not required but are provided.

  Note: 907.2.12.2, "Emergency voice/alarm communication system," is cited as governing the locations and characteristics of such systems.

402.14 Plastic signs

- Plastic signs are restricted in size and detail in covered mall buildings as follows:
  - Within every store as follows:
      On every level.
  - From side wall to side wall of each tenant space facing the mall.
  - By requirements of this section.

402.14.1 Area

- Plastic signs are limited to ≤ 20% of the tenant façade facing the mall.

402.14.2 Height and width

- The size of plastic signs is limited as follows:
  - Vertical dimension must be ≤ 36" for horizontal signs.
  - Vertical dimension must be ≤ 96" for vertical signs.
  - Horizontal dimension must be ≤ 36" for vertical signs.

402.14.3 Location

- Plastic signs must be ≥ 18" from adjacent tenants:
  - Measured to the center of the common wall between tenants.

402 Covered Mall Buildings

402.14.4 Plastics other than foam plastics

- Such plastics are to be light-transmitting plastics complying with one of the following:
  - Specifications listed elsewhere in the code.
  - Specifications as follows:
      Self-ignition temperature ≥ 650°F.
      Flame spread index ≤ 75.
      Smoke-developed index ≤ 450.

    Note: 2606.4, "Specifications," is cited as a set of acceptable properties listed elsewhere in the code. These include all properties in the group specified above plus additional properties.
    The following are cited as describing tests for verifying the properties specified above:
    ASTM D 1929, "Standard Test Method for Determining Ignition Temperature of Plastics."
    ASTM E84, "Standard Test Methods for Surface Burning Characteristics of Building Materials."

402.14.4.1 Encasement

- The backs and edges of plastic signs in the mall must be enclosed with metal.

402.14.5 Foam plastics

- Foam plastics are must have the following properties:
  - Maximum heat release of 150 kilowatts.
  - Density must be ≥ 20 lbs/cu ft.
  - Thickness of foam plastic panels and signs must be ≤ ½".

    Note: UL 1975, "Fire Test of Foamed Plastic Used for Decorative Purposes," is cited as describing the test verifying head release.

402.14.5.1 Density

- The density of foam plastic must be ≥ 20 lbs/cu ft.

402.14.5.2 Thickness

- The thickness of foam plastic signs must be ≤ ½".

402.15 Fire department access to equipment

- Areas housing the following controls are to be identified for use by the fire department:
  - Controls for air-conditioning systems.
  - Controls for automatic fire-extinguishing systems.
  - Controls for other detection, suppression, or control elements.

403 High-Rise Buildings

403.1 Applicability

- Buildings not governed by this section include the following:
  - Airport traffic control towers.
  - Open parking garages.
  - Occupancy A-5 buildings.
  - Occupancy F-2 buildings that require large heights to accommodate equipment such as the following:
    - Craneways.
    - Rolling mills.
    - Structural metal fabrication.
    - Production and distribution of power.
  - Buildings with the following occupancies:
    - H-1, H-2, H-3.

  Note: The following are cited as governing the buildings above:
  - *Section 412, "Aircraft-Related Occupancies."*
  - *406.3, "Open parking garages."*
  - *303.1, "Assembly Group A."*
  - *503.1.2, "Special industrial occupancies," for buildings with large equipment.*
  - *Section 415, "Groups H-1, H-2, H-3, H-4 and H-5."*

- Otherwise, buildings governed by this section are as follows:
  - Buildings with occupied floors > 75' above lowest level of fire department vehicle access.

403.2 Automatic sprinkler system

- Sprinklers are not required in buildings used only to house telecommunications equipment as follows, with the conditions listed below:
  - Equipment:
    - Telecommunications equipment.
    - Electrical power distribution equipment.
    - Batteries.
    - Standby engines.
  - Conditions:
    - Automatic fire detection system is required in equipment spaces.
    - Fire barriers must separate equipment spaces from remainder of building as follows:
      - Walls must have a fire-resistance rating ≥ 1 hr.
      - Floor/ceiling assemblies must have a fire resistance rating ≥ 2 hrs.
- Other high-rise buildings are required to be sprinklered as per NFPA 13.
- Secondary water systems for sprinklers are required as follows:
  - For high-rise buildings in Seismic Design Categories C, D, E, or F as follows:
    - To equal the hydraulically calculated demand.
    - To have a duration ≥ 30 minutes.

  Note: 903.3.5.2, "Secondary water supply," is cited as the source of requirements.

403 High-Rise Buildings

403.3 Reduction in fire-resistance rating

- Reduction in requirements for fire-resistance ratings is permitted as follows:
  - Where sprinkler control valves are equipped as follows for specified conditions:
    Valves have supervisory initiating devices for each floor.
    Valves have water-flow initiating devices for each floor.

  Note: The following are cited as indicating the rating reductions permitted. They also define additional conditions required for such reductions.
  403.3.1, "Type of construction."
  403.3.2, "Shaft enclosures."

403.3.1 Type of construction

- Required fire resistance may be reduced as follows:
  - Where specified devices are provided for valves:
    Type IA may be reduced to Type IB.
    Type IB may be reduced to Type IIA in the following occupancies:
    A, B, E, F-2, H, I, R, S-2, U.

  Note: The following are cited as pertaining to the reductions described above:
  IBC Table 601, "Fire-Resistance Rating Requirements for Building Elements," lists construction types and their fire-resistance ratings that may be reduced.
  404.3, "Reduction in fire-resistance rating," is cited as the source of conditions required for rating reductions.

403.3.2 Shaft enclosures

- This section does not apply to the following enclosures:
  - Exit enclosures.
  - Elevator hoistway enclosures.
- The fire-resistance rating required for other fire barriers enclosing vertical shafts may be reduced as follows:
  - Rating reduced to ≥ 1 hr in the following case:
    Where sprinklers are provided in the shaft at the following locations:
    At the top.
    At every other floor.

  Note: 403.3, "Reduction in fire-resistance rating," lists the conditions permitting the reduction described in this section.

403.4 Emergency escape and rescue

- Such openings are not required in high-rise buildings.

  Note: Section 1009, "Emergency Escape and Rescue," is cited as the source for opening requirements waived by this section.

403 High-Rise Buildings

403.5 Automatic fire detection

- Smoke detection is required in high-rise buildings.

    Note: 907.2.12, "High-rise buildings," is cited as the source of requirements for smoke detection in this type of building.

403.6 Emergency voice/alarm communication

- An emergency voice/alarm communication system is required in high-rise buildings.

    Note: 907.2.12.2, "Emergency voice/alarm communication system," is cited as the source of requirements for such systems.

403.7 Fire department communications system

- A 2-way communication system is required in high-rise buildings for fire department use as follows:
  - The system must connect the fire command center to the following locations:
    Elevators.
    Every lobby.
    Emergency and standby power rooms.
    Fire pump rooms.
    Areas of refuge.
    Within enclosed exit stairways:
      At each floor level.

    Note: 907.2.12.3, "Fire department communication system," is cited as the source of requirements for such systems. A partial summary of requirements is provided above.

403.8 Fire command

- A fire command center is required in high-rise buildings as follows:
  - Location to be approved by the fire department.

  Note: Section 911, "Fire Command Center," is cited as the source of requirements for such a facility.

403 High-Rise Buildings

403.10.1 Standby power

- A standby power system is required in high-rise buildings.
- The following apply where a generator located inside the building serves as standby power:
  - The generator system must be located in its own room.
  - The generator room must be enclosed as follows:
    With fire barrier assemblies having a fire-resistance rating ≥ 2 hrs.

  Note: Section 2702, "Emergency and Standby Power Systems," is cited as governing such systems.

- The fire command center must provide the following:
  - System supervision.
  - Manual start capability.
  - Transfer features.

403.10.1.1 Fuel supply

- An on-premises fuel supply for a standby power system is governed as follows:
  - It is not required in the following case:
    Where an approved natural gas pipeline is provided.
  - It is required in other cases as follows:
    It must supply fuel to operate the system at full demand for ≤ 2 hrs.

403.10.1.2 Capacity

- The standby system must have a capacity as follows:
  - As necessary to power all equipment that must run simultaneously in an emergency.
  - In the following case, power is not required to run all equipment, including that which is nonessential in the emergency:
    Where automatic load-shedding capability is provided.

403 High-Rise Buildings

403.10.1.3 Connected facilities

- The following must be automatically transferable to the standby power system:
  - Power and lighting for the fire command center.
  - Electrically powered fire pumps.

    Note: 403.8, "Fire command," is cited as the source of requirements for a fire command center. It establishes the need for such and refers to Section 911, "Fire Command Center," for its requirements.

- Elevators are governed as follows:
  - ≥ 1 elevator able to serve all floors must have standby power.
  - Standby power must be transferable to any elevator.
  - Transfer of elevators to the standby power system must be possible by both the following:
    Automatic transfer.
    Manual transfer.
  - Where 1 elevator is provided, the following applies:
    Standby power must transfer automatically within 60 seconds of power failure.
  - Where ≥ 2 elevators are controlled by a single operating system, the following apply:
    Where standby power can serve all elevators simultaneously:
    They must transfer to standby power within 60 seconds of power failure.
    Where standby power cannot serve all elevators simultaneously:
    They must transfer to standby power in turn to return to the designated level.
    When all elevators are at the designated level ≥ 1 must remain on standby power.
    Others at the designated level must disconnect from standby power.

    Note: 403.9, "Elevators," defers to Chapter 30, "Elevators and Conveying Systems," for requirements, most of which are summarized above.

403.10.2 Separate circuits and fixtures

- Emergency lighting is governed as follows:
  - Fixtures must be on circuits separate from normal power.
  - Fixtures must be separate from fixtures providing normal lighting.
  - ≥ 1 footcandle must be provided at floor level in the following locations:
    Means of egress corridors.
    Stairways.
    Smoke proof enclosures.
    Elevator cars and lobbies.
    Other areas that are a part of the escape route.

403.10.2.1 Other circuits

- Lighting for the following spaces must be transferable to the standby power system:
  - Fire command station.
  - Mechanical rooms.

403 High-Rise Buildings

403.10.3 Emergency systems

- The following lighting may be supplied by a standby system in the occupancies listed below:
  - Lighting:
    Exit signs.
    Exit lighting.
    Means of egress lighting.
  - Occupancies:
    F, S.
- Each of the following lighting is classified as an emergency system, with both of the requirements listed below:
  - Lighting:
    Exit signs.
    Exit lighting.
    Elevator car lighting.
  - Requirements:
    Lighting must activate ≤ 10 seconds after power failure.
    Lighting must be transferable to the standby source.

  Note: Chapter 10," Means of Egress," is cited as the source of requirements related to lighting at exits.

403.11 Stairway door operation

This section addresses stairway doors that are not exit discharge doors.

- Such doors may be locked so as to prevent opening from the stairway side in the following case:
  - Where the doors can be unlocked as follows:
    Simultaneously.
    Without being unlatched.
    By a signal from the fire command station.

403.11.1 Stairway communications system

This section addresses stairways where doors are locked from the stairway side.

- A 2-way communication system is required in the stairway as follows:
  - To be connected to an approved and continuously attended station.
  - To be located at every 5th floor or at more frequent intervals.

404 Atriums

404.1 General

- Enclosure of vertical openings complying with this section is not required in the following occupancies:
  - A, B, E, F, I, M, R, S, U.

404.1.1 Definition

- **Atrium**
  - Does not include openings through floors dedicated to any of the following:
    Enclosed stairways.
    Elevators.
    Hoistways.
    Escalators.
    Plumbing.
    Electrical services.
    Air conditioning.
    Other equipment.
  - Does not include openings through floors defined as a mall.
  - Includes other openings through ≥ 2 floor levels as follows:
    Such openings are closed at the top.
    The following are not counted as floor levels for this definition:
      Balconies in an assembly area.
      Mezzanines.

  Note: Section 505, "Mezzanines," is cited as the source of requirements for qualifying mezzanines.

404.2 Use

- Atrium floors may serve any use where both of the following apply:
  - Use is approved.
  - Individual space is sprinklered as per NFPA 13.
- Otherwise, atrium floors may serve only the following:
  - Low-fire-hazard uses.
- The following components of an atrium must be approved:
  - Materials.
  - Decorations.

  Note: International Fire Code is cited as the source of requirements with which materials and decorations must comply.

404 Atriums

404.3 Automatic sprinkler protection

- The following areas are not required to be sprinklered with the condition listed below:
  - Areas:
    - Above an atrium.
    - On levels adjacent to an atrium.
  - Condition:
    - Where separated from the atrium as follows:
      - By fire barriers with a fire-resistance rating ≥ 2 hrs.
- Sprinklers at the ceiling of an atrium are not required as follows:
  - Where the ceiling is > 55 ft above the floor.
- Otherwise, a sprinkler system is required as follows:
  - Required throughout a building containing an atrium.
  - Must be approved.

404.4 Smoke control

- Smoke control is not required for openings in floors with the following conditions:
  - Where the opening does not connect > 2 floors.
  - Other conditions.

  Note: 707.2, "Shaft enclosure required," is cited. Exception 7 is referred to as the source of additional conditions necessary to omit smoke control.

- Smoke control is not required for the following where specified conditions are present:
  - Open escalators.
  - Open stairs.
  - Automobile ramps in parking garages.
  - Between a mezzanine and the floor below.

  Note: 707.2, "Shaft enclosure required," is cited. Exceptions 2, 8, and 9 are referred to as describing the conditions necessary to omit smoke control in the locations listed above.

- In other cases, smoke control is required in atriums.

  Note: Section 909, "Smoke Control Systems," is cited as governing such systems.

404.5 Enclosure of atriums *(part 1 of 2)*

- The adjacent spaces of any 3 floors at the atrium do not require separation from it as follows:
  - Where the smoke control design includes the following in the calculation of the atrium volume:
    - The volumes of such nonseparated floors.
- In other cases, atrium spaces must be separated from adjacent spaces by one of the following:
  - By a fire barrier wall with a fire-resistance rating of 1 hr..
  - By a glass wall as described in this subsection.

404 Atriums

404.5 Enclosure of atriums *(part 2 of 2)*

- An atrium is permitted to be separated from adjacent spaces by a glass wall as follows:
  - Glass wall must function as a smoke partition.
  - Sprinklers must be located along the glass wall in one of the following arrangements:
    On both the atrium side and the room side of the glass wall.
    On only the room side of the glass wall in the following case:
      Where there is no walkway on the atrium side.
  - Sprinklers along the sides of the glass wall must be located as follows:
    Spaced ≤ 6' apart.
    ≥ 4" and ≤ 12" from the glass wall.
  - Sprinklers must wet the entire surface of the glass upon activation.
  - The glass wall must have one of the following details:
    Glass is to be set a gasketed frame to act as follows:
      Frame must be able to deflect prior to sprinkler activation as follows:
        So as to prevent glass breakage.
    Glass wall is to be glass blocks with a ¾-hour fire resistance rating.

  Note: Section 2110, "Glass Unit Masonry," is cited as the source of requirements for the glass block option above.

404.6 Automatic fire detection system

- Automatic smoke detection is required in atriums.

  Note: 907.2.13, "Buildings with an atrium," is cited as the source of requirements smoke detection in atriums.

404.7 Standby power

- Smoke control equipment must be connected to standby power.

  Note: 909.11, "Power systems," is cited as the source of requirements for smoke control system power supply.

404.8 Interior finish

- ≥ Class B finishes are required for walls in atriums as follows:
  - Sprinklers do not warrant a reduction of this class.

404.9 Travel distance in atriums

- Means of egress travel through an atrium is governed as follows:
  - On levels other than the lowest level:
    Travel distance within the atrium is limited to ≤ 150'.

406 Motor-Vehicle-Related Occupancies

406.1 Private garages and carports

406.1.1 Classification

- Occupancy U buildings or parts of buildings are limited as follows:
  - Area must be $\leq$ 1000 sf where area increases are not permitted.
  - Height must be $\leq$ 1 story.

  Note: 406.1.2, "Area increase," is cited as the source of increases permitted to the area limit.

406.1.2 Area increase

- An occupancy U storage of the following vehicles may be $\leq$ 3000 sf where the conditions listed below apply:
  - Vehicles:
    Private motor vehicles.
    Pleasure-type motor vehicles.
  - Conditions:
    No repair work is done.
    No fuel is dispensed.
    For a mixed-occupancy building, the following is required:
      The exterior wall for the occupancy U area is governed as follows:
        It must meet requirements for the major occupancy.
        Openings must be protected as per requirements of the major occupancy.
      The floor area permitted for the building is governed as follows:
        The area is that permitted by the major occupancy.
    For a building housing only occupancy U, the following is required:
      The exterior wall is governed as follows:
        It must meet requirements for R-1 or R-2.
        Openings must be protected as per requirements for R-1 or R-2.
- More than one occupancy U area $\leq$ 3000 sf is allowed in the same building as follows:
  - Where each 3000 sf of occupancy U is isolated from the occupancies listed below by fire walls with the fire-resistance ratings indicated:

Table 406.1.2   Occupancy U: Fire-Resistance Rating for Separation

Occupancy	Construction type	Rating
A, B, E, F-2, H-4, I, R, S-2, U	II, V	$\geq$ 2 hr
A, B, E, F-2, H-4, I, R, S-2, U	I, III, IV	$\geq$ 3 hr
F-1, H-3, H-5, M, S-1	I, II, III, IV, V	$\geq$ 3 hr
H-2	I, II, III, IV, V	$\geq$ 4 hr

Source: IBC Table 705.4.

Note: Section 705, "Fire-Resistance-Rated Construction," is cited as the source of requirements for fire walls applicable to this occupancy U separation.

406 Motor-Vehicle-Related Occupancies

406.2 Parking garages

406.2.1 Classification

- Parking garages are classified as one of the following:
  - Open parking garage.
  - Enclosed parking garage.

  Note: The following are cited as sources of requirements for parking garages:
       406.3, "Open parking garages."
       406.4, "Enclosed parking garages."
       Section 508, "Special Provisions," which addresses, for the most part, parking
          garages in relationship to specific occupancies.

406.2.2 Clear height

- A clear height of ≥ 7' is required at each floor level of a parking garage in the following areas:
  - Vehicle traffic areas.
  - Pedestrian traffic areas.
- Areas serving required van-accessible parking must comply with accessibility requirements.

  Note: The following are cited as sources of requirements for van-accessible parking:
       1106.4, "Van spaces."
       ICC/ANSI A117.1, "Accessible and Usable Buildings and Facilities."

406.2.3 Guards

This subsection addresses guards in parking garages:

- Guards are required at locations with all the following characteristics:
     At interior or exterior vertical openings:
        On the floors or roofs.
        Where vehicles parked or moved.
     Where the vertical distance to the adjacent surface directly below is > 2'-6".

  Note: 1003.2.12, "Guards," is cited as the source of applicable requirements.

Case study: Fig. 406.2.2. There are two levels of parking under the living units of this building. The upper parking level has headroom dictated by the significant floor to floor height of the first floor which houses retail shops. Here clear height in the parking garage is never less than 13'-1". The lower level of parking has a reduced floor to floor dimension with retail space spanning over the ramp. The lowest clear height on the ramp under the retail shop mezzanine is 7'-1⁵⁄₈". 7' - 11" is provided under the lowest beam elsewhere. Headroom under the ramp drops to 7' at the end of 2 parking spaces beyond which vehicles may not pass due to the presence of wheel-stops. The parking garage complies with the code requirement to provide 7' clear height in vehicle and pedestrian traffic areas.

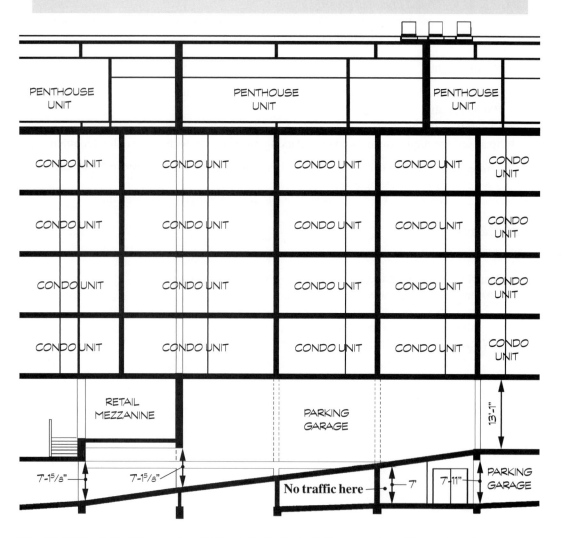

Fig. 406.2.2. Partial building section. McKenzie Lofts. Portland, Oregon. Ankrom Moisan Associated Architects. Portland, Oregon.

406 Motor-Vehicle-Related Occupancies

406.2.4 Vehicle barriers

This subsection addresses barriers in parking garages.

- Parking areas must be provided with the following as applicable where pedestrian or vehicular access is not obstructed:
  - Interior walls.
  - Exterior walls.
  - Vehicle barriers.
- Vehicle barriers are to be provided at the following locations:
  - At the ends of drive lanes.
  - At the ends of parking spaces where the floor elevation changes > 12".
- Vehicle barriers are to be ≥ 2' high.

  Note: 1607.7, "Loads on handrails, guards, grab bars and vehicular barriers," is cited as the source of structural requirements for vehicle barriers.

406.2.5 Ramps

- Vehicle ramps in parking garages do not provide means of egress.

  Note: Chapter 10, "Means of Egress," is cited as the source of requirements governing enclosed ramps.

406.2.6 Floor surfaces

This subsection addresses surfaces in parking garages.

- The parking surface at ground level must be one of the following:
  - Asphalt.
  - Concrete.
  - Surface similar to concrete as follows:
    Nonabsorbent.
    Noncombustible.
- The parking surface at other levels must be one of the following:
  - Concrete.
  - Surface similar to concrete as follows:
    Nonabsorbent.
    Noncombustible.

406.2.7 Mixed separation

- Parking garages are to be separated from other occupancies according to the fire-resistance separation requirement for each individual occupancy.

  Note: 302.3.1, "Two or more uses," is cited as the source of requirements for separating parking garages from other occupancies.

406 Motor-Vehicle-Related Occupancies

406.2.8 Special hazards

- The connection of a parking garage to a room containing a fuel-fired appliance is governed as follows:
  - Where the source of appliance ignition is < 18" above the floor:
    A vestibule providing 2 doors between the spaces is required.
  - Where the source of appliance ignition is ≥ 18" above the floor:
    1 door is permitted in lieu of a vestibule.

406.2.9 Attached to rooms

- A parking garage may not open directly to a sleeping room.

406.3 Open parking garages

406.3.1 Scope

- Parking garages must comply with other requirements of the code as follows:
  - Where they are not superceded by this section.

406.3.2 Definitions *(part 1 of 2)*

- **Open parking garage**
  - Used only for parking and/or storage of private vehicles as follows:
    Includes ≤ 1000 sf of accessory functions on grade-level tier as follows:
    Office.
    Waiting room.
    Toilet.
    Includes mechanical room serving the building.
    May be constructed under occupancies A, I, B, M, R.
  - Vehicles are moved to and from street level by their own power.
  - Openings in exterior walls for natural ventilation at each level are required as follows:
    To be on ≥ 2 sides of the building.
    To be uniformly distributed.
    Area of openings to be ≥ 20% of the total building perimeter wall area at each tier.
    Total length of openings at each level to be ≥ 40% of the building perimeter as follows:
      Where they are not evenly distributed on opposite sides of the building:
    Total length of openings at each level does not have a minimum in the following case:
      Where they are evenly distributed on opposite sides of the building.
  - Interior walls are to be open as follows:
    Open area to be > 20% of the wall area.
    Open area to be evenly distributed.

406 Motor-Vehicle-Related Occupancies

406.3.2 Definitions *(part 2 of 2)*

- **Mechanical-access open parking garages**
  - Machines similar to the following move vehicles to and from street level:
    Parking machines.
    Lifts.
    Elevators.
    Mechanical devices.
  - The public is not permitted above street level.

- **Ramp-access open parking garages**
  - An open parking garage with one of the following configurations:
    Parking floors are sloped and serve as ramps between levels.
    Ramps provide access between floors for vehicles.
  - Vehicles travel between floors and the street by their own power.

406.3.3 Construction

- Open parking garages must be one of the following types of construction:
  - Type I.
  - Type II.
  - Type IV.

406.3.3.1 Openings

- Openings in exterior walls for natural ventilation at each level are required as follows:
  - To be on ≥ 2 sides of the building.
  - To be uniformly distributed.
  - Area of openings to be ≥ 20% of the total building perimeter wall area at each tier.
  - Total length of openings at each level to be ≥ 40% of the building perimeter as follows:
    Where they are not evenly distributed on opposite sides of the building.
  - Total length of openings at each level does not have a minimum in the following case:
    Where they are evenly distributed on opposite sides of the building.
- Interior walls are to be open as follows:
  - Open area to be > 20% of the wall area.
  - Open area to be evenly distributed.

406 Motor-Vehicle-Related Occupancies

406.3.4 Uses

- Open parking garages may be used only for the following functions:
  - Parking and storage of private motor vehicles.
  - The following accessory uses are permitted with the conditions indicated below:
    Uses:
      Office.
      Waiting room.
      Toilets.
    Conditions:
      Restricted to the grade-level tier.
      Limited to a total of ≤ 1000 sf.
      Not required to be separated from the parking garage.
  - A mechanical room serving the building is permitted.
- Open parking garages may be constructed under the following occupancies:
  - A, I, B, M, R.

  Note: The following are cited as requirements for other uses in open parking garages, a partial summary of which is provided above:
  508.3, "Group S-2 enclosed parking garage with Group S-2 open parking garage above."
  508.8, "Open parking garage beneath Groups A, I, B, M and R."

406.3.5 Area and height (*part 1 of 2*)

This subsection addresses open parking garages meeting minimum opening requirements.

- In garages with a spiral floor or sloped floor, area limited as follows:
  - The area of the projected plan at any horizontal section is limited to that for a parking tier.
- In garages with a continuous spiral type floor, a tier is defined as follows:
  - Each 9'-6" height or portion thereof constitutes a parking tier.
- Parking tier clear heights are governed as follows:
  - Height must be ≥ 7' where mechanical parking-access devices are not used.
  - Height < 7' is permitted where approved and where mechanical parking-access devices are used.
- Areas of garages are governed as follows:
  - Area in Type I construction is not limited.
  - Area per tier in other permitted construction types is as follows:
    Limited to ≤ 50,000 sf.
- Heights of garages are governed as follows:
  - Not limited in Type IA construction.
  - In other types of construction height is limited as indicated in the following table:

406 Motor-Vehicle-Related Occupancies

406.3.5 Area and height (*part 2 of 2*)

Table 406.3.5	Height Limits of Open Parking Garages		
Type of construction	Height of garages with ramp access	Height of garages with mechanical access	
		without sprinklers	with sprinklers
IB	12 tiers	12 tiers	18 tiers
IIA	10 tiers	10 tiers	15 tiers
IIB	8 tiers	8 tiers	12 tiers
IV	4 tiers	4 tiers	4 tiers

Source: IBC Table 406.3.5.

Note: 406.3.6, "Area and height increases," provides higher limits on height and area based on increased open area of garages.

406.3.6 Area and height increases (*part 1 of 2*)

This subsection addresses open parking garages with openings in excess of the minimum.

- Area is unlimited in garages with the following characteristics:
  - Type IB or Type II construction.
  - Opening on each side must be ≥ 50% of the inside wall area as follows:
    Openings to be uniformly distributed on each side.
  - Height ≤ 75'.
  - Every point on the tier must be ≤ 200' from such openings measured horizontally.
- For garages with the following openings, height and area limitations are indicated below:
  - Openings:
    ≥ ¾ of the building perimeter must have sides open.
    A side that is open must have ≥ 50% of its area open as measured inside the wall.
    An open side must have its openings uniformly distributed along its length.
  - Area per tier:
    Area is unlimited for garages of Type I construction.
    Area per tier for other permitted construction types is limited as follows:
      Where ¾ of the building perimeter is open, area must be ≤ 62,500 sf.
      Where all the building perimeter is open, area must be ≤ 75,000 sf.
  - Height:
    Height is unlimited for garages of Type IA construction.
    Height limitations for other construction types are listed below:

Table 406.3.6a	Increased Height Limits of Open Parking Garages		
Type of construction	Height of garages with ramp access	Height of garages with mechanical access	
		without sprinklers	with sprinklers
IB	13 tiers	13 tiers	19 tiers
IIA	11 tiers	11 tiers	16 tiers
IIB	9 tiers	9 tiers	13 tiers
IV	5 tiers	5 tiers	5 tiers

06 Motor-Vehicle-Related Occupancies

406.3.6 Area and height increases *(part 2 of 2)*

- For the following conditions, tier areas may be increased above the maximum otherwise required and as indicated below:
  - Conditions:
    - Garage height must be ≤ 1 tier less than the maximum otherwise permitted.
    - Openings must be located on ≥ 3 sides of the garage.
    - Openings must a clear height ≥ 30".
    - Openings must extend for ≥ 80% of the length of each side where they are located.
    - Every point on the tier must be ≤ 200' from such an opening measured horizontally.
    - Openings must face one of the following:
      - Street ≥ 30' wide for the full opening length.
      - Yard ≥ 30' wide for the full opening length as follows:
        - Yard must have access to a street.
    - Standpipes are required on each such tier.
  - Tier areas are limited only by the total garage areas indicated in the following tables:

Table 406.3.6b   Limitations for Total Garage Area with Ramp Access

Type of construction	Height of garage with ramp access	Total garage area
IIA	≤ 9 tiers	≤ 500,000 sf
IIB	≤ 7 tiers	≤ 400,000 sf
IV	≤ 3 tiers	≤ 200,000 sf

Table 406.3.6c   Limitations for Total Garage Area with Mechanical Access

Type of construction	Height of garage with mechanical access	Total garage area
Without sprinklers:		
IIA	≤ 9 tiers	≤ 500,000 sf
IIB	≤ 7 tiers	≤ 400,000 sf
IV	≤ 3 tiers	≤ 200,000 sf
With sprinklers:		
IIA	≤ 14 tiers	≤ 750,000 sf
IIB	≤ 11 tiers	≤ 600,000 sf
IV	≤ 3 tiers	≤ 200,000 sf

406 Motor-Vehicle-Related Occupancies

406.3.7 Location on property

This subsection addresses open parking garages.

- Exterior walls and openings must have fire resistance as required for other building types based on the following conditions:
  ○ Construction type.
  ○ Occupancy
  ○ Fire separation distance.

    Note: The following are cited as the source of requirements for the components above:
    IBC Table 601, "Fire-Resistance Rating Requirements for Building Elements."
    IBC Table 602, "Fire-Resistance Rating Requirements for Exterior Walls Based on Fire Separation Distance."

- The distance required between a garage and its property lines is similar to that for any building type based on the following:
  ○ The fire resistance of exterior walls and openings.
  ○ Construction type.
  ○ Occupancy.
  ○ Fire separation distance.

    Note: The following are cited as sources for determining distance to property line:
    IBC Table 602, "Fire-Resistance Rating Requirements for Exterior Walls Based on Fire Separation Distance."
    Section 704, "Exterior Walls."

406.3.8 Stairs and exits

This section addresses open parking garages.

- Stairs and exits are governed as follows:
  ○ Where only parking attendants have access:
    ≥ 2 stairs are required.
    Stairs must be ≥ 3' wide.
  ○ Where persons other than parking attendants have access:
    Stairs and exits must meet means of egress requirements typical for the occupancy.

    Note: Chapter 10, "Means of Egress," is cited as the source of requirements for stairs and exits where the public has access.

- Lifts are governed as follows:
  ○ May be provided for employee-use only.
  ○ Must be enclosed by noncombustible materials.

406 Motor-Vehicle-Related Occupancies

406.3.9 Standpipes

- Standpipes are required in open parking garages as for any building type based on the following:
  - Building height.
  - Building area.
  - Occupant load.
  - Nature of building.

  Note: Chapter 9, "Fire Protection Systems," is cited as the source of requirements for standpipes. Section 905, "Standpipe Systems," contains requirements for this component.

406.3.10 Sprinkler systems

- Where sprinklers are required in open parking garages, they must comply with requirements similar to those for most other occupancies.

  Note: Chapter 9, "Fire Protection Systems," is cited as the source of requirements governing sprinklers.

406.3.11 Enclosure of vertical openings

This section addresses open parking garages.

- The following vertical openings must be enclosed where occupied by the public:
  - Stairs.
  - Exits.
- Any lifts provided for staff must be enclosed.
- Other vertical openings are not required to be enclosed.

  Note: Chapter 10, "Means of Egress," governs stairs and exits, and provides variations on enclosure requirements.

406.3.12 Ventilation

- Ventilation in open parking garages is not required beyond that provided by required openings.

  Note: 406.3.3.1, "Openings," is cited as the source of requirements for openings.

406 Motor-Vehicle-Related Occupancies

406.3.13 Prohibitions

This subsection addresses open parking garages.

- The following uses are not permitted:
  - Vehicle repairs.
  - Parking of the following vehicles:
    Buses.
    Trucks.
    Similar vehicles.
  - Partial or complete closing of required openings in exterior walls as follows:
    By tarpaulins.
    By any other means.
  - Dispensing fuel.

406.4 Enclosed parking garages

406.4.1 Heights and areas

This subsection addresses enclosed parking garages.

- Garages and parts of garages that do not qualify as an open parking garage are governed as follows:
  - They must meet height and area limitations based on construction type.
- Parking is permitted on the roofs of enclosed parking garages.

  Note: IBC Table 503, "Allowable Height and Building Areas," is cited as the source of requirements with which enclosed parking garages must comply.

406.4.2 Ventilation

- Mechanical ventilation is required for enclosed parking garages.

  Note: International Mechanical Code is cited as the source governing such ventilation.

406.5 Motor vehicle service station

406.5.1 Construction

- Motor vehicle service stations are governed by the following:
  - This section.
  - Other standards.

  Note: International Fire Code is cited as the source governing motor vehicle service stations for aspects not addressed in this section.

406 Motor-Vehicle-Related Occupancies

406.5.2 Canopies

This subsection addresses canopies over fuel dispensing pumps.

- Canopies and canopy supports must be constructed of one or more of the following:
  - Noncombustible materials.
  - Fire-retardant-treated wood.
  - Heavy timber as follows:
    - Sizes must comply with Type IV construction.
  - Construction having a 1-hr fire-resistance rating.

    Note: Chapter 23, "Wood," is cited as the source of requirements for fire-retardant treated wood.

- Combustible materials at canopies must comply with one of the following:
  - They must be shielded from the pumps by one or more of the following:
    Noncombustible materials.
    Heavy timber as follows:
      Sizes must comply with Type IV construction.
  - Plastics are governed as follows:
    Must be covered by one of the following:
      Aluminum ≥ 0.020" thick.
      Corrosion-resistant steel with a base metal thickness ≥ 0.016".
    Must be tested in the same form as installed as follows:
      Must have a flame spread ≤ 25.
      Must have a smoke-developed index ≤ 450.
      Must have a self-ignition temperature ≥ 650°F.

    Note: The following are cited as the standards with which the plastics must comply:
      ASTM E 84, "Standard Test Method for Surface Burning Characteristics of Building Materials."
      ASTM D 1929, "Standard Test Method for Determining Ignition Temperature of Plastics."

  - Light-transmitting plastics are governed as follows:
    Panels must be located ≥ 10' from any building on the same property.
    Panels must face yards or streets ≥ 40' wide on other sides.
    Total area of all panels must be ≤ 1000 sf.
    Area of a single panel must be ≤ 100 sf.
- Canopy height is governed as follows:
  - Clear height in the drive area must be ≥ 13'-6".

407 Group I-2

407.1 General

- Occupancy I-2 is governed by the following:
  - This section.
  - Other sections of the code.

407.2 Corridors

- The enclosure of occupancy I-2 corridors is governed as follows:
  - Each corridor must be continuous to an exit.
  - Corridors may be open to the spaces indicated below where design and construction meet minimum requirements for fire safety:
    Waiting areas.
    Nurses' stations.
    Mental health treatment areas.
    Gift shops.
  - Otherwise, corridors must be separated from other spaces for purposes of smoke protection.

  Note: The following are cited as sources of requirements for space opening to a corridor:
  407.2.1, "Spaces of unlimited area," which addresses waiting rooms.
  407.2.2, "Nurses' stations."
  407.2.3, "Mental health treatment areas."
  407.2.4, "Gift shops."
  407.3, "Corridor walls," for walls required to separate corridors from other spaces.

407.2.1 Spaces of unlimited area

- Waiting and similar areas may be open to a corridor where all of the following apply:
  - The areas may not be used for the following:
    Patient sleeping rooms.
    Treatment rooms.
    Hazardous uses.
    Incidental uses having their own separation requirements.
  - The open space must be protected by a fire detection system.
  - The areas must have construction as required for corridors.
  - One of the following is required for a smoke compartment with space is open to a corridor:
    The corridor must be protected by a fire detection system.
    The smoke compartment must be protected throughout by quick-response sprinklers.
  - The layout of the area may not obstruct access to required exits.

  Note: The following are cited as sources of requirements and data as indicated:
  302.1.1, "Incidental use areas," defines incidental areas that this section prohibits being open to corridors.
  Section 907, "Fire Alarm and Detection Systems," provides requirements for the fire detection systems required by this section.
  903.3.2, "Quick-response and residential sprinklers," refers to NFPA standards.

407 Group I-2

407.2.2 Nurses' stations

- Where the following areas are open to corridors, the requirement below applies:
  - Areas:
    Doctor's and nurses' charting and communications areas.
    Related clerical areas.
  - Requirement:
    Areas must be constructed according to requirements for the corridor.

407.2.3 Mental health treatment areas

- Where any of the following spaces are open to the corridor, they must comply with the all of the requirements indicated below:
  - Spaces:
    Spaces housing patients who are not capable of self-preservation.
    Group meeting spaces.
    Multipurpose therapeutic spaces.
  - Requirements:
    Space must have continuous supervision by staff.
    Each space must be ≤ 1500 sf.
    Space layout does not obstruct access to required exits.
    Space must have a fire detection system.
    Only 1 such space is allowed in each smoke compartment.
    Walls and ceilings are constructed as required for corridors.

  Note: The following are cited as sources of applicable requirements and data:
  302.1.1, "Incidental use areas," defines incidental areas that this section
  prohibits being open to corridors.
  Section 907, "Fire Alarm and Detection Systems," provides requirements for the
  fire detection systems required by this section.

407.2.4 Gift shops

- Gift shops open to the corridor must be ≤ 500 sf.
- Where gift shop storage > 100 sf the following applies:
  - Gift shop and storage require separation from the rest of the building ≥ 1 hr.

407.3 Corridor walls

This subsection governs corridor walls in occupancy I-2.

- Walls must provide a barrier to limit the transfer of smoke.
- Walls must extend from the floor to one of the following:
  - Underside of floor above.
  - Underside of roof deck above.
  - Underside of ceiling membrane constructed to limit the transfer of smoke.
- Wall materials must conform to building construction type.

407 Group I-2

407.3.1 Corridor doors

This subsection governs corridor doors in occupancy I-2.

- The following doors must meet protection requirements consistent with the fire-resistance rating of their walls:
  - Doors in walls enclosing the following:
    Incidental-use spaces.
    Vertical opening.
    Exits.

    Note: 302.1.1, "Incidental use areas," is cited as the source listing incidental areas requiring protected doors.
    714.2, "Fire door and shutter assemblies," is cited as the source of protection requirements for doors in fire-resistance-rated walls.

- Doors in other corridor walls are governed as follows:
  - A fire-protection rating is not required.
  - Self-closing devices are not required.
  - Automatic closing devices are not required.
  - Doors must limit the transfer of smoke.
  - Positive latching is required.
  - Roller latches are prohibited.

407.3.2 Locking devices

This subsection governs locking devices in occupancy I-2.

- The following locking devices are governed as indicated below:
  - Locking devices:
    Those restricting access to the patient room from the corridor.
    Those operable only by staff from the corridor side.
  - Requirements:
    In mental health facilities:
      Such locks may restrict the means of egress for patient rooms.
    In other facilities:
      Such locks may not restrict the means of egress for patient rooms.

407 Group I-2

407.4 Smoke barriers

This subsection addresses the requirement for smoke barriers in occupancy I-2.

- The following stories must be divided as indicated below:
  - Stories:
    Where patients sleep.
    Where patients receive treatment.
    Other stories where the occupant load is $\geq$ 50.
  - Requirements:
    Story must be divided by smoke barriers.
    Story must have $\geq$ smoke compartments:
      Area of compartment must be $\leq$ 22,500 sf.
      Travel in the compartment is limited as follows:
        From any point to a smoke-barrier door must be $\leq$ 200 ft.

  Note: Section 709, "Smoke Barriers," is cited as the source of requirements for such components.

407.4.1 Refuge area

This subsection addresses refuge area requirements in smoke compartments of occupancy I-2.

- The area required for refuge in a smoke compartment is computed as follows:
  - For floors where patients are confined to a bed or litter:
    Refuge area required per patient is $\geq$ 30 sf:
      Patient count includes only those from the adjoining compartment.
  - For floors where patients are not confined to a bed or litter:
    Refuge area required per occupant is $\geq$ 6 sf:
      Occupant count includes only those from the adjoining compartment.
- The refuge area required in smoke compartments is to be distributed in one or more of the following locations:
  - Corridors.
  - Patient rooms.
  - Treatment rooms.
  - Lounges.
  - Dining areas.
  - Other low-hazard areas.

  Note: The area required for refuge is in addition to the area required to meet means of egress minimums.

407.4.2 Independent egress

This subsection addresses means of egress from smoke compartments in occupancy I-2.

- Each smoke compartment requires a means of egress as follows:
  - Egress may not return to the compartment of origin.

407 Group I-2

407.5 Automatic sprinkler system

- Smoke compartments with patient sleeping rooms must be sprinklered as follows:
  - As per NFPA 13 and sprinkler listings.
  - One of the following is required:
    Quick-response sprinklers.
    Residential sprinklers.

  Note: 903.3.2, "Quick response and residential sprinklers," is cited as requiring these sprinklers and referring to standards for them as indicated above.

407.6 Automatic fire detection

- This subsection addresses smoke detection in the following locations:
  - Corridors in nursing homes:
    Intermediate-care facilities.
    Skilled nursing facilities.
  - Corridors in detoxification facilities.
  - Spaces open to corridors in occupancy I-2.
- Smoke detection is not required in the abovelisted areas with the following conditions:
  - Where each patient sleeping room has a smoke detector as follows:
    Detector meets minimum standards.
    Provides a visual display on the corridor side of the room.
    Provides the following alarms at the attending nurses station:
      Audible alarm.
      Visual alarm.
  - Where doors to patient rooms are equipped as follows:
    Doors have automatic closing devices:
      Closing devices have integral smoke detectors as follows:
        On the room side.
        Installed according to their listing.
        That perform the necessary alert function.

  Note: The following are cited as sources of data and requirements as indicated:
  407.2, "Corridors," identifies spaces permitted to be open to corridors.
  UL 268, "Smoke Detectors for Fire Protective Signaling Systems," is the standard governing the smoke detectors to be provided in patient sleeping rooms.

- All other corridors and spaces open to corridors must have an automatic fire detection system.

  Note: Section 907, "Fire Alarm and Detection Systems," is cited as governing the required fire detection system.

408 Group I-3

408.1 General

- Occupancy I-3 must comply with the following:
  - This section.
  - Other applicable sections of the code.

    Note: 308.4, "Group I-3," is cited as a section applicable to this occupancy.

408.2 Mixed occupancies

- The following applies where an I-3 space occurs in an area with a different occupancy designation:
  - The larger area must meet requirements for its occupancy designation.
  - The following applies where means of egress must be locked for security purposes:
    The release of occupants must be possible at all times.
- Where means of egress from the following I-3 occupancies pass through other use designations, the requirements indicated below apply:
  - I-3 occupancies:
    Detention.
    Correctional.
  - Requirements:
    Egress through a horizontal exit into an occupancy that does not meet I-3 egress requirements is permitted as follows:
      The other occupancy must meet its own egress requirements.
      The other occupancy may not be a high-hazard use.
    In all other cases the means of egress must comply with I-3 requirements.

408.3 Means of egress

- Means of egress for I-3 occupancies are governed by the following:
  - This section governs those aspects addressed.
  - Other code requirements govern aspects not addressed in this section.

    Note: Chapter 10, "Means of Egress," is cited as governing egress issues not covered in this section.

408.3.1 Door width

- I-3 resident sleeping room doors must have a clear width of $\geq$ 2'-4".

408.3.2 Sliding doors

- Horizontal sliding doors in an occupancy I-3 means of egress are governed as follows:
  - Doors must fully open under the following conditions:
    With an opening force $\leq$ 50 lbs in either of the following circumstances:
      Simultaneously with a force $\leq$ 50 lbs applied $\perp$ to the door.
      With no other force applied to the door.

408 Group I-3

408.3.3 Spiral stairs

- Spiral stairs may be used in occupancy I-3 for staff operational purposes.

    Note: 1003.3.3.9, "Spiral stairways," is cited as governing such stairs.

408.3.4 Exit discharge

- Exits may discharge from an I-3 occupancy into one of the following areas with the requirements indicated below:
    - Areas:
        Fenced courtyard.
        Walled courtyard.
    - Requirements:
        Enclosed yard must accommodate all occupants in a zone as follows:
            Zone to be located ≥ 50' from the building.
            Size of zone must provide ≥ 15 sf per person.

408.3.5 Sallyports

- Sallyports may be located in an occupancy I-3 means of egress as follows:
    - Where unobstructed travel through them is possible during emergencies.

408.3.6 Vertical exit enclosures

- A vertical exit enclosure of an I-3 occupancy may have glazing where all the following conditions apply:
    - Only one required vertical exit enclosure per building may have glazing.
    - Glazing is permitted only in the following:
        In doors at landings.
        In interior walls at landings serving enclosure access.
    - Stairway is limited to serving ≤ 4 floor levels.
    - Doors must be fire doors with the larger fire-protection rating of the following:
        ≥ that required for the fire-resistance rating of their wall.
        ≥ ¾ hour.
    - Total glazed area at each floor must be ≤ 5000 sq in.
    - Individual panels of glazing must be ≤ 1296 sq in.
    - Sprinklers must protect both sides of the glazing by wetting the entire surfaces.
    - Glazing must be in a gasketed frame as follows:
        Frame must be able to deflect prior to sprinkler activation without breaking the glass.
    - Obstructions such as the following are not allowed between the sprinklers and the glazing:
        Curtains and curtains rods.
        Drapes and drapery traverse rods.
        Similar obstructions.

    Note: 714.2, "Fire door and shutter assemblies," is cited as the source of fire-protection ratings for fire doors as based on the fire-resistance rating of their walls.

408 Group I-3

408.4.1 Remote release

- In occupancy I-3, remote control of locks is not required where all of the following apply:
  - In restraint condition 4.
  - Locks that must be opened to move occupants to an area of refuge from a smoke compartment are governed as follows:
    They must number ≤ 10.
    The number of separate keys needed for all the locks is limited to ≤ 2.
    Movement of all occupants to the area of refuge must be possible in ≤ 3 minutes.
- Otherwise, locks on required doors in a means of egress of occupancy I-3 must have a remote release capability as follows:
  - Devices activating lock releases must be in a location remote from the resident living areas.
  - Locks preventing egress in the following conditions of restraint must meet the requirement indicated below:
    Conditions of restraint:
    Condition 3.
    Condition 4.
    Requirement:
    Locks must be releasable in ≤ 2 minutes as follows:
    By the minimum staff available.
    At any time.

408.4.2 Power-operated doors and locks

- Emergency power for the following door mechanisms is not required in occupancy I-3 for the conditions indicated below:
  - Mechanisms:
    Power-operated sliding doors.
    Power-operated locks for swinging doors.
  - Conditions:
    In occupancy I-3 restraint condition 4.
    ≤ 10 locks must be opened to move occupants to an area of refuge.
    ≤ 2 separate keys are needed for all the locks.
    Movement of all occupants to the area of refuge must be possible in ≤ 3 minutes.
- Otherwise, the following door mechanisms must comply with requirements indicated below:
  - Mechanisms:
    Power-operated sliding doors.
    Power-operated locks for swinging doors.
  - Requirements:
    Manual release mechanism at the door must be provided.
    One of the following must be provided:
    Remote mechanical release for the door mechanisms.
    Emergency power to door mechanisms.

408 Group I-3

408.4.3 Redundant operation

- In occupancy I-3, the following mechanisms must have the redundant systems listed below:
  - Locks:
    Remote release, mechanically operated sliding doors.
    Remote release, mechanically operated locks.
  - Redundant systems:
    Mechanically operated release mechanism at each door.
    Redundant remote release mechanism.

408.4.4 Relock capability

- Doors in occupancy I-3 that are unlocked remotely in an emergency are governed as follows:
  - Doors may not relock automatically upon closing without the following action:
    Specific action is required at the control location to permit relocking.

408.5 Vertical openings

This subsection addresses occupancy I-3 resident's housing areas.

- Floor levels of such areas may be open to the same space without vertical enclosure where all the following apply:
  - Staff can observe the normally occupied areas on all levels open to the same open space.
  - The means of egress can accommodate the egress of all occupants from the interconnected spaces at the same time.
  - The vertical distance between the highest and lowest floor surfaces of the interconnected levels is $\leq 23'$.
  - $\geq \frac{1}{2}$ the means of egress capacity of each story are through exits that do not open to another story open to the interconnected spaces.
- All other openings through floors must be enclosed.

  Note: Section 707, "Shaft and Vertical Exit Enclosures," is cited as the source of requirements for enclosing openings through floors.

408 Group I-3

408.6 Smoke barrier

This subsection addresses the division of occupancy I-3 stories into smoke compartments.

- Spaces with the following characteristics are not required to be protected by smoke barriers:
  - Spaces must exit directly to one of the following locations:
    A public way.
    A building separated from resident housing by one of the following:
    Construction with a fire-resistance rating ≥ 2 hours.
    50' of open space.
    A secure yard or court with a holding space as follows:
    Holding space provides ≥ 6 sf per occupant including the following:
    Staff.
    Residents.
    Visitors.
    Holding space is located ≥ 50' from resident housing.
  - The locking methods for doors in the exit system must meet the following:
    Restraint-condition requirements for the space.
- Otherwise, each of the following stories must be subdivided as indicated below:
  - Stories:
    Where residents sleep.
    With an occupant load ≥ 50 persons.
  - Division requirements:
    Each story must be divided into ≥ 2 smoke compartments by smoke barriers.

  Note: Section 709, "Smoke Barriers," is cited as the source of requirements for these components.

408.6.1 Smoke compartments

- Smoke compartments in occupancy I-3 must have the following characteristics:
  - Number of residents in each compartment must be ≤ 200.
  - Travel distance between the following must be ≤ 150':
    Any room door required for exit access.
    The nearest door in a smoke barrier.
  - Travel distance between the following must be ≤ 200':
    Any point in the smoke compartment.
    The nearest door in a smoke barrier.

408 Group I-3

408.6.2 Refuge area

This subsection addresses refuge areas in occupancy I-3 smoke compartments.

- A refuge area is required in each smoke compartment as follows:
    - ≥ 6 sf is required for each occupant seeking refuge:
    - The occupant count for computing refuge area is based on the following:
        The occupant load of the adjacent smoke compartment.
    - The occupant count for computing refuge area does not include the following:
        Original occupants in the smoke compartment housing the refuge area.
    - The refuge area must be immediately available for occupation in a fire emergency.

    Note: The required refuge area is in addition to the area required for the original occupants of the smoke compartment.

408.6.3 Independent egress

This subsection addresses smoke compartments formed by smoke barriers in occupancy I-3.

- A means of egress is required from each smoke compartment as follows:
    - Means of egress may not require occupants to return to the smoke compartment from which they departed.

408.7.1 Occupancy conditions 3 and 4

This subsection addresses the separation required in occupancy I-3 restraint conditions 3 and 4.

- Where travel distance on the following routes is > 50', the requirement indicated applies:
    - Route:
        Beginning in a sleeping area.
        Passing through the common space.
        To an access corridor.
    - Requirement:
        Common spaces and adjacent sleeping areas must be separated as follows:
            By a smoke-tight partition.

408.7.2 Occupancy condition 5

This subsection addresses separations required in occupancy I-3 restraint condition 5.

- Each sleeping area must be separated from the following adjacent spaces by smoke-tight partitions:
    - Other sleeping areas.
    - Corridors.
    - Common spaces.
- A smoke-tight partition must separate the following areas from each other:
    - Exit access corridor.
    - Common space.

408 Group I-3

408.7.3 Openings in room face

This subsection addresses sleeping rooms in occupancy I-3 restraint conditions 2, 3, 4, and 5.

- Openings in the solid face of sleeping rooms must meet the following requirements:
    Area of openings includes the following:
        Grilles.
        Food passages.
        Door undercuts.
        All other openings.
    ○ Area of all openings combined is limited to ≤ 120 sq in:
    ○ Openings must be located ≤ 3' above the floor.
    ○ In restraint condition 5, openings must be closeable from the room side.

408.7.4 Smoke-tight doors

- Doors in smoke-tight partitions are governed as follows:
    ○ Doors must be substantial.
    ○ Doors must resist the passage of smoke.
    ○ The following are not required on cell doors:
        Latches.
        Door closers.

    Note: The following specify smoke-tight partitions in which smoke-tight doors are
    required:
    408.7.1, "Occupancy conditions 3 and 4."
    408.7.2, "Occupancy condition 5."

408.8 Windowless buildings

- A windowless building or part of a building is defined as having one or more of the following characteristics:
    ○ The building has windows that do not open.
    ○ The building has windows that are not readily breakable.
    ○ The building does not have windows.
- Each windowless building requires an engineered smoke control system as follows:
    ○ Windowless smoke compartments must be provided with one of the following types of ventilation:
        Mechanical.
        Natural.

    Note: Section 909, "Smoke Control Systems," is cited as the source of requirements for
    ventilating smoke control compartments.

410 Stages and Platforms

410.2 Definitions *(part 1 of 2)*

- **Fly gallery**
  - A floor level above a stage:
    - For the movement of scenery.
    - For controlling other stage effects.

- **Gridiron**
  - Structural framing over a stage supporting equipment:
    - For hanging and flying scenery.
    - For supporting other stage effects.

- **Pinrail**
  - A rail on or above a stage:
    - For holding belaying pin to which lines are fastened.

- **Platform**
  - A raised area within a building.
  - Used for any of the following purposes:
    - Worship.
    - Music.
    - Plays.
    - Entertainment.
    - Head table for special guests.
    - Lecturers or speakers.
    - Boxing ring.
    - Wrestling ring.
    - Theater-in-the-round stage.
    - Similar activities.
  - None of the following devices are present:
    - Overhead hanging curtains.
    - Drops.
    - Scenery.
    - Stage effects other than lighting and sound.

- **Platform, temporary**
  - A platform installed for $\leq$ 30 days.

- **Proscenium wall**
  - A wall between the stage and one of the following:
    - Auditorium.
    - Spectator seating.

410 Stages and Platforms

410.2 Definitions *(part 2 of 2)*

- **Stage**
  - A space in a building used for either of the following:
    Entertainment.
    Presentations.
  - Includes the following spaces:
    Performance area.
    Spaces adjacent to performance area as follows:
      Not separated by fire-resistance-rated construction:
      Backstage.
      Support areas.
  - Stage height is measured from the lowest point on the stage floor to the following:
    The highest point on the underside of one of the following:
      Roof deck above the stage.
      Floor deck above the stage.

410 Stages and Platforms

410.3.1 Stage construction

- Stage floors may be constructed as follows where all the conditions indicated below apply:
  - Construction:
    Wood deck.
    Nominal thickness $\geq$ 2".
  - Conditions:
    Stage is separated from other areas by fire-resistance-rated construction.
    Stage floor construction is one of the following types:
      Type II B.
      Type IV.

  Note: The following sections provide the requirements for separation of the stage from other areas as applicable to the conditions above:
      410.3.4, "Proscenium wall."
      410.3.5, "Proscenium curtain."
      410.5.1, "Separation from stage."

- A stage floor is not required to have a fire-resistance rating where all the following conditions apply:
  - Building is one of the following construction types:
    Type II A.
    Type III A.
    Type V A.
  - The space below the stage is provided with the following:
    An automatic fire-extinguishing system.

  Note: The following are cited as governing the options for the fire-extinguishing system required above:
      Section 903, "Automatic Sprinkler Systems."
      Section 904, "Alternative Automatic Fire-Extinguishing Systems."

- Stage finished floors may be constructed out of one of the following materials where the condition below applies:
  - Materials:
    Wood.
    Approved noncombustible materials.
  - Condition:
    Openings in stage floors must have trap doors with the following characteristics:
      Tight fitting.
      Solid wood.
      With approved safety locks.
- In all other cases, stages must be constructed as follows:
  - Using materials required for the building construction type.

410 Stages and Platforms

410.3.2 Galleries, gridirons, catwalks and pinrails

- Floors of the following may be constructed out of any approved material:
  - Fly galleries.
  - Catwalks.
- Materials for beams supporting only the following elements are governed as indicated below:
  - Elements:
    - Theater equipment:
      - Portable.
      - Fixed.
    - Gridirons.
    - Galleries.
    - Catwalks.
  - Beam materials:
    - Must be approved.
    - Must meet requirements of the construction type for the building.
    - Are not required to have a fire-resistance rating.
- For application of code requirements, the following elements do not constitute any of the components listed below:
  - Elements:
    - Fly galleries.
    - Gridirons.
    - Catwalks.
  - Components:
    - Floors.
    - Stories.
    - Mezzanines.
    - Levels.

410.3.3 Exterior stage doors *(part 1 of 2)*

- Where protection is required for the following openings, the requirement below applies:
  - Openings:
    - Exterior exit doors from the stage.
  - Requirement:
    - Such doors must be fire doors.

  Note: Section 714, "Opening Protectives," is cited as governing fire doors as required above.

410 Stages and Platforms

410.3.3 Exterior stage doors *(part 2 of 2)*

- The following exterior openings from a stage are governed as indicated below:
  - ○ Openings:
    - Exterior exit doors.
    - Exterior doors for loading and unloading.
  - ○ Requirements:
    - Vestibules required as follows:
      - Where doors may be open while the theater is occupied.
      - To prevent air drafts into the auditorium.

410.3.4 Proscenium wall

- The following applies where stage height is > 50'.
  - ○ All areas of the stage must be separated from the seating area as follows:
    - By a proscenium wall:
      - Wall must have a fire-resistance rating ≥ 2 hr.
    - Wall must be continuous between the foundation and roof.

410.3.5 Proscenium curtain

- This subsection applies to stages with a height > 50'.
- One of the following curtains is required for the proscenium opening:
  - ○ A water curtain as per NFPA 13.
  - ○ A curtain of approved material to function as follows:
    - Curtain must intercept the following:
      - Hot gases.
      - Flames.
      - Smoke.
    - A glow in the curtain from a stage fire is limited as follows:
      - Glow must not show on the auditorium side for ≤ 20 minutes.
    - Curtain must close from completely open as follows:
      - Must close in ≤ 30 seconds.
      - The last 8' of closing must take ≥ 5 seconds.

410.3.7 Scenery

- Materials for stage sets and scenery are governed as follows:
  - ○ Combustible materials must be flame resistant.
  - ○ Foam plastics are regulated by other provisions.

  Note: The following are cited as governing the above listed materials as indicated:
  Section 805, "Decorations and Trim," for combustible materials.
  Section 2603, "Foam Plastic Insulation," for foam plastics.
  International Fire Code for combustible materials and foam plastics.

410 Stages and Platforms

410.4 Platform construction

This subsection governs permanent platforms.

- Fire-retardant-treated wood may be used for platforms where all the following conditions are present:
  - The building of one of the following types of construction:
      Type I.
      Type II.
      Type IV.
    The platform is ≤ 30" above the main floor.
    The platform is ≤ $\frac{1}{3}$ the room area.
    The platform is ≤ 3000 sf.
- In other cases, platform materials must be consistent with that required for the construction type of the building.
- Platform floors must have a fire-resistance rating ≥ 1 hr in the following case:
  - Where the space under the floor is used for the following:
      Storage.
      Purpose other than the following:
        Equipment.
        Wiring.
        Plumbing.
  - The underside of the platform floor need not be protected in the following case:
      Where the space under the floor is used only for the following:
        Equipment.
        Wiring.
        Plumbing.

410.4.1 Temporary platforms

This section addresses platforms installed for ≤ 30 days.

- Any material allowed by the other provisions of the code may be used for temporary platforms.
- The space under a temporary platform and above the building floor is not permitted to be used for any purposes except the following service to platform equipment:
  - Plumbing.
  - Electrical wiring.

410 Stages and Platforms

410.5.1 Separation from stage

- Stages must be separated from the following spaces as indicated below:
  - Spaces:
      Dressing rooms.
      Scene docks.
      Property rooms and storerooms.
      Workshops.
      Compartments appurtenant to the stage.
      Other parts of the building.
  - Where the stage height is > 50':
      The following separations are required with the characteristics indicated below:
        Separations:
          Fire barrier walls.
          Horizontal assemblies.
        Characteristics required:
          Fire-resistance rating ≥ 2 hrs.
          Approved opening protectives.
  - Where the stage height is ≤ 50':
      The following separations are required with the characteristics indicated below:
        Separations:
          Fire barrier walls.
          Horizontal assemblies.
        Characteristics required:
          Fire-resistance rating ≥ 1 hr.
          Approved opening protectives.

410.5.2 Separation from each other

- The following spaces must be separated from each other as indicated below:
  - Spaces:
      Dressing rooms.
      Scene docks.
      Property rooms and storerooms.
      Workshops.
      Compartments appurtenant to the stage.
  - Separation:
      The following separations are required with the characteristics listed below:
        Separations:
          Fire barrier walls.
          Horizontal assemblies.
        Characteristics required:
          Fire-resistance rating ≥ 1 hr.
          Approved opening protectives.

410 Stages and Platforms

410.5.3 Opening protectives

This subsection governs doorways to dressing and appurtenant rooms.

- Doorways other than the following may not connect dressing rooms and appurtenant spaces to the stage:
  - Doors to trunk rooms.
  - Doors other than those necessary at stage level.
- Doorways must be protected with fire door assemblies.

    Note: Section 714, "Opening Protectives," is cited as governing fire door assemblies as required above.

410.5.4 Stage exits

- ≥ 1 approved means of egress is required from the following locations:
  - Each side of the stage.
  - Each side of the space under the stage.
- ≥ 1 means of escape is required from the following locations:
  - Each fly gallery.
  - The gridiron.
- The gridiron may have one of the following access devices to a scuttle in the stage roof:
  - Steel ladder.
  - Alternating tread stairway.
  - Spiral stairway.

410.6 Automatic sprinkler system (*part 1 of 2*)

- Sprinklers are not required under stages areas with all of the following characteristics:
  - The space has a clear height < 4'.
  - The space is used only for storage of tables and chairs.
  - Concealed space is separated from other spaces by Type X gypsum board ≥ $^5/_8$" thick.
- Sprinklers are not required for stages with all of the following characteristics:
  - Stages with ≤ 1000 sf.
  - Stages ≤ 50' in height as follows:
    - Where the following are not retractable vertically:
      - Curtains.
      - Scenery.
      - Other combustible hangings.
  - Combustible hangings are limited to the following:
    - One main curtain.
    - Borders.
    - Legs.
    - One backdrop.

410 Stages and Platforms

410.6 Automatic sprinkler system (*part 2 of 2*)

- Otherwise, stages require an automatic fire-extinguishing system in the following locations:
  - Under the roof above the gridiron.
  - Under the gridiron.
  - In tie and fly galleries.
  - Behind the proscenium wall of the stage.
  - In spaces accessory to the stage as follows:
    Dressing rooms.
    Lounges.
    Workshops.
    Storerooms.

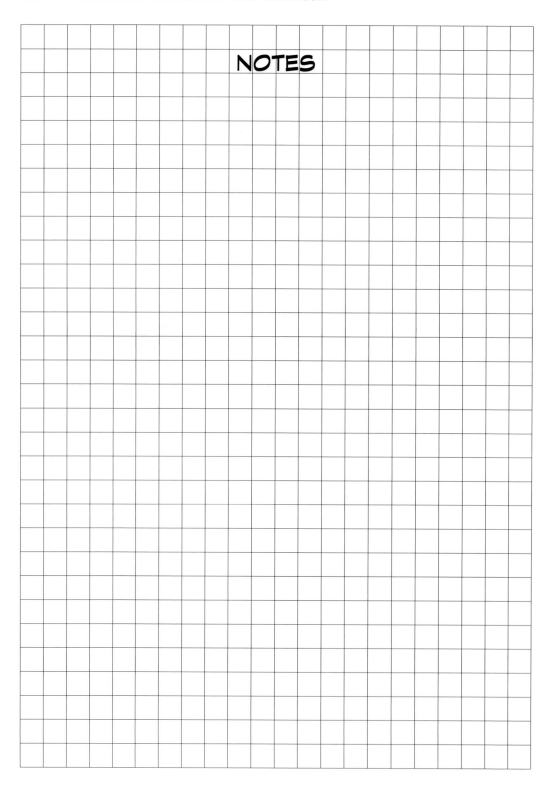

NOTES

5

General Building Heights and Areas

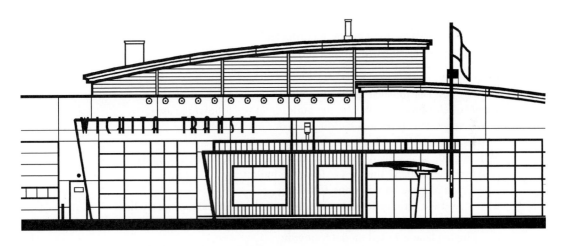

Wichita Transit Storage, Administration, and Maintenance Facility.
Wichita, Kansas. *(partial elevation)*
Wilson Darnell Mann, P.A., Architects. Wichita, Kansas.

502 Definitions

502.1 Definitions *(part 1 of 2)*

- **Area, building**
  - ○ Area within the inside surfaces of the following perimeters as applicable:
    - Exterior walls.
    - Exterior walls and fire walls.
  - ○ Areas of the following elements are not included:
    - Vent shafts.
    - Courts.
  - ○ Usable area outside the exterior walls is included where is under the following:
    - Roof above.
    - Floor above.

- **Basement**
  - ○ A story that is below the grade plane as follows:
    - Partly.
    - Completely.
  - ○ A basement is considered a story above the grade plane as follows:
    - Where the finished floor above the basement is > any of the following:
      - 6' above the grade plane.
      - 6' above the finished grade as follows:
        - For > half the total building perimeter.
      - 12' above the finished ground surface at any point.

- **Grade plane**
  - ○ Average level of finished grade at the building.
  - ○ Points of elevation are taken at the building in the following cases:
    - Where grade is level to a building façade.
    - Where grade slopes down to a building façade.
  - ○ Where grade slopes away from a building façade, the following apply:
    - Where the property line is ≤ 6' from the building:
      - Grade plane is based on the following:
        - Average level of lowest points between building and property line.
    - Where the property line is > 6' from the building:
      - Grade plane is based on the following:
        - Average level of lowest points ≤ 6' from the building.

  Note: When more than 4 corner points are used to determine the grade plane, points should be evenly distributed along any façade.

502 Definitions

502.1 Definitions *(part 2 of 2)*

- **Height, building**
  - Vertical distance between the following points:
    Grade plane.
    Roof:
      The top of a flat roof.
      A level halfway between the highest and lowest points of a sloped roof.

- **Height, story**
  - Floors below the top floor:
    Vertical distance between the following:
      Top of a finished floor.
      Top of the finished floor next above it.
  - Top floor:
    Vertical distance between the following:
      Top of the finished floor and one of the following as applicable:
        The top of the ceiling joists.
        The top of the roof rafters as follows:
          Where there is no ceiling.

- **Industrial equipment platform**
  - A platform and associated components as follows:
    Elevated walkways.
    Stairs.
    Ladders.
  - Platform is unoccupied.
  - Located in occupancy F.
  - Used exclusively for one or both of the following:
    Mechanical systems.
    Industrial process equipment.
  - Not part of a mezzanine.

- **Mezzanine**
  - A level or levels between the following:
    Floor of a story.
    Ceiling of a story.
  - Has a total floor area as follows:
    $\leq \frac{1}{3}$ that of the space where it is located.

- **Story**
  - The space between the following:
    The top surface of a floor and one of the following:
      The top surface of the next floor above.
      The top surface of the roof as follows:
        Where there is no floor above.

503 General Height and Area Limitations

503.1 General *(part 1 of 3)*

- Building height and area are limited by this section as per construction type and occupancy.
- Each part of a building enclosed is considered to be a separate building as follows:
  - Within the exterior walls.
  - Within the exterior walls and fire walls where applicable.
- Height and area limitations are subject to modification elsewhere in the code.
- Maximum area per floor and building height by occupancy are as follows:

Table 503.1a   **Maximum Building Height and Area per Floor**

Occ.	Height	Type of construction								
		IA	IB	IIA	IIB	IIIA	IIIB	IV	VA	VB
Occupancy A: maximum height in stories and feet										
A	Feet	UL	160	65	55	65	55	65	50	40
A-1	Stories	UL	5	3	2	3	2	3	2	1
A-2	"	UL	11	3	2	3	2	3	2	1
A-3	"	UL	11	3	2	3	2	3	2	1
A-4	"	UL	11	3	2	3	2	3	2	1
A-5	"	UL	UL	UL	UL	UL	UL	UL	UL	UL
Occupancy A: maximum area per floor in square feet										
A-1	SF	UL	UL	15,500	8,500	14,000	8,500	15,000	11,500	5,500
A-2	"	UL	UL	15,500	9,500	14,000	9,500	15,000	11,500	6,000
A-3	"	UL	UL	15,500	9,500	14,000	9,500	15,000	11,500	6,000
A-4	"	UL	UL	15,500	9,500	14,000	9,500	15,000	11,500	6,000
A-5	"	UL	UL	UL	UL	UL	UL	UL	UL	UL
Occupancy B: maximum area in square feet										
B	Feet	UL	160	65	55	65	55	65	50	40
B	Stories	UL	11	5	4	5	4	5	3	2
Occupancy B: maximum area per floor in square feet										
B	SF	UL	UL	37,500	23,000	28,500	19,000	36,000	18,000	9,000
Occupancy E: maximum height in stories and feet										
E	Feet	UL	160	65	55	65	55	65	50	40
E	Stories	UL	5	3	2	3	2	3	1	1
Occupancy E: maximum area per floor in square feet										
E	SF	UL	UL	26,500	14,500	23,500	14,500	25,500	18,500	9,500

Source: IBC Table 503.
UL = unlimited, Occ. = occupancy, SF = square feet.

Case study: Fig. 503.1A. The occupancy B building is Type IIB construction and is not sprinklered. A maximum height of 55' and 4 stories is permitted for this category of building. The building is 2 stories and 38'-4" high, measured to the average height of the highest roof; thus, it is in compliance with the code regarding height.

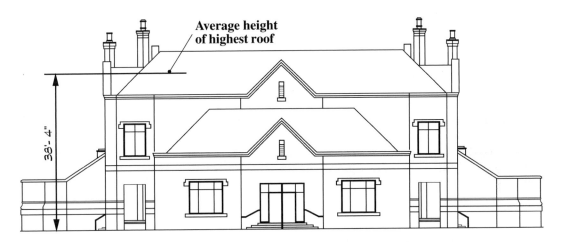

Fig. 503.1A. East elevation. Country Club Park Building One. Wichita, Kansas. Gossen Livingston Associates, Inc., Architecture. Wichita, Kansas.

503 General Height and Area Limitations

503.1 General *(part 2 of 3)*

Table 503.1b   Maximum Building Height and Area per Floor

Occ.	Height	Type of construction								
		IA	IB	IIA	IIB	IIIA	IIIB	IV	VA	VB
Occupancy F: maximum height in stories and feet										
F	Feet	UL	160	65	55	65	55	65	50	40
F-1	Stories	UL	11	4	2	3	2	4	2	1
F-2	Stories	UL	11	5	3	4	3	5	3	2
Occupancy F: maximum area per floor in square feet										
F-1	SF	UL	UL	25,000	15,500	19,000	12,000	35,500	14,000	8,500
F-2	SF	UL	UL	37,500	23,000	28,500	18,000	50,500	21,500	13,000
Occupancy H: maximum height in stories and feet										
H	Feet	UL	160	65	55	65	55	65	50	40
H-1	Stories	1	1	1	1	1	1	1	1	NP
H-2	"	UL	3	2	1	2	1	2	1	1
H-3	"	UL	6	4	2	4	2	4	2	1
H-4	"	UL	7	5	3	5	3	5	3	2
H-5	"	3	3	3	3	3	3	3	3	2
Occupancy H: maximum area per floor in square feet										
H-1	SF	21,000	16,500	11,000	7,000	9,500	7,000	10,500	7,500	NP
H-2	"	21,000	16,500	11,000	7,000	9,500	7,000	10,500	7,500	3,000
H-3	"	UL	60,000	26,500	14,000	17,500	13,000	25,500	10,000	5,000
H-4	"	UL	UL	37,500	17,500	28,500	17,500	36,000	18,000	6,500
H-5	"	UL	UL	37,500	23,000	28,500	19,000	36,000	18,000	9,000
Occupancy I: maximum height in stories and feet										
I	Feet	UL	160	65	55	65	55	65	50	40
I-1	Stories	UL	9	4	3	4	3	4	3	2
I-2	"	UL	4	2	1	1	NP	1	1	NP
I-3	"	UL	4	2	1	2	1	2	2	1
I-4	"	UL	5	3	2	3	2	3	1	1
Occupancy I: maximum area per floor in square feet										
I-1	SF	UL	55,000	19,000	10,000	16,500	10,000	18,000	10,500	4,500
I-2	"	UL	UL	15,500	11,000	12,000	NP	12,000	9,500	NP
I-3	"	UL	UL	15,000	10,000	10,500	7,500	12,000	7,500	5,000
I-4	"	UL	60,500	26,500	13,000	23,500	13,000	25,500	18,500	9,000

Source: IBC Table 503.
UL = unlimited, Occ. = occupancy, SF = square feet, NP = not permitted.

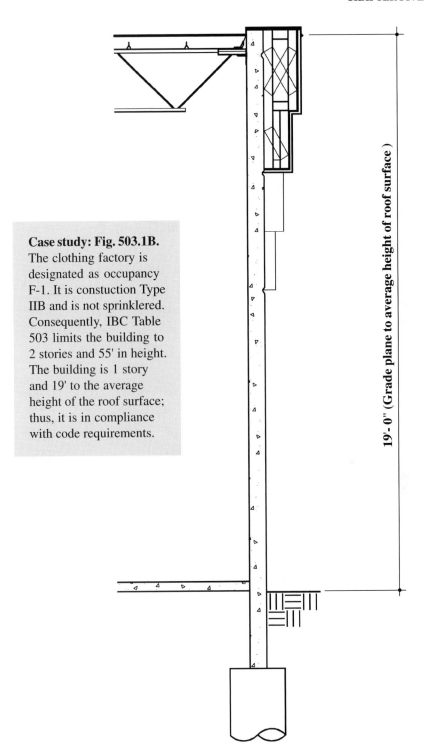

Case study: Fig. 503.1B.
The clothing factory is designated as occupancy F-1. It is constuction Type IIB and is not sprinklered. Consequently, IBC Table 503 limits the building to 2 stories and 55' in height. The building is 1 story and 19' to the average height of the roof surface; thus, it is in compliance with code requirements.

19'- 0" (Grade plane to average height of roof surface)

Fig. 503.1B. Wall section. Garments to Go. Bastrop, Texas. Spencer Godfrey Architects. Round Rock, Texas.

503 General Height and Area Limitations

503.1 General *(part 3 of 3)*

Table 503.1c   Maximum Building Height and Area per Floor

Occ.	Height	IA	IB	IIA	IIB	IIIA	IIIB	IV	VA	VB
Occupancy M: maximum height in stories and feet										
M	Feet	UL	160	65	55	65	55	65	50	40
M	Stories	UL	11	4	4	4	4	4	3	1
Occupancy M: maximum area per floor in square feet										
M	SF	UL	UL	21,500	12,500	18,500	12,500	20,500	14,000	9,000
Occupancy R: maximum height in stories and feet										
R	Feet	UL	160	65	55	65	55	65	50	40
R-1	Stories	UL	11	4	4	4	4	4	3	2
R-2	"	UL	11	4	4	4	4	4	3	2
R-3	"	UL	11	4	4	4	4	4	3	3
R-4	"	UL	11	4	4	4	4	4	3	2
Occupancy R: maximum area per floor in square feet										
R-1	SF	UL	UL	24,000	16,000	24,000	16,000	20,500	12,000	7,000
R-2	"	UL	UL	24,000	16,000	24,000	16,000	20,500	12,000	7,000
R-3	"	UL	UL	UL	UL	UL	UL	UL	UL	UL
R-4	"	UL	UL	24,000	16,000	24,000	16,000	20,500	12,000	7,000
Occupancy S: maximum height in stories and feet										
S	Feet	UL	160	65	55	65	55	65	50	40
S-1	Stories	UL	11	4	3	3	3	4	3	1
S-2	Stories	UL	11	5	4	4	4	5	4	2
Occupancy S: maximum area per floor in square feet										
S-1	SF	UL	48,000	26,000	17,500	26,000	17,500	25,500	14,000	9,000
S-2	SF	UL	79,000	39,000	26,000	39,000	26,000	38,500	21,000	13,500
Occupancy U: maximum height in stories and feet										
U	Feet	UL	160	65	55	65	55	65	50	40
U	Stories	UL	5	4	2	3	2	4	2	1
Occupancy U: maximum area per floor in square feet										
U	SF	UL	35,500	19,000	8,500	14,000	8,500	18,000	9,000	5,500

Source: IBC Table 503.
UL = unlimited, Occ. = occupancy, SF = square feet.

503 General Height and Area Limitations

503.1.1 Basements

- Basement areas are not included in the total area permitted as follows:
  - Where the basement area < that allowed for a 1-story building.

503.1.2 Special industrial occupancies

- The following buildings and structures are not required to meet height and area limitations based on occupancy and construction type:
  - Those containing low-hazard industrial processes as follows:
    Processes requiring large areas and heights to accommodate the following:
    Building with craneways.
    Rolling mills.
    Structural metal fabrication shops and foundries.
    Production and distribution of power as follows:
    Electric.
    Gas.
    Steam.

  Note: IBC Table 503, "Allowable Height and Building Areas," is cited as listing the limitations from which these buildings are exempt.

503.1.3 Buildings on same lot

- Multiple buildings on the same lot may be considered to be either of the following:
  - Separate buildings.
  - A single building where all of the following apply:
    Height of each building meets the following:
    Height limits based on occupancy and construction type as modified.
    Sum of areas of the buildings meets the following:
    Area limits based on occupancy and construction type as modified.
    The individual structures meet applicable code requirements.
    The group of structures meet applicable code requirements as a single building.

Note: The following are cited as providing limits for the buildings described above:
  IBC Table 503, "Allowable Height and Building Areas," provides the base limits.
  Section 504, "Height Modifications," alters the limits based on conditions.
  Section 506, "Area Modifications," alters the limits based on conditions.

503 General Height and Area Limitations

503.1.4 Type I construction

- Buildings of Type I construction, which are allowed unlimited height or area based on occupancy and construction type, are governed as follows:
  - These buildings are not subject to the conditions that are required for unlimited or increased height or area in other cases or construction types.

  Note: Section 504, "Height Modifications," provides conditions for height increases that are not required of Type I construction to have unlimited height.
  503.1.2, "Special industrial occupancies," is cited as a source of conditions that are not required of Type I construction to have unlimited height.
  Section 507, "Unlimited Area Buildings," is cited as a source of conditions that are not required of Type I construction in order to warrant unlimited area.

503.2 Party walls

- A party wall must be constructed as a fire wall as follows:
  - Where located on a property line.
  - When located between adjacent buildings.
  - When used for joint service by the two buildings.
- Fire walls serving as party walls define separate buildings on each side.

  Note: Section 705, "Fire Walls," is cited as governing such construction.

503.3 Area determination

- This section does not apply to buildings of unlimited area.

  Note: Section 507, "Unlimited Area Buildings," is cited as the source of requirements for the unlimited area buildings excluded from this section.

- The total area allowed for a building is calculated as follows:

  Area per floor permitted by occupancy and construction type.
  + Additional area permitted due to the availability of minimum frontage.
  + Additional area permitted by the presence of sprinklers.

  Increased area permitted per floor.

  Total building area allowed is as follows:

  Area for 1-story buildings = Increased area permitted per floor.
  Area for 2-story buildings = Increased area permitted per floor × 2 floors.
  Area for ≥ 3-story buildings = Increased area permitted per floor × 3 floors.

  Note: IBC Table 503, "Allowable Height and Building Areas," provides the area per floor permitted by occupancy and construction type.
  506.2, "Frontage increase," provides the method for determining the increase in area permitted based on frontage..
  506.3, "Automatic sprinkler system increase," provides the method for determining the increase in area permitted based on sprinklers.

504 Height Modifications

504.1 General

- The height of the following aircraft buildings is unlimited where the conditions indicated below apply:
  - Buildings:
    Aircraft hangars.
    Aircraft paint hangars.
    Buildings in which aircraft are manufactured.
  - Conditions:
    Automatic fire-extinguishing system is required.
    Building is surrounded by public ways or yards as follows:

    ### Width is ≥ 1½ × hangar height.

    Note: Chapter 9, "Fire Protection Systems," is cited as the source of requirements for the fire-extinguishing system required above.

- Height limits of other buildings based on occupancy and construction type may be increased only as permitted in this section.

504.2 Automatic sprinkler increase *(part 1 of 4)*

- This section lists maximum heights of buildings sprinklered as per NFPA 13 as follows:
  - Maximums listed for the following do not constitute limit increases over those required for building without sprinklers:
    Occupancy I-2 in construction Type IIB, III, IV, V.
    Occupancies H-1, H-2, H-3, H-5.
    Buildings having unlimited height without sprinklers.
- These heights are allowed in addition to permitted area increases.

  Note: Table 503, "Allowable Height and Building Areas," is cited as the source of height limits for buildings without sprinklers.

- Maximum height in feet and stories by occupancy are as follows:

Table 504.2a   Maximum Height of Sprinklered Buildings

| Occ. | Height | Type of construction | | | | | | | | |
		IA	IB	IIA	IIB	IIIA	IIIB	IV	VA	VB
Occupancy A:										
A	Feet	UL	180	85	75	85	75	85	70	60
A-1	Stories	UL	6	4	3	4	3	4	3	2
A-2	"	UL	12	4	3	4	3	4	3	2
A-3	"	UL	12	4	3	4	3	4	3	2
A-4	"	UL	12	4	3	4	3	4	3	2
A-5	"	UL	UL	UL	UL	UL	UL	UL	UL	UL

UL = unlimited, Occ. = occupancy.

504 Height Modifications

504.2 Automatic sprinkler increase *(part 2 of 4)*

- This section lists maximum heights of buildings sprinklered as per NFPA 13.

Table 504.2b   **Maximum Height of Sprinklered Buildings**

Occ.	Height	Type of construction								
		IA	IB	IIA	IIB	IIIA	IIIB	IV	VA	VB
Occupancy B:										
B	Feet	UL	180	85	75	85	75	85	70	60
B	Stories	UL	11	6	5	6	5	6	4	3
Occupancy E:										
E	Feet	UL	180	85	75	85	75	85	70	60
E	Stories	UL	6	4	3	4	3	4	2	2

UL = unlimited, Occ. = occupancy.

Case study: Fig.504.2A. The occupancy B building is sprinklered and is Type VB construction. This qualifies the builidng for an increase in height from limits of 40' and 2 stories for buildings that are unsprinklered to limits of 60' and 3 stories. The building is 2 stories and 30'-8" high, measured to the average height of the roof behind the parapet (just below the top of the spandrel glass). Thus, the building complies with the code requirements for height.

Fig. 504.2A. Partial elevation. AmberGlen Business Center. Hillsboro, Oregon. Ankrom Moisan Associated Architects. Portland, Oregon.

504 Height Modifications

504.2 Automatic sprinkler increase *(part 3 of 4)*

• This section lists maximum heights of buildings sprinklered as per NFPA 13.

Table 504.2c   Maximum Height of Sprinklered Buildings

Occ.	Height	IA	IB	IIA	IIB	IIIA	IIIB	IV	VA	VB
					Type of construction					
Occupancy F:										
F	Feet	UL	180	85	75	85	75	85	70	60
F-1	Stories	UL	12	5	3	4	3	5	3	2
F-2	Stories	UL	12	6	4	5	4	6	4	3
Occupancy H:										
H	Feet	UL	160	65	55	65	55	65	50	40
H-1	Stories	1	1	1	1	1	1	1	1	NP
H-2	"	UL	3	2	1	2	1	2	1	1
H-3	"	UL	6	4	2	4	2	4	2	1
H-5	"	3	3	3	3	3	3	3	3	2
Occupancy H-4:										
H-4	Feet	UL	180	85	75	85	75	85	70	60
H-4	Stories	UL	8	6	4	6	4	6	4	3
Occupancy I:										
I	Feet	UL	180	85	75	85	75	85	70	60
I-1	Stories	UL	10	5	4	5	4	5	4	3
I-3	"	UL	5	3	2	3	2	3	3	2
I-4	"	UL	6	4	3	4	3	4	2	2
Occupancy I-2:										
I-2	Feet	UL	180	85	55	65	55	65	50	40
I-2	Stories	UL	5	3	1	1	NP	1	1	NP
Occupancy M:										
M	Feet	UL	180	85	75	85	75	85	70	60
M	Stories	UL	12	5	5	5	5	5	4	2

UL = unlimited, NP = not permitted, Occ. = occupancy.

504 Height Modifications

504.2 Automatic sprinkler increase *(part 4 of 4)*

- This section lists maximum heights of buildings sprinklered as per NFPA 13.

Table 504.2d   Maximum Height of Sprinklered Buildings

Occ.	Height	IA	IB	IIA	IIB	IIIA	IIIB	IV	VA	VB
Occupancy R:										
R	Feet	UL	160	65	65	65	60	65	60	60
R-1	Stories	UL	11	4	4	4	4	4	4	3
R-2	"	UL	11	4	4	4	4	4	4	3
R-3	"	UL	11	4	4	4	4	4	4	4
R-4	"	UL	11	4	4	4	4	4	4	3
Occupancy S:										
S	Feet	UL	180	85	75	85	75	85	70	60
S-1	Stories	UL	12	5	4	4	4	5	4	2
S-2	Stories	UL	12	6	5	5	5	6	5	3
Occupancy U:										
U	Feet	UL	180	85	75	85	75	85	70	60
U	Stories	UL	6	5	3	4	3	5	3	2

UL = unlimited, Occ. = occupancy.

Case study: Fig. 504.2B. The structure houses an occupancy B area separated from an occupancy S-1 warehouse by a fire wall. Construction is Type IIIA. The warehouse is limited to 4 stories and 85' in height based on the fact that it is sprinklered. The height of the 1-story warehouse from the grade plane to the average height of the roof is 42'. The warehouse is within height limitations for a sprinklered S-1 building of this type of construction.

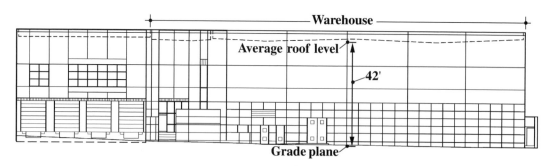

Fig. 504.2B. Elevation. New Warehouse Addition. Los Angeles, California. Stephen Wen + Associates, Architects, Inc. Pasadena, California.

504 Height Modifications

504.3 Roof structures *(part 1 of 2)*

- The following applies to penthouses on buildings of Type I and II construction:
  - Where exterior walls and roofs are > 5' and < 20' from a common property line:
    A fire-resistance rating of ≥ 1 hr is required for the following:
      Exterior walls and roofs.
    Noncombustible construction is required for the following:
      Exterior walls and roofs.
      Interior walls and framing.
  - Where exterior walls and roofs are > 20' from a common property line:
    Noncombustible construction is required for the following:
      Exterior walls and roofs.
      Interior walls.
- For penthouses on buildings of type III, IV, and V construction, the following apply:
  - Where exterior walls > 5' and < 20' from a common property line:
    Exterior walls require a fire-resistance rating of ≥ 1 hr.
  - Where exterior walls are > 20' from a common property line:
    Exterior walls are required to be at least one of the following:
      Type IV construction.
      Noncombustible construction.
  - Interior walls are required to be at least one of the following:
      Type IV construction.
      Noncombustible construction.
  - Roofs are to have materials and fire-resistance ratings required for the construction type.

    Note: IBC Table 601, "Fire-Resistance Rating Requirements for Building Elements," includes requirements for roofs as indicated above.

- The following enclosures may be unprotected noncombustible construction:
  - When containing only mechanical equipment.
  - When located ≥ 20' from property lines.
- Mechanical equipment screens may be combustible where the following conditions exist:
  - Building must be 1 story.
  - No roof may be present on the screens.
  - Screens must be located ≥ 20' from property lines.
  - Screens must be ≤ 4' in height above the roof surface.
- Dormers must be the same type of construction as one of the following:
  - The roof of which they are a part.
  - The exterior walls of the building.
- Other penthouses are to have walls, floors, and roof as required for the building.

504 Height Modifications

504.3 Roof structures *(part 2 of 2)*

- Other constructions on roofs of the following types are governed as indicated below:
  - Constructions:
    - Towers.
    - Spires and steeples.
    - Other constructions.
  - Requirements:
    - Materials as per the building construction type are required.
    - The constructions may not be used for habitation.
    - The constructions may not be used for storage.
    - Height of constructions of noncombustible materials is unlimited.
    - Height of constructions of combustible materials is as follows:
      - Limited to ≤ 20' above allowable building height.

  Note: Chapter 15, "Roof Assemblies and Rooftop Structures," is cited as the source for additional requirements.

505 Mezzanines

505.1 General

- Mezzanines are considered to be a part of the floor below.
- The areas of mezzanines are included in the computation of fire areas.
- The clear height above a mezzanine floor must be $\geq 7'$.
- The clear height below a mezzanine floor construction must be $\geq 7'$.
- The areas of mezzanines are not included in the area limit per floor as based on occupancy and construction type.
- Mezzanines are not considered to be a story when computing the number of stories in the height of a building as limited by occupancy and construction type.

> *Note: The following are cited as sources of requirements applicable as indicated:*
> > *503.1, "General," which includes IBC Table 503, "Allowable Height and Building Areas."*
> > *Section 702, "Definitions," defines fire area as referred to above.*

505.2 Area limitations

- Mezzanine areas in industrial space that are exempt from the height and area limitations are governed as follows:
  - In Type 1 and 2 construction:
    The total area of all mezzanines in a space must be $\leq {}^2/_3$ the area of the space.
- Mezzanine areas in all other occupancies are governed as follows:
  - The total area of all mezzanines in a space must be $\leq {}^1/_3$ the area of the space.
- The following are not included in determining the size of a space containing a mezzanine:
  - Enclosed areas within the space.
  - The area of the mezzanine.

> *Note: 503.1.2, "Special industrial occupancies," is cited as defining the spaces exempt from height and area limitations.*

505 Mezzanines

505.3 Egress

- ≥ 2 means of egress are required from a mezzanine as follows:
  ○ Where its occupant load exceeds that listed below.
  ○ Where its common path of travel would otherwise exceed that listed below.

Table 505.3   Length Limits for Common Path of Egress Travel

Occupancy	Occupant load	Common path with sprinklers	without sprinklers
A, E, M, U	50	75'	75'
B, F	50	75'	100'
B tenant space, S, U	30	100'	100'
H-1, H-2, H-3	3	not permitted	25'
H-4, H-5	10	not permitted	75'
I-1, I-4, R	10	75'	75'
I-3	10	100'	100'

> Note: 1004.2.5, "Common path of egress travel," is cited as the source of limits for egress travel, a partial summary of which is provided above.
>
> 1004.2.3.2, "Group I-2," addresses egress travel and means of egress requirements in occupancy I-2.

- The length of egress travel on a mezzanine stairway is included in the travel distance as follows:
  ○ As measured on a line connecting the tread nosings.

505.4 Openness (*part 1 of 2*)

- Mezzanines are not required to be open to the space in which they are located in any of the following cases:
  ○ Where the total occupant load of all the enclosed mezzanine areas totals ≤ 10.
  ○ Where both of the following apply:
    The mezzanine has ≥ 2 means of egress.
    ≥ 1 means of egress has direct access to an exit from the mezzanine.
  ○ Where enclosed portions are ≤ 10% of the total of the mezzanine areas.
- Mezzanines with both of the following conditions may be glazed on all sides:
  ○ Located in an industrial facility.
  ○ Used for control of equipment.

505 Mezzanines

505.4 Openness (*part 2 of 2*)

- Mezzanines are not required to be open to the surrounding space where all of the following conditions apply:
  - In occupancy F.
  - The building qualifies for having unlimited area.
  - The building is sprinklered as per NFPA 13.
  - The building is adjacent to public ways or yards ≥ 60' wide on all sides.
  - A fire alarm system is provided throughout the building.
  - Notification devices are located throughout the mezzanine.
  - In addition to any other required methods, fire alarms are also initiated by the following:
    Sprinkler flow.
    Manually.

  > *Note: The following are cited as the sources of requirements applicable to this section.*
  >   *507.2, "Sprinklered, one-story," provides requirements for buildings qualifying to be unlimited in area, a partial summary of which is provided above.*
  >   *507.3, "Two-story," provides requirements for buildings qualifying to be unlimited in area, a partial summary of which is provided above.*
  >   *NFPA 72, " National Fire Alarm Code," governs the fire alarm systems.*

- All other mezzanines must be open to the surrounding space as follows:
  - The following are permitted:
    Walls ≤ 42" above the mezzanine floor.
    Columns.
    Posts.

505.5 Industrial equipment platforms

- Platforms are not considered to be a part of the floor below.
- The areas of platforms are not included in the area limit per floor based on occupancy and construction type.
- Platforms are not considered to be a story when computing the number of stories in the height of a building as limited by occupancy and construction type.

  > *Note: 503.1, "General," which includes IBC Table 503, "Allowable Height and Building Areas," is cited as the source of heights and areas based on occupancy and construction type as indicated above.*

- The areas of platforms are not included in the computation of fire areas.
- Platforms may not be a part of a mezzanine.
- Platforms and the following components may not serve as a means of egress from a building:
  - Components providing access to platforms:
    Walkways.
    Stairs.
    Ladders.

505 Mezzanines

505.5.1 Area limitations

This subsection addresses industrial equipment platforms.

- The combined-areas platforms in a space is limited as follows:
  Area must be $\leq \frac{2}{3}$ the area of the space.
- The combined areas of platforms and mezzanines in the same space is limited as follows:
  Area must be $\leq \frac{2}{3}$ the area of the space.

  Note: 505.2, "Area limitation," is cited as the source of the limit on mezzanine area, which also applies when mezzanines are in the same space as a platform.

505.5.2 Fire suppression

- Sprinklers are required above and below industrial equipment platforms.

  Note: 903.3, "Installation requirements," is cited as the source of requirements for the sprinklers.

505.5.3 Guards

- Guards are required along the open sides of platforms as follows:
  - Where an open side is > 30" above the floor below.
  - Guards must be $\geq$ 42" above the floor surface of the platform.
  - Guards must meet the other requirements as follows:
    Structural requirements.
    Limitations on openings therein.

  Note: 1003.2.12, "Guards," is cited as the source of requirements for guards. Included are other requirements for guards, a partial summary of which is provided above.

506 Area Modifications

506.1 General

- Area per floor limits based on occupancy and construction type may be increased as follows:

> **Limit of area per floor**
> **+ Additional square footage allowed due to frontage**
> **+ Additional square footage allowed due to the presence of sprinklers**
>
> **Increased limit of area per floor**

- Additional square footage allowed is determined by the % increase allowed as follows:

Additional square footage allowed = (% increase added ÷ 100) ✕ Limit of area per floor

Note: The following are cited as sources of applicable requirements:
IBC Table 503, "Allowable Height and Building Areas."
506.2, "Frontage increase," describes area increases permitted by frontage.
506.3, "Automatic sprinkler system increases," lists increases based on sprinklers.

506.1.1 Basements

- The area of a single basement need not be included in the total building area as follows:
  - Where the basement area is ≤ that permitted for a 1-story building.

506.2 Frontage increase *(Part 1 of 4)*

This section addresses increases to limits to area per floor based on occupancy and construction type as permitted by minimum frontage requirements.

- The area limit may be increased where the following frontage conditions exist:
  - \> 25% of the building perimeter must adjoin a public way or an open space as follows:
    The space must be ≥ 20' wide measured ⊥ to the property line.
- The % increase in area permitted by frontage is listed in the following tables as follows:
  - Tables are based on the following equation:

% increase in area = (% of open perimeter - 25%) ✕ (width of open space ÷ 30)

"Open perimeter" = perimeter adjoining a public way or open space.
"Width of open space ÷ 30" is limited to a value ≤ 2 for buildings of unlimited area.
"Width of open space ÷ 30" is limited to a value ≤ 1 for other buildings.

Note: 506.2.1, "Width limits" establishes a maximum to the % increase in area as determined by the above equation by limiting the value of "width of open space ÷ 30" as indicated above.

506 Area Modifications

506.2 Frontage increase *(Part 2 of 4)*

- The table below indicates the permitted % increase to the limit of area per floor as follows:
    - Based on % of open perimeter from 26% to 49%.
    - For frontage widths 20' to 30'.

Table 506.2a   % Increase in Area per Floor Due to Frontage

% open	20'	21'	22'	23'	24'	25'	26'	27'	28'	29'	30'
26	0.67	0.70	0.73	0.77	0.80	0.83	0.87	0.90	0.93	0.97	1.00
27	1.33	1.40	1.47	1.53	1.60	1.67	1.73	1.80	1.87	1.93	2.00
28	2.00	2.10	2.20	2.30	2.40	2.50	2.60	2.70	2.80	2.90	3.00
29	2.67	2.80	2.93	3.07	3.20	3.33	3.47	3.60	3.73	3.87	4.00
30	3.33	3.50	3.67	3.83	4.00	4.17	4.33	4.50	4.67	4.83	5.00
31	4.00	4.20	4.40	4.60	4.80	5.00	5.20	5.40	5.60	5.80	6.00
32	4.67	4.90	5.13	5.37	5.60	5.83	6.07	6.30	6.53	6.77	7.00
33	5.33	5.60	5.87	6.13	6.40	6.67	6.93	7.20	7.47	7.73	8.00
34	6.00	6.30	6.60	6.90	7.20	7.50	7.80	8.10	8.40	8.70	9.00
35	6.67	7.00	7.33	7.67	8.00	8.33	8.67	9.00	9.33	9.67	10.00
36	7.33	7.70	8.07	8.43	8.80	9.17	9.53	9.90	10.27	10.63	11.00
37	8.00	8.40	8.80	9.20	9.60	10.00	10.40	10.80	11.20	11.60	12.00
38	8.67	9.10	9.53	9.97	10.40	10.83	11.27	11.70	12.13	12.57	13.00
39	9.33	9.80	10.27	10.73	11.20	11.67	12.13	12.60	13.07	13.53	14.00
40	10.00	10.50	11.00	11.50	12.00	12.50	13.00	13.50	14.00	14.50	15.00
41	10.67	11.20	11.73	12.27	12.80	13.33	13.87	14.40	14.93	15.47	16.00
42	11.33	11.90	12.47	13.03	13.60	14.17	14.73	15.30	15.87	16.43	17.00
43	12.00	12.60	13.20	13.80	14.40	15.00	15.60	16.20	16.80	17.40	18.00
44	12.67	13.30	13.93	14.57	15.20	15.83	16.47	17.10	17.73	18.37	19.00
45	13.33	14.00	14.67	15.33	16.00	16.67	17.33	18.00	18.67	19.33	20.00
46	14.00	14.70	15.40	16.10	16.80	17.50	18.20	18.90	19.60	20.30	21.00
47	14.67	15.40	16.13	16.87	17.60	18.33	19.07	19.80	20.53	21.27	22.00
48	15.33	16.10	16.87	17.63	18.40	19.17	19.93	20.70	21.47	22.23	23.00
49	16.00	16.80	17.60	18.40	19.20	20.00	20.80	21.60	22.40	23.20	24.00

506 Area Modifications

506.2 Frontage increase *(Part 3 of 4)*

- The table below indicates the permitted % increase to the limit of area per floor as follows:
  - Based on % of open perimeter from 50% to 79%.
  - For frontage widths 20' to 30'.

Table 506.2b   % Increase in Area per Floor Due to Frontage

% open	20'	21'	22'	23'	24'	25'	26'	27'	28'	29'	30'
50	16.67	17.50	18.33	19.17	20.00	20.83	21.67	22.50	23.33	24.17	25.00
51	17.33	18.20	19.07	19.93	20.80	21.67	22.53	23.40	24.27	25.13	26.00
52	18.00	18.90	19.80	20.70	21.60	22.50	23.40	24.30	25.20	26.10	27.00
53	18.67	19.60	20.53	21.47	22.40	23.33	24.27	25.20	26.13	27.07	28.00
54	19.33	20.30	21.27	22.23	23.20	24.17	25.13	26.10	27.07	28.03	29.00
55	20.00	21.00	22.00	23.00	24.00	25.00	26.00	27.00	28.00	29.00	30.00
56	20.67	21.70	22.73	23.77	24.80	25.83	26.87	27.90	28.93	29.97	31.00
57	21.33	22.40	23.47	24.53	25.60	26.67	27.73	28.80	29.87	30.93	32.00
58	22.00	23.10	24.20	25.30	26.40	27.50	28.60	29.70	30.80	31.90	33.00
59	22.67	23.80	24.93	26.07	27.20	28.33	29.47	30.60	31.73	32.87	34.00
60	23.33	24.50	25.67	26.83	28.00	29.17	30.33	31.50	32.67	33.83	35.00
61	24.00	25.20	26.40	27.60	28.80	30.00	31.20	32.40	33.60	34.80	36.00
62	24.67	25.90	27.13	28.37	29.60	30.83	32.07	33.30	34.53	35.77	37.00
63	25.33	26.60	27.87	29.13	30.40	31.67	32.93	34.20	35.47	36.73	38.00
64	26.00	27.30	28.60	29.90	31.20	32.50	33.80	35.10	36.40	37.70	39.00
65	26.67	28.00	29.33	30.67	32.00	33.33	34.67	36.00	37.33	38.67	40.00
66	27.33	28.70	30.07	31.43	32.80	34.17	35.53	36.90	38.27	39.63	41.00
67	28.00	29.40	30.80	32.20	33.60	35.00	36.40	37.80	39.20	40.60	42.00
68	28.67	30.10	31.53	32.97	34.40	35.83	37.27	38.70	40.13	41.57	43.00
69	29.33	30.80	32.27	33.73	35.20	36.67	38.13	39.60	41.07	42.53	44.00
70	30.00	31.50	33.00	34.50	36.00	37.50	39.00	40.50	42.00	43.50	45.00
71	30.67	32.20	33.73	35.27	36.80	38.33	39.87	41.40	42.93	44.47	46.00
72	31.33	32.90	34.47	36.03	37.60	39.17	40.73	42.30	43.87	45.43	47.00
73	32.00	33.60	35.20	36.80	38.40	40.00	41.60	43.20	44.80	46.40	48.00
74	32.67	34.30	35.93	37.57	39.20	40.83	42.47	44.10	45.73	47.37	49.00
75	33.33	35.00	36.67	38.33	40.00	41.67	43.33	45.00	46.67	48.33	50.00
76	34.00	35.70	37.40	39.10	40.80	42.50	44.20	45.90	47.60	49.30	51.00
77	34.67	36.40	38.13	39.87	41.60	43.33	45.07	46.80	48.53	50.27	52.00
78	35.33	37.10	38.87	40.63	42.40	44.17	45.93	47.70	49.47	51.23	53.00
79	36.00	37.80	39.60	41.40	43.20	45.00	46.80	48.60	50.40	52.20	54.00

506 Area Modifications

506.2 Frontage increase *(Part 4 of 4)*

- The table below indicates the permitted % increase to the limit of area per floor as follows:
  - o Based on % of open perimeter from 80% to 100%.
  - o For frontage widths 20' to 30'.

Table 506.2c   % Increase in Area per Floor Due to Frontage

% open	Width of frontage										
	20'	21'	22'	23'	24'	25'	26'	27'	28'	29'	30'
80	36.67	38.50	40.33	42.17	44.00	45.83	47.67	49.50	51.33	53.17	55.00
81	37.33	39.20	41.07	42.93	44.80	46.67	48.53	50.40	52.27	54.13	56.00
82	38.00	39.90	41.80	43.70	45.60	47.50	49.40	51.30	53.20	55.10	57.00
83	38.67	40.60	42.53	44.47	46.40	48.33	50.27	52.20	54.13	56.07	58.00
84	39.33	41.30	43.27	45.23	47.20	49.17	51.13	53.10	55.07	57.03	59.00
85	40.00	42.00	44.00	46.00	48.00	50.00	52.00	54.00	56.00	58.00	60.00
86	40.67	42.70	44.73	46.77	48.80	50.83	52.87	54.90	56.93	58.97	61.00
87	41.33	43.40	45.47	47.53	49.60	51.67	53.73	55.80	57.87	59.93	62.00
88	42.00	44.10	46.20	48.30	50.40	52.50	54.60	56.70	58.80	60.90	63.00
89	42.67	44.80	46.93	49.07	51.20	53.33	55.47	57.60	59.73	61.87	64.00
90	43.33	45.50	47.67	49.83	52.00	54.17	56.33	58.50	60.67	62.83	65.00
91	44.00	46.20	48.40	50.60	52.80	55.00	57.20	59.40	61.60	63.80	66.00
92	44.67	46.90	49.13	51.37	53.60	55.83	58.07	60.30	62.53	64.77	67.00
93	45.33	47.60	49.87	52.13	54.40	56.67	58.93	61.20	63.47	65.73	68.00
94	46.00	48.30	50.60	52.90	55.20	57.50	59.80	62.10	64.40	66.70	69.00
95	46.67	49.00	51.33	53.67	56.00	58.33	60.67	63.00	65.33	67.67	70.00
96	47.33	49.70	52.07	54.43	56.80	59.17	61.53	63.90	66.27	68.63	71.00
97	48.00	50.40	52.80	55.20	57.60	60.00	62.40	64.80	67.20	69.60	72.00
98	48.67	51.10	53.53	55.97	58.40	60.83	63.27	65.70	68.13	70.57	73.00
99	49.33	51.80	54.27	56.73	59.20	61.67	64.13	66.60	69.07	71.53	74.00
100	50.00	52.50	55.00	57.50	60.00	62.50	65.00	67.50	70.00	72.50	75.00

Case study: Fig. 506.2. The sports and fine arts center is divided into three buildings, A, B, and C by fire walls. Building A contains A-1, A-3, and B occupancies. Building B is occupancy A-3. Building C contains A-3 and B occupancies. The occupancies within buildings A and C are not separated by 2-hr walls as per IBC Table 302.3.3 so the buildings have "nonseparated uses" governed by 302.3.2. In this case, the most restrictive area limitation of the occupancies in each building dictates the area permitted.

Building A is construction Type IIB and is sprinklered. IBC Table 503 permits 8500 sf per floor for occupancy A-1 (the most restrictive case in this building). 506.1 allows this limit to be increased due to open area around the building and to the presence of sprinklers. Building A has an open frontage ≥ 30' deep at 90% of its perimeter. 506.2 permits an area increase of 65% or 5525 sf based on the frontage. 506.3 permits an area increase equal to twice the original limit, or 17,000 sf. The new limit of area per floor is, therefore, *8500 sf + 5525 sf + 17,000 sf = 31,025 sf.* Building A has 31,010 sf on the 1st floor and less on the 2nd floor; thus, it complies with the limit of 31,025 sf per floor.

Building B is construction Type IIB and is sprinklered. IBC Table 503 permits 9500 sf for occupancy A-3. 506.1 allows this limit to be increased due to open area around the builidng and to the presence of sprinklers. Building B has an open frontage ≥ 30' deep at 58% of its perimeter. 506.2 permits an area increase of 33% or 3135 sf based on the frontage. 506.3 permits an area increase equal to twice the original limit, or 19,000 sf. The new limit of area per floor is, therefore, *9500 sf + 3135 sf + 19,000 sf = 31,635 sf.* Building B has 7176 sf on the 1st floor and less on the 2nd floor; thus, it complies with the limit of 31,635 sf per floor.

Building C is construction Type IIA and is not sprinklered. IBC Table 503 permits 15,500 sf per floor for occupancy A-3 (the more restrictive case in this building). Building C has an open frontage ≥ 30' deep at 85% of its perimeter. 506.2 permits an area increase of 60% or 9300 sf based on the frontage. The new limit of area per floor is, therefore, *15,500 sf + 9300 sf = 24,800 sf.* Building C has 23,365 sf on the 1st floor and less on the 2nd floor; thus, it complies with the limit of 24,800 sf per floor.

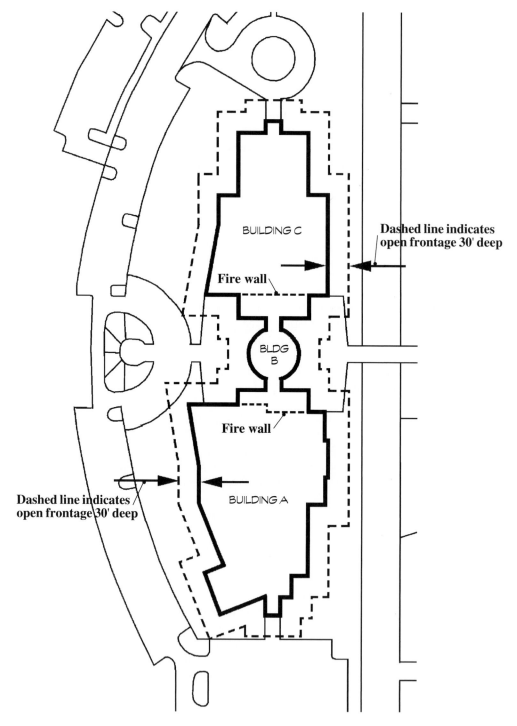

Fig. 506.2. Site plan. Newman University Sports and Fine Arts Center. Wichita, Kansas. Gossen Livingston Associates, Inc., Architecture. Wichita, Kansas.

506 Area Modifications

506.2.1 Width limits

This subsection addresses the % of increase based on frontage permitted for floor areas limits.

- The minimum width of the public way or open space must be ≥ 20' in the following case:
  - For a frontage to be considered as a basis for an area limit increase.
- In the computation of % of area increases permitted the following apply:
  - "Width of open space ÷ 30" is limited to a value ≤ 2 for buildings of unlimited area.
  - "Width of open space ÷ 30" is limited to a value ≤ 1 for other buildings.

  Note: The following are cited as sources of qualifications for warranting unlimited area.
  503.1.2, "Special industrial occupancies."
  Section 507, "Unlimited Area Buildings."
  Section 508, "Special Provisions."
  506.2 includes the equation wherein "width of open space ÷ 30" is used.

506.2.2 Open space limits

This subsection addresses the frontage used as a basis for increasing the limits of area per floor.

- Open space qualifying as frontage is governed as follows:
  - It must be one of the following:
    Located on the same lot.
    Dedicated for public use.
  - It must be accessed by one of the following:
    From a street.
    By an approved fire lane.

506 Area Modifications

506.3 Automatic sprinkler system increase *(part 1 of 2)*

- No increase in area is allowed due to sprinklers in H-1, H-2, or H-3 occupancies.
- In multistory buildings of other occupancies, the limit of area per floor is increased by the square footages listed in the table below where buildings are sprinklered as per NFPA 13.

Table 506.3a   Maximum Area per Floor in SF for Sprinklered Multistory Buildings

Occ.	IA	IB	IIA	IIB	IIIA	IIIB	IV	VA	VB
					Type of construction				
A-1	UL	UL	31,000	17,000	28,000	17,000	30,000	23,000	11,000
A-2	UL	UL	31,000	19,000	28,000	19,000	30,000	23,000	12,000
A-3	UL	UL	31,000	19,000	28,000	19,000	30,000	23,000	12,000
A-4	UL	UL	31,000	19,000	18,000	19,000	30,000	23,000	12,000
A-5	UL	UL	UL	UL	UL	UL	30,000	UL	UL
B	UL	UL	75,000	46,000	57,000	38,000	72,000	36,000	18,000
E	UL	UL	53,000	29,000	47,000	29,000	51,000	37,000	19,000
F-1	UL	UL	50,000	31,000	38,000	24,000	71,000	28,000	17,000
F-2	UL	UL	75,000	46,000	57,000	36,000	101,000	43,000	26,000
H-4	UL	UL	75,000	35,000	57,000	35,000	72,000	36,000	13,000
H-5	UL	UL	75,000	46,000	57,000	38,000	72,000	36,000	18,000
I-1	UL	110,000	38,000	20,000	33,000	20,000	36,000	21,000	9,000
I-2	UL	UL	31,000	22,000	24,000	NP	24,000	19,000	NP
I-3	UL	UL	30,000	20,000	21,000	15,000	24,000	15,000	10,000
I-4	UL	121,000	53,000	26,000	47,000	26,000	51,000	37,000	18,000
M	UL	UL	43,000	25,000	37,000	25,000	41,000	28,000	18,000
R-1	UL	UL	48,000	32,000	48,000	32,000	41,000	24,000	14,000
R-2	UL	UL	48,000	32,000	48,000	32,000	41,000	24,000	14,000
R-3	UL	UL	UL	UL	UL	UL	UL	UL	UL
R-4	UL	UL	48,000	32,000	48,000	32,000	41,000	24,000	14,000
S-1	UL	96,000	52,000	35,000	52,000	35,000	51,000	28,000	18,000
S-2	UL	158,000	78,000	52,000	78,000	52,000	77,000	42,000	27,000
U	UL	71,000	38,000	17,000	28,000	17,000	36,000	18,000	11,000

SF = square feet, NP = not permitted, UL = unlimited, Occ. = occupancy.

506 Area Modifications

506.3 Automatic sprinkler system increase *(part 2 of 2)*

- No increase in area is allowed due to sprinklers in H-1, H-2, or H-3 occupancies.
- In 1-story buildings of other occupancies, the limit of area per floor is increased by the square footages listed in the table below where buildings are sprinklered as per NFPA 13.

Table 506.3b   Maximum Area per Floor in SF for Sprinklered 1-Story Buildings

Occ.	IA	IB	IIA	IIB	IIIA	IIIB	IV	VA	VB
A-1	UL	UL	46,500	25,500	42,000	25,500	45,000	34,500	16,500
A-2	UL	UL	46,500	28,500	42,000	28,500	45,000	34,500	18,000
A-3	UL	UL	46,500	28,500	42,000	28,500	45,000	34,500	18,000
A-4	UL	UL	46,500	28,500	42,000	28,500	45,000	34,500	18,000
A-5	UL	UL	UL	UL	UL	UL	45,000	UL	UL
B	UL	UL	112,500	69,000	85,500	57,000	108,000	54,000	27,000
E	UL	UL	79,500	43,500	70,500	43,500	76,500	55,500	28,500
F-1	UL	UL	75,000	46,500	57,000	36,000	106,500	42,000	25,500
F-2	UL	UL	112,500	69,000	57,000	54,000	151,500	64,500	39,000
H-4	UL	UL	112,500	52,500	85,500	52,500	108,000	54,000	19,500
H-5	UL	UL	112,500	69,000	85,500	57,000	108,000	54,000	27,000
I-1	UL	165,000	57,000	30,000	49,500	30,000	54,000	31,500	13,500
I-2	UL	UL	46,500	33,000	36,000	NP	36,000	28,500	NP
I-3	UL	UL	45,000	30,000	31,500	22,500	36,00	22,500	15,000
I-4	UL	181,500	79,500	39,000	70,500	39,000	76,500	55,500	27,000
M	UL	UL	64,500	37,500	55,500	37,500	61,500	42,000	27,000
R-1	UL	UL	72,000	48,000	72,000	48,000	61,500	36,000	21,000
R-2	UL	UL	72,000	48,000	72,000	48,000	61,500	36,000	21,000
R-3	UL	UL	UL	UL	UL	UL	UL	UL	UL
R-4	UL	UL	72,000	48,000	72,000	48,000	61,500	36,000	21,000
S-1	UL	144,000	78,000	52,500	78,000	52,5000	76,500	42,000	27,000
S-2	UL	237,000	117,000	78,000	117,000	78,000	115,500	63,000	49,500
U	UL	106,500	57,000	25,500	42,000	25,500	54,000	27,000	16,500

NP = not permitted, SF = square feet, UL = unlimited, Occ. = occupancy.

507 Unlimited Area Buildings

507.1 Unsprinklered, one-story

- Buildings in the following occupancies are not limited in area where they meet both of the criteria indicated below:
  - Occupancies:
    F-2, S-2.
  - Requirements:
    The building must be 1 story.
    One or both of the following open areas must contact the entire perimeter of the building:
      Public ways and yards ≥ 60' wide.

507.2 Sprinklered, one-story

- Rack storage facilities meeting all the following criteria are not limited in area or height:
  - Building must be Type I or Type II construction.
  - Public does not have access to the building.
  - Building must be sprinklered as per NFPA 13.
  - One or both of the following open areas must contact the entire perimeter of the building:
    Public ways and yards ≥ 60' wide.
  - The building must conform to other rack storage requirements.

  Note: NFPA 231C, "Rack Storage of Materials," is cited as a source of requirements.

- Areas housing indoor participant sports such as the following need not be sprinklered where the conditions indicated below apply:
  - Sports areas:
    Tennis
    Skating
    Swimming
    Equestrian activities.
  - Conditions:
    Sports areas are equipped with exit doors opening directly to the outdoors.
    The building has a fire alarm system with manual fire alarm activation switches.

  Note: Section 907, "Fire Alarm and Detection Systems" is cited as the source of requirements for the system required above.

- In other cases, buildings in the following occupancies may have unlimited area if they meet all the conditions listed below:
  - Occupancies:
    A-4, B, F, M, S.
  - Conditions:
    Building must be 1 story.
    Building must be sprinklered as per NFPA 13.
    One or both of the following open areas must contact the entire building perimeter:
      Public ways and yards ≥ 60' wide.

507 Unlimited Area Building

507.3 Two-story

- 2-story buildings in the following occupancies are not limited in areas where both of the conditions below apply:
  - Occupancies:
    B, F, M, S.
  - Conditions:
    Building must be sprinklered as per NFPA 13.
    One or both of the following open areas must contact the entire perimeter of the building:
      Public ways and yards ≥ 60' wide.

507.4 Reduced open space

This subsection addresses the reduction of width for the open space required at the perimeter of unlimited area buildings.

- Such open space may be reduced from ≥ 60' to ≥ 40' as follows:
  - Reduced width may occur on ≤ 75% of the building perimeter.
  - A fire-resistance rating of ≥ 3 hrs is required as follows:
    For exterior walls facing the reduced width.
    For protectives at openings in exterior walls facing the reduced width.
- Reduced width is permitted for the facilities listed below where they comply with the following requirements:
  - Requirements:
    Facilities must meet the requirements of this section.
    Facilities must meet the requirements for having unlimited area.
  - Facilities:
    1-story buildings as follows:
      Occupancy F-2 or S-2:
        Unsprinklered.
      Occupancies A-4, B, F, M, S:
        Sprinklered.
    2-story buildings as follows:
      Occupancies B, F, M, S:
        Sprinklered.

> *Note: The following are cited as sources of requirements defining buildings of unlimited area that otherwise require a perimeter of open space 60' wide. A partial summary of such requirements is provided above.*
> *507.1, "Unsprinklered, one-story."*
> *507.2, "Sprinklered, one-story."*
> *507.3, "Two-story."*

Case study: Fig. 507.3. The 2-story office building is not limlited in area based on the facts that it is occupancy B, it is sprinklered, and it has the necessary open space around it. The dashed line shown is 60' from the structure, thus, indicating that the yards and public ways surrounding the building are all larger than the 60' minimum required.

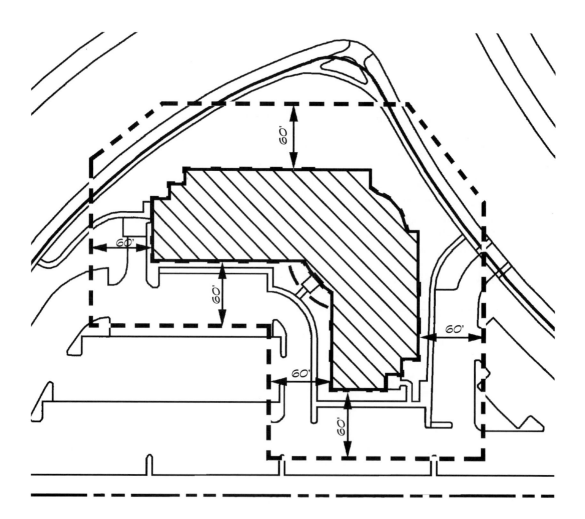

Fig. 507.3. Site plan. AmberGlen Business Center. Hillsboro, Oregon. Ankrom Moisan Associated Architects. Portland, Oregon.

507 Unlimited Area Buildings

507.5 High-hazard use groups

This section addresses H-2, H-3, or H-4 fire areas where located in unlimited area buildings of occupancy F or S.

- Where an H-2, H-3 or H-4 fire area is located at the perimeter of the building, the following applies:
  - The area of the occupancy H fire area is limited to the smaller of the following:
    - ≤ 10% of the F or S building area.
    - ≤ the following area limit to be increased as indicated below:
      - Area limit as based on the following:
        - The occupancy of the fire area.
        - The construction type of the F or S building.
      - Area limit may be increased due to open frontage as follows:
        - The "% of open perimeter" used in the computation is based on the following:
          - Length of fire area walls facing the required frontage ÷ perimeter of fire area.

  Note: IBC Table 503, "Allowable Height and Building Areas," is cited as the source of area limit based on the fire area occupancy and the construction type of the F or S building.

  506.2, "Frontage increase," is cited as the source of method for increasing the area limit from Table 503.

- Where an H-2, H-3 or H-4 fire area is located away from the perimeter of a building, the following applies:
  - The area of the occupancy H fire area is limited as follows:
    - Area must be ≤ 25% of the area limit based on the following:
      - The occupancy of the fire area.
      - The construction type of the F or S building.

  Note: IBC Table 503, "Allowable Height and Building Areas," is cited as the source of area limit based on the fire area occupancy and the construction type of the F or S building.

507.7 Group E buildings

- Occupancy E buildings may have unlimited area where all of the following apply:
  - Building is 1 story.
  - Building is one of the following types of construction:
    - Type II.
    - Type IIIA.
    - Type IV.
  - Each classroom has ≥ 2 means of egress.
  - Each classroom has ≥ 1 means of egress with a direct exit to the exterior.
  - The building is sprinklered as per NFPA 13.
  - One or both of the following open areas must contact the entire perimeter of the building:
    - Public ways and yards ≥ 60' wide.

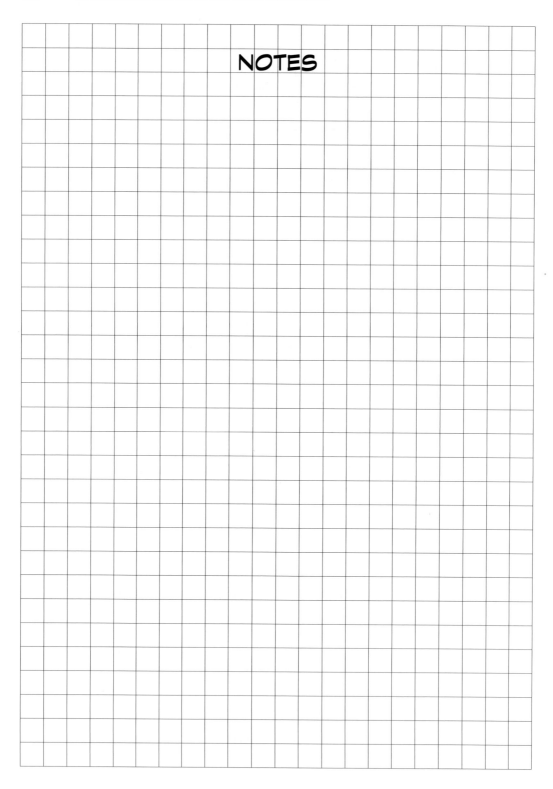

NOTES

6

Types of Construction

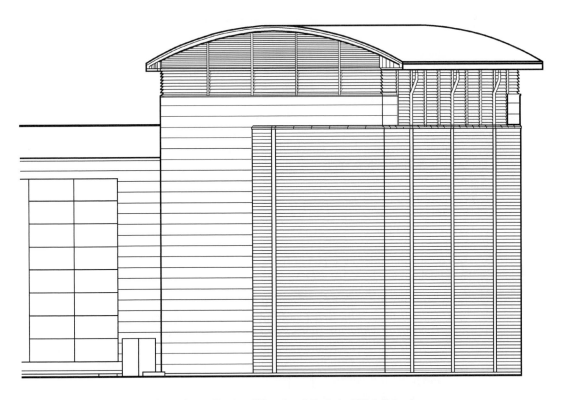

Montachusett Regional Vocational-Technical High School.
Fitchburg, Massachusetts. *(partial elevation)*
HKT Architects, Inc. Somerville, Massachusetts.

602 Construction Classification

602.1 General *(part 1 of 10)*

- The following buildings and structures are governed by this section:
  - New construction.
  - Alterations.
  - Additions to height.
  - Additions to area.
- The following apply to buildings and structures governed by this section:
  - They must be classified in 1 of the 5 construction types described in this section.
  - Where all elements of the roof construction are > 20' above the floor directly below, the guidelines listed below apply to the following occupancies and construction types:
    Occupancies:
        A, B, E, F-2, I, R, S-2, and U.
    Construction types:
        I, II, III A, IV, VA.
    Guidelines:
        The following roof members do not require fire protection:
            Structural members.
            Framing and decking.
        The following roof members may be fire-retardant-treated wood:
            Structural members.
            Framing and decking.
  - Heavy timber is permitted in roof construction where the fire-resistance rating required is ≤ 1 hr..
  - Fire-retardant-treated wood may be used in the following components where all the conditions indicated below apply:
    Components:
        Roof girders.
        Roof trusses.
        Roof construction.
    Conditions:
        The construction must be Type I or II.
        The building must be ≤ 2 stories.

Note: The following are cited as applying to this section:
IBC Table 601, "Fire-Resistance Rating Requirements for Building Elements," the contents of which are summarized above and on the following pages.
IBC Table 602, "Fire-Resistance Rating Requirements for Exterior Walls Based on Fire Separation Distance," the contents of which are summarized above and on the following pages.
The following sections supplement requirements for the 5 construction types:
602.2, "Types I and II."
602.3, "Type III."
602.4, "Type IV."
602.5, "Type V."

602 Construction Classification

602.1 General *(part 2 of 10)*

- Type IA buildings and structures must have the fire-resistance ratings listed below:

Table 602.1a   Fire-Resistance Ratings for Type IA Buildings and Structures

Construction Type IA components	Fire-resistance rating
Structural frame supporting a floor:	
Columns	≥ 3 hr
Members connected to columns:	
Girders, trusses, beams, spandrels	≥ 3 hr
Bracing members for gravity loads	≥ 3 hr
Structural frame supporting only a roof:	
Columns	≥ 2 hr
Members connected to columns:	
Girders, trusses, beams, spandrels	≥ 2 hr
Bracing members for gravity loads	≥ 2 hr
Exterior load-bearing walls other than party walls	≥ 3 hr
Interior load-bearing walls:	
Supporting a floor	≥ 3 hr
Supporting only a roof	≥ 2 hr
Exterior nonload-bearing walls other than party walls:	
All occupancies:	
Fire separation $\geq 30'$	≥ 0 hr
Occupancy R-3 and U where serving R-3:	
Fire separation distance $< 3'$	≥ 1 hr
Fire separation distance $\geq 3'$	≥ 0 hr
Occupancies A, B, E, F-2, I, R-1, R-2, R-4, S-2, U:	
Fire separation distance $< 30'$	≥ 1 hr
Occupancies F-1, M, S-1:	
Fire separation distance $< 10'$	≥ 2 hr
Fire separation distance $\geq 10' < 30'$	≥ 1 hr
Occupancy H:	
Fire separation distance $< 10'$	≥ 3 hr
Fire separation distance $\geq 10' < 30'$	≥ 2 hr
Floor construction:	
Beams and joists not connected to columns	≥ 2 hr
Other construction	≥ 2 hr
Roof construction:	
Beams and joists not connected to columns	$\geq 1\frac{1}{2}$ hr
Other construction	$\geq 1\frac{1}{2}$ hr

Source: IBC Tables 601 and 602.

> *Note: 503.2, "Party walls," defines the wall and requires that it be a fire wall.*
> *Section 705, "Fire Walls," provides fire-resistance ratings and other requirements.*

602 Construction Classification

602.1 General *(part 3 of 10)*

- Type IB buildings and structures must have the fire-resistance ratings listed below:

Table 602.1b   Fire-Resistance Ratings for Type IB Buildings and Structures

Construction Type IB components	Fire-resistance rating
Structural frame supporting a floor:	
Columns	≥ 2 hr
Members connected to columns:	
Girders, trusses, beams, spandrels	≥ 2 hr
Bracing members for gravity loads	≥ 2 hr
Structural frame supporting only a roof:	
Columns	≥ 1 hr
Members connected to columns:	
Girders, trusses, beams, spandrels	≥ 1 hr
Bracing members for gravity loads	≥ 1 hr
Exterior load-bearing walls other than party walls:	
Occupancy H:	
Fire separation distance < 5'	≥ 3 hr
Fire separation distance ≥ 5'	≥ 2 hr
All other occupancies	≥ 2 hr
Interior load-bearing walls:	
Supporting a floor	≥ 2 hr
Supporting only a roof	≥ 1 hr
Exterior nonload-bearing walls other than party walls:	
All occupancies:	
Fire separation ≥ 30'	≥ 0 hr
Occupancy R-3 and U where serving R-3:	
Fire separation distance < 3'	≥ 1 hr
Fire separation distance ≥ 3'	≥ 0 hr
Occupancies A, B, E, F-2, I, R-1, R-2, R-4, S-2, U:	
Fire separation distance < 30'	≥ 1 hr
Occupancies F-1, M, S-1:	
Fire separation distance < 5'	≥ 2 hr
Fire separation distance ≥ 5' < 30'	≥ 1 hr
Occupancy H:	
Fire separation distance < 5'	≥ 3 hr
Fire separation distance ≥ 5' < 30'	≥ 2 hr
Floor construction:	
Beams and joists not connected to columns	≥ 2 hr
Other construction	≥ 2 hr
Roof construction:	
Beams and joists not connected to columns	≥ 1 hr
Other construction	≥ 1 hr

Source: IBC Tables 601 and 602.

Note: 503.2, "Party walls," defines the wall and requires that it be a fire wall.
Section 705, "Fire Walls," provides fire-resistance ratings and other requirements.

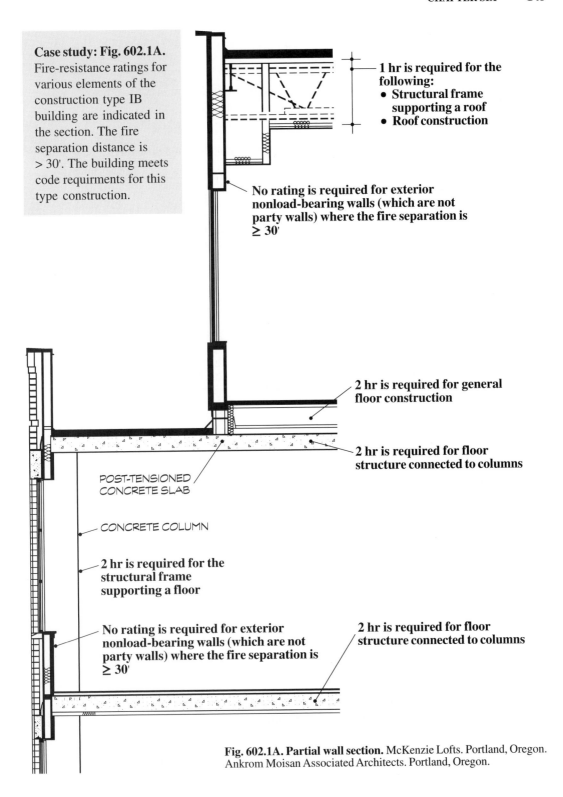

Case study: Fig. 602.1A. Fire-resistance ratings for various elements of the construction type IB building are indicated in the section. The fire separation distance is > 30'. The building meets code requirments for this type construction.

1 hr is required for the following:
- **Structural frame supporting a roof**
- **Roof construction**

No rating is required for exterior nonload-bearing walls (which are not party walls) where the fire separation is ≥ 30'

2 hr is required for general floor construction

2 hr is required for floor structure connected to columns

POST-TENSIONED CONCRETE SLAB

CONCRETE COLUMN

2 hr is required for the structural frame supporting a floor

No rating is required for exterior nonload-bearing walls (which are not party walls) where the fire separation is ≥ 30'

2 hr is required for floor structure connected to columns

Fig. 602.1A. Partial wall section. McKenzie Lofts. Portland, Oregon. Ankrom Moisan Associated Architects. Portland, Oregon.

602 Construction Classification

602.1 General *(part 4 of 10)*

- Type IIA buildings and structures must have the fire-resistance ratings listed below:
  - Reduction based on sprinklers is for sprinklers as follows:
    Sprinklers not otherwise required or used to increase area or height.

Table 602.1c   Fire-Resistance Ratings for Type IIA Buildings and Structures

Construction Type IIA components	With sprinklers	Other conditions
Structural frame supporting a floor or roof:		
Columns	≥ 0 hr	≥ 1 hr
Members connected to columns:		
Girders, trusses, beams, spandrels	≥ 0 hr	≥ 1 hr
Bracing members for gravity loads	≥ 0 hr	≥ 1 hr
Exterior load-bearing walls other than party walls:		
Occupancies A, B, E, F-2, I, R, S-2, U	≥ 1 hr	≥ 1 hr
Occupancies F-1, M, S-1:		
Fire separation distance < 5'	≥ 2 hr	≥ 2 hr
Fire separation distance ≥ 5' < 30'	≥ 1 hr	≥ 1 hr
Occupancy H:		
Fire separation distance < 5'	≥ 3 hr	≥ 3 hr
Fire separation distance ≥ 5' < 10'	≥ 2 hr	≥ 2 hr
Fire separation distance ≥ 10' < 30'	≥ 1 hr	≥ 1 hr
Interior load-bearing walls	≥ 0 hr	≥ 1 hr
Exterior nonload-bearing walls other than party walls:		
All occupancies:		
Fire separation distance ≥ 30'	≥ 0 hr	≥ 0 hr
Occupancy R-3 and U where serving R-3:		
Fire separation distance < 3'	≥ 1 hr	≥ 1 hr
Fire separation distance ≥ 3'	≥ 0 hr	≥ 0 hr
Occupancies A, B, E, F-2, I, R-1, R-2, R-4, S-2, U:		
Fire separation distance < 30'	≥ 1 hr	≥ 1 hr
Occupancies F-1, M, S-1:		
Fire separation distance < 5'	≥ 2 hr	≥ 2 hr
Fire separation distance ≥ 5' < 30'	≥ 1 hr	≥ 1 hr
Occupancy H:		
Fire separation distance < 5'	≥ 3 hr	≥ 3 hr
Fire separation distance ≥ 5' < 10'	≥ 2 hr	≥ 2 hr
Fire separation distance ≥ 10' < 30'	≥ 1 hr	≥ 1 hr
Floor construction:		
Beams and joists not connected to columns	≥ 0 hr	≥ 1 hr
Other construction	≥ 0 hr	≥ 1 hr
Roof construction:		
Beams and joists not connected to columns	≥ 0 hr	≥ 1 hr
Other construction	≥ 0 hr	≥ 1 hr

Source: IBC Tables 601 and 602.

Note: 503.2, "Party walls," defines the wall and requires that it be a fire wall.
Section 705, "Fire Walls," provides fire-resistance ratings and other requirements.

602 Construction Classification

602.1 General *(part 5 of 10)*

- Type IIB buildings and structures must have the fire-resistance ratings listed below:

Table 602.1d   Fire-Resistance Rating for Type IIB Buildings and Structures

Construction Type IIB components	Fire-resistance rating
Structural frame supporting a floor or roof:	
Columns	≥ 0 hr
Members connected to columns:	
Girders, trusses, beams, spandrels	≥ 0 hr
Bracing members for gravity loads	≥ 0 hr
Exterior walls other than party walls:	
Load-bearing walls and nonload-bearing walls:	
Occupancy R-3 and U where serving R-3:	
Fire separation distance < 3'	≥ 1 hr
Fire separation distance $\geq$ 3'	≥ 0 hr
Occupancies A, B, E, F-2, I, R-1, R-2, R-4, S-2, U:	
Fire separation distance < 10'	≥ 1 hr
Fire separation distance $\geq$ 10'	≥ 0 hr
Occupancies F-1, M, S-1:	
Fire separation distance < 5'	≥ 2 hr
Fire separation distance $\geq$ 5' <10'	≥ 1 hr
Fire separation distance $\geq$ 10'	≥ 0 hr
Occupancy H:	
Fire separation distance < 5'	≥ 3 hr
Fire separation distance $\geq$ 5' < 10'	≥ 2 hr
Fire separation distance $\geq$ 10' < 30'	≥ 1 hr
Fire separation distance $\geq$ 30'	≥ 0 hr
Interior load-bearing walls	≥ 0 hr
Floor construction:	
Beams and joists not connected to columns	≥ 0 hr
Other construction	≥ 0 hr
Roof construction:	
Beams and joists not connected to columns	≥ 0 hr
Other construction	≥ 0 hr

Source: IBC Tables 601 and 602.

> *Note: 503.2, "Party walls," defines the wall and requires that it be a fire wall.*
> *Section 705, "Fire Walls," provides fire-resistance ratings and other requirements.*

602 Construction Classification

602.1 General *(part 6 of 10)*

- Type IIIA buildings and structures must have the fire-resistance ratings listed below:
  - Reduction based on sprinklers is for sprinklers as follows:
    Sprinklers not otherwise required or used to increase area or height.

Table 602.1e   Fire-Resistance Ratings for Type IIIA Buildings and Structures

Construction Type IIIA components	With sprinklers	Other conditions
Structural frame supporting a floor or roof:		
Columns	≥ 0 hr	≥ 1 hr
Members connected to columns:		
Girders, trusses, beams, spandrels	≥ 0 hr	≥ 1 hr
Bracing members for gravity loads	≥ 0 hr	≥ 1 hr
Exterior load-bearing walls other than party walls:		
Occupancy H:		
Fire separation distance < 5'	≥ 3 hr	≥ 3 hr
Fire separation distance $\geq$ 5'	≥ 2 hr	≥ 2 hr
All other occupancies	≥ 2 hr	≥ 2 hr
Interior load-bearing walls	≥ 0 hr	≥ 1 hr
Exterior non-bearing walls other than party walls:		
All occupancies:		
Fire separation distance $\geq$ 30'	≥ 0 hr	≥ 0 hr
Occupancy R-3 and U where serving R-3:		
Fire separation distance < 3'	≥ 1 hr	≥ 1 hr
Fire separation distance $\geq$ 3'	≥ 0 hr	≥ 0 hr
Occupancies A, B, E, F-2, I, R-1, R-2, R-4, S-2, U:		
Fire separation distance < 30'	≥ 1 hr	≥ 1 hr
Occupancies F-1, M, S-1:		
Fire separation distance < 5'	≥ 2 hr	≥ 2 hr
Fire separation distance $\geq$ 5' < 30'	≥ 1 hr	≥ 1 hr
Occupancy H:		
Fire separation distance < 5'	≥ 3 hr	≥ 3 hr
Fire separation distance $\geq$ 5' < 10'	≥ 2 hr	≥ 2 hr
Fire separation distance $\geq$ 10' < 30'	≥ 1 hr	≥ 1 hr
Floor construction:		
Beams and joists not connected to columns	≥ 0 hr	≥ 1 hr
Other construction	≥ 0 hr	≥ 1 hr
Roof construction:		
Beams and joists not connected to columns	≥ 0 hr	≥ 1 hr
Other construction	≥ 0 hr	≥ 1 hr

Source: IBC Tables 601 and 602.

Note: 503.2, "Party walls," defines the wall and requires that it be a fire wall.
Section 705, "Fire Walls," provides fire-resistance ratings and other requirements.

Case study: Fig. 602.1B. The sprinklered construction Type IIIA occupancy S-1 warehouse meets the fire-resistance-rating requirements of IBC Table 601 as indicated in the illustration.

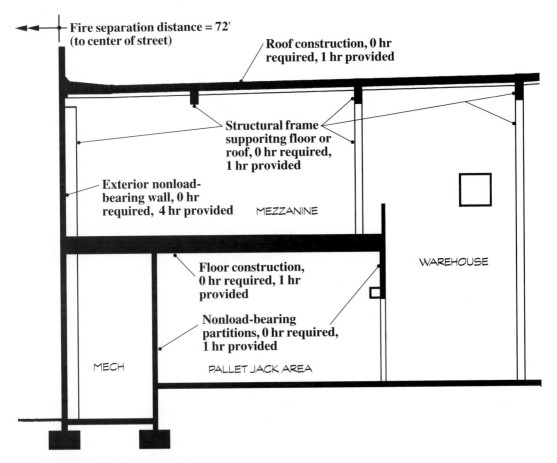

Fire separation distance = 72'
(to center of street)

Roof construction, 0 hr required, 1 hr provided

Structural frame supporitng floor or roof, 0 hr required, 1 hr provided

Exterior nonload-bearing wall, 0 hr required, 4 hr provided

MEZZANINE

WAREHOUSE

Floor construction, 0 hr required, 1 hr provided

Nonload-bearing partitions, 0 hr required, 1 hr provided

MECH

PALLET JACK AREA

Fig. 602.1B. Partial section. New Warehouse Addition. Los Angeles, California. Stephen Wen + Associates, Architects, Inc. Pasadena, California.

602 Construction Classification

602.1 General *(part 7 of 10)*

- Type IIIB buildings and structures must have the fire-resistance ratings listed below:

Table 602.1f   Fire-Resistance Rating for Type IIIB Buildings and Structures

Construction Type IIIB components	Fire-resistance rating
Structural frame supporting a floor or roof:	
Columns	≥ 0 hr
Members connected to columns:	
Girders, trusses, beams, spandrels	≥ 0 hr
Bracing members for gravity loads	≥ 0 hr
Exterior load-bearing walls other than party walls:	
Occupancy H:	
Fire separation distance $< 5'$	≥ 3 hr
Fire separation distance $\geq 5'$	≥ 2 hr
All other occupancies:	≥ 2 hr
Interior load-bearing walls	≥ 0 hr
Exterior nonload-bearing walls other than party walls:	
All occupancies:	
Fire separation distance $\geq 30'$	≥ 0 hr
Occupancy R-3 and U where serving R-3:	
Fire separation distance $< 3'$	≥ 1 hr
Fire separation distance $\geq 3'$	≥ 0 hr
Occupancies A, B, E, F-2, I, R-1, R-2, R-4, S-2, U:	
Fire separation distance $< 30'$	≥ 1 hr
Occupancies F-1, M, S-1:	
Fire separation distance $< 5'$	≥ 2 hr
Fire separation distance $\geq 5' < 30'$	≥ 1 hr
Occupancy H:	
Fire separation distance $< 5'$	≥ 3 hr
Fire separation distance $\geq 5' < 10'$	≥ 2 hr
Fire separation distance $\geq 10' < 30'$	≥ 1 hr
Floor construction:	
Beams and joists not connected to columns	≥ 0 hr
Other construction	≥ 0 hr
Roof construction:	
Beams and joists not connected to columns	≥ 0 hr
Other construction	≥ 0 hr

Source: IBC Tables 601 and 602.

Note: 503.2, "Party walls," defines the wall and requires that it be a fire wall.
Section 705, "Fire Walls," provides fire-resistance ratings and other requirements.

602 Construction Classification

602.1 General *(part 8 of 10)*

- Type IV buildings and structures must have the fire-resistance ratings or meet Heavy Timber requirements as listed below:

Table 602.1g   Fire-Resistance Rating or Heavy Timber Requirements for Type IV Buildings and Structures

Construction Type IV components	Fire-resistance rating or Heavy timber requirements
Structural frame supporting a floor or roof:	
Columns	Heavy timber
Members connected to columns:	
Girders, trusses, beams, spandrels	Heavy timber
Bracing for gravity loads	Heavy timber
Exterior load-bearing walls other than party walls:	
Occupancy H:	
Fire separation distance < 5'	≥ 3 hr
Fire separation distance ≥ 5'	≥ 2 hr
All other occupancies	≥ 2 hr
Interior load-bearing walls	≥ 1 hr or Heavy timber
Exterior nonload-bearing walls other than party walls:	
All occupancies:	
Fire separation distance ≥ 30'	≥ 0 hr
Occupancy R-3 and U where serving R-3:	
Fire separation distance < 3'	≥ 1 hr
Fire separation distance ≥ 3'	≥ 0 hr
Occupancies A, B, E, F-2, I, R-1, R-2, R-4, S-2, U:	
Fire separation distance < 30'	≥ 1 hr
Occupancies F-1, M, S-1:	
Fire separation distance < 5'	≥ 2 hr
Fire separation distance ≥ 5' < 30'	≥ 1 hr
Occupancy H:	
Fire separation distance < 5'	≥ 3 hr
Fire separation distance ≥ 5' < 10'	≥ 2 hr
Fire separation distance ≥ 10' < 30'	≥ 1 hr
Floor construction:	
Beams and joists not connected to columns	Heavy timber
Other construction	Heavy timber
Roof construction:	
Beams and joists not connected to columns	Heavy timber
Other construction	Heavy timber

Source: IBC Tables 601 and 602.

Note: 503.2, "Party walls," defines the wall and requires that it be a fire wall.

Section 705, "Fire Walls," provides fire-resistance ratings and other requirements.

602 Construction Classification

602.1 General *(part 9 of 10)*

- Type VA buildings and structures must have the fire-resistance ratings listed below:
  - Reduction based on sprinklers is for sprinklers as follows:
    Sprinklers not otherwise required or used to increase area or height.

Table 602.1h   Fire-Resistance Ratings for Type VA Buildings and Structures

Construction Type VA components	With sprinklers	Other conditions
Structural frame supporting a floor or roof :		
Columns	≥ 0 hr	≥ 1 hr
Members connected to columns:		
Girders, trusses, beams, spandrels	≥ 0 hr	≥ 1 hr
Bracing members for gravity loads	≥ 0 hr	≥ 1 hr
Exterior load-bearing walls other than party walls:		
Occupancies A, B, E, F-2, I, R, S-2, U	≥ 1 hr	≥ 1 hr
Occupancies F-1, M, S-1:		
Fire separation distance < 5'	≥ 2 hr	≥ 2 hr
Fire separation distance ≥ 5'	≥ 1 hr	≥ 1 hr
Occupancy H:		
Fire separation distance < 5'	≥ 3 hr	≥ 3 hr
Fire separation distance ≥ 5' < 10'	≥ 2 hr	≥ 2 hr
Fire separation distance ≥ 10'	≥ 1 hr	≥ 1 hr
Interior load-bearing walls	≥ 0 hr	≥ 1 hr
Exterior nonload-bearing walls other than party walls:		
All occupancies:		
Fire separation distance ≥ 30'	≥ 0 hr	≥ 0 hr
Occupancy R-3 and U where serving R-3:		
Fire separation distance < 3'	≥ 1 hr	≥ 1 hr
Fire separation distance ≥ 3'	≥ 0 hr	≥ 0 hr
Occupancies A, B, E, F-2, I, R-1, R-2, R-4, S-2, U:		
Fire separation distance < 30'	≥ 1 hr	≥ 1 hr
Occupancies F-1, M, S-1:		
Fire separation distance < 5'	≥ 2 hr	≥ 2 hr
Fire separation distance ≥ 5' < 30'	≥ 1 hr	≥ 1 hr
Occupancy H:		
Fire separation distance < 5'	≥ 3 hr	≥ 3 hr
Fire separation distance ≥ 5' < 10'	≥ 2 hr	≥ 2 hr
Fire separation distance ≥ 10' < 30'	≥ 1 hr	≥ 1 hr
Floor construction:		
Beams and joists not connected to columns	≥ 0 hr	≥ 1 hr
Other construction	≥ 0 hr	≥ 1 hr
Roof construction:		
Beams and joists not connected to columns	≥ 0 hr	≥ 1 hr
Other construction	≥ 0 hr	≥ 1 hr

Source: IBC Tables 601 and 602.

> *Note: 503.2, "Party walls," defines the wall and requires that it be a fire wall.*
> *Section 705, "Fire Walls," provides fire-resistance ratings and other requirements.*

602 Construction Classification

602.1 General *(Part 10 of 10)*

- Type VB buildings and structures must have the fire-resistance ratings listed below:

Table 602.1i   Fire-Resistance Rating for Type VB Buildings and Structures

Construction Type VB components	Fire-resistance rating
Structural frame supporting a floor or roof:	
Columns	≥ 0 hr
Members connected to columns:	
Girders, trusses, beams, spandrels	≥ 0 hr
Bracing members for gravity loads	≥ 0 hr
Exterior walls other than party walls:	
Load-bearing walls and nonload-bearing walls:	
Occupancy R-3 and U where serving R-3:	
Fire separation distance < 3'	≥ 1 hr
Fire separation distance ≥ 3'	≥ 0 hr
Occupancies A, B, E, F-2, I, R-1, R-2, R-4, S-2, U:	
Fire separation distance < 10'	≥ 1 hr
Fire separation distance ≥ 10'	≥ 0 hr
Occupancies F-1, M, S-1:	
Fire separation distance < 5'	≥ 2 hr
Fire separation distance ≥ 5' < 10'	≥ 1 hr
Fire separation distance ≥ 10'	≥ 0 hr
Occupancy H:	
Fire separation distance < 5'	≥ 3 hr
Fire separation distance ≥ 5' < 10'	≥ 2 hr
Fire separation distance ≥ 10' < 30'	≥ 1 hr
Fire separation distance ≥ 30'	≥ 0 hr
Interior load-bearing walls	≥ 0 hr
Floor construction:	
Beams and joists not connected to columns	≥ 0 hr
Other construction	≥ 0 hr
Roof construction:	
Beams and joists not connected to columns	≥ 0 hr
Other construction	≥ 0 hr

Source: IBC Tables 601 and 602.

Note: 503.2, "Party walls," defines the wall and requires that it be a fire wall.
Section 705, "Fire Walls," provides fire-resistance ratings and other requirements.

602 Construction Classification

602.1.1 Minimum requirements

- The following applies to detailing that complies with a construction type higher than required:
  - Other components of the occupancy need not comply with the higher construction type.

602.2 Type I and II

- Construction Types I and II require noncombustible materials for the following:
  - Structural frame:
    Columns.
    Members connected to columns:
      Girders.
      Trusses.
      Spandrels.
    Bracing members for gravity loads.
  - Load-bearing walls:
    Exterior.
    Interior.
  - Nonload-bearing walls and partitions:
    Exterior.
    Interior.
  - Floor construction including the following:
    Beams not connected to columns.
    Joists not connected to columns.
    Other construction.
  - Roof construction including the following:
    Beams not connected to columns.
    Joists not connected to columns.
    Other construction.

602.3 Type III

- In construction Type III, building elements are of the following materials:
  - Noncombustible materials are required for exterior walls as follows:
    Where exterior wall assemblies have fire-resistance rated at ≤ 2 hrs:
      Fire-retardant-treated wood is allowed therein.
  - The following materials are allowed for interior building elements:
    Any material permitted by the code.

  Note: 2303.2, "Fire-retardant-treated wood," is cited as the source of requirements for this material.

602 Construction Classification

602.4 Type IV

- Construction Type IV consists of Heavy timber (HT) construction as follows:
  - Noncombustible materials are required for exterior walls as follows:
    - Where exterior wall assemblies have fire-resistance rated at ≤ 2 hrs:
      - Fire-retardant-treated wood is allowed therein.
  - Interior building elements are required as follows:
    - Solid or laminated wood.
    - Contain no concealed spaces.
  - Details are governed by this section.

    Note: 2303.2, "Fire-retardant-treated wood," is cited as the source of requirements for this material.

602.4.1 Columns

- Construction Type IV wood columns are governed as follows:
  - Columns must be continuous or stacked with approved connections.
  - Columns must sawn as a single piece or be glue-laminated.
  - Column dimensions are required as follows:

Loads supported	Width	Depth
Floor loads	≥ 8"	≥ 8"
Roof and ceiling loads only	≥ 6"	≥ 8"

602.4.2 Floor framing

- Construction Type IV wood beams and girders are governed as follows:
  - Members must be sawn as a single piece or be glue-laminated.
  - Minimum nominal member dimensions are as follows:

Component	Width	Depth
Beams and girders	≥ 6"	≥ 10"
Arches springing from floor line and supporting floor loads	≥ 8"	≥ 8"
Members of trusses supporting floor loads	≥ 8"	≥ 8"

602 Construction Classification

602.4.3 Roof framing

- Construction Type IV roof framing members are governed as follows:
  - Parallel members spaced on either side of another member must have all of the following characteristics:
    - Assembled of ≥ 2 members.
    - Each member must have a nominal thickness ≥ 3".
    - Open space between spaced members requires the following:
      - Space must be closed by one of the following means:
        - Continuous blocking between spaced members as follows:
          - Nominal thickness ≥ 2".
        - Continuous wood cover plate as follows:
          - Nominal thickness ≥ 2".
          - Applied to underside of members.
  - Splice plates must have a nominal thickness ≥ 3".
  - Other roof framing members are governed as follows:
    - Required widths may be reduced with sprinklers as follows:
      - Sprinklers must be located under the roof deck.
    - Individual framing members must have the nominal dimensions listed below:

Table 602.4.3   Nominal Dimensions of Individual Roof Framing Members

Components supporting no floor loads	Width with sprinklers	Width with no sprinklers	Depth
Framed or glue-laminated arches:			
Where they spring from floor line or grade:			
In the upper half of height	≥ 6"	≥ 6"	≥ 6"
In the lower half of height	≥ 6"	≥ 6"	≥ 8"
Where they spring from the following:			
Top of walls or wall abutments	≥ 3"	≥ 4"	≥ 6"
Framed timber trusses	≥ 3"	≥ 4"	≥ 6"
Other roof framing	≥ 3"	≥ 4"	≥ 6"

602 Construction Classification

602.4.4 Floors

This section addresses floors in Type IV construction.

- No concealed spaces in floors are permitted.
- The wood decking system must be one of the following:
  - Structural decking laid flat:
    Nominal thickness in the vertical dimension must be ≥ 3".
    Either sawn or glue-laminated is required.
    One of the following edge details for decking members is required:
      Splined.
      Tongue-and-groove.
    One of the following types of subflooring is required:
      Nominal 1" tongue-and-groove flooring laid $\perp$ to or diagonally across decking.
      ½" particle board.
  - Structural decking laid on edge:
    Nominal dimensions required:
      Thickness in the vertical dimension must be ≥ 4".
    Horizontal dimension must be < the vertical dimension.
    Adjacent members must have continuous contact.
    Members must be securely spiked together.
    One of the following types of sub-flooring is required:
      Nominal 1" wood flooring.
      ½" wood structural panel.
      ½" particle board.
- Butt-joints of lumber must be staggered as follows:
  - So joints are not aligned at locations other than on supports.
- A gap $\geq$ ½" is required between floors and walls as follows:
  - Gaps must be closed by one of the following means:
    Molding attached to the wall as follows:
      Molding must permit movement in the floor due to expansion and contraction.
    Masonry wall corbeling below the floor edge.

602 Construction Classification

602.4.5 Roofs

This section addresses roofs in Type IV construction.

- Concealed spaces are not permitted in roof systems.
- Wood roof decks must be one of the following types:
  - Decking laid flat as follows:
    Either sawn or glue-laminated is required.
    One of the following edge details for plank decking is required:
    Splined.
    Tongue-and-groove.
    Nominal thickness in the vertical dimension must be ≥ 2".
  - Decking laid on edge as follows:
    Nominal thickness in the vertical dimension must be ≥ 3".
    Horizontal dimension must be < the vertical dimension.
    Adjacent members must have continuous contact.
    Members must be securely spiked together.
  - Wood structural panels with both of the following characteristics:
    Thickness ≥ $1^{1}/_{8}$".
    Exterior glue.
  - Other types of decking with both of the following characteristics:
    ≥ the fire resistance as the other options above.
    ≥ structural properties as the other options above.

602.4.6 Partitions

- Partitions in Type IV construction must be one of the following:
  - Solid wood with ≥ 2 layers of one of the following:
    1" thick matched boards.
    4" thick laminated construction.
  - Construction with a fire-resistance rating of 1 hr.

602.4.7 Exterior structural members

- Construction Type IV requires exterior wood columns and arches to have both the following:
  - A fire separation distance ≥ 20'.
  - Sizes complying with heavy timber size requirements.

602.5 Type V

- Construction Type V permits any material otherwise allowed by the code for the following:
  - Structural elements.
  - Exterior and interior walls.

Case study: Fig. 602.5. The building is an example of Type V construction. In this category, materials are neither restricted nor specified so long as they are permitted by the code for building construction. This applies to both exterior and interior walls as well as structural components. Type V construction is not limited to the materials in this example. This represents only one particular combination.

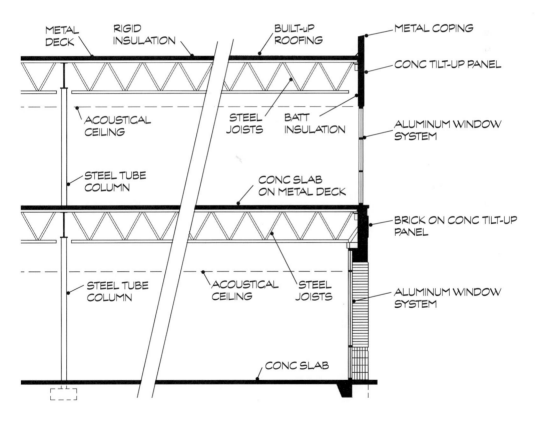

Fig. 602.5. Partial building section. AmberGlen Business Center. Hillsboro, Oregon. Ankrom Moisan Associated Architects. Portland, Oregon.

603 Combustible Material in Types I and II Construction

603.1 Allowable uses *(part 1 of 4)*

This section lists combustible materials permitted in Types I and II construction.

- Fire-retardant-treated wood in the following applications:
  - Nonload-bearing construction as follows:
      Partitions with a required fire-resistance rating ≤ 2 hrs.
      Exterior walls with no fire-resistance rating required.
  - Buildings ≤ 2 stories as follows:
      Roof construction including the following:
        Girders.
        Trusses.
- Insulation with the following conditions:
  - Layered between noncombustible materials as follows:
      No air space.
      Flame spread index is ≤ 100.
  - Layered between the following components with the conditions indicated below:
      Components:
        Finished floor.
        Solid decking.
      Conditions:
        No air space.
        Flame spread index is ≤ 200.
  - Other insulation as follows:
      Other than foam.
      With a flame spread index ≤ 25.
      Either of the following types:
        Thermal insulation.
        Acoustical insulation.
- Plastics regulated by the code as follows:
  - Foam plastics.
  - Light-transmitting plastics.

    Note: Chapter 26, "Plastic," is cited as the source of requirements for the plastics.

- Roof coverings in one of the following classifications:
  - Class A.
  - Class B.
  - Class C.
- Interior finishes as follows:
  - Floor finishes.
  - Other finishes.
- Interior trim and millwork such as the following:
  - Doors and door frames.
  - Window sash and window frames.

603 Combustible Material in Types I and II Construction

603.1 Allowable uses *(part 2 of 4)*

- In the following applications located ≤ 15' above grade:
    - Show windows including the following related elements:
        Nailing or furring strips.
        Wood bulkheads below show windows.
        Frames.
        Aprons.
        Show cases.
- This section lists combustible materials permitted in Types I and II construction.
- Finish flooring applied to one of the following is permitted:
    - Directly to a floor slab.
    - To wood sleepers in gymnasiums with no blocking of sleeper spaces required.
    - To wood sleepers in bowling facilities as follows:
        Spaces between sleepers are fire blocked in the following locations:
            At the juncture of alternate lanes.
            At the ends of each lane.
    - To wood sleepers, the following fire-resistance-rated floors with fire blocking as indicated:
        Floors:
            Masonry.
            Concrete.
        Blocking:
            Spaces between sleepers must be sealed in one of the following ways:
                Spaces filled with an approved material to obstruct the free flow of the following:
                    Flames.
                    Products of combustion.
                Spaces divided into areas ≤ 100 sf by fire blocking including the following:
                    Spaces filled solid under permanent partitions.
- Partitions with the following characteristics may be constructed of the materials listed below:
    - Characteristics:
        Used to subdivide the following of a single tenant:
            Store.
            Offices.
            Similar spaces.
        Partitions may not create a corridor serving ≥ 30 occupants.
    - Materials:
        Any of the following are permitted for partitions ≤ 6' high:
            Fire-retardant-treated wood.
            1-hr fire-resistant-rated construction.
            Wood panels.
            Similar light construction.

603 Combustible Materials in Types I and II Construction

603.1 Allowable uses *(part 3 of 4)*

- Platforms.

  Note: Section 410, "Stages and Platforms," is cited as the source of requirements for platforms permitted in combustible materials.

- Materials associated with building service and located in plenums.

  Note: International Mechanical Code Section 602, "Plenums," is cited as the source of combustible materials permitted.

- Blocking such as for the following is permitted:
  Handrails.
  Millwork.
  Cabinets.
  Window frames.
  Door frames.
- The following materials at exterior walls are permitted:
  - Combustible exterior wall coverings.
  - Appendages such as follows:
    Balconies.
    Bay windows.
    Oriel windows.
    Similar appendages.

  Note: Chapter 14, "Exterior Walls," is cited as the source of requirements for combustible materials permitted at exterior walls.

- This subsection lists combustible materials permitted in Types I and II construction.
- Sealing materials between materials of exterior walls as follows:
  - Mastics.
  - Caulking.
- Exterior plastic veneer.

  Note: 2605.2, "Exterior use," is cited as the source of requirements for plastic veneer on building exteriors.

- Nailing or furring strips.

  Note: 803.3, "Application," is cited as the source of requirements for furring.

603 Combustible Materials in Types I and II Construction

603.1 Allowable uses *(part 4 of 4)*

- Heavy timber in the following locations:
  - In roof construction where a fire-resistance rating ≤ 1 hr is required.
  - Columns and arches outside a building as follows:
    Where a fire-separation distance ≥ 20' is provided.
  - In balconies and similar projections outside the building.

  Note: The following are cited a sources of requirements applicable to the heavy timber:
  Footnote C of IBC Table 601, "Fire-Resistance Rating Requirements For Building Elements."
  602.4.7, "Exterior structural members."
  1406.3, "Balconies and similar projections."

- Combustible ingredients or components as follows:
  - Aggregates in gypsum concrete mixtures.
  - Aggregates in portland cement concrete mixtures.
  - Approved materials in assemblies meeting required fire-resistance ratings as follows:
    Admixtures.
    Component materials.

  Note: 703.2.2, "Combustible components," is cited as the source establishing the acceptability of combustible ingredients, a summary of which is provided above.

- Sprayed fire-resistive cementitious and mineral fiber materials.

  Note: 1704.11, "Sprayed fire-resistant materials," is cited as the source of requirements for such materials."

- Materials protecting penetrations in fire-resistance-rated assemblies.

  Note: Section 711, "Penetrations," is cited as the source of requirements for materials sealing penetrations against fire hazard.

- Materials in joints between components of assemblies with fire-resistance ratings.

  Note: Section 712, "Fire-Resistant Joint Systems," is cited as the source of requirements.

- Materials as follows:
  - Class A finish materials.
  - Combustible piping.
  - Combustible materials relating to building services.

  Note: 716.5, "Combustibles in concealed spaces in Types I and II construction," is cited as listing materials permitted in concealed spaces, a partial summary of which is provided above.

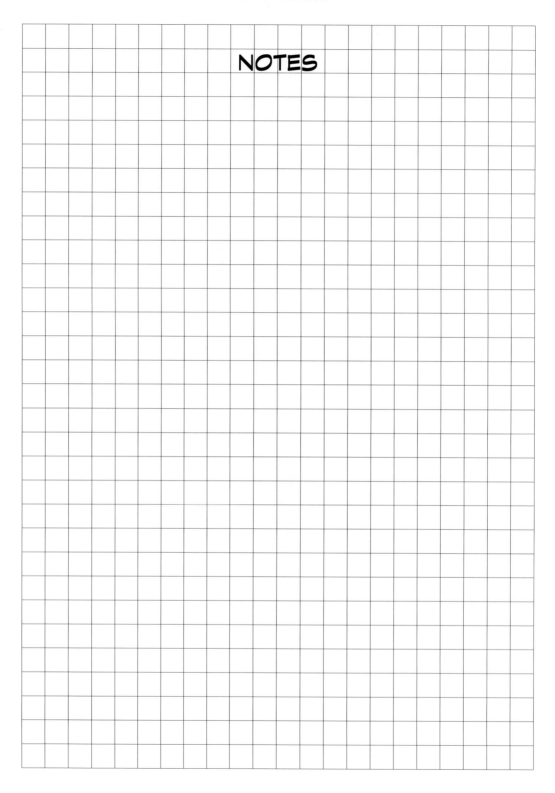

NOTES

7

Fire-Resistance-Rated Construction

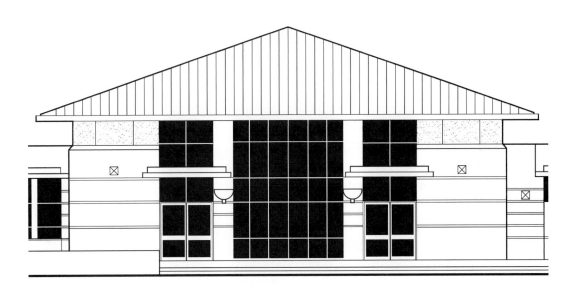

Lee's Summit Police and Court Facility. Lee's Summit, Missouri. *(partial elevation)*
The Hollis and Miller Group, Inc. Lee's Summit, Missouri.

702 Definitions

702.1 Definitions *(part 1 of 9)*

- **Annular space**
  - The gap around a component that is penetrating an assembly.

- **Combination fire/smoke damper**
  - A listed device.
  - Installed in any of the following locations:
    Air ducts.
    Air transfer openings.
  - Closes automatically upon detection of the following:
    Heat.
    Smoke.
  - Inhibits the flow of the following:
    Air.
    Smoke.
  - Capable of being adjusted from a remote command station where required.

- **Concrete, carbonate aggregate**
  - Aggregates are mainly one or both of the following substances:
    Calcium carbonate.
    Magnesium carbonate.
  - Examples of aggregates include the following:
    Limestone.
    Dolomite.
  - Aggregates consist of ≤ 40% of the following substances:
    Quartz.
    Chert.
    Flint.

- **Concrete, lightweight aggregate**
  - Aggregates are one or more of the following types:
    Expanded clay.
    Expanded shale.
    Expanded slag.
    Expanded slate.
    Sintered fly ash.
    Natural lightweight aggregates as follows:
      With the same fire-resistive properties as those listed above.
      ≥ 85 and ≤ 115 pcf.

  Note: ASTM C 330, "Specifications for Lightweight Aggregates for Structural Concrete," is cited as governing aggregate properties listed above.

702 Definitions

702.1 Definitions *(part 2 of 9)*

- **Concrete, sand-lightweight**
  - Aggregates are one or more of the following types mixed with natural sand:
    Expanded clay.
    Expanded shale.
    Expanded slag.
    Expanded slate.
    Sintered fly ash.
    Natural lightweight aggregates as follows:
    With the same fire-resistive properties as those listed above.
    ≥ 105 and ≤ 120 pcf.

  Note: ASTM C 330, "Specifications for Lightweight Aggregates for Structural Concrete," is cited as governing aggregate properties listed above.

- **Concrete siliceous aggregate**
  - Aggregates are normal weight.
  - Aggregates are mainly in one of the following substances:
    Silica.
    Compounds other than the following:
    Calcium carbonate.
    Magnesium carbonate.
  - Aggregates contain > 40% of the following substances:
    Quartz.
    Chert.
    Flint.

- **Draft stop**
  - One of the following:
    A material.
    A device.
    A construction.
  - Installed to limit the movement of air within the following types of concealed spaces:
    Crawl spaces.
    Floor-ceiling assemblies.
    Roof-ceiling assemblies.
    Attics.
    Similar spaces.

702 Definitions

702.1 Definitions *(part 3 of 9)*

> **Case study: Fig. 702.1A**. TJI joists rest on 2"× 4" bearing plates which sit on a concrete slab. An air space results between the slab and each joist through which air can flow in the concealed space. Draft stop materials placed under periodic joists isolate small areas of continuous air space between which no air can move.

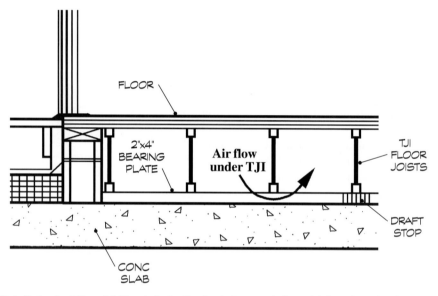

Fig. 702.1A. Detail at raised floor. McKenzie Lofts. Portland, Oregon. Ankrom Moisan Associated Architects. Portland, Oregon.

- **Fire area**
  - The area surrounded by one or more of the following barriers:
    Fire walls.
    Fire barriers.
    Exterior walls.
    Horizontal fire-resistance-rated assemblies.

- **Fire barrier**
  - A fire-resistance-rated assembly in either of the following orientations:
    Vertical.
    Horizontal.
  - Designed to limit the spread of fire.
  - Any openings in the barrier protected.

702 Definitions

702.1 Definitions *(part 4 of 9)*

- **Fire damper**
  - A listed device.
  - Installed in any of the following locations:
    - Air ducts.
    - Air distribution systems.
    - Smoke control systems.
  - Closes automatically upon detection of heat.
  - Limits air flow and passage of flame.
  - Categorized as one of two types:
    - A static system closes in case of fire.
    - A dynamic system continues to operate during a fire:
      - Tested for closure during airflow.
      - Rated for closure during airflow.

- **Fire door**
  - The door in a fire door assembly.

- **Fire door assembly**
  - An assembly of the following:
    - Fire door and door frame.
    - Hardware and accessories.
  - Provides fire protection to an opening at a defined level.

- **Fire partition**
  - A vertical assembly.
  - Limits the spread of fire.
  - Any openings in the partition are protected.

- **Fire-protection rating**
  - Pertains to an assembly protecting an opening.
  - The length of time an assembly can contain a fire as follows:
    - Measured in one of the following units:
      - Hours.
      - Minutes.

  Note: Section 714, "Opening Protectives," is cited as the source of requirements or tests used to determine fire-protection rating.

- **Fire-resistance rating**
  - The length of time an assembly or component can function in a fire as follows:
    - Confine a fire.
    - Perform assigned structural task.

  Note: Section 703, "Fire-Resistance Ratings and Fire Tests," is cited as the source of methods for determining fire-resistance ratings.

Case study: Fig. 702.1B. The selection of walls are among several types used at the hospital. The fire-resistance-rated walls shown are similar to those tested by Underwriters Laboratories, Inc.® and described in their publication, *Fire Resistance Directory,* or those listed in the Gypsum Association's *Fire Resistance Design Manual,* which are tested by several agencies. The numbers under the fire-resistance ratings shown in the wall sections indicate the index number under which descriptions of the walls are provided in the reference publications. Wall assemblies and horizontal assemblies are not considered to have a fire-resistance rating unless they have been tested by a recognized agency. Two walls without fire-resistance ratings are also shown.

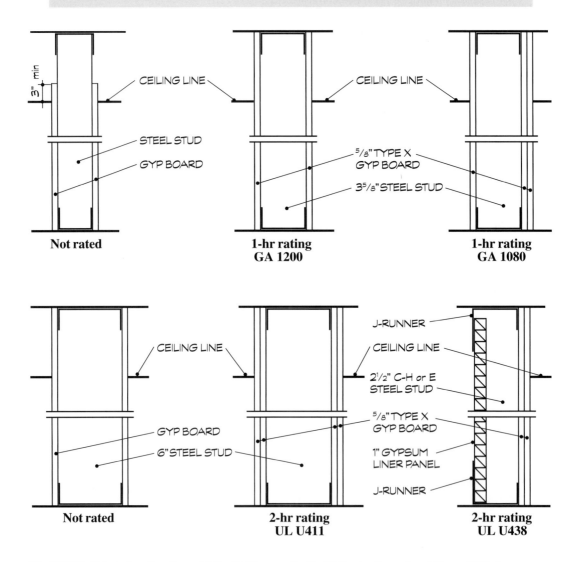

Fig. 702.1B. Selected wall sections. Methodist Community Health Center. Sugar Land, Texas. HKS, Inc., Architects, Engineers, Planners. Dallas, Texas.

702 Definitions

702.1 Definitions *(part 5 of 9)*

- **Fire separation distance**
  - ○ The dimension from the face of a building to one of the following:
    - To an imaginary line between two buildings on the same property.
    - To one of the following measured ⊥ to the lot line.
      - The closest interior lot line.
      - The centerline of a street.
      - The centerline of an alley.
      - The centerline of a public way.

> **Case study:Fig. 702.1C**. Measurement of fire separation distance ⊥ to interior lot lines and to the center of the street yields the distances indicated at the corners of the builidng and at the corners of the future expansion.

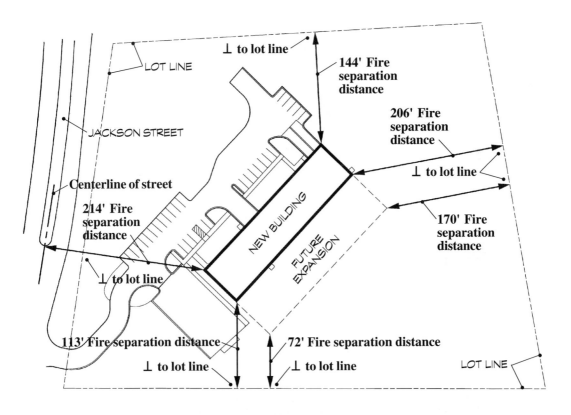

Fig. 702.1C. Site plan. Garments to Go. Bastrop, Texas. Spencer Godfrey Architects. Round Rock, Texas.

702 Definitions

702.1 Definitions *(part 6 of 9)*

- **Fire wall**
  - Wall with a fire-resistance rating.
  - Openings in wall are protected.
  - Wall retards the spread of fire.
  - Wall extends from foundation to or through roof.
  - Wall is detailed so as to remain standing as follows:
    In case of construction collapse on either side.

- **Fire window assembly**
  - A window that resists the passage of fire due to the following:
    Its construction.
    Its glazing.

- **Fireblocking**
  - Building materials installed in concealed spaces to prevent the spread of fire.

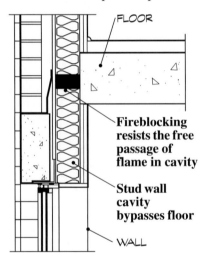

Fig. 702.1D. Detail at floor-wall intersection. McKenzie Lofts. Portland, Oregon. Ankrom Moisan Associated Architects. Portland, Oregon.

- **Floor fire door assembly**
  - An assembly including the following:
    Fire door.
    Frame.
    Hardware.
    Accessories.
  - Installed horizontally.
  - Provides fire protection at a defined level as follows:
    To an opening through a floor with a fire-resistance rating.

702 Definitions

702.1 Definitions *(part 7 of 9)*

- **Joint**
  - A linear gap in fire-resistance-rated construction.
  - Allows independent movement in any plane resulting from any of the following:
    Thermal expansion and contraction.
    Seismic activity.
    Wind.
    Other loading.

- **Membrane penetration**
  - An opening through any of the following surface membranes:
    Wall.
    Floor.
    Ceiling.

- **Membrane-penetration firestop**
  - Any of the following:
    A material.
    A device.
    A construction.
  - Prohibits the passage of flame and heat as follows:
    Through membrane openings serving the following:
      Cables.
      Cable trays.
      Conduit.
      Tubing.
      Pipes.
      Similar items.
  - Is effective for a specified length of time.

- **Penetration firestop**
  - A material or assembly protecting either of the following openings:
    An opening passing through an entire assembly.
    An opening through a membrane on one side of an assembly.

- **Self-closing**
  - A door equipped with a device as follows:
    Device closes the door after it is opened.
    Device must be approved.

- **Shaft**
  - An enclosed space.
  - Extends through ≥ 1 stories.
  - Connects vertical openings in any of the following:
    Floors.
    Floor and roof.

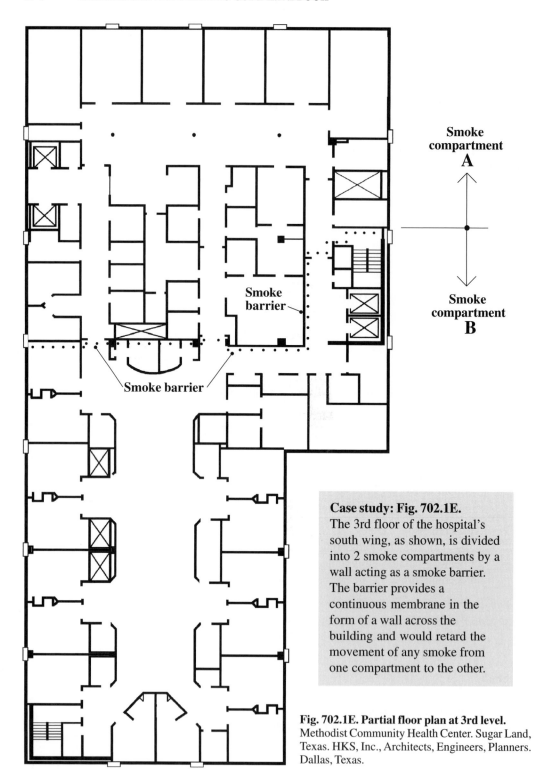

Smoke compartment
A

Smoke compartment
B

Smoke barrier

Smoke barrier

Case study: Fig. 702.1E.
The 3rd floor of the hospital's south wing, as shown, is divided into 2 smoke compartments by a wall acting as a smoke barrier. The barrier provides a continuous membrane in the form of a wall across the building and would retard the movement of any smoke from one compartment to the other.

Fig. 702.1E. Partial floor plan at 3rd level.
Methodist Community Health Center. Sugar Land, Texas. HKS, Inc., Architects, Engineers, Planners. Dallas, Texas.

702 Definitions

702.1 Definitions *(part 8 of 9)*

- **Shaft enclosure**
  - Any of the following elements surrounding a shaft:
    Walls.
    Other construction.

- **Smoke barrier**
  - A continuous membrane.
  - Oriented vertically or horizontally.
  - Examples include the following assemblies:
    Wall.
    Floor.
    Ceiling.
  - Limits the movement of smoke.

- **Smoke compartment**
  - A space surrounded by smoke barriers as follows:
    All sides.
    Above.
    Below.

- **Smoke damper**
  - A listed device.
  - Installed in any of the following locations:
    Air ducts.
    Openings for the transfer of air.
  - Limits the passage of the following:
    Air.
    Smoke.
  - Operates automatically upon detection of smoke.
  - Can be adjusted from a remote location where required.

- **Splice**
  - Connection of fire-resistant joint systems as follows:
    To form a continuous system by either of the following methods:
      Factory process.
      Field process.

702 Definitions

702.1 Definitions *(part 9 of 9)*

- **T Rating**
  - The length of time that a penetration firestop system is able to limit temperature rise as follows:
    Temperature rise through the penetration is limited by the firestop.
    The rise above initial temperature on the nonfire side is as follows:
      Rise limited to 325°F.

  Note: ASTM E 814, "Standard Test Method of Fire Tests of Through-Penetration Fire Stops," is cited as governing the method for determining T ratings.

- **Through-penetration**
  - An opening completely through an assembly.

- **Through-penetration firestop system**
  - Either of the following that prevents the spread of fire through penetrations:
    Materials.
    Products.
  - The system is fire-resistance rated.
  - The system is effective for a specified length of time.
  - The system the following ratings:
    F rating.
    T rating.

  Note: ASTM E 814, "Standard Test Method of Fire Tests of Through-Penetration Fire Stops," is cited as governing the method for determining T ratings.

704 Exterior Walls

704.2 Projections

- This subsection governs building projections extending beyond the floor area as follows:
  - Cornices and eave overhangs.
  - Exterior balconies and stairways.
  - Similar architectural projections.
- Combustible projections must comply with requirements for combustible materials.

  Note: Section 1406, "Combustible Materials on the Exterior Side of Exterior Walls," is cited as governing the projections listed above.
  1004.3.3, "Egress balconies," is cited as providing additional requirements.
  1005.3.6, "Exterior exit stairways," is cited as providing additional requirements.

- Projections may not extend closer to the property line than either of the following points:
  - A point > 12" into the zone in which openings are not permitted.
  - A point $2/3$ the distance from the property line to a point requiring protection for openings.

  Note: 704.8, "Allowable area of openings," is cited a applicable to this subsection.

Case study: Fig. 704.2. A projection from the warehouse faces a street. The fire separation distance is 67'- 6". IBC Table 704.8 indicates that for distances > 30', openings are not regulated by the table; thus, the extent of this projection on the second floor is not limited. Because the building is Type III construction, the projection may be constructed of any approved material. It is constructed of noncombustible materials.

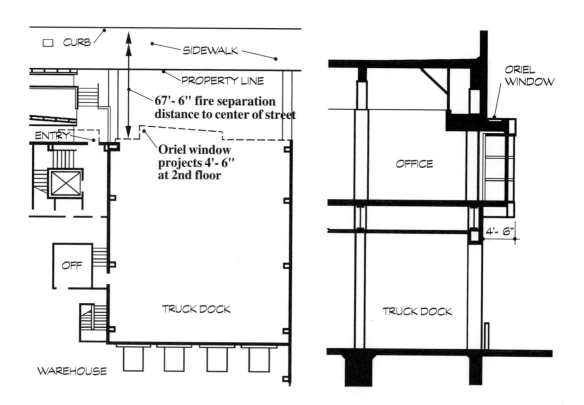

Fig. 704.2. Partial plan and section at truck dock. New Warehouse Addition. Los Angeles, California. Stephen Wen + Associates, Architects, Inc.. Pasadena, California.

704 Exterior Walls

704.2.1 Types I and II construction

This subsection addresses projections from walls of Types I and II construction.

- Combustible materials complying with the requirements listed below are permitted for the following types of projections:
  - Projections:
    Balconies.
    Porches
    Decks.
    Exterior stairways that are not required exits.
    Similar projections.
  - Requirements:
    Projections must be ≤ 50% of the building perimeter at each floor.
    Heavy timber is permitted.
    Combustible materials are permitted with the following fire-resistance ratings:
      ≥ 2 hours for projections from walls of Type I construction.
      ≥ 1 hour for projections from walls of Type II A construction.
      ≥ 0 hours for projections from walls of Type II B construction.
    Fire-retardant-treated wood is permitted on buildings ≤ 3 stories high.
    Untreated wood is permitted for the following elements where they are ≤ 42" in height:
      Pickets.
      Rails.
      Similar guardrail devices.

  Note: 1406.3, "Balconies and similar projections," is cited as governing projections of combustible materials, a partial summary of which is provided above.

- The following windows are governed as indicated below:
  - Windows:
    Bay windows.
    Oriel windows.
  - Requirements:
    For buildings ≤ 3 stories:
      Fire-retardant-treated wood is permitted.
    For other buildings:
      Window construction must match the building construction type.

  Note: 1406.4, "Bay windows and oriel windows," is cited as the source of requirements for such projections, a partial summary of which is provided above.

- Otherwise, noncombustible materials are required for projections.

704 Exterior Walls

704.2.2 Types III, IV and V construction

- Any approved material is permitted for projections as follows:
  - From walls of Types III, IV, and V construction.

704.2.3 Combustible projections

- This subsection applies to combustible projections in the following locations:
  - Where openings are not allowed.
  - Where openings are required to be protected.
- Combustible projections in occupancy R-3 may be Type V construction.
- In other cases, combustible projections must comply with one of the following:
  - Have ≥ 1 hour fire-resistance rating.
  - Be Heavy Timber construction.
  - Requirements listed below for the following types of projections:
      Projections:
        Balconies.
        Porches.
        Decks.
        Exterior stairways that are not required exits.
        Similar projections.
      Requirements:
        Projections must be ≤ 50% of the building perimeter at each floor.
        Combustible materials must have the following fire-resistance ratings:
          ≥ 2 hrs for projections from walls of Type I construction.
          ≥ 1 hr for projections from walls of the following construction types:
            II A, III A, IV, V A.
          ≥ 0 hr for sprinklered projections from walls of the following construction types:
            III A, IV, V A.
          ≥ 0 hr for projections from walls of the following construction types:
            II B, III B, V B.
        Fire-retardant-treated wood is permitted on buildings ≤ 3 stories high.
        Untreated wood is permitted for the following elements where they are ≤ 42" in height:
          Pickets.
          Rails.
          Similar guardrail devices.

Note: 1406.3, "Balconies and similar projections," is cited as the third option for combustible materials, a partial summary of which is provided above.

704 Exterior Walls

704.3 Buildings on the same property and buildings containing courts

- Where opening protection is otherwise required in court walls:
  - Such protection is not required where all the following conditions apply:
    ≤ 2 levels open onto the court.
    The sum of the following areas is $\leq$ the allowable area for the building:
    Building area.
    Court area.
    Building is not occupancy I.
- In other courts > 1 story, the following applies:
  - A property line is assumed to be located between facing walls as follows:
    To determine the wall protection required.
    To determine the opening protection required.
    To determine the requirements for roof covering.
- ≥ 2 buildings may be regulated as 1 building where they meet the following conditions:
  - They are located on the same property.
  - The sum of their areas is $\leq$ the area limit for 1 building as follows:
    Where the following differs among buildings, the smallest area limit governs:
    Occupancy classification.
    Construction type.
- In other cases where buildings are on the same property, the following applies:
  - A property line is assumed to be located between buildings > 1 story as follows:
    So that requirements for the following can be determined:
    Wall protection.
    Opening protection.
    Roof covering.
    Where a new building is adjacent to an existing building:
    The assumed property line is located as follows:
    Adjacent wall and openings of the existing building must comply with the following:
    Fire resistance based on construction type.
    Fire resistance based on fire separation distance.
    Opening size limitations based on the following:
    Protection.
    Fire separation distance.

> *Note: The following are cited as sources of requirements for the adjacent walls and openings of existing buildings indicated above:*
> *704.5, "Fire-resistance ratings."*
> *704.8, "Allowable area of openings."*

704.4 Materials

- Exterior walls are required to be of materials as follows:
  Materials within the designated construction type.

704 Exterior Walls

704.5 Fire-resistance ratings *(part 1 of 5)*

- Exterior walls are rated with regard to fire separation distance as follows:
    Where fire separation distance >5':
      Walls are rated for fire exposure on the inside.
    Where fire separation distance ≤ 5':
      Walls are rated for fire exposure on both sides.
- Type I construction exterior walls must have the fire-resistance ratings listed below:

Table 704.5a   Fire-Resistance Ratings for Type I Construction Exterior Walls

Exterior walls	Fire-resistance rating
Type I A load-bearing walls	≥ 3 hr
Type I A nonload-bearing walls:	
All occupancies:	
Fire separation distance ≥ 30'	≥ 0 hr
Occupancies R-3 and U where serving R-3:	
Fire separation distance < 3'	≥ 1 hr
Fire separation distance ≥ 3'	≥ 0 hr
Occupancies A, B, E, F-2, I, R-1, R-2, R-4, S-2, U:	
Fire separation distance < 30'	≥ 1 hr
Occupancies F-1, M, S-1:	
Fire separation distance < 10'	≥ 2 hr
Fire separation distance ≥ 10' < 30'	≥ 1 hr
Occupancy H:	
Fire separation distance < 10'	≥ 3 hr
Fire separation distance ≥ 10' < 30'	≥ 2 hr
Type I B load-bearing walls:	
Occupancy H:	
Fire separation distance < 5'	≥ 3 hr
Fire separation distance ≥ 5'	≥ 2 hr
All other occupancies	≥ 2 hr
Type I B nonload-bearing walls:	
All occupancies:	
Fire separation distance ≥ 30'	≥ 0 hr
Occupancies R-3 and U where serving R-3:	
Fire separation distance < 3'	≥ 1 hr
Fire separation distance ≥ 3'	≥ 0 hr
Occupancies A, B, E, F-2, I, R-1, R-2, R-4, S-2, U:	
Fire separation distance < 30'	≥ 1 hr
Occupancies F-1, M, S-1:	
Fire separation distance < 5	≥ 2 hr
Fire separation distance ≥ 5 < 30'	≥ 1 hr
Occupancy H:	
Fire separation distance < 5'	≥ 3 hr
Fire separation distance ≥ 5' < 30'	≥ 2 hr

Source: IBC Tables 601 and 602.

704 Exterior Walls

704.5 Fire-resistance ratings *(part 2 of 5)*

- Type II construction exterior walls must have the fire-resistance ratings listed below:

Table 704.5b   Fire-Resistance Ratings for Type II Construction Exterior Walls

Exterior walls	Fire-resistance rating
Type II A load-bearing walls:	
Occupancies A, B, E, F-2, I, R, S-2, U	≥ 1 hr
Occupancies F-1, M, S-1:	
Fire separation distance $< 5'$	≥ 2 hr
Fire separation distance $\geq 5'$	≥ 1 hr
Occupancy H:	
Fire separation distance $< 5'$	≥ 3 hr
Fire separation distance $\geq 5' < 10'$	≥ 2 hr
Fire separation distance $\geq 10'$	≥ 1 hr
Type II A nonload-bearing walls:	
All occupancies:	
Fire separation distance $\geq 30'$	≥ 0 hr
Occupancies R-3 and U where serving R-3:	
Fire separation distance $< 3'$	≥ 1 hr
Fire separation distance $\geq 3'$	≥ 0 hr
Occupancies A, B, E, F-2, I, R-1, R-2, R-4, S-2, U:	
Fire separation distance $< 30'$	≥ 1 hr
Fire separation distance $\geq 30'$	≥ 0 hr
Occupancies F-1, M, S-1:	
Fire separation distance $< 5'$	≥ 2 hr
Fire separation distance $\geq 5' < 30'$	≥ 1 hr
Occupancy H:	
Fire separation distance $< 5'$	≥ 3 hr
Fire separation distance $\geq 5' < 10'$	≥ 2 hr
Fire separation distance $\geq 10' < 30'$	≥ 1 hr
Type II B load-bearing walls and nonload-bearing walls:	
Occupancies R-3 and U where serving R-3:	
Fire separation distance $< 3'$	≥ 1 hr
Fire separation distance $\geq 3'$	≥ 0 hr
Occupancies A, B, E, F-2, I, R-1, R-2, R-4, S-2, U:	
Fire separation distance $< 10'$	≥ 1 hr
Fire separation distance $\geq 10'$	≥ 0 hr
Occupancies F-1, M, S-1:	
Fire separation distance $< 5'$	≥ 2 hr
Fire separation distance $\geq 5' < 10'$	≥ 1 hr
Fire separation distance $\geq 10'$	≥ 0 hr
Occupancy H:	
Fire separation distance $< 5'$	≥ 3 hr
Fire separation distance $\geq 5' < 10'$	≥ 2 hr
Fire separation distance $\geq 10' < 30'$	≥ 1 hr
Fire separation distance $\geq 30'$	≥ 0 hr

Source: IBC Tables 601 and 602.

704 Exterior Walls

704.5 Fire-resistance ratings *(part 3 of 5)*

- Type III construction exterior walls must have the fire-resistance ratings listed below:

Table 704.5c   Fire-Resistance Ratings for Type III Construction Exterior Walls

Exterior walls	Fire-resistance rating
Type III A load-bearing walls:	
Occupancy H:	
Fire separation distance < 5'	$\geq$ 3 hr
Fire separation distance $\geq$ 5'	$\geq$ 2 hr
All other occupancies	$\geq$ 2 hr
Type III A nonload-bearing walls:	
All occupancies:	
Fire separation distance $\geq$ 30'	$\geq$ 0 hr
Occupancies R-3 and U where serving R-3:	
Fire separation distance < 3'	$\geq$ 1 hr
Fire separation distance $\geq$ 3'	$\geq$ 0 hr
Occupancies A, B, E, F-2, I, R-1, R-2, R-4, S-2, U:	
Fire separation distance < 30'	$\geq$ 1 hr
Occupancies F-1, M, S-1:	
Fire separation distance < 5'	$\geq$ 2 hr
Fire separation distance $\geq$ 5' < 30'	$\geq$ 1 hr
Occupancy H:	
Fire separation distance < 5'	$\geq$ 3 hr
Fire separation distance $\geq$ 5' < 10'	$\geq$ 2 hr
Fire separation distance $\geq$ 10' < 30'	$\geq$ 1 hr
Type III B load-bearing walls:	
Occupancy H:	
Fire separation distance < 5'	$\geq$ 3 hr
Fire separation distance $\geq$ 5'	$\geq$ 2 hr
All other occupancies	$\geq$ 2 hr
Type III B nonload-bearing walls:	
All occupancies:	
Fire separation distance $\geq$ 30'	$\geq$ 0 hr
Occupancies R-3 and U where serving R-3:	
Fire separation distance < 3'	$\geq$ 1 hr
Fire separation distance $\geq$ 3'	$\geq$ 0 hr
Occupancies A, B, E, F-2, I, R-1, R-2, R-4, S-2, U:	
Fire separation distance < 30'	$\geq$ 1 hr
Occupancies F-1, M, S-1:	
Fire separation distance < 5'	$\geq$ 2 hr
Fire separation distance $\geq$ 5' <30'	$\geq$ 1 hr
Occupancy H:	
Fire separation distance < 5'	$\geq$ 3 hr
Fire separation distance $\geq$ 5' < 10'	$\geq$ 2 hr
Fire separation distance $\geq$ 10' < 30'	$\geq$ 1 hr

Source: IBC Tables 601 and 602.

704 Exterior Walls

704.5 Fire-resistance ratings *(part 4 of 5)*

- Type IV construction exterior walls must have the fire-resistance ratings listed below:

Table 704.5d   Fire-Resistance Ratings for Type IV Construction Exterior Walls

Exterior walls	Fire-resistance rating
Type IV load-bearing walls:	
Occupancy H:	
Fire separation distance $< 5'$	≥ 3 hr
Fire separation distance $\geq 5'$	≥ 2 hr
All other occupancies:	≥ 2 hr
Type IV nonload-bearing walls:	
All occupancies:	
Fire separation distance $\geq 30'$	≥ 0 hr
Occupancies R-3 and U where serving R-3:	
Fire separation distance $< 3'$	≥ 1 hr
Fire separation distance $\geq 3'$	≥ 0 hr
Occupancies A, B, E, F-2, I, R-1, R-2, R-4, S-2, U:	
Fire separation distance $< 30'$	≥ 1 hr
Occupancies F-1, M, S-1:	
Fire separation distance $< 5'$	≥ 2 hr
Fire separation distance $\geq 5' < 30'$	≥ 1 hr
Occupancy H:	
Fire separation distance $< 5'$	≥ 3 hr
Fire separation distance $\geq 5' < 10'$	≥ 2 hr
Fire separation distance $\geq 10' < 30'$	≥ 1 hr

Source: IBC Tables 601 and 602.

704 Exterior Walls

704.5 Fire-resistance ratings *(part 5 of 5)*

- Type V construction exterior walls must have the fire-resistance ratings listed below:

Table 704.5e   Fire-Resistance Ratings for Type V Construction Exterior Walls

Exterior walls	Fire-resistance rating
Type V A load-bearing walls:	
Occupancies A, B, E, F-2, I, R, S-2, U	≥ 1 hr
Occupancies F-1, M, S-1:	
Fire separation distance < 5'	≥ 2 hr
Fire separation distance ≥ 5'	≥ 1 hr
Occupancy H:	
Fire separation distance < 5'	≥ 3 hr
Fire separation distance ≥ 5' < 10'	≥ 2 hr
Fire separation distance ≥ 10'	≥ 1 hr
Type V A nonload-bearing walls:	
All occupancies:	
Fire separation distance ≥ 30'	≥ 0 hr
Occupancies R-3 and U where serving R-3:	
Fire separation distance < 3'	≥ 1 hr
Fire separation distance ≥ 3'	≥ 0 hr
Occupancies A, B, E, F-2, I, R-1, R-2, R-4, S-2, U:	
Fire separation distance < 30'	≥ 1 hr
Occupancies F-1, M, S-1:	
Fire separation distance < 5'	≥ 2 hr
Fire separation distance ≥ 5' < 30'	≥ 1 hr
Occupancy H:	
Fire separation distance < 5'	≥ 3 hr
Fire separation distance ≥ 5' < 10'	≥ 2 hr
Fire separation distance ≥ 10' < 30'	≥ 1 hr
Type V B load-bearing walls and nonload-bearing walls:	
Occupancies R-3 and U where serving R-3:	
Fire separation distance < 3'	≥ 1 hr
Fire separation distance ≥ 3'	≥ 0 hr
Occupancies A, B, E, F-2, I, R-1, R-2, R-4, S-2, U:	
Fire separation distance < 10'	≥ 1 hr
Fire separation distance ≥ 10'	≥ 0 hr
Occupancies F-1, M, S-1:	
Fire separation distance < 5'	≥ 2 hr
Fire separation distance ≥ 5' < 10'	≥ 1 hr
Fire separation distance ≥ 10'	≥ 0 hr
Occupancy H:	
Fire separation distance < 5'	≥ 3 hr
Fire separation distance ≥ 5' < 10'	≥ 2 hr
Fire separation distance ≥ 10' < 30'	≥ 1 hr
Fire separation distance ≥ 30'	≥ 0 hr

Source: IBC Tables 601 and 602.

704 Exterior Walls

704.6 Structural stability

- Exterior walls must be detailed to remain standing during a fire as follows:
  - For a length of time equal to its fire-resistance rating.
- Exterior walls must extend above the roof or to a lower height as per the fire hazard.

  Note: 704.11, "Parapets," is cited as governing exterior wall height.

704.7 Unexposed surface temperature *(part 1 of 4)*

- This section addresses a surface of an exterior wall as follows:
  - Surface is subject to a rise in surface temperature due to fire on the other side of the wall.
  - Surface is not directly exposed to fire.
- In the following cases the rise of temperature on the unexposed surface is not limited to 250°F as otherwise required:
  - Where the fire separation distance is > 20'.
  - Where the fire separation distance is ≤ 20':

    The allowable area of protected openings is reduced by subtracting the following amount:

    Amount subtracted = Wall area not including openings × Equivalent Opening Factor

    Equivalent Opening Factors are based on the following equation:

$$\textbf{Factor} \; = \; \frac{(\textbf{Average °F of surface not exposed to fire} + \textbf{460 °F})^4}{(\textbf{Fire-resistance temperature coefficient} + \textbf{460 °F})^4}$$

Fire-resistance temperature coefficients are as follows:

Wall fire-resistance rating	Fire-resistance temperature coefficient
1 hr	1700 °F
2 hr	1850 °F
3 hr	1925 °F
4 hr	2000 °F

Equivalent Opening Factors as derived from the equation above are provide as follows:
In parts 2, 3, and 4 of this section.
For every 10°F of unexposed surface temperature.
From 410°F to 2000°F.

Note: ASTM E 119, "Standard Test Methods for Fire Tests of Building Construction and Materials," is cited as the standard that requires a 250°F limit of temperature rise on an unexposed surface.

704 Exterior Walls

704.7 Unexposed surface temperature *(part 2 of 4)*

- Reduced allowable area of protected openings is calculated as follows:

  Allowable area – (Wall area not including openings × Equivalent Opening Factor)

- Equivalent Opening Factors are provided in the table below as follows:
  - From 410°F to 940°F.
  - Based on the following:

    Average temperature in °F of the unexposed wall surface.

    Fire-resistance rating of the wall.

Table 704.7a   Equivalent Opening Factors for Exterior Walls (410°F–940°F)

Surface Temp.°F	Wall fire-resistance rating				Surface Temp.°F	Wall fire-resistance rating			
	1 hr	2 hr	3 hr	4 hr		1 hr	2 hr	3 hr	4 hr
410	0.026	0.020	0.018	0.016	680	0.078	0.059	0.052	0.046
420	0.028	0.021	0.019	0.016	690	0.080	0.061	0.054	0.048
430	0.029	0.022	0.019	0.017	700	0.083	0.064	0.056	0.049
440	0.030	0.023	0.020	0.018	710	0.086	0.066	0.058	0.051
450	0.032	0.024	0.021	0.019	720	0.089	0.068	0.060	0.053
460	0.033	0.025	0.022	0.020	730	0.092	0.070	0.062	0.055
470	0.034	0.026	0.023	0.020	740	0.095	0.073	0.064	0.057
480	0.036	0.027	0.024	0.021	750	0.098	0.075	0.066	0.059
490	0.037	0.029	0.025	0.022	760	0.102	0.078	0.068	0.060
500	0.039	0.030	0.026	0.023	770	0.105	0.080	0.071	0.063
510	0.041	0.031	0.027	0.024	780	0.109	0.083	0.073	0.065
520	0.042	0.032	0.029	0.025	790	0.112	0.086	0.075	0.067
530	0.044	0.034	0.030	0.026	800	0.116	0.089	0.078	0.069
540	0.046	0.035	0.031	0.027	810	0.120	0.091	0.080	0.071
550	0.048	0.037	0.032	0.028	820	0.123	0.094	0.083	0.073
560	0.050	0.038	0.033	0.030	830	0.127	0.097	0.086	0.076
570	0.052	0.040	0.035	0.031	840	0.131	0.100	0.088	0.078
580	0.054	0.041	0.036	0.032	850	0.135	0.103	0.091	0.080
590	0.056	0.043	0.038	0.033	860	0.139	0.107	0.094	0.083
600	0.058	0.044	0.039	0.034	870	0.144	0.110	0.097	0.085
610	0.060	0.046	0.041	0.036	880	0.148	0.113	0.100	0.088
620	0.063	0.048	0.042	0.037	890	0.153	0.117	0.103	0.091
630	0.065	0.050	0.044	0.039	900	0.157	0.120	0.106	0.093
640	0.068	0.051	0.045	0.040	910	0.162	0.124	0.109	0.096
650	0.070	0.053	0.047	0.041	920	0.167	0.127	0.112	0.099
660	0.072	0.055	0.049	0.043	930	0.171	0.131	0.115	0.102
670	0.075	0.057	0.050	0.045	940	0.176	0.135	0.119	0.105

704 Exterior Walls

704.7 Unexposed surface temperature *(part 3 of 4)*

- Reduced allowable area of protected openings is calculated as follows:
    Allowable area – (Wall area not including openings × Equivalent Opening Factor)
- Equivalent Opening Factors are provided in the table below as follows:
    - From 950°F to 1480°F.
    - Based on the following:
        Average temperature in °F of the unexposed wall surface.
        Fire-resistance rating of the wall.

Table 704.7b   Equivalent Opening Factors for Exterior Walls (950°F–1480°F)

Surface Temp.°F	Wall fire-resistance rating				Surface Temp.°F	Wall fire-resistance rating			
	1 hr	2 hr	3 hr	4 hr		1 hr	2 hr	3 hr	4 hr
950	0.182	0.139	0.122	0.108	1220	0.366	0.280	0.246	0.218
960	0.187	0.143	0.126	0.111	1230	0.375	0.286	0.252	0.223
970	0.192	0.147	0.129	0.114	1240	0.384	0.293	0.258	0.228
980	0.198	0.151	0.133	0.117	1250	0.393	0.300	0.264	0.233
990	0.203	0.155	0.137	0.121	1260	0.402	0.307	0.270	0.239
1000	0.209	0.160	0.140	0.124	1270	0.411	0.315	0.277	0.245
1010	0.215	0.164	0.144	0.128	1280	0.421	0.322	0.283	0.250
1020	0.220	0.168	0.148	0.131	1290	0.431	0.329	0.290	0.256
1030	0.226	0.173	0.152	0.135	1300	0.441	0.337	0.297	0.262
1040	0.233	0.178	0.156	0.138	1310	0.451	0.345	0.303	0.268
1050	0.239	0.183	0.161	0.142	1320	0.461	0.352	0.310	0.274
1060	0.245	0.187	0.165	0.146	1330	0.472	0.361	0.317	0.280
1070	0.252	0.192	0.169	0.150	1340	0.482	0.369	0.324	0.287
1080	0.258	0.198	0.174	0.154	1350	0.493	0.377	0.332	0.293
1090	0.265	0.203	0.178	0.158	1360	0.504	0.385	0.339	0.300
1100	0.272	0.208	0.183	0.162	1370	0.515	0.394	0.347	0.306
1110	0.279	0.213	0.189	0.166	1380	0.527	0.403	0.354	0.313
1120	0.286	0.219	0.193	0.170	1390	0.538	0.411	0.362	0.320
1130	0.294	0.224	0.198	0.175	1400	0.550	0.420	0.370	0.327
1140	0.301	0.230	0.203	0.179	1410	0.562	0.429	0.378	0.334
1150	0.309	0.236	0.208	0.183	1420	0.574	0.439	0.386	0.341
1160	0.316	0.242	0.213	0.188	1430	0.586	0.448	0.394	0.348
1170	0.324	0.248	0.218	0.193	1440	0.599	0.458	0.403	0.356
1180	0.332	0.254	0.224	0.198	1450	0.611	0.467	0.411	0.363
1190	0.341	0.260	0.229	0.202	1460	0.624	0.477	0.420	0.371
1200	0.349	0.267	0.235	0.207	1470	0.637	0.487	0.429	0.379
1210	0.357	0.273	0.240	0.212	1480	0.651	0.497	0.438	0.387

704 Exterior Walls

704.7 Unexposed surface temperature *(part 4 of 4)*

- Reduced allowable area of protected openings is calculated as follows:
  Allowable area – (Wall area not including openings × Equivalent Opening Factor).
- Equivalent Opening Factors are provided in the table below as follows:
  - From 1490°F to 2000°F.
  - Based on the following:
    Average temperature in °F of the unexposed wall surface.
    Fire-resistance rating of the wall.

Table 704.7c   Equivalent Opening Factors for Exterior Walls (1490°F–2000°F)

Surface Temp.°F	Wall fire-resistance rating				Surface Temp.°F	Wall fire-resistance rating			
	1 hr	2 hr	3 hr	4 hr		1 hr	2 hr	3 hr	4 hr
1490	0.664	0.508	0.447	0.395	1750	NA	0.838	0.737	0.651
1500	0.678	0.518	0.456	0.403	1760	NA	0.853	0.751	0.663
1510	0.692	0.529	0.465	0.411	1770	NA	0.869	0.764	0.675
1520	0.706	0.540	0.475	0.420	1780	NA	0.884	0.778	0.687
1530	0.720	0.551	0.485	0.428	1790	NA	0.900	0.792	0.700
1540	0.735	0.562	0.495	0.437	1800	NA	0.916	0.806	0.712
1550	0.750	0.573	0.504	0.446	1810	NA	0.933	0.821	0.725
1560	0.765	0.585	0.515	0.455	1820	NA	0.949	0.835	0.738
1570	0.780	0.596	0.525	0.464	1830	NA	0.966	0.850	0.751
1580	0.796	0.608	0.535	0.473	1840	NA	0.983	0.865	0.764
1590	0.811	0.620	0.546	0.482	1850	NA	1.000	0.880	0.778
1600	0.827	0.632	0.557	0.492	1860	NA	NA	0.895	0.791
1610	0.843	0.645	0.567	0.501	1870	NA	NA	0.911	0.805
1620	0.860	0.657	0.578	0.511	1880	NA	NA	0.927	0.819
1630	0.877	0.670	0.590	0.521	1890	NA	NA	0.943	0.833
1640	0.893	0.683	0.601	0.531	1900	NA	NA	0.959	0.847
1650	0.911	0.696	0.613	0.541	1910	NA	NA	0.975	0.861
1660	0.928	0.709	0.624	0.552	1920	NA	NA	0.992	0.876
1670	0.946	0.723	0.636	0.562	1930	NA	NA	NA	0.891
1680	0.963	0.737	0.648	0.573	1940	NA	NA	NA	0.906
1690	0.982	0.750	0.660	0.583	1950	NA	NA	NA	0.921
1700	1.000	0.764	0.673	0.594	1960	NA	NA	NA	0.937
1710	NA	0.779	0.685	0.605	1970	NA	NA	NA	0.952
1720	NA	0.793	0.698	0.617	1980	NA	NA	NA	0.968
1730	NA	0.808	0.711	0.628	1990	NA	NA	NA	0.984
1740	NA	0.823	0.724	0.640	2000	NA	NA	NA	1.000

704 Exterior Walls

704.8 Allowable area of openings *(part 1 of 2)*

This part of the subsection addresses the allowable area of unprotected openings in exterior walls of buildings without sprinklers.

- Unprotected openings are not limited in buildings as follows:
  - Where the following components are not required to have fire-resistance ratings:
    Exterior bearing walls.
    Exterior nonload-bearing walls.
    Exterior structural frame.
- For other cases, the % of an exterior wall in each story that may be occupied by unprotected openings varies with the fire separation distance as follows:

Table 704.8a　　% of an Exterior Wall That May Be Occupied by Unprotected Openings

Occupancy	Fire separation distance	Unprotected openings limit of coverage
R-3, accessory to R-3	≤ 3'	Not permitted
R-3	> 3' ≤ 5'	≤ 25%
"	> 5'	Not limited
H-2, H-3	≤ 15'	Not permitted
"	> 15' ≤ 20'	25%
"	> 20' ≤ 25'	45%
"	> 25' ≤ 30'	70%
"	> 30'	Not limited
Open parking garages	≤ 5'	Not permitted
"	> 5' ≤ 10'	10%
"	> 10'	Not limited
Other occupancies	≤ 5'	Not permitted
"	> 5' ≤ 10'	10%
"	> 10' ≤ 15'	15%
"	> 15' ≤ 20'	25%
"	> 20' ≤ 25'	45%
"	> 25' ≤ 30'	70%
"	> 30'	Not limited

Source: IBC Table 704.8.

- Where a fire wall separates buildings of different heights, the following applies:
  - Where the fire wall does not extend above the lower roof:
    Openings in the lower roof are not permitted ≤ 10' from the fire wall.

  Note: 705.6.1, "Stepped buildings," is cited as the source of requirements for buildings of different heights.

704 Exterior Walls

704.8 Allowable area of openings *(part 2 of 2)*

This part of the subsection addresses the allowable area of protected openings and combinations of protected and unprotected openings in exterior walls of buildings without sprinklers.

- Where a fire wall separates buildings of different heights, the following applies:
  - Where the fire wall extends above the lower roof:
    The wall plane within 15' of the lower roof is governed as follows:
    Openings must have a ¾-hr fire-protection rating.
  - Where the fire wall stops below the lower roof:
    Openings are not permitted in the lower roof ≤ 10' from the fire wall.
- For other cases, the % of an exterior wall in each story that may be occupied by protected openings varies with the fire separation distance as follows:

Table 704.8b   % of an Exterior Wall That May Be Occupied by Protected Openings

Occupancy	Fire separation distance	Protected openings limit of coverage
R-3, accessory to R-3	≤ 3'	Not permitted
R-3	> 3' ≤ 5'	≤ 25%
"	> 5'	Not limited
Open parking garages	≤ 3' Not permitted	
"	> 3' ≤ 5'	15%
"	> 5' ≤ 10'	25%
"	> 10'	Not limited
Other occupancies	≤ 3'	Not permitted
"	> 3' ≤ 5'	15%
"	> 5' ≤ 10'	25%
"	> 10' ≤ 15'	45%
"	> 15' ≤ 20'	75%
"	> 20'	Not limited

Source: IBC Table 704.8.

- Protected and unprotected openings in the same wall of a story are governed as follows:
  - The sum of their areas, each in % of that allowed, may not be > 100%.
  - Where a surface of an exterior wall on the side away from a fire has a temperature rise > 250°F, the following applies:
    Where fire separation distance is ≤ 20':
    Allowable areas of protected and unprotected openings are reduced as shown below:

Allowable area – (Wall area not including openings × Equivalent Opening Factor)

Note: 704.7, "Unexposed surface temperature," provides Equivalent Opening Factors.
ASTM E 119, "Standard Test Methods for Fire Tests of Building Construction and Materials," is the standard limiting temperature rise on unexposed surfaces.

704 Exterior Walls

704.8.1 Automatic sprinkler system

- This subsection addresses allowable areas of unprotected openings in exterior walls of sprinklered buildings as per NFPA 13.
- The % of an exterior wall in each story that may be occupied by unprotected openings varies with the fire separation distance as follows:

Table 704.8.1   % of an Exterior Wall That May Be Occupied by Unprotected Openings: with Sprinklers

Occupancy	Fire separation distance	Unprotected openings, building sprinklered
R-3, accessory to R-3	≤ 3'	Not permitted
R-3	> 3' ≤ 5'	≤ 25%
"	> 5'	Not limited
H-1	≤ 5'	Not permitted
"	> 5' ≤ 10'	10%
"	> 10' ≤ 15'	15%
"	> 15' ≤ 20'	25%
"	> 20' ≤ 25'	45%
"	> 25' ≤ 30'	70%
	> 30'	Not limited
H-2, H-3	≤ 15'	Not permitted
"	> 15' ≤ 20'	25%
"	> 20' ≤ 25'	45%
"	> 25' ≤ 30'	70%
"	> 30'	Not limited
Open parking garages	≤ 3'	Not permitted
"	> 3' ≤ 5'	15%
"	> 5' ≤ 10'	25%
"	> 10'	Not limited
Other occupancies	≤ 3'	Not permitted
"	> 3' ≤ 5'	15%
"	> 5' ≤ 10'	25%
"	> 10' ≤ 15'	45%
"	> 15' ≤ 20'	75%
"	> 20'	Not limited

Source: IBC Table 704.8.

704 Exterior Walls

704.8.2 First story

- This section applies to buildings other than occupancy H.
- Unprotected opening area in exterior walls is not limited where all of the following apply:
  - In the 1st story.
  - Where the wall faces either of the following open spaces:
    A street with a fire separation distance >15'.
    An unoccupied open space ≥ 30' wide with all the following characteristics:
      Has access from a street by a posted fire line.
      With one of the following conditions:
        Located on the same lot.
        Dedicated to public use.

  Note: International Fire Code is cited as the source governing posted fire lanes.

704.9 Vertical separation of openings

- This section does not apply to the following:
  - Buildings ≤ 3 stories.
  - Sprinklered buildings as per NFPA 13.
  - Open parking garages.
- Other buildings where both of the following conditions exist are governed as indicated below:
  - Conditions:
    The horizontal distance between an upper and lower opening is ≤ 5'.
    The opening in the lower story is not protected.
  - Requirements:
    Vertical separation of upper and lower windows is required by one of the following:
      A vertical assembly as follows:
        Provides ≥ 3' between openings.
        Has a fire-resistance rating ≥ 1 hr.
        Is one of the following components:
          Spandrel girder.
          Exterior wall.
          Other similar assembly.
      Flame barrier as follows:
        Extends ≥ 30" horizontally beyond the exterior wall plane.
        Has a fire-resistance rating ≥ 1 hr.
    The rise of temperature on the barrier surface not exposed to a fire is not limited to 250°F by this section.

  Note: ASTM E 119, "Standard Test Methods for Fire Tests of Building Construction and Materials," is cited as the standard limiting temperature rise on unexposed surfaces.

Case study: Fig. 704.8.2. The extent of the canopy on this building is subject to restriction based on the fire hazard associated with the proximity of adjacent buildings. Since openings are also vulnerable to such a fire hazard, the need for protected openings is used as a measure of the hazard. In this case, the canopy is on the first story (most accessible to the fire department), thus, qualifying the building to be without protected openings if the fire separation distance is > 15'. The fire separation distance is measured to the center of the street on a line ⊥ to a tangent at the property line. This distance is 95'. Consequently, the projection of the canopy is not limited. Since the canopy is constructed of noncombustible materials it is not subject to limitations for combustible materials. The canopy, therefore, complies with the code in all respects.

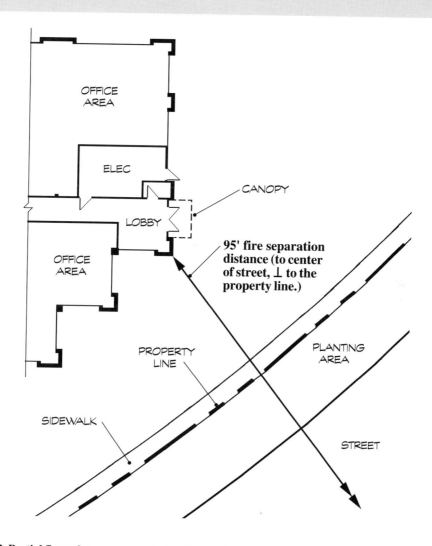

Fig. 704.8.2. Partial floor plan at canopy. AmberGlen Business Center. Hillsboro, Oregon. Ankrom Moisan Associated Architects. Portland, Oregon.

704 Exterior Walls

704.10 Vertical exposure

- This subsection addresses buildings on the same lot.
- The following applies to openings above the roof of an adjoining building:
    - Openings do not require approved protectives as follows:
        Where the lower roof has all the following characteristics:
        Construction has a fire-resistance rating ≥ 1 hr.
        Rated construction extends ≥ 10' from the wall with the window.
        Supporting structure for the rated construction complies with the following:
        It has a fire-resistance rating ≥ 1 hr for its full length.
- In other cases, windows above a roof with all of the following conditions are governed as indicated below:
    - Conditions:
        The window is in one of the following locations:
        An adjacent building.
        An adjoining building.
        The window is < 15' vertically from the lower roof.
        The lower roof and/or the higher wall is within a 15' fire separation distance.
    - Requirements:
        The openings must be provided with approved protectives.

    Note: The 15' fire separation distance is measured from each building to an imaginary line between them; thus, buildings closer than 30' to each other would cause one or both to be within the 15' fire separation distance by a literal interpretation.

704.11 Parapets *(part 1 of 2)*

- Parapets are not required on exterior walls in any of the following cases:
    - Where walls need not have a fire-resistance rating based on fire separation distance.

    Note: IBC Table 602, "Fire-Resistance Rating Requirements for Exterior Walls Based on Fire Separation Distance," is cited as the source applicable to the above walls.

    - Where no floor of the building has an area > 1000 sf.
    - Where walls terminate at either of the following roofs:
        Roofs having a fire-resistance rating ≥ 2 hrs.
        Roofs with construction of noncombustible materials including the following:
        Roof deck.
        Supporting construction.
    - Where fire separation distance permits ≥ 25% of the wall to have unprotected openings.

    Note: 704.8, "Allowable area of openings," is cited as the source governing % of wall coverage permitted for openings based on fire separation distance.

704 Exterior Walls

704.11 Parapets *(part 2 of 2)*

- Parapets are not required on exterior walls in any of the following cases:
  - Where walls terminate at the bottom of the roof deck with all the following conditions:
    Wall has a fire-resistance rating ≥ 1 hr.
    Roof/ceiling framing and supports have a fire-resistance rating ≥ 1 hr as follows:
      Where roof framing is ‖ to the exterior wall:
        Rating extends ≥ 4' from interior face of exterior wall for the following occupancies:
          R, U.
        Rating extends ≥ 10' from interior face of exterior wall for other occupancies.
      Where roof framing is not ‖ to the exterior wall:
        The entire span and its supports have a fire-resistance rating ≥ 1 hr.
    Roof openings are > 5' from the rated wall in the following occupancies:
      R, U.
    Roof openings are > 10' from the rated wall in other occupancies.
    The entire roof covering is ≥ Class B.
  - Where walls terminate at the bottom of the roof deck with all of the following conditions:
    In one of the following occupancies:
      R-2, R-3.
    In one of the following construction types:
      Types III, IV, V.
    Roof deck is constructed of one of the following for a distance of ≥ 4' from the wall:
      Approved noncombustible materials.
      Fire-retardant treated wood.
    Roof covering is ≥ Class C.
    Roof is protected with Type X ⁵⁄₈" gypsum board as follows:
      Board is mounted immediately under the roof deck.
      Board is supported by ≥ nominal 2" ledgers attached to sides of roof framing.
      Board protection is installed a distance ≥ 4' from the wall.
- Other exterior walls must have parapets.

704.11.1 Parapet construction

- Parapets must have the same fire-resistance rating as required for the wall below.
- Parapets must have noncombustible surfaces subject to both of the following conditions:
  - On sides adjacent to a roof surface.
  - Covering the area within 18" from the top of the parapet including the following:
    Coping and counterflashing.
- Parapet height must be ≥ 30" above its intersection with the roof surface.
- Where the roof slopes toward the parapet at a slope > 2:12, the following applies:
  - Parapet height must be the greater of the following:
    A height ≥ 30" above the intersection of parapet and roof surface.
    A height ≥ the highest point of the roof as follows:
      Within a distance from the parapet equal to the following fire separation distance:
        The fire separation distance requiring protection of wall openings.

704 Exterior Walls

704.12 Opening protection

- This section addresses openings required to be protected as follows:
  - Based on fire separation distance.
  - Based on relationships to openings above and below.
  - Based on relationships to lower roofs.

  Note: The following sections are cited as regulating openings governed by this section:
  704.8, "Allowable area of openings," limits size vs. fire separation distance.
  704.9, "Vertical separation of openings."
  705.10, "Vertical exposure," addresses openings exposed to lower roofs.

- Where both of the following conditions apply, openings are not required to have fire protective assemblies:
  - The building is sprinklered as per NFPA 13.
  - The exterior openings are protected by an approved water curtain as follows:
    Must be as per NFPA 13.
    Must utilize automatic sprinklers approved for use in water curtains.
- In other cases, windows must be protected as follows:
  - Where walls must have a fire-resistance rating > 1 hr based on fire separation distance:
    Windows must have a fire-protection rating ≥ 1½ hrs.
  - Where walls must have a fire-resistance rating ≥ 1 hr based on fire separation distance:
    Windows must have a fire-protection rating ≥ ¾ hr.
  - Where windows are required to be protected due to exposure to one of the following, the requirement below applies:
    Exposure conditions:
      To windows above or below.
      To a roof below.
    Requirement:
      Windows must have a fire-protection rating of ≥ ¾ hr.
  - Where windows in walls not fire-resistance-rated are required to be protected due to exposure based on one of the following, the requirement below applies:
    Exposure conditions:
      Due to fire separation distance.
      To windows above or below.
      To a roof below.
    Requirement:
      Windows must have a fire-protection rating of ≥ ¾ hr.
- Other openings governed by this section must be protected with fire doors or shutters.

  Note: 714.2, "Fire door and shutter assemblies," is cited as governing these protectives.

704 Exterior Walls

704.12.1 Unprotected openings

- Where protected openings are not required:
  - The following may be constructed of any approved material.
    Windows.
    Doors.
  - The following must meet applicable code requirements:
    Glass and glazing.
    Plastic.

  Note: Section 704, "Exterior Walls," is cited as the source requiring protected openings. Chapter 24, "Glass and Glazing," is cited as the source governing these materials. Chapter 26, "Plastic," is cited as the source governing this material.

704.13 Joints

- Where exterior walls may have unprotected openings, the following applies:
  - Joints in the walls need not comply with fire-resistant joint system requirements.
- Where exterior walls are required by this section to have a fire-resistance rating:
  - Joints in or between such walls must comply with fire-resistant joint system requirements.

  Note: Section 712, "Fire-Resistant Joint Systems," is cited as the source of requirements for joints in walls with a fire-resistance rating.

704.13.1 Voids

This section addresses the void created by the intersection of an exterior curtain wall assembly and a floor/ceiling assembly.

- The void must be sealed as follows:
  - With an approved material.
  - Sealant material must be installed securely.
  - Sealant material must prevent the passage of the following:
    Flame.
    Hot gasses.

  Note: 712.4, "Exterior curtain wall/floor intersection," is cited as the source of requirements governing the protection of such voids, a partial summary of which is provided above.

705 Fire Walls

705.1 General

- The following applies to each part of a building completely separated from adjacent parts by a fire wall:
  - Each part is considered to be a separate building.
- Where a fire wall occurs where a fire barrier wall is also required, the following applies:
  - The more restrictive requirements of each governs.
- Fire walls serving as party walls on property lines may not have openings.

  Note: 503.2, "Party walls," is cited as a source of requirements for such walls, the content of which is summarized above.

705.2 Structural stability

- Fire walls must be constructed to remain standing during a fire as follows:
  - For a time period equal to its fire-resistance rating.
  - Regardless of any collapse of adjacent construction.

705.3 Materials

- In the following types of construction, fire walls must be built of an approved noncombustible material:
  - Types I, II, III, IV.

705.4 Fire-resistance rating

- Fire-resistance ratings required for fire walls are as follows:

Table 705.4   Fire-Resistance Ratings Required for Fire Walls

Construction type	Occupancy	Fire-resistance rating
II, V	A, B, E, H-4, I, R-1, R-2, U	$\geq$ 2 hr
I, III, IV	A, B, E, H-4, I, R-1, R-2, U	$\geq$ 3 hr
I, II, III, IV, V	F-1, H-3, H-5, M, S-1	$\geq$ 3 hr
I, II, III, IV, V	H-1, H-2	$\geq$ 4 hr
I, II, III, IV, V	F-2, R-3, R-4, S-2	$\geq$ 2 hr

Source: IBC Table 705.4.

  Note: The following are cited as sources of additional requirements for H occupancies as indicated by titles:
  415.4, "Special provisions for Group H-1 occupancies," which addresses building size and configuration, roof and floor construction, and materials with multiple hazards.
  415.5, "Special provisions for Group H-2 and H-3 occupancies," which addresses building size, configuration, construction, and special requirements pertaining to protection from water.

705 Fire Walls

705.5 Horizontal continuity

- Fire walls must be continuous between exterior walls.
- Fire walls must terminate at exterior walls in one of the following configurations:
  - Fire walls may extend past the exterior surface of the exterior as follows:
    For a distance ≥ 18".
  - Fire walls may terminate at the interior surface of the following where all of the conditions indicated below apply to the exterior wall:
    Surfaces:
    Combustible exterior sheathing.
    Combustible exterior siding.
    Conditions:
    Wall has a fire-resistance rating ≥ 1 hr as follows:
    Extending ≥ 4' on both sides of the fire wall.
    Openings in this 4' length must have fire assemblies as follows:
    With a fire-protection rating ≥ ¾ hr.
  - Fire walls may terminate at the interior surface of the following where the condition indicated below applies:
    Surfaces:
    Noncombustible sheathing.
    Noncombustible siding.
    Noncombustible exterior material.
    Conditions:
    The noncombustible extends ≥ 4' on both sides of the fire wall.
  - Fire walls may terminate at the interior surface of the following where the condition indicated below applies:
    Surface:
    Noncombustible exterior sheathing.
    Condition:
    Where the building on each side of the fire wall is sprinklered as per NFPA 13.

705.5.1 Exterior walls

This section addresses exterior walls on each side of a fire wall that meet each other at the end of the fire wall.

- The angle formed by the exterior walls meeting each other is measured as follows:
  - From outside face to outside face across the exterior of the building.
- Exterior walls that meet at an angle < 180° require protection as follows:
  - A fire-resistance rating ≥ 1 hr is required in the following location:
    Extending ≥ 4' on both sides of the fire wall:
    Openings in this 4' length must be protected as follows:
    With a fire-protection rating ≥ ¾ hr.
- Exterior walls that meet at an angle ≥ 180° are governed as follows:
  - They do not require the fire-resistance rating otherwise required by this section.

705 Fire Walls

705.5.2 Horizontal projecting elements

- This subsection addresses the relationship between fire walls and horizontal projecting elements as follows in the location indicated below:
  - Projections:
    - Balconies.
    - Roof overhangs.
    - Canopies.
    - Marquees.
    - Architectural projections.
  - Location:
    - Where they occur ≤ 4' from a fire wall.
- Fire walls need not extend to the outer edge of projecting elements in the following cases:
  - o Where projections without concealed spaces comply with the following:
    - Exterior wall behind and below the projection must be as follows:
      - The wall must have a fire-resistance rating ≥ 1 hr:
        - Rating must extend along both sides of the fire wall as follows:
          - For a distance ≥ the depth of the projection.
        - Openings in this rated zone must have the following:
          - A fire-protection rating ≥ ¾ hr.
  - o Where noncombustible projections with concealed spaces comply with the following:
    - A wall with a fire resistance rating ≥ 1 hr must extend through the concealed space.
    - The projecting element must be separated from the building as follows:
      - Separating construction must have a fire-resistance rating ≥ 1 hr:
        - Rating must extend along both sides of the fire wall as follows:
          - For a distance ≥ the depth of the projection.
    - The 1-hr-rated wall need not extend under the projected element in the following case:
      - Where the exterior wall has a fire resistance rating ≥ 1 hr:
        - Rating must extend along both sides of the fire wall as follows:
          - For a distance ≥ the depth of the projection.
        - Openings in this rated zone must have the following:
          - A fire-protection rating ≥ ¾ hr.
  - o Where combustible projections with concealed spaces comply with the following:
    - Fire wall must extend through the concealed space to outer edge of projection.
    - Exterior wall behind and below the projecting element must comply with the following:
      - The wall must have a fire-resistance rating ≥ 1 hr:
        - Rating must extend along both sides of the fire wall as follows:
          - For a distance ≥ the depth of the projection.
        - Openings in this rated zone must have the following:
          - A fire-protection rating ≥ ¾ hr.
- In other cases fire walls must extend to the outer edge of projecting elements.

705 Fire Walls

705.6 Vertical continuity *(part 1 of 2)*

- Where buildings of the following occupancies are located above enclosed parking garages, the conditions indicated below apply:
  - Occupancies:
    A, B, M, R.
  - Condition:
    The bottom of the fire wall may terminate at the following location:
    At the horizontal separation between the garage and the building above.
    The construction meets fire-resistance rating and other requirements of the code.

  Note: 508.2(1), "Group S-2 enclosed parking garage with Groups A, B, M or R above," is cited as the source of requirements qualifying garages for this type of fire wall termination.

- The bottoms of fire walls in other buildings terminate at the foundations.
- This subsection does not address the upper termination fire walls as follows:
  - Where fire walls separate buildings with different roof levels.

  Note: 705.6.1, "Stepped buildings," is cited as the source governing the tops of fire walls separating such buildings.

- Fire walls may terminate at the following roof elements where all the conditions indicated in any one of the groups of conditions listed below apply:
  - Roof elements:
    Roof sheathing.
    Roof deck.
    Roof slab.
  - Conditions:
    Fire walls must have a fire-resistance rating of 2 hrs.
    No roof openings may occur in a distance $\leq 4'$ from the fire wall.
    The following components must have a fire resistance rating ≥ 1 hr:
      Lower part of the roof assembly as follows:
        For a distance $\leq 4'$ from the fire wall.
      The components supporting the rated roof assembly as follows:
        For their entire length.
    Each building must have a roof covering $\geq$ Class B.
  - Conditions:
    Buildings must be one or more of the following construction types:
      Type I or II.
    The roof elements listed above must be noncombustible.
    Each building must have a roof covering $\geq$ Class B.
    No roof openings may occur in a distance $\leq 4'$ from the fire wall.
- In cases other than those listed in part 1 and 2 of this section permitting fire walls to terminate under the roof, the following applies:
  - Fire walls must extend to a level $\geq 30"$ above both adjacent roofs.

705 Fire Walls

705.6 Vertical continuity *(part 2 of 2)*

- Fire walls may terminate at the following roof elements where all the conditions indicated in any one of the groups of conditions listed below apply:
  - Roof elements:
    - Roof sheathing.
    - Roof deck.
  - Conditions:
    - Buildings must be one or more of the following types of construction:
      - Type III, IV, or V.
    - The roof elements as listed above must be noncombustible.
    - Each building must have a roof covering ≥ Class B.
    - No roof openings may occur in a distance ≤ 4' from the fire wall.
  - Conditions:
    - Buildings must be one or more of the following types of construction:
      - Type III, IV, or V.
    - The roof element as listed above must be fire-retardant-treated wood.
    - The fire-retardant-treated wood must extend ≥ 4' on both sides of the fire wall.
    - Each building must have a roof covering ≥ Class B.
    - No roof openings may occur in a distance ≤ 4' from the fire wall.
  - Conditions:
    - Building occupancy must be as follows:
      - R-2 or R-3.
    - Buildings must be of one of the following types of construction:
      - Type III, IV, or V.
    - Roof elements listed above must be one of the following materials as indicated below:
      - Materials:
        - Approved noncombustible materials.
        - Fire-retardant treated wood.
      - Requirement:
        - Material must extend ≥ 4' on both sides of the fire wall.
    - Roof elements listed above must be protected as follows:
      - By ⁵⁄₈" Type X gypsum board on the underneath side.
      - Gypsum board must be detailed as follows:
        - Supported by nominal ≥ 2" ledgers attached to sides of roof framing.
        - Extending ≥ 4' on both sides of the fire wall.
    - No roof openings may occur in a distance ≤ 4' from the fire wall.
    - Each building must have a roof covering ≥ Class C.
- In cases other than those listed in part 1 and 2 of this section permitting fire walls to terminate under the roof, the following applies:
  - Fire walls must extend to a level ≥ 30" above both adjacent roofs.

705 Fire Walls

705.6.1 Stepped buildings

- This section addresses fire walls with both of the following characteristics:
    - The fire wall serves as an exterior wall.
    - The fire wall separates buildings with roofs at different levels.
- Such fire wall must terminate at its top in one of the following ways:
    - The fire wall must terminate at a level ≥ 30" above the lower roof as follows:
        The exterior wall above the lower roof is governed as follows:
            It must have a fire-resistance rating ≥ 1 hr from both sides:
                This rated zone must extend for a height ≥ 15' above the lower roof:
                    Openings in this zone must have a fire-protection rating ≥ ¾ hr.
- Such a fire wall must terminate at the underside of one of the following elements of the lower roof with other conditions meeting all the requirements listed below:
    - Roof elements:
        Roof sheathing.
        Roof deck.
        Roof slab.
    - Conditions:
        The lower roof assembly must have a fire-resistance rating ≥ 1 hr as follows:
            The rating must extend for a distance ≥ 10' from the fire wall.
        The support system for the rated roof assembly is governed as follows:
            It must have a fire-resistance rating ≥ 1 hr for its full length.
        No openings are permitted in the lower roof ≤ 10' from the fire wall.

705.7 Combustible framing in fire walls

- The wall thickness between combustible members penetrating a fire wall from opposite sides is governed as follows:
    - Where the fire wall is concrete or masonry:
        A wall thickness ≥ 4" between embedded ends of members is required.
- Where the fire wall is hollow or has hollow units:
    - Hollow spaces must be filled solid as follows:
        For the full thickness of the wall.
        For a distance ≥ 4" in the following locations:
            Above members.
            Below members.
            Between members.
        Filler materials to be as follows:
            Noncombustible.
            Approved for fireblocking.

705 Fire Walls

705.8 Openings

- Openings are not allowed in fire walls serving as party walls.

    Note: 503.2, "Party walls," is cited as governing fire walls acting as party walls, the requirements of which are summarized above.

- Openings through other fire walls are governed as follows:
    - The sum of opening widths at a floor level must be ≤ 25% of the wall length.
    - Area of each opening must be ≤ 120 sf where either building is without sprinklers.
    - Area of each opening is not limited where the building is sprinklered as per NFPA 13.
    - Openings must be protected.

    Note: 714.2, "Fire door and shutter assemblies," governs the protection of openings in fire walls.

706 Fire Barriers

706.1 General

- This section governs fire barriers used for the following:
  - To separate different uses from each other.
  - To subdivide an occupancy.
  - To separating the following from other areas:
    Vertical exit enclosures.
    Exit passageways.
    Horizontal exits.
    Incidental use areas.

706.2 Materials

- Materials of the following fire barriers must conform to the building construction type:
  - Walls.
  - Floor assemblies.

706.3.1 Vertical exit enclosure

- Fire resistance ratings are required for fire barriers separating vertical exit enclosures from other areas as follows:

Number of stories	Fire-resistance rating
< 4	≥ 1 hr
≥ 4	≥ 2 hr

Note: 1005.3.2, "Vertical exit enclosures," is cited as the source of fire-resistance ratings for such enclosures, a partial summary of which is provided above.

706.3.2 Exit passageway

- The following fire barriers that separate exit passageways from other building areas must comply with the requirements indicated below:
  - Barriers:
    Walls.
    Floors.
    Ceilings.
  - Requirements:
    The fire barriers must have the larger of the following fire-resistance ratings:
    ≥ 1 hr.
    $\geq$ the rating required for any connecting exit enclosure.

Note: 1005.3.3, "Exit passageway," is cited as the source of applicable requirements, a partial summary of which is provided above.

706 Fire Barriers

706.3.3 Horizontal exit

- The separation between areas provided by an horizontal exit must have a fire-resistance rating ≥ 2 hr.

    Note: 1005.3.5, "Horizontal exits," is cited as governing such elements.

706.3.4 Incidental use areas

- Fire barriers separating incidental use areas from other areas are governed as follows:
  - They must have fire-resistance ratings based on the function of the incidental space.

    Note: IBC Table 302.1.1, "Incidental Use Areas," is cited as the source of fire-resistance ratings for the areas.

706.3.5 Separation of occupancies

- The following fire barriers must have fire-resistance ratings based on the uses separated.
  - Barriers separating different occupancies.
  - Barriers subdividing an occupancy.

    Note: 302.3.3, "Separated uses," is cited as the source of fire-resistance ratings required for the separations indicated above.

706.4 Continuity *(1 of 2)*

- Shaft enclosures may terminate at some distance below the underside of a roof as follows:
  - The fire-resistance rating of the top closure of the shaft must be $\geq$ the larger of the following:

    The fire-resistance rating of the highest floor penetrated by the shaft.
    The fire-resistance rating of the shaft walls.

    Note: 707.12, "Enclosure at the top," is cited as governing the top of a shaft, a partial summary of which is provided above.

- In all other cases, fire barrier walls must extend continuously between the following levels:
  - Top of floor/ceiling assembly below.
  - Underside of one of the following elements as applicable:

    Floor slab or deck above.
    Roof slab or deck above.
- Fire barrier walls must be securely attached to construction at upper and lower terminations.
- Fire barrier walls must be continuous through concealed spaces such as follows:
  - Space above a suspended ceiling.

706 Fire Barriers

706.4 Continuity *(2 of 2)*

- Construction supporting fire barrier walls with all of the following characteristics are not required to have a fire-resistance rating ≥ than the barrier supported:
  - Walls separating incidental use areas from other building areas.
  - Walls with a fire-resistance rating = 1 hr.
  - Walls located in the following types of construction:
    Type IIB.
    Type IIIB.
    Type VB.

    Note: IBC Table 302.1.1, "Incidental Use Areas," is cited as the source listing incidental use areas requiring 1-hr rated walls.

- Construction supporting fire barriers that separate storage tank areas of H-2 occupancies from other uses must have a fire-resistance rating ≥ the larger of the following:
  - ≥ 2 hr.
  - ≥ fire-resistance rating required for building elements based on construction type.

    Note: 415.7.2.1, "Mixed occupancies," is cited as the source of requirements for tank storage.
    IBC Table 601, "Fire-Resistance Rating Requirements for Building Elements," is cited as the source for ratings based on construction type.

- In all other cases, construction supporting fire barrier walls is governed as follows:
  - It must have a fire-resistance rating ≥ that of the fire barrier supported.
- At each floor, fire stops are required in any hollow vertical spaces within a fire barrier wall.

706.5 Exterior walls

- Exterior walls separating an exterior exit stairway from the interior are governed as follows:
  - The walls must have the following fire-resistance rating:

Building height	Fire-resistance rating
< 4 stories	≥ 1 hr
≥ 4 stories	≥ 2 hr

- Exterior walls as part of a required fire-resistance rated enclosure are governed as follows:
  - Fire-resistance rated enclosure requirements do not apply to the walls.
  - The walls must comply with fire-resistance rating requirements for exterior walls.

    Note: The following are cited as sources of applicable requirements:
    1005.3.6.5, "Exterior stairway protection." A partial summary is provided above.
    Section 704, "Exterior Walls," for exterior wall fire-resistance requirements.

706 Fire Barriers

706.6 Openings

- This section does not apply to fire doors serving an exit enclosure.
- Openings in a fire barrier must be protected.

  Note: Section 714, "Opening Protectives," is cited as governing such protectives.

- Openings in a fire barrier must meet one of the following conditions:
  - Openings must comply with both of the following:
    Buildings on both sides of the fire barrier must be sprinklered as per NFPA 13.
    The sum of opening widths is limited to 25% of the wall length.
  - Openings must have both of the following:
    An opening protective assembly tested by applicable standards.
    A fire-resistance rating ≥ the wall.

  Note: ASTM E 119, "Standard Test Methods for Fire Tests of Building Construction and Materials," is cited as the applicable test for opening protective assemblies.

  - Openings must meet both of the following size restrictions:
    Each opening is limited to an area ≤ 120 sf.
    The sum of openings widths is limited to ≤ 25% of the wall length.
- Openings in exit enclosures must meet additional requirements specific to their location.

  Note: 1005.3.4, "Openings and penetrations," is cited as the source of additional requirements for openings in exit enclosures.

706.7.1 Prohibited penetrations

- Required exit doors are permitted in an exit enclosure fire barrier.
- The following penetrations of an exit enclosure fire barrier must meet the requirements for preventing the passage of fire:
  - Equipment and ductwork necessary for independent pressurization of the enclosure.
  - Sprinkler piping.
  - Standpipes.
  - Electrical conduit serving the enclosure must terminate in a steel box ≤ 16 sq in.

  Note: 1005.3.4.1, "Penetrations," is cited as the source of applicable requirements.

- Other penetrations into an exit enclosure are not permitted.

707 Shaft and Vertical Exit Enclosures

707.1 General

- This section addresses vertical shafts as follows:
  - Where required to protect openings and penetrations through the following:
    Floor/ceiling assemblies.
    Roof/ceiling assemblies.

707.2 Shaft enclosure required *(part 1 of 3)*

- A shaft enclosure is not required for the following case:
  - For an opening through a floor/ceiling assembly with both of the following characteristics:
    The opening is contained entirely within an individual dwelling unit.
    The opening connects ≤ 4 stories.
- A shaft enclosure is not required for the following case:
  - For an opening through a floor/ceiling assembly meeting all of the following conditions:
    The building is sprinklered as per NFPA 13.
    The opening serves one of the following:
      An escalator.
      A stairway not required for means of egress.
    The area of the opening is limited to one of the following:
      ≤ 2 × the projected area of the escalator.
      ≤ 2 × the projected area of the stairway.
    The opening is protected by a draft curtain.
    The opening is protected by closely spaced sprinklers as per NFPA 13.
    The opening ≤ 4 stories in the following occupancies:
      A, E, F, H, I, R, S, U.
- A shaft enclosure is not required for the following:
  - An opening through a floor/ceiling assembly meeting all of the following conditions:
    The building is sprinklered as per NFPA 13.
    The opening serves one of the following:
      An escalator.
      A stairway not required for means of egress.
    Power-operated automatic shutters protect the opening at every floor as follows:
      Shutters are approved.
      Shutters are of noncombustible materials.
      Shutters have a fire-resistance rating ≥ 1½ hr.
      Shutters close immediately upon detection of smoke.
      Shutters completely surround and seal the opening well.
      Shutters move ≤ 30 fpm.
      Shutters have a leading edge that controls movement as follows:
        Shutters stop upon meeting an obstacle.
        Shutters resume movement when the obstacle is removed.
      Escalator stops when shutters begin to close.

Note: 907.10, "Fire safety functions," is cited as the source governing smoke detectors.

707 Shaft and Vertical Exit Enclosures

707.2 Shaft enclosure required *(part 2 of 3)*

- A shaft enclosure is not required for the following:
  - Penetrations as follows through a floor/ceiling assembly meeting the requirement indicated below:
    - Penetrations:
      - Pipe.
      - Tube.
      - Conduit.
      - Wire.
      - Cable.
      - Vents.
    - Requirement:
      - Penetrations must meet requirements for protection against the passage of fire.

  Note: 711.4, "Horizontal assemblies," is cited as the source of protection requirements for the penetrations listed above.

- A shaft enclosure is not required for the following:
  - Duct penetrations through a floor/ceiling assembly as follows:
    - Ducts are required to have dampers or meet protection requirements in lieu of dampers.

  Note: 711.4.4, "Ducts and air transfer openings," is cited as the source of applicable requirements.

  - Grease ducts are governed by other standards.

  Note: The International Mechanical Code is cited as governing grease ducts.

- A shaft enclosure is not required for the following:
  - An opening through a floor/ceiling assembly meeting the requirements for the following locations:
    - Covered malls.
    - Atriums.
- A shaft enclosure is not required for the following:
  - Masonry chimneys as follows:
    - Where approved.
    - Where the annular space is protected at each floor.

  Note: 716.2.5, "Ceiling and floor openings," is cited as the source of requirements for fireblocking at openings around chimneys.

707 Shaft and Vertical Exit Enclosures

707.2 Shaft enclosure required *(part 3 of 3)*

- A shaft enclosure is not required for the following:
  - An opening through a floor/ceiling assembly meeting the following requirements:
    Opening is located in an occupancy other than the following:
    I-2, I-3.
    Opening connects ≤ 2 stories.
    Opening is not concealed in the building construction.
    Opening is not open to a corridor in the following locations:
    In occupancy I, R.
    On a nonsprinklered floor in any occupancy.
    Opening is separated from openings in other floors as follows:
    By construction meeting shaft enclosure requirements.
    Opening does not serve a required means of egress in other than special cases.

    Note: 1005.3.2, "Vertical exit enclosures," is cited as the source listing special cases where stairways serving a means of egress need not be enclosed.

- A shaft enclosure is not required for the following:
  - Automobile ramps as follows:
    In open parking garages.
    In enclosed closed parking garages.

    Note: The following are cited as governing the construction of the garages listed above:
    406.3, "Open parking garages."
    406.4, "Enclosed parking garages."

- A shaft enclosure is not required for the following:
  - A floor opening connecting a floor and a mezzanine above.
- A shaft enclosure is not required for the following:
  - Joints with a fire-resistant joint protection system.

    Note: Section 712, "Fire-Resistant Joint Systems," is cited as governing the joints indicated above.

- A shaft enclosure is not required as follows:
  - Where other sections of the code permit its omission.
- In all other cases, the following applies:
  - Openings through floor/ceiling assemblies require the following:
    A shaft enclosure meeting the requirements of this section.

707.3 Materials

- Materials for shaft construction must be as follows:
  - Consistent with the type of construction for the building.

707 Shaft and Vertical Exit Enclosures

707.4 Fire-resistance rating

- Shaft enclosures including exit enclosures are governed as follows:
  - Where they connect < 4 stories:
    The greater of the following fire-resistance ratings is required up to a maximum of 2 hrs:
    ≥ 1 hr.
    ≥ the fire-resistance rating of the floor penetrated.
  - Where they connect ≥ 4 stories:
    A fire-resistance rating ≥ 2 hrs is required.

707.5 Continuity

- Shaft enclosures must extend continuously between the following levels:
  - Top of floor/ceiling assembly below.
  - Underside of one of the following elements above:
    Floor slab or deck.
    Roof slab or deck.
- Shaft enclosures must be securely attached.
- Shaft enclosures must be continuous through concealed spaces such as follows:
  - Space above a suspended ceiling.
- Construction supporting shaft enclosures is governed as follows:
  - It must have a fire-resistance rating ≥ that of the shaft enclosure supported.
- Where shaft enclosure walls have hollow vertical spaces:
  - Fire stops are required at each floor level.

707.6 Exterior walls

- Exterior walls separating an exterior exit stairway from a building interior are governed as follows:
  - The walls must have the following fire-resistance rating:

Building height	Fire-resistance rating
< 4 stories	≥ 1 hr
≥ 4 stories	≥ 2 hr

- Exterior walls that are part of a shaft enclosure are governed as follows:
  - Fire-resistance-rated enclosure requirements do not apply to the walls.
  - The walls must comply with fire-resistance rating requirements for exterior walls.

  Note: The following are cited as sources of applicable requirements:
  1005.3.6.5, "Exterior stairway protection." A partial summary of requirements is provided above.
  Section 704, "Exterior Walls," for fire-resistance requirements of such walls.

707 Shaft and Vertical Exit Enclosures

707.7 Openings

- Openings in shaft enclosures must be one of the following:
  - Self-closing.
  - Automatic closing by smoke detection.
- Openings in shaft enclosures must meet opening protective requirements:

  Note: Section 714, "Opening Protectives," is cited as the source of requirements for opening protectives.

707.7.1 Prohibited openings

- The only openings permitted in a shaft enclosure are those required for the function of the shaft.

707.8 Penetrations

- Penetrations in shaft enclosures must be protected as required for fire barriers.

  Note: Section 714, "Opening Protectives," is cited as governing protection of penetrations in shaft enclosures.

707.8.1 Prohibited penetrations

- The only penetrations permitted in a shaft enclosure are those required for the function of the shaft.
- The only ducts permitted to penetrate a shaft enclosure are those necessary for independent pressurization of the shaft.

  Note: 1005.3.4.1, "Penetrations," is cited as the source permitting pressurization ducts to penetrate a shaft enclosure.

707.10 Enclosure at the bottom *(part 1 of 3)*

This subsection addresses shafts that terminate at a point above the bottom of the building.

- The room in which a shaft terminates is not required to have the following characteristics where the shaft meets all the requirements indicated below:
  - Characteristics:
    The room need not be separated from the building as follows:
    By fire-resistance rated construction.
    The bottom of the shaft need not have opening protectives.
  - Requirements:
    The shaft must contain no combustibles.
    There may be no openings in the shaft enclosure as follows:
    To the interior of the building.
    There may be no penetrations through the shaft enclosure as follows:
    To the interior of the building.

707 Shaft and Vertical Exit Enclosures

707.10 Enclosure at the bottom *(part 2 of 3)*

- The room in which a shaft terminates is not required to have the following characteristics where the shaft meets all the requirements indicated below:
  - ○ Characteristics:
    The room need not be separated from the building as follows:
    By fire-resistance rated construction.
  - ○ Requirements:
    There may be no openings into the shaft enclosure as follows:
    To the interior of the building other than at the bottom.
    There may be no penetrations of the shaft enclosure as follows:
    To the interior of the building other than at the bottom.
    One of the following conditions must be provided:
    The room must have an approved automatic fire-suppression system.
    Draftstopping materials as follows must be provided in the location indicated below:
    Materials:
    ½" gypsum board.
    ³/₈" wood structural panel.
    ³/₈" particleboard.
    Other approved materials.
    Location:
    Materials must seal around penetrating items at the bottom of the shaft.

  Note: 716.3.1, "Draftstopping materials," is cited as the source of materials permitted for this function, a summary of which is provided above.

- A shaft enclosure containing either of the following functions must comply with the requirements indicated below:
  - ○ Functions:
    Laundry chute.
    Refuse chute.
  - ○ Requirements:
    The shaft may not be used for any other purpose.
    The shaft must terminate at the bottom in a room as follows:
    Room must be separated from the rest of the building as follows:
    By construction with a fire-resistance rating ≥ 1 hr.
    Openings into the room must be protected as follows:
    By protectives with a fire-protection rating ≥ ¾ hr.
    Openings into the room must be one of the following:
    Self-closing.
    Automatic-closing activated by smoke detection.
    Refuse chutes may not terminate in the following room:
    An incinerator room.

  Note: 707.12.4, "Termination room," is cited as the source of requirements for the termination room serving laundry and refuse chutes.

<u>707 Shaft and Vertical Exit Enclosures</u>

707.10 Enclosure at the bottom *(part 3 of 3)*

- Other shafts must comply with one of the following requirements:
  - The shaft must be enclosed at the lowest level as follows:
    - By construction with the greater of the following fire-resistance ratings:
      - That of the lowest floor through which the shaft penetrates.
      - That required for the shaft enclosure.
  - The shaft must terminate in a room as follows:
    - The room function must relate to the function of the shaft.
    - The room must be separated from the rest of the building as follows:
      - By construction with the following:
        - A fire-resistance rating ≥ that required for the shaft enclosure.
        - Opening protectives providing the following fire protection:
          - ≥ than the fire protection required for the shaft enclosure.
  - The shaft must be protected with a fire damper as follows:
    - Dampers must be approved.
    - Dampers must be installed as per their listing.
    - Dampers must be installed in the shaft enclosure at the lowest floor level penetrated.

707.12 Enclosure at the top

- Shaft enclosures terminating at a point lower than the roof deck are governed as follows:
  - They must be enclosed at the top with construction as follows:
    - Construction having the greater of the following:
      - Fire-resistance rating ≥ that of the highest floor penetrated.
      - Fire-resistance rating ≥ that required for the shaft enclosure.

707.13 Refuse and laundry chutes

- This section addresses the following:
  - Chutes other than those contained in a single dwelling unit as follows:
    - Laundry chutes.
    - Refuse chutes.
  - Access to chutes.
  - Termination rooms.
  - Incinerator rooms.

707 Shaft and Vertical Exit Enclosures

707.13.1 Refuse and laundry chute enclosures

- This section addresses shaft enclosures for the following:
  - Refuse chute.
  - Laundry chute.
- Such shaft enclosure may not be used for other purposes:
- Fire-resistance ratings required for such shaft enclosures are as follows:
  - Where they connect < 4 stories:
    The greater of the following fire-resistance ratings is required up to a maximum of 2 hrs:
    ≥ 1 hr.
    ≥ the fire-resistance rating of the floor penetrated.
  - Where they connect ≥ 4 stories:
    A fire-resistance rating ≥ 2 hrs is required.

    Note: 707.4, "Fire-resistance rating," is cited as the source of applicable requirements, a summary of which is provided above.

- Openings into such shafts as follows required fire protection:
  - Openings from access rooms.
  - Openings from termination rooms.
  - All other openings.

    Note: Section 714, "Opening Protectives," is cited as the source of requirements for protecting the openings indicated above, in addition to requirements of this section.

- Exit access corridors may not have openings into chutes.
- Protection for shaft openings must be one of the following:
  - Self-closing.
  - Automatic-closing by one of the following means:
    Activated by heat or smoke as follows:
    Between the shaft and termination room.

    Note: 907.10, "Fire safety functions," is cited as the source of requirements for fire detectors.

707.13.2 Materials

- Shaft enclosures for the following types of chutes require materials as indicated below:
  - Chutes:
    Laundry chute.
    Refuse chute.
  - Materials:
    Must be consistent with the building construction type.

707 Shaft and Vertical Exit Enclosures

707.13.3 Refuse and laundry chute access rooms

- Chute access openings must be in rooms enclosed as follows:
  - ○ Room construction must have a fire-resistance rating ≥ 1 hr.
  - ○ Openings to access rooms must have protectives as follows:
    With a fire-protection rating ≥ ¾ hr.
    Which close by one of the following means:
    Self-closing.
    Automatic-closing when activated by smoke.

707.13.4 Termination room

- This subsection governs the following rooms with functions as indicated below:
  - ○ Rooms:
    Laundry.
    Refuse.
  - ○ Functions:
    Receives discharge from chutes.
    Does not receive discharge from chutes.
- Rooms receiving chutes discharge are governed as follows:
  - ○ Room must be separated from the rest of the building as follows:
    Room construction must have a fire-resistance rating ≥ 1 hr.
    Openings to the room must have protectives as follows:
    With a fire-protection rating ≥ ¾ hr.
    Opening protectives must close by one of the following means:
    Self-closing.
    Automatic-closing activated by smoke.
  - ○ Incinerator rooms may not receive refuse by chute.
- Rooms that do not receive chute discharge are governed as follows:
  - ○ Incinerators rooms require the following:
    Must be separated from the rest of the building as follows:
    By ≥ 2 hr fire-resistance-rated construction.
    Room must be sprinklered.
  - ○ The following rooms where > 100 sf are governed as indicated below:
    - ○ Rooms:
      Laundry rooms.
      Waste collection.
      Linen collection.
    - ○ Requirement:
      Must be separated from the rest of the building as follows:
      By ≥ 1-hr fire-resistance rated construction.
  - *Note: IBC Table 302.1, "Incidental Use Areas," is cited as the source for fire protection requirements for refuse and laundry rooms without chutes, a partial summary of which is provided above.*

707 Shaft And Vertical Exit Enclosures

707.13.6 Automatic fire sprinkler system

- The following chutes must be sprinklered:
  - Rubbish chutes.
  - Linen chutes.
- Sprinklers for chutes must comply with the following:
  - Characteristics:
    - Must be approved.
    - Must be automatic.
    - Must have access for servicing.
  - Locations:
    - Required at the top of chutes.
    - Required at alternate floors in the following case:
      - Where chutes pass through $\geq$ 3 floors.

> *Note: 903.2.12.2, "Rubbish and linen chutes," is cited as the source of requirements for sprinklers in chutes, a summary of which is provided above.*

707.14 Elevator and dumbwaiter shafts

- Elevator hoistways and dumbwaiter enclosures are governed by this subsection.
- Shaft enclosures are governed as follows:
  - Where they connect < 4 stories:
    - The greater of the following fire-resistance ratings is required up to a maximum of 2 hrs:
      - $\geq$ 1 hr.
      - $\geq$ the fire-resistance rating of the floor penetrated.
  - Where they connect $\geq$ 4 stories:
    - A fire-resistance rating $\geq$ 2 hrs is required.

> *Note: The following are cited as sources of requirements pertaining to the above shafts:*
> *707.4, "Fire-resistance rating," a summary of which is provided above.*
> *Chapter 30, "Elevators and Conveying Systems."*

707 Shaft And Vertical Exit Enclosures

707.14.1 Elevator lobby

- A fire-resistance-rated separation between an elevator lobby and the connecting corridor is not required where all the following conditions are present:
  - The building is an office building.
  - The lobby is on the street-level floor.
  - The entire street-level floor is sprinklered as per NFPA 13.
- This section does not apply where elevators are not required to have a shaft enclosure.

  Note: 707.2, "Shaft enclosure required," is cited as the source of conditions that do not require a shaft enclosure for an elevator.

- Requirements of this section do not apply to elevator lobbies where additional doors are provided as follows:
  - Additional doors are in addition to hoistway doors and car doors.
  - Additional doors are located at the point of access to elevators as follows:
    Between the hoistway doors and the lobby or corridor.
  - Additional doors must be readily openable from car side as follows:
    Without a key or tool.
    Without special knowledge.
    Without special effort.

  Note: 3002.6, "Prohibited doors," is cited as the source of additional requirements.

- A fire-resistance-rated separation between an elevator lobby and the connecting corridor is not required where all the following conditions are present:
  - The building is among the following occupancies:
    A, B, E, F, H, I-1, I-4, M, R, S, U.
  - The building is ≤ 4 stories above the lowest level of fire department vehicle access.
  - The building is sprinklered throughout as follows as per NFPA 13 or 13R:
    The elevator lobby is included.
    Corridors leading to the elevator lobby are included.
- In all other cases, elevators opening into a fire-resistance-rated corridor require an elevator lobby as follows:
  - A lobby is required at each floor where elevators open into such a corridor.
  - The lobby must separate the elevators from the corridor with fire barriers as follows:
    With the required opening protection.
  - The lobby must have ≥ 1 means of egress.

  Note: The following are cited as sources of requirements applicable to elements above:
  1004.3.2.1, "Construction," governs fire-resistance ratings for corridors.
  Chapter 10, "Means of Egress," governs the means of egress for the lobby.

708 Fire Partitions

708.1 General

- This section governs the following walls, which are required elsewhere in the code to have fire-resistance ratings:
  - Walls between dwelling units in the same building.
  - Walls in occupancy R-1 between guestrooms.
  - Walls in covered malls between tenant spaces.
  - Corridor walls.

    Note: The following are cited as sources requiring fire-resistance ratings for the elements indicated above:
    310.3, "Required dwelling unit and guest room separation."
    402.7.2, "Tenant separations."
    1004.3.2.1, "Construction," which addresses corridors.

708.2 Materials

- Fire partitions must be constructed of materials as follows:
  - Consistent with building construction type.

708.3 Fire-resistance rating *(part 1 of 2)*

- Fire-resistance ratings are not required for the following corridors:
  - Corridors with all the following characteristics:
    In occupancy E.
    $\geq$ 1 door in each instruction room opens as follows:
    Directly to the outside at ground level.
    $\geq$ half the required egress doors in assembly rooms open as follows:
    Directly to outside at ground level.
  - Corridors in occupancy R as follows:
    Within dwelling units.
    Within guest rooms.
  - Corridors in open parking garages.
  - Corridors with both the following characteristics:
    In occupancy B.
    Where only one means of egress is required.
  - Corridors with all the following characteristics:
    Building sprinklered as per NFPA 13.
    Located in one of the following occupancies:
    A, B, E, F, I-2, I-4, M, S, U.
    I-3 resident housing.
  - Corridors with occupant loads as follows:
    $\leq$ 30 in A, B, E, F, H-4, H-5, M, S, and U.
    $\leq$ 10 in R.

708 Fire Partitions

708.3 Fire-resistance rating *(part 2 of 2)*

- Fire partitions as follows must have a fire-resistance rating ≥ ½ hr:
  - ○ Walls with all the following characteristics:
    - Serving as separations between either of the following:
      - Dwelling units.
      - Guestrooms.
    - Located in one of the following construction types:
      - Type II B.
      - Type III B.
      - Type V B.
    - Located in sprinklered buildings as per NFPA 13.
- All other fire partitions must have a fire-resistance rating ≥ 1 hr.

708.4 Continuity *(part 1 of 3)*

This subsection addresses the upper and lower points of termination for a fire partition.

- A fire partition is not required to extend into a crawl space as follows:
  - ○ Where the floor above the crawl space has the following:
    - A fire-resistance rating ≥ 1 hr.
- Requirements listed below apply to the corridor ceiling adjacent to the following membrane:
  - ○ Membrane:
    - Membrane is located on the room-side of the corridor wall.
    - Membrane is fire-resistance rated.
    - Membrane extends to the underside of one of the following as applicable:
      - Fire-resistance rated floor above.
      - Fire resistance rated roof above.
  - ○ Requirements:
    - Corridor ceiling may be protected by ceiling materials as follows:
      - As required for a fire-resistance rating ≥ 1 hr for one of the following:
        - A roof system.
        - A floor system.
- Corridor walls may terminate as follows:
  - ○ At the upper membrane of the corridor ceiling in the following case:
    - Where the corridor ceiling complies with the same requirements as for the walls.

708 Fire Partitions

708.4 Continuity *(part 2 of 3)*

- Fire partitions between mall tenant spaces are governed as follows:
  - They are not required to extend above the following height:
    - The underside of a ceiling in the following case:
      - Where the ceiling is not part of a fire-resistance-rated assembly.
  - A wall is not required in the following spaces:
    - In the attic above tenant separation walls.
    - In the ceiling spaces above tenant separation walls.

    Note: 402.7.2, "Tenant separations," is cited as the source requiring tenant spaces to be separated by fire partitions.

- Fireblocking or draftstopping is not required in the following locations:
  - At the line of a fire partition in either of the following cases:
    - In occupancy R-2 buildings where all the following conditions apply:
      - In buildings ≥ 4 stories.
      - Where the attic has draftstops isolating areas ≤ the smaller of the following:
        - Area above every two dwelling units.
        - 3000 sf.
    - In buildings sprinklered as follows as per NFPA 13 or 13R:
      - Automatic sprinklers are also installed in the following spaces:
        - Combustible floor/ceiling spaces.
        - Combustible roof/ceiling spaces.
- Construction supporting a fire partition is governed as follows:
  - Supporting construction need not have a fire-resistance rating ≥ that of the partition supported in the following cases:
    - Tenant separation walls.
    - Guestroom, separation walls.
    - Exit access corridor walls in buildings of the following construction types:
      - Types II B, III B, V B.
  - Supporting construction must have a fire-resistance rating ≥ that of the partition supported in the following types of construction:
    - Types I, II A, III A, IV, V A.

708 Fire Partitions

708.4 Continuity *(part 3 of 3)*

- In all other cases, fire-partition continuity is required as follows:
  - Partitions must extend to the following termination levels:
    - Top of floor assembly below.
    - Underside of one of the following above:
      - Floor slab or deck.
      - Roof slab or deck.
      - Fire-resistance rated floor/ceiling assembly.
      - Fire-resistance rated roof/ceiling assembly.
  - Partitions must be securely attached to the termination points.
  - Combustible partitions that do not reach the deck above are governed as follows:
    - One of the following is required in the gap between the partition and the deck:
      - Space is to be fireblocked with one of the following materials held securely in place:
        - 2" nominal lumber.
        - 2 layers of 1" nominal lumber with staggered joints.
        - 0.719" wood structural panel with joints backed by the same material.
        - 0.75" particle board with joints backed by the same material.
        - Gypsum board.
        - Cement fiber board.
        - Batts of mineral wool or glass fiber.
        - Blankets of mineral wool or glass fiber.
        - Loose-fill insulation only as follows:
          - Must be specifically tested in the form and manner of the actual application.
          - Ability to remain in place must be demonstrated.
          - Ability to retard the spread of fire and hot gasses must be demonstrated.
        - Other approved material.
      - Space is to be draftstopped with one of the following materials adequately supported:
        - 0.5" gypsum board.
        - 0.375" wood structural panel.
        - 0.375" particle board.
        - Other approved material.

    Note: The following are cited as sources of fireblocking and draftstopping materials, a summary of which is provided above:
    716.2.1, "Fireblocking materials."
    716.3.1, "Draftstopping materials."

708.5 Exterior walls

- Exterior walls as part of a required fire-resistance-rated enclosure are governed as follows:
  - Such walls must comply with fire-resistance requirements for exterior walls.
  - Fire-resistance-rated enclosure requirements do not apply.

  Note: Section 704, "Exterior Walls," is cited as governing fire-resistance requirements.

709 Smoke Barriers

709.2 Materials

- Materials for smoke barriers must conform to the construction type for the building.

709.3 Fire-resistance rating

- Smoke barriers with both the following characteristics are not required to have a fire-resistance rating ≥ 1 hr:
  - Located in occupancy I-3.
  - Constructed of ≥ 0.10" thick steel.
- Other smoke barriers must have a fire-resistance rating ≥ 1 hr.

709.4 Continuity

- Smoke barriers must form a membrane continuous between the following points:
  - From exterior wall to exterior wall.
  - From floor slab to floor or roof deck above.
- Smoke barriers must be continuous through the following spaces where applicable:
  - Concealed spaces such as above suspended ceilings.
  - Interstitial structural or mechanical space in the following case:
    - Where ceilings do not resist the passage of fire and smoke to the following degree:
      - To a degree equal that of the smoke barrier walls.
- Construction supporting smoke barriers must have a fire-resistance rating ≥ that of the wall or floor supported in the following construction types:
  - Types I, II A, III A, IV, V A.

Case study: Fig. 709.4. The 2nd floor of the hospital's south wing, as shown, is separated into 2 smoke compartments by a wall acting as a smoke barrier. The barrier provides a continuous membrane in the form of a wall across the building and from the 2nd floor to the floor above. It is continuous through the space above the suspended ceiling. Construction supporting the smoke barrier has a fire-resistance rating ≥ the barrier as required.

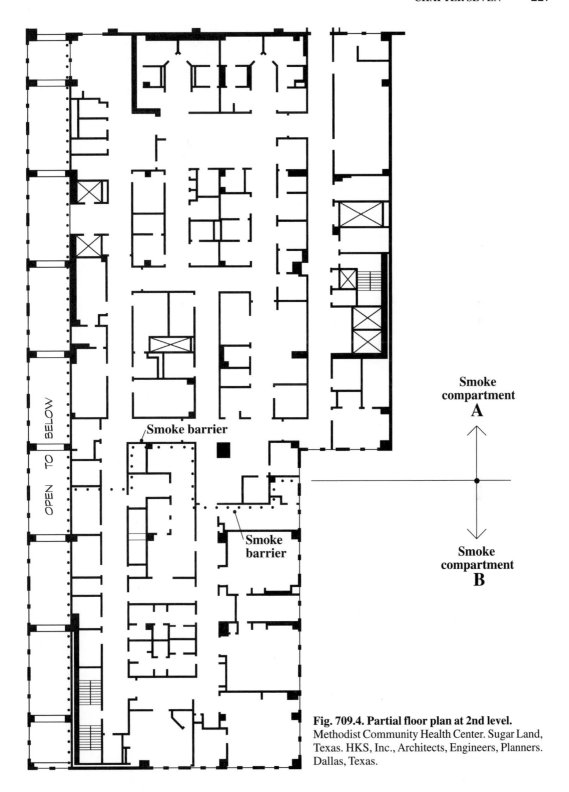

Fig. 709.4. Partial floor plan at 2nd level.
Methodist Community Health Center. Sugar Land,
Texas. HKS, Inc., Architects, Engineers, Planners.
Dallas, Texas.

709 Smoke Barriers

709.5 Openings

- Doors with all the following characteristics need not meet the requirements indicated below:
  - Characteristics:
    - In occupancy I-2.
    - Located across a corridor.
    - In a smoke barrier.
    - Opposite swinging with no center mullion.
    - With vision panels as follows:
      - Approved fire-resistance-rated glazing and frames.
      - With an area ≤ that tested.
    - Close fitting within operational tolerances.
    - With none of the following:
      - Undercuts.
      - Louvers or grilles.
    - With all the following:
      - Head stops.
      - Jamb stops.
      - Astragals at meeting edges.
      - Rabbets at meeting edges.
      - Automatic-closing devices.
  - Requirements:
    - Doors need not have meet other opening protection requirements.
    - Doors need not have a fire-protection rating of 20 min.
    - Positive-latching devices are not required.
- All other openings in smoke barriers must meet both the following requirements:
  - Openings must comply with opening protective requirements.
  - Openings must have a fire-protection rating ≥ 20 min.

  Note: Section 714, "Opening Protectives," is cited as governing the opening protective requirements for openings in smoke barriers.

710 Horizontal Assemblies

710.2 Materials

- Construction for the following must be consistent with the building construction type:
  - Floor assemblies.
  - Roof assemblies.

710.3 Fire-resistance rating

- Floor and roof assemblies must have fire-resistance ratings as follows:
  - ≥ the requirements of the building construction type.
- Floor assemblies as follows must meet the requirement indicated below:
  - Floor assemblies:
    Separating occupancies.
    Dividing an occupancy into separate fire areas.
  - Requirement:
    Assemblies must have a fire-resistance rating as follows:
    ≥ that required for occupancy separations.

  Note: 302.3.3, "Separated uses," is cited as the source of fire-resistance ratings required for separating occupancies.

- Fire-resistance ratings required for floor assemblies separating the following are listed below:
  - Dwelling units.
  - Guestrooms.

Building construction type	Sprinklered as per NFPA 13	Floor assembly fire-resistance rating
II B, III B, V B	Yes	≥ ½ hr
II B, III B, V B	No	≥ 1 hr
I, II A, III A, IV, V A	Yes	≥ 1 hr
I, II A, III A, IV, V A	No	≥ 1 hr

710.3.1 Ceiling panels

- Lay-in ceiling panels must resist upward displacement as follows:
  - From a force ≤ 1 psf by one of the following methods:
    Self-weight.
    One of the following restraining systems above the panel:
    Wire system.
    Other approved system.

710.3.1.1 Access doors

- Access doors in a fire-resistance-rated ceiling must have the following characteristics:
  - They must be approved.
  - They must be listed for their purpose.

710 Horizontal Assemblies

710.3.2 Unusable space

- The following membranes may be omitted from 1-hr fire-resistance-rated horizontal assemblies:
  - The ceiling membrane as follows:
    At floor construction directly over an unusable crawl space.
  - The floor membrane as follows:
    At ceiling construction directly below unusable attic space.

710.4 Continuity

- Supporting construction must have a fire-resistance rating as follows:
  - ≥ the horizontal assembly supported.
- Horizontal assemblies must be continuous as follows:
  - Discontinuity is permitted as follows only where indicated by the code.
    Openings.
    Penetrations.
    Joints.
  - Discontinuity is governed as follows:
    Shaft enclosures are required for most openings through a horizontal assembly.
    Penetrations must be detailed to maintain the integrity of the horizontal assembly.
    Joints must be detailed to maintain the integrity of the horizontal assembly.

  Note: The following are cited as sources of applicable requirements:
  707.2, "Shaft enclosure required," governs openings in horizontal assemblies,
  indicating where they are required and where not required.
  711.4, "Horizontal assemblies," governs penetrations.
  Section 712, "Fire-Resistant Joint Systems," governs joints.

  - Skylights and other penetrations in fire-resistance-rated roof construction are governed as follows:
    They must be protected where they would create a fire hazard as follows:
      To a higher wall of an adjacent building on the same lot.
    The structural integrity of the roof construction must be maintained.

  Note: 704.10, "Vertical exposure," is cited as the source of conditions defining a fire
  hazard for adjacent buildings on the same lot.

    Otherwise, skylights need not be protected as follows:
      Where the structural integrity of the fire-resistance-rated roof assembly is maintained.

711 Penetrations

711.1 Scope

- This section governs the protection of the following penetrations:
  - Penetrations passing entirely through assemblies.
  - Penetrations passing through membranes of assemblies.

711.2 Installation details

- Sleeves in penetrations are governed as follows:
  - Sleeves must be secured to the assembly penetrated.
  - The following spaces must be protected as per requirements of this section:
    Between a sleeve and the component inside the sleeve.
    Between a sleeve and the opening through which the sleeve passes.
- Insulation or covering as part of a penetrating element is governed as follows:
  - The materials may not penetrate an assembly except for the following case:
    Where they have been tested with the assembly as per requirements of this section.

711.3 Fire-resistance-rated walls

- This section governs penetrations into or through the following:
  - Fire walls.
  - Fire barriers.
  - Smoke barrier walls.
  - Fire partitions.

711.3.1 Through penetrations *(part 1 of 2)*

- This subsection addresses protection penetrations through fire-resistive-rated walls.
- The following penetrating items must comply with one of the alternative protection methods indicated in this subsection or with the other requirements of this section:
  - Penetrating items:
    Steel pipes.
    Steel condiuts.
    Ferrous pipes
    Copper pipes.

711 Penetrations

711.3.1 Through penetrations *(part 2 of 2)*

- Alternative protection for the metallic penetrating items listed in this subsection is as follows:
  - Where concrete or masonry walls are penetrated:
    Annular space may filled with concrete, mortar, or grout in the following conditions:
    The penetrating item must be ≤ 6" nominal diameter.
    The opening must be ≤ 144 sq in.
    Annular space must be filled to one of the following extents:
    Filled to the full thickness of the wall.
    Filled to a thickness adequate to maintain the fire-resistance rating of the wall.
  - Where other walls are penetrated:
    The annular space may be filled with a substance able to perform as follows:
    Prevents passage of the following fire hazards for the time period indicated below:
    Fire hazards:
    Flame.
    Gasses as follows:
    Hot enough to ignite cotton waste in the following conditions:
    With a positive pressure differential at penetration ≥ 0.01" of water.
    Time period:
    For a length of time = the fire-resistance rating of the wall penetrated.

  Note: ASTM E 119, "Standard Test Methods for Fire Tests of Building Construction and Materials," is cited as governing the substance filling the annular space.

- Other through penetrations must comply with the other requirements of this section.

711.3.1.1 Fire-resistance-rated assemblies

- Penetrations must be installed as follows:
  - In an approved fire-resistance-rated assembly.
  - In the same detailing as tested.

711.3.1.2 Through-penetration firestop system

- Through penetrations must be protected as follows:
  - By a penetration firestop system with the following conditions:
    Must be approved and installed as tested.
    Must be tested with a positive pressure differential ≥ 0.01" of water.
    Must have an F rating ≥ the required fire-resistance rating of the wall penetrated.

  Note: ASTM E 814, "Standard Test Method of Fire Tests of Through-Penetration Fire Stops," is cited as governing the required test.

711 Penetrations

711.3.2 Membrane penetrations

- Steel electrical boxes may penetrate a membrane as follows:
  - The area of the box must be ≤ 16 sq in.
  - The sum of opening areas in any 100 sf of wall must be ≤ 100 sq in.
  - Outlet boxes located on opposite faces of a wall must be separated by one of the following:
    By one of the following horizontal distances:
      ≥ the depth of the wall cavity where filled with in either of the following:
        Cellulose loose-fill insulation.
        Mineral fiber insulation.
      ≥ 24" in other cases.
    By solid fire-blocking with one of the following materials held securely in place:
      2" nominal lumber.
      2 layers of 1" nominal lumber with staggered joints.
      0.719" wood structural panel with joints backed by the same material.
      0.75" particle board with joints backed by the same material.
      Gypsum board.
      Cement fiber board.
      Batts of mineral wool or glass fiber.
      Blankets of mineral wool or glass fiber.
      Loose-fill insulation only as follows:
        Must be specifically tested in the form and manner of the actual application.
        Ability to remain in place must be demonstrated.
        Ability to retard the spread of fire must be demonstrated.
        Ability to retard the spread of hot gasses must be demonstrated.
      Other approved material.
    By other materials and methods where materials are listed.
- Electrical boxes of any material may penetrate a membrane where meeting the following conditions:
  - Boxes must be listed.
  - Boxes must be tested for use in a fire-resistance-rated wall.
  - Boxes must be installed according to their listing.
- A metal escutcheon plate must cover the annular space of a fire-sprinkler pipe penetration.
- Recessed fixtures may not reduce the fire-resistance rating of the following:
    Walls or partitions with a minimum required fire-resistance rating of 1 hr.
- Other membrane penetrations must be protected as are through penetrations.

  Note: 711.3.1, "Through penetrations," is cited as the source for the necessary protection methods for membrane penetrations.

711 Penetrations

711.3.3 Ducts and air transfer openings

- This section governs the penetrations of fire-resistance rated walls by the following components where no fire dampers are provided:
  - Ducts.
  - Air transfer openings.

711.3.4 Dissimilar materials

- The following connection is permitted only with the condition indicated below:
  - Connection:
    Between the following components at a point beyond the firestopping:
    Noncombustible penetrating component.
    Combustible component.
  - Condition:
    It must be shown that the required fire resistance of the wall is not diminished.

711.4 Horizontal assemblies

- Penetrations of the following must meet requirements for shaft and vertical exit enclosures:
  - Floor.
  - Floor/ceiling assembly.
  - Ceiling membrane of a roof/ceiling assembly.

  Note: Section 707, "Shaft and Vertical Exit Enclosures," is cited as governing the assemblies above.

- Penetrations by the following components must meet the requirements of this section:
  - Pipes.
  - Tubes.
  - Conduits.
  - Wire.
  - Cable.
  - Vents.
  - Ducts.

  Note: 707.2, "Shaft enclosure required." Exceptions 3 and 5 are cited as the source of penetrating components governed by the following sections, a summary of which is provided above.
  The following are cited as governing the penetrations listed above:
  711.4.1, "Through penetrations."
  711.4.2, "Membrane penetrations."
  711.4.3, "Nonfire-resistance-rated assemblies."
  711.4.4, "Ducts and air transfer openings."

711 Penetrations

711.4.1 Through penetrations *(part 1 of 2)*

This subsection addresses penetrations passing entirely through fire-resistance-rated horizontal assemblies.

- Requirements for penetrations of single fire-resistance-rated floors are indicated below for the following penetrating items:
  - Penetrating items:
    The following components in the materials indicated below:
      Components:
        Conduits, tubes, and pipes.
        Vents.
      Materials:
        Steel and ferrous metals.
        Copper.
      Concrete and masonry elements.
  - Requirements:
    The annular space must be filled with a substance able to perform as follows:
      Prevents passage of the following fire hazards for the time period indicated below:
        Fire hazards:
          Flame.
          Gasses as follows:
            Hot enough to ignite cotton waste in the following condition:
              With a positive pressure differential at penetration ≥ 0.01" of water.
        Time period:
          For a length of time = the fire-resistance rating of the wall penetrated.

  Note: ASTM E 119, "Standard Test Methods for Fire Tests of Building Construction and Materials," is cited as governing the substance filling the annular space.

  - Penetrations are not limited to a single floor where both of the following conditions are met:
    The penetrating component is ≤ 6" nominal diameter.
    The area of penetration is ≤ 144 sq in.
- Electrical outlet boxes of any material may be used as follows:
  - They must be tested for use in such assemblies.
  - They must be installed as tested in such assemblies.

711 Penetrations

711.4.1 Through penetrations *(part 2 of 2)*

- Requirements are indicated below for penetrations of a single concrete floor by the following items:
  - Penetrating items:
    - The following components in the materials indicated below:
      - Components:
        - Conduits, tubes, and pipes.
        - Vents.
      - Materials:
        - Steel and ferrous metals.
        - Copper.
  - Requirements:
    - Diameter of penetrating item must be ≤ 6".
    - The annular space must be filled with one of the following:
    - Concrete.
    - Grout.
    - Mortar.
    - The extent of the fill in the annular space must be one of the following:
      - For the full thickness of the floor.
      - ≥ a thickness which does not diminish the required fire-resistance rating.
  - Penetrations are not limited to a single floor where area of the penetration is ≤ 144 sq in.
- Other penetrations must comply with one of the following:
  - They must be installed as they were tested in the approved fire-resistance-rated assembly.
  - They must be protected by an approved through-penetration firestop system.

  Note: The following are cited as sources of requirements for other penetrations, partial summaries of which are provided above:
  711.4.1.1, "Fire-resistance-rated assemblies."
  711.4.1.2, "Through-penetration firestop system."

711.4.1.1 Fire-resistance-rated assemblies

- Through-penetrations of fire-resistance-rated horizontal assemblies are governed as follows:
  - Penetrations must be installed in the manner tested in the approved assembly.

  Note: 711.4.1, "Through penetrations," requires compliance with either this subsection or 711.4.1.2, "Through-penetration firestop system."

711.4.1.2 Through-penetration firestop system *(part 1 of 2)*

- Through penetrations of fire-resistance-rated horizontal assemblies must be protected by an approved through-penetration firestop system tested and installed as follows:
  - System must be tested as follows:
    - With a positive pressure differential of ≥ 0.01" of water.
  - System must be installed as tested.

711 Penetrations

711.4.1.2 Through-penetration firestop system *(part 2 of 2)*

- Through penetrations of fire-resistance-rated horizontal assemblies must be protected by a firestop system with the following F and T ratings.
  - ○ System must have an F rating ≥ the larger of the following:
    1 hr.
    The rating of the floor penetrated.
  - ○ System T rating is governed as follows:
    No T rating is required for a floor penetration within the cavity of a wall.
    Otherwise, T rating must be ≥ the larger of the following:
    1 hr.
    The rating of the floor penetrated.

  Note: ASTM E 814, "Standard Test Method of Fire Tests of Through-Penetration Fire Stops," is cited as governing the firestop test required above.

711.4.2 Membrane penetrations *(part 1 of 2)*

- This subsection addresses membrane penetrations in horizontal assemblies with a fire-resistance rating.
- Requirements for penetrations by the following items are listed below:
  - ○ Penetrating items:
    The following components are included in the materials listed below:
    Components:
    Conduits.
    Electrical outlet boxes.
    Tubes.
    Pipes.
    Vents.
    Materials:
    Steel.
    Ferrous metals.
    Copper.
    Concrete elements
    Masonry elements.
  - ○ Requirements:
    Penetrations must comply with one of the following:
    Must be as tested in the approved fire-resistance-rated assembly.
    Must be protected by an approved through-penetration firestop system.
    Must be protected to prevent the passage of the following:
    Flame.
    Products of combustion.
    Where assemblies were tested without penetrations:
    The sum of penetration areas is limited as follows:
    ≤ 100 sq in in any 100 sf of ceiling area.

711 Penetrations

711.4.2 Membrane penetrations *(part 2 of 2)*

- Penetrations by electrical outlet boxes of any material are allowed as follows:
  - Boxes must be listed.
  - Boxes must be tested for use in assemblies with fire-resistance ratings.
  - Boxes must be installed as per instructions dictated by their listing.
- A metal escutcheon plate must cover the following:
  - The annular space of a fire-sprinkler pipe penetration.
- Other penetrations must comply with one of the following:
  - Must be as tested in the approved fire-resistance-rated assembly.
  - Must be protected by an approved through-penetration firestop system.

  > *Note: The following are cited as governing the requirements for other penetrations, a partial summary of which is provided above:*
  > *711.4.1.1, "Fire-resistance-rated assemblies."*
  > *711.4.1.2, "Through-penetration firestop system."*

- Recessed fixtures may not reduce the fire-resistance rating of the following assembly:
  - Floor/ceiling assemblies with a minimum required fire-resistance rating of 1 hr.

711.4.3 Nonfire-resistance-rated assemblies

This subsection addresses penetrations of horizontal assemblies that are not required to have a fire-resistance rating.

- Penetrations must meet one of the following requirements:
  - Penetrations as follows must meet the requirements indicated below:
    Penetrations:
      Noncombustible items.
      Connecting ≤ 3 stories.
    Requirement:
      Annular space must be filled with a material as follows:
        Must be approved.
        Must be noncombustible.
        Must restrict the passage of flame.
        Must restrict the passage combustion products.
  - Penetrations connecting ≤ 2 stories are governed as follows:
    Annular space must be filled with a material as follows:
      Must be approved.
      Must restrict the passage of flame.
      Must restrict the passage combustion products.
  - Penetrations must be protected by a shaft enclosure.

  > *Note: Section 707, "Shaft and Vertical Exit Enclosures," is cited as the source for shaft enclosure requirements.*

711 Penetrations

711.4.3.1 Noncombustible penetrating items

- Penetrations as follows must meet the requirements indicated below:
  Penetrations:
    Noncombustible items.
    Connecting ≤ 3 stories.
  Requirement:
    Annular space must be filled with an approved noncombustible material as follows:
      Must restrict the passage of flame and combustion products.

711.4.3.2 Penetrating items

- Penetrations connecting ≤ 2 stories are governed as follows:
  Annular space must be filled with an approved material as follows:
    Must restrict the passage of flame and combustion products.

711.4.4 Ducts and air transfer openings

- Penetrations of horizontal assemblies by ducts and air transfer openings must meet the following requirements:
  - Where not required to have dampers:
    Penetrations must comply with this section.
  - Where provided with dampers:
    Penetrations must comply with requirements as follows:
      Those addressing ducts and air-transfer openings elsewhere in the code.

  Note: Section 715, "Ducts and Air Transfer Openings," is cited as governing penetrations by these components with dampers.

711.4.5 Dissimilar materials

- The following connection is permitted only with the condition indicated below:
  - Connection:
    Between the following components at a point beyond the firestopping:
      Noncombustible penetrating component.
      Combustible component.
  - Condition:
    It must be shown that the required fire-resistance of the assembly is not diminished.

711.4.6 Floor fire doors

- Fire doors in floors with a fire-resistance rating must comply with the following:
  - Doors must be tested in a horizontal position.
  - Doors must have a fire-resistance rating ≥ the assembly penetrated.
  - Doors must be labeled by an approved agency.

  Note: ASTM E 119, "Standard Test Methods for Fire Tests of Building Construction and Materials," is cited as the required test.

714 Opening Protectives

714.2 Fire door and shutter assemblies

- Approved fire door and shutter assemblies are governed as follows:
  - They may be of any material verified by specified fire tests.
  - They meet test requirements listed in this and subsequent sections.
  - They must be installed by the standards identified in this subsection.

    > *Note:* NFPA 80, *"Fire Doors and Windows,"* is cited as governing fire door installation.
    > *The following are cited as specifying required tests:*
    > *714.2.1, "Side-hinged or pivoted swinging doors."*
    > *714.2.2, "Other types of doors."*
    > *714.2.3, "Doors in corridors and smoke barriers."*
    > *The following are cited as governing tin clad fire doors:*
    > *UL 10A, "Tin Clad Fire Doors."*
    > *UL 14B, "Sliding Hardware for Standard Horizontally Mounted Tin Clad Fire Doors."*
    > *UL 14C, "Swinging Hardware for Standard Tin Clad Fire Doors Mounted Single and in Pairs."*

- Approved fire door and shutter assemblies must have the following fire-protection ratings:*
  - ≥ 20 minutes where located in the following:
    1-hr fire-resistance-rated fire partitions as exit access corridor walls.
  - ≥ ¾ hr where located in one of the following:
    1-hr fire-resistance-rated walls as follows:
      Exterior walls.
      Fire partitions other than exit-access corridor enclosures.
      Fire barriers other than shaft and exit enclosures.
  - ≥ 1 hr where located in one of the following:
    1-hr fire-resistance-rated fire barriers as follows:
      Shaft and exit enclosures.
  - ≥ 1½ hr where located in one of the following:
    1½-hr fire-resistance-rated fire walls and fire-barrier walls.
  - ≥ 1½ hr where located in one of the following:
    2-hr fire-resistance-rated walls as follows:
      Fire walls.
      Fire barriers.
      Exterior walls.
  - ≥ 1½ hr where located in one of the following:
    3-hr fire-resistance-rated exterior walls.
  - ≥ 1½ hr each where 2 doors or shutters are located as follows:
    At the same opening with one on each side of a wall with the following rating:
      3-hr fire-resistance-rated fire walls and fire-barrier walls.
  - ≥ 3 hr when located in one of the following:
    4-hr fire-resistance rated fire walls and fire-barrier walls.

Source: IBC Table 714.2.

714 Opening Protectives

714.2.4.1 Glazing in doors

- Glazing larger than 100 sq in is allowed in fire door assemblies as follows:
  - Glazing must have a fire-protection rating.
  - Glazing must be tested as follows:
    As a component of the door assembly, not as a glass light.
    The transmitted temperature end point is governed as follows:
    $\leq 450°F$ above ambient after ½ hr of testing.
    Not limited as follows:
    Where the building is sprinklered as per NFPA 13 or 13R.

  Note: NFPA 252, "Standard Method of Fire Tests of Door Assemblies," is cited as governing the test required above for glazing.

714.2.6 Glazing material

- Fire-door assemblies may have glazing that conforms to the following:
  - Glazing must have a fire-protection rating.
  - Glazing must conform to opening protection requirements.

  Note: 714.2, "Fire door and shutter assemblies," is cited as the source of opening protection requirements.

714.2.6.1 Size limitations

- Glazing in fire doors in fire walls is governed as follows:
  - Where doors are serving as a horizontal exit, the following applies:
    A glazed vision panel is permitted as follows:
    Door must be swinging type.
    Door must be self-closing.
    Glazing must have a fire-protection rating.
    Glazing area is limited to ≤ 100 sq in.
    Glazing dimensions are limited to ≤ 10 in.
  - In other cases, glazing is not permitted.
- Glazing in fire doors in fire barriers is governed as follows:
  - Glazing must have a fire-protection rating.
  - Where such doors have a 1½-hr rating:
    Glazing area is limited to ≤ 100 sqin.
- In other cases, glazing in fire doors shall comply with one of the following:
  - Wired glass is limited in size based on its fire-protection rating.
  - Fire-protection-rated glass other than wired glass is governed as follows:
    It must comply with size requirements of the applicable standard.

  Note: The following are cited as governing the glass above:
  NFPA 80, "Fire Doors and Windows," for glass that is not wired glass.
  IBC Table 714.3.2, "Limiting Sizes of Wired Glass Panels," for wired glass.

Case study: Fig. 714.2.6.1. Wired glass is provided in the 1-hr fire door at the exit enclosre. IBC Table 714.3.2 limits the area of such glass to 100 sq in where the fire-protection rating of the opening is 1 hr. The height of the glass is limited to 33" and the maximum width permitted by the table is 10". The 10"x10" glass meets these requirements.

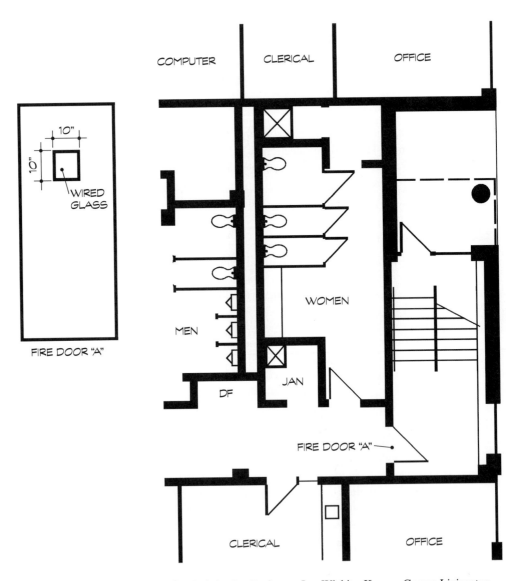

Fig. 714.2.6.1. Fire door elevation and plan. Lubrication Engineers, Inc. Wichita, Kansas. Gossen Livingston Associates, Inc., Architecture. Wichita, Kansas.

714 Opening Protectives

714.3.2 Wired glass

- A ¾-hr fire window assembly has the following characteristics:
  - The window frame is one of the following materials:
    - ≥ 0.125" thick solid steel.
    - ≥ 0.048" thick formed sheet steel.
  - The window frame is fabricated by any of the following methods:
    - Pressing.
    - Mitering.
    - Riveting.
    - Interlocking.
    - Welding.
  - The window frame is able to receive ¼" wired glass.
  - The window frame is secured into the building construction.
  - The glazing is ¼" thick wired glass.
  - The glazing is labeled.
- Wired glass size limitations are as follows:*
  - Where located in openings requiring the following:
    - 3-hr fire-protection rating:
      - Not permitted.
  - Where located in doors of exterior walls requiring the following:
    - 1½-hr fire-protection rating:
      - Not permitted.
  - Where located in openings requiring the following:
    - 1-hr fire-protection rating:
      - Area must be ≤ 100 sq in.
      - Height must be ≤ 33".
      - Width must be ≤ 10".
  - Where located in openings requiring the following:
    - 1½-hr fire-protection rating:
      - Area must be ≤ 100 sq in.
      - Height must be ≤ 33".
      - Width must be ≤ 10".
  - Where located in openings requiring the following:
    - ¾-hr fire-protection rating:
      - Area must be ≤ 1296 sq in.
      - Each dimension must be ≤ 54".
  - Where located in openings requiring the following:
    - 20-minute fire-protection rating:
      - Area not limited.
      - Dimensions not limited.
  - Fire window assemblies:
    - Area must be ≤ 1296 sq in.
    - Each dimension must be ≤ 54".

*Source: IBC Table 714.3.2

714 Opening Protectives

714.3.3 Nonwired glass

- Glazing other than wired glass where used in fire window assemblies is governed as follows:
  - It must be fire-protection rated.
  - It must comply with standards other than this code for installation and size.

  Note: NFPA 80, "Fire Doors and Windows," is cited as governing glazing other than wired glass used in fire window assemblies.

714.3.4 Installation

- Glazing with a fire-protection rating must comply with the following:
  - Frames must be approved.
  - Glazing must be fixed or automatic-closing.

714.3.5 Window mullions

- The following metal mullions must comply with the requirement indicated below:
  - Mullions:
    Serving glazing with a fire-protection rating.
    > 12' tall.
  - Requirement:
    Mullion fire-resistance rating must be ≥ that of their wall.

714.3.6 Interior fire window assemblies

This subsection governs glazing with a fire-protection rating as used in fire window assemblies.

- Such glazing is limited to use the following components:
  - Fire partitions with a fire-resistance rating ≤ 1 hr.
  - Fire barriers with a fire-resistance rating ≤ 1 hr.

714.3.6.1 Where permitted

This subsection governs glazing with a fire-protection rating.

- Such glazing may be used only in the following applications:
  - Fire partitions with a fire-resistance rating of 1 hr.
  - Fire barriers as follows:
    With a fire resistance rating of 1 hr.
    Separating the following:
    Incidental use areas from the rest of the building.
    Mixed occupancies from each other.
    A single occupancy into different fire areas.

  Note: The following are cited as governing the partitions and barriers indicated above:
  Section 708, "Fire Partitions."
  706.3.4, "Incidental use areas," addresses fire barriers.
  706.3.5, "Separation of occupancies," addresses fire barriers.

714 Opening Protectives

714.3.6.2 Size limitations

- The sum of window areas is limited to ≤ 25% of the following walls between rooms:
  - Fire partitions and fire barriers.

714.3.7 Exterior fire window assemblies *(part 1 of 2)*

- Exterior openings require a fire-protection rating ≥ 1½ hr as follows:
  - Where all the following conditions apply:
    Openings that are not doors.
    Openings that are required to be protected based on the following:
      Size.
      Relationship to other openings above and below.
      Relationship to a lower roof on the same property.
    Openings in walls required to have a fire-resistance rating as follows:
      >1 hr based on fire-separation distance.

  Note: The following are cited as sources of requirements applicable to the openings indicated above:
  > *704.12, "Opening protection," identifies openings that require protection based on size, relationships to other openings above and below, and to a lower roof on the same property.*
  > *IBC Table 602, "Fire-Resistance Rating Requirements for Exterior Walls Based on Fire Separation Distance."*

- Exterior openings require a fire-protection rating ≥ ¾ hr as follows:
  - Where all the following conditions apply:
    Openings that are required to be protected based on size.
    Openings in walls required to have a fire-resistance rating as follows:
      1 hr based on fire-separation distance.

  Note: The following are cited as sources of applicable requirements:
  > *704.8, "Allowable area of openings," identifies openings that require protection based on size.*
  > *IBC Table 602, "Fire-Resistance Rating Requirements for Exterior Walls Based on Fire Separation Distance."*

- Exterior openings require a fire-protection rating ≥ ¾ hr as follows:
  - Where openings are required to be protected based on the following:
    Relationship to other openings above and below.
    Relationship to a lower roof on the same property.

  Note: The following are cited as sources of requirements applicable to openings:
  > *704.9, "Vertical separation of openings," identifies openings that require protection based on relationships to other openings above and below.*
  > *704.10, "Vertical exposure," identifies openings that required protection based on relationships to a lower roof on the same property.*

714 Opening Protectives

714.3.7 Exterior fire window assemblies *(part 2 of 2)*

- Exterior openings with the following conditions require a fire-protection rating ≥ ¾ hr:
  - Openings that are in a wall without a fire-resistance rating.
  - Openings that are required to be protected based on the following:
    Size.
    Relationship to other openings above and below.
    Relationship to a lower roof on the same property.

> *Note: The following are cited as sources of requirements applicable to openings:*
> *704.8, "Allowable area of openings," identifies openings that require protection.*
> *704.9, "Vertical separation of openings," identifies openings that require protection based on relationships to other openings above and below.*
> *704.10, "Vertical exposure," identifies openings that required protection based on relationships to a lower roof on the same property.*

716 Concealed Spaces

716.1 General

- The following are required in combustible concealed spaces:
  - Fireblocking at the following locations:
    In walls at floor and ceilings.
    In stair construction.
    At penetrations.
    In exterior wall finish systems.
    Between sleepers.
  - Draftstopping at the following locations:
    Floor/ceiling spaces.
    Attic spaces.
  - Where buildings are required to be noncombustible:
    The use of combustible materials in concealed spaces is limited as follows:
    To locations with conditions specified by the code.

  Note: The following are cited as sources of applicable requirements:
  716.2, "Fireblocking."
  716.3, "Draftstopping in floors."
  716.4, "Draftstopping in attics."
  716.5, "Combustibles in concealed spaces in Types I and II construction."

716.2 Fireblocking

- Fireblocking is required to seal openings to restrict drafts as follows:
  - In combustible construction in concealed spaces as follows:
    Vertical openings.
    Horizontal openings.
- Fireblocking is required to form a barrier between the following elements:
  - Between floors.
  - Between the top story and a roof.
  - Between the top story and an attic.

  Note: The following are cited as the source for specific locations requiring fireblocking:
  716.2.2, "Concealed wall spaces."
  716.2.3, "Connections between horizontal and vertical spaces."
  716.2.4, "Stairways."
  716.2.5, "Ceiling and floor openings."
  716.2.6, "Architectural trim."
  716.2.7, "Concealed sleeper spaces."

716 Concealed Spaces

716.2.1 Fireblocking materials

- Fireblocking must be one of the following materials:
  - 2" nominal lumber or 2 layers of 1" nominal lumber with staggered joints.
  - 0.719" wood structural panel with joints backed by the same material.
  - 0.75" particle board with joints backed by the same material.
  - Gypsum board.
  - Cement fiber board.
  - Batts or blankets of mineral wool or glass fiber.
  - Loose-fill insulation where all the following apply:
    - Must be tested in the form and manner of the actual application.
    - Ability to remain in place must be demonstrated.
    - Ability to retard the spread of fire must be demonstrated.
    - Ability to retard the spread of hot gasses must be demonstrated.
  - Other approved material.
- Fireblocking must be held securely in place.

716.2.1.1 Double stud walls

- The following nonrigid materials may serve as fireblocking in the walls indicated below:
  - Materials:
    - Batts or blankets of mineral fiber.
    - Batts of or blankets of glass fiber.
    - Other approved nonrigid materials.
  - Walls:
    - Double walls with parallel rows of studs.
    - Walls with cavity space wider than stud width as follows:
      - Alternate studs are flush with opposite sides of the wall.

716.2.2 Concealed wall spaces

- Fireblocking is required in stud walls and partitions as follows:
  - In concealed spaces at the ceiling level:
    - Includes furred spaces.
  - In concealed spaces at the floor level:
    - Includes furred spaces.
  - At ≤ 10' intervals vertically.
  - At ≤ 10' intervals horizontally.

716 Concealed Spaces

716.2.3 Connections between horizontal and vertical spaces

- Fireblocking is required to seal through connections as follows:
  - Between the concealed spaces in stud walls or partitions and the following:
    Concealed spaces created by floor joists.
    Concealed spaces created by trusses.
  - Between vertical and horizontal spaces occurring at the following and similar locations:
    Soffits.
    Drop ceilings.
    Cove ceilings.

716.2.4 Stairways

- Fireblocking is required in concealed spaces as follows:
  - Between stair stringers at the top and bottom of a stair run.
  - Between studs along stair stringers where walls beneath the stairs are not finished.

716.2.5 Ceiling and floor openings

- Fireblocking is required at annular space of the following penetrations at locations indicated:
  - Penetrations:
    Vents.
    Pipes.
    Chimneys.
    Ducts.
    Conduits.
    Fireplaces.
  - Locations:
    Ceilings.
    Floors.

  *Note: The following are cited as sources listing penetrations requiring fireblocking, a
  partial summary of which is provided above:*
  707.2, "Shaft enclosure required," Exception 6.
  711.4.2, "Membrane penetrations," Exception 1.
  711.4.3, "Nonfire-resistance-rated assemblies."

- Fireblocking must be an approved material.
- Fireblocking must resist the passage of the following:
  Flame and combustion products.
- Fireblocking for prefabricated fireplaces and chimneys is governed by other standards.

  Note: The following are cited as governing prefabricated fireplaces and chimneys:
  *UL 103, "Chimneys, Factory-Built, Residential Type and Building Heating
  Appliance."*
  UL 127, "Factory-Built Fireplaces."

716 Concealed Spaces

716.2.6 Architectural trim

- Fireblocking is required in cornices at the party wall of duplexes.
- Fireblocking is not required in the following cases:
  - At locations in cornices other than at the party wall of duplexes.
  - In cornices of single-family dwellings.
  - Where both the following conditions are present:
      The architectural trim is installed on noncombustible framing.
      The exterior wall finish exposed to the concealed space is one of the following:
        Aluminum ≥ 0.019" thick.
        Steel as follows:
          Corrosion-resistant.
          Base metal thickness is ≥ 0.016" at thinnest point.
        Other approved noncombustible materials.
- Fireblocking is required in concealed spaces of the following components as indicated:
  - Components:
      With combustible construction or framing as follows:
        Exterior wall finish.
        Exterior architectural elements.
  - Requirements:
      Continuous concealed spaces must be fireblocked at a spacing ≤ 20'.
      Noncontinuous concealed spaces must have both the following:
        Closed ends.
        Separation between sections ≥ 4".

  Note: Section 1406, "Combustible Materials on the Exterior Side of Exterior Walls," is cited as governing the combustible materials at exterior walls indicated above.

716.2.7 Concealed sleeper spaces

- Slab-on-grade gymnasium floors do not require fireblocking:
- Bowling alley lanes require blocking only at the following locations:
  - At the juncture of every other lane.
  - At the ends of each lane.
- In other cases, space between wood sleepers on floors as follows are governed as indicated:
  - Floors:
      Masonry or concrete floors with a fire-resistance rating.
  - Sleeper space:
      Space between flooring and floor slab must be detailed in one of the following ways:
        Fireblocked to limit the air space to ≤ 100 sf.
        Filled with an approved material as follows:
          That will prevent passage of the following:
            Flame and combustion products.
      Space between flooring and slab must be completely filled in the following location:
        Under permanent partitions between rooms.

716 Concealed Spaces

716.3 Draftstopping in floors

- This section addresses draftstopping in the following locations:
  - In combustible construction.
  - In floor/ceiling assemblies.

    Note: The following are cited as sources of specific locations where draftstopping is
    required:
    716.3.2, "Groups R-1, R-2, R-3 and R-4."
    716.3.3, "Other groups."

716.3.1 Draftstopping materials

- The following qualify as draftstopping materials:
  - Gypsum board $\geq \frac{1}{2}$" thick.
  - Wood structural panel $\geq \frac{3}{8}$" thick.
  - Particle board $\geq \frac{3}{8}$" thick.
  - Other approved materials.
- Draftingstopping materials must be adequately supported.

716.3.2 Groups R-1, R-2, R-3 and R-4

- This section applies to draftstopping in concealed spaces as follows:
  - Combustible floor/ceiling assemblies in the following occupancies:
    R-1.
    R-2 with $\geq$ 3 dwelling units.
    R-3 with 2 dwelling units.
    R-4.
- Draftstopping is not required as follows:
  - In buildings sprinklered as per NFPA 13.
  - In buildings sprinklered as per NFPA 13R as follows:
    Sprinklers provided in combustible concealed spaces.
- In other cases, draftstopping is required in the following locations:
  - On the line of separation between dwelling units.
  - On the line of separation between tenants.

716 Concealed Spaces

716.3.3 Other groups

- This section applies to draftstopping in concealed spaces as follows:
  - Combustible floor/ceiling assemblies in the following:
    Occupancies other R.
- Draftstopping is not required as follows:
  - In buildings sprinklered as per NFPA 13.
- In other buildings, draftstopping is required as follows:
  - Horizontal air space must be limited to ≤ 1000 sf of floor area.

716.4 Draftstopping in attics

- This subsection series addresses draftstopping in the following locations of combustible construction:
  - In attics.
  - In concealed roof spaces.

  Note: The following sections are cited as sources of specific locations required for draftstopping:
  716.4.2, "Groups R-1 and R-2."
  716.4.3, "Other groups."

- Ventilation of concealed spaces under the roof must be provided.

  Note: 1202.2, "Attic spaces," is cited as the source for ventilation requirements.

716.4.1 Draftstopping materials

- The following qualify as draftstopping materials:
  - Gypsum board ≥ $1/2$" thick.
  - Wood structural panel ≥ $3/8$" thick.
  - Particle board ≥ $3/8$" thick.
  - Other approved materials.
- Draftstopping materials must be adequately supported.

716.4.1.1 Openings

- Openings in draftstopping attic partitions must be protected as follows:
  - With self-closing doors.
  - Doors must have automatic latches.

716 Concealed Spaces

716.4.2 Groups R-1 and R-2

- This subsection applies to draftstopping where required as follows:
  - In combustible concealed spaces of the following occupancies in locations listed below:
    Occupancies:
    R-1.
    R-2 with ≥ 3 dwellings.
    Locations:
    General locations:
    Attics.
    Mansards.
    Overhangs.
    Other concealed roof spaces.
    Specific locations:
    On line with separation walls which do not reach the roof sheathing as follows:
    Between dwelling units.
    Between tenants.
- Draftstopping is required above only one of the two corridor walls in the following case:
  - Where corridor walls provide the following separations:
    Between dwelling units.
    Between tenants.
- Draftstopping is not required as follows:
  - In buildings sprinklered as per NFPA 13.
  - In buildings sprinklered as per NFPA 13R as follows:
    Sprinklers provided in combustible concealed spaces.
- Draftstopping is required as indicated below in the following occupancy:
  - Occupancy:
    R-2 ≤ 4 stories.
  - Requirement:
    Draftstops must divide attic space into the smaller of the following areas:
    ≤ 3000 sf.
    ≤ area above every two dwellings.
- Draftstopping is otherwise required in the general and specific locations specified in this section.

716 Concealed Spaces

716.4.3 Other groups

- This subsection applies to draftstopping in the following:
  - Combustible concealed spaces of occupancies other than the following:
    R-1.
    R-2 with ≥ 3 dwellings.
- Draftstopping is not required in attics and concealed roof spaces as follows:
  - In buildings sprinklered as per NFPA 13.
- Draftstopping is otherwise required in the following locations as indicated below:
  - Locations:
    Attics.
    Concealed roof spaces.
  - Requirement:
    Horizontal areas must be limited to ≤ 3000 sf.

716.5 Combustibles in concealed spaces in Types I and II construction

- The following combustible materials may be used in concealed spaces of Types I and II construction:
  - Combustible materials permitted in other locations of Type I and II construction.
  - Combustible materials permitted in plenums.
  - Class A finish materials.
  - Combustible piping as follows:
    In the following locations as otherwise governed by this code.
      Partitions.
      Enclosed shafts.
    In concealed spaces where installed as per applicable codes.

  Note: The following are cited as sources of requirements for combustible materials permitted in concealed spaces of Types I and II construction:
  Section 603, "Combustible Material in Types I and II Construction," lists material permitted in other locations in Types I and II construction.
  Section 602 of the International Mechanical Code governs materials in plenums.
  The following provide requirements for combustible piping in concealed spaces:
  International Mechanical Code.
  International Plumbing Code.

- Otherwise combustible materials are not allowed in concealed spaces of the following:
  - Type I construction.
  - Type II construction.

Case study: Fig. 716.4.3. The attic of the occupancy E building is divided by walls providing draftstops. One draftstopping wall separates the new attic (not sprinklered) from the existing attic. A second draftstopping wall separates the new attic into areas of 2780 sf and 1670 sf, both within the 3000 sf limit.

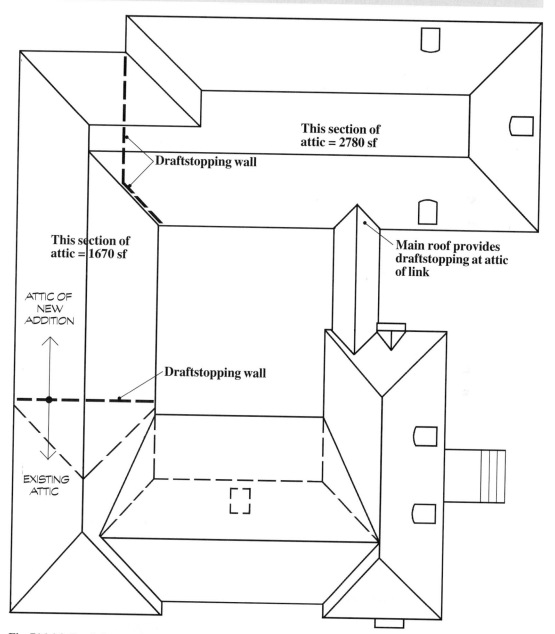

This section of attic = 2780 sf

Draftstopping wall

Main roof provides draftstopping at attic of link

This section of attic = 1670 sf

ATTIC OF NEW ADDITION

Draftstopping wall

EXISTING ATTIC

Fig. 716.4.3. Roof plan. Multipurpose Building Addition to Children's Home. Wilkes-Barre, Pennsylvania. C. Allen Mullins, Architect. Bear Creek, Pennsylvania.

717 Fire-Resistance Requirements for Plaster

717.1 Thickness of plaster

- The thickness required for the following types of plaster is determined by specified fire tests:
  - Gypsum plaster. and portland cement plaster
- Where applied to the following, plaster thickness is measured to the face of the lath:
  - Gypsum lath and metal lath.

717.2 Plaster equivalents

- The following are considered to have equal fire resistance:
  - 0.5" unsanded gypsum plaster.
  - 0.75" 1:3 gypsum sand plaster.
  - 1" of portland cement sand plaster.

717.3 Noncombustible furring

- In Types I and II construction plaster must be applied directly to one of the following:
  - Concrete or masonry.
  - Approved noncombustible plastering base and furring.

717.4 Double reinforcement

- The following plaster systems do not require supplementary reinforcement:
  - Solid plaster partitions.
  - Assemblies where it is deemed by fire test to be unnecessary.
- Other plaster as follows requires supplementary reinforcement as indicated below:
  - Plaster:
    - With both the following characteristics:
      - Plaster used as fire protection.
      - Plaster > 1" thick.
  - Requirement:
    - An additional layer of approved lath is required as follows:
      - Lath must be embedded ≥ 0.75" from outer surface of plaster.
      - Lath must be fastened securely in place.

717.5 Plaster alternatives for concrete

- This subsection addresses concrete cover protection in reinforced concrete construction.
- The following plaster types may substitute for concrete cover as indicated below:
  - Plaster types:
    - Gypsum plaster. and portland cement plaster.
  - Substitution:
    - Up to ½" of concrete cover may be replaced with plaster as follows:
      - Concrete cover may not be reduced below the following:
        - $^3/_8$" for poured reinforced concrete floors in addition to the plaster.
        - 1" for reinforced concrete columns in addition to the plaster.

718 Thermal- and Sound-Insulating Materials

718.1 General

- This section does not apply to the following materials:
  - Fiberboard insulation.
  - Foam plastic insulation.
  - Foam plastic insulation.
  - Duct insulation.
  - Insulation in plenums.

    Note: The following are cited as governing the materials listed above:
    Chapter 23, "Wood Governs Fiberboard Insulation."
    Chapter 26, "Plastic," governs foam plastic insulation.
    International Mechanical Code governs duct and plenum insulation.

- This section governs the following materials:
  - Other insulating materials.
  - Facings such as follows:
    Vapor retarders.
    Breather papers.
    Similar coverings.
  - All layers of the following:
    Single-layer reflective foil insulation.
    Multilayer reflective foil insulation.
- Materials are not allowed as follows:
  - Where the following factors increase indexes as indicated below:
    Factors:
    Age.
    Moisture.
    Other atmospheric conditions.
    Indexes:
    Where either of the following increase to surpass prescribed limits:
    Flame spread index.
    Smoke-developed index.

    Note: ASTM E 84, "Standard Test Methods for Surface Burning Characteristics of Building Materials," is cited as governing flame spread and smoke-developed indexes where required in this section.

718 Thermal- and Sound-Insulating Materials

718.2 Concealed installation

- Concealed cellulose insulation as follows must have a smoke-developed index ≤ 450:
  - Loose-fill insulation.
  - Insulation that is not spray-applied.
  - Complies with applicable third-party standards.

  Note: 718.6, "Cellulose loose-fill insulation," is cited as the course for required standards.

- Other concealed insulating materials must comply with the following indexes:
  - Flame spread index ≤ 25.
  - Smoke-developed index ≤ 450.

718.2.1 Facings

- This section applies to the following facings installed as indicated below:
  - Facings:
    As follows on insulation installed in concealed spaces governed by this section:
    Facings.
    Coverings.
    Layers of reflective foil insulation.
  - Installation:
    Where installed in the following construction types:
    Types III, IV, and V.
    Where concealed behind and in substantial contact with the following elements:
    Ceiling finish.
    Wall finish.
    Floor finish.
- The following indexes are not limited for facings addressed in this section:
  - Flame spread index.
  - Smoke-developed index.

718.3 Exposed installation

- Exposed cellulose insulation as follows must have a smoke-developed index ≤ 450:
  - Loose-fill insulation.
  - Insulation that is not spray-applied.
  - Complies with applicable third-party standards.

  Note: 718.6, "Cellulose loose-fill insulation," is cited as the course for required standards.

- Other exposed insulating materials must comply with the following indexes:
  - Flame spread index ≤ 25.
  - Smoke-developed index ≤ 450.

718 Thermal- and Sound-Insulating Materials

718.3.1 Attic floors

- Insulation materials exposed on attic floors must have the following property:
  - A critical radiant flux ≥ 0.12 watt/sq cm.

  Note: ASTM E 970, "Standard Test Method for Critical Radiant Flux of Exposed Attic Floor Insulation Using a Radiant Heat Energy Source," is cited as the required test method.

718.4 Loose-fill insulation

- Cellulose loose-fill insulation is not required to comply with the standard surface burning tests where it complies with applicable Consumer Product Safety Commission standards.

  Note: 718.6, "Cellulose loose-fill insulation," is cited as the sourse of standards.

- In the following case, other loose-fill insulation may be tested by an alternate surface burning test instead of the standard test applicable to this section:
  - Where insulation materials require one of the following in order to be mounted in the standard test apparatus:

    A screen or artificial supports.

  Note: ASTM E 84, "Standard Test Methods for Surface Burning Characteristics of Building Materials," is cited as the standard test for this section.
  CAN/ULC S102, "Surface Burning Characteristics of Building Materials and Assemblies," is cited as the acceptable substitution.

  - Cellulose loose-fill insulation must comply with the following limit:

    Smoke-developed index ≤ 450.
  - Other loose-fill insulation must comply with the following limits:

    Flame spread index ≤ 25.
    Smoke-developed index ≤ 450.

718.5 Roof insulation

- Combustible roof insulation need not comply with the following standards where the conditions indicated below apply:
  - Standards:

    Flame spread index is not required to be ≤ 25.
    Smoke-developed index is not required to be ≤ 450.
  - Conditions:

    Where insulation is covered with an approved roof covering.
    Where the roof covering is applied directly to the insulation.

  Note: The following are cited as the sources of requirements which are waived for the insulation addressed in this section, a partial summary of which is provided above:
  718.2, "Concealed insulation," which limits flame spread and smoke developed index.
  718.3, "Exposed insulation," which limits flame spread and smoke developed index.

718 Thermal- and Sound-Insulating Materials

718.6 Cellulose loose-fill insulation

- Cellulose loose-fill insulation must comply with the following:
  - Meet standards of the Consumer Product Safety Commission.
  - Have packaging labeled as per the standards.

    Note: The following Consumer Product Safety Commission are cited as governing cellulose loose-fill insulation:
      CPSC 16 CFR, 1209, "Interim Safety Standard for Cellulose Insulation."
      CPSC 16 CFR, 1404, "Cellulose Insulation."

718.7 Insulation and covering on pipe and tubing

- Insulation and coverings on pipe and tubing must comply with the following standards:
  - Flame spread index must be ≤ 25.
  - Smoke-developed index must be ≤ 450.

719 Prescriptive Fire Resistance

719.1 General

- This subsection provides details with assigned fire-resistance ratings.

   Note: The following are cited as sources of details with fire-resistance ratings:
   IBC Table 719.1(1), "Minimum Protection of Structural Parts Based on Time Periods for Various Noncombustible Insulating Materials."
   IBC Table 719.1(2), "Rated Fire-Resistance Periods for Various Walls and Partitions."
   IBC Table 719.1(3), "Minimum Protection for Floor and Roof Systems."

- Where changes are made to the details provided herein, the following applies:
  - Where changes affect the heat dissipation potential of the detail:
    Documentation must be made available as follows:
    Type:
       Fire tests.
       Other data.
    Content:
       Verifying that the fire-resistance period of the detail is not reduced.
    Availability:
       Must be made available to the building official.

719.1.1 Thickness of protective coverings

- Thickness of fire-resistant materials protecting structure must be one of the following:
  - As indicated in details provided in this section.
  - As otherwise indicated in this section.

   Note: IBC Table 719.1(1), "Minimum Protection of Structural Parts Based on Time Periods for Various Noncombustible Insulating Materials," is cited as the source of details.

- Protective covering thickness indicated in this section is defined as follows:
  - Net thickness of protecting materials.
  - Thickness does not include air space behind the protecting material.

719.1.2 Unit masonry protection

- Where required, metal ties must be installed as follows:
  - In bed joints of masonry protecting steel columns.
  - Ties must be one of the following:
    As shown in details provided in this section.
    Equivalent to that shown in details of this section.

   Note: IBC Table 719.1(1), "Minimum Protection of Structural Parts Based on Time Periods for Various Noncombustible Insulating Materials," is cited as the source of details.

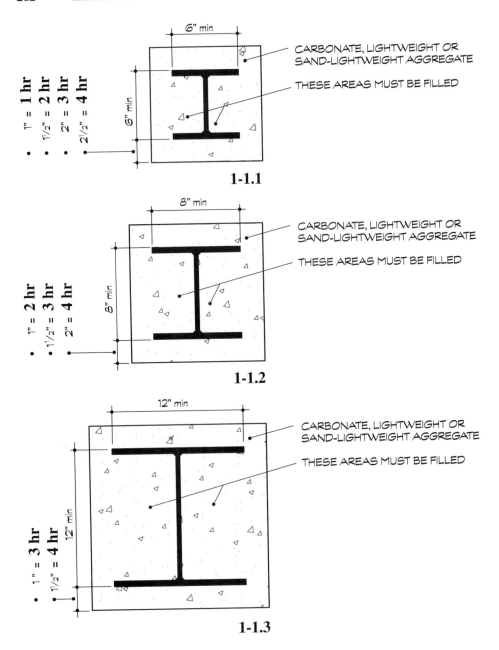

Fig. 719.1(1) 1A. Minimum protection of steel columns and all members of primary trusses. Minimum thicknesses of noncombustibule insulating materials are indicated as required for the fire-resistance ratings shown. Such thicknesses are the same on all sides where insulating materials occur. *[Source: IBC Table 719.1(1).]*

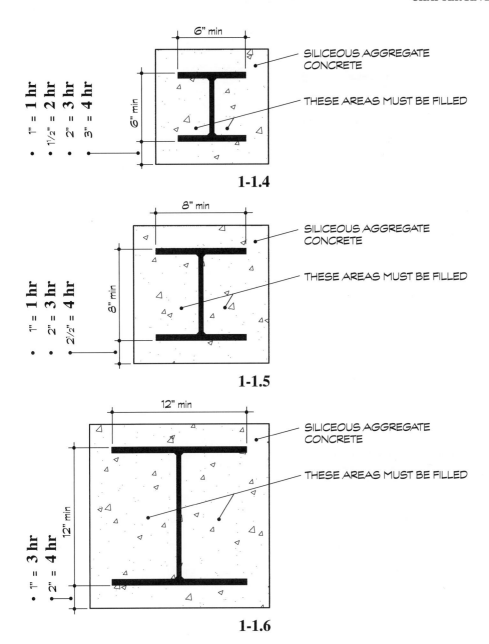

Fig. 719.1(1) 1B. Minimum protection of steel columns and all members of primary trusses. Minimum thicknesses of noncombustibule insulating materials are indicated as required for the fire-resistance ratings shown. Such thicknesses are the same on all sides where insulating materials occur. *[Source: IBC Table 719.1(1).]*

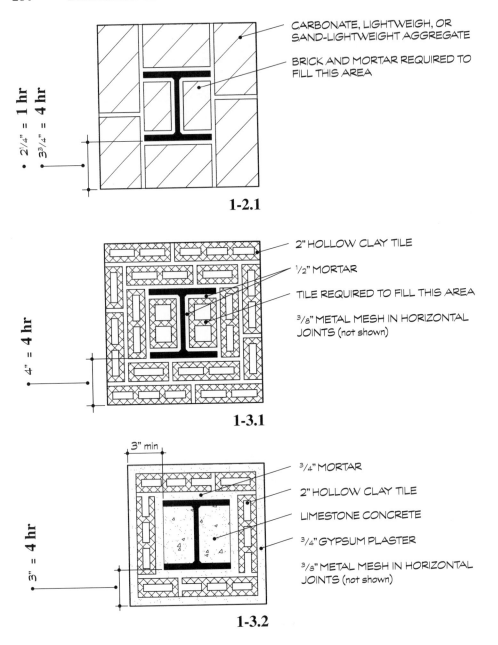

Fig. 719.1(1) 1C. Minimum protection of steel columns and all members of primary trusses. Minimum thicknesses of noncombustibule insulating materials are indicated as required for the fire-resistance ratings shown. Such thicknesses are the same on all sides where insulating materials occur. *[Source: IBC Table 719.1(1).]*

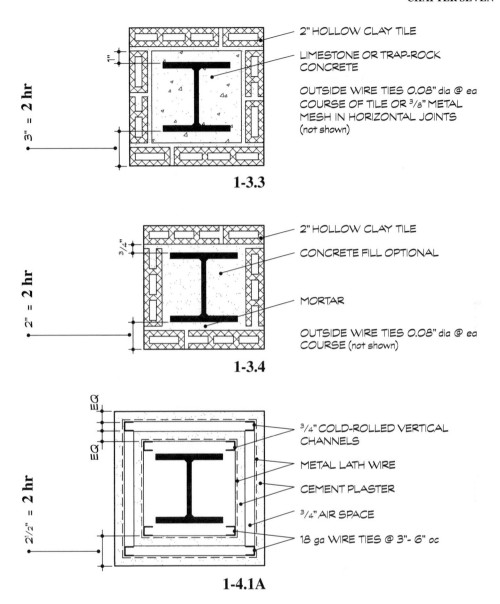

Fig. 719.1(1) 1D. Minimum protection of steel columns and all members of primary trusses. Minimum thicknesses of noncombustibule insulating materials are indicated as required for the fire-resistance ratings shown. Such thicknesses are the same on all sides where insulating materials occur. *[Source: IBC Table 719.1(1).]*

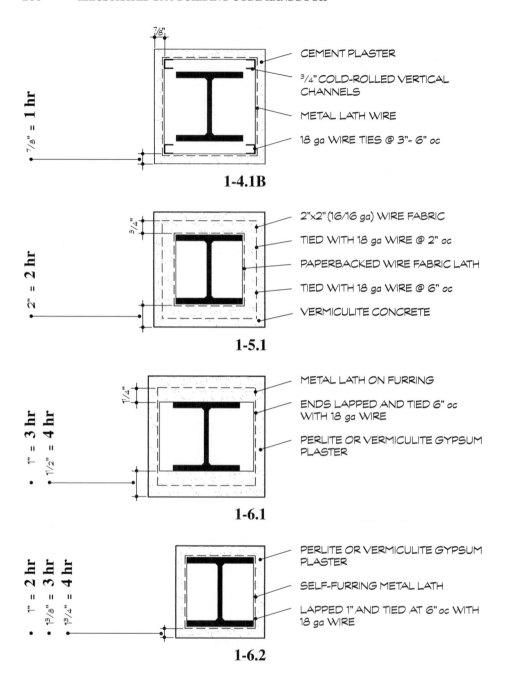

Fig. 719.1(1) 1E. Minimum protection of steel columns and all members of primary trusses. Minimum thicknesses of noncombustibule insulating materials are indicated as required for the fire-resistance ratings shown. Such thicknesses are the same on all sides where insulating materials occur. *[Source: IBC Table 719.1(1).]*

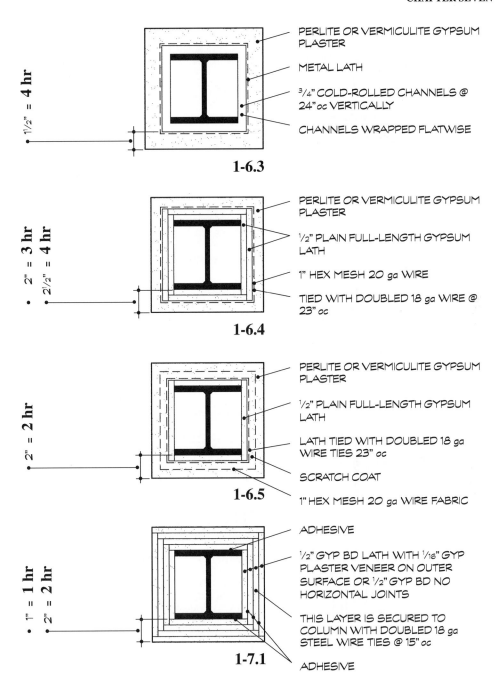

1/2" = 4 hr

1-6.3

PERLITE OR VERMICULITE GYPSUM PLASTER

METAL LATH

3/4" COLD-ROLLED CHANNELS @ 24" oc VERTICALLY

CHANNELS WRAPPED FLATWISE

2" = 3 hr
2 1/2" = 4 hr

1-6.4

PERLITE OR VERMICULITE GYPSUM PLASTER

1/2" PLAIN FULL-LENGTH GYPSUM LATH

1" HEX MESH 20 ga WIRE

TIED WITH DOUBLED 18 ga WIRE @ 23" oc

2" = 2 hr

1-6.5

PERLITE OR VERMICULITE GYPSUM PLASTER

1/2" PLAIN FULL-LENGTH GYPSUM LATH

LATH TIED WITH DOUBLED 18 ga WIRE TIES 23" oc

SCRATCH COAT

1" HEX MESH 20 ga WIRE FABRIC

1" = 1 hr
2" = 2 hr

1-7.1

ADHESIVE

1/2" GYP BD LATH WITH 1/16" GYP PLASTER VENEER ON OUTER SURFACE OR 1/2" GYP BD NO HORIZONTAL JOINTS

THIS LAYER IS SECURED TO COLUMN WITH DOUBLED 18 ga STEEL WIRE TIES @ 15" oc

ADHESIVE

Fig. 719.1(1) 1F. Minimum protection of steel columns and all members of primary trusses. Minimum thicknesses of noncombustibule insulating materials are indicated as required for the fire-resistance ratings shown. Such thicknesses are the same on all sides where insulating materials occur. *[Source: IBC Table 719.1(1).]*

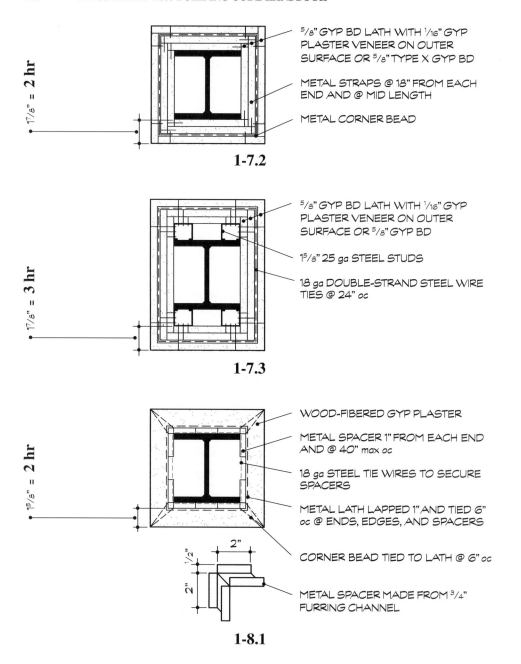

1-7.2

17/8" = 2 hr

- 5/8" GYP BD LATH WITH 1/16" GYP PLASTER VENEER ON OUTER SURFACE OR 5/8" TYPE X GYP BD
- METAL STRAPS @ 18" FROM EACH END AND @ MID LENGTH
- METAL CORNER BEAD

1-7.3

17/8" = 3 hr

- 5/8" GYP BD LATH WITH 1/16" GYP PLASTER VENEER ON OUTER SURFACE OR 5/8" GYP BD
- 15/8" 25 ga STEEL STUDS
- 18 ga DOUBLE-STRAND STEEL WIRE TIES @ 24" oc

1-8.1

15/8" = 2 hr

- WOOD-FIBERED GYP PLASTER
- METAL SPACER 1" FROM EACH END AND @ 40" max oc
- 18 ga STEEL TIE WIRES TO SECURE SPACERS
- METAL LATH LAPPED 1" AND TIED 6" oc @ ENDS, EDGES, AND SPACERS
- CORNER BEAD TIED TO LATH @ 6" oc
- METAL SPACER MADE FROM 3/4" FURRING CHANNEL

2"
1/2"
2"

Fig. 719.1(1) 1G. Minimum protection of steel columns and all members of primary trusses. Minimum thicknesses of noncombustibule insulating materials are indicated as required for the fire-resistance ratings shown. Such thicknesses are the same on all sides where insulating materials occur. *[Source: IBC Table 719.1(1).]*

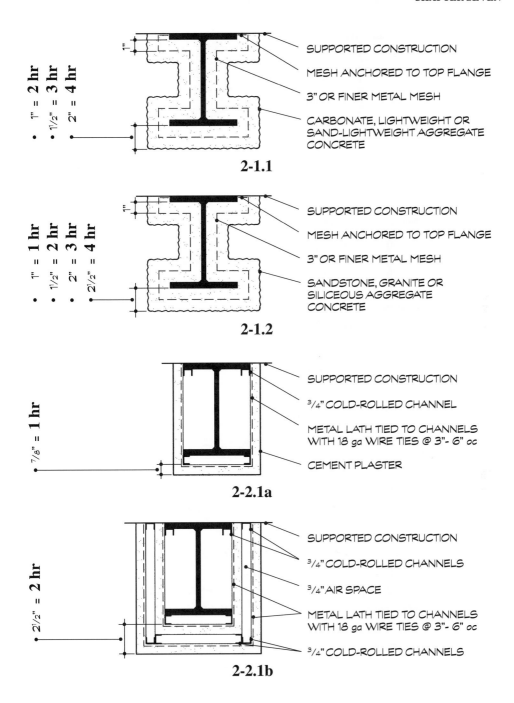

- 1" = **2 hr**
- 1½" = **3 hr**
- 2" = **4 hr**

SUPPORTED CONSTRUCTION

MESH ANCHORED TO TOP FLANGE

3" OR FINER METAL MESH

CARBONATE, LIGHTWEIGHT OR SAND-LIGHTWEIGHT AGGREGATE CONCRETE

2-1.1

- 1" = **1 hr**
- 1½" = **2 hr**
- 2" = **3 hr**
- 2½" = **4 hr**

SUPPORTED CONSTRUCTION

MESH ANCHORED TO TOP FLANGE

3" OR FINER METAL MESH

SANDSTONE, GRANITE OR SILICEOUS AGGREGATE CONCRETE

2-1.2

⅞" = **1 hr**

SUPPORTED CONSTRUCTION

¾" COLD-ROLLED CHANNEL

METAL LATH TIED TO CHANNELS WITH 18 ga WIRE TIES @ 3"- 6" oc

CEMENT PLASTER

2-2.1a

2½" = **2 hr**

SUPPORTED CONSTRUCTION

¾" COLD-ROLLED CHANNELS

¾" AIR SPACE

METAL LATH TIED TO CHANNELS WITH 18 ga WIRE TIES @ 3"- 6" oc

¾" COLD-ROLLED CHANNELS

2-2.1b

Fig. 719.1(1) 2A. Minimum protection of webs and flanges of steel beams and girders. Minimum thicknesses of noncombustibule insulating materials are indicated as required for the fire-resistance ratings shown. Such thicknesses are the same on all sides where insulating materials occur. *[Source: IBC Table 719.1(1).]*

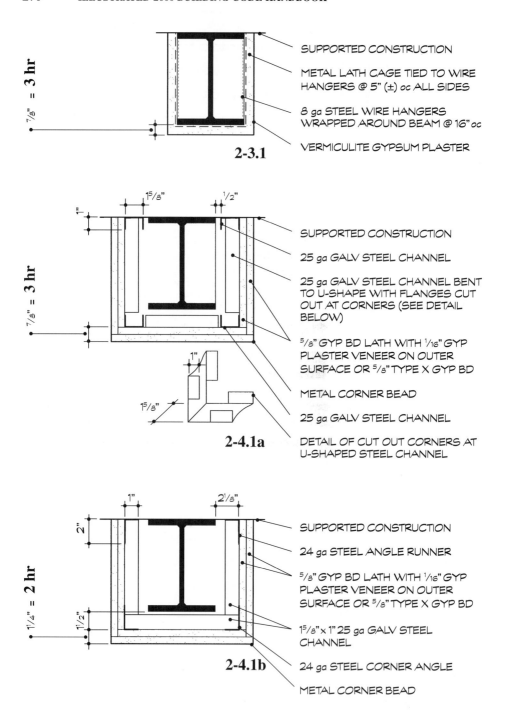

Fig. 719.1(1) 2B. Minimum protection of webs and flanges of steel beams and girders. Minimum thicknesses of noncombustibule insulating materials are indicated as required for the fire-resistance ratings shown. Such thicknesses are the same on all sides where insulating materials occur. *[Source: IBC Table 719.1(1).]*

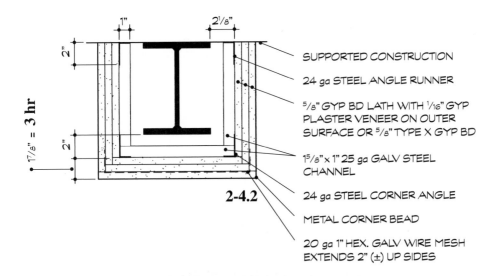

Fig. 719.1(1) 2C. Minimum protection of webs and flanges of steel beams and girders. Minimum thicknesses of noncombustibule insulating materials are indicated as required for the fire-resistance ratings shown. Such thicknesses are the same on all sides where insulating materials occur. *[Source: IBC Table 719.1(1).]*

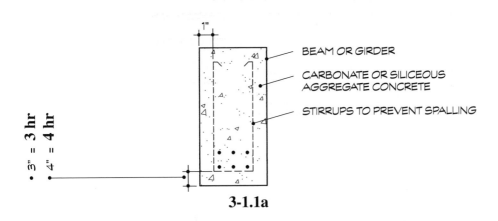

Fig. 719.1(1) 3A. Minimum protection of bonded pretensioned reinforcement in prestressed concrete. Minimum thicknesses of concrete cover are indicated as required for the fire-resistance ratings shown. Such minimum thicknesses are the same on all sides. *[Source: IBC Table 719.1(1).]*

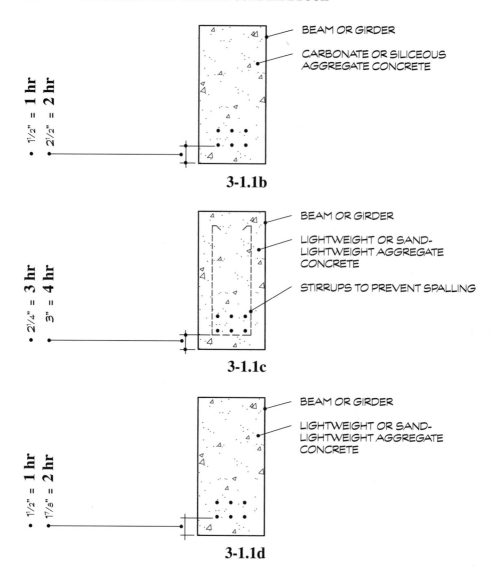

Fig. 719.1(1) 3B. Minimum protection of bonded pretensioned reinforcement in prestressed concrete. Minimum thicknesses of concrete cover are indicated as required for the fire-resistance ratings shown. Such minimum thicknesses are the same on all sides. *[Source: IBC Table 719.1(1).]*

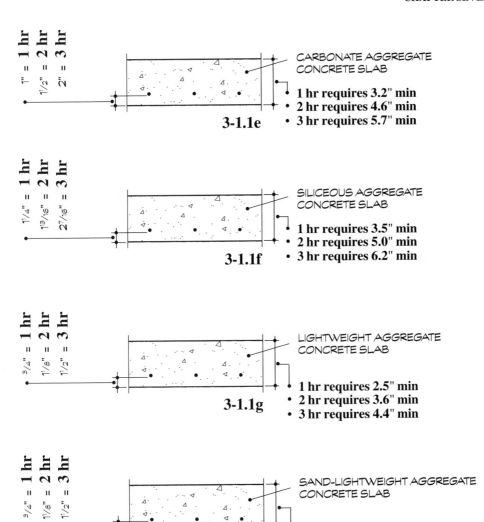

Fig. 719.1(1) 3C. Minimum protection of bonded pretensioned reinforcement in prestressed concrete.
Minimum thicknesses of concrete cover are indicated as required for the fire-resistance ratings shown. Such minimum thicknesses are the same on all sides. *[Source: IBC Table 719.1(1).]*

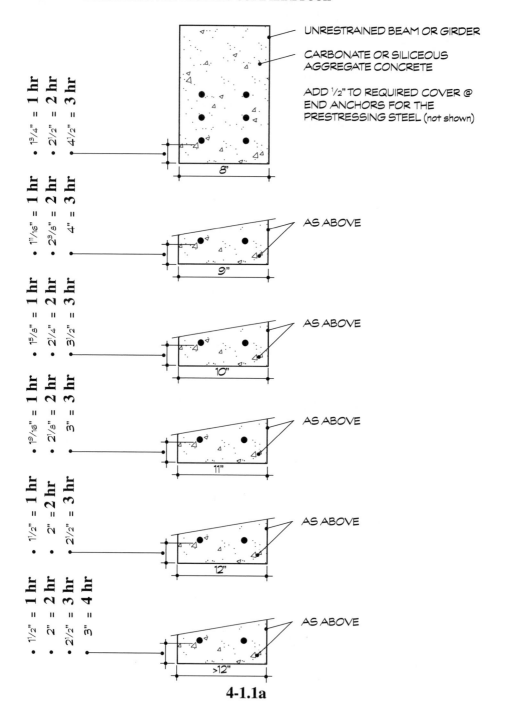

4-1.1a

Fig. 719.1(1) 4A. Minimum protection of bonded or unbonded post-tensioned tendons in prestressed concrete. Minimum thicknesses of concrete cover are indicated as required for the fire-resistance ratings shown. Such minimum thicknesses are the same on all sides. *[Source: IBC Table 719.1(1).]*

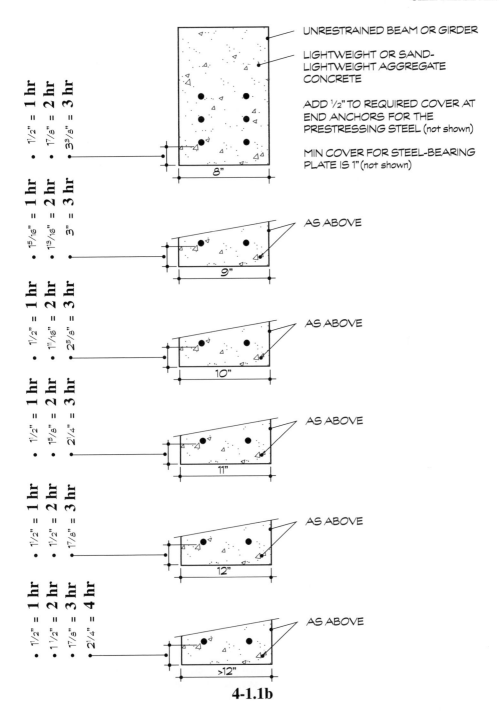

Fig. 719.1(1) 4B. Minimum protection of bonded or unbonded post-tensioned tendons in prestressed concrete. Minimum thicknesses of concrete cover are indicated as required for the fire-resistance ratings shown. Such minimum thicknesses are the same on all sides. *[Source: IBC Table 719.1(1).]*

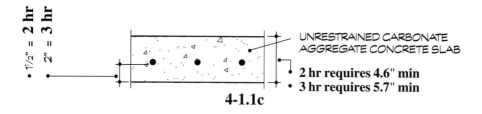

- $1/2" = $ **2 hr**
- $2" = $ **3 hr**

UNRESTRAINED CARBONATE
AGGREGATE CONCRETE SLAB

- **2 hr requires 4.6" min**
- **3 hr requires 5.7" min**

4-1.1c

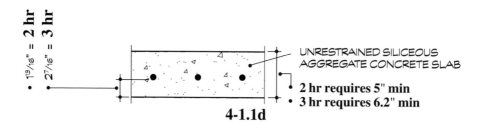

- $1 3/16" = $ **2 hr**
- $2 7/16" = $ **3 hr**

UNRESTRAINED SILICEOUS
AGGREGATE CONCRETE SLAB

- **2 hr requires 5" min**
- **3 hr requires 6.2" min**

4-1.1d

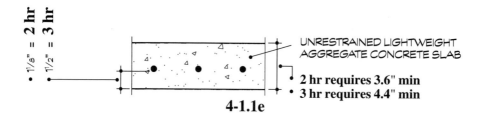

- $1/8" = $ **2 hr**
- $1/2" = $ **3 hr**

UNRESTRAINED LIGHTWEIGHT
AGGREGATE CONCRETE SLAB

- **2 hr requires 3.6" min**
- **3 hr requires 4.4" min**

4-1.1e

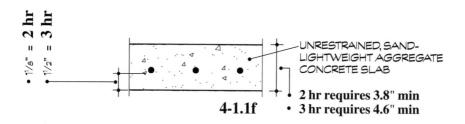

- $1/8" = $ **2 hr**
- $1/2" = $ **3 hr**

UNRESTRAINED, SAND-
LIGHTWEIGHT AGGREGATE
CONCRETE SLAB

- **2 hr requires 3.8" min**
- **3 hr requires 4.6" min**

4-1.1f

Fig. 719.1(1) 4C. Minimum protection of bonded or unbonded post-tensioned tendons in prestressed concrete. Minimum thicknesses of concrete cover are indicated as required for the fire-resistance ratings shown. Such minimum thicknesses are the same on all sides. *[Source: IBC Table 719.1(1).]*

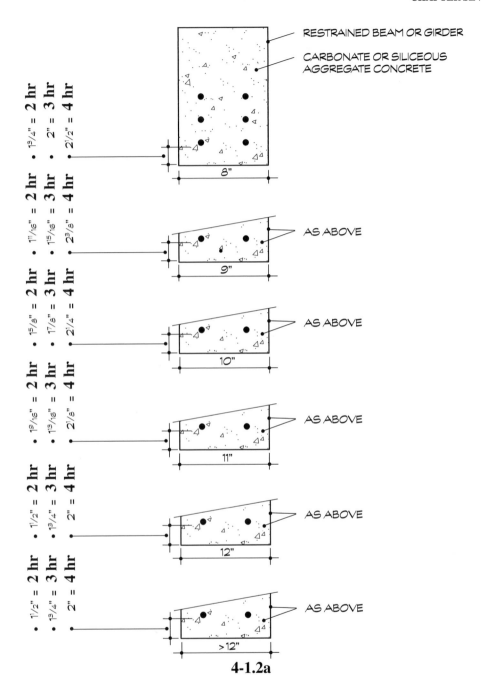

4-1.2a

Fig. 719.1(1) 4D. Minimum protection of bonded or unbonded post-tensioned tendons in prestressed concrete. Minimum thicknesses of concrete cover are indicated as required for the fire-resistance ratings shown. Such minimum thicknesses are the same on all sides. *[Source: IBC Table 719.1(1).]*

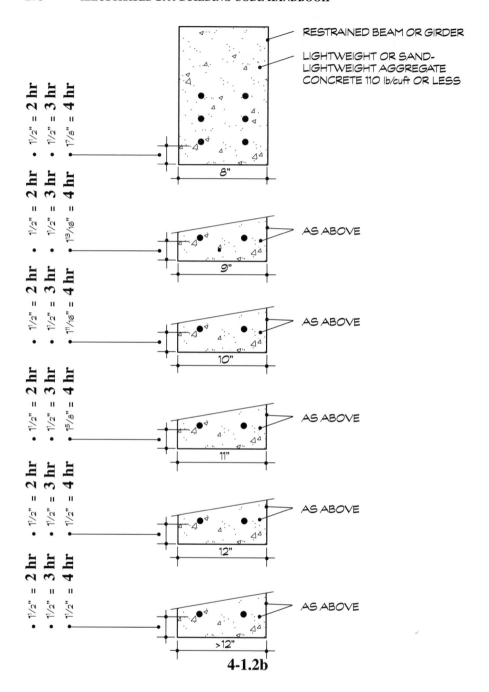

4-1.2b

Fig. 719.1(1) 4E. Minimum protection of bonded or unbonded post-tensioned tendons in prestressed concrete. Minimum thicknesses of concrete cover are indicated as required for the fire-resistance ratings shown. Such minimum thicknesses are the same on all sides. [Source: IBC Table 719.1(1).]

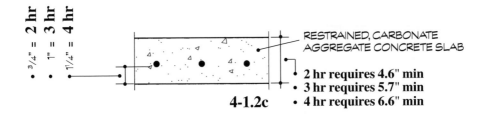

• ³/₄" = **2 hr**
• 1" = **3 hr**
• 1¹/₄" = **4 hr**

RESTRAINED, CARBONATE
AGGREGATE CONCRETE SLAB

4-1.2c

• **2 hr requires 4.6" min**
• **3 hr requires 5.7" min**
• **4 hr requires 6.6" min**

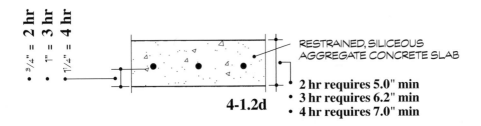

• ³/₄" = **2 hr**
• 1" = **3 hr**
• 1¹/₄" = **4 hr**

RESTRAINED, SILICEOUS
AGGREGATE CONCRETE SLAB

4-1.2d

• **2 hr requires 5.0" min**
• **3 hr requires 6.2" min**
• **4 hr requires 7.0" min**

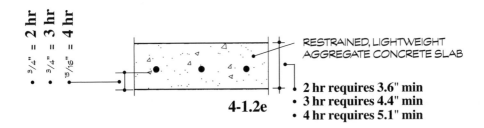

• ³/₄" = **2 hr**
• ³/₄" = **3 hr**
• ¹⁵/₁₆" = **4 hr**

RESTRAINED, LIGHTWEIGHT
AGGREGATE CONCRETE SLAB

4-1.2e

• **2 hr requires 3.6" min**
• **3 hr requires 4.4" min**
• **4 hr requires 5.1" min**

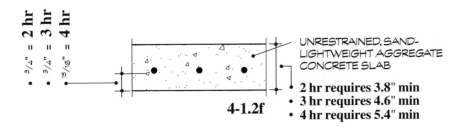

• ³/₄" = **2 hr**
• ³/₄" = **3 hr**
• ¹⁵/₁₆" = **4 hr**

UNRESTRAINED, SAND-
LIGHTWEIGHT AGGREGATE
CONCRETE SLAB

4-1.2f

• **2 hr requires 3.8" min**
• **3 hr requires 4.6" min**
• **4 hr requires 5.4" min**

Fig. 719.1(1) 4F. Minimum protection of bonded or unbonded post-tensioned tendons in prestressed concrete. Minimum thicknesses of concrete cover are indicated as required for the fire-resistance ratings shown. Such minimum thicknesses are the same on all sides. *[Source: IBC Table 719.1(1).]*

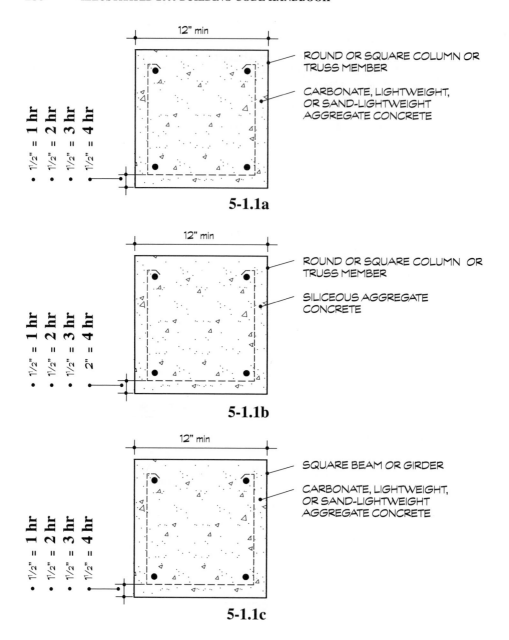

Fig. 719.1(1) 5A. Minimum protection of reinforcing steel in reinforced concrete columns, beams, girders, and trusses. Minimum thicknesses of concrete cover are indicated as required for the fire-resistance ratings shown. Such minimum thicknesses are the same on all sides. *[Source: IBC Table 719.1(1).]*

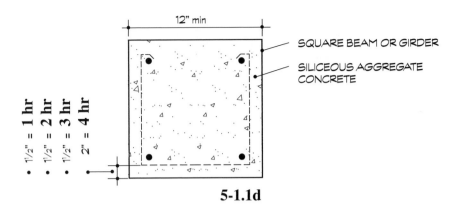

5-1.1d

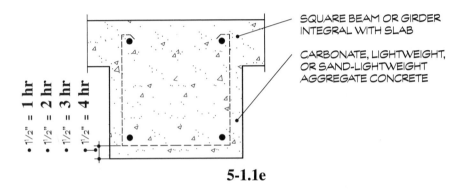

5-1.1e

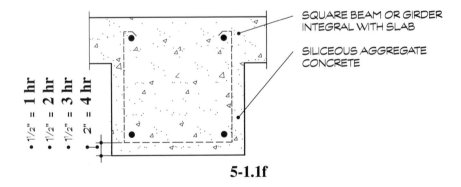

5-1.1f

Fig. 719.1(1) 5B. Minimum protection of reinforcing steel in reinforced concrete columns, beams, girders, and trusses. Minimum thicknesses of concrete cover are indicated as required for the fire-resistance ratings shown. Such minimum thicknesses are the same on all sides. *[Source: IBC Table 719.1(1).]*

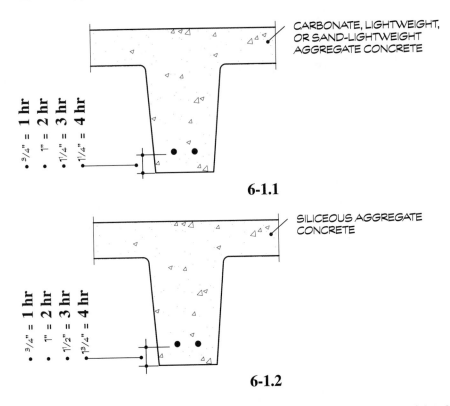

Fig. 719.1(1) 6A. Minimum protection of reinforcing steel in reinforced concrete joists. Minimum thicknesses of concrete cover are indicated as required for the fire-resistance ratings shown. Such minimum thicknesses are the same on all sides. *[Source: IBC Table 719.1(1).]*

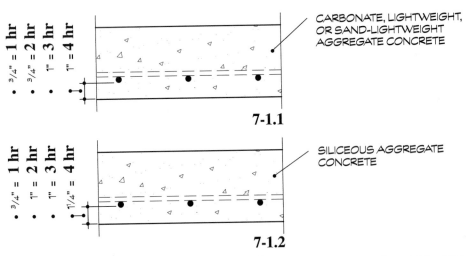

Fig. 719.1(1) 7A. Minimum protection of reinforcing and tie rods in floor and roof slabs. Minimum thicknesses of concrete cover are indicated as required for the fire-resistance ratings shown. Such minimum thicknesses are the same on all sides. *[Source: IBC Table 719.1(1).]*

Note: Acceptable fill materials for voids in details 1-1.1 and 1-1.3 are as follows:

Silicone-treated loose fill insulation   Expanded shale lightweight aggregate
Vermiculite loose fill insulation   Expanded lightweight aggregate
Expanded clay lightweight agggregate   Grout

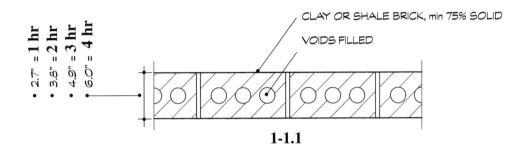

1-1.1

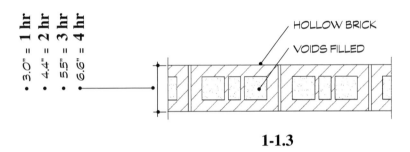

1-1.3

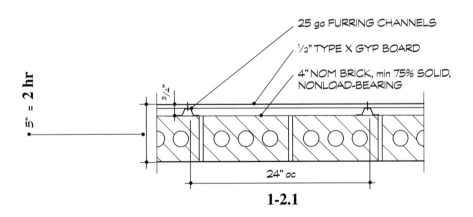

1-2.1

Fig. 719.1(2) 1A. Fire-resistance ratings for clay or shale brick walls and partitions. Minimum thickness of assembly is indicated as required for the fire-resistance rating shown. *[Source: IBC Table 719.1(2).]*

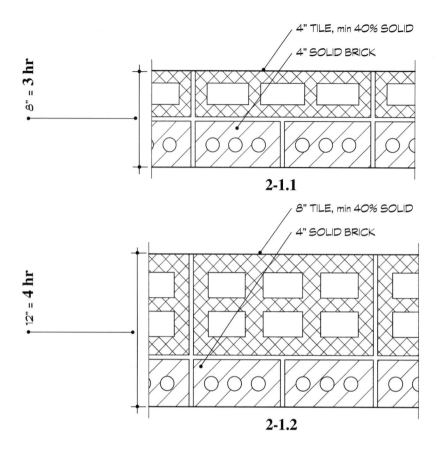

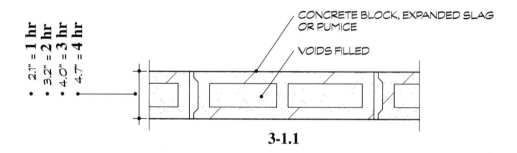

Fig. 719.1(2) 2A. Fire-resistance ratings for clay brick and load-bearing hollow clay tile walls and partitions. Minimum thickness of assembly is indicated as required for the fire-resistance rating shown. *[Source: IBC Table 719.1(2).]*

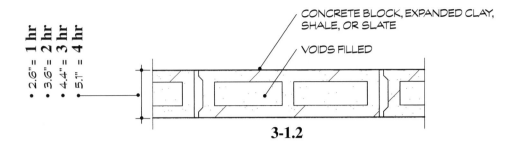

3-1.2

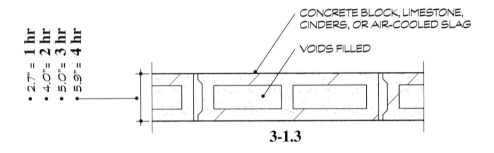

3-1.3

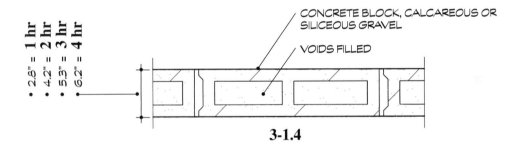

3-1.4

Fig. 719.1(2) 3A. Fire-resistance ratings for concrete masonry walls and partitions. Minimum thickness of assembly is indicated as required for the fire-resistance rating shown. *[Source: IBC Table 719.1(2).]*

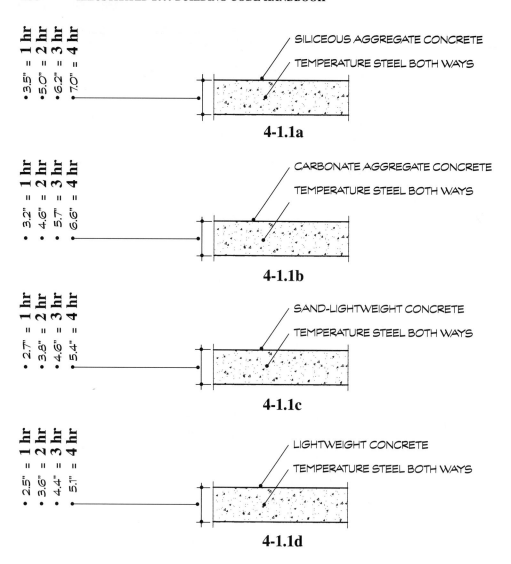

Fig. 719.1(2) 4A. Fire-resistance ratings for solid concrete walls and partitions. Minimum thickness of assembly is indicated as required for the fire-resistance rating shown. *[Source: IBC Table 719.1(2).]*

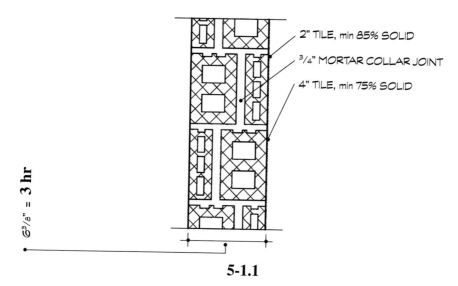

6³/₈" = 3 hr

2" TILE, min 85% SOLID

³/₄" MORTAR COLLAR JOINT

4" TILE, min 75% SOLID

5-1.1

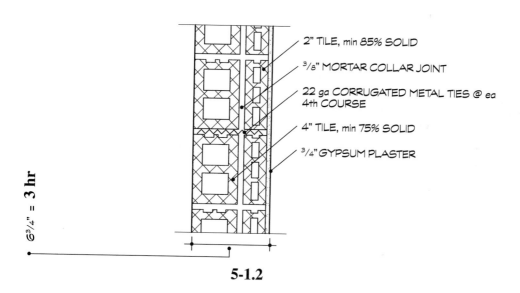

6³/₄" = 3 hr

2" TILE, min 85% SOLID

³/₈" MORTAR COLLAR JOINT

22 ga CORRUGATED METAL TIES @ ea 4th COURSE

4" TILE, min 75% SOLID

³/₄" GYPSUM PLASTER

5-1.2

Fig. 719.1(2) 5A. Fire-resistance ratings for glazed or unglazed nonload-bearing facing tile walls and partitions. Minimum thickness of assembly is indicated as required for the fire-resistance rating shown. *[Source: IBC Table 719.1(2).]*

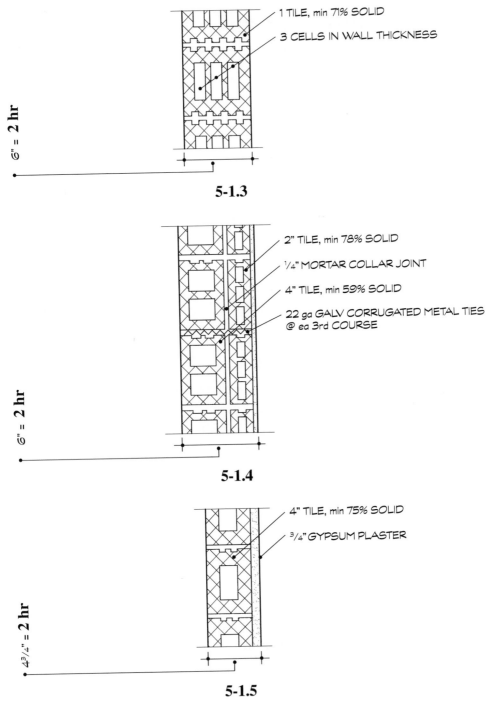

6" = 2 hr

1 TILE, min 71% SOLID

3 CELLS IN WALL THICKNESS

5-1.3

6" = 2 hr

2" TILE, min 78% SOLID

¼" MORTAR COLLAR JOINT

4" TILE, min 59% SOLID

22 ga GALV CORRUGATED METAL TIES @ ea 3rd COURSE

5-1.4

4³/₄" = 2 hr

4" TILE, min 75% SOLID

³/₄" GYPSUM PLASTER

5-1.5

Fig. 719.1(2) 5B. Fire-resistance ratings for glazed or unglazed nonload-bearing facing tile walls and partitions. Minimum thickness of assembly is indicated as required for the fire-resistance rating shown. *[Source: IBC Table 719.1(2).]*

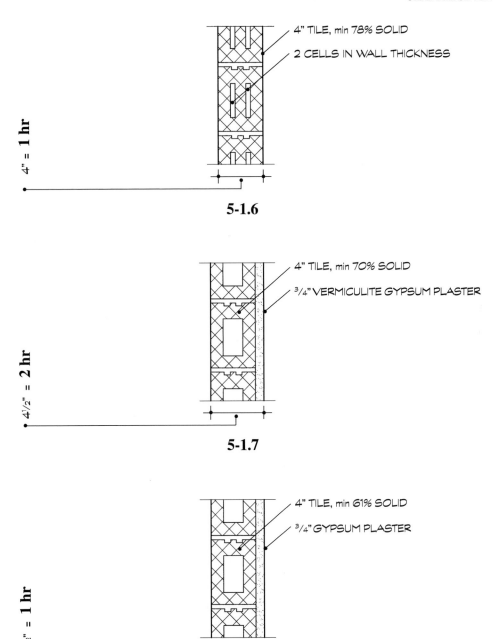

Fig. 719.1(2) 5C. Fire-resistance ratings for glazed or unglazed nonload-bearing facing tile walls and partitions. Minimum thickness of assembly is indicated as required for the fire-resistance rating shown. *[Source: IBC Table 719.1(2).]*

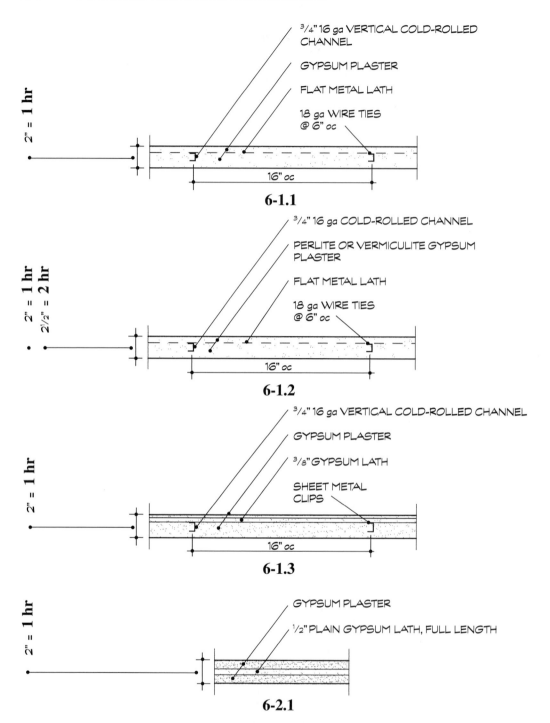

Fig. 719.1(2) 6A. Fire-resistance ratings for solid gypsum plaster nonload-bearing walls and partitions.
Minimum thickness of assembly is indicated as required for the fire-resistance rating shown. *[Source: IBC Table 719.1(2).]*

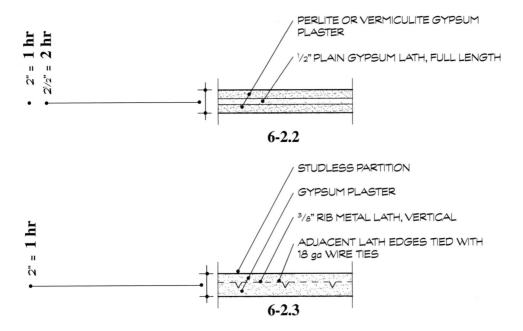

Fig. 719.1(2) 6B. Fire-resistance ratings for solid gypsum plaster nonload-bearing walls and partitions. Minimum thickness of assembly is indicated as required for the fire-resistance rating shown. *[Source: IBC Table 719.1(2).]*

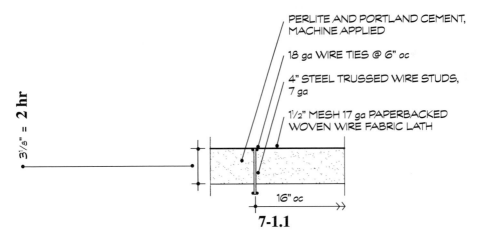

Fig. 719.1(2) 7A. Fire-resistance ratings for solid perlite and portland cement nonload-bearing walls and partitions. Minimum thickness of assembly is indicated as required for the fire-resistance rating shown. *[Source: IBC Table 719.1(2).]*

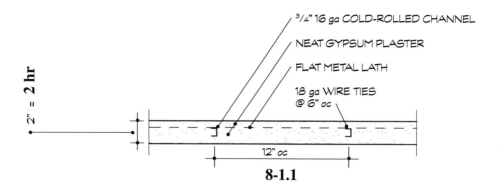

Fig. 719.1(2) 8A. Fire-resistance Ratings for Solid Neat Wood Fibered Gypsum Plaster Nonload-bearing Walls and Partitions. Minimum thickness of assembly is indicated as required for the fire-resistance rating shown. *[Source: IBC Table 719.1(2).]*

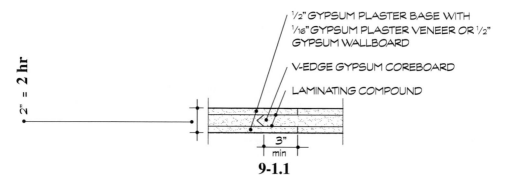

Fig. 719.1(2) 9A. Fire-resistance ratings for solid gypsum wallboard nonload-bearing walls and partitions. Minimum thickness of assembly is indicated as required for the fire-resistance rating shown. *[Source: IBC Table 719.1(2).]*

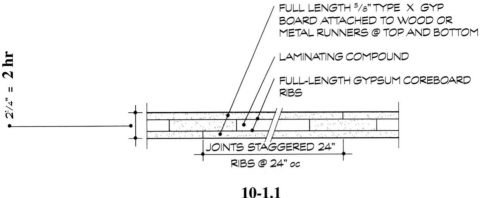

2¹/₄" = 2 hr

FULL LENGTH ⁵/₈" TYPE X GYP
BOARD ATTACHED TO WOOD OR
METAL RUNNERS @ TOP AND BOTTOM

LAMINATING COMPOUND

FULL-LENGTH GYPSUM COREBOARD
RIBS

JOINTS STAGGERED 24"

RIBS @ 24" oc

10-1.1

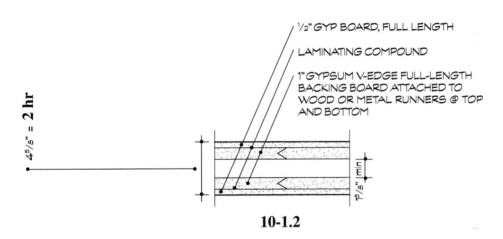

4⁵/₈" = 2 hr

¹/₂" GYP BOARD, FULL LENGTH

LAMINATING COMPOUND

1" GYPSUM V-EDGE FULL-LENGTH
BACKING BOARD ATTACHED TO
WOOD OR METAL RUNNERS @ TOP
AND BOTTOM

1⁵/₈" min

10-1.2

Fig. 719.1(2) 10A. Fire-resistance ratings for hollow (studless) gypsum wallboard nonload-bearing walls and partitions. Minimum thickness of assembly is indicated as required for the fire-resistance rating shown. *[Source: IBC Table 719.1(2).]*

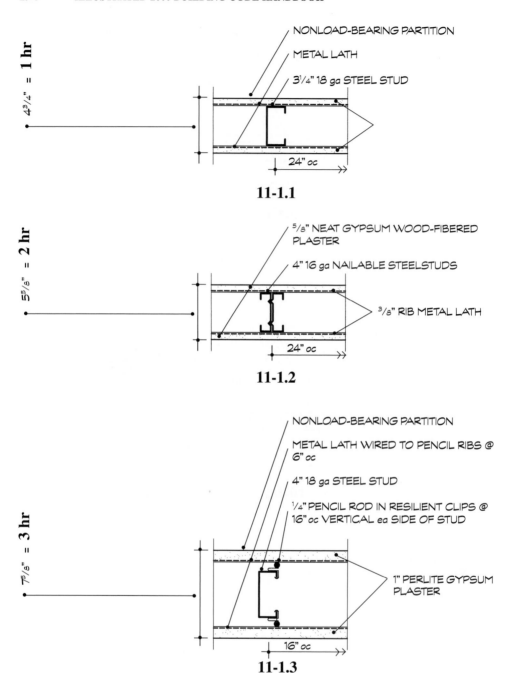

Fig. 719.1(2) 11A. Fire-resistance ratings for interior partitions with noncombustible studs and pluster.
Minimum thickness of assembly is indicated as required for the fire-resistance rating shown. *[Source: IBC Table 719.1(2).]*

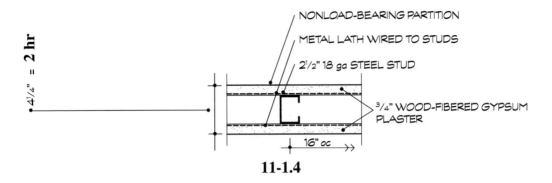

Fig. 719.1(2) - 11B. Fire-resistance Ratings for Interior Partitions with Noncombustible Studs and Pluster.. Minimum thickness of assembly is indicated as required for the fire-resistance rating shown. *[Source: IBC Table 719.1(2).]*

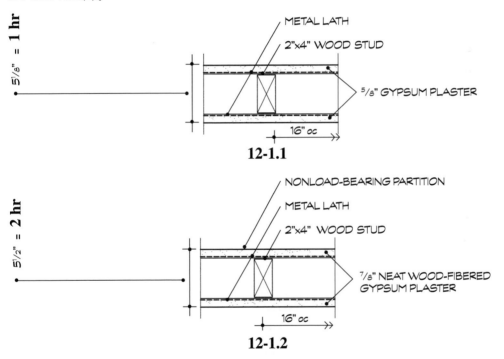

Fig. 719.1(2) 12A. Fire-resistance ratings for interior partitions with wood studs and pluster. Minimum thickness of assembly is indicated as required for the fire-resistance rating shown. *[Source: IBC Table 719.1(2).]*

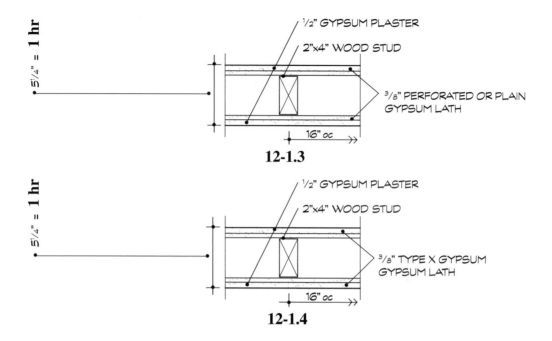

Fig. 719.1(2) 12B. Fire-resistance ratings for interior partitions with wood studs and pluster. Minimum thickness of assembly is indicated as required for the fire-resistance rating shown. *[Source: IBC Table 719.1(2).]*

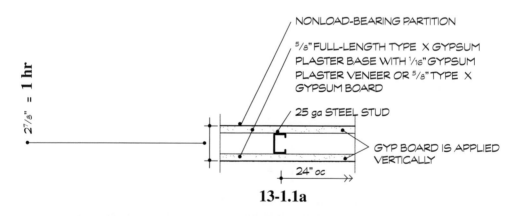

Fig. 719.1(2) 13A. Fire-resistance ratings for interior partitions with noncombustible studs and gypsum board. Minimum thickness of assembly is indicated as required for the fire-resistance rating shown. *[Source: IBC Table 719.1(2).]*

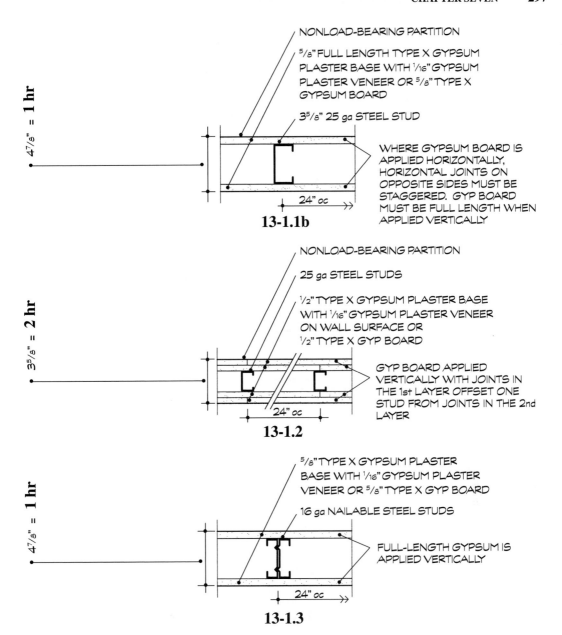

4⁷⁄₈" = 1 hr

NONLOAD-BEARING PARTITION

⁵⁄₈" FULL LENGTH TYPE X GYPSUM
PLASTER BASE WITH ¹⁄₁₆" GYPSUM
PLASTER VENEER OR ⁵⁄₈" TYPE X
GYPSUM BOARD

3⁵⁄₈" 25 ga STEEL STUD

WHERE GYPSUM BOARD IS
APPLIED HORIZONTALLY,
HORIZONTAL JOINTS ON
OPPOSITE SIDES MUST BE
STAGGERED. GYP BOARD
MUST BE FULL LENGTH WHEN
APPLIED VERTICALLY

24" oc

13-1.1b

3⁵⁄₈" = 2 hr

NONLOAD-BEARING PARTITION

25 ga STEEL STUDS

¹⁄₂" TYPE X GYPSUM PLASTER BASE
WITH ¹⁄₁₆" GYPSUM PLASTER VENEER
ON WALL SURFACE OR
¹⁄₂" TYPE X GYP BOARD

GYP BOARD APPLIED
VERTICALLY WITH JOINTS IN
THE 1st LAYER OFFSET ONE
STUD FROM JOINTS IN THE 2nd
LAYER

24" oc

13-1.2

4⁷⁄₈" = 1 hr

⁵⁄₈" TYPE X GYPSUM PLASTER
BASE WITH ¹⁄₁₆" GYPSUM PLASTER
VENEER OR ⁵⁄₈" TYPE X GYP BOARD

16 ga NAILABLE STEEL STUDS

FULL-LENGTH GYPSUM IS
APPLIED VERTICALLY

24" oc

13-1.3

Fig. 719.1(2) 13B. Fire-resistance ratings for interior partitions with noncombustible studs and gypsum board. Minimum thickness of assembly is indicated as required for the fire-resistance rating shown. *[Source: IBC Table 719.1(2).]*

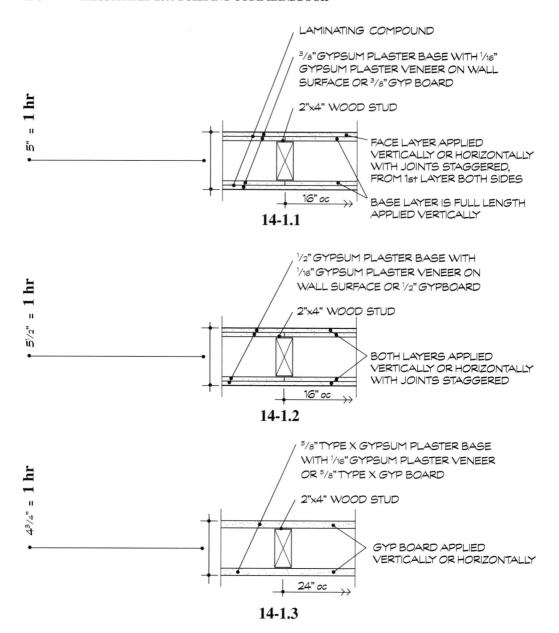

Fig. 719.1(2) 14A. Fire-resistance ratings for interior partitions with wood studs and gypsum board.
Minimum thickness of assembly is indicated as required for the fire-resistance rating shown. *[Source: IBC Table 719.1(2).]*

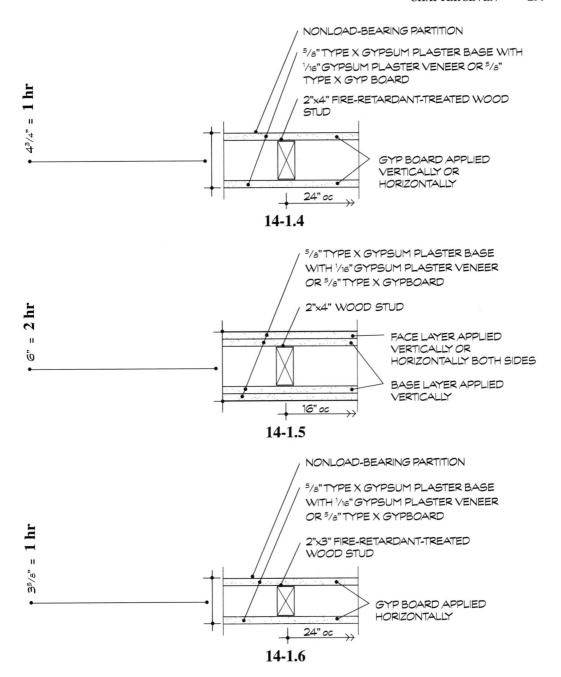

$4^3/4" = 1$ hr

NONLOAD-BEARING PARTITION

⁵/₈" TYPE X GYPSUM PLASTER BASE WITH
¹/₁₆" GYPSUM PLASTER VENEER OR ⁵/₈"
TYPE X GYP BOARD

2"x4" FIRE-RETARDANT-TREATED WOOD
STUD

GYP BOARD APPLIED
VERTICALLY OR
HORIZONTALLY

24" oc

14-1.4

$6" = 2$ hr

⁵/₈" TYPE X GYPSUM PLASTER BASE
WITH ¹/₁₆" GYPSUM PLASTER VENEER
OR ⁵/₈" TYPE X GYPBOARD

2"x4" WOOD STUD

FACE LAYER APPLIED
VERTICALLY OR
HORIZONTALLY BOTH SIDES

BASE LAYER APPLIED
VERTICALLY

16" oc

14-1.5

$3^5/8" = 1$ hr

NONLOAD-BEARING PARTITION

⁵/₈" TYPE X GYPSUM PLASTER BASE
WITH ¹/₁₆" GYPSUM PLASTER VENEER
OR ⁵/₈" TYPE X GYPBOARD

2"x3" FIRE-RETARDANT-TREATED
WOOD STUD

GYP BOARD APPLIED
HORIZONTALLY

24" oc

14-1.6

Fig. 719.1(2) 14B. Fire-resistance ratings for interior partitions with wood studs and gypsum board.
Minimum thickness of assembly is indicated as required for the fire-resistance rating shown. *[Source: IBC Table 719.1(2).]*

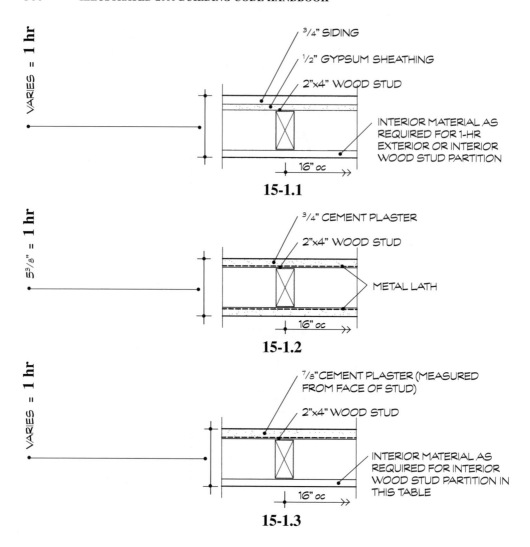

Fig. 719.1(2) 15A. Fire-resistance ratings for exterior or interior walls. Minimum thickness of assembly is indicated as required for the fire-resistance rating shown. *[Source: IBC Table 719.1(2).]*

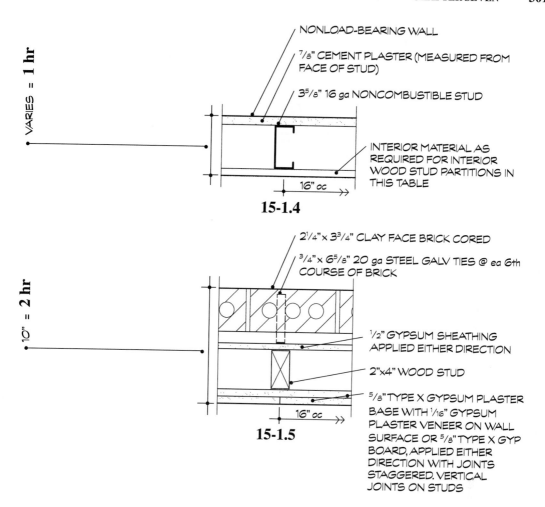

Fig. 719.1(2) 15B. Fire-resistance ratings for exterior or interior walls. Minimum thickness of assembly is indicated as required for the fire-resistance rating shown. *[Source: IBC Table 719.1(2).]*

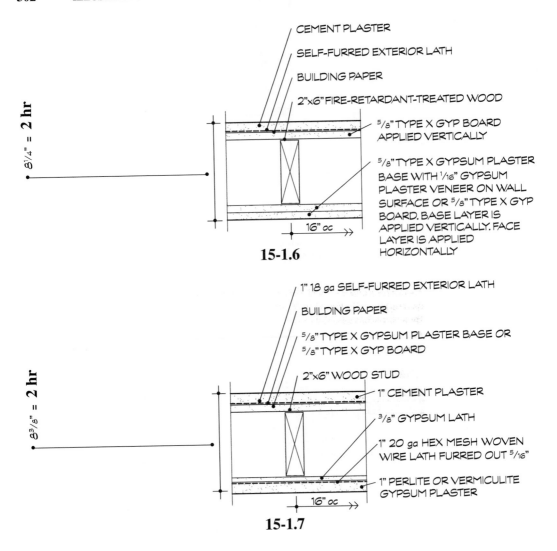

Fig. 719.1(2) 15C. Fire-resistance ratings for exterior or interior walls. Minimum thickness of assembly is indicated as required for the fire-resistance rating shown. *[Source: IBC Table 719.1(2).]*

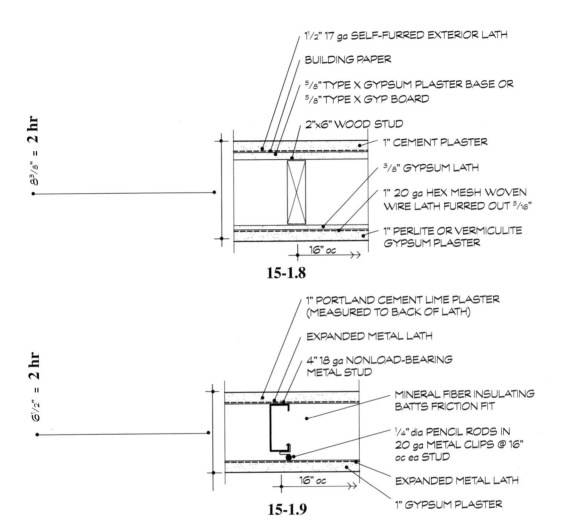

8³/₈" = 2 hr

1¹/₂" 17 ga SELF-FURRED EXTERIOR LATH

BUILDING PAPER

⁵/₈" TYPE X GYPSUM PLASTER BASE OR
⁵/₈" TYPE X GYP BOARD

2"x6" WOOD STUD

1" CEMENT PLASTER

³/₈" GYPSUM LATH

1" 20 ga HEX MESH WOVEN
WIRE LATH FURRED OUT ⁵/₁₆"

1" PERLITE OR VERMICULITE
GYPSUM PLASTER

16" oc

15-1.8

6¹/₂" = 2 hr

1" PORTLAND CEMENT LIME PLASTER
(MEASURED TO BACK OF LATH)

EXPANDED METAL LATH

4" 18 ga NONLOAD-BEARING
METAL STUD

MINERAL FIBER INSULATING
BATTS FRICTION FIT

¹/₄" dia PENCIL RODS IN
20 ga METAL CLIPS @ 16"
oc ea STUD

EXPANDED METAL LATH

16" oc

1" GYPSUM PLASTER

15-1.9

Fig. 719.1(2) 15D. Fire-resistance ratings for exterior or interior walls. Minimum thickness of assembly is indicated as required for the fire-resistance rating shown. *[Source: IBC Table 719.1(2).]*

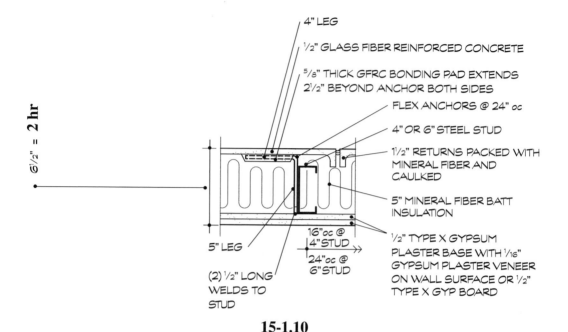

15-1.10

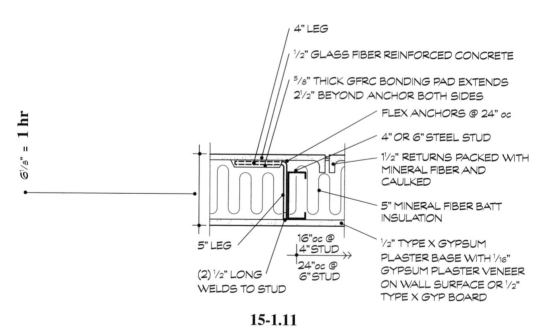

15-1.11

Fig. 719.1(2) 15E. Fire-resistance ratings for exterior or interior walls. Minimum thickness of assembly is indicated as required for the fire-resistance rating shown. *[Source: IBC Table 719.1(2).]*

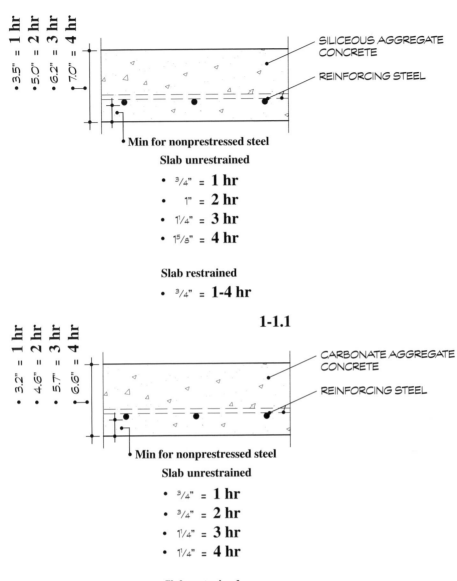

Fig. 719.1(3) 1–5A. Minimum protection for concrete floor and roof systems. Minimum thickness of assembly is indicated as required for the fire-resistance rating shown. *[Source: IBC Table 719.1(3).]*

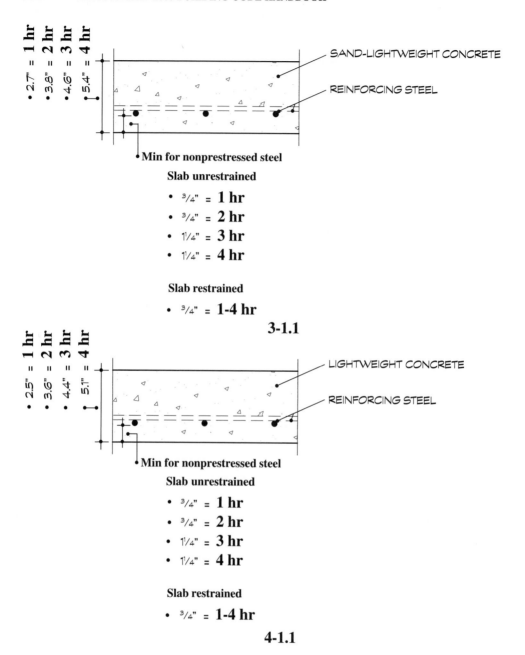

Fig. 719.1(3) 1–5B. Minimum protection for concrete floor and roof systems. Minimum thickness of assembly is indicated as required for the fire-resistance rating shown. *[Source: IBC Table 719.1(3).]*

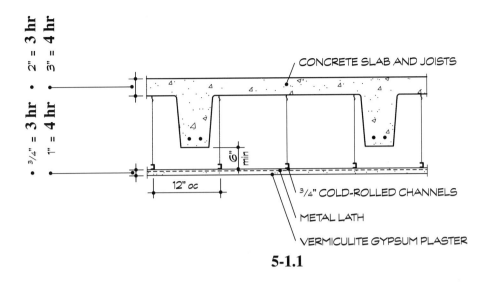

Fig. 719.1(3) 1–5C. Minimum protection for concrete floor and roof systems. Minimum thickness of assembly is indicated as required for the fire-resistance rating shown. *[Source: IBC Table 719.1(3).]*

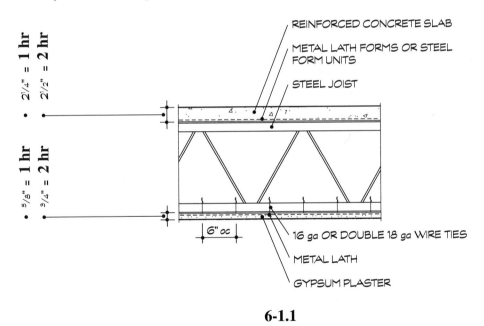

Fig. 719.1(3) 6–12A. Minimum protection for concrete and steel floor and roof systems. Minimum thickness of assembly is indicated as required for the fire-resistance rating shown. *[Source: IBC Table 719.1(3).]*

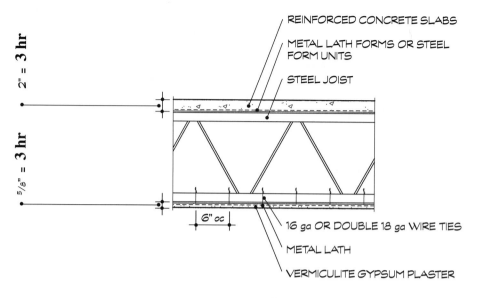

2" = 3 hr

5/8" = 3 hr

REINFORCED CONCRETE SLABS

METAL LATH FORMS OR STEEL FORM UNITS

STEEL JOIST

6" oc

16 ga OR DOUBLE 18 ga WIRE TIES

METAL LATH

VERMICULITE GYPSUM PLASTER

6-2.1

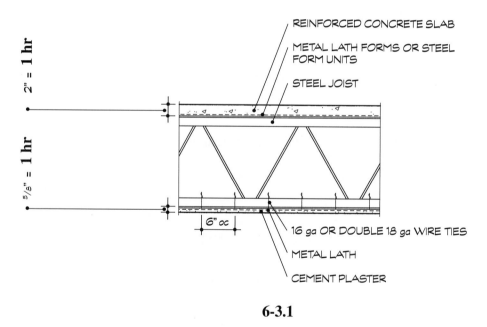

2" = 1 hr

5/8" = 1 hr

REINFORCED CONCRETE SLAB

METAL LATH FORMS OR STEEL FORM UNITS

STEEL JOIST

6" oc

16 ga OR DOUBLE 18 ga WIRE TIES

METAL LATH

CEMENT PLASTER

6-3.1

Fig. 719.1(3) 6–12B. Minimum protection for concrete and steel floor and roof systems. Minimum thickness of assembly is indicated as required for the fire-resistance rating shown. *[Source: IBC Table 719.1(3).]*

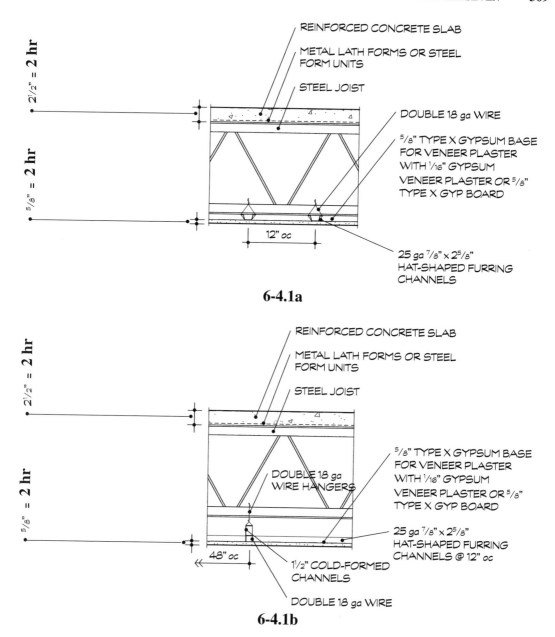

6-4.1a

6-4.1b

Fig. 719.1(3) 6–12C. Minimum protection for concrete and steel floor and roof systems. Minimum thickness of assembly is indicated as required for the fire-resistance rating shown. *[Source: IBC Table 719.1(3).]*

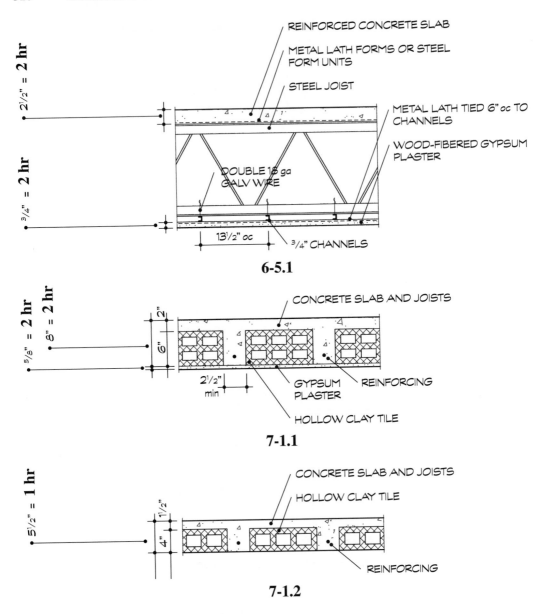

Fig. 719.1(3) 6–12D. Minimum protection for concrete and steel floor and roof systems. Minimum thickness of assembly is indicated as required for the fire-resistance rating shown. *[Source: IBC Table 719.1(3).]*

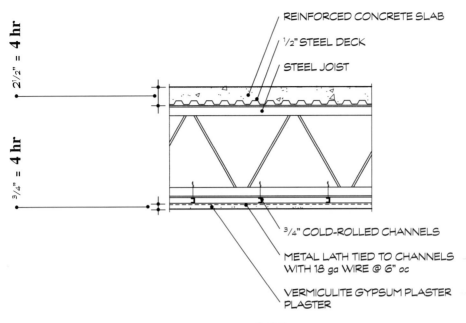

2½" = 4 hr

¾" = 4 hr

REINFORCED CONCRETE SLAB

½" STEEL DECK

STEEL JOIST

¾" COLD-ROLLED CHANNELS

METAL LATH TIED TO CHANNELS
WITH 18 ga WIRE @ 6" oc

VERMICULITE GYPSUM PLASTER
PLASTER

8-1.1

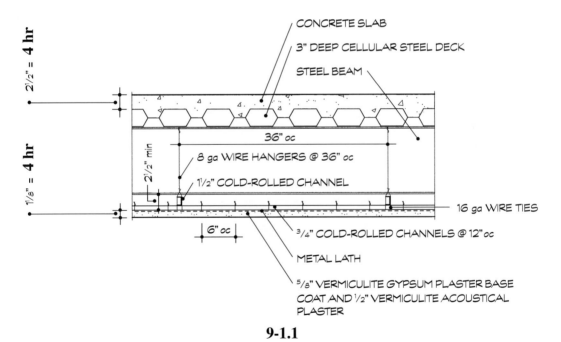

2½" = 4 hr

⅛" = 4 hr

CONCRETE SLAB

3" DEEP CELLULAR STEEL DECK

STEEL BEAM

36" oc

2½" min

8 ga WIRE HANGERS @ 36" oc

1½" COLD-ROLLED CHANNEL

16 ga WIRE TIES

6" oc

¾" COLD-ROLLED CHANNELS @ 12" oc

METAL LATH

⅝" VERMICULITE GYPSUM PLASTER BASE
COAT AND ½" VERMICULITE ACOUSTICAL
PLASTER

9-1.1

Fig. 719.1(3) 6–12E. Minimum protection for concrete and steel floor and roof systems. Minimum
thickness of assembly is indicated as required for the fire-resistance rating shown. *[Source: IBC Table 719.1(3).]*

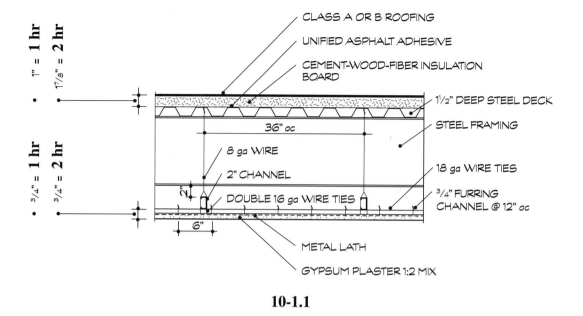

10-1.1

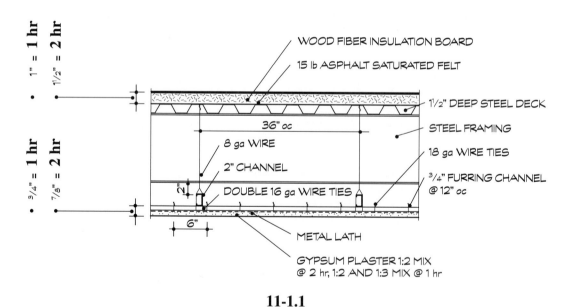

11-1.1

Fig. 719.1(3) 6–12F. Minimum protection for concrete and steel floor and roof systems. Minimum thickness of assembly is indicated as required for the fire-resistance rating shown. *[Source: IBC Table 719.1(3).]*

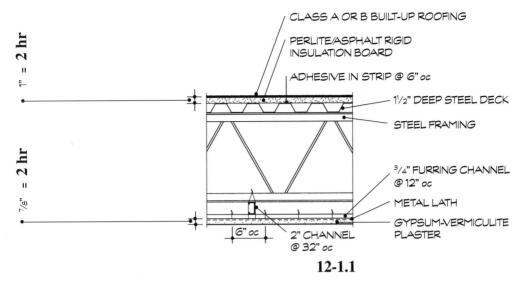

1" = 2 hr

7/8" = 2 hr

CLASS A OR B BUILT-UP ROOFING

PERLITE/ASPHALT RIGID INSULATION BOARD

ADHESIVE IN STRIP @ 6" oc

1½" DEEP STEEL DECK

STEEL FRAMING

¾" FURRING CHANNEL @ 12" oc

METAL LATH

GYPSUM-VERMICULITE PLASTER

6" oc   2" CHANNEL @ 32" oc

12-1.1

Fig. 719.1(3) 6–12G. Minimum protection for concrete and steel floor and roof systems. Minimum thickness of assembly is indicated as required for the fire-resistance rating shown. *[Source: IBC Table 719.1(3).]*

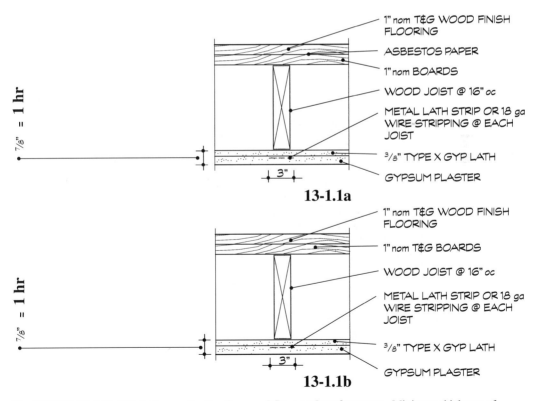

7/8" = 1 hr

1" nom T&G WOOD FINISH FLOORING

ASBESTOS PAPER

1" nom BOARDS

WOOD JOIST @ 16" oc

METAL LATH STRIP OR 18 ga WIRE STRIPPING @ EACH JOIST

⅜" TYPE X GYP LATH

GYPSUM PLASTER

3"

13-1.1a

7/8" = 1 hr

1" nom T&G WOOD FINISH FLOORING

1" nom T&G BOARDS

WOOD JOIST @ 16" oc

METAL LATH STRIP OR 18 ga WIRE STRIPPING @ EACH JOIST

⅜" TYPE X GYP LATH

GYPSUM PLASTER

3"

13-1.1b

Fig. 719.1(3) 13–14A. Minimum protection for wood floor and roof systems. Minimum thickness of assembly is indicated as required for the fire-resistance rating shown. *[Source: IBC Table 719.1(3).]*

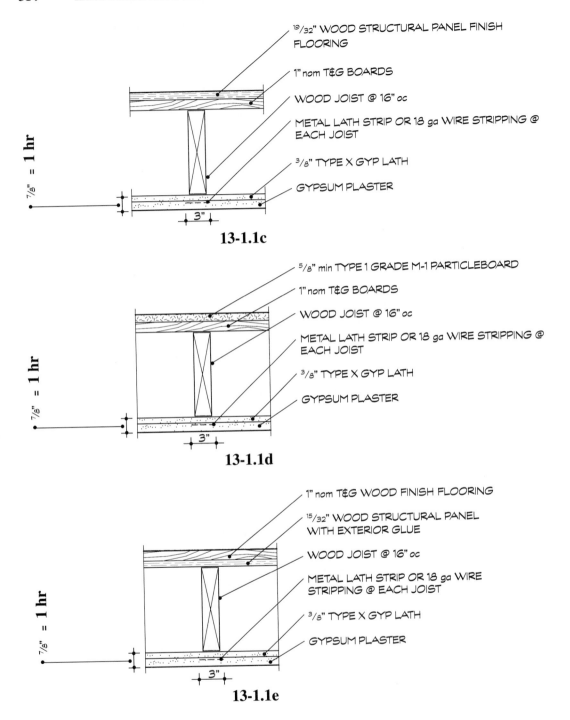

13-1.1c

13-1.1d

13-1.1e

Fig. 719.1(3) 13–14B. Minimum protection for wood floor and roof systems. Minimum thickness of assembly is indicated as required for the fire-resistance rating shown. *[Source: IBC Table 719.1(3).]*

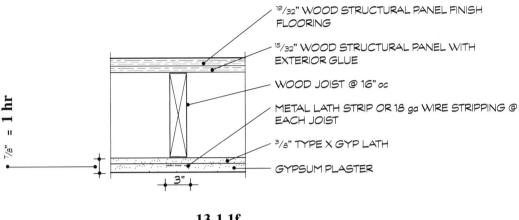

13-1.1f

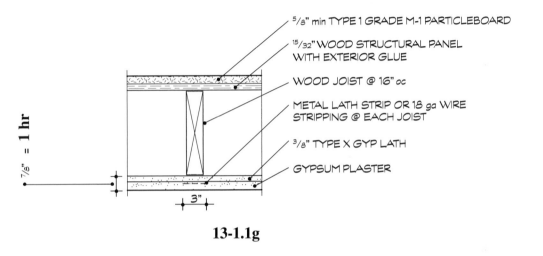

13-1.1g

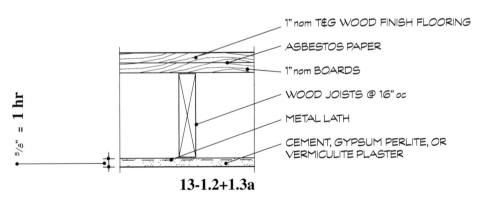

13-1.2+1.3a

Fig. 719.1(3) 13–14C. Minimum protection for wood floor and roof systems. Minimum thickness of assembly is indicated as required for the fire-resistance rating shown. *[Source: IBC Table 719.1(3).]*

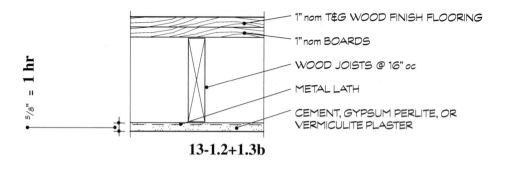

13-1.2+1.3b

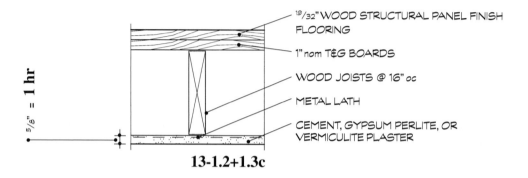

13-1.2+1.3c

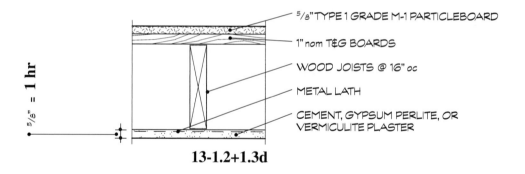

13-1.2+1.3d

Fig. 719.1(3) 13–14D. Minimum protection for wood floor and roof systems. Minimum thickness of assembly is indicated as required for the fire-resistance rating shown. *[Source: IBC Table 719.1(3).]*

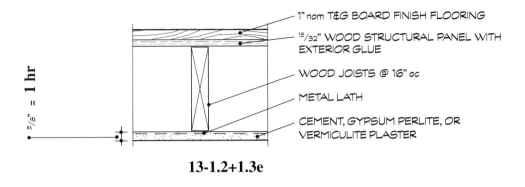

5/8" = 1 hr

1" nom T&G BOARD FINISH FLOORING

¹⁵/₃₂" WOOD STRUCTURAL PANEL WITH EXTERIOR GLUE

WOOD JOISTS @ 16" oc

METAL LATH

CEMENT, GYPSUM PERLITE, OR VERMICULITE PLASTER

13-1.2+1.3e

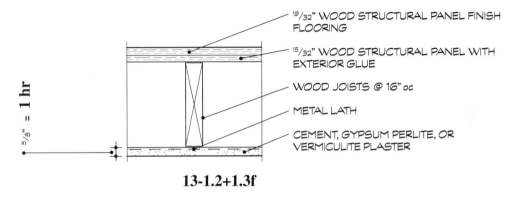

5/8" = 1 hr

¹⁹/₃₂" WOOD STRUCTURAL PANEL FINISH FLOORING

¹⁵/₃₂" WOOD STRUCTURAL PANEL WITH EXTERIOR GLUE

WOOD JOISTS @ 16" oc

METAL LATH

CEMENT, GYPSUM PERLITE, OR VERMICULITE PLASTER

13-1.2+1.3f

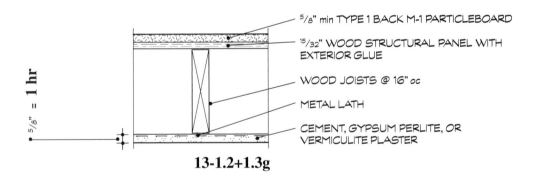

5/8" = 1 hr

⁵/₈" min TYPE 1 BACK M-1 PARTICLEBOARD

¹⁵/₃₂" WOOD STRUCTURAL PANEL WITH EXTERIOR GLUE

WOOD JOISTS @ 16" oc

METAL LATH

CEMENT, GYPSUM PERLITE, OR VERMICULITE PLASTER

13-1.2+1.3g

Fig. 719.1(3) 13–14E. Minimum protection for wood floor and roof systems. Minimum thickness of assembly is indicated as required for the fire-resistance rating shown. *[Source: IBC Table 719.1(3).]*

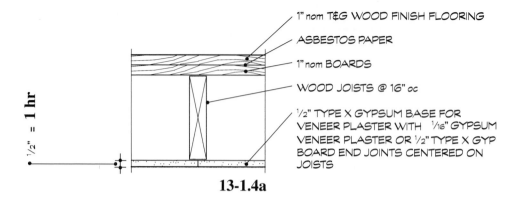

13-1.4a

$\frac{1}{2}" = 1 \text{ hr}$

- 1" nom T&G WOOD FINISH FLOORING
- ASBESTOS PAPER
- 1" nom BOARDS
- WOOD JOISTS @ 16" oc
- $\frac{1}{2}$" TYPE X GYPSUM BASE FOR VENEER PLASTER WITH $\frac{1}{16}$" GYPSUM VENEER PLASTER OR $\frac{1}{2}$" TYPE X GYP BOARD END JOINTS CENTERED ON JOISTS

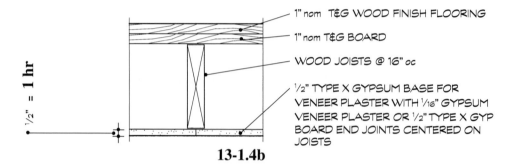

13-1.4b

$\frac{1}{2}" = 1 \text{ hr}$

- 1" nom T&G WOOD FINISH FLOORING
- 1" nom T&G BOARD
- WOOD JOISTS @ 16" oc
- $\frac{1}{2}$" TYPE X GYPSUM BASE FOR VENEER PLASTER WITH $\frac{1}{16}$" GYPSUM VENEER PLASTER OR $\frac{1}{2}$" TYPE X GYP BOARD END JOINTS CENTERED ON JOISTS

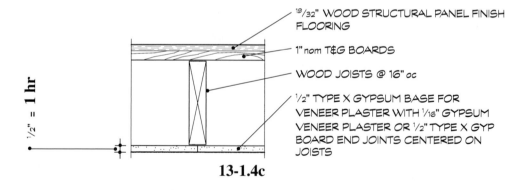

13-1.4c

$\frac{1}{2}" = 1 \text{ hr}$

- $\frac{19}{32}$" WOOD STRUCTURAL PANEL FINISH FLOORING
- 1" nom T&G BOARDS
- WOOD JOISTS @ 16" oc
- $\frac{1}{2}$" TYPE X GYPSUM BASE FOR VENEER PLASTER WITH $\frac{1}{16}$" GYPSUM VENEER PLASTER OR $\frac{1}{2}$" TYPE X GYP BOARD END JOINTS CENTERED ON JOISTS

Fig. 719.1(3) 13–14F. Minimum protection for wood floor and roof systems. Minimum thickness of assembly is indicated as required for the fire-resistance rating shown. *[Source: IBC Table 719.1(3).]*

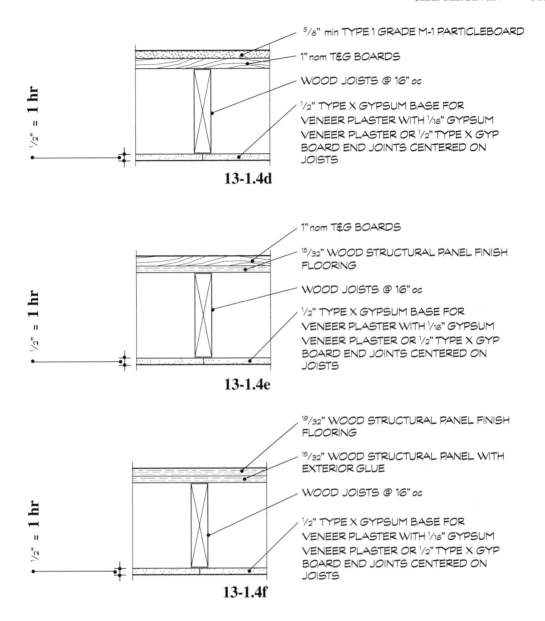

13-1.4d

⅝" min TYPE 1 GRADE M-1 PARTICLEBOARD

1" nom T&G BOARDS

WOOD JOISTS @ 16" oc

½" TYPE X GYPSUM BASE FOR VENEER PLASTER WITH ¹⁄₁₆" GYPSUM VENEER PLASTER OR ½" TYPE X GYP BOARD END JOINTS CENTERED ON JOISTS

½" = 1 hr

13-1.4e

1" nom T&G BOARDS

¹⁵⁄₃₂" WOOD STRUCTURAL PANEL FINISH FLOORING

WOOD JOISTS @ 16" oc

½" TYPE X GYPSUM BASE FOR VENEER PLASTER WITH ¹⁄₁₆" GYPSUM VENEER PLASTER OR ½" TYPE X GYP BOARD END JOINTS CENTERED ON JOISTS

½" = 1 hr

13-1.4f

¹⁹⁄₃₂" WOOD STRUCTURAL PANEL FINISH FLOORING

¹⁵⁄₃₂" WOOD STRUCTURAL PANEL WITH EXTERIOR GLUE

WOOD JOISTS @ 16" oc

½" TYPE X GYPSUM BASE FOR VENEER PLASTER WITH ¹⁄₁₆" GYPSUM VENEER PLASTER OR ½" TYPE X GYP BOARD END JOINTS CENTERED ON JOISTS

½" = 1 hr

Fig. 719.1(3) 13–14G. Minimum protection for wood floor and roof systems. Minimum thickness of assembly is indicated as required for the fire-resistance rating shown. *[Source: IBC Table 719.1(3).]*

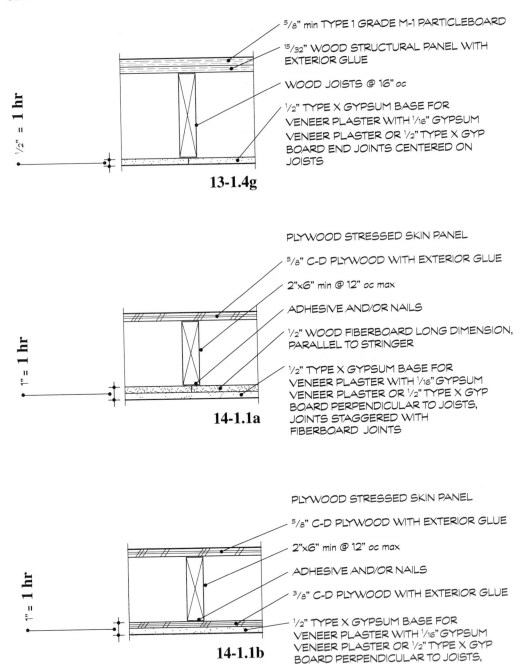

5/8" min TYPE 1 GRADE M-1 PARTICLEBOARD

15/32" WOOD STRUCTURAL PANEL WITH EXTERIOR GLUE

WOOD JOISTS @ 16" oc

1/2" TYPE X GYPSUM BASE FOR VENEER PLASTER WITH 1/16" GYPSUM VENEER PLASTER OR 1/2" TYPE X GYP BOARD END JOINTS CENTERED ON JOISTS

1/2" = 1 hr

13-1.4g

PLYWOOD STRESSED SKIN PANEL

5/8" C-D PLYWOOD WITH EXTERIOR GLUE

2"x6" min @ 12" oc max

ADHESIVE AND/OR NAILS

1/2" WOOD FIBERBOARD LONG DIMENSION, PARALLEL TO STRINGER

1/2" TYPE X GYPSUM BASE FOR VENEER PLASTER WITH 1/16" GYPSUM VENEER PLASTER OR 1/2" TYPE X GYP BOARD PERPENDICULAR TO JOISTS, JOINTS STAGGERED WITH FIBERBOARD JOINTS

1" = 1 hr

14-1.1a

PLYWOOD STRESSED SKIN PANEL

5/8" C-D PLYWOOD WITH EXTERIOR GLUE

2"x6" min @ 12" oc max

ADHESIVE AND/OR NAILS

3/8" C-D PLYWOOD WITH EXTERIOR GLUE

1/2" TYPE X GYPSUM BASE FOR VENEER PLASTER WITH 1/16" GYPSUM VENEER PLASTER OR 1/2" TYPE X GYP BOARD PERPENDICULAR TO JOISTS,

1" = 1 hr

14-1.1b

Fig. 719.1(3) 13–14H. Minimum protection for wood floor and roof systems. Minimum thickness of assembly is indicated as required for the fire-resistance rating shown. *[Source: IBC Table 719.1(3).]*

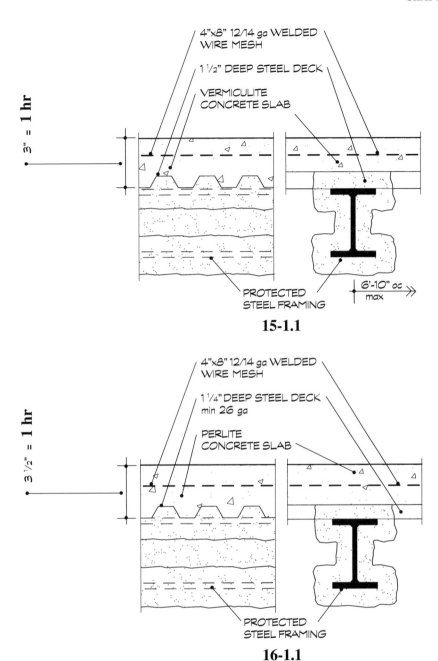

3" = 1 hr

4"x8" 12/14 ga WELDED WIRE MESH

1 ½" DEEP STEEL DECK

VERMICULITE CONCRETE SLAB

PROTECTED STEEL FRAMING

6'-10" oc max

15-1.1

3 ½" = 1 hr

4"x8" 12/14 ga WELDED WIRE MESH

1 ¼" DEEP STEEL DECK min 26 ga

PERLITE CONCRETE SLAB

PROTECTED STEEL FRAMING

16-1.1

Fig. 719.1(3) 15–20A. Minimum protection for concrete and steel floor and roof systems. Minimum thickness of assembly is indicated as required for the fire-resistance rating shown. *[Source: IBC Table 719.1(3).]*

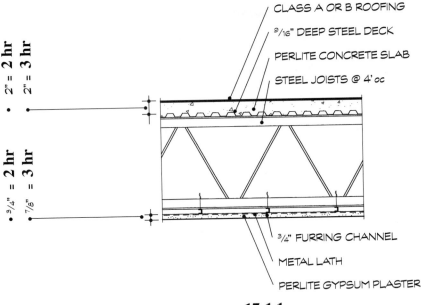

2″ = 2 hr
2″ = 3 hr

¾″ = 2 hr
⅞″ = 3 hr

- CLASS A OR B ROOFING
- ⁹/₁₆″ DEEP STEEL DECK
- PERLITE CONCRETE SLAB
- STEEL JOISTS @ 4′ oc

- ¾″ FURRING CHANNEL
- METAL LATH
- PERLITE GYPSUM PLASTER

17-1.1

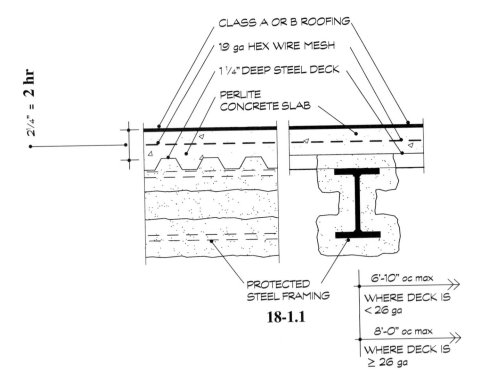

2¼″ = 2 hr

- CLASS A OR B ROOFING
- 19 ga HEX WIRE MESH
- 1¼″ DEEP STEEL DECK
- PERLITE CONCRETE SLAB

PROTECTED
STEEL FRAMING

18-1.1

6′-10″ oc max
WHERE DECK IS
< 26 ga

8′-0″ oc max
WHERE DECK IS
≥ 26 ga

Fig. 719.1(3) 15–20B. Minimum protection for concrete and steel floor and roof systems. Minimum thickness of assembly is indicated as required for the fire-resistance rating shown. *[Source: IBC Table 719.1(3).]*

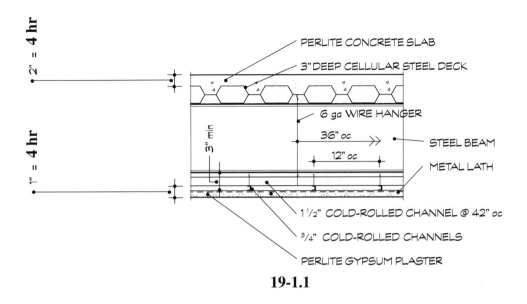

2" = 4 hr

1" = 4 hr

PERLITE CONCRETE SLAB

3" DEEP CELLULAR STEEL DECK

6 ga WIRE HANGER

36" oc

12" oc

STEEL BEAM

METAL LATH

3" min

1 1/2" COLD-ROLLED CHANNEL @ 42" oc

3/4" COLD-ROLLED CHANNELS

PERLITE GYPSUM PLASTER

19-1.1

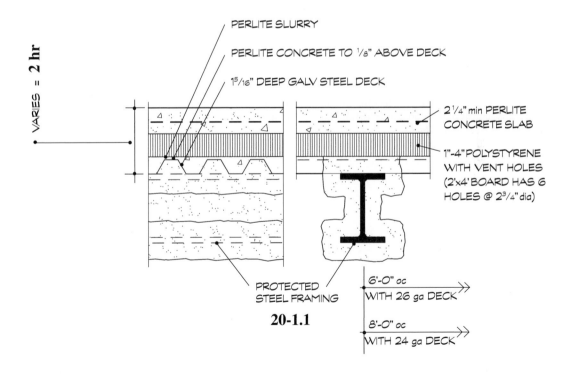

VARIES = 2 hr

PERLITE SLURRY

PERLITE CONCRETE TO 1/8" ABOVE DECK

1 5/16" DEEP GALV STEEL DECK

2 1/4" min PERLITE CONCRETE SLAB

1"-4" POLYSTYRENE WITH VENT HOLES (2'x4' BOARD HAS 6 HOLES @ 2 3/4" dia)

PROTECTED STEEL FRAMING

20-1.1

6'-0" oc WITH 26 ga DECK

8'-0" oc WITH 24 ga DECK

Fig. 719.1(3) 15–20C. Minimum protection for concrete and steel floor and roof systems. Minimum thickness of assembly is indicated as required for the fire-resistance rating shown.[*Source: IBC Table 719.1(3).]*

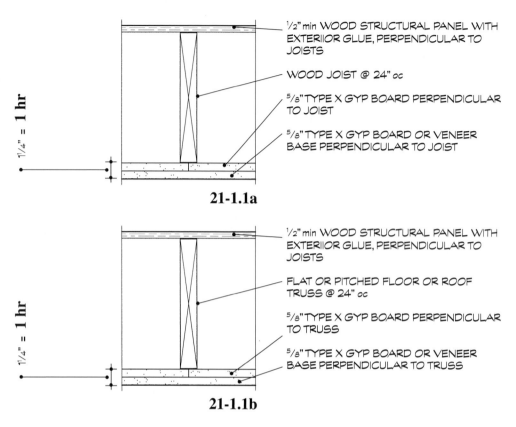

21-1.1a

21-1.1b

Fig. 719.1(3) 21A. Minimum protection for wood truss floor and roof systems. Minimum thickness of assembly is indicated as required for the fire-resistance rating shown. *[Source: IBC Table 719.1(3).]*

719 Prescriptive Fire Resistance

719.1.3 Reinforcement for cast-in-place concrete column protection

- Cast-in-place concrete protection for steel columns requires the following or equivalent:
  - Wire ties as follows:
    To have a diameter ≥ 0.18".
    To be located a the edges of the column.
    To be wound around the column in a spiral path with a pitch ≤ 8".

719.1.4 Plaster application

- A finish coat of a protective plaster cover is not required in the following case:
  - Where the following meet the requirements of details provided in this section:
    Plaster design mix.
    Total plaster thickness indicated.

  Note: The following tables are cited as listing minimum requirements:
  IBC Table 719.1(1), "Minimum Protection of Structural Parts Based on Time
  Periods for Various Noncombustible Insulating Materials."
  IBC Table 719.1(2), "Rated Fire-Resistance Periods for Various Walls and
  Partitions."
  IBC Table 719.1(3), "Minimum Protection for Floor and Roof Systems."

719.1.5 Bonded prestressed concrete tendons

- The concrete cover for prestressed tendons must be as required by details provided in this section as follows:
  - Where there are single tendons.
    Cover is measured from the nearest surface.
- Multiple tendons with different concrete covers are governed for fire protection as follows:
  - The average cover must be ≥ that required by details provided in this section as follows:
    The average cover is based the following:
      The clear distance from each tendon to the nearest surface.
    The cover for any tendon may not be less than the following:
      That specified by details provided in this section.
    Required cover for slabs with any type aggregate is ≥ ¾".
    Required cover for beams with any type aggregate is ≥ ¾".
    Tendons with cover less than required are governed as follows:
      They must provide ≤ 50% of the ultimate moment capacity in the following case:
        Where members have a cross-sectional area < 350 sq in.
      They must provide ≤ 65% of the ultimate moment capacity in the following case:
        Where members have a cross-sectional area ≥ 350 sq in.
    The following assumption is made regarding reduced cover permitted for fire protection:
      Structural integrity is not affected.

  Note: IBC Table 719.1(1), "Minimum Protection of Structural Parts Based on Time
  Periods for Various Noncombustible Insulating Materials," is cited as
  governing the above requirements.

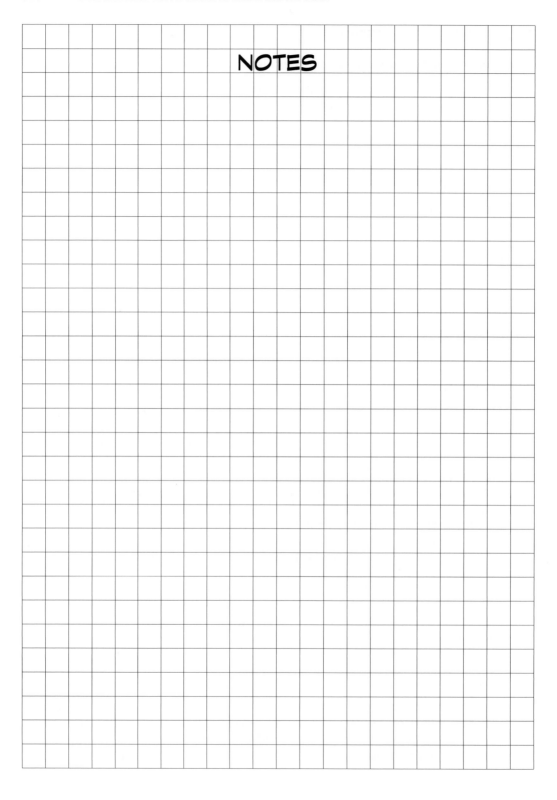

NOTES

8

Interior Finishes

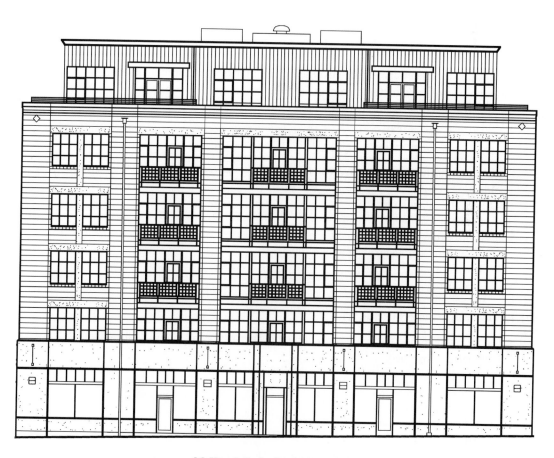

McKenzie Lofts. Portland, Oregon.
Ankrom Moisan Associated Architects. Portland, Oregon.

801 General

801.1 Scope

- This chapter governs materials used for the following:
  - Interior finishes.
  - Interior trim.
  - Interior decorative materials.

801.1.1 Interior finishes

- The following standards required by this chapter do not apply to the materials listed below:
  - Standards not applicable to materials below:
    Flame spread index.
    Smoke-developed index.
  - Materials with the following characteristics are not governed by the standards listed above:
    With a thickness < 0.036".
    Applied directly to the following surfaces:
    Walls.
    Ceilings.
- The following materials are not governed by interior finish requirements:
  - Exposed parts of structural members as follows:
    Those meeting requirements of Type IV construction.

    Note: 602.4, "Type IV," is cited as defining the pertinent requirements of Type IV construction.

- Other interior materials are governed by the following standards based on the criteria listed below:
  - Applicable standards:
    Flame spread index.
    Smoke-developed index.
  - Criteria affecting indexes of above standards:
    Location.
    Occupancy.

801.1.2 Decorative materials and trim

- The following properties are governed by this chapter for the materials listed below:
  - Properties governed:
    Combustibility.
    Flame resistance.
  - Materials governed:
    Decorative materials.
    Trim.

  Note: Section 805, "Decorations and Trim," is cited as governing these materials.

801 General

801.1.3 Applicability

- This subsection addresses the following materials in a flood hazard area:
  - Interior finishes.
  - Trim.
  - Decorative materials.

  > *Note: 1612.3, "Establishment of flood hazard areas," is cited as the source of guidelines*
  > *for establishing such an area.*
  > *1612.2, "Definitions," defines a flood hazard area as the greater of the following:*
  > *Area in a floodplain with a chance of flooding ≥ 1% each year.*
  > *One of the following areas:*
  > *Area designated as a flood hazard on the flood hazard map of the community.*
  > *Area otherwise legally designated as a flood hazard.*

- Where such materials are below the design flood elevation, they must be resistant to flood damage as follows:
  - They must be able to withstand lengthy contact with floodwaters.
  - They must not sustain damage from floodwaters requiring more than cosmetic repair.

801.2 Application

- Combustible materials may be used as a finish for the following interior surfaces:
  - Walls.
  - Ceilings.
  - Floors.
  - Other interior surfaces.

801.2.1 Windows

- 1st story show windows may be of the following materials:
  - Wood.
  - Unprotected metal framing.

801.2.2 Foam plastics

- Where foam plastics are used as interior finish or trim, they must comply with large-scale tests and other standards and property limitations.

  > *Note: 2603.7, "Special approval," and Section 2604, "Interior Finish and Trim," are cited*
  > *as the applicable sources of requirements for foam plastics.*

802 Definitions

802.1 General *(part 1 of 2)*

- **Expanded vinyl wall covering**
  - Woven textile backing.
  - Expanded vinyl base coat layer:
    A homogeneous vinyl layer.
    Contains a blowing agent:
      Agent decomposes during processing, causing the layer to expand:
        Closed cells are formed in this process.
  - Nonexpanded vinyl skin coat.
  - Total thickness is ≥ 0.055"(±) , ≤ 0.070"(±).

- **Flame resistance**
  - The ability of a material or combination thereof to resist the spread of flame.

    Note: NFPA 701, "Methods of Fire Test for Flame-Resistant Textiles and Films," is cited as the measure of this ability.

- **Flame spread**
  - The expansion of flame over a surface.

- **Flame spread index**
  - A number signifying relative speed of the spread of flame on a surface determined by testing.

    Note: ASTM E 84, "Standard Test Methods for Surface Burning Characteristics of Building Materials," is cited as the governing test.

- **Interior finish**
  - Interior wall finish.
  - Interior ceiling finish.
  - Interior floor finish.

- **Interior floor finish**
  - Exposed floor surfaces.
  - Coverings applied over the following:
    A finished floor.
    Stair treads.
    Stair risers.
    Stair landings.

802 Definitions

802.1 General *(part 2 of 2)*

- **Interior wall and ceiling finish**
  - Interior exposed surfaces of a building including but not limited to the following:
    Walls:
      Fixed.
      Mobile.
    Partitions:
      Fixed.
      Mobile.
    Columns.
    Ceilings.
    Wainscoting.
    Paneling.
    Other finish applied structurally.
    Other finish applied decoratively.
    Acoustical materials.
    Surface insulation.
    Structural fire resistance or similar function.
  - Trim is not included.

- **Smoke-developed index**
  - A number signifying relative speed of the propagation of smoke determined by testing.

    Note: ASTM E 84, "Standard Test Methods for Surface Burning Characteristics of Building Materials," is cited as the governing test.

- **Trim**
  - The following components used in fixed applications:
    Picture molding.
    Chair rails.
    Baseboards.
    Handrails.
    Door frames.
    Window frames.
    Similar decorative materials.
    Similar protective materials.

803 Wall and Ceiling Finishes

803.1 General

- The following interior finishes are classified as indicated below:
  - Interior finishes to be classified:
    Wall finishes.
    Ceiling finishes.
  - Classifications of interior finishes:

Class	Flame spread index	Smoke-developed index
A	0 – 25	0 – 450
B	26 – 75	0 – 450
C	76 – 200	0 – 450

803.2 Stability

- Interior finish materials governed by this chapter must comply with the following:
  - They must remain securely attached under the conditions:
    In room temperatures $\leq 200°F$.
    For a time of 30 minutes minimum.

803.3.1 Direct attachment and furred construction

- This subsection governs the following elements requiring either property listed below:
  - Elements:
    Walls.
    Ceilings.
  - Properties required by other sections of the code:
    A fire-resistance rating.
    To be noncombustible.
- Interior finish materials applied to the elements governed by this subjection must comply with one of the following:
  - It must be applied directly against the element.
  - It must be applied to furring strips as follows:
    The furring strips must be $\leq 1\frac{3}{4}$" thick.
    The furring strips must be applied directly to the element.
- Spaces between furring strips must be detailed in one of the following ways:
  - Spaces must be filled with one of the following materials:
    Inorganic.
    Class A.
  - Spaces must be fireblocked so as to isolate air space $\leq 8'$ in length in any direction.

    Note: Section 716, "Concealed Spaces," is cited as the source of requirements for fireblocking.

803 Wall and Ceiling Finishes

803.3.2 Set-out construction

- This subsection governs the following interior building elements where they require one of the properties listed below:
  - Building elements:
    Walls where the finished surface is set out from the wall structure > 1¾".
    Ceilings that are dropped >1¾" from the ceiling structure.
  - Properties required by other sections of the code:
    A fire-resistance rating.
    To be noncombustible.
- Walls and ceilings governed by this section require one of the following:
  - Class A finish materials.
  - Finish materials protected on both sides by sprinklers.
  - Finish materials with all of the following characteristics:
    Attached to noncombustible backing or furring strips.
    Any air space behind finish materials is detailed in one of the following ways:
      Filled with inorganic materials.
      Filled with Class A materials.
      Fireblocked so as to isolate air space ≤ 8' in length in any direction.
- In dropped ceilings the following components are governed as indicated below:
  - Components below the main ceiling line:
    Hangers.
    Assembly members.
  - The components below the main ceiling line must be one of the following:
    Noncombustible materials.
    Fire-retardant treated wood in the following types of construction only:
      Type III.
      Type V.
- Set-out wall construction must be fire-resistance-rated as per other code requirements.

803.3.3 Heavy timber construction

- The following wall and ceiling finishes must be fireblocked as indicated below:
  - Finishes applied in Type IV construction as follows:
    Directly to wood decking or planking.
    To furring strips that are applied directly to wood decking or planking.
  - Any airspace behind the finishes must be detailed in one of the following ways:
    Fill with inorganic material.
    Fill with Class A material.
    Fireblock so as to isolate airspace in ≤ 8' in length in any direction.

803 Wall and Ceiling Finishes

803.3.4 Materials

- This subsection applies to materials ≤ ¼" thick used as follows:
    - Used as interior wall finish.
    - Used as interior ceiling finish.
- The following materials are not required to be applied directly to a noncombustible backing:
    - Class A materials.
    - Materials successfully tested while set out from the noncombustible backing.
- All other materials must be applied directly to a noncombustible backing.

803.4 Interior finish requirements based on group *(part 1 of 5)**

- This subsection dictates the minimum flame-spread class of finish materials required for interior walls and ceilings.
- This subsection does not restrict the flame-spread class for materials in occupancy U.
- Sprinklers cited in this section must comply with NFPA 13 or NFPA 13R.
- Vertical exits and passageways require the following flame-spread class:
    - ≥ Class C finish materials are required for the following conditions:
        Materials are ≤ 1000 sf of surface area of wainscot or paneling.
        Materials are used in the grade-level lobby.
        Materials are applied to one of the following:
            Directly to a noncombustible base.
            To furring on a noncombustible base and fireblocked by one of the following methods:
                Airspace filled with inorganic materials.
                Airspace filled with Class A materials.
                Airspace fireblocked so as to isolate air spaces ≤ 8' in length in any direction.
    - Flame-spread class for other conditions are listed with occupancy designations subsequently in this subsection.
- Vertical exits in other than occupancy I-3 require materials with the following flame spreads:
    - ≥ Class C in buildings ≤ 3 stories in sprinklered buildings.
    - ≥ Class B in buildings ≤ 3 stories in buildings not sprinklered.
    - Flame-spread class for other buildings are reported with occupancy designations subsequently listed in this subsection.
- Rooms and enclosed spaces are defined by partitions that run from the floor to the ceiling in the following case:
    Where the structure requires a fire-resistance rating.

    Note: In these cases, a room or enclosed space does not terminate at any partition that does not reach the ceiling, but continues into the adjacent area to a point where a partition reaches the ceiling. Where more than one occupancies occupy such a room or enclosed space, the most restrictive governs flame-spread class.

*Source: IBC Table 803.4.

803 Wall and Ceiling Finishes

803.4 Interior finish requirements based on group *(part 2 of 5)**

Occupancies A-1 and A-2

- Vertical exits and passageways:
  - ≥ Class B finish materials are required where spaces are sprinklered.
  - ≥ Class A finish materials are required where spaces are not sprinklered.
- Exit access corridors and other exitways:
  - ≥ Class B finish materials are required where spaces are sprinklered.
  - Where spaces are not sprinklered:
    - ≥ Class B finish materials are required in lobbies.
    - ≥ Class A finish materials are required in other spaces.
- Rooms and enclosed spaces:
  - ≥ Class C finish materials are required where spaces are sprinklered.
  - Where spaces are not sprinklered:
    - ≥ Class C finish materials are required for occupancy loads ≤ 300.
    - ≥ Class B finish materials are required for occupancy loads > 300.

Occupancies A-3, A-4, and A-5

- The following applies to occupancy A-3:
  - In places of worship, wood may be used for the following:
    - Ornamental purposes.
    - Trusses.
    - Paneling.
    - Chancel furnishing.
  - Other spaces and buildings in A-3 are governed by other requirements of this subsection.
- Vertical exits and passageways:
  - ≥ Class B finish materials are required where spaces are sprinklered.
  - ≥ Class A finish materials are required where spaces are not sprinklered.
- Exit access corridors and other exitways:
  - ≥ Class B finish materials are required where spaces are sprinklered.
  - Where spaces are not sprinklered:
    - ≥ Class B finish materials are required in lobbies.
    - ≥ Class A finish materials are required in other spaces.
- Rooms and enclosed spaces:
  - ≥ Class C finish materials are required.

Source: IBC Table 803.4.

803 Wall and Ceiling Finishes

803.4 Interior finish requirements based on group *(part 3 of 5)**

Occupancies B, E, M, R-1, and R-4

- Vertical exits and passageways:
  - ≥ Class B finish materials are required where spaces are sprinklered.
  - ≥ Class A finish materials are required where spaces are not sprinklered.
- Exit access corridors and other exitways:
  - ≥ Class C finish materials are required where spaces are sprinklered.
  - ≥ Class B finish materials are required where spaces are not sprinklered.
- Rooms and enclosed spaces:
  - ≥ Class C finish materials are required.

Occupancy F

- Vertical exits and passageways:
  - ≥ Class C finish materials are required where spaces are sprinklered.
  - ≥ Class B finish materials are required where spaces are not sprinklered.
- Exit access corridors and other exitways:
  - ≥ Class C finish materials are required.
- Rooms and enclosed spaces:
  - ≥ Class C finish materials are required.

Occupancy H

- Vertical exits and passageways:
  - ≥ Class B finish materials are required where spaces are sprinklered.
  - ≥ Class A finish materials are required where spaces are not sprinklered.
- Exit access corridors and other exitways:
  - ≥ Class B finish materials are required where spaces are sprinklered.
  - ≥ Class A finish materials are required where spaces are not sprinklered.
- Rooms and enclosed spaces:
  - ≥ Class C finish materials are required where both of the following conditions are present:
    Where the spaces are sprinklered.
    Where the building is ≤ 2 stories.
  - ≥ Class B finish materials are required in either of the following cases:
    Where the building is not sprinklered.
    Where the building is > 2 stories.

Source: IBC Table 803.4.

803 Wall and Ceiling Finishes

803.4 Interior finish requirements based on group *(part 4 of 5)**

Occupancy I-1

- Vertical exits and passageways:
  - ≥ Class B finish materials are required where spaces are sprinklered.
  - ≥ Class A finish materials are required where spaces are not sprinklered.
- Exit access corridors and other exitways:
  - ≥ Class C finish materials are required where spaces are sprinklered.
  - ≥ Class B finish materials are required where spaces are not sprinklered.
- Rooms and enclosed spaces:
  - ≥ Class C finish materials are required where spaces are sprinklered.
  - ≥ Class B finish materials are required where spaces are not sprinklered.

Occupancy I-2

- Vertical exits and passageways:
  - ≥ Class B finish materials are required where spaces are sprinklered.
  - ≥ Class A finish materials are required where spaces are not sprinklered.
- Exit access corridors and other exitways:
  - ≥ Class B finish materials are required where spaces are sprinklered.
  - ≥ Class A finish materials are required where spaces are not sprinklered.
- Rooms and enclosed spaces:
  - Where spaces are sprinklered:
    - ≥ Class C finish materials are required in administrative spaces.
    - ≥ Class C finish materials are required in rooms having a capacity ≤ 4 persons.
    - ≥ Class B finish materials are required for other conditions.
  - ≥ Class B finish materials are required where spaces are not sprinklered.

Occupancy I-3

- Vertical exits and passageways:
  - ≥ Class A finish materials are required.
- Exit access corridors and other exitways:
  - ≥ Class B finish materials are required in sprinklered spaces as follows:
    Where used as a wainscot ≤ 48" above the finished floor in exit access corridors.
  - ≥ Class A finish materials are required for all other conditions.
- Rooms and enclosed spaces:
  - ≥ Class C finish materials are required where spaces are sprinklered.
  - ≥ Class B finish materials are required where spaces are not sprinklered.

*Source: IBC Table 803.4.

803 Wall and Ceiling Finishes

803.4 Interior finish requirements based on group *(part 5 of 5)**

Occupancy I-4

- Vertical exits and passageways:
  - ≥ Class B finish materials are required where spaces are sprinklered.
  - ≥ Class A finish materials are required where spaces are not sprinklered.
- Exit access corridors and other exitways:
  - ≥ Class B finish materials are required where spaces are sprinklered.
  - ≥ Class A finish materials are required where spaces are not sprinklered.
- Rooms and enclosed spaces:
  - Where spaces are sprinklered:
    - ≥ Class C finish materials are required in administrative spaces.
    - ≥ Class C finish materials are required in rooms having a capacity ≤ 4 persons.
    - ≥ Class B finish materials are required for other conditions.
  - ≥ Class B finish materials are required where spaces are not sprinklered.

Occupancies R-2 and S

- Vertical exits and passageways:
  - ≥ Class C finish materials are required where spaces are sprinklered.
  - ≥ Class B finish materials are required where spaces are not sprinklered.
- Exit access corridors and other exitways:
  - ≥ Class C finish materials are required where spaces are sprinklered.
  - ≥ Class B finish materials are required where spaces are not sprinklered.
- Rooms and enclosed spaces:
  - ≥ Class C finish materials are required.

Occupancy R-3

- Vertical exits and passageways:
  - ≥ Class C finish materials are required.
- Exit access corridors and other exitways:
  - ≥ Class C finish materials are required.
- Rooms and enclosed spaces:
  - ≥ Class C finish materials are required.

Source: IBC Table 803.4.

803 Wall and Ceiling Finishes

803.5 Textiles

- Textiles, including the following, are governed by this subsection series where they are used as interior wall or ceiling finishes:
  - Materials with a woven surface.
  - Materials with a surface that is not woven.
  - Materials with a napped surface.
  - Materials with a tufted surface.
  - Materials with a looped surface.
  - Materials with a surface similar to those listed above.

803.5.1 Textile wall coverings

- Textile wall coverings must meet one of the following sets of conditions:
  - Conditions specified by this subsection include both of the following:
    Coverings must be protected by a sprinkler system as per NFPA 13 or 13R.
    Coverings must have a Class A flame spread index.

    Note: ASTM E 84, "Standard Test Methods for Surface Burning Characteristics of Building Materials," is cited as the standard governing the flame spread index.

  - Conditions specified by other standards and subsections.

    Note: The following subsections and standard are cited as governing alternative test methods for textile wall coverings:
    803.5.1.1, "Method A test protocol."
    803.5.1.2, "Method B test protocol."
    NFPA 265, "Standard Methods of Fire Texts for Evaluating Room Fire Growth Contribution of Textile Wall Coverings."

803.5.2 Textile ceiling finish

- This subsection addresses the following materials used as ceiling finishes:
  - Textiles.
  - Carpet.
  - Similar textile materials.
- Such ceiling finishes must comply with both of the following:
  The materials must be protected by sprinklers.
  The materials must have a Class A flame spread index.

  Note: ASTM E 84, "Standard Test Methods for Surface Burning Characteristics of Building Materials," is cited as the standard governing the flame spread index.

803 Wall and Ceiling Finishes

803.6 Expanded vinyl wall coverings

- Expanded vinyl wall coverings must comply with the same requirements as do textiles.
- Expanded vinyl wall coverings must meet one of the following sets of conditions:
  - Coverings must meet both of the following conditions:
    Coverings must be protected by a sprinkler system as per NFPA 13 or 13R.
    Coverings must have a Class A flame spread index.

    Note: ASTM E 84, "Standard Test Methods for Surface Burning Characteristics of Building Materials," is cited as the standard governing the flame spread index.

  - Coverings must meet alternate conditions specified by other standards and subsections.

    Note: The following subsections and standard are cited as governing alternative test methods for textile wall coverings:
    803.5.1.1, "Method A test protocol."
    803.5.1.2, "Method B test protocol."
    NFPA 265, "Standard Methods of Fire Texts for Evaluating Room Fire Growth Contribution of Textile Wall Coverings."

803.8.1 Materials and installation

- Acoustical materials for ceiling systems must comply with the following:
  - Manufacturer's instructions.
  - Provisions of this section regarding the application of interior finish.

803.8.1.1 Suspended acoustical ceilings

- Suspended acoustical ceilings must be installed according to standards of the American Society for Testing and Materials.

  Note: The following standards are cited as governing suspended acoustical ceilings:
  ASTM C 635, "Specifications for the Manufacture, Performance, and Testing of Metal Suspension Systems for Acoustical Tile and Lay-in Panel Ceilings."
  ASTM C 636, "Standard Practice for Installation of Metal Ceiling Suspension Systems for Acoustical Tile and Lay-in Panels."

803.8.1.2 Fire-resistance-rated construction

- Acoustical ceiling systems that constitute the part of construction which is fire rated must comply with the following:
  - Such systems must be installed in the same format as tested.
  - Such systems must comply with fire-resistance-rated requirements.

Note: Chapter 7, "Fire-Resistance-Rated Construction," is cited as the source for requirements for acoustical ceiling systems in such construction.

804 Interior Floor Finish

804.1 General

- The following traditional floors and coverings are not governed by this section:
  - Wood.
  - Vinyl.
  - Linoleum.
  - Terrazzo.
  - Resilient coverings not composed of fibers.

804.2 Classification

- Materials required by this section to be Class I or Class II must have a heat threshold preventing the advent of flame spread as follows:
  - Class I materials must have a critical radiant flux ≥ 0.45 watts/sq cm.
  - Class II materials must have a critical radiant flux ≥ 0.22 watts/sq cm.

  Note: NFPA 253, "Test for Critical Radiant Flux of Floor Covering Systems Using a Radiant Energy Heat Source," is cited as the standard for determining heat thresholds.

  804.5.1, "Minimum critical radiant flux," is the subsection cited for requiring minimum heat thresholds for interior floor finishes.

804.3 Testing and identification

- Floor covering materials must be tested as follows:
  - By an approved agency.
  - To determine classification according to critical radiant flux.
  - Carpet-type coverings must be tested in the manner installed, including any underlayment.

  Note: NFPA 253, "Test for Critical Radiant Flux of Floor Covering Systems Using a Radiant Energy Heat Source," is cited as the standard for testing.

- Floor covering materials must be identified in the following manner, providing the information listed below:
  - Methods of identification:
    Hang tag.
    Other suitable method.
  - Information required:
    Manufacturer or supplier.
    Style.
    Classification of critical radiant flux as follows:
    Class I materials must have a critical radiant flux ≥ 0.45 watts/sq cm.
    Class II materials must have a critical radiant flux ≥ 0.22 watts/sq cm.
- Reports of test must be provided to the building official upon request.

804 Interior Floor Finish

804.4 Application

- This subsection does not apply to the following:
  - Stage.
  - Platforms.

    Note: 410.3, "Stages," is cited as the source defining the stages omitted from this subsection.
    410.4, "Platform construction," is cited as the source defining the platforms omitted from this section.

- This subsection series governs other combustible floor materials in the following:
  - Type I construction.
  - Type II construction.

804.4.1 Subfloor construction

- This subsection applies to the following floor components in Type I and II construction:
  - Sleepers.
  - Bucks.
  - Nailing blocks.
- Such floor components must be noncombustible unless the following is provided:
  - The space between the flooring and the floor construction with a fire-resistance rating must be detailed by one of the following methods:
    Space to be filled solid with approved noncombustible materials.
    Space must be fire blocked.

    Note: Section 716, "Concealed Spaces," is cited as the source for fireblocking requirements.

  - Open space between flooring and floor construction may not pass by the following:
    Permanent partitions.
    Permanent walls.

804.4.2 Wood finish flooring

- Wood finish flooring in Types I and II construction may be attached as follows:
  - Directly to wood sleepers of the following type:
    Embedded wood sleepers.
    Fire-blocked wood sleepers.
  - Cemented directly to the top surface of the floor construction of the following type:
    Approved.
    With a fire-resistance rating.
  - Directly to a wood subfloor that is attached to sleepers.

  Note: 804.4.1, "Subfloor construction," is cited as the source of requirements for sleepers.

804 Interior Floor Finish

804.4.3 Insulating boards

- Combustible insulating boards may be used in flooring of Types I and II construction as follows:
  - Boards must be ≤ 0.5" thick.
  - Boards must be covered with an approved finish flooring.
  - Boards must be attached by one of the following details:
    Directly to a noncombustible floor assembly.
    To wood subflooring attached to sleepers.

    Note: 804.4.1, "Subfloor construction," is cited as the source for sleeper requirements.

804.5.1 Minimum critical radiant flux

- The minimum critical radiant flux for interior floor finishes in the following locations is required for specific occupancies as shown below:
  - Floor locations:
    Vertical exits.
    Exit passageways.
    Exit access corridors.
    Rooms or spaces not separated from exit access corridors by the following:
    Partitions running from the floor to the underside of the ceiling.
  - Buildings not sprinklered:
    ≥ Class I finish materials are required for the following occupancies:
    I-2, I-3.
    ≥ Class II finish materials are required for the following occupancies:
    A, B, E, H, I-4, M, R-1, R-2, S.
  - Sprinklered buildings:
    ≥ Class II finish materials are required for the following occupancies:
    I-2, I-3.
    ≥ Class II materials and those meeting the "pill test" test are permitted in the following:
    Occupancies A, B, E, H, I-4, M, R-1, R-2, S.

    Note: DOC FF-1, "Pill test" – 16 CFT 1630, "Standard for the Surface Flammability of Carpets and Rugs," are cited as the required test.

- In all other areas, the interior floor finish must meet the requirements of the "pill test" as noted above.

805 Decorations and Trim

805.1 General

- This subsection addresses the following decorations:
  - Curtains and draperies.
  - Hangings and other decorative materials.
- Decorative materials must be flame resistant or noncombustible in the following locations:
  - Occupancies A, E, I, R-1.
  - Dormitories in occupancy R-2.

  Note: NFPA 701, "Methods of Fire Test for Flame-Resistant Textiles and Films," is cited as the source for defining flame resistance.

- Combustible decorations are governed in occupancies I-1 and I-2 as follows:
  - The following decorations are not governed if their quantity is too small to be a hazard:
    Photographs.
    Paintings.
    Similar decorations.
  - Other combustible decorations must be flame retardant.
- Combustible decorations in occupancy I-3 are not permitted.

805.1.1 Noncombustible materials

- Noncombustible decorative materials are not limited in quantity.

805.1.2 Flame-resistant materials

- Flame-resistant decorative material in occupancy A auditoriums in sprinklered buildings is limited as follows:
  - The decorative material is limited to half the sum of wall and ceiling areas as follows:
    Material must compy with wall and ceiling application requirements.

    Note: 803.3 "Application," is cited as the source for application requirements.

- In other locations, flame-resistant decorative material is limited to the following:
  - 10% of the sum of wall and ceiling areas.

805.2 Acceptance criteria and reports

- Decorative materials required to be flame resistant must comply with one of the following:
  - They must be noncombustible.
  - They must pass applicable fire tests for establishing flame resistance:
    Test results are to be available to the code official.

    Note: NFPA 701, "Methods of Fire Test for Flame-Resistant Textiles and Films," is cited as the source, for establishing flame resistance. Test 1 or Test 2 of this standard is to be used as applicable.

805 Decorations and Trim

805.4 Pyroxylin plastic

- The following is prohibited in occupancy A:
  - Materials involving pyroxylin plastic such as imitation leather and other materials.
  - Materials involving a substance equally as hazardous as pyroxylin plastic.

805.5 Trim

- Interior trim must have a flame and smoke-developed index ≥ Class C.
- Combustible trim is governed as follows:
  - This subsection does not limit the area of handrails or guardrails.
  - Other combustible trim is limited to the following:
    - ≤ 10% of the sum of wall and ceiling areas in the space where located.

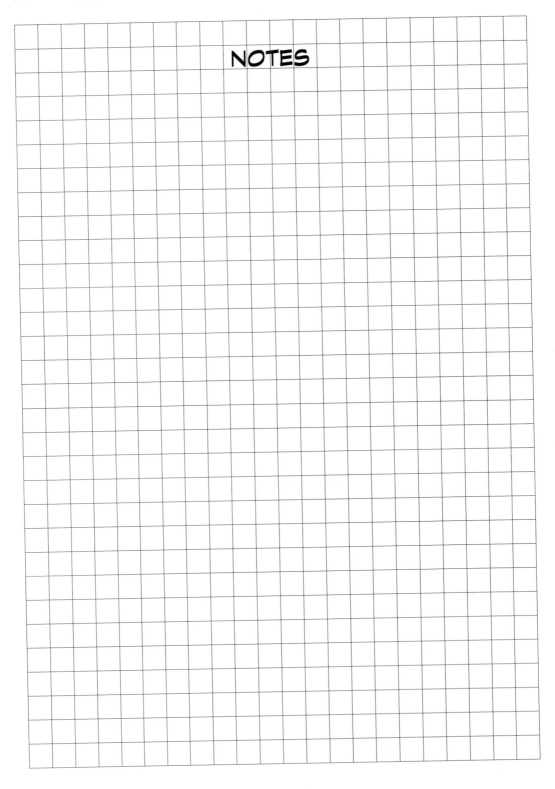

NOTES

9

Fire Protection Systems

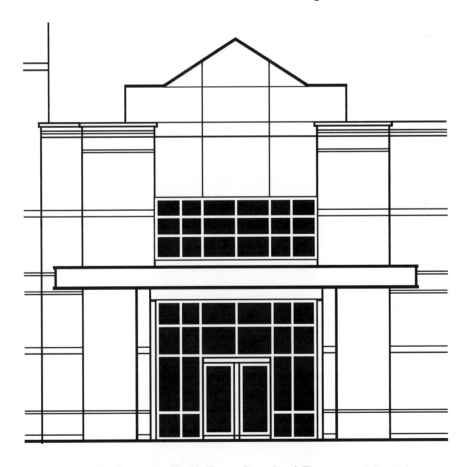

Methodist Community Health Center. Sugar Land, Texas. *(partial elevation)*
HKS, Inc., Architects, Engineers, Planners. Dallas, Texas.

903 Automatic Sprinkler Systems

903.1.1 Alternative protection

- Other automatic fire-protection systems may be substituted for automatic sprinklers where the following apply:
  - Must be approved.
  - Must meet applicable standards.

  Note: Section 904, "Alternative Automatic Fire-Extinguishing Systems," is cited as the source of requirements for such systems.

903.2.1 Group A

- Sprinklers are required in the following locations:
  - Throughout the floor containing an occupancy A area.
  - Throughout all floors between the occupancy A area and the exit discharge level.

903.2.1.1 Group A-1

- Sprinklers are required in an A-1 occupancy fire area with any of the following characteristics:
  - Fire area is > 12,000 sf.
  - Fire area occupant load is ≥ 300.
  - Fire area is not on the exit discharge level.
  - Fire area contains multiple motion picture theaters.

903.2.1.2 Group A-2

- Sprinklers are required in an A-2 occupancy fire area with any of the following characteristics:
  - Fire area is > 5000 sf.
  - Fire area occupant load is ≥ 300.
  - Fire area is not on the exit discharge level.

903.2.1.3 Group A-3

- This section does not apply to areas used exclusively for participant sports as follows:
  - Main floor and main entrance/exit is on exit discharge level.
- Otherwise, sprinklers are required in an A-3 occupancy fire area with any of the following characteristics:
  - Fire area is > 12,000 sf.
  - Fire area occupant load is ≥ 300.
  - Fire area is not on the exit discharge level.

903 Automatic Sprinkler Systems

903.2.1.4 Group A-4

- This section does not apply to areas used exclusively for participant sports as follows:
  - Main floor and main entrance/exit is on exit discharge level.
- Sprinklers are required in an A-4 occupancy fire area with any of the following characteristics:
  - Fire area is > 12,000 sf.
  - Fire area occupant load is ≥ 300.
  - Fire area is not on the exit discharge level.

903.2.1.5 Group A-5

- Sprinklers are required in the following functions where areas are > 1000 sf:
  - Concession stands.
  - Retail areas.
  - Press boxes.
  - Other accessory use areas.

903.2.2 Group E

- Sprinklers are not required in an occupancy E fire area as follows:
  - Where each classroom has ≥ 1 exterior exit door at ground level.
- Otherwise, sprinklers are required in an occupancy E as follows:
  - Throughout all fire areas > 20,000 sf.
  - Throughout all parts of buildings below exit discharge level.

903.2.3 Group F-1

- Sprinklers are required throughout buildings in all of the following cases:
  - Where a fire area has an F-1 occupancy with any of the following characteristics:
    Fire area is > 12,000 sf.
    Fire area is > 3 stories.
  - Where the sum of all fire areas in a building with an F-1 occupancy is as follows:
    Total area including mezzanines is > 24,000 sf.

903.2.3.1 Woodworking operations

- Sprinklers are required in all F-1 fire areas that have all of the following characteristics:
  - Woodworking operations are present.
  - Woodworking operations are > 2500 sf.
  - Fine combustible particles are present in either of the following formats:
    As waste.
    As materials used in the process.

903 Automatic Sprinkler Systems

903.2.4.1 General

- An automatic sprinkler system is required in occupancy H facilities.

903.2.4.2 Group H-5 occupancies

- Where an H-5 occupancy is present, automatic sprinklers are required throughout the building as follows:
  - System design must comply with both of the following:
    Code requirements according to the following hazard classifications:
    Ordinary Hazard Group 2 applies to the following:
    Fabrication areas.
    Corridors and service corridors.
    Storage rooms without dispensing functions.
    Extra Hazard Group 2 applies to the following:
    Storage rooms with dispensing functions.

  Note: IBC Table 903.2.4.2, "Group H-5 Sprinkler Design Criteria," is cited as the source of requirements based on hazard level, the content of which is summarized above.

  - Corridors with one row of sprinklers are governed as follows:
    ≤ 13 sprinklers are required based on calculations.

903.2.4.3 Pyroxylin plastics

- Sprinklers are required where the following substances are present in amounts > 100 lbs in any of the activities indicated below:
  - Substances:
    Cellulose nitrate film.
    Pyroxylin plastics.
  - Activities:
    The plastics are manufactured.
    The plastics are stored or handled.

903.2.5 Group I

- One of the following sprinkler systems is required in the following occupancy I-1 fire areas:
  - Sprinklers as per NFPA 13.
  - Sprinklers as per NFPA 13R.
  - Sprinklers as per NFPA 13D.
- Otherwise, where a building has an occupancy I fire area, the following applies:
  - Sprinklers are required throughout the building as per NFPA 13.

  Note: The following are cited as sources of requirements for the systems required above as indicated by their titles:
  903.3.1.2, "NFPA 13R sprinkler systems."
  903.3.1.3, "NFPA 13D sprinkler systems."

903 Automatic Sprinkler Systems

903.2.6 Group M

- Sprinklers are required throughout buildings in all of the following cases:
  - Where a fire area has an M occupancy with any of the following characteristics:
       Fire area > 12,000 sf.
       Fire area is > 3 stories.
  - The sum of all fire areas in a building with M occupancies is as follows:
       Total area including mezzanines is > 24,000 sf.

903.2.7 Group R-1

- Sprinklers are not required in occupancy R-1 as follows:
  - Where guestrooms are ≤ 3 stories above lowest level of exit discharge.
  - Each guestroom has ≥ 1 door opening to an exterior exit access as follows:
       The exit access leads directly to an exit.
- Otherwise, sprinklers are required throughout buildings as follows:
  - Buildings with an occupancy R-1 fire area.
  - Sprinklers must be one of the following:
       Sprinklers as per NFPA 13R.
       Sprinklers as per NFPA 13.

    Note: 903.3.1.2, "NFPA 13R sprinkler systems," is cited as the source of requirements for such systems.

903.2.8 Group R-2

- Sprinklers are required throughout buildings with an occupancy R-2 fire area as follows:
  - Where either of the following conditions apply:
       Fire area is > 2 stories as follows:
         A basement not high enough to be a story does not count in the two stories.
       Fire area has > 16 dwelling units
  - In buildings ≤ 4 stories, sprinklers must be one of the following types:
       Sprinklers as per NFPA 13.
       Sprinklers as per NFPA 13R.
  - In buildings > 4 stories, sprinklers must be as per NFPA 13.

    Note: 903.3.1.2, "NFPA 13R sprinkler systems," is cited as the source of requirements for such systems.

903.2.9 Group R-4 *(part 1 of 2)*

- One of the following types of sprinklers is required in occupancy I-1 facilities:
  - NFPA 13, 13R, or 13D.

    Note: The following are cited as sources of requirements for sprinkler systems as indicated by section titles:
         903.3.1.2, "NFPA 13R sprinkler systems."
         903.3.1.3, "NFPA 13D sprinkler systems."

903 Automatic Sprinkler Systems

903.2.9 Group R-4 *(part 2 of 2)*

- Otherwise, sprinklers are required throughout buildings with an occupancy R-4 fire area as follows:
  - Where fire area occupant count is > 8.
  - Sprinklers must be as per NFPA 13.

903.2.10 Group S-1

- Sprinklers are required throughout buildings as follows:
  - Where a fire area has an S-1 occupancy with any of the following characteristics:
    Fire area > 12,000 sf.
    Fire area is > 3 stories.
    The sum of fire areas in the building is as follows:
      The total area including mezzanines is > 24,000 sf.

903.2.10.1 Repair garages

- Sprinklers are required throughout buildings housing repair garages as follows:
  - Buildings where a repair garage is in the basement.
  - 1-story buildings with the following:
    A repair garage in a fire area > 12,000 sf.
  - Buildings ≥ 2 stories including basements with the following:
    A repair garage in a fire area > 10,000 sf.

    Note: 406.6, "Repair garages," is cited as the source defining and providing requirements for such facilities.

903.2.11 Group S-2

- This subsection does not govern enclosed parking garages below occupancy R-3.
- Otherwise, sprinklers are required throughout all enclosed parking garages as follows:
  - Those meeting height and area limitations based on occupancy and construction type.
  - Those under other occupancies.

    Note: 406.4, "Enclosed parking garages," is cited as the source of requirements.

903.2.11.1 Commercial parking garages

- Sprinklers are required throughout commercial parking garages as follows:
  - Where fire areas containing the following are > 5000 sf:
    Commercial truck or bus storage.

903 Automatic Sprinkler Systems

903.2.12.1 Stories and basements without openings

This subsection addresses occupancies other than R-3 and U.

- Sprinklers are required in stories and basements with both of the following characteristics:
  - Where floor area is > 15,000 sf.
  - Where there are no provided openings meeting either of the following conditions:
    Openings totally above adjacent grade:
    Must be located within each segment of wall length ≤ 50':
    Sum of opening areas in each segment must be ≥ 20 sf.
    Must be located on ≥ 1 side of the basement.
    Openings with any part below adjacent grade:
    Must lead directly to grade level as follows:
    Access must be by an exterior stairway or ramp.
    Must be located as follows:
    Within each segment of wall length ≤ 50'.
    On ≥ 1 side of the basement.

  Note: The following are cited as governing the stairways and ramps required above:
  1003.3.3, "Stairways."
  1003.3.4, "Ramps."

903.2.12.1.1 Opening dimensions and access

This subsection addresses stories and basements in occupancies other than R-3 and U.

- Openings provided in lieu of sprinklers must have all of the following characteristics:
  - Dimensions must be ≥ 2'-6".
  - Must comply with one of the following:
    Must provide access from the outside for the fire department.
    Must provide the possibility of the following from the outside:
    Fire fighting.
    Rescue.

903.2.12.1.2 Openings on one side only

This subsection addresses stories in occupancies other than R-3 and U.

- Sprinklers are required where openings are not provided as follows:
  - Openings as required in lieu of sprinklers must meet one of the following conditions:
    Openings are on ≥ 2 sides of the story.
    Openings are on 1 side of the story as follows:
    The wall opposite the side with openings is ≤ 75' away.

  Note: The following sections provide the requirements for openings where they may be
  provided in lieu of sprinklers:
  903.2.12.1, "Stories and basements without openings."
  903.2.12.1.1, "Opening dimensions and access."

903 Automatic Sprinkler Systems

903.2.12.1.3 Basements

This subsection addresses occupancies other than R-3 and U.

- An approved sprinkler system is required in basements as follows:
  - Where any point is > 75' from the following opening:
    An opening qualifying to be provided in lieu of sprinklers.

  Note: 903.2.12.1, "Stories and basements without openings," is cited as the source of requirements for openings qualifying to substitute for sprinklers.

903.2.12.2 Rubbish and linen chutes

This subsection addresses rubbish and linen chutes in occupancies other than R-3 and U.

- Sprinklers are required as follows:
  - At the top of chutes.
  - In the terminal rooms of chutes.
  - In chutes through ≥ 3 stories as follows:
    At alternate floors.
    At the top of chutes.
    In the terminal rooms of chutes.
  - Sprinklers must be accessible for servicing.

903.2.12.3 Buildings over 55 feet in height

This section addresses occupancies other than R-3 and U.

- The following high-rise occupancies are not governed by this section:
  - Airport control towers.
  - Open parking garages.
  - Occupancy F-2.
- Other buildings as follows require sprinklers throughout:
  - Buildings with a floor level as follows:
    Occupant load ≥ 30.
    Located ≥ 55' above lowest level of fire department vehicle access.

903 Automatic Sprinkler Systems

903.2.15 Other required suppression systems

- The following facilities are among others having requirements pertaining to fire suppression systems:
  - Covered malls.

    Note: 402.8, "Automatic sprinkler system," is cited as the source of requirements.

  - High-rise buildings.

    Note: The following are cited as sources of requirements:
    403.2, "Automatic sprinkler system."
    403.3, "Reduction in fire-resistance rating."

  - Atriums.

    Note: 404.3, "Automatic sprinkler protection," is cited as the source of requirements.

  - Underground structures.

    Note: 405.3, "Automatic sprinkler system," is cited as the source of requirements.

  - Occupancy I-2.

    Note: 407.5, "Automatic sprinkler system," is cited as the source of requirements.

  - Stages.

    Note: 410.6, "Automatic sprinkler system," is cited as the source of requirements.

  - Special amusement buildings.

    Note: 411.1, "Automatic sprinklers," is cited as the source of requirements.

  - Aircraft hangers.

    Note: The following are cited as sources of requirements:
    412.2.5, "Finishing."
    412.2.6, "Fire suppression."

  - Occupancy H-2.

    Note: 415.7.2.4, "Suppression," is cited as the source of requirements.

  - Flammable finishes.

    Note: 416.4, "Fire protection," is cited as the source of requirements.

  - Drying rooms.

    Note: 417.4, "Fire protection," is cited as the source of requirements.

  - Unlimited area buildings.

    Note: Section 507, "Unlimited Area Buildings," is cited as the source of requirements.

*Source: IBC Table 903.2.15.

903 Automatic Sprinkler Systems

903.3.1.1 NFPA 13 sprinkler systems

- Sprinklers required for buildings or parts of buildings must comply with the following:
  - Sprinklers are to be as per NFPA 13 unless otherwise noted.
  - Sprinklers are to be automatic.
  - Sprinklers are to be installed throughout the building or area specified.

    Note: The following are cited as sources of requirements for sprinklers:
    NFPA 13, "Installation of Sprinkler Systems," addresses the sprinklers required unless otherwise specified.
    903.3.1.1.1, "Exempt locations," lists locations where sprinklers are not required.
    903.3.1.2 , "NFPA 13R sprinkler systems," provides requirements for such sprinklers for locations where specified in lieu of NFPA 13 sprinklers.
    903.3.1.3, "NFPA 13D sprinkler systems," provides requirements for such sprinklers for locations where specified in lieu of NFPA 13 sprinklers.

903.3.1.1.1 Exempt locations *(part 1of 2)*

- The following conditions do not justify the omission of sprinklers from a space:
  - Space is damp.
  - Space is of construction with a fire-resistance rating.
  - Space contains electrical equipment.
- Sprinklers are not required in any of the following spaces:
  - Where protected by an approved fire-detection system as follows:
    Automatic.
    Detects visible and invisible products of combustion.
  - Where the application of the following substances results in the hazards indicated below:
    Substances:
    Water.
    Flame and water.
    Hazards:
    Hazard to life.
    Fire hazard.
  - Where both of the following conditions apply:
    Nature of contents render sprinklers undesirable.
    Omission of sprinklers is approved.
  - In both of the following rooms where the condition indicated below applies:
    Rooms:
    Generator rooms.
    Transformer rooms.
    Condition:
    Rooms are separated from rest of building as follows:
    By the following assemblies as applicable with a fire-resistance rating $\geq$ 2 hrs:
    Walls.
    Floor/ceiling assemblies.
    Roof/ceiling assemblies.

903 Automatic Sprinkler Systems

903.3.1.1.1 Exempt locations *(part 2of 2)*

- Sprinklers are not required in any of the following spaces:
  - In spaces of telecommunications buildings as follows with the conditions indicated below:
    - Spaces used only for the following:
      - Telecommunications equipment.
      - Related electrical power distribution equipment.
      - Batteries.
      - Standby engines.
    - Conditions:
      - Spaces have an automatic fire alarm system.
      - Spaces are separated from rest of building as follows:
        - Wall has a fire-resistance rating $\geq$ 1 hr.
        - Floor/ceiling assembly has a fire-resistance rating $\geq$ 2 hr.
  - Where spaces are as follows:
    - Constructed of noncombustible construction.
    - Has noncombustible contents.

903.3.1.2 NFPA 13R sprinkler systems

- Sprinklers must meet the requirements of NFPA 13R where permitted as follows:
  - In occupancy R buildings $\leq$ 4 stories.

  Note: NFPA 13R, "Installation of Sprinkler Systems in Residential Occupancies up to and Including Four Stories in Height," is cited as the standard for the sprinklers.

903.3.1.3 NFPA 13D sprinkler systems

- Sprinklers must meet the requirements of NFPA 13D where permitted as follows:
  - In 1- and 2-family dwellings.

  Note: NFPA 13D, "Installation of Sprinkler Systems in One- and Two-Family Dwellings and Manufactured Homes," is cited as the standard for the sprinklers.

=

903 Automatic Sprinkler Systems

903.3.2 Quick-response and residential sprinklers

- Where sprinklers are required by the code, the sprinkler types specified by this subsection must be installed in the following locations:
  - Locations required:
    - In occupancy I-2 as follows:
      - Throughout all spaces within a smoke compartment with sleeping rooms.
    - In the following rooms in the occupancies R and I-1:
      - Dwelling units.
      - Guest rooms.
      - Sleeping rooms.
    - In light-hazard occupancies as follows:
      - Buildings with the following characteristics:
        - Quantity of combustible material is low.
        - Combustibility of contents is low.
        - Low rates of heat are anticipated from any fire.
      - Typical building types:
        - Churches.
        - Libraries excluding large stack rooms.
        - Clubs.
        - Educational buildings.
        - Offices.
        - Nursing homes, convalescent homes, and hospitals.
        - Institutional buildings.
        - Restaurant seating.
        - Auditoriums and theaters excluding stages and prosceniums.
        - Museums.
        - Unused attics.
        - Residential buildings.

  Note: NFPA 13, "Installation of Sprinkler Systems," is cited as the source of light-hazard occupancies, a partial summary of which is provided above.

- Where sprinklers are required by the code, the following types must be installed in locations specified in this subsection.
  - Types:
    - Residential sprinklers as follows:
      - Where permitted as per their listing.
      - As per the following as applicable:
        - NFPA 13R or 13D.
    - Quick response sprinklers as follows:
      - Where residential sprinklers are not permitted.
      - As per their listing.
      - As per NFPA 13.

903 Automatic Sprinkler Systems

903.3.3 Obstructed locations

- Kitchen equipment located under exhaust hoods that are protected by a fire-extinguishing system are not governed by this section.

    Note: Section 904, "Alternative Automatic Fire-Extinguishing Systems," is cited as the source of requirements for the facilities indicated above.

- Sprinklers must be installed so that obstructions will not hinder their function as follows:
    ○ Water distribution may not be obstructed.
    ○ Activation may not be delayed.
- Sprinklers must be installed in or under the following covered locations:
    ○ Kiosks and concession stands.
    ○ Displays and booths.
    ○ Equipment > 4' wide.
- Clearance of ≥ 3' is required between sprinklers and the top of stacks of combustible fibers.

903.3.4 Actuation

- Sprinkler systems must be activated automatically unless otherwise specifically permitted.

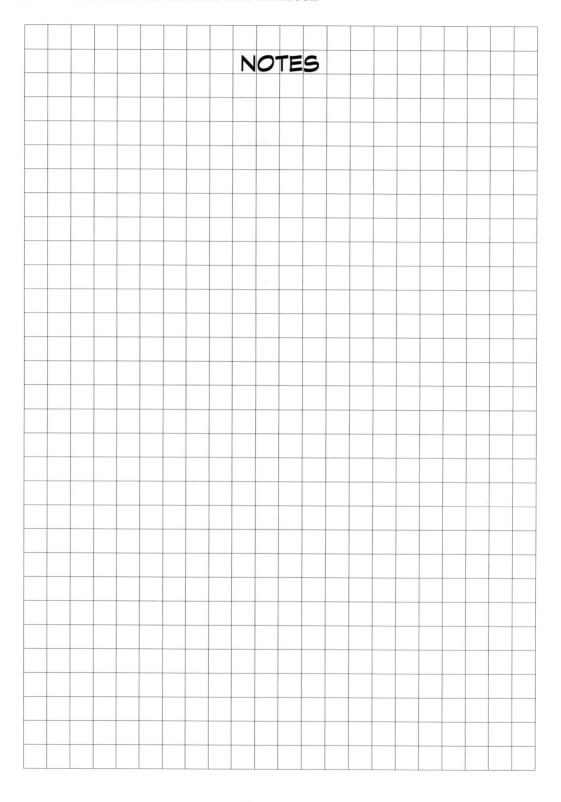

NOTES

10

Means of Egress

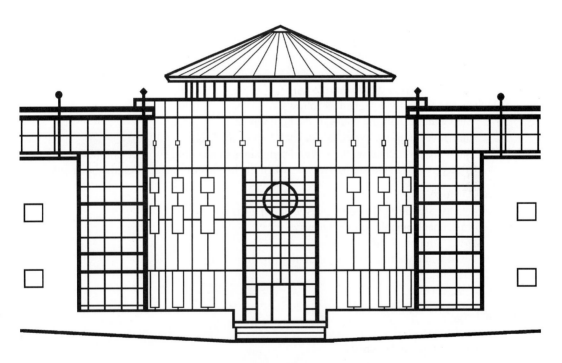

Newman University Sports and Fine Arts Center. Wichita, Kansas. *(partial elevation)*
Gossen Livingston Associates, Inc., Architecture. Wichita, Kansas

1002 Definitions

1002.1 Definitions *(part 1 of 7)*

- **Accessible means of egress**
  - A route of travel as follows:
    - In either of the following:
      - A building.
      - A facility.
    - Route is continuous.
    - Route is unobstructed.
    - Route is from any point in an accessible route to one of the following:
      - An area of refuge.
      - A horizontal exit.
      - A public way.

- **Aisle accessway**
  - A segment of an exit access path as follows:
    - The path leads to an aisle.

- **Alternating tread device**
  - A component with a series of steps as follows:
    - Angle of travel is as follows:
      - $\geq 50°$ and $\leq 70°$.
      - Angle is measured from horizontal
    - Steps are typically designed as follows:
      - Step width is half the width of the component.
      - Individual steps are provided for each foot of the user.
      - Steps are positioned on the left and right sides of a central support as follows:
        - Steps on one side are halfway between the heights of the steps on the other side.

- **Area of refuge**
  - An area for use during emergency evacuation as follows:
    - For occupants unable to use stairways.
    - Affords temporary protection:
      - Used while waiting for one or both of the following:
        - Instructions.
        - Assistance.

- **Bleachers**
  - A grandstand as follows:
    - Seats are without backrests.

1002 Definitions

1002.1 Definitions *(part 2 of 7)*

- **Common path of egress travel**
  - A route of travel as follows:
    Toward an exit.
    Provides the only option for a route of travel.
    Terminates at the following location:
      At the point where more than one option of travel toward an exit is provided.
  - Routes that are initially separate, but which merge at some point, are common paths.

> **Case study: Fig. 1002.1 A.** A common path of egress travel is measured on the most direct route available to occupants. The rectangular paths shown in the figure approximate the distance around objects such as furniture and fixtures, the locations of which may vary over time. Some jurisdictions don't require egress paths to follow the rectangular geometry.
>
> **Retail 107:** Path AD is a common path, there being only one choice of travel. Some jurisdictions may not include toilet rooms in common path measurements. Path BDE and BC are not common paths but "exit access travel distance." This is due to the fact that from point B, there are two choices of travel.
>
> **Retail 106A and 106B:** All paths of egress travel in these rooms are common paths since all routes merge at point B and since there is a single choice of path from B to the exit door.
>
> **Storage 108:** All paths in the room are common paths since they must merge at some point prior to leaving the room. The common path extends to point C, which is the first opportunity for more than one choice of travel to an exit. The one diagonal segment is shown since this area is for circulation only, permitting no furnishings to be located there.

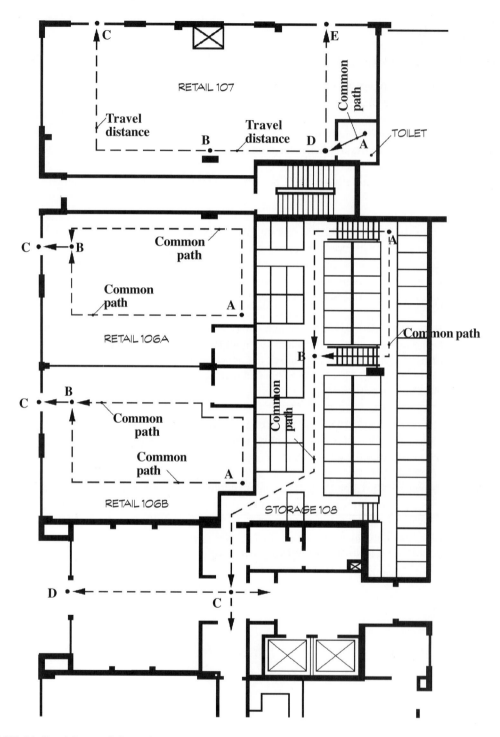

Fig. 1002.1A. Partial ground floor plan, east building. Hoyt Street Properties, Portland, Oregon. Ankrom Moisan Associated Architects. Portland, Oregon.

1002 Definitions

1002.1 Definitions *(part 3 of 7)*

- **Corridor**
  - An exit access component as follows:
    Enclosed.
    Provides a route to an exit.

- **Egress court**
  - One of the following elements providing access to a public way.
    Court.
    Yard.

- **Emergency escape and rescue opening**
  - The following openings providing a means of escape or rescue.
    Operable window.
    Door.
    Other similar element.

- **Exit**
  - A route of travel from an exit access to an exit discharge.
  - Separated from interior building spaces:
    By fire-resistance-rated construction.
    By opening protectives.
  - May include the following elements:
    Exterior exit doors at ground level.
    Exit enclosures.
    Exit passageways.
    Exterior exit stairs.
    Exterior exit ramps.
    Horizontal exits.
  - A part of a means of egress.

- **Exit access**
  - A route of travel from any occupiable point in a building to an exit.
  - A part of a means of egress.

- **Exit discharge**
  - A route between the following:
    The termination of an exit.
    A public way.
  - A part of a means of egress.

- **Exit discharge, level of**
  - A horizontal plane.
  - Located at the termination of an exit.
  - Located at the beginning of an exit discharge.

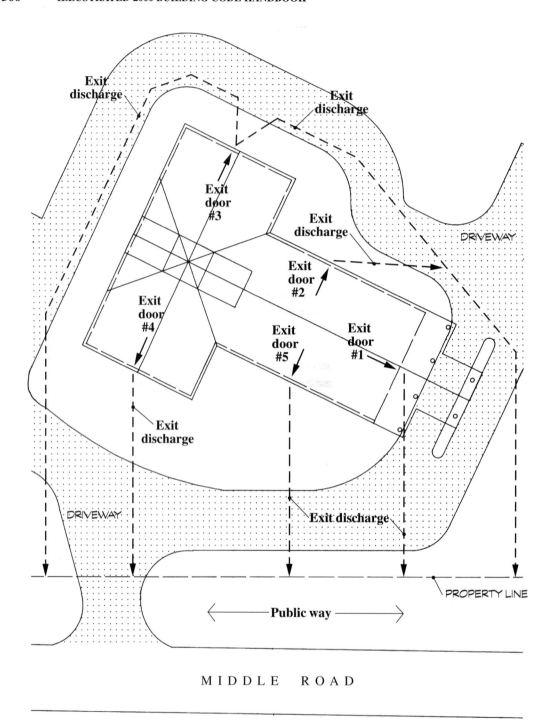

Fig. 1002.1B. Site plan. Glad Tidings Assembly of God Church. Naticoke, Pennsylvania. Mullins and Weida, Architect and Associate. Bear Creek, Pennsylvania.

1002 Definitions

1002.1 Definitions *(part 4 of 7)*

- **Exit enclosure**
    - A component of an exit.
    - Separated from interior building spaces:
        By fire-resistance-rated construction.
        By opening protectives.
    - A protected route of travel to one of the following:
        Exit discharge.
        Public way.
    - May be in either of the following directions:
        Horizontal.
        Vertical.

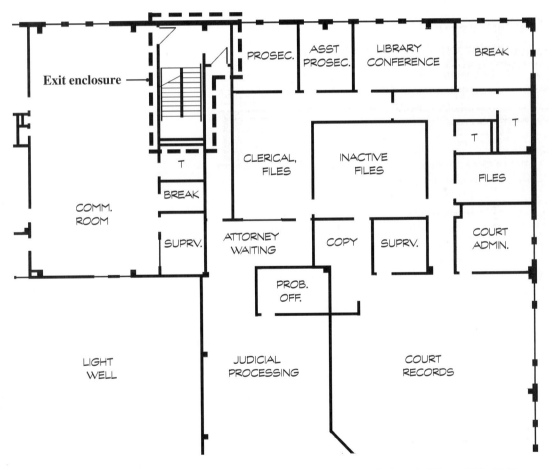

Fig. 1002.1C. Partial floor plan. Lee's Summit Police and Court Facility. Lee's Summit, Missouri. The Hollis and Miller Group, Inc. Lee's Summit, Missouri.

1002 Definitions

1002.1 Definitions *(part 5 of 7)*

- **Exit, horizontal**
  - A route of egress travel.
  - Between either of the following:
    - Two buildings on approximately the same level.
    - Two areas in the same building approximately on the same level.
  - Through an assembly providing protection from fire and smoke.

- **Exit passageway**
  - A component of an exit.
  - Separated from interior building spaces:
    - By fire-resistance-rated construction.
    - By opening protectives.
  - A protected route of travel to one of the following:
    - Exit discharge.
    - Public way.
  - A horizontal route of travel.

- **Fire exit hardware**
  - Panic hardware as follows:
    - Listed for fire door assemblies.

- **Floor area, gross**
  - Area within the inside perimeter of the exterior walls.
  - Does not include the following:
    - Vent shafts.
    - Shafts with no openings.
    - Interior courts.
  - Includes space occupied by the following:
    - Corridors.
    - Stairways.
    - Closets.
    - Interior walls.
    - Columns.
    - Other interior elements.
  - Space not enclosed with exterior walls is included as follows:
    - Usable area under the following horizontal projections:
      - Roof above.
      - Floor above.

1002 Definitions

1002.1 Definitions *(part 6 of 7)*

- **Floor area, net**
  - ○ Occupied area.
  - ○ Unoccupied accessory areas, such as the following, are not included:
    - Corridors.
    - Stairways.
    - Toilet rooms.
    - Mechanical rooms.
    - Closets.

- **Folding and telescopic seating**
  - ○ A structure for seating as follows:
    - Seating is tiered.
    - Size can be reduced without dismanteling for the following purposes:
      - For moving.
      - For storing.

- **Footboards**
  - ○ The walking surface of aisle accessways in the following:
    - Reviewing stands.
    - Grandstands.
    - Bleachers.

- **Grandstand**
  - ○ A structure for one of the following types of seating:
    - Stepped.
    - Tiered.

- **Guard**
  - ○ A barrier as follows:
    - Located at the open edge of walking surfaces where there is an elevation change.
    - Minimizes chances for falling from the walking surface to the lower level.

- **Handrail**
  - ○ A rail for grasp by the hand as follows:
    - Rail can be in either of the following positions:
      - Horizontal.
      - Sloping.
    - For either of the following purposes:
      - Guidance.
      - Support.

1002 Definitions

1002.1 Definitions *(part 7 of 7)*

- **Means of egress**
  - A route of travel from any point in a building to a public way:
    Route is continuous.
    Route is unobstructed.
  - Consists of 3 separate segments:
    Exit access.
    Exit.
    Exit discharge.

- **Nosing**
  - The leading edge of the following stair components:
    Treads.
    Landings at the top of stair runs.

- **Occupant load**
  - The number of people for which a means of egress is designed.

- **Panic hardware**
  - A door-latching assembly as follows:
    Latch releases upon application of a force in the direction of egress.

- **Public way**
  - Any of the following that leads to a street dedicated to public use:
    Street.
    Alley.
    Parcel of land.
  - Has clear dimensions as follows:
    ≥ 10' in height.
    ≥ 10' in width.

- **Ramp**
  - A walking surface sloping > 1:20 in the direction of travel.

- **Stair**
  - A change in elevation consisting of ≥ 1 riser.

- **Stairway, exterior**
  - Open to the exterior on at least one side:
    Where required, the following are permitted at open sides:
    Structural columns and beams.
    Guards and handrails.
  - Open to one of the following:
    Yard.
    Court.
    Public way.

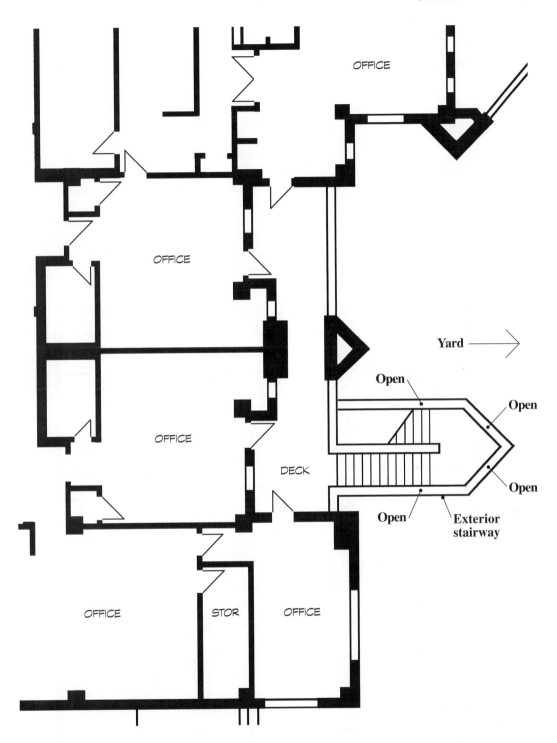

OFFICE

OFFICE

Yard ⟶

Open

Open

Open

OFFICE

DECK

Open

Open

Exterior
stairway

OFFICE

STOR

OFFICE

Fig. 1002.1D. Partial second floor plan. Country Club Park Building One. Wichita, Kansas. Gossen Livngston Associates, Inc., Architecture. Wichita, Kansas.

1003 General Means of Egress

1003.2.1. Multiple occupancies

- This subsection applies to buildings containing more than one occupancy.
- Means of egress within an occupancy are governed by the occupancy requirements.
- Where more than one occupancy shares parts of the same means of egress, shared portions are governed by the more restrictive requirements of the occupancies served.

> **Case study: Fig. 1003.2.1A.** IBC Table 1004.3.2.1 requires that corridors serving I-3 occupancies with sprinklers have walls with a fire-resistance rating of 1 hr, although the walls of corridors serving A and B occupancies with sprinklers need have no fire-resistance rating. The corridor between the I-3 and A or B occupancies in the case study serves all these occupancies and, therefore, must have a minimum of 1-hr-rated walls in compliance with the more restrictive I-3 requirement. (In this case, the stair walls and the I-3 corridor wall are rated at 2 hrs, although the other corridor walls are 1 hr.)

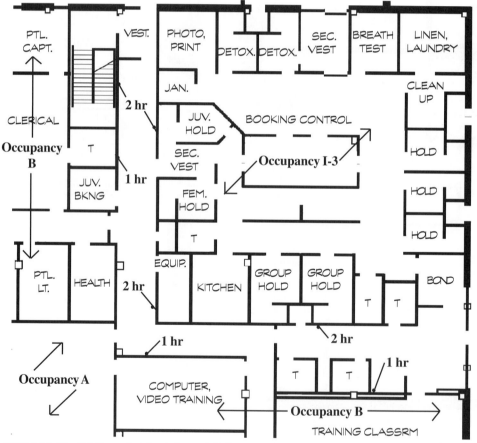

Fig. 1003.2.1A. Partial floor plan. Lee's Summit Police and Court Facility. Lee's Summit, Missouri. The Hollis and Miller Group, Inc. Lee's Summit, Missouri.

Case study: Fig. 1003.2.1B. Each exit door in the plan is indicated by a dot with its maximum egress capacity listed in number of occupants. The doors in occupancies B and S have a larger capacity than do doors in the H-2 occupancy for the same width. IBC Table 1003.2.3 indicates that in sprinklered buildings, occupancies B and S require a minimum of 0.15" width per occupant served. In H occupancies the minimum width is 0.2" per occupant. Consequently, the 36" exterior doors have capacities of 240 occupants each in the B and S occupancies, but only 180 occupants in the H occupancy. This is an example of separate means of egress in different occupancies subject to differing occupancy-specific requirements.

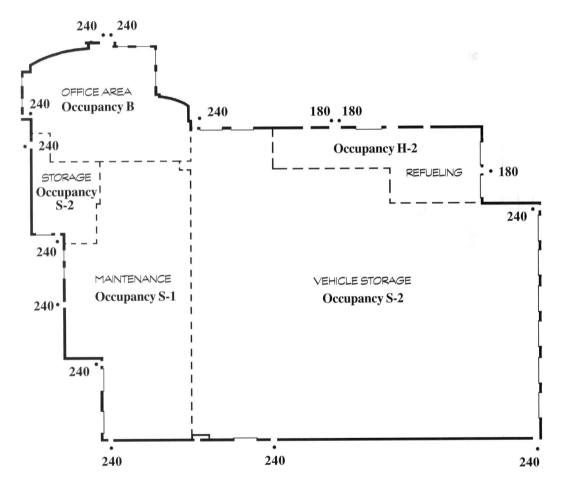

Fig. 1003.2.1B. Floor plan. Wichita Transit Storage, Administration, and Maintenance Facility. Wichita, Kansas. Wilson Darnell Mann, P.A., Architects. Wichita, Kansas.

1003 General Means of Egress

1003.2.2 Design occupant load

- The occupant load assigned to a space for purposes of providing adequate egress is the largest of the three methods of determination defined in this subsection series.

  Note: The following are cited as sources of the three methods of load determination:
  1003.2.2.1, "Actual number."
  1003.2.2.2, "Number by Table 1003.2.2.2."
  1003.2.2.3, "Number by combination."

1003.2.2.1 Actual number

- Occupant load used to determine egress requirements is as follows:
  - Use the actual number for which the area is designed.

1003.2.2.2 Number by Table 1003.2.2.2 *(part 1 of 2)*

- Occupant load in fixed seating areas is determined in one of the following ways:
  - For individual seats, *occupant load = number of seats.*
  - For continuous seating without arms, *occupant load = length of seating ÷ 18".*
  - For booth seating, *occupant load = length of seating ÷ 24"* as follows:
      Length is measured at the backrest.
- Occupant load used to determine egress requirements is as follows:
  - Divide the floor area served by the following square feet per occupant:

Table 1003.2.2.2   Maximum Floor Area per Occupant

Function	SF/ occupant	Function	SF/occupant
Agricultural		**Assembly**	
Barns	300 gross	Gambling areas	11 gross
Outbuildings	300 gross	No fixed seats	
Storage	300 gross	Concentrated	
Maintenance	50 gross	(chairs only)	7 net
Aircraft		Standing space	5 net
Hangars	500 gross	Not concentrated	
Fabrication	100 gross	(tables, chairs)	15 net
Office	100 gross	**Bowling centers**	
Airport terminal		5 occupants per	
Concourse	100 gross	lane including 15'	
Waiting area	15 gross	of lane-approach	
Baggage claim	20 gross	Lane service area	300 gross
Baggage handling	300 gross	Other areas	7 net
Newsstand	30 gross	**Business areas**	
Gift shop	30 gross	Offices	100 gross
Lounge	7 net	Computer mainframe	300 gross
Snack bar	7 net	Computer room	100 gross
Ticket area	7 net	Copy room	100 gross
Office	100 gross	Conference room	
Car rental	20 gross	(table, chairs)	15 net

Sources: IBC Table 1003.2.2.2; and survey data.

1003 General Means of Egress

1003.2.2.2 Number by Table 1003.2.2.2 *(part 2 of 2)*

Table 1003.2.2.2 —*Continued*

Function	SF/ occupant	Function	SF/ occupant
Courthouses		**Institutional areas**	
Hearing room		In patient treatment	240 gross
(No fixed seats)	40 net	Outpatient areas	100 gross
Courtroom		Sleeping areas	120 gross
(No fixed seats)	40 net	Admitting	100 gross
Waiting space	15 net	Waiting	15 net
Jury room	15 net	Offices	100 gross
Attorney lounge	15 net	**Kitchens, commercial**	200 gross
Press room	15 net	**Library**	
Witness isolation	100 gross	Reading rooms	50 net
Attorney workspace	100 gross	Stack area	100 gross
Detention cell	120 gross	**Mercantile**	
Dormitories	50 gross	Basement	30 gross
Lounge	7 net	Grade floor	30 gross
Recreation	7 net	Other floors	60 gross
Kitchenette	3 net	Storage, shipping	300 gross
Vending area	3 net	**Parking garages**	200 gross
Dining	15 net	**Residential**	200 gross
Laundry	15 net	**Skating rink**	
Seminar room	15 net	Rink	50 gross
Library reading room	50 net	Deck	15 gross
Mail room	100 gross	**Swimming pool**	
Student rooms	200 gross	Pool	50 gross
Educational		Deck	15 gross
Classroom	20 net	**Stages and platforms**	15 net
Shops	50 net	**Storage** (accessory)	300 gross
Vocational areas	50 net	**Mechanical room**	300 gross
Offices	100 gross	**University center**	
Electrical room	300 gross	Steam room	100 net
Elevator machinery	300 gross	Gymnasium	5 net
Exercise rooms	50 gross	Game room	15 net
H-5 Fabrication and		Dance studio	7 net
manufacturing areas	200 gross	Group study	100 net
Industrial areas	100 gross	Individual study	200 net
		Gymnastics	15 net
		Indoor archery	100 net
		Handball	100 net

Sources: IBC Table 1003.2.2.2; and survey data.

1003.2.2.3 Number by combination

• Where occupants in an accessory space egress through a primary area, the calculated occupant load of the primary area is the sum of the following:
  ○ The occupant load of the primary area.
  ○ The occupant load egressing through the primary area from the accessory space.

Case study: Fig. 1003.2.2.2A. The office area is designated as occupancy B for purposes of determining occupant load. IBC Table 1003.2.2.2 indicates that the area allowance for occupants is 100 sf (gross) per person. Since the allowance is in gross sf, interior wall thicknesses, toilets, closets, and hall are included in the area computation. The area allowance for the 2 storage rooms is 300 sf (gross) per person. In this example, computing occupants for the storage rooms separately from the business area would result in 1 less occupant for the complex. Since the means of egress serving this occupant load is larger than required, treating the storage rooms separately is not justified. The occupant count for the business area, including storage, is, therefore, determined by the conservative following calculation:

3210 gross sf ÷ 100 sf/occupant = 33 occupants.

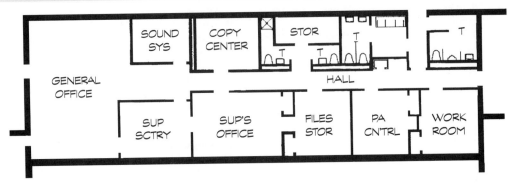

Fig. 1003.2.2.2A. Partial floor plan. Montachusett Regional Vocational-Technical High School. Fitchburg, Massachusetts. HKT Architects, Inc. Somerville, Massachusetts.

Case study: Fig. 1003.2.2.2B. Gross (gr) and net square foot (sf) allowances from IBC Table 1003.2.2.2 are applied to the case study example as follows:

415 Electric room	Mechanical: 985 gr sf	÷ 300 gr sf/occ	=	4 occupants
416 Storage	Storage: 675 gr sf	÷ 300 gr sf/occ	=	3 occupants
417 Utility and storage	Storage: 390 gr sf	÷ 300 gr sf/occ	=	2 occupants
418 Emergency generator	Mechanical: 300 gr sf	÷ 300 gr sf/occ	=	1 occupant
419 Maintenance office	Office: 480 gr sf	÷ 100 gr sf/occ	=	5 occupants
423 Storage	Storage: 1642 gr sf	÷ 300 gr sf/occ	=	6 occupants
424 Incinerator	Mechanical: 350 gr sf	÷ 300 gr sf/occ	=	2 occupants
426 Office	Office: 470 gr sf	÷ 100 gr sf/occ	=	5 occupants
431 Restaurant	Assembly: 2440 net sf	÷ 15 net sf/occ	=	163 occupants
433 Culinary arts	Vocational: 3870 net sf	÷ 50 net sf/occ	=	78 occupants
440 Solarium	Assembly: 184 net sf	÷ 15 net sf/occ	=	13 occupants
448 Nonfood storage	Storage: 144 gr sf	÷ 300 gr sf/occ	=	1 occupant
449 Food storage	Storage: 172 gr sf	÷ 300 gr sf/occ	=	1 occupant
450 Classroom	Classroom: 750 net sf	÷ 20 net sf/occ	=	38 occupants
451 Receiving	Storage: 920 gr sf	÷ 300 gr sf/occ	=	4 occupants

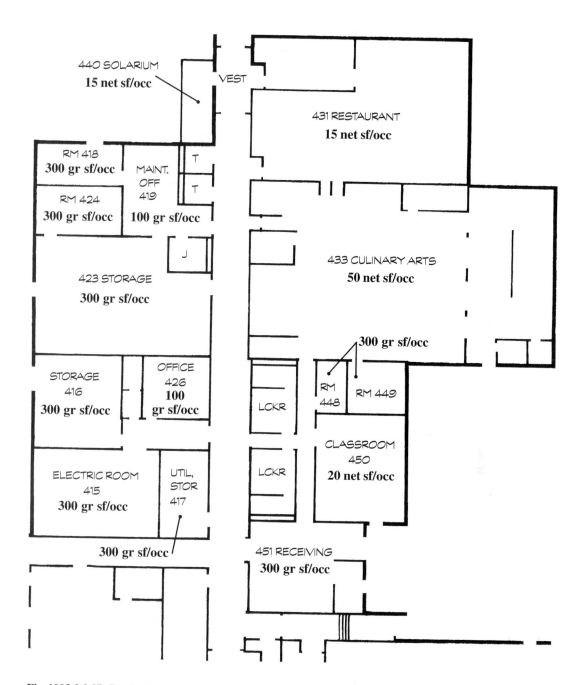

Fig. 1003.2.2.2B. Partial floor plan. Montachusett Regional Vocational-Technical High School. Fitchburg, Massachusetts. HKT Architects, Inc. Somerville, Massachusetts.

1003 General Means of Egress

1003.2.2.6 Exiting from multiple levels

- This subsection addresses exits serving ≥ 1 floor.
- The capacity of the exit at each floor is serves occupants of each floor only:
- Occupant loads are not summed from each floor in the direction of egress.
- The capacity of the exit may not decrease along the route of egress.

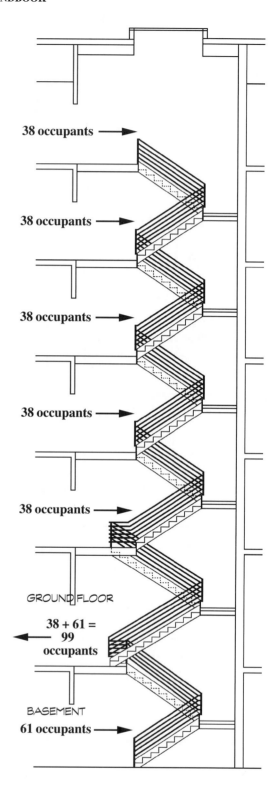

38 occupants →

38 occupants →

38 occupants →

38 occupants →

38 occupants →

Case study: Fig. 1003.2.2.6. The occupant load entering the exit stairway at each floor above grade level is 38. The occupant load used to determine the minimum requirements for the stairway down to the ground floor is, therefore, 38. It is assumed that the occupants from each floor enter the stairway at the same time and vacate each segment of the stairway as the following group enters it behind them. Thus, no segment of the stair has more than 38 occupants in it at any time. Should a larger number have been assigned to any floor, all stairway segments below that floor would have to serve the larger number. (1003.2.2.6)

The occupant load entering the stairway from the basement parking area is 61. These occupants merge with the 38 from the 2nd floor, placing both groups in the means of egress at the 1st floor (the intermediate floor) at the same time. The means of egress at the point of convergence must, therefore, serve *38 + 61 = 99 occupants*. (1003.2.2.7)

GROUND FLOOR

← **38 + 61 = 99 occupants**

BASEMENT

61 occupants →

Fig. 1003.2.2.6. Stairway section. Hoyt Street Properties, Portland, Oregon. Ankrom Moisan Associated Architects, Portland, Oregon.

1003 General Means of Egress

1003.2.2.7 Egress convergence

- Where the means of egress from a floor above, converges with that of the floor below, at a level in between, the following applies:
  - Egress capacity in the direction of travel from the point of convergence is as follows: Capacity must be ≥ the sum of the capacities of the converging means of egress.

1003.2.2.8 Mezzanine levels

- This subsection governs the exit capacity of a space with mezzanine egress through it.
- The exit capacity of such space is based on the sum of occupant loads of the following:
  - The mezzanine.
  - The space.

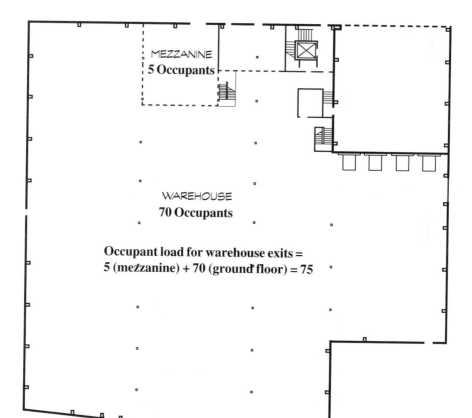

Fig. 1003.2.2.8 Floor plan. New Warehouse Addition. Los Angeles, California. Stephen Wen + Associates, Architects, Inc. Pasadena, California.

1003 General Means of Egress

1003.2.2.9 Fixed seating

- Occupant load in fixed seating areas is determined in one of the following ways:
  - For individual seats, *occupant load = number of seats*.
  - For continuous seating without arms, *occupant load = length of seating ÷ 18"*.
  - For booth seating, *occupant load = length of seating ÷ 24,"* as follows:
    Length is measured at the backrest.

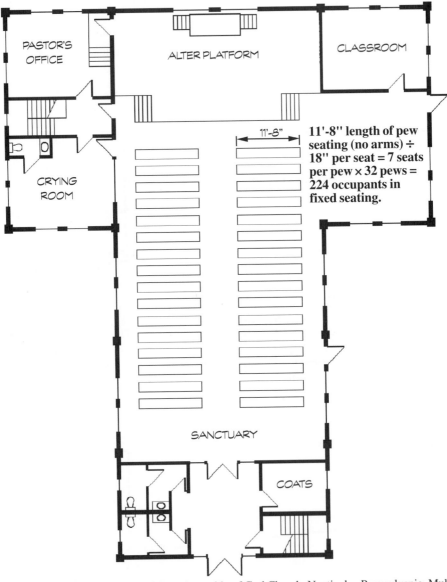

11'-8" length of pew seating (no arms) ÷ 18" per seat = 7 seats per pew × 32 pews = 224 occupants in fixed seating.

Fig. 1003.2.2.9. First floor plan. Glad Tidings Assembly of God Church. Nanticoke, Pennsylvania. Mullins and Weida, Architect and Associate. Bear Creek, Pennsylvania.

1003 General Means of Egress

1003.2.2.10 Outdoor areas

- This section does not apply to the following outdoor areas:
  - Outdoor areas of occupancy R-3.
  - Outdoor areas of individual dwelling units of occupancy R-2.
- Outdoor areas used only for building service are required to have only one means of egress.
- Other outdoors areas usable by building occupants, such as the following, must have a means of egress complying with this chapter:
  - Yards.
  - Patios.
  - Courts.
  - Similar outdoor areas.
- The occupant load of outdoor areas is assigned by the building official as per expected use.
- Means of egress of outdoor areas passing through a building are governed as follows:
  - Where an outdoor area serves persons other than building occupants, the following applies:
    - Requirements for the means of egress based on the sum of the following occupants:
      - Occupant load from the building.
      - Occupant load from outside the building.

> **Case study: Fig. 1003.2.2.10.** If 102 occupants from adjoining rooms egress through those rooms, 1125 of the courtyard occupant load of 1227 will pass through the auditorium lobby. Total capacity of doors to the lobby is 1440. 566 of the auditorium occupants also egress through the lobby, thus, its means of egress serves 1691. Total capacity of exit doors serving the lobby is 2400. To omit the courtyard load from the lobby means of egress, it would have to be shown that the auditorium and courtyard would not be occupied simultaneously. This scenario reflects one set of assumptions about use of the courtyard.

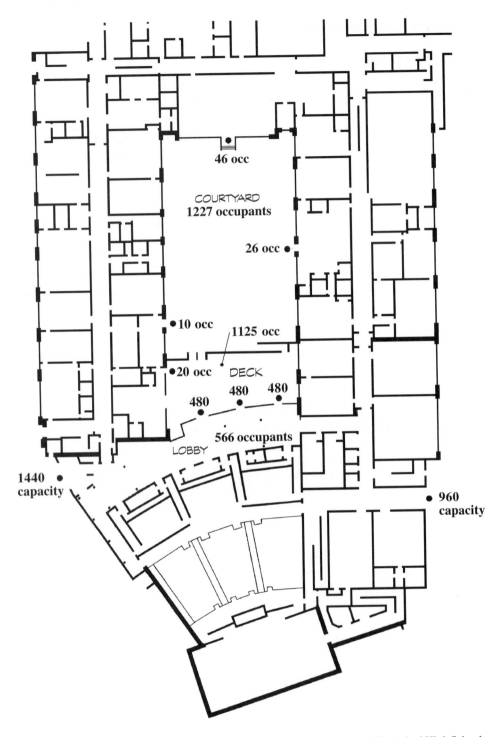

Fig. 1003.2.2.10 Partial floor plan at courtyard. Montachusett Regional Vocational-Technical High School. Fitchburg, Massachusetts. HKT Architects, Inc. Somerville, Massachusetts.

1003 General Means of Egress

1003.2.3 Egress width

- Requirements for means of egress listed in the assembly section supercede any conflicting requirements of this section.

  Note: Section 1008, "Assembly," is cited as the source governing certain aspects of means of egress for assembly occupancies. Aisle widths are the pertinent issue.

- In other cases, means of egress widths must be ≥ the greater of the following:
  - Minimums required elsewhere in the code.
  - Number of occupants served × the factors below.

Table 1003.2.3   Means of Egress Width

Minimum width of stairway per occupant served:	
Occupancy	Building sprinklered as per NFPA 13 or 13R
A, B, E, F, H-5, I-1, I-3, I-4, M, R, S, U	0.2"
H-1, H-2, H-3, H-4, I-2	0.3"
	Building not sprinklered
A, B, E, F, H-5, I-1, I-3, I-4, M, R, S, U	0.3"
I-2	0.4"
H-1, H-2, H-3, H-4	0.7"

Minimum width of other egress components per occupant served:	
Occupancy	Building sprinklered as per NFPA 13 or 13R
A, B, E, F, H-5, I-1, I-3, I-4, M, R, S, U	0.15"
H-1, H-2, H-3, H-4, I-2	0.2"
	Building not sprinklered
A, B, E, F, H-5, I, M, R, S, U	0.2"
H-1, H-2, H-3, H-4	0.4"

Source: IBC Table 1003.2.3

- A loss of a means of egress may not reduce the total egress capacity by > ¹/₂ that required.
- Means of egress capacity must be ≥ the largest required from any point to its termination.

Case study: Fig. 1003.2.3A. Minimum width per occupant for a stairway in occupancy E with sprinklers = 0.2" from IBC Table 1003.2.3. Stairway occupant load = 435. Actual width of stairway is 7'-3 ¹/₂". *Minimum width of stairway = 0.2" × 435 = 7'-3".*

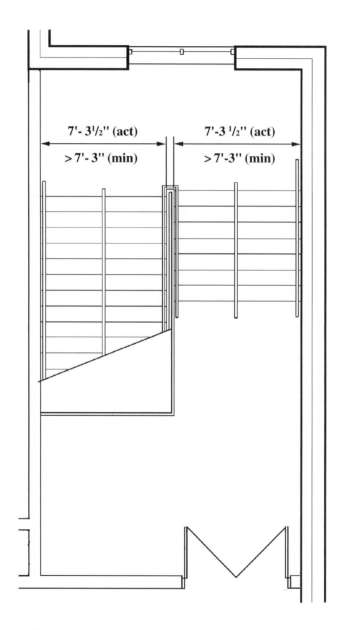

Fig. 1003.2.3A. Stairway plan. Montachusett Regional Vocational-Technical High School. Fitchburg, Massachusetts. HKT Architects, Inc. Sommerville, Massachusetts.

Case study: Fig. 1003.2.3B. The auditorium requires a total means of egress width ≥ 102", based on IBC Table 1003.2.3. While other requirements are also applicable, this section prohibits a layout wherein the loss of one means of egress would reduce the total width to less than 51". The actual means of egress width available (as limited by exit access doors) is 276". The auditorium meets this requirement because the loss of the largest doorway (72") would leave 204" available. 204" > 51", the minimum permitted to remain upon the loss of a doorway.

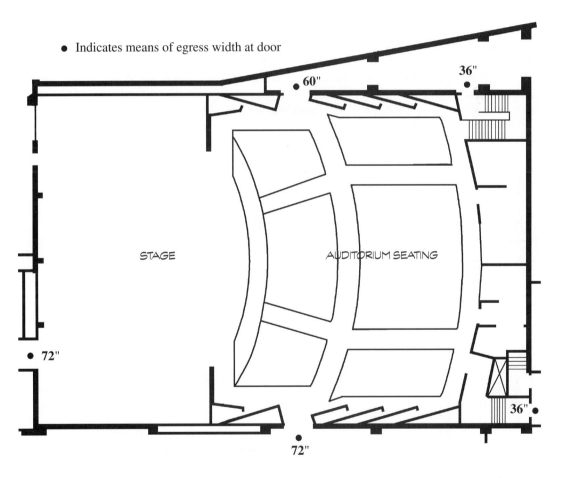

● Indicates means of egress width at door

36"

60"

STAGE

AUDITORIUM SEATING

72"

36"

72"

Fig. 1003.2.3B. Partial floor plan. Newman University Sports and Fine Arts Center. Wichita, Kansas. Gossen Livingston Associates, Inc., Architecture. Wichita, Kansas.

1003 General Means of Egress

1003.2.3.1 Door encroachment

- Door swing restrictions of this subsection do not apply to doors within individual dwelling units of the following occupancies:
  - R-2, R-3.
- In other cases, doors that open into the route of egress travel may not reduce the required egress width more than the following:
  - ½ the required width during the process of swinging open.
  - Doors and hardware may not project > 7" into the required width when fully open.

Case study: Figure 1003.2.3.1. The required egress width of corridor 368 is 6' based on occupant load. The actual width is 8'. It is assumed that the required width is centered in the corridor, although other locations are feasible. When door E05.1 swings 90°, it can open no further. Therefore, the two limitations of its projection into required egress width are applied to the door fully open. When fully open it projects 6" into the required egress width, which is < the 7" maximum and < ½ the required width. The greatest projection of double doors 368.2 into required egress width during their swing is 6", which is < ½ the required width. Although, due to the column, one door is not flush to the wall when fully open, neither door encroaches on the required egress width in the open position.

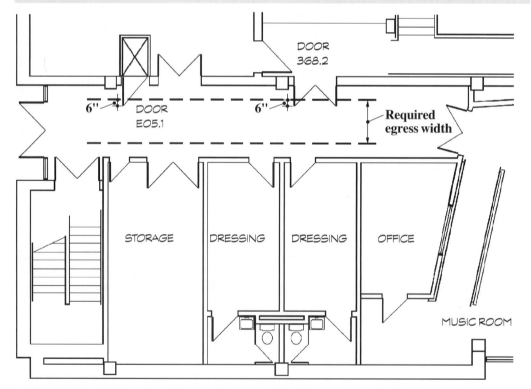

Fig. 1003.2.3.1. Partial floor plan. Newman Elementary School Renovations. Needham, Massachusetts. HKT Architects, Inc. Sommerville, Massachusetts.

1003 General Means of Egress

1003.2.4 Ceiling height

- The height minimum of this subsection does not apply to the following:
    - Sloped ceilings.
    - Ceilings of dwelling units in occupancy R.
    - Projections where permitted.
    - Headroom at stairs.
    - Height at doors.

    Note: The following are cited as governing the heights listed above:
    1207.2, "Minimum ceiling heights," for sloped and residential ceilings.
    1003.2.5, "Protruding objects," for protrusions into headroom.
    1003.3.3.2, "Headroom," for stairway headroom.
    1003.3.1.1, "Size of doors," for door headroom.

- Otherwise, ceiling height must be ≥ 7' in a means of egress.

1003.2.5.1 Headroom

- Door stops and closers may not reduce headroom to < 6'-6".
- Other protrusions below minimum ceiling height are governed as follows:
    - ≥ 6'-8"headroom is required at walking surfaces including the following:
    Walks.
    Corridors.
    Aisles.
    Passageways.
    - ≤ ½ the ceiling area in a means of egress may be reduced below required height.

    Note: 1003.2.4, "Ceiling height," is cited as governing minimum ceiling height.

- A barrier is required where headroom is reduced to < 6'-8" as follows:
    - The leading edge must be ≤ 2'-3" above the floor.
    - At locations other than doorways.

> **Case study: Fig. 1003.2.5.1 A.** The soffit of the stair landing at 7'-4" is above the 7' minimum ceiling height in a means of egress. A wall flush with the stringer of the lower flight provides the barrier required where protrusions below the 7' minimum ceiling height would otherwise reduce headroom below 6'-8". Doors B5 and B6 at 7'-2" meet the 6'-8" minimum headroom. Their ⅝" stops are above the 6'-6" minimum in doorways.

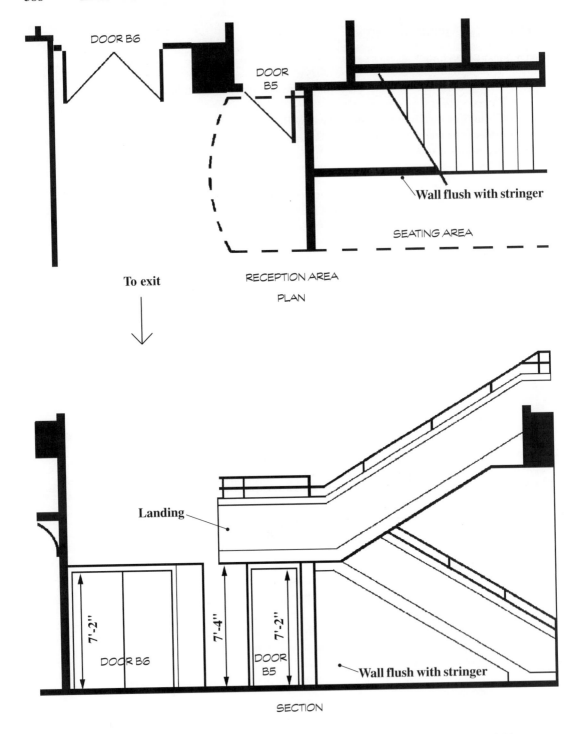

Fig. 1003.2.5.1A. Partial floor plan and section at reception area. Lubrication Engineers, Inc. Wichita, Kansas. Gossen Livingston Associates, Inc., Architecture. Wichita, Kansas.

Case study: Fig. 1003.2.5.1B. The detailing complies with the requirement to provide a barrier ≤ 2'-3" high to protect a protrusion which reduces headroom to < 6'-8". In this case, the protrusion is the lower flight of the stairway, and the barrier is a rail.

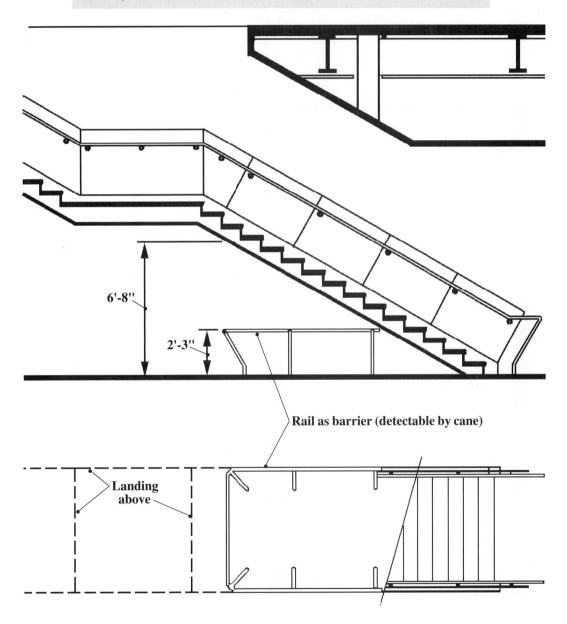

Rail as barrier (detectable by cane)

Landing above

Fig. 1003.2.5.1. Partial plan and section of stair in the first floor concourse. University of Connecticut New Downtown Campus at Stamford, Connecticut. Perkins Eastman Architects, P.C. New York, New York.

Case study: Fig. 1003.2.5.1C. The ceiling height of the corridor is 11'-4", well over the minimum. The light alcoves at the walls and those spanning across the corridor at the columns have soffits at 7'-4". Thus, the required 6'-8" minimum is maintained for headroom under objects extending below the ceiling.

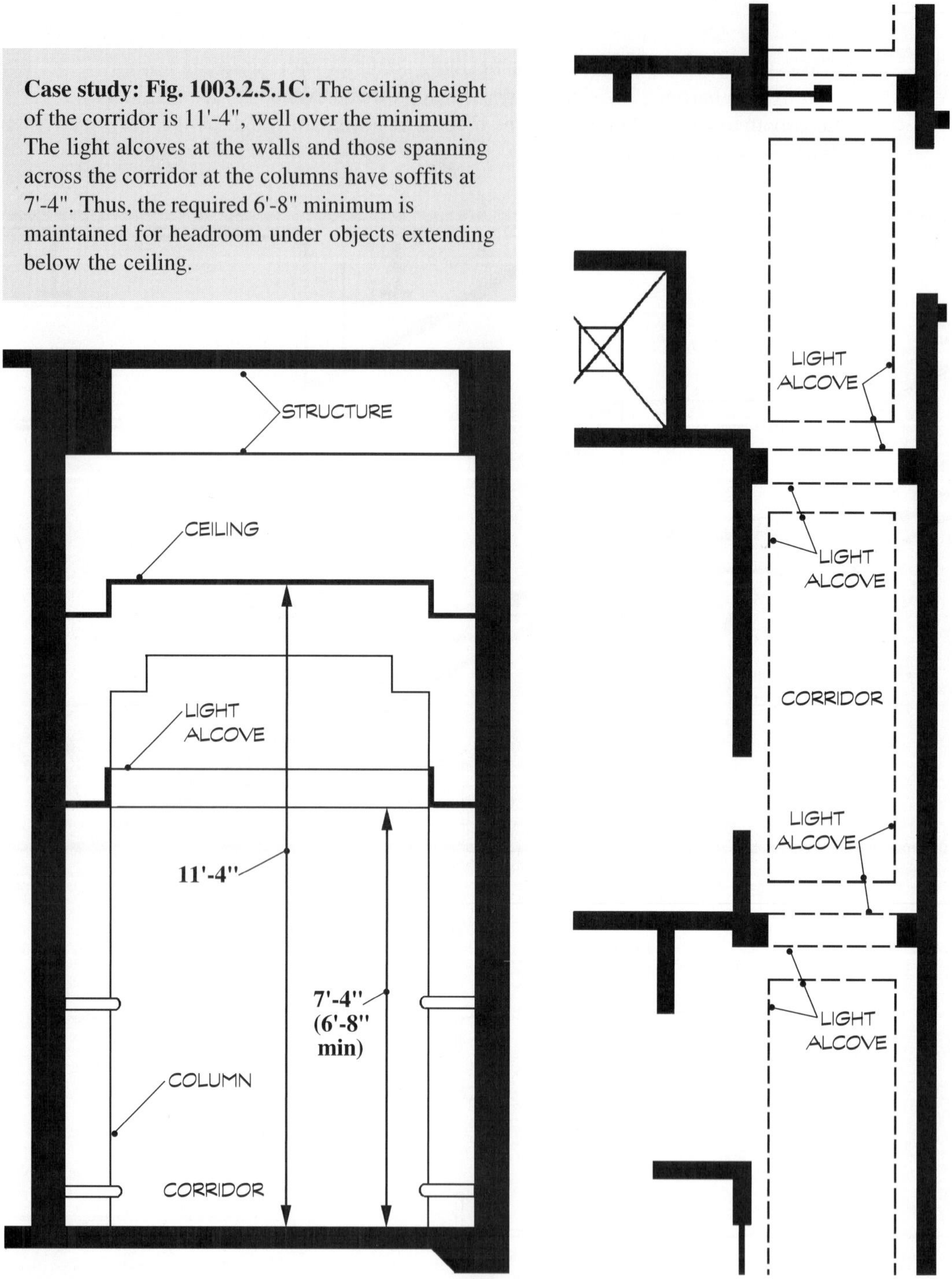

STRUCTURE

CEILING

LIGHT ALCOVE

11'-4"

7'-4" (6'-8" min)

COLUMN

CORRIDOR

LIGHT ALCOVE

LIGHT ALCOVE

CORRIDOR

LIGHT ALCOVE

LIGHT ALCOVE

Fig. 1003.2.5.1C. Partial floor plan and section at corridor. Lubrication Engineers, Inc. Wichita, Kansas. Gossen Livingston, Associates, Inc., Architecture. Wichita, Kansas.

1003 General Means of Egress

1003.2.5.2 Freestanding objects

- A freestanding object may not overhang the post on which it is mounted by > 12" as follows:
  - Where the lowest point of the overhanging object is > 2'-3" and < 6'-8" above the floor.

1003.2.5.3 Horizontal projections

- Handrails for the following may protrude ≤ 4½" from the wall:
  - Stairs.
  - Ramps.
- The following objects may not project horizontally from either side over a walking surface > 2'-3" or < 6'-8" above the floor:
  - Structural elements.
  - Fixtures.
  - Furnishings.

1003.2.5.4 Clear width

- Protruding objects may not reduce the minimum required clear width of accessible routes.

  Note: Section 1104, "Accessible Route," is cited as the source of requirements for such routes.

1003.2.6 Floor surface

- Means of egress walking surface must have the following characteristics:
  - Surface must be slip resistant.
  - Surface must be securely attached.

Case study: Fig. 1003.2.5.3A. The fire hose cabinet and fire extinguisher cabinet comply with the limit of protrusions to 4" over a walking surface, at a height > 2'-3" and < 6'-8".

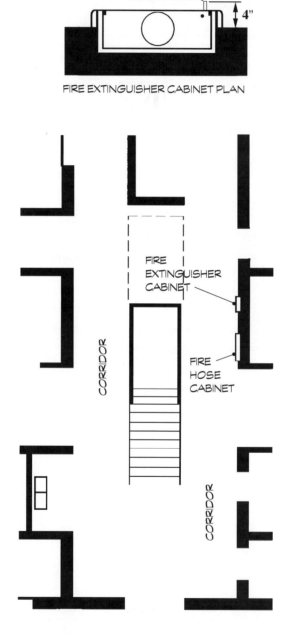

Fig. 1003.2.5.3A. **Partial plan and detail.** Newman University Sports and Fine Arts Center. Wichita, Kansas. Gossen Livingston Associates, Inc., Architecture. Wichita, Kansas.

Case study: Fig. 1003.2.5.3B. The wall mounted light fixtures protrude only 4" into the corridor, thus, complying with the 4" limitation for horizontal projections at heights > 2'-3" and < 6'-8". The wall mass projects 6" into the corridor at point A, but since it extends below the 2'-3" height, it is detectable by a cane and complies with the code.

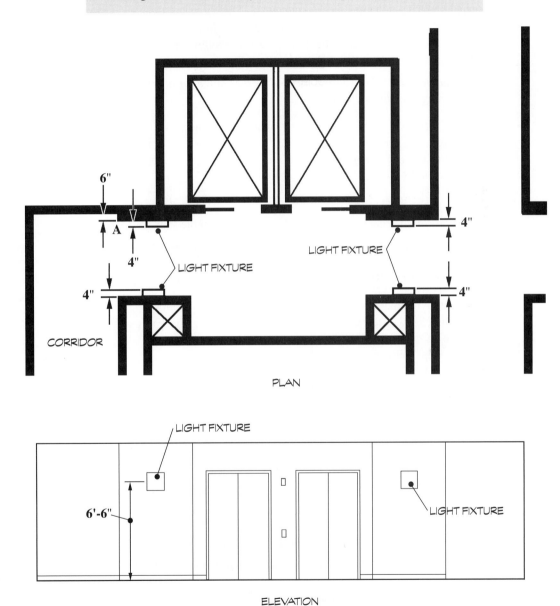

Fig. 1003.2.5.3B. Partial floor plan and interior elevation at elevators. Methodist Community Health Center. Sugar Land, Texas. HKS, Inc., Architects, Engineers, Planners. Dallas, Texas.

1003 General Means of Egress

1003.2.7 Elevation change

- A sloped floor is required for any changes in elevation where both the following apply:
  - In occupancy I-2.
  - In corridors serving nonambulatory occupants.
- A single riser ≤ 7" may be used in a means of egress as follows:
  - At exterior doors not required to be accessible in the following locations:
    In occupancies F, H, R-2, R-3, S, U.

    Note: Chapter 11, "Accessibility," is cited as the source for accessibility requirements throughout this subsection.

- A stair with ≤ 2 risers is allowed with the following conditions:
  - At locations not required to be accessible.
  - Step sizes must be as follows:
    Risers ≥ 4" and ≤ 7".
    Treads ≥ 13".
  - ≥ 1 handrail must be provided as follows:
    Within 2'-6" of the center of anticipated egress travel on the stair.

    Note: The following are cited as sources for requirements as noted:
    1003.3.3.3, "Stair treads and risers," step requirements.
    1003.3.3.11, "Handrails," for handrail requirements.

- Aisles for seating not required to be accessible are governed as follows:
  - Where seating has a difference in elevation < 12", aisles may have steps as follows:
    Treads to be ≥ 11".
    Risers to be as follows:
      Same gradient as seating.
      ≥ 4" and ≤ 8".
  - Aisle must have a handrail.

    Note: The following are cited as the source for requirements as noted:
    1008.9, "Assembly aisle walking surfaces," for stairs in aisles.
    1008.11, "Handrails," for aisle handrails.

- In other means of egress, a ramp is required for changes in elevation < 12" as follows:
  - Where elevation change is ≤ 6", one of the following is required:
    Handrails.
    Floor surface contrasting with adjacent floor surfaces.

    Note: 1003.3.4, "Ramps," is cited as governing ramps with a slope > 1:20.

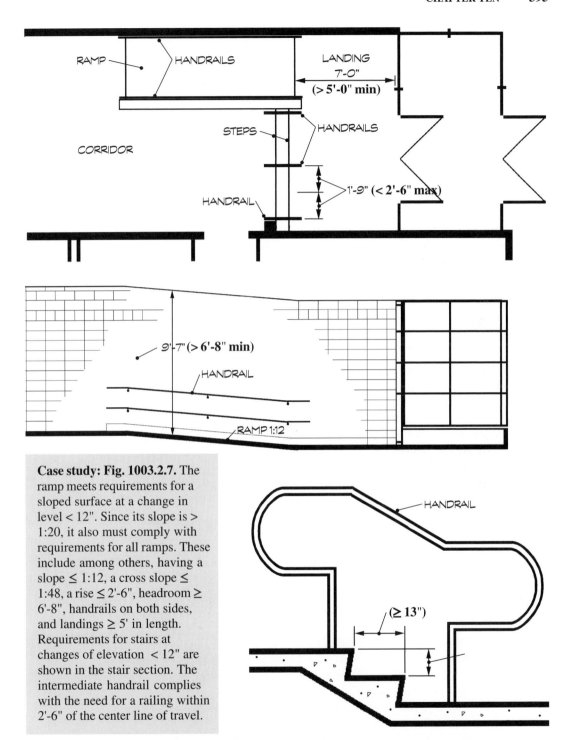

RAMP — HANDRAILS

LANDING
7'-0"
(> 5'-0" min)

CORRIDOR

STEPS — HANDRAILS

HANDRAIL

1'-9" (< 2'-6" max)

9'-7" (> 6'-8" min)

HANDRAIL

RAMP 1:12

Case study: Fig. 1003.2.7. The ramp meets requirements for a sloped surface at a change in level < 12". Since its slope is > 1:20, it also must comply with requirements for all ramps. These include among others, having a slope ≤ 1:12, a cross slope ≤ 1:48, a rise ≤ 2'-6", headroom ≥ 6'-8", handrails on both sides, and landings ≥ 5' in length. Requirements for stairs at changes of elevation < 12" are shown in the stair section. The intermediate handrail complies with the need for a railing within 2'-6" of the center line of travel.

HANDRAIL

(≥ 13")

Fig. 1003.2.7. Partial plan and sections at corridor. Montachusett Regional Vocational-Technical High School. Fitchburg, Massachusetts. HKT Architects, Inc. Sommerville, Massachusetts.

1003 General Means of Egress

1003.2.8 Means of egress continuity

- Continuity of the travel route in a means of egress is required as follows:
  - Only means of egress building components are permitted to interrupt the travel route.
  - The only obstructions permitted in the route are protrusions allowed by this chapter.
- The capacity required for a means of egress may not diminish in the direction of egress.

1003.2.9 Elevators, escalators, and moving walks

- Elevators may serve as an accessible means of egress.

  Note: 1003.2.13.3, "Elevators," is cited as the source of requirements.

- Otherwise, the following may not serve a required means of egress:
  - Elevators and escalators.
  - Moving walks.

  Note: The components listed above may become a means of egress for persons already using them at the time of an emergency.

1003.2.10.1 Where required

- Exit signs are not required in the following locations:
  - In spaces requiring only one exit or exit access.
  - At main exterior exit doors or gates as follows:
    Where their identity as exits is obvious.
    Where approved by the building official.
  - In the following occupancies and locations:
    I-3 sleeping areas
    R-1 guestrooms
    R-2 dwelling units
    Occupancy R-3
    Sleeping rooms
    Occupancy U
  - On seating side of vomitories or openings to seating areas, where all the following apply:
    In occupancies A-4 and A-5.
    Where there is grandstand seating.
    Where exit signs are provided as follows:
      In the concourse.
      Exit signs are readily apparent from vomitories.
    Where vomitories or openings are identified by emergency egress lighting.
- In other locations, approved exit signs are required as follows:
  - At exit and exit access doors as follows:
    Signs must be readily visible from any direction of egress travel.
  - Where exit access is not readily apparent to occupants.
  - Exit signs must be visible from every point in an exit access corridor as follows:
    No point may be > 100' from the nearest sign.

Case study: Fig. 1003.2.9. The escalators shown on this hospital floor do not serve as a means of egress as per code limitations. Exits are provided with exit access travel distances in compliance with code requirements. The elevators qualify as an accessible means of egress by virtue of the building being sprinklered and by their size, which meets required standards.

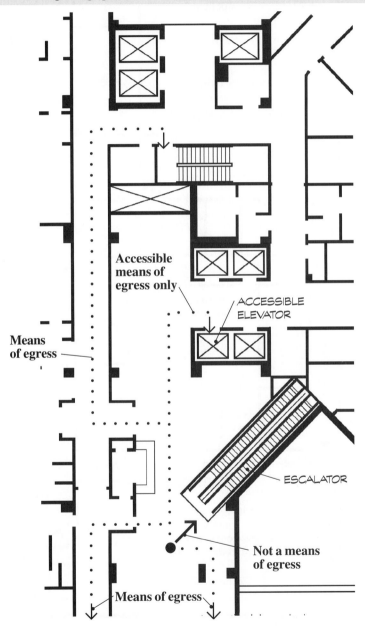

Fig. 1003.2.9. Partial floor plan. Christus St. Michael Health Care Center. Texarkana, Texas. Watkins Hamilton Ross Architects, Inc. Houston, Texas.

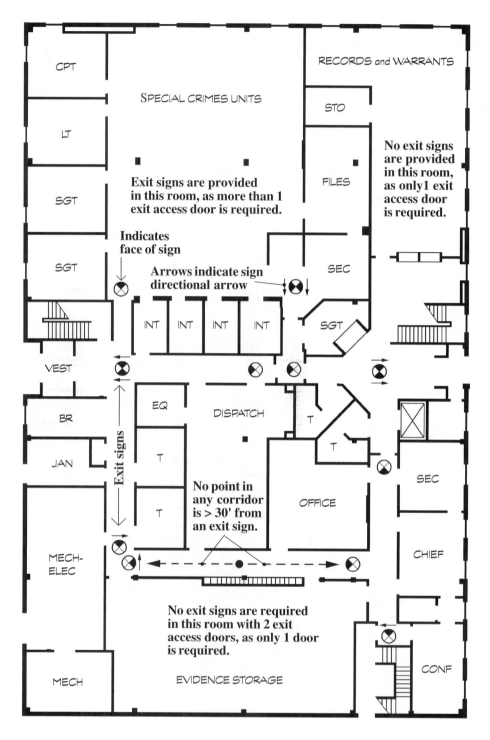

Fig. 1003.2.10.1. First floor plan. Hot Springs Police Department New Headquaraters. Hot Springs National Park, Arkansas. Cromwell Architects Engineers. Little Rock, Arkansas.

General Means of Egress

1003.2.10.2 Graphics

- Graphics for exit signs is governed as follows:
  - Direction of any arrow must not be readily changeable.
  - Letters in the word "EXIT" must have high contrast with background.
  - Must be clearly discernable when illuminated or not.
  - Proportions of letters larger than minimum must be the same as required for minimum size.
- Required sizes of letters in the word "EXIT" are as follows:

Table 1003.2.10.2	Exit Sign Graphics
Graphics	Dimension
Height	≥ 6"
Width of letter strokes	≥ ¾"
Width of letters E, X, and T	≥ 2"
Width of letter I	≥ ¾"
Spacing between letters	≥ ³/₈"

Fig. 1003.2.10.2A. Exit sign letter dimensions. Required minimums for letter sizes and spacing are shown for exit signs.

Fig. 1003.2.10.2B. Typical exit signs. Emergi-Lite. St. Matthews, South Carolina.

Case study: Fig. 1003.2.10.2B. The signs meet letter size and spacing minimums and other requirements. The arrow direction is not readily changeable, as it is available as a "snap-out" section in the sign face. As required, sign letters (in red) contrast with the sign face (aluminum) when the LED lights are on or off.

1003 General Means of Egress

1003.2.10.3 Stairway exit signs

- A tactile sign is required by each door to an egress stairway as follows:
  - Sign must state the word "EXIT" as follows:
    In raised letters.

1003.2.10.4 Exit sign illumination

- Internal or external illumination is required for exit signs.
- External illumination must provide at least 5 footcandles on sign face.
- Internal illumination must meet one of the following sets of conditions:
  - Sign face must have a luminance = to that produced by 5 footcandles of lighting.
  - Sign letters must have a luminance = to a minimum of 0.06 foot lamberts.
- Internally illuminated signs must comply with the following:
  - Signs must be listed for the purpose.
  - Signs must be approved.

1003.2.10.5 Power source

- Exit signs must be illuminated at all times.
- If primary power fails, signs must remain illuminated for a minimum of 90 minutes.
- Sign lighting that is not dependent on the primary power source need not be connected to an emergency power system.
- Sign lighting that is dependent on the primary power source must also be connected to one of the following emergency electrical systems:
  Storage batteries.
  Unit equipment.
  On site generator.

  Note: The ICC Electrical Code is cited as the source of requirements governing emergency power systems.

1003.2.11 Means of egress illumination

- Illumination requirements are shown below for means of egress, including exit discharge, during times when the portion of the building using the means of egress is occupied:

Table 1003.2.11	Egress Illumination
Occupancy	Illumination required
U	no
Aisle accessways in A	no
R-1 guest rooms	no
R-2 and R-3 dwelling units	no
R-2 and R-3 sleeping rooms	no
Sleeping rooms in I	no
All other	yes

General Means of Egress

1003.2.11.1 Illumination level

• Requirements for illumination at floor level in a means of egress are as follows:

Table 1003.2.11.1   **Egress Illumination at Floor Level**

Location and time	Illumination required if no fire alarm is activated	Illumination required if a fire alarm is activated
During performances in auditoriums, theaters, opera halls, and similar assembly occupancies	≥ 0.2 footcandle	≥ 1.0 footcandle
All other	≥ 1.0 footcandle	≥ 1.0 footcandle

1003.2.11.2 Illumination emergency power

• Normal power for means of egress illumination is to be the building's electrical source.
• An emergency power system must illuminate the following areas in case of power failure:
  ○ In areas requiring ≥ 2 means of egress:
     Exit access corridors.
     Exit access passageways.
     Aisles.
  ○ In buildings requiring ≥ 2 means of egress:
     Exit access corridors.
     Exit stairways.
     Exterior exit discharge elements immediately adjacent to exit discharge doors.
     Exit discharge elements that are within the building interior.

   Note: 1006.1, "General," is cited as governing exit discharge to the interior of a building.

• The emergency power system is governed as follows:
  ○ It must provide power for ≥ 90 minutes.
  ○ It must consist of one of the following:
     Storage batteries.
     Unit equipment.
     On-site generator.

   Note: ICC Electrical Code is cited as the source of requirements for emergency systems.

1003 General Means of Egress

Case study: Fig. 1003.2.11.2. The example shows a typical emergency lighting fixture and the symbol used on floor plans to indicate location. The many fixtures available for this purpose are similar in their surface mounting and two adjustible lamps. The battery powered units meet code performance requirements.

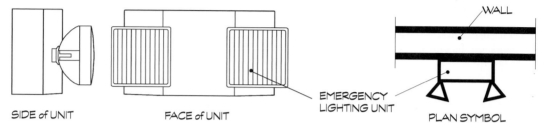

SIDE of UNIT   FACE of UNIT   EMERGENCY LIGHTING UNIT   WALL   PLAN SYMBOL

Fig. 1003.2.11.2. Elevations and symbol. Emergency lighting unit. Emergi-Lite. St. Matthews, South Carolina.

1003.2.12 Guards *(part 1 of 2)*

- Guards are not required in the following locations:
  - On the loading side of the following:
    Docks and piers.
  - On the audience side of the following:
    Stages stages and raised platforms.
  - At steps leading up to the following:
    Stages and raised platforms.
  - On the following, where used for entertainment or presentations:
    Runways.
    Ramps.
    Side stages.
  - At openings in the floors of the following:
    Performance area of stages.
    Performance area of platforms.
  - At the following elevated walkways for access to equipment listed below:
    Walkways:
      Serving stages and platforms.
    Equipment:
      Special lighting.
      Special equipment.
  - Along vehicle service pits as follows:
    Where not accessed by the public.
  - At cross aisles in assembly seating.

    Note: 1008.12, "Assembly guards," is cited as the source of requirements for guards in assembly seating that are not governed by this subsection.

1003 General Means of Egress

1003.2.12 Guards *(part 2 of 2)*

- Guards are required in other locations as follows:
    - Along the following which are > 2'-6" above an adjacent level:
        Open-sided walking surfaces.
        Mezzanines.
        Industrial equipment platforms.
        Stairways.
        Ramps.
        Landings.
- Guards are required along glazed sides of the following elements where all the conditions indicated below apply:
    - Elements:
        Stairways.
        Ramps.
        Landings.
    - Conditions:
        Where walking surfaces are > 2'-6" above an adjacent level.
        Where glazing does not meet the strength requirements of a guard.
- Guards must meet minimum strength requirements.

    Note: 1607.7, "Loads on handrails, guards, grab bars and vehicle barriers," is cited as the source of applied loading requirements that guards must be able to withstand.

1003.2.12.1 Height

- Guards serving as handrails in the following locations are governed as listed below:
    - Applicable locations:
        Occupancy R-3.
        Within dwelling units of occupancy R-2.
    - Required heights:
        ≥ 38" where adjacent to stairs:
            Measured vertically from the leading edge of the tread nosing.
        ≥ 34" where located elsewhere:
            Measured vertically from one of the following:
                Adjacent walking surface.
                Adjacent seatboard.
- Other guards must have a height ≥ 42" as follows:
    - Measured vertically from the following lower points as applicable:
        Leading edge of tread.
        Adjacent walking surface.
        Adjacent seatboard.

> **Case study: Fig. 1003.2.12.1.** 4", 6", and 8" spheres cannot pass through the guard at heights specified by 1003.2.12.2. Circles superimposed on the illustration are to scale and illustrate their relationship to openings. The centerline of the top rail is at 42" above tread nosings, thus, meeting the minimum height requirement of 42" to the top of the rail, as specified in 1003.2.12.1. The guard is in full compliance with the code.

1003.2.12.2 Opening limitations

- Sizes of openings in guards are limited based on their ability to restrict the passage of spheres of the sizes indicated below.

  Note: This method of measure accounts for space between elements that may not be in a vertical plane.

Table 1003.2.12.2	Sizes of Spheres That May Not Pass through a Guard	
Location	Sphere size	Height within guard
Assembly seating at ends of aisles terminating at fascias of boxes, balconies, galleries	4"	To a height of 26"
"	8"	Between heights of 26" and 42"
Other occupancy A areas and occupancy B, E, I-1, I-2, I-4, M, R, U	4"	To a height of 34"
"	6"	In triangular space between bottom rail and treads and risers
"	8"	Between heights of 34" and 42"
Occupancy I-3, F, H, S	21"	Entire guard area
Access to mechanical electrical, and plumbing in all occupancies	21"	Entire guard area

1003.2.13 Accessible means of egress

- Alterations to existing buildings do not require an accessible means of egress.
- Other buildings require the following accessible means of egress:
  - Accessible spaces require ≥ 1 accessible means of egress.
  - A minimum of 2 means of egress are required from the following space:
    The space requires ≥ 2 means of egress.
    The space is accessible.

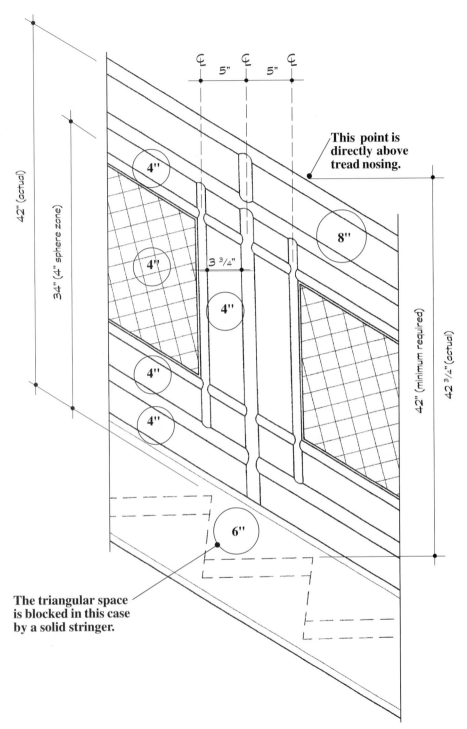

Fig. 1003.2.12.1. Elevation of guard at stairs. Montacahusett Regional Vocational-Technical High School. Fitchburg, Massachusetts. HKT Architects, Inc. Sommerville, Massachusetts.

1003 General Means of Egress

1003.2.13.1 General

- An exterior area for assisted rescue is required in the following case:
  - Where exit discharge is not accessible.

    Note: 1003.2.13.7, "Exterior area for assisted rescue," is cited as the source of requirements for this feature.

- Where the exit stairway is open to the exterior, the accessible means of egress must include one of the following:
  - An area of refuge.
  - An exterior area for assisted rescue.

    Note: The following are cited as sources of requirements for the features listed above:
    1003.2.13.5, "Areas of refuge."
    1003.2.13.7, "Exterior area for assisted rescue."

- Otherwise, required accessible means of egress must comply with the following:
  - They must be continuous to a public way.
  - They must consist of ≥ 1 of the following:
    Accessible routes.
    Stairways within exit enclosures.
    Elevators.
    Horizontal exits.
    Smoke barriers.

    Note: The following are cited as governing the above listed elements as per titles:
    Section 1104, "Accessible Route."
    1003.2.13.2, "Enclosed stairways."
    1005.3.2, "Vertical exit enclosures."
    1003.2.13.3, "Elevators."

1003.2.13.1.1 Buildings with four or more stories

- This subsection applies to buildings where a required accessible floor is ≥ 4 stories above or below the level of exit discharge.
- An elevator serving as an accessible means of egress is not required where all of the following conditions apply:
  - The building is sprinklered as per NFPA 13 or 13R.
  - The floor has a horizontal exit.
  - The floor is at or above the level of exit discharge.
- An elevator serving as an accessible means of egress is not required where all of the following conditions apply:
  - The building is sprinklered as per NFPA 13 or 13R.
  - The floor has a ramp serving as an accessible means of egress.

    Note: 1003.3.4, "Ramps," is cited as governing ramps as means of egress.

Case study: Fig. 1003.2.13. The 1242 occupants of the gymnasium require 4 eixts. Therefore, ≥ 2 accessible means of egress are required. The gymnasium is in compliance, as 4 accessible exits are provided.

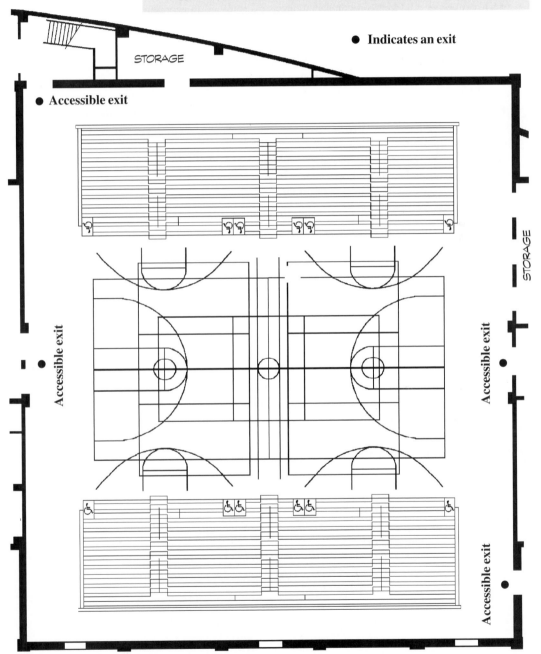

● **Indicates an exit**

● **Accessible exit**

Fig. 1003.2.13. Gymnasium floor plan. Newman University Sports and Fine Arts Center. Wichita, Kansas. Gossen Livingston, Associates, Inc., Architecture. Wichita, Kansas.

1003 General Means of Egress

1003.2.13.2 Enclosed stairways

- This subsection addresses enclosed stairways serving as an accessible means of egress.
- The following stairways do not require a clear space $\geq$ 4' between handrails:
  - Where serving one guestroom or dwelling unit.
  - In buildings sprinklered as per NFPA 13 or 13R.
  - For stairways that are accessed from a horizontal exit.
  - Where serving open parking garages.
- In other cases, stairways serving an accessible means of egress must have the following:
  - A clear width $\geq$ 4' between handrails.
  - One of the following is required:

    An area of refuge within a floor-level landing.

    To be accessed from a horizontal exit.

    To be accessed from an area of refuge.

    Note: 1003.2.13.5, "Areas of refuge," is cited as governing areas of refuge from which the stairway is to be accessed where this option is employed.

1003.2.13.3 Elevators

- Accessible elevators need not be accessed from one of the following in open parking garages:
  - Area of refuge.
  - Horizontal exit.
- Accessible elevators need not be accessed from one of the following in buildings sprinklered as per NFPA 13 or 13R:
  - Area of refuge.
  - Horizontal exit.
- Otherwise, elevators must comply with the following to be considered accessible:
  - They must meet emergency operation and signaling device requirements.
  - They must have standby power.
  - They must be accessed from one of the following:

    Area of refuge.

    Horizontal exit.

    Note: The following are cited as governing the elements listed above:

    Section 211 of ASME A17.1, "Safety Code for Elevators and Escalators," for emergency operations and signaling requirements.

    Section 2702, "Emergency and Standby Power Systems," for standby power.

    Section 3003, "Emergency Operations," for standby power.

    1003.2.13.5, "Areas of refuge."

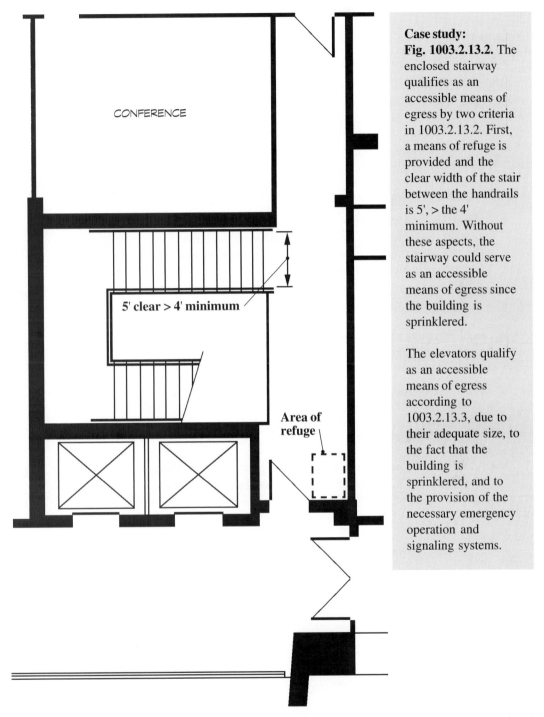

CONFERENCE

5' clear > 4' minimum

Area of refuge

Case study:
Fig. 1003.2.13.2. The enclosed stairway qualifies as an accessible means of egress by two criteria in 1003.2.13.2. First, a means of refuge is provided and the clear width of the stair between the handrails is 5', > the 4' minimum. Without these aspects, the stairway could serve as an accessible means of egress since the building is sprinklered.

The elevators qualify as an accessible means of egress according to 1003.2.13.3, due to their adequate size, to the fact that the building is sprinklered, and to the provision of the necessary emergency operation and signaling systems.

Fig. 1003.2.13.2. Partial plan at stairway and elevators. University of Connecticut New Downtown Campus at Stamford, Connecticut. Perkins Eastman Architects, P.C. New York, New York.

1003 General Means of Egress

1003.2.13.4 Platform lifts

- Platform lifts, such as for wheelchairs lifts, may serve as an accessible means of egress only in certain limited applications.

    Note: The following are cited as governing platform lifts:
    1108.7, "Lifts," lists limited applications where wheelchair lifts are permitted to serve in an accessible means of egress.
    ASME A17.1, "Safety Code for Elevators and Escalators," governs the installation of platform lifts.

1003.2.13.5 Areas of refuge

- A required area of refuge must be accessible from the space it serves as follows:
    - Access must be provided by an accessible means of egress.
    - The accessible route from an accessible space to the nearest area of refuge must be ≤ travel distance, as limited by the occupancy.

    Note: 1004.2.4, "Exit access travel distance," is cited as governing travel distance length and other characteristics.

- A required area of refuge must have direct access to one of the following:
    - An enclosed stairway.
    - An elevator.

    Note: The following are cited as governing the elements listed above:
    1003.2.13.2, "Enclosed stairways."
    1005.3.2, "Vertical exit enclosures."
    1003.2.13.3, "Elevators."

- An elevator lobby serving as an area of refuge must comply with one of the following:
    - Shaft and lobby must meet smokeproof enclosure requirements.
    - Elevators must be in an area of refuge formed by one of the following:
        Horizontal exit.
        Smoke barrier.

    Note: 1005.3.2.5, "Smokeproof enclosures," is cited as the source of requirements for such elements.

Case study: Fig. 1003.2.13.5. Access to the area of refuge is provided by an accessible means of egress. The area of refuge has direct access to the elevator. The elevator lobby, including the telephone area, which serves as the area of refuge, meets smokeproof enclosure requirements. The area of refuge is, therefore, in compliance with the code.

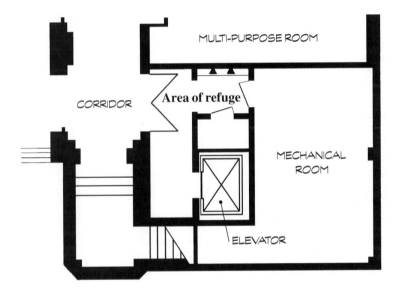

Fig. 1003.2.13.5. Plan of elevator with refuge area. Lady Bird Johnson Wildflower Center. Austin, Texas. Overland Partners, Inc. San Antonio, Texas.

1003 General Means of Egress

1003.2.13.5.1 Size

- This subsection addresses wheelchair spaces in an area of refuge.
- Wheelchair spaces may not protrude into the minimum required width of the means of egress.
- Wheelchairs may be positioned no more than two deep from the path of travel.
- Occupant load for determining the number of wheelchairs required is as follows:
  - The sum of the occupant load of the area of refuge plus that of the area served.
- The minimum size of a wheelchair space is 30" × 48".
- Wheelchair spaces required, as listed below, are based on the following equation:

Occupant load ÷ 200 = number of wheelchair spaces required

Table 1003.2.13.5.1   Wheelchair Spaces Required

Occupant load	Spaces required	Occupant load	Spaces required
1 – 200	1	1001 – 1200	6
201 – 400	2	1201 – 1400	7
401 – 600	3	1401 – 1600	8
601 – 800	4	1601 – 1800	9
801 – 1000	5	etc.	etc.

1003.2.13.5.2 Separation

- The subsection does not apply to the following areas of refuge:
  - Where located within a stairway enclosure.
  - Where the areas of refuge and areas served are sprinklered as per NFPA 13 or 13R.
- Other areas of refuge must be separated from the rest of the story by a smoke barrier.

  Note: Section 709, "Smoke Barriers," is cited as governing those elements.

- Areas of refuge must be designed to minimize the penetration of smoke.

1003.2.13.5.3 Two-way communication

- Areas of refuge must have a communication system as follows:
  - Where a central point is continuously attended, the following is required:
    2-way communication between the area of refuge and the central point.
  - Where a central point is not continuously attended, both of the following are required:
    2-way communication between the area of refuge and the central point.
    A public telephone system available though controlled access.
- The central point for the communication system must be approved by the fire department.
- The 2-way communication system must include audible signals.
- The 2-way communication system must include visual signals.

Case study: Fig. 1003.2.13.5.1. The areas of refuge in the enclosed stairway do not encroach on the minimum width required for egress. They are no more than 2 deep from the path of travel. They are 30" × 48", thus, meeting size requirements. The areas of refuge are in compliance.

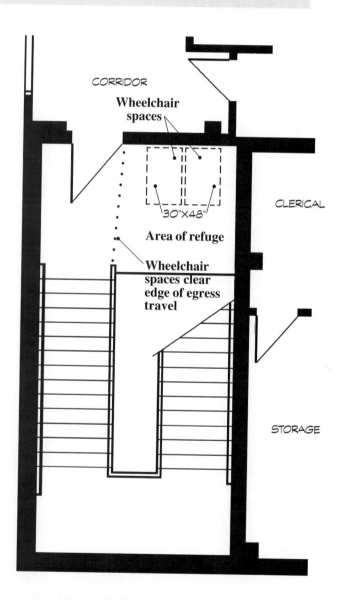

Fig. 1003.2.13.5.1. Plan of stair with area of refuge. University of Connecticut New Downtown Campus at Stamford, Connecticut. Perkins Eastman Architects, P.C. New York, New York.

1003 General Means of Egress

1003.2.13.5.4 Instructions

- The following instructions for emergencies must be posted in an area of refuge next to the communications system:
  - Directions to other means of egress.
  - Instructions advising ambulatory persons, who are not assisting others, to use the exit's stairway as soon as possible.
  - A description of how assistance will be provided for use of the stairway or elevator.
  - Instructions on how to call for assistance.
  - Instructions on how to use the communications system.
  - Instructions on how to use the area of refuge.

1003.2.13.5.5 Identification

- Doors to areas of refuge from the adjacent floor area must be identified by a sign as follows:
  - Sign must state "AREA OF REFUGE."
  - Sign must have the International Symbol of Accessibility.
  - The area of refuge sign must be illuminated where exit sign illumination is required.

    Note: 1003.2.10.4, "Exit sign illumination," is cited as governing sign illumination.

- Tactile signage is required at doors to areas of refuge.

    Note: ICC/ANSI A117.1, "Accessible and Usable Buildings and Facilities," is cited as governing the signage required by this subsection.

1003.2.13.6 Signage

- Signage, with directions to accessible means of egress, is required at the following locations:
  - At exits and elevators serving an accessible space but which do not provide an approved accessible means of egress.

1003.3.1 Doors

- Means of egress doors must be apparent as follows:
  - They must be easily distinguished from adjacent construction.
  - They must be readily recognizable as means of egress doors.
  - They may not be covered with reflective materials such as mirrors.
  - They may not be concealed by the following:
    Curtains.
    Drapes.
    Decorations.
    Similar materials.

    Note: 1005.3.1, "Exterior exit doors." is cited as providing additional requirements.

- Doors provided that are in excess of the minimum required must meet the same requirements as those of required doors.

1003 General Means of Egress

1003.3.1.1 Size of doors

- Clear width for swinging doors is measured as follows:
  - From the stop to the face of the door when it is open at 90°.
- The following doorway must have a width ≥ 32" when only one leaf is open:
  - A door with two leafs.
  - A door required to have a width ≥ 32".
- Minimum door width is the greater of the following:
  - Minimum width established by occupant load.
  - Minimum width listed below:

Table 1003.3.1.1a   Minimum Width of Doors

Doors	Minimum clear width	Maximum width of swinging door
Serving other than means of egress in R-2 and R-3	none	none
To storage closets < 10 sf other than R-2 and R-3	none	48"
To resident sleeping rooms in I-3	28"	48"
For moving beds in means of egress in I-2	41½"	48"
Revolving doors	none	none
Interior egress doors in dwelling units not required to be accessible or adaptable	none	none
Doors required to be accessible in Type B dwelling units (units adaptable to accessibility)	31¾"	48"
Other means of egress doors	32"	48"

Note: 1003.3.1.3.1, "Revolving doors." is cited as providing requirements for revolving doors.

- Minimum door heights required are as listed below:

Table 1003.3.1.1b   Minimum Door Height

Doors	Minimum height
Required exit door of a dwelling unit	6'-8"
Doors within dwelling units	6'-6"
Exterior doors other than the required exit	6'-4"
Interior egress doors in dwelling units not required to be accessible or adaptable	none
Other means of egress doors	6'-8"

1003.3.1.1.1 Projections into clear width

- Projections permitted into the clear width of a door opening are as shown below:

Height in door opening	Projection allowed
≥ 2'-10" and ≤ 6'-8"	≤ 4"
< 2'-10"	none

1003 General Means of Egress

1003.3.1.2 Door swing

- The following means of egress doors are not governed by this subsection:
  - The following locations with an occupant load ≤ 10:
    - Private garages.
    - Office areas.
    - Factory areas.
    - Storage areas.
  - In occupancy I-3 used as a place of detention.
  - Within or serving a single dwelling unit in occupancies R-2 and R-3.
  - Revolving doors in occupancies other than H.
  - Horizontal sliding doors in occupancies other than H.
  - Power-operated doors.

    Note: The following are cited as sources of requirements for the door types indicated:
    1003.3.1.3.1, "Revolving doors."
    1003.3.1.3.3, "Horizontal sliding doors."
    1003.3.1.3.2, "Power-operated doors."

- Other egress doors are required to be side-hinged swinging as follows:
  - Doors must swing in the direction of travel in either of the following cases:
    - Where the occupant load > 50.
    - Where the occupancy is high-hazard.
- At the latch side, the force necessary to open the door is limited as follows:

Table 1003.3.1.2   Force Required at Door

Door type	Door action	Force necessary for door action
Side-swinging, interior, no closer	To open	≤ 5 lbs
Side-swinging, sliding, folding	Release of latch	≤ 15 lbs
"	Start door in motion	≤ 30 lbs
"	Swing to full-open position	≤ 15 lbs

1003 General Means of Egress

1003.3.1.3.1 Revolving doors

- Revolving doors must have all the following characteristics:
  - Be collapsible into a bookfold position as follows:
      Provide parallel paths of travel.
      Travel paths to total 36" in width.
  - Be a minimum distance of 10' from the following:
      Stairs.
      Escalator.
  - Be separated from the following by a dispersal area:
      Stairs.
      Escalator.
  - Be within 10' of a side-swinging door in the same wall.

    Note: 1003.3.1, "Doors," is cited as the source of requirements for side-swinging doors.

  - Have a maximum speed in revolutions per minute as follows:

Table 1003.3.1.3.1   Maximum Speed for Revolving Doors

Speed control type	Inside diameter of door							
	6.5'	7.0'	7.5'	8.0'	8.5'	9.0'	9.5'	10'
RPM for power-driven speed control	11	10	9	9	8	8	7	7
RPM for manual speed control	12	11	11	10	9	9	8	8

Source: IBC Table 1003.3.1.3.1.

1003.3.1.3.1.1 Egress component

This subsection addresses revolving doors serving in a means of egress.

- Such revolving doors must comply with the following:
  - Have collapsible doors of adequate size.
  - Have the necessary relationship to the following:
      Stairs.
      Escalators.
      A swinging door.
  - Have RPM limits as appropriate.

    Note: 1003.3.1.3.1, "Revolving doors," is cited as requiring compliance. A summary of its requirements are shown above.

- They may not be assigned more than half the required egress capacity.

- Revolving doors may be assigned only ≤ 50 occupants each.

- Must be collapsible into a bookfold position as follows:
  - With a force of ≤ 130 lbs.
  - With the force applied ≤ 3" from the outer edge of a door leaf.

1003 General Means of Egress

1003.3.1.3.1.2 Other than egress component

This subsection addresses revolving doors not serving in a means of egress.

- Such revolving doors must comply with the following:
  - Have collapsible doors of adequate size.
  - Have the necessary relationship to the following:
    Stairs and escalators.
    A swinging door.
  - Have RPM limits as appropriate.

    Note: 1003.3.1.3.1, "Revolving doors," is cited as requiring compliance. A summary of its requirements are shown above.

- The force necessary to collapse the doors may be >180 lbs as follows:
  - Where it is reduced to ≤ 130 lbs in at least one of the following circumstances:
    Loss of power that holds doors in position.
    Activation of sprinklers.
    Activation of smoke detection system as follows:
      System covers the area inside the building within 75' of the revolving doors.
    Activation of manual control switch reducing the necessary force to < 130 lbs:
      The switch must be in an approved location.
      The switch must be clearly defined.

    Note: Section 907, "Fire Alarm and Detection Systems," is cited as governing the smoke detection system indicated above.

- In other cases, the force necessary to collapse a revolving door must be ≤ 180 lbs.

1003.3.1.3.2 Power-operated doors (*part 1 of 2*)

- Doors in I-3 are not subject to this subsection.
- Certain horizontal sliding doors are not subject to this subsection.

    Note: 1003.3.1.3.3, "Horizontal sliding doors," is cited as defining sliding doors that are not governed by this subsection.

- This subsection addresses other doors serving in a means of egress as follows:
  - Operated by power.
  - Doors with a photoelectric-actuated mechanism as follows:
    Opens door upon approach of a person.
  - Manual doors with power-assistance.

    Note: The following are cited as governing the types of doors indicated:
    BHMA A156.10, "Power Operated Pedestrian Doors."
    BHMA A156.19, "Power Assist and Low Energy Operated Doors."

- Such doors must have the following capability upon loss of power:
  - Able to be opened or closed manually.

1003 General Means of Egress

1003.3.1.3.2 Power-operated doors (*part 2 of 2*)

- At the side latch, the maximum force necessary for manual operation of the doors is as follows:

Manual operation of door	Force
Release of latch	$\leq$ 15 lbs
Start door in motion	$\leq$ 50 lbs
Swing to full-open position	$\leq$ 15 lbs

- Upon application of force in the direction of egress, the door must perform as follows:
  - Swing to full opening width from any position.
- The following applies to biparting doors in the emergency break-out position:
  - The requirement for a 32" width applies to the opening with both doors open.

    Note: 1003.3.1.1, "Size of doors," is cited as requiring the 32" width when one door of a double door is open in other cases.

1003.3.1.3.3 Horizontal sliding doors

This subsection addresses horizontal sliding doors serving in a means of egress.

- Such doors may serve in a means of egress in other than occupancy H.
- Power requirements are as follows:
  - Doors must be power operated.
  - Doors must have an integrated standby power supply.
  - Door power must be supervised electronically.
- Manual requirements are as follows:
  - Doors must operate manually if power is lost as follows:
    By a simple method from both sides.
    Without special knowledge or effort.
  - The force necessary to operate the doors manually is limited as follows:
    $\leq$ 30 lbs to set door in motion.
    $\leq$ 15 lbs to open door to minimum width required for opening.
    $\leq$ 15 lbs to close door.
    $\leq$ 15 lbs to open door in the following case:
    When 250-lb force is applied $\perp$ to door at a point adjacent to operating device.
- Where fire-protection rating is required, the door is governed as follows:
  - Must have applicable fire-protection rating.
  - Must be automatically closed by smoke detection system.

    Note: The following are cited as governing the fire protection afforded by the doors:
    NFPA 80, "Fire Doors and Windows."
    Section 714, "Opening Protectives."

- Doors must open to required width as follows:
  - Within 10 seconds of activating operating device.

Case study: Fig. 1003.3.1.3.3. Power-operated sliding doors become manually operated doors upon a loss of power to the doors. As manually operated doors, they are required in many locations by section 1003.3.1.2, "Door swing," to be side-hinged doors that swing in the direction of egress travel. The horizontal sliding doors in the hospital of the example below are such a case. They comply with the power and force requirements, as well as having the capability to swing from the side in an emergency. They are in compliance with all code requirements.

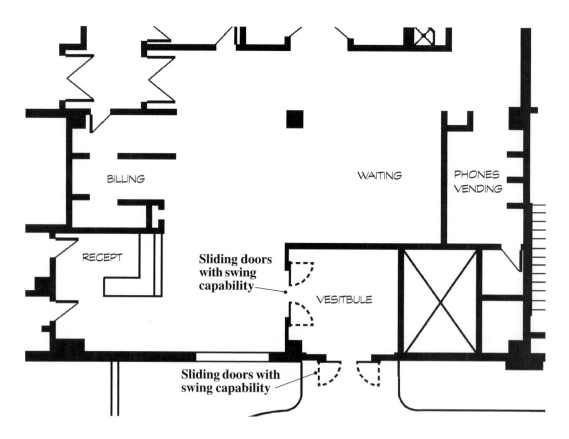

Fig. 1003.3.1.3.3. Partial floor plan. Christus St. Michael Health Care Center. Texarkana, Texas. Watkins Hamilton Ross Architects, Inc. Houston, Texas.

1003 General Means of Egress

1003.3.1.3.4 Access-controlled egress doors

- • The subsection addresses entrance doors in a means of egress.
- • The following doors may have an entrance and egress access control system:
  - ○ Doors in occupancy A, B, E, M, R-1, R-2 as follows:
    Entrance doors.
    Entrance doors to tenant spaces.
- • Access control systems are governed as follows:
  - ○ They must be approved.
  - ○ A sensor is required on the egress side as follows:
    Sensor detects an approaching person.
    Doors unlock upon a signal from the sensor.
    Doors unlock upon loss of power to the sensor.
  - ○ Doors must unlock upon loss of power to door locks.
  - ○ A manual unlocking device must be provided as follows:
    Located $\geq$ 3'-4" and $\leq$ 4' above floor.
    Located $\leq$ 5' from locked doors.
    Must be readily accessible
    Must be identified by a sign.
    Device activation must interrupt power to lock.
    Device must operate independently of access control electronics.
    Device activation must leave doors unlocked for $\geq$ 30 seconds.
  - ○ Doors must unlock upon activation of a fire-protection system as follows:
    Building fire alarm system.
    Building sprinkler system.
    Building fire detection system.
    Doors to remain unlocked until the fire alarm system is reset.
- • The following applies to occupancies A, B, E, and M:
  - ○ Entrance doors may not be locked as follows:
    From the egress side.
    During times the building is open to the public.

1003.3.1.3.5 Security grilles

- • Security grilles are permitted at the main exit of the following occupancies:
  - ○ B, F, M, S.
- • The following types of security grilles are permitted:
  - ○ Horizontal sliding.
  - ○ Vertical.
- • Grilles must be operable, as follows, during the time the space is occupied:
  - ○ From inside without the use of a key.
  - ○ Without special knowledge or effort.
- • Grilles must remain in full-open position as follows:
  - ○ During times the space is occupied by the general public.

1003 General Means of Egress

1003.3.1.4 Floor elevation

- This subsection addresses floor elevations on each side of a door.
- This subsection does not apply to exterior doors complying with both of the following:
  - Not on an accessible route.
  - Meeting size and functional requirements of the code.

  > Note: 1005.3.1, "Exterior exit doors," is cited as defining the exit doors excluded. This subsection and its referenced subsections describe size and functional requirements for exterior doors, thus, encompassing virtually all such doors permitted in a building.

- The following locations have requirements indicated below:
  - Locations:
    Occupancy R-3 > 3 stories.
    Individual units of occupancy R-2.
  - Requirements:
    Door at interior stairs:
      Door may open at the top step as follows:
        Door may not swing over the top step.
    Screen doors and storm doors may swing over the following:
      Stairs and landings.
- A single step is permitted at exterior doors where all the following apply:
  - In occupancies F, H, R-2, R-3, S, U.
  - Door is not required to be accessible.
  - Step is ≤ 7" high.
- Variation in elevation on each side of a door is permitted where both of the following apply:
  - Where caused by differences in finish materials.
  - Where the difference is ≤ ½".
- Variation in elevation on each side of certain doors are limited as indicated below for the following location:
  - In Type B dwelling units (adaptable to accessibility) as follows:
    At exterior decks.
    At exterior patios.
    At exterior balconies.
  - Limitations for exterior surface:
    Must be impervious.
    Must be ≤ 4" below adjacent interior finished floor of the unit.
- The following applies to all other cases:
  - One of the following is required on each side of a door at the same elevation:
    A floor.
    A landing as follows:
      Interior landings must be level.
      Exterior landings may slope ≤ 1:48.

1003 General Means of Egress

1003.3.1.5 Landings at doors

- Landing length in the direction of travel is governed as follows:
  - In the following locations such length is not required to be >36":
    - Occupancy R-3.
    - Occupancy U.
    - Within individual units of R-2.
  - Landings in other locations must have a length ≥ 44" in the direction of travel.
- Landings must have a width equal to the larger of the following:
  - Equal to the width of the stairway.
  - Equal to the width of the door.
- A door may protrude ≤ 7" into the required width of a landing as follows:
  - Where the door is fully open.
  - Door hardware is included.
- A door may protrude ≤ ½ the required width of a landing where all the following apply:
  - The occupant load is ≥ 50.
  - With the door in any position.
  - Door hardware is included.

Case study: Fig. 1003.3.1.5. The landing width at the turn is measured as a radius which must be ≥ the 3'-11" width of the stair. In this case, the landing at the door is 4'-0" wide. The length of the landing in the direction of travel is > than the 44" minimum. The width of the landing is greater than the 3' width of the door. The door (including hardware) protrudes 7" into the landing radius when fully open, thus, complying with the maximum permitted. The door does not protrude into the required landing width more than half the required width, as indicated by the arc in the illustration. The landings comply with the code.

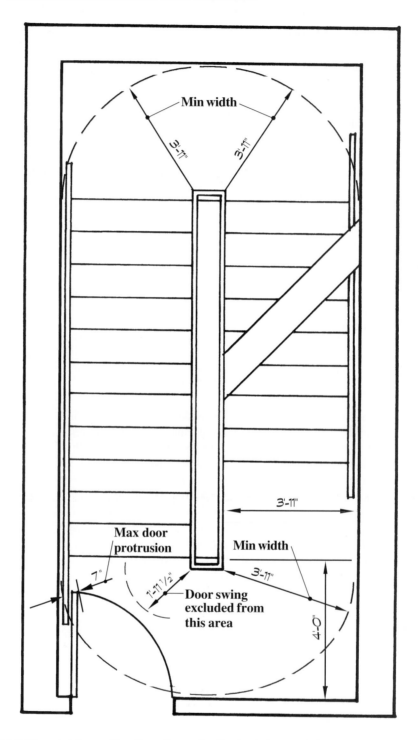

Fig. 1003.3.1.5. Plan at stairway. Hoyt Street Properties. Portland, Oregon. Ankrom Mosian Associated Architects. Portland, Oregon.

1003 General Means of Egress

1003.3.1.6 Thresholds

- Doorway thresholds are limited in height as follows:

Location	Height
Dwelling unit sliding doors	≤ ¾"
Other doors	≤ ½"

- A beveled edge is required at doorways for changes in floor level > ¼" as follows:
  - The higher floor material must be beveled at a slope ≤ 1:2 for the following:
    Thresholds.
    Floor elevation variations.

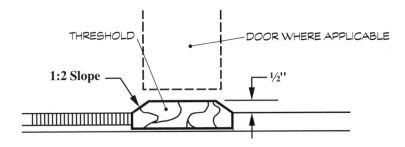

Fig. 1003.3.1.6. Threshold detail. Hot Springs Police Department New Headquarters. Hot Springs National Park, Arkansas. Cromwell Architects Engineers. Little Rock, Arkansas.

1003.3.1.7 Door arrangement

This subsection addresses the distance between multiple doors in sequence as encountered in the direction of travel.

- Space required between horizontal sliding power-operated doors in a series is ≥ 4'.
- Spacing of multiple doors in the direction of travel is governed as follows:
  - The following doors are not required to be spaced ≥ 4' apart:
    Exterior doors with storm doors for individual dwelling units in the following locations:
    Occupancy R-2.
    Occupancy R-3.
    Doors within dwelling units that are not Type A (accessible) as follows:
    Occupancy R-2.
    Occupancy R-3.
- Other swinging doors in a series must be spaced the following distance apart:
  - 4' + the width of the door swinging into the space.
- Doors in a series must swing in one of the following patterns:
  - In the direction of travel.
  - Away from the space between the doors.

1003 General Means of Egress

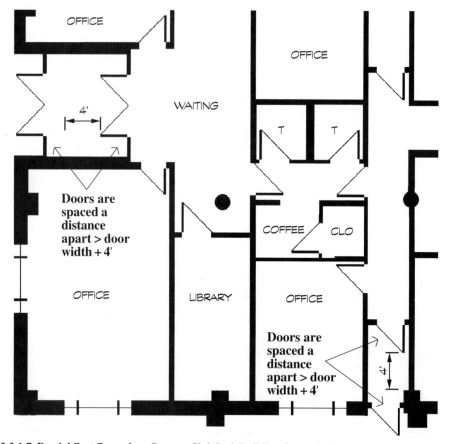

Fig. 1003.3.1.7. Partial first floor plan. Country Club Park Building One. Wichita, Kansas. Gossen Livingston Associats, Inc., Architecture. Wichita, Kansas.

1003.3.1.8.3 Hardware height

- Locks not used for routine operation but only for security purposes may be mounted at any height.
- Otherwise, the following door hardware must be positioned at the height indicated below:
  - Door hardware:
    Handles.
    Pulls.
    Latches.
    Locks.
    Other operating devices.
  - Required height:
    $\geq 2'\text{-}10''$ and $\leq 4'$.

1003 General Means of Egress

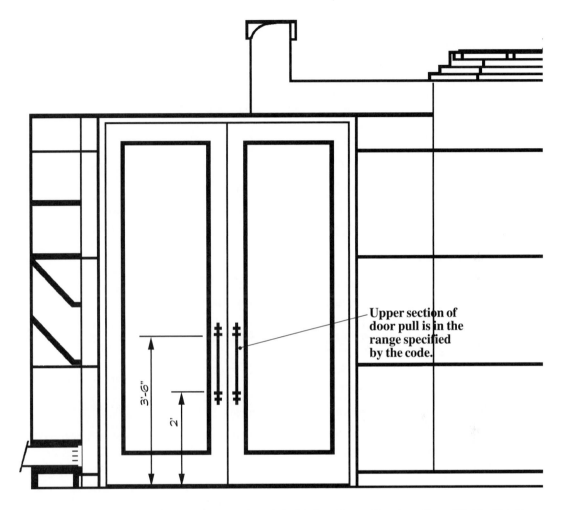

Upper section of door pull is in the range specified by the code.

Fig. 1003.3.1.8.3. Door elevation. Christus St. Michael Health Care Center. Texarkana, Texas. Watkins Hamilton Ross Architects, Inc. Houston, Texas.

1003.3.2 Gates

- Gates > 4' wide as follows are allowed in fences and walls around a stadium:
  - Horizontal sliding gates.
  - Swinging gates.
- Other gates in a means of egress must comply with requirements for doors that are applicable.

1003 General Means of Egress

1003.3.2.1 Stadiums

- Panic hardware is not required on gates where the following conditions exist:
  - Gates are around stadiums.
  - Gates are continually supervised when the public is present.
  - A dispersal area is provided as follows:

    Area is located between the fence and enclosed space.

    Area is $\geq$ 50' from enclosed space.

    Area must be $\geq$ the following size:

    ### Occupant load × 3 sf (per occupant)

- Dispersal area must meet means of egress requirements.

    Note: Section 1005, "Exits," is cited as the source of requirements for means of egress requirements from safe dispersal areas.

1003.3.2.2 Educational uses

- School grounds may have fences with gates.
- Gates in such fences may have locks in the following case:
  - Where a dispersal area is provided as follows:

    Area is located between the fence and the school.

    Area is $\geq$ 50' from school buildings.

    Area must be $\geq$ the following size:

    ### Occupant load × 3 sf (per occupant)

- Dispersal area must meet means of egress requirements.

    Note: Section 1005, "Exits," is cited as the source of requirements for means of egress requirements from safe dispersal areas.

Case study: Fig. 1003.3.2.2. The school complex is fenced with several gates. To the south of the multipurpose building and within the fenced area are playing fields. To the east within the fenced area are more campus buildings and open land. The two new buildings are 100' apart; thus, a line half way between them divides the plaza into to potential dispersal areas, each the required minimum of 50' from the builidng served. The dispersal area north of the dividing line serves the multipurpose building while the area south of the dividing line serves the new classroom building. Larger dispersal areas at greater distances from the buildings served are available to the east and south of the complex shown in the illustration. These are available for use by any of the buildings around the plaza.

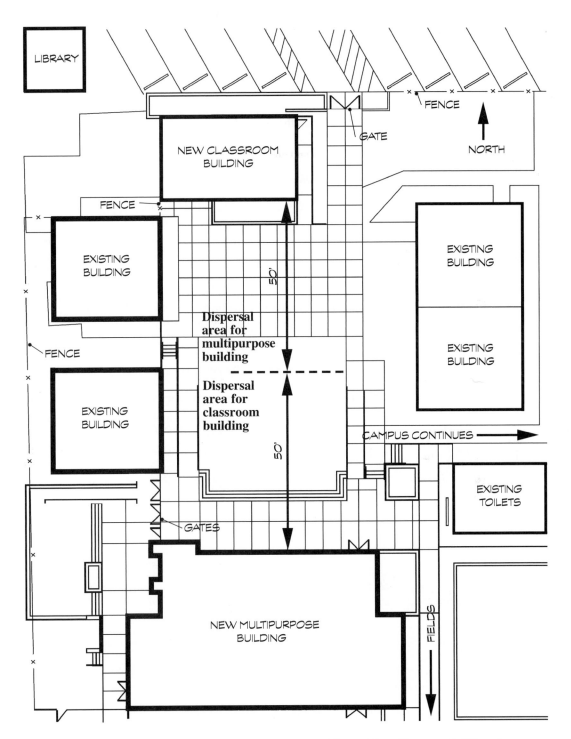

LIBRARY

NEW CLASSROOM
BUILDING

FENCE

GATE

NORTH

FENCE

EXISTING
BUILDING

EXISTING
BUILDING

FENCE

50'

**Dispersal
area for
multipurpose
building**

EXISTING
BUILDING

EXISTING
BUILDING

**Dispersal
area for
classroom
building**

EXISTING
BUILDING

CAMPUS CONTINUES

50'

GATES

EXISTING
TOILETS

NEW MULTIPURPOSE
BUILDING

FIELDS

Fig. 1003.3.2.2. Site plan. Creston Elementary Multipurpose Building and New Classroom Building. Creston, California. Phillips Metsch Sweeney Moore Architects. Santa Barbara, California.

1003 General Means of Egress

1003.3.3.1 Stairway width

- Spiral stairways are not governed by this section.

    Note: 1003.3.3.9, "Spiral stairways," is cited as the source of requirements for this type of stairway.

- Assembly aisle stairs are not governed by this section.

    Note: Section 1008, "Assembly," is cited as governing aisle stairs.

- A clear passage ≥ 1'-8" is required on stairways where both the following apply:
    ○ Where a stairway lift is installed.
    ○ In the following occupancies:
        R-3.
        Within dwelling units of R-2.
- In other cases, stairway width must be the larger of the following:
    ○ ≥ 4' clear width between handrails where required to be accessible.
    ○ For stairs not required to be accessible, the following widths apply:
        ≥ 3' for occupant loads ≤ 50.
        ≥ 3'-8" for occupant loads > 50.
    ○ ≥ Number of occupants served × the minimum width per occupant served as follows:

    Table 1003.3.3.1   Minimum Width of Stairway per Occupant Served

Occupancy	Building sprinklered as per NFPA 13 or 13R
A, B, E, F, H-5, I-1, I-3, I-4, M, R, S, U	0.2"
H-1, H-2, H-3, H-4, I-2	0.3"
	Building not sprinklered
A, B, E, F, H-5, I-1, I-3, I-4, M, R, S, U	0.3"
I-2	0.4"
H-1, H-2, H-3, H-4	0.7"

    Source: IBC Table 1003.2.3.

Note: 1003.2.13.2, "Enclosed stairways," is cited as the source of requirements for accessible stairways.

1003 General Means of Egress

1003.3.3.2 Headroom

- Spiral stairways may have a headroom clearance of 6'-6".

  Note: 1003.3.3.9, "Spiral stairways," is cited as the source of requirements for spiral stairways with this headroom minimum.

- Other stairways require a headroom clearance ≥ 6'-8" as follows:
  - Measured vertically from a line tangent to tread nosings.
  - Required headroom must be continuous to a point directly above the following:
    The point where the line tangent to the nosings intersects the landing below the stair run:
    This point is located a distance away from the bottom riser equal to one tread depth.
- The minimum headroom clearance is required for the full width of the landing and stairway.

1003.3.3.3 Stair treads and risers *(part 1 of 2)*

- The following stairways are not governed by this subsection:
  - Circular stairways.
  - Winders.
  - Spiral stairways.
  - Stairways replacing existing stairways are not required to meet dimensional requirements of this subsection where existing conditions do not permit.

  Note: The following are cited as governing the tread and riser dimensions of the stairways listed above:
  1003.3.3.7, "Circular stairways."
  1003.3.3.8, "Winders."
  1003.3.3.9, "Spiral stairways."

- In assembly seating areas, the following applies:
  - Where aisle gradient is dictated by sightlines, stair dimensions are required as follows:
    Risers ≥ 4" and ≤ 8".
    Treads ≤ 11".

  Note: 1008.9.2, "Risers," is cited as the source of requirements for aisles in assembly seating. The above dimensions, variations, and other requirements are included.

- For the following locations and conditions, the requirements indicated below apply:
  - Locations:
    R-3.
    Within dwelling units of R-2.
    U where serving R-3.
  - Conditions:
    Stairs with solid risers.
    Treads < 11" in depth.
  - Requirements:
    A nosing ≥ ¾" is required.

1003 General Means of Egress

1003.3.3.3 Stair treads and risers *(part 2 of 2)*

- Other tread and riser sizes requirements are as follows:

Table 1003.3.3.3   Tread and Riser Heights

Occupancy	Riser	Tread
R-3	$\geq 4"$ and $\leq 7\,\frac{3}{4}"$	$\geq 10"$
Within dwelling units of R-2	$\geq 4"$ and $\leq 7\,\frac{3}{4}"$	$\geq 10"$
U where serving R-3	$\geq 4"$ and $\leq 7\,\frac{3}{4}"$	$\geq 10"$
All other	$\geq 4"$ and $< 7"$	$\geq 11"$

- Riser height is measured vertically between leading edges of adjacent treads.
- Tread depth is measured horizontally as follows:
  - Between points directly above adjacent nosings.
  - $\perp$ to the leading edge of the tread.

1003.3.3.3.1 Dimensional uniformity

- Aisle risers serving assembly seating where the gradient is dictated by sightlines are not required to be uniform within certain limits.

  Note: 1008.9.2, "Risers" is cited as the source of requirements for aisle risers.

- Winders may differ from rectangular treads in the same stairway flight as follows:
  - Winders must be consistent in shape among themselves.
  - Winder tread depth must be $\geq 11"$ as follows:
    At a point $\leq 12"$ from the narrow edge.
    Tread depth must be $\geq 6"$ at all points.
  - Winders are not permitted in a means of egress in other than dwelling units.
- Top or bottom stairway risers abutting a sloped surface are governed as follows:
  - Sloped surfaces as follows permitted to serve as landings must have an fixed gradient.
    Public way.
    Walkway.
    Driveway.
  - The abutting riser may follow the slope of the landing to a height $< 4"$ as follows:
    Slope must be $\leq 1{:}12$ across the stairway width.
  - The leading edge of the abutting riser must be identified with a marking stripe as follows:
    Marking stripe to be distinctive.
    Marking stripe to differ from any other nosing marking in the flight.
    Marking stripe to be visible when traveling down the stairs.
    Marking stripe to have a slip-resistant surface.
    Marking stripe to have a width $\geq 1"$ and $\leq 2"$.
- Other stair treads and risers are governed as follows:
  - They must be uniform in size and shape.
  - The difference in size between the largest and smallest tread in a flight must be $\leq \frac{3}{8}"$.
  - The difference in size between the largest and smallest riser in a flight must be $\leq \frac{3}{8}"$.

1003 General Means of Egress

1003.3.3.3.2 Profile

- Solid risers in stairways are governed as follows:
  - ○ Solid risers are not required for stairways in occupancy I-3.
  - ○ Stairways not required to be an enclosed accessible means of egress need not have solid risers as follows:

    Where the opening between treads will not pass a 4" sphere.

  Note: 1003.2.13.2, "Enclosed stairways," is cited as the source for these and other requirements governing accessible stairways.

- Other stairways must have solid risers in one of the following positions:
  - ○ Vertical.
  - ○ Sloped at ≤ 30° from the vertical as follows:

    Adjoins the underside of the leading edge of the tread above.
- Other aspects of stairways are governed as follows:
  - ○ The leading edge of the treads may not have a radius > ½".
  - ○ Nosings may not be beveled > ½".
  - ○ Nosings may not project > 1¼" over the tread below.
  - ○ Nosings must be uniform in size, including the following:

    The nosing of the floor at the top of a stair run.

1003.3.3.4 Stairway landings

- Aisle stairs are not governed by this section where they comply with requirements for aisles in assembly occupancies.

  Note: Section 1008, "Assembly" is cited as the source of requirements for aisle stairs.

- Other stairway landings are governed as follows:
  - ○ One of the following is required at the top and bottom of a stairway:

    Floor.

    Landing.
  - ○ The landing width must be ≥ the stairway width.
  - ○ Landings located in other than straight runs must have the following dimension in the direction of travel:

    A dimension ≥ the stair width.
  - ○ Landings located in straight runs must have the smaller of the following dimensions in the direction of travel:

    A dimension ≥ the stair width.

    ≥ 48".
  - ○ Doors opening onto landings may protrude into the required width as follows:

    A distance ≤ ½ the required width at any point while opening.

    A distance ≤ 7" when the door is fully open.

    The protrusion of a door includes its hardware.

1003 General Means of Egress

1003.3.3.5 Stairway construction

- Wood handrails are allowed in stairways in all types of building construction.
- Otherwise, stairway materials must conform to the construction-type requirements for the building.

1003.3.3.5.1 Stairway walking surface

- The walking surface of the following stairway components must not slope > 1:48 in any direction:
  - Landings.
  - Treads.
- The surfaces of treads and landings are governed as follows:

Table 1003.3.5.1   Surfaces of Treads and Landings

Locations	Tread and landing surfaces
Occupancies A, B, E, I, M, R, U	Solid surfaces required.
Parking structure public areas	Solid surfaces required.
Occupancies F, H	Openings allowed which cannot pass a $1^1/8$" sphere.
Occupancy S other than public areas of parking structures	Openings allowed which cannot pass a $1^1/8$" sphere.

1003.3.3.5.2 Outdoor conditions

- The following outdoor walking surfaces must not accumulate water:
  - Outdoor stairways.
  - Outdoor approaches to stairways.
- The following surfaces in locations shown must be protected as indicated below:
  - Surfaces that are a part of exterior stairways:
    Treads.
    Platforms.
    Landings.
  - Locations:
    In the following occupancies:
      A, B, E, F, H, I, M, R-1, R-2, R-4, S.
      U not serving R-3.
    In the following climates:
      Subject to snow or ice.
  - Requirements:
    Surfaces must be protected to prevent the accumulation of snow or ice.

1003 General Means of Egress

> **Case study: Fig. 1003.3.3.5.2.** The surfaces of the stairway slope 2% to shed water. Snow melting mats are embedded in the landing and the steps to prevent the accumulationof snow or ice. The stairway meets requirements for exterior conditions as required for a B occupancy.

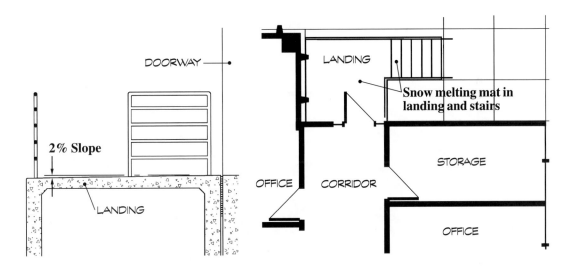

Fig. 1003.3.3.5.2. Plan and section at exterior stair. Lubrication Engineers, Inc. Wichita, Kansas. Gossen Livingston, Associates, Inc., Architecture. Wichita, Kansas.

1003.3.3.6 Vertical rise

- Aisle stairs are not governed by this subsection.

    Note: Section 1008, "Assembly," is cited as the source of requirements for aisle stairs.

- Other stairs are limited in their vertical rise to ≤ 12'.

1003 General Means of Egress

1003.3.3.7 Circular stairways

- Tread and riser dimensions of circular stairs are governed as indicated below:

Table 1003.3.3.7   **Treads and Risers of Circular Stairways**

Stairway location	Riser height	Tread depth at 12" from narrow end	Depth of tread at narrow end	Smaller radius of stairway
In R-3 and within R-2 dwelling units	≥ 4" ≤ 7"	≥ 11"	≥ 6"	Not governed
All other locations	≥ 4" ≤ 7"	≥ 11"	≥ 10"	≥ 2 × stair width

Case study: Fig. 1003.3.3.7. The tower stairway meets requirements for radius as well as tread depth at the narrow end and at a point 12" from the narrow end as indicated in the illustration. The adjacent steps are not circular in the strictest sense, but meet the same requirements.

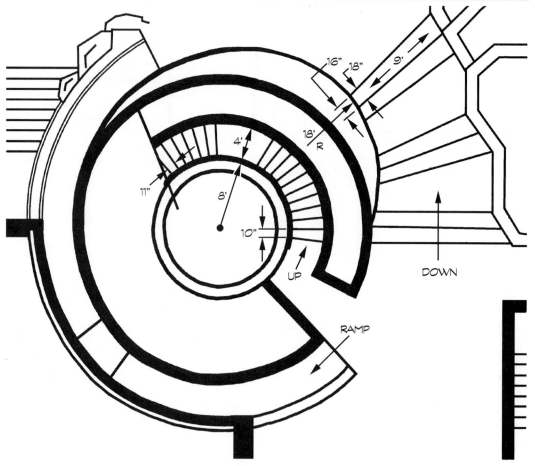

Fig. 1003.3.3.7 Plan at tower. Lady Bird Johnson Wildflower Center. Austin, Texas. Overland Partners, Inc. San Antonio, Texas.

1003 General Means of Egress

1003.3.3.8 Winders

- Winders in a means of egress are governed as follows:
  - Permitted within a dwelling unit.
  - Not permitted in other locations.
- Winder dimensions are governed as follows:
  - Tread depth at ≤ 12" from narrow end must be ≥ 11".
  - Tread depth at any point ≥ 6".

1003.3.3.9 Spiral stairways

- This subsection does not govern the following:
  - Catwalks.
  - Galleries.
  - Gridirons.

    Note: 1007.5, "Stage means of egress," is cited as the source of requirements for the components listed above.

- Use of spiral stairways in a means of egress is governed as follows:
  - Permitted in the following locations:
    Within a dwelling unit:
      From a space as follows:
        Area ≤ 250 sf.
        Occupant load ≤ 5 persons.
  - Not permitted in other locations.
- Dimensions required of a spiral stairway are as follows:
  - Tread width at 12" from narrow end must be ≥ 7 ½".
  - Headroom ≥ 6'-6".
  - Riser height ≤ 9 ½".
  - Width of stairway ≥ 2'-2".

1003.3.3.10 Alternating tread devices

- Use of alternating tread devices in a means of egress is governed as follows:
  - Permitted in the following locations:
    From mezzanines in occupancies F, H, and S as follows:
      Mezzanine area ≤ 250 sf.
      Mezzanine occupants ≤ 5.
    In I-3 areas ≤ 250 sf as follows:
      Guard towers.
      Observation stations.
      Control rooms.
    For access to unoccupied roofs.
  - Not permitted in other locations.

1003 General Means of Egress

1003.3.3.10.1 Handrails of alternating tread devices

- Handrails for alternating tread devices must comply with the same requirements as do handrails for stairways.

  Note: 1003.3.3.11, "Handrails," is cited as the source of requirements for stairway handrails.

1003.3.3.10.2 Treads of alternating tread devices

- The initial tread of an alternating tread device must be at the same elevation as the following:
  - Landing or floor surface.
  - Platform.
- Alternating tread device dimensions are governed as follows:

Table 1003.3.3.10.2   Alternating Tread Devices

Device location	Projected tread	Tread depth	Tread width	Rise to next tread
Means of egress from a mezzanine of ≤ 250 sf and ≤ 5 occupants	≥ 8 ½"	≥ 10 ½"	≤ 7"	≤ 8"
Other locations	≥ 5"	≥ 8 ½"	≥ 7"	≤ 9 ½"

Note: "Projected tread" is that visible beyond the tread above in a plan view.

1003.3.3.11 Handrails

- Additional handrails are not required at an aisle stair with a center handrail.
- The following may have a handrail on one side only:
  - Stairways within dwelling units.
  - Spiral stairways.
  - Aisle stairs with seating only on one side.
- Handrails are not required for the following components where conditions indicated apply:
  - Components:
    Decks and patios.
    Walkways.
  - Conditions:
    At a single change in elevation.
    Landing depth on each side of elevation change is greater than required.
- Handrails are not required at the following:
  - At a single riser at the following occupancy R-3 locations:
    Entrance and egress doors.
  - At a single riser in a room within a dwelling unit as follows:
    In occupancies R-2 and R-3.
- Other stairways require a handrail on each side as follows:
  - Handrails must have adequate strength and attachment.

  Note: 1607.7, "Loads on handrails, guards, grab bars and vehicle barriers," is cited as the source for handrail and attachment strength requirements.

General Means of Egress

1003.3.3.11.1 Height

- The height of a handrail must be $\geq$ 2'-10" and $\leq$ 3'-2" measured as follows:
  - Above stair tread nosings.
  - Above ramp finished surface.
- Handrail height must be uniform.

1003.3.3.11.2 Intermediate handrails

- Intermediate handrails are required at stairways where necessary as follows:
  - So that all points in the required width are $\leq$ 2'-6" away from a handrail.
  - Intermediate handrails necessary for selected required widths are indicated below:

Table 1003.3.3.11.2   Intermediate Handrails Required

Required egress width (less handrail protrusions)	Intermediate handrails required	Required egress width (less handrail protrusions)	Intermediate handrails required
$\leq$ 5'	0	> 15' and $\leq$ 20'	3
> 5' and $\leq$ 10'	1	> 20' and $\leq$ 25'	4
> 10' and $\leq$ 15'	2	> 25' and $\leq$ 30'	5

- Handrails must be located on monumental stairs as follows:
  - Along the most direct path of egress travel.

1003.3.3.11.3 Handrail graspability

- Circular handrails meet one of the following requirements:
  - Have an outside diameter $\geq$ 1 ¼" and $\leq$ 2".
  - Have equivalent graspability to the above diameter range.
- Other handrail shapes must comply with the following:
  - Have a perimeter $\geq$ 4" and $\leq$ 6 ¼".
  - Have all cross-section dimensions $\leq$ 2¼".
  - Have edges with a radius $\geq$ ⅛".

General Means of Egress

1003.3.3.11.4 Continuity

- Handrail-gripping surface continuity is governed as follows:
  - Within a dwelling unit, the following applies:
    - A newel post may interrupt a handrail at a stair landing.
    - The following details are permitted at the lowest tread:
      - Volute.
      - Turnout.
      - Starting easing.
  - The following attachments to handrails are permitted where they comply with the restrictions listed below:
    - Attachments:
      - Brackets.
      - Balusters.
    - Restrictions:
      - They may not project beyond the sides of the handrail as follows:
        - Within a distance $\leq 1\frac{1}{2}"$ down from the bottom of the handrail.
  - Otherwise, handrails must be continuous as follows:
    - Without interruptions by the following:
      - Newel posts.
      - Other obstructions.

1003.3.3.11.5 Handrail extensions

- Handrails serving aisles in occupancy A are not governed by this subsection.

  Note: 1008.11, "Handrails," is cited as defining the pertinent handrails.

- Handrails in nonaccessible dwelling units are required to extend between the following extremities:
  - Between points above the top and bottom riser.
- Other handrails are governed as follows:
  - They must return to one of the following points:
    - A wall.
    - A guard.
    - The walking surface.
    - Be continuous to the handrail of the adjacent stair run.
  - Handrails that are not continuous between stair runs must terminate as follows:
    - They must extend horizontally >12" beyond the top riser.
    - They must continue to slope beyond the bottom riser equal to a distance of one tread.

General Means of Egress

1003.3.3.11.6 Clearance

- Clear space ≥ 1½" is required between a handrail and the following:
  - Wall.
  - Other surface.
- The following surfaces must be without sharp or abrasive elements:
  - Handrail surfaces.
  - Surfaces adjacent to handrail.

1003.3.3.11.7 Stairway projections

- Projections into the required width of a stairway are limited as follows:

Height	Projection permitted
At handrail height	≤ 4½"
Below handrail height	≤ 4 ½"
Above 6'-8"	Not limited

1003.3.3.12 Stairway to roof

- A stairway is required to extend to the roof where both of the following apply:
  - In buildings ≥ 4 stories above grade.
  - Where the roof slopes ≤ 4:12.
- Access to unoccupied roof from the top floor may be by the following:
  - An alternating tread device.

1003.3.3.12.1 Roof access

- Access to unoccupied roofs may be through a roof hatch as follows:
  - Area of hatch must be ≥ 16 sf.
  - Dimensions of hatch must be ≥ 2'.
- Access provided to other roofs must be by way of a penthouse.

  Note: 1509.2, "Penthouses," is cited as the source of applicable requirements.

1003.3.4 Ramps

- This subsection series does not govern the following ramps:
  - Ramped aisles.
  - Curb ramps.

  Note: The following are cited as governing ramps omitted from this subsection series:
  1008.9, "Assembly aisle walking surfaces."
  ICC/ANSI A 117.1, "Accessible and Usable Buildings and Facilities," for curb
  ramp requirements.

1003 General Means of Egress

1003.3.4.1 Slope

- Aisle ramp slope in occupancy A is not governed by this subsection.

  Note: 1008.9, "Assembly aisle walking surfaces," is cited as governing aisle ramp slope.

- Other ramps are governed as follows:
  - Ramps in a means of egress must have a slope ≤ 1:12.
  - Other ramps must have a slope < 1:8.

1003.3.4.2 Cross slope

- The slope of a ramp ⊥ to direction of travel must be ≤ 1:48.

1003.3.4.3 Rise

- Rise of any ramp is limited to ≤ 2'-6".

1003.3.4.4.1 Width

- The width required for a means of egress ramp is the same as that required for corridors.

  Note: 1004.3.2.2, "Corridor width," is cited as the source governing applicable widths.

- ≥ 3' clear width is required for ramps in a means of egress.
- ≥ 3' clear width is required between handrails on ramps in a means of egress.

1003.3.4.4.2 Headroom

- Headroom required for all parts of a ramp in a means of egress is ≥ 6'-8".

1003.3.4.4.3 Restrictions

- Means of egress ramps are governed as follows:
  - Width may not reduce in direction of egress travel.
  - Projections are not permitted into required width of ramps.
  - Projections are not permitted into required width of landings.
  - Door swing onto a landing must leave ≥ 3'-6" clear width unobstructed.

1003.3.4.5 Landings

- Landings are required for ramps at the following locations:
  - Bottom of ramp.
  - Top of ramp.
  - At changes of direction.
  - At doors.
  - At entrances.
  - At exits

1003 General Means of Egress

1003.3.4.5.1 Slope

- Changes of level on a ramp landing are not permitted.
- Ramp landings may not slope ≥ 1:48 in any direction.

1003.3.4.5.2 Width

- The width of a landing must be ≥ the width of adjoining ramps.

1003.3.4.5.3 Length

- The lengths required for ramp landings are as follows:
  - ≥ 3' in the following locations:
    In nonaccessible dwelling units of the following occupancies:
      R-2, R-3.
  - ≥ 5' in other locations.

1003.3.4.5.4 Change in direction

- Dimensions of ramp landings at changes in direction are required as follows:
  - ≥ 3' in all dimensions in the following locations:
    In nonaccessible dwelling units of the following occupancies:
      R-2, R-3.
  - ≥ 5' in other locations.

1003.3.4.5.5 Doorways

- Clearances required for accessibility at doorways may overlap required landing dimensions.

    Note: ICC/ANSI A 117.1, "Accessible and Usable Buildings and Facilities," is cited as the source of maneuvering requirements at doorways.

1003.3.4.6 Ramp construction

- Ramp materials are governed as follows:
  - Wood handrails are allowed at ramps in all building construction types.
  - Otherwise, all ramp construction must conform to that required for the building construction type.
- Ramps used as exits must meet the same requirements as do vertical exit enclosures.

    Note: The following are cited as governing requirements for vertical exit enclosures.
    1005.3.2, "Vertical exit enclosures."
    1005.3.4, "Openings and penetrations."

1003.3.4.6.1 Ramp surface

- Materials on surfaces must comply with the following:
  - Must be slip-resistant.
  - Must be securely attached.

1003 General Means of Egress

1003.3.4.6.2 Outdoor conditions

- Outdoor ramps must not accumulate water.
- Outdoor approaches to ramps must not accumulate water.
- The following surfaces in locations indicated must minimuze accumulation of snow or ice.
  - Exterior ramp surfaces.
  - Exterior ramp landing surfaces.
  - Locations:
    In the following occupancies:
    A, B, E, F, H, I, M, R-1, R-2, R-4, S.
    U not serving R-3.
    In climates subject to snow or ice.

1003.3.4.7 Handrails

- Ramps with a rise > 6" must meet the following requirements:
  - Handrails are required on both sides as follows:
    Handrails must meet the same requirements as do stairways.

  Note: 1003.3.3.11, "Handrails," is cited as the source of stairway handrail requirements.

1003.3.4.8 Edge protection

- Edge protection is not required on the following:
  - At ramps where both of the following conditions apply:
    Handrails are not required.
    Ramps have flared sides meeting curb ramp requirements.

  Note: ICC/ANSI A117.1, "Accessible and Usable Buildings and Facilities," is cited as governing the pertinent curb ramps.

  - At the sides of ramp landings that meet either of the following:
    A ramp.
    A stairway.
  - At the sides of ramp landings with the following condition:
    Vertical drop at the ramp edge is ≤ ½" over the following distance:
    A 10" distance measured horizontally from the edge of the required landing area.
- Other ramps and landings must have one of the following edge protections:
  - Railing.
  - Curb.
  - Barrier.

  Note: The following are cited as providing the requirements for the edge protection listed above.
    1003.3.4.8.1, "Railings."
    1003.3.4.8.2, "Curb or barrier."

1003 General Means of Egress

1003.3.4.8.1 Railings

- The following meets the requirement for ramp or landing edge protection:
  - A rail mounted below the handrail as follows:
    At a distance ≥ 17" and ≤ 19" above the ramp or landing surface.

1003.3.4.8.2 Curb or barrier

- The following meets the requirements for ramp or landing edge protection:
  - Curb or barrier that prevents the passage of a 4" sphere as follows:
    Within 8" of the floor or ground surface.

1003.3.4.9 Guards

- Guards are required along ramps and landings more than 2'-6" above floor or grade.
- Guards for ramps and landings must comply with the same construction requirements as for stairways.

  Note: 1003.2.12, "Guards," is cited as the source of requirements for the location and construction of guards for ramps, stairways, and other locations.

1004 Exit Access

1004.2.1 Exit or exit access doorways required

- Exit and exit access doorways for occupancy I-2 are not governed by this section.

    Note: 1004.2.3.2, "Group I-2," is cited as the source of requirements for this occupancy.

- Other access doorways are governed as follows:
    - ≥ 2 exit or exit access doorways are required from a space where either of the following conditions applies:
        Where the common path of egress travel exceeds that permitted.
        Where the occupant load is as follows:

Table 1004.2.1	Spaces Requiring ≥ 2 Means of Egress
Occupancy	Occupants
A, B, E, F, M, U	> 50
H-1, H-2, H-3	> 3
H-4, H-5	> 10
I-1, I-3, I-4	> 10
R	> 10
S	> 30

Source: IBC Table 1004.2.1.

Note: 1004.2.5, "Common path of egress travel," is cited as the source of path limits.

1004.2.1.1 Three or more exits

- Access to exits from a floor is required as follows:*
    - Access to ≥ 3 exits is required as follows:
        Where a floor has an occupant load ≥ 501 and ≤ 1000.
    - Access to ≥ 4 exits is required as follows:
        Where a floor has an occupant load > 1000.

    Note: 1005.2.1, "Minimum number of exits," is cited as the source of requirements for number of exits required.

1004.2.2 Exit or exit access doorway arrangement

- Required exits must be clearly available for their purpose.
- Exits may not be obstructed at any time.
- Exits and exit access doorways must be separated by the following distance:
    - A distance large enough to prevent the loss of more than one in an emergency.

    Note: The following are cited as sources of requirements for separation distances:
    1004.2.2.1, "Two exit or exit access doorways."
    1004.2.2.2, "Three or more exits or exit access doorways."

Source: IBC Table 1005.2.1.

Case study: Fig. 1004.2.1. The church organ loft has an occupant load of 5 based on gross area. Since this is < 50 and the common path distance is < the 75' maximum for the occupancy B space, only 1 exit or exit door is required.

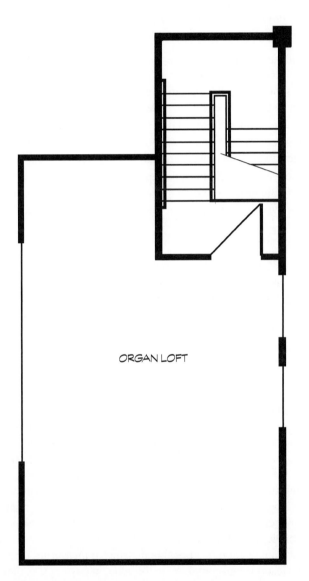

ORGAN LOFT

Fig. 1004.2.1. Floor plan of organ loft. Glad Tidings Assembly of God Church. Naticoke, Pennsylvania. Mullins and Weida, Architect and Associate. Bear Creek, Pennsylvania.

1004 Exit Access

1004.2.2.1 Two exit or exit access doorways

- Where there are exit enclosures meeting the following conditions, separation is required as indicated below:
  - Exit enclosures connected to each other by the following:
    A corridor with a fire-resistance rating of 1 hr.

    Note: 1004.3.2, "Corridors," is cited as the source of additional requirements with which the connecting corridor must comply.

  - Requirements:
    The required distance separating the exits is measured as follows:
    On the line of travel in the corridor.
    Exit enclosures must be ≥ 30' apart from each other as follows:
    Measured in a straight line between nearest walls.
- In buildings sprinklered as per NFPA 13 or 13R, the following applies:
  - The distance between exit or exit access doors is required to be as follows:
    ≥ $\frac{1}{3}$ the greatest overall diagonal dimension of the area served.
- Other exit or exit access doorways must be separated as follows:
  - By a distance ≥ ½ the greatest overall diagonal dimension of the building or area served:
    The distance is measured on a straight line between the exit or exit access doorways.

1004.2.2.2 Three or more exits or exit access doorways

- The following apply where access is required to ≥ 3 exits:
  - ≥ 2 exit or exit access doorways must be separated as follows:
    By a distance ≥ ½ the greatest overall diagonal dimension of the building or area served:
    The distance is measured on a straight line between the exit or exit access doorways.
  - The separation of additional exits or exit access doorways is required as follows:
    Separation distance must be adequate to assure the following:
    That a single emergency will not block > 1 exit or exit access doorway.

Case study: Fig. 1004.2.2.1. Since the space on each side of the folding partition in the multipurpose room requires an exit access door, the whole space with the open partition will have 2 doors regardless of its occupant load. To determine whether or not the distance between the 2 doors must meet the code minimum, the whole space is analyzed as a single room with the partition open. As an assembly space with chairs and tables, the occupant load would be 98. The storage room adds 1 additional occupant. Consequently, 2 exit access doors are required and must be spaced a minimum distance apart. In this sprinklered building, the minimum distance is $\frac{1}{3}$ the diagonal of the area or 28'-4". Since double doors are provided and, in this example only a single door is required at each location, an argument could be made for measuring between the most remote doors. The closest doors comply with the code, in any case, as they are 38' apart.

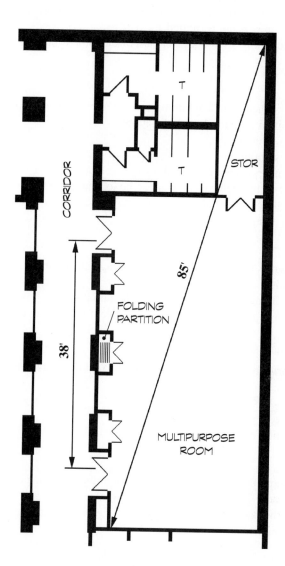

Fig. 1004.2.2.1. Partial floor plan. Lady Bird Johnson Wildflower Center. Austin, Texas. Overland Partners, Inc. San Antonio, Texas.

1004 Exit Access

1004.2.3 Egress through intervening spaces

- Egress through a high-hazard space from an adjoining space is governed as follows:
  - Egress is permitted where the spaces involved are the same occupancy.
  - In other cases, egress is not permitted.
- Egress from an adjoining space may not pass through the following spaces:
  - Store rooms.
  - Closets.
  - Similar spaces.
- Egress though a kitchen from a adjoining space is governed as follows:
  - Egress is permitted in the following locations:
    Within a dwelling unit.
    Within a guest room.
  - In other cases, egress is not permitted.
- Egress may not pass through a room that can be locked to obstruct egress.
- Egress from dwelling units or sleeping areas may not pass through the following:
  - Other sleeping areas.
  - Toilet rooms.
  - Bathrooms.
- In other cases, egress from a space may pass through an adjoining space where both of the following conditions apply:
  - Where the adjoining space is accessory to the initial space.
  - Where adjoining space provides a readily apparent route to an exit.

1004.2.3.1 Multiple tenants

- Where more than one tenant occupies a floor, the requirements indicated below apply to the following spaces:
  - Spaces:
    Tenant space.
    Dwelling units.
    Guestrooms.
  - Requirements:
    Access to required exits may not pass through the following adjacent spaces:
    Tenant space.
    Dwelling units.
    Guestrooms.

Case study: Fig. 1004.2.3 A – F. Examples on the following pages indicate a variety of intervening rooms in several occupancies though which egress travel may pass or may not pass. Those rooms through which egress travel is not permitted cannot be counted as a required means of egress in order to meet the number required, the total width required, in measuring minimum travel distances, or for other purposes. In all cases illustrated, means of egress requirements are met by the plans with appropriate routes some of which are marked and some of which are not indicated. Arbitrary starting points are marked with a dot, and each means of egress analysis applies only to the room so marked.

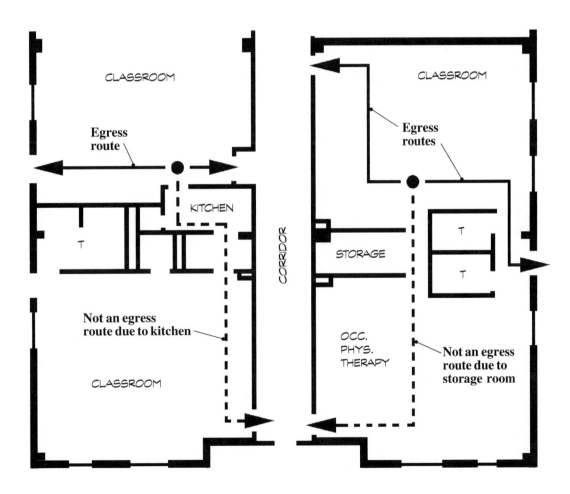

Fig. 1004.2.3A. Partial floor plan. New Jasper Pre-K – 2nd Grade School. Jasper, Texas. PBK Architects, Inc. Houston, Texas.

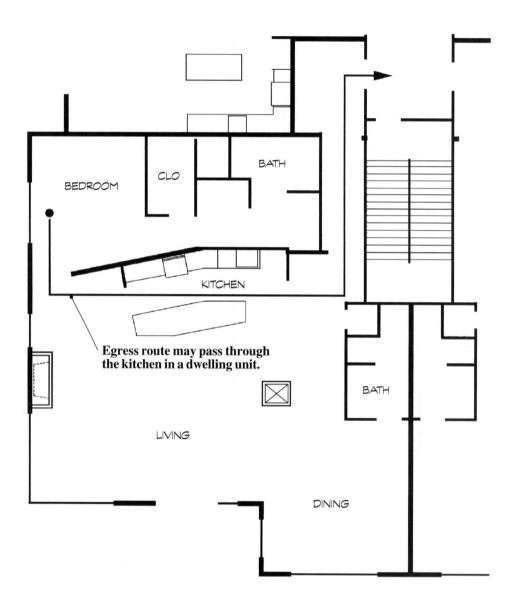

Fig. 1004.2.3B. Apartment floor plan. McKenzie Lofts. Portland, Oregon. Ankrom Moisan Associated Architects. Portland, Oregon.

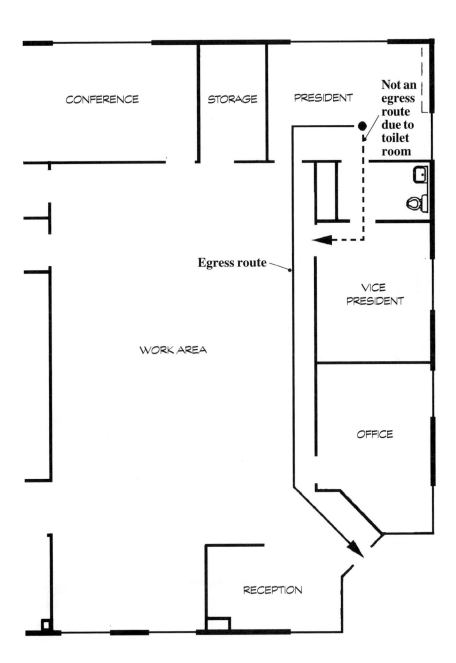

CONFERENCE

STORAGE

PRESIDENT

Not an egress route due to toilet room

Egress route

VICE PRESIDENT

WORK AREA

OFFICE

RECEPTION

Fig. 1004.2.3C. Partial floor plan. Garments to Go. Bastrop, Texas. Spencer Godfrey Architects, Round Rock, Texas.

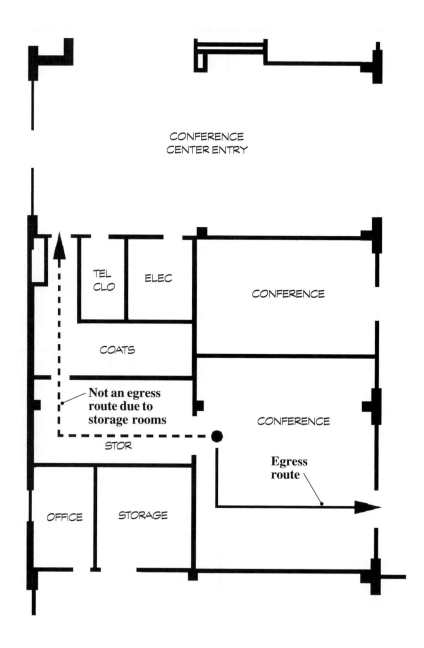

CONFERENCE
CENTER ENTRY

TEL
CLO

ELEC

CONFERENCE

COATS

Not an egress
route due to
storage rooms

CONFERENCE

STOR

Egress
route

OFFICE

STORAGE

Fig. 1004.2.3D. Partial floor plan at conference center. University of Connecticut New Downtown Campus at Stamford, Connecticut. Perkins Eastman Architects, New York, New York.

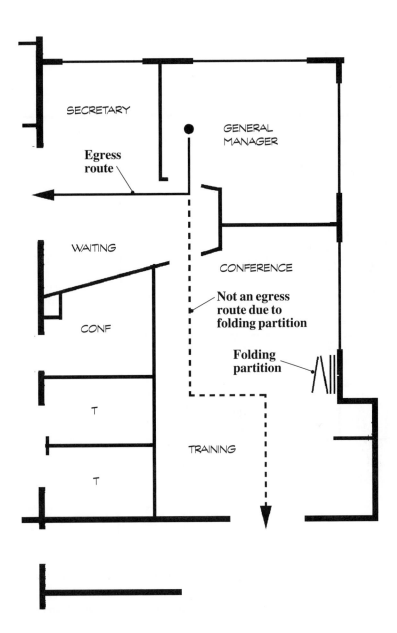

Fig. 1004.2.3E. Partial floor plan. Wichita Transit Storage Administration, and Maintenance Facility. Wichita, Kansas. Wilson Darnell Mann, P.A., Architects. Wichita, Kansas.

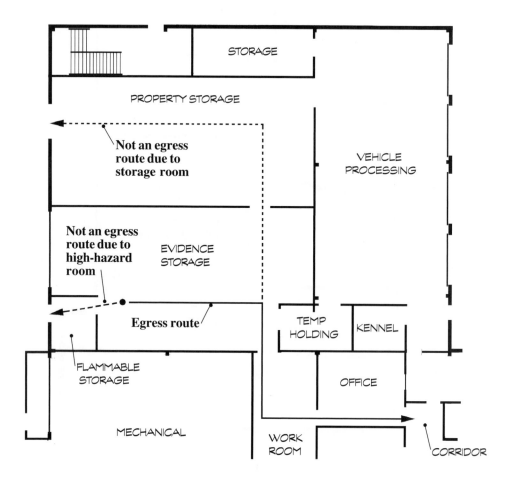

Fig. 1004.2.3F. Partial floor plan. Lee's Summit Police and Court Facility. Lee's Summit, Missouri. The Hollis and Miller Group, Inc. Lee's Summit, Missouri.

1004 Exit Access

1004.2.3.2 Group I-2

- Exit access doors leading directly to an exit access corridor are not required as follows:
  - For rooms with exit doors as follows:
    Opening directly to the exterior.
    Opening at ground level.
  - Patient sleeping rooms may have 1 intervening room as follows:
    Intervening room may not serve as exit access for > 8 patient beds.
  - Special nursing suites may have 1 intervening room as follows:
    Direct continual visual supervision by nursing staff is required.
  - Suites without patient sleeping may have 1 intervening room as follows:
    Travel distance is ≤ 100' as follows:
      Within the suite to the exit access door.
  - Suites without patient sleeping may have 2 intervening rooms as follows:
    Travel distance is ≤ 50' as follows:
      Within the suite to the exit access door.
- In other habitable rooms or suites in occupancy I-2, the following is required:
  - An exit access door leading directly to an exit access corridor.
- Where ≥ 2 exits or exit access doors are required, they must be remote from each other.
- The following is a summary of requirements for habitable rooms or suites in occupancy I-2:

Table 1004.2.3.2   Egress for I-2 Rooms and Suites

Rooms	Distance to door in room	Exit or exit access doors required based on square footage of room			
		≤ 1000 sf	> 1000 sf	≤ 2500 sf	> 2500 sf
With sleeping	≤ 50'	≥ 1	≥ 2	≥ 2	≥ 2
Other	≤ 50'	≥ 1	≥ 1	≥ 1	≥ 2

Suites	Size	Distance to door in suite	Exit or exit access doors required based on square footage of suite			
			≤ 1000 sf	>1000 sf	≤ 2500 sf	>2500 sf
With sleeping	≤ 5,000 sf	≤ 100'	≥ 1	≥ 2	≥ 2	≥ 2
No sleeping	≤ 10,000 sf	NA	≥ 1	≥ 1	≥ 1	≥ 2

1004.2.4 Exit access travel distance *(part 1 of 2)*

- Exit access travel distance is measured as follows:
  - Along a normal unobstructed route of circulation.
  - From any occupiable location in a building to one of the following points:
    To the nearest riser of an open stair in an open parking garage.
    To the nearest exit in other locations.
  - Where open stairs are on the route, travel is measured as follows:
    On the centerline along the slope tangent to tread nosings.
  - Where open ramps are on the route, travel is measured as follows:
    On the centerline along the surface of the slope.

1004 Exit Access

1004.2.4 Exit access travel distance *(part 2 of 2)*

- In the following, travel distance limitations vary from those specified in this subsection:
  - Malls.
  - Atriums.
  - Buildings with 1 exit.
  - Assembly seating.
  - Assembly open-air seating.

  Note: The following are cited as governing travel distances in the above areas:
  Section 402, "Covered Mall Buildings."
  Section 404, "Atriums."
  1008.6, "Travel distance," addresses indoor and outdoor assembly seating.
  1005.2.2, "Buildings with one exit."

- In F-1 or S-1 buildings, exit access travel is limited to ≤ 400' where all the following apply:
  - Building is 1 story.
  - Building is sprinklered as per NFPA 13.
  - Building has automatic heat and smoke vents.

  Note: Section 910, "Smoke and Heat Vents," is cited as the source of requirements.

- In temporary structures, exit access travel is limited to ≤ 100'.

  Note: Section 3103, "Temporary Structures," is the source of requirements.

- In other locations, exit access travel distance is limited as follows:

Table 1004.2.4   Exit Access Travel Distance Limits

Buildings sprinklered:

Occupancy	Travel distance	Occupancy	Travel distance
A, E, F-1, I-1, M, R, S-1	≤ 250'	H-2	≤ 100'
B	≤ 300'	H-3	≤ 150'
F-2, S-2, U	≤ 400'	H-4	≤ 175'
H-1	≤ 75'	H-5, I-2, I-3, I-4	≤ 200'

Buildings not sprinklered:

Occupancy	Travel distance	Occupancy	Travel distance
A, B, E, F-1, I-1, M, R, S-1	≤ 200'	F-2, S-2, U	≤ 300'
		I-2, I-3, I-4	≤ 150'

Source: IBC Table 1004.2.4.

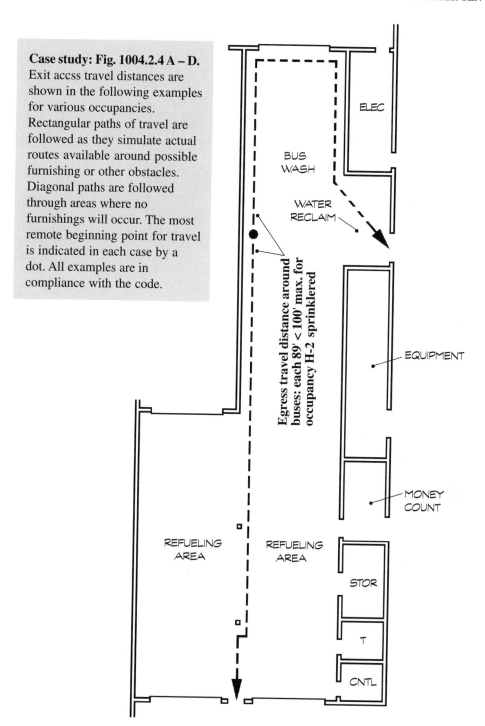

Case study: Fig. 1004.2.4 A – D. Exit access travel distances are shown in the following examples for various occupancies. Rectangular paths of travel are followed as they simulate actual routes available around possible furnishing or other obstacles. Diagonal paths are followed through areas where no furnishings will occur. The most remote beginning point for travel is indicated in each case by a dot. All examples are in compliance with the code.

Egress travel distance around buses: each 89' < 100' max. for occupancy H-2 sprinklered

ELEC

BUS WASH

WATER RECLAIM

EQUIPMENT

MONEY COUNT

REFUELING AREA

REFUELING AREA

STOR

T

CNTL

Fig. 1004.2.4A. Partial floor plan. Wichita Transit Storage, Adiminstration, and Maintenance Facility. Wichita, Kansas. Wilson Darnell Mann, P.A. Wichita, Kansas.

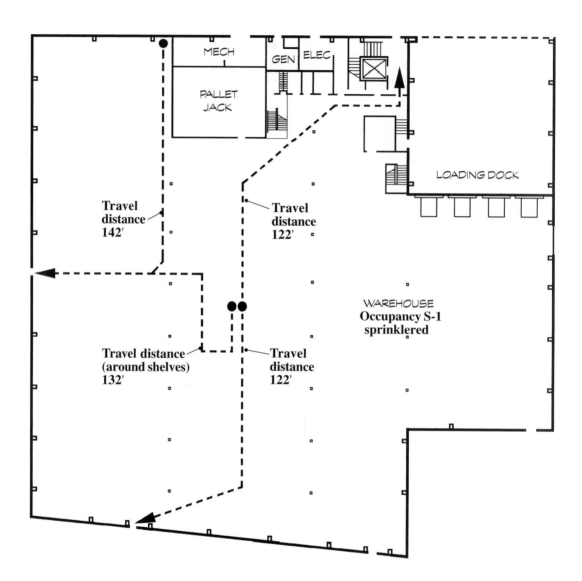

Fig. 1004.2.4B. Floor plan. New Warehouse Addition. Los Angeles, California. Stephen Wen + Associates, Architects, Inc. Pasadena, California.

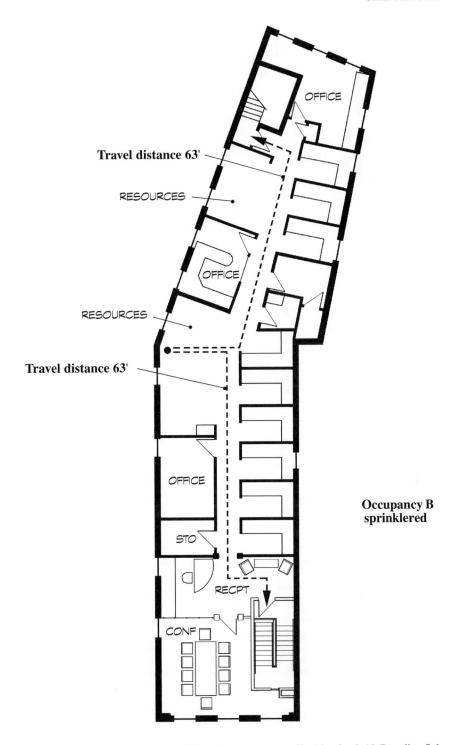

Travel distance 63'

RESOURCES

RESOURCES

OFFICE

OFFICE

Travel distance 63'

OFFICE

STO

RECPT

CONF

**Occupancy B
sprinklered**

Fig. 1004.2.4C. 2nd floor plan. Alterations to 209 MainStreet. Annapolis, Maryland. Alt Breeding Schwarz Architects, LLC. Annapolis, Maryland.

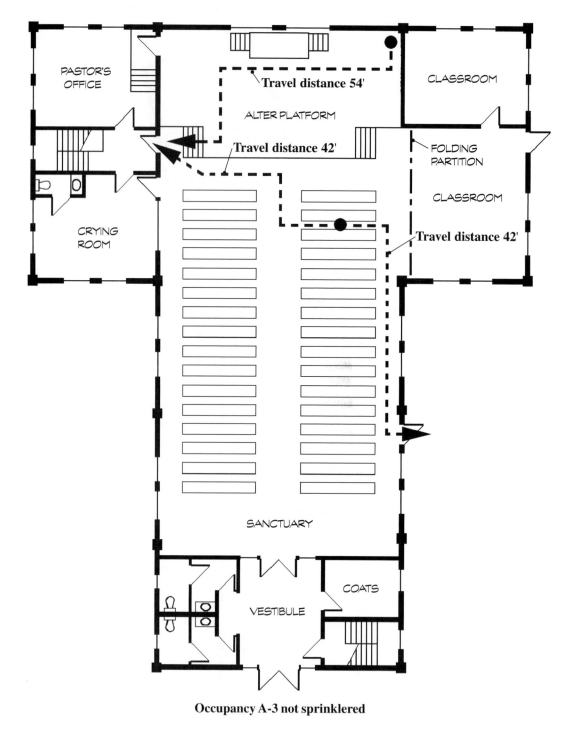

Occupancy A-3 not sprinklered

Fig. 1004.2.4D. Floor plan. Glad Tidings Assembly of God Church. Naticoke, Pennsylvania. Mullins and Weida, Architect and Associate. Bear Creek, Pennsylvania.

1004 Exit Access

1004.2.5 Common path of egress travel

- The length of common path egress travel is limited as shown below:
  - Sprinklered buildings are as per NFPA 13.

Table 1004.2.5   Common Path Distance Limits

Tenant spaces:

		Common path distance	
Occupancy	Occupant load	Buildings sprinklered	Buildings not sprinklered
B, S, U	≤ 30	≤ 100'	≤ 100'
B, S	> 30	≤ 100'	≤ 75'
U	> 30	≤ 75'	≤ 75'

Locations other than tenant spaces:

	Common path distance	
Occupancy	Buildings sprinklered	Buildings not sprinklered
A, E, I-1, I-2, I-4, M, R, U	≤ 75'	≤ 75'
B, F, S	≤ 100'	≤ 75'
H-1, H-2, H-3,	≤ 25'	--
H-4, H-5	≤ 75'	--
I-3	≤ 100'	≤ 100'

Occupancy M sprinklered

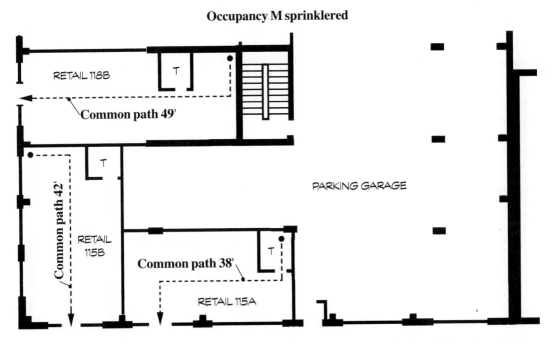

Fig. 1004.2.5A. Partial floor plan at shops. McKenzie Lofts. Portland, Oregon. Ankrom Moisan Associated Architects. Portland, Oregon.

Case study: Fig. 1004.2.5 A – B. The shortest common paths of egress travel are shown from remote points in each area. Where a room or area has a single exit door or a single exit access door, all routes in the space are common paths. The termination of a common path arrow indicates the point at which the common path ends. Where this occurs prior to reaching an exit, it indicates the first point encountered in the path at which the occupant has a choice of two routes to separate exits. Diagonal paths are through spaces where no furnishings will block such a route. Otherwise, travel is measured on a rectangular pattern.

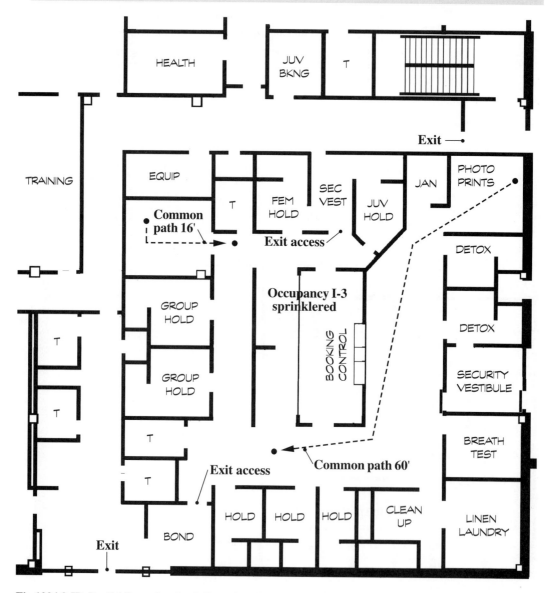

Fig.1004.2.5B. Partial floor plan. Lee's Summit Police and Court Facility. Lee's Summit, Missouri. The Hollis and Miller Group, Inc. Lee's Summit, Missouri.

1004 Exit Access

1004.3.1 Aisles

This subsection addresses aisles serving in a means of egress.

- The following aisles are not addressed by this subsection:
    - In assembly other than seating at tables.
    - In reviewing stands.
    - In grandstands.
    - In bleachers.
- Aisles are required for occupied areas containing the following:
    - Seats.
    - Tables.
    - Furnishing.
    - Displays.
    - Similar fixtures or equipment.
- Obstructions in required aisle width are limited to the following:
    - The following elements may protrude a total ≤ 7" into the required width:
        Fully opened doors.
        Handrails.

        Note: The protrusion limit describes the sum of protrusions where they are directly opposite each other across an aisle. Handrails on each side of an aisle, for example, may each protrude ≤ 3½" so that the total protrusion would be ≤ 7" at point of width measurement in the aisle.

    - Doors in any position may not reduce the required aisle width to < ½.
    - The following nonstructural items may protrude into required width ≤ 1 ½" from each side:
        Trim.
        Similar decorations.

1004.3.1.1 Public areas Group B and M

- In public areas of Group B and M, aisle width is governed as follows:
    - Required aisle width varies as indicated below based on the sides of the aisle occupied by the following:
        Fixtures.
          Seats.
          Tables.
          Furnishings.
          Displays.
          Similar features or equipment.
        Width must be ≥ 36" where fixtures are one side of the aisle only.
        Width must be ≥ 44" where fixtures are on both sides of the aisle.

1004 Exit Access

1004.3.1.2 Nonpublic areas

- Width of other nonpublic aisles must be ≥ 36".
- Width of aisles must be ≥ 2'-4" where all the following conditions apply:
  ○ Aisles are not public.
  ○ Occupant load ≤ 50.
  ○ Aisle is not required to be accessible.

    Note: Chapter 11, "Accessibility," is cited as the source defining aisles required to be accessible.

1004.3.1.3 Seating at tables

- The clear width of an aisle or aisle accessway along the following seating is measured as indicated below:
  ○ Movable seating:
    At tables.
    At counters.
  ○ Width measurement:
    Aisle width is measured to a line 19" away from and ‖ to the edge of the following:
      Table.
      Counter.
    The 19" distance is measured ⊥ to the edge of the table or counter.
- The clear width of an aisle or aisle accessway along the following seating is measured as indicated below:
  ○ Fixed seating:
    At tables.
    At counters.
  ○ Width measurement is made to the back of the fixed seating.
- Other aisle or aisle accessway width measurements are to bypass any handrails and continue to the bordering element such as follows:
  ○ Walls.
  ○ Edges of seating.
  ○ Tread edges.

1004 Exit Access

1004.3.1.3.1 Aisle accessway for tables and seating

- An aisle accessway for seating at tables or counters must have a width ≥ the larger of the following:
  - o Egress width required for means of egress.

    Note: 1003.2.3, "Egress width," is cited as the source of width requirements for means of egress. Minimum width is calculated by an allocation of inches per occupant.

  - o Accessway width required for seating at tables and counters.

    Note: 1004.3.1.3.2, "Table and seating accessway width," is cited as the source of width requirements. Minimum width is calculated based on accessway length.

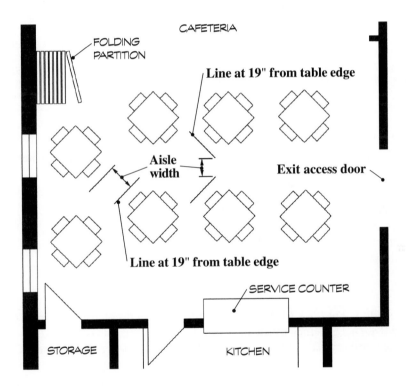

Fig. 1004.3.1.3. Partial floor plan at cafeteria. Multipurpose Building Addition to Children's Home. Wilkes-Barre, Pennsylvania. C. Allen Mullins, Architect. Bear Creek, Pennsylvania.

1004 Exit Access

1004.3.1.3.2 Table and seating accessway width

- Segments of an aisle accessway with the both of the following characteristics is not governed by this subsection:
  - Length $\leq 6'$.
  - Occupant load ≤ 4.
- Other aisle accessways must have a width as follows:
  - $\geq 12"$ where accessways are $\leq 12'$.
  - For accessways $> 12'$ and $\leq 30'$ in length, a table of widths is provided below:
    Aisle accessway length is measured to the center of the seat most remote from the aisle.

Table 1004.3.1.3.2   Aisle Accessway Widths

Length	Width	Length	Width	Length	Width
$> 12' \leq 13'$	$\geq 12.5"$	$> 18' \leq 19'$	$\geq 15.5"$	$> 24' \leq 25'$	$\geq 18.5"$
$> 13' \leq 14'$	$\geq 13.0"$	$> 19' \leq 20'$	$\geq 16.0"$	$> 25' \leq 26'$	$\geq 19.0"$
$> 14' \leq 15'$	$\geq 13.5"$	$> 20' \leq 21'$	$\geq 16.5"$	$> 26' \leq 27'$	$\geq 19.5"$
$> 15' \leq 16'$	$\geq 14.0"$	$> 21' \leq 22'$	$\geq 17.0"$	$> 27' \leq 28'$	$\geq 20.0"$
$> 16' \leq 17'$	$\geq 14.5"$	$> 22' \leq 23'$	$\geq 17.5"$	$> 28' \leq 29'$	$\geq 20.5"$
$> 17' \leq 18'$	$\geq 15.0"$	$> 23' \leq 24'$	$\geq 18.0"$	$> 29' \leq 30'$	$\geq 21.0"$

Above table is based on the following equation:

Minimum clear width = 12" + 0.5" × [(length in ft –12') rounded up to next foot]

1004.3.1.3.3 Table and seating aisle accessway length

- Travel distance in an aisle accessway is limited to $\leq 30'$ as follows:
  - The distance is measured between the following points:
    From any seat.
    To the point providing a choice of ≥ 2 routes to separate exits.

Case study 1: Fig.1004.3.1.3.2. Table group 1: The widths of aisle accessways A and B are not governed as length of travel in these segments is < 6' and occupant load is 4 each. Width E of the aisle accessway between table ends is governed by length of travel. It is assumed that once an occupant enters this accessway, travel continues to an aisle. In this case, longest travel is 10' requiring a width of 12" which is < the 18" provided. Other travel patterns can be assumed which place > 4 occupants in the A or B segments, thus, requiring widths to meet minimums based on length. Such width D is measured between lines that are 19" (dimension C) from the table edges. Width D is 12", which is adequate for travel up to 12'. Travel in this scenario is 10'.

Case study 2: Fig. 1004.3.1.3.2. Table group 2: Aisle accessways A and B are 7' -6" in length, thus, requiring a minimum width D of 12" which is provided. Width D is measured between lines at 19" (dimension C) from the table edges.

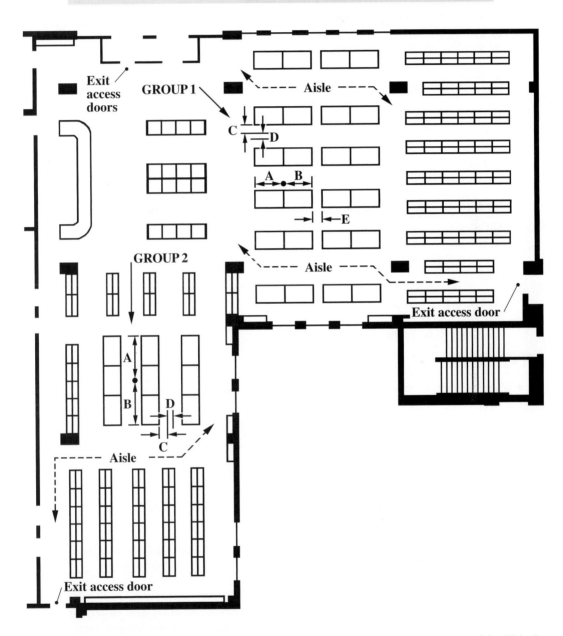

Fig. 1004.3.1.3.2. Partial floor plan at library. High School 6, Cypress-Fairbanks Independent School District. Harris County, Texas. PBK Architects, Inc. Houston, Texas.

1004 Exit Access

1004.3.2.2 Corridor width

- The following widths are required for corridors serving the locations noted:

Table 1004.3.2.2 a   **Minimum Corridor Widths**

Width	Occupants	Location
≥ 24"	Not limited	Access to building service equipment
≥ 36"	≤ 50	All locations
≥ 36"	Not limited	Within a dwelling unit
≥ 72"	≥ 100	Occupancy E
≥ 72"	Not limited	Occupancy I – surgical, health-care centers for ambulatory outpatients incapable of self-preservation
≥ 96"	Not limited	Occupancy I-2 where bed movement is required

- In other locations, corridors must be the larger of the following widths:
  - ≥ 3'-8".
  - ≥ occupant load × the widths per occupant listed below.

Table 1004.3.2.2b   **Minimum Required Width for Corridors per Occupant Served**

Occupancy	Building sprinklered as per NFPA 13 or 13R
A, B, E, F, H-5, I-1, I-3, I-4, M, R, S, U	0.15"
H-1, H-2, H-3, H-4, I-2	0.2"
	Building not sprinklered
A, B, E, F, H-5, I, M, R, S, U	0.2"
H-1, H-2, H-3, H-4	0.4"

Source: IBC Table 1003.2.3

1004.3.2.3 Dead ends

- Where > 1 exit or exit access doorway is required, the following applies:
  - Dead end corridor length is limited as follows:

Table 1004.3.2.3   **Dead-End Length Limits**

Occupancy	Conditions	Length
B, F	No sprinklers	≤ 20'
B, F	Sprinklered as per NFPA 13	≤ 50'
I-3	Condition 1 or 5	≤ 20'
I-3	Condition 2, 3, or 4	≤ 50'
A, E, H, I-1, I-2, 1-4, M, R, S, U	Width at narrowest point	≤ 20' or < 2.5 × width of dead end, whichever is longer

Note: 308.4 "Group I-3," is cited as the source of characteristics for I-3 conditions. Condition 1 and 5 require the least and most restraint of resident movement. Conditions 2, 3, and 4 require restraint for residents between the extremes.

Case study: Fig. 1004.3.2.3A. The dead-end corridor at the storage room in the occupancy E building is 14'- 0" long and 7'- 4" wide. The length of a dead end must be < 2.5 × its width or ≤ 20', whichever is greater. Since *2.5 × 7'- 4" = 18'- 4"* which is < 20', maximum length is 20'. The 14'- 0" length is < 20'; thus, the dead end is in compliance with the code.

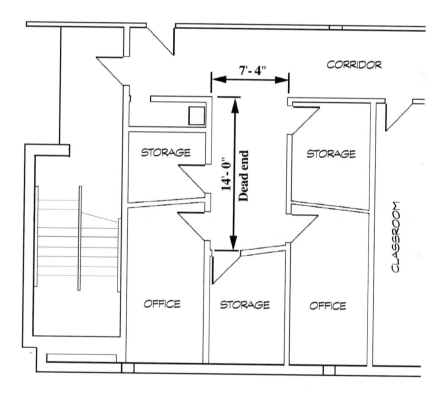

Fig. 1004.3.2.3A. Partial floor plan. Newman Elementary School Renovations. Needham, Massachusetts. HKT Architects, Inc. Sommerville, Massachusetts.

Case study: Fig.1004.3.2.3B. The elevator lobby of the occupancy B sprinklered building is a dead end 13' in length. This is in compliance with the 50' maximum for sprinklered buildings of this occupancy.

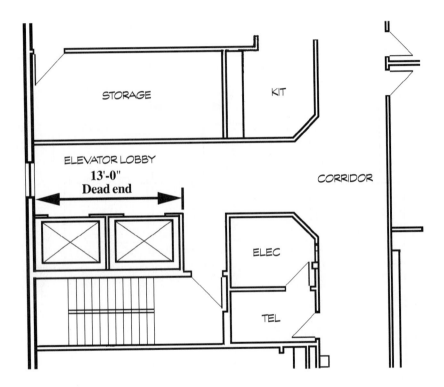

Fig. 1004.3.2.3B. Partial floor plan at elevator lobby. South Texas Blood and Tissue Center. San Antonio, Texas. Overland Partners, Inc. San Antonio, Texas.

1004 Exit Access

1004.3.2.5 Corridor continuity

This subsection addresses corridors with a fire-resistant rating.

- Corridors may pass through the following rooms in the condition indicated below:
  - Intervening rooms:
    Foyers and lobbies.
    Reception rooms.
  - Condition:
    Rooms to be constructed with fire resistance $\geq$ that of the connecting corridor.
- Corridors may pass through an elevator lobby where all of the following conditions apply:
  - In occupancy B.
  - Building is sprinklered as per NFPA 13.
  - Elevator lobby is enclosed.
  - All points in the building have access to a required exit which does not pass through the elevator lobby.
- Otherwise, corridors must comply with both of the following:
  - They must be continuous from their beginning to an exit.
  - They may not pass through intervening rooms.

1004.3.3 Egress balconies

- Balconies in a means of egress must comply with corridor requirements as follows:
  - Width and headroom.
  - Dead ends.
  - Projections.
- Protection against the accumulation of snow or ice is governed as follows:
  - Such protection is not required on exterior balconies and concourses at outdoor stadiums.
  - Such protection is required for all other exterior balconies in a means of egress.

1004.3.3.1 Wall separation

This section addresses the separation of a means of egress balcony from the building interior.

- Separation is not required where both of the following conditions apply:
  - The egress balcony is served by $\geq$ 2 stairs.
  - Travel from a dead end does not pass an unprotected opening en route to a stair.
- Otherwise, such a balcony must be separated from the interior of the building as follows:
  - By the walls as required for corridors.
  - By opening protectives as required for corridors.

1004.3.3.2 Openness

- The area on the long side of the egress balcony must be open to exterior as follows:
  - $\geq$ 50 % openness is required.
- Open area above guards must be distributed to minimize the collection of smoke and gases.

1005 Exits

1005.1 General

- Any use of an exit that interferes with its function is prohibited.
- A level of protection at any point in an exit may not diminish until the exit discharge.

1005.2.1 Minimum number of exits

- Occupied roofs have the same requirements for exits as do floors.
- The required number of exits from the following must be provided from the point required throughout the means of egress to grade or public way:
  - A story.
  - A basement.
  - A space.
- The following number of exits are required from every floor based on number of occupants:*

Occupants	< 500	> 500 and ≤ 1000	> 1000
Exits required	≥ 2	≥ 3	≥ 4

Note: The following are cited as modifying the number of exits required:
> *1004.2.1, "Exit or exit access doorways required."*
> *1005.2.2, "Buildings with one exit."*

> **Case study: Fig. 1005.2.1.** 646 occupants in this occupancy E building require 3 exits. The building complies with the code by providing 8 exits. Exits are numbered in the illustration.

1005.2.1.1 Open parking structures

- Where vehicles are mechanically parked, exits required are as follows:
  - Only 1 exit is required from each parking level.
- In other parking structures, exits are required as follows:
  - ≥ 2 exits are required from each parking level.
- Open vehicle ramps without pedestrian facilities are not considered exits.
- Open vehicle ramps with pedestrian facilities are considered exits.
- Stairways need not be enclosed.

* *Source*: IBC Table 1005.2.1.

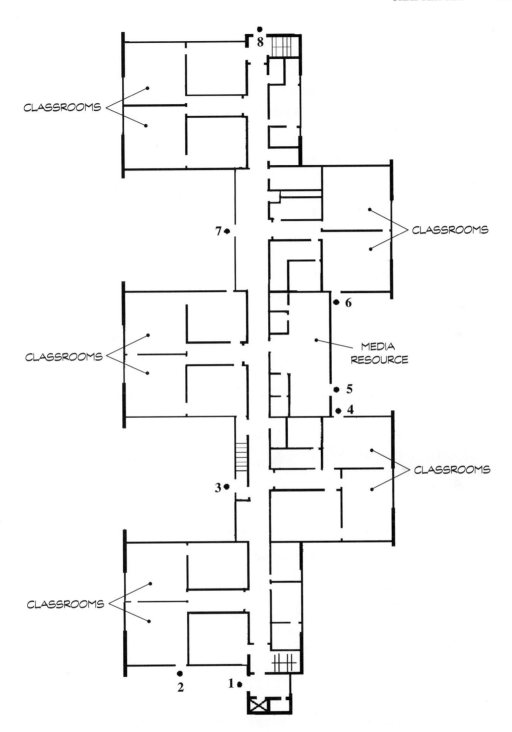

Fig. 1005.2.1. Floor plan of classroom wing. Newman Elementary School Renovations. Needham, Massachusetts. HKT Architects, Inc. Somerville, Massachusetts.

1005 Exits

1005.2.2 Buildings with one exit *(part 1 of 2)*

- Only 1 exit is required in occupancy R-3.
- Buildings meeting all the following criteria require only 1 exit:
  - The building has only one level.
  - Occupied space is on the level of discharge.
  - Occupant load is under the required limit.
  - Common path egress travel distance is under the required limit.

  Note: 1004.2.1, "Exit or exit access doorways required," is cited as defining occupant loads and common path distances over which ≥ 2 exits are required.

- Only 1 exit is required from air traffic control towers meeting the following criteria:
  - ≤ 15 occupants.
  - Requirements for the stairway location, construction, and operation.

  Note: 412.1, "Airport traffic control towers," is cited as providing exit requirements for these structures.

- Exits in open parking garages are required from each parking level as follows:
  - ≥ 1 where vehicles are mechanically parked.
  - > 2 in other cases.

  Note: 1005.2.1.1, "Open parking structures," is cited as providing requirements for exits from parking garages including the above and other criteria.

Case study: Figure 1005.2.2A. The modular classroom builidng is occupancy E, 1 story, and has no basement. Its 45 occupants and exit access travel distance ≤ 58' require only 1 exit.

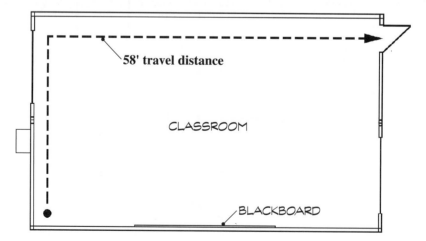

Fig. 1005.2.2A. Floor plan. Modular Classroom Building, Creston Elementary School. Creston, California. Phillips Metsch Sweeney Moore Architects. Santa Barbara, Calfornia.

1005 Exits

1005.2.2 Buildings with one exit *(part 2 of 2)*

- In other cases, only 1 exit is required where the criteria below is met:

Table 1005.2.2   Conditions Permitting 1 Exit from a Building

Occupancy	Occupants per floor	Travel distance
1-story buildings with ≤ 1 level below it:		
A, E, F, M, U	≤ 50	≤ 75'
B sprinklered as per NFPA 13	≤ 50	≤ 100'
B not sprinklered	≤ 50	≤ 75'
H-2, H-3	≤ 3	≤ 25'
H-4, H-5, I, R	≤ 10	≤ 75'
S	≤ 30	≤ 75'
2-story buildings with ≤ 1 level below the 1st story:		
B, F, M, S	≤ 30	≤ 75'

Multistory buildings with ≤ 1 level below the 1st story:

Occupancy	Sprinklered as per NFPA 13 and 13R	Escape & rescue openings	Stories permitted	Dwelling units	Travel distance
R-2	no	no	2	≤ 4	≤ 50'
R-2	no	yes	2	≤ 4	≤ 50'
R-2	yes	no	2	≤ 4	≤ 50'
R-2	yes	yes	3	≤ 4	≤ 50'

Source: IBC Table 1005.2.2.

Note: Section 1009, "Emergency Escape and Rescue," is cited as providing requirements for openings necessary to permit 1 exit in 3 stories in occupancy R-2.

Case study: fig. 1005.2.2B. The occupancy B pavilion is 1 story with no basement. The space is used by staff only for refreshment preparation. Customers are served at pass-through windows and do not enter the building. With 10 occupants and no sprinklers, the building qualifies for 1 exit since no exit access travel distance is > 54' from any point to either of the 2 exits provided. Since only 1 exit is required, the 2 provided do not have to be located a minimum distance apart. Travel distances shown are those applicable, if either door was omitted. With 2 exits, the distances are shorter.

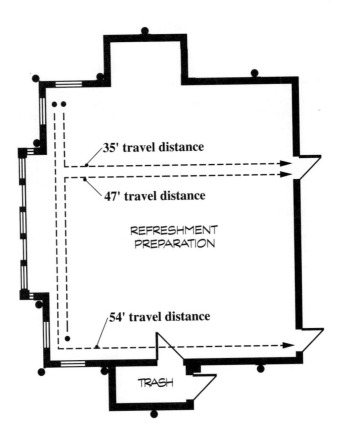

Fig. 1005.2.2B. Floor plan. Visitor Services Pavilions at Clarence Buckingham Memorial Fountain. Chicago Park District. Chicago, Illinois. David Woodhouse, Architects. Chicago, Illinois.

1005 Exits

1005.2.3 Exit continuity

- Exits must be continuous from their beginning to the exit discharge.

1005.3.1 Exterior exit doors

- ≥ 1 exterior exit door is required as follows:
  - In any building for human occupancy.
  - Must meet size requirements for means of egress doors.

    Note: 1003.3.1.1, "Size of doors," is cited as the source of size requirements for means of egress doors.

1005.3.1.1 Detailed requirements

- Exterior exit doors must meet the applicable requirements for means of egress doors.

  Note: 1003.3.1, "Doors," is cited as the source of requirements for means of egress doors.

1005.3.1.2 Arrangement

- Exterior exit doors must open directly to one of the following:
  - An exit discharge.
  - A public way.

1005.3.2 Vertical exit enclosures *(part 1 of 2)*

- Exits do not require an enclosure where all of the following conditions are present:
  - In occupancy A-5.
  - Where all parts of the means of egress are essentially open to the exterior.
- Stairways do not require an enclosure in the following cases:
  - Where all of the following conditions are present:
    In occupancies A, B, E, F, M, R, S, U.
    Occupant load < 10.
    Stairway serves ≤ 1 story above the level of exit discharge.
  - In any of the following locations:
    Within a dwelling unit of the following occupancies:
      R-2,R-3.
    Guestrooms in occupancy R-1.
    Individual suites in occupancy R-1.
  - Where the stairway is not a required means of egress as follows:
    The opening through the floor/ceiling is protected by a shaft enclosure where required.

    Note: 707.2, "Shaft enclosure required," is cited as the source of requirements for shaft protection where floor/ceiling assemblies are penetrated.

  - Where the stairway serves only an open parking structure and is located within it.
  - Where the stairway is serving a stage area.

    Note: 410.5.4, "Stage exits," is cited as identifying stairways associated with a stage..

1005 Exits

1005.3.2 Vertical exit enclosures *(part 2 of 2)*

- Stairway enclosures are not required as follows:
  - For ≤ ¹/₂ the egress stairways where all of the following conditions apply:
    In occupancies A, B, E, F, M, R, S, U.
    The stairways serve only 1 adjacent floor.
    ≥ 2 means of egress exist from both floors served by an open stairway.
    The 2 floors connected by the open stairway are not open to other floors.

  - 1 required stairway enclosure in a building is not required to meet all the enclosure requirements of this subsection where both of the following conditions apply:
    - Where located in occupancy I-3.
    - Where complying with requirements permitting glazing in a stairway enclosure.

    Note: 408.3.6, "Vertical exit enclosures," is cited as the source of modifications for egress stairways in occupancy I-3.

  - All other interior exit stairways must be enclosed as follows:
    - Enclosures must be constructed as fire barriers.

    Note: Section 706, "Fire Barriers," is cited as the source of requirements for this component.

    - Enclosure fire-resistance ratings are required as follows:

Number of stories: mezzanines are not counted; basements are counted	Fire-resistance rating required
< 4 stories	≥ 1 hr
≥ 4 stories	≥ 2 hr

  - Interior exit ramps must meet the requirements of this subsection.
  - An exit enclosure may be used only as a means of egress.

1005.3.2.1 Vertical enclosure exterior walls *(part 1 of 2)*

- Vertical exit enclosure walls that are exterior walls must meet fire-resistance requirements for exterior walls.

  Note: Section 704, "Exterior Walls," is cited as the source of fire-resistance requirements for exterior walls.

1005 Exits

1005.3.2.1 Vertical enclosure exterior walls *(part 2 of 2)*

- In the following circumstances, the conditions listed below are required:
  - Circumstances applying to the exterior wall of a stairway enclosure:
    The wall has one or both the following characteristics:
      It does not have a fire-resistance rating.
      It has unprotected openings.
    The wall is exposed to another exterior wall of the building at an angle < 180°.
  - Conditions required:
    The building exterior wall so exposed must be constructed as follows:
      It must have a fire-resistance rating ≥ 1 hr.
      It must have opening protectives > ¾ hr.
    Required fire-resistant construction must cover an area as follows:
      ≤ 10' horizontally from the stairway wall as defined above.
      From grade to the lower of the two upper limits described as follows:
        A level 10' above the highest landing of the stairway.
        The roof line.

1005.3.2.2 Enclosures under stairways

- The space under a stairway in a dwelling unit is not governed by this subsection as follows:
  - In ccupancies R-2 and R-3.
- In other locations, space under stairways with the following characteristics is governed as indicated below:
  - Stairway characteristics:
    Interior stairway.
    Stairway enclosed or not enclosed.
  - Space characteristics:
    Space is enclosed and usable.
  - Requirements:
    Walls and soffits of the space must have the larger of the following:
      ≥ 1-hr fire-resistance rating.
      Fire-resistance rating ≥ that of the stairway enclosure.
    Access to the space must be from outside the stair enclosure.
- Open space below exterior stairways may not be used for any purpose.
- The following space under exterior stairways is governed as indicated below:
  - Space characteristics:
    Space is enclosed and usable.
  - Space enclosure must have one of the following fire-resistance ratings:

Number of stories served	Fire resistance rating required
< 4	1 hr
≥ 4	2 hr

- Open space below exterior stairways may not be used for any purpose.

Case study: Fig. 1005.3.2.2. A meter room is located under an interior stairway as shown in the illustration. The walls of the space and the soffit of the landing above it have a 1-hr fire-resistance rating. The room is accessed from outside the stairway enclosure. The meter room is in compliance with code requirements.

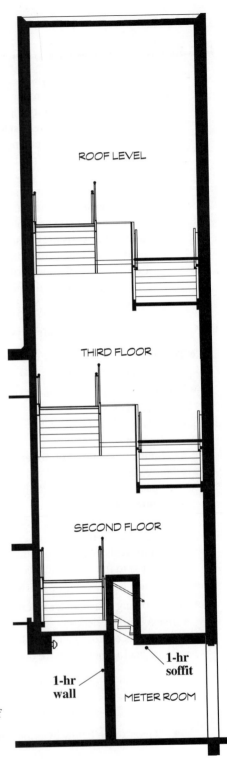

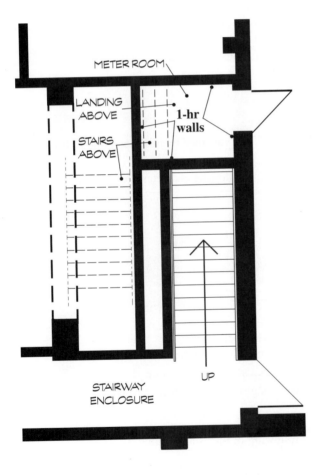

Fig. 1005.3.2.2. Plan and section at meter room. University of Connecticut New Downtown Campus at Stamford, Connecticut. Perkins Eastman Architects, P.C. New York, New York.

1005 Exits

1005.3.2.3 Discharge identification

- Enclosed exit stairways continuing to below level of exit discharge are governed as follows:
  - An approved barrier is required at the level of exit discharge as follows:
    Barrier must prevent accidental egress travel to below the level of exit discharge.
  - Directional exit signs are required.

    Note: 1003.2.10, "Exit signs," is cited as the source of exit sign requirements.

1005.3.2.4 Stairway floor number signs

- Signs described below are required at floor landings in the following enclosures:
  - Enclosures with both of the following characteristics:
    Interior vertical exit enclosures.
    Enclosure connects > 3 stories.
  - Sign information required:
    Floor level.
    Identifying the termination of the stairway enclosure at the top and bottom.
    Stairway identification.
    Story of the exit discharge.
    Direction to the exit discharge.
    Availability of fire department roof access.
- Required signs are to be positioned as follows:
  - 5' above the floor landing.
  - To be visible when the doors are open or closed.

1005.3.2.5 Smokeproof enclosures

- This subsection addresses exits serving the following floor levels:
  - In high-rise buildings as follows:
    Floor surface > 75' above lowest level of fire department vehicle access.
  - In underground buildings as follows:
    Floor surface > 30' below level of exit discharge.

    Note: The following sections are cited as defining the buildings in this subsection:
    Section 403, "High-Rise Buildings."
    Section 405, "Underground Buildings."

- Exits serving such floors must be one of the following:
  - A smokeproof enclosure.
  - A pressurized stairway.

    Note: 909.20, "Smokeproof enclosures," is cited as a source of requirements.

1005 Exits

1005.3.2.5.1 Enclosure exit

- This subsection addresses the following enclosures:
  - Smokeproof enclosures.
  - Pressurized stairways.
- Such enclosures must discharge to one of the following:
  - A public way.
  - One of the following with direct access to a public way:
    Exit passageway.
    Yard.
    Open space.
- An exit passageway serving the enclosures is governed as follows:
  - Passageway must be separated from the rest of the building as follows:
    By construction with a 2-hr fire-resistant rating.
  - Openings are permitted only with the following conditions:
    Where passageways serve a smokeproof enclosure:
    Passageway equals the enclosure with regard to the following:
    Fire protection.
    Pressurization.
    Openings are protected at access from other floors.
    Where passageways serve a pressurized stairway:
    Passageway equals the stairway with regard to the following:
    Fire protection.
    Pressurization.

1005.3.2.5.2 Enclosure access

- Access to stairways in smokeproof enclosures by one of the following components is governed as indicated below:
  - Components:
    Vestibule.
    Open exterior balcony.
  - Requirements:
    Access via the vestibule or balcony is not required where the stairway is pressurized.
    Otherwise, access via the vestibule or balcony is required.

  Note: 909.20.5, "Stair pressurization alternative," is cited as the source of requirements for stairway pressurization.

1005.3.3 Exit passageway

- An exit passageway may be used only for a means of egress.

1005 Exits

1005.3.3.1 Width

- The width of an exit passageway must be the larger of the following:
  - One of the following dimensions as applicable:
    - ≥ 44" for occupant load ≥ 50.
    - ≥ 36" for occupant load < 50.
  - As calculated by occupant load based on occupancy.

    Note: 1003.2.3, "Egress width," is cited as the source of width allocations per occupant and occupancy.

- Protrusions into the required width of an exit passageway are limited as follows:

  Table 1005.3.3.1   Protrusions into Exit Passageways

Protruding elements	Protrusion permitted
Handrails	≤ 7"
Doors at full open position	≤ 7"
Doors in any position	≤ ½ required width
Nonstructural trim and similar decorative features	≤ 1½" from each side

  Note: Where not specified as being from each side, permitted protrusions, as listed above, are the sum of protrusions from both sides at any point of width measurement. For example, the sum of door swing protrusion into the required width from locations directly opposite each other may not be greater than ½ the required width. Thus, at least ½ the required width would remain unobstructed with both doors extended to their fullest protrusion.

1005.3.3.2 Construction

- The fire-resistance rating for the following exit passageway enclosure components must be as indicated below:
  - Components:
    Walls.
    Floors.
    Ceilings.
  - Fire-resistance rating must be the larger of the following:
    1 hr.
    The rating required for any connecting exit enclosure.
- An exit passageway must be constructed as a fire barrier.

  Note: Section 706, "Fire Barriers," is cited as the source of requirements for those components.

1005 Exits

1005.3.4 Openings and penetrations

- This subsection addresses openings into the following enclosures:
  - Exit passageways.
  - Exit enclosures.
- Such openings must be protected.

  Note: Section 714, "Opening Protectives," is cited as the source of requirements by which openings must be protected.

- Openings in an exit passageway to the following service areas are permitted where the requirement listed below is met:
  - Service areas:
    Mechanical and electrical rooms.
    Building service areas.
    Service elevators.
  - The fire-resistance rating of the passageway may not be compromised.
- Other than service elevators may not open into an exit passageway.
- Unexposed exterior openings are permitted in the enclosures.

  Note: Exposure of exterior openings occurs when they are exposed to fire hazard due to their proximity to certain other exterior walls. Such exposure is mentioned in 1005.3.2.1, "Vertical enclosure exterior walls."

- The only other openings permitted in the enclosures are as follows:
    Those required for exit access from routinely occupied spaces.
    Those required for egress from the enclosure.
- A fire door is required as follows:
  - Where an interior exit enclosure connects to an exit passageway.

  *Note: The following are cited as governing fire doors:
    714.2, "Fire door and shutter assemblies," is cited as the source of requirements for fire doors.*

1005.3.4.1 Penetrations

- Penetrations or openings are not permitted between adjacent exit enclosures.
- Only components of the following devices where serving an exit enclosure are permitted to penetrate the enclosure:
  - Required exit doors.
  - Equipment and duct work necessary for independent pressurization.
  - Sprinkler piping.
  - Standpipes.
  - Electrical conduit terminating in a steel box not exceeding 16 sq in.
- Penetrations and openings are required to be protected.

  Note: Section 711, "Penetrations," is cited as the source of requirements for penetrations.

1005 Exits

1005.3.5 Horizontal exits

- All required exits may be horizontal exits in occupancy I-3 as follows:
    - The space on each side of a horizontal exit must have the following occupant capacity:
        Area ≥ 6 sf × (sum of occupants from both sides of the horizontal exit).
    - A fire compartment defined by a horizontal exit is not required to have the following egress components where the conditions indicated below are present:
        Egress components:
            Stairway leading directly to the exterior.
            Door leading directly to the exterior.
        Conditions:
            An adjoining fire compartment must have one of the egress components listed above.
            Egress does not return to the compartment of origin.
- ≤ ²/₃ of required exits in occupancy I-2 may be horizontal exits as follows:
    - From a building or a floor.
- In other occupancies, horizontal exits are limited as follows:
    - They may not provide the only means of exit from any part of a building.
    - They may provide ≤ ½ the required exits.
    - They may provide ≤ ½ the required exit width.
- Exits serving the area receiving occupants through a horizontal exit are governed as follows:
    - Exit capacity is required for original occupants of the area.
    - Exit capacity is not required for occupants entering the area through a horizontal exit.
    - In other than I-3 ≥ 1 exit must lead to one of the following:
        To the outdoors or to an exit enclosure.

1005.3.5.1 Separation

- This subsection governs separation walls between the following:
    - Buildings connected by a horizontal exit.
    - Areas of refuge connected by a horizontal exit.
- The separation wall must be one of the following types:
    - A fire wall.
    - A fire barrier as follows:
        Walls must completely divide the floor served by the horizontal exit.
        Walls must be continuous between exterior walls.

    Note: Section 705, "Fire Walls," is cited as a source of separation wall requirements.
            Section 706, "Fire Barriers," is cited as a source of separation wall requirements.

- The separation wall must have a fire-resistance rating ≥ 2 hr.
- Separation wall must extend vertically through entire building in either of the following:
    - Where fire-resistance rating of floor assemblies is < 2 hr.
    - Where floor assemblies have unprotected openings.
- Openings in the separation wall must be protected.

    Note: Section 714, "Opening Protectives," is cited as the pertinent source of requirements.

1005 Exits

1005.3.5.2 Opening protectives

- Opening protectives in horizontal exits must be as per the wall fire-resistance rating.
- Fire doors in horizontal exits must close when activated by a smoke detector.
- Fire doors in a cross-corridor configuration must close when activated by a smoke detector.

  Note: 907.10, "Fire safety functions," is cited as a source of smoke detector requirements.

1005.3.5.3 Capacity of refuge area

- Refuge areas of a horizontal exit must be one of the following:
  - Areas occupied by the same tenant.
  - Public areas.
- A refuge area must be able to hold the sum of the following:
  - Its original occupants.
  - Occupants expected from the area connected by the horizontal exit.
- The number of occupants expected to travel to an area of refuge through a horizontal exit is based on the following:
  - By the capacity of the horizontal exit doors through which they must pass.
- The space required to house people in a refuge area is governed as follows:
  - Required area ≥ floor area per person × total number of occupants to be accommodated.
  - Area required for housing occupants does not include the following:
    Stairways.
    Elevators or other shafts.
    Courts.
  - Floor areas required per person are based on occupancy as follows:

    Table 1005.3.5.3   Refuge Area Capacity

Occupancy	Net floor area per person
I-2 housing nonambulatory occupants	30 sf
I-2 housing ambulatory occupants	15 sf
I-3	6 sf
All other occupancies	3 sf

1005.3.6 Exterior exit stairways

- Exterior exit stairways at outdoor stadiums as follows are not governed by this section:
  - Where all portions of the means of egress are essentially open to the exterior.

1005.3.6.1 Use in a means of egress

- The use of exterior exit stairways in a required means of egress is governed as follows:
  - Not permitted in occupancy I-2.
  - Permitted in other occupancies where both of the following apply:
    Building is ≤ 6 stories.
    Building is ≤ 75' in height.

1005 Exits

1005.3.6.2 Open side

- Exterior exit stairways serving in a means of egress must have ≥ 1 side open as follows in the locations indicated below:
  - A total of ≥ 35 sf must be open.
  - Required open area must be located ≤ 42" above each of the following:
    Each adjacent floor level.
    Each adjacent intermediate landing.

1005.3.6.3 Side yards

- The required open side of an exterior exit stairway must adjoin one of the following:
  - Yard.
  - Court.
  - Public way.
- Closed sides of an exterior exit stairway may be exterior walls of the building.

1005.3.6.4 Location

- Exterior exit stairways must be must be positioned as follows:
  - ≥ 10' from lot lines.
  - ≥ 10' from other buildings on the same lot as follows:
    Where adjacent, the exterior building walls and openings are not protected as follows:
    As per exterior wall requirements vs. fire separation distance.

  Note: Section 704, "Exterior Walls," is cited as the source of requirements for adjacent walls within 10' of the stairway according to fire separation distance.

Case study: Fig. 1005.3.6.2. 100% of the exterior stairway is open above the 42" level on both sides of the intermediate landing and on all sides of the 2nd floor landing. The east side of the stairway is 100% open at the first floor landing, thus, providing 38 $\frac{1}{2}$ sf of opening above the 42" level. This is > than the 35 sf minimum. The open sides face yards and are > 10' from lot lines. The stairway serves the power plant and is not part of the I-2 occupancy building. The stairway is in compliance with the code.

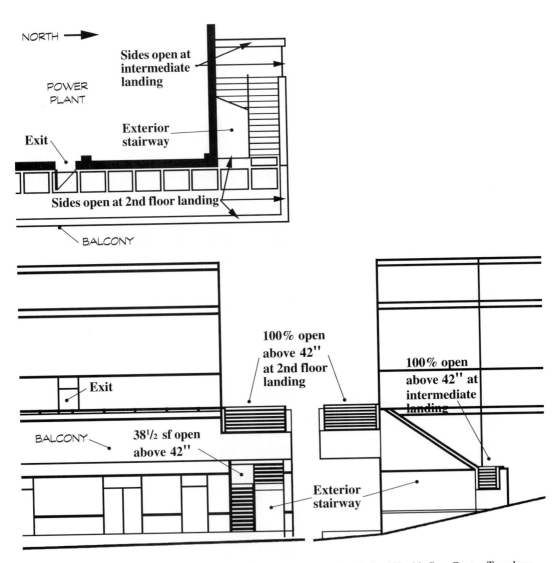

Fig. 1005.3.6.2. Plan and elevations of exterior stairway. Christus St. Michael Health Care Center. Texarkana, Texas. Watkins Hamilton Ross Architects, Inc. Houston, Texas.

1005 Exits

1005.3.6.5 Exterior stairway protection

This subsection addresses the separation of an exterior exit stairway from the building interior.

- Separation is not required where all of the following conditions apply:
  - In occupancies A, B, E, F, H, I, M, R-3, R-4, S, and U.
  - Buildings are ≤ 2 stories above grade.
  - Level of exit discharge is the 1st story above grade.
- Separation is not required where the stairway is served by an exterior balcony meeting all of the following conditions:
  - Balcony connects 2 remote exits that are of the following types:
    Exterior stairways.
    Other approved exits.
  - Balcony has a perimeter that is ≥ 50% open as follows:
    Open area is ≥ half the height of the enclosing wall.
    Top of the open area ≥ 7' above the floor of the balcony.
- Separation is not required at buildings where enclosures are not required for interior stairways.

  Note: 1005.3.2, "Vertical exit enclosures," is cited as the source of requirements permitting open interior stairs.

- Separation is not required where the exterior exit stairway is connected to an open-ended corridor meeting all of the following conditions:
  - Building is sprinklered as per NFPA 13 or 13R, including the following:
    The corridors.
    The stairs.
  - Open-ended corridor complies with dimensional, fire-resistance, and other requirements for interior corridors.

  Note: 1004.3.2, "Corridors," is cited as the source of requirements for interior corridors.

  - Each end of the open-ended corridor connects to an exterior exit stairway.

  Note: 1005.3.6, "Exterior exit stairways," is cited as the pertinent source of requirements.

  - One of the following is provided at any change of direction > 45°:
    A clear opening to the exterior ≥ 35 sf as follows:
      Opening minimizes accumulation of smoke and toxic gases.
    An exterior exit stairway.
- For all other cases, the walls separating exterior exit stairways from the interior of the building must comply with the following:
  - They must meet fire-resistance and other requirements for vertical exit enclosures.

  Note: 1005.3.2, "Vertical exit enclosures," is cited as the source of applicable requirements.

  - Only openings necessary for egress are permitted in the separating walls.

1006 Exit Discharge

1006.1 General

- Egress from an exit enclosure may pass through an interior space only with all of the following conditions present:
  - The space is at the level of exit discharge.
  - Egress from ≤ 50% of the capacity of enclosures passes through interior space.
  - Egress from ≤ 50% of the number enclosures passes through interior space.
  - The space provides a path to the exterior as follows:
    Path must be unobstructed.
    Path must be readily apparent from the terminal of the exit enclosure.
  - Level of discharge must be separated from areas below as follows:
    Separation construction has a fire-resistance rating = to that of the exit enclosure.
  - Level of discharge is sprinklered as per NFPA 13 or 13R.
  - Areas at discharge level with access to exit discharge area must have one of the following:
    A sprinkler system as per NFPA 13 or 13R.
    Separation from the rest of the building as per exit enclosure requirements.
- Egress from an exit enclosure may pass through a vestibule only with all the following conditions present:
  - Egress from ≤ 50% of the capacity of enclosures passes through interior space.
  - Egress from ≤ 50% of the number of enclosures passes through interior space.
  - The vestibule must have all of the following characteristics:
    It is separated from areas below it as follows:
    Separation construction has a fire-resistance rating = to that of the exit enclosure.
    Depth of vestibule measured from exterior of building is ≤ 10'.
    It is separated from rest of exit discharge level as follows:
    Separation construction is equivalent to the following:
    To that provided by wire glass in steel frames:
    Wire glass must be approved.
    Vestibule is used as a means of egress only.
    Vestibule discharges directly to the exterior.
- All other exit discharges must comply with all of the following:
  Discharge must be directly to the outside.
  Discharge must occur in one of the following ways:
  At grade.
  At direct access to grade.
  Discharge may not return to the building.

1006.2.1 Exit discharge capacity

- Exit discharge capacity must be ≥ the required capacity of exits being discharged.

1006 Exit Discharge

1006.2.2 Exit discharge location

- The following elements must be located as indicated below:
    - Elements:
        Exterior balconies.
        Exterior stairways.
        Exterior ramps.
    - Location requirements:
        ≥ 10' from lot lines.
        ≥ 10' from other buildings on the same lot in the following circumstance:
            Where adjacent exterior building walls and openings are not protected as follows:
                As per exterior wall requirements based on fire separation distance.

    Note: Section 704, "Exterior Walls," is cited as the source of requirements for adjacent walls within 10' of the stairway, according to fire separation distance.

> **Case study: Fig. 1006.2.2.** The 5 exterior stairways are > 10' from lot lines ranging from 160' to 240' away. The 10' minimum distance is indicated at each stairway. The 6 exterior balconies are further from the lot lines. There are no other buldings on the site.

1006.3 Exit discharge components

- Exit discharge components must be open to the exterior as follows:
    To a degree that minimizes the accumulation of smoke and toxic gases.
- Exit discharge components in a means of egress must meet exit discharge requirements.

    Note: Section 1006, "Exit Discharge," is cited as the source of applicable requirements.

1006.3.1 Egress courts

- An egress court as a component of the exit discharge in a means of egress must comply with exit discharge requirements:

    Note: Section 1006, "Exit Discharge," is cited as the source of applicable requirements.

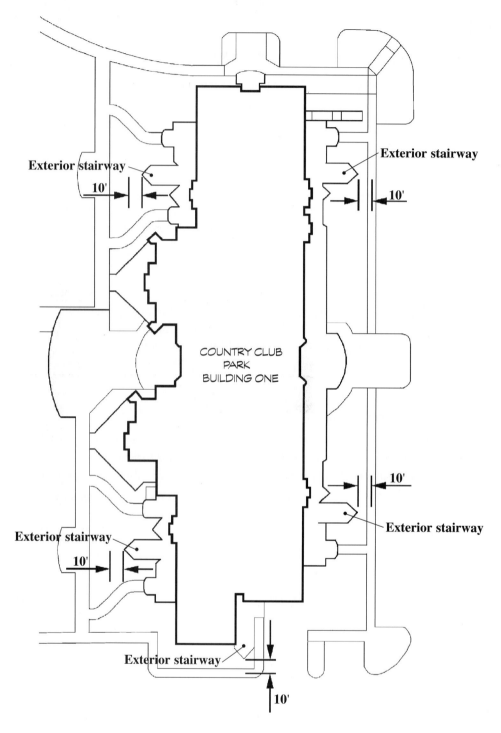

Fig. 1006.2.2. Partial site plan. Country Club Park Building One. Wichita, Kansas. Gossen Livingston Associates, Inc. Architecture. Wichita, Kansas.

1006 Exit Discharge

1006.3.1.1 Width

- The width of an egress court must be ≥ the larger of the following:
  - The width required for means of egress.

    Note: 1003.2.3, "Egress width," is cited as the source of required width.

  - Widths as follows:

Occupancy	Width
R-3, U	≥ 3'
Other	≥ 3'-8"

- Unobstructed height of an egress court within required width must be ≥ 7'.
  - Only the following protrusions are permitted into the required width of an egress court:

Table 1006.3.1.1	Protrusions into Egress Courts
Protruding elements	Protrusion permitted
Handrails	≤ 7"
Doors at full open position	≤ 7"
Doors in any position	≤ ½ required width
Nonstructural trim and similar decorative features	≤ 1½" from each side

    Note: The 7" protrusions listed above are the sum of protrusions on both sides of the court at any point. The ½ width into which doors may protrude is the sum of door protrusions on both sides of a court at any point.

  - An egress court may diminish in width in the direction of egress only as follows:
    - Width may not diminish to < the required width.
    - The transition must be gradual.
    - The transition may not form an angle > 30° with the line of travel.
    - The transition must be bordered by a guard ≥ 36" high.

1006.3.1.2 Construction and openings

- The following egress occupancy R-3 courts are not governed by this subsection:
  - Where the occupant load is < 10.
- In other cases, where an egress court is < 10' wide, the following applies:
  - Egress court walls must comply with both the following:
    Comply with exterior wall requirements.
    Have a fire-resistance rating of ≥ 1 hr as follows:
    Rated construction must extend ≥ 10' above the court floor.
    Openings ≤ 10' high have one of the following:
    Fixed opening protective ≥ ¾ hr.
    Self-closing opening protective ≥ ¾ hr.

  Note: Section 704, "Exterior Walls," is cited as the source of requirements.

1007 Miscellaneous Means of Egress Requirements

1007.1 Boiler, incinerator and furnace rooms

- The following rooms require ≥ 2 exit access doorways where both of the conditions listed below apply:
  - Rooms:
    Boiler.
    Incinerator.
    Furnace.
  - Conditions:
    Area > 500 sf.
    Fuel-fire equipment > 400,000 Btu input capacity.
- Where ≥ 2 exit access doorways are required, the following applies:
  - 1 exit access doorway may be accessed by the following:
    By a fixed ladder.
    By an alternating tread stair.
  - Exit access doorways must be separated by a horizontal distance as follows:
    By a distance ≥ ½ the greatest horizontal dimension of the room.

1007.2 Refrigeration machinery rooms

- ≥ 2 exits or exit access doors are required in machinery rooms > 1000 sf.
- Where ≥ 2 exit access doorways are required, the following apply:
  - 1 may be accessed by the following:
    By a fixed ladder.
    By an alternating tread stair.
  - Doorways must be separated by a horizontal distance as follows:
    By a distance ≥ ½ the greatest horizontal dimension of the room.
- Travel distance in the room to an exit or exit access doorway must be ≤ the larger of the following:
  - 150'.
  - 150' + permitted increases.

  Note: 1004.2.4, "Exit access travel," is cited as the source of potential increases to the 150' travel distance limit.

- Doors must swing in the direction of egress travel for any occupant load.
- Doors must fit tightly.
- Doors must be self-closing.

1007 Miscellaneous Means of Egress Requirements

1007.3 Refrigerated rooms or spaces

- Room with limited amounts of refrigerants are not governed by this subsection.

    Note: The International Mechanical Code is cited as the source of limits on refrigerant volume applicable to the waiver for compliance with this subsection.

- Otherwise, ≥ 2 exits or exit access doors are required in rooms with all of the following characteristics:
    - ≥ 1000 sf.
    - Contains a refrigerant evaporator.
    - Has a room temperature < 68°.
- Egress travel may pass through adjoining refrigerated spaces.
- Where not sprinklered, travel distance in the room to an exit or exit access doorway must be ≤ the smaller of the following:
    - 150'.
    - As required for building occupancy.

    Note: 1004.2.4, "Exit access travel," is cited as the source of travel distance limitations.

1007.4 Cellulose nitrate film handling

- Access to ≥ 2 exits or exit access doors is required where cellulose nitrate film is handled in the following places:
    - Film laboratories.
    - Projection rooms.
    - Film processing rooms.
- Doors to such rooms must be protected as follows:
    - Have a fire-resistance rating of ≥ 1 hr.
    - Be self-closing.

1007.5 Stage means of egress

- A means of egress must be located on each side of a stage as follows:
    - Where ≥ 2 are required based on either of the following:
        Stage size.
        Occupant load.

1007 Miscellaneous Means of Egress Requirements

1007.5.1 Gallery, gridiron, and catwalk means of egress

- This section addresses the means of egress from the following:
  - Lighting catwalks.
  - Access catwalks.
  - Galleries.
  - Gridirons.
- Lighting and access catwalks must have a width ≥ 22".
- The following are permitted in the means of egress:
  - Spiral stairs.
  - Open stairs.
  - Stairs with width ≥ 22".
  - Ladders.
- > 1 means of egress are not required as follows:
  - Where a means of escape is provided to the following locations by the devices indicated below:
        Locations:
          To a roof.
          To a floor.
        Devices:
          Ladders.
          Alternating tread stairs.
          Spiral stairs.
- Otherwise, means of egress requirements are the same as those for occupancy F-2.

1008 Assembly

1008.1 Assembly main exit

This subsection governs buildings and spaces in occupancy A.

- Exits may be distributed on the perimeter of buildings where all of the following conditions apply:
  - Exits have a total egress width $\geq$ the required width.
  - One of the following cases applies:
      There are no well-defined main exits.
      Multiple main exits are provided.

    Note: Stadiums and arenas are typical of this condition.

- Where the following conditions apply, other buildings and spaces must have a main exit as indicated below:
  - Where the occupant load > 300.
  - Main exit requirement:
      Width must accommodate $\geq$ ½ the total occupant load.
      Width must accommodate all means of egress served by the exit.
- Where the building is designated as occupancy A, the main exit must face one of the following:
  - A street.
  - An unoccupied space with both the following characteristics:
      $\geq$ 10' wide.
      Adjoins a street or public way.

1008.2 Assembly other exits

This subsection governs buildings and spaces in occupancy A.

- Exits may be distributed on the perimeter of buildings where all of the following conditions apply:
  - Exits have a total egress width $\geq$ the required width.
  - One of the following cases applies:
      There are no well-defined main exits.
      Multiple main exits are provided.

    Note: Stadiums and arenas are typical of this condition.

- Other buildings and spaces with an occupant load > 300 are governed as follows:
  - Exits in addition to the main exit are required for each level of occupancy A as follows:
      Egress capacity must $\geq$ ½ the total occupant load of the level served.
      Exits must comply with exit access location requirements.

    Note: 1004.2.2, "Exit or exit access doorway arrangement," is cited as the applicable requirements for exit access location.

1008 Assembly

1008.3 Foyers and lobbies

This subsection addresses theaters and similar functions in occupancy A.

- Lobbies and similar spaces where people wait for seating to be available must comply with the following:
  - Waiting spaces may not overlap into the means of egress required width.
  - Waiting spaces must be separated from the required means of egress by one of the following:
      Substantial permanent partitions.
      Fixed rigid railings ≥ 42" high.
  - Waiting spaces must have one of the following relationships to a public street:
      Be connected directly by all the main entrances/exits.
      Have a straight, unobstructed corridor or passage to every main entrance/exit.

1008.4 Interior balcony and gallery means of egress

This subsection addresses balcony and gallery seating in occupancy A.

- Where seating is provided for > 50, the following applies:
  - ≥ 2 means of egress are required as follows:
      ≥ 1 means of egress must be located at each side of the seating area.
      ≥ 1 means of egress must lead directly to an exit.

1008.4.1 Enclosure of balcony openings

- Stairways may be open between balconies and the main assembly floor in assembly spaces such as the following:
  - Theaters.
  - Churches.
  - Auditoriums.
- In other assembly spaces, the following openings at balconies must be enclosed in vertical exit enclosures:
  - Interior stairways.
  - Other vertical openings.

  Note: 1005.3.2, "Vertical exit enclosures," is cited as the source of applicable requirements.

1008.5 Width of means of egress for assembly

- Clear width of aisles and other means of egress is measured to the following:
  - Walls.
  - Edges of seating.
  - Edges of treads.
- A requirement for a specified clear width does not preclude protrusions into the clear width where permitted.

Case study: Fig. 1008.4. The swimming pool balcony seats 86 occupants, thus, requiring ≥ 2 means of egress. The balcony meets the requirement with the provision of a stairway at each side of the seating as stipulated by the code. Both means of egress lead directly to an exit.

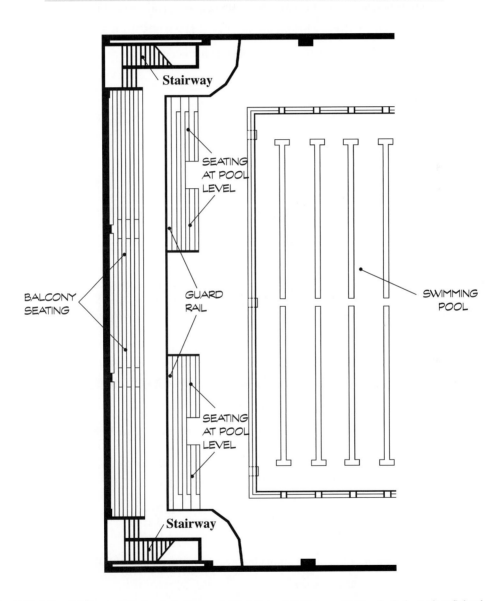

Fig. 1008.4. Partial floor plan at swimming pool. High School 6, Cypress-Fairbanks Independent School District. Harris County, Texas. PBK Architects, Inc. Houston, Texas.

1008 Assembly

1008.5.1 Without smoke protection

- This subsection addresses means of egress clear width where no smoke protection is provided.
- A width per occupant ≥ 0.3" is required on stairways with the following profile:
  - ◦ Riser height ≤ 7".
  - ◦ Tread depth ≥ 11".
- Where the riser height is > 7", the required width per occupant is as follows:

Width per occupant ≥ {[(riser height minus 7") ÷ 0.1] × 0.005"} + 0.3"

This equation yields the following required widths per occupant for riser heights up to 8".

Table 1008.5.1a   Stairway Width Based on Riser Height

Riser height	Width per occupant	Riser height	Width per occupant	Riser height	Width per occupant	Riser height	Width per occupant
7.05"	≥ 0.3025"	7.30"	≥ 0.3150"	7.55"	≥ 0.3275"	7.80"	≥ 0.3400"
7.10"	≥ 0.3050"	7.35"	≥ 0.3175"	7.60"	≥ 0.3300"	7.85"	≥ 0.3425"
7.15"	≥ 0.3075"	7.40"	≥ 0.3200"	7.65"	≥ 0.3325"	7.90"	≥ 0.3450"
7.20"	≥ 0.3100"	7.45"	≥ 0.3225"	7.70"	≥ 0.3350"	7.95"	≥ 0.3475"
7.25"	≥ 0.3125"	7.50"	≥ 0.3250"	7.75"	≥ 0.3375"	8.00"	≥ 0.3500"

- A width per occupant ≥ 0.375" is required as follows:
  - ◦ Where egress requires going down stairs.
  - ◦ Where risers are ≤ 7".
  - ◦ Required for the segment of stairs > 30" from a handrail.
- The width indicated below is required where all of the following conditions apply:
  - ◦ Conditions:
    - Where egress requires going down stairs.
    - Where risers are > 7".
    - Required for the segment of stairs > 30" from a handrail.
  - ◦ The width required per occupant is defined by the following equation:

Width per occupant ≥ {[(riser height minus 7") ÷ 0.1] × 0.005"} + 0.375" required

This equation yields the following required widths per occupant for riser heights up to 8".

Table 1008.5.1b   Descending Egress Stairway Width Based on Riser Height

Riser height	Width per occupant	Riser height	Width per occupant	Riser height	Width per occupant	Riser height	Width per occupant
7.05"	≥ 0.3775"	7.30"	≥ 0.3900"	7.55"	≥ 0.4025"	7.80"	≥ 0.4150"
7.10"	≥ 0.3800"	7.35"	≥ 0.3925"	7.60"	≥ 0.4050"	7.85"	≥ 0.4175"
7.15"	≥ 0.3825"	7.40"	≥ 0.3950"	7.65"	≥ 0.4075"	7.90"	≥ 0.4200"
7.20"	≥ 0.3850"	7.45"	≥ 0.3975"	7.70"	≥ 0.4100"	7.95"	≥ 0.4225"
7.25"	≥ 0.3875"	7.50"	≥ 0.4000"	7.75"	≥ 0.4125"	8.00"	≥ 0.4250"

- Ramped or level means of egress require clear widths per occupant as follows:

Slope	Width per occupant
> 1:12	≥ 0.22"
≤ 1:12	≥ 0.20"

1008 Assembly

1008.5.2 Smoke-protected seating *(part 1 of 3)*

This subsection addresses the clear width required for means of egress in smoke-protected assembly seating.

- Width required is calculated as follows:
  - *Total width = (width required per seat served) × (number of seats served)* as follows:
    Seats must be within one assembly space.
    Seats must be exposed to same smoke-protected environment.
  - Factors for inches of width required per seat served, as provided by the code, may be interpolated.
- A Life Safety Evaluation is required for seating utilizing egress widths stipulated by this subsection.

  Note: NFPA 101, "Code for Safety to Life from Fire in Buildings and Structures," is cited as the source of requirements for the Life Safety Evaluation.

- Required widths for means of egress elements are provided in the tables below as follows:
  - Equations for interpolating factors for width per seat served as required by the code.
  - Tables of required total egress widths for selected quantities of seats.

Table 1008.5.2a	Width of Stairs and Aisle Steps ≤ 30" from a Handrail

Method of calculating inches per seat served for the table of minimum widths below:

Seats	Calculation
1 – 2,000	0.300" a fixed number
2,001 – 5,000	0.300" – [0.0000333" × (number of seats > 2,000)]
5,001 – 10,000	0.200" – [0.0000140" × (number of seats > 5,000)]
10,001 – 15,000	0.130" – [0.0000068" × (number of seats > 10,000)]
15,001 – 20,000	0.096" – [0.0000040" × (number of seats > 15,000)]
20,001 – 25,000	0.076" – [0.0000032" × (number of seats > 20,000)]
25,000 – up	0.060" a fixed number

Minimum width per seat served :

Seats	Width	Seats	Width	Seats	Width	Seats	Width
500	≥ 0.300"	7,000	≥ 0.172"	14,000	≥ 0.103"	21,000	≥ 0.073"
1,000	≥ 0.300"	8,000	≥ 0.158"	15,000	≥ 0.096"	22,000	≥ 0.696"
2,000	≥ 0.300"	9,000	≥ 0.144"	16,000	≥ 0.092"	23,000	≥ 0.066"
3,000	≥ 0.268"	10,000	≥ 0.130"	17,000	≥ 0.088"	24,000	≥ 0.063"
4,000	≥ 0.233"	11,000	≥ 0.123"	18,000	≥ 0.084"	25,000	≥ 0.060"
5,000	≥ 0.200"	12,000	≥ 0.116"	19,000	≥ 0.080"	26,000	≥ 0.060"
6,000	≥ 0.186"	13,000	≥ 0.110"	20,000	≥ 0.076"	27,000	≥ 0.060"

Source: IBC Table 1008.5.2.

1008 Assembly

1008.5.2 Smoke-protected seating *(part 2 of 3)*

Table 1008.5.2b   Width of Stairs and Aisle Steps > 30" from a Handrail

Method of calculating inches per seat served for the table of minimum widths below:

Seats	Calculation
1 – 2,000	0.375" a fixed number
2,001 – 5,000	0.375" – [0.0000416" × (number of seats > 2,000)]
5,001 – 10,000	0.250" – [0.0000174" × (number of seats > 5,000)]
10,001 – 15,000	0.163" – [0.0000086" × (number of seats > 10,000)]
15,001 – 20,000	0.120" – [0.0000050" × (number of seats > 15,000)]
20,001 – 25,000	0.095" – [0.0000040" × (number of seats > 20,000)]
25,000 – up	0.075" a fixed number

Minimum width per seat served:

Seats	Width	Seats	Width	Seats	Width	Seats	Width
500	≥ 0.375"	7,000	≥ 0.215"	14,000	≥ 0.129"	21,000	≥ 0.091"
1,000	≥ 0.375"	8,000	≥ 0.198"	15,000	≥ 0.120"	22,000	≥ 0.087"
2,000	≥ 0.375"	9,000	≥ 0.180"	16,000	≥ 0.115"	23,000	≥ 0.083"
3,000	≥ 0.333"	10,000	≥ 0.163"	17,000	≥ 0.110"	24,000	≥ 0.079"
4,000	≥ 0.292"	11,000	≥ 0.154"	18,000	≥ 0.105"	25,000	≥ 0.075"
5,000	≥ 0.250"	12,000	≥ 0.146"	19,000	≥ 0.100"	26,000	≥ 0.075"
6,000	≥ 0.233"	13,000	≥ 0.137"	20,000	≥ 0.095"	27,000	≥ 0.075"

Source: IBC Table 1008.5.2.

Table 1008.5.2c   Width of Passageways, Doorways, and Ramps ≤ 1:10 Slope

Method of calculating inches per seat served for the table of widths below:

Seats	Calculation
1 – 2,000	0.200" a fixed number
2,001 – 5,000	0.200" – [0.0000166" × (number of seats > 2,000)]
5,001 – 10,000	0.150" – [0.0000100" × (number of seats > 5,000)]
10,001 – 15,000	0.100" – [0.0000060" × (number of seats > 10,000)]
15,001 – 20,000	0.070" – [0.0000028" × (number of seats > 15,000)]
20,001 – 25,000	0.056" – [0.0000024" × (number of seats > 20,000)]
25,000 – up	0.044" a fixed number

Minimum width per seat served:

Seats	Width	Seats	Width	Seats	Width	Seats	Width
500	≥ 0.200"	7,000	≥ 0.130"	14,000	≥ 0.076"	21,000	≥ 0.054"
1,000	≥ 0.200"	8,000	≥ 0.120"	15,000	≥ 0.070"	22,000	≥ 0.051"
2,000	≥ 0.200"	9,000	≥ 0.110"	16,000	≥ 0.067"	23,000	≥ 0.049"
3,000	≥ 0.183"	10,000	≥ 0.100"	17,000	≥ 0.064"	24,000	≥ 0.046"
4,000	≥ 0.167"	11,000	≥ 0.094"	18,000	≥ 0.062"	25,000	≥ 0.044"
5,000	≥ 0.150"	12,000	≥ 0.088"	19,000	≥ 0.059"	26,000	≥ 0.044"
6,000	≥ 0.140"	13,000	≥ 0.082"	20,000	≥ 0.056"	27,000	≥ 0.044"

Source: IBC Table 1008.5.2.

1008 Assembly

1008.5.2 Smoke-protected seating *(part 3 of 3)*

Table 1008.5.2d   Width of Ramps > 1:10 Slope

Method of calculating inches per seat served for the table of widths below:

Seats	Calculation
1 – 2,000	0.220" a fixed number
2,001 – 5,000	0.220" – [0.0000183" × (number of seats > 2,000)]
5,001 – 10,000	0.165" – [0.0000110" × (number of seats > 5,000)]
10,001 – 15,000	0.110" – [0.0000066" × (number of seats > 10,000)]
15,001 – 20,000	0.077" – [0.0000030" × (number of seats > 15,000)]
20,001 – 25,000	0.062" – [0.0000028" × (number of seats > 20,000)]
25,000 – up	0.048" a fixed number

Minimum width per seat served:

Seats	Width	Seats	Width	Seats	Width	Seats	Width
500	≥ 0.220"	7,000	≥ 0.143"	14,000	≥ 0.084"	21,000	≥ 0.059"
1,000	≥ 0.220"	8,000	≥ 0.132"	15,000	≥ 0.077"	22,000	≥ 0.056"
2,000	≥ 0.220"	9,000	≥ 0.121"	16,000	≥ 0.074"	23,000	≥ 0.054"
3,000	≥ 0.202"	10,000	≥ 0.110"	17,000	≥ 0.071"	24,000	≥ 0.051"
4,000	≥ 0.183"	11,000	≥ 0.103"	18,000	≥ 0.068"	25,000	≥ 0.048"
5,000	≥ 0.165"	12,000	≥ 0.097"	19,000	≥ 0.065"	26,000	≥ 0.048"
6,000	≥ 0.154"	13,000	≥ 0.090"	20,000	≥ 0.062"	27,000	≥ 0.048"

Source: IBC Table 1008.5.2.

1008.5.2.1 Smoke control

This subsection addresses the means of egress from smoke-protected seating in an assembly area.

- The means of egress must be protected from smoke by one of the following methods:
  - A smoke control system.

    Note: Section 909, "Smoke Control Systems," is cited as the source of requirements.

  - Natural ventilation as follows:
    Smoke must be held to ≥ 6 feet above the floor.

1008.5.2.2 Roof height

This subsection addresses the roof height in a smoke-protected assembly area.

- In an outdoor stadium, the following applies:
  - A canopy < 15' above the highest aisle or aisle accessway is permitted as follows:
    Where a height < 6'-8" is clear of any object.
- In other locations, the lowest roof deck must be ≥ 15' above the following:
  - The highest aisle.
  - The highest aisle accessway.

1008 Assembly

1008.5.2.3 Automatic sprinklers

This subsection addresses smoke-protected assembly seating enclosed with ceiling and walls.

- This subsection does not apply to outdoor seating facilities as follows:
  - Where seating is essentially open to the exterior.
  - Where means of egress in seating areas are essentially open to the exterior.
- Sprinklers are not required for the following floor areas where the conditions below apply:
  - Floor areas used for the following:
    Competition.
    Performance.
    Entertainment.
  - Conditions:
    Roof construction must be > 50' above the floor level.
    Only low-hazard uses occur.
- Sprinklers are not required for the following where < 1000 sf.:
  - Press boxes.
  - Storage.
- In other cases the seating must be protected with sprinklers as per NFPA 13.

1008.5.3 Width of means of egress for outdoor smoke-protected assembly

- Means of egress in an outdoor-smoke-protected assembly area must comply with one of the following width requirements:
  - Width required for indoor smoke-protected assembly.

    Note: 1008.5.2, "Smoke-protected seating," is cited as a source of width requirements.

  - *Width = (Number of occupants served) × (required width per occupant)* as follows:

Table 1008.5.3	Egress Width in Outdoor Smoke-Protected Assembly		
Means of egress	Width/occupant	Means of egress	Width/occupant
Aisles	≥ 0.08"	Stairs	≥ 0.08"
Ramps	≥ 0.06"	Corridors	≥ 0.06"
Tunnels	≥ 0.06"	Vomitories	≥ 0.06"

1008 Assembly

1008.6 Travel distance

- Travel distance is measured along aisles and aisle accessways as follows:
  - Without crossing over seats.
- Travel distance is limited in assembly occupancies as indicated below:

Table 1008.6   Travel Distance in Assembly Spaces

Location and description of egress route	Travel distance
From each seat to outside the building:	
In open-air seating on Type I or II construction	not limited
In open-air seating of Type III, IV, and V construction	≤ 400'
In smoke-protected seating:	
From each seat to nearest entrance to a vomitory	≤ 200'
From vomitory entrance to outside the building:	
To a stair, ramp, or walk	≤ 200'
From each seat to nearest entrance to the concourse	≤ 200'
From concourse entrance outside the building:	
To a stair, ramp, or walk	≤ 200'
In sprinklered buildings to exit door	≤ 250'
In unsprinklered buildings to an exit door	≤ 200'

1008.7 Assembly aisles are required (*part 1 of 2*)

- An aisle is not required for assembly seating where all of the following conditions are met:
  - Seats have no backrests.
  - Rise is ≤ 6" per row.
  - Row spacing is ≤ 28" as follows:
    Where seat boards are not at the same level as the foot boards in the next higher row.
  - Number of rows ≤ 16.
  - The lowest seat board is ≤ 12" above one of the following:
    The ground.
    The floor.
    A cross aisle.
  - Seat boards surface is as follows:
    Continuous.
    Flat.
  - Seat boards provide a walking surface ≥ 11" wide.
  - Seating egress is not restricted by any of the following:
    Rails.
    Guards.
    Other obstructions.

1008 Assembly

1008.7 Assembly aisles are required (*part 2 of 2*)

- Other occupied parts of occupancy A facilities with the following fixtures have requirements as indicated below:
  - Fixtures:
    Seats and/or tables.
    Displays.
    Similar fixtures or equipment.
  - Requirements:
    Aisles leading to one or both the following are required:
      Exits and exit access doors.
    Aisle accessways for tables and seating must meet dimensional requirements.

  Note: 1004.3.1.3, "Seating at tables," is cited as the source of dimension requirements.

1008.7.1 Minimum aisle widths

- Required aisle width in assembly areas are required as follows:

Table 1008.7.1   Aisle Width in Assembly Spaces

Description	Width
Aisle stairs:	
With seats on both sides totaling > 50	≥ 48"
With seats on both sides totaling ≤ 50	≥ 36"
With seats on one side only	≥ 36"
With ≤ 5 rows of seats on one side only	≥ 23" between rail and seating
Aisle stairs divided by handrail:	
With seats on both sides	≥ 23" between rail and seating
Level or ramped aisles:	
With seats on both sides totaling > 50	≥ 42"
With seats on both sides totaling ≤ 50	≥ 36"
With seats on one side only	≥ 36"

1008.7.2 Aisle width

- An aisle must have sufficient width to serve as egress for its assigned portion of the space.
- The required capacity of aisles is based on balanced use of all means of egress.

1008.7.3 Converging aisles

- A means of egress receiving occupant loads of converging aisles must have the following capacity:
  - ≥ the sum of the required capacities of the converging aisles.

1008.7.4 Uniform width

- The parts of aisles where egress travel is in either direction must have uniform width.

1008 Assembly

1008.7.5 Assembly aisle termination

- A dead-end aisle may be > 20' only as follows:
  - Seats beyond a point 20' into a dead-end must comply with both of the following:
    Seats must be ≤ 24 seats from another aisle counted along the row of seats.
    Required clear width between rows is as follows:

    ### Width ≥ 12" + [(number of seats – 7) × 0.6"]

    This equation yields the following required clear widths between rows:

Table 1008.7.5a   Row Width at Long Dead-End Aisles

Seats	Width	Seats	Width	Seats	Width	Seats	Width	Seats	Width
1–7	≥ 12.0"	11	≥ 14.4"	15	≥ 16.8"	19	≥ 19.2"	23	≥ 21.6"
8	≥ 12.6"	12	≥ 15.0"	16	≥ 17.4"	20	≥ 19.8"	24	≥ 22.2"
9	≥ 13.2"	13	≥ 15.6"	17	≥ 18.0"	21	≥ 20.4"		
10	≥ 13.8"	14	≥ 16.2"	18	≥ 18.6"	22	≥ 21.0"		

- In smoke-protected seating, a dead-end vertical aisle (⊥ to rows) is governed as follows:
  - It may be > than 21 rows in length only:
    Where seats beyond the 21 rows comply with both of the following:
    Seats must be ≤ 40 seats from another aisle counted along the row of seats.
    Required clear width between rows served by this part of the dead end is:

    ### Width ≥ 12" + [(number of seats – 7) × 0.3"]

    This equation yields the following required clear widths between rows:

Table 1008.7.5b   Clear Width between Rows of Assembly Seating

Seats	Width	Seats	Width	Seats	Width	Seats	Width	Seats	Width
1–7	≥ 12.0"	14	≥ 14.1"	21	≥ 16.2"	28	≥ 18.3"	35	≥ 20.4"
8	≥ 12.3"	15	≥ 14.4"	22	≥ 16.5"	29	≥ 18.6"	36	≥ 20.7"
9	≥ 12.6"	16	≥ 14.7"	23	≥ 16.8"	30	≥ 18.9"	37	≥ 21.0"
10	≥ 12.9"	17	≥ 15.0"	24	≥ 17.1"	31	≥ 19.2"	38	≥ 21.3"
11	≥ 13.2"	18	≥ 15.3"	25	≥ 17.4"	32	≥ 19.5"	39	≥ 21.6"
12	≥ 13.5"	19	≥ 15.6"	26	≥ 17.7"	33	≥ 19.8"	40	≥ 21.9"
13	≥ 13.8"	20	≥ 15.9"	27	≥ 18.0"	34	≥ 20.1"		

- All other dead-end vertical aisles in smoke-protected seating must be ≤ 21 rows in length.
- All other dead-end aisles must be ≤ 20' in length.
- All other aisles must terminate at both ends as follows:
  - Termination must be at one of the following having access to an exit:
    Cross aisle.
    Vomitory or concourse.
    Doorway.
    Foyer.

1008 Assembly

1008.7.6 Assembly aisle obstructions

- Handrails are the only obstructions permitted within the required aisle width.

  Note: 1008.11, "Handrails," is cited as the source of applicable requirements.

1008.8 Clear width of aisle accessways serving seating

- Clear aisle-accessway width is measured between the following points:
  - From the back of a row of seats to the closest element of the row of seats behind it.
- Width is measured with the seats up where chairs have self-rising seats.
- Width is measured with the seat down for any chair without a self-rising seat.
- Width is measured with the tablet arm down as follows for seats with folding tablet arms.
- For ≤ 14 seats in a row, the the clear aisle-accessway width required is ≥ 12".

Case study: Fig. 1008.8. The central area of the auditorium has 14 seats or fewer seats per row. Since they are self-rising the aisle accessway width is measured with the seat up at 1'-6 ³/₄". This meets the code minimum of 12" for this number of seats.

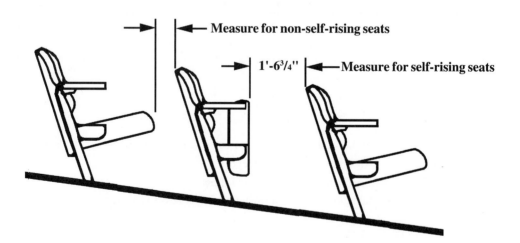

← Measure for non-self-rising seats

1'-6³/₄" ← Measure for self-rising seats

Fig. 1008.8. Elevation of auditorium seating. High School 6, Cypress-Fairbanks Independent School District. Harris County, Texas. PBK Architects, Inc. Houston, Texas.

1008 Assembly

1008.8.1 Dual access *(part 1 of 3)*

- Rows of seating served by aisles or doorways at each side are limited as follows:
  - Limited to ≤ 100 seats per row.
- A clear width of ≥ 12" is required for rows with 1–14 seats.
- Clear width between rows > 22" is not required for rows of any length.
- For rows with > 14 seats, required width is as follows:

Width ≥ 12" + [(number of seats – 14)] × 0.3":

This equation yields the following required clear widths up to 22":

Table 1008.8.1a   **Required Width between Rows for Seating Not Smoke-Protected, Access from 2 Sides**

Seats	Width	Seats	Width	Seats	Width	Seats	Width	Seats	Width
1–14	≥ 12.0"	21	≥ 14.1"	28	≥ 16.2"	35	≥ 18.3"	42	≥ 20.4"
15	≥ 12.3"	22	≥ 14.4"	29	≥ 16.5"	36	≥ 18.6"	43	≥ 20.7"
16	≥ 12.6"	23	≥ 14.4"	30	≥ 16.8"	37	≥ 18.9"	44	≥ 21.0"
17	≥ 12.9"	24	≥ 15.0"	31	≥ 17.1"	38	≥ 19.2"	45	≥ 21.3"
18	≥ 13.2"	25	≥ 15.3"	32	≥ 17.4"	39	≥ 19.5"	46	≥ 21.6"
19	≥ 13.5"	26	≥ 15.6"	33	≥ 17.7"	40	≥ 19.8"	47	≥ 21.9"
20	≥ 13.8"	27	≥ 15.9"	34	≥ 18.0"	41	≥ 20.1"	48	≥ 22.0"

Source: IBC Table 1008.8.1.

- A clear width of ≥ 12" is required for rows with lengths varying from 14–17 seats and to which 0.3" per seat is added for longer rows as follows:

Table 1008.8.1b   **Required Width between Rows for Smoke-Protected Seats, Access from 2 Sides**

Seats	Width	Seats	Width	Seats	Width	Seats	Width	Seats	Width
< 4000 smoke-protected seats:									
1–14	≥ 12.0"	21	≥ 14.1"	28	≥ 16.2"	35	≥ 18.3"	42	≥ 20.4"
15	≥ 12.3"	22	≥ 14.4"	29	≥ 16.5"	36	≥ 18.6"	43	≥ 20.7"
16	≥ 12.6"	23	≥ 14.4"	30	≥ 16.8"	37	≥ 18.9"	44	≥ 21.0"
17	≥ 12.9"	24	≥ 15.0"	31	≥ 17.1"	38	≥ 19.2"	45	≥ 21.3"
18	≥ 13.2"	25	≥ 15.3"	32	≥ 17.4"	39	≥ 19.5"	46	≥ 21.6"
19	≥ 13.5"	26	≥ 15.6"	33	≥ 17.7"	40	≥ 19.8"	47	≥ 21.9"
20	≥ 13.8"	27	≥ 15.9"	34	≥ 18.0"	41	≥ 20.1"	48	≥ 22.0"
4000–6999 smoke-protected seats:									
1–15	≥ 12.0"	22	≥ 14.1"	29	≥ 16.2"	36	≥ 18.3"	43	≥ 20.4"
16	≥ 12.3"	23	≥ 14.4"	30	≥ 16.5"	37	≥ 18.6"	44	≥ 20.7"
17	≥ 12.6"	24	≥ 14.4"	31	≥ 16.8"	38	≥ 18.9"	45	≥ 21.0"
18	≥ 12.9"	25	≥ 15.0"	32	≥ 17.1"	39	≥ 19.2"	46	≥ 21.3"
19	≥ 13.2"	26	≥ 15.3"	33	≥ 17.4"	40	≥ 19.5"	47	≥ 21.6"
20	≥ 13.5"	27	≥ 15.6"	34	≥ 17.7"	41	≥ 19.8"	48	≥ 21.9"
21	≥ 13.8"	28	≥ 15.9"	35	≥ 18.0"	42	≥ 20.1"	49	≥ 22.0"

Source: IBC Table 1008.8.1.

1008 Assembly

1008.8.1 Dual access *(part 2 of 3)*

Table 1008.8.1b *–Continued*

Seats	Width	Seats	Width	Seats	Width	Seats	Width	Seats	Width
7000 –9999 smoke-protected seats:									
1–16	≥ 12.0"	23	≥ 14.1"	30	≥ 16.2"	37	≥ 18.3"	44	≥ 20.4"
17	≥ 12.3"	24	≥ 14.4"	31	≥ 16.5"	38	≥ 18.6"	45	≥ 20.7"
18	≥ 12.6"	25	≥ 14.4"	32	≥ 16.8"	39	≥ 18.9"	46	≥ 21.0"
19	≥ 12.9"	26	≥ 15.0"	33	≥ 17.1"	40	≥ 19.2"	47	≥ 21.3"
20	≥ 13.2"	27	≥ 15.3""""	34	≥ 17.4"	41	≥ 19.5"	48	≥ 21.6"
21	≥ 13.5"	28	≥ 15.6"	35	≥ 17.7"	42	≥ 19.8"	49	≥ 21.9"
22	≥ 13.8"	29	≥ 15.9"	36	≥ 18.0"	43	≥ 20.1"	50	≥ 22.0"
10,000 –12,999 smoke-protected seats:									
1–17	≥ 12.0"	24	≥ 14.1"	31	≥ 16.2"	38	≥ 18.3"	45	≥ 20.4"
18	≥ 12.3"	25	≥ 14.4"	32	≥ 16.5"	39	≥ 18.6"	46	≥ 20.7"
19	≥ 12.6"	26	≥ 14.4"	33	≥ 16.8"	40	≥ 18.9"	47	≥ 21.0"
20	≥ 12.9"	27	≥ 15.0"	34	≥ 17.1"	41	≥ 19.2"	48	≥ 21.3"
21	≥ 13.2"	28	≥ 15.3"	35	≥ 17.4"	42	≥ 19.5"	49	≥ 21.6"
22	≥ 13.5"	29	≥ 15.6"	36	≥ 17.7"	43	≥ 19.8"	50	≥ 21.9"
23	≥ 13.8"	30	≥ 15.9"	37	≥ 18.0"	44	≥ 20.1"	51	≥ 22.0"

Source: IBC Table 1008.8.1.

- A clear width of ≥ 12" is required for rows with lengths varying from 18–21 seats and to which 0.3" per seat is added for longer rows as follows:

Table 1008.8.1c   Required Width between Rows for Smoke-Protected Seats, Access from 2 Sides

Seats	Width	Seats	Width	Seats	Width	Seats	Width	Seats	Width
13,000 –15,999 smoke-protected seats:									
1–18	≥ 12.0"	25	≥ 14.1"	32	≥ 16.2"	39	≥ 18.3"	46	≥ 20.4"
19	≥ 12.3"	26	≥ 14.4"	33	≥ 16.5"	40	≥ 18.6"	47	≥ 20.7"
20	≥ 12.6"	27	≥ 14.4"	34	≥ 16.8"	41	≥ 18.9"	48	≥ 21.0"
21	≥ 12.9"	28	≥ 15.0"	35	≥ 17.1"	42	≥ 19.2"	49	≥ 21.3"
22	≥ 13.2"	29	≥ 15.3"	36	≥ 17.4"	43	≥ 19.5"	50	≥ 21.6"
23	≥ 13.5"	30	≥ 15.6"	37	≥ 17.7"	44	≥ 19.8"	51	≥ 21.9"
24	≥ 13.8"	31	≥ 15.9"	38	≥ 18.0"	45	≥ 20.1"	52	≥ 22.0"
16,000 –18,999 smoke-protected seats:									
1–19	≥ 12.0"	26	≥ 14.1"	33	≥ 16.2"	40	≥ 18.3"	47	≥ 20.4"
20	≥ 12.3"	27	≥ 14.4"	34	≥ 16.5"	41	≥ 18.6"	48	≥ 20.7"
21	≥ 12.6"	28	≥ 14.4"	35	≥ 16.8"	42	≥ 18.9"	49	≥ 21.0"
22	≥ 12.9"	29	≥ 15.0"	36	≥ 17.1"	43	≥ 19.2"	50	≥ 21.3"
23	≥ 13.2"	30	≥ 15.3"	37	≥ 17.4"	44	≥ 19.5"	51	≥ 21.6"
24	≥ 13.5"	31	≥ 15.6"	38	≥ 17.7"	45	≥ 19.8"	52	≥ 21.9"
25	≥ 13.8"	32	≥ 15.9"	39	≥ 18.0"	46	≥ 20.1"	53	≥ 22.0"

Source: IBC Table 1008.8.1.

1008 Assembly

1008.8.1 Dual access *(part 3 of 3)*

Table 1008.8.1c *– Continued*

Seats	Width	Seats	Width	Seats	Width	Seats	Width	Seats	Width
19,000–21,999 smoke-protected seats:									
1–20	≥ 12.0"	27	≥ 14.1"	34	≥ 16.2"	41	≥ 18.3"	48	≥ 20.4"
21	≥ 12.3"	28	≥ 14.4"	35	≥ 16.5"	42	≥ 18.6"	49	≥ 20.7"
22	≥ 12.6"	29	≥ 14.4"	36	≥ 16.8"	43	≥ 18.9"	50	≥ 21.0"
23	≥ 12.9"	30	≥ 15.0"	37	≥ 17.1"	44	≥ 19.2"	51	≥ 21.3"
24	≥ 13.2"	31	≥ 15.3"	38	≥ 17.4"	45	≥ 19.5"	52	≥ 21.6"
25	≥ 13.5"	32	≥ 15.6"	39	≥ 17.7"	46	≥ 19.8"	53	≥ 21.9"
26	≥ 13.8"	33	≥ 15.9"	40	≥ 18.0"	47	≥ 20.1"	54	≥ 22.0"
≥ 22,000 smoke-protected seats:									
1–21	≥ 12.0"	28	≥ 14.1"	35	≥ 16.2"	42	≥ 18.3"	49	≥ 20.4"
22	≥ 12.3"	29	≥ 14.4"	36	≥ 16.5"	43	≥ 18.6"	50	≥ 20.7"
23	≥ 12.6"	30	≥ 14.4"	37	≥ 16.8"	44	≥ 18.9"	51	≥ 21.0"
24	≥ 12.9"	31	≥ 15.0"	38	≥ 17.1"	45	≥ 19.2"	52	≥ 21.3"
25	≥ 13.2"	32	≥ 15.3"	39	≥ 17.4"	46	≥ 19.5"	53	≥ 21.6"
26	≥ 13.5"	33	≥ 15.6"	40	≥ 17.7"	47	≥ 19.8"	54	≥ 21.9"
27	≥ 13.8"	34	≥ 15.9"	41	≥ 18.0"	48	≥ 20.1"	55	≥ 22.0"

Source: IBC Table 1008.8.1.

1008.8.2 Single access *(part 1 of 3)*

- Where rows of seats in an assembly area are served by an aisle or doorway only at one end, the following apply:
  - Egress travel distance is limited to ≤ 30' from any seat to a point where there is a choice of 2 paths to separate exits.
  - Where 1 of these 2 paths crosses an aisle and passes between rows of seats to another aisle, the following applies to the rows between the 2 aisles:
    The number of seats is limited to ≤ 24.
    Clear width required between the rows is as follows:
    For rows ≤ 7 seats, required width is ≥ 12".
    For rows > 7 seats, required width is determined by the following equation:

$$\text{Width} \geq 12" + [(\text{number of seats} - 7) \times 0.6"]:$$

This equation yields the clear widths in the table below:

Table 1008.8.2a   **Required Clear Width between Rows Used for Egress between Aisles**

Seats	Width	Seats	Width	Seats	Width	Seats	Width	Seats	Width
1–7	≥ 12.0"	11	≥ 14.4"	15	≥ 16.8"	19	≥ 19.2"	23	≥ 21.6"
8	≥ 12.6"	12	≥ 15.0"	16	≥ 17.4"	20	≥ 19.8"	24	≥ 22.2"
9	≥ 13.2"	13	≥ 15.6"	17	≥ 18.0"	21	≥ 20.4"		
10	≥ 13.8"	14	≥ 16.2"	18	≥ 18.6"	22	≥ 21.0"		

Source: IBC Table 1008.8.1.

1008 Assembly

1008.8.2 Single access *(part 2 of 3)*

- Clear width required between rows with an aisle or doorway at one side only, where not smoke protected, is as follows:
  - For rows ≤ 7 seats, required width is ≥ 12".
  - Clear width between rows of any length is not required to be > 22".
  - For rows > 7 seats, required width is determined by the following equation:

    Width ≥ 12" + [(number of seats − 7) × 0.6"]:

    This equation yields the clear widths in the table below:

Table 1008.8.2b   **Required Clear Width between Rows for Seating Not Smoke-Protected, Access 1 Side**

Seats	Width	Seats	Width	Seats	Width	Seats	Width	Seats	Width
1–7	≥ 12.0"	11	≥ 14.4"	15	≥ 16.8"	19	≥ 19.2"	23	≥ 21.6"
8	≥ 12.6"	12	≥ 15.0"	16	≥ 17.4"	20	≥ 19.8"	24	≥ 22.0"
9	≥ 13.2"	13	≥ 15.6"	17	≥ 18.0"	21	≥ 20.4"	25	≥ 22.0"
10	≥ 13.8"	14	≥ 16.2"	18	≥ 18.6"	22	≥ 21.0	26	≥ 22.0"

Source: IBC Table 1008.8.1.

- A clear width of ≥ 12" is required for rows with lengths varying from 7–11 smoke-protected seats and to which 0.6" per seat is added for longer rows as in the table below:

Table 1008.8.2c   **Required Clear Width between Rows for Smoke-Protected Seats, Access 1 Side**

Seats	Width	Seats	Width	Seats	Width	Seats	Width	Seats	Width
< 7000 smoke-protected seats:									
1–7	≥ 12.0"	11	≥ 14.4"	15	≥ 16.8"	19	≥ 19.2"	23	≥ 21.6"
8	≥ 12.6"	12	≥ 15.0"	16	≥ 17.4"	20	≥ 19.8"	24	≥ 22.0"
9	≥ 13.2"	13	≥ 15.6"	17	≥ 18.0"	21	≥ 20.4"	25	≥ 22.0"
10	≥ 13.8"	14	≥ 16.2"	18	≥ 18.6"	22	≥ 21.0"	26	≥ 22.0"
7000 – 12,999 smoke-protected seats:									
1–8	≥ 12.0"	12	≥ 14.4"	16	≥ 16.8"	20	≥ 19.2"	24	≥ 21.6"
9	≥ 12.6"	13	≥ 15.0"	17	≥ 17.4"	21	≥ 19.8"	25	≥ 22.0"
10	≥ 13.2"	14	≥ 15.6"	18	≥ 18.0"	22	≥ 20.4"	26	≥ 22.0"
11	≥ 13.8"	15	≥ 16.2"	19	≥ 18.6"	23	≥ 21.0"	27	≥ 22.0"
13,000 – 18,999 smoke-protected seats:									
1–9	≥ 12.0"	13	≥ 14.4"	17	≥ 16.8"	21	≥ 19.2"	25	≥ 21.6"
10	≥ 12.6"	14	≥ 15.0"	18	≥ 17.4"	22	≥ 19.8"	26	≥ 22.0"
11	≥ 13.2"	15	≥ 15.6"	19	≥ 18.0"	23	≥ 20.4"	27	≥ 22.0"
12	≥ 13.8"	16	≥ 16.2"	20	≥ 18.6"	24	≥ 21.0"	28	≥ 22.0"

Source: IBC Table 1008.8.1.

1008 Assembly

1008.8.2 Single access *(part 3 of 3)*

Table 1008.8.2c – *Continued*

Seats	Width	Seats	Width	Seats	Width	Seats	Width	Seats	Width
19,000 – 21,999 smoke-protected seats:									
1–10	≥ 12.0"	14	≥ 14.4"	18	≥ 16.8"	22	≥ 19.2"	26	≥ 21.6"
11	≥ 12.6"	15	≥ 15.0"	19	≥ 17.4"	23	≥ 19.8"	27	≥ 22.0"
12	≥ 13.2"	16	≥ 15.6"	20	≥ 18.0"	24	≥ 20.4"	28	≥ 22.0"
13	≥ 13.8"	17	≥ 16.2"	21	≥ 18.6"	25	≥ 21.0"	29	≥ 22.0"
≥ 22,000 smoke-protected seats:									
1–11	≥ 12.0"	15	≥ 14.4"	19	≥ 16.8"	23	≥ 19.2"	27	≥ 21.6"
12	≥ 12.6"	16	≥ 15.0"	20	≥ 17.4"	24	≥ 19.8"	28	≥ 22.0"
13	≥ 13.2"	17	≥ 15.6"	21	≥ 18.0"	25	≥ 20.4"	29	≥ 22.0"
14	≥ 13.8"	18	≥ 16.2"	22	≥ 18.6"	26	≥ 21.0"	30	≥ 22.0"

Source: IBC Table 1008.8.1.

1008.9 Assembly aisle walking surfaces

- Aisles with a gradient must have the following configurations:

Aisle Slope	Aisle configuration required
≤ 1:8	Ramp with slip-resistant surface
> 1:8	Treads and risers = to width of aisle

1008.9.1 Treads

- Treads in aisle steps must comply with the following:
  - Depth required is ≥ 11".
  - Variation in adjacent tread depth is limited to ≤ $^3/_{16}$".

1008.9.2 Risers

- Risers of aisle stairs with the same gradient as adjacent seating are governed as follows:
  - Required riser height is ≥ 4".
  - Required riser height is ≤ 8" where sightlines permit.
  - Required riser height is ≤ 9" where required by sightlines.
- Variations in riser height are limited to those necessary for changes in the slope of seating.
- Riser height is to be uniform in each flight.
- Adjacent riser heights which vary more than $^3/_{16}$" must be identified as follows:
  - A distinctive stripe must be on the nosing of a tread next to a nonuniform riser as follows:
    Width of stripe to be ≥ 1" and ≤ 2".
    Appearance of stripe to be distinctly different from strips marking other tread edges.

1008 Assembly

1008.9.3 Tread contrasting marking stripe

- Tread edges which are not readily apparent during descent must be marked as follows:
  - A stripe contrasting with the appearance of the tread is required on each nosing as follows:
    Width of marking stripe is to be ≥ 1" and ≤ 2".
    Marking must make treads readily apparent during descent.

1008.10 Seat stability

- Seats are not required to be fastened to the floor in the following applications:
  - ≤ 200 seats without ramped or tiered floors for the seating.
  - > 200 seats where both of the following apply:
    Where floors for seating are neither ramped nor tiered.
    Where seats are joined together in groups ≥ 3 seats.
  - Seating at tables without ramped or tiered floors for the seating.
  - ≤ 200 seats where all of the following apply:
    Where flexibility of seating layout is integral with the function of the space.
    Where seating is on tiered levels.
    Where plans for seating, tiers, and aisles are submitted for approval.
  - Groups ≤ 14 seats with both of the following conditions:
    Where the seats are separated from other seating by any of the following:
      Railings or guards.
      Low walls or similar barriers.
    Where floors are level.
  - Seats for musicians or other performers with the following conditions:
    Where the seats are separated from other seating by any of the following:
      Railings or guards.
      Low walls or similar barriers.
- In all other places of assembly, seats must be fastened to the floor.

1008.11 Handrails

- This subsection addresses the following in places of assembly:
  - Ramped aisles.
  - Stepped aisles.
- Handrails are not required as follows:
  - Where a guard meets handrail, the graspability requirement is as follows:
    The guard is located at the side of the aisle.
- Handrails are not required for ramped aisles where both of the following apply:
  - Where the slope is ≤ 1:8.
  - Where seating is on both sides.
- In other cases, handrails are required as follows:
  - For aisle stairs.
  - For ramped aisles sloping ≥ 1:15.

1008 Assembly

1008.11.1 Discontinuous handrails

This subsection addresses aisles where handrails are required.

- The following applies where seating is on both sides of an aisle:
  - Handrails must be discontinuous as follows:
      Gaps in handrails must be spaced as follows:
        At intervals ≤ 5 rows of seating.
      Clear width in handrail gaps is to be as follows:
        ≥ 22" and ≤ 36".
        Measured horizontally.
      The following handrail details are to be rounded:
        Terminations.
        Bends.

1008.11.2 Intermediate handrails

- Where handrails occur in the center of aisle stairs, the following applies:
  - A second handrail is required at 12" (±) below the main handrail.

Case study: Fig. 1008.11.2. The handrail complies with requirements of 1008.11, 1008.11.1, and 1008.11.2. It is provided in the center of stepped aisles where seats are on both sides; it has a 2nd handrail below the top; and it is discontinuous with rounded corners. The intermediate handrail is 12" lower than the main handrail as required.

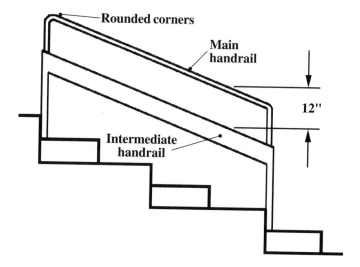

Fig. 1008.11.2. Elevation of handrail. Newman University Sports and Fine Arts Center. Wichita, Kansas. Gossen Livingston Associates, Inc., Architecture. Wichita, Kansas.

1008 Assembly

1008.12.1 Cross aisles

- Cross aisles > 30" above an adjacent level require guards as follows:
  - Guards must be ≥ 42" high.
  - Guards must meet opening and other requirements.
- Cross aisles ≤ 30" above an adjacent lower level are governed as follows:
  - Guards are not required in the following case:
    Where the backs of seats on the lower level extend ≥ 24" above the aisle.
  - In other cases, guards ≥ 26" high are required.

  Note: 1003.2.12, "Guards," is cited as the source of requirements for guards required by this subsection.

1008.12.2 Sightline-constrained guard heights

This subsection applies to the edge of a walking surface other than at the ends of aisles.

- Barriers meeting guard requirements are required as follows:
  - Where a floor or foot board is > 30" above the adjacent level.
- Such barriers must be ≥ 26" high in the following location:
  - Where a higher barrier would obstruct sightlines of adjacent seating.

  Note: The following are cited as governing requirements related to this subsection:
  1008.12.3, "Guards at the end of aisles," is cited as governing the barriers at the end of aisles that are not addressed in this subsection.
  1003.2.12, "Guards," is cited as the source of requirements for guards required by this subsection.

1008.12.3 Guards at the end of aisles

- Where the end of an aisle is > 30" above the adjacent level, a barrier is required as follows:
  - Barrier must meet guard requirements.
  - Barrier must extend the full width of the aisle.
  - Barrier must be ≥ 36" high.
  - The diagonal distance between the following points must be ≥ 42":
    The top of the barrier and the nosing of the nearest tread.

  Note: 1003.2.12, "Guards," is cited as the source of requirements for barriers required by this subsection.

Case study: Fig. 1008.12.1. The floor of the balcony cross aisle is 8'-11" above the floor of the adjacent lower level seating, which is greater than the 30" maximum. The edge of the cross aisle, therefore, requires a guard ≥ 3'-6" high as provided.

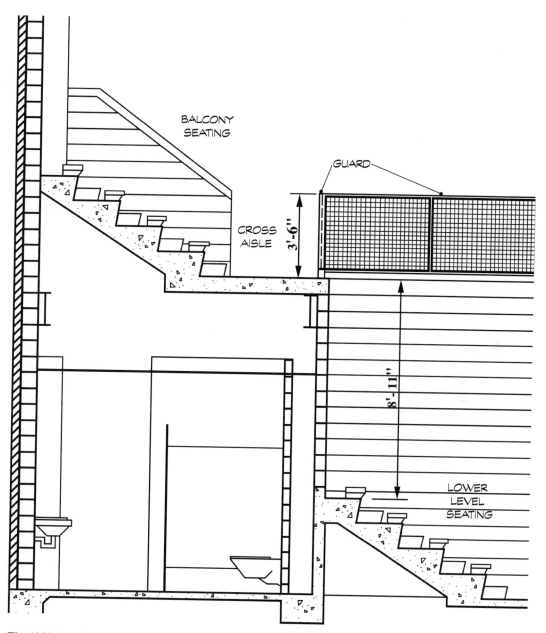

Fig. 1008.12.1. Section of seating at swimming pool. High School 6, Cypress-Fairbanks Independent School District. Harris County, Texas. PBK Architects, Inc. Houston, Texas.

1008 Assembly

1008.13 Bleacher footboards

- Individual bleacher footboards are required for either of the following:
  - For seats above the 3rd row.
  - For seats where the seatboard is > 24" above the floor or grade.
- Individual bleacher footboards are not required where both of the following conditions are present:
  - Seatboards are ≥ 24" wide.
  - Seatboards serve as footboards.
- Gaps between seatboards and adjacent footboards are limited to ≤ $^1/_4$" as follows:
  - Measured horizontally as projected to a horizontal plane.
- Where footboards are > 30" above the floor or grade, the following applies:
  - A sphere > 4" diameter must not be able to pass between seatboard and footboard.

1008.14 Bench seating

- The capacity of bench seating is determined as follows:
  - *Number of seats = bench length ÷ 18".*

1009 Emergency Escape and Rescue

1009.1 General

This subsection addresses openings required for emergency escape and rescue.

- Such openings are not required in the following cases:
  - In buildings other than R-3, where either of the following conditions apply:
    Where the building is sprinklered as per NFPA 13 and 13R.
    Where sleeping rooms with a door to a corridor having a fire-resistance rating as follows:
      Corridor provides access in opposite directions to 2 remote exits.
- Such openings may open to a balcony in an atrium where all of the following apply:
  - Where the balcony serves one of the following:
    Dwelling unit.
    Sleeping room.
  - Where the balcony provides access to an exit.
  - Where a means of egress not open to the atrium is provided.

    Note: Section 404, "Atriums," is cited as the source of requirements defining applicable atriums.

- Otherwise, at least one escape and rescue opening is required as follows:
  - In the following locations within R and I-1 occupancies:
    Basements with ceiling height $\geq$ 6'-8".
    Sleeping rooms below the 4th story.
  - Openings must open directly into one of the following:
    Public street.
    Public alley.
    Yard.
    Court.

1009.2 Minimum size

- Sizes required for emergency escape and rescue openings are as follows:

Location	Clear area required
At grade floor	$\geq$ 5.0 sf
Other locations	$\geq$ 5.7 sf

1009.2.1 Minimum dimensions

- Dimensions required for emergency escape and rescue openings are as follows:

Clear height required	Clear width required
$\geq$ 2'	$\geq$ 1'-8"

- Normal operation of the opening must yield the required clear dimensions.

1009 Emergency Escape and Rescue

1009.3 Maximum height from floor

- Height of emergency escape and rescue openings is limited as follows:
  - The bottom of the clear opening must be ≤ 3'-8" from the floor..

1009.4 Operational constraints

- Emergency escape and rescue openings must be operable as follows:
  - From inside the room.
  - Without the use of keys or tools.
- The following devices may cover such openings where the conditions indicated apply:
  - Devices:
    Bars.
    Grilles.
    Grates.
    Similar devices.
  - Required conditions:
    The size requirements for the opening may not be reduced.
    The device must be openable from inside the room as follows:
      Without keys or tools.
      Without a force greater than that required for the opening itself.
    Smoke detectors must be provided in the following case:
      Where devices are installed in existing buildings for all alterations.

  Note: The following are cited as the sources of additional requirements:
  1009.2, "Minimum size," governs the size of the opening that must remain
  available after any covering device is installed.
  907.2.10, "Single- and multiple-station smoke alarms," governs the smoke
  detector required where covering devices are installed in existing buildings.

1009.5 Window wells

This section addresses emergency escape and rescue openings below grade.

- Where the finished sill is below adjacent grade, a window well is required.

  Note: 1009.5.1, "Minimum size," is cited as a source of requirements for window wells.
  1009.5.2 ,"Ladders or steps," is cited as a source of requirements for window wells.

1009.5.1 Minimum size

- Window wells serving emergency escape and rescue openings must have the following size:
  - Window well must allow escape and rescue opening to fully open.
  - All horizontal dimensions of the window well to be ≥ 3'.
  - Window well must provide a clear opening ≥ 9 sf.

1009 Emergency Escape and Rescue

1009.5.2 Ladders or steps

This subsection addresses ladders or steps in window wells serving emergency escape and rescue openings.

- Ladders or steps required by this subsection are not governed by stair requirements.

    Note: 1003.3.3, "Stairways," is cited as the requirements that are waived for ladders and steps required by this section.

- Approved ladders or steps must be provided in window wells ≥ 3'-8" in depth as follows:
    - Must be permanently affixed.
    - Must have an inside width ≥ 12".
    - Must project ≥ 3" from the wall.
    - Rungs or steps must be spaced ≤ 1'-6" center to center vertically.
    - Must extend full height of well.
    - Must not protrude > 6" into required dimensions of well.
    - Must not be obstructed by the escape and rescue opening.

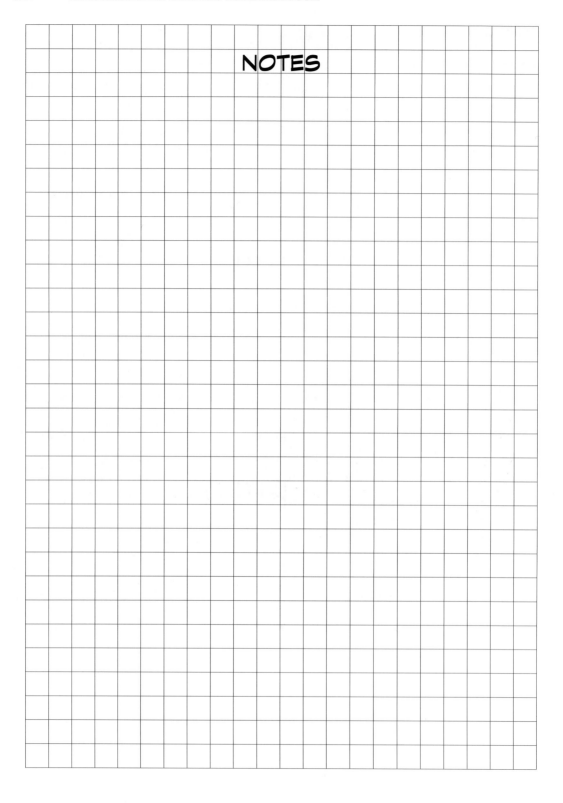

NOTES

11

Accessibility

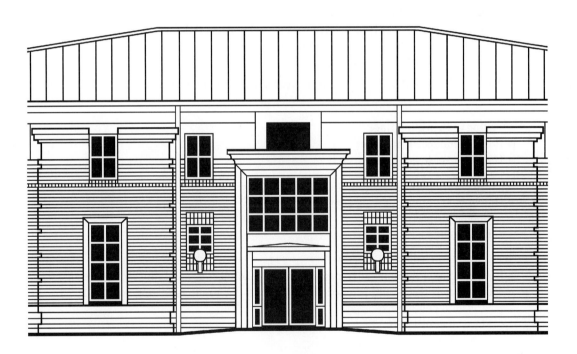

Hot Springs Police Department New Headquarters.
Hot Springs National Park, Arkansas. *(partial elevation)*
Cromwell Architects Engineers. Little Rock, Arkansas.

1102 Definitions

1102.1 General

- **Detectable warning**
  - A standardized feature warning of hazards:
    - On a walking surface.
    - On other elements.
  - Detectable by visually impaired persons.

- **Dwelling unit, Type A**
  - Has full compliance for accessibility requirements.

  Note: ICC/ANSI A 117.1, "Accessible and Usable Buildings and Facilities," is cited as the source of accessibility requirements.

- **Dwelling unit, Type B**
  - Consistent with the following:
    - Fair Housing Amendments Act.
    - Fair Housing Accessibility Guidelines (FHAG):
      - U.S. Department of Housing and Urban Development (HUD).
  - Potentially adaptable to full accessibility requirements.
  - Less accessible than dwelling unit, Type A.

  Note: ICC/ANSI A 117.1, "Accessible and Usable Buildings and Facilities," is cited as the source of accessibility requirements.

- **Dwelling unit, ground floor**
  - Primary entrance is at grade.
  - Habitable space is at grade.

- **Dwelling unit, multistory**
  - One or both of the following are on > 1 story:
    - Habitable space.
    - Bathroom.

- **Technically infeasible**
  - Regarding modifications to an existing building to meet accessibility requirements.
  - Modifications that would be excessively difficult due to the following constraints:
    - Structural constraints.
    - Physical constraints.
    - Site constraints.

- **Wheelchair space cluster**
  - $\geq$ 2 wheelchair spaces in assembly spaces:
    - With companion seating.

1103 Scoping Requirements

1103.1 Where required

- Certain facilities designated by this section are not required to be accessible.
- Other constructions in the categories indicated below are required to be accessible to persons with physical disabilities as follows:
  - Constructions:
      Temporary.
      Permanent.
  - Categories:
      Buildings.
      Structures.
      Associated sites.
      Associated facilities.

1103.2.2 Existing buildings

- Accessibility of existing buildings is governed elsewhere in the code.

  Note: Chapter 34, "Existing Structures," is cited as governing accessibility of such buildings.

1103.2.3 Work areas

- Individual work stations are governed as follows:
  - They are not required to be accessible.
  - They are required to be on an accessible route.

1103.2.4 Detached dwellings

- The following are not required to be accessible:
  - Detached 1-family dwellings:
      Including associated sites.
      Including associated facilities.
  - Detached 2-family dwellings:
      Including associated sites.
      Including associated facilities.

1103.2.5 Utility buildings

- The following are required to be accessible in agricultural buildings:
  - Paved work areas.
  - Areas open to the general public.
  - The following accessible parking is required in the following:
      Private garages.
      Private carports.
- Other occupancy U facilities are not required to be accessible.

1103 Scoping Requirements

1103.2.6 Construction sites

- The following elements of construction sites are not required to be accessible:
  - Structures.
  - Sites.
  - Equipment.
  - Materials storage.
  - Scaffolding.
  - Bridging.
  - Materials hoists.
  - Construction trailers.

1103.2.7 Raised areas

- Raised areas similar to the types listed below and used primarily for the following are not required to be accessible or on an accessible route:
  - Uses:
    Security.
    Life safety.
    Fire safety.
  - Types:
    Observation galleries.
    Lifeguard stands.
    Prison guard towers.
    Fire towers.

1103.2.8 Limited access spaces

- Nonoccupiable spaces with access only by the following:
  - Catwalks.
  - Ladders.
  - Freight elevators.
  - Crawl spaces.
  - Tunnels.
  - Very narrow passageways.

1103 Scoping Requirements

1103.2.9 Equipment spaces

- Spaces such as the types indicated below that are accessed only for the following functions are not required to be accessible:
  - Functions:
    Maintenance.
    Repair.
    Monitoring.
  - Types:
    Communication equipment rooms.
    Electric substations.
    Elevator penthouses.
    Elevator pits.
    Equipment catwalks.
    Highway utility facilities.
    Mechanical equipment rooms.
    Piping catwalks.
    Sewage treatment stations.
    Sewage treatment pump rooms.
    Transformer vaults.
    Tunnel utility facilities.
    Water treatment stations.
    Water treatment pump rooms.

1103.2.10 Single occupant structures

- Facilities occupied by a single person such as the example indicated below and accessed only as follows are not required to be accessible:
  - Access:
    By passageways elevated above grade.
    By passageways below grade.
  - Example:
    Tollbooths.

1103.2.11 Residential Group R-1

- Buildings in occupancy R-1 meeting both of the following conditions:
  - ≤ 5 rooms for rent.
  - Serves as the residence of the proprietor.

1103.2.12 Fuel-dispensing systems

- Devices that dispense fuel are not required to be accessible.

1104 Accessible Route

1104.1 Site arrival points

- Accessible routes are required to an accessible building entrance from the following:
    - Accessible passenger loading areas.
    - Accessible parking.
    - Public streets.
    - Public transportation stops.
    - Public sidewalks.

Case study: Fig. 1104.1. An accessible route is provided as required by the code from accessible parking to the accessible entrance of the building. Included is a ramp sloped within the limits for accessibility.

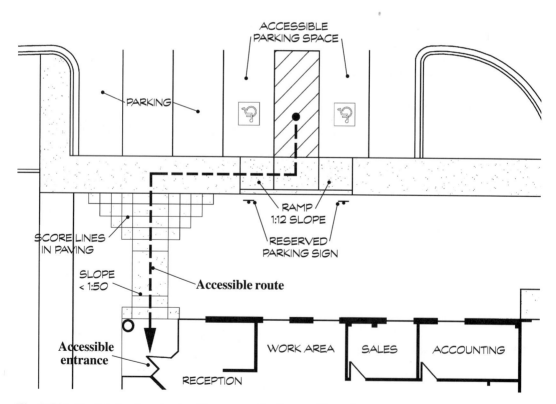

Fig. 1104.1. Partial site plan at entry. Garments to Go. Bastrop, Texas. Spencer Godfrey Architects. Round Rock, Texas.

1104 Accessible Route

1104.2 Within a site

- Accessible routes are not required between accessible facilities in the following case:
  - Where the only means of access between facilities is vehicular as follows:
      No pedestrian access is provided.
- Otherwise, ≥ 1 accessible route is required connecting the following within a site:
  - Accessible buildings.
  - Accessible facilities.
  - Accessible elements.
  - Accessible spaces.

1104.3 Connected spaces

- An accessible route is required to connect the following:
  - Each part of a building required to be accessible.
  - Building entrances required to be accessible.
  - Pedestrian walkways required to be accessible.
  - The public way.
- The following applies where only 1 accessible route is provided:
  - In an accessible dwelling unit the route may pass through the following:
      A kitchen.
      A storage room.
  - Otherwise, the route may not pass through the following or similar spaces:
      A kitchen.
      A storage room.
      A closet.
      A restroom.

1104.4 Multilevel buildings and facilities *(part 1 of 2)*

This section addresses access to floors directly above and below accessible levels.

- Such floors need not be connected to the adjacent accessible level by an accessible route if they meet all of the following conditions:
  - The sum of their areas is ≤ 3000 sf.
  - They contain none of the following uses:
      In occupancy B or I:
        Offices of health care providers.
      In occupancy A3 or B:
        Passenger transportation facilities.
        Airport facilities.
      In occupancy M:
        Multiple tenant facilities.

Case study: Fig. 1104.2. All buildings on the site are accessible, and all are on accessible routes as indicated in the illustration. The site plan complies with the code regarding accessibility.

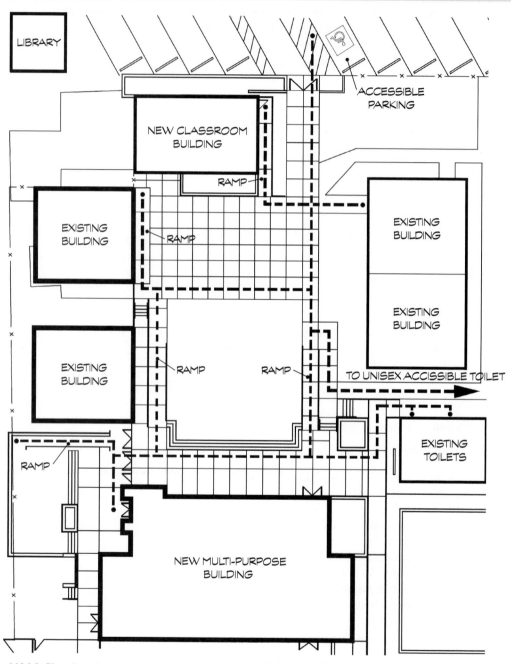

Fig. 1104.2. Site plan. Creston Elementary Multipurpose Building and New Classroom Building. Creston, California. Phillips Metsch Sweeney Moore Architects. Santa Barbara, California.

1104 Accessible Route

1104.4 Multilevel buildings and facilities *(part 2 of 2)*

- Such floors need not be connected to the adjacent accessible level by an accessible route if they meet all of the following conditions:
  - Located in any of the following occupancies:
    A, I, R, S.
    Care facilities.
  - They contain no spaces or elements required to be accessible.

    Note: The following are cited as sources of applicable requirements:
    1107.4, "Care facilities," defines these facilities as indicated above.
    Section 1107, "Special Occupancies," defines additional spaces or elements
    required to be accessible.

- Otherwise, the following applies to multiple levels:
  - ≥ 1 accessible route is required to connect each accessible level as follows:
    Including mezzanines.

1104.5 Location

- Accessible routes must have one of the following relationships to general circulation:
  - Accessible routes must coincide with general circulation routes.
  - Accessible routes must be located in the same area as general circulation routes.
- The location of accessible routes is governed as follows:
  - Accessible routes are not required to be interior in the following case:
    From parking garages contained within and serving Type B dwelling units.
  - In other locations, the accessible route must be interior as follows:
    Where the general circulation path is interior.

1105 Accessible Entrances

1105.1 Required

- Entrances are not required to be accessible in the following cases:
  - To spaces not required to be accessible.
  - Loading and service entrances that are not the sole entrance to the following:
    A building.
    A tenant space.

    Note: Section 1107, "Special Occupancies," is cited as the source identifying spaces that are not required to be accessible.

- In other locations, indicated below, accessible entrances are required as follows:
  - Accessible entrances:
    The number of entrances required to be accessible is the larger of the following:
    $\geq$ 50% of the entrances provided.
    $\geq$ 1 entrance.
  - Locations:
    Buildings.
    Structures.
    Individual tenant spaces.

1105.2 Multiple accessible entrances

- Where a building has entrances serving any of the following facilities, the requirement below applies:
  - Facilities:
    Accessible parking.
    Transportation facilities.
    Passenger loading zones.
    Taxi stands.
    Public streets.
    Public sidewalks.
    Tunnels.
    Elevated walkways.
    Interior accessible vertical access.
  - Requirement:
    $\geq$ 1 entrance serving each facility must be accessible.

1106 Parking and Passenger Loading Facilities

1106.1 Required

- This section does not govern accessible parking in the following parking facilities:
  - Where accessible dwelling units are required in the following occupancies:
    R-2, R-3.
  - Rehabilitation facilities.

    Note: The following are cited as sources of parking requirements applicable to the facilities indicated above:
    1106.2, "Groups R-2 and R-3."
    1106.3, "Rehabilitation facilities and outpatient physical therapy facilities."

- In other parking, the number required to be accessible is as follows:

Table 1106.1   Accessible Parking Other Than R-2 and R-3

Total spaces	Accessible required	Total spaces	Accessible required	Total spaces	Accessible required
1–25	≥ 1	651–700	≥ 14	1501–1600	≥ 26
26–50	≥ 2	701–750	≥ 15	1601–1700	≥ 27
51–75	≥ 3	751–800	≥ 16	1701–1800	≥ 28
76–100	≥ 4	801–850	≥ 17	1801–1900	≥ 29
101–150	≥ 5	851–900	≥ 18	1901–2000	≥ 30
151–200	≥ 6	901–950	≥ 19	2001–2100	≥ 31
201–300	≥ 7	951–1000	≥ 20	2101–2200	≥ 32
301–400	≥ 8	1001–1100	≥ 21	2201–2300	≥ 33
401–500	≥ 9	1101–1200	≥ 22	2101–2400	≥ 34
501–550	≥ 11	1201–1300	≥ 23	2401–2500	≥ 35
551–600	≥ 12	1301–1400	≥ 24	2501–2600	≥ 36
601–650	≥ 13	1401–1500	≥ 25	2601–2700	≥ 37

Source: IBC Table 1106.1.

- The number of accessible parking places required in parking > 2700 total spaces is determined indicated below:
  - Fractions of accessible spaces required are rounded up to the next higher whole number.

    Number of accessible parking spaces = [(Total spaces – 2700) ÷ 100] + 37

Case study: Fig. 1106.1. The parking lot in front of the occupancy B building has 26 parking spaces. IBC Table 1106.1 requires 2 spaces to be accessible where 26 to 50 regular spaces are provided. 3 accessible spaces are provided, which meets the code requirement. Subsection 1106.4 requires that 1 of every 8 accessible spaces be van-accessible. 1 van-accessible space is provided in the front parking lot as required.

The parking lot in back of the building has 150 parking spaces. IBC Table 1106.1 requires that 5 spaces be accessible where 101 to 150 regular spaces are provided. 6 accessible parking spaces are provided, which supercede the minimum requirement. 1 van-accessible space is needed since $\leq$ 8 accessible spaces are provided. 2 van-accessible spaces are provided which is > the minimum requirement.

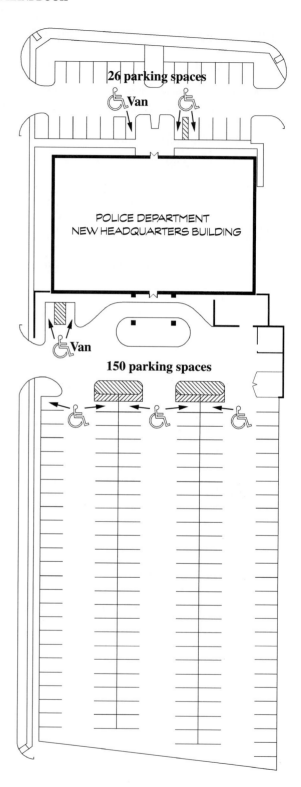

Fig. 1106.1. Site plan. Hot Springs Police Department New Headquarters. Hot Springs National Park, Arkansas. Cromwell Architects Engineers. Little Rock, Arkansas.

1106 Parking and Passenger Loading Facilities

1106.2 Groups R-2 and R-3

- Where accessible dwelling units are required:
  - $\geq 2\%$ of total parking spaces provided are required to be accessible as listed below:
    Fractions of accessible spaces required are rounded up to the next higher whole number.

Table 1106.2   Accessible Parking in R-2 and R-3

Total spaces	Accessible required	Total spaces	Accessible required	Total spaces	Accessible required
1–50	≥ 1	451–500	≥ 10	901–950	≥ 19
51–100	≥ 2	501–550	≥ 11	951–1000	≥ 20
101–150	≥ 3	551–600	≥ 12	1001–1050	≥ 21
151–200	≥ 4	601–650	≥ 13	1051–1100	≥ 22
201–250	≥ 5	651–700	≥ 14	1101–1150	≥ 23
251–300	≥ 6	701–750	≥ 15	1151–1200	≥ 24
301–350	≥ 7	751–800	≥ 16	1201–1250	≥ 25
351–400	≥ 8	801–850	≥ 17	1251–1300	≥ 26
401–450	≥ 9	851–900	≥ 18	etc.	

- Accessible parking is required to be within or beneath a building in the following case:
  - Where general parking is provided within or beneath a building.

1106.3 Rehabilitation facilities and outpatient physical therapy facilities

- 20% of visitor and patient parking spaces are required to be accessible as listed below:
  - Fractions of accessible spaces required are rounded up to the next higher number.

Table 1106.3   Accessible Parking at Rehabilitation and Outpatient Physical Therapy Facilities

Total spaces	Accessible required	Total spaces	Accessible required	Total spaces	Accessible required
1–5	≥ 1	31–35	≥ 7	61–65	≥ 13
5–10	≥ 2	36–40	≥ 8	66–70	≥ 14
11–15	≥ 3	41–45	≥ 9	71–75	≥ 15
16–20	≥ 4	46–50	≥ 10	76–80	≥ 16
21–25	≥ 5	51–55	≥ 11	81–85	≥ 17
26–30	≥ 6	56–60	≥ 12	etc.	

Case study: Fig. Fig. 1106.2. This occupancy R-2 building provides 136 parking spaces in the parking plan shown. At least 2% of these must be accessible. 4 accessible parking spaces are provided, thus, meeting the minimum requirement of 3. Subsection 1106.4 requires at least 1 van-accessible space for every 8 or fraction of 8 accessible spaces. 2 van-accessible spaces are provided, thus, meeting the minimum of 1 required. Since parking is provided beneath the building, accessible parking must be provided there as well. The parking garage also meets this requirement and is, therefore, in compliance with the code in all respects.

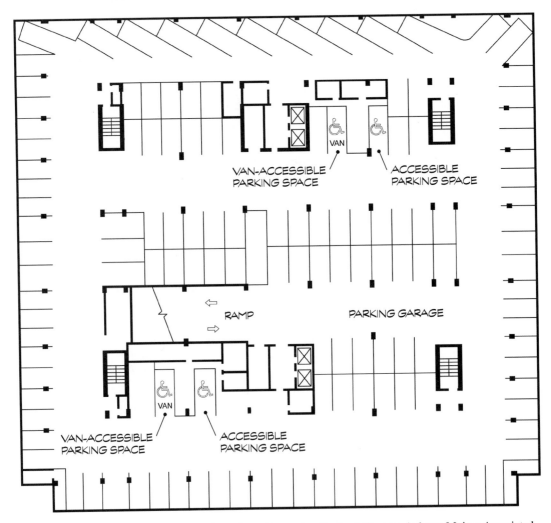

Fig. 1106.2. Parking garage floor plan. Hoyt Street Properties. Portland, Oregon. Ankrom Moisan Associated Architects. Portland, Oregon.

1106 Parking and Passenger Loading Facilities

1106.4 Van spaces

- ≥ 12½ % of accessible parking spaces must be van-accessible as listed below:
  - Fractions of accessible van spaces required are rounded up to the next higher whole number.

Accessible spaces	Accessible van spaces required
1–8	≥ 1
8–16	≥ 2
17–24	≥ 3
etc.	

1106.5 Location

- Where parking serves a particular building, the following applies:
  - Accessible parking spaces must be located as follows:
    On the shortest accessible route to the following:
    An accessible building entrance.
- Where parking does not serve a particular building, the following apply:
  - Accessible parking must be located as follows:
    On the shortest accessible route to the following:
    An accessible pedestrian entrance to the parking facility.
- Where parking serves multiple accessible entrances, the following applies:
  - Where parking is on a single level:
    Accessible spaces must be distributed near accessible entrances.
  - Where parking is multilevel:
    Van-accessible spaces are allowed to be on 1 level.
    Other accessible spaces must be distributed near accessible entrances.

1106.6.1 Medical facilities

- A passenger loading zone is required as follows:
  - At an accessible entrance to the following facilities, which function as indicated below:
    Facilities:
    Licensed medical facilities.
    Licensed long-term care facilities.
    Functions:
    People stay > 24 hours per visit.
    People receive the following treatment or care:
    Physical.
    Medical.

1106.6.2 Valet parking

- An accessible passenger loading zone is required as follows:
  - Where valet parking is provided.

1107 Special Occupancies

1107.2.1 Services

This section addresses assembly areas with fixed seating.

- The following functions are required on an accessible level and must be accessible in the location indicated below:
  - Functions:
      Services.
      Facilities.
  - Location:
      Where such functions are provided in areas not required to be accessible.

1107.2.2 Wheelchair spaces

- This section addresses the following assembly areas with fixed seating:
  - Theaters.
  - Bleachers.
  - Grandstands.
  - Other fixed seating.
- Accessible wheelchair spaces as follows are required in the quantities listed below:
  - Each wheelchair space must have ≥ 1 companion seat adjacent.

Table 1107.2.2   Wheelchair Spaces in Assembly Areas

Total seats	Wheelchair spaces required	Total seats	Wheelchair spaces required
4–25	≥ 1	1301–1500	≥ 11
26–50	≥ 2	1501–1700	≥ 12
51–100	≥ 4	1701–1900	≥ 13
101–300	≥ 5	1901–2100	≥ 14
301–500	≥ 6	2101–2300	≥ 15
501–700	≥ 7	2301–2500	≥ 16
701–900	≥ 8	2501–2700	≥ 17
901–1100	≥ 9	2701–2900	≥ 18
1101–1300	≥ 10	2901–3100	≥ 19

Source: IBC Table 1107.2.2.

- Number of wheelchair spaces required where fixed seats are > 3100 is determined by the equation indicated below:
  - Fractions of wheelchair spaces required are rounded up to the next higher whole number.

Wheelchair spaces = [(Total seats − 3100) ÷ 200] + 19

Case study: Fig. 1107.2.2. The auditorium seats 120. IBC Table 1107.2.2 indicates that 5 wheelchair spaces are required where seating totals 101 through 300. The auditorium provides 8 wheelchair spaces, thus, meeting this requirement. The 4 wheelchair spaces in the front of the auditorium are provided by way of removable standard seats. As required, a companion seat is provided by every wheelchair space.

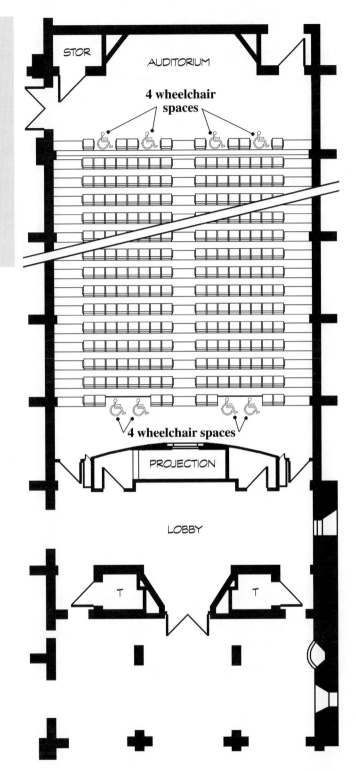

Fig. 1107.2.2. Partial floor plan at auditorium. Lady Bird Johnson Wildflower Center. Austin, Texas. Overland Partners, Inc. San Antonio, Texas.

1107 Special Occupancies

1107.2.2.1 Wheelchair space clusters

This section addresses assembly areas with fixed seating.

- In areas where there is not > 1 step rise between rows, the following applies:
  - The number of wheelchair clusters required is listed below:

Table 1107.2.2.1a   Wheelchair Clusters with ≤ 1 Step between Rows

Total seats	Wheelchair clusters required	Total seats	Wheelchair clusters required
1–300	≥ 1	3001–4000	≥ 7
301–600	≥ 2	4001–5000	≥ 8
601–900	≥ 3	5001–6000	≥ 9
901–1500	≥ 4	6001–7000	≥ 10
1501–2100	≥ 5	7001–8000	≥ 11
2101–3000	≥ 6	8001–9000	≥ 12

Source: IBC Table 1107.2.2.1.

- The number of wheelchair space clusters where fixed seats are > 9000 is determined by the equation indicated below:
  - Fractions of wheelchair space clusters required are rounded up to the next higher whole number.

  Wheelchair space clusters = [(Total seats − 9000) ÷ 1000] + 12

- In areas where there is > 1 step rise between rows, the following applies:
  - The number of wheelchair clusters required is listed below:

Table 1107.2.2.1b   Wheelchair Clusters with > 1 Step between Rows

Total seats	Wheelchair clusters required	Total seats	Wheelchair clusters required
1–600	≥ 1	3001–5000	≥ 4
601–1500	≥ 2	5001–7000	≥ 5
1501–3000	≥ 3	7001–9000	≥ 6

- The number of wheelchair space clusters where fixed seats are > 9000 is determined by the equation indicated below:
  - Fractions of wheelchair space clusters required are rounded up to the next higher whole number.

  Wheelchair space clusters = [(Total seats − 9000) ÷ 2000] + 6

1107 Special Occupancies

1107.2.3 Dispersion of wheelchair space clusters

- Distribution of wheelchair space clusters is based on the availability of accessible routes.

1107.2.3.1 Multilevel assembly seating areas

- Wheelchair space clusters are required on the main floor level.
- All wheelchair space clusters may be on the main floor where all of the following apply:
  - The space is used for worship services.
  - The upper level contains ≤ 25% of the total seating capacity.
- All wheelchair space clusters may be on the main floor where all of the following apply:
  - The upper level contains ≤ 25% of the total seating capacity.
  - The upper level contains ≤ 300 seats.
- For other conditions of multilevel assembly seating, the following applies:
  - Wheelchair space clusters are required on one of each two upper levels as follows:
    In addition to locations on the main floor level.

1107.2.3.2 Separation between clusters

This section addresses wheelchair space clusters in assembly areas with fixed seating.

- Wheelchair space clusters must meet both of the following requirements:
  - Separation of clusters by ≥ 5 rows of seating is required.
  - Separation of clusters by ≥ 10 seats in a row is required.
- Separation of individual wheelchair spaces within any one cluster is governed as follows:
  - Separation by a row of seats is prohibited.
  - Separation by > 2 seats in a row is prohibited.
  - Separation by a height change > 7" is permitted where necessary to maintain sight lines.
  - Separation by a height change > 7" is prohibited where sight lines do not require it.

1107.2.4 Assistive listening systems

- Where sound is integral to the function of assembly areas with fixed seating as follows, the requirement indicated below applies:
  - Assembly areas:
    Stadiums.
    Theaters.
    Auditoriums.
    Lectures halls.
    Similar assembly areas with fixed seating.
  - Requirement:
    An assistive listening system is required in either of the following cases:
    Where the area is equipped with an audio amplification system.
    Where the area has a capacity ≥ 50 people.

1107 Special Occupancies

1107.2.4.1 Receivers

- Receivers are required for assistive listening in assembly areas with fixed seating.
- Receivers are required as follows:
  - The number of standard receivers required are listed in the table below.
  - The number of required receivers that must also be hearing-aid compatible is listed in the table below:

Table 1107.2.4.1   Number of Receivers for Assistive Listening

Total seats	Receivers required	Hearing-aid compatible	Total seats	Receivers required	Hearing-aid compatible
1–50	≥ 2	≥ 2	1101–1200	≥ 39	≥ 10
51-150	≥ 6	≥ 2	1201–1300	≥ 41	≥ 11
151–250	≥ 10	≥ 3	1301–1400	≥ 43	≥ 11
251–350	≥ 14	≥ 4	1401–1500	≥ 45	≥ 12
351–450	≥ 18	≥ 5	1501–1600	≥ 47	≥ 12
451–500	≥ 20	≥ 5	1601–1700	≥ 49	≥ 13
501–600	≥ 23	≥ 6	1701–1800	≥ 51	≥ 13
601–700	≥ 26	≥ 7	1801–1900	≥ 53	≥ 14
701–800	≥ 29	≥ 8	1901–2000	≥ 55	≥ 14
801–900	≥ 32	≥ 8	2001–2100	≥ 56	≥ 14
901–1000	≥ 35	≥ 9	2101–2200	≥ 57	≥ 15
1001–1100	≥ 37	≥ 10	2201–2300	≥ 58	≥ 15

Source: IBC Table 1107.2.4.1.

- The number of receivers required for > 2300 seats is determined as indicated below:
  - Fractions of receivers required are rounded up to the next whole number.

  Receivers required = [(Total seats – 2300) ÷ 100] + 58

- The number of receivers that must be hearing-aid compatible for > 2300 seats is as follows:
  - ≥ 25% of the standard receivers required:
    Fractions of receivers required are rounded up to the next whole number.

1107.2.5 Dining areas

- An accessible route to a mezzanine is not required where both of the following apply:
  - The mezzanine has < 25% the total dining area.
  - The building has no elevator.
  - The same services provided on the mezzanine are provided in the accessible area.
- Otherwise, the total dining area for tables and seating must be accessible.

1107 Special Occupancies

1107.2.5.1 Fixed or built-in seating or tables

- The requirements indicated below apply where the following facilities are provided:
  - Facilities:
    Fixed seating or tables.
    Built-in seating or tables.
  - Requirements:
    The number of seats or tables required to be accessible is listed below:

Total seats or tables	Seats or tables to be accessible	Total seats or tables	Seats or tables to be accessible
1 - 20	≥ 1	61 - 80	≥ 4
21 - 40	≥ 2	81 - 100	≥ 5
41 - 60	≥ 3	101 - 120	≥ 6

- Where the total number of fixed seats or tables is > 120, the following applies:
  - The number required to be accessible is ≥ 5% of the total provided.
- The fixed seating or tables must be dispersed throughout the dining area.

1107.2.5.2 Dining counters

- Counters with all of the following characteristics must have a 5' length that is accessible:
  - Characteristics:
    Located where the following is served for consumption:
    Food.
    Drink.
    Where counters provide the only seating.
    Where the counter is > 2'-10" high.

1107.3.1 Group I-1

- The following facilities must be accessible in the quantity indicated below.
  - Residential sleeping rooms, including bathing and toilet facilites.

Table 1107.3.1   Accessible Residential Sleeping Rooms

Total number of sleeping rooms	Number to be accessible	Total number of sleeping rooms	Number to be accessible
1–25	≥ 1	151–175	≥ 7
26–50	≥ 2	176–200	≥ 8
51–75	≥ 3	201–225	≥ 9
76–100	≥ 4	226–250	≥ 10
101–125	≥ 5	251–275	≥ 11
126–150	≥ 6	276–300	≥ 12

- Where the total number of sleeping rooms is > 300, the following applies:
  - The number required to be accessible is ≥ 4% of the total number of rooms provided.

1107 Special Occupancies

1107.3.2 Group I-2

- The following facilities in nursing homes must be accessible in the quantity indicated below:
  - Facilities:
    Patient sleeping rooms, including bathing and toilet facilities.
  - Quantity:
    The number of facilities that must be accessible is the larger of the following:
    $\geq 50\%$ of the total number.
    ≥ 1.
- The facilities listed below for the following units must be accessible in the quantity indicated:
  - Units:
    General-purpose hospitals.
    Psychiatric facilities.
    Detoxification facilities.
  - Facilities:
    Patient sleeping rooms, including bathing and toilet facilities.
  - Quantity:
    The number of facilities that must be accessible is the larger of the following:
    $\geq 10\%$ of the total number.
    ≥ 1.
- The facilities listed below for the following units must be accessible in the quantity indicated:
  - Units:
    Units specializing in mobility limitations as follows:
    Hospitals.
    Units within hospitals.
    Rehabilitation facilities.
    Units within rehabilitation facilities.
  - Facilities:
    Patient sleeping rooms, including bathing and toilet facilities.
  - Quantity:
    100% must be accessible.

1107.3.3 Group I-3

- The following facilities must be accessible in the quantity indicated below:
  - Facilities:
    Residential unit:
    Including bathing facilities.
    Including toilet facilities.
  - Quantity:
    The number of facilities that must be accessible is the larger of the following:
    $\geq 5\%$ of the total number.
    ≥ 1.

1107 Special Occupancies

1107.4 Care facilities

- Where a care facility is part of a dwelling unit, the following applies:
    - Only the areas serving the care facility need be accessible.
- Otherwise, the following occupancies containing care facilities must be accessible:
    - A-3, E, I-4, R-3.

1107.5.1 Accessible sleeping accommodations *(part 1 of 2)*

- Where sleeping accommodations occur in occupancies R-1 and R-2, the following applies:
    - Accessible sleeping accommodations must be provided as follows:
        Sleeping accommodations in the numbers indicated require a roll-in shower as follows:
        Roll-in showers must have a permanent folding seat.
        The number of accessible sleeping accommodations required is based the following:
        The total number of sleeping accommodations provided on the site.
- The number of accessible sleeping accommodations required in R-1 and R-2 is listed below:

Table 1107.5.1	Accessible Sleeping Accommodations in R-1 and R-2		
Total sleeping accommodations on the site	Accommodations to be accessible and requiring a roll-in shower	Accommodations to be accessible but not requiring a roll-in shower	Total accessible sleeping accommodations required
1–25	≥ 0	≥ 1	≥ 1
26–50	≥ 0	≥ 2	≥ 2
51–75	≥ 1	≥ 3	≥ 4
76–100	≥ 1	≥ 4	≥ 5
101–150	≥ 2	≥ 5	≥ 7
151–200	≥ 2	≥ 6	≥ 8
201–300	≥ 3	≥ 7	≥ 10
301–400	≥ 4	≥ 8	≥ 12
401–500	≥ 4	≥ 9	≥ 13
501–533	≥ 6	≥ 10	≥ 16
534–566	≥ 6	≥ 11	≥ 17
567–600	≥ 6	≥ 12	≥ 18
601–633	≥ 7	≥ 12	≥ 19
634–666	≥ 7	≥ 13	≥ 20
667–700	≥ 7	≥ 14	≥ 21
701–733	≥ 8	≥ 14	≥ 22
734–766	≥ 8	≥ 15	≥ 23
767–800	≥ 8	≥ 16	≥ 24
801–833	≥ 9	≥ 16	≥ 25
834–866	≥ 9	≥ 17	≥ 26
867–900	≥ 9	≥ 18	≥ 27

Source: IBC Table 1107.5.1.

1107 Special Occupancies

1107.5.1 Accessible sleeping accommodations *(part 2 of 2)*

- The number of accessible sleeping accommodations required in R-1 and R-2 is listed below:

Table 1107.5.1—*Continued*

Total sleeping accommodations on the site	Accommodations to be accessible and requiring a roll-in shower	Accommodations to be accessible but not requiring a roll-in shower	Total accessible sleeping accommodations required
901–933	≥ 10	≥ 18	≥ 28
934–966	≥ 10	≥ 19	≥ 29
967–1000	≥ 10	≥ 20	≥ 30
1001–1100	≥ 11	≥ 21	≥ 32
1101–1200	≥ 12	≥ 22	≥ 34
1201–1300	≥ 13	≥ 23	≥ 36
1301–1400	≥ 14	≥ 24	≥ 38
1401–1500	≥ 15	≥ 25	≥ 40
1501–1600	≥ 16	≥ 26	≥ 42
1601–1700	≥ 17	≥ 27	≥ 44
1701–1800	≥ 18	≥ 28	≥ 46
1801–1900	≥ 19	≥ 29	≥ 48
1901–2000	≥ 20	≥ 30	≥ 50
2001–2100	≥ 21	≥ 31	≥ 52
2101–2200	≥ 22	≥ 32	≥ 54
2201–2300	≥ 23	≥ 33	≥ 56
2301–2400	≥ 24	≥ 34	≥ 58
2401–2500	≥ 25	≥ 35	≥ 60

Source: IBC Table 1107.5.1.

- The number of accessible sleeping accommodations for a total number of sleeping accommodations on a site > 2500 is determined as follows:
  - Accommodations to be accessible and requiring a roll-in shower:
    Fractions of accommodations required round up to the next higher whole number.

    Accommodations = [(Total accommodations on site – 2500) ÷100] + 25

  - Accommodations to be accessible and not requiring a roll-in shower:
    Fractions of accommodations required round up to the next higher whole number.

    Accommodations = [(Total accommodations on site – 2500) ÷ 100] + 35

  - Total accessible sleeping accommodations required:
    Fractions of accommodations required round up to the next higher whole number.

    Accommodations = {[(Total accommodations on site – 2500) ÷ 100] × 2} + 60

1107 Special Occupancies

1107.5.2 Accessible spaces

- The following rooms and spaces in occupancy R-1 and R-2 must comply with the requirement indicated below:
  - Spaces:
    Such as the following where used by occupants of accessible sleeping accommodations:
      Toilet and bathing rooms.
      Kitchens.
      Living areas.
      Dining areas.
      Exterior spaces such as follows:
        Patios.
        Terraces.
        Balconies.

1107.5.3 Dispersion

- Accessible sleeping accommodations in occupancy R-1 and R-2 are to be distributed as follows:
  - Among all classes of accommodations.

1107.5.4 Accessible dwelling units *(part 1 of 2)*

This section addresses occupancy R-2 and R-3 dwelling units.

- Type A and B dwelling units are not required above the ground floor in the following case:
  - Where the building has no elevator.
- Where both of the following conditions apply, the requirement indicated below governs:
  - Conditions:
    The building has no elevator.
    The ground floor does not contain dwelling units.
  - Requirement:
    The only units required to comply with this section are as follows:
      The lowest floor of dwelling units.
- Multistory dwelling units are governed as follows:
  - Where no elevator service is provided to the unit:
    Units need not meet Type B dwelling unit requirements.
  - Where an elevator serves only one floor of the unit:
    Only the floor served need meet Type B dwelling units requirements.
    A toilet is required on the floor served.
- Where there are more than one building on a site with no elevator:
    The number of Type B dwelling units required is the larger of the following:
      ≥ 20% of all ground floor units on the site.
      A % of ground floor units equal to the following:
        The % of the site with predeveloped slopes ≤ 10%.

1107 Special Occupancies

11107.5.4 Accessible dwelling units *(part 2 of 2)*

- The number of Type A and Type B units required does not apply to the following site:
  - Where a base flood elevation forces the lowest floor level to a height with one of the following relationships to grade as measured between the two points indicated below:
    Relationships:
      A difference in elevation >30" between the two points.
      A slope >10% between the two points.
    Two points:
      Minimum floor elevation required at primary entrances.
      Elevation of vehicular and pedestrian arrival points within 50' or as follows:
        Where no arrival point is within 50' of a primary entrance:
          The closest arrival point is used.
- Otherwise, Type A and Type B dwelling units are required as follows:
  - In occupancy R-2 and R-3 with ≥ 4 dwelling units in one building:
    All units must be Type B dwelling units.
  - In occupancy R-2 with >20 dwelling units:
    The number of Type A dwelling units is the larger of the following:
      ≥ 2% of the total number of units.
      ≥ 1 unit.
  - Type A units may be substituted where Type B units are required.

    Note: ICC/ANSI A117.1, "Accessible and Usable Buildings and Facilities," is cited as governing Type A and Type B dwelling units.

1107.5.5 Accessible route *(part 1 of 2)*

This section addresses occupancies R-2 and R-3.

- The following may substitute for an accessible route for the conditions indicated below:
  - Substitute:
    A vehicular route with parking at each accessible facility or building.
  - Conditions:
    Where the slope of finished grade between accessible facilities and buildings is > 1:12.
    Where physical barriers prevent installation of an accessible route.
- The following facilities may have a floor surface ≤ 4" below the adjacent interior floor where the conditions below apply:
  - Facilities:
    Exterior decks.
    Patios.
    Balconies.
  - Conditions:
    At Type B dwelling units.
    The facility must have an impervious surface.

1107 Special Occupancies

1107.5.5 Accessible route *(part 2 of 2)*

- In all other cases, ≥ 1 accessible route is required between accessible building or facility entrances and the following locations:
  - Primary entrances of accessible dwelling units.
  - Exterior and interior spaces serving accessible dwelling units.

1107.5.6 Accessible spaces

This section addresses occupancies R-2 and R-3.

- The larger of the following numbers of recreational facilities serving accessible dwelling units must be accessible:
  - ≥ 25% of each type in each occupancy group of facilities as follows:
    Based on the total number of each type of a site.
  - ≥ 1 of each type in each occupancy group of facilities.
- All other rooms and spaces serving accessible dwelling units must be accessible as follows:
  - Those available to the general public.
  - Those available to residents.

  Note: 1108.14, "Recreational facilities," is cited as governing such facilities.

1107.5.7 Group R-4

- ≥ 1 sleeping room must be accessible, including the following:
  - Related toilet.
  - Related bathing facility.

1107 Special Occupancies

1107.6 Self-service storage facilities

- The numbers of self-storage units required to be accessible are listed below:

Table 1107.6   Accessible Self-Storage Units

Total number of units provided	Number to be accessible	Total number of units provided	Number to be accessible
1–20	≥ 1	301–350	≥ 13
21–40	≥ 2	351–400	≥ 14
41–60	≥ 3	401–450	≥ 15
61–80	≥ 4	451–500	≥ 16
81–100	≥ 5	501–550	≥ 17
101–120	≥ 6	551–600	≥ 18
121–140	≥ 7	601–650	≥ 19
141–160	≥ 8	651–700	≥ 20
161–180	≥ 9	701–750	≥ 21
181–200	≥ 10	751–800	≥ 22
201–250	≥ 11	801–850	≥ 23
251–300	≥ 12	851–900	≥ 24

Source: IBC Table 1107.6.

- The number of self-storage units required to be accessible in a facility with > 900 units is determined as indicated below:

  Required accessible units = [(Total number of units – 900) × 0.02] + 24

1107.6.1 Dispersion

- Where there are fewer accessible self-storage units required than there are classes of storage, the following applies:
  - The number of accessible units provided need not be > the number otherwise required for the following purpose:
    To distribute accessible units among all classes of storage.
- Otherwise, accessible self-storage units must be distributed among all classes of storage spaces provided.
- In a multibuilding storage facility, accessible self-storage units may be distributed in a single building.

1108 Other Features and Facilities

1108.1 General

- Type A and Type B dwelling units are not governed by this section.

    Note: ICC/ANSI A117.1, "Accessible and Usable Buildings and Facilities," is cited as governing Type A and B dwelling units.

1108.2 Toilet and bathing facilities *(part 1 of 2)*

- Alternatives to the accessibility requirements of this section for the following facilities are provided below:
    - Facilities:
        Toilet rooms or bathing facilities where all the following conditions apply:
        Facilities accessed only through a private office.
        Facilities not for public use.
        Facilities intended for use by a single occupant.
    - Alternatives:
        Doors may swing into the clear floor space in the following case:
        Where it can be reversed to meet other accessibility standards.
        Height requirements of other accessibility standards do not apply for the water closet.
        Toilet room grab bars not required in the following case:
        Where backing is provided in walls suitable for their installation.
        The following requirements at the lavatory do not apply:
        Height minimum.
        Knee clearance.
        Toe clearance.

    Note: ICC/ANSI A117.1, "Accessible and Usable Buildings and Facilities," is cited as the accessibility standard that applies to the above alternatives or which is waived as indicated.

- This section does not apply to the following facilities:
    - Those not required to be accessible as follows:
        In dwelling units.
        In sleeping accommodations.
        Patient toilets.
        Patient bathing facilities.

    Note: Section 1107, "Special Occupancies," is cited as the source that does not require certain facilities to be accessible as indicated above.

1108 Other Features and Facilities

1108.2 Toilet and bathing facilities *(part 2 of 2)*

- Where there is a group of ≥ 2 toilet rooms or bathing facilities as follows, the requirements listed below apply:
  - Facilities:
      Each is designed for use by a single occupant.
      Where such facilities combined have more fixtures than the total required.
  - Requirement:
      The larger of the following number of rooms or bathing facilities must be accessible:
        For men's facilities:
          ≥ 5% of the rooms.
          ≥ 1 room.
        For women's facilities:
          ≥ 5% of the rooms.
          ≥ 1 room.
        For unisex facilities:
          ≥ 5% of the rooms.
          ≥ 1 room.
- This section does not apply to the following facilities:
  - Where toilet room fixtures have all the following characteristics:
      They are in excess of those required by the plumbing code.
      They are for use by children in either of the following:
        Day care.
        Primary school.
- Other toilet rooms and bathing facilities are governed as follows:
  - Such rooms and facilities are required to be accessible.
  - ≥ 1 of the following in each accessible room or facility must be accessible:
      Fixture.
      Element.
      Control.
      Dispenser.
  - Where such rooms or facilities are the only ones in a building, the following applies:
      They may not be located on a floor without an accessible route.

1108 Other Features and Facilities

1108.2.1 Unisex toilet and bathing rooms

- A unisex bathing room is not required in the following case:
  - Where fixtures in each separate-sex bathing room are limited as follows:
    Where a bathtub is provided, there is only 1.
    Where a shower is provided, there is only 1.
- In other cases, the following requirements apply:
  - An accessible unisex toilet room is required where all the following conditions apply:
    In occupancies A and M.
    Where the sum of male and female water closets required is ≥ 6.
  - Where A or M occupancies are mixed with others, the following applies:
    An accessible unisex toilet room is required for the following condition:
    Where the sum of male and female water closets required is ≥ 6 as follows:
    In the A or M occupancies only.
- An accessible unisex toilet room is required in recreational facilities as follows:
  - Where separate-sex bathing rooms are provided.
- Fixtures in unisex toilet and bathing rooms count toward the following minimum:
  - The total number of fixtures required.

1108.2.1.1 Standard

- Unisex toilet rooms and bathing facilities must comply with this section and other standards.

  Note: ICC/ANSI A117.1, "Accessible and Usable Buildings and Facilities," is cited as the other standard governing unisex facilities as indicated above.

1108.2.1.2 Unisex toilet rooms

- Toilet rooms meet the requirements of a unisex toilet in the following cases:
  - Where they have no more and no fewer than the plumbing fixtures listed below:
    A unisex toilet room with the following:
    1 lavatory.
    1 water closet.
    A separate-sex toilet room with the following:
    1 lavatory.
    ≤ 2 water closets.
    A separate-sex toilet room with the following:
    1 lavatory.
    1 water closet.
    1 urinal.
    A unisex bathing room with the following:
    1 lavatory.
    1 water closet .
    1 shower or bathtub.

  Note: 1108.2.1.2, "Unisex bathing rooms," is cited as the source of bathing rooms that qualify as unisex toilets.

1108 Other Features and Facilities

1108.2.1.3 Unisex bathing rooms

- Unisex bathing rooms must include no more and no fewer of the following plumbing fixtures:
  - One bathtub or shower.
  - One water closet.
  - One lavatory.
- Accessible storage facilities are required for unisex bathing rooms in the following case:
  - Where storage is provided for separate-sex bathing rooms.

1108.2.1.4 Location

- Unisex toilet and bathing rooms must be on an accessible route.
- Unisex toilet rooms must be placed in one of the following locations:
  - ≤ 1 story above separate-sex toilet rooms.
  - ≤ 1 story below separate-sex toilet rooms.
- The accessible route between the following points is limited to $\leq 500'$:
  Any separate-sex toilet room.
  A unisex toilet room.

1108.2.1.5 Prohibited location

This section addresses passenger transportation facilities and airports.

- The accessible route between the following facilities is governed as indicated below:
  - Facilities:
    Separate-sex toilet rooms.
    A unisex to toilet room.
  - Requirement:
    The route may not pass through a security checkpoint.

1108.2.1.6 Clear floor space

- Where doors swing into the following rooms, the following clear space is required:
  - Rooms:
    Unisex toilet room.
    Unisex bathing rooms.
  - Requirement:
    Clear floor space must be available in the room beyond the door swing as follows:
      $\geq 30" \times \geq 48"$.

1108.2.1.7 Privacy

- Doors to the following rooms must be securable from inside the rooms:
  - Unisex toilet rooms.
  - Unisex bathing rooms.

1108 Other Features and Facilities

1108.2.2 Water closet compartment

This section addresses toilet rooms and bathing rooms.

- Where water closet compartments are provided, the following is required:
  - ≥ 1 wheelchair-accessible water closet compartment.
- Where the sum of the following facilities is ≥ 6, the requirement indicated below applies:
  - Facilities:
    Water closet compartments.
    Urinals.
  - Requirement:
    ≥ 1 wheelchair-accessible water closet compartment is required.
    ≥ 1 ambulatory-accessible water closet compartment is required.

  Note: ICC/ANSI A117.1, "Accessible and Usable Buildings and Facilities," is cited as governing wheelchair-accessible and ambulatory-accessible compartments.

1108.3 Sinks

- The following sinks are not governed by this section:
  Mop sinks.
  Service sinks.
  Children's sinks in the following locations:
    Day care.
    Primary school.
- In other cases where other sinks are provided, the number required to comply with accessibility requirements are listed below:

Total number of sinks provided	Sinks required to meet accessibility requirements
1–20	≥ 1
21–40	≥ 2
41–60	≥ 3

- Where > 60 sinks are provided, $\geq 5\%$ must meet accessibility requirements.

  Note: ICC/ANSI A117.1, "Accessible and Usable Buildings and Facilities," is cited as governing the sinks indicated above.

Case study: Fig. 1108.3. Where 1–20 sinks are provided, ≥ 1 must meet accessibility requirements. In this classroom laboratory, 4 sinks are provided. 1 meets accessibility requirements; thus, the sinks are in compliance with the code.

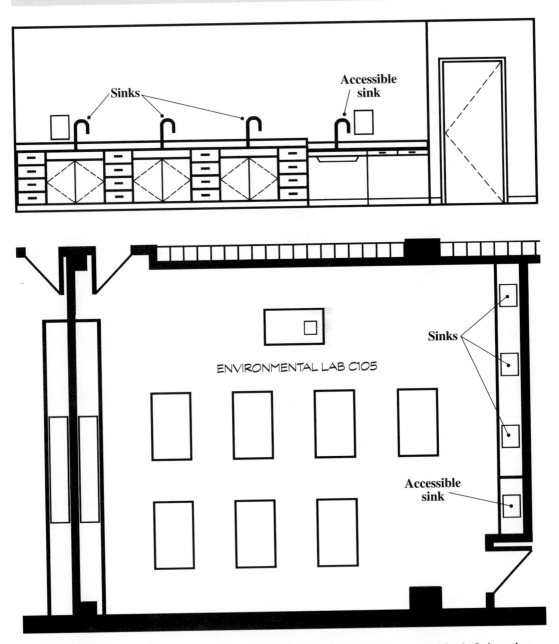

Fig. 1108.3. Plan and elevation at environmental lab C105. High School 6, Cypress-Fairbanks Independent School District. Harris County, Texas. PBK Architects, Inc. Houston, Texas.

1108 Other Features and Facilities

1108.4 Kitchens, kitchenettes and wet bars

- Where provided in accessible spaces, the following must meet accessibility requirements:
  - Kitchens.
  - Kitchenttes.
  - Wet bars.

    Note: ICC/ANSI A117.1, "Accessible and Usable Buildings and Facilities," is cited as governing the facilities indicated above.

1108.5 Drinking fountains

- Where drinking fountains are provided, the following applies:
  - The larger of the following numbers of drinking fountains must be accessible:
    ≥ 1.
    $\geq 50\%$ of the drinking fountains provided.

1108.6 Elevators

- Passenger elevators on an accessible route must be accessible.

    Note: 3001.3, "Accessibility," is cited as governing passenger elevators, which refers to ICC/ANSI A117.1, "Accessible and Usable Buildings and Facilities," for all requirements.

1108.7 Lifts

- Platform (wheelchair) lifts are permitted in the following accessible routes:
  - In occupancy A, as follows:
    To a performing area.
    To required wheelchair spaces.
  - To spaces meeting both of the following conditions:
    Not open to the general public.
    Having an occupant load ≤ 5.
  - Within a dwelling unit.
  - In occupancy A-5, with all of the following conditions:
    Route is to wheelchair seating spaces.
    Route is to outdoor dining.
    Means of egress as follows is open to the outdoors:
      From the outdoor dining to a public way.
- Otherwise, platform (wheelchair) lifts are not permitted as follows:
  - In required accessible routes in new construction.

Case study: Fig. 1108.5.
Two drinking fountains are provided on the 2nd floor of the building. Half of those provided or a minimum of 1 is required to be accessible. The drinking fountains meet this requirement.

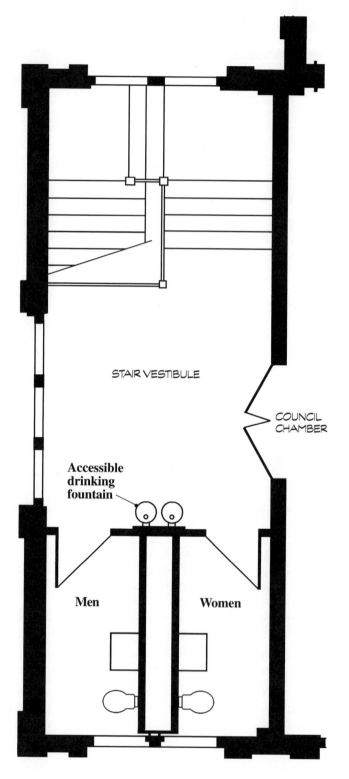

Fig.1108.5. Plan at south stair. Lake Forest City Hall Renovation and Addition. Lake Forest, Illinois. David Woodhouse Architects. Chicago, Illinois.

1108 Other Features and Facilities

1108.8 Storage

- Where fixed or built-in storage units such as the following are provided in a required accessible space, the requirement below applies:
  - Storage units:
    Cabinets.
    Shelves.
    Medicine cabinets.
    Closets.
    Drawers.
    Similar storage components
  - Requirements:
    ≥ 1 of each type must comply with accessibility requirements.

  Note: ICC/ANSI A117.1, "Accessible and Usable Buildings and Facilities," is cited as the source of accessibility requirements for the units indicated above.

1108.8.1 Lockers

- Where lockers are provided in accessible spaces, the following numbers must be accessible:

Total number of lockers provided	Lockers required to be accessible	Total number of lockers provided	Lockers required to be accessible
1–20	≥ 1	61–80	≥ 4
21–40	≥ 2	81–100	≥ 5
41–60	≥ 3	101–120	≥ 6

- Where > 120 lockers are provided, ≥ 5% are required to be accessible.

1108.8.2 Shelving and display units

- The requirements indicated below apply to the following shelving:
  - Shelving:
    Self-service and display units in occupancy M.
    Shelving in stack areas of libraries.
  - Requirements:
    Shelving must be on an accessible route.
    Shelving need not comply with reach-range provisions.

1108 Other Features and Facilities

1108.8.3 Coat hooks and folding shelves

- The following accessible spaces require ≥ 1 of each device listed below when similar devices are provided for similar spaces that are inaccessible:
  - Spaces:
    Toilet rooms and compartments.
    Dressing and fitting rooms.
    Locker rooms.
  - Devices:
    Coat hooks.
    Folding shelves.

1108.11 Seating at tables, counters and work surfaces

- Where there is seating at the following, the number required to be accessible is listed below:
  - At fixed or built-in tables.
  - At fixed or built-in counters.
  - At fixed or built-in work surfaces.

Total seats	Seats to be accessible	Total seats	Seats to be accessible
1–20	≥ 1	61–80	≥ 4
21–40	≥ 2	81–100	≥ 5
41–60	≥ 3	101–120	≥ 6

- Where the number of seats at the built-in locations is > 120, the following applies:
  - The number required to be accessible is ≥ 5% of the total provided.

1108.11.1 Dispersion

- Where accessible seating provided at the following locations, it must be distributed throughout the seating area:
  - At fixed or built-in tables.
  - At fixed or built-in counters.
  - At fixed or built-in work surfaces.

1108 Other Features and Facilities

1108.12.1 Dressing, fitting and locker rooms

- Where the following facilities are provided, the number required to be accessible in each group is as listed below:
  - Dressing rooms.
  - Fitting rooms.
  - Locker rooms.

Total of each facility type	Number of each to be accessible
1–20	≥ 1
21–40	≥ 2
41–60	≥ 3

- Where the number of such facilities is > 60, the following applies:
  - The number required to be accessible is $\geq 5\%$ of the total number provided.

1108.12.2 Check-out aisles

- Where the area of selling space is < 5000 sf, the following applies:
  - Only 1 checkout aisle must be accessible.
- For selling space $\geq$ 5000 sf, the following applies:
  - Accessible checkout aisles must be distributed throughout a facility in the following case:
    Where inaccessible checkout aisles are distributed throughout the facility.
  - The following devices located in accessible check-out aisles must be accessible:
    Traffic control devices.
    Security devices.
    Turnstiles.
  - Where checkout aisles serve different functions, the following applies:
    ≥ 1 accessible checkout aisle must be provided for each function.
  - Where checkout aisles are provided following number for each sales function must be accessible:

Table 1108.12.2   **Accessible Checkout Aisles**

Checkout aisles at each function	Checkout aisles at each function to be accessible	Checkout aisles at each function	Checkout aisles at each function to be accessible
1–4	≥ 1	16–20	≥ 4
5–8	≥ 2	21–25	≥ 5
9–15	≥ 3	26–30	≥ 6

Source: IBC Table 1108.12.2.

- Where checkout aisles are > 30, the number to be accessible is determined as follows:

  Number to be accessible = [(Checkout aisles provided – 30) × 0.2] + 6

1108 Other Features and Facilities

1108.12.3 Point of sales and service counters

- Counters for sales and distribution of goods and services are governed as follows:
  - Where such counters are provided the following applies:
    - ≥ 1 of each type must be accessible.
  - Where such counters are distributed throughout the facility, the following applies:
    The accessible counters must be distributed throughout the facility.

1108.12.4 Food service lines

- Food service lines must be accessible.
- Where self-service shelves are provided, the following applies:
  - The greater of the following numbers of shelves must be accessible:
    - ≥ 1 of each type.
    - ≥ 50% of each type.

1108.12.5 Queue and waiting lines

- Queue and waiting lines for the following facilities must be accessible:
  - Accessible counters.
  - Accessible checkout aisles.

1108.13 Controls, operating mechanisms and hardware

- Devices used by occupants such as follows must be accessible where located as shown below:
  - Devices:
    Controls.
    Operating mechanisms and hardware.
    Light and ventilation switches.
    Switches for electrical convenience outlets.
  - Locations:
    In accessible spaces.
    Along accessible routes.
    As parts of accessible elements.

1108 Other Features and Facilities

1108.13.1 Operable windows

- Accessible windows are not required in the following rooms:
  - Bathrooms.
  - Kitchens
- In other rooms, listed below, the following operable windows must be accessible:
  - Windows:
    ≥ 1 operable window in each room where operable windows are provided.
    Every required operable window.
  - Locations:
    In required accessible residential sleeping rooms of occupancy I-1.
    In required accessible patient sleeping rooms of occupancy I-2.
    In required accessible sleeping rooms of occupancy R-1 and R-2.

  Note: The following are cited as sources listing rooms that must be accessible, a partial summary of which is provided above:
  1107.3.1, "Group I-1."
  1107.3.2, "Group I-2."
  1107.5.1, "Accessible sleeping accommodations," which addresses R-1 and R-2.

1108.14.1 Groups R-2 and R-3

- Recreational facilities serving accessible dwelling units are governed as follows:
  - The larger of the following number must be accessible:
    ≥ 1 facility of each type provided in each occupancy group of such facilities.
    ≥ 25% of each type of facility provided in each occupancy group of such facilities.
  - All facilities of each type on a site are considered to determine the accessible number.

1108.14.2 Other occupancies

- All recreational facilities provided must be accessible in other than occupancies R-2 and R-3.

1109 Signage

1109.1 Signs

- Required accessible elements require the International Symbol of Accessibility as follows:
  - For accessible parking spaces where > 5 total parking spaces are provided.
  - For accessible loading zones for passengers.
  - For accessible areas of refuge.
  - For accessible toilet and bathing rooms as follows:
    Single-user rooms grouped at a single location.
  - For accessible entrances where not all entrances are accessible.
  - For accessible checkout aisles where not all aisles are accessible as follows:
    Signage must be located above the aisle as is other checkout aisle identification.
  - For unisex toilet and bathing rooms.
  - For the following facilities where not all similar facilities are accessible:
    Dressing rooms.
    Fitting rooms.
    Locker rooms.

  Note: The following are cited as sources of applicable requirements as indicated:
  1106.1, "Required," requires accessible parking spaces as indicated above.
  1003.2.13.5, "Areas of refuge," provides requirements for areas of refuge.

Case study: Fig. 1109.1. The International symbol for accessibility, as shown in the illustration, is painted on the pavement at each accessible parking space in this project and is applied to signs reserving the spaces. The symbol is also used on the sign beside the door of the unisex toilet room. In addition, the toilet room is identified as being unisex by the symbol on the door and by the wording on the accessibility sign, which includes Braille. The signs at the toilet room are mounted 5' above the floor. The signage complies with code requirements.

1109.2 Directional signage

- Signage with the following information is required at the locations indicated below:
  - Information:
    Indicates route to nearest similar facility that is accessible.
    Exhibits the International Symbol of Accessibility.
  - Location:
    At inaccessible building entrances.
    At inaccessible public toilets and bathing facilities.
    At elevators not serving an accessible route.
    At each separate-sex toilet and bathing room indicating the following:
      The location of nearest unisex toilet or bathing room.

  Note: 1108.2.1, "Unisex toilet and bathing rooms," is cited as the source providing
  requirements for such rooms.

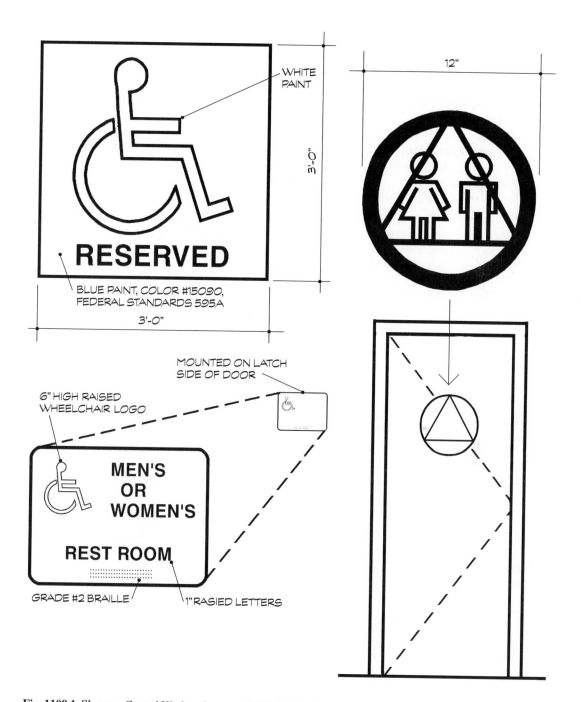

Fig. 1109.1. Signage. Central Kitchen. Lompoc Unified School District. Lompoc, California. Phillips Metsch Sweeney Moore Architects. Santa Barbara, California.

1109 Signage

1109.3 Other signs

- Signage reporting assistive listening system availability to the public is required as follows:
    - Where assistive listening systems are required in assembly.
    - Signage is to be placed at ticket offices or similar locations.
- Tactile signage with all the following characteristics is required as indicated below:
    - Characteristics:
        Signs to have raised letters.
        Signs to have Braille.
        Signs to state "EXIT".
    - Requirement:
        To be located at each exit stairway door.
- Signage indicating the location of an accessible means of egress is required as follows:
    - At the following, where they are not an accessible means of egress:
        Exits serving a required accessible space.
        Elevators serving a required accessible space.

    Note: 1107.2.4, "Assistive listing systems," is cited as the source requiring such systems.

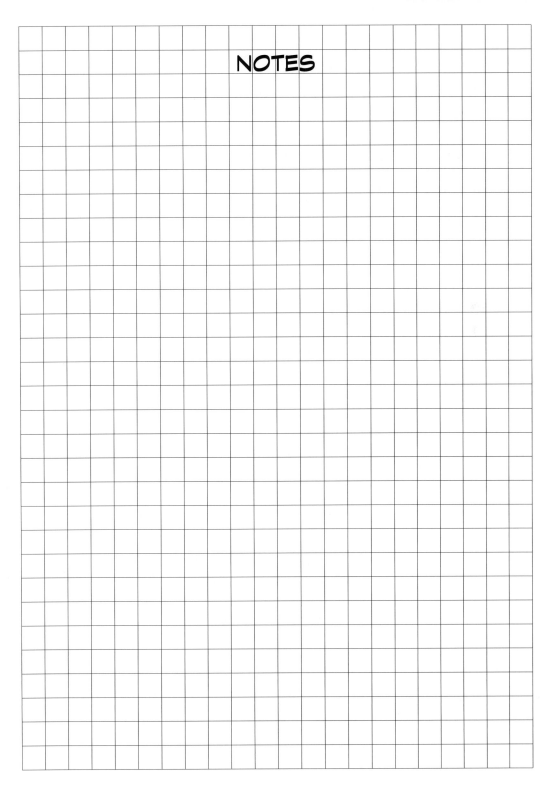

NOTES

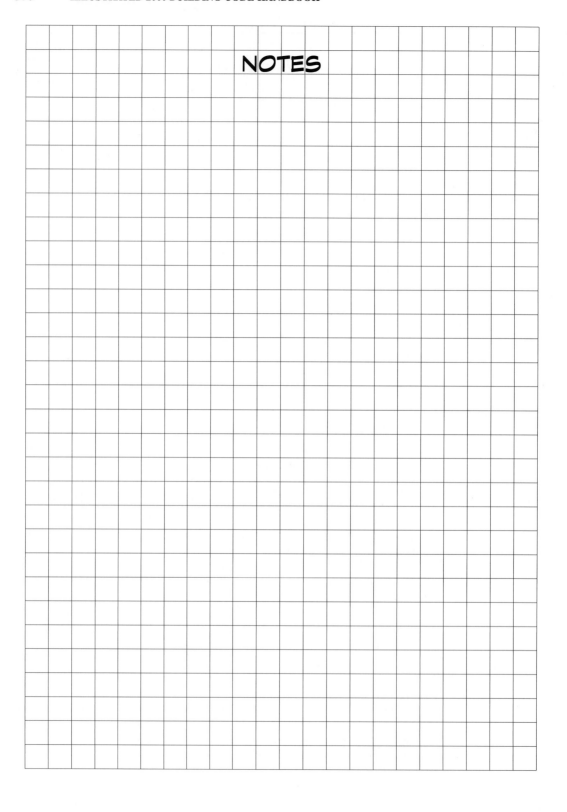

NOTES

12

Interior Environment

Multipurpose Building Addition to Children's Home. Wilkes-Barre, Pennsylvania. *(partial elevation)*
C. Allen Mullins, Architects. Bear Creek, Pennsylvania.

1202 Ventilation

1202.1 General

- One of the following types of ventilation is required for buildings:
  - Natural ventilation as governed by this chapter.
  - Mechanical ventilation.

    Note: "International Mechanical Code" is cited as governing mechanical ventilation.

1202.2 Attic spaces

- Spaces between rafters enclosed as follows must be ventilated as indicated below:
  - Rafter spaces:
    Enclosed by attaching a ceiling directly to the underside of rafters.
  - Requirements:
    Each separate rafter space must be ventilated.
    Air space required for ventilation is $\geq 1"$ as follows:
      Between the insulation and roof sheathing.
    Area of rafter space is measured on the plane of rafter slope.
- Enclosed attics and enclosed rafter spaces must be ventilated as follows:
  - Net clear open area for ventilation must be the following size:
    $\geq \frac{1}{300}$ of the area ventilated:
      Where a vapor retarder is provided as follows:
        Retarder must have a transmission rate ≤ 1 perm.
        Retarder is placed on the warm side of the attic insulation.
    $\geq \frac{1}{150}$ of the area ventilated:
      Where a vapor retarder is not provided as required.
  - $\frac{1}{2}$ the required vents must be located as follows:
    In the upper part of the ventilated space.
    $\geq 3'$ above the eave or cornice vents.
  - $\frac{1}{2}$ the required vents must be at the eave or cornice.

    Note: ASTM E 96, "Standard Test Method for Water Vapor Transmission of Materials."

- Openings ventilation may not permit penetration by the following:
  - Rain.
  - Snow.
- The following may not interfere with ventilation air flow:
  - Blocking.
  - Bridging.

Case study: Fig. 1202.2. Spaces, between rafters enclosed by the attachment of a ceiling to the bottom of the rafters, are ventilated. Metal soffit vents are provided under the eave and blocking is cut to permit the through-flow of air. A 1" air space is provided between the top of the insulation and the bottom of the roof sheathing for air flow as required. Ventilation of the rafter spaces is in compliance with the code.

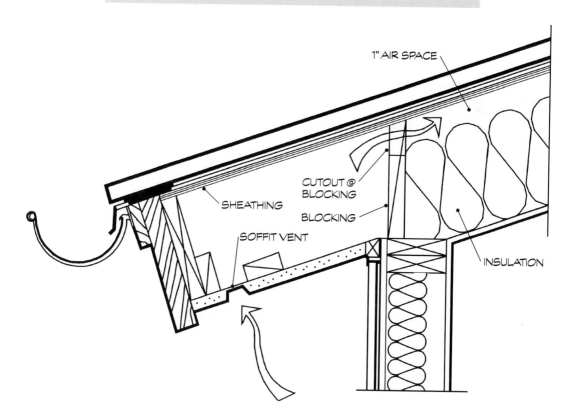

1" AIR SPACE

CUTOUT @ BLOCKING

BLOCKING

SHEATHING

SOFFIT VENT

INSULATION

Fig. 1202.2. Detail at eave. Central Kitchen. Lompoc Unified School District. Lompoc, California. Phillips Metsch Sweeney Moore Architects. Santa Barbara, California.

1202 Ventilation

1202.2.1 Openings into attic

This section addresses attics in buildings for human occupancy.

- Openings into attics from the outside must be covered as follows:
  - Corrosion resistant materials such as the following are required:
    Wire cloth screening.
    Hardware cloth.
    Perforated vinyl.
    Similar material.
  - Coverings must prevent entry of the following and similar creatures:
    Birds.
    Squirrels.
    Rodents.
    Snakes.
  - Openings in the coverings to be $\geq \frac{1}{8}"$ and $\leq \frac{1}{4}"$.
- Combustion air taken from the attic is not governed by this section.

  Note: International Mechanical Code, Chapter 7, is cited governing combustion air taken from the attic.

1202.3 Under-floor ventilation

This section addresses crawl spaces for which conditions require natural ventilation.

- Space between the earth and floor joists, other than the following, must be ventilated as indicated below:
  - Spaces not governed by this section:
    Basements.
    Cellars.
  - Requirements:
    Spaces must be ventilated by openings through the following as applicable:
      Foundation walls.
      Exterior walls.
    Ventilation openings must be located to provide cross-ventilation of the space.

  Note: 1202.3.2, "Exceptions," lists conditions that do not require ventilation or natural ventilation.

1202 Ventilation

1202.3.1 Openings for under-floor ventilation

This section addresses ventilation of crawl spaces where no vapor retarder is used.

- The net clear open area required for ventilating crawl spaces is as follows:
  - $\geq \frac{1}{150}$ of the crawl space area.
- Openings providing ventilation must be covered with one of the following:
  - Materials with openings $\leq \frac{1}{4}$" are as follows:
    Perforated sheet metal ≥ 0.070"thick.
    Expanded sheet metal ≥ 0.047" thick.
    Cast iron grille or grating.
    Extruded load bearing vents.
    Hardware cloth:
      Wire diameter ≥ 0.035".
  - Corrosion resistant wire mesh:
    Openings $\leq \frac{1}{8}$".

Note: 1201.3.2, "Exceptions," addresses ventilation requirements where a vapor retarder is used in the crawl space.

Case study: Fig. 1202.2.1. A corrosion resistant screen is provided at the attic opening to prevent the entry of birds and other creatures. Openings in the screen are between $\frac{1}{8}$" and $\frac{1}{4}$" as required. The sleeve surrounding the passage to the mechanical louvers is lined with sheet metal, and the bottom surface slopes to the exterior for drainage. Protection of the opening into the attic is in compliance with the code.

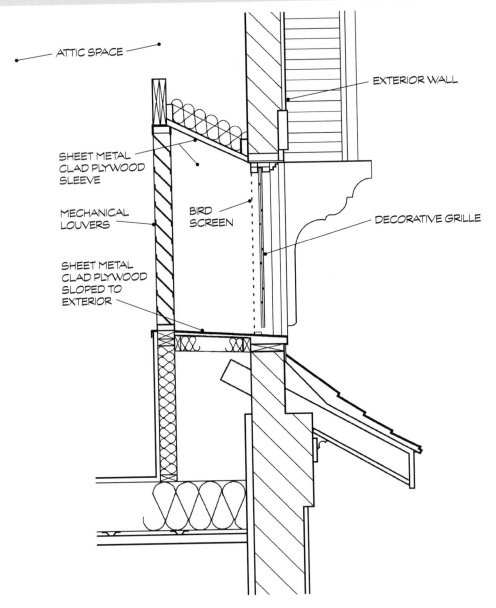

Fig. 1202.2.1. Detail at attic vent. Lake Forest City Hall Renovation and Addition. Lake Forest, Illinois. David Woodhouse Architects. Chicago, Illinois.

1202 Ventilation

1202.3.2 Exceptions

This section addresses conditions that do not require ventilation or natural ventilation or that permit reduced ventilation in crawl spaces.

- Openings providing ventilation are not required to the exterior in the following case:
  - Where the climate permits vent openings to the interior of the building.
- The required net area of ventilation openings is as follows:
  - $\geq \frac{1}{1500}$ of the crawl-space area where the following are provided:
    The ground is covered with an approved vapor retarder.
    Openings must be positioned to provide cross-ventilation of the space:
      Openings with operable louvers are permitted.
- Openings providing ventilation are not required in the following case:
  - Where mechanical ventilation is provided as follows:
    Mechanical ventilation must be continuous.
    1.0 cfm per 50 sf of crawl-space area must be provided.
    The ground must be covered as follows:
      With an approved vapor retarder.
- Openings providing ventilation are not required where both of the following apply:
  - Where the ground in the crawl space is covered as follows:
    With an approved vapor retarder.
  - Where the surrounding walls are insulated.
  - Where the space is conditioned.

    Note: International Energy Conservation Code is cited as governing conditioning of the insulated crawl space.

- Openings providing ventilation in flood hazard areas are governed as follows:
  - They may be designed according to flood resistance principles.

    Note: 1612.3, "Establishment of flood hazard areas," is cited as the source of requirements for establishing such areas.
    ASCE 24, "Flood Resistance Design and Construction Standard," is cited as governing the design of openings in flood hazard areas.

1202.4 Natural ventilation

- Where natural ventilation is provided to occupied space, it must be through one or more of the following openings to the exterior:
  - Windows.
  - Doors.
  - Louvers.
  - Other openings.

1202 Ventilation

1202.4.1 Ventilation area required

- Area of ventilating openings must be as follows:
  - ○ ≥ 4% of the area of the space ventilated.

1202.4.1.1 Adjoining spaces

- Space ventilated through an adjoining space is governed as follows:
  - ○ The area of the opening between spaces must be the larger of the following:
    - ≥ 8% of the area of the space being ventilated through an adjoining space.
    - ≥ 25 sf.
  - ○ The size of the ventilating openings to the exterior are based on the following:
    - The total area of all spaces ventilated.

1202.4.1.2 Openings below grade

- The following openings are governed as indicated below:
  - ○ Openings:
    - Providing natural ventilation.
    - Located all or partly below grade.
  - ○ Requirement:
    - Clear space outside the opening must have the following size:
      - Horizontal dimension ⊥ to the opening:
        - Must be ≥ 1.5 × opening depth:
          - Opening depth is measured as follows:
            - Vertically from average adjacent grade to opening bottom.

1202.4.2.1 Bathrooms

- Spaces with the following fixtures must be mechanically ventilated:
  - ○ Bathtubs.
  - ○ Showers.
  - ○ Spas.
  - ○ Similar bathing fixtures.

    Note: *International Mechanical Code is cited as governing such ventilation.*

1204 Lighting

1204.1 General

- All occupiable space must have lighting by one of the following means:
  - Artificial.
  - Natural:
    Openings providing light must open to one of the following:
    Public way.
    Yard.
    Court.
    Other space as permitted by the code.

    Note: The following are cited as sources of applicable requirements:
    1204.2, "Natural light."
    1204.3, "Artificial light."
    Section 1205, "Yards or Courts."
    1204.2.2, "Exterior openings," describes other space that openings may face.

1204.2 Natural light

- Net glazed area providing natural light must be the following size:
  - $\geq 8\%$ of floor area served.

1204.2.1 Adjoining spaces

- A space may receive required natural light through an adjoining space as follows:
  - $\geq 50\%$ the common wall must be open.
  - The opening in the common wall must be the larger of the following:
    $\geq 10\%$ of the interior space floor area.
    ≥ 25 sf.

1204.2.2 Exterior openings

- Exterior openings providing required natural light must comply with one of the following:
  - Openings must open directly to one of the following:
    Public way.
    Yard or court.
    A roofed porch with all the following characteristics:
    Porch abuts one of the following:
    Public way.
    Yard or court.
    Porch ceiling is $\geq 7'$ high.
    Longer side of porch is $\geq 65\%$ open.
  - The opening is a skylight.

    Note: The following are cited as sources of applicable requirements:
    1204.2, "Natural light."
    Section 1205, "Yards or Courts."

1204 Lighting

1204.3 Artificial light

- Artificial light must provide the following illumination:
  - An average intensity ≥ 10 footcandles is required as follows:
    At a level 2'-6" high across the room.

1205 Yards or Courts

1205.1 General

This section addresses yards and courts next to openings for ventilation or natural light.

- The following must be located on the same property as the building served:
  - Yards.
  - Courts.

1205.2 Yards

- The width of a yard measured ⊥ to the building façade is required indicated below:

Table 1205.2   Minimum Yard Width

Building height	Yard width	Building height	Yard width	Building height	Yard width
1 story	≥ 3'	6 stories	≥ 7'	11 stories	≥ 12'
2 stories	≥ 3'	7 stories	≥ 8'	12 stories	≥ 13'
3 stories	≥ 4'	8 stories	≥ 9'	13 stories	≥ 14'
4 stories	≥ 5'	9 stories	≥ 10'	14 stories	≥ 15'
5 stories	≥ 6'	10 stories	≥ 11'	>14 stories	≥ 15'

1205.3 Courts *(part 1 of 2)*

- Courts with windows on any two opposite sides require widths as listed below:
  - Width is measured between walls with facing windows.
  - Where all walls have facing windows:
    Either dimension is designated as width:
      The other dimension is designated as length:
        Length is governed by Table 1205.3c.

Table 1205.3a   Courts with Windows on Opposite Sides

Building height	Court width	Building height	Court width	Building height	Court width
1 story	≥ 6'	6 stories	≥ 10'	11 stories	≥ 15'
2 stories	≥ 6'	7 stories	≥ 11'	12 stories	≥ 16'
3 stories	≥ 7'	8 stories	≥ 12'	13 stories	≥ 17'
4 stories	≥ 8'	9 stories	≥ 13'	14 stories	≥ 18'
5 stories	≥ 9'	10 stories	≥ 14'	>14 stories	≥ 18'

- Courts without windows on opposite sides require widths as listed below:
  - Where courts are open on one end to a public way or yard:
    Width is measured between facing walls.
  - Where courts are not open on one side to a public way or yard:
    Either dimension is designated as width:
      The other dimension is designated as length:
        Length is governed by Table 1205.3c.

1205 Yards or Courts

1205.3 Courts *(part 2 of 2)*

Table 1205.3b   Courts without Windows on Opposite Sides

Building height	Court width	Building height	Court width	Building height	Court width
1 story	≥ 3'	6 stories	≥ 7'	11 stories	≥ 12'
2 stories	≥ 3'	7 stories	≥ 8'	12 stories	≥ 13'
3 stories	≥ 4'	8 stories	≥ 9'	13 stories	≥ 14'
4 stories	≥ 5'	9 stories	≥ 10'	14 stories	≥ 15'
5 stories	≥ 6'	10 stories	≥ 11	>14 stories	≥ 15'

- Courts not open on one end to a public way or yard require lengths as listed below:
  - Length is ⊥ to the required widths governed by Table 1205.3a and 1205.3b.

Table 1205.3c   Minimum Length of Courts

Building height	Court length	Building height	Court length	Building height	Court length
1 story	≥ 10'	6 stories	≥ 18'	11 stories	≥ 28'
2 stories	≥ 10'	7 stories	≥ 20'	12 stories	≥ 30'
3 stories	≥ 12'	8 stories	≥ 22'	13 stories	≥ 32'
4 stories	≥ 14'	9 stories	≥ 24'	14 stories	≥ 34'
5 stories	≥ 16'	10 stories	≥ 26'	>14 stories	≥ 34'

1205.3.1 Court access

- Access is required to the bottom of a court for cleaning.

1205.3.2 Air intake

- Courts require a way to bring in air at the bottom as follows:
  - Air intake is required for the following courts:
    Courts which do not abut a yard or public way.
    Courts > 2 stories high.
  - Air intake requires the following characteristics:
    Must be horizontal.
    Must be located at the bottom of the court.
    Must be ≥ 10 sf in area.
    Must lead to the exterior.

1205.3.3 Court drainage

- The following is required for drainage of a court:
  - Court must be graded for adequate drainage.
  - Court must be drained to one of the following:
    A public sewer.
    Other approved disposal system.

  Note: International Plumbing Code is cited as the source governing drainage disposal systems as required above.

Case study: Fig. 1205.3. All walls facing the courtyard of this 2-story building have windows. One corner of the courtyard is open to the public way on the ground level only. The minimum width of the courtyard is 6'. The minimum length of the courtyard between walls is 10'. The courtyard is 27'-9" wide and 33' long, thus, meeting size minimums. The courtyard is graded and drained as required by the code. The courtyard is in compliance with code requirements.

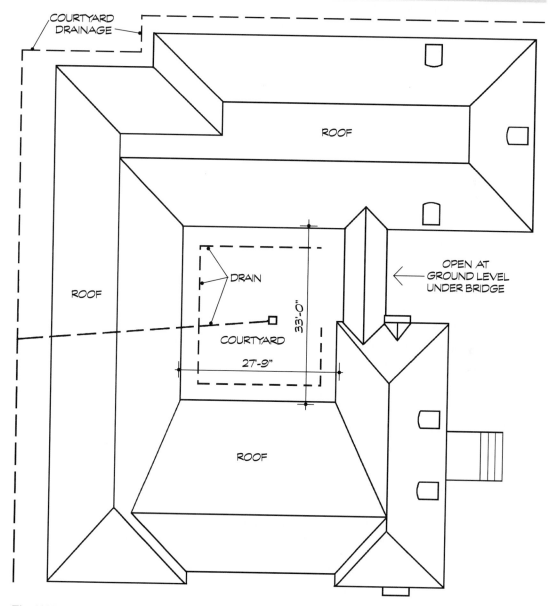

Fig. 1205.3. Courtyard plan. Multipurpose Building Addition to Children's Home. Wilkes-Barre, Pennsylvania. C. Allen Mullins, Architect. Bear Creek, Pennsylvania.

1206 Sound Transmission

1206.1 Scope

- This section provides sound transmission requirements indicated below as applicable to elements of dwelling units as follows:
  - Elements:
    Common interior walls between adjacent units.
    Interior walls between units and adjacent public areas:
    Halls.
    Corridors.
    Stairs.
    Service areas.
    Floor/ceiling assemblies between adjacent units.
    Floor/ceiling assemblies between units and adjacent public areas:
    Halls.
    Corridors.
    Stairs.
    Service areas.

1206.2 Air-borne sound

- Dwelling unit entrance doors are governed for air-borne sound as follows:
  - Tight fit to the frame and sill are required.
  - A required Sound Transmission Class (STC) rating is not specified.
- One of the following STC ratings is required for walls and floors governed by this section:
  - STC $\geq$ 50 is required where not verified by field test.
  - STC $\geq$ 45 is required where verified by field test.

  Note: ASTM E 90, "Standard Test Method for Laboratory Measurement of Airborne Sound Transmission Loss of Building Partitions and Elements," is cited as governing the method for determining STC ratings.
  1206.1, "Scope," lists walls and floors governed by this section.

1206.3 Structure-borne sound

- One of the following Impact Insulation Class (IIC) ratings is required for floor/ceiling assembles governed by this section:
  - IIC $\geq$ 50 is required where not verified by field test.
  - IIC $\geq$ 45 is required where verified by field test.

  Note: ASTM E 492, "Standard Test Method for Laboratory Measurement of Impact Sound Transmission Through Floor-Ceiling Assemblies Using the Tapping Machine," is cited as governing the method for determining IIC ratings.
  1206.1, "Scope," lists floor/ceiling assemblies governed by this section.

1207 Interior Space Dimensions

1207.1 Minimum room widths

- Habitable spaces other than kitchens require the following size:
  - ≥ 7' for any room dimension in plan.
- Kitchens require ≥ 3' clear space as follows:
  - Between counter fronts and any of the following:
      Appliances.
      Other counter fronts.
      Walls.

1207.2 Minimum ceiling heights

- Mezzanines are not governed by this section.

    Note: 505.1, "General," is cited as governing mezzanines.

- In 1- and 2-family dwellings, the following applies:
  - Ceiling height in basements is governed as follows:
      ≥ 6'-4" is required under the following:
        Beams.
        Girders.
        Ducts.
        Similar obstructions.
      Otherwise, ≥ 6'-8" is the required ceiling height.
  - On other floors, beams and girders may project below the required the ceiling height as follows:
      Where spaced ≥ 4' on center.
      Where projecting ≤ 6" below required ceiling height.
- In all occupancies, the following applies:
  - ≥ 7'-0" is the required ceiling height in the following spaces:
      Bathrooms.
      Toilet rooms.
      Kitchens.
      Storage rooms.
      Laundry rooms.
  - ≥ 7'-6" is the required ceiling height for other spaces as follows:
      Habitable space.
      Occupiable space.
      Corridors,
- The following applies to sloped ceilings:
  - The required ceiling height must be provided for ≥ ½ the area.
  - Floor area counted in minimum area requirements must have the following height:
      Ceiling height ≥ 5'.

Case study: Fig. 1207.1. The kitchen complies with the requirement that at least 3' of space be provided between counters and other objects and walls as indicated in the plan.

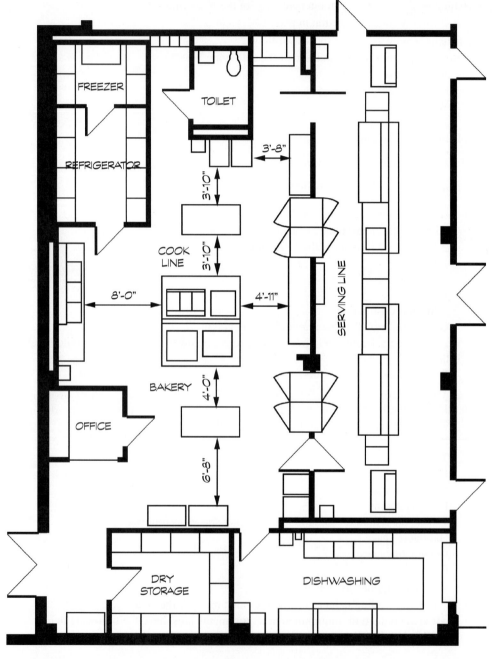

Fig. 1207.1. Partial floor plan at kitchen. New Jasper Pre-K–2nd Grade School. Jasper, Texas. PBK Architects, Inc. Houston, Texas.

1207 Interior Space Dimensions

1207.2.1 Furred ceiling

- Furred ceilings are governed as follows:
  - A furred ceiling must have the required ceiling height as follows:
    In ²/₃ the room area.
  - Otherwise, a furred ceiling may not have a height < 7'.

1207.3 Room area

This section addresses rooms in dwelling units other than kitchens.

- A net floor area ≥ 150 sf is required in ≥ 1 room.
- Other habitable rooms require a net floor area ≥ 70 sf.

1207.4 Efficiency dwelling units

- A living room ≥ 220 sf is required for units with ≤ 2 occupants:
  - 100 sf is added to this requirement for each additional occupant.
- A separate closet is required.
- The following appliances and clearances are required:

Appliance	Clearance in front of appliance
Cooking	≥ 2'-6"
Refrigerator	≥ 2'-6"

- A separate bathroom is required with the following:
  - Water closet.
  - Lavatory.
  - Bathtub or shower.
- Units must conform to the requirements of the code as follows:
  - For light.
  - For ventilation.
  - All other requirements as applicable.

1208 Access to Unoccupied Spaces

1208.1 Crawl spaces

- Crawl spaces required ≥ 1 access opening as follows:
  - Dimensions must be as follows:
    Width ≥ 1'-6".
    Length ≥ 2'.

1208.2 Attic spaces

- Attic space with a clear height ≥ 2'-6" has the following access requirements:
  - Dimensions of an access opening must be as follows:
    Width ≥ 1'-8".
    Length ≥ 2'-6".
  - Headroom ≥ 2'-6" is required at the access opening.

1208.3 Mechanical appliances

- Access to mechanical appliances in the following locations is not governed by this code:
  - In crawl spaces.
  - In attic spaces.
  - On roofs.
  - On elevated structures.

  Note: International Mechanical Code is cited as governing such access.

Case study: Fig. 1208.2. The clear height of the attic is > 2'-6"; thus, it must meet minimum access requirements. The headroom at the attic access is 4'-3" which is > than the 2'-6" minimum required. The access opening is 3' × 3' which complies with the minimum size requirements of 1'-8" × 2'-6". Access to the attic is in compliance with code requirements.

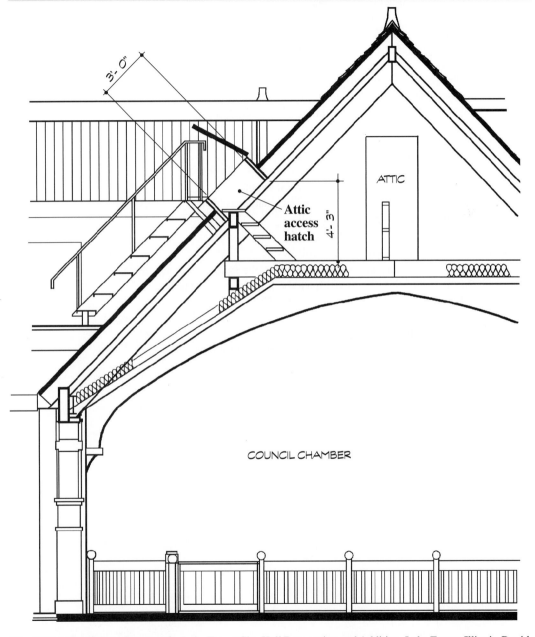

Fig. 1208.2. Partial section at attic. Lake Forest City Hall Renovation and Addition. Lake Forest, Illinois. David Woodhouse Architects. Chicago, Illinois.

1209 Surrounding Materials

1209.1 Floors

- The following applies to other than dwelling units:
  - ○ Floors of the following rooms are governed as indicated below:
    Rooms:
      Toilets.
      Bathing rooms.
    Floors:
      Smooth surface required.
      Hard nonabsorbent surface required.
      Floor surface material must extend up walls $\geq 6"$.

1209.2 Walls

- Requirements indicated below do not apply to the following:
  - ○ Toilet rooms in dwelling units and guest rooms.
  - ○ Toilet rooms with both of the following characteristics:
    Rooms not accessible to the public.
    Rooms with < 2 water closets.
- Other toilet rooms are governed as follows:
  - ○ Walls $\leq 2'$ of urinals and water closets have the following requirements:
    Surface to a height $\geq 4'$ must have the following characteristics:
      Smooth.
      Hard.
      Nonabsorbent.
    Materials other than structure are governed as follows:
      Must not be affected by moisture.
  - ○ Accessories as follows must be installed as indicated below:
    Accessories:
      Grab bars.
      Towel bars.
      Paper dispensers.
      Soap dishes.
      Similar accessories.
    Requirement:
      Installed and sealed to protect structure from moisture.

Case study: Fig. 1209.2. The wall of the toilet room within 2' of the water closet is covered with tile to a height of 7'. The floor is tile, and tile is provided as a base at the wall. These surfaces meet the minimum requirement wherein a smooth, hard, and non-absorbent material must reach a height ≥ 4' on the wall, cover the floor, and reach ≥ 6" up the wall from the floor. As required, accessories such as grab bars and toilet paper holder are sealed where they connect to the wall to prohibit the penetration of moisture. This toilet room complies with all code requirements.

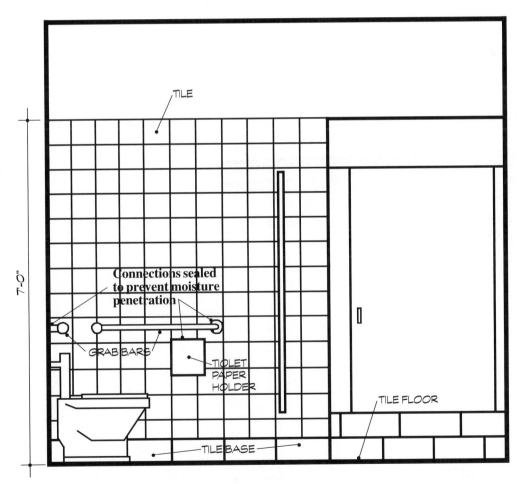

Fig. 1209.2. Toilet room elevation. AmberGlen Business Center. Hillsboro, Oregon. Ankrom Moisan Associated Architects. Portland, Oregon.

1209 Surrounding Materials

1209.3 Showers

- Finish materials in the following shower areas are governed as indicated below:
  - Shower areas:
    Shower stalls.
    Showers in bathtubs.
  - A surface as follows is required to a height ≥ 5'-10" above the drain inlet:
    Smooth.
    Hard.
    Nonabsorbent.

1209.4 Waterproof joints

- The joint between the following components must be waterproof:
  - A built-in bathtub with a shower.
  - The adjacent wall.

1209.5 Toilet rooms

- Toilet rooms may not open directly to the following space:
  - A space where food for service to the public is prepared.

Case study: Fig. 1209.5. Toilet rooms are prohibited from opening into a space where food is prepared for the public. The staff toilet room for this kitchen opens into an alcove, thus, complying with this code restriction.

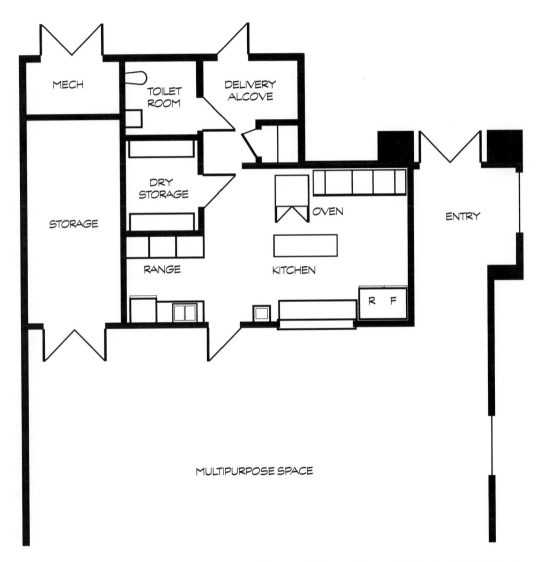

Fig. 1209.5. Partial floor plan. Creston Elementary Multipurpose Building. Creston, California. Phillips Metsch Sweeney Moore Architects. Santa Barbara, California.

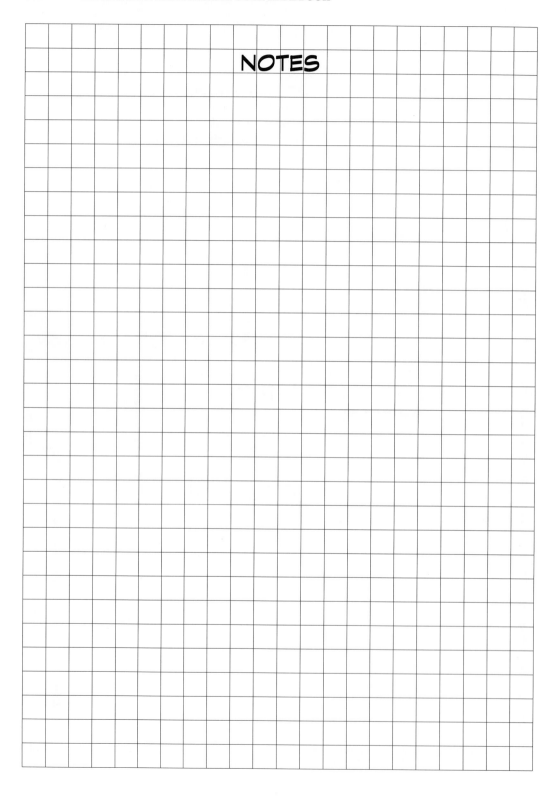

NOTES

13

Energy Efficiency

Alterations to 209 Main Street. Annapolis, Maryland.
Alt Breeding Schwarz Architects, LLC. Annapolis, Maryland.

1301 General

1301.1.1

- For purposes of energy efficiency, buildings must comply with the following code:
  - *International Energy Conservation Code.*

NOTES

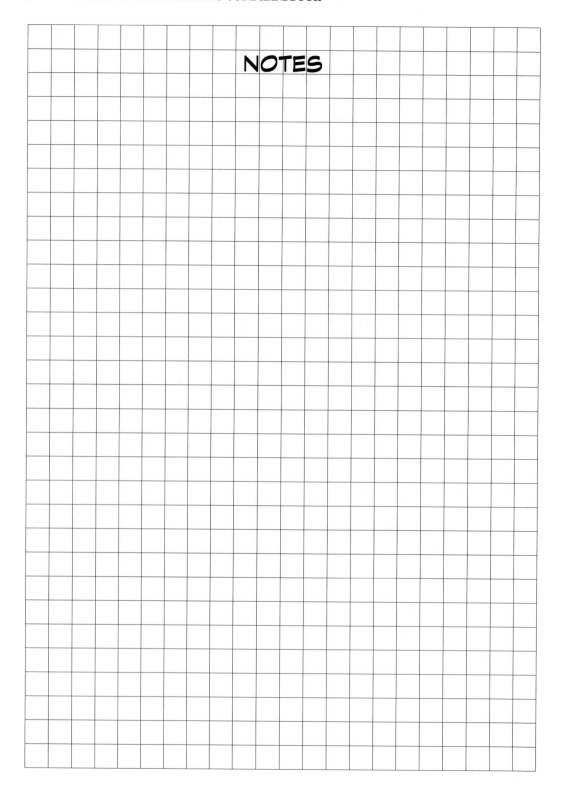

NOTES

14

Exterior Walls

New Warehouse Addition. Los Angeles, California. *(partial elevation)*
Stephen Wen + Associates, Architects, Inc. Pasadena, California.

1403 Performance Requirements

1403.1 General

- This section applies to the following:
  - Exterior walls.
  - Exterior wall coverings.
  - Components of exterior walls.

1403.2 Weather protection *(part 1 of 2)*

This section addresses detailing of the exterior wall.

- A weather-resistant exterior wall envelope is not required on the following:
  - Concrete walls.
  - Masonry walls.

   Note: The following are cited as governing the walls indicated above:
   Chapter 19, "Concrete."
   Chapter 21, "Masonry."

- Otherwise, the following is required for exterior walls:
  - A weather-resistant exterior wall envelope including the following:
    Flashing.

   Note: 1405.3, "Flashing," is cited as governing required flashing.

- The following detailing may be omitted in lieu of testing the exterior wall envelope as indicated below:
  - Details:
    The following details as specified in this chapter may be omitted:
    Drainage.
    Weather protection.
    Flashing.
  - Testing:
    Test must demonstrate the following:
    Ability of alternative detailing to resist wind-driven rain.

   Note: The following are cited as governing the detailing that may be omitted in lieu of testing:
   1405.2, "Weather protection," specifies acceptable exterior surface materials.
   1405.3, "Flashing."
   ASTM E 331, "Standard Test Method for Water Penetration of Exterior Windows, Curtain Walls, and Doors by Uniform Static Air Pressure Difference," is cited as governing the required testing.

1403 Performance Requirements

1403.2 Weather protection *(part 2 of 2)*

- Where water penetration would compromise building performance:
  - The following detailing must be provided to perform as indicated below:
    Detailing:
    A water-resistant barrier behind the exterior veneer.
    A method for drainage.
    Flashing.
    Performance:
    Must prevent collection of water within the assembly.

    Note: 1404.2, "Water-resistive barrier," is cited as governing such components.

- The wall must be protected against condensation.

    Note: International Energy Conservation Code is cited providing requirements applicable to condensation.

1403.3 Vapor retarder

- A vapor retarder as specified in this section is not required in an exterior wall in the following cases:
  - Where other approved methods are provided to prevent the following:
    Condensation.
    Moisture leakage.
  - In concrete walls.
  - In masonry walls.

    Note: The following are cited as governing concrete and masonry walls in lieu of this section:
    Chapter 19, "Concrete."
    Chapter 21, "Masonry."

- Otherwise, an interior vapor retarder must be provided in exterior walls as follows:
  - Must be approved.
  - Must not be subject to corrosion.

    Note: ASTM E 96, "Standard Test Method for Water Vapor Transmission of Materials," is cited as governing vapor barriers.

1403 Performance Requirements

1403.6 Flood resistance

- The following applies to buildings in flood hazard areas:
  - Exterior walls below design flood elevation are governed as follows:
    They must resist water damage.
    Wood must be one of the following:
    Pressure treated with preservative.
    Decay-resistant heartwood of one of the following:
    Redwood.
    Black locust.
    Cedar.

  Note: The following are cited as governing pressure-treated wood as required above:
  AWPA C1, "All Timber Products-Preservative Treatment by Pressure Processes."
  AWPA C2, "Lumber, Timber, Bridge Ties and Mine Ties-Preservative Treatment by Pressure Processes."
  AWPA C3, "Piles-Preservative Treatment by Pressure Processes."
  AWPA C4, "Poles- Preservative Treatment by Pressure Processes."
  AWPA C9, "Plywood-Preservative Treatment by Pressure Processes."
  AWPA C15, "Wood for Commercial-Residential Construction Preservative Treatment by Pressure Processes."
  AWPA C18, "Standard for Pressure Treated Material in Marine Construction."
  AWPA C22, "Lumber and Plywood for Permanent Wood Foundations-Preservative Treatment by Pressure Processes."
  AWPA C24, "Sawn Timber Piles Used for Residential and Commercial Building."
  AWPA C28, "Standard for Preservative Treatment of Structural Glued Laminated Members and Lamination before Gluing of Southern Pine, Coastal Doubles-Fir, Hemfir and Western Hemlock by Pressure Processes."
  AWPA P1, "Standard for Coal Tar Creosote for Land and Fresh Water and Marine (Costal Water) Use."
  AWPA P2, "Standard for Creosote Solutions."

1405 Installation of Wall Coverings

1405.2 Weather protection

- Exterior walls must provide the following for a building:
  - Protection from the weather.
- The following materials are acceptable as weather coverings on exterior walls:
  - Materials having the nominal thickness in details provided with this subsection.

  Note: IBC Table 1405.2, "Minimum Thickness of Weather Coverings," is cited as the source of acceptable materials as required above.

1405.3 Flashing

- Flashing is required to prevent moisture penetration of an exterior wall at the following locations:
  - At exterior windows as follows:
      At the top and sides.
  - At exterior doors as follows:
      At the top and sides.
  - At the intersection of the following components with the elements indicated below:
      Components:
        Masonry chimneys.
        Other masonry construction.
      Elements:
        Frame walls.
        Stucco walls.
  - Under stucco copings as follows:
      On both sides.
      With projecting flanges.
  - At the following components of the materials indicated and at the locations listed below:
      Components:
        Copings and sills.
      Materials:
        Masonry.
        Wood.
        Metal.
      Locations:
        At edges and joints.
        At the ends.
  - Above projecting wood trim as follows:
      Flashing to be continuous.
  - At the intersection of exterior walls with the following:
      Porches and decks.
  - At the intersection of walls and roofs as follows:
      Using the step-flashing format.
  - At built-in gutters.

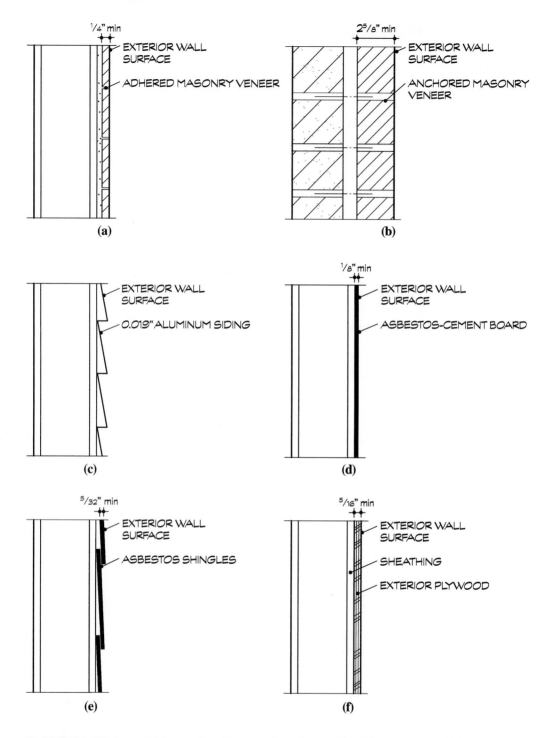

Fig. 1405.2A. Minimum thickness of weather coverings. Acceptable minimum nominal thickness of various types of cladding are shown in the wall sections.

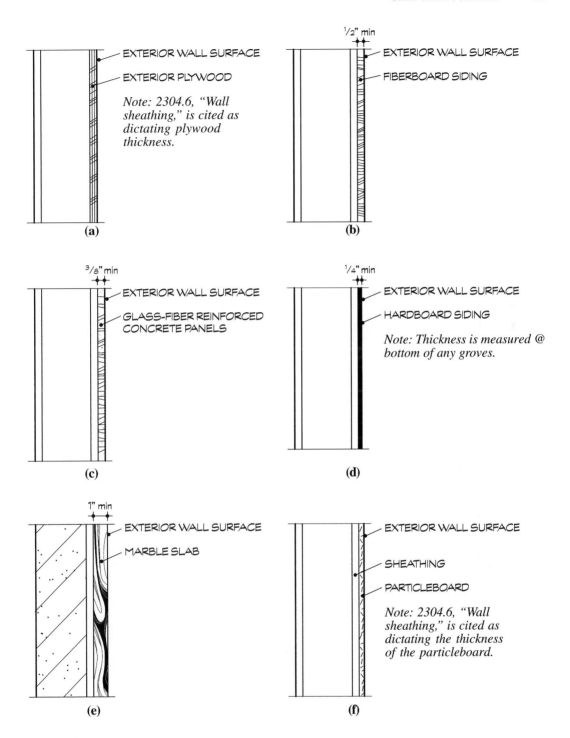

Fig. 1405.2B. Minimum thickness of weather coverings. Acceptable minimum nominal thickness of various types of cladding are shown in the wall sections.

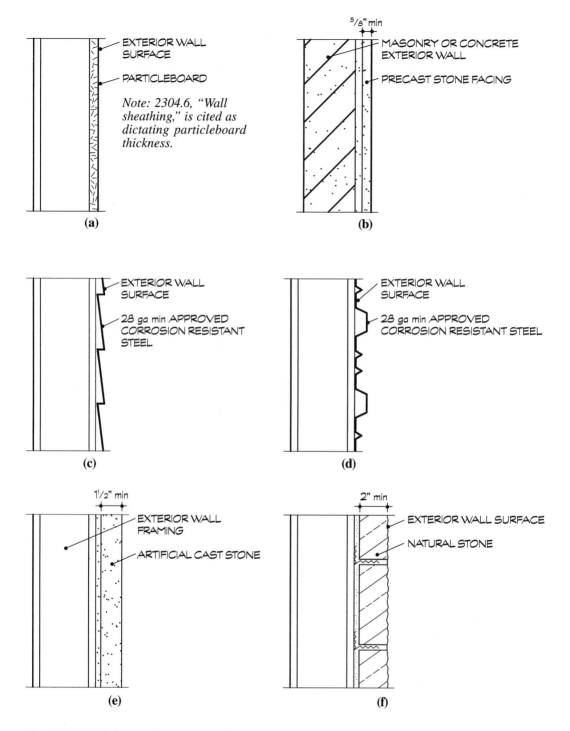

Fig. 1405.2C. Minimum thickness of weather coverings. Acceptable minimum nominal thickness of various types of cladding are shown in the wall sections.

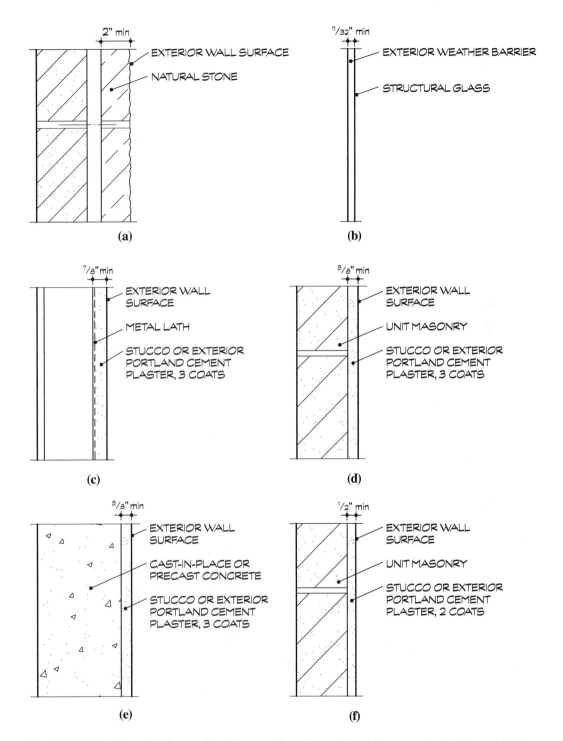

Fig. 1405.2D. Minimum thickness of weather coverings. Acceptable minimum nominal thickness of various types of cladding are shown in the wall sections.

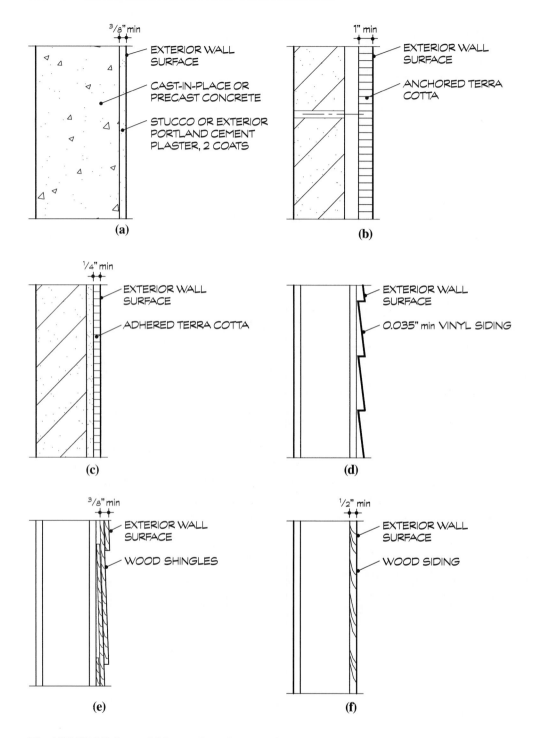

Fig. 1405.2E. Minimum thickness of weather coverings. Acceptable minimum nominal thickness of various types of cladding are shown in the wall sections.

1405 Installation of Wall Coverings

> **Case study: Fig. 1405.3.** The intersection of the entry canopy roof and the building wall is required to have flashing in the step-configuration. Such flashing is provided; thus, the detailing is in compliance with the code.

Fig. 1405.3. Partial elevation at east entry. Hot Springs Police Department New Headquarters. Hot Springs National Park, Arkansas. Cromwell Architects Engineers. Little Rock, Arkansas.

1405.3.1 Exterior wall pockets

- Detailing at exterior walls that permits moisture to collect is governed as follows:
  - Such is not permitted without the following protection:
    Devices to prevent water damage as follows:
    Caps.
    Drips.
    Other approved protection.

1405 Installation of Wall Coverings

1405.3.2 Masonry

- The following detailing is required in anchored masonry veneers at the locations indicated:
  - Detailing:
    Flashing.
    Weep holes.
  - Locations:
    Above grade and in the first course of masonry above the following:
    Foundation wall.
    Slab.
    Points of masonry support such as the following:
    Structural floors.
    Shelf angles.
    Lintels.

    Note: 1405.5, "Anchored masonry veneer," is cited as a source of requirements.

1405.4 Wood veneers

This section addresses exterior wood veneers in construction other than Type V.

- The following materials are required for such veneers:
  - ≥ 1" wood.
  - $\geq \frac{7}{16}$" exterior hardboard siding.
  - $\geq \frac{3}{8}$" exterior wood structural panels.
  - $\geq \frac{3}{8}$" exterior particleboard.
- Such wood veneers must comply with all of the following:
  - The height of the veneer measured from grade is limited as follows:
    Fire-retardant-treated wood must be ≤ 4 stories.
    Other wood must be ≤ 3 stories.
  - The veneer must be attached as follows to a backing as indicated below:
    Attachment:
    To a noncombustible backing.
    To furring on a noncombustible backing.
    Backing:
    Must have the fire-resistance rating as required elsewhere in the code.
  - Open or spaced veneers without concealed spaces are governed as follows:
    Veneer not projecting $> 2'$ from the building wall.

1405 Installation of Wall Coverings

1405.5.1 Support

- The exterior masonry veneers are allowed to be supported on wood construction as follows:
  - Where the veneer weighs ≤ 40 lbs/sf.
  - Where the detailing complies with this section.
- Detailing where wood supports a masonry veneer must comply with the following:
  - A joint permitting vertical differential movement is required as follows:
    Between the following veneers:
      That supported by wood.
      That supported by the foundation.
  - Devices on which the veneer bears must be attached to wood studs as follows:
    By lag screws.
  - Horizontal span members supporting the veneer must be designed as follows:
    To limit deflection to $1/600$ of the span.
  - Wood construction supporting a veneer must be designed for the following loading:
    Weight of the veneer.
    Other loads as applicable.

1405.6 Stone veneer *(part 1 of 2)*

- Stone veneer ≤ 10" thick must be anchored directly to the following construction:
  - Concrete or masonry backing:
    Anchor ties are required as follows:
      One of the following is required:
        Corrosion-resistant wire:
          ≥ 0.1055" diameter (12 gage).
        Approved equal.
      Anchor ties to be formed in loops:
        Legs ≥ 6" bent at right angles for embedding in the backing wall.
        Loop extends beyond the face of the backing wall.
        Loops are spaced ≤ 12" on center in both directions.
    Masonry ties are required as follows:
      One of the following is required:
        Corrosion-resistant wire:
          ≥ 0.1055" diameter (12 gage).
        Approved equal.
      Masonry ties to be formed into loops:
        Threaded through anchor tie loops as follows:
          ≥ 1 masonry tie is required for every ≤ 2 sf of stone.
        Legs ≥ 15" bent to lie in joint of stone veneer:
          Last 2" of each leg must be bent at a right angle.
    ≥ 1" cement grout must be placed as follows:
      Between stone and backing.

1405 Installation of Wall Coverings

1405.6 Stone veneer *(part 2 of 2)*

- Stone veneer ≤ 10" thick must be anchored directly to the following construction:
  - Stud backing:
    Wood studs to be spaced ≤ 16" on center.
    2 layers of waterproof paper backing are applied to the studs.
    Wire mesh is attached to the studs over the paper backing as follows:
    Mesh to be corrosion-resistant wire:
    Wire to be ≥ 0.0625" diameter (16 gage).
    Mesh to be 2" × 2".
    Mesh is attached to studs as follows:
    With 2" steel wire furring nails:
    Nails at 4" on center.
    Nails to penetrate studs ≥ $1^1/_8$".
    Mesh is attached to top and bottom plates as follows:
    With 8d common nails or equivalent wire ties:
    Nails at 8" on center.
    Masonry ties are required as follows:
    One of the following is required:
    Corrosion-resistant wire:
    ≥ 0.1055" diameter (12 gage).
    Approved equal.
    Masonry ties to be formed into loops:
    Threaded through the wire mesh as follows:
    ≥ 1 masonry tie is required for every ≤ 2 sf of stone.
    Legs ≥ 15" bent to lie in joint of stone veneer:
    Last 2" of each leg must be bent at a right angle.
    ≥ 1" cement grout must be placed as follows:
    Between stone and backing.

1405.7 Slab-type veneer *(part 1 of 2)*

- Slab-shaped masonry veneer units must be anchored directly to the following construction:
  - Masonry.
  - Concrete.
  - Stud.
- Slab-shaped masonry veneer units must comply with the following size limits:
  - Thickness must be ≤ 2".
  - Face area must be ≤ 20 sf.

1405 Installation of Wall Coverings

1405.7 Slab-type veneer *(part 2 of 2)*

- The requirements indicated below apply to the following veneer units:
  - ○ Units:
    - Marble.
    - Travertine.
    - Granite.
    - Other slab-shaped stone.
  - ○ Requirements:
    - Corrosion-resistant dowels are required to secure ties to slabs.
    - ≥ 4 dowels and ties for each veneer unit are required.
    - Dowels are to be located as follows:
      - In holes drilled in the middle $^1/_3$ of the edge thickness:
        - Holes to be spaced around the perimeter of the unit as follows:
          - At $\leq 2'$ on center.
        - Holes to be one of the following:
          - Tight-fitting around dowel.
          - With a diameter $\leq {}^1/_{16}"$ > dowel diameter as follows:
            - Hole is countersunk as follows:
              - With a diameter $2 \times$ that of the dowel.
              - To a depth $2 \times$ that of the dowel diameter.
            - Hole is grouted with cement mortar around dowel.
    - Ties are to be as follows:
      - Corrosion-resistant metal.
      - Able to resist tensile or compressive forces as follows:
        - $\geq 2 \times$ the weight of the veneer unit attached.
      - In one of the following shapes:
        - Sheet metal $\geq 0.0336"$ (22 gage) $\times 1"$ in cross section.
        - Wire $\geq 0.1483"$ diameter (9 gage).

1405.8 Terra cotta *(part 1 of 2)*

This section addresses terra cotta or ceramic units anchored directly to backing walls.

- Veneer units specified in this section must be anchored directly to the following construction:
  - ○ Masonry.
  - ○ Concrete.
  - ○ Stud.
- Veneer units must have the following physical properties:
  - ○ Ribbed profile as follows:
    - Dovetail ribs at 8"($\pm$) on center.
  - ○ $\geq 1^5/_8"$ thick including the ribs.

1405 Installation of Wall Coverings

1405.8 Terra cotta *(part 2 of 2)*

- Veneer units are tied to the backing as follows:
  - ○ Ties are corrosion-resistant wire as follows:
      Diameter ≥ 0.162" (8 gage).
  - ○ Ties are installed into the top of each unit:
      In horizontal bed joints as follows:
          ≥ 12" and ≤ 18" on center.
  - ○ Ties are connected to ¼" diameter steel rods as follows:
      Rods are vertical.
      Rods pass through loops of anchors secured in the backing wall.
  - ○ Ties must have the following strength:
      To support the full weight of the veneer in tension.
- Veneer units must be installed as follows:
  - ○ With ≥ 2" space behind the units as follows:
      Between the face of the ribs and the backing wall.
  - ○ Space must be grouted solid with the following:
      Portland cement grout.
      Pea gravel.
  - ○ Just prior to setting, the following must be thoroughly wetted with clean water:
      Veneer units.
      Backing wall.
  - ○ The following must be visibly damp when the veneer units are set:
      Veneer units.
      Backing wall.

1405.9.1.1 Interior masonry veneers

- Interior masonry veneers fastened in place by being adhered to the backing wall are governed as follows:
  - ○ Veneer weight is limited to ≤ 20 lbs/sf.
  - ○ Where supported by wood construction, the following applies:
      Supporting members which have a span must be designed as follows:
          Deflection is limited to ≤ $1/600$ of the span.

  Note: 1405.9, "Adhered masonry veneer," is cited as the source of requirements for the installation of such components.

1405 Installation of Wall Coverings

1405.10 Metal veneers

- Metal veneers must be one of the following:
  - Of approved corrosion-resistant materials.
  - Be protected with porcelain enamel as follows:
    On the front.
    On the back.
  - Be processed to provided corrosion resistance.
- Metal veneers must be as follows:
  - ≥ 0.0149" thick (28 gage) sheet steel.
  - Mounted on one of the following:
    Wood furring strips.
    Metal furring strips.
    Approved sheathing on wood construction.

1405.10.1 Attachment

- Exterior metal veneers must be attached to the following construction as indicated below:
  - Construction:
    Masonry.
    Framing.
  - Attachment:
    One of the following attachment methods is required:
      Corrosion-resistant fastenings.
      Metal ties.
      Other approved methods.
    Spacing of attachments must be ≤ 2' as follows:
      Vertically.
      Horizontally.
    Where units are > 4 sf:
      ≥ 4 attachments per unit are required.
    Attachment devices must have the following cross-sectional area:
      ≥ that provided by W 1.7 wire (0.017 sq in) .
    Attachments and their supports must have strength as per the larger of the following:
      They must be able to resist applicable wind loads.
      They must be able to resist a horizontal load ≥ 20 lbs/sf.

  Note: Section 1609, "Wind Loads," is cited as the source of applicable wind loading for the metal veneer.

1405 Installation of Wall Coverings

1405.10.2 Weather protection

- Metal supports for exterior metal veneer must be protected by one of the following:
  - Painting.
  - Galvanizing.
  - Other equivalent method.
- The following wood supports must be protected from moisture as indicated below:
  - Supports:
    Studs.
    Furring strips.
    Other wood supports.
  - Moisture protection:
    One of the following is required:
    Supports must be approved pressure-treated wood.
    Must be protected from moisture contact.
    The following details must be protected as indicated below:
    Details:
    Joints exposed to the weather.
    Edges exposed to the weather.
    Protection:
    Must be caulked by one of the following to prevent moisture penetration:
    With a durable waterproofing material.
    Other approved material.

  Note: 1403.2, "Weather protection," is cited as the source of methods to protect wood supports from moisture contact.

1405.11 Glass veneer

- The area limitations of exterior glass veneer panels as follows is indicated below:
  - Structural glass veneer as follows:
    Single sections of thin glass:

Height above grade	Glass area
≤ 15'	≤ 10 sf
> 15'	≤ 6 sf

1405.11.1 Length and height

- Thin exterior structural glass veneer dimensions are governed as follows:
  - All dimensions are limited to ≤ 4'.

1405.11.2 Thickness

- Thin exterior structural glass veneer thickness is governed as follows:
  - Thickness must be ≥ 0.344".

1405 Installation of Wall Coverings

1405.11.3 Application

- Thin exterior structural glass veneer must be set in the following conditions:
  - Backing must be dry.
  - An approved bond coat applied to the backing as follows:
    Bond coat must be evenly distributed.
    Backing surface must be completely sealed.
  - Glass panels must be installed as follows:
    With an approved mastic cement.
    So that ≥ 50% of each glass panel is bonded to the backing as follows:
    By mastic ≥ ¼" and ≤ ⅝" thick.
    Compatibility of mastic with bond coat must be verified.
    Mastic must adhere securely to backing.

1405.11.4 Installation at sidewalk level

- Glass veneer at sidewalk level must be detailed as follows:
  - Glass panels must set in a metal molding as follows:
    Must be approved.
    Space between molding and sidewalk must be treated as follows:
    Caulked for watertightness.
  - Glass panels must be set ≥ ¼" above the following:
    The highest point of the sidewalk.

1405.11.4.1 Installation above sidewalk level

- This section applies to thin exterior structural glass veneer as follows:
  - Where installed ≥ higher than one of the following levels:
    The level of the top of a bulkhead facing.
    A level > 36" above the sidewalk.
- In such cases the following are required in addition to mastic behind the glass:
  - Shelf angles:
    With all of the following characteristics:
    Approved.
    Nonferrous metal.
    ≥ 0.0478" thick.
    ≥ 2" long ‖ to the glass.
    Installed as follows:
    Spaced at approved intervals.
    ≥ 2 angles per glass panel.
    Secured to the backing by one of the following:
    Expansion bolts.
    Toggle bolts.
    Other approved means.

1405 Installation of Wall Coverings

1405.11.5 Joints

- This section applies to thin exterior structural glass veneer.
- The abutting edges of such glass panels must be square as follows:
  - Miters are not permitted as follows:
       Where not specifically approved for obtuse-angled surfaces.
  - Other shapes are not permitted unless approved.
- An approved jointing compound must be applied uniformly to joints.
- Horizontal joints must be $\geq \frac{1}{16}$" as follows:
     Spaced by approved nonrigid materials.
- Where glass panels abut rigid materials the following is required:
     Expansion joints $\geq \frac{1}{4}$" as follows:
       At the sides of the glass.
       At the top of the glass.

1405.11.6 Mechanical fastenings

- This section applies to thin exterior structural glass veneer.
- Glass veneer panels installed at the following heights is governed as indicated below:
  - Heights:
       Above the level of heads of show windows.
       > 12' above the sidewalk.
  - Requirements:
       Fastenings required include all the following:
         Mastic as required at lower levels.
         Shelf angles as required at lower levels.
         Mechanical fasteners are required as follows:
           At one of the following locations of each glass panel:
             At each horizontal edge.
             At each vertical edge.
             At each corner.
         Fasteners must be fixed to the backing by one of the following:
           Expansion bolts.
           Toggle bolts.
           Other methods.
         Fasteners must support the glass as follows:
           In a vertical plane without assistance from the mastic.
         Shelf angles that also serve as mechanical fasteners are acceptable.

1405.11.7 Flashing

- This section applies to thin exterior structural glass veneer.
- Exposed edges of the glass veneer panels must be detailed as follows:
  - Covered with overlapping flashing of the following material:
       Corrosion-resistant metal.
  - Made moisture tight as follows:
       By caulking with a waterproof substance.

1406 Combustible Materials on the Exterior Side of Exterior Walls

1406.2.2 Architectural trim

- This section applies to the following construction types:
    Types I, II, III, IV.
- Exterior wall coverings may be of the following materials where the conditions indicated below apply:
    - Materials:
        Wood.
        Materials of equivalent combustibility.
    - Conditions:
        Building ≤ 3 stories.
        Such wall coverings other than fire-retardant treated wood are governed as follows:
            Limited to ≤ 10% of the exterior wall surface in the following case:
                Where the fire separation distance is ≤ 5'.
- Architectural trim ≥ 40' above the grade plane is governed as follows:
    - Approved noncombustible materials are required.
    - Must be fastened to the wall with the one of the following:
        Metal brackets.
        Other approved noncombustible brackets.

    Note: The following are cited as sources of applicable requirements:
    1405.4, "Wood veneers," provides requirements for exterior wall coverings that
    are permitted to be constructed of wood.
    2303.2, "Fire-retardant-treated wood," governs such material.

1406.2.3 Location

- Combustible wall covering may not extend above the exterior wall.
- Combustible wall covering may not extend over the top of the exterior wall.
- Combustible wall covering at the top of an exterior wall is governed as follows:
    - The wall must be behind the combustible covering at every point.

1406.2.4 Fireblocking *(part 1 of 2)*

- Fireblocking is not required in the following locations:
    - In cornices of single-family dwellings.
    - Where the following two conditions are present:
        The architectural trim is installed on noncombustible framing.
        The exterior wall finish exposed to the concealed space is one of the following:
            Aluminum ≥ 0.019" thick.
            Corrosion-resistant steel as follows:
                Base metal thickness is ≥ 0.016" at thinnest point.
            Other approved noncombustible materials.

1406 Combustible Materials on the Exterior Side of Exterior Walls

1406.2.4 Fireblocking *(part 2 of 2)*

- In other cases, the following applies:
  - Concealed furred space thus formed by combustible wall coverings is governed as follows:
    The dimension between the back of the wall covering and the wall must be $\leq 1^5/8$".
    The furred space must be fireblocked as follows:
      So that no air space will be > 100 square feet in area.
    Wood furring must be one of the following:
      Approved wood of natural decay resistance.
      Preservative-treated wood.

  Note: Section 716, "Concealed Spaces," is cited as the source of requirements for fireblocking in the furred spaces indicated above.

1406.3 Balconies and similar projections *(part 1 of 2)*

- This subsection addresses the following elements where they are of combustible construction:
  - Balconies.
  - Similar projections from buildings.
- Fire-retardant-treated wood may be used as follows:
  - For the following elements in construction Type I and II where the conditions below apply:
    Elements:
      Balconies.
      Porches.
      Decks.
      Exterior stairways.
    Conditions:
      Building must be ≤ 3 stories.
      Elements may not be required exits.
- Wood that is not fire-retardant treated may be used in guardrail systems that are ≤ 42" in height as follows:
  - As pickets.
  - As rails.
  - For similar components.
- Balconies and similar projections on the following construction types are governed as indicated below:
  - Construction Types:
    II, III and IV.
  - Requirements:
    They may be Type V construction.
    They are not required to have a fire-resistance rating as follows:
      Where the element is protected by sprinklers.

1406 Combustible Materials on the Exterior Side of Exterior Walls

1406.3 Balconies and similar projections *(part 2 of 2)*

- In other cases, balconies and similar projections are governed as follows:
  - They must comply with one of the following:
    Must have the fire-resistance rating required floors in the building construction type.
    Must be Type IV construction.
  - The total length of these on a building is limited as follows:
    Must be ≤ ½ the building perimeter at each floor.

  Note: IBC Table 601, "Fire-Resistance Rating Requirements for Building Elements," is cited as the source of such requirements for the floor construction noted above. 602.4, "Type IV," is cited as the source of requirements for Type IV construction.

Case study: Fig. 1406.3. Type V construction is permitted for the balcony of the Type IIIB building. The balcony must meet the fire-resistance requirements for floor construction as specified in IBC Table 601 for Type IIIB construction for which there is no fire-resistance-rating required. Wood that is not fire-retardant treated is permitted for the guardrail system. The balcony length is 8% of the building perimeter which is less than the 50% maximum. The balcony is in compliance with the code.

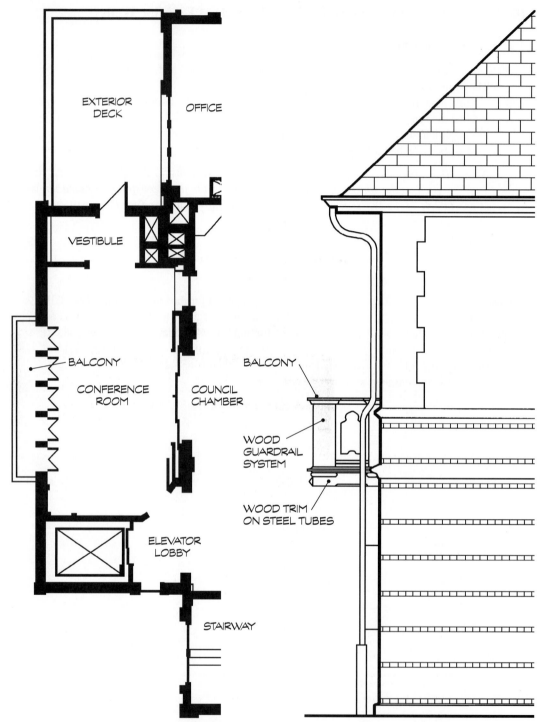

Fig. 1406.3. Partial elevation and plan at balcony. Lake Forest City Hall Renovation and Addition. Lake Forest, Illinois. David Woodhouse Architects. Chicago, Illinois.

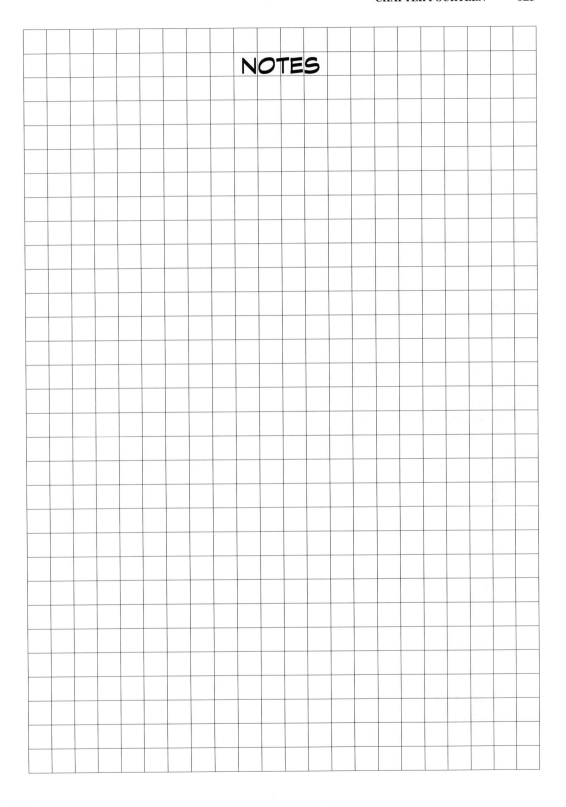

NOTES

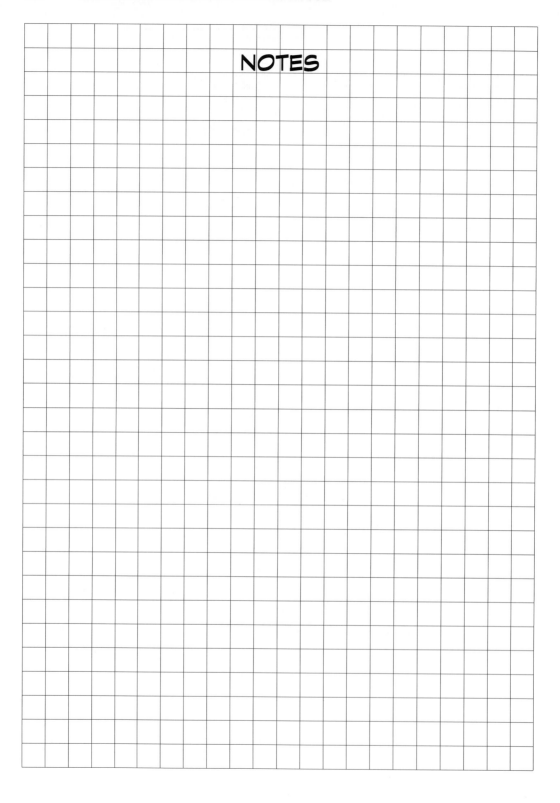

NOTES

15

Roof Assemblies and Rooftop Structures

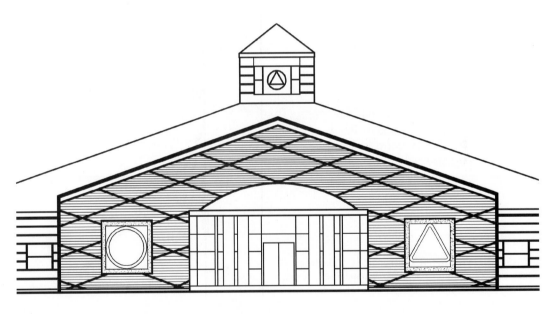

New Jasper Pre-K–2nd Grade School. Jasper, Texas. *(partial elevation)*
PBK Architects, Inc. Houston, Texas.

1503 Weather Protection

1503.2 Flashing

- Flashing must be installed to prohibit moisture penetration as follows:
  - ○ Through the wall at the following locations:
    - Joints in the coping.
    - Through materials permeable to moisture.
    - At intersections with the roof.
    - At parapet intersections with the roof.

1503.2.1 Locations

- Flashing must be installed at the following locations:
  - ○ At intersections of walls and roofs.
  - ○ At gutters.
  - ○ At changes in roof slope.
  - ○ At changes in roof direction.
  - ○ Around openings in the roof.
- Where flashing is metal, it must be as follows:
  - ○ Corrosion resistant.
  - ○ $\geq 0.019"$ thick.

> **Case study: Fig. 1503.2.1.**
> Flashing is installed at the intersection of the wall and the roof as required by the code. It meets corrosion resistance and thickness requirements.

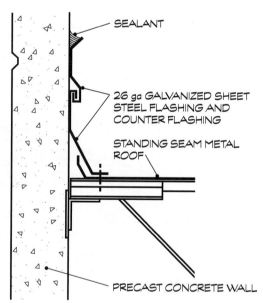

SEALANT

26 ga GALVANIZED SHEET STEEL FLASHING AND COUNTER FLASHING

STANDING SEAM METAL ROOF

PRECAST CONCRETE WALL

Fig. 1503.2.1. Wall detail. Garments to Go. Bastrop, Texas. Spencer Godfrey Architects. Round Rock, Texas.

1503.3 Coping

- Parapet walls must be coped with materials as follows:
  - ○ Noncombustible.
  - ○ Weatherproof.
  - ○ With a width $\geq$ the thickness of the parapet.

1503 Weather Protection

1503.4.1 Gutters

- This section does not apply to the following:
  - Occupancy R-3.
  - Private garages.
  - Buildings of Type IV construction.
- The following devices are governed as indicated below:
  - Devices:
    - Gutters.
    - Leaders.
  - Requirement:
    - Devices must be one of the following materials:
      - Noncombustible.
      - Schedule 40 plastic pipe.

Case study: Fig. 1503.4.1. The gutters and leaders on this building are metal and, thus, meet the code requirements for these components by being noncombustible.

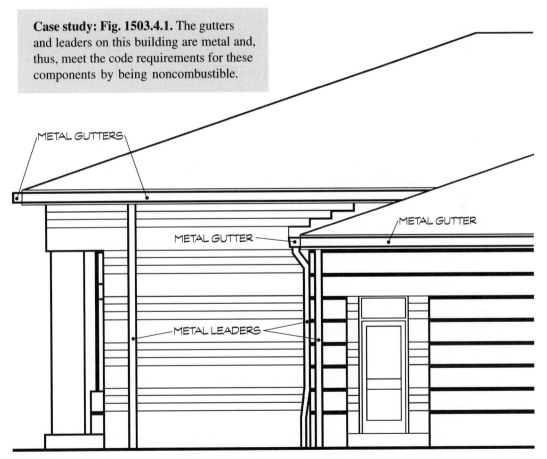

Fig. 1503.4.1. Partial elevation. New Jasper Pre-K–2nd Grade School. Jasper, Texas. PBK Architects, Inc. Houston, Texas.

1505 Fire Classification

1505.2 Class A roof assemblies

- Class A roof assemblies perform as follows:
  - Effective against severe fire test.
- Such assemblies and roof coverings must have the following characteristics:
  - They must be listed by an approved testing agency.
  - They must be identified as Class A by an approved testing agency.
- Class A roof assemblies may be used in all types of construction.

1505.3 Class B roof assemblies

- Class B roof assemblies perform as follows:
  - Effective against moderate fire test.
- Class B roof assemblies include the following:
  - Metal sheets.
  - Metal shingles.
- Otherwise, such assemblies and roof coverings must have the following characteristics:
  - They must be listed by an approved testing agency.
  - They must be identified as Class B by an approved testing agency.

1505.4 Class C roof assemblies

- Class C roof assemblies perform as follows:
  - Effective against light fire test.
- Such assemblies and roof coverings must have the following characteristics:
  - They must be listed by an approved testing agency.
  - They must be identified as Class C by an approved testing agency.

1505.7 Special purpose roofs

- The following special-purpose roofing are governed as indicated below:
  - Roofing:
    Wood shingles.
    Wood shakes.
  - Requirements:
    One of the following sheathings is required under the roofing:
    ≥ ½" wood structural panel solid sheathing.
    ≥ Nominal 1" boards spaced sheathing.
    Gypsum backing board or sheathing is required under the wood sheathing as follows:
    ≥ ⅝" Type X.
    Water resistant.

  Note: The following are cited as sources of requirements for special purpose roofing:
  1507.8, "Wood shingles."
  1507.9, "Wood shakes."

1507 Requirements for Roof Coverings

1507.2.1 Deck requirements

- Asphalt shingles must be secured to the following:
  - ○ Solidly sheathed deck.

Case study: Fig. 1507.2.1. A solid deck is required for the asphalt shingles on the roof of the example below. Such a deck is provided. The minimum slope of the shingles is 2:12. This roof slopes 3:12 and, thus, meets this code requirement. Since the slope is < 4:12, double underlayment is provided as required.

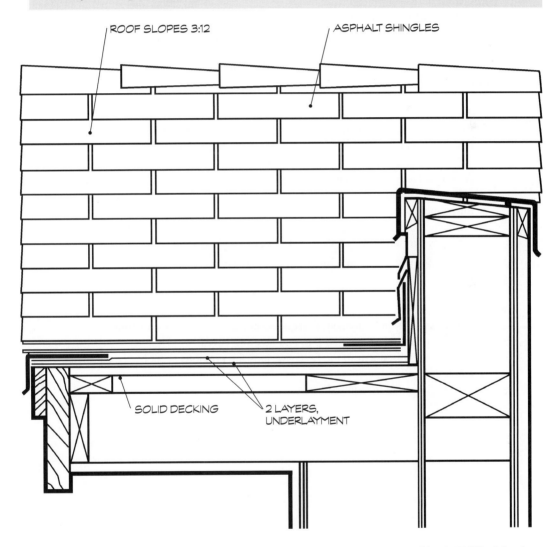

Fig. 1507.2.1. Detail at roof. Creston Elementary Multipurpose Building. Creston, California. Phillips Metsch Sweeney Moore Architects. Santa Barbara, California.

1507 Requirements for Roof Coverings

1507.2.2 Slope

- The slope required for asphalt shingles is as follows:
  - $\geq$ 2:12 slope.
- Double underlayment is required for asphalt shingles at the following range of slopes:
  - 2:12 $\leq$ slope < 4:12 slope.

  Note: 1507.2.8, "Underlayment application," is cited as governing the application of two layers of underlayment.

1507.2.8 Underlayment application

This section governs the application of underlayment for asphalt shingles.

- Where roof slopes are in the following range, the requirements below apply:
  - Slope:
    - 2:12 $\leq$ slope < 4:12.
  - Requirement:
    - Two layers of underlayment are required in the following installation:
      - Underlayment felt is applied $\parallel$ to and meeting eaves as follows:
        - Felt is $\geq$ 1'-7" wide.
      - A second layer of underlayment is applied on top of the first at the eaves as follows:
        - Felt is $\geq$ 3' wide.
      - Subsequent sheets of underlayment are applied as follows:
        - Sheets are $\geq$ 3' wide.
        - Sheets overlap previous sheet $\geq$ 1'-7".
- Where roof slopes are as follows, the requirements below apply:
  - Slope:
    - $\geq$ 4:12.
  - Requirements:
    - A single layer of underlayment is required in the following installation:
      - Underlayment felt is applied $\parallel$ to and meeting eaves.
      - Each sheet subsequent to the first, overlaps the previous sheet by the following amount:
        - $\geq$ 2" overlap is required.

1507 Requirements for Roof Coverings

1507.2.8.2 Ice dam protection

This section applies to asphalt shingles.

- For any of the following conditions, the underlayment indicated below is required:
  - Conditions:
    Average daily temperature in January is $\leq 25°F$.
    Ice can form along the eaves that accumulate water.
  - Underlayment:
    One of the following ice barriers is required in lieu of standard underlayment:
    $\geq$ 2 layers of underlayment cemented together.
    Self-adhering polymer modified bitumen sheet.
    Ice barriers must be applied as follows:
    Barrier meets the eave.
    Barrier extends over the interior of the building as follows:
    $\geq$ 2' inside the exterior wall.

1507.2.9.1 Base and cap flashing

- This section applies to asphalt shingles.
- Base and cap flashing are required as follows:
  - Installed as per manufacturer's instructions.
  - Base flashing must be one of the following:
    Corrosion-resistant metal $\geq$ nominal 0.019" thick.
    Mineral-surfaced roll roofing as follows:
    $\geq$ 77 lbs/100 sf.
  - Cap flashing must be the following:
    Corrosion-resistant metal $\geq$ nominal 0.019" thick.

1507 Requirements for Roof Coverings

1507.2.9.2 Valleys

- Valley linings for asphalt shingles are required as follows:
  - Installed as per manufacturer's instructions.
  - The following materials are acceptable for the valley types indicated below:
    Materials:
    Metal as follows:
    ≥ 1'-4" wide.
    Any of the following are permitted:
    Copper.
    Aluminum.
    Stainless steel.
    Painted terne.
    Lead.
    Zinc alloy.
    Galvanized steel.
    Two plies of mineral surface roll roofing as follows:
    Bottom layer to be ≥ 1'-6" wide.
    Top layer to be ≥ 3' wide.
  - Valleys:
    Where valley lining is exposed (open valleys).
    Where valley lining is covered with shingles (closed valleys).
- The following material may be used where valley lining is covered with shingles:
  1-ply smooth roll roofing ≥ 3' wide.

  Note: The following are cited as sources of applicable requirements:
  IBC Table 1507.2.9.2 lists acceptable valley lining metals and metal thickness.
  ASTM D 224, "Specification for Smooth-Surfaced Asphalt Roll Roofing (Organic Felt)," addresses lining for closed valleys.
  ASTM D 1970, "Specification for Self-Adhering Polymer Modified Bituminous Sheet Materials Used as Steep Roof Underlayment for Ice Dam Protection," addresses underlayment for closed valley linings.

1507.2.9.3 Drip edge *(part 1 of 2)*

- A drip edge for asphalt shingles is required on shingled roofs at the following locations:
  - Eaves.
  - Gables.
- A drip edge must be detailed as follows:
  - Extend ≥ 2" onto the roof under the shingles.
  - Extend downward past the bottom edge of sheathing ≥ ¼".
  - Attached with mechanical fasteners ≤ 12" on center.

1507 Requirements for Roof Coverings

1507.2.9.3 Drip edge *(part 2 of 2)*

- A chimney requires a cricket or saddle as follows:
  - On the side of the chimney where the roof is higher in the following case:
    Where water will drain toward an ≥ 2'-6" width of chimney.
  - Coverings must be one of the following:
    Sheet metal.
    Same material as roofing.

1507.3.1 Deck requirements

- The following roofing must be installed on one of the sheathing materials listed below:
  - Roofing:
    Concrete tile.
    Clay tile.
  - Sheathing:
    Solid sheathing.
    Spaced structural sheathing boards.

1507.3.2 Deck slope

- Clay and concrete roof tile must be installed on slopes as follows:
  - ≥ 2½:12 slope.
- Slopes < 4:12 require the following:
  - Double underlayment.

  Note: 1507.3.3, "Underlayment," is cited as the source providing requirements applicable to double underlayment.

1507.3.3.1 Low slope roofs

This section addresses clay and concrete tile roofing.

- ≥ 2 layers of underlayment are required for roofs as follows:
  - Where the slope is 2½:12 ≤ slope < 4:12 the following is required:
    First strip of underlayment:
      ≥ 1'-7" wide.
      Applied ∥ to and meeting the eave.
    Second strip of underlayment:
      ≥ 3' wide.
      Applied over the 1st strip meeting the eave.
    Subsequent strips of underlayment:
      Applied overlapping previous strips as follows:
        ≥ 1'-7" overlap.

1507 Requirements for Roof Coverings

1507.3.3.2 High slope roofs

This section addresses clay and concrete tile roofing.

- Roof slopes ≥ 4:12 require the following underlayment:
  - 1 layer of underlayment felt as follows:
    First strip applied ‖ to and meeting the eaves.
    Subsequent strips lap previous strips ≥ 2".

1507.3.9 Flashing

This section addresses flashing for clay and concrete tile roofing.

- Flashing and counterflashing is required as follows:
  - At the intersection of the roof with vertical surfaces.
- Where flashing is metal, the following is required:
  - Corrosion-resistant metal ≥ 0.019" thick.
- Flashing must be installed according to manufacturer's instructions.
- Valley flashing is governed as follows:
  - It must extend ≥ 11" in to each side of the valley centerline.
  - It must have a splash diverter rib ≥ 1" high as follows:
    At the centerline of the valley.
    Integrally formed with the flashing.
- Flashing sections must overlap each other ≥ 4" where ends meet.
- For roof slopes ≥ 3:12, valley flashing is governed as follows:
  - The following valley underlayment is required:
    ≥ 3' wide.
    Type I underlayment.
    Extending the full length of the valley.
    Provided in addition to other underlayment required for the roof.
- Where all of the following conditions apply, the detailing indicated below is required:
  - Conditions:
    Roof slope is < 7:12.
    One of the following applies:
      Average daily January temperature is ≤ 25°F.
      Where ice can form to accumulate water along the eaves.
  - Requirement:
    The underlayment for the metal valley flashing is detailed as follows:
      It is cemented across its entire surface to the roofing underlayment.

1507 Requirements for Roof Coverings

1507.4.1 Deck requirements

- Metal roof panels must be applied to one of the following types of decks:
  - Solid deck.
  - Closely fitted deck.
  - Spaced decking as follows:
    Where the metal roofing is specifically designed for such application.

1507.4.2 Deck slope

- The following metal roofing requires the slope indicated below:
  - Roofing:
    Nonsoldered seam metal roofing.
    Lapped sections.
    No lap sealant.
  - Slope:
    Required slope is $\geq$ 3:12.
- The following metal roofing requires the slope indicated below:
  - Roofing:
    Nonsoldered seam metal roofing.
    Lapped sections.
    With lap sealant.
  - Slope:
    Required slope is $\geq$ 1½:12.
- Standing seam metal roofing requires the following slope:
  - ¼:12.

1507.5.1 Deck requirements

- Metal roof shingles must be applied to one of the following types of decks:
  - Solid deck.
  - Closely fitted deck.
  - Spaced decking as follows:
    Where the metal shingles are specifically designed for such application.

1507.5.2 Deck slope

- Metal roof shingles require the following slope:
  - $\geq$ 3:12.

Case study: Fig. 1507.4.2A. The batten seam metal roofing requires a minimum slope of 3:12 according to manufacturer's recommendations and code requirements. The actual slope of the roofs is 4:12; thus, the roofing is in compliance with the code.

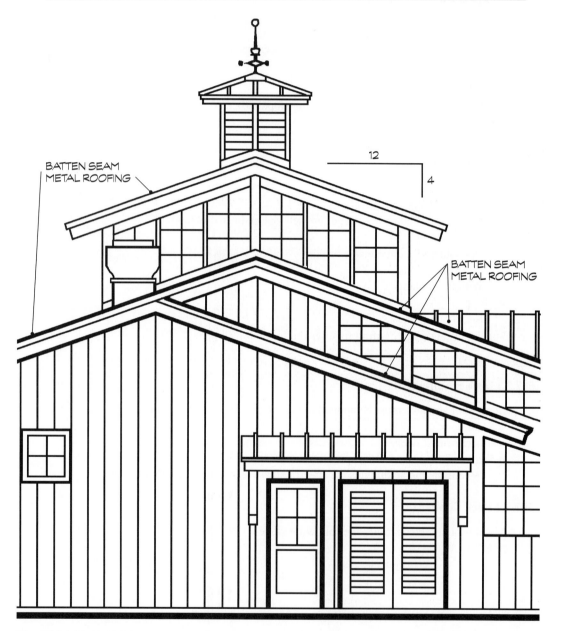

Fig. 1507.4.2A. Partial elevation. Central Kitchen. Lompoc Unified School District. Lompoc, California. Phillips Metsch Sweeney Moore Architects. Santa Barbara, California.

Case study: Fig. 1507.4.2B. The standing seam roof on the cupola of the tower slopes 2:12 which is $> \frac{1}{4}$:12, the minimum required slope. The standing seam roof is, therefore, in compliance with code requirements for slope.

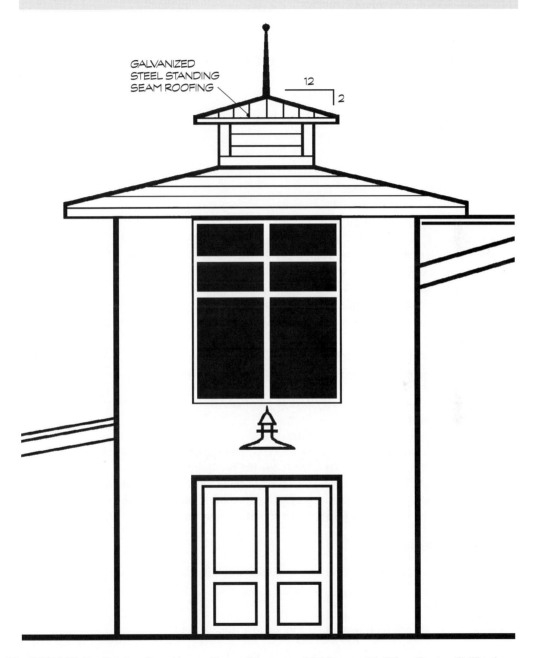

GALVANIZED
STEEL STANDING
SEAM ROOFING

12

2

Fig. 1507.4.2B. Partial elevation at tower. Creston Elementary Multipurpose Building. Creston, California. Phillips Metsch Sweeney Moore Architects. Santa Barbara, California.

1507 Requirements for Roof Coverings

1507.5.6 Flashing

This section addresses metal roof shingles.

- Valley flashing must be one of the following materials:
  - Galvanized steel.
  - Corrosion-resistant metal matching the roof shingle material.
  - Prepainted steel.
  - Aluminum-zinc alloy coated steel.
  - Copper.
  - Lead-coated copper.
  - Hard lead.
  - Soft lead.
  - Terne (tin).
  - Terne-coated stainless steel.
  - Aluminum.
- Valley flashing must be detailed as follows:
  - Extend ≥ 8" on both sides of the valley center line.
  - Have a splash diverter rib ≥ ¾" high as follows:
    At the center line of the valley.
    Formed as an integral part of the flashing.
  - Flashing sections must lap ≥ 4" where ends meet.
- Where either of the following conditions apply, the detailing indicated below is required:
  - Conditions:
    Average daily January temperature is ≤ 25°F.
    Where ice can form to accumulate water along the eaves.
  - Requirement:
    The following valley underlayment is required:
      ≥ 3' wide.
      Extending the full length of the valley.
      Provided in addition to other underlayment required for the roof shingles.
    Where the roof slope is < 7:12, the following is required:
      The underlayment for the metal valley flashing must be one of the following:
      Cemented across its entire surface to the roofing underlayment.
      It must be self-adhering polymer modified bitumen sheet.

1507.6.1 Deck requirements

- Mineral-surfaced roll roofing must be applied to a solidly sheathed surface.

1507.6.2 Deck slope

- Mineral-surface roll roofing must be applied to a slope ≥ 1:12.

1507 Requirements for Roof Coverings

1507.6.3 Underlayment

- Where one of the following conditions applies, the detailing indicated below is required:
  - Conditions:
    Average daily January temperature is $\leq 25°F$.
    Where ice can form to accumulate water along the eaves.
  - Requirement:
    An ice barrier is required as follows:
       One of the following is required:
          ≥ 2 layers of underlayment cemented together.
          A self-adhering polymer modified bitumen sheet.
       Ice barrier must extend from the eave to the following point above the interior:
          $\geq 2'$ inside the exterior wall.

  Note: ASTM D 226, "Specification for Asphalt-Saturated Organic Felt Used in Roofing and Waterproofing," is cited as the standard required for the underlayment, which is to be Type I.

1507.7.1 Deck requirements

- Slate shingles must be applied to the following:
  - A solidly sheathed surface.

1507.7.2 Deck slope

- Slate shingles must be applied to the following slope:
  - $\geq 4:12$.

1507.7.3 Underlayment

- Underlayment for slate shingles is Type II.
- Where one of the following conditions applies, underlayment for slate shingles is detailed as indicated below:
  - Conditions:
    Average daily January temperature is $\leq 25°F$.
    Where ice can form to accumulate water along the eaves.
  - Requirement:
    An ice barrier is required as follows:
       One of the following is required:
          ≥ 2 layers of underlayment cemented together.
          A self-adhering polymer modified bitumen sheet.
       Ice barrier must extend from the eave to the following point above the interior:
          $\geq 2'$ inside the exterior wall.

  Note: ASTM D 226, "Specification for Asphalt-Saturated Organic Felt Used in Roofing and Waterproofing," is cited as governing the underlayment.

1507 Requirements for Roof Coverings

1507.7.5 Application

- Slate shingles must have the headlap shown in the details provided.
- Slate shingles must be applied to the roof as follows:
  - With 2 fasteners for each piece.

1507.7.6 Flashing

- Flashing and counterflashing for slate shingles must be of the following material:
  - Sheet metal as follows:
    - ≥ 0.0179" uncoated thickness zinc coated G90.
- Valley flashing is governed as follows:
  - Sheet metal as follows:
    - ≥ 0.0179" uncoated thickness zinc coated G90.
  - Must be ≥ 1'-3" wide.
- Intersections between the roof and the following vertical surfaces require the cap flashing indicated below:
  - Vertical surfaces:
    - Chimneys.
    - Stucco walls.
    - Brick walls.
  - Cap flashing:
    - Two plies of felt are required as follows:
      - 4" wide strips of felt set in plastic cement.
      - Top felt extends 1" above the bottom felt.
      - Top coating of plastic cement.
      - Felts overlaps the base flashing 2".

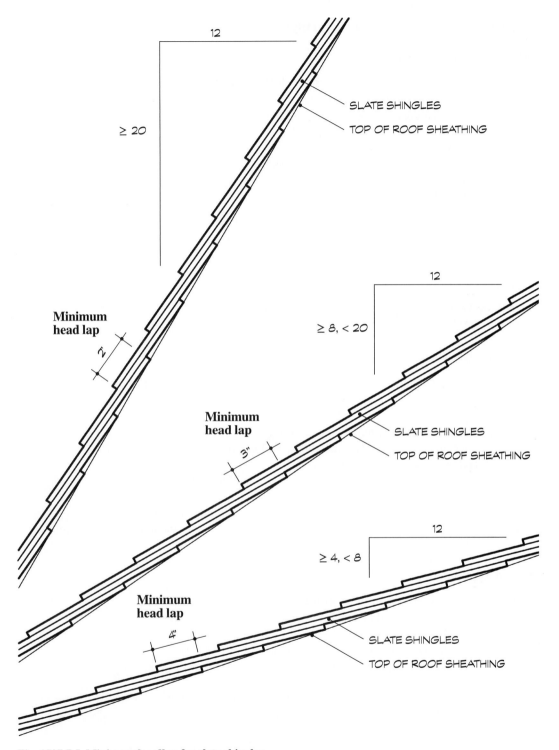

12

≥ 20

SLATE SHINGLES

TOP OF ROOF SHEATHING

Minimum head lap

2"

12

≥ 8, < 20

SLATE SHINGLES

TOP OF ROOF SHEATHING

Minimum head lap

3"

12

≥ 4, < 8

SLATE SHINGLES

TOP OF ROOF SHEATHING

Minimum head lap

4"

Fig. 1507.7.5. Minimum headlap for slate shingles.

1507 Requirements for Roof Coverings

1507.8.1 Deck requirements

- Wood shingles must be applied to one of the following:
  - Solidly sheathed surface.
  - Spaced sheathing as follows:
    - ≥ nominal 1"×4" boards are required.
    - Spacing must = the following:
      - Length of shingle exposed to the weather.

1507.8.1.1 Solid sheathing required

- Wood shingles require solid sheathing in either of the following cases:
  - Where average daily temperature in January is ≤ 25°F.
  - Where ice can form to accumulate water along the eaves.

1507.8.2 Deck slope

- Wood shingles must be applied to the following slope:
  - ≥ 3:12.

1507.8.3 Underlayment

- Wood shingles require underlayment as indicated below, where either of the following conditions apply:
  - Conditions:
    - Where average daily temperature in January is ≤ 25°F.
    - Where ice can form to accumulate water along the eaves.
  - Underlayment:
    - ≥ 2 layers of underlayment are adhered in one of the following ways :
      - Layers must be cemented together.
      - Layers must be self-adhering polymer modified bitumen sheet.
    - Underlayment must extend from eave edge to a point over the interior space as follows:
      - To a point ≥ 24" inside the exterior wall.

1507.8.6 Application

- Wood shingles must be installed as follows:
  - With a lap between side joints in adjacent courses as follows:
    - ≥ 1½" lap is required.
  - Shingles in alternate courses may not align.
  - Spacing between adjacent shingles in the same course must be as follows:
    - ≥ ½" and ≤ ³/₈".
  - The length of naturally durable wood shingles that may be exposed to the weather is as per details provided.

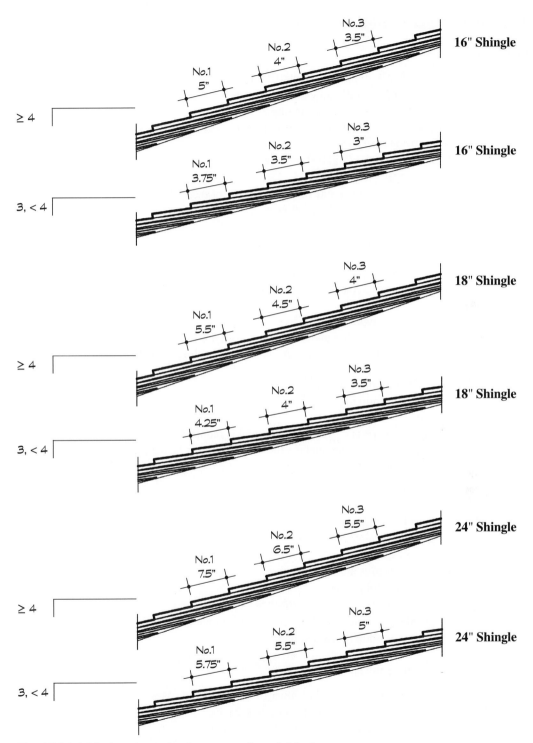

Fig. 1507.8.6. Maximum permitted exposure of wood shingles.

1507 Requirements for Roof Coverings

1507.8.7 Flashing

- Wood shingles require flashing and counterflashing as follows:
  - At the intersection of the roof and vertical surfaces.
  - Installed as per manufacturer's instructions.
  - Where flashing is metal, the following is required:
    Must be corrosion-resistant.
    Must be ≥ 0.019" thick (26 galvanized sheet gage).
- Valley flashing is governed as follows:
  - It must extend ≥ 11" on either side of the centerline of the valley.
  - It must have a splash diverter rib as follows:
    ≥ 1" high.
    Located at the centerline of the valley.
    Formed as part of the valley flashing.
  - Flashing sections must lap ≥ 4" where ends meet.
  - Valley flashing requires Type I underlayment as follows:
    ≥ 3' wide.
    Extending the full length of the valley.
    Provided in addition to other underlayment required for the roof shingles.
  - Where either of the following conditions apply, the detailing indicated below is required:
    Conditions:
    Average daily January temperature is ≤ 25°F.
    Where ice can form to accumulate water along the eaves.
    Requirement:
    Where the roof slope is < 7:12, the following is required:
    The underlayment for the metal valley flashing must be detailed as follows:
    It is cemented across its entire surface to the roofing underlayment.

1507.9.1 Deck requirements

- Wood shakes must be applied to one of the following:
  - Solidly sheathed surface.
  - Spaced sheathing as follows:
    ≥ nominal 1"×4" boards are required.
    Spacing must = the following:
    Length of shingle exposed to the weather.
- Where 1"×4" sheathing is spaced 10" on center, the following applies:
  - 1"×4" boards must be added between them.

1507.9.1.1 Solid sheathing required

- Wood shakes require solid sheathing in either of the following cases:
  - Where average daily temperature in January is ≤ 25°F.
  - Where ice can form to accumulate water along the eaves.

1507 Requirements for Roof Coverings

1507.9.2 Deck slope

- Wood shakes must be applied to the following slopes:
  - ≥ 4:12.

1507.9.3 Underlayment

- Wood shakes require underlayment as indicated for either of the following conditions:
  - Conditions:
    Where average daily temperature in January is ≤ 25°F.
    Where ice can form to accumulate water along the eaves.
  - Underlayment:
    ≥ 2 layers of underlayment are required in one of the following details:
    Layers must be cemented together.
    Layers must be self-adhering polymer modified bitumen sheet.
    Underlayment must extend from eave edge to a point over the interior space as follows:
    To a point ≥ 24" inside the exterior wall.
- Wood shakes require Type 1 underlayment.

  Note: ASTM D 226, "Specifications for Asphalt-Saturated Organic Felt Used in Roofing and Waterproofing," is cited as governing the underlayment as required above.

1507.9.7 Application

- Wood shakes must be installed as follows:
  - With a lap ≥ 1½" between side joints in adjacent courses.
  - Shakes in alternate courses may not align.
  - Spacing between adjacent shakes in the same course must be as follows:
    ≥ ³/₈" and ≤ ⁵/₈" for the following:
    Shakes.
    Taper-sawn shakes of naturally durable wood.
    ≥ ¼" and ≤ ³/₈" for the following:
    Taper-sawn shakes that are preservative treated.
  - The length of shakes that may be exposed to the weather is as shown in the detail provided.

1507 Requirements for Roof Coverings

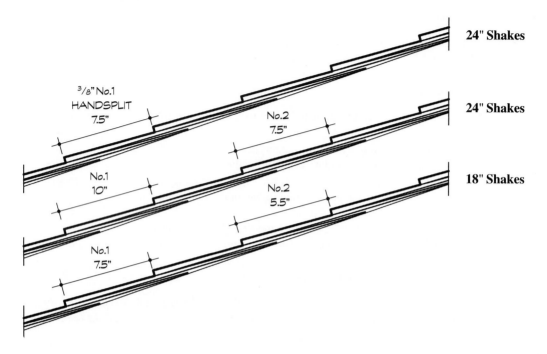

Fig. 1507.9.7. Maximum permitted exposure of wood shakes.

1507.9.8 Flashing *(part 1 of 2)*

- Wood shakes require flashing and counterflashing as follows:
  - At the intersection of the roof and vertical surfaces.
  - Installed as per manufacturer's instructions.
  - Where flashing is metal, the following is required:
    Must be corrosion-resistant.
    Must be ≥ 0.019" thick (26 galvanized sheet gage).

1507 Requirements for Roof Coverings

1507.9.8 Flashing *(part 2 of 2)*

- Valley flashing for wood shakes is governed as follows:
  - It must extend ≥ 11" on either side of the centerline of the valley.
  - It must have a splash diverter rib as follows:
    - ≥ 1" high.
    - Located at the centerline of the valley.
    - Formed as part of the valley flashing.
  - Flashing sections must lap ≥ 4" where ends meet.
  - Valley flashing requires Type I underlayment as follows:
    - ≥ 3' wide.
    - Extending the full length of the valley.
    - Provided in addition to other underlayment required for the roof shingles
  - Where either of the following conditions apply, the detailing indicated below is required:
    - Conditions:
      - Average daily January temperature is ≤ 25°F.
      - Where ice can form to accumulate water along the eaves.
    - Requirement:
      - Where the roof slope is < 7:12, the following is required:
        - The underlayment for the metal valley flashing must be detailed as follows:
          - It is cemented across its entire surface to the roofing underlayment.

1507.10.1 Slope

- Coal-tar built-up roofs must have a slope as follows:
  - ≥ $^1/_8$:12.
- Other built-up roofs must have a slope as follows:
  - ≥ ¼:12.

1507.12.1 Slope

- Thermoset single-ply membrane roofs must have a slope as follows:
  - ≥ ¼:12.

1507.13.1 Slope

- Thermoplastic single-ply membrane roofs must have a slope as follows:
  - ≥ ¼:12.

1507.14.1 Slope

- Sprayed polyurethane foam roofs must have the following slope:
  - ≥ ¼:12.

1507.15.1 Slope

- Liquid-applied roofs must have the following slope:
  - ≥ ¼:12.

1509 Rooftop Structures

1509.2 Penthouses

- This section addresses the following roof structures on buildings of Type I construction:
  Penthouses.
  Other projections above the roof.
- The following constructions may project above the roof a height as indicated below:
  - Constructions:
    Housing the following:
      Tanks.
      Elevators stopping at roof level.
  - Height:
    Required height is ≤ 28'.
- Other constructions may project above the roof the following height:
  - Required height is ≤ 12'.
- The following constructions above the roof are limited to the uses noted and the detailing indicated below:
  - Constructions:
    Penthouses.
    Bulkheads.
    Similar constructions.
  - Uses:
    Shelter of mechanical equipment.
    Shelter of vertical shaft openings in the roof.
  - Detailing:
    Such constructions require the following as applicable to protect equipment and the building interior.
      Louvers.
      Louver blades.
      Flashing.
      Similar provisions.
- The following constructions above the roof used for purposes other than allowed by this section are governed indicated below:
  - Constructions:
    Penthouses.
    Bulkheads.
  - Requirement:
    Such constructions must meet code requirements for an additional story.
- The following devices are permitted above the roof:
  - Wood flagpoles.
  - Similar structures.

1509 Rooftop Structures

1509.2.1 Type of construction

- The following applies to penthouses on buildings of Type I and II construction:
    - Where exterior walls and roofs are > 5' and < 20' from a common property line:
        They require the following:
            A fire-resistance rating of ≥ 1 hr is required.
            Noncombustible construction is required.
    - Where exterior walls and roofs are > 20' from a common property line:
        Noncombustible construction is required.
    - The following must be noncombustible construction:
        Interior framing.
        Interior walls.
    - The following apply to penthouses on buildings of Types III, IV, and V construction:
    - Where exterior walls are > 5' and < 20' from a common property line:
        They must have a fire-resistance rating of ≥ 1 hr.
    - Where exterior walls are > 20' from a common property line:
        They must be ≥ one of the following:
            Type IV construction.
            Noncombustible construction.
    - Interior walls are required to be ≥ one of the following:
        Type IV construction.
        Noncombustible construction.
    - Roofs must have materials and fire-resistance ratings required for the construction type.

    Note: IBC Table 601, "Fire-Resistance Rating Requirements for Building Elements," is cited as the source of requirements for roofs as indicated above.

- Enclosures on the roof as follows may be unprotected, noncombustible construction:
    - Containing only mechanical equipment.
    - Located ≥ 20' from property lines.
- Mechanical equipment screens on the roof may be combustible where all of the following apply:
    - Building must be 1 story.
    - No roof may be present on the screens.
    - Screens must be located ≥ 20' from property lines.
    - Screens must be ≤ 4' in height above the roof surface.
- Dormers must be the same type construction as one of the following:
    - The roof of which they are a part.
    - The exterior walls of the building.
- Other penthouses must have the following constructed as required for the building.
    - Walls.
    - Floors.
    - Roof.

1509 Rooftop Structures

1509.5 Towers, spires, domes and cupolas

- The following is required where such elements are ≤ 60' above grade;
  - They must have a fire-resistance rating ≥ that of the building.
- Where such elements have the following characteristics, the construction indicated below is required:
  - Characteristics:
    - Height is > 60' above grade and either of the following also apply:
      - Area at any horizontal section is > 200 sf.
      - The elements are used for anything other than the following:
        - A belfry.
        - An architectural embellishment.
  - Requirements:
    - The following must be Type I or II construction:
      - Such elements.
      - The construction on which such elements are supported.

1509.5.1 Noncombustible construction required *(part 1 of 2)*

- This section addresses the following elements:
  - Towers.
  - Spires.
  - Domes.
  - Cupolas.
- Where such elements have any of the following characteristics, the requirements below apply:
  - Characteristics:
    - > 25' high above the following point:
      - Highest point of contact with the roof.
    - > 200 sf at any horizontal section.
    - To be used for any purpose other than the following:
      - A belfry.
      - An architectural embellishment.
  - Requirements:
    - Constructed entirely of noncombustible materials.
    - Supported by noncombustible materials.
    - Separated from the building below by construction as follows:
      - With a fire-resistance rating ≥ 1½ hrs .
      - With openings having a fire-protection rating ≥ 1½ hrs.

509 Rooftop Structures

509.5.1 Noncombustible construction required *(part 2 of 2)*

- The requirements listed below apply to elements on the roofs of buildings that are > 50' high other than the following:
  - Elements:
    The following elements are not included in the requirements below:
    Aerial supports ≤ 12' high.
    Flag poles.
    Water tanks.
    Cooling towers.
  - Requirements:
    Other types of elements must comply with the following:
    Elements must be noncombustible.
    Construction supporting the elements must be noncombustible.

1509.5.2 Towers and spires

- Where such structures are enclosed, the following applies:
  - The exterior walls must be constructed as required for the building.
- The roof covering of spires is governed as follows:
  - It must be the class of roofing required for the main roof of the building.

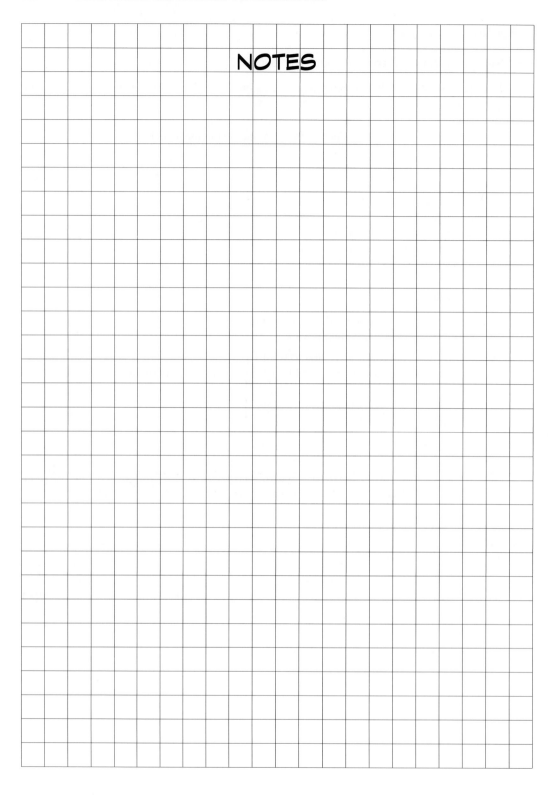

NOTES

16

Structural Design

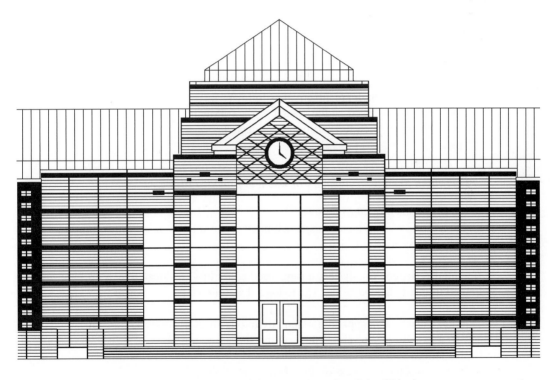

High School 6, Cypress-Fairbanks Independent School District.
Harris County, Texas. *(partial elevlation)*
PBK Architects, Inc. Houston, Texas.

1604 General Design Requirements

1604.3.6 Limits *(part 1 of 2)*

- Deflection in metal building components is governed as follows:
    - Total load deflection of the following cladding is limited as indicated below:
        Structural roofing of formed metal sheets:
            Span ÷ 60.
        Structural siding of formed metal sheets:
            Span ÷ 60.
    - Live load deflection of the following roof structure is limited as indicated below:
        Secondary roof structure supporting the following:
            Formed metal roofing with no roof covering:
                Span ÷ 150.
    - Wind load deflection of the following wall structure is limited as indicated below:
        Secondary roof structure supporting formed metal siding:
            Span ÷ 90.
- Interior partitions are governed as follows:
    - The following interior partitions are not regulated by this section:
        Partitions ≤ 6' high.
        Flexible partitions.
        Folding partitions.
        Portable partitions.
    - Interior partitions > 6' high are governed as follows:
        Actual deflection is based on the greater of the following lateral loads:
            Actual loads to which the partition is subjected.
            5 psf.

    Note: 1607.13, "Interior walls and partitions," is cited as the source of requirements for partition loading, a summary of which is provided above.

- Deflection of glass is limited as follows:
    - Deflection of the edge of a glass sheet is limited to the smaller of the following:
        Length of glass edge ÷ 175.
        ¾".
    - Differential deflection of adjacent unsupported edges of glass located by a walking surface is limited to that indicated below, where loaded as follows:
        Loading:
            50 lbs/linear foot is applied horizontally to one sheet as follows:
                At any point ≤ 3'-6" above the walking surface.
        Deflection:
            Limited to ≤ the thickness of the glass.

    Note: Section 2403, "General Requirements for Glass," is cited as governing glass deflection, a partial summary of which is provided above.

1604 General Design Requirements

1604.3.6 Limits *(part 2 of 2)*

- Wood structural members with all of the following characteristics are governed as indicated below:
  - Characteristics:
    Moisture content < 16% at time of installation.
    Used in dry conditions.
  - Deflection:
    Actual total deflection is permitted to be based on the following:
    Live load + half the dead load.
- Where roof drainage is not assured, the possibility of ponding must be investigated as follows:
  - The deflection limits of this section do not necessarily prevent ponding.

  Note: The following sections are cited as sources of applicable requirements:
  Section 1611, "Rain Loads."
  Section 1503.4, "Roof drainage."

- In computing actual deflection, wind load may be taken as the following:
  - 0.7 × "component and cladding" loads.
- In computing actual total load deflection, dead load of steel structural members is taken as zero.
- Otherwise, deflection of structural members is limited to a fraction of span as indicated below:

Table 1604.3.6   Deflection Limit for Structural Members

Deflection of structural members	Fraction of span
Deflection based on live load:	
Roof members:	
Supporting a plaster ceiling	Span ÷ 360
Supporting a ceiling not plaster	Span ÷ 240
Not supporting a ceiling	Span ÷ 180
Floor members	Span ÷ 360
Deflection based on snow or wind load:	
Roof members:	
Supporting a plaster ceiling	Span ÷ 360
Supporting a ceiling not plaster	Span ÷ 240
Not supporting a ceiling	Span ÷ 180
Exterior walls and interior partitions:	
With brittle finishes	Span ÷ 240
With flexible finishes	Span ÷ 120
Deflection based on total load (dead load + live load):	
Roof members:	
Supporting a plaster ceiling	Span ÷ 240
Supporting a ceiling not plaster	Span ÷ 180
Not supporting a ceiling	Span ÷ 120
Floor members	Span ÷ 240
Farm buildings	Span ÷ 180
Greenhouses	Span ÷ 120

Source: IBC Table 1604.3.

1607 Live Loads

1607.3 Uniform live loads *(part 1 of 3)*

- Lives loads for structural design are to be the larger of the following:
  - The maximum anticipated.
  - The minimums listed in this section.
- Decks:
  - Live load to be the same as the occupancy served.

  Note: 1604.8.3, "Decks," is cited as a source of related requirements.

- Horizontal swaying forces ∥ and ⊥ to seating must be considered in addition to vertical live loads for the following:
  - Gymnasiums.
  - Reviewing stands.
  - Grandstands.
  - Bleachers.
  - Fixed stadium seats.
  - Fixed arena seats.

  Note: NFPA 102, "Assembly Seating, Tents and Membrane Structures," is cited as governing the design of such loading.

- Library stacks:
  - The live load for library stack areas is the larger of the following:
    The volume of book shelving at 65 lb/cu ft converted to a uniform floor load.
    150 psf.
- The following uses are cited for special consideration of live loads that may be higher than those listed herein:
  - Uses subject to trucking as follows:
    Sidewalks.
    Driveways.
    Yards.
  - Office building spaces as follows:
    File rooms.
    Computer rooms.
  - Storage warehouses.
  - Uses subject to snow load.

  Note: Section 1608 ,"Snow Loads," is cited as the source of applicable requirements.
  The following are cited as sources of requirements not covered by this section:
  1607.6, "Truck and bus garage live load application."
  1607.7, "Loads on handrails, guards, grab bars and vehicle barriers."
  1607.11, "Roof loads."

1607 Live Loads

1607.3 Uniform live loads *(part 2 of 3)*

• For other than special cases, minimum uniformly distributed live loads are to be as follows:

Table 1607.3   Minimum Uniformly Distributed Live Loads

Use	psf	Use	psf
Access-floors		**Corridors**—*continued*	
Computer	100	Libraries:	
Office	50	1st floor	100
		Upper floors	80
Apartments		Office buildings:	
Corridors serving public rooms	100	1st floor	100
Private rooms	40	Upper floors	80
Public rooms	100	Penal institutions	100
		Schools:	
Arenas		1st floor	100
Bleachers	100	Upper floors	80
Fixed seats	60	Other locations	100
Armories and drill rooms	150	**Dance halls**	100
		Dining rooms	100
Assembly		**Driveways subject to trucks**	250
Catwalks	40		
Control rooms	50	**Fire escapes**	
Fixed seat area	60	1-family dwellings	40
Follow-spot floors	50	Other locations	100
Lobbies	100		
Movable seat area	100	**Garages, passenger cars**	50
Platforms (similar to stage)	125	**Grandstands**	100
Projection rooms	50		
Stages	125	**Gymnasiums**	
		Main floor	100
Balconies, exterior		Balconies	100
≤ 100 sf, 1- & 2-family dwelling	60		
Other sizes and locations	100	**Hospitals**	
		Corridors:	
Bleachers	100	1st floor	100
Ballrooms	100	Upper floors	80
Bowling alleys	75	Laboratories	60
Canopies	75	Operating rooms	60
		Private rooms	40
Corridors		Wards	40
Hospitals:			
1st floor	100	**Hotels**	
Upper floors	80	Corridors serving public rooms	100
Hotels, serving public rooms	100	Private rooms	40
		Public rooms	100

Source: IBC Table 1607.1.

1607 Live Loads

1607.3 Uniform live loads *(part 3 of 3)*

- For other than special cases, minimum uniformly distributed live loads are to be as follows:

Table 1607.3—*Continued*

Use	psf	Use	psf
Libraries		**Residential** – *Continued*	
Corridors:		Multi-family dwellings:	
Upper floors	80	Corridors serving public rooms	100
Reading rooms	60	Private rooms	40
Stacks	150	Public rooms	100
		Stairs and exits	100
Manufacturing			
Light	125	**Restaurants**	100
Heavy	250	**Reviewing stands**	100
Marquees	75	**Schools**	
		Classrooms	40
Office buildings		Corridors:	
Corridors:		1st floor	100
1st floor	100	Upper floors	80
Upper floors	80		
Lobbies	100	**Sidewalks subject to trucks**	250
Offices	50	**Skating rinks**	100
Penal institutions		**Stadium bleachers**	100
Cell blocks	40	**Stadium fixed seats**	60
Corridors	100		
		Stairs and exits	
Platforms, elevated	60	1- & 2-family dwellings	40
(not exitway, not similar to stage)		Other locations	100
Residential		**Storage warehouses**	
1-family dwellings:		Light	125
Fire escapes	40	Heavy	250
1- & 2-family dwellings:			
Stairs and exits	40	**Stores**	
Balconies, exterior ≤ 100 sf	60	Retail:	
R-3:		1st floor	100
Balconies, exterior	100	Upper floors	75
Habitable attics	30	Wholesale, all floors	125
Sleeping rooms	30		
Stairs and exits	100	**Terraces, pedestrian**	100
Uninhabitable attics:		**Walkways** (not exitways)	60
No storage	10		
With storage	20	**Yards**	
Other areas (other than decks)	40	Pedestrian	100
		Subject to trucks	250

Source: IBC Table 1607.1.

1607 Live Loads

1607.4 Concentrated loads

- Floors and similar surfaces must be designed to support the live loads indicated below:
  - The following load that produces greater stresses in the structure is required:
    Uniformly distributed loads as specified in the code.
    The following concentrated loads as follows:
       To be evenly distributed over 2½ sf.
       To be located to yield the greatest stresses in the structure.

Table 1607.4   Minimum Concentrated Live Loads

Use	Concentrated load in lbs	Use	Concentrated load in lbs
Access-floors		**Office buildings**	
Computer	2000	Corridors	2000
Office	2000	Lobbies	2000
		Offices	2000
Ceilings			
Able to be accessed	200	**Schools**	
		Classrooms	1000
Driveways		Corridors	1000
Subject to trucks	8000		
		Scuttles	200
Hospitals			
Corridors, upper floors	1000	**Sidewalks**	
Laboratories	1000	Subject to trucks	8000
Operating rooms	1000		
Private rooms	1000	**Skylight ribs**	200
Wards	1000		
		Stores	
Libraries		Retail	1000
Corridors, upper floors	1000	Wholesale	1000
Reading rooms	1000		
Stacks	1000	**Yards**	
		Subject to trucks	8000
Manufacturing			
Light	2000		
Heavy	2000		

Source: IBC Table 1607.1.

1607.5 Partition loads

- In the following buildings, the additional live load must be added as indicated below:
  - Buildings:
    Office buildings.
    Buildings where partition locations change.
  - Load:
    Where the required live load is ≤ 80 psf:
       20 psf must be added to the required live load.

1607 Live Loads

1607.7.1 Handrails and guards

- This section does not apply to 1- and 2-family dwellings.
- In other locations, the following components and their supports must resist the loading indicated below:
  - ○ Components:
    - Handrail assemblies.
    - Guards.
  - ○ ≥ 50 lb/linear foot as follows:
    - Applied in any direction at the top.
    - Load is not applied simultaneously with other loads.

1607.7.1.1 Concentrated load

- The following components and their supports must resist the loading indicated below:
  - ○ Components:
    - Handrail assemblies.
    - Guards.
  - ○ A single concentrated load ≥ 200 lbs as follows:
    - Applied in any direction at any point at the top.
    - Load is not applied simultaneously with other loads.

1607.7.1.2 Components

- The following components of a handrail assembly or guard must resist the loading indicated below:
  - ○ Components:
    - All rails other than the top handrail.
    - Balusters.
    - Panel fillers.
  - ○ ≥ 50 lbs as follows:
    - Applied horizontally ⊥ to the component.
    - Applied to an area ≤ 1 sf including the following:
      - Openings.
      - Space between rails.
    - Load is not applied simultaneously with other loads.

1607.7.2 Grab bars, shower seats and dressing room bench seats

- Such components must resist 250 lbs as follows:
  - ○ Applied at any point.
  - ○ Applied in any direction.

NOTES

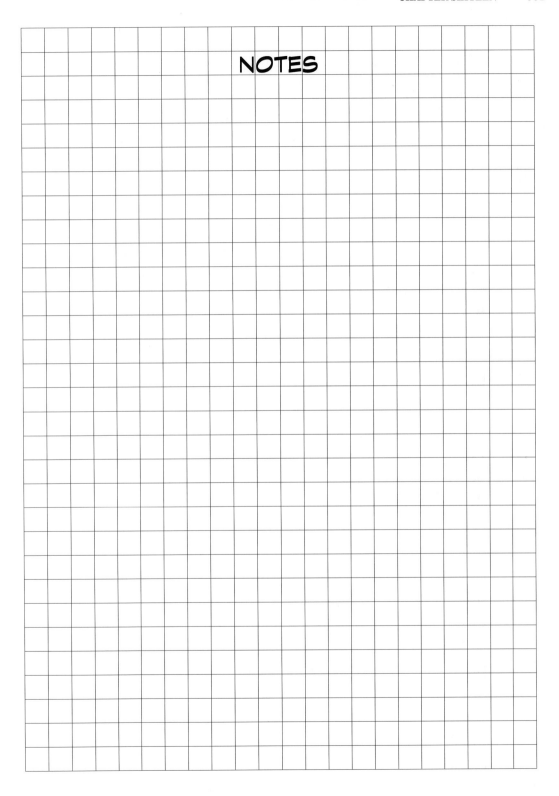

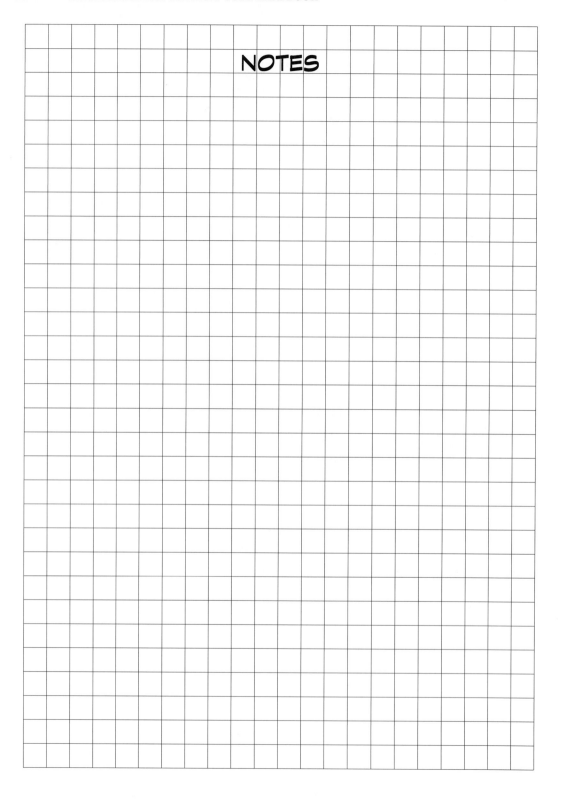

NOTES

17

Structural Tests and Special Inspections

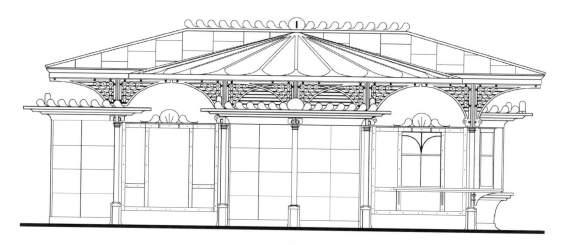

Visitor Services Pavilions at Clarence Buckingham Memorial Fountain.
Chicago Park District. Chicago, Illinois
David Woodhouse Architects. Chicago, Illinois.

1703 Approvals

1703.5 Labeling

- Where the following components are to be labeled, the requirements indicated below apply:
  - Components:
    Materials.
    Assemblies.
  - Requirements:
    Such components must be labeled by an approved agency.
    Such components must be labeled according to the requirements of this section.

  > *Note: Section 1703, "Approvals," is cited as governing the approved agency indicated.*
  > *The following are cited as governing the labeling of components indicated above:*
  > *1703.5.1, "Testing."*
  > *1703.5.2," Inspection and identification."*
  > *1703.5.3, "Label information."*

1703.5.1 Testing

This section addresses a part of the labeling process.

- An approved agency must test an example of the component to be labeled as follows:
  - Tests must be based on relevant standards.
  - The agency must maintain a record of tests performed as follows:
    Adequate information must be recorded to verify compliance with the relevant standards.

1703.5.2 Inspection and identification

This section addresses a part of the labeling process.

- The approved agency must inspect the components subsequently labeled as follows:
  - Inspections must be periodic.
  - Inspections of the component fabrication must be done where necessary.
  - Inspections must verify that the labeled component is representative of that tested.

1703.5.3 Label information

- Labels must include the following information.
  - Identification of one of the following:
    Manufacturer.
    Distributor.
  - One of the following types of information:
    Description of the components performance properties.
    Both identification numbers as follows:
      Model number.
      Serial number.
  - Identification of the approved agency issuing the label.

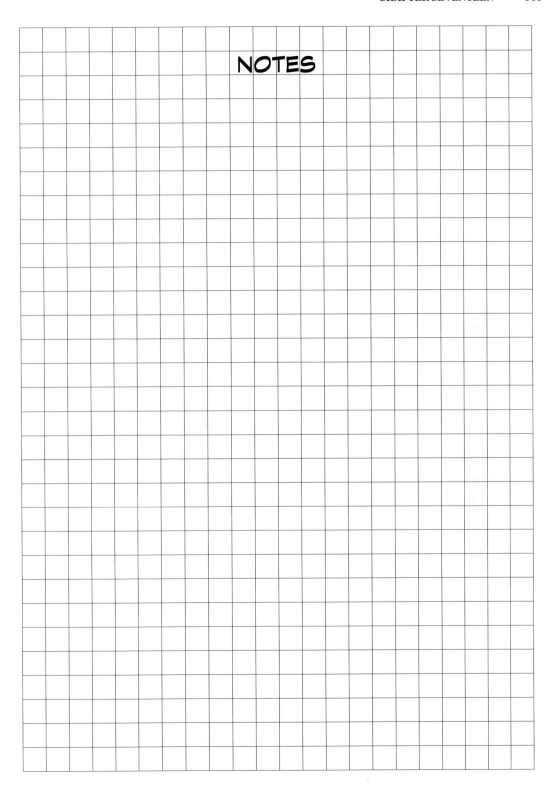

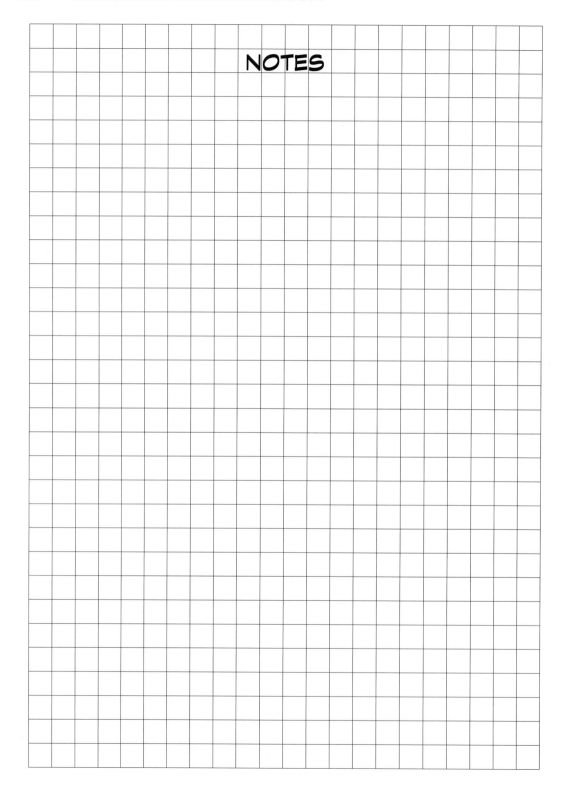

NOTES

18

Soil and Foundations

Lake Forest City Hall Renovation and Addition. Lake Forest, Illinois.
David Woodhouse Architects. Chicago, Illinois.

1803 Excavation, Grading and Fill

1803.3 Site grading

- Water is to be directed away from the foundation by one of the following methods:
  - ○ Grade must slope away from the foundation as per one of the following:
    - At a slope ≥ 1:20 as follows:
      - For a distance ≥ 10' from the foundation.
    - At a slope ≥ 1:48 as follows:
      - For a distance ≥ 10' from the foundation.
      - Where this slope is adequate based on the following:
        - Climatic conditions.
        - Soil conditions.
  - ○ An approved method.
- Settlement of backfill must be considered in determining final grade.

1805 Footings and Foundations

1805.1 General

- The top of a footing must be level.
- The bottom of a footing may slope ≤ 1:10.
- Footing surfaces must be stepped as follows:
  - At the top where required for to change level.
  - At the bottom where grade slopes > 1:10.
- The following components must be constructed on the soil indicated below:
  - Components:
    Foundations.
    Footings.
  - Soil:
    Undisturbed.
    Compacted.

  Note: 1803.4, "Compacted fill material," is cited as the source of applicable requirements for compacted soils as indicated above.

1805.2.1 Frost protection

- The following foundations must be detailed as indicated below:
  - Foundations:
    The following components of the buildings indicated below are included:
      Components:
        Foundation walls.
        Piers.
        Other permanent building supports.
      Buildings:
        Buildings with any of the following characteristics:
          > 400 sf.
          > 10' high.
  - Detailing:
    - Components must extend below the local frost line as follows:
        Where constructed on other than bedrock.
        Where not otherwise protected from frost.
    - One of the following must be provided:
        Spread footings sized as follows:
          To distribute the load.
          According to soil strength.
        Piles where neither of the following is available:
          Solid earth.
          Solid rock.
  - Footings may not bear on frozen soil as follows:
    Where the soil is not permanently frozen.

1805 Footings and Foundations

1805.2.2 Isolated footings

This subsection applies to footings on granular soil.

- Isolated footings must be detailed as per one of the following:
  - Footings must be positioned in one of the following ways:
    So that a line between near bottom edges of adjacent footings has the following slope:
    - ≤ 30° to the horizontal.
    - A slope determined appropriate by engineering analysis.
  - Soil supporting the higher footing must be detailed in one of the following ways:
    - It must be braced.
    - It must be retained.
    - It must be laterally supported in an approved way.

1805.3.1 Building clearance from ascending slopes

- Buildings near the bottom of a slope with a gradient > 1:3 are governed as follows:
  - Buildings must be located far enough from such a slope to be protected from the following:
    - Drainage.
    - Erosion.
    - Sloughing.
  - The distance required between building face and toe of slope is to be one of the following:
    - That verified to be adequate by engineering analysis.
    - ≥ the smaller of the following distances as defined below:
      Distance:
      - ½ the rise of the slope.
      - 15'.
      Definitions:
      - Where the slope is > 1:1, the toe is defined as follows:
        The toe is located at the intersection of the following lines:
        - A 45° line tangent to the top of the slope.
        - A horizontal line at the top of the foundation.
      - Rise of slope is measured vertically between the following points:
        - Top of the slope.
        - Toe of slope if there is no retaining wall.
        - Top of any retaining wall at the toe of the slope.

    Note: The following are cited as sources of pertinent requirements:
    1805.3.5, "Alternate setback and clearance," addresses requirements pertaining to the engineering analysis as indicated above.
    Figure 1805.3.1, "Foundation clearances from slopes," includes setback requirements, a summary of which is provided above.

1805 Footings and Foundations

1805.3.2 Footing setback from descending slope surface

- This section applies to buildings on or near a slope with a gradient > 1:3.
- Footings of such buildings are governed as follows:
  - They must be embedded in firm material.
  - They must be set back from the sloped surface as follows:
    So as to avoid damaging settlement by the following:
      Adequate vertical support.
      Adequate lateral support.
  - They must be set back equal to one of the following distances:
    That verified to be adequate by engineering analysis.
    ≥ the smaller of the following distances measured as defined below:
    Distance:
      $^1/_3$ the rise.
      40'.
    Measurement:
      The setback distance is measured from the near face of the footing as follows:
        From the footing at bearing level on a horizontal line to one of the following:
          Where the slope is ≤ 1:1:
            To a point on the surface of the slope.
          Where the slope is > 1:1:
            To a point on a line as follows:
              A 45° line connecting to the bottom of the slope.
      Rise of slope is measured vertically between the following points:
        Top of the slope.
        Bottom of slope.

  Note: The following are cited as sources of pertinent requirements:
    1805.3.5, "Alternate setback and clearance," addresses requirements pertaining to the engineering analysis as indicated above.
    Figure 1805.3.1, "Foundation clearances from slopes," includes setback requirements, a summary of which is provided above.

1805.3.3 Pools

- This section addresses pools near a slope with a gradient > 1:3 as follows:
  - Pools regulated by the code.
- The required setback between pools and slopes is as follows:
  - ½ the setback required for building footings.
- Any part of a pool wall which is ≤ 7' from the top of a slope is governed as follows:
  - The wall must be able to support the water contained without the following:
    Assistance from the soil.

1805 Footings and Foundations

1805.3.4 Foundation elevation

- On all sites, the top of the foundation wall must be at one of the following heights:
  - ≥ a height equal to the sum of the following dimensions:
    - 12".
    - 2% of the distance between the building and either of the following:
      - The surface of the street gutter as follows:
        - At the point where the site drains into it.
      - An approved drainage device as follows:
        - At the inlet where the site drains into it.
  - A height as follows:
    - Approved by the building official.
    - Where the following drainage is verified at all points on the site:
      - Site drainage is to the point of discharge.
      - Site drainage is away from the structure.

1805.3.5 Alternate setback and clearance

- The following dimensional requirements for construction near slopes may vary from those specified in this section as indicated below:
  - Requirements:
    - Setbacks.
    - Clearances.
  - Variations:
    - Building official approval is required.
    - Building official may require the following:
      - Investigation and recommendation as follows:
        - By a registered design professional verifying the following:
          - That the intent of the setbacks and clearances is met.
        - Investigation must include consideration of the following:
          - Slope material.
          - Slope height.
          - Slope gradient.
          - Loading.
          - Erosion characteristics of slope material.

1805.4.1 Design

- Footings must be sized as follows:
  - So that the soil bearing capacity is not surpassed.
- A width ≥ 12" is required for footings.
- Footings in expansive soils must be designed as follows:
  - To accommodate the expansive soil.

  Note: 1805.8, "Design for expansive soils," is cited as governing such footing design.

1805 Footings and Foundations

1805.4.2 Concrete footings

- Concrete footings supporting walls of light-frame construction may be designed according to details provided in this section.
- Otherwise, the following aspects of concrete footings must comply with this section and the concrete design requirements of the code:
  - Design.
  - Materials.
  - Construction.

  Note: The following are cited as sources of requirements for concrete footing design:
  The 6 subsections of this section.
  Chapter 19, "Concrete."
  IBC Table 1805.4.2, "Footings Supporting Walls of Light-Frame Construction."

1805.4.2.3 Plain concrete footings

- The edge thickness for such footings is governed as follows for conditions indicated below:
  - Edge thickness:
    May be ≥ 6".
  - Conditions:
    In either of the following locations:
      Occupancy R-3.
      Under light-frame construction < 2 stories.
    With the following detailing:
      Footing extends beyond foundation wall as follows:
        ≤ wall thickness.
      Bearing on soil.
- For other plain concrete footings, the edge thickness is governed as follows:
  - Must be ≥ 8" as follows:
    Where bearing on soil.

1805.4.3. Masonry-unit footings

- Masonry-unit footings supporting walls of light-frame construction may be designed according to details in Fig. 1805.4.2 A–G.
- Otherwise, the following aspects of masonry-unit footings must comply with this section and the masonry design requirements of the code:
  - Design.
  - Materials.
  - Construction.

  Note: The following are cited as sources of requirements for concrete footing design:
  The 2 subsections of this section.
  Chapter 21, "Masonry."
  IBC Table 1805.4.2, "Footings Supporting Walls of Light-Frame Construction."

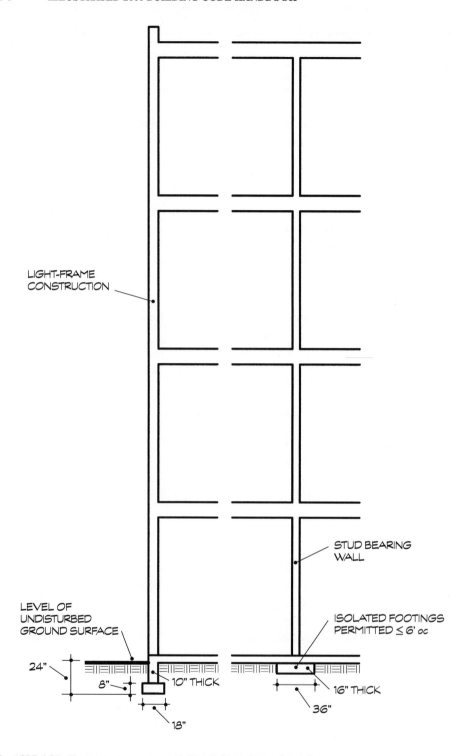

Fig. 1805.4.2A. Concrete or masonry-unit foundations supporting 3 floors.

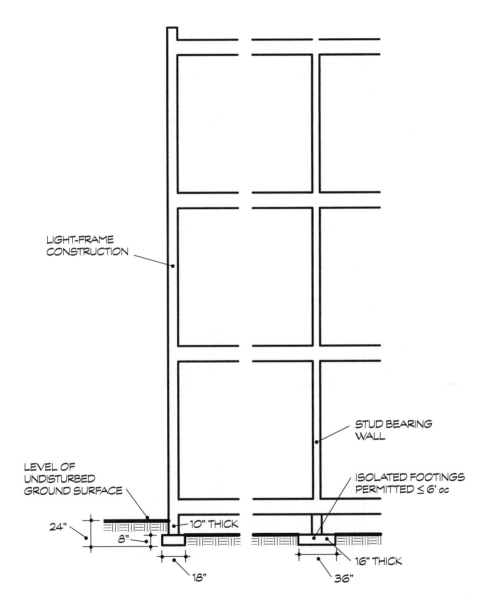

Fig. 1805.4.2B. Concrete or masonry-unit foundations supporting 3 floors.

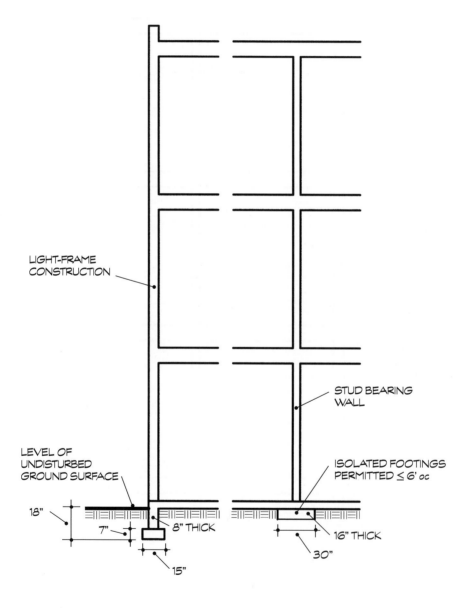

Fig. 1805.4.2C. Concrete or masonry-unit foundations supporting 2 floors.

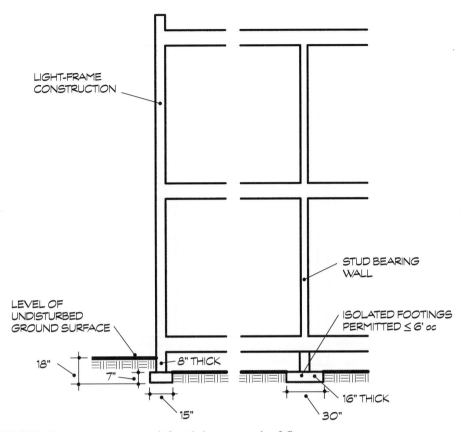

Fig. 1805.4.2D. Concrete or masonry-unit foundations supporting 2 floors.

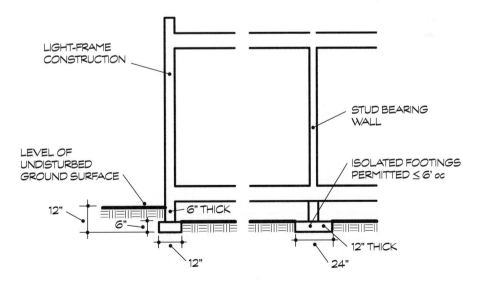

Fig. 1805.4.2E. Concrete or masonry-unit foundations supporting 1 floor.

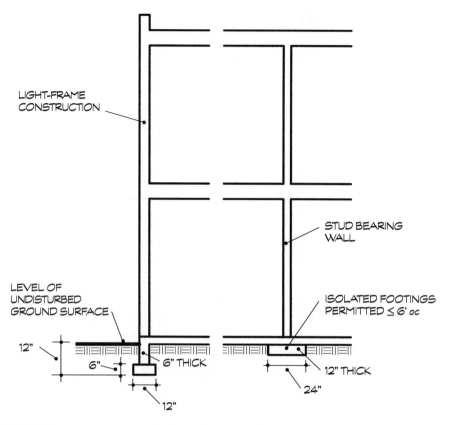

Fig. 1805.4.2F. Concrete or masonry-unit foundations supporting 1 floor.

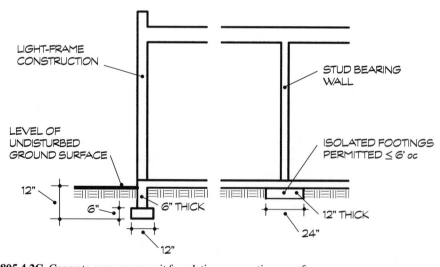

Fig. 1805.4.2G. Concrete or masonry-unit foundations supporting a roof.

1805 Footings and Foundations

1805.4.3.1 Dimensions

- •Masonry-unit footings are governed as follows:
  - ○ Footing depth (thickness) required is as follows:
    - $\geq 2 \times$ footing projection beyond the following:
      Wall.
      Pier.
      Column.
  - ○ Footing width required is as follows:
    - $\geq 8"$ wider than the foundation wall supported.
  - ○ Masonry must be set in one of the following mortar types:
    M, S.

  Note: 2103.7, "Mortar," is cited as governing this material as indicated above.

1805.4.3.2 Offsets

- • This section governs brick foundations as follows:
  - ○ Where successive brick courses step back from a wider footing to approach the thickness of the foundation wall.
- • Where such foundations step back with each course, the following applies:
  - ○ Courses must be set back $\leq 1\frac{1}{2}"$ from the course below.
- • Where each step back consists of two courses flush with each other, the following applies:
  - ○ Pairs of flush courses must be set back $\leq 3"$ from the pair of courses below.

1805.4.4 Steel grillage footings

- • Structural steel sections in grillage footings are governed as follows:
  - ○ Components must be separated by approved steel spacers.
  - ○ Components must be completely encased in concrete as follows:
    - $\geq 6"$ thick on the bottom.
    - $\geq 4"$ elsewhere.
  - ○ Space between components must be filled with one of the following:
    Concrete.
    Cement grout.

1805 Footings and Foundations

1805.5 Foundations walls

- This section addresses concrete and masonry foundation walls.
- Walls meeting the following conditions may be constructed according to this section:
  - Walls laterally supported at top and bottom.
  - Walls conforming to the details provided in this section.
- Other foundation walls must meet design requirements of this code.

   Note: The following are cited as governing foundation walls as indicated above:
   Chapter 19, "Concrete."
   Chapter 21, "Masonry."
   The 5 subsections of this section.
   IBC Table 1805.5 (1), "Plain Masonry and Plain Concrete Foundation Walls."
   IBC Table 1805.5 (2), "8-Inch Reinforced Concrete and Masonry Foundation Walls Where d ≥ 5 Inches."
   IBC Table 1805.5 (3), "10-Inch Reinforced Concrete and Masonry Foundation Walls Where d ≥ 6.75 Inches."
   IBC Table 1805.5 (4), "12-Inch Reinforced Concrete and Masonry Foundation Walls Where d ≥ 8.75 Inches."

1805.5.1.1 Thickness based on walls supported

- This section addresses concrete and masonry foundation walls.
- Foundation walls ≥ 8" nominal thickness may support the following walls where meeting requirements indicated below:
  - Walls:
     Frame walls with brick veneers.
     10"-wide cavity walls.
  - Requirements:
     A corbeled 8" wall is governed as follows:
       The top corbel must be the following:
         A full course of headers ≥ 6" long.
       Height of the wall is limited as follows:
         ≤ that of the bottom of the floor framing.

   Note: The following are cited as sources of applicable requirements:
   1805.5.1.2, "Thickness based on soil loads, unbalanced backfill height and wall height," provides requirements for the 8" walls indicated above.
   2104.2, "Corbeled masonry," governs such detailing.

- Otherwise, foundation wall thickness is governed as follows:
  - It must be ≥ the thickness of the wall it supports.

1805 Footings and Foundations

1805.5.1.2 Thickness based on soil loads, unbalanced backfill height and wall height

- The following applies to the details of foundation walls provided for this section:
  - Where the walls are masonry, they are based on the following:
    Masonry set in the following type M or S mortar.
  - The height of unbalanced backfill is measured as follows:
    Between the following two levels:
    The finished exterior grade.
    One of the following interior levels:
    Interior grade where there is no concrete slab.
    Top of concrete slab where provided.
  - Foundation wall thickness must comply with the details provided in
    Figures 1805.5.1.2 (A–D).

  Note: The following are cited as sources of required wall thickness:
  IBC Table 1805.5 (1), "Plain Masonry and Plain Concrete Foundation Walls."
  IBC Table 1805.5 (2), "8-Inch Reinforced Concrete and Masonry Foundation Walls Where d ≥ 5 Inches."
  IBC Table 1805.5 (3), "10-Inch Reinforced Concrete and Masonry Foundation Walls Where d ≥ 6.75 Inches."
  IBC Table 1805.5 (4), "12-Inch Reinforced Concrete and Masonry Foundation Walls Where d ≥ 8.75 Inches."

1805.5.1.3 Rubble stone

- Foundation walls of random rubble stone are governed as follows:
  - Thickness must be ≥ 1'-4".
  - Such walls may not be used in the following Seismic Design Categories:
    C, D, E, F.

1805.5.3 Alternative foundation wall reinforcement

- Reinforcement indicated in details provided in this section may be varied as follows:
  - Bar sizes and spacing may be adjusted providing the following is met:
    Cross-sectional area of steel per linear foot of wall must remain the same.
  - Bar spacing must be ≤ 6'.
  - Bar size must be ≤ #11.

  Note: The following are cited as sources of required wall reinforcing:
  IBC Table 1805.5 (2), "8-Inch Reinforced Concrete and Masonry Foundation Walls Where d ≥ 5 Inches."
  IBC Table 1805.5 (3), "10-Inch Reinforced Concrete and Masonry Foundation Walls Where d ≥ 6.75 Inches."
  IBC Table 1805.5 (4), "12-Inch Reinforced Concrete and Masonry Foundation Walls Where d ≥ 8.75 Inches."

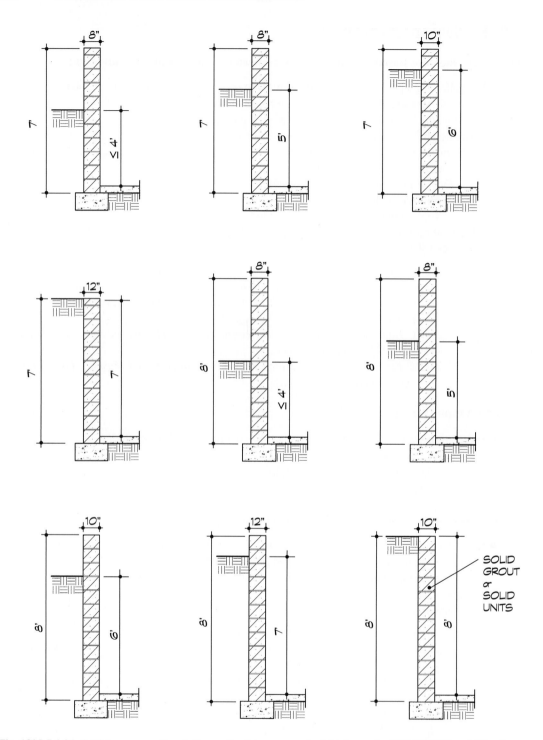

Fig. 1805.5.1.2A-1. Plain masonry foundation wall minimum, nominal thickness for GW, GP, SW, and SP soils. *[IBC Table 1805.5(1)]*

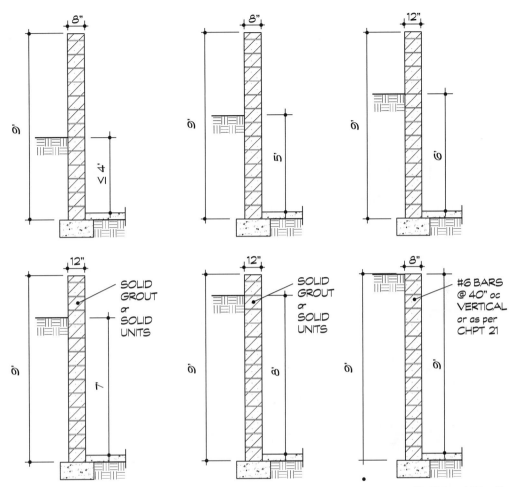

Fig. 1805.5.1.2A-2. Plain masonry foundation wall minimum, nominal thickness for GW, GP, SW, and SP soils. *[IBC Table 1805.5(1)]*

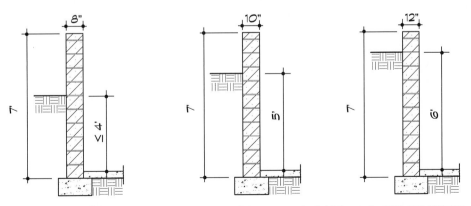

Fig. 1805.5.1.2A-3. Plain masonry foundation wall minimum, nominal thickness for GM, GC, SM-SC, and ML soils. *[IBC Table 1805.5(1)]*

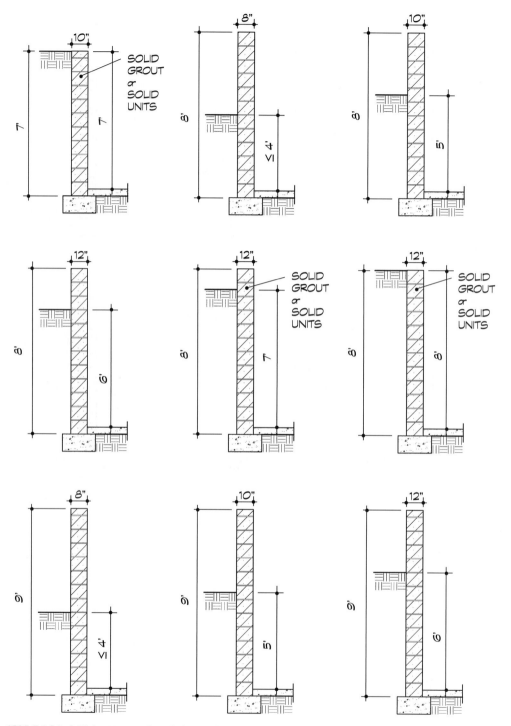

Fig. 1805.5.1.2A-4. Plain masonry foundation wall minimum, nominal thickness for GM, GC, SM, SM-SC, and ML soils. *[IBC Table 1805.5(1)]*

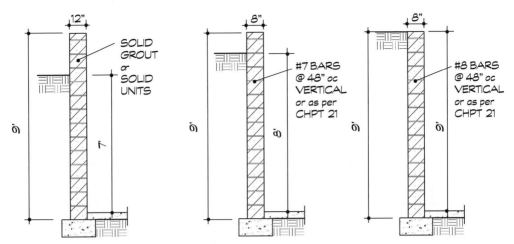

Fig. 1805.5.1.2A-5. Plain masonry foundation wall minimum, nominal thickness for GM, GC, SM, SM–SC, and ML soils. *[IBC Table 1805.5(1)]*

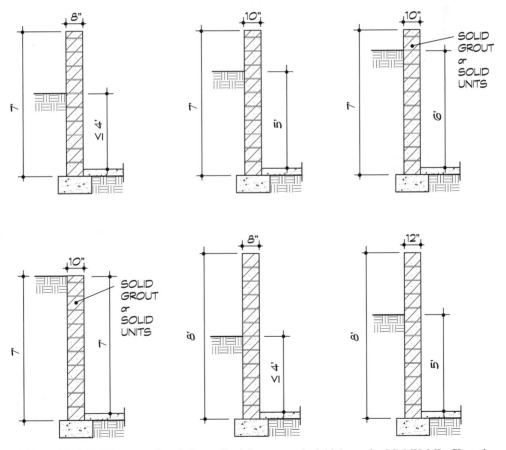

Fig. 1805.5.1.2A-6. Plain masonry foundation wall minimum, nominal thickness for SC, MH, ML–CL, and inorganic CL soils. *[IBC Table 1805.5(1)]*

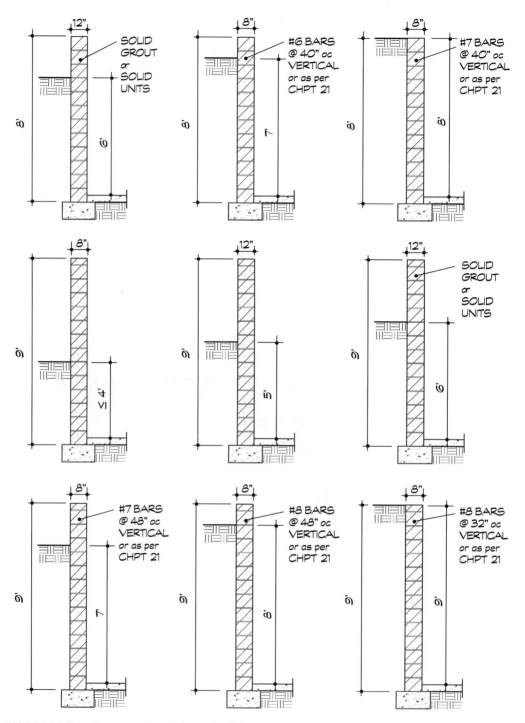

Fig. 1805.5.1.2A-7. Plain masonry foundation wall minimum, nominal thickness for SC, MH, ML–CL, and inorganic CL soils. *[IBC Table 1805.5(1)]*

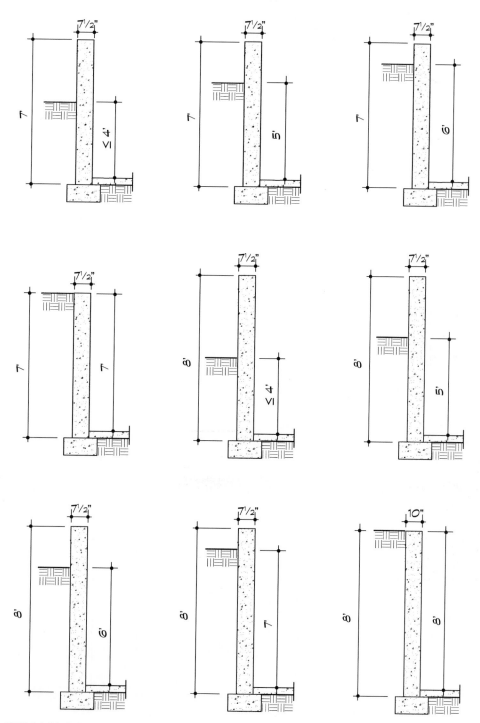

Fig. 1805.5.1.2A-8. Plain masonry foundation wall minimum, nominal thickness for GW, GP, SW, and SP soils.
[IBC Table 1805.5(1)]

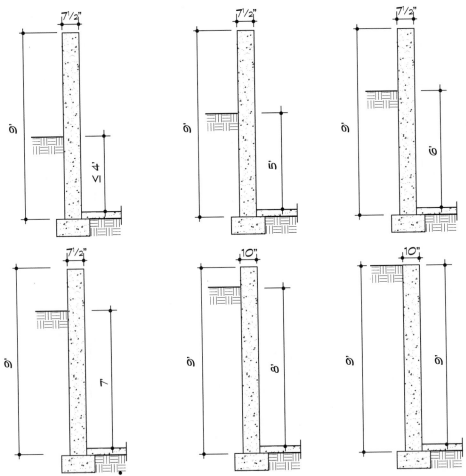

Fig. 1805.5.1.2A-9. Plain concrete foundation wall minimum, nominal thickness for GW, GP, SW, and SP soils. *[IBC Table 1805.5(1)]*

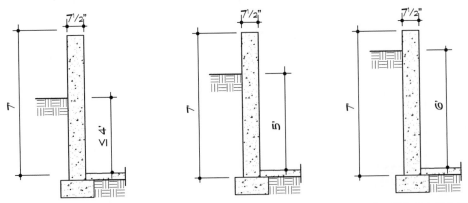

Fig. 1805.5.1.2A-10. Plain masonry foundation wall minimum, nominal thickness for GM, GC, SM, SM–SC, and ML soils. *[IBC Table 1805.5(1)]*

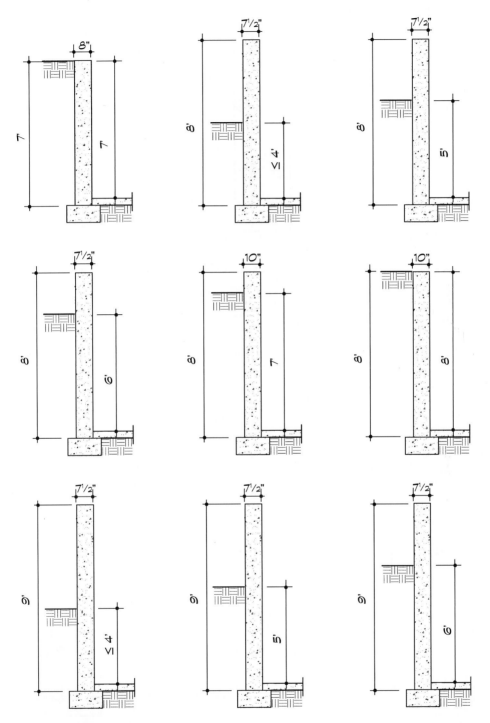

Fig. 1805.5.1.2A-11. Plain concrete foundation wall minimum, nominal thickness for GM, GC, SM, SM–SC, and ML soils. *[IBC Table 1805.5(1)]*

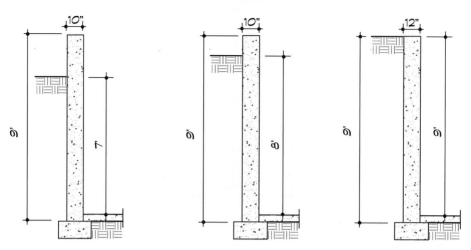

Fig. 1805.5.1.2A-12. Plain concrete foundation wall minimum, nominal thickness for GM, GC, SM, SM–SC, and ML soils. *[IBC Table 1805.5(1)]*

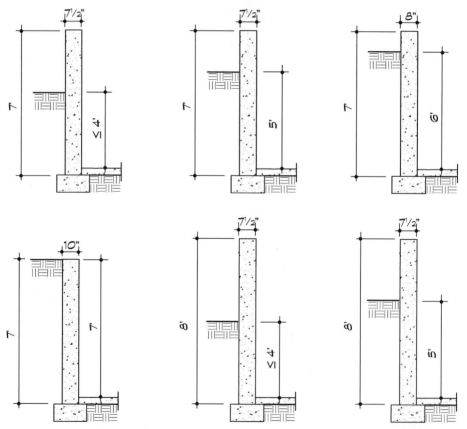

Fig. 1805.5.1.2A-13. Plain concrete foundation wall minimum, nominal thickness for SC, MH, ML–CL and inorganic CL soils. *[IBC Table 1805.5(1)]*

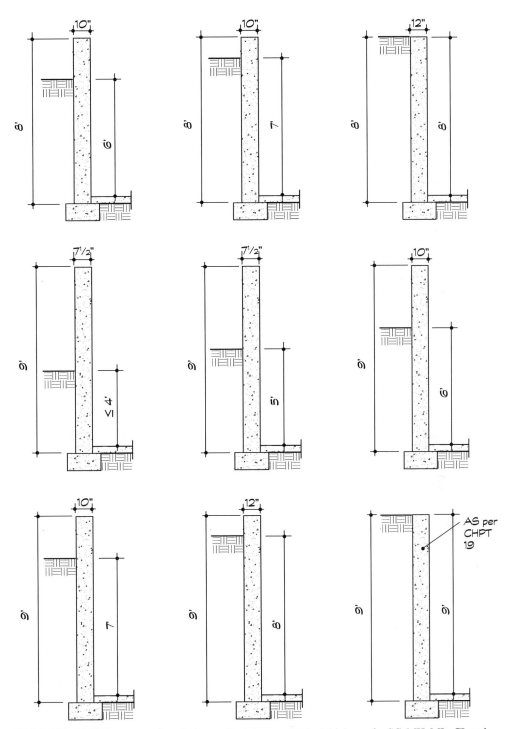

Fig. 1805.5.1.2A-14. Plain concrete foundation wall minimum, nominal thickness for SC, MH, ML–CL and inorganic CL soils. *[IBC Table 1805.5(1)]*

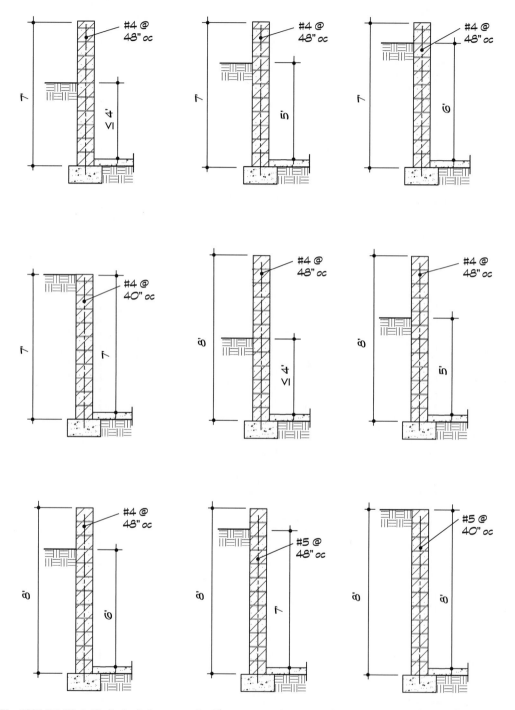

Fig. 1805.5.1.2B-1. Vertical reinforcement for 8" concrete and masonry foundation walls with d ≥ 5" . Soil is GW, GP, SW, or SP. *[IBC Table 1805.5(2)]*

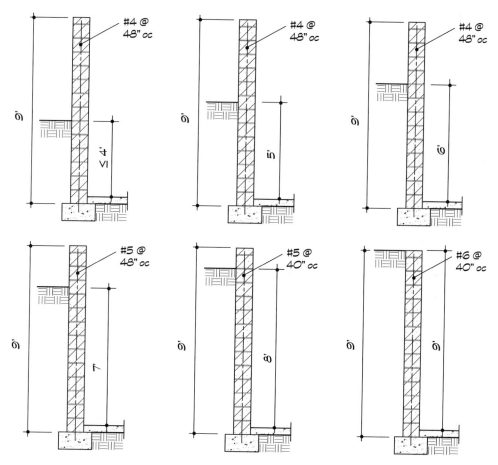

Fig. 1805.5.1.2B-2. Vertical reinforcing for 8" concrete and masonry foundation walls with d ≥ 5" . Soil is GW, GP, SW, or SP. *[IBC Table 1805.5(2)]*

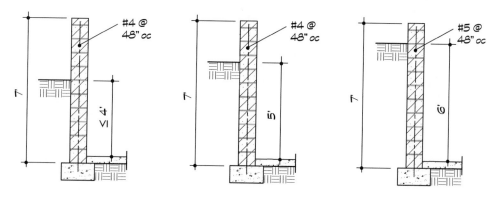

Fig. 1805.5.1.2B-3. Vertical reinforcing for 8" concrete and masonry foundation walls with d ≥ 5" . Soil is GM, GC, SM, SM–SC, or ML. *[IBC Table 1805.5(2)]*

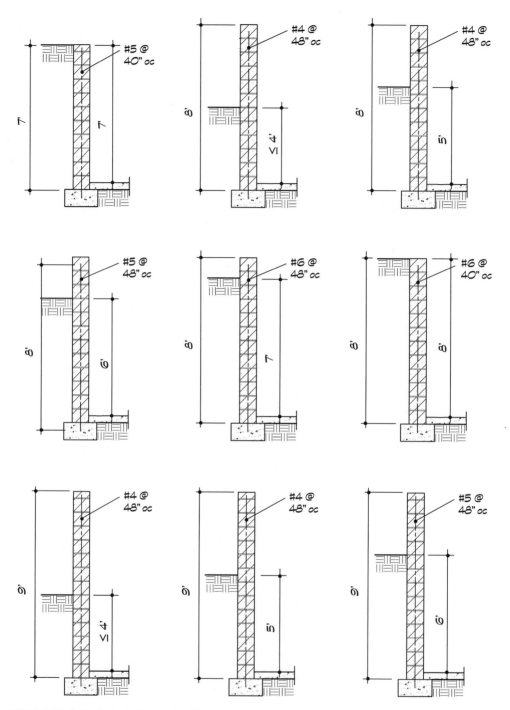

Fig. 1805.5.1.2B-4. Vertical reinforcing for 8" concrete and masonry foundation walls with d ≥ 5". Soil is GM, GC, SM, SM–SC, or ML. *[IBC Table 1805.5(2)]*

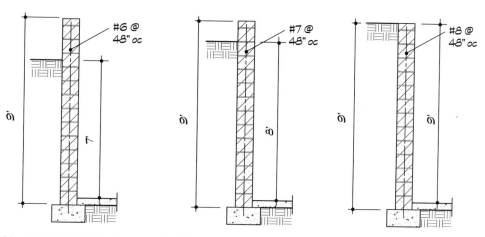

Fig. 1805.5.1.2B-5. Vertical reinforcing for 8" concrete and masonry foundation walls with d ≥ 5" . Soil is GM, GC, SM, SM–SC, or ML. *[IBC Table 1805.5(2)]*

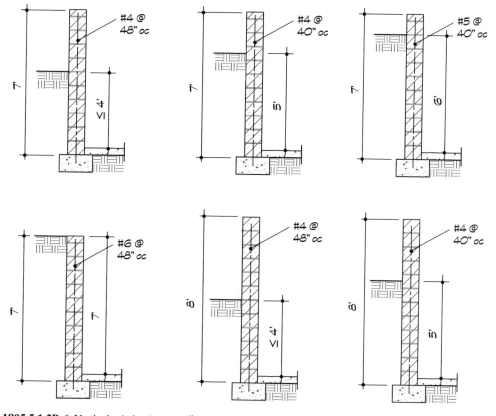

Fig. 1805.5.1.2B-6. Vertical reinforcing for 8" concrete and masonry foundation walls with d ≥ 5" . Soil is SC, MH, ML–CL, or inorganic CL. *[IBC Table 1805.5(2)]*

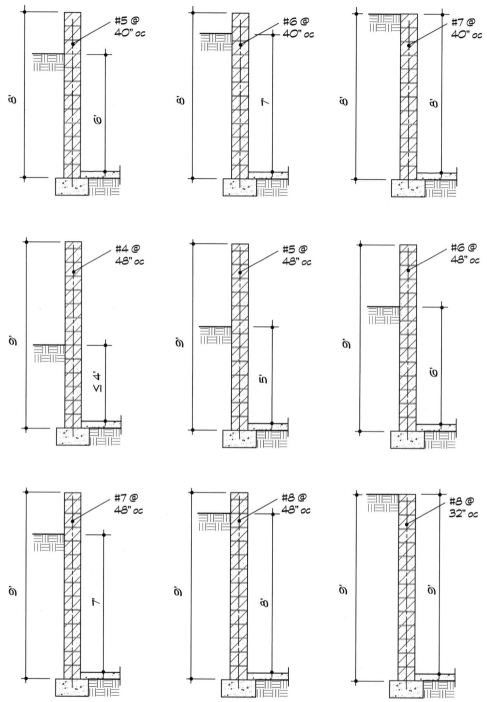

Fig. 1805.5.1.2B-7. Vertical reinforcing for 8" concrete and masonry foundation walls with d ≥ 5" . Soil is SC, MH, ML–CL, or inorganic CL. *[IBC Table 1805.5(2)]*

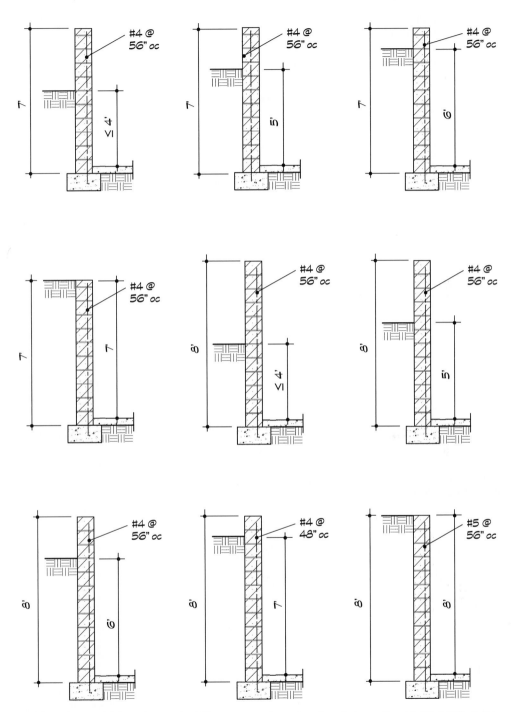

Fig. 1805.5.1.2C-1. Vertical reinforcing for 10" concrete and masonry foundation walls with d ≥ 6.75" . Soil is GW, GP, SW, or SP. *[IBC Table 1805.5(3)]*

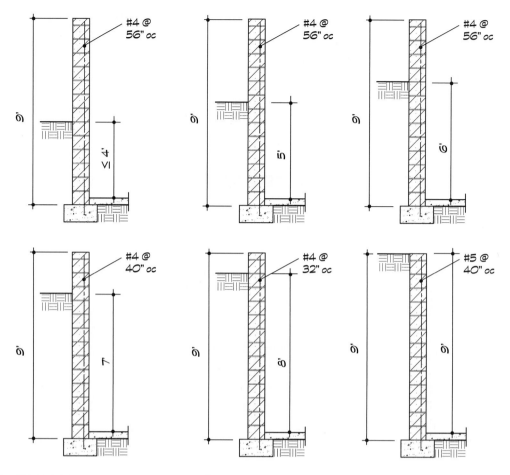

Fig. 1805.5.1.2C-2. Vertical reinforcing for 10" concrete and masonry foundation walls with d ≥ 6.75" . Soil is GW, GP, SW, or SP. *[IBC Table 1805.5(3)]*

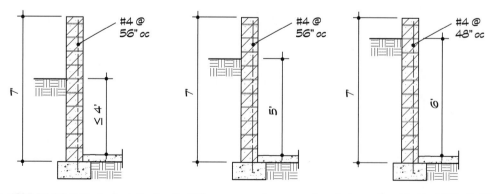

Fig. 1805.5.1.2C-3. Vertical reinforcing for 10" concrete and masonry foundation walls with d ≥ 6.75" . Soil is GM, GC, SM, SM–SC, and ML. *[IBC Table 1805.5(3)]*

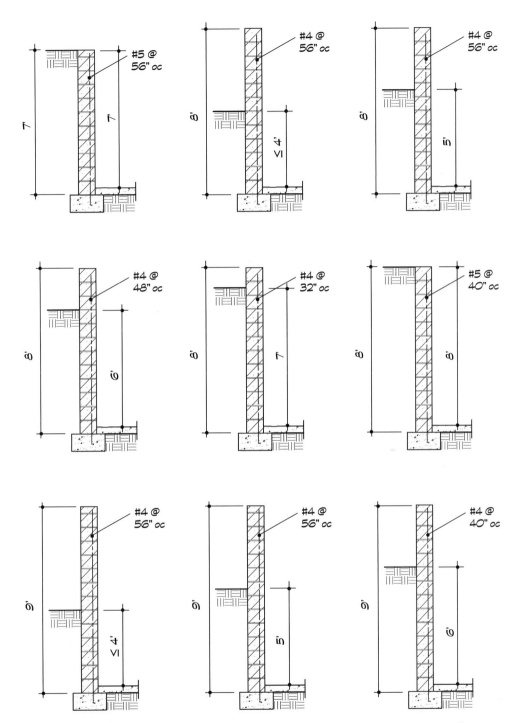

Fig. 1805.5.1.2C-4. Vertical reinforcing for 10″ concrete and masonry foundation walls with d ≥ 6.75″ . Soil is GM, GC, SM, SM–SC, and ML. *[IBC Table 1805.5(3)]*

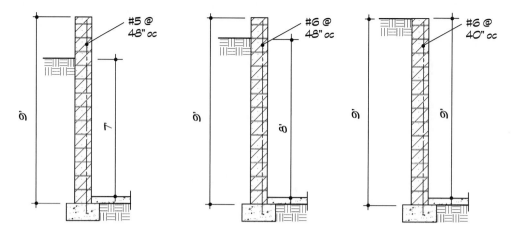

Fig. 1805.5.1.2C-5. Vertical reinforcing for 10" concrete and masonry foundation walls with d ≥ 6.75". Soil is GM, GC, SM, SM–SC, and ML. *[IBC Table 1805.5(3)]*

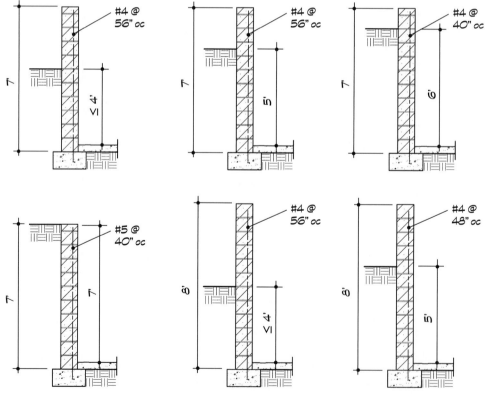

Fig. 1805.5.1.2C-6. Vertical reinforcing for 10" concrete and masonry foundation walls with d ≥ 6.75". Soil is SC, MH, ML–CL, or inorganic CL. *[IBC Table 1805.5(3)]*

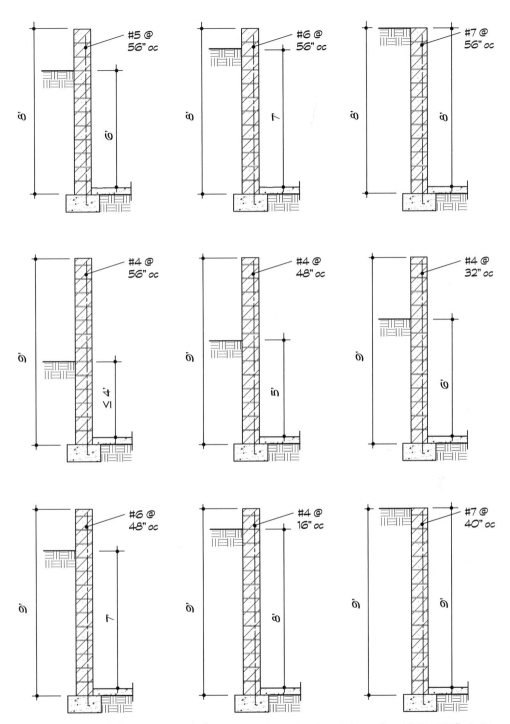

Fig. 1805.5.1.2C-7. Vertical reinforcing for 10" concrete and masonry foundation walls with d ≥ 6.75" . Soil is SC, MH, ML–CL, or inorganic CL. *[IBC Table 1805.5(3)]*

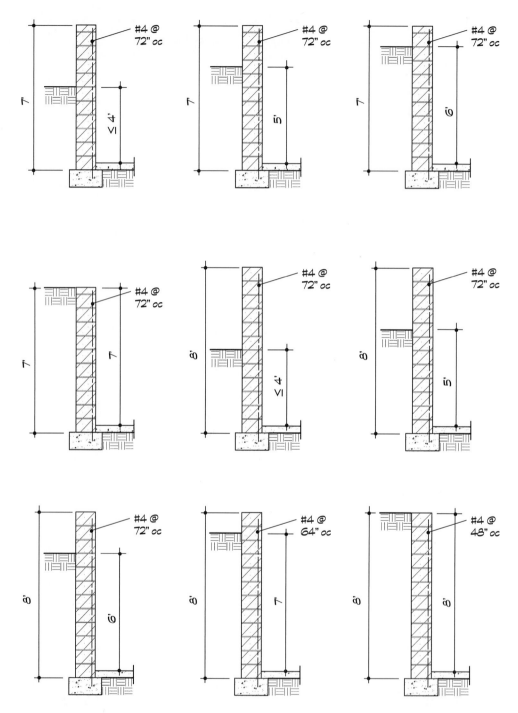

Fig. 1805.5.1.2D-1. Vertical reinforcing for 12" concrete and masonry foundation walls with $d \geq 8.75"$. Soil is GW, GP, SW, or SP. *[IBC Table 1805.5(4)]*

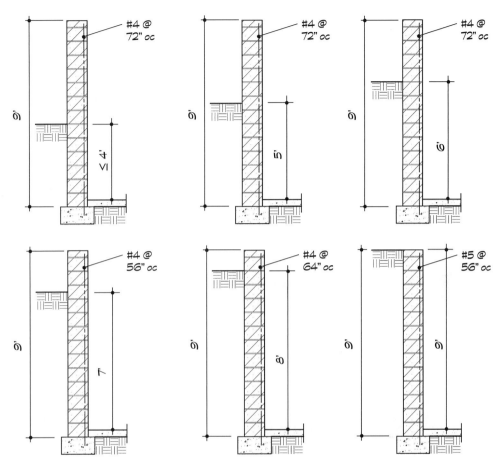

Fig. 1805.5.1.2D-2. Vertical reinforcing for 12" concrete and masonry foundation walls with d ≥ 8.75" . Soil is GW, GP, SW, or SP. *[IBC Table 1805.5(4)]*

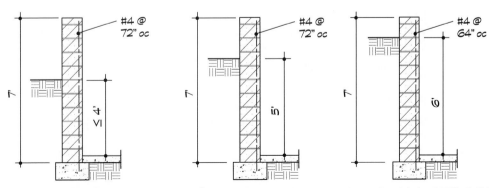

Fig. 1805.5.1.2D-3. Vertical reinforcing for 12" concrete and masonry foundation walls with d ≥ 8.75" . Soil is GM, GC, SM, SM–SC, or ML. *[IBC Table 1805.5(4)]*

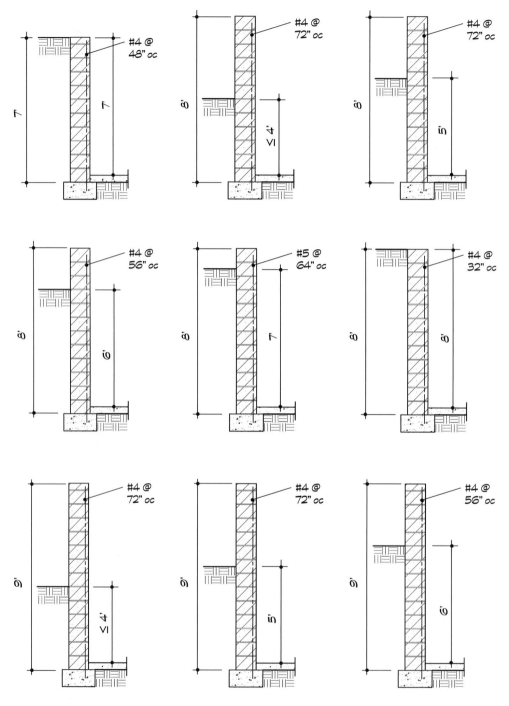

Fig. 1805.5.1.2D-4. Vertical reinforcing for 12" concrete and masonry foundation walls with d ≥ 8.75". Soil is GM, GC, SM, SM–SC, or ML. *[IBC Table 1805.5(4)]*

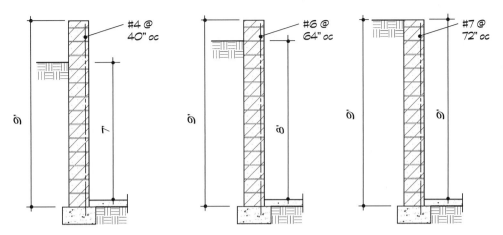

Fig. 1805.5.1.2D-5. Vertical reinforcing for 12" concrete and masonry foundation walls with d ≥ 8.75". Soil is GM, GC, SM, SM–SC, or ML. *[IBC Table 1805.5(4)]*

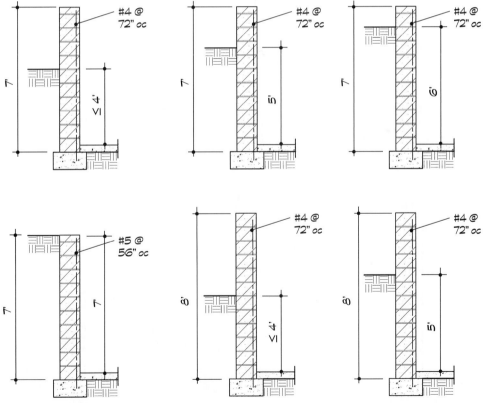

Fig. 1805.5.1.2D-6. Vertical reinforcing for 12" concrete and masonry foundation walls with d ≥ 8.75". Soil is SC, MH, ML–CL, or inorganic CL. *[IBC Table 1805.5(4)]*

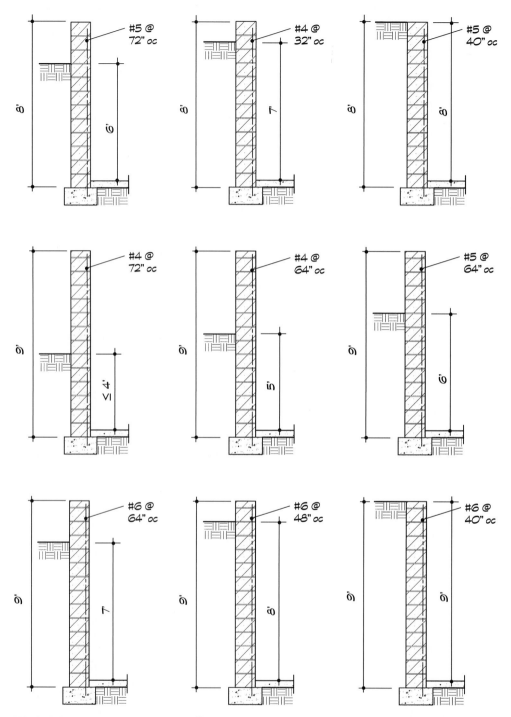

Fig. 1805.5.1.2D-7. Vertical reinforcing for 12" concrete and masonry foundation walls with d ≥ 8.75" . Soil is SC, MH, ML–CL, or inorganic CL. *[IBC Table 1805.5(4)]*

1805 Footings and Foundations

1805.5.4 Hollow masonry walls

- The following is required for foundation walls of hollow masonry units:
  - ≥ 4" of solid masonry as follows:
    - At the tops of walls.
    - At girder supports.

1805.5.6 Pier and curtain wall foundations *(part 1 of 2)*

- Pier and curtain wall foundations may be used as follows where the conditions indicated in this section apply:
  - In locations other than the following Seismic Design Categories:
    - D, E, F.
  - For light-frame construction as follows:
    - ≤ 2 stories.
- Load-bearing walls must meet the following requirements:
  - They must bear on continuous footings with the following detail:
    - Footings must tie into exterior wall footings.
  - Thickness must be one of the following:
    - ≥ 4" nominal.
    - ≥ 3⅝" actual.
  - They must be integral with piers as follows:
    - Spaced ≤ 6' on center.
- Piers must meet the following requirements:
  - Unsupported height of masonry piers is limited as follows:
    - Height must be ≤ 10 × the least pier dimension.
  - The following units supporting beams and girders must meet requirements shown below:
    - Units:
      - Structural clay tile.
      - Hollow concrete masonry.
    - Requirements:
      - Where unsupported height of piers is > 4 × least dimension:
        - Cellular spaces must be filled with the following:
          - Type M or S mortar.
      - Where unsupported height of piers is ≤ 4 × least dimension:
        - Cellular spaces need not be filled.
      - Hollow piers must be capped by one of the following methods:
        - With ≥ 4" of solid masonry.
        - With ≥ 4" of concrete.
        - By filling the cells of the top course with concrete or grout.

1805 Footings and Foundations

1805.5.6 Pier and curtain wall foundations *(part 2 of 2)*

- The height of a 4" load-bearing masonry wall is limited as follows:
    - To ≤ 4' where supporting the following:
        - Wood-framed walls.
        - Wood-framed floors.
- The height of unbalanced fill for 4" foundation walls is limited as follows:
    - To ≤ 2' for solid masonry.
    - To ≤ 1' for hollow masonry.

1806 Dampproofing and Waterproofing

1806.1 Where required

- The following components must be detailed as indicated below:
    - Components:
        Walls or parts of walls with both the characteristics:
            In contact with earth.
            Enclose interior space.
        Floors below grade.
    - Detailing:
        Components in locations indicated below must be treated with one of following systems:
            Systems:
                Dampproofing as per requirements of this section.
                Waterproofing as per requirements of this section.
            Locations:
                Occupancy R, I.
                Other occupancies where omission of the systems would be detrimental as follows:
                    To the building.
                    To the occupancy.

    Note: 1202.4, "Natural ventilation," is cited as the source governing ventilation for crawl spaces.

1806.1.1 Story above grade

- This section applies to a basement that qualifies as a story above grade.
- Where finished grade is as follows, the requirements below apply:
    - Grade:
        Located below the basement floor for $\geq \frac{1}{4}$ of the perimeter.
    - Requirements:
        The walls below grade must be dampproofed.
        The floor must be dampproofed.
        A foundation drain is required around the walls below grade.
- A subsurface soil investigation is not required as follows:
    - To determine the height of the water table.
- Such a basement need not be waterproofed.
- A base course is not required under such a basement floor.

    Note: The following are cited as sources of requirements which may be omitted for the basement described in this section:
    1802.2.3, "Groundwater table," describes the soil investigation otherwise required.
    1806.3, "Waterproofing required," describes waterproofing otherwise required.
    1806.4.1,"Floor base course," describes the base course otherwise required.
    The following are cited as sources of requirements applicable to this section:
    1806.2, "Dampproofing required."
    1806.4.2, "Foundation drain."

1806 Dampproofing and Waterproofing

1806.1.2 Underfloor space

- Ground surface in a crawl space is governed as follows:
  - It may not be below footing bearing level.
- One of the following details must be provided where either condition indicated applies:
  - Details:
      Ground surface in a crawl space must be at the following height:
          ≥ the height of exterior finished grade.
      An approved drainage system must be provided.
    Conditions:
      Groundwater table rises to ≤ 6" of finished grade at building perimeter.
      Surface groundwater does not readily drain from the site.
- Where a crawl space is as follows, the conditions listed below may be omitted:
  - Crawl space:
      Where ground surface is ≥ the height of exterior finished grade.
  - Conditions:
      The following requirements may be omitted:
      A subsurface soil investigation to determine the height of the water table.
      Dampproofing.
      Waterproofing.
      A subsoil drainage system.

    Note: The following are cited as sources of requirements which may be omitted for the basement described in this section:
    1802.2.3, "Groundwater table," describes soil investigation requirements.
    1806.2, "Dampproofing required."
    1806.3, "Waterproofing required."
    1806.4, "Subsoil drainage system."

1806.1.2.1 Flood hazard areas

- Where located in a flood hazard area, the following applies:
  - Ground surface in a crawl space must be as follows:
      ≥ the height of exterior finished grade.

    Note: 1612.3, "Establishment of flood hazard areas," is cited as the source defining the conditions that establish the area indicated above.

1806 Dampproofing and Waterproofing

1806.1.3 Ground-water control

- • This section addresses the following components:
  - Walls or parts of walls with both the following characteristics:
    - In contact with earth.
    - Enclose interior space.
  - Floors below grade.
- • Such walls and floors must be dampproofed in the following case:
  - ○ Where the groundwater table is lowered as follows:
    - Lowered and maintained at < 6" below the bottom of lowest floor.
- • Systems utilized to lower the groundwater table must be in consideration of the following:
  - ○ Accepted principles of engineering.
  - ○ Permeability of the soil.
  - ○ Rate of water flow into the drainage system.
  - ○ Capacity of pumps.
  - ○ Pressure against which pumps must perform.
  - ○ Capacity of disposal area for the system.
  - ○ Other applicable conditions.

  > *Note: 1806.2, "Dampproofing required," is cited as the source of requirements for dampproofing.*

1806.2 Dampproofing required

- • This section does not apply to wood foundations.
- • This section applies to walls and floors qualifying for one of the following:
  - ○ Waterproofing.
  - ○ Dampproofing.
- • Such walls and floors must be dampproofed in the following case:
  - ○ Where there is no hydrostatic pressure.

  > *Note: The following are cited as sources of applicable requirements:*
  > *1802.2.3, "Groundwater table," describes conditions where no hydrostatic pressure will occur.*
  > *AFPA TR7, "Basic Requirements for Permanent Wood Foundation System," provides requirements by which such foundations must be designed.*

1806 Dampproofing and Waterproofing

1806.2.1 Floors

- This section applies to floors requiring dampproofing.
- Where there is no separate floor above a slab, dampproofing is installed as follows:
  - Dampproofing must be installed between the floor and base course.

    Note: 1806.4.1, "Floor base course," is cited as the source of requirements for the base course indicated above.

- Where located below a slab, dampproofing is governed as follows:
  - One of the following systems is required:
    $\geq$ 6-mil polyethylene as follows:
    With joints lapped $\geq$ 6".
    Other approved materials and methods.
- Where located on top a slab, dampproofing is governed as follows:
  - One of the following systems is required:
    Dampproofing is to be mopped-on-bitumen.
    $\geq$ 4-mil polyethylene.
    Other approved materials and methods.
  - Joints in the dampproofing membrane are governed as follows:
    To be lapped and sealed as per manufacturer's instructions.

1806.2.2 Walls

- This section applies to walls requiring dampproofing.
- Dampproofing must be installed as follows:
  - On the exterior surface of the wall.
  - From the top of footing to above grade.
- Dampproofing must be one of the following materials:
  - Bituminous material.
  - Acrylic modified cement at 3 lbs/square yard.
  - $^1/_8$" coat of surface-bonding mortar.
  - Any waterproofing material as follows:
    Two-ply hot mopped felts.
    $\geq$ 6-mil polyvinyl chloride.
    $\geq$ 40-mil polymer-modified asphalt.
    $\geq$ 6-mil polyethylene.
    Other approved materials and methods.

Note: The following are cited as sources of applicable requirements:
ASTM C 887, "Specification for Packaged, Dry Combined Materials for Surface Bonding Mortar," governs surface bonding mortar as indicated above.
1806.3.2, "Walls," lists waterproofing materials as summarized above.

1806 Dampproofing and Waterproofing

1806.2.2.1 Surface preparation of walls

- Walls to receive dampproofing must be prepared as follows:
  - Concrete walls:
    Form tie holes and recesses must be sealed with one of the following:
      Bituminous material.
      Other approved material or method.
  - Unit masonry:
    Where dampproofing is not approved for direct application:
      Walls must be parged as follows:
        On the exterior surface below grade.
        With $\geq \frac{3}{8}$" portland cement mortar.
        Parging is to be coved at the footing.
    Where dampproofing is approved for direct application:
      Parging is not required.

1806.3 Waterproofing required

- This section applies to walls and floors qualifying for one of the following:
  - Waterproofing.
  - Dampproofing.
- Such walls and floors must be waterproofed as follows:
  - Where both of the following conditions apply:
    Where there is hydrostatic pressure.
    Where a groundwater control system is not provided.

  Note: The following are cited as sources of applicable requirements:
  1802.2.3, "Groundwater table," describes the conditions where hydrostatic pressure will occur.
  1806.1.3, "Groundwater control," provides requirements for the control system indicated above.

1806.3.1 Floors

- Concrete floors required to be waterproofed must use the following material:
  - Material designed to resist the hydrostatic pressure against it.
- One of the following or other approved waterproofing material must be placed under the slab:
  - Rubberized asphalt membrane.
  - Butyl rubber membrane.
  - $\geq$ 60-mil polyvinyl chloride as follows:
    Joints lapped $\geq$ 6".
  - Membrane joints must be lapped and sealed as per manufacturer's instructions.

1806 Dampproofing and Waterproofing

1806.3.2 Walls

- Walls and parts of walls required to be waterproofed are governed as follows:
  - They must be one of the following:
    Concrete.
    Masonry.
  - They must be designed to resist the following:
    Hydrostatic pressure applied.
    Lateral loads applied.
  - They must have waterproofing between the following points:
    The bottom of the wall.
    A point $\geq 12"$ above the highest groundwater table level.
  - They must have dampproofing as follows:
    On the remainder of the wall below grade.
  - Waterproofing must consist of one of the following:
    Two-ply hot mopped felts.
    $\geq$ 6-mil polyvinyl chloride.
    $\geq$ 40-mil polymer-modified asphalt.
    $\geq$ 6-mil polyethylene.
    Other approved materials and methods.
  - Joints in the waterproofing membrane must be detailed as follows:
    Lapped and sealed as per manufacturer's instructions.

    Note: 1806.2.2, "Walls," is cited as the source of requirements for dampproofing as required above.

1806.3.2.1 Surface preparation of walls

- Walls to receive waterproofing must be prepared as follows:
  - Concrete walls:
    Form tie holes and recesses must be sealed with one of the following:
      Bituminous material.
      Other approved material or method.
  - Unit masonry:
    Where waterproofing is not approved for direct application:
      Walls must be parged as follows:
        On the exterior surface below grade.
        With $\geq$ $^3/_8"$ portland cement mortar.
        Parging is to be coved at the footing.
    Where waterproofing is approved for direct application:
      Parging is not required.

    Note: 1806.2.2.1, "Surface preparation of walls," is cited as the source of requirements for wall preparation, a summary of which is provided above.

1806 Dampproofing and Waterproofing

1806.4 Subsoil drainage system

This section addresses floors below grade and walls enclosing space and contacting earth.

- Where hydrostatic pressure is not present, the following applies:
  - Dampproofing is required.
  - A base is required under the floor.
  - A drain is required at the perimeter of the foundation.
  - The water table may be lowered by the subsoil drainage system described in this section.

  Note: 1806.1.3, "Groundwater control," is cited as the source of requirements for the subsoil drainage system indicated above.

1806.4.1 Floor base course

- The following basement floors are not subject to the requirements indicated below:
  - Excluded floors:
    Basements with both the following characteristics:
    The basement qualifies as a story above grade.
    The finished grade is below ≥ ¼ of the basement wall perimeter.
    Where the site has either of the following conditions:
    Site soil is well-drained gravel mixture.
    Site soil is well-drained sand/gravel mixture.
  - Requirements:
    Other basement floors must be on a base course as follows:
    ≥ 4" of gravel crushed stone.
    Base must have ≤ 10% material passing a #4 sieve.

1806.4.2 Foundation drain

- This section addresses foundation drains where required.
- One of the following foundation drains is required at the perimeter of the foundation:
  - Gravel or crushed stone as follows:
    With ≤ 10% material passing a #4 sieve.
    Drain must extend horizontally ≥ 12" beyond the outside edge of the footing.
    Bottom of drain must be ≤ the height of the bottom of the base under floor.
    Top of drain must be ≥ 6" above top of footing.
    Top of drain must be covered with an approved membrane filter.
  - Drain tile or perforated pipe as follows:
    Drain invert elevation must be ≤ that of the floor.
    Top of joints or perforations must be covered with an approved membrane filter.
    Drain must be placed on ≥ 2" of gravel or crushed stone.
    Drain must be covered with ≥ 6" of gravel or crushed stone.

  Note: 1806.4.1, "Floor base course," is cited as governing the gravel or crushed stone required for the drain tile or pipe above.

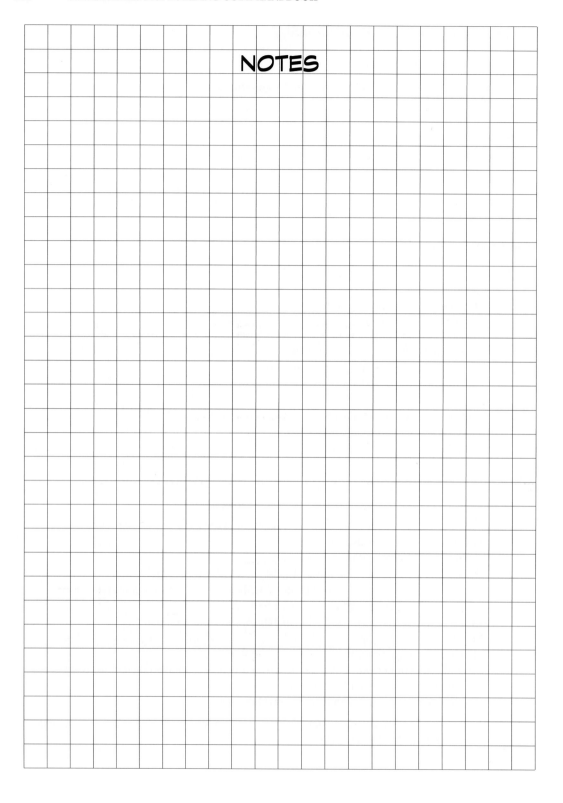

NOTES

19

Concrete

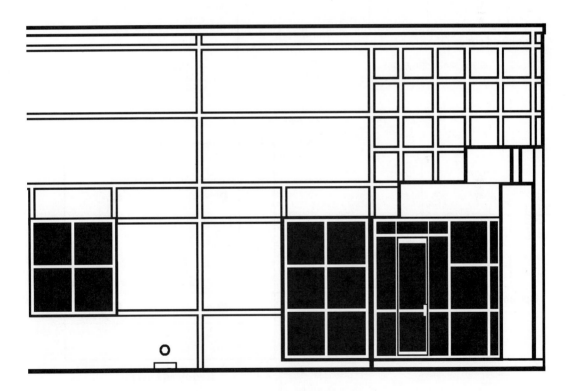

Garments to Go. Bastrop, Texas. *(partial elevlation)*
Spencer Godfrey Architects, Round Rock, Texas.

1907 Details of Reinforcement

1907.5.2.1 Depth and cover

- Tolerances permitted for the following are as shown in the details provided in this section:
  - Placement of reinforcing in the following concrete components:
    Flexural members.
    Walls.
    Compression members.
- Tolerance may not reduce cover > $^1/_3$ that required by construction documents.

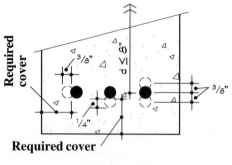

FLEXURAL MEMBER

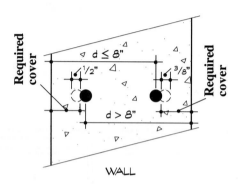

WALL

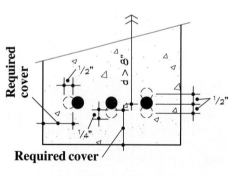

FLEXURAL MEMBER

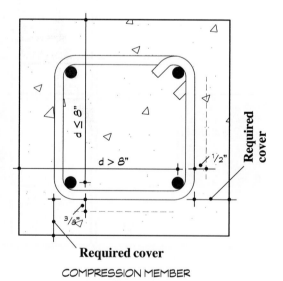

COMPRESSION MEMBER

Fig. 1907.5.2.1. Tolerances for steel in concrete. Maximum tolerances for placing reinforcement, prestressing tendons, and prestressing ducts in concrete are shown.

1907 Details of Reinforcement

1907.5.2.2 Bends and ends

- Tolerances permitted for the following are as shown in the detail provided in this section:
  - Bends in reinforcement.
  - Ends of reinforcement.

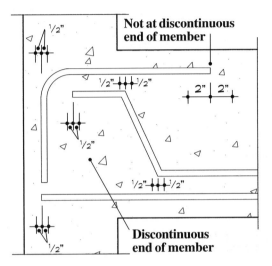

Fig. 1907.5.2.2. Tolerances for location of bends and ends of concrete reinforcing.

1907.7.1 Cast-in-place concrete (nonprestressed)

- Details provided in this section show the concrete cover required for reinforcement in the following:
  - Nonprestressed, cast-in-place concrete.

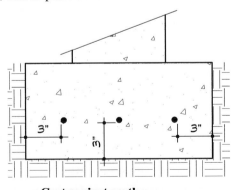

**Cast against earth,
permanent contact to earth**

Fig. 1907.7.1A. Minimum concrete cover for nonprestressed steel in cast-in-place concrete.

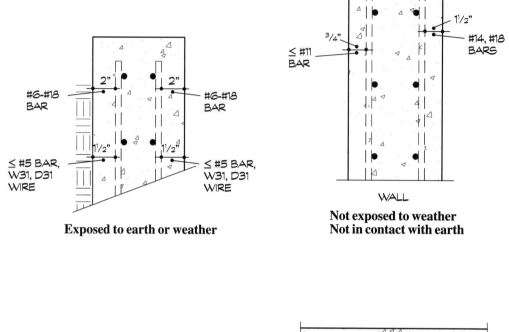

Exposed to earth or weather

Not exposed to weather
Not in contact with earth

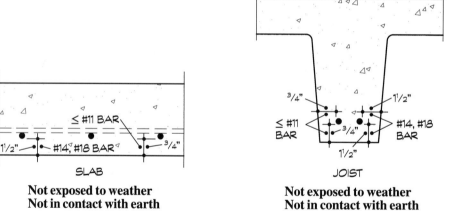

Not exposed to weather
Not in contact with earth

Not exposed to weather
Not in contact with earth

Fig. 1907.7.1B. Minimum concrete cover for nonprestressed steel in cast-in-place concrete.

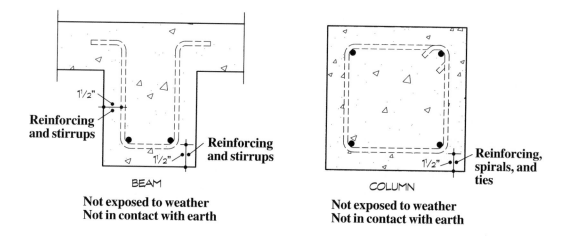

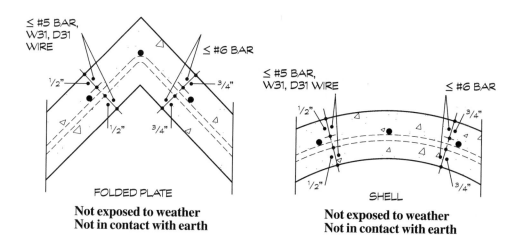

Fig. 1907.7.1C. Minimum concrete cover for nonprestressed steel in cast-in-place concrete.

1909 Structural Plain Concrete

1909.6.1 Basement walls

- The detail provided in this section indicates the thickness required for the following:
  - ○ Structural plain concrete walls as follows:
    Exterior basement walls.
    Foundation walls.
- Such walls need not comply with the following requirements of this chapter:
  - ○ Water-cement ratios based on exposure conditions.
  - ○ Compressive strength based on exposure conditions.

    Note: 1904.2.2, "Concrete properties," is cited as the source of requirements which are waived for the walls above.
    Chapter 22 of ACI 318, "Building Code Requirements for Structural Concrete," is the source of requirements with which the walls above must comply in addition to this section.

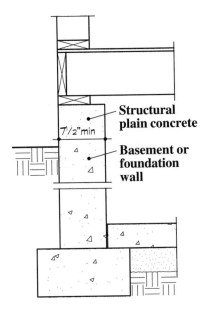

Fig. 1909.6.1. Minimum thickness of exterior basement or foundation wall of structural plain concrete.

1909 Structural Plain Concrete

1909.6.2 Other walls

- This section addresses concrete bearing walls other than the following:
  - Basement and foundation walls.
- The thickness of other structural plain concrete bearing walls is governed as follows:
  - Required thickness is based on unsupported dimensions as follows:
      Length or height.
  - Required thickness of walls with an unsupported dimension ≤ 11' is ≥ 5½".
  - Required thickness of walls with an unsupported dimension > 11' is as follows:
      Unsupported dimension ÷ 24.
- A partial list of minimum thickness for plain concrete bearing walls is provided below:

Table 1909.6.2   Minimum Thickness of Plain Concrete Bearing Walls

Dimension	Thickness	Dimension	Thickness	Dimension	Thickness
11'-0"	5-$^1/_2$"	15'-0"	7-$^1/_2$"	19'-0"	9-$^1/_2$"
11'-2"	5-$^9/_{16}$"	15'-2"	7-$^9/_{16}$"	19'-2"	9-$^9/_{16}$"
11'-4"	5-$^{11}/_{16}$"	15'-4"	7-$^{11}/_{16}$"	19'-4"	9-$^{11}/_{16}$"
11'-6"	5-$^3/_4$"	15'-6"	7-$^3/_4$"	19'-6"	9-$^3/_4$"
11'-8"	5-$^{13}/_{16}$"	15'-8"	7-$^{13}/_{16}$"	19'-8"	9-$^{13}/_{16}$"
11'-10"	5-$^{15}/_{16}$"	15'-10"	7-$^{15}/_{16}$"	19'-10"	9-$^{15}/_{16}$"
12'-0"	6-0"	16'-0"	8-0"	20'-0"	10-0"
12'-2"	6-$^1/_6$"	16'-2"	8-$^1/_6$"	20'-2"	10-$^1/_6$"
12'-4"	6-$^3/_{16}$"	16'-4"	8-$^3/_{16}$"	20'-4"	10-$^3/_{16}$"
12'-6"	6-$^1/_4$"	16'-6"	8-$^1/_4$"	20'-6"	10-$^1/_4$"
12'-8"	6-$^5/_{16}$"	16'-8"	8-$^5/_{16}$"	20'-8"	10-$^5/_{16}$"
12'-10"	6-$^7/_{16}$"	16'-10"	8-$^7/_{16}$"	20'-10"	10-$^7/_{16}$"
13'-0"	6-$^1/_2$"	17'-0"	8-$^1/_2$"	21'-0"	10-$^1/_2$"
13'-2"	6-$^9/_{16}$"	17'-2"	8-$^9/_{16}$"	21'-2"	10-$^9/_{16}$"
13'-4"	6-$^{11}/_{16}$"	17'-4"	8-$^{11}/_{16}$"	21'-4"	10-$^{11}/_{16}$"
13'-6"	6-$^3/_4$"	17'-6"	8-$^3/_4$"	21'-6"	10-$^3/_4$"
13'-8"	6-$^{13}/_{16}$"	17'-8"	8-$^{13}/_{16}$"	21'-8"	10-$^{13}/_{16}$"
13'-10"	6-$^{15}/_{16}$"	17'-10"	8-$^{15}/_{16}$"	21'-10"	10-$^{15}/_{16}$"
14'-0"	7-0"	18'-0"	9-0"	22'-0"	11-0"
14'-2"	7-$^1/_6$"	18'-2"	9-$^1/_6$"	22'-2"	11-$^1/_6$"
14'-4"	7-$^3/_{16}$"	18'-4"	9-$^3/_{16}$"	22'-4"	11-$^3/_{16}$"
14'-6"	7-$^1/_4$"	18'-6"	9-$^1/_4$"	22'-6"	11-$^1/_4$"
14'-8"	7-$^5/_{16}$"	18'-8"	9-$^5/_{16}$"	22'-8"	11-$^5/_{16}$"
14'-10"	7-$^7/_{16}$"	18'-10"	9-$^7/_{16}$"	22'-10"	11-$^7/_{16}$"

1909 Structural Plain Concrete

1909.6.3 Openings in walls

This section addresses structural plain concrete walls.

- Reinforcing required around openings is shown in the detail below:

  Note: Chapter 22 of ACI 318, "Building Code Requirements for Structural Concrete," governs plain concrete walls as indicated above.

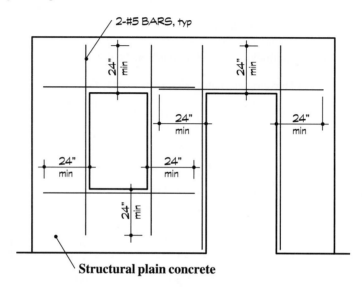

Fig. 1909.6.3. Reinforcing required around openings in structural plain concrete walls.

1910 Seismic Design Provisions

1910.4.4.2 Footings

This section addresses structural plain concrete foundations in Seismic Design Category C.

- The details provided in this section show reinforcing requirements for foundations.
- Plain concrete footings under walls must be reinforced as follows:
  - Footing must have ≥ #4 bars.
  - Footing must have ≥ 2 bars.
  - Area of reinforcing required in footing is as follows:
    ≥ 0.002 × gross cross-sectional area of the footing as follows:
    A partial list of reinforcing meeting this requirement is provided below:

Table 1910.4.4.2   Reinforcing Required in Plain Concrete Footings

Footing height (")	Footing width (")	Area of section (sq in)	Steel area required (sq in)	Number of reinforcing bars required			
				#4	#5	#6	#7
8.0	16	128.0	0.256	2	2	2	2
8.5	17	144.5	0.289	2	2	2	2
9.0	18	162.0	0.324	2	2	2	2
9.5	19	180.5	0.361	2	2	2	2
10.0	20	200.0	0.400	2	2	2	2
10.5	21	220.5	0.441	3	2	2	2
11.0	22	242.0	0.484	3	2	2	2
11.5	23	264.5	0.529	3	2	2	2
12.0	24	288.0	0.576	3	2	2	2
12.5	25	312.5	0.625	4	3	2	2
13.0	26	338.0	0.676	4	3	2	2
13.5	27	364.5	0.729	4	3	2	2
14.0	28	392.0	0.784	4	3	2	2
14.5	29	420.5	0.841	5	3	2	2
15.0	30	450.0	0.900	5	3	3	2
15.5	31	480.5	0.961	5	4	3	2
16.0	32	512.0	1.024	6	4	3	2
16.5	33	544.5	1.089	6	4	3	2

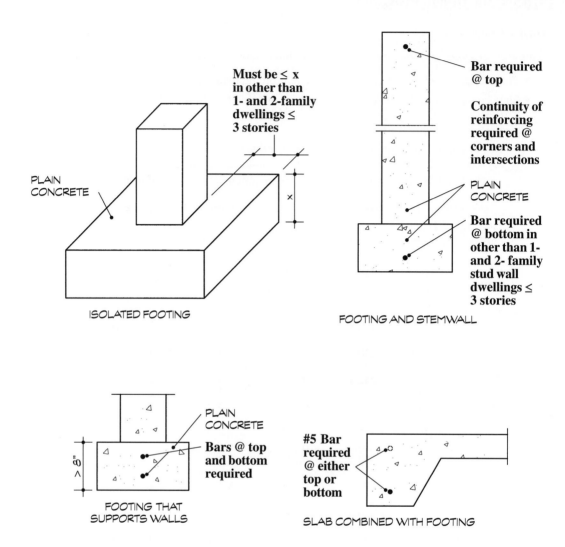

Fig. 1910.4.4.2B. Plain concrete footings in Seismic Design Category C.

1911 Minimum Slab Provisions

1911.1 General

- Requirements for concrete floor slabs-on-grade are shown in the detail provided in this section.
- A vapor retarder is not required under a slab in the following locations:
  - In detached buildings which are accessory to occupancy R-3 such as follows:
    Garages.
    Utility buildings.
    Other unheated facilities.
  - In unheated storage rooms as follows:
    < 70 sf in area.
  - In unheated carports attached to occupancy R-3 buildings.
  - In buildings of occupancies other than R-3 as follows:
    Where moisture migrating to the surface of the slab will not be detrimental.
  - Where the following slabs will remain unenclosed:
    Driveways.
    Walks.
    Patios.
    Other similar slabs.
  - Where local site conditions permit as follows:
    Must be approved.

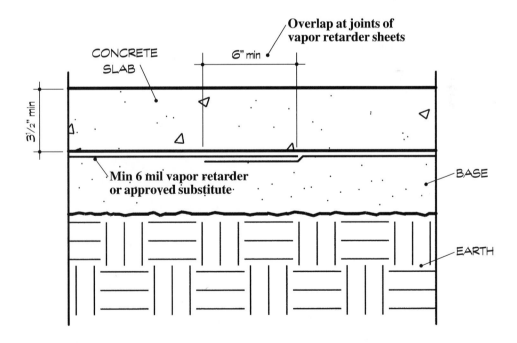

Fig. 1911.1A. Detail at concrete slab. The detail shows code requirements for concrete slabs on grade.

Case study: Fig. 1911.1B. The concrete slab is 4" thick which is > than the 3^1/$_2$" required minimum. The 8 mil vapor retarder is thicker than the minimum 6 mils required. The concrete slab is in compliance with code requirements.

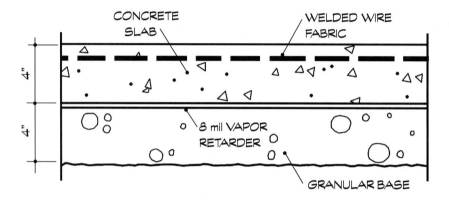

Fig. 1911.1B. Detail at concrete slab. Multipurpose Building Addition to Children's Home. Wilkes-Barre, Pennsylvania. C. Allen Mullins, Architect. Bear Creek, Pennsylvania.

1914 Shotcrete

1914.4.1 Size

- Required reinforcing for shotcrete construction is one of the following:
  - ≤ #5 bars.
  - Any size for which preconstruction tests verify that adequate encasement will be provided.

1914.4.2 Clearance

- Required clearances between reinforcing bars are shown in the details provided in this section as follows:
  - Required clearances may be reduced where both of the following apply:
    Where preconstruction tests verify that adequate encasement will be provided.
    Where approved by the building official.

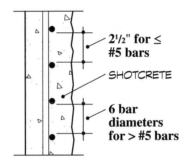

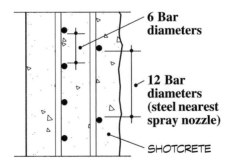

Fig. 1914.4.2. Minimum clearance required between reinforcing for shotcrete.

1915 Reinforced Gypsum Concrete

1915.2 Minimum thickness

- The thickness required for reinforced gypsum concrete is shown in the details provided in this section as follows:
  - ○ Requirements for the reduced thickness include those indicated on the detail and the following:

    Diaphragm action must not be required of the assembly.

    The live load may not > 40 psf.

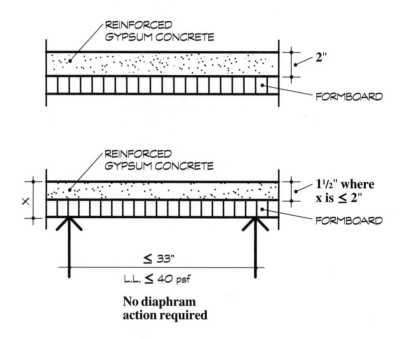

Fig. 1915.2. Minimum thickness of reinforced gypsum concrete.

1916 Concrete-Filled Pipe Columns

1916.4 Reinforcement

- Reinforcing in concrete-filled pipe columns is governed as follows:
  - Reinforcing is to be one of the following.
    Rods.
    Structural shapes.
    Pipe.
  - Structural shapes must be milled to provide bearing on the following:
    Cap plate.
    Base plate.
  - Adequate clearance between pipe wall and reinforcing is required for composite action.
  - Minimum clearance between pipe wall and reinforcing is shown in the details provided.

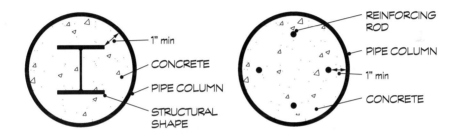

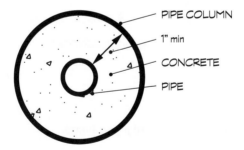

Fig. 1916.4. Clearance for reinforcement in concrete-filled pipe columns.

1916 Concrete-Filled Pipe Columns

1916.5 Fire-resistance-rating protection

- Pipe columns must have the fire-resistance rating required for the building type.
- Where a steel shell surrounds the fire-resistive covering, it may not be assumed to carry a structural load.
- Required sizes are shown in the details provided.

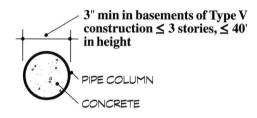

3" min in basements of Type V construction ≤ 3 stories, ≤ 40' in height

PIPE COLUMN

CONCRETE

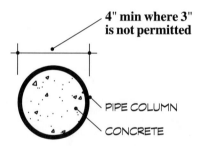

4" min where 3" is not permitted

PIPE COLUMN

CONCRETE

Fig. 1916.5. Minimum diameter of concrete-filled pipe columns.

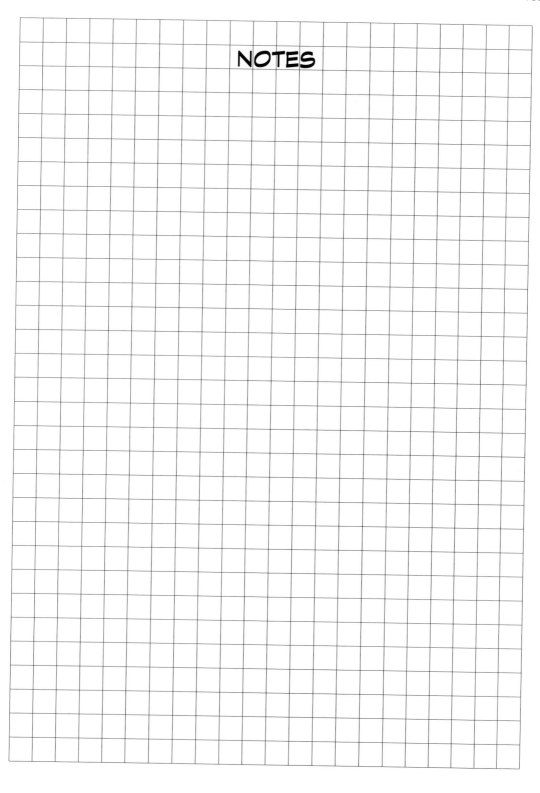

NOTES

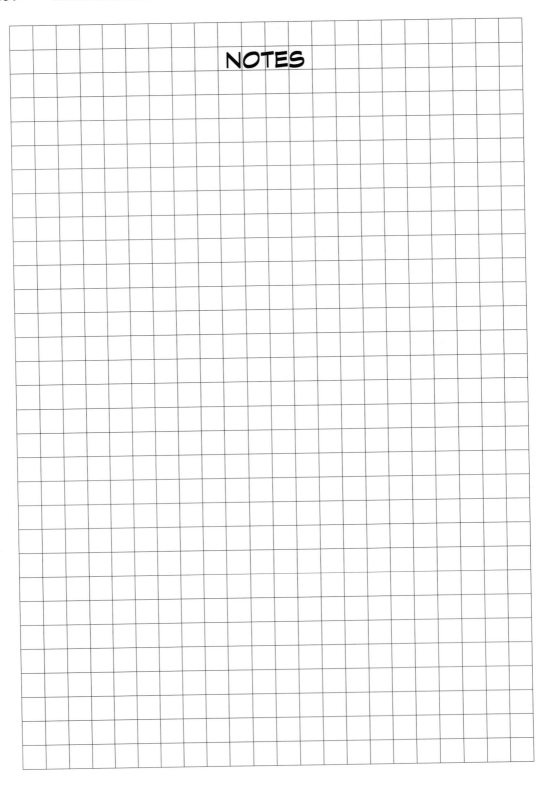

NOTES

20

Aluminum

Multipurpose Building Addition to Children's Home. Wilkes-Barre, Pennsylvania. *(partial elevation)*
C. Allen Mullins, Architects. Bear Creek, Pennsylvania.

2002 <u>Materials</u>

2002.1 General

- Design of aluminum components for structural application is governed as follows:
  - Design must comply with structural load requirements of the code.
  - Design must comply with industry standards.

  Note: The following are cited as governing the design of aluminum components:
    Chapter 16, "Structural Design."
    AA ASM 35, "Aluminum Sheet Metal Work in Building Construction."
    AA Aluminum Design Manual, Part 1-A, "Aluminum Structures, Allowable Stress Design."
    AA Aluminum Design Manual, Part 1-B, "Aluminum Structures, Load and Resistance Factor Design of Buildings and Similar Type Structures."

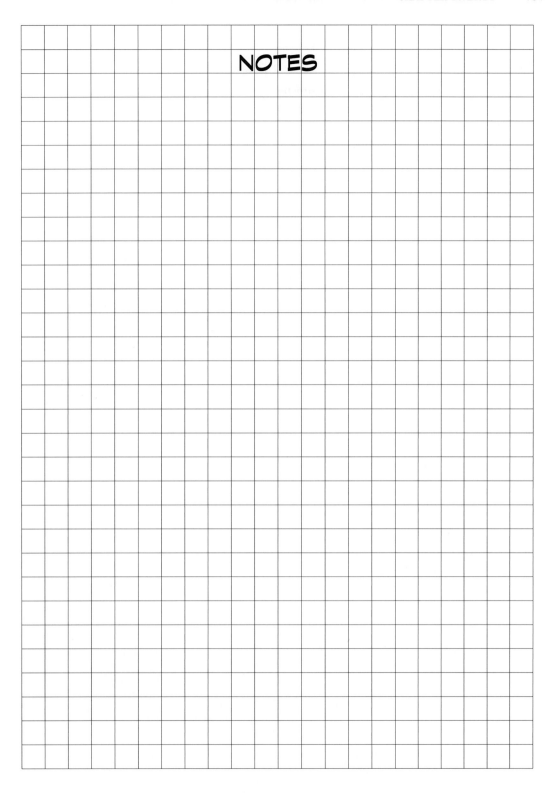

NOTES

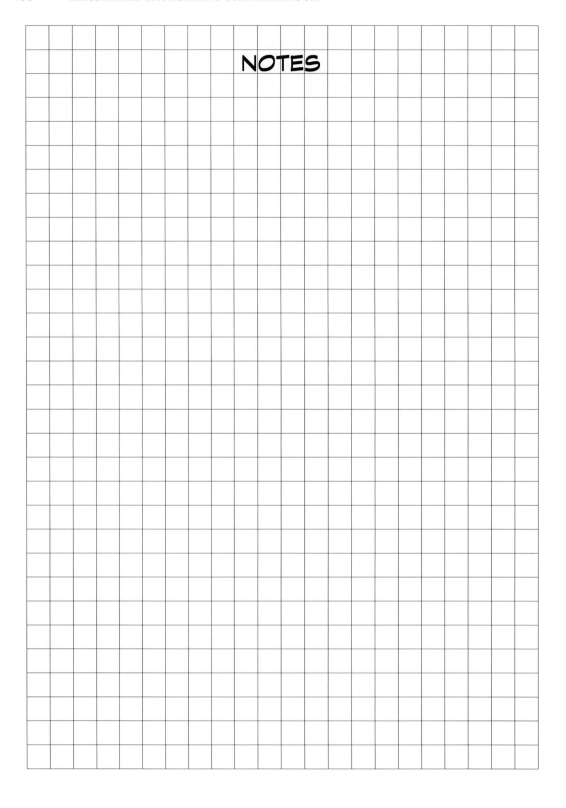

21

Masonry

Country Club Park Building One. Wichita, Kansas. *(partial elevation)*
Gossen Livingston Associates, Inc., Architecture. Wichita, Kansas.

2103 Masonry Construction Materials

2103.5 Glass unit masonry

- Requirements for hollow glass blocks are as follows:
  - Reclaimed units may not be used.
  - Other requirements are shown on the detail provided.

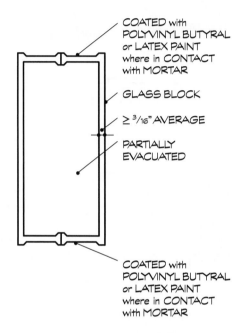

Fig. 2103.5. Section through hollow glass block.

2104 Construction

2104.1.2.1 Bed and head joints

- Unless superceded by other requirements, sizes required for the following masonry joints are shown in the detail provided:
  - Head joints.
  - Bed joints.

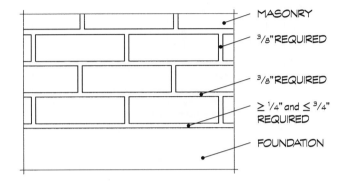

Fig. 2104.1.2.1. Masonry joint sizes.

2104.1.2.1.1 Open-end units

- Grout requirements for open-end masonry units are shown in the detail provided.

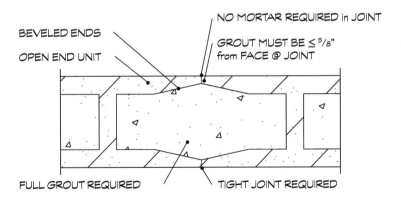

Fig. 2104.1.2.1.1. Grouted open-end masonry units.

2104 Construction

2104.1.2.2 Hollow units

- Fill requirements for head and bed joints of hollow masonry units are shown in the details provided.

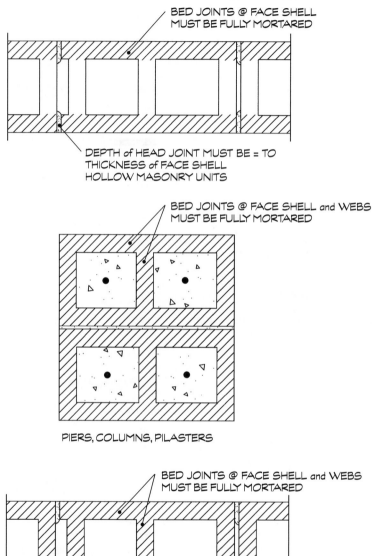

Fig. 2104.1.2.2A. Mortar joint requirements for hollow masonry.

2104 Construction

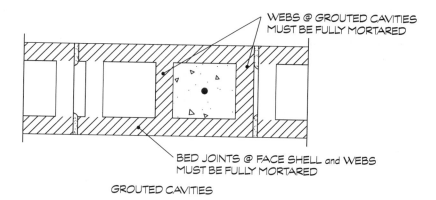

Fig. 2104.1.2.2B. Mortar joint requirements for hollow masonry.

2104.1.2.3 Solid units

- Joint requirements for head and bed joints of solid masonry units are shown in the detail provided, where not superceded by the following:
  - Directions in construction documents.
  - Other requirements.
- Head joints must be fully buttered.
- "Slushing" mortar to fill head joints is not permitted.
- Head joints must be formed by pushing mortar against the adjacent unit.

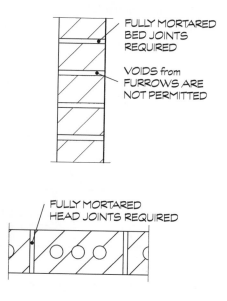

Fig. 2104.1.2.3. Mortar joint requirements for solid masonry.

2104 Construction

2104.1.2.4 Glass unit masonry

- Size and other joint requirements for glass block are shown in the detail provided.

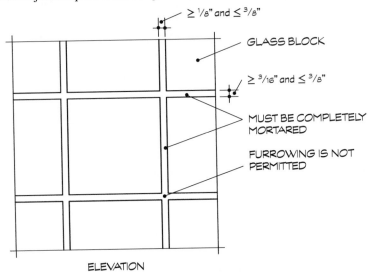

Fig. 2104.1.2.4. Mortar joint requirements for glass unit masonry.

2104.1.3 Installation of wall ties

- Requirements for embedding wall ties in masonry are as follows:
  - Wall ties must be embedded in mortar joint.
  - Wall ties may not be bent once they are embedded in grout or mortar.
  - Other requirements are shown in the details provided.

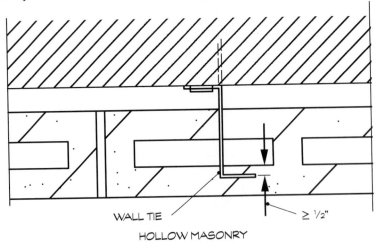

Fig. 2104.1.3A. Requirements for embedment of wall ties in masonry.

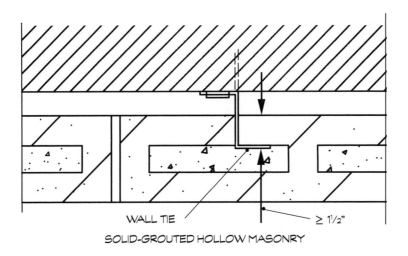

SOLID-GROUTED HOLLOW MASONRY

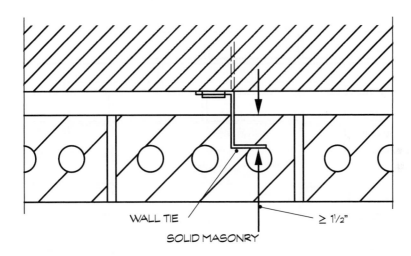

SOLID MASONRY

Fig. 2104.1.3B. Requirements for embedment of wall ties in masonry.

2104 Construction

2104.1.4 Chases and recesses

- Where the following occur in masonry construction, they are to be constructed as the masonry units are set:
  - Chases.
  - Recesses.
- A lintel is required for masonry above chases or recesses > 12".

2104.1.5 Lintels

- Masonry lintels are to be designed by one of the following methods:
  - Working stress design.
  - Strength design.

    Note: The following are cited as governing the design of masonry lintels:
    Section 2107, "Working Stress Design."
    Section 2108, "Strength Design of Masonry."

- The bearing requirement for lintels in masonry construction is shown in the detail provided.

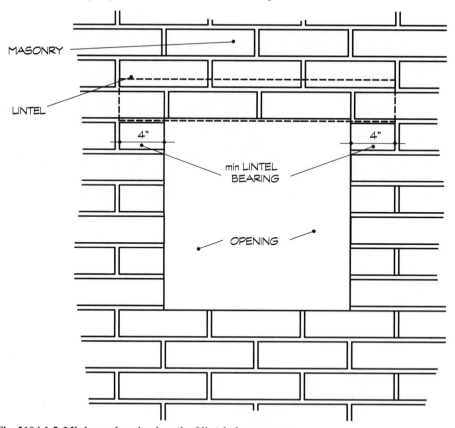

Fig. 2104.1.5. Minimum bearing length of lintels for masonry.

2104 Construction

2104.1.8 Weep holes

- Requirements for weep holes in masonry are shown in the detail provided.

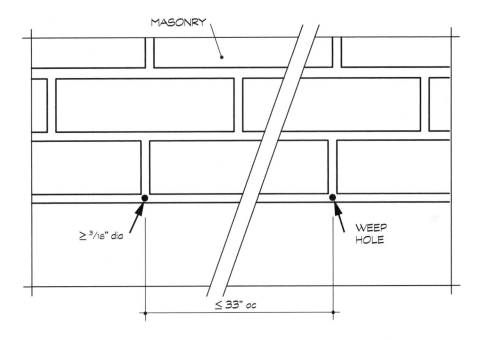

Fig. 2104.1.8. Weep hole size and spacing for masonry.

2104 Construction

2104.2 Corbeled masonry

- Projection limitations for corbeled masonry are shown in the details provided.

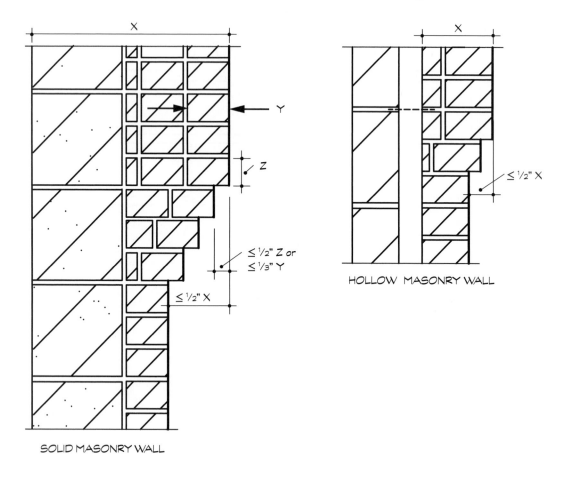

Fig. 2104.2. Projection limitations for corbeled masonry.

2106 Seismic Design

2106.4.1.2 Masonry partition walls

This section addresses masonry walls in Seismic Design Category C.

- This section governs the following walls with the characteristics indicated below:
  - Walls:
    Partitions.
    Screen walls.
    Other similar elements.
  - Characteristics:
    Walls do not resist loads other than those due to their own mass as follows:
    Vertical loads.
    Lateral loads.
- Requirements for isolation from the structure are shown in the detail provided.

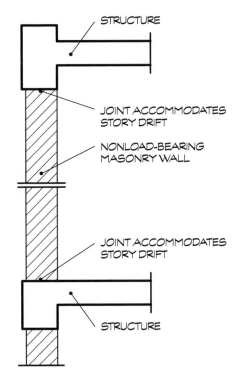

Fig. 2106.4.1.2. Isolation of nonload-bearing masonry walls.

2106 Seismic Design

2106.4.1.3 Reinforcement requirements for masonry elements

This section addresses masonry walls in Seismic Design Category C.

- Nonload-bearing masonry walls and partitions must be reinforced as follows:
  - Either vertically or horizontally as follows:
    Direction varies with the location of lateral supporting elements of the building structure.
  - Reinforcing requirements are shown in the details provided.

Note: 2106.4.1.2, "Masonry partition walls," is cited as the source defining walls to which this section applies.

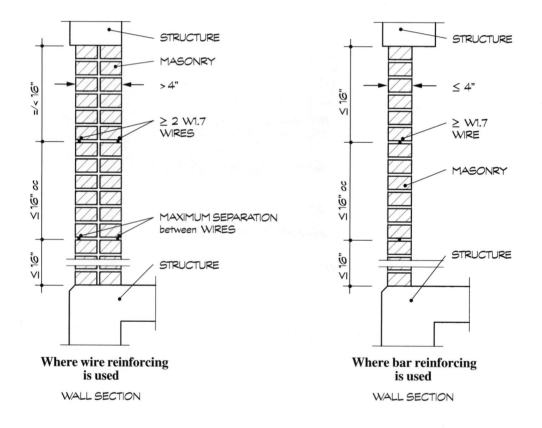

Where wire reinforcing is used

WALL SECTION

Where bar reinforcing is used

WALL SECTION

Fig. 2106.4.1.3A. Reinforcing for masonry partitions in Seismic Design Category C.

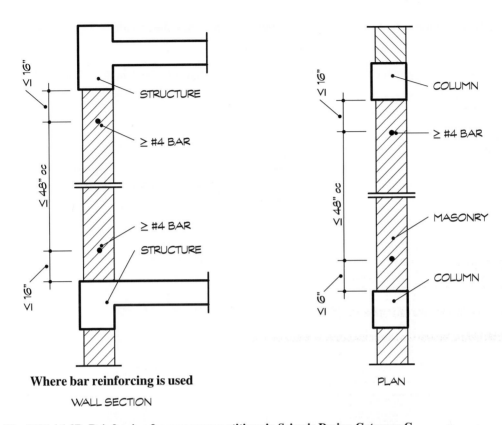

Where bar reinforcing is used

WALL SECTION

PLAN

Fig. 2106.4.1.3B. Reinforcing for masonry partitions in Seismic Design Category C.

2106 Seismic Design

2106.4.2.3.1 Minimum reinforcement requirements for masonry shear walls

This section addresses masonry walls in Seismic Design Category C.

- Reinforcing requirements for masonry shear walls are shown in the details provided.

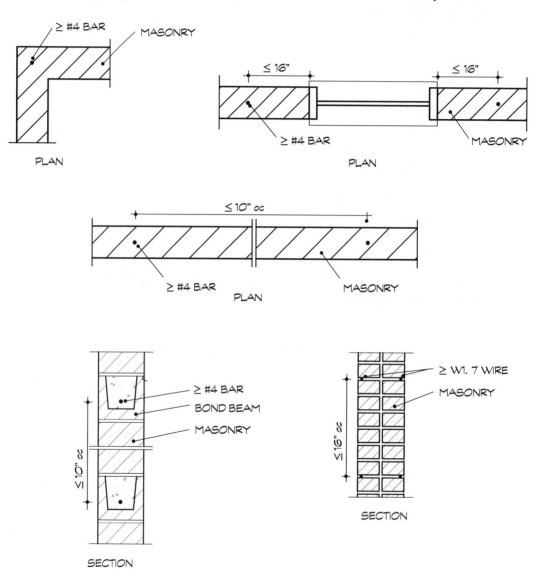

Fig. 2106.4.2.3.1A. Minimum reinforcement requirements for masonry shear walls.

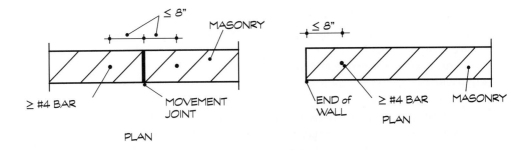

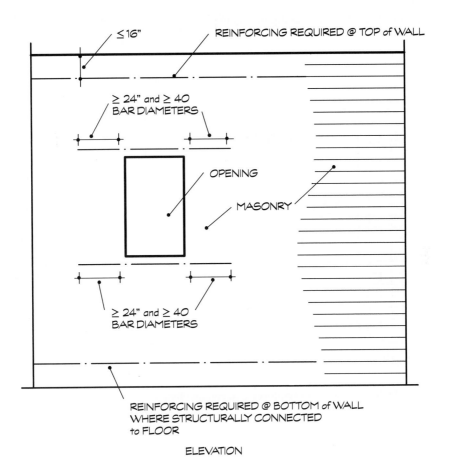

Fig. 2106.4.2.3.1B. Minimum reinforcement requirements for masonry shear walls.

2106 Seismic Design

2106.5.2 Minimum reinforcement requirements for masonry walls *(part 1 of 4)*

- This subsection applies to Seismic Design Category D.
- This subsection does not apply to building components which are not part of the lateral force-resisting system:
  - Vertical and horizontal reinforcing are required.
- The tables in part 2 list reinforcing that meets the following minimum cross-sectional area requirements for steel in running bond:
  - (Area of vertical steel) ÷ (gross cross-sectional area of wall) must be ≥ 0.007.
  - (Area of horizontal steel) ÷ (gross cross-sectional area of wall) must be ≥ 0.007.
  - (Area of vertical steel + area of horizontal steel) ÷ (gross cross-sectional area of wall) must be ≥ 0.002.
- Maximum spacing of reinforcing in running bond is shown in the following detail:

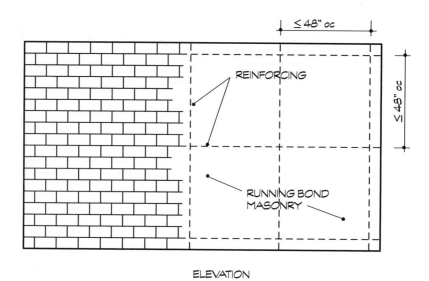

ELEVATION

Fig. 2106.5.2A. Maximum spacing of reinforcing in running bond.

2106 Seismic Design

2106.5.2 Minimum reinforcement requirements for masonry walls *(part 2 of 4)*

This part addresses running bond masonry.

- Maximum spacing of vertical and horizontal deformed-bar reinforcing (inches):
  - Bar size and spacing are the same in both directions.

Table 2106.5.2a **Spacing (") for Reinforcing in Running Bond Masonry**

Bar	Nominal wall thickness					
	4"	6"	8"	10"	12"	16"
#4	48.00	33.33	25.00	20.00	16.67	12.50
#5	48.00	48.00	38.75	31.00	25.83	19.38
#6	48.00	48.00	48.00	44.00	36.67	27.50
#7	48.00	48.00	48.00	48.00	48.00	37.50
#8	48.00	48.00	48.00	48.00	48.00	48.00
#9	48.00	48.00	48.00	48.00	48.00	48.00

- Maximum spacing of deformed bars $\perp$ to the minimum reinforcing permitted (inches):
  - Bar size is the same in both directions.
  - Bar spacing in one direction varies with bar spacing in the $\perp$ direction as follows:
    Column A: Minimum reinforcing permitted in horizontal or vertical direction.
    Column B: Maximum spacing of steel $\perp$ to the reinforcing spaced as shown in column A.

Table 2106.5.2b **Spacing (") for Reinforcing in Running Bond Masonry**

Bar	Nominal wall thickness					
	4"		6"		8"	
	A	B	A	B	A	B
#3	39.29	21.15	26.19	14.10	19.64	10.58
#4	48.00	38.46	47.62	25.64	35.71	19.23
#5	48.00	48.00	48.00	39.74	48.00	29.81
#6	48.00	48.00	48.00	48.00	48.00	42.31
#7	48.00	48.00	48.00	48.00	48.00	48.00
#8	48.00	48.00	48.00	48.00	48.00	48.00

Bar	Nominal wall thickness					
	10"		12"		16"	
	A	B	A	B	A	B
#3	15.71	8.46	13.10	7.05	9.82	5.29
#4	28.57	15.38	23.81	12.82	17.86	9.62
#5	44.29	23.85	36.90	19.87	27.68	14.90
#6	48.00	33.85	48.00	28.21	39.29	21.15
#7	48.00	46.15	48.00	38.46	48.00	28.85
#8	48.00	48.00	48.00	48.00	48.00	37.98

2106 Seismic Design

2106.5.2 Minimum reinforcement requirements for masonry walls *(part 3 of 4)*

- This part applies to the following pattern bonds:
  - Stack bond.
  - Any bond other than running bond.
- Stack bond units and units in any bond other than running bond must be constructed of one of the following:
  - Fully grouted hollow open-end units.
  - Fully grouted hollow units laid with full head joints.
  - Solid units.
- The tables in part 4 lists reinforcing that meets the following minimum cross-sectional area requirements for steel in stack bond or any bond other than running bond:
  - Area of vertical steel ÷ gross cross-sectional area of wall must be ≥ 0.007.
  - Area of horizontal steel ÷ gross cross-sectional area of wall must be ≥ 0.007.
  - (Area of vertical steel + area of horizontal steel) ÷ (gross cross-sectional area of wall) must be ≥ 0.002.
- Maximum spacing of reinforcing in the following bonds is shown in the detail below:
  - Stack bond.
  - Any bond other than running bond.

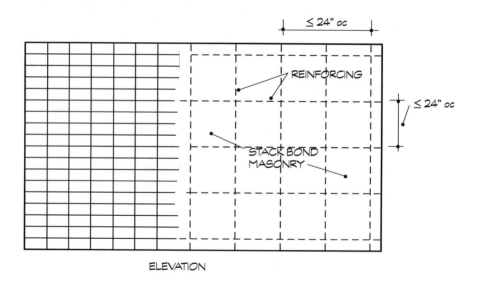

ELEVATION

Fig. 2106.5.2B. Maximum spacing of reinforcing in stack bond.

2106 Seismic Design

2106.5.2 Minimum reinforcement requirements for masonry walls *(part 4 of 4)*

This part addresses stack bond masonry and any bond other than running bond.

- Maximum spacing of vertical and horizontal deformed-bar reinforcing (inches):
  - Bar size and spacing are the same in both directions.

Table 2106.5.2c   Maximum Spacing (") for Reinforcing in Stack Bond Masonry

Bar	4"	6"	8"	10"	12"	16"
#4	24.00	24.00	24.00	20.00	16.67	12.50
#5	24.00	24.00	24.00	24.00	24.00	19.38
#6	24.00	24.00	24.00	24.00	24.00	24.00
#7	24.00	24.00	24.00	24.00	24.00	24.00
#8	24.00	24.00	24.00	24.00	24.00	24.00
#9	24.00	24.00	24.00	24.00	24.00	24.00

Nominal wall thickness

- Maximum spacing of deformed bars $\perp$ to the minimum reinforcing permitted (inches):
  - Bar size is the same in both directions.
  - Bar spacing in one directions varies with bar spacing in the $\perp$ direction as follows:
    Column A: Minimum reinforcing permitted in horizontal or vertical direction.
    Column B: Maximum spacing of steel $\perp$ to the reinforcing spaced as shown in column A.

Table 2106.5.2d   Maximum Spacing (") for Reinforcing in Stack Bond Masonry

Nominal wall thickness

Bar	4" A	4" B	6" A	6" B	8" A	8" B
#3	24.00	21.15	24.00	14.10	19.64	10.58
#4	24.00	24.00	24.00	24.00	24.00	19.23
#5	24.00	24.00	24.00	24.00	24.00	24.00
#6	24.00	24.00	24.00	24.00	24.00	24.00
#7	24.00	24.00	24.00	24.00	24.00	24.00
#8	24.00	24.00	24.00	24.00	24.00	24.00

Nominal wall thickness

Bar	10" A	10" B	12" A	12" B	16" A	16" B
#3	15.71	8.46	13.10	7.05	9.82	5.29
#4	24.00	15.38	23.81	12.82	17.86	9.62
#5	24.00	23.85	24.00	19.87	24.00	14.90
#6	24.00	24.00	24.00	24.00	24.00	21.15
#7	24.00	24.00	24.00	24.00	24.00	24.00
#8	24.00	24.00	24.00	24.00	24.00	24.00

2106 Seismic Design

2106.5.3.1 Shear wall reinforcement requirements

This subsection addresses masonry shear walls in Seismic Design Category D.

- Walls must be reinforced as per requirements of Seismic Category D for the following and this section:
  - Running bond.
  - Stack bond.
  - Bonds other than running bond.

  Note: 2106.5.2, "Minimum reinforcement requirements for masonry walls," is cited as governing minimum reinforcing requirements for shear walls as indicated above.

- Cross-sectional area of vertical steel must be as follows:
  - $\geq \frac{1}{3}$ that required for shear reinforcement.
- Shear reinforcing must be anchored around vertical reinforcing with a standard hook.
- Maximum spacing of reinforcement is shown on the detail provided.

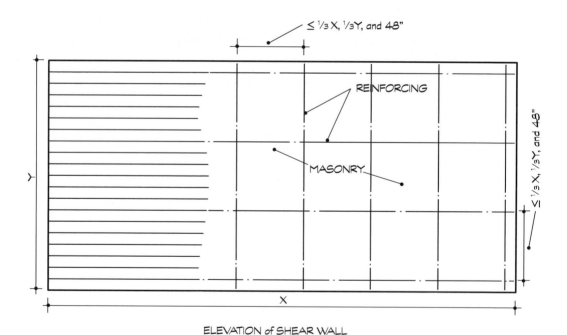

ELEVATION of SHEAR WALL

Fig. 2106.5.3.1. Maximum spacing of reinforcement in masonry shear walls in Seismic Design Category D.

2106 Seismic Design

2106.5.4 Minimum reinforcement for masonry columns

This subsection addresses masonry columns in Seismic Design Category D.

- Lateral ties in masonry columns are governed as follows:
  - Spacing must be $\leq 8"$ oc.
  - Diameter must be $\leq {}^{3}/_{8}"$.
  - Must be embedded in grout.

2106.6.1 Design of elements that are not part of the lateral-force-resisting system *(part 1 of 2)*

This subsection addresses stack bond masonry in Seismic Design Categories E and F.

- Units must be one of the following:
  - Solid grouted hollow open-ended units.
  - Double-wythe solid units.
- The spacing of vertical deformed-bar reinforcing (inches) shown below meets the minimum requirement as follows:
  - Area of steel must be $\geq 0.0015 \times$ gross cross-sectional area of wall.

Table 2106.6.1 **Maximum Spacing (") for Reinforcing in Stack Bond Masonry**

Bar	Nominal wall thickness					
	4"	6"	8"	10"	12"	16"
#4	33.33	22.22	16.66	13.33	11.11	8.33
#5	48.00	34.44	25.83	20.66	17.22	12.91
#6	48.00	48.00	36.66	29.33	24.44	18.33
#7	48.00	48.00	48.00	40.00	33.33	25.00
#8	48.00	48.00	48.00	48.00	43.80	32.91
#9	48.00	48.00	48.00	48.00	48.00	41.66

2106 Seismic Design

2106.6.1 Design of elements that are not part of the lateral-force-resisting system *(part 2 of 2)*

• Maximum spacing for horizontal reinforcement is shown on the detail provided.

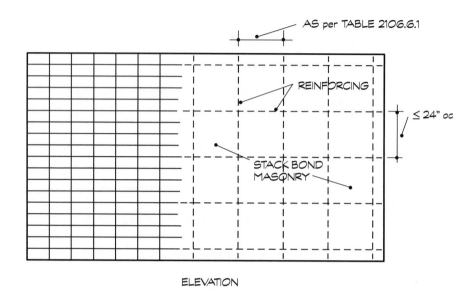

ELEVATION

Fig. 2106.6.1. Maximum spacing for horizontal reinforcement in masonry not part of the lateral-force-resisting system in Seismic Design Categories E and F.

2106.6.2 Design of elements that are part of the lateral-force-resisting system *(part 1 of 2)*

This section addresses stack bond masonry in Seismic Design Categories E and F.

- • Units must be one of the following:
  - ○ Solid grouted hollow open-ended units.
  - ○ Double-wythe solid units.
- • The spacing of vertical deformed-bar reinforcing (inches) shown below meets the minimum requirement as follows:
  - ○ Area of steel must be ≥ 0.0025 × gross cross-sectional area of wall.

2106 Seismic Design

2106.6.2 Design of elements that are part of the lateral-force-resisting system *(part 2 of 2)*

Table 2106.6.2	**Maximum Spacing (") for Reinforcing in Stack Bond Masonry**					
	Nominal wall thickness					
Bar	4"	6"	8"	10"	12"	16"
#4	20.00	13.33	10.00	8.00	6.66	5.00
#5	24.00	20.66	15.50	12.40	10.33	7.75
#6	24.00	24.00	22.00	17.60	14.66	11.00
#7	24.00	24.00	24.00	24.00	20.00	15.00
#8	24.00	24.00	24.00	24.00	24.00	19.75
#9	24.00	24.00	24.00	24.00	24.00	24.00

• Maximum spacing for horizontal reinforcement is shown on the detail provided.

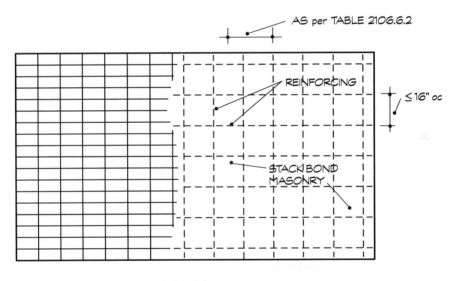

Fig. 2106.6.2. Maximum spacing for horizontal reinforcement in masonry that are part of the lateral-force-resisting system in Seismic Design Categories E and F.

2107 Working Stress Design

2107.2.2 ACI 530/ASCE 5/TMS 402, Section 2.1.4

This section addresses masonry columns in Seismic Design Categories A, B, and C.

- Where columns support only the following, the requirements indicated below apply:
  - Roofs of carports.
  - Roofs of porches.
  - Roofs of sheds.
  - Roofs of similar light structures.
- Masonry materials must meet minimum specification of this chapter.

  Note: The following are cited as sources of material specifications:
  2103.1, "Concrete masonry units."
  2103.2, "Clay or shale masonry units."

- Where columns must resist uplift, the following applies:
  - The sum of the following must ≥ 1.5 × uplift load.
    Weight of column.
    Weight of footing.

  Note: Chapter 16, "Structural Design," is cited as the source of requirements for loading
  that the anchorage must resist.

- Other requirements are indicated in the details provided.

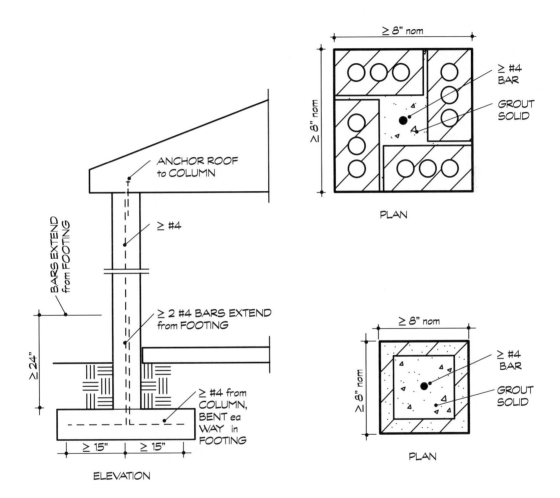

≥ 8" nom

≥ 8" nom

≥ #4
BAR

GROUT
SOLID

PLAN

ANCHOR ROOF
to COLUMN

≥ #4

BARS EXTEND
from FOOTING

≥ 2 #4 BARS EXTEND
from FOOTING

≥ 24"

≥ #4 from
COLUMN,
BENT ea
WAY in
FOOTING

≥ 15"   ≥ 15"

ELEVATION

≥ 8" nom

≥ 8" nom

≥ #4
BAR

GROUT
SOLID

PLAN

Fig. 2107.2.2. Masonry columns supporting light structures in Seismic Design Categories A, B, and C.

2108 Strength Design of Masonry

2108.9.2.1 Reinforcing bar size

- The largest reinforcing bar permitted in masonry is as follows:
  - ≤ #11.
- Bar diameter must be ≤ the following and as shown in details provided:
  - $1/8$ nominal wall thickness.
  - $1/4$ the least dimension of the following locations in which the steel is placed:
    Cell.
    Collar joint.
    Course.
- Other reinforcing bar limitations are shown in details provided.

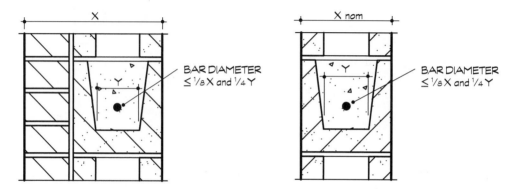

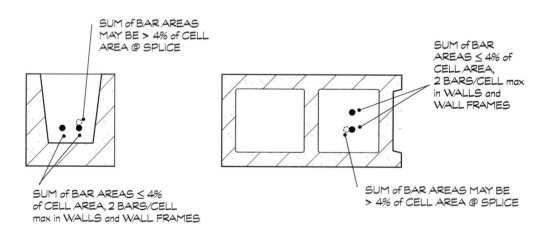

Fig. 2108.9.2.1. Reinforcing bar limitations in masonry.

2108 Strength Design of Masonry

2108.9.2.2 Joint reinforcement

- Joint reinforcing does not provide shear reinforcing in Seismic Design Categories D, E, and F.
- Requirements for joint reinforcement are shown on the details provided.

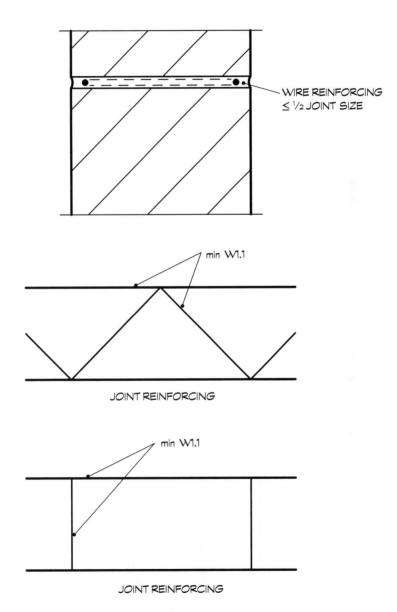

Fig. 2108.9.2.2. Joint reinforcement requirements.

2108 Strength Design of Masonry

2108.9.2.3 Clear distance between parallel bars

- Minimum clear distance between parallel bars is shown on the details provided.

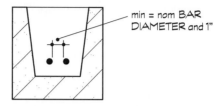

Fig. 2108.9.2.3. Clear distance between parallel reinforcing bars in masonry.

2108.9.2.4 Clear distance between vertical bars in columns and piers

- Required clear distances for reinforcing in columns and piers is shown in the details provided.

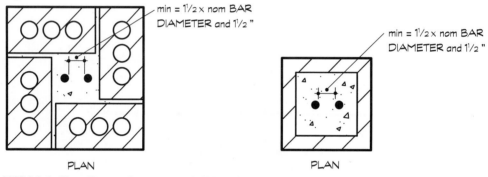

Fig. 2108.9.2.4. Clear distance between vertical bars in columns and piers.

2108.9.2.5 Clear distance between spliced bars

- Required clear distance between spliced reinforcing bars is shown in the details provided.

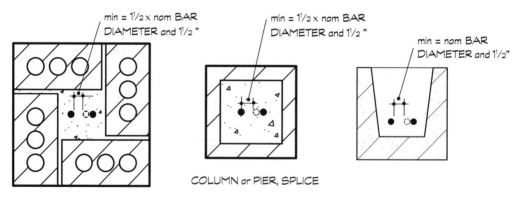

Fig. 2108.9.2.5. Clear distance between spliced bars in masonry.

2108 Strength Design of Masonry

2108.9.2.6 Bundling of reinforcing bars

- Bundling of reinforcing bars is not permitted.

2108.9.2.7 Reinforcing bar cover

- Required cover for reinforcing bars is shown in the details provided.

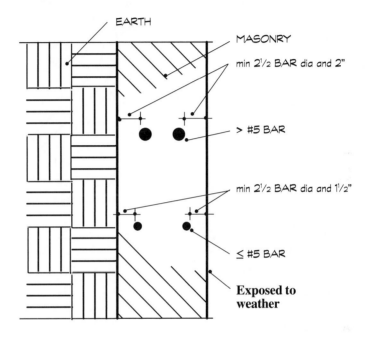

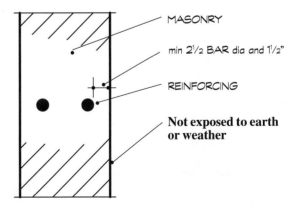

Fig. 2108.9.2.7. Required cover for reinforcing bars in masonry.

2108 Strength Design of Masonry

2108.9.2.8 Standard hooks

- Requirements for standard hook configuration are shown in the details provided.

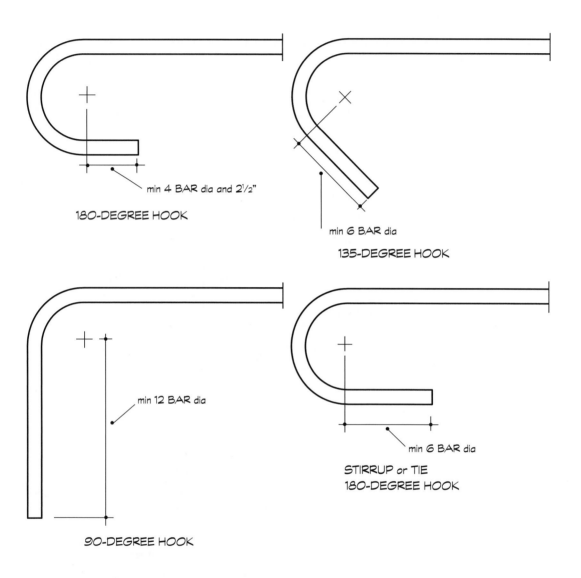

Fig. 2108.9.2.8A. Requirements for standard hooks in masonry reinforcement.

2108 Strength Design of Masonry

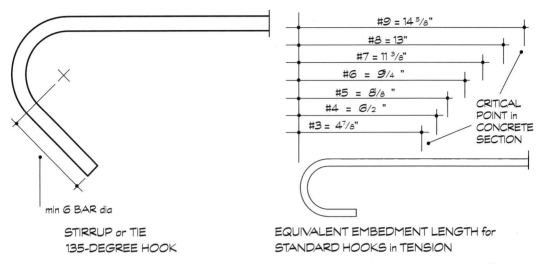

Fig. 2108.9.2.8B. Requirements for standard hooks in masonry reinforcement.

2108.9.2.9 Minimum bend diameter for reinforcing bars

- Minimum diameters for bending reinforcing bars other than the following are shown on the details provided:
  - The following reinforcing is not included:
    Stirrups.
    Ties.

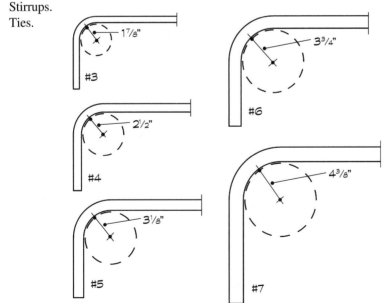

GRADE 40 REINFORCING BARS

Fig. 2108.9.2.9A. Minimum bend diameter for reinforcing bars in masonry.

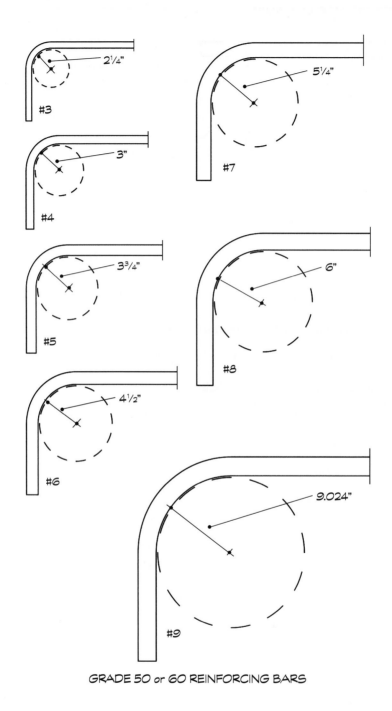

GRADE 50 or 60 REINFORCING BARS

Fig. 2108.9.2.9B. Minimum bend diameter for reinforcing bars in masonry.

2108 Strength Design of Masonry

2108.9.3.8 Dimensional limits *(part 1 of 2)*

- A partial list of maximum clear spacing between lateral bracing for masonry beams as follows is provided in the table below:
  - Bracing at the compression side of beams.
  - Clear distance must be ≤ 32 × the smallest width at the compressive zone.

Table 2108.9.3.8a   Maximum Spacing for Lateral Bracing for Masonry Beams

Beam width (")	Maximum bracing spacing	Beam width (")	Maximum bracing spacing
6	16'-0"	15	40'-0"
7	18'-8"	16	42'-8"
8	21'-4"	17	45'-4"
9	24'-0"	18	48'-0"
10	26'-8"	19	50'-8"
11	29'-4"	20	53'-4"
12	32'-0"	21	56'-0"
13	34'-8"	22	58'-8"
14	37'-4"	23	61'-4"

- A partial list of maximum clear spacing between lateral bracing for piers and columns as follows is shown in the table below:
  - Lateral bracing for piers as follows:
    - Piers with lateral spacing greater than that listed must be designed as follows:
      - According to methods for wall design for out-of-plane loads.
  - Lateral bracing for columns begins with 12", the smallest permitted column dimension.

Table 2108.9.3.8b   Maximum Spacing for Lateral Bracing for Masonry Piers and Columns

Member width	Maximum bracing spacing	Member width	Maximum bracing spacing
6	15'-0"	15	37'-6"
7	17'-6"	16	40'-0"
8	20'-0"	17	42'-6"
9	22'-6"	18	45'-0"
10	25'-0"	19	47'-6"
11	27'-6"	20	50'-0"
12	30'-0"	21	52'-6"
13	32'-6"	22	55'-0"
14	35'-0"	23	57'-6"

Note: 2108.9.4, "Wall design for out-of-plane loads," is cited as the source of requirements for pier design where lateral bracing spacing is greater than that listed above.

2108 Strength Design of Masonry

2108.9.3.8 Dimensional limits *(part 2 of 2)*

- Pier width is permitted = pier length where factored axial load at the point of maximum moment is as follows:

  Force < pier capacity ÷ 20.

- Other requirements for beams, piers and columns are shown in the details provided.

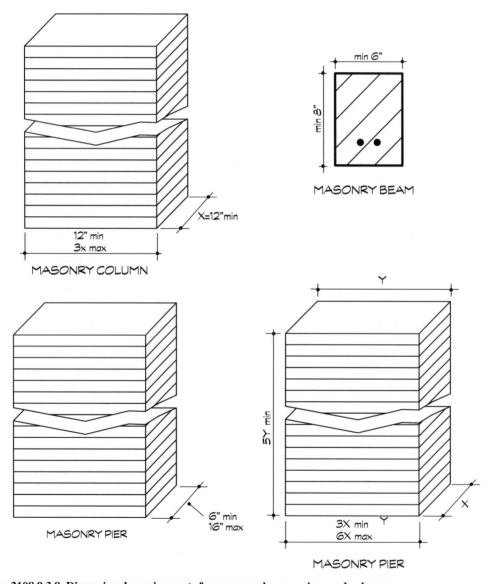

Fig. 2108.9.3.8. Dimensional requirements for masonry beams, piers and columns.

2108 Strength Design of Masonry

2108.9.6.3.3 Minimum clear span

This section addresses masonry moment-frame (wall frame) beams.

- Clear span requirements for wall frame beams is shown in the detail provided.

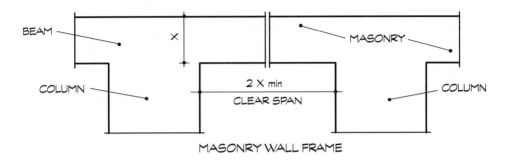

Fig. 2108.9.6.3.3 Minimum clear span for masonry moment-frame (wall frame) beams.

2108.9.6.3.4 Beam depth

- A partial list of maximum wall-frame beam depths based on the following relationship to width is provided below:
    - Depth may not be > 6 × width.
- Other requirements for wall-frame beam depth are shown in the details provided.

Table 2108.9.6.3.4   Maximum Wall-Frame Masonry Beam Depths

Beam depth	Clear span	Beam depth	Clear span	Beam depth	Clear span
8"	4'-0"	14"	7'-0"	20"	10'-0"
9"	4'-6"	15"	7'-6"	21"	10'-6"
10"	5'-0"	16"	8'-0"	22"	11'-0"
11"	5'-6"	17"	8'-6"	23"	11'-6"
12"	6'-0"	18"	9'-0"	24"	12'-0"
13"	6'-6"	19"	9'-6"	25"	12'-6"

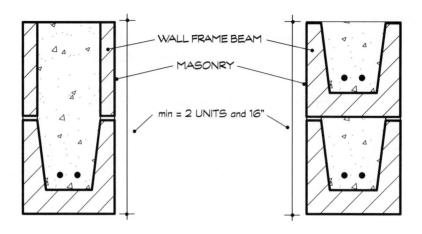

Fig. 2108.9.6.3.4A. Wall-frame beam depth requirements.

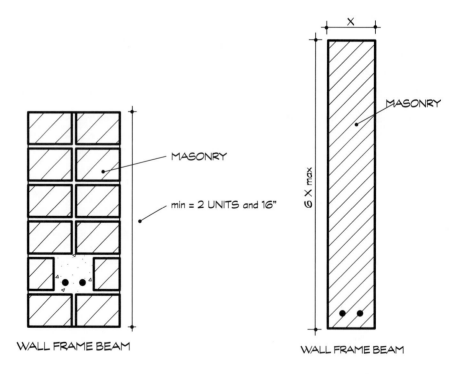

Fig. 2108.9.6.3.4 B. Wall-frame beam depth requirements.

2108 Strength Design of Masonry

2108.9.6.3.5 Beam width

This section addresses masonry moment-frame (wall frame) beams.

- Nominal beam width must be the larger of the following:
  - ○ ≥ 8".
  - ○ ≥ width listed in the table below as based on clear span ÷ 26:

Table 2108.9.6.3.5   Maximum Widths for Masonry Wall-Frame Beams

Clear span	Beam width	Clear span	Beam width
17'-4"	8"	30'-4"	14"
19'-6"	9"	32'-6"	15"
21'-8"	10"	34'-8"	16"
23'-10"	11"	36'-10"	17"
26'-0"	12"	39'-0"	18"
28'-2"	13"	41'-2"	19"

Note: 2108.9.3.8, "Dimensional limits," is cited as a source of a minimum beam depth applicable to this section. The 6" depth therein specified is < the 8" minimum of this section and, therefore, does not affect this section.

2108 Strength Design of Masonry

2108.9.6.6.2 Parallel column dimension

This section addresses masonry moment-frame (wall frame) columns.

- Dimensional requirements for columns are shown in the detail provided.

2108.9.6.6.3 Height-to-depth ratio

This section addresses masonry moment-frame (wall frame) columns.

- Dimensional requirements for columns are shown in Figure 2108.9.6.6.2.

2108.9.6.6.4 Height-to-depth ratio

This section addresses masonry moment-frame (wall frame) columns.

- Dimensional requirements for columns are shown in Figure 2108.9.6.6.2.

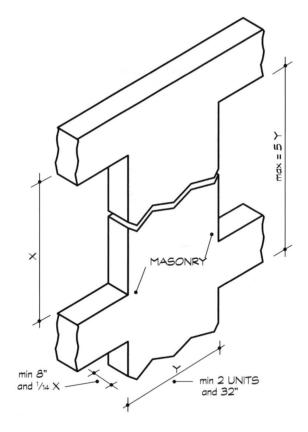

Fig. 2108.9.6.6.2. Dinemsional requirements for masonry wall-frame columns.

2109 Empirical Design of Masonry

2109.2.1.1 Shear wall thickness

- Minimum thickness of masonry shear walls is shown on the detail provided.

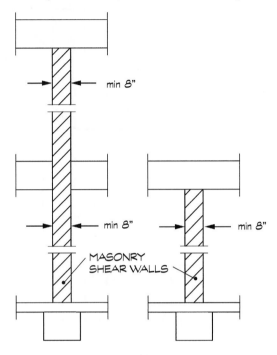

Fig. 2109.2.1.1. Minimum thickness of masonry shear walls.

2109.2.1.2 Cumulative length of shear walls

- The length of shear walls where required is governed as follows:
  - Shear wall length does not include openings.
  - The sum of individual shear wall lengths in any direction must total the following:
    $\geq 0.4 \times$ the long dimension of the building as shown in the detail provided.

Case study: Fig. 2109.2.1.2. The illustration shows a shear wall system in each direction. The minimum length in each direction where a shear wall is required is indicated in the summation of the segments as shown below: Dimension "x" indicates the long dimension of the building.

Where shear walls are required in the long dimension of the building:
   A + B + C + D + E + F + G + H + I + J + K + L ≥ 0.4x.

Where shear walls are required in the short direction of the building:
   M + N + O + P + Q + R + S ≥ 0.4x.

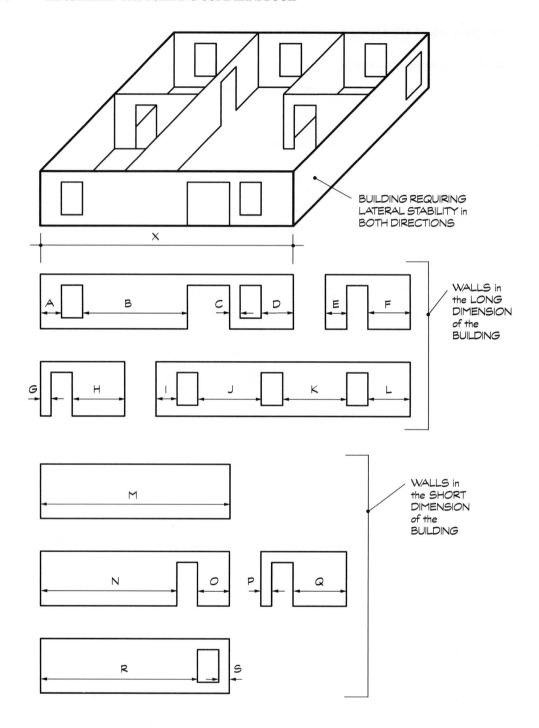

Fig. 2109.2.1.2. Cumulative length of shear walls.

2109 Empirical Design of Masonry

2109.2.1.3 Maximum diaphragm ratio

- Masonry shear walls are required in the following locations:
  - Locations that will maintain span to width ratios as follows:
    - As shown in the details provided for the following building elements:
      - Roofs.
      - Floors.

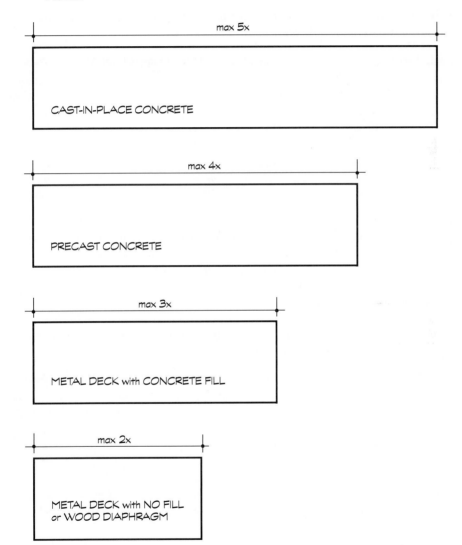

Fig. 2109.2.1.3. Maximum diaphragm ratios of various floor and roof systems as defined by shear wall locations.

2109 Empirical Design of Masonry

2109.4.1 General *(part 1 of 2)*

- A partial list of maximum dimensions between lateral support is provided below for the following walls:
  - Load-bearing masonry walls with solid units or fully grouted as follows:
    Length must be $\leq 20 \times$ thickness.
    Width must be $\leq 20 \times$ thickness.

  Note: IBC Table 2109.4.1, "Wall Lateral Support Requirements," is cited as the source of ratios governing wall dimensions.

Table 2109.4.1a   Maximum Distance between Lateral Supports for Masonry Walls

Wall thickness	Max. length Max. height	Wall thickness	Max. length Max. height	Wall thickness	Max. length Max. height
4"	6'-8"	12"	20'-0"	18"	30'-0"
6"	10'-0"	13"	21'-8"	19"	31'-8"
8"	13'-4"	14"	23'-4"	20"	33'-4"
9"	15'-0"	15"	25'-0"	21"	35'-0"
10"	16'-8"	16"	26'-8"	22"	36'-8"
11"	18'-4"	17"	28'-4"	23"	38'-4"

- A partial list of maximum dimensions between lateral support is provided below for the following walls:
  - Load-bearing walls other than solid units or fully grouted.
    Length must be $\leq 18 \times$ thickness.
    Width must be $\leq 18 \times$ thickness.

  Note: IBC Table 2109.4.1, "Wall Lateral Support Requirements," is cited as the source of ratios governing wall dimensions.

Table 2109.4.1b   Maximum Distance between Lateral Supports for Masonry Walls

Wall thickness	Max. length Max. height	Wall thickness	Max. length Max. height	Wall thickness	Max. length Max. height
4"	6'-0"	12"	18'-0"	18"	27'-0"
6"	9'-0"	13"	19'-6"	19"	28'-6"
8"	12'-0"	14"	21'-0"	20"	30'-0"
9"	13'-6"	15"	22'-6"	21"	31'-6"
10"	15'-0"	16"	24'-0"	22"	33'-0"
11"	16'-6"	17"	25'-6"	23"	34'-6"

2109 Empirical Design of Masonry

2109.4.1 General *(part 2 of 2)*

- A partial list of maximum dimensions between lateral support is provided below for the following walls:
  - Exterior nonload-bearing walls:
    Length must be ≤ 18 × thickness.
    Width must be ≤ 18 × thickness.

  Note: IBC Table 2109.4.1, "Wall Lateral Support Requirements," is cited as the source of ratios governing wall dimensions.

Table 2109.4.1c   Maximum Distance between Lateral Supports for Masonry Walls

Wall thickness	Max. length Max. height	Wall thickness	Max. length Max. height	Wall thickness	Max. length Max. height
4"	6'-0"	12"	18'-0"	18"	27'-0"
6"	9'-0"	13"	19'-6"	19"	28'-6"
8"	12'-0"	14"	21'-0"	20"	30'-0"
9"	13'-6"	15"	22'-6"	21"	31'-6"
10"	15'-0"	16"	24'-0"	22"	33'-0"
11"	16'-6"	17"	25'-6"	23"	34'-6"

- A partial list of maximum dimensions between lateral support is provided below for the following walls:
  - Interior nonload-bearing walls:
    Length must be ≤ 36 × thickness.
    Width must be ≤ 36 × thickness.

  Note: IBC Table 2109.4.1, "Wall Lateral Support Requirements," is cited as the source of ratios governing wall dimensions.

Table 2109.4.1d   Maximum Distance between Lateral Support for Masonry Walls

Wall thickness	Max. length Max. height	Wall thickness	Max. length Max. height	Wall thickness	Max. length Max. height
4"	12'-0"	12"	36'-0"	18"	54'-0"
6"	18'-0"	13"	39'-0"	19"	57'-0"
8"	24'-0"	14"	42'-0"	20"	60'-0"
9"	27'-0"	15"	45'-0"	21"	63'-0"
10"	30'-0"	16"	48'-0"	22"	66'-0"
11"	33'-0"	17"	51'-0"	23"	69'-0"

2109 Empirical Design of Masonry

2109.4.2 Thickness

- Wall thickness is measured as shown in the details provided.
- The ratio of height to thickness for cantilever walls is as indicated in the details provided.

> *Note: 2109.5.5, "Parapet walls," is cited as the source of thickness requirements for such walls in lieu of those in this section.*

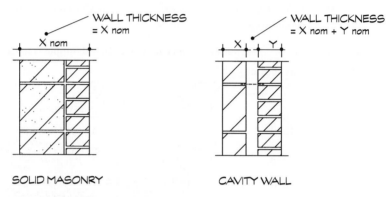

Fig. 2109.4.2A. Measurement of masonry wall thickness.

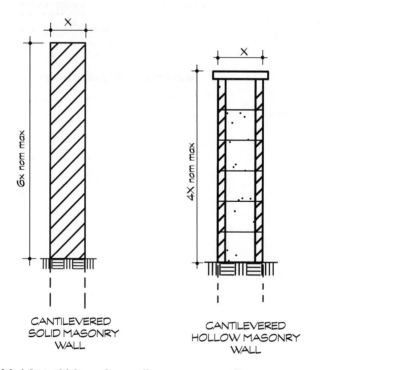

Fig. 2109.4.2B. Ratio of height to thickness for cantilever masonry walls.

2109 Empirical Design of Masonry

2109.4.3 Lateral support

- Lateral support must be provided to masonry walls as follows and as indicated in the details provided:
  - Where the horizontal dimension is limited by thickness:
    Lateral support is to be provided by the following elements:
    Cross walls.
    Pilasters.
    Buttresses.
    Structural frame members.
  - Where the vertical dimension is limited by thickness:
    Lateral support is to be provided by the following elements:
    Floors acting as diaphragms.
    Roofs acting as diaphragms.
    Structural frame members

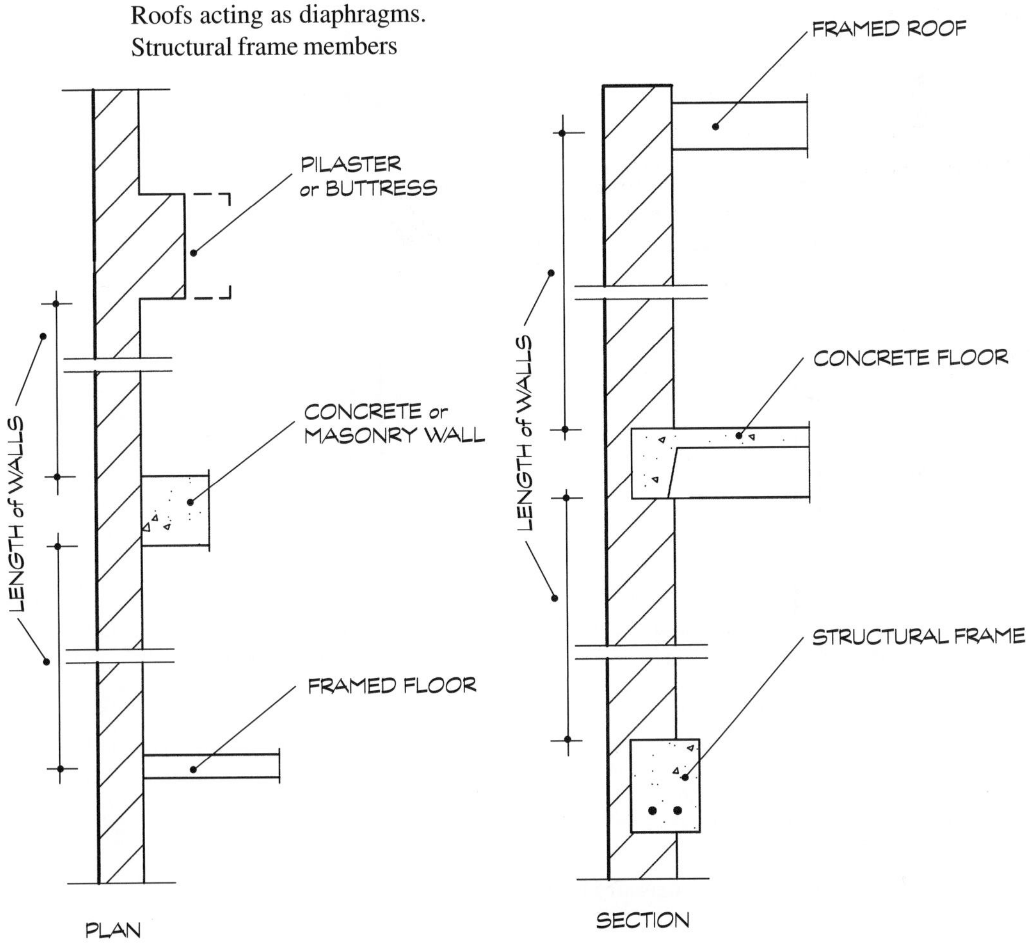

Fig. 2109.4.3. Lateral support for masonry walls.

2109 Empirical Design of Masonry

2109.5.2 Minimum thickness

- The minimum thickness of masonry bearing walls is shown in the details provided.

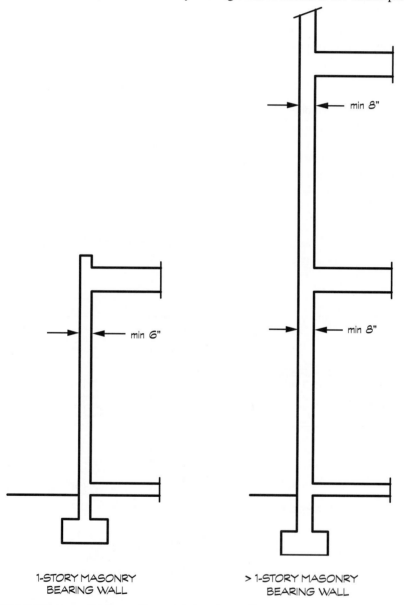

min 8"

min 6"

min 8"

1-STORY MASONRY
BEARING WALL

> 1-STORY MASONRY
BEARING WALL

Fig. 2109.5.2. Minimum thickness of masonry bearing walls.

2109.5.3 Rubble stone walls

- The required thickness of rubble stone walls is ≥ 16".

2109 Empirical Design of Masonry

2109.5.4 Change in thickness

- Where a higher part of a masonry wall with the following units is thinner than a lower part, the requirement indicated below applies:
  - Walls:
    - Hollow units.
    - Bonded hollow walls.
  - Requirement:
    - One of the following is required at the transition to transfer loads:
      - One or more courses of solid masonry as required.
      - Special units as shown in the detail provided.
      - Special construction.

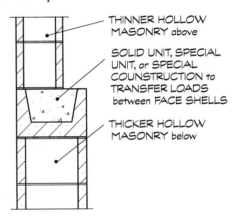

Fig. 2109.5.4. Change in masonry wall thickness at a grouted U-block.

2109.5.5.1 Minimum thickness

- The thickness required for unreinforced masonry parapet walls is shown in details provided.

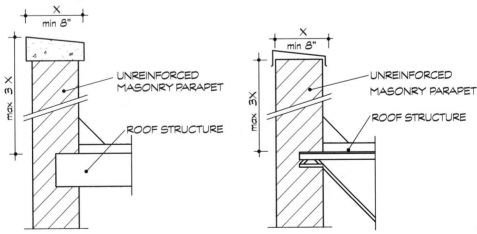

Fig. 2109.5.5.1. Minimum thickness required for unreinforced masonry parapet walls.

2109 Empirical Design of Masonry

2109.6.2.1 Solid units

This section addresses solid masonry units.

- Where adjacent wythes are bonded with masonry headers, the following is required:
    - Vertical and horizontal distance between headers must be ≤ 24".
    - ≥ 4% of the wall surface must be headers, acceptable examples of which are shown in the elevations provided.
    - Other requirements are shown in the details provided.

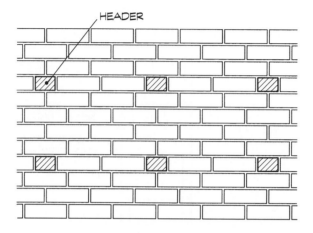

Fig. 2109.6.2.1A. Bond pattern providing headers at the minimum 4% of wall surface.

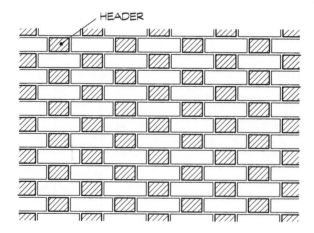

Fig. Fig. 2109.6.2.1B. Flemish bond providing headers at 33% of the wall surface.

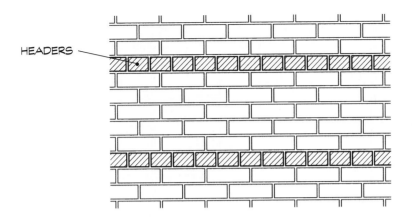

Fig. 2109.6.2.1C. Common bond with 6th course headers providing headers at 16% of the wall surface.

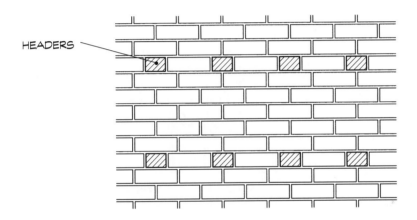

Fig. 2109.6.2.1D. Common bond with 6th course Flemish headers providing headers @ 5% of the wall surface.

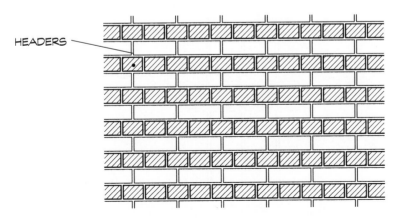

Fig. 2109.6.2.1E. English bond providing headers at 50% of the wall surface.

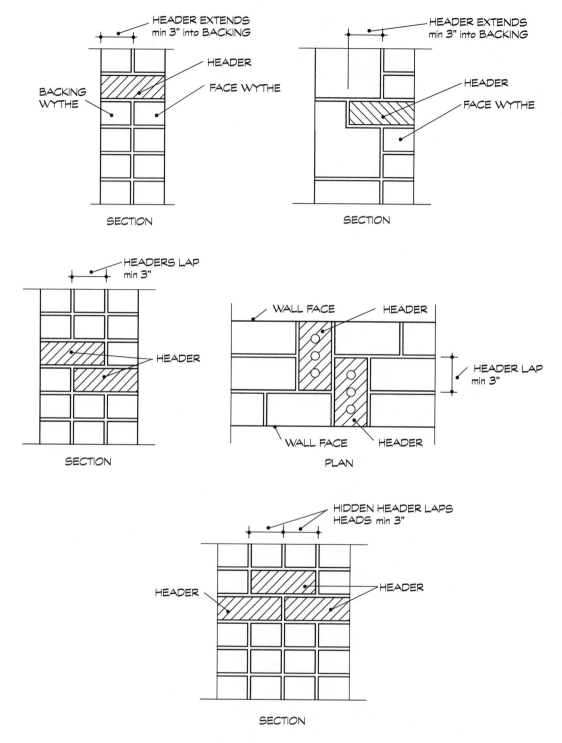

Fig. 2109.6.2.1F. Overlap requirements for headers used to bond masonry walls.

2109 Empirical Design of Masonry

2109.6.2.2 Hollow units

This section addresses hollow masonry units.

- Where adjacent wythes are bonded with masonry headers, the requirements shown in the details provided apply:

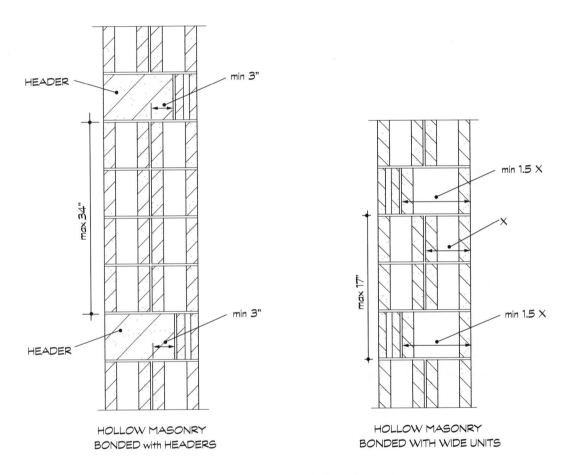

HOLLOW MASONRY
BONDED with HEADERS

HOLLOW MASONRY
BONDED WITH WIDE UNITS

Fig. 2109.6.2.2. Requirements for bonding masonry walls with hollow units.

2109.6.2.3 Masonry bonded hollow walls

This section addresses hollow masonry walls.

- Where adjacent wythes are bonded with masonry headers, the requirements are as follows:
  - Headers must constitute $\geq 4\%$ of the wall surface.
  - Other requirements are as shown in the details provided.

2109 Empirical Design of Masonry

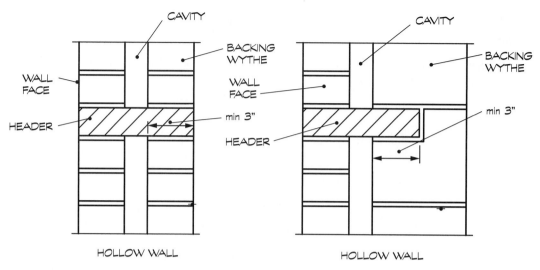

Fig. 2109.6.2.3. Requirements for masonry bonding hollow walls.

2109.6.3.1 Bonding with wall ties

- This section addresses rigid metal ties for masonry walls as follows:
  - Adjustable wall ties are not included.
- Requirements are shown in the details provided.

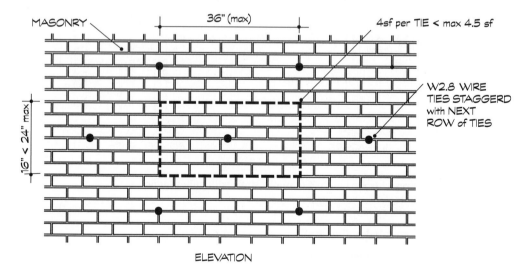

Fig. 2109.6.3.1A. Bonding masonry walls with metal ties. Wire ties at the maximum horizontal spacing of 36"and at 16" vertical spacing results in ties at ea 4 sf of wall surface which is less than the maximum permitted 4¹/₂ sf. 24" vertical spacing (max permitted) and 24" horizontal spacing also yield 4 sf of wall surface per tie.

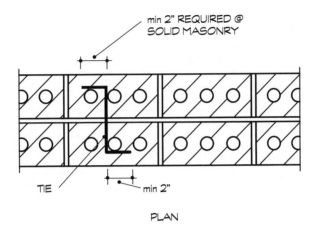

min 2" REQUIRED @
SOLID MASONRY

TIE   min 2"

PLAN

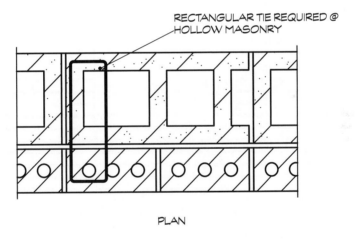

RECTANGULAR TIE REQUIRED @
HOLLOW MASONRY

PLAN

Fig. 2109.6.3.1B. Bonding masonry walls with metal ties.

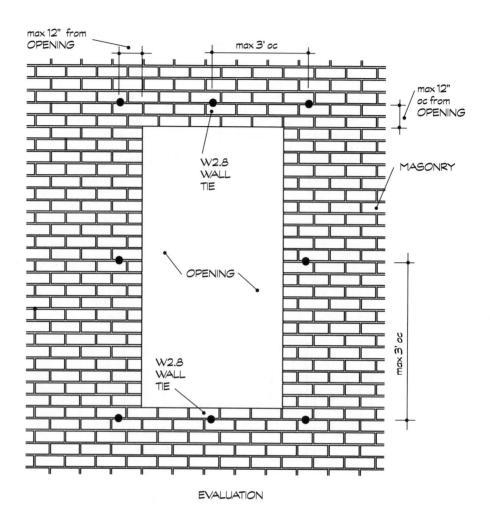

Fig. 2109.6.3.1C. Bonding masonry walls with metal ties.

2109 Empirical Design of Masonry

2109.6.3.1.1 Bonding with adjustable wall ties

- This section addresses adjustable wall ties, as follows, where used to bond masonry walls:
  - Where pintle legs are used:
    Ties must have ≥ 2 legs ≥ W2.8 wire.
- Other requirements are shown on the details provided.

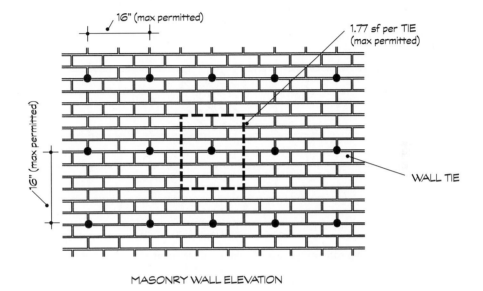

MASONRY WALL ELEVATION

Fig. 2109.6.3.1.1A. Bonding with adjustable wall ties. Adjustable wall ties @ 16" oc in both directions limits the area of wall face served by a tie to 1.77 sf, which is the maximum permitted.

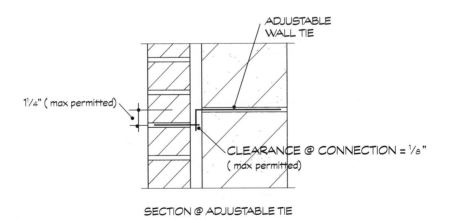

SECTION @ ADJUSTABLE TIE

Fig. 2109.6.3.1.1B. Bonding with adjustable wall ties.

2109 Empirical Design of Masonry

2109.6.3.2 Bonding with prefabricated joint reinforcement

- Requirements for masonry walls bonded with prefabricated joint reinforcement are shown in the details provided.

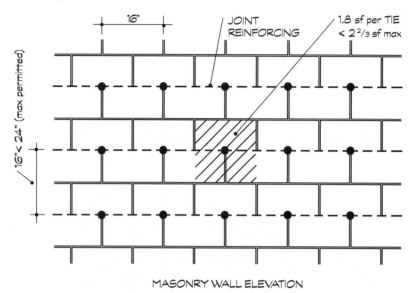

Fig. 2109.6.3.2A. Bonding with prefabricated joint reinforcement. Cross wires @ 16" oc horizontally and joint reinforcement @ 16" oc vertically yield 1.8 sf of wall surface per cross wire. This is $< 2^2/_3$ sf per cross wire, the maximum permitted.

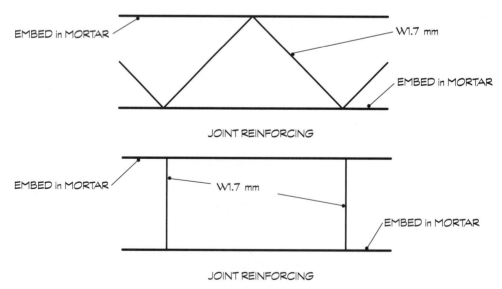

Fig. 2109.6.3.2B. Minimum wire sizes for bonding with prefabricated joint reinforcement.

2109 Empirical Design of Masonry

2109.6.4.1 Ashlar masonry

- Requirements for bonding ashlar natural or cast stone masonry are shown in the details provided.

BOND UNITS @ min 10% of WALL FACE

BOND UNITS

NATURAL or CAST STONE WALL ELEVATION

Fig. 2109.6.4.1A. Bonding ashlar masonry with masonry units. Units used to bond ashlar masonry must =10% minimum of the wall face and be uniformly distributed.

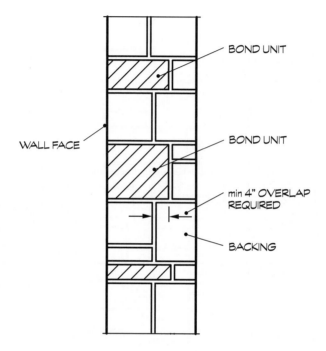

NATURAL or CAST STONE WALL ELEVATION

Fig. 2109.6.4.1B. Required overlap for bonding ashlar masonry with masonry units.

2109 Empirical Design of Masonry

2109.6.4.2 Rubble stone masonry

- Requirements for bonding with rubble stone masonry are shown in the details provided.

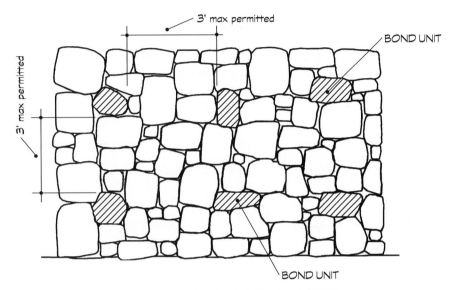

max 24" THICK RUBBLE STONE MASONRY

ELEVATION

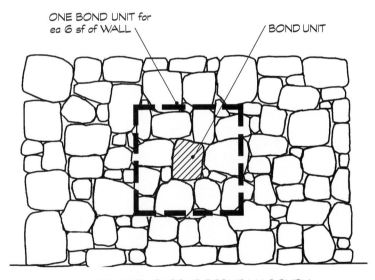

> 24" THICK RUBBLE STONE MASONRY

ELEVATION

Fig. 2109.6.4.2. Bonding with rubble stone masonry.

2109 Empirical Design of Masonry

2109.6.5.1 Masonry laid in running bond

- Masonry laid in running bond must meet the unit overlap requirements shown in the detail provided.
- Masonry with overlaps < ¼ unit length must be reinforced longitudinally.

  Note: 2109.6.5.2, "Masonry laid in stack bond," is cited as the source of requirements for units laid with less than ¼ unit length overlap.

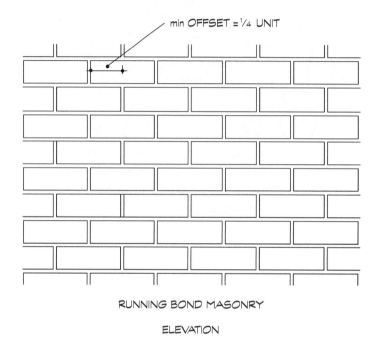

min OFFSET = ¼ UNIT

RUNNING BOND MASONRY

ELEVATION

Fig. 2109.6.5.1. Masonry laid in running bond.

2109 Empirical Design of Masonry

2109.6.5.2 Masonry laid in stack bond

- Masonry laid with units overlapping < ¼ unit length are governed as follows:
  - Area of reinforcing must ≥ 0.0003 × the vertical cross-sectional area of the wall.
  - Reinforcing is required in bed joints or bond beams.
- Horizontal reinforcing may not spaced vertically > 4'.
- The tables below provide partial lists of reinforcing that meet the requirements of this section:
  - Table for wire reinforcing includes allowance for cross-wires.

Table 2109.6.5.2a   **Maximum Vertical Spacing of Wire Joint-Reinforcing**

	Nominal wall thickness					
Longitudinal wire size	4"	6"	8"	10"	12"	16"
Truss-type wire joint-reinforcing:						
2 - W1.7	42.50"	27.77"	20.00"	15.66"	12.50"	8.95"
2 - W2.8	48.00"	39.44"	28.75"	22.66"	18.33"	13.33"
3 - W1.7	na	na	27.50"	21.33"	17.50"	12.50"
3 - W2.8	na	na	40.41"	31.66"	26.11"	19.16"
4 - W1.7	na	na	na	27.00"	22.22"	16.25"
4 - W2.8	na	na	na	41.00"	33.88"	24.79"
Ladder-type wire joint-reinforcing:						
2 - W1.7	28.33"	18.89"	14.17"	11.33"	9.44"	7.08"
2 - W2.8	46.67"	31.11"	23.33"	18.67"	15.56"	11.67"
3 - W1.7	na	na	21.25"	17.00"	14.17"	10.63"
3 - W2.8	na	na	35.00"	28.00"	23.33"	17.50"
4 - W1.7	na	na	na	22.67"	18.89"	14.17"
4 - W2.8	na	na	na	37.33"	31.11"	23.33"

Table 2109.6.5.2b   **Maximum Vertical Spacing of Deformed Reinforcing Bars in Bond Beams**

	Nominal wall thickness					
Bar	4"	6"	8"	10"	12"	16"
#3	48.00"	48.00"	45.83"	36.67"	30.56"	22.92"
#4	48.00"	48.00"	48.00"	48.00"	48.00"	41.67"
#5	48.00"	48.00"	48.00"	48.00"	48.00"	48.00"
#6	48.00"	48.00"	48.00"	48.00"	48.00"	48.00"
#7	48.00"	48.00"	48.00"	48.00"	48.00"	48.00"
#8	48.00"	48.00"	48.00"	48.00"	48.00"	48.00"

2109 Empirical Design of Masonry

2109.7.2.1 Bonding pattern

This section addresses the intersection of masonry walls that provide lateral support to each other.

- Such walls must be anchored to each other as follows:
  - 2 acceptable methods with masonry bond anchorage are shown in the details provided.

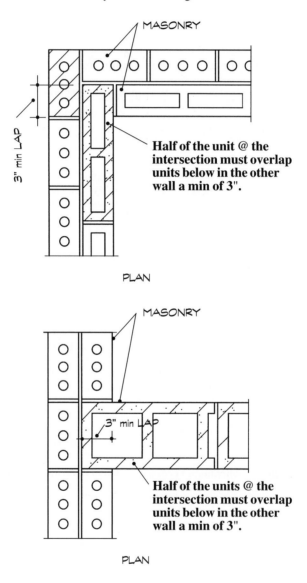

Fig. 2109.7.2.1. Bonding requirements at intersection of masonry walls.

2109 Empirical Design of Masonry

2109.7.2.2 Steel connectors

This section addresses the intersection of masonry walls that provide lateral support to each other.

- Such walls must be anchored to each other as follows:
  - ○ One acceptable method with steel connectors is shown in the detail provided.

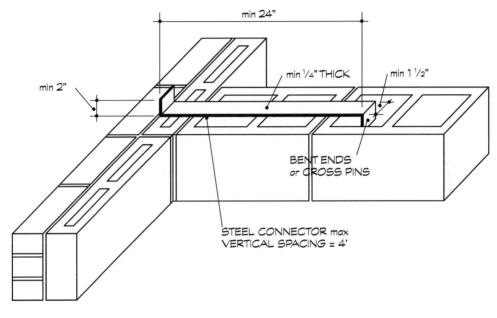

INTERSECTING MASONRY WALLS

Fig. 2109.7.2.2. Steel connectors at intersections of masonry walls.

2109.7.2.3 Joint reinforcement

This section addresses the intersection of masonry walls that provide lateral support to each other.

- Such walls must be anchored to each other as follows:
  - ○ Acceptable methods with joint reinforcement are shown in the details provided.

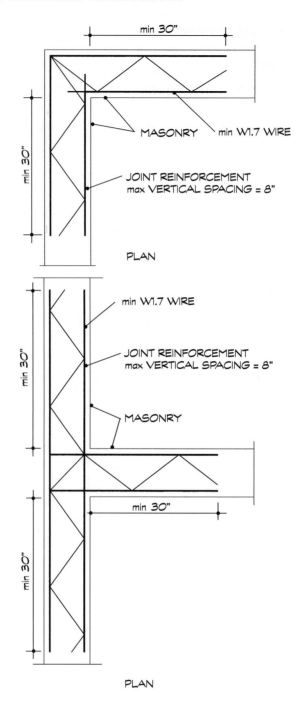

Fig. 2109.7.2.3. Joint reinforcement at intersection masonry walls.

2109 Empirical Design of Masonry

2109.7.2.4 Interior nonload-bearing walls

This section addresses the intersection of masonry walls that provide lateral support to each other.

- Such walls must be anchored to each other as follows:
  - One acceptable method for walls with both the following characteristics is shown in the detail provided:
    Interior.
    Nonload-bearing.

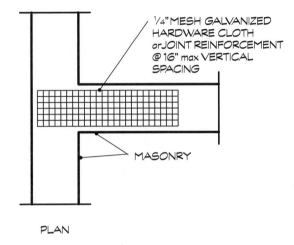

¼" MESH GALVANIZED HARDWARE CLOTH or JOINT REINFORCEMENT @ 16" max VERTICAL SPACING

MASONRY

PLAN

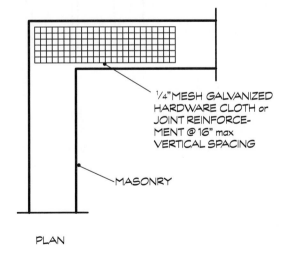

¼" MESH GALVANIZED HARDWARE CLOTH or JOINT REINFORCE-MENT @ 16" max VERTICAL SPACING

MASONRY

PLAN

Fig. 2109.7.2.4. Anchorage at intersections of interior nonload-bearing walls.

2109 Empirical Design of Masonry

2109.7.3.1 Wood floor joists

This section address wood floor diaphragms providing lateral stability to masonry walls.

- The floor joists must be anchored to the wall as shown in the details provided.

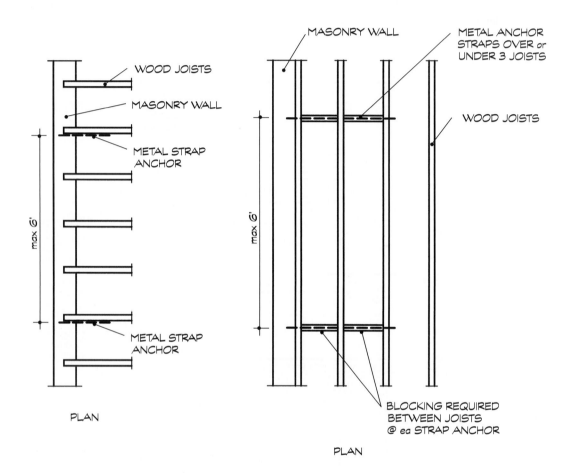

Fig. 2109.7.3.1. Anchorage of wood floor diaphragms providing lateral stability to masonry walls.

2109 Empirical Design of Masonry

2109.7.3.2 Steel floor joists

This section addresses steel floor joist diaphragms providing lateral stability to masonry walls.

• The floor joists must be anchored to the wall as shown in the details provided.

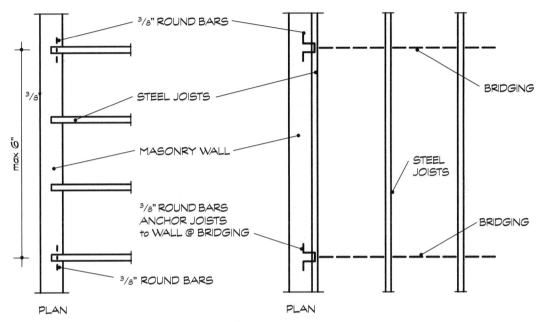

Fig. 2109.7.3.2. Anchorage of steel floor joist diaphragms providing lateral stability to masonry walls.

2109.7.3.3 Roof diaphragms

This section addresses roof diaphragms providing lateral stability to masonry walls.

• The roof must be anchored to the wall as shown in the details provided.

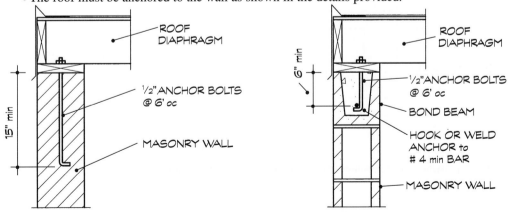

Fig. 2109.7.3.3. Anchorage of roof diaphragms providing lateral stability to masonry walls.

2109 Empirical Design of Masonry

2109.7.4 Walls adjoining structural framing

- Walls dependent on the structural frame for lateral support must be anchored to the frame as shown in the details provided.

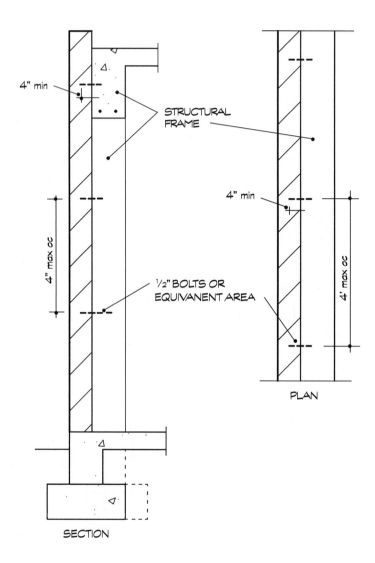

Fig. 2109.7.4. Anchorage of masonry walls adjoining structural framing.

2110 Glass Unit Masonry

2110.2.1 Standard units

- The thickness of standard units is shown in the detail provided.

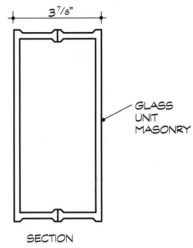

Fig. 2110.2.1. Minimum thickness of standard glass masonry units.

2110.2.2 Thin units

- The thickness of thin units are shown in the details provided.

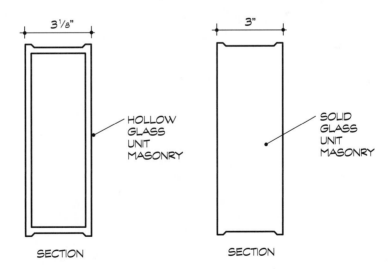

Fig. 2110.2.1. Minimum thickness of thin glass masonry units.

2110 Glass Unit Masonry

2110.3.1 Exterior standard-unit panels *(part 1 of 4)*

This section addresses exterior glass block panels with standard units.

- Maximum panel height between structural supports is 20'.
- Maximum panel width between structural supports is 25'.
- Maximum panel area varies with wind load as follows:
  - The tables below provide a partial list of width and height combinations that yield an area within the maximum permitted for the wind pressure indicated:
    Width and height are multiples of standard glass block dimensions.
    Either or both dimensions in any combination may be smaller than those listed.

  Note: Figure 2110.3.1, "Glass Masonry Design Wind Load Resistance," is cited as the source of glass block panel area limits. The following tables are based on this graph.

Table 2110.3.1   Maximum Dimensions of Glass Block Panels

Width	Height	Width	Height	Width	Height	Width	Height
Widths and heights ≤ 57 sf as permitted by a wind pressure of 60 psf:							
24'-8"	2'-0"	18'-8"	2'-8"	12'-8"	4'-0"	7'-4"	7'-4"
24'-0"	2'-0"	18'-0"	2'-8"	12'-0"	4'-8"	6'-8"	8'-0"
23'-4"	2'-0"	17'-4"	2'-8"	11'-4"	4'-8"	6'-0"	9'-4"
22'-8"	2'-0"	16'-8"	3'-4"	10'-8"	5'-4"	5'-4"	10'-8"
22'-0"	2'-0"	16'-0"	3'-4"	10'-0"	5'-4"	4'-8"	12'-0"
21'-4"	2'-8"	15'-4"	3'-4"	9'-4"	6'-0"	4'-0"	14'-0"
20'-8"	2'-8"	14'-8"	3'-4"	8'-8"	6'-0"	3'-4"	16'-8"
20'-0"	2'-8"	14'-0"	4'-0"	8'-0"	6'-8"	2'-8"	20'-0"
19'-4"	2'-8"	13'-4"	4'-0"				
Widths and heights ≤ 62 sf as permitted by a wind pressure of 55 psf:							
24'-8"	2'-0"	18'-8"	2'-8"	12'-8"	4'-8"	7'-4"	8'-0"
24'-0"	2'-0"	18'-0"	3'-4"	12'-0"	4'-8"	6'-8"	8'-8"
23'-4"	2'-0"	17' 4"	3'-4"	11'-4"	5'-4"	6'-0"	10'-0"
22'-8"	2'-8"	16'-8"	3'-4"	10'-8"	5'-4"	5'-4"	11'-4"
22'-0"	2'-8"	16'-0"	3'-4"	10'-0"	6'-0"	4'-8"	12'-8"
21' 4"	2'-8"	15'-4"	4'-0"	9'-4"	6'-0"	4'-0"	15'-4"
20'-8"	2'-8"	14'-8"	4'-0"	8'-8"	6'-8"	3'-4"	18'-0"
20'-0"	2'-8"	14'-0"	4'-0"	8'-0"	7'-4"	2'-8"	20'-0"
19'-4"	2'-8"	13'-4"	4'-0"				

2110 Glass Unit Masonry

2110.3.1 Exterior standard-unit panels *(part 2 of 4)*

Table 2110.3.1—*Continued.*

Width	Height	Width	Height	Width	Height	Width	Height
Widths and heights ≤ 70 sf as permitted by a wind pressure of 50 psf:							
24'-8"	2'-8"	18'-8"	3'-4"	13'-4"	4'-8"	8'-0"	8'-8"
24'-0"	2'-8"	18'-0"	3'-4"	12'-8"	5'-4"	7'-4"	9'-4"
23'-4"	2'-8"	17'-4"	4'-0"	12'-0"	5'-4"	6'-8"	10'-0"
22'-8"	2'-8"	16'-8"	4'-0"	11'-4"	6'-0"	6'-0"	11'-4"
22'-0"	2'-8"	16'-0"	4'-0"	10'-8"	6'-0"	5'-4"	12'-8"
21'-4"	2'-8"	15'-4"	4'-0"	10'-0"	6'-8"	4'-8"	14'-8"
20'-8"	3'-4"	14'-8"	4'-8"	9'-4"	7'-4"	4'-0"	17'-4"
20'-0"	3'-4"	14'-0"	4'-8"	8'-8"	8'-0"	3'-4"	20'-0"
19'-4"	3'-4"						
Widths and heights ≤ 77 sf as permitted by a wind pressure of 45 psf:							
24'-8"	2'-8"	18'-8"	4'-0"	13'-4"	5'-4"	8'-0"	9'-4"
24'-0"	2'-8"	18'-0"	4'-0"	12'-8"	6'-0"	7'-4"	10'-0"
23'-4"	2'-8"	17'-4"	4'-0"	12'-0"	6'-0"	6'-8"	11' 4"
22'-8"	3'-4"	16'-8"	4'-0"	11'-4"	6'-8"	6'-0"	12'-8"
22'-0"	3'-4"	16'-0"	4'-8"	10'-8"	6'-8"	5'-4"	14'-0"
21'-4"	3'-4"	15'-4"	4'-8"	10'-0"	7'-4"	4'-8"	16'-0"
20'-8"	3'-4"	14'-8"	4'-8"	9'-4"	8'-0"	4'-0"	18'-8"
20'-0"	3'-4"	14'-0"	5'-4"	8'-8"	8'-8"	3'-4"	20'-0"
19'-4"	3'-4"						
Widths and heights ≤ 84 sf as permitted by a wind pressure of 40 psf:							
24'-8"	3'-4"	19'-4"	4'-0"	14'-0"	6'-0"	8'-8"	9- 4"
24'-0"	3'-4"	18'-8"	4'-0"	13' 4"	6'-0"	8'-0"	10'-0"
23'-4"	3'-4"	18'-0"	4'-8"	12'-8"	6'-0"	7'-4"	11'-4"
22'-8"	3'-4"	17'-4"	4'-8"	12'-0"	6'-8"	6'-8"	12'-0"
22'-0"	3'-4"	16'-8"	4'-8"	11'-4"	7'-4"	6'-0"	14'-0"
21'-4"	3'-4"	16'-0"	4'-8"	10'-8"	7'-4"	5'-4"	15'-4"
20'-8"	4'-0"	15'-4"	5'-4"	10'-0"	8'-0"	4'-8"	17'-4"
20'-0"	4'-0"	14'-8"	5'-4"	9'-4"	8'-8"	4'-0"	20'-0"

2110 Glass Unit Masonry

2110.3.1 Exterior standard-unit panels *(part 3 of 4)*

Table 2110.3.1—*Continued.*

Width	Height	Width	Height	Width	Height	Width	Height
Widths and heights ≤ 94 sf as permitted by a wind pressure of 35 psf:							
24'-8"	3'-4"	19'-4"	4'-8"	14'-0"	6'-8"	8'-8"	10'-8"
24'-0"	3'-4"	18'-8"	4'-8"	13'-4"	6'-8"	8'-0"	11'-4"
23'-4"	4'-0"	18'-0"	4'-8"	12'-8"	7'-4"	7'-4"	12'-8"
22'-8"	4'-0"	17'-4"	5'-4"	12'-0"	7'-4"	6'-8"	14'-0"
22'-0"	4'-0"	16'-8"	5'-4"	11'-4"	8'-0"	6'-0"	15'-4"
21'-4"	4'-0"	16'-0"	5'-4"	10'-8"	8'-8"	5'-4"	17'-4"
20'-8"	4'-0"	15'-4"	6'-0"	10'-0"	9'-4"	4'-8"	20'-0"
20'-0"	4'-8"	14'-8"	6'-0"	9'-4"	10'-0"		
Widths and heights ≤ 104 sf as permitted by a wind pressure of 30 psf:							
24'-8"	4'-0"	19'-4"	5'-4"	14'-0"	7'-4"	8'-8"	11'-4"
24'-0"	4'-0"	18'-8"	5'-4"	13'-4"	7'-4"	8'-0"	12'-8"
23'-4"	4'-0"	18'-0"	5'-4"	12'-8"	8'-0"	7'-4"	14'-0"
22'-8"	4'-0"	17'-4"	6'-0"	12'-0"	8'-8"	6'-8"	15'-4"
22'-0"	4'-8"	16'-8"	6'-0"	11'-4"	8'-8"	6'-0"	17'-4"
21'-4"	4'-8"	16'-0"	6'-0"	10'-8"	9'-4"	5'-4"	19'-4"
20'-8"	4'-8"	15'-4"	6'-8"	10'-0"	10'-0"	4'-8"	20'-0"
20'-0"	4'-8"	14'-8"	6'-8"	9'-4"	10'-8"		
Widths and heights ≤ 119 sf as permitted by a wind pressure of 25 psf.							
24'-8"	4'-8"	18'-8"	6'-0"	12'-8"	9'-4"	8'-8"	13'-4"
24'-0"	4'-8"	18'-0"	6'-0"	12'-0"	9'-4"	8'-0"	14'-8"
23'-4"	4'-8"	17'-4"	6'-8"	11' 4"	10'-0"	7'-4"	16'-0"
22'-8"	4'-8"	16'-8"	6'-8"	10'-8"	10'-8"	6'-8"	17'-4"
22'-0"	5'-4"	16'-0"	7'-4"	10'-0"	11'-4"	6'-0"	19'-4"
21'-4"	5'-4"	15'-4"	7'-4"	9'-4"	12'-8"	5'-4"	20'-0"
20'-8"	5'-4"	14' 8"	8'-0"				
20'-0"	5'-4"	14'-0"	8'-0"				
19'-4"	6'-0"	13'-4"	8' 8"				

2110 Glass Unit Masonry

2110.3.1 Exterior standard-unit panels *(part 4 of 4)*

Table 2110.3.1—*Continued.*

Width	Height	Width	Height	Width	Height	Width	Height
Widths and heights ≤ 144 sf as permitted by a wind pressure of 20 psf.							
24-8"	5'-4"	20'-0"	6'-8"	15'-4"	9'-4"	10'-8"	13'-4"
24'-0"	6'-0"	19' 4"	7'-4"	14'-8"	9'-4"	10'-0"	14'-0"
23'-4"	6'-0"	18'-8"	7'-4"	14'-0"	10'-0"	9'-4"	15' 4"
22'-8"	6'-0"	18'-0"	8'-0"	13'-4"	10'-8"	8'-8"	16'-0"
22'-0"	6'-0"	17'-4"	8'-0"	12'-8"	11'-4"	8'-0"	18'-0"
21' 4"	6'-8"	16'-8"	8'-0"	12'-0"	12'-0"	7'-4"	19'-4"
20'-8"	6'-8"	16'-0"	8'-8"	11' 4"	12'-8"	6'-8"	20'-0"
Widths and heights ≤ 182 sf as permitted by a wind pressure of 15 psf.							
24'-8"	7'-4"	20'-0"	8'-8"	16'-0"	11'-4"	12'-0"	14'-8"
24'-0"	7'-4"	19'-4"	9'-4"	15'-4"	11'-4"	11'-4"	16'-0"
23'-4"	7'-4"	18'-8"	9'-4"	14'-8"	12'-0"	10'-8"	16'-8"
22'-8"	8'-0"	18'-0"	10'-0"	14'-0"	12'-8"	10'-0"	18'-0"
22'-0"	8'-0"	17'-4"	10'-0"	13'-4"	13'-4"	9'-4"	19'-4"
21'-4"	8'-0"	16'-8"	10'-8"	12'-8"	14'-0"	8'-8"	20'-0"
20'-8"	8'-8"						
Widths and heights ≤ 235 sf as permitted by a wind pressure of 10 psf.							
24'-8"	9'-4"	20'-8"	11'-4"	17'-4"	13'-4"	14'-0"	16'-8"
24'-0"	9'-4"	20'-0"	11'-4"	16'-8"	14'-0"	13'-4"	17'-4"
23'-4"	10'-0"	19'-4"	12'-0"	16'-0"	14'-8"	12'-8"	18'-0"
22'-8"	10'-0"	18'-8"	12'-0"	15'-4"	14'-8"	12'-0"	19'-4"
22'-0"	10'-8"	18'-0"	12'-8"	14'-8"	16'-0"	11'-4"	20'-0"
21'-4"	10'-8"						

2110 Glass Unit Masonry

2110.3.2 Exterior thin-unit panels

This section addresses exterior glass block panels with standard units.

- Panels may not be subjected to wind pressure > 20 psf.
- Maximum panel height between structural supports is 10'.
- Maximum panel width between structural supports is 15'.
- Maximum panel area between structural supports is 85 sf.
- The table below provides a partial list of widths and heights which yield an area within the maximum permitted as follows:
  - Width and height are multiples of standard glass block dimensions.
  - Either or both dimensions in any combination may be smaller than those listed.

Table 2110.3.2   **Thin Glass Block Units: Widths × Heights ≤ 85 sf**

Width	Height		Width	Height
14'-8"	5'-4"		11'-4"	7'-4"
14'-0"	6'-0"		10'-6"	7'-4"
13'-4"	6'-0"		10'-0"	8'-0"
12'-8"	6'-8"		9'-4"	8'-8"
12'-0"	6'-8"		8'-8"	9'-4"

2110 Glass Unit Masonry

2110.3.3 Interior panels

This section addresses interior glass block panels.

- Maximum panel height between structural supports is 20'.
- Maximum panel width between structural supports is 25'.
- Standard units are governed as follows:
  - Maximum panel area between structural supports is 250 sf.
- Thin units are governed as follows:
  - Maximum panel area between structural supports is 150 sf.
- The tables below provide a partial list of widths and heights which yield an area within the maximum permitted as follows:
  - Width and height are multiples of standard glass block dimensions.
  - Either or both dimensions in any combination may be smaller than those listed.

Table 2110.3.3a   Standard Glass Block Units: Width × Height ≤ 250 sf

Width	Height	Width	Height	Width	Height	Width	Height
24-'8"	10'-0"	21'-4"	11'-4"	18'-0"	13'-4"	14'-8"	16'-8"
24'-0"	10'-0"	20'-8"	12'-0"	17'-4"	14'-0"	14'-0"	17'-4"
23'-4"	10'-8"	20'-0"	12'-0"	16'-8"	14'-8"	13'-4"	18'-8"
22'-8"	10'-8"	19'-4"	12'-8"	16'-0"	15'-4"	12'-8"	19'-4"
22'-0"	11'-4"	18'-8"	13'-4"	15'-4"	16'-0"	12'-0"	20'-0"

Table 2110.3.3b   Thin Glass Block Units: Width × Height ≤ 150 sf

Width	Height	Width	Height	Width	Height
24-'8"	6'-0"	18'-8"	8'-0"	12'-8"	11'-4"
24'-0"	6'-0"	18'-0"	8'-0"	12'-0"	12'-0"
23'-4"	6'-0"	17'-4"	8'-0"	11'-4"	12'-8"
22'-8"	6'-0"	16'-8"	8'-8"	10'-8"	14'-0"
22'-0"	6'-8"	16'-0"	9'-4"	10'-0"	14'-8"
21'-4"	6'-8"	15'-4"	9'-4"	9'-4"	16'-0"
20'-8"	6'-8"	14'-8"	10'-0"	8'-8"	16'-8"
20'-0"	7'-4"	14'-0"	10'-8"	8'-0"	18'-8"
19'-4"	7'-4"	13'-4"	10'-8"	7'-4"	20'-0"

2110.3.4 Solid units

- Solid glass-block wall panels are governed as follows:
  - Maximum area is ≤ 100 sf in the following locations:
    Outside.
    Inside.

2110 Glass Unit Masonry

2110.3.5 Curved panels

- The width of curved glass-block panels must comply with the same dimensional limitations that govern straight panels.

  Note: The following are cited as sources of width requirements governing curved-block panels:

  2110.3.1, "Exterior standard-unit panels."
  2110.3.2, "Exterior thin-unit panels."
  2110.3.3, "Interior panels."

- Additional structural supports are required an the following locations as shown in the details provided:
  - At the connection of a curved panel to a straight panel.
  - At inflection points of serpentine curves.

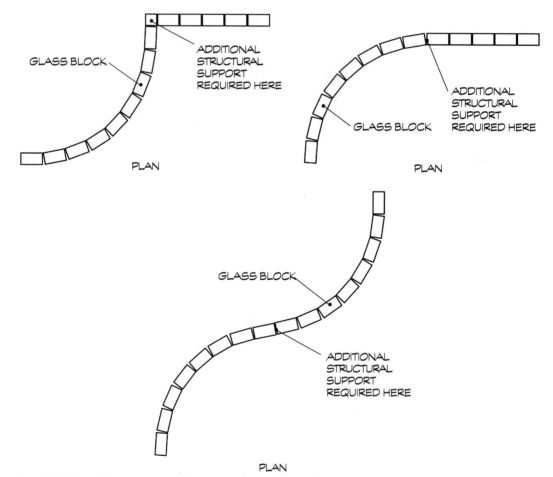

Fig. 2110.3.5. Additional structural support in curved glass block panels.

2110 Glass Unit Masonry

2110.4.3 Lateral

- Lateral support for glass block is required as follows.
  - At the top of a panel as follows:
    Where the panel is more than one block wide.
    Lateral support is not required where the panel is only 1 block wide.
  - At the sides of a panel as follows:
    Where the panel is more than one block high.
    Lateral support is not required where the panel is only 1 block high.
- Lateral supports must resist the greater of the following loads:
  - Actual loads applied.
  - 200 lbs/lineal foot.
- Dimensional requirements for lateral support is shown in the details provided.

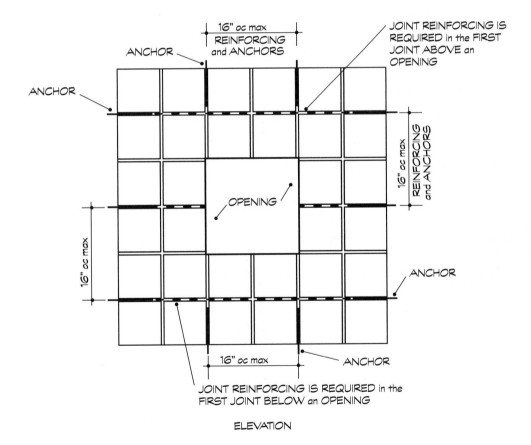

Fig. 2110.4.3A. Lateral support for glass block.

2110 Glass Unit Masonry

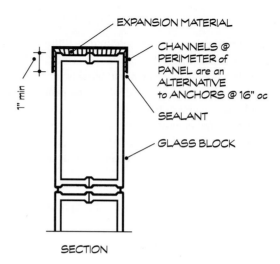

Fig. 2110.4.3B. Lateral support for glass block.

2110.7 Reinforcement

- Glass block panels require joint reinforcing as follows and as shown in the detail provided:
  - Reinforcing does not cross expansion joints.

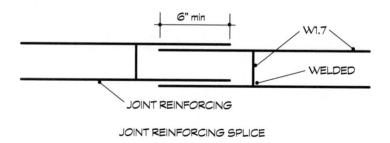

Fig. 2110.7. Size and splice requirements for joint reinforcement.

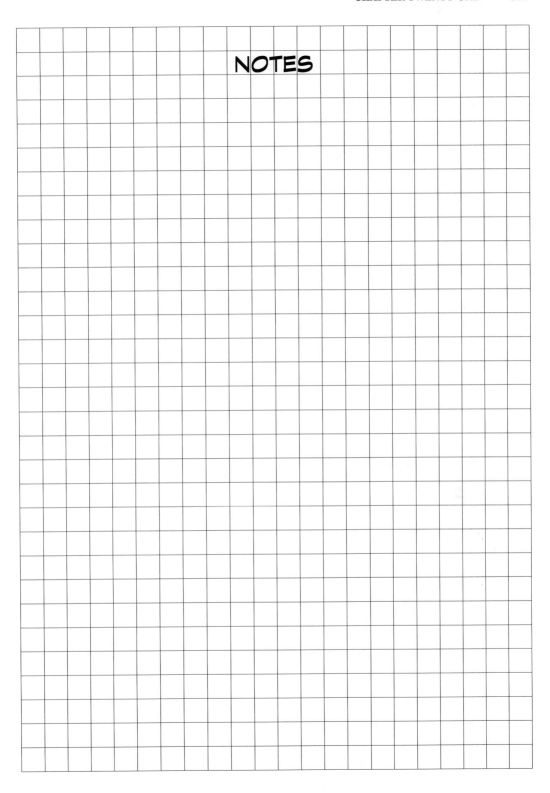

NOTES

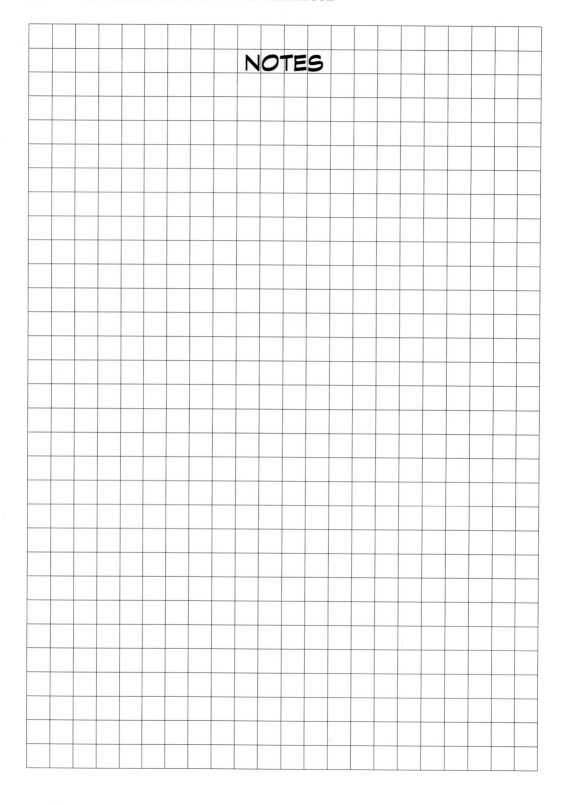

NOTES

22

Steel

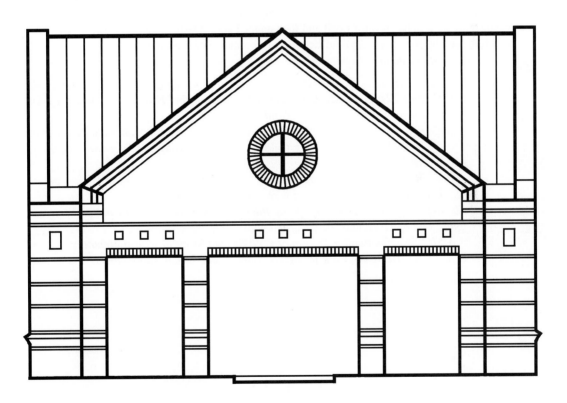

Christus St. Michael Health Care Center. Texarkana, Texas. *(partial elevation)*
Watkins Hamilton Ross Architects, Inc. Houston, Texas.

2211 Wind and Seismic Requirements for Light-Framed Cold-Formed Steel Walls

2211.1 General

- This section addresses the strength of shear walls as follows:
  - Walls framed with of one of the following light-gage steels:
    Cold-formed carbon steel.
    Cold-formed low-alloy steel.
  - Walls resisting shear due to the following:
    Wind.
    Seismic loading.
- Shear strength in lbs/ft of shear-wall length is shown in the details provided in the following formats.
  - Nominal shear strength is shown.
  - Shear strength to be used for allowable stress design (ASD) is shown as determined by the following modification of nominal shear strength:
    ASD shear strength = Nominal shear strength ÷ safety factor 2.5.
  - Shear strength to be used for Load and Resistance Factor Design (LRFD) is shown as determined by the following modification of nominal shear strength:
    LFRD shear strength = Nominal shear strength × resistance factor 0.55.

  Note: The following are cited as sources of shear values for light-gage steel framed walls:
    IBC Table 2211.1(1), "Nominal Shear Values for Wind Forces in Pounds per Foot for Shear Walls Framed with Cold-Formed Steel Studs."
    IBC Table 2211.1(2), "Nominal Shear Values for Wind Forces in Pounds per Foot for Shear Walls Framed with Cold-Formed Steel Studs and Faced with Gypsum Board."
    IBC Table 2211.1(3), "Nominal Shear Values for Seismic Forces in Pounds per Foot for Shear Walls Framed with Cold-Formed Steel Studs."
  The following are cited as governing the design of walls to resist wind and seismic loads, one of which must be complied with:
    AISI, "Specification for Design of Cold-formed Steel Structural Members.".
    ASCE 8, "Design of Cold-formed Stainless Steel Structural Members."

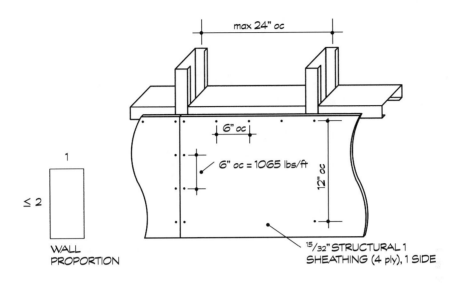

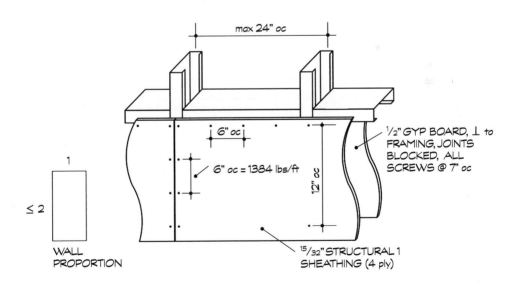

Fig. 2211.1 (A-1). Nominal shear value of shear walls framed with cold-framed steel studs, and subject to wind. *[IBC Table 2211.1(1)]*

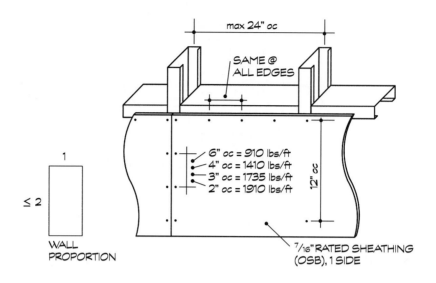

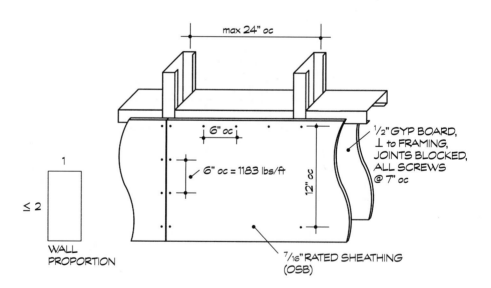

Fig. 2211.1 (A-3). Nominal shear value of shear walls framed with cold-framed steel studs, and subject to wind. *[IBC Tabl2 2211.1(1)]*

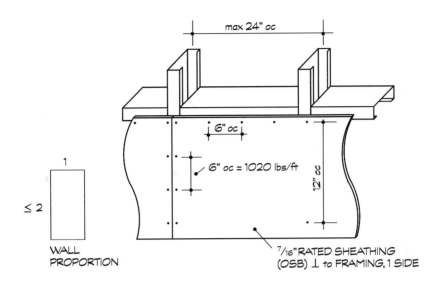

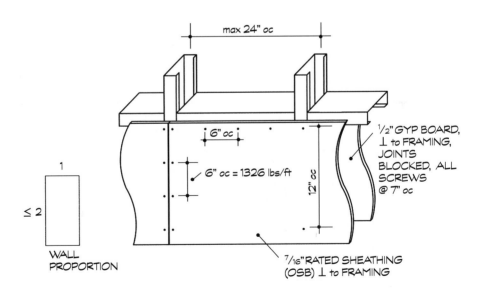

Fig. 2211.1 (A-3). Nominal shear value of shear walls framed with cold-framed steel studs, and subject to wind. *[IBC Table 2211.1(1)]*

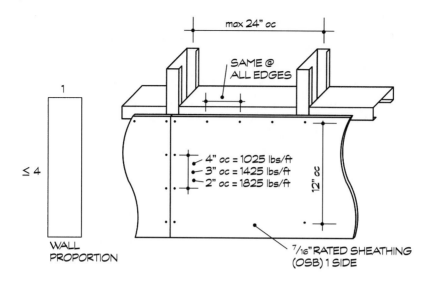

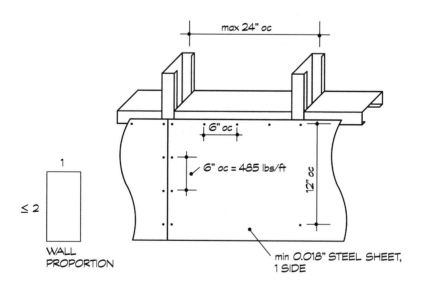

Fig. 2211.1 (A-4). Nominal shear value of shear walls framed with cold-framed steel studs, and subject to wind. *[IBC Table 2211.1(1)]*

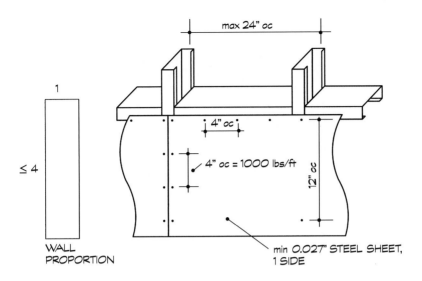

Fig. 2211.1 (A-5). Nominal shear value of shear walls framed with cold-framed steel studs, and subject to wind. *[IBC Table 2211.1(1)]*

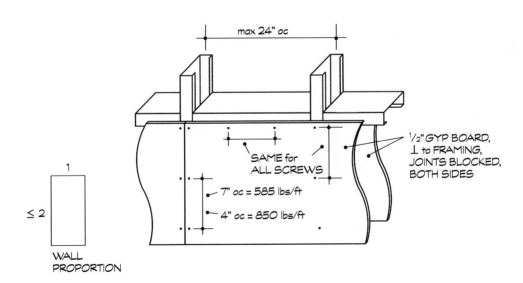

Fig. 2211.1 (B). Nominal shear value of shear walls framed with cold-framed steel studs and gypsum board, and subject to wind. *[IBC Table 2211.1(2)]*

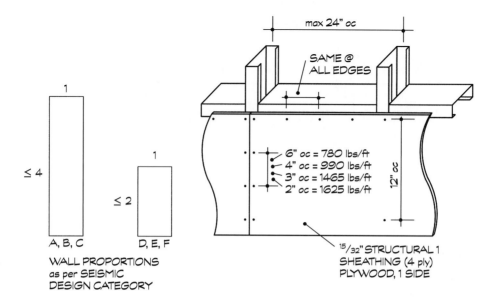

WALL PROPORTIONS
as per SEISMIC
DESIGN CATEGORY

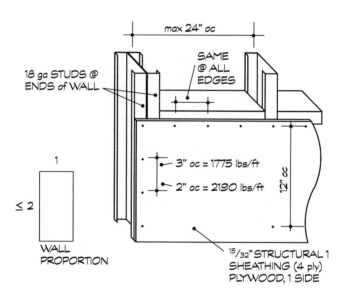

Fig. 2211.1 (C-1). Nominal shear value of shear walls framed with cold-framed steel studs, and subject to seismic forces. *[IBC Table 2211.1(3)]*

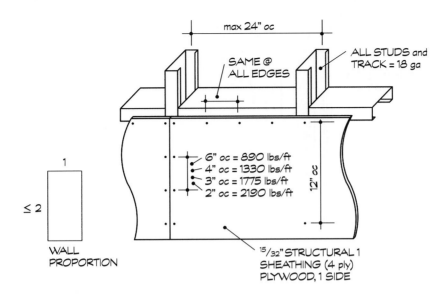

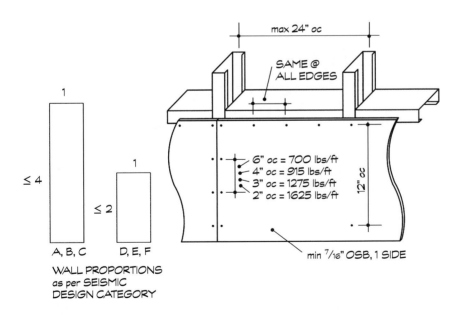

Fig. 2211.1 (C-2). Nominal shear value of shear walls framed with cold-framed steel studs, and subject to seismic forces. *[IBC Table 2211.1(3)]*

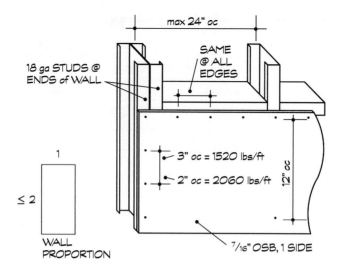

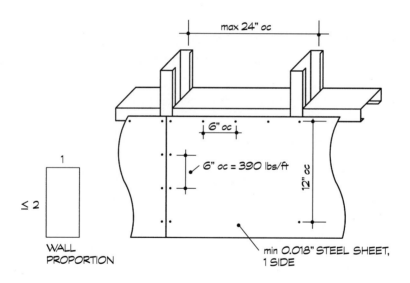

Fig. 2211.1 (C-3). Nominal shear value of shear walls framed with cold-framed steel studs, and subject to seismic forces. *[IBC Table 2211.1(3)]*

2211 Wind and Seismic Requirements for Light-Framed Cold-Formed Steel Walls

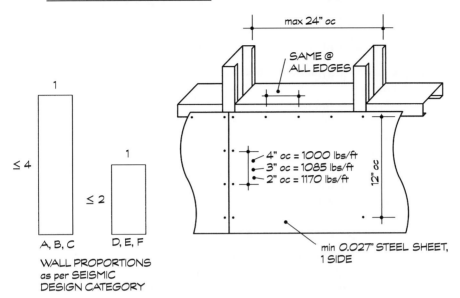

Fig. 2211.1 (C-4). Nominal shear value of shear walls framed with cold-framed steel studs, and subject to seismic forces. *[IBC Table 2211.1(3)]*

2211.2.1 Limitations for systems in Tables 2211.1(1), 2211.1(2) and 2211.1(3)

This section addresses light-gage steel framing members used in the shear walls specified in this chapter.

- Light-gage steel studs and track are governed as follows:
  - Thickness must be $\geq 0.033"$ (20 gage) as follows:
    Uncoated base metal thickness.

> *Note: The steel as indicated above must be SS Grade 33 as per one of the following:*
>
> *ASTM A 653, "Specification for Steel Sheet, Zinc-Coated (Galvanized) or Zinc-Iron Alloy-Coated (Galvannealed) by the Hot-Dip Process."*
>
> *ASTM A 792, "Specification for Steel Sheet, 55% Aluminum-Zinc Alloy-Coated by the Hot-Dip Process."*
>
> *ASTM A 875, "Specification for Steel Sheet, Zinc-5% Aluminum Alloy-Coated by the Hot-Dip Process."*
>
> *The following are cited as the sources of shear values to which this section applies:*
>
> *IBC Table 2211.1(1), "Nominal Shear Values for Wind Forces in Pounds per Foot for Shear Walls Framed with Cold-Formed Steel Studs."*
>
> *IBC Table 2211.1(2), "Nominal Shear Values for Wind Forces in Pounds per Foot for Shear Walls Framed with Cold-Formed Steel Studs and Faced with Gypsum Board."*
>
> *IBC Table 2211.1(3), "Nominal Shear Values for Seismic Forces in Pounds per Foot for Shear Walls Framed with Cold-Formed Steel Studs."*

2211 Wind and Seismic Requirements for Light-Framed Cold-Formed Steel Walls

2211.3.1 Shear values

This section addresses shear walls of light-gage steel framing.

- Shear-wall strength may be determined by structural calculations as follows:
  - By use of the following:
      Structural wood panels as follows:
        Panels with exterior quality glue.
      Approved fasteners.
  - Such values may be used in lieu of shear values shown in the details provided in this chapter.
  - Strength increases based on duration of load are not allowed.
  - Strength increases based on application of sheathing to both sides of the wall are governed as follows:
      Allowed only where specifically permitted by the code.

  Note: The following are cited as governing wood structural panels:
  > *DOC PS 1, "Construction and Industrial Plywood."*
  > *DOC PS 2, "Performance Standard for Wood-Based Structural-Use Panels."*
  > *The following are cited as sources of shear values to which this section applies:*
  > *IBC Table 2211.1(1), "Nominal Shear Values for Wind Forces in Pounds per Foot for Shear Walls Framed with Cold-Formed Steel Studs."*
  > *IBC Table 2211.1(3), "Nominal Shear Values for Seismic Forces in Pounds per Foot for Shear Walls Framed with Cold-Formed Steel Studs."*

- $^{15}/_{32}$" structural 1 sheathing (plywood) may substitute for the following:
  - $^{7}/_{16}$" oriented strand board (OSB) where specified.

2211.3.2 Orientation

This section addresses shear walls of light-gage steel framing.

- Permitted orientations of structural panels on shear walls are shown in the details provided.

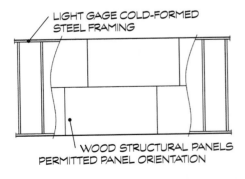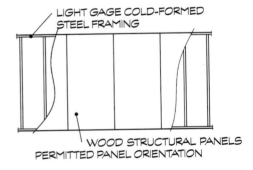

Fig. 2211.3.2. Permitted orientations of structural panels on shear-wall framing.

2211 Wind and Seismic Requirements for Light-Framed Cold-Formed Steel Walls

2211.3.3 Attachment

This section addresses shear walls of light-gage steel framing.

- Screws attaching plywood and oriented strand board (OSB) to framing are governed as follows:
  - Screws must be approved.
  - Other screw requirements are shown in the detail provided.

    Note: SAE J78, "Steel Self-Drilling Tapping Screws," is cited as governing the screws indicated above.

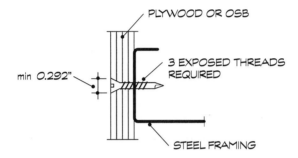

Fig. 2211.3.3. Required size and penetration of screws in shear walls of light-gage steel framing.

2211 Wind and Seismic Requirements for Light-Framed Cold-Formed Steel Walls

2211.4.2 Orientation

This section addresses shear walls of light-gage steel framing.

- Gypsum board must be applied to shear walls as indicated in the detail provided.

  Note: IBC Table 2211.1(2), "Nominal Shear Values for Wind Forces in Pounds per Foot for Shear Walls Framed with Cold-Formed Steel Studs and Faced with Gypsum Board," is cited as governing the walls addressed in this section.

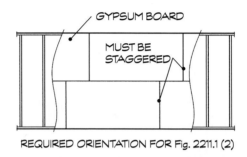

Fig. 2211.4.2. Required orientation of gypsum board on shear-wall framing.

2211.4.3 Attachment

This section addresses shear walls of light-gage steel framing.

- Gypsum board must attached to shear walls as indicated in the detail provided.

  Note: ASTM C 954, "Specification for Steel Drill Screws for the Application of Gypsum Panel Products or Metal Plaster Bases to Steel Studs from 0.033" (0.84mm) to 0.112" (2.84mm) in Thickness," is cited as governing the fasteners in the detail provided.

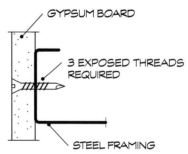

Fig. 2211.4.3. Required size and penetration of screws in shear walls of light-gage steel framing.

2211 Wind and Seismic Requirements for Light-Framed Cold-Formed Steel Walls

2211.5.2 Orientation

This section addresses shear walls of light-gage steel framing.

- Permitted orientations of steel sheet on shear walls are shown in the details provided.

    The following govern the shear walls to which this section applies:
    IBC Table 2211.1(1), "Nominal Shear Values for Wind Forces in Pounds Per Foot for Shear Walls Framed With Cold-Formed Steel Studs."
    IBC Table 2211.1(3), "Nominal Shear Values for Seismic Forces in Pounds Per Foot for Shear Walls Framed With Cold-Formed Steel Studs."

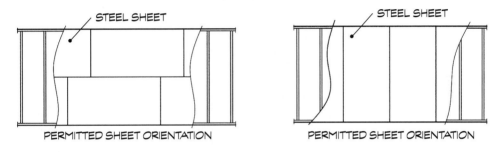

Fig. 2211.5.2. Permitted orientations of structural panels on shear-wall framing.

2211.5.3 Attachment

This section addresses shear walls of light-gage steel framing.

- Steel sheet must be attached to wall framing as shown in the details provided.

    The following govern the shear walls to which this section applies:
    IBC Table 2211.1(1), "Nominal Shear Values for Wind Forces in Pounds per Foot for Shear Walls Framed with Cold-Formed Steel Studs."
    IBC Table 2211.1(3), "Nominal Shear Values for Seismic Forces in Pounds per Foot for Shear Walls Framed with Cold-Formed Steel Studs."

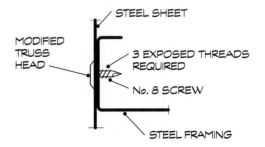

Fig. 2211.5.3. Required size, shape and penetration of screws in shear walls of light-gage steel framing.

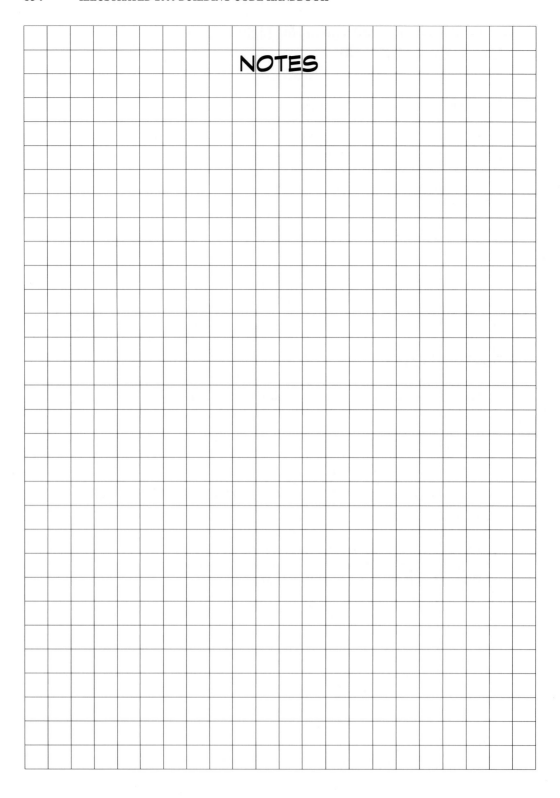

NOTES

23

Wood

Central Kitchen. Lompoc Unified School District.
Lompoc, California. *(partial elevation)*
Phillips Metsch Sweeney Moore Architects. Santa Barbara, California.

2304 General Construction Requirements

2304.6.1 Wall sheathing

This section addresses wall sheathing in wood-framed construction.

- Framing for buildings must be sheathed by one of the following materials:
  - The following materials specified elsewhere in the code:
    Weather boarding.
    Stucco.
  - Materials shown in details provided in this section.
  - Other material as follows:
    Approved.
    Of equal strength and durability.

> *Note: The following are cited as sources of requirements for sheathing indicated above:*
> *Section 1405, "Installation of Wall Coverings."*
> *Section 2510, "Lathing and Furring for Cement Plaster (Stucco)."*
> *IBC Table 2304.6.1, "Minimum thickness of wall sheathing" is the basis of the details provided.*

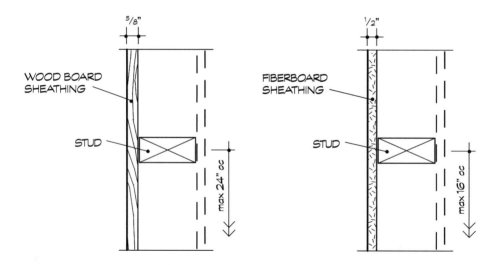

Fig. 2304.6.1A. Minimum thickness of wall sheathing.

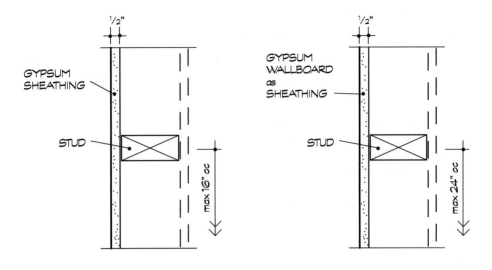

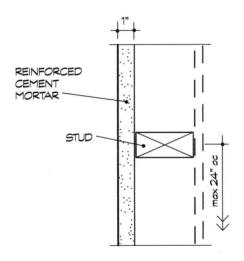

Fig. 2304.6.1A. Minimum thickness of wall sheathing.

2304 General Construction Requirements

2304.7.1 Structural floor sheathing

- Thicknesses required for structural floor sheathing are shown in the details provided.

    Note: IBC Table 2304.7(2), "Sheathing Lumber, Minimum Grade Requirements: Board Grade," is cited as governing floor sheathing. The table lists grading rules. The following are cited as the sources of requirements for the structural floor sheathing indicated above and are the basis of the details provided:
    IBC Table 2304.7(1), "Allowable Spans for Lumber Floor and Roof Sheathing."
    IBC Table 2304.7(3), "Allowable Spans and Loads for Wood Structural Panel Sheathing and Single-Floor Grades Continuous over Two or More Spans with Strength Axis Perpendicular to Supports."
    IBC Table 2304.7(4), "Allowable Span for Wood Structural Panel Combination Subfloor-Underlayment (Single Floor)."

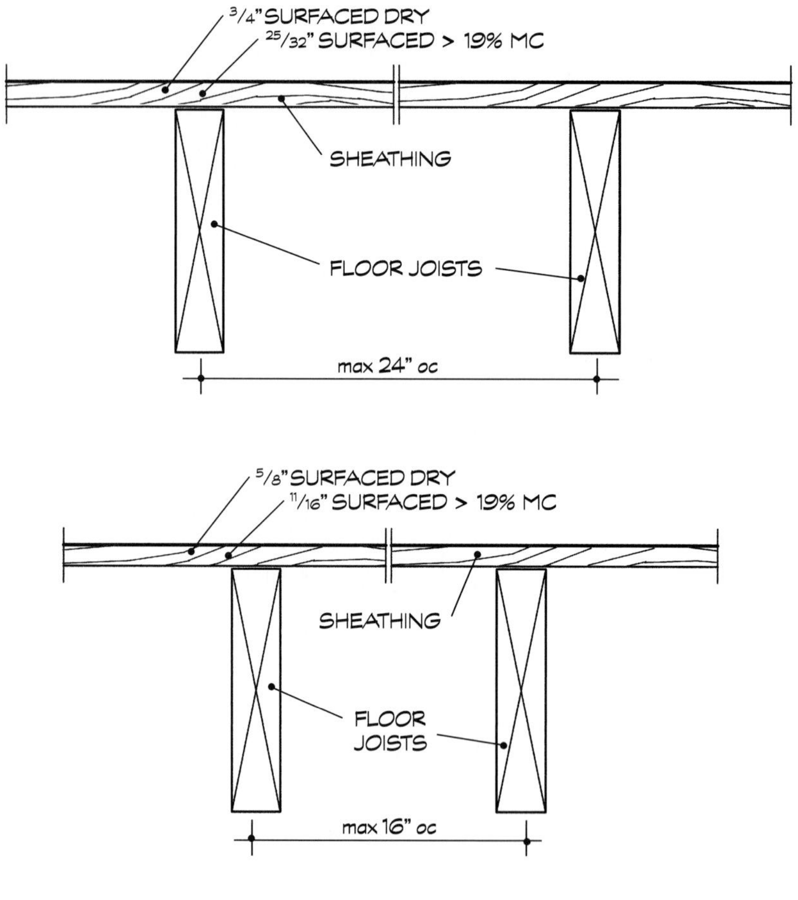

Fig. 2304.7.1A. Spans and minimum thicknesses for floor sheathing. *[IBC Table 2304.7(1)]*

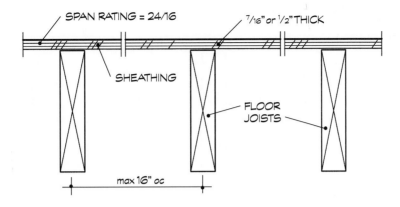

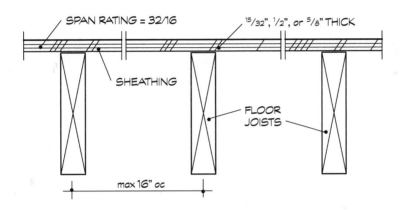

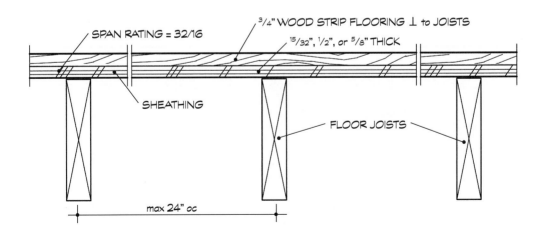

Fig. 2304.7.1B-1. Spans, loads, and minimum thicknesses for wood structural panel floor sheathing continuous over ≥ 2 spans, ⊥ to supports. *[IBC Table 2304.7(3)]*

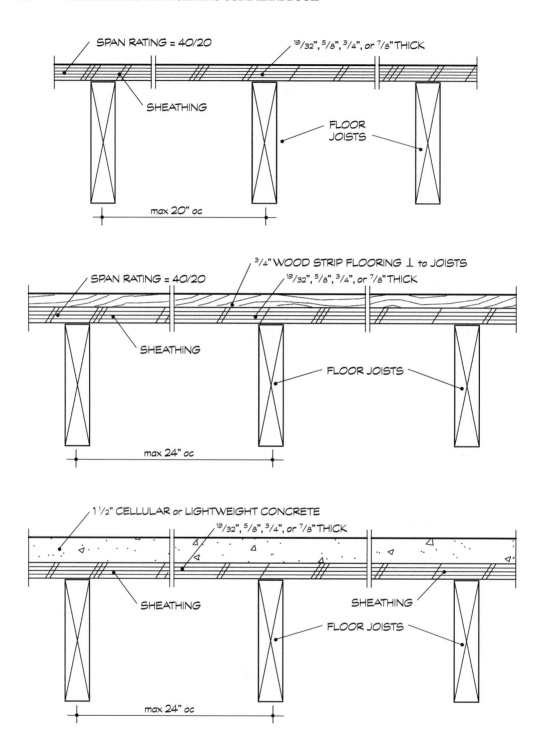

Fig. 2304.7.1B-2. Spans, loads, and minimum thicknesses for wood structural panel floor sheathing continuous over ≥ 2 spans, ⊥ to supports. *[IBC Table 2304.7(3)]*

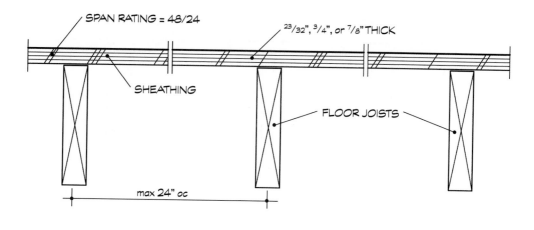

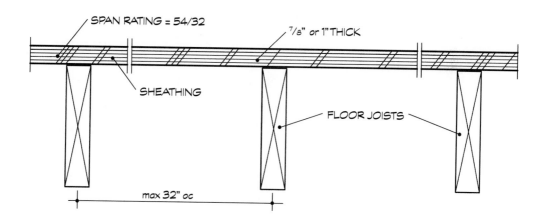

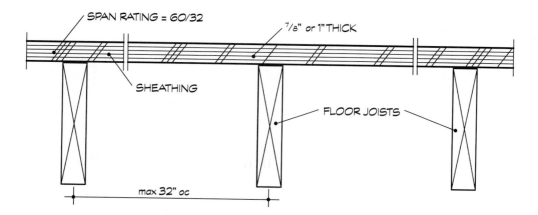

Fig. 2304.7.1B-3. Spans, loads, and minimum thicknesses for wood structural panel floor sheathing continuous over ≥ 2 spans, ⊥ to supports. *[IBC Table 2304.7(3)]*

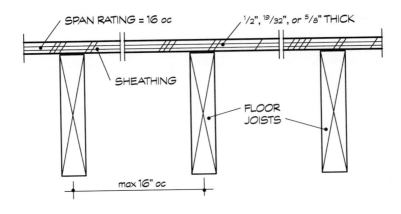

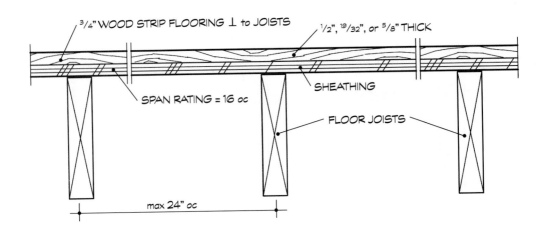

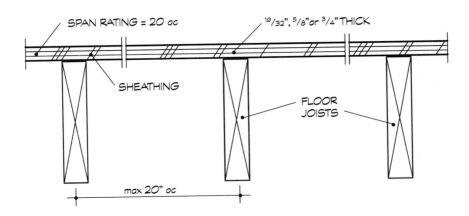

Fig. 2304.7.1B-4. Spans, loads, and minimum thicknesses for wood structural panel floor sheathing continuous over ≥ 2 spans, ⊥ to supports. *[IBC Table 2304.7(3)]*

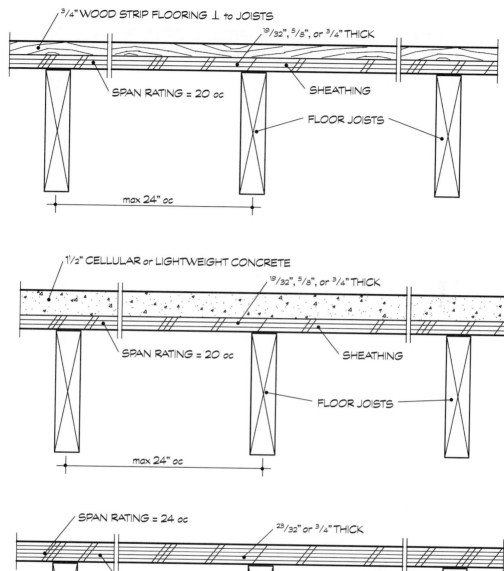

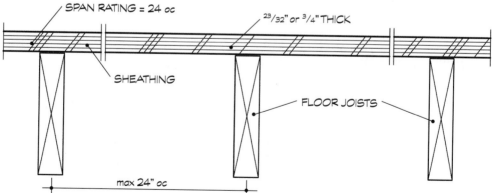

Fig. 2304.7.1B-5. Spans, loads, and minimum thicknesses for wood structural panel floor sheathing continuous over ≥ 2 spans, ⊥ to supports. *[IBC Table 2304.7(3)]*

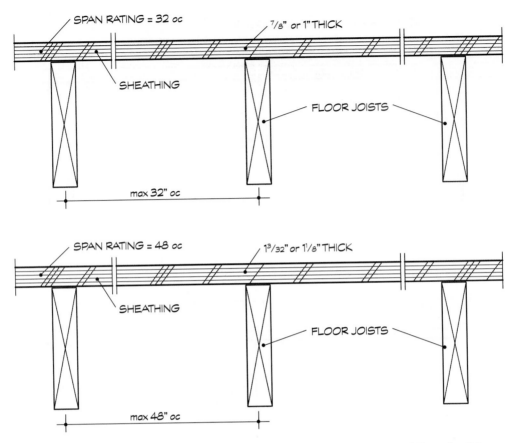

Fig. 2304.7.1B-6. Spans, loads, and minimum thicknesses for wood structural panel floor sheathing continuous over ≥ 2 spans, ⊥ to supports. *[IBC Table 2304.7(3)]*

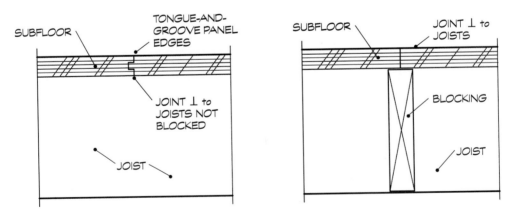

Fig. 2304.7.1C-1. Options for required edge support at subfloor panels. Subfloor panels in IBC Table 2304.7(4) require one of the edge support details shown in Figure 2304.71C-1 and C-2.

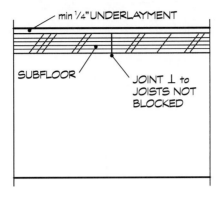

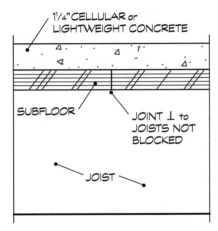

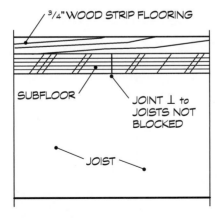

Fig. 2304.7.1C-2. Options for required edge support at subfloor panels. Subfloor panels in IBC Table 2304.7(4) require one of the edge support details shown in Figure 2304.71C-1 and C-2.

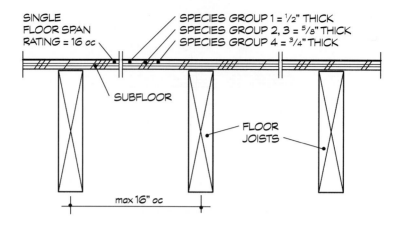

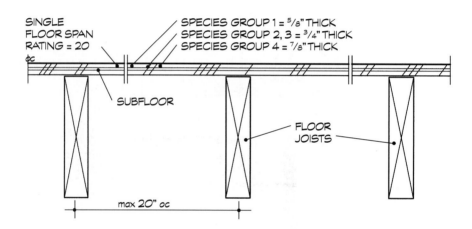

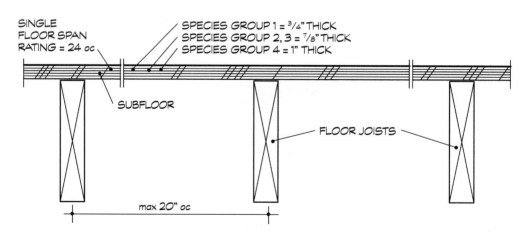

Fig. 2304.7.1D. Spans and minimum thicknesses of combination subfloor-underlayment (single floor) panels continuous over ≥ 2 spans, ⊥ to supports. *[IBC Table 2304.7(4)]*

2304 General Construction Requirements

2304.7.2 Structural roof sheathing

- Thicknesses required for structural roof sheathing are shown in the details provided.
- Wood structural panel roof sheathing must be bonded as follows:
  - With exterior grade glue.

> *Note: IBC Table 2304.7(2), "Sheathing Lumber, Minimum Grade Requirements: Board Grade," is cited as governing roof sheathing. The table lists grading rules.*
> *The following are cited as the sources of requirements for the structural roof sheathing indicated above and are the basis of the details provided:*
> *IBC Table 2304.7(1), "Allowable Spans for LumberFloor and Roof Sheathing."*
> *IBC Table 2304.7(3), "Allowable Spans and Loads for Wood Structural Panel Sheathing and Single-Floor Grades Continuous over Two or More Spans with Strength Axis Perpendicular to Supports."*
> *IBC Table 2304.7(5), "Allowable Load (psf) for Wood Structural Panel Roof Sheathing Continuous over Two or More Spans and Strength Axis Parallel to Supports."*

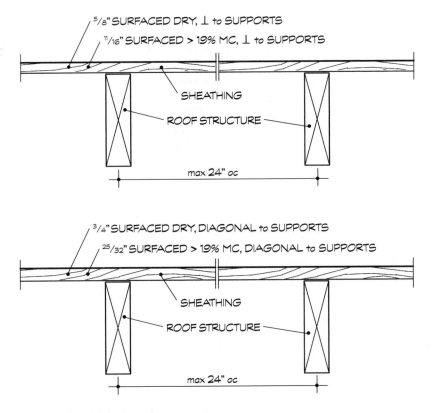

Fig. 2304.7.2A. Spans and minimum thicknesses for roof sheathing. *[IBC Table 2304.7(1)]*

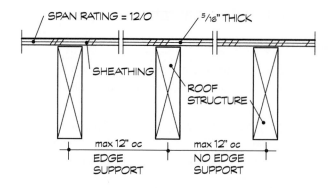

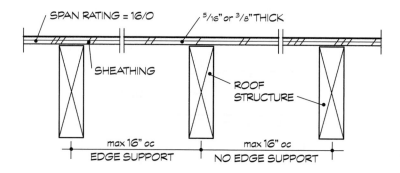

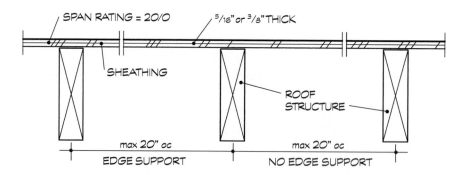

Fig. 2304.7.2B-1. Spans, loads, and minimum thicknesses for wood structural panel roof sheathing continuous over ≥ 2 spans, ⊥ to supports. *[IBC Table 2304.7(3)]*

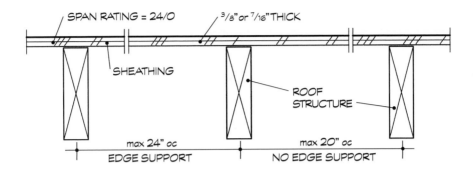

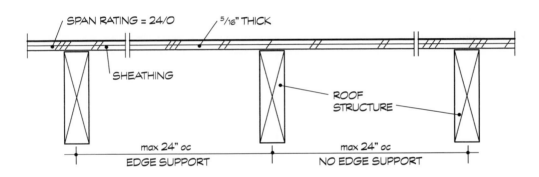

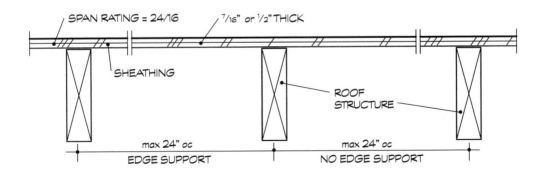

Fig. 2304.7.2B-2. Spans, loads, and minimum thicknesses for wood structural panel roof sheathing continuous over ≥ 2 spans, ⊥ to supports. *[IBC Table 2304.7(3)]*

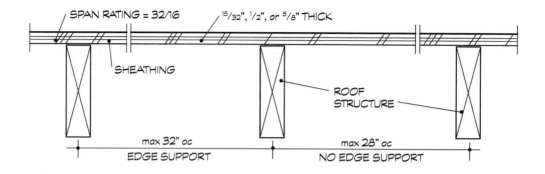

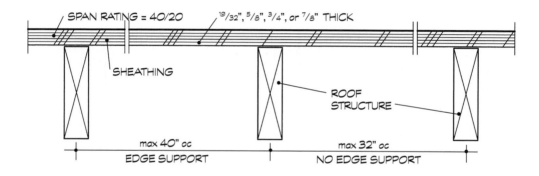

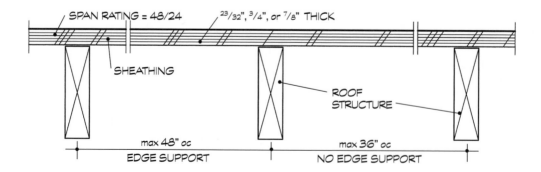

Fig. 2304.7.2B-3. Spans, loads, and minimum thicknesses for wood structural panel roof sheathing continuous over ≥ 2 spans, ⊥ to supports. *[IBC Table 2304.7(3)]*

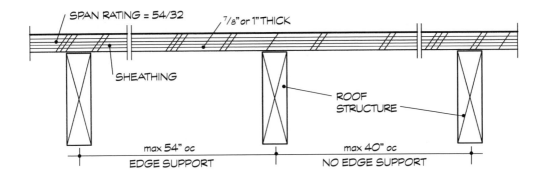

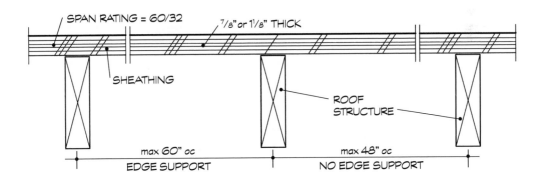

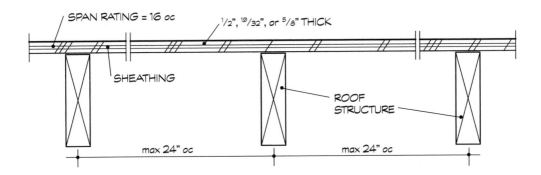

Fig. 2304.7.2B-4. Spans, loads, and minimum thicknesses for wood structural panel roof sheathing continuous over ≥ 2 spans, ⊥ to supports. *[IBC Table 2304.7(3)]*

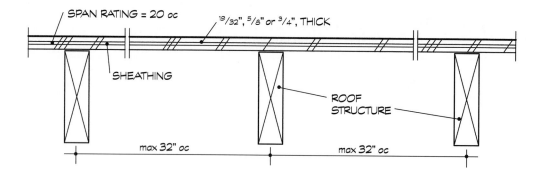

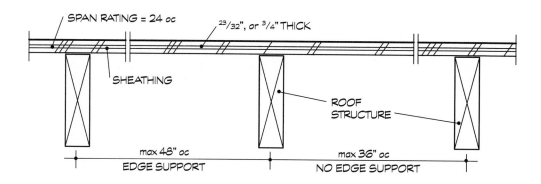

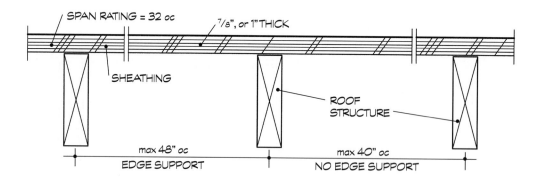

Fig. 2304.7.2B-5. Spans, loads, and minimum thicknesses for wood structural panel roof sheathing continuous over ≥ 2 spans, ⊥ to supports. *[IBC Table 2304.7(3)]*

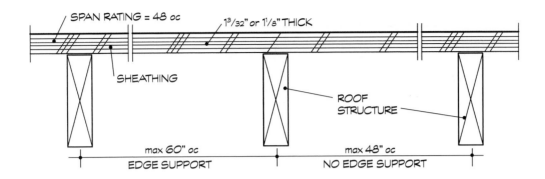

Fig. 2304.7.2B-6. Spans, loads, and minimum thicknesses for wood structural panel roof sheathing continuous over ≥ 2 spans, ⊥ to supports. *[IBC Table 2304.7(3)]*

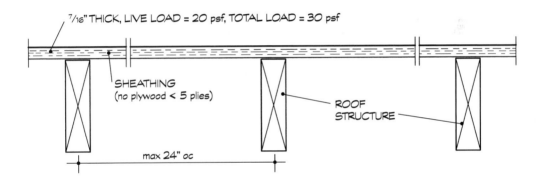

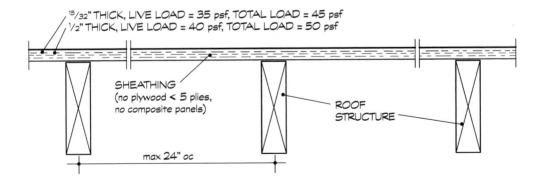

Fig. 2304.7.2C-1. Spans, loads, and minimum thicknesses for wood structural 1 roof sheathing panels continuous over ≥ 2 spans, ⊥ to supports. *[IBC Table 2304.7(5)]*

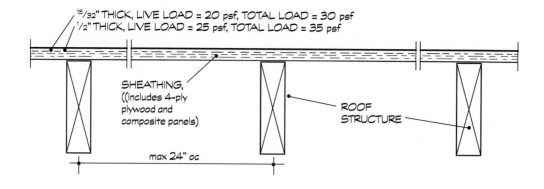

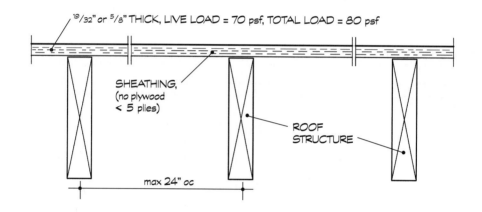

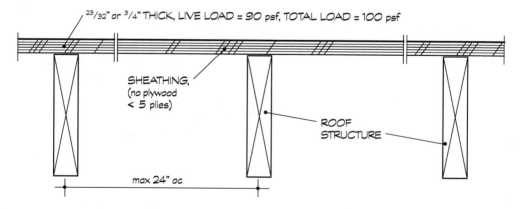

Fig. 2304.7.2C-2. Spans, loads, and minimum thicknesses for wood structural 1 roof sheathing panels continuous over ≥ 2 spans, ⊥ to supports. *[IBC Table 2304.7(5)]*

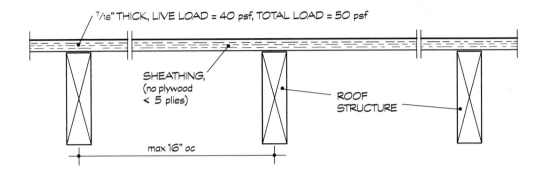

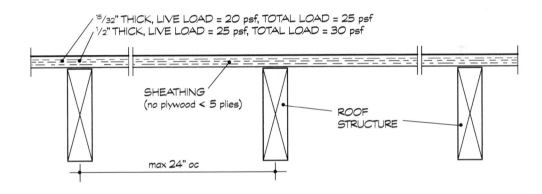

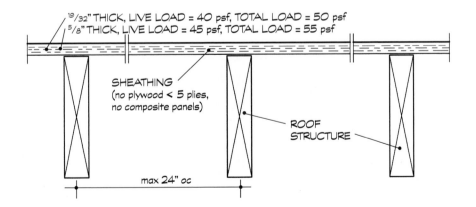

Fig. 2304.7.2C-3. Spans, loads, and minimum thicknesses for wood panel roof sheathing (other than structural 1 sheathing) continuous over ≥ 2 spans, ⊥ to supports. *[IBC Table 2304.7(5)]*

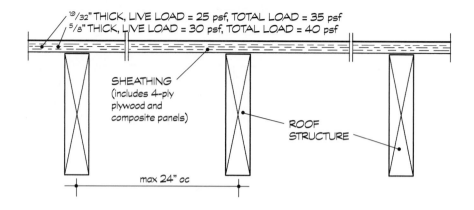

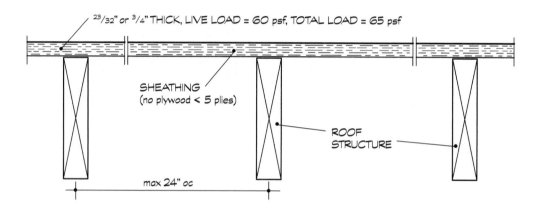

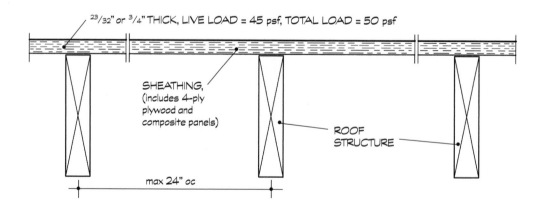

Fig. 2304.7.2C-4. Spans, loads, and minimum thicknesses for wood panel roof sheathing (other than structural 1 sheathing) continuous over ≥ 2 spans, ⊥ to supports. *[IBC Table 2304.7(5)]*

2308 Conventional Light-Frame Construction

2308.9.1 Size, height and spacing

- Utility-grade studs are governed as follows:
    - Spacing must be ≤ 16" on center.
    - They may not support more than the following:
        A ceiling and a roof.
    - Length is limited as follows:
        ≤ 8' for exterior walls.
        ≤ 8' for load-bearing walls.
        ≤ 10' for interior walls.
        ≤ 10' for nonload-bearing walls.
- Other studs are governed as shown in the details provided.

> *Note: IBC Table 2308.9.1, "Size, Height and Spacing of Wood Studs," is cited as the source of requirements and is the basis for the details provided.*

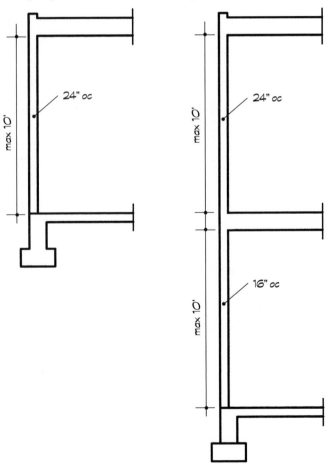

2308.9.1A. Maximum height between lateral supports for 2"× 4" wood studs in load-bearing walls.

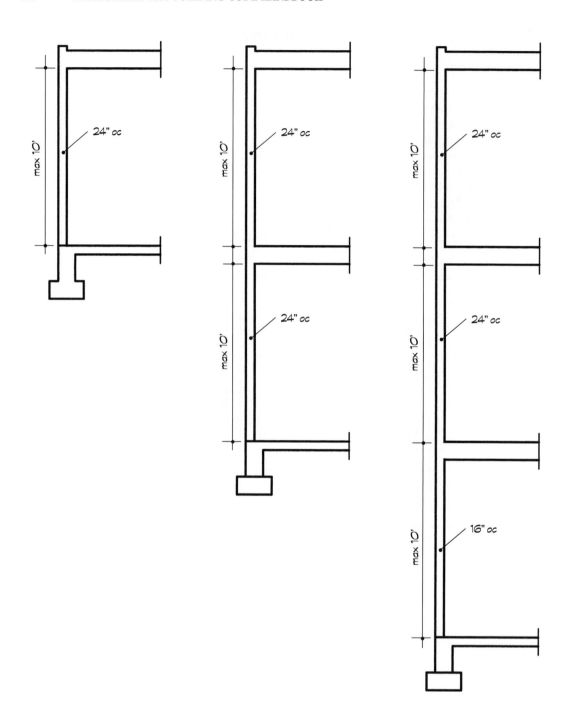

2308.9.1B. Maximum height between lateral supports for 3"x 4" wood studs in load-bearing walls.

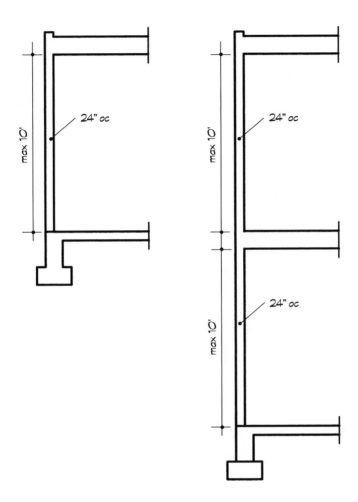

2308.9.1C. Maximum height between lateral supports for 2"× 5" wood studs in load-bearing walls.

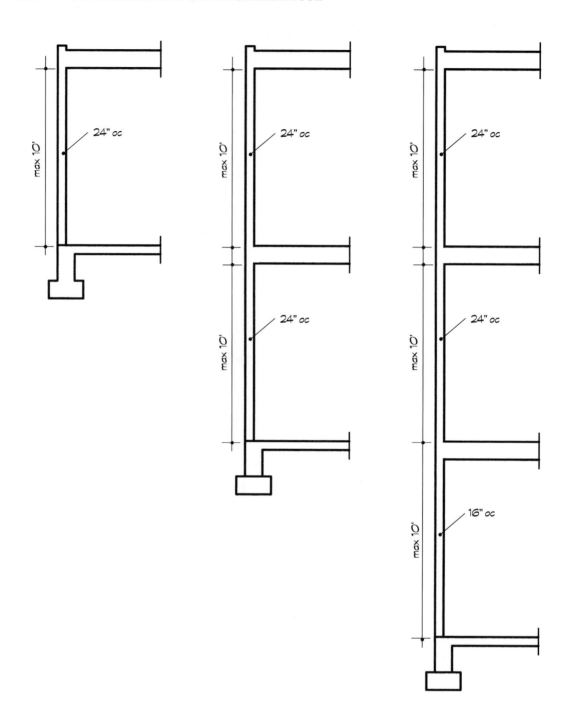

2308.9.1D. Maximum height between lateral supports for 2"x 6" wood studs in load-bearing walls.

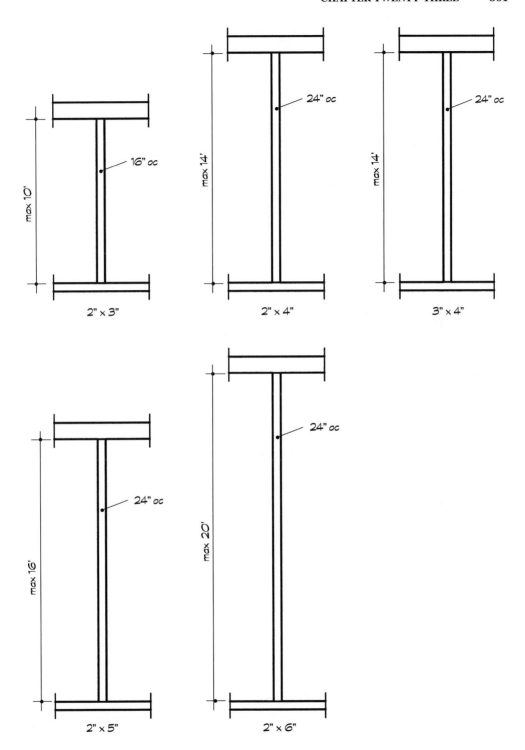

2308.9.1E. Maximum height between lateral supports for wood studs in nonload-bearing walls.

2308 Conventional Light-Frame Construction

2308.9.3 Bracing *(part 1 of 3)*

- Braced wall lines must consist of the following:
  - Braced wall panels as follows:
    - Panels must meet the following requirements of this section:
      - Location within the wall.
      - Type of bracing.
      - Amount of bracing.

  Note: IBC Table 2308.9.3(1), "Braced Wall Panels," is cited as the source of requirements for braced wall panels as indicated above.

- Braced wall panels must be located as follows:
  - In one of the following positions:
    - Aligned with each other.
    - Offset ≤ 4'.
  - ≤ 8' from each end of a braced wall line.
  - ≤ 12'- 6" from each end of a braced wall line as follows:
    - Where a designed collector is provided.
- Braced wall panels must be identified on construction drawings.
- Braced wall panels must be detailed as follows:
  - Vertical joints of panel sheathing must fall on studs.
  - Adjacent panels must be fastened to the same framing member as follows:
    - Where edges meet.
  - Horizontal joints must fall on blocking or other framing as follows:
    - Blocking or other framing must be one of the following:
      - The same size as the studs.
      - The size specified by installation requirements for the sheathing material.
  - Blocking is required under braced wall lines in the following case:
    - Where the joists below are ‖ to braced wall lines.
  - Sole plates must be nailed to floor framing.
  - Top plates must be nailed to the framing above.

  Note: 2308.3.2, "Braced wall panel connections," is cited as governing sole plate and top plate connections to adjacent framing.

- Cripple walls must meet the following bracing requirements:
  - Where stud height ≥ 1'-2":
    - Where located in Seismic Design Category A, B, or C:
      - Requirements are the same for full height walls.
    - Where located in Seismic Design Category D or E:
      - Requirements other than those for full height walls apply.

  Note: 2308.9.4.1, "Bracing," is cited as the source of requirements for cripple walls as indicated above.

2308 Conventional Light-Frame Construction

2308.9.3 Bracing *(part 2 of 3)*

- Braced wall panels must be constructed as one of the following systems:
    - Continuous diagonal lumber braces with the following characteristics:
        Nominal 1"× 4".
        Let into the following:
            Top plates.
            Bottom plates.
            Intervening studs.
        Installed at an angle as follows:
            ≥ 45° and ≤ 60° from the horizontal.

    Note: IBC Table 2304.9.1, "Fastening Schedule," is cited as governing the size, type, and location of fastener required for the bracing system indicated above.

    - Wood boards with the following characteristics:
        ≥ ⁵/₈" net thickness.
        Installed diagonally on studs as follows:
            Studs spaced ≤ 24" on center.
        Length of panel (measured horizontally) must be ≥ 4'.
        Where studs are spaced ≤ 16" on center:
            Panel must span ≥ 3 stud spaces.
        Where studs are spaced ≤ 24" on center:
            Panel must span ≥ 2 stud spaces.
    - Wood structural panel sheathing as shown on the details provided.

    Note: The following are cited as governing the structural panels indicated above and are the basis of the details provided:
        IBC Table 2308.9.3(2), "Exposed Plywood Panel Siding."
        IBC Table 2309.9.3(3), "Wood Structural Panel Wall Sheathing."

    - Fiberboard sheathing panels with the following characteristics:
        ≥ ½" thickness.
        Installed vertically on studs as follows:
            Studs spaced ≤ 16" on center.
        Length of panel (measured horizontally) must be ≥ 4'.
        Panel must span ≥ 3 stud spaces.

    Note: The following are cited as governing the fastening of the fiberboard panels indicated above:
        2306.4.3, "Particleboard shear walls."
        IBC Table 2308.9.3(4), "Allowable Shear Values (plf) for Wind or Seismic Loading on Vertical Diaphragms of Fiberboard Sheathing Board Construction for Type V Construction Only."

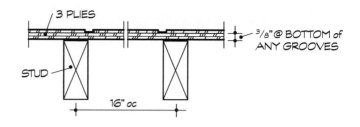

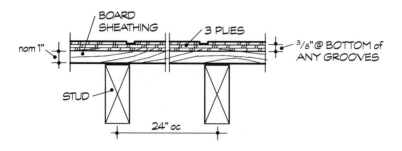

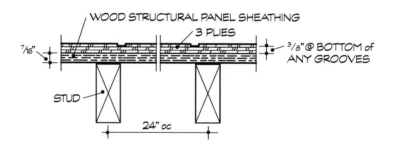

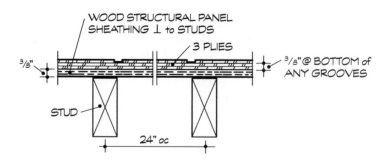

Fig. 2308.9.3A-1. Span, plies, and minimum thickness of exposed plywood siding applied directly to studs or over sheathing. *[IBC Table 2308.9(2)]*

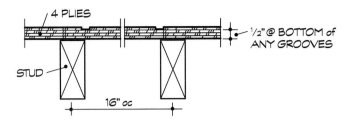

Fig. 2308.9.3A-2. Span, plies, and minimum thickness of exposed plywood siding applied directly to studs or over sheathing. *[IBC Table 2308.9(2)]*

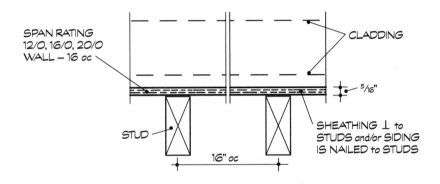

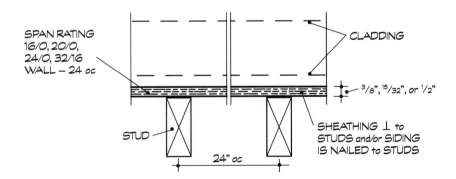

Fig. 2308.9.3B-1. Span and minimum thickness of wood structural wall sheathing not exposed to weather. *[IBC Table 2308.9(3)]*

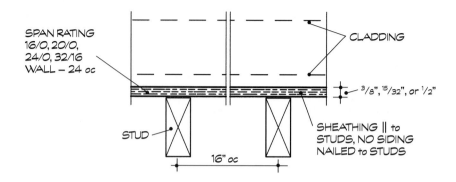

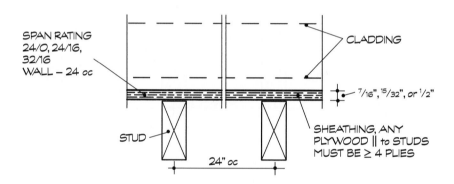

Fig. 2308.9.3B-2. Span and minimum thickness of wood structural wall sheathing not exposed to weather. *[IBC Table 2308.9(3)]*

2308 Conventional Light-Frame Construction

2308.9.3 Bracing *(part 3 of 3)*

- Gypsum board as follows:
    Types:
        Sheathing.
        Wallboard.
        Veneer base.
    Requirements:
        ½" thick.
        4' wide.
        On studs ≤ 24" on center.
        Nailed 7" on center.
        Where applied to one side of a bracing panel:
            Length must be ≥ 8' (measured horizontally).
        Where applied to both sides of a bracing panel:
            Length must be ≥ 4' (measured horizontally).

    Note: IBC Table 2306.4.5, "Shear Walls Sheathed with Other Materials," is cited as the source of requirements for fastening the gypsum board indicated above.

- Particleboard wall sheathing panels with the following characteristics as shown in the details provided:
    Length of panel (measured horizontally) must be ≥ 4':
        Where studs are spaced ≤ 16" on center:
            Panel must span ≥ 3 stud spaces.
        Where studs are spaced ≤ 24" on center:
            Panel must span ≥ 2 stud spaces.

    Note: IBC Table 2308.9.3(5), "Allowable Spans for Particleboard Wall Sheathing," is cited as governing particleboard wall sheathing and is the basis of the details provided.

- Portland cement plaster as follows:
    On studs ≤ 16" on center.
    Length of panel (measured horizontally) must be ≥ 4'.
    Panel must span ≥ 3 stud spaces.

    Note: Section 2510, "Lathing and Furring for Cement Plaster (Stucco)," is cited as governing the application of portland cement plaster as indicated above.

- Hardboard panel siding as follows:
    Length of panel (measured horizontally) must be ≥ 4'.
    Where studs are spaced ≤ 16" on center:
        Panel must span ≥ 3 stud spaces.
    Where studs are spaced ≤ 24" on center:
        Panel must span ≥ 2 stud spaces.

    Note: 2303.1.6, "Hardboard." is cited as a source of requirements.
    IBC Table 2308.9.3(6), "Hardboard Siding," is cited as a source of requirements.

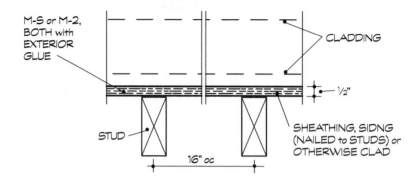

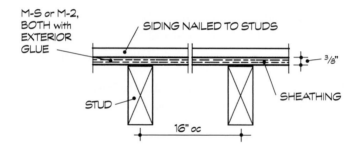

Fig. 2308.9.3A. Span and minimum thickness of particleboard wall sheathing not exposed to weather.
[IBC Table 2308.9(5)]

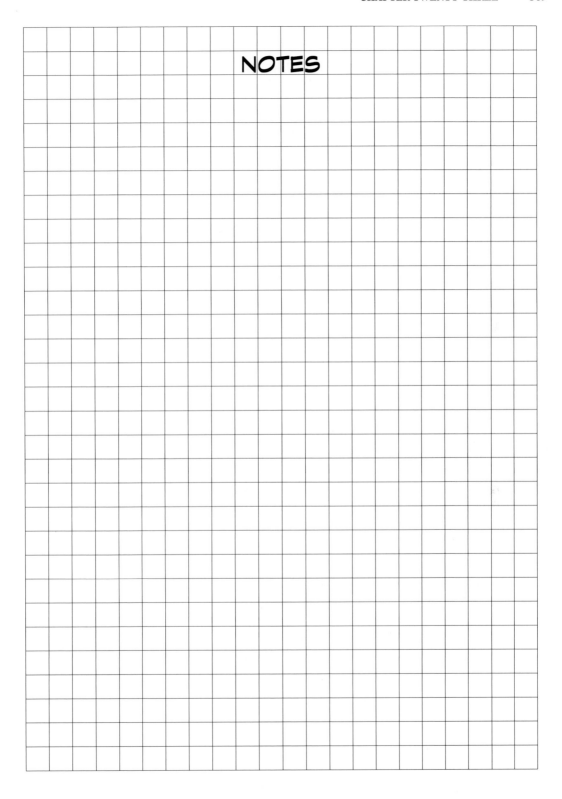

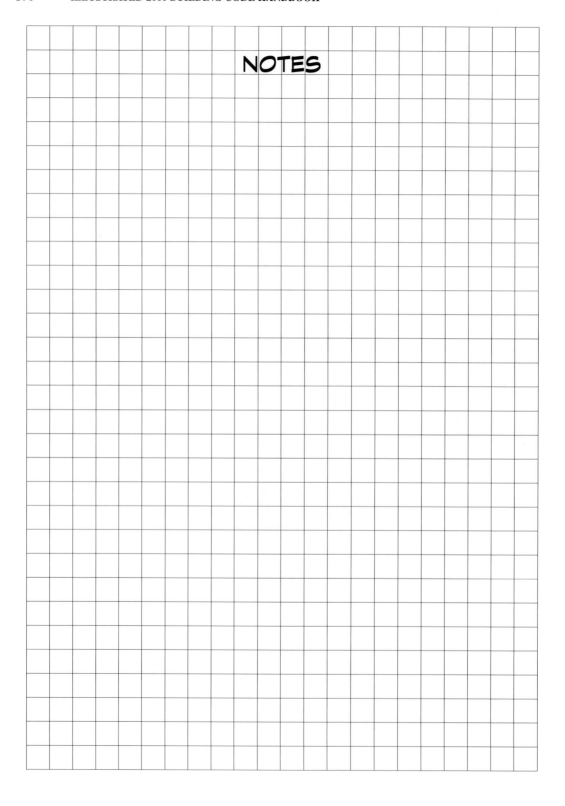

NOTES

24

Glass and Glazing

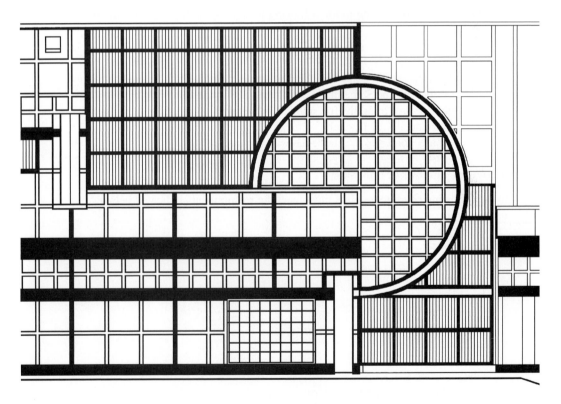

Lubrication Engineers, Inc. Wichita, Kansas. *(partial elevation)*
Gossen Livingston Associates, Inc. Architecture. Wichita, Kansas.

2403 General Requirements for Glass

2403.3 Framing

- A glass edge qualifies as having a firm support where deflection due to the loading indicated below is limited as follows:
  - Deflection:
    The edge deflection ⊥ to a pane of glass may not be > either of the following:
      $^1/_{175}$ the length of the glass edge.
      ¾".
  - Loading:
    Where the larger of the following loads is applied where loads are combined:
      The positive load.
      The negative load.

  Note: Section 1605, "Load Combinations."

2403.4 Interior glazed areas

- Deflection of interior glazing in the following location is limited as indicated below:
  - Location:
    Adjacent to a walking surface.
  - Deflection:
    The differential deflection of adjacent unsupported edges is governed as follows:
      Deflection must be ≤ the thickness of the glass in the following case:
        Where a force of 50 lbs/ft is applied as follows:
          Horizontally to 1 panel.
          At any point ≤ 3'-6" above the walking surface.

2403.5 Louvered windows or jalousies

- In the following conditions, glass must meet the requirements indicated below:
  - Conditions:
    Glass:
      Float.
      Wired.
      Patterned.
    Locations:
      Louvered windows.
      Jalousies.
  - Requirements:
    Glass must be ≥ $^3/_{16}$" thick.
    Glass must be ≤ 4' long.
    Exposed edges of glass must be smooth.
    Wire glass may not be used as follows:
      Where wire is exposed on longitudinal edges.
    Where other glass types are used, the following applies:
      Design must be provided to the building official for approval.

2405 Sloped Glazing and Skylights

2405.1 Scope

- This section applies to the following glazing where sloped as indicated below:
  - Glazing:
    Glass.
    Transparent materials.
    Translucent materials.
    Opaque glazing materials.
    Glazing materials in the following:
      Skylights.
      Roofs.
      Sloped walls.
  - Slope:
    Where sloped > 15 degrees from vertical plane.

2405.2 Allowable glazing materials and limitations

- The following materials are permitted in sloped glazing:
  - Laminated glass with one of the following:
    A polyvinyl butyral interlayer ≥ 30 mils thick.
    An equivalent interlayer.
  - Wired glass.
  - Light-transmitting plastics.
  - Heat-strengthened glass.
  - Fully tempered glass.
  - Annealed glass as follows:
    Where there is no walking surface below.
    Where any walking surface below is protected from falling glass.
    In commercial or detached noncombustible greenhouses as follows:
      Used only for growing plants.
      Closed to the public.
      Height of greenhouse at ridge is ≤ 30' above grade.

  Note: Section 2610, "Light-Transmitting Plastic Skylight Glazing," is cited as the source
  of additional requirements for plastic skylights.
  2101.2.4, "Glass masonry," is cited as governing glass block installations.

2405 Sloped Glazing and Skylights

2405.3 Screening *(part 1 of 2)*

- Screens are not required under fully tempered glass in the following case:
    - Where the glazing occurs between floors as follows:
        Glazing is sloped ≤ 30 degrees from a vertical plane.
        Highest point of glass is ≤ 10' above the walking surface.
- Screens are not required below the following glazing for the conditions indicated below:
    - Glazing:
        Any glazing including annealed glass.
    - Conditions:
        Where one of the following conditions applies:
        Where there is no walking surface below.
        Where any walking surface below is protected from falling glass.
- Screens are not required below the following glazing in the locations indicated below:
    - Glazing:
        Any glazing including annealed glass.
    - Locations:
        In commercial or detached noncombustible greenhouses as follows:
        Used only for growing plants.
        Closed to the public.
        Height of greenhouse at ridge is ≤ 30' above grade.
- Screens are not required in the following locations for the conditions indicated below:
    - Locations:
        In occupancies R-2, R-3, R-4.
    - Conditions:
        Area of each pane of glass is ≤ 16 sf.
        Highest point of glass is ≤ 12' above either of the following:
        A walking surface.
        Any other area which may be accessed.
        Where glazing is fully tempered glass:
        Glass thickness is ≤ $^3/_{16}$".
        Where glazing is laminated glass:
        One of the following interlayers must be provided:
        Polyvinyl butyral ≥ 15 mils thick.
        An equivalent interlayer.

2405 Sloped Glazing and Skylights

2405.3 Screening *(part 2 of 2)*

- Screens as indicated below are required under the following sloped glazing:
  - Glazing:
    Includes the following glass in the formats listed below:
      Glass:
        Heat-strengthened glass.
        Fully tempered glass.
      Formats:
        Glazing with a single layer of glass.
        The bottom layer among multiple layers of glass.
  - Screens:
    Must be able to support 2 × the weight of the glazing.
    Must be securely fastened to framing.
    Must be installed ≤ 4" of the glass.
    Must be noncombustible.
    Must be ≥ #12 B&S gage (0.0808") mesh ≤ 1" × 1".
    Where located in a corrosive atmosphere:
      Equivalent noncorrosive screening is required.

2405.4 Framing

- The following must be noncombustible in Type I and II construction:
  - Frames for sloped glazing.
  - Frames for skylights.
- In environments with acid fumes that damage metals, the following applies:
  - The following components may be constructed of the materials listed below:
    Components:
      Sash and frames of skylights.
      Sash and frames of sloped glazing.
    Materials:
      Approved pressure-treated wood.
      Other approved noncorrosive material.
- Curbs for skylights are governed as follows:
  - Curbs are not required for skylights in occupancy R-3 as follows:
    Where installed in a roof with a slope ≥ 3:12.
  - In other locations, the following is required:
    Where the roof slope is < 45°:
      Skylights may not be installed in the plane of the roof.
      Curbs ≥ 4" high are required for skylights.
- Skylights and sloped glazing must be designed as follows:
  - To resist tributary roof loads assigned by the code.

  Note: Chapter 16, "Structural Design," is cited as the source of tributary roof loads.

Case study: Fig. 2405.4. The roof of the occupancy B building slopes 4:12, thus requiring a 4" curb at skylights. Such a curb is provided as indicated in the illustration. Consequently the skylight is in compliance with code requirements.

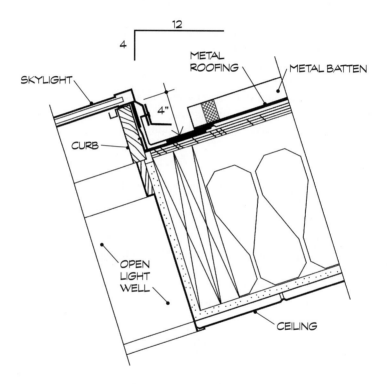

Fig. 2405.4. Detail at skylight. Central Kitchen. Lompoc Unified School District. Lompoc, California. Phillips Metsch Sweeney Moore Architects. Santa Barbara, California.

2406 Safety Glazing

2406.2 Hazardous locations *(part 1 of 3)*

This section addresses the requirement for safety glazing where glazing is used.

- Safety glazing is not required in locations that are not considered to be hazardous as specified elsewhere in this chapter.

  Note: 2406.2.1, "Exceptions," lists locations not considered to be hazardous for glazing.

- The following locations require safety glazing:
  - Sliding door units as follows:
    - Sliding panels.
    - Fixed panels.
  - Sliding and bifold closet doors.
  - Storm doors.
  - Unframed swinging doors.
  - In the following elements at the bathing-type locations listed below:
    - Elements:
      - Doors.
      - Enclosures.
      - Any building wall serving as an enclosure as follows:
        - Where the lowest exposed glazing is < 5' above the standing surface.
    - Locations:
      - Hot tubs.
      - Whirlpools.
      - Saunas.
      - Steam rooms.
      - Bathtubs
      - Showers.
- The following glazing near doors is governed as indicated below:
  - Glazing:
    - Any of the following types:
      - Fixed glazing.
      - Operable glazing.
    - Adjacent to a door with both the following characteristics:
      - Exposed glazing is ≤ 2' from the door as follows:
        - Measured on the shortest line to the nearest edge of the closed door.
      - Lowest exposed glazing is < 5' above the walking surface.
  - Requirements:
    - The following conditions do not require safety glazing:
      - Where the glazing is decorative glass.
      - Where there is a wall or barrier as follows:
        - Between the door and the glazing.
      - Where the glazing is ⊥ to the closed door as follows:
        - In 1- and 2-family dwellings.
        - In occupancy R-2.
    - Other conditions require safety glazing.

Case study: Fig. 2406.2. Safety glazing is required on either side of the entry doors since it is within 2' of the door. The glazing above the door is not required to be safety glazing as it is above a height of 5'. Safety glazing is required in the swingnig doors. Tempered glass is provided in the doors and on each side of the doors, thus, the entry is in compliance with the code.

Fig. 2406.2. Partial elevation at east entry. Hot Springs Police Department New Headquarters. Hot Springs National Park, Arkansas. Cromwell Architects Engineers. Little Rock, Arkansas.

2406 Safety Glazing

2406.2 Hazardous locations *(part 2 of 3)*

- Safety glazing in swinging doors is governed as follows:
  - It is not required in swinging jalousie doors.
  - It is not required where the glazing is decorative glass.
  - It is required in other swinging doors.

    Note: 2406.2.1, "Exceptions," is cited as the source of requirements for jalousies without safety glazing.

- The following glazing is governed as indicated:
  - The following glazing is not required to be safety glazing:
    That which is protected by a bar as follows:
      Bar has a vertical dimension ≥ 1½".
      Bar is able to resist a 50-lb/ft load applied horizontally as follows:
        Without deflecting to contact the glazing.
      Bar is located as follows:
        On the side of glazing to which there is access.
        ≥ 2'-10" and ≤ 3'-2" above the walking surface.
    The exterior pane of multiple layers of glazing as follows:
      Where the lowest exposed glazing is ≥ 25' above the following:
        Above any of the following surfaces adjacent to the exterior of the glazing:
          Grade.
          Roof.
          Walking surface.
          Other horizontal or sloped surface.
  - The following glazing is governed elsewhere in this section:
    That which is required by this section to have safety glazing as follows:
      Where glazing is < 5' above a standing surface in the following locations:
        Bathing-type locations.
        Near doors.
  - Glazing in locations other than those indicated above is governed as follows:
    Decorative glass is not required to be safety glazing.
    Otherwise, safety glazing is required where all of the following conditions apply:
      Exposed surface has all the following characteristics:
        Area of any pane is > 9 sf.
        Bottom edge is < 1'-6" above the floor.
        Top edge is > 3' above the floor.
      Plane of glazing is ≤ 3' from a walking surface as follows:
        Measured horizontally.

2406 Safety Glazing

2406.2 Hazardous locations *(part 3 of 3)*

- Safety glazing is required for the following components in the locations listed below:
  - ○ Components:
    - The following components with any area or height are included:
      - Structural baluster panels.
      - Nonstructural in-fill panels.
  - ○ Locations:
    - Guards.
    - Railings.
- Safety glazing is required in the following locations where the conditions listed below apply:
  - ○ Locations:
    - Walls and fences as follows:
      - Enclosing the following both indoors and outdoors:
        - Swimming pools.
        - Hot tubs.
        - Spas.
  - ○ Conditions:
    - Where all of the following conditions apply:
      - Bottom edge of glazing is < 5' above the walking surface as follows:
        - On the side where water is contained.
      - Glazing is ≤ 5' from the edge of the water as follows:
        - Measured horizontally.
    - Glazing adjacent to the following elements is governed as indicated below:
      - Elements:
        - Stairways.
        - Landings.
        - Ramps.
      - Requirements:
        - Safety glazing is not required where the following conditions apply:
          - The side of the element has the following:
            - Guard or handrail as follows:
              - With one of the following components:
                - Balusters.
                - In-fill panels.
              - Located ≥ 1'-6" from the glazing.
        - Safety glazing is required where the glazing is located with all of the following:
          - Glazing is ≤ 3' from a walking surface.
          - Glazing is ≤ 5' from the bottom stairway tread as follows:
            - Measured horizontally.
          - Bottom edge of glazing is < 5' above the adjacent walking surface as follows:
            - Measured from the tread nosing where applicable to a stairway.

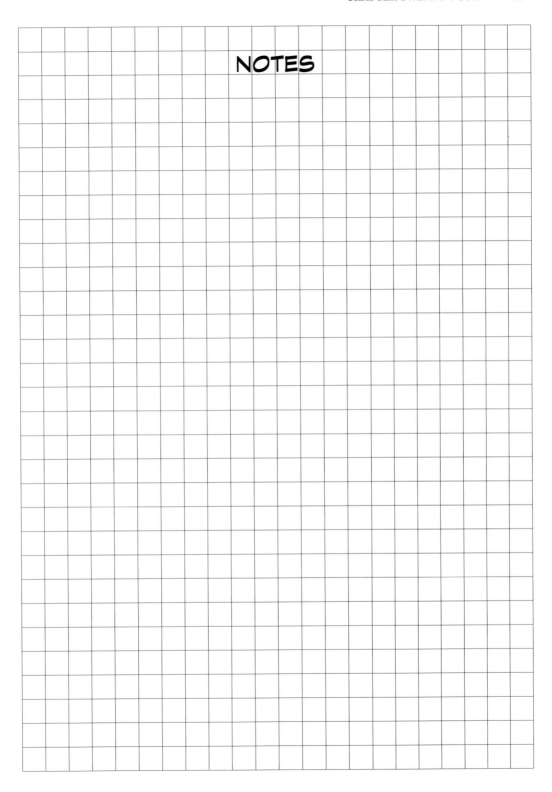

NOTES

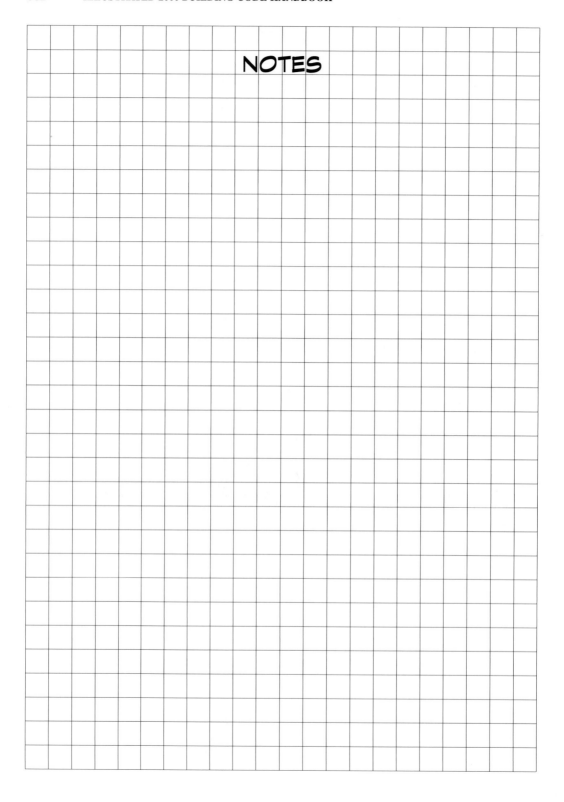

25

Gypsum Board and Plaster

Hoyt Street Properties. Portland Oregon. *(partial elevlation)*
Ankrom Moisan Associated Architects. Portland, Oregon.

2502 Definitions

2502.1 Definitions

- **Cement plaster**
  - One of the following mixtures:
    - Portland cement, aggregate, other approved materials.
    - Portland cement, hydrated lime, aggregate, other approved materials.
    - Blended cement, aggregate or other approved materials.
    - Blended cement, hydrated lime, aggregate, other approved materials.
    - Masonry cement, aggregate, other approved materials.
    - Plastic cement, aggregate, other approved materials.
  - Other approved materials are as specified in the code.
- **Gypsum veneer plaster**
  - Gypsum plaster as follows:
    - Applied to an approved base.
    - Applied in 1 or more layers.
    - Usually $\leq \frac{1}{4}$" thick.
- **Weather-exposed surfaces**
  - The following surfaces are not included:
    - Ceilings and roof soffit surfaces as follows:
      - Enclosed by the following components that extend ≥ 12" below such surfaces:
        - Walls.
        - Fascia.
        - Bulkheads.
        - Beams.
    - Walls or parts of walls under a roof as follows:
      - In an area that is not enclosed.
      - Set back from the roof edge as follows:
        - A distance $\geq 2 \times$ the height of the open space under the roof edge.
    - Parts of ceilings and roof soffits located as follows:
      - A horizontal distance $\geq 10'$ from the outer edges of the following:
        - The ceiling or roof soffit.
  - Otherwise, the following surfaces where exposed to the weather are included:
    - Walls.
    - Ceilings.
    - Floors.
    - Roofs.
    - Soffits.
    - Similar surfaces.
- **Wire backing:**
  - Horizontal strands of wire as follows:
    - Attached to surfaces of vertical supports.
    - Wire is taut.
    - Covered with building paper.
    - Serves as a backing for cement plaster.

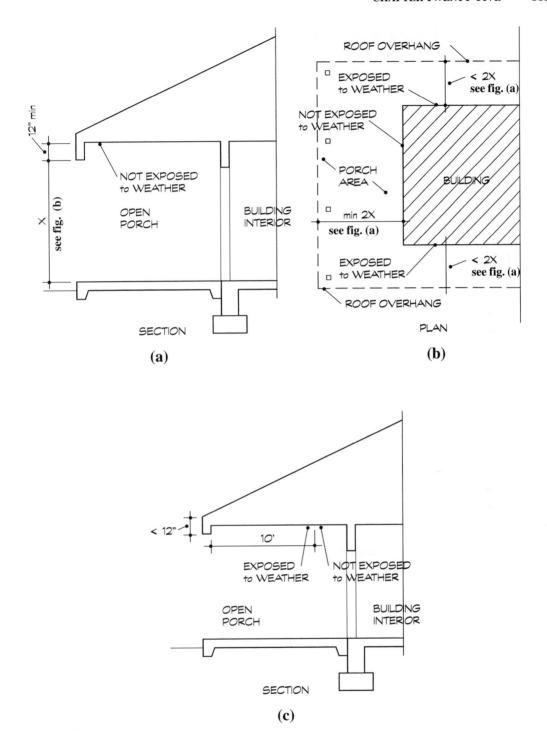

Fig. 2502.1. Conditions of exposure conditions for ceilings, soffits, and walls.

2504 Vertical and Horizontal Assemblies

2504.1.1 Wood framing

- The wood supports for the following be ≥ 2" in any dimension:
  - Lath.
  - Gypsum board.
- Wood stripping or furring is governed as follows:
  - Where applied to solid backing the following size is required:
    - 1"× 2" or greater.
  - Otherwise, the following size is required:
    - ≥ 2" in any dimension.

2504.1.2 Studless partitions

- The required thicknesses of the following vertical studless partitions are ≥ 2":
  - Solid plaster on the following:
    - $^3/_8$" rib metal lath.
    - ¾" rib metal lath.
    - ½" long-length gypsum lath.
  - Gypsum board partitions.

2509 Gypsum Board in Showers and Water Closets

2509.2 Base for tile

This section addresses the base required under tile and or panels.

- Water-resistant gypsum backing board is required as a substrate in the following case:
  - Where gypsum board is used as a base in the following locations:
    Bathtub areas.
    Shower compartment walls.
    Water closet compartment walls.
  - At other walls and ceilings, the following applies:
    Regular gypsum board may be used as a base.

2509.3 Limitations

This section addresses water-resistant gypsum backing board.

- Such boards may not be used as follows:
  - Over a vapor retarder in the following areas:
    Bathtub compartments.
    Shower compartments.
  - In areas with continuous high humidity, such as follows:
    Saunas.
    Steam rooms.
    Gang shower rooms.
    Indoor pools.
- Such boards ½" thick may not be used as follows:
  - On ceilings where supports are > 12" on center.
- Such boards $^5/_8$" thick may not be used as follows:
  - On ceilings where supports are 16" on center.

2510 Lathing and Furring for Cement Plaster (Stucco)

2510.5.1 Support of lath

- Solid backing is required for lath and attachments as follows:
  - Where lath on a vertical surface extends between the following:
    Rafters or similar projections.

2510.5.2.1 Use of gypsum board as a backing board

- Use of the following materials as backing board is governed as indicated below:
  - Materials:
    Gypsum lath or wallboard.
  - Requirements:
    Such materials may be used as a backing for cement plaster as follows:
    Where the following materials are used in the locations indicated below:
    Materials:
    Weather-resistant barrier between lath and sheathing.
    One of the following types lath:
    Self-furred metal lath.
    Self-furred wire fabric lath.
    Locations:
    On horizontal supports of ceilings or roof soffits.
    On interior walls.
    Such materials may not be used as backing for cement plaster in other cases.

2510.5.2.2 Use of gypsum sheathing backing

- Gypsum sheathing may be used as a backing for cement plaster where the following are used:
  - Weather-resistant barrier between lath and sheathing.
  - Metal or wire fabric lath.

    Note: 2510.6, "Weather-resistant barriers," is cited as governing such barriers.

2510.5.3 Backing not required

- Wire backing is not required behind the following:
  - Expanded metal lath.
  - Paperbacked wire fabric lath.

2510.6 Weather-resistant barriers

- Where such barriers are installed over wood-based sheathing, the following applies:
  - A weather-resistive vapor permeable barrier as follows must be included:
    Performance to be ≥ 2 layers of Grade D paper.
  - Weather-resistant barriers are to be installed as specified elsewhere in the code.

    Note: 1404.2, "Weather-resistive barrier," is cited as governing such barriers.

2511 Interior Plaster

2511.2 Limitations

- Plaster may not be applied directly to the following:
  - Fiber insulation board.
- Cement plaster applied to the following materials is governed as indicated below:
  - Materials:
    Gypsum lath.
    Gypsum plaster.
  - Requirements:
    Such materials must be protected by a water-resistive barrier.
    Direct application to such materials is not permitted.

  Note: The following are cited as sources of applicable requirements, a partial summary of which is provided above:
  2510.5.1, "Support of lath."
  2510.5.2, "Use of gypsum backing board."

2511.3 Grounds

- Where used, grounds must establish the required thickness for plaster.
- Plaster thickness is measured from the following:
  - Face of lath.
  - Face of other bases as applicable.

  Note: The following are cited as governing the required thickness of plaster:
  ASTM C 842, "Specification for Application of Gypsum Veneer Plaster."
  ASTM C 926, "Specification for Application of Portland Cement Based Plaster."

2511.5.1 Wet areas

- Showers and public toilets require the following wall surfaces:
  - Smooth.
  - Nonabsorbent.

  Note: The following are cited as sources of applicable requirements, a partial summary of which is provided above:
  1209.2, "Walls."
  1209.3, "Showers."

- Wood framing must be protected with an approved moisture barrier as follows:
  - Where the interior of walls and partitions have all of the following characteristics:
    Covered with one of the following materials:
    Cement plaster.
    Tile of similar material.
    Subject to splashed water.

2512 Exterior Plaster

2512.1.2 Weep screeds

- Weep screeds are required for exterior cement plaster as follows:
  - Screeds must drain trapped water to the exterior.
  - Screed requirements are shown on the detail provided.

  Note: ASTM C 926, "Specification for Application of Portland Cement Based Plaster," is cited as governing weep screeds.

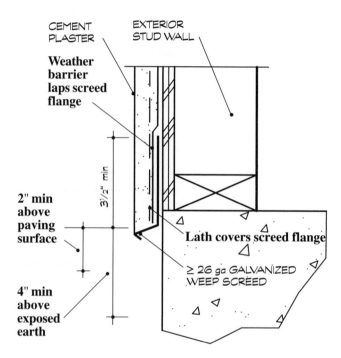

Fig. 2512.1.2. Cement plaster weep screed requirements.

2512.3 Limitations

- Gypsum plaster is not permitted as follows:
  - In exterior applications.

2512.5 Second coat application

- The second coat of exterior cement plaster is governed as follows:
  - It must be applied to the required thickness.
  - It must be rodded and floated to a roughness as follows:
    Adequate for bonding with the finish coat.
    Roughness is limited to $^1/_4$" variation under a 5' straight edge in any direction.

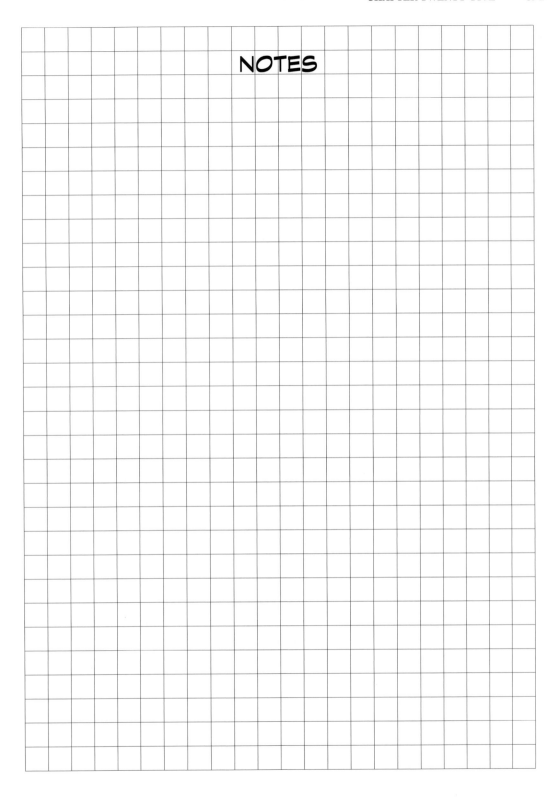

NOTES

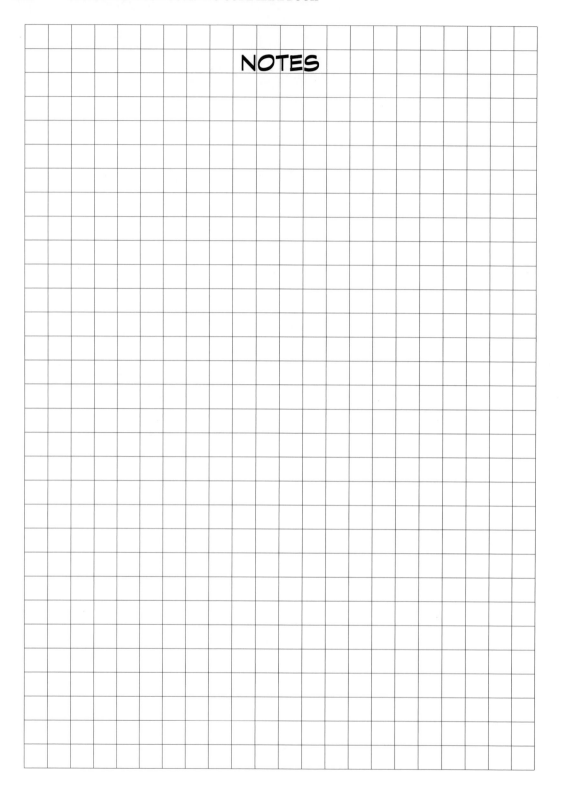

NOTES

26

Plastic

Alterations to 209 Main Street. Annapolis, Maryland.
Alt Breeding Schwarz, Architects, LLC. Annapolis, Maryland.

2603 Foam Plastic Insulation

2603.4 Thermal barrier

- Foam plastic insulation need not be separated from the interior of a building where specifically permitted by the code.

  Note: The following are cited as sources of conditions wherein such insulation need not be separated from the interior:
  2603.4.1, "Thermal barrier not required."
  2603.7, "Special approval."

- Otherwise, foam plastic insulation must be separated from the interior of a building as follows:
  - By the following thermal barrier:
    Barrier must limit temperature rise as follows:
      Average temperature rise on the unexposed surface is limited by the following:
        ≤ 250°F after 15 minutes of fire exposure.
    Barrier must remain in place for ≥ 15 minutes of fire exposure.
  - Other requirements are shown in the detail provided.

  Note: ASTM E 119, "Standard Test Methods for Fire Tests of Building Construction and Materials," is cited as governing temperature rise as indicated above.
  Section 716, "Concealed Spaces," is cited as governing such spaces.
  The following are cited as governing a barrier's ability to remain in place during fire exposure:
  FM 4880, "Approval Standard for Class 1: a) Insulated Wall or Wall and Roof/ Ceiling Panels, b) Plastic Interior Finish Materials, c) Plastic Exterior Building Panels, d) Wall/Ceiling Coating Systems and e) Interior or Exterior Finish Systems."
  UL 1040, "Fire Test of Insulated Wall Construction."
  UL 1715, "Fire Test of Interior Finish Material."

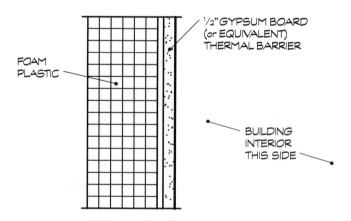

Fig. 2603.4. Thermal barrier.

2603 Foam Plastic Insulation

2603.4.1.1 Masonry or concrete construction

This subsection addresses thermal barriers between foam plastic insulation and building interiors.

- Such a thermal barrier is not required in the following walls where conditions indicated below apply:
  - Walls:
    Concrete.
    Masonry.
  - Conditions:
    Where the insulation is covered on both sides by ≥ 1" of one of the the following materials:
    Concrete.
    Masonry.

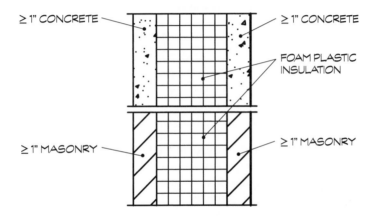

Fig. 2603.4.1A. Alternative to thermal barrier.

2603.4.1.2 Cooler and freezer walls

This subsection addresses thermal barriers between foam plastic insulation and building interiors.

- Such a thermal barrier is not required in walls of cooler and freezer walls where all of the following conditions apply:
  - The foam plastic insulation is tested in a thickness ≥ 4" to have the following properties:
    Flame spread index ≤ 25.
    Smoke-developed index ≤ 450.
  - The foam plastic insulation has the following temperature thresholds:
    Flash ignition temperature is ≥ 600°F.
    Self-ignition temperature is ≥ 800°F.
  - Cooler or freezer is spinklered.
  - Where located in a building:
    The portion of the building containing the cooler or freezer is sprinklered.
  - Other requirements are shown on the illustration provided.

2603 Foam Plastic Insulation

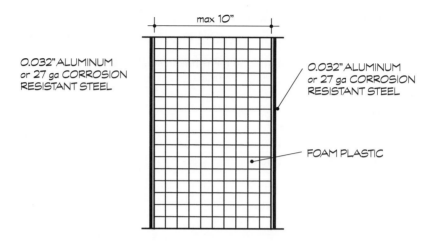

Fig. 2603.4.1.2. Alternative to thermal barriers in cooler and freezer walls.

2603.4.1.3 Walk-in coolers

This subsection addresses thermal barriers between foam plastic insulation and building interiors.

- Where buildings are not sprinklered, the following applies to walk-in coolers and freezers:
  - A thermal barrier is not required where all of the following conditions are present:
    The sum of cooler and/or freezer floor areas is ≤ 400 sf.
    The foam plastic flame spread is ≤ 75.
    The foam plastic conforms to requirements shown in the detail provided.
  - Thicker foam plastic is permitted where meeting requirements shown in the detail provided.

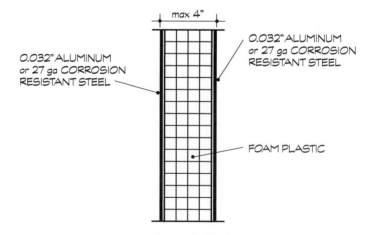

Fig. 2603.4.1.3A. Alternative to thermal barrier in walk-in collers.

2603 Foam Plastic Insulation

2603.4.1.4 Exterior walls — one story buildings

This subsection addresses thermal barriers between foam plastic insulation and building interiors.

- Such barriers are not required where all of the following conditions apply:
  - The foam plastic has the following properties:
    Flame spread index is ≤ 25.
    Smoke-developed index is ≤ 450.
  - Building is sprinklered as per NFPA 13.
  - Other requirements are met as shown in the detail provided.

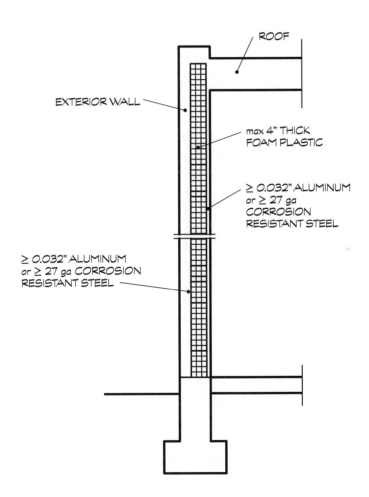

ROOF

EXTERIOR WALL

max 4" THICK
FOAM PLASTIC

$\geq$ 0.032" ALUMINUM
or $\geq$ 27 ga
CORROSION
RESISTANT STEEL

$\geq$ 0.032" ALUMINUM
or $\geq$ 27 ga CORROSION
RESISTANT STEEL

Fig. 2603.4.1.4. Alternative to a thermal barrier in exterior walls of 1-story buildings.

2603 Foam Plastic Insulation

2603.4.1.5 Roofing

This subsection addresses thermal barriers between foam plastic insulation and building interiors.

- Such a barrier is not required where foam plastic insulation is used as follows:
  - Where the plastic is part of a roof assembly meeting all of the following conditions:
    Assembly is one of the following:
      Class A.
      Class B.
      Class C.
    The assembly with the plastic insulation passes required tests.

    Note: The following tests are cited as applicable. The assembly indicated above must pass either of the tests:
    FM 4450, "Approved Standard for Class 1 Insulated Steel Deck Roofs."
    UL 1256, "Fire Test of Roof Deck Construction."

- The insulation does not require a thermal barrier for conditions shown in the detail provided.

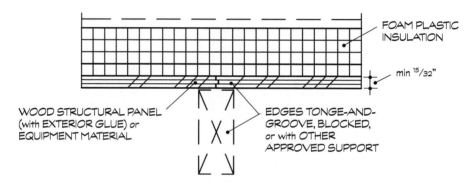

Fig. 2603.4.1.5. Roof sheathing not requiring a thermal barrier.

2603.4.1.6 Attics and crawl spaces

This subsection addresses thermal barriers between foam plastic insulation and building interiors.

- Such a barrier is not required in the following spaces for conditions indicated below:
  - Spaces:
    The following locations where accessed only for utility service:
      Attics.
      Crawl spaces.
  - Conditions:
    Foam insulation is protected against ignition as shown in the details provided.

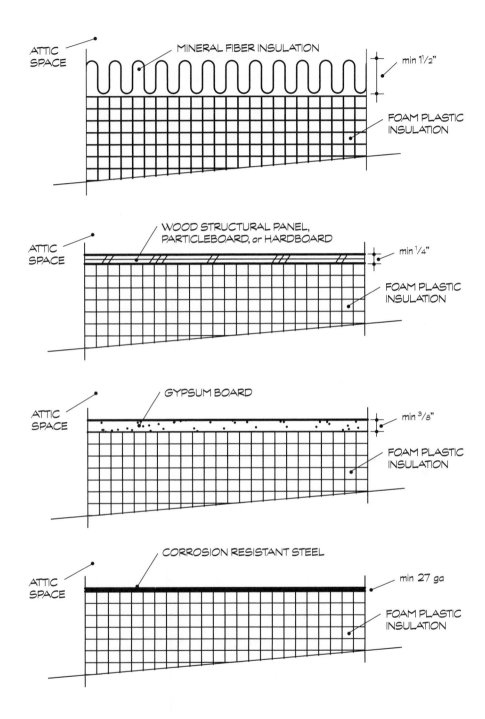

Fig. 2603.4.1.6. Alternatives to a thermal barrier at attics and crawl spaces. Orientation varies for crawl spaces and some attics.

2603 Foam Plastic Insulation

2603.4.1.7 Doors not required to have a fire-protection rating

This subsection addresses thermal barriers between foam plastic insulation and building interiors.

- Such a barrier is not required in doors with the following insulation and as shown in the detail provided:
  - Foam plastic insulation must have the following properties:
    Flame spread index ≤ 75.
    Smoke-developed index ≤ 450.

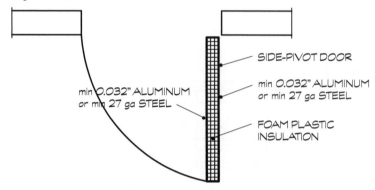

Fig. 2603.4.1.7. Door facing material where no fire-protection rating is required.

2603.4.1.8 Exterior doors in buildings of Groups R-2 or R-3

This subsection addresses thermal barriers between foam plastic insulation and building interiors.

- Such barriers are not required in doors filled with foam insulation as follows:
  - Entrance doors as follows:
    In the following occupancies:
      R-2, R-3.
    To individual dwelling units.
    That do not require a fire-resistance rating.
    As shown in the detail provided.

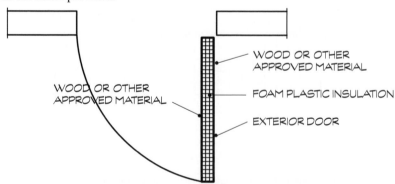

Fig. 2603.4.1.8. Exterior door facing at R2 and R3 where no fire-resistance rating is required.

2603 Foam Plastic Insulation

2603.4.1.9 Garage doors

This subsection addresses thermal barriers between foam plastic insulation and building interiors.

- Such barriers are not required in garage doors filled with foam insulation where all of the following conditions are met:
  - Insulation has the following properties:
    - Flame spread index is ≤ 75.
    - Smoke developed index is ≤ 450.
  - Garage serves 1- or 2-family dwelling.
  - Garage may be either of the following:
    - Attached.
    - Detached.

  Note: 2603.3, "Surface-burning characteristics," is cited as governing foam insulation, a partial summary of which is provided above.

- A thermal barrier is not required for the following garage doors filled with foam insulation:
  - Garage doors that do not require a fire-resistance rating as follows:
    - With facing materials shown in the detail provided.
    - Other facing materials must meet required standards.

  Note: ANSI/DASMA 107, "Room Fire Test Standard for Garage Doors Using Foam Plastic Insulation," is cited as the standard that other facings must meet.

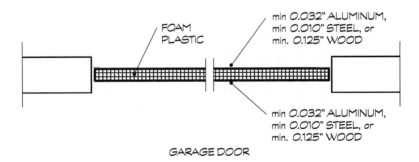

Fig. 2603.4.1.9.

2603 Foam Plastic Insulation

2603.4.1.10 Siding backer board

This subsection addresses thermal barriers between foam plastic insulation and building interiors.

- Such a barrier is not required for foam plastic insulation with all of the following characteristics:
  - Insulation of $\leq$ 2000 Btu/sf.
  - Used as a backing for siding.
  - Meeting conditions shown in the detail provided.

  Note: NFPA 259, "Test Method for Potential Heat of Building Materials," is cited as the test for determining BTU/sf.

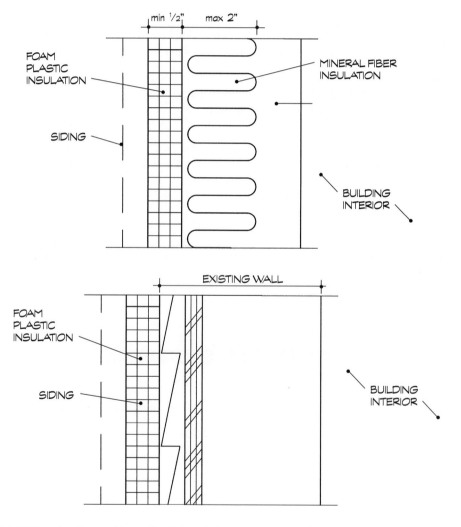

Fig. 2603.4.1.10. Permitted uses of foam plastic insulation as a backing for siding.

2604 Interior Finish and Trim

2604.2.2 Thickness

- Size limitations of interior trim of foam plastic are shown on the illustration provided.

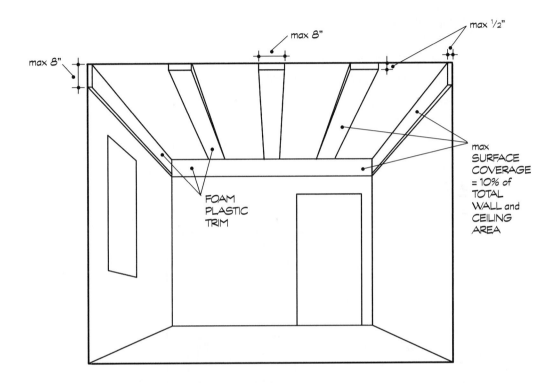

Fig. 2604.2.2. Foam plastic as interior trim

2604.2.3 Area limitation

- Limitations of surface coverage for trim of foam plastic are shown in Figure 2604.2.2.

2605 Plastic Veneer

2605.2 Exterior use

- Plastic veneer on building exteriors must meet the following requirements:
  - Plastic must be one of the following types:
    Thermoplastic.
    Thermosetting plastic.
    Reinforced thermosetting plastic.
  - Physical aspects are governed as follows:
    In Type VB construction:
    The following are not limited where the walls do not have a fire-resistance rating:
    Area of plastic panel.
    Minimum separation distance between panels.
    Smoke-density.
    Otherwise, plastic must meet the requirements shown on the detail provided.

Note: Section 2602, "Definitions," is cited as defining plastaic veneer.

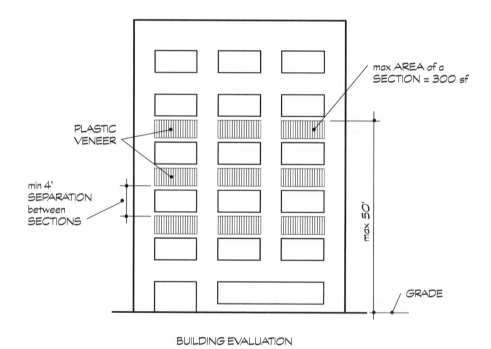

BUILDING EVALUATION

Fig. 2605.2.

2606 Light-Transmitting Plastics

2606.7.1 Support

- Light-transmitting plastic diffusers must be supported from overhead construction as follows:
  - By hangers as shown in the detail provided.

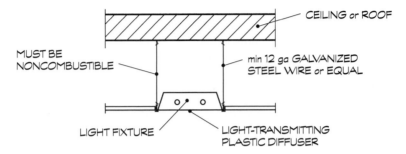

Fig. 2606.7.1. Supports for right-transmitting plastic diffusers.

2606.7.3 Size limitations

- Individual panels of light-transmitting plastics are limited in size as follows:
  - Length must be ≤ 10'.
  - Area must be ≤ 30 sf.
- A partial list of dimensions meeting size limitations is provided below:

Table 2606.7.3		Maximum Sizes of Light-Transmitting Plastic Panels			
Width	Length	Width	Length	Width	Length
3'-0"	10'-0"	3'-10"	7'-9"	4'-8"	6'-5"
3'-1"	9'-8"	3'-11"	7'-7"	4'-9"	6'-3"
3'-2"	9'-5"	4'-0"	7'-6"	4'-10"	6'-2"
3'-3"	9'-2"	4'-1"	7'-4"	4'-11"	6'-1"
3'-4"	9'-0"	4'-2"	7'-2"	5'-0"	6'-0"
3'-5"	8'-9"	4'-3"	7'-0"	5'-1"	5'-10"
3'-6"	8'-6"	4'-4"	6'-11"	5'-2"	5'-9"
3'-7"	8'-4"	4'-5"	6'-9"	5'-3"	5'-8"
3'-8"	8'-2"	4'-6"	6'-8"	5'-4"	5'-7"
3'-9"	8'-0"	4'-7"	6'-6"	5'-5"	5'-6"

2606 Light-Transmitting Plastics

2606.7.5 Electrical lighting fixtures

- Light-transmitting plastic diffusers in light fixtures located in the following areas are governed as indicated below:
  - Areas:
    - Required exits.
    - Required corridors.
  - Requirements:
    - Where the building is not sprinklered as per NFPA 13:
      - Area of plastic must be ≤ 30% of the ceiling area as follows:
        - A partial list of minimum on-center spacing of various fixtures is provided below.
        - Details showing common layouts that meet minimums are provided.

  Note: The following are cited, one of which must govern the plastic panels above:
  Chapter 8, "Interior Finishes."
  2606.7.2, "Installation," which governs service temperatures.

Table 2606.7.5   Minimum Center-to-Center Spacing of Plastic Diffusers in Ceilings of Exits and Corridors

Diffuser size	Width of ceiling					
	3'	4'	5'	6'	7'	8'
1' x 4'	4'-5"	3'-4"	2'-8"	2'-3"	1'-11"	1'-8"
1' x 8'	8'-11"	6'-8"	5'-4"	4'-5"	3'-10"	3'-4"
2' x 2'	4'-5"	3'-4"	2'-8"	2'-3"	1'-11"	1'-8"
2' x 4'	8'-11"	6'-8"	5'-4"	4'-5"	3'-10"	3'-4"
2' x 8'	17'-9"	13'-4"	10'-8"	8'-11"	7'-7"	6'-8"
4' x 4'	17'-9"	13'-4"	10'-8"	8'-11"	7'-7"	6'-8"

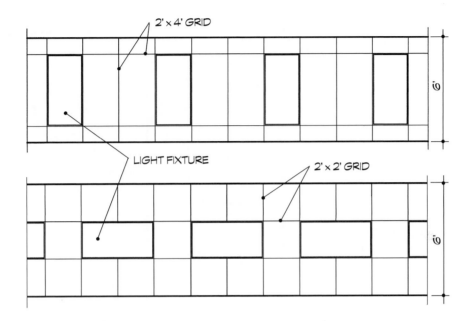

Fig. 2606.7.5. Reflected ceiling plans with 22% fixture coverage.

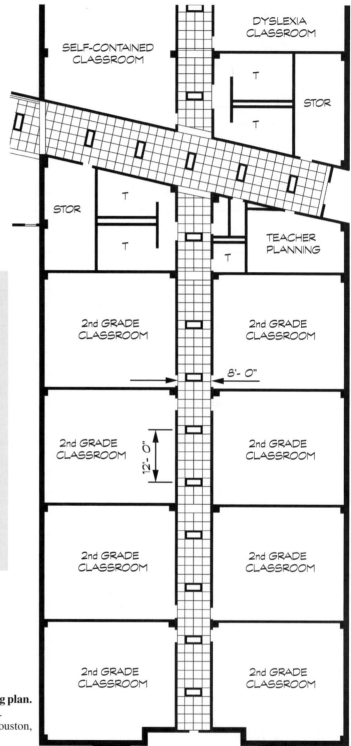

Case study: Fig. 2606.7.5.
Plastic diffusers at the ceiling light fixtures are limited to 30% of the ceiling area. The corridor shown in this school is 8' wide. This means that the difussers cannot be closer than 3'- 4" as indicated in the handbook Table 2606.7.5. Since the actual spacing of the fixtures is 12' oc, they comply with the code requirement. The actual ceiling coverage of the fixtures is < 9%.

Fig. 2606.7.5. Partial reflected ceiling plan.
New Jasper Pre-K–2nd Grade School. Jasper, Texas. PBK Architects, Inc. Houston, Texas.

2606 Light-Transmitting Plastics

2606.12 Solar collectors

This subsection addresses light-transmitting plastics as covers on solar collectors.

- Such plastic covers are limited in area as follows:
  - Where thickness is ≤ 0.010":
    The total area of any type plastic must be ≤ ¹/₃ the roof area.
  - Where thickness is > 0.010":
    The total area of type CC1 plastics as follows must be ≤ ¹/₃ the roof area:
    Such as polycarbonate.
    The total area of type CC2 plastics as follows must be ≤ ¼ the roof area:
    Such as acrylic.
- Other requirements are shown on the illustration provided.

  Note: 2606.4, "Specifications," lists the properties and standards for CC1 and CC2 plastics, which are based on burning characteristics.

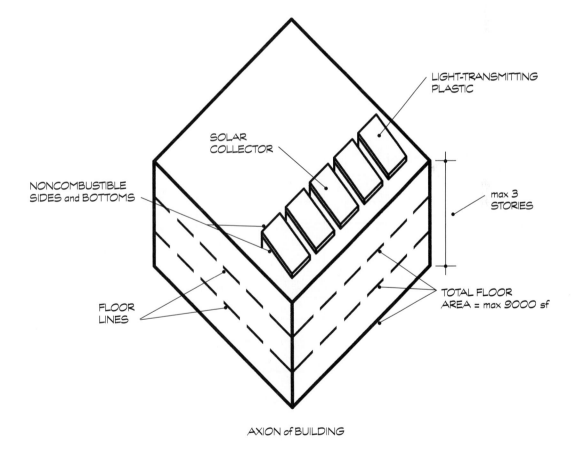

AXION of BUILDING

Fig. 2606.12. Building limits for roof-top solar collectors with light-transmitting plastic covers.

2607 Light-Transmitting Plastic Wall Panels

2607.3 Height limitation

This subsection addresses light-transmitting plastic panels on exterior building walls.

- The height of such panels is not limited where all of the following apply:
  - Where building is sprinklered as per NFPA 13.
  - Where panel size is limited according to the following:
      Fire separation distance.
      Class of plastic.

    Note: 2607.5, "Automatic sprinkler system," is cited as the source of requirements necessary for panels to have unlimited height as indicated above.

- Height requirement of other exterior wall panels is shown on the illustration provided.

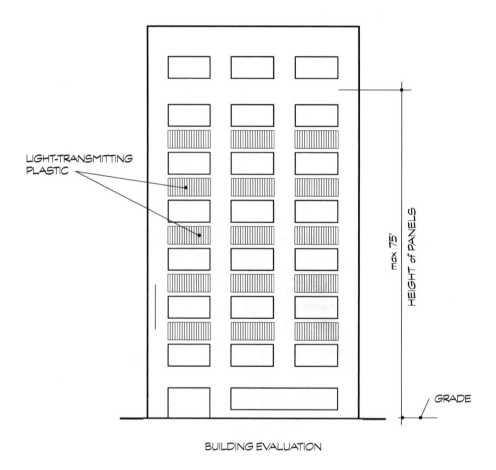

Fig. 2607.3. Maximum height for light-transmitting plastic on a building façade.

2607 Light-Transmitting Plastic Wall Panels

2607.4 Area limitation and separation

This subsection addresses light-transmitting plastic panels on exterior building walls.

- This subsection does not apply to plastic veneers used as exterior siding in Type V construction.

    Note: Section 1406, "Combustible Materials on the Exterior Side of Exterior Walls," is cited as the source of requirements for the plastic siding as indicated above.

- This subsection does not apply to plastic wall panels in greenhouses.

    Note: 704.8, "Allowable area of openings," is cited as the source of requirements for unprotected openings which governs greenhouses.

- The following are shown on the illustrations provided:
  - Maximum area of an individual plastic panel on a building façade.
  - Minimum vertical and horizontal distances between panels as follows:
      Separation may be provided by either of the following:
      Distances shown in the illustrations provided.
      A flame barrier as shown in the illustration provided.
- The maximum % of wall area in any story that a plastic panel may cover is the smaller of the following:
  - The maximum % of unprotected openings permitted by the code.
  - The maximum % shown in the illustrations provided.

    Note: 704.8, "Allowable area of openings," is cited as the source listing the maximum % of unprotected openings permitted in a building façade.

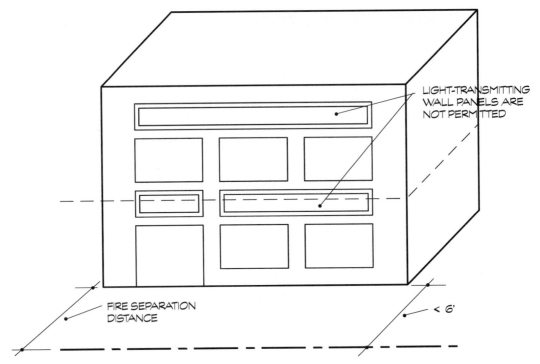

Fig. 2607.4A. Building with fire separationg distance < 6'.

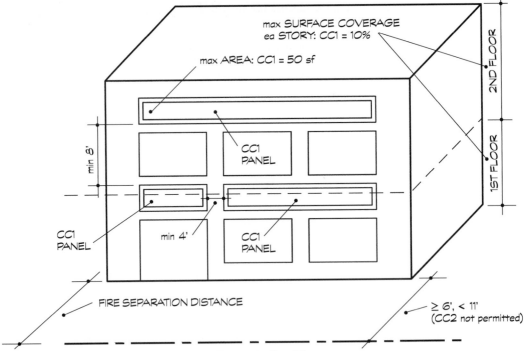

Fig. 2607.4B. Building with fire separation distance ≥ 6', < 11'.

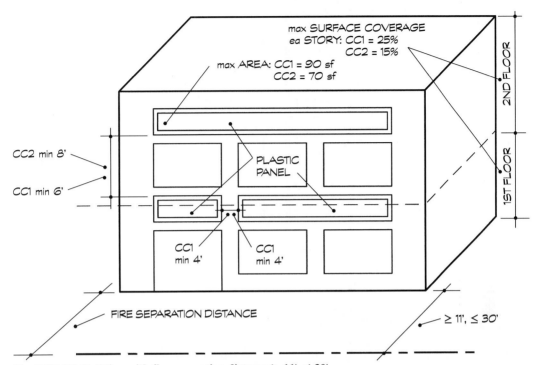

Fig. 2607.4C. Building with fire separation distance ≥ 11', ≤ 30'.

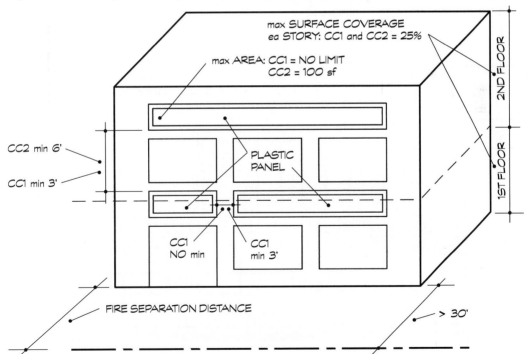

Fig. 2607.4D. Building with fire separation distance > 30'.

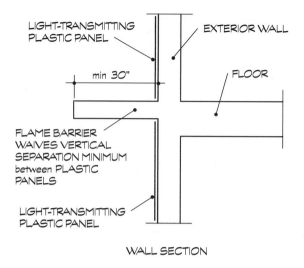

Fig. 2607.4E. Flame barrier at exterior wall.

Case study: Fig. 2607.4A. The CC1 light-transmitting plastic wall panels located above the lower roof are in a wall of high 1st-floor space. Neither the distance between panels nor the area of the panels is governed for this type plastic, as indicated by IBC Table 2607.4. The panel coverage is < 50% of the exterior wall area (which continues beyond the elevation shown), thus, meeting this code limitation.

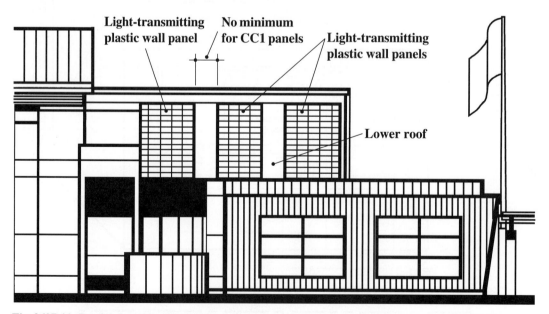

Fig. 2607.4A. Partial elevation. Wichita Transit Storage, Administration, and Maintenance Facility. Wichita, Kansas. Wilson Darnell Mann, P.A., Architects. Wichita, Kansas.

2607 Light-Transmitting Plastic Wall Panels

2607.5 Automatic sprinkler system

This subsection addresses light-transmitting plastic panels on exterior building walls.

- The maximum % of wall area in any story that a plastic panel may cover is the smaller of the following:
  - The maximum % of unprotected openings permitted by the code.
  - The maximum % shown in the illustrations provided.
  - 50%

    Note: 704.8, "Allowable area of openings," is cited as the source listing the maximum % of unprotected openings permitted in a building façade.

  - There are no height limitations to the plastic panels meeting the above requirements.

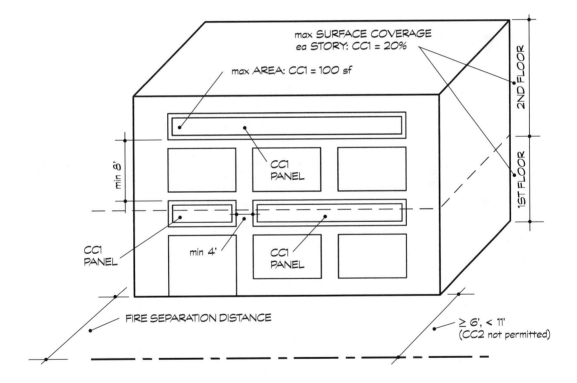

max SURFACE COVERAGE
ea STORY: CC1 = 20%

max AREA: CC1 = 100 sf

2ND FLOOR

1ST FLOOR

CC1 PANEL

min 8'

CC1 PANEL

min 4'

CC1 PANEL

FIRE SEPARATION DISTANCE

≥ 6', < 11'
(CC2 not permitted)

Fig. 2607.5A. Building with fire separation distance ≥ 6', < 11'; building sprinklered

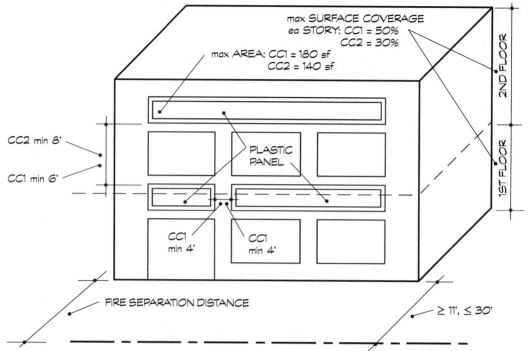

Fig. 2607.5B. Building with fire separation distance ≥ 11', ≤ 30'.

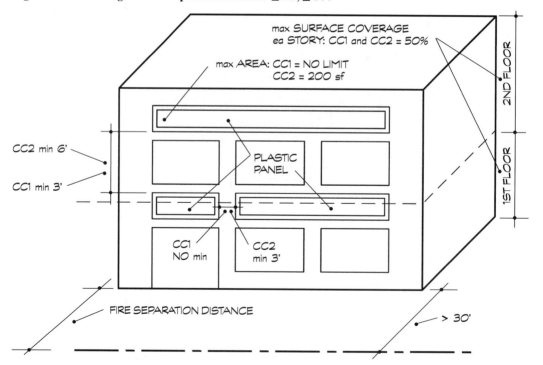

Fig. 2607.5C. Building with fire separation distance > 30'; building sprinklered.

2608 Light-Transmitting Plastic Glazing

2608.2 Buildings of other types of construction

This subsection addresses light-transmitting plastic glazing in buildings other than Type VB construction.

- Where the openings in exterior walls are not required to be protected, the following applies:
  - Requirements for light-transmitting plastic glazing are shown on the illustrations provided as follows:

    Required vertical separation may be provided by either of the following:

    Distances shown in the illustrations provided.

    A flame barrier as shown in the illustration provided.

  Note: *Section 704, "Exterior Walls," is cited as the source specifying conditions wherein exterior walls must be protected.*

  Section 2606, "Light-Transmitting Plastics," is cited as the source of requirements with which the light-transmitting glazing indicated above must comply.

  903.3.1.1, NFPA 13, "Sprinkler Systems," is cited as the source governing the sprinklers required for reduced restrictions on the plastic glazing.

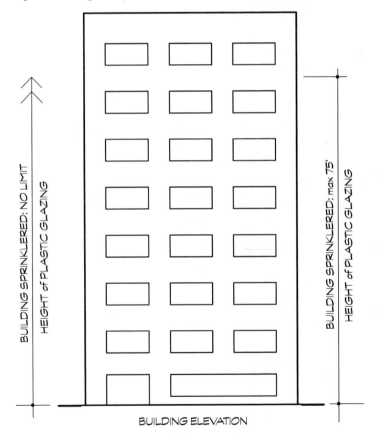

Fig. 2608.2A. Height limit for plastic glazing on building façades.

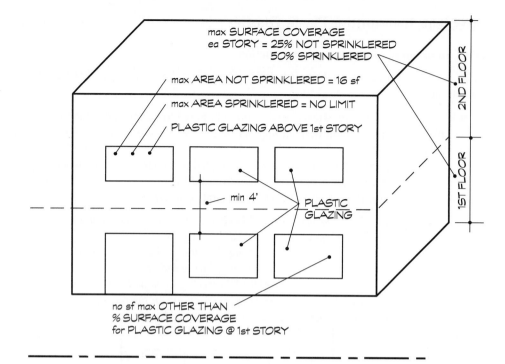

max SURFACE COVERAGE
ea STORY = 25% NOT SPRINKLERED
50% SPRINKLERED

max AREA NOT SPRINKLERED = 16 sf

max AREA SPRINKLERED = NO LIMIT

PLASTIC GLAZING ABOVE 1st STORY

2ND FLOOR

1ST FLOOR

min 4'

PLASTIC
GLAZING

no sf max OTHER THAN
% SURFACE COVERAGE
for PLASTIC GLAZING @ 1st STORY

Fig. 2608.2B. Plastic glazing limits.

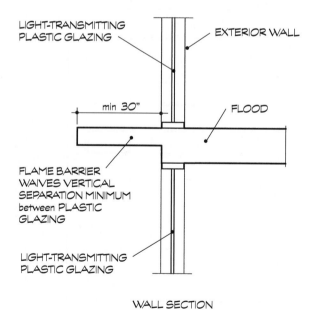

LIGHT-TRANSMITTING
PLASTIC GLAZING

EXTERIOR WALL

min 30"

FLOOD

FLAME BARRIER
WAIVES VERTICAL
SEPARATION MINIMUM
between PLASTIC
GLAZING

LIGHT-TRANSMITTING
PLASTIC GLAZING

WALL SECTION

Fig. 2608.2B. Plastic glazing limits.

2609 Light-Transmitting Plastic Roof Panels

2609.2 Separation

This subsection addresses light-transmitting plastic roof panels.

- The separation of plastic roof panels is not required in the following cases:
  - In low-hazard buildings such as the following:
    The following swimming pool buildings:
    $\leq$ 5000 sf.
    With a fire separation distance $\geq$ 10'.
    The following greenhouses:
    Used to grow plants for one of the following purposes:
    On a production basis.
    For research.
    No public access.
    With a fire separation distance $\geq$ 4'.
- Otherwise, separation requirements for plastic roof panels are as shown in the illustrations provided.

  Note: 2609.4, "Area limitations," is cited as the source waiving the requirements for roof-panel separation for the cases indicated above by way of its Exceptions 2 and 3.
  903.3.1.1, NFPA 13, "Sprinkler Systems," is cited as the source governing the sprinklers required for waiving separation requirements for plastic roof panels.

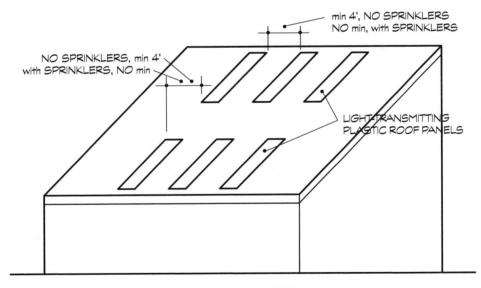

BUILDING ELEVATION

Fig. 2609.2A. Minimum separation of light-transmitting plaster roof panels measured in a horizontal plane.

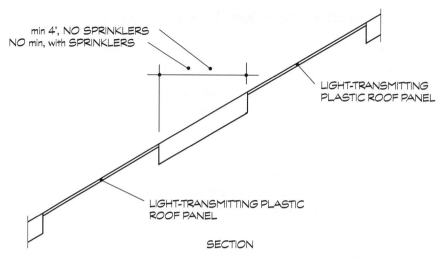

Fig. 2609.2B. Minimum separation of light-transmitting plastic roof p anels measured in a horizontal plane.

2609.3 Location

This subsection addresses light-transmitting plastic roof panels.

- The requirement for locating plastic roof panels is shown in the illustration provided for the following case:
  ○ Where exterior wall openings are required to be protected.

  Note: 704.8, "Allowable area of openings," is cited as the source defining conditions wherein exterior wall openings must be protected.

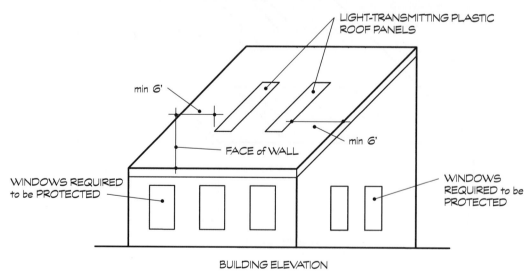

Fig. 2609.3. Plastic roof panels near walls where windows need to be protected.

2609 Light-Transmitting Plastic Roof Panels

2609.4 Area limitations *(part 1 of 5)*

This subsection addresses light-transmitting plastic roof panels.

- This section does not apply to the following structures:
  - Low-hazard structures such as the following:
    The following swimming pool buildings:
      ≤ 5000 sf.
      With a fire separation distance ≥ 10'.
  - The following greenhouses:
    Used to grow plants for one of the following purposes:
      On a production basis.
      For research.
    No public access.
    With a fire separation distance ≥ 4'.
  - Roof coverings over the following:
    In occupancy R-3:
      Terraces.
      Patios.
- Otherwise, areas of plastic roof panels are limited as shown in the tables and illustration provided.

  Note: IBC Table 2609.4, "Area Limitations for Light-Transmitting Plastic Roof Panels,"
  is cited as the source of area limitations as shown in the tables provided.
  903.3.1.1, NFPA 13, "Sprinkler Systems," is cited as the source governing the
  sprinklers required for increasing area limitations for plastic roof panels.

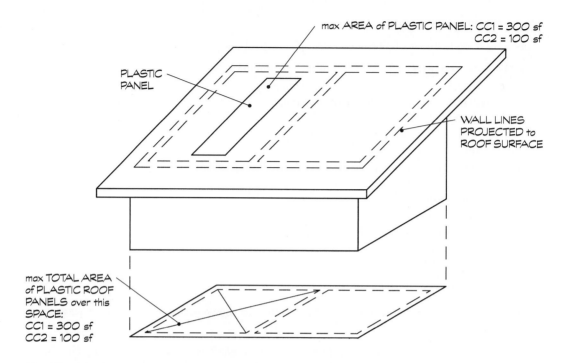

Fig. 2609.4. Maximum size of light-transmitting plastic roof panels.

2609 Light-Transmitting Plastic Roof Panels

2609.4 Area limitations *(part 2 of 5)*

- A partial list of maximum sizes for the following CC1-class plastic roof panels is shown below:
  - Panels must be ≤ 300 sf each for buildings with no sprinklers.

Table 2609.4a   Maximum Roof Panel Sizes for CC1 Plastics with No Sprinklers

Given width	Max. length	Given width	Max. length	Given width	Max. length	Given width	Max. length
1'-0"	300'-0"	6'-0"	50'-0"	11'-0"	27'-3"	16'-0"	18'-9"
1'-4"	225'-6"	6'-4"	47'-4"	11'-4"	26'-5"	16'-4"	18'-4"
1'-8"	180'-0"	6'-8"	45'-0"	11'-8"	25'-8"	16'-8"	18'-0"
2'-0"	150'-0"	7'-0"	42'-10"	12'-0"	25'-0"	17'-0"	17'-7"
2'-4"	128'-6"	7'-4"	40'-11"	12'-4"	24'-3"	17'-4"	17'-3"
2'-8"	112'-6"	7'-8"	39'-1"	12'-8"	23'-8"	17'-8"	16'-11"
3'-0"	100'-0"	8'-0"	37'-6"	13'-0"	23'-0"	18'-0"	16'-8"
3'-4"	90'-0"	8'-4"	36'-0"	13'-4"	22'-6"	18'-4"	16'-4"
3'-8"	81'-9"	8'-8"	34'-7"	13'-8"	21'-11"	18'-8"	16'-0"
4'-0"	75'-0"	9'-0"	33'-4"	14'-0"	21'-5"	19'-0"	15'-9"
4'-4"	69'-3"	9'-4"	32'-1"	14'-4"	20'-11"	19'-4"	15'-6"
4'-8"	64'-3"	9'-8"	31'-0"	14'-8"	20'-5"	19'-8"	15'-3"
5'-0"	60'-0"	10'-0"	30'-0"	15'-0"	20'-0"	20'-0"	15'-0"
5'-4"	56'-3"	10'-4"	29'-0"	15'-4"	19'-6"	20'-4"	14'-9"
5'-8"	52'-11"	10'-8"	28'-1"	15'-8"	19'-1"	20'-8"	14'-6"

- A partial list of maximum sizes for the following CC1-class plastic roof panels is shown below:
  - Panels must be ≤ 600 sf each for sprinklered buildings.

Table 2609.4b   Maximum Roof Panel Sizes for CC1 Plastics on Sprinklered Buildings

Given width	Max. length	Given width	Max. length	Given width	Max. length	Given width	Max. length
1'-0"	600'-0"	7'-0"	85'-8"	13'-0"	46'-1"	19'-0"	31'-7"
1'-6"	400'-0"	7'-6"	80'-0"	13'-6"	44'-5"	19'-6"	30'-9"
2'-0"	300'-0"	8'-0"	75'-0"	14'-0"	42'-10"	20'-0"	30'-0"
2'-6"	240'-0"	8'-6"	70'-7"	14'-6"	41'-4"	20'-6"	29'-3"
3'-0"	200'-0"	9'-0"	66'-8"	15'-0"	40'-0"	21'-0"	28'-6"
3'-6"	171'-5"	9'-6"	63'-1"	15'-6"	38'-8"	21'-6"	27'-10"
4'-0"	150'-0"	10'-0"	60'-0"	16'-0"	37'-6"	22'-0"	27'-3"
4'-6"	133'-4"	10'-6"	57'-1"	16'-6"	36'-4"	22'-6"	26'-8"
5'-0"	120'-0"	11'-0"	54'-6"	17'-0"	35'-3"	23'-0"	26'-1"
5'-6"	109'-1"	11'-6"	52'-2"	17'-6"	34'-3"	23'-6"	25'-6"
6'-0"	100'-0"	12'-0"	50'-0"	18'-0"	33'-4"	24'-0"	25'-0"
6'-6"	92'-3"	12'-6"	48'-0"	18'-6"	32'-5"	24'-6"	24'-5"

2609 Light-Transmitting Plastic Roof Panels

2609.4 Area limitations *(part 3 of 5)*

- A partial list of maximum areas for the following CC1-class plastic roof panels is shown below:
  - Sum of panel areas must be ≤ 30% of floor area served in buildings with no sprinklers.

Table 2609.4c   Maximum Total Area Permitted for Roof Panels of CC1 Plastics with No Sprinklers

Floor area (sf)	Maximum panel area (sf)	Floor area (sf)	Maximum panel area (sf)	Floor area (sf)	Maximum panel area (sf)	Floor area (sf)	Maximum panel area (sf)
100	30	1300	390	2500	750	3700	1110
200	60	1400	420	2600	780	3800	1140
300	90	1500	450	2700	810	3900	1170
400	120	1600	480	2800	840	4000	1200
500	150	1700	510	2900	870	4100	1230
600	180	1800	540	3000	900	4200	1260
700	210	1900	570	3100	930	4300	1290
800	240	2000	600	3200	960	4400	1320
900	270	2100	630	3300	990	4500	1350
1000	300	2200	660	3400	1020	4600	1380
1100	330	2300	690	3500	1050	4700	1410
1200	360	2400	720	3600	1080	4800	1440

- A partial list of maximum areas for the following CC1-class plastic roof panels is shown below:
  - Sum of panel areas must be ≤ 60% of floor area served in sprinklered buildings.

Table 2609.4d   Total Aggregate Area Permitted for Roof Panels of CC1 Plastics with Sprinklers

Floor area (sf)	Maximum panel area (sf)	Floor area (sf)	Maximum panel area (sf)	Floor area (sf)	Maximum panel area (sf)	Floor area (sf)	Maximum panel area (sf)
100	60	1300	780	2500	1500	3700	2220
200	120	1400	840	2600	1560	3800	2280
300	180	1500	900	2700	1620	3900	2340
400	240	1600	960	2800	1680	4000	2400
500	300	1700	1020	2900	1740	4100	2460
600	360	1800	1080	3000	1800	4200	2520
700	420	1900	1140	3100	1860	4300	2580
800	480	2000	1200	3200	1920	4400	2640
900	540	2100	1260	3300	1980	4500	2700
1000	600	2200	1320	3400	2040	4600	2760
1100	660	2300	1380	3500	2100	4700	2820
1200	720	2400	1440	3600	2160	4800	2880

2609 Light-Transmitting Plastic Roof Panels

2609.4 Area limitations *(part 4 of 5)*

- A partial list of maximum sizes of the following CC2-class plastic roof panels is shown below:
  - Panels must be ≥ 100 sf each for buildings with no sprinklers.

Table 2609.4e   Maximum Roof Panel Sizes for CC2 Plastics with No Sprinklers

Given width	Max. length	Given width	Max. length	Given width	Max. length	Given width	Max. length
1'-0"	100'-0"	3'-6"	28'-6"	6'-0"	16'-8"	8'-6"	11'-9"
1'-2"	85'-8"	3'-8"	27'-3"	6'-2"	16'-2"	8'-8"	11'-6"
1'-4"	75'-0"	3'-10"	26'-1"	6'-4"	15'-9"	8'-10"	11'-3"
1'-6"	66'-8"	4'-0"	25'-0"	6'-6"	15'-4"	9'-0"	11'-1"
1'-8"	60'-0"	4'-2"	24'-0"	6'-8"	15'-0"	9'-2"	10'-10"
1'-10"	54'-6"	4'-4"	23'-1"	6'-10"	14'-7"	9'-4"	10'-8"
2'-0"	50'-0"	4'-6"	22'-2"	7'-0"	14'-3"	9'-6"	10'-6"
2'-2"	46'-1"	4'-8"	21'-5"	7'-2"	13'-11"	9'-8"	10'-4"
2'-4"	42'-10"	4'-10"	20'-8"	7'-4"	13'-7"	9'-10"	10'-2"
2'-6"	40'-0"	5'-0"	20'-0"	7'-6"	13'-4"	10'-0"	10'-0"
2'-8"	37'-6"	5'-2"	19'-4"	7'-8"	13'-0"	10'-2"	9'-10"
2'-10"	35'-3"	5'-4"	18'-9"	7'-10"	12'-9"	10'-4"	9'-8"
3'-0"	33'-4"	5'-6"	18'-2"	8'-0"	12'-6"	10'-6"	9'-6"
3'-2"	31'-7"	5'-8"	17'-7"	8'-2"	12'-2"	10'-8"	9'-4"
3'-4"	30'-0"	5'-10"	17'-1"	8'-4"	12'-0"	10'-10"	9'-2"

- A partial list of maximum sizes for the following CC2-class plastic roof panels is shown below:
  - Panels must be ≤ 200 sf each for sprinklered buildings.

Table 2609.4f   Maximum Roof Panel Sizes for CC2 Plastics on Sprinklered Buildings

Given width	Max. length	Given width	Max. length	Given width	Max. length	Given width	Max. length
1'-0"	200'-0"	5'-0"	40'-0"	9'-0"	22'-2"	13'-0"	15'-4"
1'-4"	150'-0"	5'-4"	37'-6"	9'-4"	21'-5"	13'-4"	15'-0"
1'-8"	120'-0"	5'-8"	35'-3"	9'-8"	20'-8"	13'-8"	14'-7"
2'-0"	100'-0"	6'-0"	33'-4"	10'-0"	20'-0"	14'-0"	14'-3"
2'-4"	85'-8"	6'-4"	31'-7"	10'-4"	19'-4"	14'-4"	13'-11"
2'-8"	75'-0"	6'-8"	30'-0"	10'-8"	18'-9"	14'-8"	13'-7"
3'-0"	66'-8"	7'-0"	28'-6"	11'-0"	18'-2"	15'-0"	13'-4"
3'-4"	60'-0"	7'-4"	27'-3"	11'-4"	17'-7"	15'-4"	13'-0"
3'-8"	54'-6"	7'-8"	26'-1"	11'-8"	17'-1"	15'-8"	12'-9"
4'-0"	50'-0"	8'-0"	25'-0"	12'-0"	16'-8"	16'-0"	12'-6"
4'-4"	46'-1"	8'-4"	24'-0"	12'-4"	16'-2"	16'-4"	12'-2"
4'-8"	42'-10"	8'-8"	23'-1"	12'-8"	15'-9"	16'-8"	12'-0"

2609 Light-Transmitting Plastic Roof Panels

2609.4 Area limitations *(part 5 of 5)*

- A partial list of maximum areas for the following CC2-class plastic roof panels is shown below:
  - Sum of panel areas must be ≤ 25% of floor area served in buildings with no sprinklers.

Table 2609.4g   **Maximum Total Area Permitted for Roof Panels of CC2 Plastics with No Sprinklers**

Floor area (sf)	Maximum panel area (sf)	Floor area (sf)	Maximum panel area (sf)	Floor area (sf)	Maximum panel area (sf)	Floor area (sf)	Maximum panel area (sf)
100	25	1300	325	2500	625	3700	925
200	50	1400	350	2600	650	3800	950
300	75	1500	375	2700	675	3900	975
400	100	1600	400	2800	700	4000	1000
500	125	1700	425	2900	725	4100	1025
600	150	1800	450	3000	750	4200	1050
700	175	1900	475	3100	775	4300	1075
800	200	2000	500	3200	800	4400	1100
900	225	2100	525	3300	825	4500	1125
1000	250	2200	550	3400	850	4600	1150
1100	275	2300	575	3500	875	4700	1175
1200	300	2400	600	3600	900	4800	1200

- A partial list of maximum areas for the following CC2-class plastic roof panels is shown below:
  - Sum of panel areas must be ≤ 50% of floor area served in sprinklered buildings.

Table 2609.4h   **Total Aggregate Area Permitted for Roof Panels of CC2 Plastics with Sprinklers**

Floor area (sf)	Maximum panel area (sf)	Floor area (sf)	Maximum panel area (sf)	Floor area (sf)	Maximum panel area (sf)	Floor area (sf)	Maximum panel area (sf)
100	50	1300	650	2500	1250	3700	1850
200	100	1400	700	2600	1300	3800	1900
300	150	1500	750	2700	1350	3900	1950
400	200	1600	800	2800	1400	4000	2000
500	250	1700	850	2900	1450	4100	2050
600	300	1800	900	3000	1500	4200	2100
700	350	1900	950	3100	1550	4300	2150
800	400	2000	1000	3200	1600	4400	2200
900	450	2100	1050	3300	1650	4500	2250
1000	500	2200	1100	3400	1700	4600	2300
1100	550	2300	1150	3500	1750	4700	2350
1200	600	2400	1200	3600	1800	4800	2400

2610 Light-Transmitting Plastic Skylight Glazing

2610.2 Mounting

This subsection addresses skylights with light-transmitting plastic glazing.

- Curbs are not required for skylights as follows:
  - Where the roof slopes ≥ 3:12 in either of the following locations:
    In occupancy R-3.
    Where unclassified roof coverings are allowed.
- Neither of the following materials is required at the edge of a skylight where the condition indicated below applies:
  - Materials:
    Metal.
    Noncombustible material.
  - Condition:
    Where unclassified roof coverings are allowed.
- Otherwise, skylights are governed as follows:
  - Curbs are required for skylights as shown in the detail provided.
  - Where edges are not constructed as per the detail provided, the following applies:
    Edge must be shown to resist combustion upon exposure to a standard test flame.

  Note: The following are cited as governing exposure of the skylight edge to a test flame. One of the standards must be used. A Class-B brand is specified for the test.
  ASTM E 108, "Standard Test Method for Fire Tests of Roof Coverings."
  UL 790, "Tests for Fire Resistance of Roof Covering Materials."

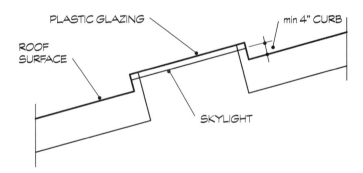

Fig. 26010.2. Required curb for light-transmitting plastic glazing in skylights.

2610 Light-Transmitting Plastic Skylight Glazing

2610.3 Slope

This section addresses skylights with light-transmitting plastic glazing.

- This section does not apply to skylights that are shown to resist combustion upon exposure to a standard test flame.

  Note: *The following are cited as governing exposure of the skylight to a test flame. One of the standards must be used. A Class-B brand is specified for the test.*
  ASTM E 108, "Standard Test Method for Fire Tests of Roof Coverings."
  UL 790, "Tests for Fire Resistance of Roof Covering Materials."

- Requirements for other skylights are shown on the details provided.
- A partial list of mounting heights required for domed skylights is provided.
- Dome-shaped skylights must have a rise ≥ 10% of its longest span as indicated in the following partial list of rise requirements.

Table 2610.3   Required Rise of Domed Skylight vs. Span

Span	Minimum rise	Span	Minimum rise	Span	Minimum rise	Span	Minimum rise
≤ 2'-6"	3"	3'-10"	4 $5/8$"	5'-2"	6 $1/4$"	6'-6"	7 $13/16$"
2'-7"	3 $1/8$"	3'-11"	4 $3/4$"	5'-3"	6 $5/16$"	6'-7"	7 $15/16$"
2'-8"	3 $1/4$"	4'-0"	4 $13/16$"	5'-4"	6 $7/16$"	6'-8"	8"
2'-9"	3 $5/16$"	4'-1"	4 $15/16$"	5'-5"	6 $1/2$"	6'-9"	8 $1/8$"
2'-10"	3 $7/16$"	4'-2"	5"	5'-6"	6 $5/8$"	6'-10"	8 $1/4$"
2'-11"	3 $1/2$"	4'-3"	5 $1/8$"	5'-7"	6 $3/4$"	6'-11"	8 $5/16$"
3'-0"	3 $5/8$"	4'-4"	5 $1/4$"	5'-8"	6 $13/16$"	7'-0"	8 $7/16$"
3'-1"	3 $3/4$"	4'-5"	5 $5/16$"	5'-9"	6 $15/16$"	7'-1"	8 $1/2$"
3'-2"	3 $13/16$"	4'-6"	5 $7/16$"	5'-10"	7"	7'-2"	8 $5/8$"
3'-3"	3 $15/16$"	4'-7"	5 $1/2$"	5'-11"	7 $1/8$"	7'-3"	8 $3/4$"
3'-4"	4"	4'-8"	5 $5/8$"	6'-0"	7 $1/4$"	7'-4"	8 $13/16$"
3'-5"	4 $1/8$"	4'-9"	5 $3/4$"	6'-1"	7 $5/16$"	7'-5"	8 $15/16$"
3'-6"	4 $1/4$"	4'-10"	5 $13/16$"	6'-2"	7 $7/16$"	7'-6"	9"
3'-7"	4 $5/16$"	4'-11"	5 $15/16$"	6'-3"	7 $1/2$"	7'-7"	9 $1/8$"
3'-8"	4 $7/16$"	5'-0"	6"	6'-4"	7 $5/8$"	7'-8"	9 $1/4$"
3'-9"	4 $1/2$"	5'-1"	6 $1/8$"	6'-5"	7 $3/4$"	7'-9"	9 $5/16$"

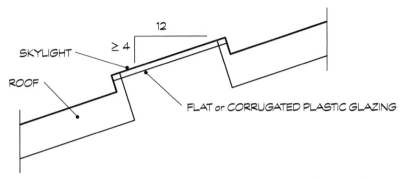

Fig. 26010.3A. Minimum slope of flat or corrugated light-transmitting plastic skylight glazing.

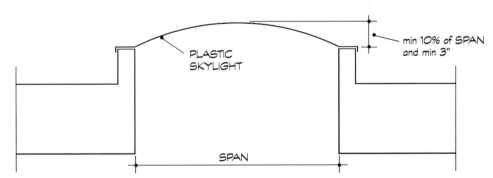

Fig. 26010.3B. Minimum rise of dome-shaped light-transmitting plastic skylight glazing.

2610 Light-Transmitting Plastic Skylight Glazing

2610.4 Maximum area of skylights

This subsection addresses skylights with light-transmitting plastic glazing.

- Area limitations of this section do not apply to skylights in the following cases:
  - Where the building is sprinklered as per NFPA 13.
  - Where the building is equipped with the following:
    Smoke vents.
    Heat vents.

    Note: Section 910, "Smoke and Heat Vents," is cited as governing such devices as indicated above.

- Otherwise, the table below provides a partial list of maximum sizes permitted for skylights as follows:
  - Area inside the curb must ≤ 100 sf for an individual skylight.

Table 2610.4   Maximum Sizes Permitted for Skylights

Given width	Max. length	Given width	Max. length	Given width	Max. length	Given width	Max. length
1'-0"	100'-0"	3'-6"	28'-6"	6'-0"	16'-8"	8'-6"	11'-9"
1'-2"	85'-8"	3'-8"	27'-3"	6'-2"	16'-2"	8'-8"	11'-6"
1'-4"	75'-0"	3'-10"	26'-1"	6'-4"	15'-9"	8'-10"	11'-3"
1'-6"	66'-8"	4'-0"	25'-0"	6'-6"	15'-4"	9'-0"	11'-1"
1'-8"	60'-0"	4'-2"	24'-0"	6'-8"	15'-0"	9'-2"	10'-10"
1'-10"	54'-6"	4'-4"	23'-1"	6'-10"	14'-7"	9'-4"	10'-8"
2'-0"	50'-0"	4'-6"	22'-2"	7'-0"	14'-3"	9'-6"	10'-6"
2'-2"	46'-1"	4'-8"	21'-5"	7'-2"	13'-11"	9'-8"	10'-4"
2'-4"	42'-10"	4'-10"	20'-8"	7'-4"	13'-7"	9'-10"	10'-2"
2'-6"	40'-0"	5'-0"	20'-0"	7'-6"	13'-4"	10'-0"	10'-0"
2'-8"	37'-6"	5'-2"	19'-4"	7'-8"	13'-0"	10'-2"	9'-10"
2'-10"	35'-3"	5'-4"	18'-9"	7'-10"	12'-9"	10'-4"	9'-8"
3'-0"	33'-4"	5'-6"	18'-2"	8'-0"	12'-6"	10'-6'	9'-6"
3'-2"	31'-7"	5'-8"	17'-7"	8'-2"	12'-2"	10'-8"	9'-4"
3'-4"	30'-0"	5'-10"	17'-1"	8'-4"	12'-0"	10'-10"	9'-2"

2610 Light-Transmitting Plastic Skylight Glazing

2610.5 Aggregate area of skylights *(part 1 of 3)*

This subsection addresses skylights with light-transmitting plastic glazing.

- The sum of the areas of skylights on a roof is limited based on the size of the floor area served as shown in the illustration provided.
- Higher limits are permitted where one of the following is present:
  - Sprinklers as per NFPA 13.
  - Smoke and heat vents.

    Note: Section 910, "Smoke and Heat Vents," is cited as governing such devices as indicated above.

- Tables are provided with partial lists of skylight sizes complying with the limits of this section.

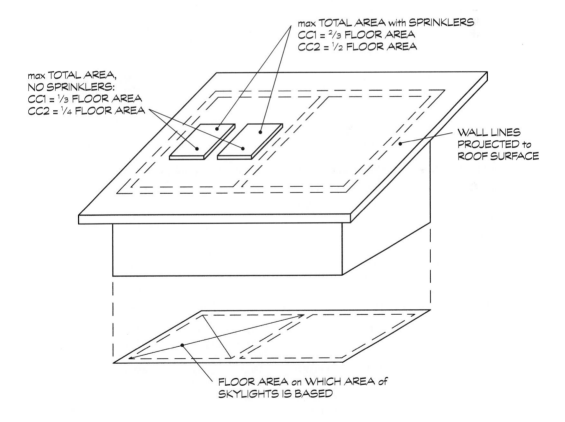

Fig. 26010.5. Maximum area of skylights with light-transmitting plastic glazing.

2610 Light-Transmitting Plastic Skylight Glazing

2610.5 Aggregate area of skylights *(part 2 of 3)*

- The maximum permitted sum of skylight areas with CC1-class plastic is as follows:
  - Total area be ≤ $^1/_3$ the floor area served where no sprinklers or vents are provided.

Table 2510.5a   Maximum Total Skylight Area for CC1 Plastics with No Sprinklers or Vents

Floor area (sf)	Maximum panel area (sf)	Floor area (sf)	Maximum panel area (sf)	Floor area (sf)	Maximum panel area (sf)	Floor area (sf)	Maximum panel area (sf)
100	33.33	1300	433.33	2500	833.33	3700	1233.33
200	66.67	1400	466.67	2600	866.67	3800	1266.67
300	100.00	1500	500.00	2700	900.00	3900	1300.00
400	133.33	1600	533.33	2800	933.33	4000	1333.33
500	166.67	1700	566.67	2900	966.67	4100	1366.67
600	200.00	1800	600.00	3000	1000.00	4200	1400.00
700	233.33	1900	633.33	3100	1033.33	4300	1433.33
800	266.67	2000	666.67	3200	1066.67	4400	1466.67
900	300.00	2100	700.00	3300	1100.00	4500	1500.00
1000	333.33	2200	733.33	3400	1133.33	4600	1533.33
1100	366.67	2300	766.67	3500	1166.67	4700	1566.67
1200	400.00	2400	800.00	3600	1200.00	4800	1600.00

- The maximum permitted sum of skylight areas with CC1-class plastic is as follows:
  - Total area be ≤ $^2/_3$ the floor area served with sprinklers or vents provided.

Table 2610.5b   Maximum Total Skylight Area for CC1 Plastics with Sprinklers or Vents

Floor area (sf)	Maximum panel area (sf)	Floor area (sf)	Maximum panel area (sf)	Floor area (sf)	Maximum panel area (sf)	Floor area (sf)	Maximum panel area (sf)
100	66.67	1300	866.67	2500	1666.67	3700	2466.67
200	133.33	1400	933.33	2600	1733.33	3800	2533.33
300	200.00	1500	1000.00	2700	1800.00	3900	2600.00
400	266.67	1600	1066.67	2800	1866.67	4000	2666.67
500	333.33	1700	1133.33	2900	1933.33	4100	2733.33
600	400.00	1800	1200.00	3000	2000.00	4200	2800.00
700	466.67	1900	1266.67	3100	2066.67	4300	2866.67
800	533.33	2000	1333.33	3200	2133.33	4400	2933.33
900	600.00	2100	1400.00	3300	2200.00	4500	3000.00
1000	666.67	2200	1466.67	3400	2266.67	4600	3066.67
1100	733.33	2300	1533.33	3500	2333.33	4700	3133.33
1200	800.00	2400	1600.00	3600	2400.00	4800	3200.00

2610 Light-Transmitting Plastic Skylight Glazing

2610.5 Aggregate area of skylights *(part 3 of 3)*

- The maximum permitted sum of skylight areas with CC2-class plastic is as follows:
  - Total area be ≤ ¼ the floor area served where no sprinklers or vents are provided.

Table 2610.5c   Maximum Total Skylight Area for CC2 Plastics with No Sprinklers or Vents

Floor area (sf)	Maximum panel area (sf)	Floor area (sf)	Maximum panel area (sf)	Floor area (sf)	Maximum panel area (sf)	Floor area (sf)	Maximum panel area (sf)
100	25	1300	325	2500	625	3700	925
200	50	1400	350	2600	650	3800	950
300	75	1500	375	2700	675	3900	975
400	100	1600	400	2800	700	4000	1000
500	125	1700	425	2900	725	4100	1025
600	150	1800	450	3000	750	4200	1050
700	175	1900	475	3100	775	4300	1075
800	200	2000	500	3200	800	4400	1100
900	225	2100	525	3300	825	4500	1125
1000	250	2200	550	3400	850	4600	1150
1100	275	2300	575	3500	875	4700	1175
1200	300	2400	600	3600	900	4800	1200

- The maximum permitted sum of skylight areas with CC2-class plastic is as follows:
  - Total area be ≤ ½ the floor area served with sprinklers or vents provided.

Table 2610.5d   Maximum Total Skylight Area for CC2 Plastics with Sprinklers or Vents

Floor area (sf)	Maximum panel area (sf)	Floor area (sf)	Maximum panel area (sf)	Floor area (sf)	Maximum panel area (sf)	Floor area (sf)	Maximum panel area (sf)
100	50	1300	650	2500	1250	3700	1850
200	100	1400	700	2600	1300	3800	1900
300	150	1500	750	2700	1350	3900	1950
400	200	1600	800	2800	1400	4000	2000
500	250	1700	850	2900	1450	4100	2050
600	300	1800	900	3000	1500	4200	2100
700	350	1900	950	3100	1550	4300	2150
800	400	2000	1000	3200	1600	4400	2200
900	450	2100	1050	3300	1650	4500	2250
1000	500	2200	1100	3400	1700	4600	2300
1100	550	2300	1150	3500	1750	4700	2350
1200	600	2400	1200	3600	1800	4800	2400

Case study: Fig. 2610.5. There are 4 light-transmitting polycarbonate (CC1) plastic skylights serving the atrium shown. The area of each 10' ×10' skylight is not limited due to the fact that the building is sprinklered. The aggregate area of the skylights is limited to $2/3$ of the area they serve (twice the $1/3$ limit for non-sprinklered buildings). In this case, the 400 sf total area of the 4 skylights is < the 1410 sf limit. Separation of the skylights is not governed since the building is sprinklered. The skylights are in compliance with code requirements.

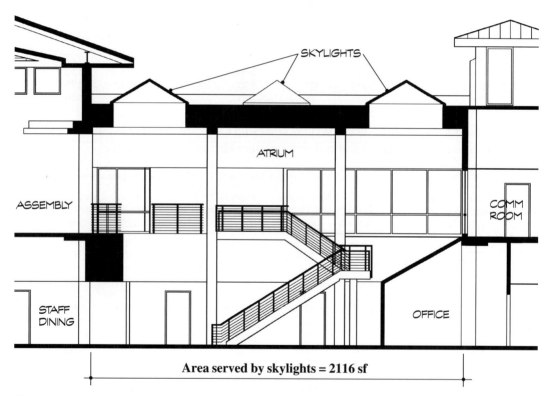

Area served by skylights = 2116 sf

Fig. 2610.5. Section at atrium. Lee's Summit Police and Court Facility. Lee's Summit, Missouri. The Hollis and Miller Group, Inc. Lee's Summit, Missouri.

2610 Light-Transmitting Plastic Skylight Glazing

2610.6 Separation

This subsection addresses skylights with light-transmitting plastic glazing.

- This section does not address the following:
  - Buildings sprinklered as per NFPA 13.
  - In occupancy R-3 with both the following characteristics:
    Multiple skylights above the same space.
    Sum of areas ≤ 100 sf.
- Otherwise, skylights must be separated as shown in the illustration provided.

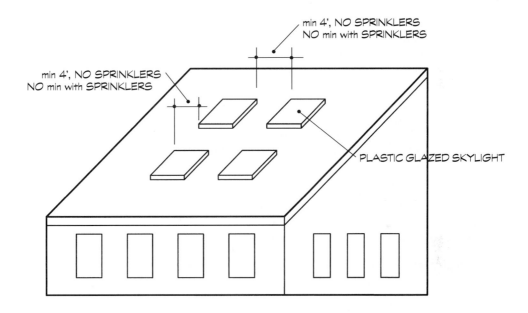

Fig. 2610.6. Minimum separation of skylights with light-transmitting plastic glazing measured in a horizontal plane.

2611 Light-Transmitting Plastic Interior Signs

2611.2 Aggregate area

- Wall signs of light-transmitting plastics in covered mall buildings may not be > 20% of the wall area as follows:
  - A partial list of signs within this limit is provided below:

Table 2611.2   **Areas of Interior Signs Permitted Based on Wall Area**

Wall area (sf)	Sign area (sf)	Wall area (sf)	Sign area (sf)	Wall area (sf)	Sign area (sf)	Wall area (sf)	Sign area (sf)
73	14.60	85	17.00	97	19.40	109	21.80
74	14.80	86	17.20	98	19.60	110	22.00
75	15.00	87	17.40	99	19.80	111	22.20
76	15.20	88	17.60	100	20.00	112	22.40
77	15.40	89	17.80	101	20.20	113	22.60
78	15.60	90	18.00	102	20.40	114	22.80
79	15.80	91	18.20	103	20.60	115	23.00
80	16.00	92	18.40	104	20.80	116	23.20
81	16.20	93	18.60	105	21.00	117	23.40
82	16.40	94	18.80	106	21.20	118	23.60
83	16.60	95	19.00	107	21.40	119	23.80
84	16.80	96	19.20	108	21.60	120	24.00

2611.3 Maximum area

- Wall signs of light-transmitting plastics in covered mall buildings may not be > 24 sf as follows:
  - A partial list of signs within this limit is provided below:

Table 2611.3   **Dimensions of Interior Signs ≤ 24 sf in Area**

Width	Length	Width	Length	Width	Length	Width	Length
1'-0"	24'-0"	2'-0"	12'-0"	3'-0"	8'-0"	4'-0"	6'-0"
1'-1"	22'-1"	2'-1"	11'-6"	3'-1"	7'-9"	4'-1"	5'-10"
1'-2"	20'-6"	2'-2"	11'-1"	3'-2"	7'-7"	4'-2"	5'-9"
1'-3"	19'-2"	2'-3"	10'-8"	3'-3"	7'-4"	4'-3"	5'-7"
1'-4"	18'-0"	2'-4"	10'-3"	3'-4"	7'-2"	4'-4"	5'-6"
1'-5"	16'-11"	2'-5"	9'-11"	3'-5"	7'-0"	4'-5"	5'-5"
1'-6"	16'-0"	2'-6"	9'-7"	3'-6"	6'-10"	4'-6"	5'-4"
1'-7"	15'-1"	2'-7"	9'-3"	3'-7"	6'-8"	4'-7"	5'-2"
1'-8"	14'-4"	2'-8"	9'-0"	3'-8"	6'-6"	4'-8"	5'-1"
1'-9"	13'-8"	2'-9"	8'-8"	3'-9"	6'-4"	4'-9"	5'-0"
1'-10"	13'-1"	2'-10"	8'-5"	3'-10"	6'-3"	4'-10"	4'-11"
1'-11"	12'-6"	2'-11"	8'-2"	3'-11"	6'-1"	4'-11"	4'-10"

2611 Light-Transmitting Plastic Interior Signs

2611.4 Encasement

This subsection addresses interior signs of light-transmitting plastic wall signs in covered mall buildings.

- Edge requirements for such signs are shown in the illustration provided.

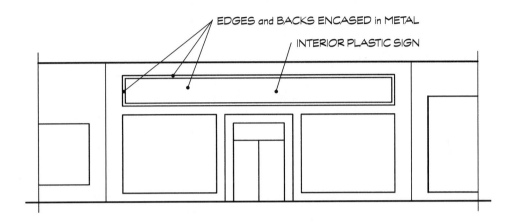

Fig. 2611.4. Light-transmitting plastic wall signs in covered mall buildings.

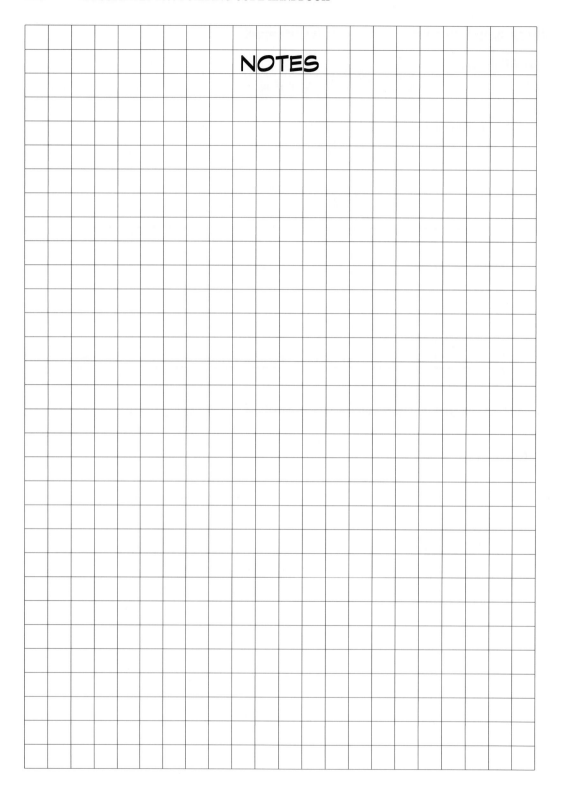

NOTES

27

Electrical

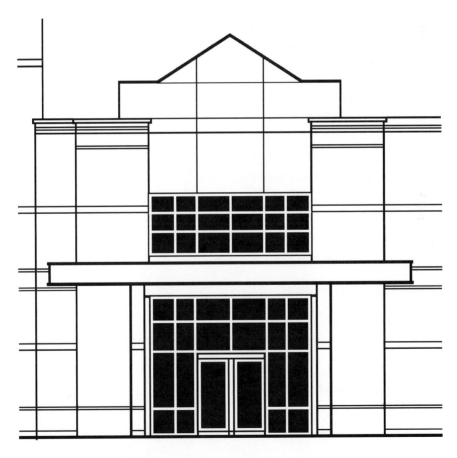

Methodist Community Health Center. Sugar Land, Texas. *(partial elevation)*
HKS, Inc., Architects, Engineers, Planners. Dallas, Texas.

2702 Emergency and Standby Power Systems

2701.2 Where required

- Emergency power systems are required for the following:
  - Voice communication systems in occupancy A.
  - Exit signs.
  - Means of egress illumination.
  - Semiconductor fabrication facilities.
  - Exit signs in temporary tents and membrane structures.
  - Occupancies with toxic or highly toxic materials.
  - Occupancies with pyrophoric materials.
  - High-rise buildings for the following:
    Fire command center.
    Fire pumps.
    Emergency voice/alarm communication systems.
    Lighting for mechanical equipment rooms.
    Elevators.
  - Underground buildings.
  - Doors in occupancy I-3.
- Standby power systems are required for the following:
  - Smoke control systems.
  - Elevators that are in an accessible means of egress.
  - Horizontal sliding doors.
  - Auxiliary inflation systems for membrane structures.
  - Occupancies with organic peroxides.
  - Emergency voice/alarm communication systems as follows:
    In covered mall buildings > 50,000 sf.
  - High-rise buildings for the following:
    Fire command center.
    Fire pumps.
    Emergency voice/alarm communication systems.
    Lighting for mechanical equipment rooms.
    Elevators.
  - Airport traffic control towers.
  - Elevators.
  - Smoke-proof enclosures.
- One of the following systems is required in the location indicated below:
  - Systems:
    Emergency power system.
    Standby power system.
  - Location:
    Occupancies with hazardous materials.

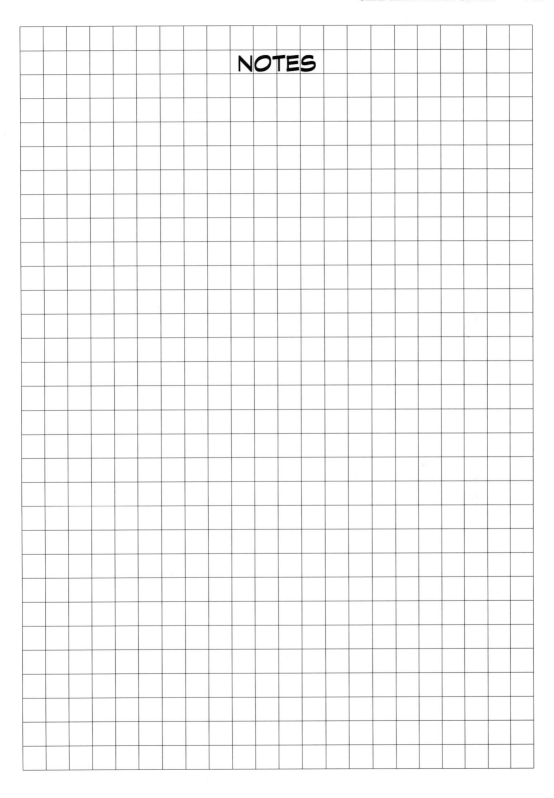

NOTES

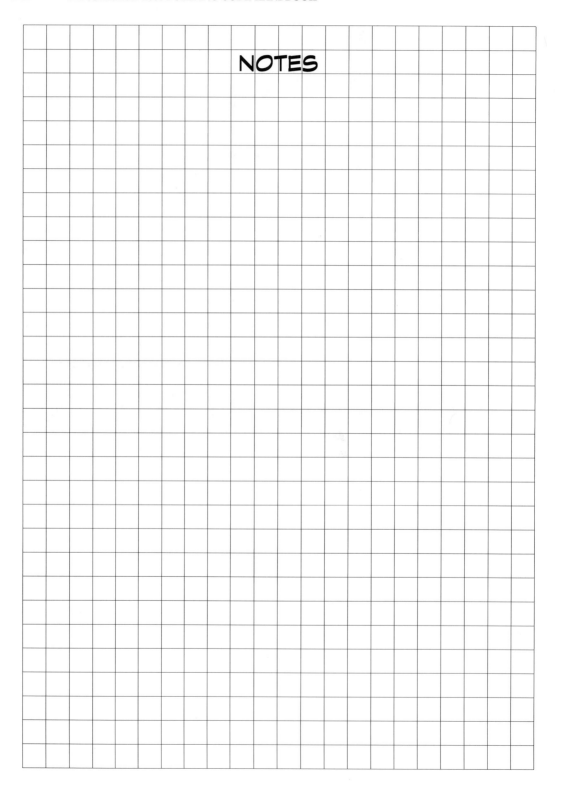

28

Mechanical Systems

Glad Tidings Assembly of God Church. Naticoke, Pennsylvania.
Mullins and Weida, Architect and Associate. Bear Creek, Pennsylvania.

2801 General

2801.1 Scope

- The following components are governed by the codes indicated below:
    - Components:
        Mechanical appliances.
        Mechanical equipment.
        Mechanical systems.
    - Codes:
        International Mechanical Code.
        International Fuel Gas Code.
- The following components are governed by the codes indicated below:
    - Components:
        Masonry chimneys.
        Fireplaces.
        Barbecues.
    - Codes:
        Chapter 21, "Masonry."
        International Mechanical Code.

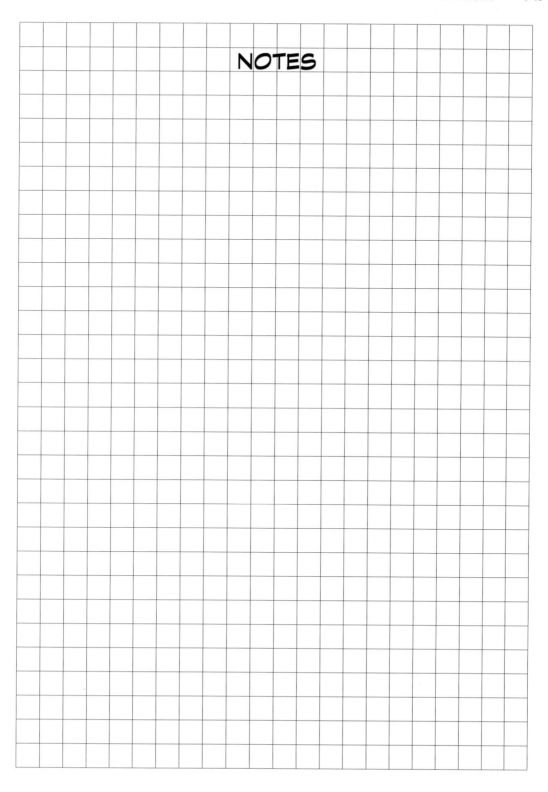

NOTES

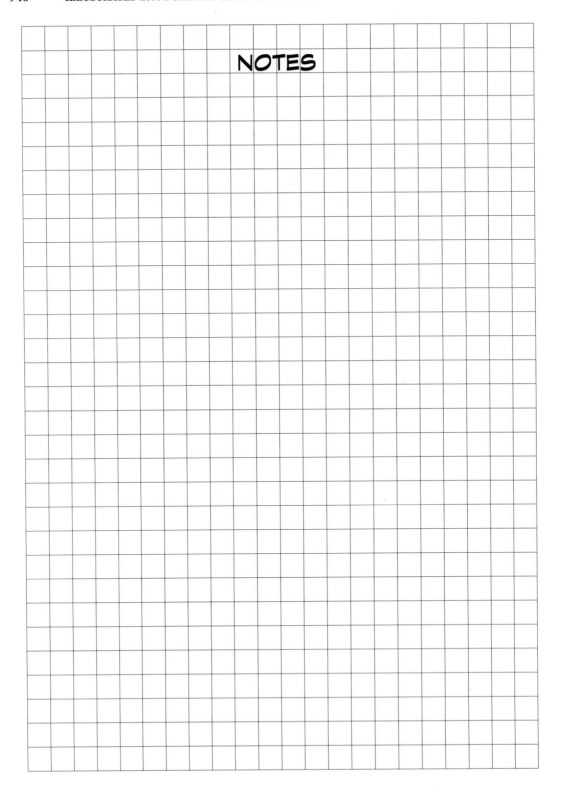

NOTES

29

Plumbing Systems

Creston Elementary Multipurpose Building. Creston, California.
Phillips Metsch Sweeney Moore Architects. Santa Barbara, California.

2902 Minimum Plumbing Facilities

2902.1 Minimum number of fixtures *(part 1 of 19)*

- Partial lists of plumbing fixtures required for various occupancies are provided in this section.
- Minimums for occupancies not listed will be determined by the building official.
- Where not indicated otherwise, ≥ 1 service sink is required for all occupancies.
- In each toilet room, urinals may be installed in lieu of ≤ ½ the required water closets.
- Drinking fountains are not required in the following locations:
  - Where restaurants serve water.
  - Where bottled-water coolers are provided.

> *Note: IBC Table 2902.1, "Minimum Number of Plumbing Facilities," is cited as governing the number of occupants served by 1 fixture of each type. See the code table where occupant counts are larger than those shown in the tables provided in this section.*
>
> *Chapter 3, "Use and Occupancy Classification," is cited as governing occupancy designations.*
>
> *The following sections of the International Plumbing Code are cited:*
>
> *419.2, "Substitution for water closets," permits the substitution of urinals for water closets as summarized above.*
>
> *410.1, "Approval," permits omitting drinking fountains as summarized above.*

Table 2902.1a   Restaurants: Minimum Plumbing Fixtures Required

Occupant count	WC men	WC women	Lavs	DF	Occupant count	WC men	WC women	Lavs	DF
1–75	1	1	1	1	376–400	6	6	2	1
76–150	2	2	1	1	401–450	6	6	3	1
151–200	3	3	1	1	451–500	7	7	3	1
201–225	3	3	2	1	501–525	7	7	3	2
226–300	4	4	2	1	526–600	8	8	3	2
301–375	5	5	2	1	601–675	9	9	4	2

Source: IBC Table 2902.1.

2902 Minimum Plumbing Facilities

2902.1 Minimum number of fixtures *(part 2 of 19)*

- The following plumbing fixtures must be made available when the church is occupied:
  - Located in adjacent buildings owned and controlled by the church.

Table 2902.1b   **Churches: Minimum Plumbing Fixtures Required**

Occupant count	WC men	WC women	Lavs	DF	Occupant count	WC men	WC women	Lavs	DF
1–75	1	1	1	1	451–525	4	7	3	1
76–150	1	2	1	1	526–600	4	8	3	1
151–200	2	3	1	1	601–675	5	9	4	1
201–225	2	3	2	1	676–750	5	10	4	1
226–300	2	4	2	1	751–800	6	11	4	1
301–375	3	5	2	1	801–825	6	11	5	1
376–400	3	6	2	1	826–900	6	12	5	1
401–450	3	6	3	1	901–975	7	13	5	1

Source: IBC Table 2902.1.

Table 2902.1c   **Nightclubs: Minimum Plumbing Fixtures Required**

Occupant count	WC men	WC women	Lavs	DF	Occupant count	WC men	WC women	Lavs	DF
1–40	1	1	1	1	226–240	6	6	4	1
41–75	2	2	1	1	241–280	7	7	4	1
76–80	2	2	2	1	281–300	8	8	4	1
81–120	3	3	2	1	301–320	8	8	5	1
121–150	4	4	2	1	321–360	9	9	5	1
151–160	4	4	3	1	361–375	10	10	5	1
161–200	5	5	3	1	376–400	10	10	6	1
201–225	6	6	3	1	401–440	11	11	6	1

Source: IBC Table 2902.1.

2902 Minimum Plumbing Facilities

2902.1 Minimum number of fixtures *(part 3 of 19)*

Table 2902.1d   Theaters, Halls, Museums, etc: Minimum Plumbing Fixtures Required

Occupant count	WC men	WC women	Lavs	DF	Occupant count	WC men	WC women	Lavs	DF
1–65	1	1	1	1	751–780	7	12	4	2
66–125	1	2	1	1	781–800	7	13	4	2
126–130	2	2	1	1	801–845	7	13	5	2
131–195	2	3	1	1	846–875	7	14	5	2
196–200	2	4	1	1	876–910	8	14	5	2
201–250	2	4	2	1	911–975	8	15	5	2
251–260	3	4	2	1	976–1000	8	16	5	2
261–325	3	5	2	1	1001–1040	9	16	6	3
326–375	3	6	2	1	1041–1105	9	17	6	3
376–390	4	6	2	1	1106–1125	9	18	6	3
391–400	4	7	2	1	1126–1170	10	18	6	3
401–455	4	7	3	1	1171–1200	10	19	6	3
456–500	4	8	3	1	1201–1235	10	19	7	3
501–520	5	8	3	2	1236–1250	10	20	7	3
521–585	5	9	3	2	1251–1300	11	20	7	3
586–600	5	10	3	2	1301–1365	11	21	7	3
601–625	5	10	4	2	1366–1375	11	22	7	3
626–650	6	10	4	2	1376–1400	12	22	7	3
651–715	6	11	4	2	1401–1430	12	22	8	3
716–750	6	12	4	2	1431–1495	12	23	8	3

Source: IBC Table 2902.1.

2902 Minimum Plumbing Facilities

2902.1 Minimum number of fixtures *(part 4 of 19)*

Table 2902.1e   Coliseums and Arenas 1–1725 Seats: Minimum Plumbing Fixtures Required

Occupant count	WC men	WC women	Lavs	DF	Occupant count	WC men	WC women	Lavs	DF
1–40	1	1	1	1	881–900	12	23	6	1
41–75	1	2	1	1	901–920	13	23	7	1
76–80	2	2	1	1	921–960	13	24	7	1
81–120	2	3	1	1	961–975	13	25	7	1
121–150	2	4	1	1	976–1000	14	25	7	1
151–160	3	4	2	1	1001–1040	14	26	7	2
161–200	3	5	2	1	1041–1050	14	27	7	2
201–225	3	6	2	1	1051–1080	15	28	8	2
226–240	4	6	2	1	1081–1120	15	29	8	2
241–280	4	7	2	1	1121–1125	15	30	8	2
281–300	4	8	2	1	1126–1160	16	30	8	2
301–320	5	8	3	1	1161–1200	16	30	8	2
321–360	5	9	3	1	1201–1240	17	31	9	2
361–375	5	10	3	1	1241–1275	17	32	9	2
376–400	6	10	3	1	1276–1280	18	32	9	2
401–440	6	11	3	1	1281–1320	18	33	9	2
441–450	6	12	3	1	1321–1350	18	34	9	2
451–480	7	12	4	1	1351–1360	19	34	10	2
481–520	7	13	4	1	1361–1400	19	35	10	2
521–525	7	14	4	1	1401–1425	19	36	10	2
526–560	8	14	4	1	1426–1440	20	36	10	2
561–600	8	15	4	1	1441–1480	20	37	10	2
601–640	9	16	5	1	1481–1500	20	38	10	2
641–675	9	17	5	1	1501–1520	21	38	11	2
676–680	10	17	5	1	1521–1560	21	39	11	2
681–720	10	18	5	1	1561–1575	21	40	11	2
721–750	10	19	5	1	1576–1600	22	40	11	2
751–760	11	19	6	1	1601–1640	22	41	11	2
761–800	11	20	6	1	1641–1650	22	42	11	2
801–825	11	21	6	1	1651–1680	23	42	12	2
826–840	12	21	6	1	1681–1720	23	43	12	2
841–880	12	22	6	1	1721–1725	23	44	12	2

Source: IBC Table 2902.1.

2902 Minimum Plumbing Facilities

2902.1 Minimum number of fixtures *(part 5 of 19)*

Table 2902.1f   Coliseums and Arenas 1726–2999 Seats: Minimum Plumbing Fixtures Required

Occupant count	WC men	WC women	Lavs	DF	Occupant count	WC men	WC women	Lavs	DF
1726–1760	24	44	12	2	2401–2440	33	61	17	3
1761–1800	24	45	12	2	2441–2475	33	62	17	3
1801–1840	25	46	13	2	2476–2480	34	62	17	3
1841–1875	25	47	13	2	2481–2500	34	63	17	3
1876–1880	26	47	13	2	2501–2520	34	63	17	3
1881–1920	26	48	13	2	2521–2550	34	64	17	3
1921–1950	26	49	13	2	2551–2560	35	64	18	3
1951–1960	27	49	14	2	2561–2600	35	65	18	3
1961–2000	27	50	14	2	2601–2625	35	66	18	3
2001–2025	27	51	14	3	2626–2640	36	66	18	3
2026–2040	28	51	14	3	2641–2680	36	67	18	3
2041–2080	28	52	14	3	2681–2700	36	68	18	3
2081–2100	28	53	14	3	2701–2720	37	68	19	3
2101–2120	29	53	15	3	2726–2760	37	69	19	3
2120–2160	29	54	15	3	2761–2775	37	70	19	3
2161–2175	29	55	15	3	2776–2800	38	70	19	3
2176–2200	30	55	15	3	2801–2840	38	71	19	3
2201–2240	30	56	15	3	2841–2850	38	72	19	3
2241–2250	30	57	15	3	2851–2880	39	72	20	3
2251–2280	31	57	16	3	2881–2920	39	73	20	3
2281–2320	31	58	16	3	2921–2925	39	74	20	3
2231–2325	31	59	16	3	2926–2960	40	74	20	3
2326–2360	32	59	16	3	2961–2980	40	75	20	3
2361–2400	32	60	16	3	2981–2999	40	75	20	3

Source: IBC Table 2902.1.

2902 Minimum Plumbing Facilities

2902.1 Minimum number of fixtures *(part 6 of 19)*

Table 2902.1g   Coliseums and Arenas > 3000 Seats: Minimum Plumbing Fixtures Required

Occupant count	WC m	WC w	Lavs m	Lavs w	DF	Occupant count	WC m	WC w	Lavs m	Lavs w	DF
3000	25	50	15	20	3	4501–4560	38	76	23	31	5
3001–3060	26	51	16	21	4	4561–4600	39	77	23	31	5
3061–3120	26	52	16	21	4	4601–4620	39	77	24	31	5
3121–3150	27	53	16	21	4	4621–4650	39	78	24	31	5
3151–3180	27	53	16	22	4	4651–4680	39	78	24	32	5
3181–3200	27	54	16	22	4	4681–4740	40	79	24	32	5
3201–3240	27	54	17	22	4	4741–4800	40	80	24	32	5
3241–3300	28	55	17	22	4	4801–4860	41	80	25	33	5
3301–3360	28	56	17	23	4	4861–4920	41	81	25	33	5
3361–3400	29	57	17	23	4	4921–4950	42	82	25	33	5
3401–3420	29	57	18	23	4	4951–4980	42	82	25	34	5
3421–3450	29	58	18	23	4	4981–5000	42	83	25	34	5
3451–3480	29	58	18	24	4	5001–5040	42	83	26	34	6
3481–3540	30	59	18	24	4	5041–5100	43	84	26	34	6
3541–3600	30	60	18	24	4	5101–5160	43	85	26	35	6
3601–3660	31	61	19	25	4	5161–5200	44	86	26	35	6
3661–3720	31	62	19	25	4	5201–5220	44	86	27	35	6
3721–3750	32	63	19	25	4	5221–5250	44	87	27	35	6
3751–3780	32	63	19	26	4	5251–5280	44	87	27	36	6
3781–3800	32	64	19	26	4	5281–5340	45	88	27	36	6
3801–3840	32	64	20	26	4	5341–5400	45	89	27	36	6
3841–3900	33	65	20	26	4	5401–5460	46	90	28	37	6
3901–3960	33	66	20	27	4	5461–5520	46	91	28	37	6
3961–4000	34	67	20	27	4	5521–5550	47	92	28	37	6
4001–4020	34	67	21	27	5	5551–5580	47	92	28	38	6
4021–4050	34	68	21	27	5	5581–5600	47	93	28	39	6
4051–4080	34	68	21	28	5	5601–5640	47	93	29	39	6
4081–4140	35	69	21	28	5	5641–5700	48	94	29	39	6
4141–4200	35	70	21	28	5	5701–5760	48	95	29	40	6
4201–4260	36	71	22	29	5	5761–5800	49	96	29	40	6
4261–4320	36	72	22	29	5	5801–5820	49	96	30	40	6
4320–4350	37	73	22	29	5	5821–5850	49	97	30	40	6
4351–4380	37	73	22	30	5	5851–5880	49	97	30	41	6
4381–4400	37	74	22	30	5	5881–5940	50	98	30	41	6
4401–4440	37	74	23	30	5	5941–6000	50	99	30	41	6
4441–4500	38	75	23	30	5	6001–6060	51	100	31	42	7

Source: IBC Table 2902.1.

2902 Minimum Plumbing Facilities

2902.1 Minimum number of fixtures *(part 7 of 19)*

Table 2902.1h   Stadiums and Pools < 3000 Seats: Minimum Plumbing Fixtures Required

Occupant count	WC men	WC women	Lavs	DF	Occupant count	WC men	WC women	Lavs	DF
1–50	1	1	1	1	1501–1550	16	31	11	2
51–100	1	2	1	1	1551–1600	16	32	11	2
101–150	2	3	1	1	1601–1650	17	33	11	2
151–200	2	4	2	1	1651–1700	17	34	12	2
201–250	3	5	2	1	1701–1750	18	35	12	2
251–300	3	6	2	1	1751–1800	18	36	12	2
301–350	4	7	3	1	1801–1850	19	37	13	2
351–400	4	8	3	1	1851–1900	19	38	13	2
401–450	5	9	3	1	1901–1950	20	39	13	2
451–500	5	10	4	1	1951–2000	20	40	14	2
501–550	6	11	4	1	2001–2050	21	41	14	3
551–600	6	12	4	1	2051–2100	21	42	14	3
601–650	7	13	5	1	2101–2150	22	43	15	3
651–700	7	14	5	1	2151–2200	22	44	15	3
701–750	8	15	5	1	2201–2250	23	45	15	3
751–800	8	16	6	1	2251–2300	23	46	16	3
801–850	9	17	6	1	2301–2350	24	47	16	3
851–900	9	18	6	1	2351–2400	24	48	16	3
901–950	10	19	7	1	2401–2450	25	49	17	3
951–1000	10	20	7	1	2451–2500	25	50	17	3
1001–1050	11	21	7	2	2501–2550	26	51	17	3
1051–1100	11	22	8	2	2551–2600	26	52	18	3
1101–1150	12	23	8	2	2601–2650	27	53	18	3
1151–1200	12	24	8	2	2651–2700	27	54	18	3
1201–1250	13	25	9	2	2701–2750	28	55	19	3
1251–1300	13	26	9	2	2751–2800	28	56	19	3
1301–1350	14	27	9	2	2801–2850	29	57	19	3
1351–1400	14	28	10	2	2851–2900	29	58	20	3
1401–1450	15	29	10	2	2901–2950	30	59	20	3
1451–1500	15	30	10	2	2951–2999	30	60	20	3

Source: IBC Table 2902.1.

2902 Minimum Plumbing Facilities

2902.1 Minimum number of fixtures *(part 8 of 19)*

Table 2902.1i   **Stadiums 17,100–21,375 Seats: Minimum Plumbing Fixtures Required**

Occupant count	WC m	WC w	Lavs m	Lavs w	DF	Occupant count	WC m	WC w	Lavs m	Lavs w	DF
17,100	114	228	86	114	18	19,201–19,275	128	257	98	128	20
17,101–17,175	115	229	86	115	18	19,276–19,350	129	258	98	129	20
17,176–17,200	115	229	86	115	18	19,351–19,400	130	258	98	130	20
17,201–17,250	115	230	87	115	18	19,401–19,425	130	259	99	130	20
17,251–17,325	116	231	87	116	18	19,426–19,500	130	260	99	130	20
17,326–17,400	116	232	87	116	18	19,501–19,575	131	261	99	131	20
17,401–17,475	117	233	88	117	18	19,576–19,600	131	261	99	131	20
17,476–17,550	117	234	88	117	18	19,601–19,650	131	262	100	131	20
17,551–17,600	117	234	88	117	18	19,651–19,725	132	263	100	132	20
17,601–17,625	118	235	89	118	18	19,726–19,800	132	264	100	132	20
17,626–17,700	118	236	89	118	18	19,801–19,875	133	265	101	133	20
17,701–17,775	119	237	89	119	18	19,876–19,950	133	266	101	133	20
17,776–17,800	119	237	89	119	18	19,951–20,000	134	266	101	134	20
17,801–17,850	119	238	90	119	18	20,001–20,025	134	267	102	134	21
17,851–17,925	120	239	90	120	18	20,026–20,100	134	268	102	134	21
17,926–18,000	120	240	90	120	18	20,101–20,175	135	269	102	135	21
18,001–18,075	121	241	91	121	19	20,176–20,200	135	269	102	135	21
18,076–18,150	121	242	91	121	19	20,201–20,250	135	270	103	135	22
18,151–18,200	122	242	91	122	19	20,251–20,325	136	271	103	136	22
18,201–18,225	122	243	92	122	19	20,326–20,400	136	272	103	136	22
18,226–18,300	122	244	92	122	19	20,401–20,475	137	273	104	137	23
18,301–18,375	123	245	92	123	19	20,476–20,550	137	274	104	137	23
18,376–18,400	123	245	92	123	19	20,551–20,600	138	274	104	138	23
18,401–18,450	123	246	93	123	19	20,601–20,625	138	275	105	138	24
18,451–18,525	124	247	93	124	19	20,626–20,700	138	276	105	138	24
18,526–18,600	124	248	93	124	19	20,701–20,775	139	277	105	139	24
18,601–18,675	125	249	94	125	19	20,776–20,800	139	277	105	139	24
18,676–18,750	125	250	94	125	19	20,801–20,850	139	278	107	139	25
18,751–18,800	126	250	94	126	19	20,851–20,925	140	279	107	140	25
18,801–18,825	126	251	95	126	19	20,926–21,000	140	280	107	140	25
18,826–18,900	126	252	95	126	19	21,001–21,075	141	281	108	141	26
18,901–18,975	127	253	95	127	19	21,076–21,150	141	282	108	141	26
18,976–19,000	127	253	95	127	19	21,151–21,200	142	282	108	142	26
19,001–19,050	127	254	97	127	20	21,201–21,225	142	283	109	142	27
19,051–19,125	128	255	97	128	20	21,226–21,300	142	284	109	142	27
19,126–19,200	128	256	97	128	20	21,301–21,375	143	285	109	143	27

Source: IBC Table 2902.1.

2902 Minimum Plumbing Facilities

2902.1 Minimum number of fixtures *(part 9 of 19)*

Table 2902.1j   Stadiums 31,050–35,325 Seats: Minimum Plumbing Fixtures Required

Occupant count	WC m	WC w	Lavs m	Lavs w	DF	Occupant count	WC m	WC w	Lavs m	Lavs w	DF
31,050	207	414	156	207	32	33,201–33,225	222	443	267	222	34
31,051–31,125	208	415	156	208	32	33,226–33,300	222	444	267	222	34
31,126–31,200	208	416	156	208	32	33,301–33,375	223	445	167	223	34
31,201–31,275	209	417	157	209	32	33,376–33,400	223	446	167	223	34
31,276–31,350	209	418	157	209	32	33,376–33,450	223	446	168	223	34
31,351–31,400	210	419	157	210	32	33,451–33,525	224	448	168	224	34
31,401–31,425	210	419	158	210	32	33,526–33,600	224	448	168	224	34
31,426–31,500	210	420	158	210	32	33,601–33,675	225	450	169	225	34
31,501–31,575	211	421	158	211	32	33,676–33,750	225	451	169	225	34
31,576–31,600	211	421	158	211	32	33,751–33,800	226	451	169	226	34
31,601–31,650	211	422	159	211	32	33,801–33,825	226	452	170	226	34
31,651–31,725	212	423	159	212	32	33,826–33,900	226	453	170	226	34
31,726–31,800	212	424	159	212	32	33,901–33,975	227	454	170	227	34
31,801–31,875	213	425	160	213	32	33,976–34,000	227	454	170	227	34
31,876–31,950	213	426	160	213	32	34,001–34,050	227	455	171	227	35
31,951–32,000	214	427	160	214	32	34,051–34,125	228	456	171	228	35
32,001–32,025	214	427	161	214	33	34,126–34,200	228	457	171	228	35
32,026–32,100	214	428	161	214	33	34,201–34,275	229	458	172	229	35
32,101–32,175	215	429	161	215	33	34,276–34,350	229	459	172	229	35
32,176–32,200	215	430	161	215	33	34,351–34,400	230	459	172	230	35
32,201–32,250	215	430	162	215	33	34,401–34,425	230	460	173	230	35
32,251–32,325	216	431	162	216	33	34,426–34,500	230	461	173	230	35
32,326–32,400	216	432	162	216	33	34,501–34,575	231	462	173	231	35
32,401–32,475	217	433	163	217	33	34,576–34,600	231	462	173	231	35
32,476–32,550	217	434	163	217	33	34,601–34,650	231	463	174	231	35
32,551–32,600	218	435	163	218	33	34,651–34,725	232	464	174	232	35
32,601–32,625	218	435	164	218	33	34,726–34,800	232	465	174	232	35
32,626–32,700	218	436	164	218	33	34,801–34,875	233	466	175	233	35
32,701–32,775	219	437	164	219	33	34,876–34,950	233	467	175	233	35
32,776–32,800	219	438	264	219	33	34,951–35,000	234	467	175	234	35
32,801–32,850	219	438	265	219	33	35,001–35,025	234	468	176	234	36
32,851–32,925	220	439	265	220	33	35,026–35,100	234	469	176	234	36
32,026–33,000	220	440	265	220	33	35,101–35,175	235	470	176	235	36
33.001–33,075	221	441	266	221	34	35,176–35,200	235	470	176	235	36
33,076–33,150	221	442	266	221	34	35,201–35,250	235	471	177	235	36
33,151–33,200	222	443	266	222	34	35,251–35,325	236	472	177	236	36

Source: IBC Table 2902.1.

2902 Minimum Plumbing Facilities

2902.1 Minimum number of fixtures *(part 10 of 19)*

Table 2902.1k   Stadiums 45,000–49,275 Seats: Minimum Plumbing Fixtures Required

Occupant count	WC m	WC w	Lavs m	Lavs w	DF	Occupant count	WC m	WC w	Lavs m	Lavs w	DF
45,000	300	600	225	300	45	47,101–47,175	315	629	236	315	48
45,001–45,075	301	601	226	301	46	47,126–47,200	315	629	236	315	48
45,076–45,150	301	602	226	301	46	47,201–47,250	315	630	237	315	48
45,151–45,200	302	602	226	302	46	47,251–47,325	316	631	237	316	48
45,201–45,225	302	603	227	302	46	47,326–47,400	316	632	237	316	48
45,226–45,300	302	604	227	302	46	47,401–47,475	317	633	238	317	48
45,301–45,375	303	605	227	303	46	47,476–47,550	317	634	238	317	48
45,376–45,400	303	605	227	303	46	47,551–47,600	318	635	238	318	48
45,401–45,450	303	606	228	303	46	47,601–47,625	318	635	239	318	48
45,451–45,525	304	607	228	304	46	47,626–47,700	318	636	239	318	48
45,526–45,600	304	608	228	304	46	47,701–47,775	319	637	239	319	48
45,601–45,675	305	609	229	305	46	47,776–47,800	319	638	239	319	48
45,676–45,750	305	610	229	305	46	47,801–47,850	319	638	240	319	48
45,751–45,800	306	610	229	306	46	47,851–47,925	320	639	240	320	48
45,801–45,825	306	611	230	306	46	47,926–48,000	320	640	240	320	48
45,826–45,900	306	612	230	306	46	48,001–48,075	321	641	241	321	49
45,901–45,975	307	613	230	307	46	48,076–48,150	321	642	241	321	49
45,976–46,000	307	613	230	307	46	48,151–48,200	322	643	241	322	49
46,001–46,050	307	614	231	307	47	48,201–48,225	322	643	242	322	49
46,051–46,125	308	615	231	308	47	48,226–48,300	322	644	242	322	49
46,126–46,200	308	616	231	308	47	48,301–48,375	323	645	242	323	49
46,201–46,275	309	617	232	309	47	48,376–48,400	323	646	242	323	49
46,276–46,350	309	618	232	309	47	48,401–48,450	323	646	243	323	49
46,351–46,400	310	618	232	310	47	48,451–48,525	324	647	243	324	49
46,401–46,425	310	619	233	310	47	48,526–48,600	324	648	243	324	49
46,426–46,500	310	620	233	310	47	48,601–48,675	325	649	244	325	49
46,501–46,575	311	621	233	311	47	48,676–48,750	325	650	244	325	49
46,576–46,600	311	622	233	311	47	48,751–48,800	326	650	244	326	49
46,601–46,650	311	622	234	311	47	48,801–48,825	326	650	245	326	49
46,651–46,725	312	623	234	312	47	48,826–48,900	326	652	245	326	49
46,726–46,800	312	624	234	312	47	48,901–48,975	327	653	245	327	49
46,801–46,875	313	625	235	313	47	48,976–49,000	327	654	245	327	49
46,876–46,950	313	626	235	313	47	49,001–49,050	327	654	246	327	50
46,951–47,000	314	627	235	314	47	49,051–49,125	328	655	246	328	50
47,001–47,025	314	628	235	314	48	49,126–49,200	328	656	246	328	50
47,026–47,100	314	629	236	314	48	49,201–49,275	329	657	247	329	50

Source: IBC Table 2902.1.

2902 Minimum Plumbing Facilities

2902.1 Minimum number of fixtures *(part 11 of 19)*

Table 2902.1l   **Mercantile: Minimum Plumbing Fixtures Required**

Occupant count	WC	Lavs	DF	Occupant count	WC	Lavs	DF
1–500	1	1	1	1501–2000	4	3	2
501–750	2	1	1	2001–2250	5	3	3
751–1000	2	2	1	2251–2500	5	4	3
1001–1500	3	2	2	2501–3000	6	4	3

Source: IBC Table 2902.1.

Table 2902.1m   **Business: Minimum Plumbing Fixtures Required**

Occupant count	WC	Lavs	DF	Occupant count	WC	Lavs	DF
1–25	1	1	1	126–150	6	4	2
26–40	2	1	1	151–160	7	4	2
41–50	2	2	1	161–175	7	5	2
51–75	3	2	1	176–200	8	5	2
76–80	4	2	1	201–225	9	6	3
81–100	4	3	1	226–240	10	6	3
101–120	5	3	2	241–250	10	7	3
121–125	5	4	2	251–275	11	7	3

Source: IBC Table 2902.1.

Table 2902.1n   **Educational: Minimum Plumbing Fixtures Required**

Occupant count	WC	Lavs	DF	Occupant count	WC	Lavs	DF
1–50	1	1	1	801–850	17	17	9
51–100	2	2	1	851–900	18	18	9
101–150	3	3	2	901–950	19	19	10
151–200	4	4	2	951–1000	20	20	10
201–250	5	5	3	1001–1050	21	21	11
251–300	6	6	3	1051–1100	22	22	11
301–350	7	7	4	1101–1150	23	23	12
351–400	8	8	4	1151–1200	24	24	12
401–450	9	9	5	1201–1250	25	25	13
451–500	10	10	5	1251–1300	26	26	13
501–550	11	11	6	1301–1350	27	27	14
551–600	12	12	6	1351–1400	28	28	14
601–650	13	13	7	1401–1450	29	29	15
651–700	14	14	7	1451–1500	30	30	15
701–750	15	15	8	1501–1550	31	31	16
751–800	16	16	8	1551–1600	32	32	16

Source: IBC Table 2902.1.

2902 Minimum Plumbing Facilities

2902.1 Minimum number of fixtures *(part 12 of 19)*

- Factory and industrial occupancies require the following facilities, where required by the manufacturer, and other fixtures as shown in the partial table below:
  - Emergency eyewash stations.
  - Emergency showers.

Table 2902.1o   Factory and Industrial: Minimum Plumbing Fixtures Required

Occupant count	WC	Lavs	DF	Occupant count	WC	Lavs	DF
1–100	1	1	1	801–900	9	9	3
101–200	2	2	1	901–1000	10	10	3
201–300	3	3	1	1001–1100	11	11	3
301–400	4	4	1	1101–1200	12	12	3
401–500	5	5	2	1201–1300	13	13	4
501–600	6	6	2	1301–1400	14	14	4
601–700	7	7	2	1401–1500	15	15	4
701–800	8	8	2	1501–1600	16	16	4

Source: IBC Table 2902.1.

Table 2902.1p   Passenger Terminals and Transportation Facilities: Minimum Fixtures Required

Occupant count	WC	Lavs	DF	Occupant count	WC	Lavs	DF
1–500	1	1	1	7,501–8,000	16	11	8
501–750	2	1	1	8,001–8,250	17	11	9
751–1,000	2	2	1	8,251–8,500	17	12	9
1,001–1,500	3	2	2	8,501–9,000	18	12	9
1,501–2,000	4	3	2	9,001–9,500	19	13	10
2,001–2,250	5	3	3	9,501–9,750	20	13	10
2,251–2,500	5	4	3	9.751–10,000	20	14	10
2,501–3,000	6	4	3	10,001–10,500	21	14	11
3,001–3,500	7	5	4	10,501–11,000	22	15	11
3,501–3,750	8	5	4	11,001–11,250	23	15	12
3,751–4,000	8	6	4	11,251–11,500	23	16	12
4,001–4,500	9	6	5	11,501–12,000	24	16	12
4,501–5,000	10	7	5	12,001–12,500	25	17	13
5,001–5,250	11	7	6	12,501–12,750	26	17	13
5,251–5,500	11	8	6	12,751–13,000	26	18	13
5,501–6,000	12	8	6	13,001–13,500	27	18	14
6,001–6,500	13	9	7	13,501–14,000	28	19	14
6,501–6,750	14	9	7	14,001–14,250	29	19	15
6,751–7,000	14	10	7	14,251–14,500	29	20	15
7,001–7,500	15	10	8	14,500–15,000	30	20	15

Source: IBC Table 2902.1.

2902 Minimum Plumbing Facilities

2902.1 Minimum number of fixtures *(part 13 of 19)*

Table 2902.1q   Residential Care: Minimum Plumbing Fixtures Required

Occupant count	WC	Lavs	Bathtub/ shower	DF		Occupant count	WC	Lavs	Bathtub/ shower	DF
1–8	1	1	1	1		41–48	5	5	6	1
9–10	1	1	2	1		49–50	5	5	7	1
11–16	2	2	2	1		51–56	6	6	7	1
17–20	2	2	3	1		57–60	6	6	8	1
21–24	3	3	3	1		61–64	7	7	8	1
25–30	3	3	4	1		65–70	7	7	9	1
31–32	4	4	4	1		71–72	8	8	9	1
33–40	4	4	5	1		73–80	8	8	10	1

Source: IBC Table 2902.1.

- Fixtures for patients in hospitals and ambulatory nursing homes are governed as follows:
  - Employee toilets are separate from patient toilets as follows:
    They are not governed by the following requirements or table below.
  - 1 toilet room may serve 2 adjacent rooms where all of the following conditions apply:
    Toilet is for 1 occupant.
    Toilet has 1 lavatory.
    Toilet has 1 water closet.
    Toilet is directly accessed from each room with provisions for privacy.
  - Otherwise, the following is required:
    1 water closet for each room.
    1 lavatory for each room.
  - 1 service sink is required for each floor.
  - Other fixtures are required as shown in the partial table below:

Table 2902.1r   Hospitals, Ambulatory Nursing Homes: Minimum Fixtures Required for Patients

Patient count	Bathtub/ shower	DF	Patient count	Bathtud/ shower	DF	Patient count	Bathtub/ shower	DF
1–15	1	1	166–180	12	2	331–345	23	4
16–30	2	1	181–195	13	2	346–360	24	4
31–45	3	1	196–200	14	2	361–375	25	4
46–60	4	1	201–210	14	3	376–390	26	4
61–75	5	1	211–225	15	3	391–400	27	4
76–90	6	1	226–240	16	3	401–405	27	5
91–100	7	1	241–255	17	3	406–420	28	5
101–105	7	2	256–270	18	3	421–435	29	5
106–120	8	2	271–285	19	3	436–450	30	5
121–135	9	2	286–300	20	3	451–465	31	5
136–150	10	2	301–315	21	4	466–480	32	5
151–165	11	2	316–330	22	4	481–495	33	5

Source: IBC Table 2902.1.

2902 Minimum Plumbing Facilities

2902.1 Minimum number of fixtures *(part 14 of 19)*

- Fixtures for patients in day nurseries and other institutional occupancies indicated below are governed as follows:
  - Employee toilets are separate from patient toilets as follows:
    They are not governed by the following requirements or table below.
  - Day nurseries require only 1 bathtub.
  - Otherwise, fixture requirements are as shown in the table below:

Table 2902.1s   Day Nurseries, Sanitariums, Nonambulatory Nursing Homes: Minimum Plumbing Fixtures Required for Patients

Patient count	WC	Lavs	Bathtub/ shower	DF	Patient count	WC	Lavs	Bathtub/ shower	DF
1–15	1	1	1	1	106–120	8	8	8	2
16–30	2	2	2	1	121–135	9	9	9	2
31–45	3	3	3	1	136–150	10	10	10	2
46–60	4	4	4	1	151–165	11	11	11	2
61–75	5	5	5	1	166–180	12	12	12	2
76–90	6	6	6	1	181–195	13	13	13	2
91–100	7	7	7	1	196–200	14	14	14	2
101–105	7	7	7	2	201–210	14	14	14	3

Source: IBC Table 2902.1.

- Fixtures for institutional employees other than residential care are governed as follows:
  - Employee toilets are separate from patient toilets.
  - A service sink is not required to serve employees.
  - Bathing facilities are not required for employees.
  - Otherwise, fixture requirements are as shown in the partial table below:

Table 2902.1t   Institutional Employees Other Than Residential Care: Minimum Fixtures Required for Employees

Employee count	WC	Lavs	DF	Employee count	WC	Lavs	DF
1–25	1	1	1	126–140	6	4	2
26–35	2	1	1	141–150	6	5	2
36–50	2	2	1	151–175	7	5	2
51–70	3	2	1	176–200	8	6	2
71–75	2	2	1	201–210	9	6	3
76–100	4	3	1	211–225	9	7	3
101–105	5	3	2	226–245	10	7	3
106–125	5	4	2	246–250	10	8	3

Source: IBC Table 2902.1.

2902 Minimum Plumbing Facilities

2902.1 Minimum number of fixtures *(part 15 of 19)*

- Fixtures for institutional visitors other than residential care are governed as follows:
  - A service sink is not required to serve visitors.
  - Bathing facilities are not required for visitors.
  - Otherwise, fixture requirements are as shown in the partial table below:

Institutional Visitors Other Than Residential Care:
Table 2902.1u   Minimum Plumbing Fixtures Required for Vistors

Visitor count	WC	Lavs	DF	Visitor count	WC	Lavs	DF
1–75	1	1	1	201–225	3	3	1
76–100	2	1	1	226–300	4	3	1
101–150	2	2	1	301–375	5	4	1
151–200	3	2	1	376–400	6	4	1

Source: IBC Table 2902.1.

- Fixtures for inmates of prisons are governed as follows:
  - Employee toilets are separate from inmate toilets and are not governed by guidelines for inmates or the table below.
  - 1 water closet for each cell.
  - 1 lavatory for each cell.
  - Other fixtures are required as shown in the partial table below:

Table 2902.1v   Prisons: Minimum Fixtures Required for Inmates

Inmate count	Bathtub/ shower	DF	Inmate count	Bathtud/ shower	DF	Inmate count	Bathtub/ shower	DF
1–15	1	1	211–225	15	3	436–450	30	5
16–30	2	1	226–240	16	3	451–465	31	5
31–45	3	1	241–255	17	3	466–480	32	5
46–60	4	1	256–270	18	3	481–495	33	5
61–75	5	1	271–285	19	3	496–500	34	5
76–90	6	1	286–300	20	3	501–510	34	6
91–100	7	1	301–315	21	4	511–525	35	6
101–105	7	2	316–330	22	4	526–540	36	6
106–120	8	2	331–345	23	4	541–555	37	6
121–135	9	2	346–360	24	4	556–570	38	6
136–150	10	2	361–375	25	4	571–585	39	6
151–165	11	2	376–390	26	4	586–600	40	6
166–180	12	2	391–400	27	4	601–615	41	7
181–195	13	2	401–405	27	5	616–630	42	7
196–200	14	2	406–420	28	5	631–645	43	7
201–210	14	3	421–435	29	5	646–660	44	7

Source: IBC Table 2902.1.

2902 Minimum Plumbing Facilities

2902.1 Minimum number of fixtures *(part 16 of 19)*

- Fixtures for inmates of asylums and other institutional occupancies indicated below are governed as follows:
  - Employee toilets are separate from inmate toilets and are not governed by the table below.
  - Otherwise, fixture requirements are as shown in the table below:

Table 2902.1w   Asylums, Reformatories, etc.: Minimum Plumbing Fixtures Required for Inmates

Inmate count	WC	Lavs	Bathtub/ shower	DF	Inmate count	WC	Lavs	Bathtub/ shower	DF
1–15	1	1	1	1	106–120	8	8	8	2
16–30	2	2	2	1	121–135	9	9	9	2
31–45	3	3	3	1	136–150	10	10	10	2
46–60	4	4	4	1	151–165	11	11	11	2
61–75	5	5	5	1	166–180	12	12	12	2
76–90	6	6	6	1	181–195	13	13	13	2
91–100	7	7	7	1	196–200	14	14	14	2
101–105	7	7	7	2	201–210	14	14	14	3

Source: IBC Table 2902.1.

Table 2902.1x   Lodges: Minimum Plumbing Fixtures Required

Occupant count	WC	Lavs	Bathtub/ shower	DF	Occupant count	WC	Lavs	Bathtub/ shower	DF
1–8	1	1	1	1	61–64	7	7	8	1
9–10	1	1	2	1	65–70	7	7	9	1
11–16	2	2	2	1	71–72	8	8	9	1
17–20	2	2	3	1	73–80	8	8	10	1
21–24	3	3	3	1	81–88	9	9	11	1
25–30	3	3	4	1	89–90	9	9	12	1
31–32	4	4	4	1	91–96	10	10	12	1
33–40	4	4	5	1	97–100	10	10	13	1
41–48	5	5	6	1	101–104	11	11	13	2
49–50	5	5	7	1	104–110	11	11	14	2
51–56	6	6	7	1	111–112	12	12	14	2
57–60	6	6	8	1	113–120	12	12	15	2

Source: IBC Table 2902.1.

- Hotels and motels require the following plumbing fixtures for each guest room:
  - 1 water closet.
  - 1 lavatory.
  - 1 bathtub/shower.

2902 Minimum Plumbing Facilities

2902.1 Minimum number of fixtures *(part 17 of 19)*

- The plumbing fixtures listed below are required for each dwelling unit of the following type:
  - ○ Dwellings:
    - Multifamily housing.
    - Attached 1- and 2-family dwellings.
    - Detached 1- and 2- family dwellings.
  - ○ Fixtures:
    - 1 water closet.
    - 1 lavatory.
    - 1 bathtub/shower.
    - 1 kitchen sink.
    - Drinking fountains are not required.
    - A service sink is not required.
    - Automatic clothes washer connections are required as follows:
      - 1 connection for each dwelling unit of the following type:
        - Detached 1- and 2- family dwellings.
      - As shown in the table below for the following types:
        - Multifamily housing.
        - Attached 1- and 2-family dwellings.

Table 2902.1y   **Multifamily Housing and Attached 1- and 2- Family Dwellings: Minimum Automatic Clothes Washer Connections Required**

Dwelling unit count	Connections requiredunit	Dwelling unit count	Connections required	Dwelling unit count	Connections required
20	1	220	9	320	17
30	2	230	10	330	18
40	3	240	11	340	19
50	4	250	12	350	20
60	5	260	13	360	21
80	6	280	14	380	22
90	7	290	15	390	23
100	8	300	16	400	24

Source: IBC Table 2902.1.

- Storage requires the following facilities where required by the function of the occupancy:
  - ○ Emergency eyewash stations.
  - ○ Emergency showers.

Table 2902.1z   **Storage: Minimum Plumbing Fixtures Required**

Occupant count	WC	Lavs	DF	Occupant count	WC	Lavs	DF
1–100	1	1	1	301–400	4	4	1
101–200	2	2	1	401–500	5	5	1
201–300	3	3	1	501–600	6	6	1

Source: IBC Table 2902.1.

2902 Minimum Plumbing Facilities

2902.1 Minimum number of fixtures *(part 18 of 19)*

Table2902.1aa   **Dormitories: Minimum Plumbing Fixtures Required for 1–360 Occupants**

Occupant count	WC	Lavs	Bathtub/ shower	DF	Occupant count	WC	Lavs	Bathtub/ shower	DF
1–8	1	1	1	1	181–184	19	19	23	2
9–10	1	1	2	1	185–190	19	19	24	2
11–16	2	2	2	1	191–192	20	20	24	2
17–20	2	2	3	1	193–200	20	20	25	2
21–24	3	3	3	1	201–208	21	21	26	3
25–30	3	3	4	1	209–210	21	21	27	3
31–32	4	4	4	1	211–216	22	22	27	3
33–40	4	4	5	1	217–220	22	22	28	3
41–48	5	5	6	1	221–224	23	23	28	3
49–50	5	5	7	1	225–230	23	23	29	3
51–56	6	6	7	1	231–232	24	24	29	3
57–60	6	6	8	1	233–240	24	24	30	3
61–64	7	7	8	1	241–248	25	25	31	3
65–70	7	7	9	1	249–250	25	25	32	3
71–72	8	8	9	1	251–256	26	26	32	3
73–80	8	8	10	1	257–260	26	26	33	3
81–88	9	9	11	1	261–264	27	27	33	3
89–90	9	9	12	1	265–270	27	27	34	3
91–96	10	10	12	1	271–272	28	28	34	3
97–100	10	10	13	1	273–280	28	28	35	3
101–104	11	11	13	2	281–288	29	29	36	3
105–110	11	11	14	2	289–290	29	29	37	3
111–112	12	12	14	2	291–296	30	30	37	3
113–120	12	12	15	2	297–300	30	30	38	3
121–128	13	13	16	2	301–304	31	31	38	4
129–130	13	13	17	2	305–310	31	31	39	4
131–136	14	14	17	2	311–312	32	32	39	4
137–140	14	14	18	2	313–320	32	32	40	4
141–144	15	15	18	2	321–328	33	33	41	4
145–150	15	15	19	2	329–330	33	33	42	4
151–152	16	16	19	2	331–336	34	34	42	4
153–160	16	16	20	2	337–340	34	34	43	4
161–168	17	17	21	2	341–344	35	35	43	4
169–170	17	17	22	2	345–350	35	35	44	4
171–176	18	18	22	2	351–352	36	36	44	4
177–180	18	18	23	2	353–360	36	36	45	4

Source: IBC Table 2902.1.

2902 Minimum Plumbing Facilities

2902.1 Minimum number of fixtures *(part 19 of 19)*

Table 2902.1bb   Dormitories: Minimum Plumbing Fixtures Required for 361–720 Occupants

Occupant count	WC	Lavs	Bathtub/ shower	DF	Occupant count	WC	Lavs	Bathtub/ shower	DF
361–368	37	37	46	4	541–544	55	55	68	6
369–370	37	37	47	4	545–550	55	55	69	6
371–376	38	38	47	4	551–552	56	56	69	6
377–380	38	38	48	4	553–560	56	56	70	6
381–384	39	39	48	4	561–568	57	57	71	6
385–390	39	39	49	4	569–570	57	7	72	6
391–392	40	40	49	4	571–576	58	58	72	6
393–400	40	40	50	4	577–580	58	58	73	6
401–408	41	41	51	5	581–584	59	59	73	6
409–410	41	41	52	5	585–590	59	59	74	6
411–416	42	42	52	5	591–592	60	60	74	6
417–420	42	42	53	5	593–600	60	60	75	6
421–424	43	43	53	5	601–608	61	61	76	7
425–430	43	43	54	5	609–610	61	61	77	7
431–432	44	44	54	5	611–616	62	62	77	7
433–440	44	44	55	5	617–620	62	62	78	7
441–448	45	45	56	5	621–624	63	63	78	7
449–450	45	45	57	5	625–630	63	63	79	7
451–456	46	46	57	5	631–632	64	64	79	7
457–460	46	46	58	5	633–640	64	64	80	7
461–464	47	47	58	5	641–648	65	65	81	7
465–470	47	47	59	5	649–650	65	65	82	7
471–472	48	48	59	5	651–656	66	66	82	7
473–480	48	84	60	5	657–660	66	66	83	7
481–488	49	49	61	5	661–664	67	67	83	7
489–490	49	49	62	5	665–670	67	67	84	7
491–496	50	50	62	5	671–672	68	68	84	7
497–500	50	50	63	5	673–680	68	68	85	7
501–504	51	51	63	6	681–688	69	69	86	7
505–510	51	51	64	6	689–690	69	69	87	7
511–512	52	52	64	6	691–696	70	70	87	7
513–520	52	52	65	6	697–700	70	70	88	7
521–528	53	53	66	6	701–704	71	71	88	8
529–530	53	53	67	6	705–710	71	71	89	8
531–536	54	54	67	6	711–712	72	72	89	8
537–540	54	54	68	6	713–720	72	72	90	8

Source: IBC Table 2902.1.

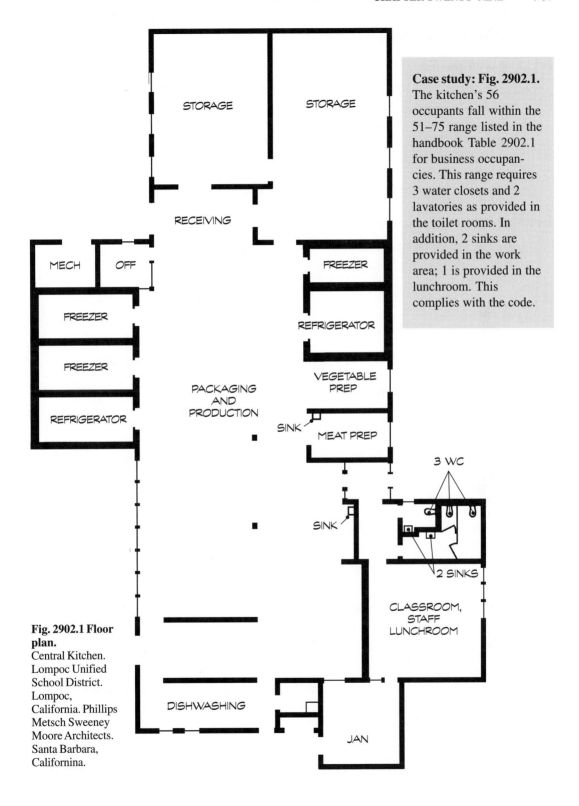

Case study: Fig. 2902.1. The kitchen's 56 occupants fall within the 51–75 range listed in the handbook Table 2902.1 for business occupancies. This range requires 3 water closets and 2 lavatories as provided in the toilet rooms. In addition, 2 sinks are provided in the work area; 1 is provided in the lunchroom. This complies with the code.

STORAGE

STORAGE

RECEIVING

MECH   OFF

FREEZER

REFRIGERATOR

FREEZER

FREEZER

VEGETABLE PREP

PACKAGING AND PRODUCTION

REFRIGERATOR

SINK

MEAT PREP

3 WC

SINK

2 SINKS

CLASSROOM, STAFF LUNCHROOM

Fig. 2902.1 Floor plan. Central Kitchen. Lompoc Unified School District. Lompoc, California. Phillips Metsch Sweeney Moore Architects. Santa Barbara, Californina.

DISHWASHING

JAN

2902 Minimum Plumbing Facilities

2902.2 Separate facilities

- Separate sex toilet facilities are not required for the following cases:
  - Private facilities.
  - For employees with ≤ 15 employees.
  - In buildings or tenant spaces where occupant load is ≤ 15 including both of the following:
    Employees.
    Customers.
- Otherwise, where toilet fixtures are required, separate sex facilities must be provided.

2902.3 Number of occupants of each sex

- Where not specified otherwise, distribution of the following facilities must be as indicated below:
  - Facilities:
    Water closets.
    Lavatories.
    Showers or bathtubs.
  - Distribution:
    Facilities must be distributed between sexes in one of the following ways:
      Equally.
      According to anticipated distribution of the sexes in the occupant load as follows:
        Supporting statistical data is required.
        Must be approved by the building official.

2902.4 Location of employee toilet facilities in occupancies other than assembly or mercantile *(part 1 of 2)*

- The following toilet facilities are governed as indicated below:
  - Toilets:
    Where provided as indicated below for employees working in the following locations:
      Work locations:
        Storage structures.
        Kiosks.
      Toilet location:
        In an adjacent structure.
  - Requirements:
    Adjacent structure must have one of the following characteristics:
      Under same ownership or lease as is the work location.
      Under same control is as the work location.
    Travel distance from the work location to the toilet facilities must be as follows:
      ≤ 500'.

2902 Minimum Plumbing Facilities

2902.4 Location of employee toilet facilities in occupancies other than assembly or mercantile *(part 2 of 2)*

- In other cases, employee toilet facilities are governed as follows:
  - In occupancies other than A or M, the following applies:
    Access to toilet facilities must be from within the employees' regular work area.
    Employee toilet facilities must be one of the following:
    Separate from public customer facilities.
    Combined with public customer facilities.

2902.4.1 Travel distance

- Occupancies A and M are not governed by this section.
- In occupancy F, required toilet facilities need not be located as indicated below, where approved by the building official:
- In other occupancies, required toilet facilities must be located as follows:
  - ≤ 1 story above or below an employee's regular work area.
  - $\leq 500'$ travel distance from an employee's regular work area.

2902.5 Location of employee toilet facilities in mercantile and assembly occupancies

- Employee toilet facilities are not required in the following location:
  - In tenant spaces where toilets are otherwise provided as follows:
    Where travel distance between the following points is $\leq 300'$:
    Main entrance to tenant space.
    Central toilet area.
    Central toilet area is located ≤ 1 story above or below the tenant space.
- In other cases, employee toilets are required in buildings and tenant spaces as follows:
  - Restaurants.
  - Nightclubs.
  - Places of public assembly.
  - Mercantile occupancies.
- Employee toilet facilities may be separate or combined with public customer facilities.
- Required toilet facilities must be located as follows:
  - ≤ 1 story above or below an employee's work area.
  - $\leq 500'$ travel distance from an employee's work area in other than a covered mall.
  - $\leq 300'$ travel distance from an employee's work area in a covered mall.

2902.6 Public facilities

- Buildings and tenant spaces for public use must have toilet facilities for the public as follows:
  - Toilet facilities must be located as follows:
    ≤ 1 story above or below the space requiring toilet facilities.
    $\leq 500'$ travel distance to the toilet facilities.

2902 Minimum Plumbing Facilities

2902.6.1 Covered malls

- Covered mall buildings require toilet facilities as follows:
  - Travel distance to toilets must be ≤ 300'.
  - Number of toilet facilities is based on total square footage.
  - Required toilet facilities must be provided in one of the following locations:
    In each individual store.
    In a central toilet area.
  - Travel distance to central toilet facilities is measured from each store or tenant space.

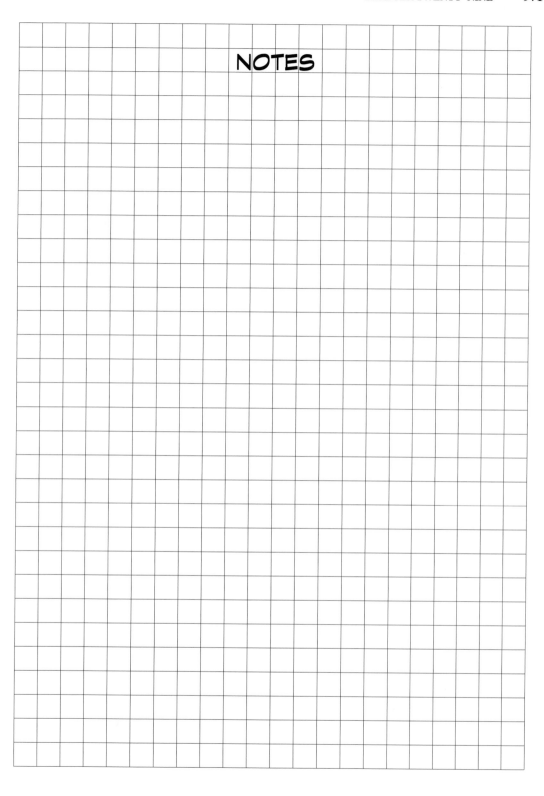

NOTES

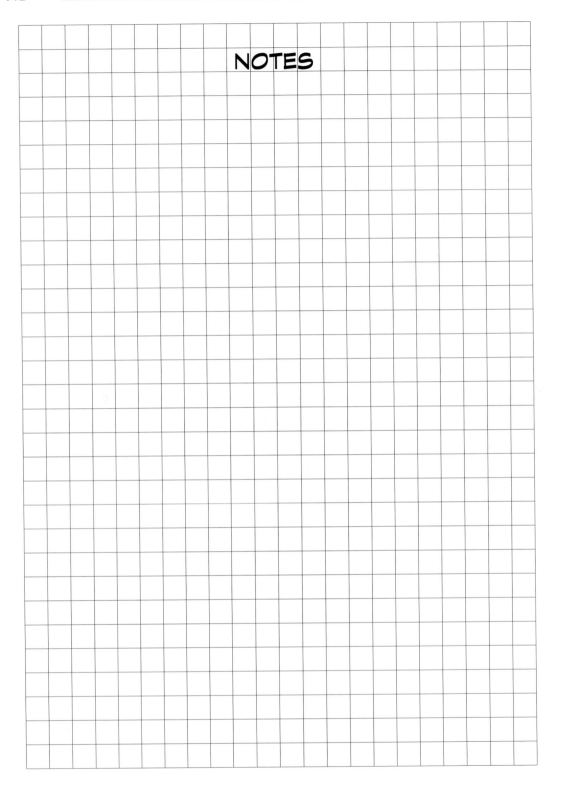

NOTES

30

Elevators and Conveying Systems

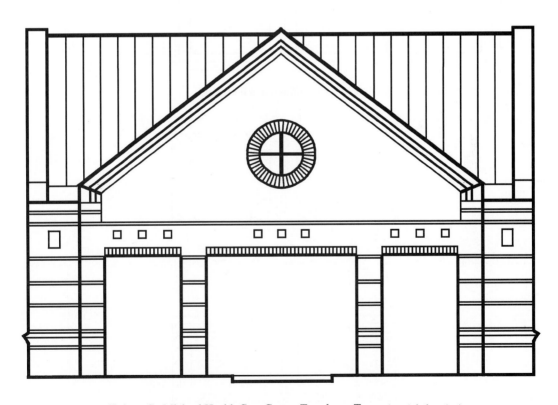

Christus St. Michael Health Care Center. Texarkana, Texas. *(partial elevation)*
Watkins Hamilton Ross Architects, Inc. Houston, Texas.

3002 Hoistway Enclosures

3002.2 Number of elevator cars in a hoistway

- The number of elevators permitted in a hoistway is shown in the details provided.

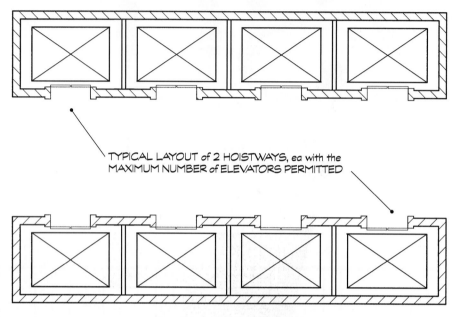

Fig. 3002.4A. Maximum number of elevators premitted in a hoistway.

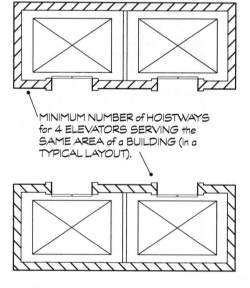

Fig. 3002.4B. Minimum number of hoistways.

3002 Hoistway Enclosures

3002.3 Emergency signs

- Signs at elevators prohibiting use of elevators during a fire are not required as follows:
  - Where elevators are part of an accessible means of egress.

    Note: 1003.2.13.3, "Elevators," is cited as governing elevators as indicated above.

- Otherwise, a sign is required by each elevator call button as follows:
  - Sign must be approved.
  - Sign must be a standardized design.
  - Sign must state the message shown on the illustration provided.

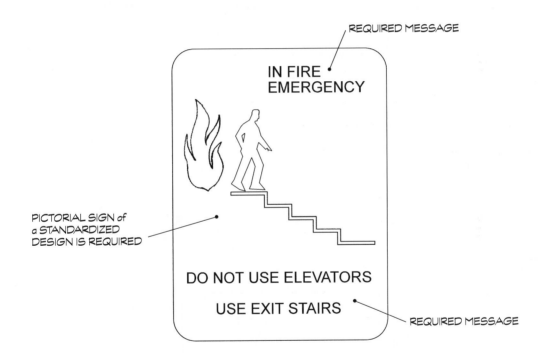

Fig. 3002.3. Acceptable pictorial design for a sign required to be posted at elevators prohibiting elevator use during fire.

3002 Hoistway Enclosures

3002.4 Elevator car to accommodate ambulance stretcher

- In buildings ≥ 4 stories, the following applies:
  - ≥ 1 elevator must be provided as follows:
    For fire department emergency access to all floors.
    Size to be as indicated in the detail provided.
    Must be identified with signs as shown in the details provided.

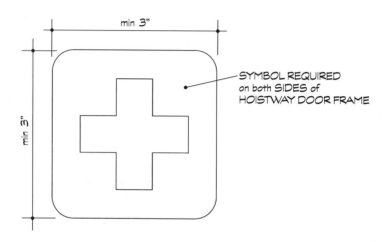

Fig. 3002.4A. Symbol required at elevator design for fire department use.

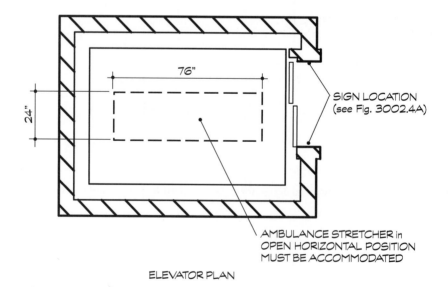

Fig. 3002.4B. Plan of elevator accommodating an ambulance stretcher.

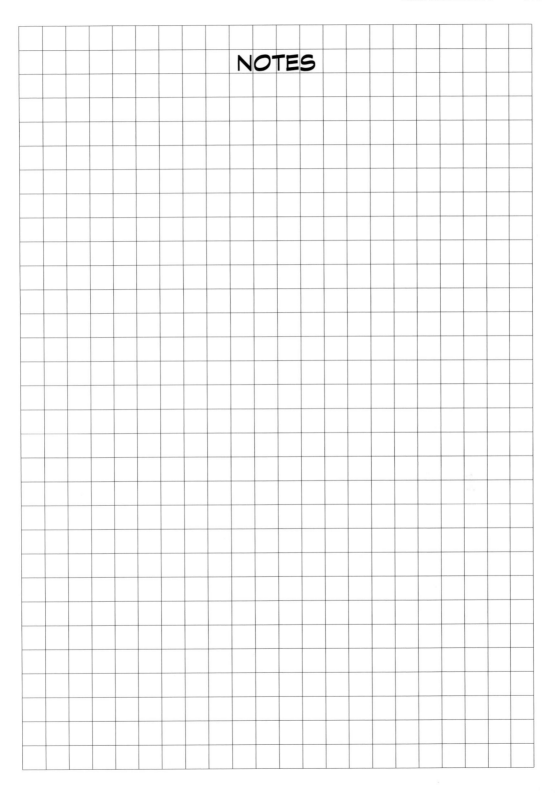

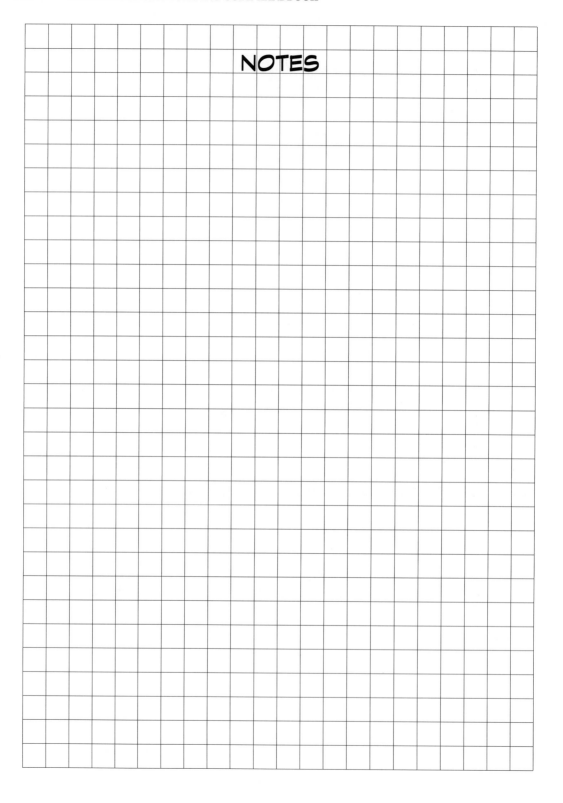

NOTES

31

Special Construction

AmberGlen Business Center. Hillsboro, Oregon. *(partial elevation)*
Ankrom Moisan Associated Architects. Portland, Oregon.

3104 Pedestrian Walkways and Tunnels

3104.5 Fire barriers between pedestrian walkways and buildings *(part 1 of 2)*

- This section applies to pedestrian walkways connecting buildings as follows:
  - At grade.
  - Above grade.
  - Below grade.
- Where exterior walls of the connected buildings are required to have a fire-resistance rating > 2 hrs, the following applies:
  - The walkway must be sprinklered as per NFPA 13.

  Note: Section 704, "Exterior Walls," is cited as the source governing the fire-resistance ratings of exterior walls.

- This section does not require a fire-resistance rating for walls of the following heights where they have any of the additional conditions indicated below:
  - Heights:
      Walls separating a pedestrian walkway from a building as follows:
        Height complies with both of the following where not sprinklered:
          ≤ 3 stories and ≤ 40'.
        Height complies with both of the following where sprinklered:
          ≤ 5 stories and 55'.
        Height is ≥ 8'.
  - Conditions:
      Where connected buildings are ≥ 10' apart and all of the following apply:
        Walkway is sprinklered as per NFPA 13.
        Any glass in the wall and doors separating the walkway from building is as follows:
          One of the following types of glass is used:
            Tempered.
            Wired.
            Laminated.
          Glass is protected by sprinklers as follows:
            As per NFPA 13.
            Sprinklers can wet the whole interior surface of the glass.
          Glass is mounted as follows:
            In a gasketed frame.
            So that the frame can deflect without breaking the glass as follows:
              Prior to activation of the sprinklers.
          No obstructions exist between sprinklers and glass.
      Where connected buildings are ≥ 10' apart and all of the following apply:
        Both side walls of the walkway must be open as follows:
          ≥ 50%.
        Open area is uniformly distributed.
        Open area prevents the accumulation of the following:
          Smoke and toxic gases.
      Where buildings are on the same lot.

  Note: 503.1.3, "Buildings on the same lot," is cited as governing such buildings.

3104 Pedestrian Walkways and Tunnels

3104.5 Fire barriers between pedestrian walkways and buildings *(part 2 of 2)*

- In other cases, walkways must be separated from the connected buildings as shown in the illustration provided.

    Note: Section 714, " Opening Protectives," is cited as governing the fire-protection rating required for windows as noted in the illustration.

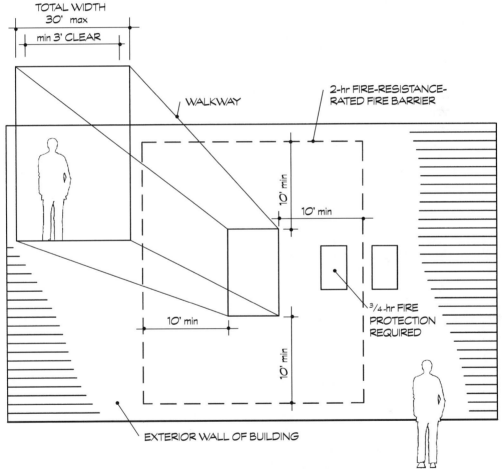

Fig. 3104.5. Pedestrian walkway, dimensions and fire barrier at building.

3104 Pedestrian Walkways and Tunnels

3104.8 Width

- Clear width and total width of pedestrian walkways must be as shown in Figure 3104.5.

3104.9 Exit access travel

This section addresses pedestrian walkways and tunnels.

- Exit access travel distance within such elements is governed as follows:

Type of walkway	Sprinklered	Not sprinklered
Tunnel	≤ 200'	≤ 200'
Pedestrian walkway	≤ 250'	≤ 200'
Pedestrian walkway, both sides open ≥ 50%	≤ 400'	≤ 300'

3106 Marquees

3106.2 Thickness

- The vertical dimension of a marquee is as shown in the illustrations provided.

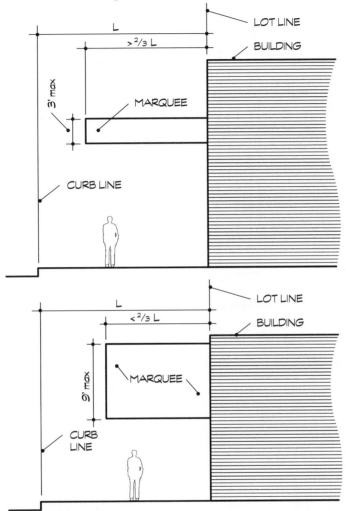

Fig. 3106.2. Maximum vertical dimension of marquees.

3106.5 Construction

- A marquee must be supported entirely from the building.
- A marquee must be constructed of noncombustible materials.
- A marquee's structure must be protected from deterioration.
- A marquee must meet structural requirements of the code.

  Note: Chapter 16, "Structural Design," is cited as governing the structure of a marquee.

3109 Swimming Pool Enclosures

3109.3 Public swimming pools

- Public swimming pools must be enclosed by a fence as shown in the detail provided.

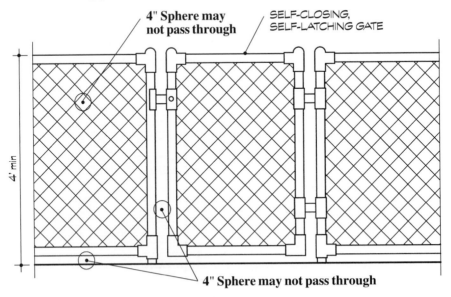

Fig. 3109.3. Barriers around public swimming pools.

3109.4.1 Barrier height and clearances

This section addresses residential swimming pools.

- Such pools must be enclosed by a barrier as shown in the details provided.

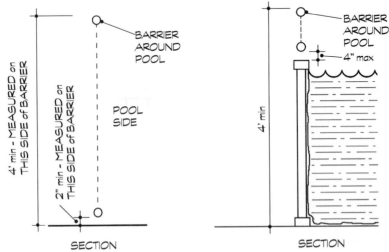

Fig. 3109.4.1. Residential swimming poor barrier height and clearances.

3109 Swimming Pool Enclosures

3109.4 1.1 Openings

This section addresses barriers enclosing residential swimming pools.

● Openings in the required barrier must be as shown in the detail provided.

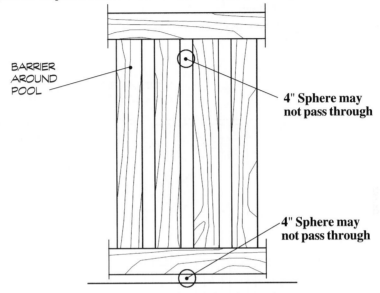

BARRIER
AROUND
POOL

**4" Sphere may
not pass through**

**4" Sphere may
not pass through**

Fig. 3109.4 1.1. Openings in barriers around residential swimming pools.

3109.4.1.2 Solid barrier surfaces

This section addresses barriers enclosing residential swimming pools.

● Where a required barrier is solid, the surface must be as shown in the detail provided.

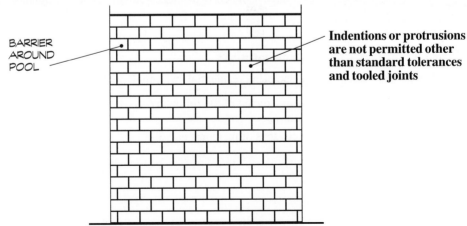

BARRIER
AROUND
POOL

**Indentions or protrusions
are not permitted other
than standard tolerances
and tooled joints**

Fig. 3109.4.1.2. Solid barrier surfaces around residential swimming pools.

3109 Swimming Pool Enclosures

3109.4.1.3 Closely spaced horizontal members

This section addresses barriers enclosing residential swimming pools.

- Requirements for barriers constructed of the following are shown in the detail provided:
  - Horizontal members as follows:
    Vertical distance between tops of members is < 3'-9".
  - Vertical members.

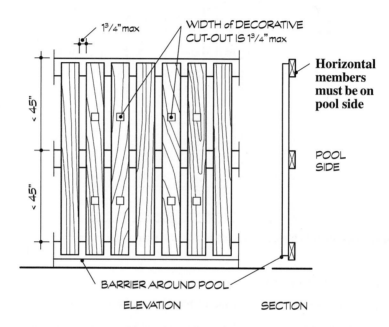

Fig. 3109.4.1.3. Closely spaced horizontal members in barriers around residential swimming pools.

3109.4.1.4 Widely spaced horizontal members

This section addresses barriers enclosing residential swimming pools.

- Requirements for barriers constructed of the following are shown in the detail provided:
  - Horizontal members as follows:
    Vertical distance between tops of members is ≥ 3'-9".
  - Vertical members.

3109 Swimming Pool Enclosures

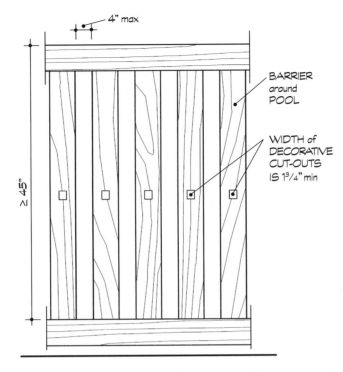

4" max

BARRIER
around
POOL

WIDTH of
DECORATIVE
CUT-OUTS
IS 1³/₄" min

≥ 45"

Fig. 3109.4.1.4. Widely spaced horizontal members in barriers around residential swimming pools.

3109.4.1.5 Chain link dimensions

This section addresses barriers enclosing residential swimming pools.

- Requirements for chain link fencing are shown on the details provided.

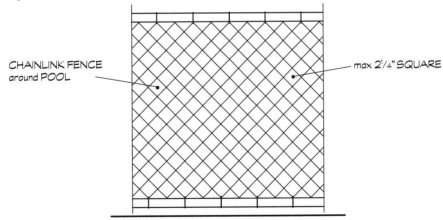

CHAINLINK FENCE
around POOL

max 2¹/₄" SQUARE

Fig. 3109.4.1.5A. Chain link dimensions in fences around residential swimming pools.

3109 Swimming Pool Enclosures

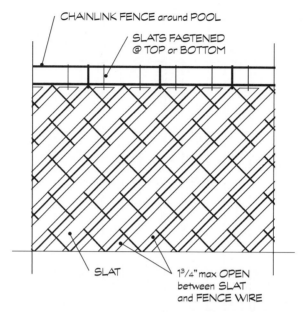

Fig. 3109.4.1.5B. Chain link dimensions at slats in fences around residential swimming pools.

3109.4.1.6 Diagonal members

This section addresses barriers enclosing residential swimming pools.

- The limitation of openings for barriers with diagonal members is shown in the detail provided.

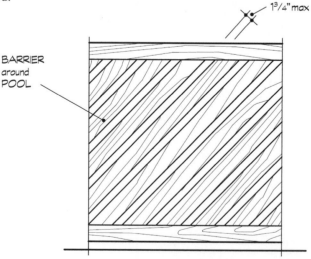

Fig. 3109.4.1.6. Diagonal members in barriers around residential swimming pools.

3109 Swimming Pool Enclosures

3109.4.1.7 Gates

- Requirements for access gates in barriers are shown in the detail provided.

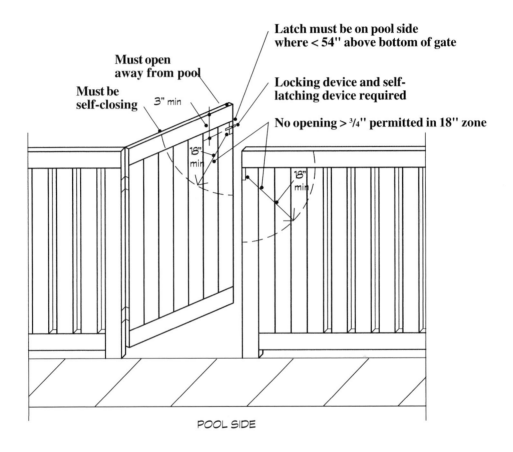

Fig. 3109.4.1.7. Gates in barriers around residential swimming pools.

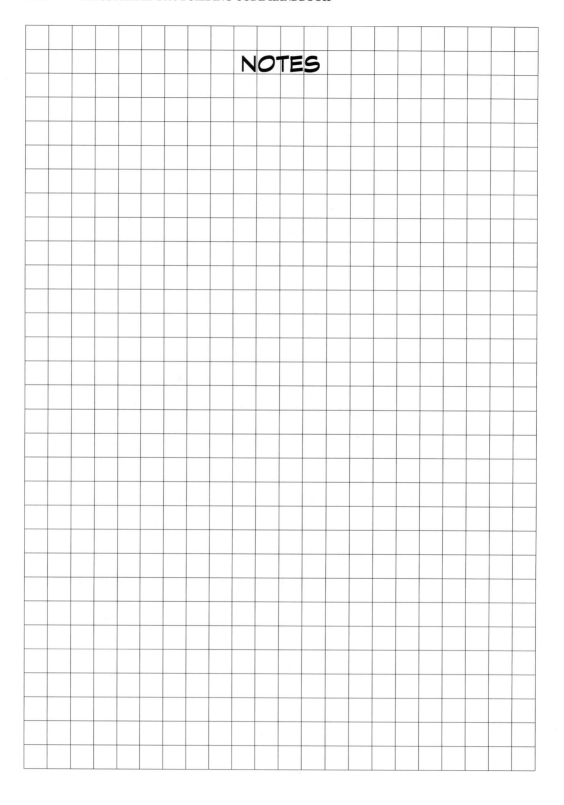

NOTES

32

Encroachments into the Public Right-of-Way

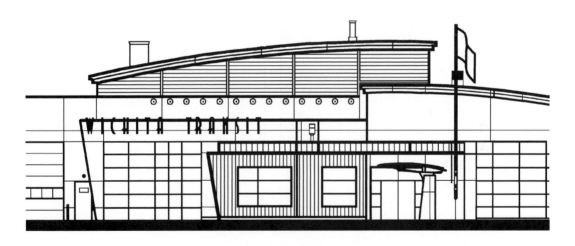

Wichita Transit Storage, Administration, and Maintenance Facility.
Wichita, Kansas. *(partial elevation)*
Wilson Darnell Mann, P.A., Architects. Wichita, Kansas.

3202 Encroachments

3202.1.1 Structural support

- The detail provided shows where a foundation may project beyond the property line.
- Otherwise, foundations may not project beyond the property line.

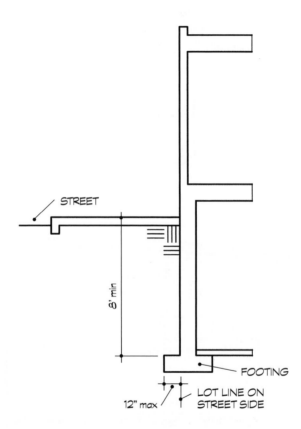

Fig. 3202.1.1. Projection of foundation over property line.

3202 Encroachments

3202.2 Encroachments above grade and below 8 feet in height

- Only the following elements may project into the public right-of-way within a height of 8'.
  - Steps.
  - Architectural features.
  - Awnings.

    Note: The following are cited as governing the elements that may project into the public right-of-way within a height of 8':
    3202.2.1, "Steps."
    3202.2.2, "Architectural features."
    3202.2.3, "Awnings."

- Doors and window may not project into the public right of way within a height of 8'.

3202.2.1 Steps

- Requirements for steps that encroach on the public right-of-way are shown in the illustration provided.

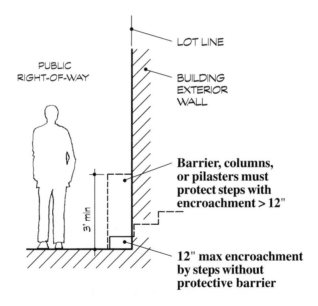

Fig. 3202.2.1. Projection of steps into the public right-of-way.

3202 Encroachments

3202.2.2 Architectural features

- Projection of the following features into the public right-of-way is limited as shown in the illustration provided:
  - The following features are limited to a projection of ≤ 12":
    - Columns.
    - Pilasters.
  - The following details are limited to a projection of ≤ 4":
    - Belt courses.
    - Lintels.
    - Sills.
    - Architraves.
    - Pediments.

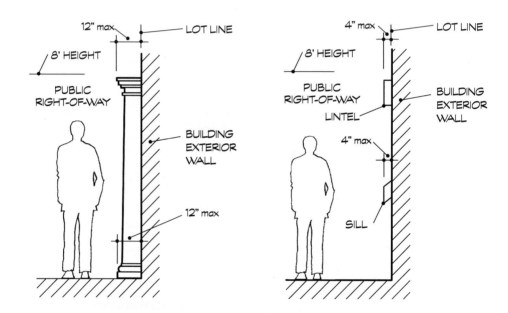

Fig. 3202.2.2. Projection of architectural features into the public right-of-way.

3202 Encroachments

3202.2.3 Awnings

- The required clearance for an awning projecting into the public right-of-way is shown in the illustration provided.

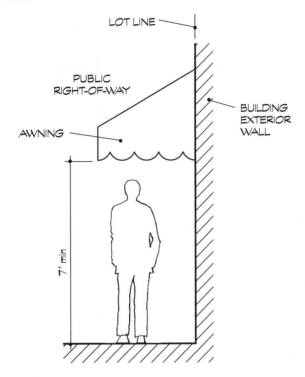

Fig. 3202.2.3. Projection of awnings into the public-right-of-way.

3202.3.1 Awnings, canopies, marquees and signs

This subsection addresses encroachments into the public-right-of way above a height of 8'.

- The following elements are governed as indicated below:
  - Elements:
      Awnings.
      Canopies.
      Marquees.
      Signs.
  - Requirements:
      Elements must meet code structural requirements.
      Clearance requirements are shown in the illustrations provided.

  Note: Chapter 16, "Structural Design," is cited as governing the structure of the elements indicated above.

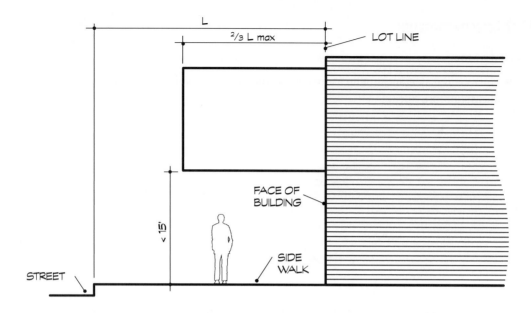

Fig. 3202.3.1A. Projection of awnings, canopies, marquees, and signs into the public right-of-way at a height ≥ 8' and < 15'.

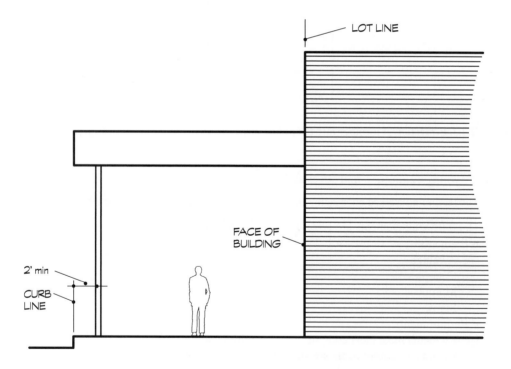

Fig. 3202.3.1B. Columns supporting awnings, canopies, marquees, and signs that project into the public right-of-way.

3202 Encroachments

3202.3.2 Windows, balconies, architectural features and mechanical equipment

- The following elements that project into the public right-of-way are governed as indicated below:
  - Elements:
    - Windows.
    - Balconies.
    - Architectural features.
    - Mechanical equipment.
  - Requirements:
    - Where located above 8', the limit of encroachment is indicated as follows:
      - In the illustration provided.
      - In the partial table below as based on the following:
        - 1" of encroachment is permitted for each 1" of height above 8'.
        - ≤ 4' of encroachment is permitted.

Table 3202.3.2   Encroachment into Public Right-of-Way Permitted: Windows, Balconies, Architectural Features, Mechanical Equipment

Vertical	Projection	Vertical	Projection	Vertical	Projection
8'-1"	0'-1"	9'-5"	1'-5"	10'-9"	2'-9"
8'-2"	0'-2"	9'-6"	1'-6"	10'-10"	2'-10"
8'-3"	0'-3"	9'-7"	1'-7"	10'-11"	2'-11"
8'-4"	0'-4"	9'-8"	1'-8"	11'-0"	3'-0"
8'-5"	0'-5"	9'-9"	1'-9"	11'-1"	3'-1"
8'-6"	0'-6"	9'-10"	1'-10"	11'-2"	3'-2"
8'-7"	0'-7"	9'-11"	1'-11"	11'-3"	3'-3"
8'-8"	0'-8"	10'-0"	2'-0"	11'-4"	3'-4"
8'-9"	0'-9"	10'-1"	2'-1"	11'-5"	3'-5"
8'-10"	0'-10"	10'-2"	2'-2"	11'-6"	3'-6"
8'-11"	0'-11"	10'-3"	2'-3"	11'-7"	3'-7"
9'-0"	1'-0"	10'-4"	2'-4"	11'-8"	3'-8"
9'-1"	1'-1"	10'-5"	2'-5"	11'-9"	3'-9"
9'-2"	1'-2"	10'-6"	2'-6"	11'-10"	3'-10"
9'-3"	1'-3"	10'-7"	2'-7"	11'-11"	3'-11"
9'-4"	1'-4"	10'-8"	2'-8"	12'-0"	4'-0"

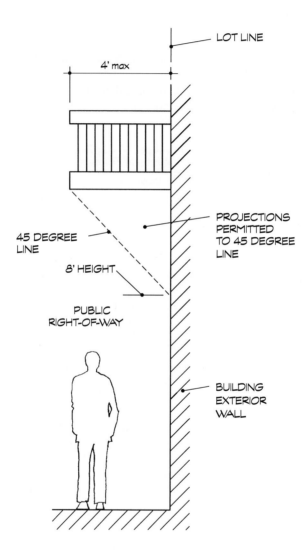

Fig. 3202.3.2. Projection of windows, balconies, architectural features and mechanical equipment into the public right-of-way.

3202 Encroachments

3202.3.3 Encroachments 15 feet or more above grade

- Encroachments ≥ 15' above grade are governed as shown in the illustration provided.

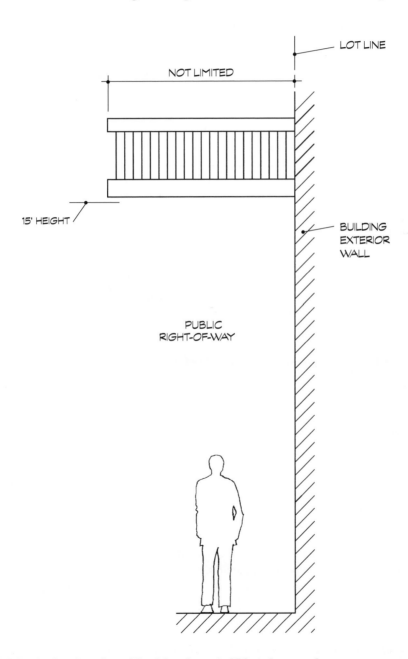

Fig. 3202.3.3. Projections into the public right-of-way ≥ 15 feet above grade.

3202 Encroachments

3202.3.4 Pedestrian walkways

- Pedestrian walkways over a public right-of-way are governed as follows:
  - Must be approved by the authority having jurisdiction.
  - Clearance required is shown in the illustration provided.

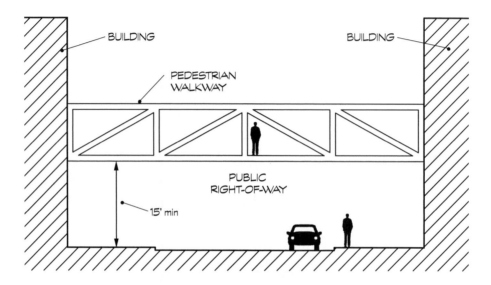

Fig. 3202.3.4 Pedestrian walkways over the public right-of-way.

3202.4 Temporary encroachments

- The following elements installed for ≤ 7 months in any calendar year are governed as indicated below:
  - Elements:
    Vestibules.
    Storm enclosures.
  - Requirements:
    Must be approved by the authority having jurisdiction.
    Encroachment permitted into a public right-of-way is shown in the illustration provided.
- Temporary entrance awnings are governed as indicated in the illustration provided.

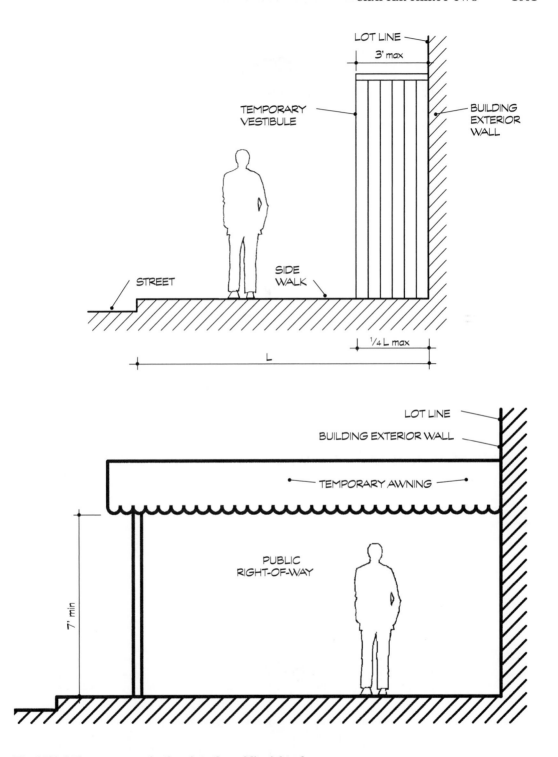

Fig. 3202.4. Temporary projections into the public right-of-way.

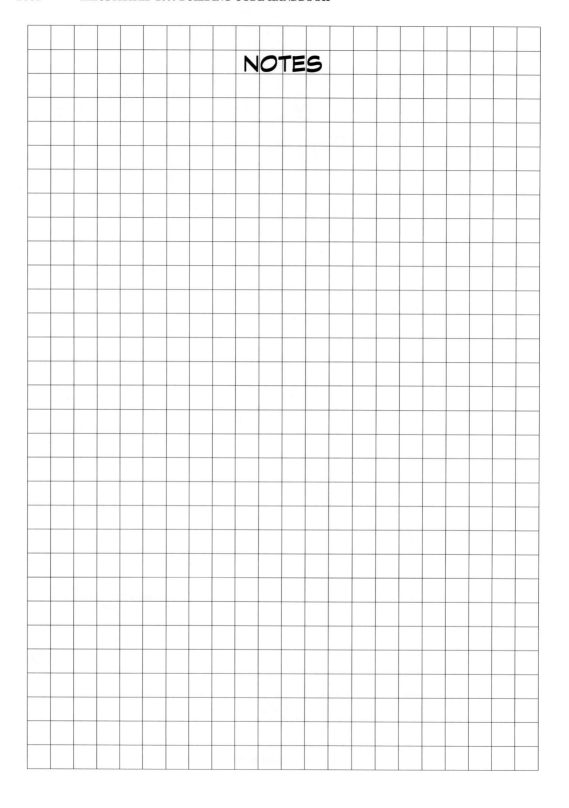

33

Safeguards
During Construction

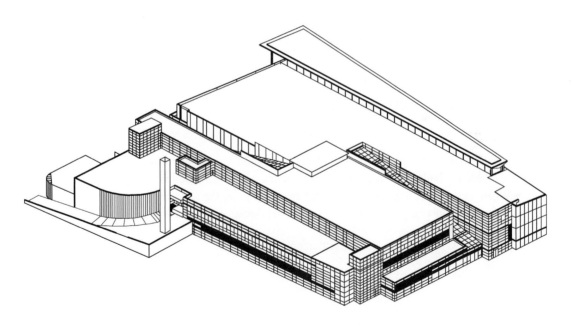

University of Connecticut New Downtown Campus at Stamford, Connecticut.
Perkins Eastman Architects, P.C. New York, New York.

3304 Site Work

3304.1 Excavation and fill

- Excavation and fill must be accommodated to protect the following:
  - Life safety.
  - Property.
- Stumps and roots must be removed as follows:
  - In the area to be occupied by the building:
    To a depth of ≥ 12" below grade.
- The following wood forms used for concrete must be removed before the building is used for any purpose:
  - Forms in the ground.
  - Forms between foundations sills and grade.
- Prior to completion of construction, the following must be removed:
  - Loose or miscellaneous wood as follows:
    Where in contact with grade under the building.

3304.1.1 Slope limits

- Permanent fill must slope as follows:
  - ≤ 1:2.
- Permanent slopes for excavated grade must comply with one of the following:
  - A gradient ≤ 1:2.
  - Other slopes are permitted where both of the following apply:
    Slope is justified by documentation from a soil investigation.
    Slope is approved by the building official.

3304.1.2 Surcharge

- Fill or other surcharge may be placed against a building only as follows:
  - Where the building is capable of resisting the additional loading.
- Where existing footings can be affected by excavation, the following applies:
  - Footings must be protected from present and future movement by one of the following:
    Underpinning.
    Otherwise protected against settlement.

NOTES

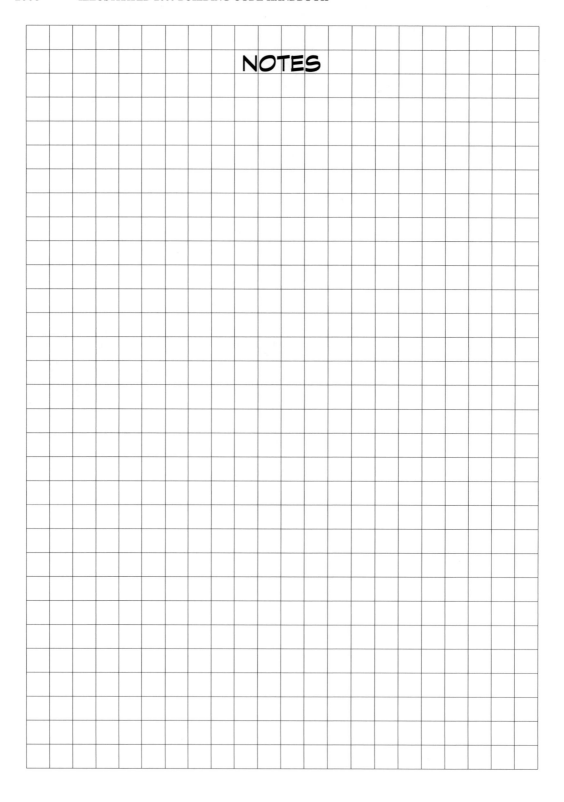

NOTES

34

Existing Structures

Lake Forest City Hall Renovation and Addition. Lake Forest, Illinois.
David Woodhouse Architects. Chicago, Illinois.

3402 Additions, Alternations or Repairs

3402.4 Stairways

- Stairway construction in an existing building is not required to meet requirements for stairways in new construction where all of the following conditions apply:
  - ° Where the stairway construction is one of the following types:
    An alteration.
    A replacement.
  - ° Where existing conditions do not permit a reduction in the following:
    Pitch.
    Slope.

Case study: Fig. 3402.4. The stairway is part of the existing portion of the renovation project. The winders, which would be prohibited in new construction by subsection 1003.3.3.8, are permitted to remain in this stairway alteration. This is possible since the stairway space is restricted by the existing construction which does not permit the additional steps that would be necessary to eliminate the winders.

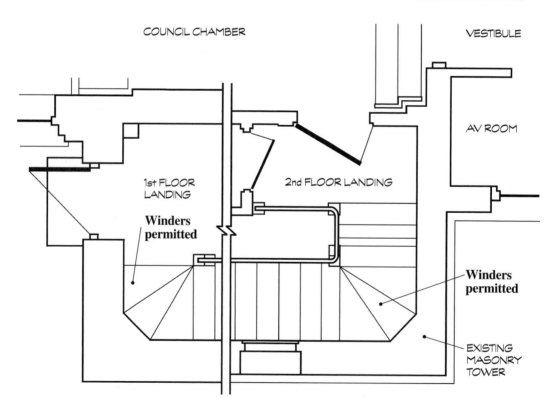

Fig. 3402.4. Partial plan at existing stairway. Lake Forest City Hall Renovation and Addition. Lake Forest, Illinois. David Woodhouse Architects. Chicago, Illinois.

3408 Accessibility for Existing Buildings

3408.7.4 Ramps

This subsection addresses alterations to existing buildings.

- Where space does not permit compliance with standard ramp slopes, ramps are governed as shown in the details provided.

   Note: 1003.3.4.1, "Slope," is cited as governing standard ramp slopes that may not be met due to space limitations.

   IBC Table 3408.7.4, "Ramps," is cited as the source of requirements for ramps that cannot meet the standard slope requirements.

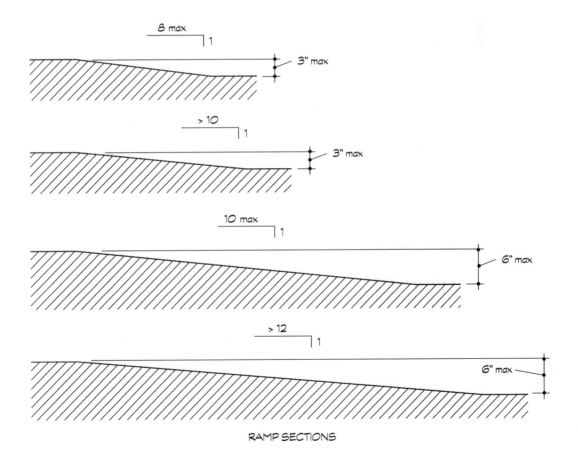

RAMP SECTIONS

Fig. 3408.7.4. Ramps for accessibility in existing buildings.

3408 Accessibility for Existing Buildings

3408.8.5 Ramps

This subsection addresses alterations to existing buildings.

- Slope requirements for ramp runs ≤ 2' is shown in the detail provided.

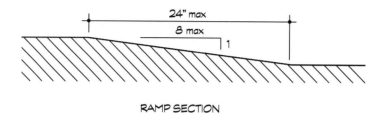

Fig. 3408.8.5. Ramps in historic buildings.

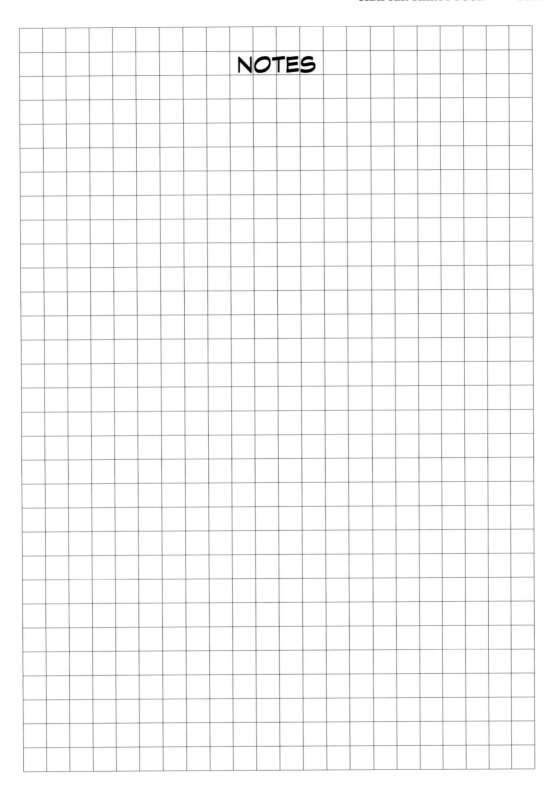

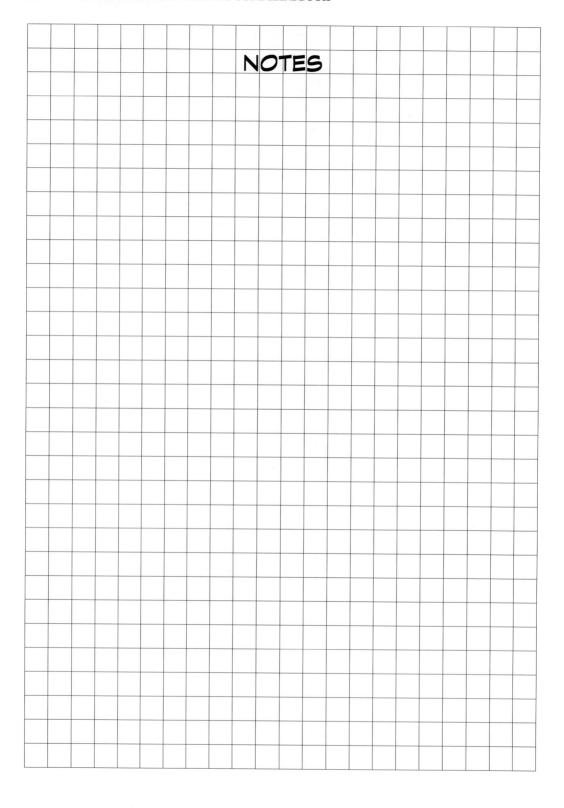

NOTES

35

Referenced Standards

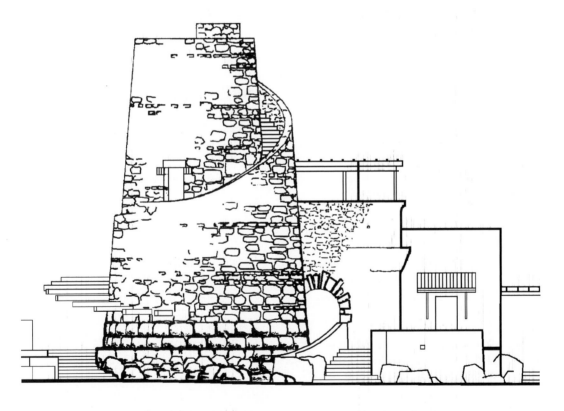

Lady Bird Johnson Wildflower Center. Austin, Texas. *(partial elevation)*
Overland Partners, Inc. San Antonio, Texas.

Referenced Standards

Below are agencies providing standards cited in the code including title abbreviations and contact information.

- **AA**

  Aluminum Association   Web site: www.aluminum.org
  900 19th Street, NW   Fax: 202-862-5164
  Washington, DC 20006   Tel: 202-862-5100

- **AAMA**

  American Architectural   Web site: www.aamanet.org
    Manufacturers Association   Fax: 847-303-5774
  1827 Walden Office Square, Suite 104   Tel: 847-303-5664
  Schaumberg, IL 60173

- **ACI**

  American Concrete Institute   Web site: www.aci-int.org
  P.O. Box 9094   Tel: 248-848-3700
  Farmington Hills, MI 48333

- **AF&PA**

  American Forest & Paper Association   Web site: www.afandpa.org
  1111 19th St., NW, Suite 800   e-mail: info@afandpa.org
  Washington, DC 20036   Fax: 202-463-2700
                                       Tel: 202-463-2471

- **AHA**

  American Hardwood Association   Tel: 847-934-8800
  1210 West NW Highway
  Palatine, IL 60067

- **AISC**

  American Institute of Steel Construction   Web site: www.aisc.org
  One East Wacker Drive, Suite 3100   Fax: 312-670-5403
  Chicago, IL 60601-2001   Tel: 312-670-2400

- **AISI**

  American Iron and Steel Institute   Tel: 202-452-7100
  1101 17th Street, NW, Suite 1300
  Washington, DC 20036-4700

Referenced Standards

- ### AITC
  American Institute of Timber Construction
  7012 S. Revere Parkway, Suite 140
  Englewood, CO 80112

  Web: www.aitc-glulam.org
  e-mail: info@aitc-glulam.org
  Fax: 303-792-0669
  Tel: 303-792-9559

- ### ALI
  Automotive Lift Institute
  P.O. Box 33116
  Indialantic, FL 32903-3116

  Web: www.autolift.org
  e-mail: autolift@iu.net
  Fax: 321-722-9993
  Tel: 321-722-9931

- ### ANSI
  American National Standards Institute
  11 West 42nd Street, 13th Floor
  New York, NY 10036

  Web: www.ansi.org
  e-mail: ansionline@ansi.org
  Fax: 212-398-0023
  Tel: 212-642-4900

- ### ASAE
  American Society of Agricultural Engineers
  2950 Niles Road
  St. Joseph, MI 49085-9659

  Web: www.asae.org
  e-mail: hq@asae.org
  Fax: 616-429-3852
  Tel: 616-429-0300

- ### ASCE
  American Society of Civil Engineers
  1801 Alexander Bell Drive
  Reston, Virginia 20191-4400

  Web: www.asce.org
  Tel: 800-548-2723

- ### ASME
  American Society of Mechanical Engineers
  Three Park Avenue
  New York, NY 10016-5990

  Web: www.asme.org
  Tel: 212-591-7000
  Tel: 800-843-2763

- ### ASTM
  American Society for Testing and Materials
  100 Barr Harbor Drive
  West Conshohocken, PA 19428-2959

  Web: www.astm.org
  e-mail: infoctr@astm.org
  Fax: 610-832-9555
  Tel: 610-832-9550

- ### AWPA
  American Wood-Preservers' Association
  P.O. Box 5690
  Grandbury, TX 76049-0690

  Web: www.awpa.com
  e-mail: awpa@itexas.net
  Fax: 817-326-6306

Referenced Standards

- **AWS**

  American Welding Society   Web: www.aws.org
  550 NW LeJeune Road   Fax: 305-443-7559
  Miami, FL 33126 Tel: Tel: 305-443-9353

- **BHMA**

  Builders Hardware Manufacturers'   Web: www.buildershardware.com
  Association   e-mail: info@buildershardware.com
  355 Lexington Avenue, 17th Floor   Fax: 212-370-9047
  New York, NY 10017-6603   Tel: 212-297-2100

- **CGSB**

  Canadian General Standards Board   Web: http//w3.pwgsc.gc.ca/
  222 Queens Street, 14th Floor, Suite 1402   e-mail: cgsb/text/welcom_e.html
  Ottawa, Ontario, Canada K1A 1G6   Fax: 819-956-5644
                                          Tel: 819-956-0425

- **CISCA**

  Ceiling and Interior Systems   Web: www.cisca.org
  Construction Association   Fax: 630-524-2003
  1500 Lincoln Highway, Suite 202   Tel: 630-584-1919
  St. Charles, IL 60174   Tel: 800-524-7228

- **CPSC**

  US Consumer Product Safety Commission   Web: www.cpsc.gov
  4330 East-West Highway   Fax: 301-504-0124
  Bethesada, MD 20814-4408   Tel: 301-504-0990
                                          Tel: 800-638-2772

- **CCSB**

  Cedar Shake and Shingle Bureau   Web: www.cedarbureau.org
  P.O. Box 1178   e-mail: info@cedarbureau.com
  Sumas, WA 98295-1178   Fax: 604-462-9386
                                    Tel: 604-462-8961

- **DASMA**

  Door and Access Systems Manufacturer's   Web: www.taol.com/dorma
  Association International   e-mail: dasma@taol.com
  1300 Summer Avenue   Tel: 216-241-7333
  Cleveland, OH 44115-2851

Referenced Standards

- **DOC**

  U.S. Department of Commerce
  National Institute of Standards
    and Technology
  100 Bureau Drive, Stop 2460
  Gaithersburg, MD 20899

  Web: www.nist.gov

- **DOL**

  U.S. Department of Labor
  c/o Superintendent of Documents
  U.S. Government Printing Office
  Washington, DC 20402-9325

  Web: www.gpo.gov

- **DOTn**

  U.S. Department of Transportation
  c/o Superintendent of Documents
  U.S. Government Printing Office
  Washington, DC 20402-9325

  Web: www.gpo.gov

- **EIA**

  Electronics Industries Alliance
  2500 Wilson Boulevard
  Arlington, VA 22201-3834

  Web: www.eia.org
  Fax: 703-907-7501
  Tel: 703-907-7500

- **EWA**

  APA — The Engineered Wood Association
  P.O. Box 11700
  Tacoma, WA 98411-0700

  Web: www.apawood.org
  e-mail: help@apawood.org
  Fax: 253-565-7265

- **FEMA**

  Federal Emergency Management Agency
  Federal Center Plaza
  500 C Street, SW, Room 824
  Washington, DC 20472-0001

  Web: www.fema.gov
  e-mail: eipa@fema.gov
  Tel: 202-646-4600

- **FM**

  Factory Mutual
  Standards Laboratories Department
  1151 Boston-Providence Turnpike
  P.O. Box 9102
  Norwood, MA 02062

  Web: www.fmglobal.com
  e-mail: information@fmglobal.com
  Fax: 781-255-4218
  Tel: 781-255-4200

Referenced Standards

- **GA**

  Gypsum Association   Web: www.gypsum.org
  810 First Street NE, #510   e-mail: info@gysum.org
  Washington, DC 20002-4268   Fax: 202-289-3707
                                        Tel: 202-289-5440

- **HPVA**

  Hardwood Plywood Veneer Association   Web: www.hpva.org
  1825 Michael Faraday Drive   e-mail: hpva@hpva.org
  P.O. Box 2789   Fax: 703-435-2537
  Reston, VA 20190-5350   Tel: 703-435-2900

- **ICC**

  International Code Council   Web: www.intlcode.org
  5203 Leesburg Pike, Suite 708   e-mail: staff@intlcode.org
  Falls Church, VA 22041   Fax: 703-379-1546
                                         Tel: 703-931-4533

- **NBS**

  National Bureau of Standards   Web: www.gpo.gov
  U.S. Department of Commerce
  Superintendent of Documents
  Government Printing Office
  Washington, DC 20401

- **NCMA**

  National Concrete Masonry Association Web: www.ncma.org
  2302 Horse Pen Road   e-mail: recepti@ncma.org
  Herndon, VA 22071-3499   Fax: 703-713-1910
                                         Tel: 703-713-1900

- **NEMA**

  National Electrical Manufacturers Association   Web: www.nema.org
  1300 North 17th Street, Suite 1847   Fax: 703-841-3300
  Rosslyn, VA 22209   Tel: 703-841-3200

- **NFPA**

  National Fire Protection Association   Web: www.nfpa.org
  1 Batterymarch Park   Fax: 617-770-0700
  P.O. Box 9101   Tel: 617-770-3000
  Quincy, MA 02269-9101

Referenced Standards

- **PCI**

  Precast/Prestressed Concrete Institute
  209 W. Jackson Boulevard
  Chicago, IL 60606-6938

  Web: www.pci.org
  e-mail: info@pci.org
  Fax: 312-786-0353
  Tel: 312-786-0300

- **PTI**

  Post-Tensioning Institute
  1717 W. Northern Avenue, Suite 114
  Phoenix, AZ 85021

  Web: www.post-tensioning.org
  e-mail: info@post-tensioning.org
  Fax: 602-870-7541
  Tel: 602-870-7540

- **RMA**

  Rubber Manufacturers Association
  1400 K Street, NW, #900
  Washington, DC 20005

  Web: www.rma.org
  Fax: 202-682-4854
  Tel: 202-682-4800
  Tel: 800-220-7622

- **RMI**

  Rack Manufacturers Institute
  8720 Red Oak Boulevard, Suite 201
  Charlotte, NC 28217

  Web: www.mhia.org/rmi/pr3.htm
  e-mail: infosinger@mhia.org
  Fax: 704-676-1199
  Tel: 704-676-1190

- **SAE**

  Society of Automotive Engineers
  400 Commonwealth Drive
  Warrendale, Pa 15096

  Web: www.sae.org
  e-mail: swiss@sae.org
  Fax: 724-776-5760
  Tel: 724-776-4841

- **SJI**

  Steel Joist Institute
  3127 10th Avenue, North Ext.
  Myrtle Beach, SC 29577-6760

  Web: www.steeljoist.org
  Fax: 843-626-5565
  Tel: 843-626-1995

- **SMACNA**

  Sheet Metal & Air Conditioning
     Contractor's National Association, Inc.
  4201 Lafayette Center Drive
  Chantilly, VA 20151-1209

  Web: www.smacna.org
  e-mail: info@smacna.org
  Fax: 703-803-3732
  Tel: 703-803-2980

- **TIA**

  Telecommunications Industry Association
  2500 Wilson Boulevard, Suite 300
  Arlington, VA 22201-3834

  Web: www.tiaonline.org
  e-mail: tia@tia.eia.org
  Fax: 703-907-7727
  Tel: 703-907-7700

<u>Referenced Standards</u>

- **TMS**

  The Masonry Society   Web: www.masonrysociety.org
  3970 Broadway, Unit 201-D   e-mail: info@masonrysociety.org
  Boulder, CO 80304-1135   Fax: 303-541-9215
                                               Tel: 303-939-9700

- **TPI**

  Truss Plate Institute   Tel: 608-833-5900
  583 D'Onofrio Drive, Suite 200
  Madison, WI 53719

- **UL**

  Underwriters Laboratories   Web: www.ul.com
  333 Pfingsten Road   e-mail: northbrook@us.ul.com
  Northbrook, IL 60062-2096   Fax: 847-272-8129
                                               Tel: 847-272-8800

- **ULC**

  Underwriters Laboratories of Canada   Web: www.ulc.ca
  7 Crouse Road   e-mail: ulcinfo@ulc.ca
  Toronto, Ontario, Canada M1R 3A9   Fax: 416-757-9540
                                               Tel: 416-757-3611
                                               Tel: 800-4636-852

- **USC**

  United States Code   Web: www.gpo.gov.
  c/o Superintendent of Documents
  U.S. Government Printing Office
  Washington, DC 20402-9325

- **WRI**

  Wire Reinforcement Institute, Inc.   Web: bright.net/~wwri/index.html
  2nd Floor, Suite 203C   e-mail: wwri@bright.net
  203 Loudon Street, SW
  Leesburg, VA 22075

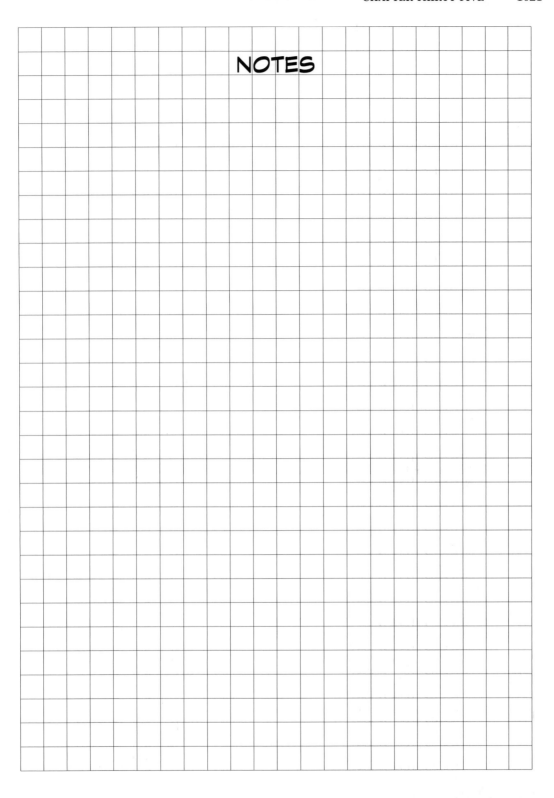

NOTES

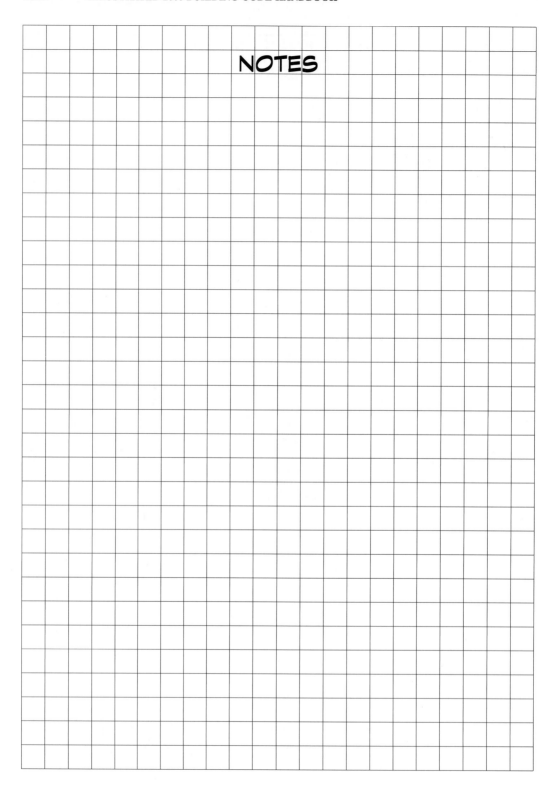

NOTES

Appendix

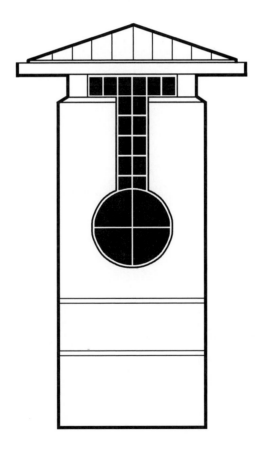

Lee's Summit Police and Court Facility. Lee's Summit, Missouri. *(partial elevation)*
The Hollis and Miller Group, Inc. Lee's Summit, Missouri.

Appendix A:
List of Abbreviations

These abbreviated terms may appear in both upper and lower case forms in the text, tables, and drawings.

act	actual	*dr*	door
admin	administration	*ea*	each
all	allowable	*elec*	electrical
bd	board	*elev*	elevation
bldg	building	*eq*	equal
bm	beam	*equip*	equipment
Btu	British thermal unit	*exist*	existing
cmu	concrete masonry unit	*ext*	exterior
col	column	*fe*	fire extinguisher
conc	concrete	*fec*	fire extinguisher cabinet
conf	conference	*fin*	finish
const	construction	*flr*	floor
cu ft	cubic foot or feet	*fdn*	foundation
cu in	cubic inch or inches	*ft*	foot or feet
df	drinking fountain	*ga*	gage
dia	diameter	*galv*	galvanized
dim	dimension	*gyp*	gypsum

horiz	horizontal	*ref*	refrigerator
ht	height	*reinf*	reinforcing
IBC	*International Building Code*	*req'd*	required
insul	insulation	*rm*	room
int	interior	*sched*	schedule
j	janitor	*sec*	secretary
jan	janitor	*sf*	square foot or feet
lav	lavatory	*sht*	sheet
lb	pound	*sq cm*	square centimeter
lbs/ft	pounds per foot	*sq in*	square inch or inches
lbs/ft	pounds per feet	*stl*	steel
m	men	*sto*	storage
max	maximum	*stor*	storage
mech	mechanical	*struct*	structural
mezz	mezzanine	*t*	toilet
mgr	manager	*typ*	typical
min	minimum	*ul*	unlimited
na	not applicable	*vert*	vertical
no.	number	*vest*	vestibule
nom	nominal	*w*	women
np	not permitted	*wc*	water closet
oc	on center	*wd*	wood
occ	occupancy	*wt*	weight
occ	occupants	*wwf*	welded wire fabric
off	office	*wwm*	welded wire mesh
opng	opening		
psf	pounds per square foot		
psi	pounds per square inch		
r	radius		
rec	reception		
recpt	*reception*		

Appendix B:
Symbols

@   at

<   less than

>   greater than

$\geq$ greater than or equal to

$\leq$ less than or equal to

$\perp$ perpendicular to

$\parallel$ parallel to

°   degrees, temperature

°   degrees, radial

÷   divide by

×   multiply by

=   equal to

%   percent

'   foot or feet

"   inch or inches

Appendix C:
List of Tables

The tables in the *Illustrated 2000 Building Code Handbook* are numbered according to the section they reference in the *International Building Code*.

Table   **Page**

Chapter 3

302.1.1.1	Maximum Undercut of Doors	12
302.3.3a	Occupancy A: Fire-Resistance Ratings for Occupancy Separations	16
302.3.3b	Occupancy B: Fire-Resistance Ratings for Occupancy Separations	17
302.3.3c	Occupancy E: Fire-Resistance for Occupancy Separations	18
302.3.3d	Occupancy F-1: Fire-Resistance Ratings for Occupancy Separations	19
302.3.3e	Occupancy F-2: Fire-Resistance Ratings for Occupancy Separations	20
302.3.3f	Occupancy H-2: Fire-Resistance Ratings for Occupancy Separations	21
302.3.3g	Occupancy H-3: Fire-Resistance Ratings for Occupancy Separations	21
302.3.3h	Occupancy H-4: Fire-Resistance Ratings for Occupancy Separations	22
302.3.3i	Occupancy H-5: Fire-Resistance Ratings for Occupancy Separations	22
302.3.3j	Occupancy I-1: Fire-Resistance Ratings for Occupancy Separations	23
302.3.3k	Occupancy I-2: Fire-Resistance Ratings for Occupancy Separations	23
302.3.3l	Occupancy I-3: Fire-Resistance Ratings for Occupancy Separations	24
302.3.3m	Occupancy I-4: Fire-Resistance Ratings for Occupancy Separations	24
302.3.3n	Occupancy M: Fire-Resistance Ratings for Occupancy Separations	25
302.3.3o	Occupancy R: Fire-Resistance Ratings for Occupancy Separations	26
302.3.3p	Occupancy S-1: Fire-Resistance Ratings for Occupancy Separations	27
302.3.3q	Occupancy S-2: Fire-Resistance Ratings for Occupancy Separations	28
302.3.3r	Occupancy U: Fire-Resistance Ratings for Occupancy Separations	29

Table		Page

Chapter 4

406.1.2	Occupancy U: Fire-Resistance Rating for Separation	72
406.3.5	Height Limits of Open Parking Garages	79
406.3.6a	Increased Height Limits of Open Parking Garages	79
406.3.6b	Limitations for Total Garage Area with Ramp Access	80
406.3.6c	Limitations for Total Garage Area with Mechanical Access	80

Chapter 5

503.1a	Maximum Building Height and Area per Floor	110
503.1b	Maximum Building Height and Area per Floor	112
503.1c	Maximum Building Height and Area per Floor	114
504.2a	Maximum Height of Sprinklered Buildings	117
504.2b	Maximum Height of Sprinklered Buildings	118
504.2c	Maximum Height of Sprinklered Buildings	119
504.2d	Maximum Height of Sprinklered Buildings	120
505.3	Length Limits for Common Path of Egress Travel	124
506.2a	% Increase in Area per Floor Due to Frontage	128
506.2b	% Increase in Area per Floor Due to Frontage	129
506.2c	% Increase in Area per Floor Due to Frontage	130
506.3a	Maximum Area per Floor in SF for Sprinklered Multistory Buildings	134
506.3b	Maximum Area per Floor in SF for Sprinklered 1-Story Buildings	135

Chapter 6

602.1a	Fire-Resistance Ratings for Type IA Buildings and Structures	143
602.1b	Fire Resistance Ratings for Type IB Buildings and Structures	144
602.1c	Fire-Resistance Ratings for Type IIA Buildings and Structures	146
602.1d	Fire-Resistance Ratings for Type IIB Buildings and Structures	147
602.1e	Fire-Resistance Ratings for Type IIIA Buildings and Structures	148
602.1f	Fire-Resistance Rating for Type IIIB Buildings and Structures	150
602.1g	Fire-Resistance Rating or Heavy Timber Requirements for Type IV Buildings and Structures	151
602.1h	Fire-Resistance Ratings for Type VA Buildings and Structures	152
602.1i	Fire-Resistance Rating for Type VB Buildings and Structures	153
602.4.3	Nominal Dimensions of Individual Roof Framing Members	156

Chapter 7

704.5a	Fire-Resistance Ratings for Type I Construction Exterior Walls	182
704.5b	Fire-Resistance Ratings for Type II Construction Exterior Walls	183
704.5c	Fire-Resistance Ratings for Type III Construction Exterior Walls	184
704.5d	Fire-Resistance Ratings for Type IV Construction Exterior Walls	185
704.5e	Fire-Resistance Ratings for Type V Construction Exterior Walls	186
704.7a	Equivalent Opening Factors for Exterior Walls	188
704.7b	Equivalent Opening Factors for Exterior Walls	189
704.7c	Equivalent Opening Factors for Exterior Walls	190

Table		Page
704.8a	% of an Exterior Wall That May Be Occupied by Unprotected Openings	191
704.8b	% of an Exterior Wall That May Be Occupied by Protected Openings	192
704.8.1	% of an Exterior Wall That May Be Occupied by Unprotected Openings: With Sprinklers	193
705.4	Fire-Resistance Ratings Required for Fire Walls	200

Chapter 10

1003.2.2.2	Maximum Floor Area per Occupant	374–375
1003.2.3	Means of Egress Width	383
1003.2.10.2	Exit Sign Graphics	399
1003.2.11	Egress Illumination	400
1003.2.11.1	Egress Illumination at Floor Level	401
1003.2.12.2	Sizes of Spheres That May Not Pass through a Guard	404
1003.2.13.5.1	Wheelchair Spaces Required	412
1003.3.1.1a	Minimum Width of Doors	415
1003.3.1.1b	Minimum Door Height	415
1003.3.1.2	Force Required at Door	416
1003.3.1.3.1	Maximum Speed for Revolving Doors	417
1003.3.3.1	Minimum Width of Stairway per Occupant Served	430
1003.3.3.3	Tread and Riser Heights	432
1003.3.5.1	Surfaces of Treads and Landings	434
1003.3.3.7	Treads and Risers of Circular Stairways	436
1003.3.10.2	Alternating Tread Devices	438
1003.3.11.2	Intermediate Handrails Required	439
1004.2.1	Spaces Requiring ≥ 2 Means of Egress	446
1004.2.3.2	Egress for I-2 Rooms and Suites	457
1004.2.4	Exit Access Travel Distance Limits	458
1004.2.5	Common Path Distance Limits	463
1004.3.1.3.2	Aisle Accessway Widths	468
1004.3.2.2 a	Minimum Corridor Widths	470
1004.3.2.2b	Minimum Required Width for Corridors per Occupant Served	470
1004.3.2.3	Dead-End Length Limits	470
1005.2.2	Conditions Permitting 1 Exit from a Building	477
1005.3.3.1	Protrusions into Exit Passageways	485
1005.3.5.3	Refuge Area Capacity	488
1006.3.1.1	Protrusions into Egress Courts	495
1008.5.1a	Stairway Width Based on Riser Height	502
1008.5.1b	Descending Egress Stairway Width Based on Riser Height	502
1008.5.2a	Width of Stairs and Aisle Steps ≤ 30" from a Handrail	503
1008.5.2b	Width of Stairs and Aisle Steps > 30" from a Handrail	504
1008.5.2c	Width of Passageways, Doorways, and Ramps ≤ 1:10 Slope	504
1008.5.2d	Width of Ramps > 1:10 Slope	505
1008.5.3	Egress Width in Outdoor Smoke-Protected Assembly	506
1008.6	Travel Distance in Assembly Spaces	507

Table		**Page**
1008.7.1	Aisle Width in Assembly Spaces	508
1008.7.5a	Row Width at Long Dead-End Aisles	509
1008.7.5b	Clear Width between Rows of Assembly Seating	509
1008.8.1a	Required Width between Rows for Seating Not Smoke-Protected, Access from 2 Sides	511
1008.8.1b	Required Width between Rows for Smoke-Protected Seats, Access from 2 Sides	511–512
1008.8.1c	Required Width between Rows for Smoke-Protected Seats, Access from 2 Sides	512–513
1008.8.2a	Required Clear Width between Rows Used for Egress between Aisles	513
1008.8.2b	Required Clear Width between Rows for Seating Not Smoke-Protected, Access 1 Side	514
1008.8.2c	Required Clear Width between Rows for Smoke-Protected Seats, Access 1 Side	514

Chapter 11

1106.1	Accessible Parking Other Than R-2 and R-3	535
1106.2	Accessible Parking in R-2 and R-3	537
1106.3	Accessible Parking at Rehabilitation and Outpatient Physical Therapy Facilities	537
1107.2.2	Wheelchair Spaces in Assembly Areas	540
1107.2.2.1a	Wheelchair Clusters with ≤ 1 Step between Rows	542
1107.2.2.1b	Wheelchair Clusters with > 1 Step between Rows	542
1107.2.4.1	Number of Receivers for Assistive Listening	544
1107.3.1	Accessible Residential Sleeping Rooms	545
1107.5.1	Accessible Sleeping Accommodations in R-1 and R-2	547–548
1107.6	Accessible Self-Storage Units	552
1108.12.2	Accessible Checkout Aisles	563

Chapter 12

1205.2	Minimum Yard Width	581
1205.3a	Courts with Windows on Opposite Sides	581
1205.3b	Courts without Windows on Opposite Sides	582
1205.3c	Minimum Length of Courts	582

Chapter 16

1604.3.6	Deflection Limit for Structural Members	655
1607.3	Minimum Uniformly Distributed Live Loads	657–658
1607.4	Minimum Concentrated Live Loads	659

Chapter 19

1909.6.2	Minimum Thickness of Plain Concrete Bearing Walls	723
1910.4.4.2	Reinforcing Required in Plain Concrete Footings	725

Table   **Page**

Chapter 21

2106.5.2a	Spacing (") for Reinforcing in Running Bond Masonry	755
2106.5.2b	Spacing (") for Reinforcing in Running Bond Masonry	755
2106.5.2c	Maximum Spacing (") for Reinforcing in Stack Bond Masonry	757
2106.5.2d	Maximum Spacing (") for Reinforcing in Stack Bond Masonry	
2106.6.1	Maximum Spacing (") for Reinforcing in Stack Bond Masonry	759
2106.6.2	Maximum Spacing (") for Reinforcing in Stack Bond Masonry	761
2108.9.3.8a	Maximum Spacing for Lateral Bracing for Masonry Beams	771
2108.9.3.8b	Maximum Spacing for Lateral Bracing for Masonry Piers and Columns	771
2108.9.6.3.4	Maximum Wall-Frame Masonry Beam Depths	773
2108.9.6.3.5	Maximum Widths for Masonry Wall-Frame Beams	775
2109.4.1a	Maximum Distance between Lateral Supports for Masonry Walls	780
2109.4.1b	Maximum Distance between Lateral Supports for Masonry Walls	780
2109.4.1c	Maximum Distance between Lateral Supports for Masonry Walls	781
2109.4.1d	Maximum Distance between Lateral Support for Masonry Walls	781
2109.6.5.2a	Maximum Vertical Spacing of Wire Joint-Reinforcing	799
2109.6.5.2b	Maximum Vertical Spacing of Deformed Reinforcing Bars in Bond Beams	799
2110.3.1	Maximum Dimensions of Glass Block Panels	808–811
2110.3.2	Thin Glass Block Units: Widths × Heights ≤ 85 sf	812
2110.3.3a	Standard Glass Block Units: Width × Height ≤ 250 sf	813
2110.3.3b	Thin Glass Block Units: Width × Height ≤ 150 sf	813

Chapter 26

2606.7.3	Maximum Sizes of Light-Transmitting Plastic Panels	905
2606.7.5	Minimum Center-to-Center Spacing of Plastic Diffusers in Ceilings of Exits and Corridors	906
2609.4a	Maximum Roof Panel Sizes for CC1 Plastics with No Sprinklers	923
2609.4b	Maximum Roof Panel Sizes for CC1 Plastics on Sprinklered Buildings	923
2609.4c	Maximum Total Area Permitted for Roof Panels of CC1 Plastics with No Sprinklers	924
2609.4d	Total Aggregate Area Permitted for Roof Panels of CC1 Plastics with Sprinklers	924
2609.4e	Maximum Roof Panel Sizes for CC2 Plastics with No Sprinklers	925
2609.4f	Maximum Roof Panel Sizes for CC2 Plastics on Sprinklered Buildings	925
2609.4g	Maximum Total Area Permitted for Roof Panels of CC2 Plastics with No Sprinklers	926
2609.4h	Total Aggregate Area Permitted for Roof Panels of CC2 Plastics with Sprinklers	926
2610.3	Required Rise of Domed Skylight vs. Span	928
2610.4	Maximum Sizes Permitted for Skylights	930
2610.5a	Maximum Total Skylight Area for CC1 Plastics with No Sprinklers or Vents	932

Table		**Page**
2610.5b	Maximum Total Skylight Area for CC1 Plastics with Sprinklers or Vents	932
2610.5c	Maximum Total Skylight Area for CC2 Plastics with No Sprinklers or Vents	933
2610.5d	Maximum Total Skylight Area for CC2 Plastics with Sprinklers or Vents	933
2611.2	Areas of Interior Signs Permitted Based on Wall Area	936
2611.3	Dimensions of Interior Signs ≤ 24 sf in Area	936

Chapter 29

2902.1a	Restaurants: Minimum Plumbing Fixtures Required	948
2902.1b	Churches: Minimum Plumbing Fixtures Required	949
2902.1c	Nightclubs: Minimum Plumbing Fixtures Required	949
2902.1d	Theaters, Halls, Museums, etc: Minimum Plumbing Fixtures Required	950
2902.1e	Coliseums and Arenas 1–1725 Seats: Minimum Plumbing Fixtures Required	951
2902.1f	Coliseums and Arenas 1726–2999 Seats: Minimum Plumbing Fixtures Required	952
2902.1g	Coliseums and Arenas > 3000 Seats: Minimum Plumbing Fixtures Required	953
2902.1h	Stadiums and Pools < 3000 Seats: Minimum Plumbing Fixtures Required	954
2902.1i	Stadiums 17,100–21,375 Seats: Minimum Plumbing Fixtures Required	955
2902.1j	Stadiums 31,050–35,325 Seats: Minimum Plumbing Fixtures Required	956
2902.1k	Stadiums 45,000–49,275 Seats: Minimum Plumbing Fixtures Required	957
2902.1l	Mercantile: Minimum Plumbing Fixtures Required	958
2902.1m	Business: Minimum Plumbing Fixtures Required	958
2902.1n	Educational: Minimum Plumbing Fixtures Required	958
2902.1o	Factory and Industrial: Minimum Plumbing Fixtures Required	959
2902.1p	Passenger Terminals and Transportation Facilities: Minimum Fixtures Required	959
2902.1q	Residential Care: Minimum Plumbing Fixtures Required	960
2902.1r	Hospitals, Ambulatory Nursing Homes: Minimum Fixtures Required for Patients	960
2902.1s	Day Nurseries, Sanitariums, Nonambulatory Nursing Homes: Minimum Plumbing Fixtures Required for Patients	961
2902.1t	Institutional Employees Other Than Residential Care: Minimum Fixtures Required for Employees	961
2902.1u	Institutional Visitors Other Than Residential Care: Minimum Plumbing Fixtures Required for Vistors	962
2902.1v	Prisons: Minimum Fixtures Required for Inmates	962
2902.1w	Asylums, Reformatories, etc.: Minimum Plumbing Fixtures Required for Inmates	962
2902.1x	Lodges: Minimum Plumbing Fixtures Required	962

Table   **Page**

2902.1y   Multifamily Housing and Attached 1- and 2- Family Dwellings:
                    Minimum Automatic Clothes Washer Connections Required   964

2902.1z   Storage: Minimum Plumbing Fixtures Required   964

2902.1aa   Dormitories: Minimum Plumbing Fixtures Required for 1–360
                    Occupants   965

2902.1bb   Dormitories: Minimum Plumbing Fixtures Required for 361–720
                    Occupants   966

Chapter 32

3202.3.2   Encroachment into Public Right-of-Way Permitted: Windows, Balconies,
                    Architectural Features, Mechanical Equipment   997

Index

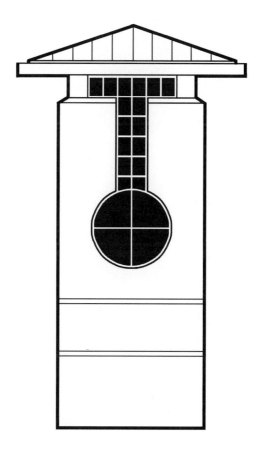

Lee's Summit Police and Court Facility. Lee's Summit, Missouri. *(partial elevation)*
The Hollis and Miller Group, Inc. Lee's Summit, Missouri.

Index A:
Tables

The tables in the *Illustrated 2000 Building Code Handbook* are italicized and in parentheses. They are numbered according to the section they reference in the *2000 International Building Code*.

A

Accessible check-out aisles *(1108.12.2)*, **563**
Accessible self-storage units *(1107.6)*, **552**
Accessible sleeping accommodations:
    residential *(1107.3.1)*, **545**
    R-1 and R-2 *(1107.5.1)*, **547–548**
Accessibility:
    assistive listening receivers *(1107.2.4.1)*, **544**
    R-2 and R-3 parking *(1106.1)*, **535;**
    other parking *(1106.2)*, **537**
    outpatient parking *(1106.3)*, **537**
    wheelchair clusters *(1107.2.2.1a–b)*, **542**
    wheelchair spaces *(1107.2.2)*, **540**
    wheelchair spaces required *(1003.2.13.5.1)*,
        412
Aisles:
    check-out, accessible *(1108.12.2)*, **563**
    steps *(1008.5.2a–b)*, **503–504**
    widths *(1004.3.1.3.2)*, **468**
Aisles:
    width *(1008.7.1)*, **508**; *(1008.8.2a)*, **513**
    width, not smoke-protected *(1008.8.1a)*, **511**;
        (1008.8.2b), **514**
    width, smoke-protected *(1008.1.1b)*, **511–512**;

(1008.8.1c), **512–513**; *(1008.8.2c)*, **514**
Aisles, dead-end:
    clear width *(1008.7.5b)*, **509**
    width *(1008.7.5a)*, **509**
Area of refuge, *see* Refuge area.
Assistive listening receivers *(1107.2.4.1)*, **544**

B

Beams, masonry:
    depth *(2108.9.6.3.4)*, **773**
    lateral bracing *(2108.9.3.8a)*, **771**
    width *(2108.9.6.3.5)*, **775**
Bracing, lateral:
    masonry beams *(2108.9.3.8a)*, **771**
    masonry columns *(2108.9.3.8a)*, **771**
    masonry piers *(2108.9.3.8a)*, **771**
Building area:
    area increase due to frontage *(506.2a-c)*,
        128–130
    occupancies A, B, E *(503.1a)*, **110**
    occupancies F, F-1, F-2, H1-5, I1-4 *(503.1b)*,
        112
    occupancies M, R1-4, S1-2, U *(503.1c)*, **114**

Building area – *continued*:
    sprinklered occupancy A *(504.2a)*, **117**
    sprinklered occupancies B, E *(504.2b)*, **118**
    sprinklered occupancies F, H, H-4, I-4, M
        (504.2c), **119**
    sprinklered occupancies R, S, U *(504.2d)*, **120**
Building height
    occupancies A, B, E *(503.1a)*, **110**
    occupancies F, F-1, F-2, H1-5, I1-4 *(503.1b)*,
        112
    occupancies M, R1-4, S1-2, U *(503.1c)*, **114**
    sprinklered occupancy A *(504.2a)*, **117**
    sprinklered occupancies B, E *(504.2b)*, **118**
    sprinklered occupancies F, H, H-4, I-4, M
        (504.2c), **119**
    sprinklered occupancies R, S, U *(504.2d)*, **120**
Buildings, multistory
    area per floor *(506.3a)*, **134**
Buildings, 1-story:
    area per floor, *(506.3b)*, **135**
    only 1 exit *(1005.2.2)*, **477**

C

Columns, masonry:
    lateral bracing *(2108.9.3.8a)*, **771**
Common path distance:
    limits *(1004.2.5)*, **463**
Concrete, plain:
    bearing walls *(1909.6.2)*, **723**
    footings *(1910.4.4.2)*, **725**
Corridors:
    widths *(1004.3.2.2a)*, **470**
    widths per occupant served*(1004.3.2.2b)*, **470**
Courts:
    minimum length *(1205.3c)*, **582**
    width *(1205.3a–b)*, **581–582**

D

Deflection: structural members *(1604.3.6)*, **655**
Diffusers:
    ceilings of exits and corridors *(2606.7.5)*, **906**
    maximum panel size *(2606.7.3)*, **905**
Dead ends:
    length limits *(1004.3.2.3)*, **470**

Doors:
    force required *(1003.3.1.2)*, **416**
    height *(1003.3.1.1a)*, **415**
    maximum undercut *(302.1.1.1)*, **12**
    revolving doors *(1003.3.1.3.1)*, **417**
    width *(1003.3.1.1a)*, **415**
Doorways: width on a slope *(1008.5.2c)*, **504**

E

Egress travel
    common path length limits *(505.3)*, **124**
Encroachments: windows, balconies, etc.
    (3202.3.2), **997**
Exit access:
    aisle widths *(1004.3.1.3.2)*, **468**
    corridor widths *(1004.3.2.2a)*, **470**
    corridor widths per occupant served
        (1004.3.2.2b), **470**
Exit passageways:
    protrusions *(1005.3.3.1)*, **485**
Exits:
    common path distance *(1004.2.5)*, **463**
    dead ends *(1004.3.2.3)*, **470**
    egress for I-2 rooms and suites *(1004.2.3.2)*,
        446
    minimum required *(1004.2.1)*, **446**
    only 1 required *(1005.2.2)*, **477**
    signs *(1003.2.10.2)*, **399**
    travel distance *(1004.2.4)*, **458**

F

Footings:
    reinforcing required *(1910.4.4.2)*, **725**
Fire-resistance ratings:
    fire walls *(705.4)*, **200**
Fire-resistance ratings, construction type:
    Type IA *(602.1a)*, **143**
    Type IB *(602.1b)*, **144**
    Type IIA *(602.1c)*, **146**
    Type IIB *(602.1d)*, **147**
    Type IIIA *(602.1e)*, **148**
    Type IIIB *(602.1f)*, **150**
    Type IV *(602.1g)*, **151**
    Type VA *(602.1h)*, **152**
    Type VB *(602.1i)*, **153**

Fire-resistance ratings, exterior walls:
    Type I *(704.5a)*, **182**
    Type II *(704.5b)*, **183**
    Type III *(704.5c)*, **184**
    Type IV *(704.5d)*, **185**
    Type V *(704.5e)*, **186**
Fire-resistance ratings, occupancy:
    A *(302.3.3a)*, **16**
    B *(302.3.3b)*, **17**
    E *(302.3.3c)*, **18**
    F-1 *(302.3.3d)*, **19**
    F-2 *(302.3.3e)*, **20**
    H-2 *(302.3.3f)*, **21**
    H-3 *(302.3.3g)*, **21**
    H-4 *(302.3.3h)*, **22**
    H-5 *(302.3.3i)*, **22**
    I-1 *(302.3.3j)*, **23**
    I-2 *(302.3.3k)*, **23**
    I-3 *(302.3.3l)*, **24**
    I-4 *(302.3.3m)*, **24**
    M *(302.3.3n)*, **25**
    R *(302.3.3o)*, **26**
    S-1 *(302.3.3p)*, **27**
    S-2 *(302.3.3q)*, **28**
    U *(302.3.3r)*, **29**
    U *(406.1.2)*, **72**
Floors:
    max area per occupant *(1003.2.2.2)*, **374-75**
Frontage:
    area per floor *(506.2a)*, **128–130**

G

Garages:
    with mechanical access *(406.3.6c)*, **80**
    with ramp access *(406.3.6b)*, **80**
Garages, open parking:
    height limits *(406.3.5)*, **79**
    increased height limits *(406.3.6a)*, **79**
    protected openings *(704.8b)*, **192**
    unprotected openings *(704.8a)*, **191**; *(704.8.1)*, **193**
Glass, block:
    panel dimensions *(2110.3.1)*, **808–811**
    widths × heights ≤ 85 sf *(2110.3.2)*, **812**
    widths × heights ≤ 250 sf *(2110.3.3a)*, **813**
    widths × heights ≤ 150 sf *(2110.3.3b)*, **813**

Guards: limitations of openings *(1003.2.12.2)*, **404**

H

Handrails: intermediate *(1003.3.11.2)*, **439**

I

Illumination:
    at floor level *(1003.2.11.1)*, **401**
    means of egress *(1003.2.11)*, **400**

L

Loads, live:
    uniform *(1607.3)*, **657–658**
    concentrated *(1607.4)*, **659**

M

Means of egress:
    common path length limits *(505.3)*, **124**
    door height *(1003.3.1.1b)*, **415**
    door width *(1003.3.1.1a)*, **415**
    exits required *(1004.2.1)*, **446**
    force at doors *(1003.3.1.2)*, **416**
    illumination *(1003.2.11)*, **400**
    I-2 rooms and suites *(1004.2.3.2)*, **457**
    protrusions *(1006.3.1.1)*, **495**
    revolving doors *(1003.3.1.3.1)*, **417**
    smoke-protected assembly space *(1008.5.3)*, **506**
    stairway width *(1003.3.3.1)*, **430**
    travel distance in assembly spaces *(1008.6)*, **507**
    width *(1003.2.3)*, **383**
    width between seating rows *(1008.8.2a)*, **513**
    width on a slope *(1008.5.2c)*, **504**
Mechanical access:
    garages *(406.3.6b)*, **80**

O

Occupancy separations
    occupancy A *(302.3.3a)*, **16**
    occupancy B *(302.3.3b)*, **17**
    occupancy E *(302.3.3c)*, **18**
    occupancy F-1 *(302.3.3d)*, **19**
    occupancy F-2 *(302.3.3e)*, **20**
    occupancy H-2 *(302.3.3f)*, **21**
    occupancy H-3 *(302.3.3g)*, **21**
    occupancy H-4 *(302.3.3h)*, **22**
    occupancy H-5 *(302.3.3i)*, **22**
    occupancy I-1 *(302.3.3j)*, **23**
    occupancy I-2 *(302.3.3k)*, **23**
    occupancy I-3 *(302.3.3l)*, **24**
    occupancy I-4 *(302.3.3m)*, **24**
    occupancy M *(302.3.3n)*, **25**
    occupancy R *(302.3.3o)*, **26**
    occupancy S-1 *(302.3.3p)*, **27**
    occupancy S-2 *(302.3.3q)*, **28**
    occupancy U *(302.3.3r)*, **29**
Openings: within guards *(1003.2.12.2)*, **404**
Openings, protected: exterior walls *(704.8b)*, **192**
Openings, unprotected: exterior walls *(704.8a)*, **191**

P

Plumbing fixtures required:
    asylums, etc. *(2902.1w)*, **962**
    business *(2902.1m)*, **958**
    churches *(2902.1b)*, B
    coliseums and areanas *(2902.1e–g)*, **951–953**
    day nurseries, etc. *(2902.1s)*, **961**
    dormitories *(2902.1aa–bb)*, **965–966**
    educational *(2902.1n)*, **958**
    factory and industrial *(2902.1o)*, **959**
    hospitals, etc. *(2902.1r)*, **960**
    institutional employees *(2902.1t)*, **961**
    institutional visitors *(2902.1u)*, **962**
    mercantile *(2902.1l)*, **958**
    lodges *(2902.1x)*, **962**
    multifamily housing etc.*(2902.1y)*, **964**
    nightclubs *(2902.1c)*, **949**
    passenger terminals etc. *(2902.1p)*, **959**
    prisons *(2902.1v)*, **962**
    residential care *(2092.1q)*, **960**
    restaurants *(2902.1a)*, **948**
    staiums and pools *(2902.1h–k)*, **954–957**
    storage *(2902.1z)*, **964**
    theaters, halls, museums, etc. *(2902.1d)*, **950**
Protrusions:
    into egress courts *(1006.3.1.1)*, **495**
    into exit passageways *(1005.3.3.1)*, **485**
Parking, accessible:
    R-2 and R-3 *(1106.1)*, **535**
    other *(1106.2)*, **537**
    outpatient *(1106.3)*, **537**
Piers, masonry: lateral bracing *(2108.9.3.8a)*,**771**

R

Ramp access:
    garages *(406.3.6b)*, **80**
Ramps: slope *(1008.5.2c–d)*, **504–505**
Refuge area:
    capacity *(1005.3.5.3)*, **488**
    wheelchair spaces required *(1003.2.13.5.1)*, **412**
Reinforcing:
    bond beams *(2109.6.5.2b)*, **799**
    joint *(2109.6.5.2a)*, **799**
    running bond *(2106.5.2a–b)*, **755**
    stack bond *(2106.5.2c–d)*, **757**
Risers, *see* Stairways.
Roof framing: dimensions *(602.4.3)*, **156**
Roof panels:
    CC1 plastic, no sprinklers *(2609.4a)*, **923**; *(2609.4c)*, **924**
    CCI plastic, with sprinklers *(2609.4b)*, **923**; *(2609.4d)*, **924**
    CC2 plastic, no sprinklers *(2609.4e)*, **925**; *(2609.4g)*, **926**
Roofs: deflection *(1604.3.6)*, **655**

S

Signs:
    area permitted *(2611.2)*, B
    dimensions *(2611.3)*, **936**
    exit *(1003.2.10.2)*, **399**
Skylights:
    CC1 plastic, no sprinklers or vents *(2610.5a)*, **932**
    CC1 plastic, with sprinklers or vents *(2610.5b)*, **932**

CC2 plastic, no sprinklers or vents
(2610.5c), **933**
CC2 plastaic, with sprinklers or vents
(2510.5d), **933**
maximum size *(2610.4)*, **928**
rise vs. span *(2610.3)*, **928**
Seating:
clear width *(1008.7.5b)*, **509**
clear width, not smoke-protected
(1008.8.2b), **514**
clear width, smoke-protected *(1008.8.2c)*,
514
wheelchair clusters *(1107.2.2.1a–b)*, **542**
wheelchair spaces *(1107.2.2)*, **540**
width *(1008.8.2a)*, **513**
width, not smoke-protected *(1008.8.1a)*,
511; *(1008.8.1c)*, **512–513**
width, smoke-protected *(1008.1.1b)*,
511–512
Sleeping accommodations, accessible:
residential *(1107.3.1)*, **545**
R-1 and R-2 *(1107.5.1)*, **547–548**
Stairways:
alternating tread devices *(1003.3.10.2)*, **438**
intermediate handrails *(1003.3.11.2)*, **439**
riser height *(1003.3.3.3)*, **430**
surface of landings *(1003.3.5.1)*, **434**
surface of treads *(1003.3.5.1)*, **434**
tread height *(1003.3.3.3)*, **430**
width *(1003.3.3.1)*, **430**; *(1008.5.1a–b)*,
502; *(1008.5.2a–b)*, **503–504**
Stairways, circular:
treads and risers *(1003.3.3.7)*, **436**
Storage units, accessible *(1107.6)*, **552**

T

Treads, *see* Stairways.

W

Walls: plain concrete *(1909.6.2)*, **723**
Walls, exterior:
deflection *(1604.3.6)*, **655**
Equivalent Opening Factors *(704.7a-c)*,
188-190
unprotected openings *(704.8a)*, **191**;

Walls, reinforcing:
running bond *(2106.5.2a–b)*, **755**
stack bond (2106.5.2c–d), **757**; *(2106.6.1)*,
759; 2106.6.2), **761**
Wheelchairs, *see* Accessibility.

Y

Yards: width *(1205.2)*, **581**

Index B:
Subject

Section numbers are italicized and in parentheses. They also correspond
to the section they reference in the the *2000 International Building Code*.

A

Access:
    courts *(1205.3.1)*, **582**
    doors *(710.3.1.1)*, **229**
    to emergency equipment *(402.15)*, **62**
    to exits *(402.4.5)*, **56**
Access to Unoccupied Spaces, **588**
Accessibility, **525**
    definitions, *(1102.1)*, **526**
    Scoping Requirements *(1103)*, **527**
    Special Occupancies *(1107)*, **540**
Accessibility for Existing Buildings, **1009**
Accessible:
    entrances *(1105.1)*, **534**; *(1105.2)*, **534**
    Parking and Passenger Loading Facilities
    (1106), **535**
    routes *(1104.1)*, **530**
    spaces *(1107.5.2)*, **549**
Accessory use area *(302.2)*, **13**
ACI 530/ASCE 5/TMS 402, Section 2.1.4
    (2107.2.2), **762**
Acoustical ceiling systems:
    fire-resistance-rated construction *(803.8.1.2)*,
    340

    materials and installation *(803.8.1)*, **340**
    suspended acoustical ceilings *(803.8.1.1)*, **340**
Additions, Alterations or Repairs, **1008**
Adult care facility *(308.5.1)*, **45**
Air transfer *(711.3.3)*, **234**; *(see also*, Ducts and
    air transfer)
Air-borne sound *(1206.2)*, **584**
Aisles *(1008.7)*, **507-508**:
    check-out *(1108.12.2)*, **563**
    converging *(1008.7.3)*, **508**
    discontinuous handrails *(1008.11.1)*, **517**
    dual access *(1008.8.1)*, **511-513**
    guards *(1008.12.3)*, **518**
    handrails *(1008.11)*, **516**
    intermediate handrails *(1008.11.2)*, **517**
    obstructions to *(1008.7.6)*, **510**
    risers *(1008.9.2)*, **515**
    serving seating *(1008.8)*, **510**
    single access *(1008.8.2)*, **513-515**
    treads *(1008.9.1)*, **515**; *(1008.9.3)*, **516**
    uniform width *(1008.7.4)*, **508**
    walking surface *(1008.9)*, **515**
    widths *(1008.7.1)*, **508**; *(1008.7.2)*, **508**
Aisles, cross *(1008.12.1)*, **518**
Alarm communication system *(402.13)*, **61**;
    (403.6), **65**

Aluminum, **735**; *(2002.1)*, **736**
Anchor building:
  means of egress *(402.4.3.1)*, **56**
  occupant load *(402.4.1.3)*, **55**
  openings *(402.7.2.1)*, **59**
Anchorage:
  masonry wall *(2109.7.2.2)*, **801**;
    (2109.7.2.3), **801**; *(2109.7.2.4)*, **803**;
    (2109.7.4), **806**
  roof *(2109.7.3.3)*, **805**
  steel floor *(2109.7.3.2)*, **805**
  wood floor *(2109.7.3.1)*, **804**
Approvals, **664**
Architectural features *(3202.2.2)*, **994**
Architectural trim:
  combustible exterior walls *(1406.2.2)*, **619**
Area Modifications, **127**
Areas:
  accessory use *(302.2)*, **13**
  incidental use *(302.1.1)*, **11–12**; *(706.3.4)*,
    208; *(302.1.1.1)*, **12**
  mixed occupancies *(302.3.1)*, **13**; *(302.3.2)*,
    14; *(302.3.3)*, **14–29**
Areas, private garages and carports *(406.1.2)*, **72**
Areas, service *(402.4.6)*, **57**
Areas of refuge:
  2-way communication *(1003.2.13.5.3)*, **412**;
    (1003.2.13.5.4), **414**
  identification *(1003.2.13.5.5)*, **414**
  means of egress *(1003.2.13.5)*, **410**;
    (1003.2.13.5.1), **412**
Ashlar masonry *(2109.6.4.1)*, **795**
Assembly *(1008)*, **499**
Assembly aisle termination *(1008.7.5)*, **509**
Assembly Group A *(303.1)*, **30 – 31**
Assistive listening systems *(1107.2.4)*, **543**:
  receivers *(1107.2.4.1)*, **544**
Atriums, **69**
Attics:
  access *(1208.2)*, **588**
  draftstopping *(716.4)*, **252**
  insulation materials in floors *(718.3.1)*, **259**
  thermal barrier *(2603.4.1.6)*, **898**
  ventilation *(1202.2)*, **572**
  ventilation openings *(1202.2.1)*, **574**
Automatic sprinkler systems, **348**
Awnings *(3202.2.3)*, **995**
Awnings, canopies, marquees and signs
  (3202.3.1), **995**

B

Backing board:
  gypsum board *(2510.5.2.1)*, **888**;
    (2510.5.2.2), **888**
Balconies:
  combustible exterior walls *(1406.3)*, **620-621**
  means of egress *(1004.3.3)*, **473**
Barriers:
  height and clearances *(3109.4.1)*, **984**
Barriers, fire *(706.1)*, **207**
Basements:
  area modifications *(506.1.1)*, **127**
  limitations *(503.1.1)*, **115**
  sprinkler system *(903.2.12.1.3)*, **354**
  walls *(1909.6.1)*, **722**
  without openings *(903.2.12.1)*, **353**
Bathing facilities:
  accessibility *(1108.2)*, **553-554, 555**
  unisex *(1108.2.1)*, **555**
Bathing rooms *(2509.2)*, **887**; *(2509.3)*, **887**
Bathing rooms, accessible:
  clear floor space *(1108.2.1.6)*, **556**
  location *(1108.2.1.4)*, **556**
  privacy *(1108.2.1.7)*, **556**
  prohibited route *(1108.2.1.5)*, **556**
  unisex *(1108.2.1.3)*, **556**
Bathrooms:
  ventilation *(1202.4.2.1)*, **578**
Beams, masonry:
  clear span *(2108.9.6.3.3)*, **773**
  columns *(2108.9.6.6.2)*, **776**; *(2108.9.6.6.3)*,
    776; *(2108.9.6.6.4)*, **776**
  depth *(2108.9.6.3.4)*, **773**
  dimensional limits *(2108.9.3.8)*, **771-772**
  width *(2108.9.6.3.5)*, **775**
Bench seating *(1008.14)*, **520**
Bleachers, footboards *(1008.13)*, **520**
Boiler, incinerator and furnace rooms *(1007.1)*,
  496
Bonding:
  ashlar masonry *(2109.6.4.1)*, **795**
  headers *(2109.6.2.1)*, **786**; *(2109.6.2.2)*, **789**
  hollow walls *(2109.6.2.3)*, **789**
  joint reinforcement *(2109.6.3.2)*, **794**
  rubble stone *(2109.6.4.2)*, **797**
  wall ties *(2109.6.3.1)*, **790**; *(2109.6.3.1.1)*,
    793
Bonding patterns:
  intersecting walls *(2109.7.2.1)*, **800**

running bond *(2109.6.5.1)*, **798**
stack bond *(2109.6.5.2)*, **799**
Building area modifications *(506.1)*, **127**
Building height modifications *(504.1)*, **117**
Building heights and areas, general limitations *(503.1)*, **110**; **107**
Buildings with one exit *(1005.2.2)*, **476-477**
Buildings, unlimited area *(507)*, **136**
Business Group B *(304.1)*, **32**

C

Canopies:
    motor vehicle service station *(406.5.2)*, **84**
Care facilities:
    accessibility *(1107.4)*, **547**
Catwalk *(410.3.2)*, **100**:
    means of egress *(1007.5.1)*, **498**
Ceilings:
    acoustical systems *(803.8.1)*, **340**; *(803.8.1.1)*, **340**; *(803.8.1.2)*, **340**
    fireblocking openings *(716.2.5)*, **249**
    heights *(1207.2)*, **585**
    means of egress *(1003.2.4)*, **387**
    panels *(710.3.1)*, **229**
Cellulose nitrate film handling *(1007.4)*, **497**
Chain link dimensions *(3109.4.1.5)*, **987**
Chases and recesses *(2104.1.4)*, **746**
Child care facility *(308.3.1)*, **43**; *(308.5.2)*, **45**
Columns:
    classification *(602.4.1)*, **155**
    concrete-filled pipe *(1916.4)*, **731**
    load-bearing *(2106.4.1.2)*, **749**
    reinforcing *(2108.9.2.4)*, **766**
Columns, masonry:
    dimensional limits *(2108.9.3.8)*, **771-772**
    reinforcement *(2106.5.4)*, **759**
Combustible Material in Types I and II Construction, **160**
Combustible Materials on the Exterior Side of Exterior Walls, **619**
Communication system:
    alarm/emergency voice *(402.13)*, **61**; *(403.6)*, **65**
    fire department *(403.7)*, **65**
    stairways *(403.11.1)*, **68**
Concealed spaces, **247**
Concrete, **717**:
    fire resistance protection *(719.1.5)*, **325**

foam plastic insulation *(2603.4.1.1)*, **895**
footings *(1805.4.2)*, **673**
tolerances *(1907.5.2.1)*, **718**; *(1907.5.2.2)*, **719**
Concrete slabs — thickness *(1911.1)*, **727**
Concrete, cast-in-place:
    fire-resistance protection for columns *(719.1.3)*, **325**
    nonprestressed *(1907.7.1)*, **719**
Concrete, gypsum:
    reinforcing *(1915.2)*, **730**
Concrete, plain:
    basement walls *(1909.6.1)*, **722**
    footings *(1805.4.2.3)*, **673**
    openings *(1909.6.3)*, **724**
    walls *(1909.6.2)*, **723**
Concrete-filled pipe columns *(1916.4)*, **731**
Connectors, masonry *(2109.7.2.2)*, **801**
Construction *(3106.5)*, **983**; **741**
Construction classification *(602.1)*, **142**
Construction Documents, *(106)*, **2**
Controls and operating mechanisms:
    accessibility *(1108.13)*, **564**
Coolers and freezers:
    insulation *(2603.4.1.2)*, **895**
    thermal barrier *(2603.4.1.2)*, **895**; *(2603.4.1.3)*, **896**
Coping *(1503.3)*, **626**
Corridors:
    continuity *(1004.3.2.5)*, **473**
        doors *(407.3.1)*, **87**
    gift shops *(407.2.4)*, **86**
    Group I-2 *(407.2)*, **85**
    locking devices *(407.3.2)*, **87**
    mental health treatment areas *(407.2.3)*, **86**
    nurses' stations *(407.2.2)*, **86**
    spaces of unlimited area *(407.2.1)*, **85**
    walls *(407.3)*, **86**
    width *(1004.3.2.2)*, **470**
Counters, point of sales and service:
    accessibility *(1108.12.3)*, **564**
Courts *(1205.1)*, **581**
Covered Mall Buildings, **54**
Crawl spaces:
    access *(1208.1)*, **588**
    thermal barrier *(2603.4.1.6)*, **898**
Cupolas (*see also* Towers, spires, domes and cupolas) *(1509.5)*, **650**
Curb or barrier:
    ramps *(1003.3.4.8.2)*, **445**

Curtain walls:
foundation*(1805.5.6)*, **707-708**

D

Dampproofing and waterproofing *(1806.1)*, **709**
Day care:
classification *(305.2)*, **34**
Group I-4 *(308.5)*, **45**
Dead ends *(1004.3.2.3)*, **470**
Decks:
asphalt roof *(1507.2.1)*, **629**
clay and concrete tile roof *(1507.3.1)*, **633**;
(1507.3.2), **633**
metal roof *(1507.5.1)*, **635**; *(1507.5.2)*,
635
metal roof panels *(1507.4.1)*, **635**;
(1507.4.2), **635**
mineral-surfaced roll roof *(1507.6.1)*, **638**;
(1507.6.2), **638**
slate roof *(1507.7.1)*, **639**; *(1507.7.2)*, **639**
solid sheathing *(1507.9.1.1)*, **644**
wood shake roof *(1507.9.1)*, **644**; *(1507.9.2)*,
645
wood shingle roof *(1507.8.1)*, **642**;
(1507.8.2), **642**
Decorations and trim *(805.1)*, **344**
Definitions:
accessibility, **526**
atriums *(404.1.1)*, **69**
building areas *(502.1)*, **108–109**
building heights *(502.1)*, **108–109**
covered mall buildings *(402.2)*, **54**
fire-resistant-rated construction *(702.1)*,
166–176
gypsum board and plaster *(2502.1)*, **884**
interior finishes, **330**
means of egress *(1002.1)*, **362-371**
open parking garages *(406.3.2)*, **76–77**
stages and platforms *(410.2)*, **97—98**
Design requirements:
limits *(1604.3.6)*, **654-655**
Details of Reinforcement, **718**
Diagonal members *(3109.4.1.6)*, **988**
Dining areas:
accessibility *(1107.2.5)*, **544**
Dining counters:
accessibility *(1107.2.5.2)*, **545**

Domes (*see also* Towers, spires, domes and
cupolas) *(1509.5)*, **650**
Door encroachment:
means of egress *(1003.2.3.1)*, **386**
Door swing:
means of egress *(1003.3.1.2)*, **416**
Door width:
means of egress *(408.3.1)*, **90**
Doors:
arrangement *(1003.3.1.7)*, **425**
corridors *(407.3.1)*, **87**
exterior exits *(1005.3.1)*, **479**
foam, plastic insulation *(2603.4.1.7)*, **900**;
(2603.4.1.8), **900**
glazing *(714.2.4.1)*, **241**
operation in stairways *(403.11)*, **68**
power operated *(408.4.2)*, **92**
projections into clear width *(1003.3.1.1.1)*,
415
resident housing *(408.7.4)*, **96**
security *(402.11)*, **60**
stage *(410.3.3)*, **100-101**
without fire-resistance rating *(2603.4.1.7)*, **900**
Doors, access:
horizontal assemblies *(710.3.1.1)*, **229**
Doors, access-controlled:
means of egress *(1003.3.1.3.4)*, **421**
Doors, fire *(714.2)*, **240**; *(711.4.6)*, **239**
Doors, garage:
without fire-resistance rating *(2603.4.1.9)*, **901**
Doors, hardware height *(1003.3.1.8.3)*, **426**
Doors, horizontal sliding doors;
means of egress *(1003.3.1.3.3)*, **419**
Doors, means of egress *(1003.3.1)*; **414**
(1003.3.1.1), **415**
Doors, power-operated:
means of egress *(1003.3.1.3.2)*, **418-419**
Doors, revolving *(1003.3.1.3.1.2)*, **418**:
means of egress *(1003.3.1.3.1)*, **417**
Doors, sliding:
means of egress *(408.3.2)*, **90**
Doorway landings *(1003.3.4.5.5)*, **443**
Draftstopping:
attics *(716.4)*, **252**
combustibles in concealed spaces in Types I
and II construction *(716.5)*, **254**
floors *(716.3)*, **251**
Groups R-1 and R-2 *(716.4.2)*, **253**
Groups R-1, R-2, R-3 and R-4 *(716.3.2)*, **251**
materials *(716.3.1)*, **251**; *(716.4.1)*, **252**

openings *(716.4.1.1)*, **252**

other groups *(716.3.3)*, **252**; *(716.4.3)*, **254**

Drain, foundation *(1806.4.2)*, **715**

Drainage:

court *(1205.3.3)*, **582**

floor base course *(1806.4.1)*, **715**

roofs *(1503.4.1)*, **627**

subsoil *(1806.4)*, **715**

Dressing rooms:

accessibility *(1108.12.1)*, **563**

openings *(410.5.3)*, **104**

separations *(410.5.2)*, **103**

Drinking fountains, accessibility *(1108.5)*, **559**

Ducts and air transfer:

openings *(711.3.3)*, **234**; *(711.4.4)*, **239**

Dumbwaiter (see, also *Elevators and dumbwaiters*) *(707.14)*, **220**

Dwelling units:

accessibility *(1107.5.4)*, **549-550**

efficiency *(1207.4)*, **587**

E

Educational Group E:

classification *(305.1)*, **34**

day care *(305.2)*, **34**

Egress:

convergence *(1003.2.2.7)*, **379**

mezzanine *(505.3)*, **124**

smoke barriers *(407.4.2)*, **88**; *(408.6.3)*, **95**

Egress courts *(1006.3.1)*, **492**:

construction and openings *(1006.3.1.2)*, **495**

width *(1006.3.1.1)*, **495**; *(1003.2.3)*, **383**

Electrical, **939**

Elevation change:

means of egress *(1003.2.7)*, **394**

Elevation, foundation *(1805.3.4)*, **672**

Elevators:

accessibility *(1108.6)*, **559**

accommodation of ambulance stretcher *(3002.4)*, **976**

lobby *(707.14.1)*, **221**

means of egress *(1003.2.13.3)*, **408**

Elevators and Conveying Systems, **973**

Elevators and dumbwaiters:

shafts *(707.14)*, **220**

Elevators, escalators, and moving walks;

means of egress *(1003.2.9)*, **396**

Emergency and Standby Power Systems *(2702.2)*, **940**

Emergency escape and rescue, **521**

high-rise buildings *(403.4)*, **64**

Emergency signs *(3002.3)*, **975**

Emergency systems *(403.10.3)*, **68**

Emergency voice communication system *(402.13)*, **61**; *(403.6)*, **65**

Empirical Design Of Masonry, **777**

Enclosures:

access *(1005.3.2.5.2)*, **484**

atriums *(404.5)*, **70–71**

balcony openings *(1008.4.1)*, **500**

exit *(706.3.1)*, **207**; *(1005.3.2.5.1)*, **484**

laundry chutes *(707.13.1)*, **218**

refuse chutes *(707.13.1)*, **218**

smokeproof *(1005.3.2.5)*, **483**

under stairways *(1005.3.2.2)*, **481**

vertical exit *(1005.3.2)*, **479-480**

vertical exterior walls *(1005.3.2.1)*, **480-481**

Enclosures, required:

shafts *(707.2)*, **211-213**

veritcal exits *(707.2)*, **211-213**

Encroachments, **992**:

15 feet or more above grade *(3202.3.3)*, **999**

above grade and below 8 feet in height *(3202.2)*, **993**

Encroachments into the Public Right of Way **991**

Energy efficiency, **595**; *(1301.1.1)*, **596**

Entrances, accessible *(1105)*, **534**

Escalators (see also, *Elevators, escalators, and moving walks*) *(1003.2.9)*, **396**

Escape routes:

circuits and fixtures *(403.10.2)*, **67**; *(403.10.2.1)*, **67**

Excavation and fill *(3304.1)*, **1004**

Excavation, Grading and Fill, **668**

Exceptions:

High Hazard Group H *(307.9)*, **39–41**

Exempt locations

sprinkler systems *(903.3.1.1.1)*, **356-357**

Existing Structures, **1007**

Exit access, **446**

Exit access travel *(3104.9)*, **982**

Exit discharge, **492**:

means of egress *(408.3.4)*, **91**

Exit enclosures:

at the bottom *(707.10)*, **215-217**

at the top *(707.12)*, **217**

exterior walls *(707.6)*, **214**

fire barriers *(706.3.1)*, **207**

fire-resistance rating *(707.4)*, **214**

materials *(707.3)*, **213**
means of egress *(408.3.6)*, **91**
openings *(707.7)*, **215**
passageway *(402.4.5.1)*, **57**
penetrations *(707.8)*, **215**
penetrations, prohibited *(707.8.1)*, **215**
prohibited openings*(707.7.1)*, **215**
required *(707.2)*, **211-213**
Exits, **474**:
    access to *(402.4.5)*, **56**
    distance to *(402.4.4)*, **56**
    main assembly *(1008.1)*, **499**
    open garage parking *(406.3.8)*, **81**
    other assembly *(1008.2)*, **499**
    stage *(410.5.4)*, **104**
Exits, fire barriers:
    horizontal *(706.3.3)*, **208**
    passageway *(706.3.2)*, **207**
Exterior Plaster, **890**
Exterior Walls, **177, 599**

F

Facilities:
    adult care *(308.5.1)*, **45**
    child care *(308.3.1)*, **43**; *(308.5.2)*, **45**
    day care *(305.2)*, **34**; *(308.5)*, **45**
Factory Group F, **35**
Factory Industrial F-1 Moderate- Hazard
    Occupancy *(306.2)*, **35**
Factory Industrial F-2 Low-Hazard Occupancy
    (306.3), **36**
Factory Industrial Group F *(306.1)*, **35**
Finishes, interior:
    floor *(804.1)*, **341**
    scope *(801.1)*, **328**
Finishes, wall and ceiling *(803.1)*, **332**
Fire Barriers, **207**
Fire barriers between pedestrian walkways and
    buildings *(3104.5)*, **980-981**
Fire Classification   628
Fire command *(403.8)*, **65**
Fire department:
    access to equipment *(402.15)*, **62**
    communications system *(403.7)*, **65**
Fire detection:
    Group I-2 *(407.6)*, **89**
    high-rise buildings *(403.5)*, **65**

Fire detection system:
    atriums *(404.6)*, **71**
Fire Partitions, **222**
Fire Protection Systems, **347**
Fire resistance:
    interior finishes *(803.4)*, **334-338**
    prescriptive *(719.1)*, **261-324**
    textile ceiling finish *(803.5.2)*, **339**
Fire Walls, **200**
Fireblocking:
    architectural trim *(716.2.6)*, **250**
    ceiling and floor openings *(716.2.5)*, **249**
    combustible exterior walls *(1406.2.4)*,
        619–620
    concealed sleeper spaces *(716.2.7)*, **250**
    concealed spaces *(716.2)*, **247**
    concealed wall spaces *(716.2.2)*, **248**
    connections between horizontal and vertical
        spaces *(716.2.3)*, **249**
    double stud walls *(716.2.1.1)*, **248**
    materials *(716.2.1)*, **248**
    stairways *(716.2.4)*, **249**
Fire-Resistant-Rated Construction, **165**
Fire-resistance rating:
    concrete-filled pipes *(1916.5)*, **732**
    fire partitions *(708.3)*, **222-223**
    garages *(402.7.1)*, **58**
    high-rise buildings *(403.3)*, **64**
    horizontal assemblies *(710.3)*, **229**
    shaft enclosures *(707.4)*, **214**
    smoke barriers *(709.3)*, **226**
    vertical exit enclosures *(707.4)*, **214**
Fire-resistance ratings *(704.5)*, **182–186**
Fire-Resistance Requirements for Plaster, **256**
Fire-resistance-rated assemblies:
    non combustible penetrating items *(711.4.3.1)*,
        239
    penetrations *(711.4.1.1)*, **236**; *(711.4.3)*, **238**
Fire-resistance-rated construction:
    acoustical ceiling systems *(803.8.1.2)*, **340**
Fire-resistant-rated materials and construction, **165**
Fire-resistance-rated separation:
    covered mall buildings *(402.7)*, **58**
Fire-resistance-rated walls:
    penetrations *(711.3)*, **231**; *(711.3.1)*, **231–232**;
        (711.3.1.1), **232**; *(711.3.1.2)*, **232**
Firestop system *(711.4.1.2)*, **236-237**
Fixed seating:
    means of egress *(1003.2.2.9)*, **380**
Flashing *(1405.3)*, **603**:
    clay and concrete tile roofs *(1507.3.9)*, **634**

glass veneer *(1405.11.7)*, **618**
masonry *(1405.3.2)*, **610**
metal roofs *(1507.5.6)*, **638**
roofs *(1503.2)*, **626**
slate roofs *(1507.7.6)*, **640**
wood shake roofs *(1507.9.8)*, **646-647**
wood shingle roofs *(1507.8.7)*, **644**
Flood hazard areas, dampproofing *(1806.1.2.1)*, **710**
Flood resistance *(1403.6)*, **602**
Floor elevation at landings *(1003.3.1.4)*, **422**
Floor joist:
    anchoring steel *(2109.7.3.2)*, **805**
    anchoring wood *(2109.7.3.1)*, **804**
Floor surface, means of egress *(1003.2.6)*, **391**
Floors *(602.4.4)*, **157**; *(1209.1)*, **590**:
    framing *(602.4.2)*, **155**
    dampproofing *(1806.2.1)*, **712**
    draftstopping *(716.3)*, **251**
    fireblocking openings*(716.2.5)*, **249**
    insulating boards *(804.4.3)*, **343**
    minimum critical radiant flux *(804.5.1)*, **343**
    parking garages *(406.2.6)*, **75**
    sheathing *(2304.7.1)*, **838**
    waterproofing *(1806.3.1)*, **713**
    wood finish *(804.4.2)*, **342**
Floors, interior finish:
    application *(804.4)*, **342**
    subfloor construction *(804.4.1)*, **342**
    testing and identification *(804.3)*, **341**
Floors, subfloors: interior finish *(804.4.1)*, **342**
Floors, under:
    ventilation *(1202.3)*, **574**
    ventilation openings *(1202.3.1)*, **575**
Foam Plastic Insulation, **894**
Food courts, occupant load *(402.4.1.4)*, **55**
Footings:
    concrete *(1805.4.2)*, **673**
    design *(1805.4.1)*, **672**
    masonry-unit *(1805.4.3)*, **673**
    on slopes *(1805.3.1)*, **670**
    plain concrete *(1805.4.2.3)*, **673**
    setback *(1805.3.2)*, **671**
    steel grillage *(1805.4.4)*, **679**
Footings and foundations:
    frost protection *(1805.2.1)*, **669**
    setback *(1805.3.5)*, **672**
    thickness *(1805.1)*, **669**
Footings, isolated *(1805.2.2)*, **670**; *(1910.4.4.2)*, **725**
Foundation drain *(1806.4.2)*, **715**

Foundation walls *(1805.5)*, **680**:
    masonry *(1805.5.4)*, **707**
    reinforcement *(1805.5.3)*, **681**
    rubble stone *(1805.5.1.3)*, **681**
    thickness *(1805.5.1.1)*, **680**; *(1805.5.1.2)*, **681**
Foundations *(1805.1)*, **669** *(see also,* Footings and Foundations):
    curtain walls *(1805.5.6)*, **707-708**
    elevations *(1805.3.4)*, **672**
    pier wall *(1805.5.6)*, **707-708**
Foyers *(1008.3)*, **500**
Framing:
    floors *(602.4.2)*, **155**
    glass *(2403.3)*, **872**
    glazing *(2405.4)*, **875**
    gypsum board *(2504.1.1)*, **886**
    lath *(2504.1.1)*, **886**
    roofs *(602.4.3)*, **156**
    wall bracing *(2308.9.3)*, **862-868**
    walls *(2308.9.1)*, **857**
Framing, combustible: fire walls *(705.7)*, **205**
Freestanding objects: means of egress *(1003.2.5.2)*, **391**
Frontage:
    increase *(506.2)*, **127—132**
    open space limits *(506.2.2)*, **133**
    width limits *(506.2.1)*, **133**

G

Galleries *(410.3.2)*, **100**:
    means of egress *(1007.5.1)*, **498**
Garage doors, without fire-resistance rating *(2603.4.1.9)*, **901**
Garages: fire-resistance rating *(402.7.1)*, **58**
Garages and carports, private:
    area *(406.1.2)*, **72**
    classification *(406.1.1)*, **72**
Garages, commercial parking: sprinkler system *(903.2.11.1)*, **352**
Garages, enclosed parking:
    areas *(406.4.1)*, **83**
    heights *(406.4.1)*, **83**
    ventilation *(406.4.2)*, **83**
Garages, open parking: sprinkler systems *(406.3.10)*, **82**
    area *(406.3.5)*, **78–79**; *(406.3.6)*, **79—80**
    construction *(406.3.3)*, **77**

definitions *(406.3.2)*, **76–77**
enclosure *(406.3.11)*, **82**
exits *(406.3.8)*, **81**
height *(406.3.5)*, **78–79**; *(406.3.6)*, **79–80**
location *(406.3.7)*, **81**
openings *(406.3.3.1)*, **77**
prohibitions *(406.3.13)*, **83**
stairs *(406.3.8)*, **81**
standpipes *(406.3.9)*, **82**
ventilation *(406.3.12)*, **82**
Garages, open parking *(406.3)*, **76**:
    uses *(406.3.4)*, **78**
Garages, parking *(406.2)*, **73**:
    attached to rooms *(406.2.9)*, **76**
    classifications *(406.2.1)*, **73**
    floor surfaces *(406.2.6)*, **75**
    guards *(406.2.3)*, **73**
    height *(406.2.2)*, **73**
    mixed separation *(406.2.7)*, **75**
    ramps *(406.2.5)*, **75**
    special hazards *(406.2.8)*, **76**
    vehicle barriers *(406.2.4)*, **75**
Garages, repair: sprinkler system *(903.2.10.1)*, **352**
Gates:
    educational uses *(1003.3.2.2)*, **428**
    means of egress *(1003.3.2)*, **427**
    stadiums *(1003.3.2.1)*, **428**
Gates: locks *(3109.4.1.7)*, **989**
Gift shops: corridors *(407.2.4)*, **86**
Glass:
    frame *(2403.3)*, **872**
    louvered windows or jalousies *(2403.5)*, **872**
Glass unit masonry *(2103.5)*, **740**
Glass blocks:
    curved *(2110.3.5)*, **814**
    exterior *(2110.3.1)*, **808-811**
    exterior *(2110.3.2)*, **812**
    interior *(2110.3.3)*, **813**
    lateral support *(2110.4.3)*, **815**
    reinforcement *(2110.7)*, **816**
    solid units *(2110.3.4)*, **813**
    standard units *(2110.2.1)*, **807**
    thin units *(2110.2.2)*, **807**
Glass veneer, exterior *(1405.11)*, **616**
Glazing:
    doors *(714.2.4.1)*, **241**
    installation *(714.3.4)*, **244**
    light-transmitting plastic *(2610.2)*, **927**;
        (2610.3), **928**; *(2610.4)*, **930**; *(2610.5)*,
        931-933; *(2610.6)*, **935**; *(2608.2)*, **917**
    material *(714.2.6)*, **241**

nonwired glass *(714.3.3)*, **244**
    size limitations *(714.2.6.1)*, **241**
    window mullions *(714.3.5)*, **244**
    wired glass *(714.3.2)*, **243**
Glazing areas: deflection *(2403.4)*, **872**
Glazing, safety: hazardous locations *(2406.2)*,
    877-880
Glazing, sloped:
    framing *(2405.4)*, **875**
    limitations *(2405.2)*, **873**
    materials *(2405.2)*, **873**
    screening *(2405.3)*, **874-875**
    scope *(2405.1)*, **873**
Grading: site *(1803.3)*, **668**
Gridiron: means of egress *(1007.5.1)*, **498**
Gridirons *(410.3.2)*, **100**
Ground water control: dampproofing *(1806.1.3)*,
    711
Grounds: interior plaster *(2511.3)*, **889**
Group E: unlimited area buildings *(507.7)*, **139**
Group H-1 structures: classification *(307.3)*, **37**
Group H-2 structures: classification *(307.4)*, **37**
Group H-3 structures: classification *(307.5)*, **38**
Group H-4 structures: classification *(307.6)*, **38**
Group H-5 structures: classification *(307.7)*, **38**
Group I-1: classification *(308.2)*, **42**
Group I-2: classification *(308.3)*, **43**
Group I-4, day care facilities: classification *(308.5)*,
    45
Group S-2 *(903.2.11)*, **352**
Guards:
    end of aisles *(1008.12.3)*, **518**
    industrial equipment platforms *(505.5.3)*,
        126
    live loads *(1607.7.1)*, **660**; *(1607.7.1.1)*, **660**;
        (1607.7.1.2), **660**
    means of egress *(1003.2.12)*, **402-403**;
        (1003.2.12.1), **403**; *(1003.2.12.2)*, **404**
    ramps *(1003.3.4.9)*, **445**
    sightline-constrained limits *(1008.12.2)*, **518**
Gutters, roofs *(1503.4.1)*, **627**
Gypsum board:
    backing board for cement plaster *(2510.5.2.1)*,
        888; *(2510.5.2.2)*, **888**
    base for tile *(2509.2)*, **887**
    framing *(2504.1.1)*, **886**
    location limitations *(2509.3)*, **887**
    partitions *(2504.1.2)*, **886**
Gypsum board and plaster: definitions *(2502.1)*, **884**

H

Handrails:
  aisle *(1008.11)*, **516**
  aisles *(1008.11.1)*, **517**; *(1008.11.2)*, **517**
  clearance *(1003.3.3.11.6)*, **441**
  continuity *(1003.3.3.11.4)*, **440**
  extensions *(1003.3.3.11.5)*, **440**
  graspability *(1003.3.3.11.3)*, **439**
  height *(1003.3.3.11.1)*, **439**
  intermediate *(1003.3.3.11.2)*, **439**
  live loads *(1607.7.1)*, **660**; *(1607.7.1.1)*, **660**;
    (1607.7.1.2), **660**
  ramps *(1003.3.4.7)*, **444**
  stairway *(1003.3.3.10.1)*, **438**
Hardware, accessibility *(1108.13)*, **564**
Hazardous Group H, classification *(307.1)*, **37**
Hazardous materials, quantity *(309.2)*, **46**
Headers, masonry: bonding *(2109.6.2.1)*, **786**;
  (2109.6.2.2), **789**
Headroom: means of egress *(1003.2.5.1)*, **387**
Heavy timber construction: wall and ceiling
  finishes *(803.3.3)*, **333**
High-Hazard use groups: unlimited area buildings
  (507.5), **139**
Horizontal projections: means of egress
  (1003.2.5.3), **391**

I

Identification: areas of refuge *(1003.2.13.5.5)*, **414**
Illumination:
  exit sign *(1003.2.10.4)*, **400**
  for means of egress *(1003.2.11)*, **400**;
    (1003.2.11.1), **401**; *(1003.2.11.2)*, **401**
Incidental use areas:
  classification *(302.1.1)*, **11—12**
  fire barriers *(706.3.4)*, **208**
  separation *(302.1.1.1)*, **12**
Institutional Group I: classification *(308.1)*, **42**
Institutional Group I, Group I-3: classification
  (308.4), **43**
Insulation:
  attic floors *(718.3.1)*, **259**
  cellulose loose-fill *(718.6)*, **260**
  concealed installation *(718.2)*, **258**
  covering on pipe and tubing *(718.7)*, **260**
  exposed installation *(718.3)*, **258**
  facings *(718.2.1)*, **258**

  loose-fill *(718.4)*, **259**
  plastic foam *(2603.4)*, **894**
  roof *(718.5)*, **259**
Insulation, foam plastic:
  attics *(2603.4.1.6)*, **898**
  concrete *(2603.4.1.1)*, **895**
  crawl spaces *(2603.4.1.6)*, **898**
  doors *(2603.4.1.7)*, **900**
  exterior walls *(2603.4.1.4)*, **897**
  masonry *(2603.4.1.1)*, **895**
  roofing *(2603.4.1.5)*, **898**
Interior finish: atriums *(404.8)*, **71**
Interior finishes
  textiles *(803.5)*, **339**
  wall coverings*(803.5.1)*, **339**
International Symbol of Accessibility *(1109.1)*, **566**;
  (1109.2), **566**

J

Joints:
  bed and head *(2104.1.2.1)*, **741**
  exterior walls *(704.13)*, **199**
  glass units *(2104.1.2.4)*, **744**
  hollow units *(2104.1.2.2)*, **742**
  open-end units *(2104.1.2.1.1)*, **741**
  reinforcement *(2108.9.2.2)* **765**; *(2109.6.3.2)*
    794; *(2109.7.2.3)* **801**
  solid units *(2104.1.2.3)*, **743**
  wall ties *(2104.1.3)*, **744**
  waterproof *(1209.4)*, **592**

K

Kiosks — covered mall buildings *(402.10)*, **60**
Kitchens, kitchenettes and wet bars — accessibility
  (1108.4), **559**

L

Ladders — emergency escape and rescue openings
  (1009.5.2), **523**
Landings:
  at doors *(1003.3.1.5)*, **423**
  change in direction *(1003.3.4.5.4)*, **443**

doorways *(1003.3.4.5.5)*, **443**

floor elevation *(1003.3.1.4)*, **422**

length *(1003.3.4.5.3)*, **443**

ramps *(1003.3.4.5)*, **442**

slope *(1003.3.4.5.1)*, **443**

stairways *(1003.3.3.4)*, **433**

width *(1003.3.4.5.2)*, **443**

Lateral-force-resisting systems *(2106.4.2.3.1)*, **752**

Lateral force-resisting system: non-elements
(2106.4.1.3), **750**; *(2106.6.1)*, **759-760**;
(2106.6.2), **760-761**

Lath *(2502.1)*, **884**; *(2510.5.1)*, **888**
(*see also*, Gypsum board and plaster)

Lath: backing board *(2510.5.2.1)*, **888**;
(2510.5.2.2), **888**

Laundry chutes *(707.13)*, **217** (*see also*, Refuse and
laundry chutes)

Lifts: accessibility *(1108.7)*, **559**

Lighting *(1204.1)*, **579**:
light-transmitting plastics *(2606.7.5)*, **906**

Lines:
accessibility *(1108.12.4)*, **564**; *(1108.12.5)*,
564

food service *(1108.12.4)*, **564**

queue and waiting lines, accessibility
(1108.12.5), **564**

Lintels *(2104.1.5)*, **746**

Live loads:
concentrated *(1607.4)*, **659**

grab bars, shower seats and dressing room
bench seats *(1607.7.2)*, **660**

handrails and guards *(1607.7.1)*, **660**;
(1607.7.1.1), **660**; *(1607.7.1.2)*, **660**

partitions *(1607.5)*, **659**

uniform *(1607.3)*, **656–658**

Load-bearing columns or frames *(2106.4.1.2)*, **749**

Lobbies *(1008.3)*, **500**

Location *(1406.2.3)*, **619**

Locker rooms: accessibility *(1108.12.1)*, **563**

Locking devices:
corridors *(407.3.2)*, **87**

power operated *(408.4.2)*, **92**

redundant operation *(408.4.3)*, **93**

relock capability *(408.4.4)*, **93**

remote release *(408.4.1)*, **92**

Low-hazard storage Group S-2: classification
(311.3), **49**

M

Malls: openings *(402.7.2.1)*, **59**

Masonry:
ashlar *(2109.6.4.1)*, **795**

chases and recesses *(2104.1.4)*, **746**

corbelling *(2104.2)*, **748**

flashing *(1405.3.2)*, **610**

foam plastic insulation *(2603.4.1.1)*, **895**

foundation walls *(1805.5.4)*, **707**

glass unit *(2103.5)*, **740**; *(2104.1.2.4)*, **744**

hollow units *(2104.1.2.2)*, **742**

hollow walls *(2109.6.2.3)*, **789**

joint reinforcement *(2108.9.2.2)*, **765**;
(2109.6.3.2), **794**

joints *(2104.1.2.1)*, **741**; *(2104.1.2.1.1)*, **741**;
(2104.1.2.2), **742**; *(2104.1.2.3)*, **743**;
(2104.1.2.4), **744**

lateral support *(2109.4.1)*, **780-781**;
(2109.4.2), **782**; *(2109.4.3)*, **783**

lintels *(2104.1.5)*, **746**

not part of lateral-force-resisting system
(2106.6.1), **759-760**; *(2106.6.2)*,
760-761

open-end units *(2104.1.2.1.1)*, **741**

parapets *(2109.5.5.1)*, **785**

reinforcement *(2106.4.1.3)*, **750**

rubble stone *(2109.6.4.2)*, **797**

rubble stone walls *(2109.5.3)*, **784**

running bond *(2109.6.5.1)*, **798**

shear walls *(2109.2.1.1)*, **777**; shear walls
(2109.2.1.2), **777**; *(2109.2.1.3)*, **779**

solid units *(2104.1.2.3)*, **743**

stack bond *(2109.6.5.2)*, **799**

thickness *(2109.5.2)*, **784**; *(2109.5.4)*, **785**

wall ties *(2104.1.3)*, **744**; *(2109.6.3.1)*, **790**;
(2109.6.3.1.1), **793**

weep holes *(2104.1.8)*, **747**

Masonry headers:
hollow units *(2109.6.2.2)*, **789**

solid units *(2109.6.2.1)*, **786**

Masonry veneers:
exterior *(1405.5.1)*, **611**

interior *(1405.9.1.1)*, **614**

Masonry, beams:
clear span *(2108.9.6.3.3)*, **773**

depth *(2108.9.6.3.4)*, **773**

width *(2108.9.6.3.5)*, **775**

Masonry, columns:
beams and piers *(2108.9.3.8)*, **771-772**

dimensions *(2108.9.6.6.2)*, **776**;
      (2108.9.6.6.3), **776**; *(2108.9.6.6.4)*, **776**
   reinforcement *(2106.5.4)*, **759**
   reinforcing *(2108.9.2.4)*, **766**
Masonry, glass block:
   solid units *(2110.3.4)*, **813**
   standard *(2110.2.1)*, **807**
   thin units *(2110.2.2)*, **807**
Masonry, glass panels:
   curved *(2110.3.5)*, **814**
   exterior *(2110.3.1)*, **808-811**; *(2110.3.2)*, **812**
   interior *(2110.3.3)*, **813**
   lateral support *(2110.4.3)*, **815**
   reinforcement *(2110.7)*, **816**
Masonry, piers: reinforcing*(2108.9.2.4)*, **766**
Masonry, reinforcing bars:
   bend diameter *(2108.9.2.9)*, **769**
   bundling *(2108.9.2.6)*, **767**
   clear distance *(2108.9.2.3)*, **766**; *(2108.9.2.4)*,
      766; *(2108.9.2.5)*, **766**
   cover *(2108.9.2.7)*, **767**
   sizes *(2108.9.2.1)*, **764**
   standard hooks *(2108.9.2.8)*, **768**
Masonry, unit:
   fire-resistance protection *(719.1.2)*, **261**
   footings*(1805.4.3)*, **673**; *(1805.4.3.2)*, **679**
Masonry, walls: reinforcement *(2106.4.2.3.1)*, **752**;
      (2106.5.3.1), **758**
Materials:
   draftstopping *(716.3.1)*, **251**; *(716.4.1)*, **252**
   exit enclosures *(707.3)*, **213**
   fire barriers *(706.2)*, **207**
   fire partitions *(708.2)*, **222**
   fire-resistance rated *(704.4)*, **181**
   glazing *(2405.2)*, **873**; *(714.2.6)*, **241**
   horizontal assemblies *(710.2)*, **229**
   plastic interior finish and trim *(2604.2.2)*, **903**;
      (2604.2.3), **903**
   refuse and laundry chutes *(707.13.2)*, **218**
   shafts enclosures *(707.3)*, **213**
   smoke barriers *(709.2)*, **226**
   wall and ceiling finishes *(803.3.4)*, **334**
Materials, decorative: interior finishes *(801.1.2)*,
   328
Materials, flame-resistant: decoration and trim
   (805.1.2), **344**
Materials, noncombustible: decorations and trim
   (805.1.1), **344**
Means of egress:
   anchor building *(402.4.3.1)*, **56**
   arrangements of *(402.4.3)*, **56**

balcony *(1008.4)*, **500**
common path of egress travel *(1004.2.5)*, **463**
covered mall buildings *(402.4)*, **55**
definitions *(1002.1)*, **362-371**
door width *(408.3.1)*, **90**
egress convergence *(1003.2.2.7)*, **379**
exit discharge *(408.3.4)*, **91**
from multiple levels *(1003.2.2.6)*, **378**
gallery *(1008.4)*, **500**
Group I-3 *(408.3)*, **90**
number *(402.4.2)*, **56**; *(1003.2.2.1)*, **374**;
      (1003.2.2.3), **375**
occupant formula *(402.4.1.1)*, **55**
outdoor smoke-protected assembly *(1008.5.3)*,
   506
sallyports *(408.3.5)*, **91**
sliding doors *(408.3.2)*, **90**
spiral stairs *(408.3.3)*, **91**
Table 1003.2.2.2 *(1003.2.2.2)*, **374-375**
through intervening spaces *(1004.2.3)*, **450**
vertical exit enclosures *(408.3.6)*, **91**
Mechanical appliances: access *(1208.3)*, **588**
Mechanical systems *(2801.1)*, **944**
Medical facilities: accessibility *(1106.6.1)*, **539**
Mental health treatment areas: corridors *(407.2.3)*,
   86
Mercantile Group M: classification *(309.1)*, **46**
Metal veneers *(1405.10)*, **615**; *(1405.10.1)*, **615**
Mezzanine: means of egress *(1003.2.2.8)*, **379**
Mixed occupancies:
   nonseparated uses *(302.3.2)*, **14**
   separated uses *(302.3.3)*, **14 — 29**
   two or more uses *(302.3.1)*, **13**
Moderate-hazard storage, Group S-1: classification
   (311.2), **48**
Moment frame, masonry:
   beam clear span *(2108.9.6.3.3)*, **773**
   beam depth *(2108.9.6.3.4)*, **773**
   beam width *(2108.9.6.3.5)*, **775**
   columns *(2108.9.6.6.2)*, **776**; *(2108.9.6.6.3)*,
      776; *(2108.9.6.6.4)*, **776**
Motor vehicle service station:
   canopies *(406.5.2)*, **84**
   construction *(406.5.1)*, **83**
   station *(406.5)*, **83**
Moving walks *(1003.2.9)*, **396** (*see also*, Elevators,
   escalators, and moving walks)
Multiple occupancies: means of egress *(1003.2.1)*,
   372
Multiple tenants; exit access *(1004.2.3.1)*, **450**

N

NFPA 13 sprinkler systems *(903.3.1.1)*, **356**
NFPA 13D sprinkler systems *(903.3.1.3)*, **357**
NFPA 13R sprinkler systems *(903.3.1.2)*, **357**
Number of elevator cars in a hoistway *(3002.2)*, **974**
Nurses' stations, corridors *(407.2.2)*, **86**

O

Occupancies:
    Group I-3 *(408.2)*, **90**
    special industrial *(503.1.2)*, **115**
Occupancy: separations *(706.3.5)*, **208**
Occupant formula: means of egress *(402.4.1.1)*, **55**
Occupant load:
    anchor buildings *(402.4.1.3)*, **55**
    determination of *(402.4.1)*, **55**
    food courts *(402.4.1.4)*, **55**
    means of egress *(1003.2.2)*, **374**
Offsets: masonry-unit footings *(1805.4.3.2)*, **679**
OLF range: covered mall buildings *(402.4.1.2)*, **55**
One-story buildings:
    sprinklered *(507.2)*, **136**
    unsprinklered *(507.1)*, **136**
Openings:
    access *(903.2.12.1.1)*, **353**
    between anchor building and mall
        (402.7.2.1), **59**
    dimensions *(903.2.12.1.1)*, **353**
    draftstopping *(716.4.1.1)*, **252**
    dressing and appurtenance rooms protectives
        (410.5.3), **104**
    ducts and air transfer *(711.4.4)*, **239**
    ducts and air transfer*(711.3.3)*, **234**
    exit passageway *(1005.3.4)*, **486**
    exterior walls *(704.8)*, **191—192**
    fire walls *(705.8)*, **206**
    fireblocking*(716.2.5)*, **249**
    Group I-3 *(408.5)*, **93**
    in concrete walls *(1909.6.3)*, **724**
    open garage parking *(406.3.11)*, **82**
    resident housing *(408.7.3)*, **96**
    separations in exterior walls *(704.9)*, **194**
    shaft enclosures *(707.7)*, **215**
    smoke barriers *(709.5)*, **228**
    vertical exit enclosures *(707.7)*, **215**

Openings *(3109.4.1.1)*, **985**
Openings, attic: ventilation *(1202.2.1)*, **574**
Openings, below grade: ventilation *(1202.4.1.2)*, **578**
Openings, emergency escape and rescue *(1009.1)*, **521**:
    dimension *(1009.2.1)*, **521**
    height from floor *(1009.3)*, **522**
    operational constraints *(1009.4)*, **522**
    size *(1009.2)*, **521**
    window well ladders or steps *(1009.5.2)*, **523**
    window wells *(1009.5)*, **522**
    window wells *(1009.5.1)*, **522**
    shaft enclosures *(707.7.1)*, **215**
    vertical exit enclosures *(707.7.1)*, **215**
Openings, protected: exterior walls *(704.12)*, **198**
Openings, under floor: ventilation *(1202.3.1)*, **575**
Openings, unprotected: exterior walls *(704.12.1)*, **199**
Openness: exit access *(1004.3.3.2)*, **473**
Outdoor areas: means of egress *(1003.2.2.10)*, **381**

P

Parapets:
    construction *(704.11.1)*, **197**
    thickness *(2109.5.5.1)*, **785**
Parking facilities:
    accessibility *(1106.1)*, **535**
    accessible parking spaces *(1106.5)*, **539**
    van-accessible *(1106.4)*, **539**
Parking garages *(406.2)*, **73**
Parking, open structures: exits *(1005.2.1.1)*, **474**
Partitions *(602.4.6)*, **158**:
    gypsum board *(2504.1.2)*, **886**
    masonry*(2106.4.1.2)*, **749**
    plaster*(2504.1.2)*, **886**
    studless *(2504.1.2)*, **886**
Partitions, fire *(708.1)*, **222**
Party walls: limitations *(503.2)*, **116**
Passageway enclosures: exit *(402.4.5.1)*, **57**
Passageway, exit *(706.3.2)*, **207**; *(1005.3.3)*, **484**:
    construction *(1005.3.3.2)*, **485**
    openings and penetrations *(1005.3.4)*, **486**
    width *(1005.3.3.1)*, **485**
Passenger loading zone:
    medical facilities *(1106.6.1)*, **539**
    valet parking *(1106.6.2)*, **539**

Passenger loading facilities: accessibility*(1106)*, **535**

Pedestrian walkways *(3202.3.4)*, **1000**

Penetrations:

  exit enclosure *(1005.3.4.1)*, **486**

  exit passageways*(1005.3.4)*, **486**

  fire-resistance-rated assemblies *(711.4.1.1)*, **236**

  fire-resistance-rated walls *(711.3)*, **231**; *(711.3.1)*, **231-232**; *(711.3.1.1)*, **232**; *(711.3.1.2)*, **232**

  firestop system *(711.4.1.2)*, **236-237**

  membrane *(711.3.2)*, **233**; *(711.4.2)*, **237-238**

  nonfire-resistance-rated assemblies *(711.4.3)*, **238**

  shaft enclosures *(707.8)*, **215**

  vertical exit enclosures *(707.8)*, **215**

Penetrations, prohibited:

  fire barriers *(706.7.1)*, **210**

  shaft enclosures *(707.8.1)*, **215**

  vertical exit enclosures *(707.8.1)*, **215**

Penthouses *(1509.2)*, **648**

Pier walls: foundation *(1805.5.6)*, **707-708**

Piers, masonry: dimensional limits*(2108.9.3.8)*, **771-772**

Piers, reinforcing *(2108.9.2.4)*, **766**

Pinrails *(410.3.2)*, **100**

Plaster:

  alternatives for concrete *(717.5)*, **256**

  backing board *(2510.5.2.1)*, **888**; *(2510.5.2.2)*, **888**

  backing not required *(2510.5.3)*, **888**

  double reinforcement *(717.4)*, **256**

  equivalents *(717.2)*, **256**

  fiber insulation board *(2511.2)*, **889**

  fire resistance protection *(719.1.4)*, **325**

  frame for lath*(2504.1.1)*, **886**

  lath support *(2510.5.1)*, **888**

  noncombustible furring *(717.3)*, **256**

  partitions*(2504.1.2)*, **886**

  thickness *(717.1)*, **256**

  weather-resistant barriers *(2510.6)*, **888**

Plaster (see also, Gypsum Board and Plaster) *(2502.1)*, **884**

Plaster, exterior:

  limitations *(2512.3)*, **890**

  second coat *(2512.5)*, **890**

  weep screeds *(2512.1.2)*, **890**

Plaster, interior:

  grounds *(2511.3)*, **889**

  limitations *(2511.2)*, **889**

  wet areas *(2511.5.1)*, **889**

Plastic:

  interior finish and trim *(2604)*, **903**; *(2604.2.2)*, **903**; *(2604.2.3)*, **903**

  veneer *(2605.2)*, **904**

Plastic signs (*see* Signs, plastic)

Plastic, foam: interior finishes *(801.2.2)*, **329**

Plastic, light-transmitting:

  glazing *(2608.2)*, **917**

  interior signs *(2611.2)*, **936**; *(2611.3)*, **936**; *(2611.4)*, **937**

  light fixtures *(2606.7.5)*, **906**

  roof panels *(2609.2)*, **919**; *(2609.3)*, **920**; *(2609.4)*, **921-926**

  size *(2606.7.1)*, **905**

  size limitations *(2606.7.3)*, **905**

  skylight glazing *(2610.2)*, **927**; *(2610.3)*, **928**; *(2610.4)*, **930**; *(2610.5)*, **931-933**; *(2610.6)*, **935**

  solar collectors *(2606.12)*, **909**

  wall panel *(2607.3)*, **910**; *(2607.4)*, **911**; *(2607.5)*, **915**

Platform lifts: means of egress *(1003.2.13.4)*, **410**

Platforms:

  construction *(410.4)*, **102**

  definitions*(410.2)*, **97—98**

  sprinkler system*(410.6)*, **104—105**

  temporary *(410.4.1)*, **102**

Platforms, industrial equipment *(505.5)*, **125**:

  area limitations *(505.5.1)*, **126**

  fire suppression *(505.5.2)*, **126**

  guards *(505.5.3)*, **126**

Plumbing:

  fixtures *(2902.1)*, **948-966**

  number of occupants *(2902.3)*, **968**

  separate facilities *(2902.2)*, **968**

Plumbing, toilet facilities:

  covered malls *(2902.6.1)*, **970**

  employee *(2902.4)*, **968-969**; *(2902.4.1)*, **969**; *(2902.5)*, **969**

  public facilities *(2902.6)*, **969**

Pools *(1805.3.3)*, **671**

Power source *(1003.2.10.5)*, **400**

Projections:

  combustible *(704.2.3)*, **180**

  fire-resistant rated *(704.2)*, **177**

  fire walls *(705.5.2)*, **202**

Proscenium curtain *(410.3.5)*, **101**

Proscenium wall *(410.3.4)*, **101**

Public swimming pools *(3109.3)*, **984**

Pyroxylin plastic *(805.4)*, **345**:

  sprinkler systems *(903.2.4.3)*, **350**

Q

Quick-response and residential sprinklers
   (903.3.2), **358**

R

Railings *(1003.3.4.8.1)*, **445**
Ramps:
   construction *(1003.3.4.6)*, **443**;
      (1003.3.4.6.1), **443**; *(1003.3.4.6.2)*, **444**
   cross slope *(1003.3.4.2)*, **442**
   curb or barrier *(1003.3.4.8.2)*, **445**
   edge protection *(1003.3.4.8)*, **444**
   guards *(1003.3.4.9)*, **445**
   handrails *(1003.3.4.7)*, **444**
   headroom *(1003.3.4.4.2)*, **442**
   landings *(1003.3.4.5)*, **442**
   means of egress *(1003.3.4)*, **441**
   parking garages *(406.2.5)*, **75**
   restrictions *(1003.3.4.4.3)*, **442**
   rise *(1003.3.4.3)*, **442**
   slope *(1003.3.4.1)*, **442**
   width *(1003.3.4.4.1)*, **442**
Ramps *(3408.7.4)*, **1009**; *(3408.8.5)*, **1010**
Reduced open space *(507.4)*, **137**
Referenced standards, **1013-1020**
Refrigerated machinery rooms *(1007.2)*, **496**
Refrigerated rooms or spaces *(1007.3)*, **497**
Refuge area:
   capacity of horizontal exit *(1005.3.5.3)*, **488**
   identification *(1003.2.13.5.5)*, **414**
   smoke barriers *(407.4.1)*, **88**; *(408.6.2)*, **95**
   2-way communication *(1003.2.13.5.3)*, **412**;
      (1003.2.13.5.4), **414**
Refuse and laundry chutes *(707.13)*, **217**:
   access rooms *(707.13.3)*, **219**
   enclosures *(707.13.1)*, **218**
   termination room *(707.13.4)*, **219**
Rehabilitation facilities and outpatient physical
   therapy facilities: accessibility *(1106.3)*, **537**
Reinforcement:
   concrete-filled pipes *(1916.4)*, **731**
   foundation walls*(1805.5.3)*, **681**
   glass masonry panels*(2110.7)*, **816**
   gypsum concrete *(1915.2)*, **730**
   masonry columns *(2106.5.4)*, **759**
   masonry elements *(2106.4.1.3)*, **750**
   masonry shear walls *(2106.4.2.3.1)*, **752**

   masonry shear walls *(2106.5.3.1)*, **758**
      masonry walls *(2106.5.2)*, **754-757**
   not part of lateral-force-resisting system
(2106.6.1), **759-760**
   not part of lateral-force-resisting system
(2106.6.2), **760-761**
      shotcrete *(1914.4.1)*, **729**
Reinforcing bars:
   size *(2108.9.2.1)*, **764**
   bend diameter *(2108.9.2.9)*, **769**
   bundling *(2108.9.2.6)*, **767**
   clear distance *(2108.9.2.3)*, **766**
   clear distance *(2108.9.2.4)*, **766**
   clear distance *(2108.9.2.5)*, **766**
   cover *(2108.9.2.7)*, **767**
   standard hooks *(2108.9.2.8)*, **768**
Reinforcing, clearance: shotcrete *(1914.4.2)*, **729**
Resident housing:
   openings *(408.7.3)*, **96**
   smoke-tight doors *(408.7.4)*, **96**
Resident housing *(408.7.1)*, **95**; *(408.7.2)*, **95**
Residential Group "R": classification *(310.1)*, **47**
Residential sprinklers *(903.3.2)*, **358**; *(see also,*
   Quick Response and Residential Sprinklers)
Risers, aisles *(1008.9.2)*, **515**
Roof panels:
   light-transmitting plastics *(2609.2)*, **919**;
      (2609.3), **920**; *(2609.4)*, **921-926**
Roof, height modifications *(504.3)*, **121—122**
Roof, stairway to *(1003.3.3.12.1)*, **441**;
   (1003.3.3.12), **441**
Roofs *(602.4.5)*, **158**:
   anchorage *(2109.7.3.3)*, **805**
   coping *(1503.3)*, **626**
   fire classifications *(1505)*, **628**
   flashing *(1503.2)*, **626**
   foam plastic insulation*(2603.4.1.5)*, **898**
   framing *(602.4.3)*, **156**
   gutters*(1503.4.1)*, **627**
   sheathing *(2304.7.2)*, **847**
   thermal- and sound-insulation materials
      (718.5), **259**
   thermal barrier *(2603.4.1.5)*, **898**
   underlayment *(1507.2.8)*, **630**
Roofs, asphalt:
   base and cap flashing *(1507.2.9.1)*, **631**
   decks *(1507.2.1)*, **629**
   drip edge *(1507.2.9.3)*, **632-633**
   ice dam protection *(1507.2.8.2)*, **631**
   slope *(1507.2.2)*, **630**
   valleys *(1507.2.9.2)*, **632**

Roofs, built-up *(1507.10.1)*, **647**
Roofs, clay and concrete tile:
  deck slope *(1507.3.2)*, **633**
  decks *(1507.3.1)*, **633**
  flashing *(1507.3.9)*, **634**
  high slope *(1507.3.3.2)*, **634**
  low slope *(1507.3.3.1)*, **633**
Roofs, liquid applied coating *(1507.15.1)*, **647**
Roofs, metal:
  deck slope *(1507.5.2)*, **635**
  decks *(1507.5.1)*, **635**
  flashing *(1507.5.6)*, **638**
Roofs, metal panel:
  deck slope *(1507.4.2)*, **635**
  decks *(1507.4.1)*, **635**
Roofs, mineral-surfaced roll:
  deck slope *(1507.6.2)*, **638**
  decks *(1507.6.1)*, **638**
  underlayment *(1507.6.3)*, **639**
Roofs, slate:
  application *(1507.7.5)*, **640**
  deck slope *(1507.7.2)*, **639**
  decks *(1507.7.1)*, **639**
  flashing *(1507.7.6)*, **640**
  underlayment *(1507.7.3)*, **639**
Roofs, sprayed polyurethane foam *(1507.14.1)*, **647**
Roofs, thermoplastic single-ply *(1507.13.1)*, **647**
Roofs, thermoset single-ply *(1507.12.1)*, **647**
Roofs, wood shake:
  application *(1507.9.7)*, **645**
  deck slope *(1507.9.2)*, **645**
  decks *(1507.9.1)*, **644**
  flashing *(1507.9.8)*, **646-647**
  solid sheathing *(1507.9.1.1)*, **644**
  underlayment *(1507.9.3)*, **645**
Roofs, wood shingle:
  application *(1507.8.6)*, **642**
  deck slope *(1507.8.2)*, **642**
  decks *(1507.8.1)*, **642**
  flashing *(1507.8.7)*, **644**
  underlayment *(1507.8.3)*, **642**
Rooftop structures, **648**
Room:
  area *(1207.3)*, **587**
  widths *(1207.1)*, **585**
Routes: accessibility *(1107.5.5)*, **550-551**
Rubbish and linen chutes: sprinkler system *(903.2.12.2)*, **354**
Rubble stone walls:
  bonding *(2109.6.4.2)*, **797**

foundation walls*(1805.5.1.3)*, **681**
thickness *(2109.5.3)*, **784**

S

Safety glazing, **877**
Sallyports: means of egress *(408.3.5)*, **91**
Scenery: stages *(410.3.7)*, **101**
Screening: glazing *(2405.3)*, **874-875**
Seating:
  accessibility *(1108.11)*, **562**
  accessway length *(1004.3.1.3.3)*, **468**
  accessway width *(1004.3.1.3.2)*, **468**
  aisle accssway *(1004.3.1.3.1)*, **467**
  roof height *(1008.5.2.2)*, **505**
  smoke control *(1008.5.2.1)*, **505**
  smoke-protected *(1008.5.2)*, **503-505**
  sprinkler system *(1008.5.2.3)*, **506**
  stability *(1008.10)*, **516**
  without smoke protection *(1008.5.1)*, **502**
Seating, bench *(1008.14)*, **520**
Seating, fixed or built-in — accessibility *(1107.2.5.1)*, **545**
Security grilles *(1003.3.1.3.5)*, **421**
Security grilles and doors *(402.11)*, **60**
Seismic design: masonry partition walls *(2106.4.1.2)*, **749**
Seismic Design, **749**
Seismic Design Provisions, **725**
Self-service storage facilities: accessibility *(1107.6)*, **552**; *(1107.6.1)*, **552**
Separations:
  dressing and appurtenance rooms *(410.5.2)*, **103**
  fire-resistance-rated *(402.7)*, **58**
  horizontal exit *(1005.3.5.1)*, **487**
  incidental use areas *(302.1.1.1)*, **12**
  means of egress *(1003.2.13.5.2)*, **412**
  occupancy *(706.3.5)*, **208**
  parking garages *(406.2.7)*, **75**
  stage *(410.5.1)*, **103**
  tenant *(402.7.2)*, **59**
Service areas: covered mall buildings *(402.4.6)*, **57**
Setback:
  footings *(1805.3.2)*, **671**
  footings and foundations *(1805.3.5)*, **672**
Shaft and vertical exit enclosures, **211**
Shaft enclosures: high-rise buildings *(403.3.2)*, **64**
Shear values: light-framed cold-formed steel walls

(2211.3.1), **830**

Shear walls:
    diaphragm ratio *(2109.2.1.3)*, **779**
    length *(2109.2.1.2)*, **777**
    thickness *(2109.2.1.1)*, **777**

Sheathing:
    sheet steel *(2211.4.2)*, **832**; *(2211.4.3)*, **832**;
       (2211.5.2), **833**; *(2211.5.3)*, **833**
    structural wood panel *(2211.3.1)*, **830**;
       (2211.3.2), **830**; *(2211.3.3)*, **831**

Sheathing, structural:
    floor *(2304.7.1)*, **838**
    roof *(2304.7.2)*, **847**

Sheathing, wall *(2304.6.1)*, **836**

Shotcrete *(1914.4.1)*, **729**; *(1914.4.2)*, **729**

Showers *(1209.3)*, **5902**

Shutters, fire *(714.2)*, **240**

Siding backer board *(2603.4.1.10)*, **902**

Signage: at means of egress *(1003.2.13.6)*, **414**

Signage, **566**

Signs:
    identifying elements accessible elements
       (1109.1), **566**
    indicating route to accessible elements
       (1109.2), **566**
    special accessibility provisions *(1109.3)*, **568**
    stairway floor number *(1005.3.2.4)*, **483**

Signs, exit *(1003.2.10.4)*, **400**

Signs, interior:
    light-transmitting plastic *(2611.2)*, **936**
    light-transmitting plastic *(2611.3)*, **936**
    light-transmitting plastic *(2611.4)*, **937**

Signs, plastic *(402.14)*, **61**:
    area *(402.14.1)*, **61**
    encasement *(402.14.4.1)*, **62**
    foam *(402.14.5-2)*, **62**
    height *(402.14.2)*, **61**
    location *(402.14.3)*, **61**
    other than foam *(402.14.4)*, **62**

Signs, stairway exit *(1003.2.10.3)*, **400**

Signs, width *(402.14.2)*, **61**

Sinks: accessibility *(1108.3)*, **557**

Site grading *(1803.3)*, **668**

Site plan *(106.2)*, **3**

Skylights:
    light-transmitting plastic *(2610.2)*, **927**;
       (2610.3), **928**; *(2610.4)* **930**; *(2610.5)*,
       931-933; *(2610.6)*, **935**

Slabs: concrete *(1911.1)*, **727**

Slab-type veneers, exteriors *(1405.7)*, **612-613**

Sleeper spaces: fireblocking *(716.2.7)*, **250**

Sleeping accommodations: accessibility *(1107.5.1)*,
    547-548; *(1107.5.3)*, **549**

Slope limits *(3304.1.1)*, **1004**

Sloped glazing and skylights, **873**

Smoke barriers, **226**:
    Group I-2 *(407.4)*, **88**
    Group I-3 *(408.6)*, **94**
    independent egress *(407.4.2)*, **88**; *(408.6.3)*,
       95
    refuge area *(407.4.1)*, **88**; *(408.6.2)*, **95**
    smoke compartments *(408.6.1)*, **94**

Smoke control:
    atriums *(404.4)*, **70**
    covered mall buildings *(402.9)*, **60**

Soils and foundations, **667**

Solar collectors: plastic covers *(2606.12)*, **909**

Solid barrier surfaces *(3109.4.1.2)*, **985**

Sound transmission, **584**

Spaces, concealed *(716.1)*, **247**

Special hazards: parking garages *(406.2.8)*, **76**

Spires *(1509.5)*, **650** *(see also*, Towers, spires,
    domes and cupolas)

Sprinkler protection: atriums *(404.3)*, **70**

Sprinkler system, **348**:
    area modifications *(506.3)*, **134—135**
    covered mall buildings *(402.8)*, **59**
    exterior walls *(704.8.1)*, **193**
    Group I-2 *(407.5)*, **89**
    height modifications *(504.2)*, **117—120**
    high-rise buildings *(403.2)*, **63**
    laundry chutes *(707.13.6)*, **220**
    light-transmitting plastic wall panels *(2607.5)*,
       915
    refuse chutes *(707.13.6)*, **220**
    seating *(1008.5.2.3)*, **506**
    stages and platforms *(410.6)*, **104—105**
    open garage parking *(406.3.10)*, **82**

Stadiums: gates *(1003.3.2.1)*, **428**

Stages:
    construction *(410.3.1)*, **99**
    definitions *(410.2)*, **97—98**
    doors *(410.3.3)*, **100-101**
    exits *(410.5.4)*, **104**
    means of egress *(1007.5)*, **497**
    scenery *(410.3.7)*, **101**
    separations *(410.5.1)*, **103**
    sprinkler system *(410.6)*, **104—105**

Stairs:
    open garage parking *(406.3.8)*, **81**
    treads and risers *(1003.3.3.3)*, **431-432**;
       (1003.3.3.3.1), **432**; *(1003.3.3.3.2)*, **433**

Stairs, spiral: means of egress *(408.3.3)*, **91**
Stairway projections *(1003.3.3.11.7)*, **441**
Stairway, to roof *(1003.3.3.12)*, **441**;
    (1003.3.3.12.1), **441**
Stairways:
    alternating tread devices *(1003.3.3.10)*, **437**
    circular *(1003.3.3.7)*, **436**
    communications system *(403.11.1)*, **68**
    construction *(1003.3.3.5)*, **434**; *(1003.3.3.5.1)*,
        434; *(1003 3.3.5.2)*, **434**
    discharge identification *(1005.3.2.3)*, **483**
    door operation *(403.11)*, **68**
    enclosures under *(1005.3.2.2)*, **481**
    fireblocking *(716.2.4)*, **249**
    floor number signs *(1005.3.2.4)*, **483**
    handrail clearance *(1003.3.3.11.6)*, **441**
    handrail continuity *(1003.3.3.11.4)*, **440**
    handrail extensions *(1003.3.3.11.5)*, **440**
    handrail graspability *(1003.3.3.11.3)*, **439**
    handrail height *(1003.3.3.11.1)*, **439**
    handrails *(1003.3.3.11)*, **438**
    handrails of alternating tread devices
(1003.3.3.10.1), **438**
    headroom *(1003.3.3.2)*, **431**
    intermediate handrails *(1003.3.3.11.2)*, **439**
    landings *(1003.3.3.4)*, **433**
    spiral *(1003.3.3.9)*, **437**
    treads of alternating tread devices
        (1003.3.3.10.2), **438**
    vertical rise *(1003.3.3.6)*, **434**
    width *(1003.3.3.1)*, **430**
    winders *(1003.3.3.8)*, **437**
Stairways *(3402.4)*, **1008**
Stairways, enclosed: means of egress
    (1003.2.13.2), **408**
Stairways, exit signs: means of egress
    (1003.2.10.3), **400**
Stairways, exterior exit:
    means of egress *(1005.3.6.1)*, **488**;
        (1005.3.6.2), **489**
Stairways, exterior exit *(1005.3.6)*, **488**;
    (1005.3.6.3), **489**; *(1005.3.6.4)*, **489**;
    (1005.3.6.5), **491**
Standby power:
    atriums *(404.7)*, **71**
    capacity *(403.10.1.2)*, **66**
    connected facilities *(403.10.1.3)*, **67**
    covered mall buildings *(402.12)*, **60**
    fuel supply *(403.10.1.1)*, **66**
    high-rise buildings *(403.10.1)*, **66**
Standpipe system: covered mall buildings *(402.8.1)*,
    59
Steel grillage: foundation walls *(1805.4.4)*, **679**
Steps: emergency escape and rescue open-
ings *(1009.5.2)*, **523**
Steps *(3202.2.1)*, **993**
Stone veneers *(1405.6)*, **611-612**
Storage: accessibility *(1108.8)*, **561**
Storage Group S: classification *(311.1)*, **48**
Storage:
    coat hooks and folding shelves *(1108.8.3)*,
        562
    lockers *(1108.8.1)*, **561**
    shelving and display units *(1108.8.2)*, **561**
Stories, without openings; sprinkler system
    (903.2.12.1), **353**
Structural stability *(704.6)*, **187**
Structural support *(3202.1.1)*, **992**
Structure-borne sound *(1206.3)*, **584**
Surcharge *(3304.1.2)*, **1004**

T

Tables:
    accessway length *(1004.3.1.3.3)*, **468**
    accessway width *(1004.3.1.3.2)*, **468**
    aisle accessway *(1004.3.1.3.1)*, **467**
    seating *(1004.3.1.3)*, **466**
Tables, fixed or built-in: accessibility *(1107.2.5.1)*,
    545
Temporary encroachments *(3202.4)*, **1000**
Terra cotta *(1405.8)*, **613-614**
Textiles:
    ceiling finish *(803.5.2)*, **339**
    interior finishes *(803.5)*, **339**
    wall coverings *(803.5.1)*, **339**
Thermal- and sound-insulating materials *(718.1)*,
    257
Thermal barrier:
    attics and crawl spaces *(2603.4.1.6)*, **898**
    cooler/freezer walls *(2603.4.1.2)*, **895**
    coolers and freezers *(2603.4.1.3)*, **896**
    roofing *(2603.4.1.5)*, **898**
Thermal barrier *(2603.4)*, **894**
Thresholds *(1003.3.1.6)*, **425**
Toilet facilities: accessibility *(1108.2)*, **553-554**
Toilet facilities, unisex: accessibility *(1108.2.1)*,
    555
Toilet rooms *(1209.5)*, **592**
Toilet rooms, accessible:

clear floor space *(1108.2.1.6)*, **556**
privacy *(1108.2.1.7)*, **556**
prohibited route *(1108.2.1.5)*, **556**
unisex *(1108.2.1.2)*, **555**
unisex, accessible location *(1108.2.1.4)*, **556**
Tolerances, concrete:
    bends and ends *(1907.5.2.2)*, **719**
    depth and cover *(1907.5.2.1)*, **718**
Towers and spires *(1509.5.2)*, **651**
Towers, spires, domes and cupolas *(1509.5)*, **650**;
    (1509.5.1), **650-651**
Travel distance *(1008.6)*, **507**:
    atriums *(404.9)*, **71**
    exit access *(1004.2.4)*, **457-458**
Treads:
    aisles *(1008.9.1)*, **515**
    alternating tread devices *(1003.3.3.10.2)*, **438**
    marking *(1008.9.3)*, **516**
Trim *(805.1)*, **344** (*see also,* Decorations and trim):
    fireblocking *(716.2.6)*, **250**
Two-way communication: areas of refuge
    (1003.2.13.5.3), **412**; *(1003.2.13.5.4)*, **414**
Type I construction: limitations *(503.1.4)*, **116**
Types of construction:
    covered mall buildings *(402.6)*, **58**
    high-rise buildings *(403.3.1)*, **64**

U

Underfloor dampproofing *(1806.1.2)*, **710**
Underlayment:
    mineral-surfaced roll roofs *(1507.6.3)*, **639**
    slate roofs *(1507.7.3)*, **639**
    wood shake roofs *(1507.9.3)*, **645**
    wood shingle roofs *(1507.8.3)*, **642**
Underlayment *(1507.2.8)*, **630**

V

Valet parking: accessibility *(1106.6.2)*, **539**
Vapor retarder: exterior wall *(1403.3)*, **601**
Veneer:
    glass *(1405.11)*, **616**
    masonry *(1405.5.1)*, **611**
    metal *(1405.10)*, **615**; *(1405.10.1)*, **615**
    slab-type *(1405.7)*, **612-613**
    stone *(1405.6)*, **611-612**
    wood *(1405.4)*, **610**

Veneer, interiors: masonry *(1405.9.1.1)*, **614**
Ventilation: open garage parking *(406.3.12)*, **82**
Ventilation *(1202.1)*, **572**
Voids: exterior walls *(704.13.1)*, **199**

W

Wall and ceiling finishes, **332**
Wall coverings:
    expanded vinyl *(803.6)*, **340**
    textiles *(803.5.1)*, **339**
    installation *(1405)*, **603**
Wall panels:
    height limitations *(2607.3)*, **910**
    light-transmitting plastic *(2607.3)*, **910**
Wall separation *(1004.3.3.1)*, **473**
Wall spaces — fireblocking *(716.2.2)*, **248**;
    (716.2.3), **249**
Walls:
    corridors *(407.3)*, **86**
    curtain *(410.3.5)*, **101**
    dampproofing *(1806.2.2)*, **712**; *(1806.2.2.1)*,
        713
    envelope *(106.1.3)*, **2**
    fireblocking *(716.2.1.1)*, **248**
    fire-resistance rated *(711.3)*, **231**; *(711.3.1)*,
        231-232; *(711.3.1.1)*, **232**; *(711.3.1.2)*,
        232
    metal veneer *(1405.10)*, **615**; *(1405.10.1)*, **615**
    parapets*(2109.5.5.1)*, **785**
    proscenium *(410.3.4)*, **101**
    rubble stone *(1805.5.1.3)*, **681**
    sheathing *(2304.6.1)*, **836**
    waterproofing *(1806.3.2)*, **714**; *(1806.3.2.1)*,
        714
Walls *(1209.2)*, **590**
Walls, concrete *(1909.6.2)*, **723**
    basement *(1909.6.1)*, **722**
Walls, exterior
    combustible materials *(1406)*, **619**
    combustible projections *(704.2.3)*, **180**
    fire barriers *(706.5)*, **209**
    fire partitions *(708.5)*, **225**
    fire-resistance ratings *(704.5)*, **182—186**
    fire-resistance-rated projections *(704.2)*, **177**
    fire walls *(705.5.1)*, **201**
    first story *(704.8.2)*, **194**
    foam plastic insulation *(2603.4.1.4)*, **897**
    glass veneer *(1405.11)*, **616**

joints *(704.13)*, **199**

    masonry veneer *(1405.5.1)*, **611**

materials *(704.4)*, **181**

opening protection *(704.12)*, **198**

openings *(704.8)*, **191—192**; *(706.6)*, **210**

parapet construction *(704.11.1)*, **197**

parapets *(704.11)*, **196—197**

shaft enclosures *(707.6)*, **214**

slab-type veneer *(1405.7)*, **612-613**

sprinkler system *(704.8.1)*, **193**

stone veneer *(1405.6)*, **611-612**

structural stability *(704.6)*, **187**

unexposed surface temperature *(704.7)*, **187—190**

unprotected openings *(704.12.1)*, **199**

vertical enclosure *(1005.3.2.1)*, **480-481**

vertical exit enclosures *(707.6)*, **214**

vertical exposure *(704.10)*, **196**

vertical separation of openings *(704.9)*, **194**

voids *(704.13.1)*, **199**

wood veneer *(1405.4)*, **610**

Walls, fire *(705.1)*, **200**:

combustible framing *(705.7)*, **205**

exterior walls *(705.5.1)*, **201**

fire-resistance rating *(705.4)*, **200**

horizontal continuity *(705.5)*, **201**

horizontal projecting elements *(705.5.2)*, **202**

materials *(705.3)*, **200**

openings *(705.8)*, **206**

structural stability *(705.2)*, **200**

vertical continuity *(705.6)*, **203—204**; *(705.6.1)*, **205**

Walls, foundation *(1805.5)*, **680**:

curtain*(1805.5.6)*, **707-708**

hollow masonry *(1805.5.4)*, **707**

pier *(1805.5.6)*, **707-708**

reinforcement *(1805.5.3)*, **681**

thickness *(1805.5.1.1)*, **680**; *(1805.5.1.2)*, **681**

Walls, framing:

bracing *(2308.9.3)*, **862-868**

framing *(2308.9.1)*, **857**

Walls, interior nonload-bearing — anchorage *(2109.7.2.4)*, **803**

Walls, intersecting — bonding pattern *(2109.7.2.1)*, **800**

Walls, light-framed cold-formed steel — shear values *(2211.3.1)*, **830**

Walls, light-framed cold-formed steel:

steel framing *(2211.5.2)*, **833**; *(2211.5.3)*, **833**

steel sheathing *(2211.4.2)*, **832**; *(2211.4.3)*, **832**

wind and seismic requirements *(2211.1)*, **820**

wood sheathing *(2211.3.2)*, **830**; *(2211.3.3)*, **831**

Walls, masonry:

anchorage *(2109.7.2.2)*, **801**; *(2109.7.2.3)*, **801**; *(2109.7.4)*, **806**

partitions *(2106.4.1.2)*, **749**

reinforcement *(2106.5.2)*, **754-757**

Walls, openings *(1909.6.3)*, **724**

Walls, partitions: masonry*(2106.4.1.2)*, **749**

Walls, party: limitations *(503.2)*, **116**

Walls, rubble stone: thickness*(2109.5.3)*, **784**

Walls, shear:

diaphragm ratio*(2109.2.1.3)*, **779**

length*(2109.2.1.2)*, **777**

reinforcement *(2106.5.3.1)*, **758**; *(2106.4.2.3.1)*, **752**

thickness*(2109.2.1.1)*, **777**

Walls:

tubs, showers or water closet compartments *(2509.2)*, **887**; *(2509.3)*, **887**

Water closet compartments:

accessibility *(1108.2.2)*, **557**

gypsum board*(2509.2)*, **887**

gypsum board*(2509.3)*, **887**

Weather protection:

exterior wall *(1403.2)*, **600-601**

wall coverings *(1405.2)*, **603**

Weather-resistant barriers: plaster *(2510.6)*, **888**

Weep holes *(2104.1.8)*, **747**

Weep screeds: exterior plaster *(2512.1.2)*, **890**

Wheelchair space clusters *(1107.2.2.1)*, **542**

dispersion *(1107.2.3)*, **543**; *(1107.2.3.1)*, **543**; *(1107.2.3.2)*, **543**

Wheelchair spaces *(1107.2.2)*, **540**

Widely spaced horizontal members *(3109.4.1.4)*, **986**

Width *(3104.8)*, **982**

Window assemblies, exterior fire *(714.3.7)*, **245-246**

Window assemblies, interior fire *(714.3.6)*, **244**:

size limitations *(714.3.6.2)*, **245**

where permitted *(714.3.6.1)*, **244**

Windowless buildings *(408.8)*, **96**

Windows:

accessibility *(1108.13.1)*, **565**

balconies, architectural features and mechani cal equipment *(3202.3.2)*, **997**

interior finishes *(801.2.1)*, **329**

jalousies *(2403.5)*, **872**

louvered *(2403.5)*, **872**

mullions *(714.3.5)*, **244**
Wood veneers, exterior *(1405.4)*, **610**

Y

Yards *(1205.1)*, **581**